D1565055

Slavery in Russia

Richard Hellie

Slavery in Russia
1450-1725

The University of Chicago Press

Chicago and London

The University of Chicago Press, Chicago 60637
The University of Chicago Press, Ltd., London

Publication of this work was made possible
in part by a grant from the Andrew W. Mel-
lon Foundation and by a grant from the
Publications Program of the National Endowment for the Humanities, an independent federal agency.

Library of Congress Cataloging in Publication Data

Hellie, Richard.
  Slavery in Russia, 1450-1725.

  Bibliography: p.
  Includes index.
  1. Slavery—Soviet Union—History. I. Title.
HT1206.H44   306'.3   81-12954
ISBN 0-226-32647-0   AACR2

Richard Hellie is professor of Russian History
at the University of Chicago and is the author
of *Enserfment and Military Change in Muscovy*,
published by The University of Chicago Press.

This work is dedicated to my father, OLE INGEMAN HELLIE, and my mother, ELIZABETH LARSEN HELLIE, who helped to teach me the value of freedom.

Contents

Maps, Figures, and Tables

Maps

Figures

Tables

Preface

My *Enserfment and Military Change in Muscovy* was published by the University of Chicago Press over a decade ago. That was followed by a Guggenheim Fellowship during whose tenure (1972-73) I read extensively in the anthropology and sociology of law, and began to consider the Muscovite law of slavery, which directed and regulated a surprisingly dynamic institution. Then I discovered that it would be possible to quantify what ultimately came to be 2,499 slavery contracts, dowries, wills, and other documents involving slaves. These documents contain the price and demographic information used in this study. The demo-. graphic material is the earliest available for Russian history and reveals a world of nuclear families and young males, and a layer of society that almost certainly practiced, on a large scale, female infanticide.

Knowledge of the existence of slavery in early modern Russia is not widespread. Many people know of the existence of serfdom, and confuse the two. A major mission of this book is to inform readers of the existence of slavery as an institution different and separate from serfdom and to reveal how serfdom was molded by the institution of slavery. Slavery is also relatively unknown because for much of the Soviet period it was the reigning dogma that slavery barely existed in Russian history and was fundamentally irrelevant. That story is discussed in my essay "Recent Soviet Historiography on Medieval and Early Modern Russian Slavery" (*The Russian Review*, 35, no. 1 [January 1976] : 1-32), which the reader is advised to consult if he is interested in that and other historiographic issues.

The parochial outlook of most Russianists and a number of peculiarities in the institution of Russian slavery led me to adopt a comparative approach, which infuses the entire work. My purpose is not to show that slavery in early modern Russia was exactly like, or nearly like, some other slave system, for it was not, but rather to demonstrate that the major features of Muscovite slavery can be found in other slave systems, and that most of the features of almost any slave system can be found in the Muscovite one. An attempt also has been made to explain the absence in Muscovy of prominent or central features of other slave systems.

The major peculiarity of Muscovite slavery was that the majority of the slaves were natives who sold themselves into slavery. The basic feature of the slave in most systems is that he is an outsider, a marginal person, someone who is distinct from the host slave-owning population. When natives fall into slavery, as a punishment, through debt or indenture, most societies insist that such servitude be temporary. Muscovy also had those forms of temporary slavery, but most of the slaves were natives who sold themselves into perpetual, hereditary slavery. An attempt is made to explain this peculiarity of Muscovite slavery—the willingness of Muscovites to enslave their own ethnos—and to consider its consequences for the subsequent course of Russian history. This is considered in the context of the notable infrequency of manumission, the absence of a transitional status for freedmen, and the high rate and ease of flight from slavery.

Another peculiarity of Muscovite slavery, at least from a New World perspective, is the presence of elite slaves, ranging from government ministers and estate managers to cavalrymen. Most of the slaves, however, were household slaves who were not engaged in the production of agricultural or other commodities for the market, and most of whom did little farming.

Most of the research for this work was completed several years ago, when I decided to embark on an examination of the slaveowners of Muscovy. There is no comparable study for any other slave system, at least that I am aware of. The prosopographical analysis shows that the vast majority of the two thousand slaveowners examined were government servitors, primarily lifelong cavalrymen, and also those who worked in government offices. Attempts are made to correlate their slaveholdings and expenditures with their landholdings and various forms of compensation. Other slaveowners were elite merchants, clergymen, and elite slaves. Ordinary townsmen and, especially, peasants rarely owned slaves. To illustrate both the lives of real people and the life of the Muscovite slave world, I have adopted a narrative strategy of summarizing court cases involving slavery issues and prefacing them with biographies of the litigating slaveowners. To my knowledge, this is the first book on the subject of slavery throughout the entire Muscovite period, and one of the most comprehensive examinations of any of the world's numerous slave systems.

The study was completed during the tenure of a National Endowment for the Humanities Fellowship (1978-79). I am greatly indebted to the National Endowment and also to the Guggenheim Foundation for their support. I am indebted to the University of Chicago Social Sciences Divisional Research Fund, which has supported my computer operations and other incidental expenses, and to the Federal College Work-Study Program, which has provided me with a work-study student assistant in many of the years during which this study was in preparation.

Every author of a work of this nature incurs a number of debts to others for their invaluable assistance and generous gifts of time. Several students should be singled out. Marc D. Zlotnik did the preliminary coding for about a third of the cases that were processed by computer. Peter B. Brown provided twenty-five documents from Soviet archives and translated several articles on Polish slavery. Brian Davies did much of the prosopographical searching and drew twenty maps. Louise McReynolds calculated the distances shown on the maps, produced the ten DISSLPA graphs in the book, and rendered other computer assistance. Other students who assisted me in numerous ways were Deborah Jones, Milan Andrejevich, Michael Levine, Gloria Gibbs, and Mikhail Khodarkovskii. University of Chicago Library Slavic Biographer Vaclav Laska has built a superb collection that provides nearly everything a Russian historian could want. Marianna Tax Choldin, Slavic Reference Librarian at the University of Illinois, furnished biographical assistance and copies of rare materials. The text was typed by Marnie Veghte, Elizabeth Bitoi, and Barbara Lewert. Mark Landerghini assisted in the proofreading of the galleys and in the compilation of the index.

I have benefited immeasurably from the advice and criticism of colleagues throughout the world. Much of this work was presented in preliminary form in fifteen papers at professional meetings and conferences, and I gained much from the critical remarks made during the discussions of the papers as well as from the written comments on the fifty copies of each that were usually sent to interested people. Also exceptionally helpful were the comparative reading suggestions brought to my office and sent to me by mail. I hope that all those who provided me with assistance on such occasions understood my genuine appreciation for their thoughtfulness and help. Lastly, my thanks must go to those who shared with me their thoughts on the entire manuscript, Jeffrey Brooks, Emmet Larkin, and Arthur Mann, and those who provided lengthy written critiques, Daniel H. Kaiser, Ann M. Kleimola, and Stanley L. Engerman. They are models of unstinting, generous collegiality.

Chapter 17 is dedicated to the memory of Arcadius Kahan, who died suddenly on February 26, 1982, as this book was about to be printed. His chance remark, "It would be nice to know how much land slaveowners had," catalyzed the investigation that resulted in this chapter.

1. Slavery in Russia, 1450-1725

This chapter will trace briefly the history of Russia between 1450 and 1725, dates chosen because the first one marks the time when documents on Muscovite slavery began to appear in any significant amount and the second the time by which slavery was abolished. The chapter will close with a discussion of definitions of slavery and the place of Muscovy in the early modern international slave trade.

The most obvious feature of the period under discussion is that it was one of almost continuous expansion, unparalleled at any other time or place in world history. In 1300, Moscow, the engine of this expansion, had been the capital of a very small, undistinguished principality covering not more than 47,000 square kilometers. During the next century and a half it expanded significantly, to a size of about 430,000 square kilometers, and became a major political force and center on the east European plain. During the reigns of Ivan III (1462-1505) and his son Vasilii III (1505-33), Muscovy expanded to a size of about 2,800,000 square kilometers and encompassed most of the northern East Slavic lands. At this time, when Moscow formally freed the northeastern Russian lands from the "Mongol-Tatar Yoke" (1480), and its focus of attention shifted from Sarai, the capital of the Golden Horde on the Lower Volga, to Italy, Muscovy became the eastern outpost of European civilization. With the movement of the center of Western civilization from the Mediterranean to northern Europe about 1550, Russia began to be attracted toward England and Holland. Simultaneously, in the 1550s, Muscovy annexed lands held by Tatars in the middle and lower Volga, opening the way to the Urals, with its storehouse of minerals, while simultaneously dividing the Turkic world in two and weakening it correspondingly. The push into Siberia began in the 1580s, and by the end of the sixteenth century Muscovy's realm covered about 5,400,000 square kilometers. After serious reverses at the beginning of the seventeenth century (the Time of Troubles), when the Poles briefly occupied Moscow and Sweden held Novgorod and much of northwest Russia, expansion was resumed in the late 1630s. By moving fortified lines further south to keep out the Crimean Tatars (who had burned Moscow in 1571 and its suburbs in 1591), much of Ukraine was gradually secured, a movement marked by the completion of the Belgorod line in 1653 and the annexation of Kiev in 1654. By the end of the seventeenth century Siberia had been swallowed up, and Moscow ruled over an area of 15,280,000 square kilometers. After initial reverses at Narva (1700), Peter the Great went on to victory in the Northern War (1721), which confirmed his conquests of the Baltic littoral from Vyborg to Riga. Peter also secured Azov on the Black Sea. The size of the Russian Empire was over 16,000,000 square kilometers, well on the way to today's size of 22,400,000 square kilometers.

The reasons for this phenomenal territorial expansion, which continues to this day, have been widely debated; but it does not appear as though the Russians have been expansionists carrying out a conscious mission. Rather, they have been rational actors who have regularly maximized their self-interest by exploiting the weakness of others while learning to keep what they have acquired. Certainly, Russian rulers were motivated by security concerns aroused by the Mongol conquest of 1236-41 and repeated Tatar raids for centuries thereafter; by Polish and Lithuanian expansionism; by battles with Germans, from Alexander Nevskii's famous encounter on the ice of Lake Chud' down through the liquidation of Livonia in the sixteenth century; and by Swedish aggression, from Alexander's encounter on the Neva in 1240 until the Peace of Nystadt in 1721. Provoked into a state of constant military preparedness, the Russians have nearly always been able martially to pursue targets of opportunity presented by the weakness of neighbors.

Precise population figures are unavailable, but the population of Muscovy in the middle of the fifteenth century may have been somewhere between two and five million, a number which rose to about 15.5 million in the early 1720s.[1] Such low population density as there was in Muscovy is often viewed as one of the necessary conditions for the existence of slavery, especially when natives perceive that there is a labor shortage.

With perhaps the exception of the first half of the sixteenth century, and maybe the years 1673-94, the entire Muscovite period was one of great stress. Warfare was nearly constant, and the progress of the gunpowder revolution was accompanied and assisted by a voracious appetite for taxes, which were collected by a government that evolved from a royal household in, say, 1475, to an organ with several dozen central chancelleries (*prikazy*) by the 1680s. These *prikazy* were primarily branches of the army, but many of them also had judicial functions. Merit and efficiency were hallmarks of sixteenth-century central administration, but these principles were sometimes compromised in the seventeenth century under the Romanov tsars. While leading figures in court cliques often headed *prikazy* in the seventeenth century, it must be stressed that the major, key chancelleries were still usually directed by professional bureaucrats, regardless of which clique was dominant at the Romanov court. Peter the Great revitalized, rationalized, and renamed the *prikazy* as "colleges" in the first quarter of the eighteenth century.

1. For various estimates, see Richard Hellie, *Enserfment and Military Change in Muscovy* (Chicago: University of Chicago Press, 1971), p. 305, n. 9; Ia. E. Vodarskii, *Naselenie Rossii za 400 let (XVI-nachalo XX vv.)* (Moscow: Prosveshchenie, 1973), pp. 27, 29, 55; idem, *Naselenie Rossii v kontse XVII-nachale XVIII veka* (Moscow: Nauka, 1977), p. 192.

Warfare was not the only stressful aspect of Muscovite life. There was also Ivan IV's mad Oprichnina, when the tsar split the state in two and ravaged much of it (1565-72), the Time of Troubles (the extinction of the 700-year-old Riurikid dynasty in 1598, in 1601-3 perhaps the worst famine Russia has ever experienced, a series of pretenders from 1605 to 1614, civil war, and Polish and Swedish invasions between 1605 and 1618), and massive rural and urban civil disorders from the time of Ivan IV down through the beginning of the reign of Peter the Great. Also stressful were the very low, pre-Carolingian grain yields (three seeds were harvested for each one sown) that resulted from the poor podzolic soil, excessive moisture, and a short growing season, and that forced most of the population to farm. The years 1645-1715 were ones of low sunspot activity, known as the Maunder minimum, which caused the "little ice age" and worsened the condition of Russian agriculture. Useful minerals were nonexistent in the Muscovite heartland, and this forced a dependence on imports, many of which were paid for by plundering Siberia of its furs.

Russia left the medieval era with none of the institutional restraints on the government that existed in the West. The Orthodox church, created by royal decree in 988, was always the state's supporter. While an occasional churchman criticized exceptional acts of official savagery in the century between 1450 and 1550, no such voice was ever again raised after Ivan IV in the 1560s ordered clerics to refrain from commenting on governmental reprisals against perceived "opponents."

Whether or not individuals actually owned land has been debated, but it is very clear that the government could and did mobilize whatever land it wanted almost at will. Partially in consequence of that fact, Muscovy had neither a meaningful aristocracy nor a gentry. Towns were undifferentiated politically from the countryside, town air made no one "free," and there were no guilds. In the first half of the sixteenth century the monarch was converted ideologically from a mortal who consulted with his boyars (men whom he of course appointed, and could remove) to an autocrat with pretensions to being God's vicegerent. (Byzantine writings, especially those of Agapetus, were used in this process.)

Early modern Russia witnessed a great explosion of interest in and use of law. Inherited from the Middle Ages was the *Russkaia Pravda*, primarily a tool for horizontal conflict resolution, which remained the major legal monument through the first half of the sixteenth century. In 1497 a *Sudebnik* was compiled, sixty-six articles primarily outlining procedures and fees for use in judicial matters, but also expressing the beginnings of vertical, triadic legal relations in which the state power assumed more of an interest than simply collecting fees from the process of conflict resolution.[2] Simultaneously, the central power in Moscow became more sophisticated and centralized and began to cancel judicial and fiscal

2. Daniel H. Kaiser, "The Transformation of Legal Relations in Old Rus' (Thirteenth-Fifteenth Centuries)" (Ph.D. diss., University of Chicago, 1977); idem, *The Growth of Law in Medieval Russia* (Princeton: Princeton University Press, 1980).

immunity charters.[3] A new redaction of the *Sudebnik* was promulgated in 1550, others in 1589 and 1606. The major monument of Muscovite legislation was the *Ulozhenie* of 1649, a quite sophisticated and comprehensive code of 967 articles divided into twenty-five chapters. The *Ulozhenie*, whose compilation was forced by urban uprisings in June 1648, systematized the practice of the Muscovite chancelleries and was printed in two editions of 1,200 copies each. This code, which was widely distributed throughout Muscovy and served as the fundamental law of Russia until 1830, was the major instrument for prescribing, enforcing, and perpetuating the dominance of the reigning political structure. This structure, with a social inequality that amounted almost to a caste society, was the hallmark of Russia between 1649 and the emancipation of 1861. Monarchical arbitrariness was prescribed in the law, particularly in instances involving members of the upper service class, for whom sanctions often were prescribed to be only what "the sovereign decrees." No official below the tsar was allowed to interpret the law, and there is a large body of evidence indicating that this injunction was taken literally. While there was no "rule of law" or *Rechtsstaat* in Russia, since the monarch was declared to be above the law, there was the kind of "legality" defined by Lon Fuller in his *Morality of Law*: the authorities achieved rules that were publicized and explicit; there was little retroactive legislation and few, if any, contradictory rules; conduct was not required that was beyond the powers of the affected parties; and those rules that were administered were those that had been announced.[4] While the Muscovites occasionally rebelled against their prescribed status, early modern Russian law ordinarily was both an effective instrument for conflict resolution and the best device for the central oligarchy to use in imposing its norms on the rest of society.

Already from the fifteenth century and before, Muscovy had a sense of hierarchy. In fact, there were several hierarchies—military-court, government, urban, church—and transfer from one to another seems to have been as possible as vertical mobility within the hierarchies. Each hierarchy had its ranks, which served as a cursus honorum through which any person with ambition, talent, luck, and perhaps proper connections might pass. The names of the ranks changed little until the Petrine reforms at the beginning of the eighteenth century. What did change was the underlying reality of the names and their relation to the social milieu. The hierarchical society became rigidly stratified. A late Muscovite conception of the social order was expressed in 1658 by members of the middle service class cavalry demanding that the government take more effective action for return of their fugitive slaves and serfs: "in your sovereign kingdom [*derzhava*] all people belong to God and to you, your Majesty, . . . and they are of four estates [*chiny*]—the clergy, the servicemen, the merchants, and the agricultural-

3. Marc D. Zlotnik, "Immunity Charters and the Centralization of the Muscovite State" (Ph.D. diss., University of Chicago, 1976).
4. Lon Fuller, *The Morality of Law* (New Haven: Yale University Press, 1964).

ists."[5] (This structure is shown in table 1.1.) This, of course, was already after 1649, the date of the formal completion of the enserfment of the peasantry, the binding of the townsmen to their station with their corresponding monopolies on the various urban handicrafts and trade, and the relative closing off of the service classes from both emigration and immigration. After 1649 Muscovy was essentially a caste society, with the living individual's status fixed by law and the place of his heirs predetermined. The ranks themselves were formalized and even quantified (by the value.of a person's honor) by the law codes of Muscovy, particularly the *Sudebnik* of 1550 and the *Ulozhenie* of 1649. A 1627 law specified the number of carts individuals of each rank had to furnish the postal system.[6] The *Ulozhenie* of 1649 also prescribed how much would be paid to ransom Muscovites from foreign captivity, which often meant slavery, and decreed the quantity of land that servicemen of different ranks were entitled to possess in Moscow province.[7] These rankings, figures, and other statements can be used to illustrate the later Muscovite system of hierarchy.[8]

To exaggerate only slightly, one might say that both the genius and the tragic flaw of this rank system, which was universally known and resorted to, was that service in Moscow was considered to be so much more prestigious than service in the provinces. The natural attraction of the capital was greatly enhanced by the ranking system, which initially facilitated the concentration and centralization of power by and in Muscovy, but in the long run it sapped the periphery, the enormous landed area from the east European plain to the Pacific, of the vitality it might have had, if the centripetal force had not been so overwhelming. These values established by government were apparently accepted by nearly everyone.

In the late fifteenth century these ranks were granted on the basis of service, and at least to a certain extent were open to anyone who could render that service. This was the period of the rapid expansion of Muscovy territorially and of the Muscovite army and officialdom. Moscow "gathered. in" most of the East Slavic lands, putting an end to the large number of principalities and the three independent republics that had existed on the east European plain for the preceding quarter-millennium. The middle service class cavalry corps, ultimately 25,000 strong, was created to provide at least a protostanding army to replace the court retinues that had been the nucleus of East Slavic military forces since

---

5. A. A. Novosel'skii, "Kollektivnye dvorianskie chelobitnye o syske beglykh krest'ian i kholopov vo vtoroi polovine XVII v.," in *Dvorianstvo i krepostnoi stroi Rossii XVI-XVIII vv. Sbornik statei, posviashchennyi pamiati Alekseia Andreevicha Novosel'skogo*, ed. N. I. Pavlenko et al. (Moscow: Nauka, 1975), p. 312.

6. PRP 5: 539-40; 1550 *Sudebnik* 26; 1649 *Ulozhenie* 10: 27-99; MS, pp. 4-15.

7. 1649 *Ulozhenie* 3: 2-7; 16: 1; MS, p. 32.

8. V. N. Storozhev, ed., "Boiarskii spisok 1610-1611. Boiarskii spisok 119-go goda sochinen do moskovskogo razoreniia pri Letve s pisma dumnogo d'iaka Mikhaila Danilova," *Chteniia* 230 (1909, bk. 3): 73-103; S. A. Belokurov, ed., "Razriadnye zapisi za Smutnoe vremia," *Chteniia* 222 (1907, bk. 3): 184.

TABLE 1.1
The Structure of Muscovite Society

Social Group	Payment for Injured Honor	Carts to be Provided to Postal Service	Moscow Province Land Entitlement	Captivity Ransom Sum
Church Hierarchy*				
Patriarch	Personal enslavement for offender			
Metropolitans	400 rubles	20		
Archbishops	300 rubles	15		
Bishops	200 rubles	11		
Archimandrites	Sum depends on rank of monastery (the *lesnitsa*)	9		
Monastery fathers superior	do.	5		
Monastery cellarers	do.			
Monastery treasurers	do.			
Archpriests	Sum depends on rank of church where employed			
Archdeacons				
Cathedral elders				
Elders				
Clavigers				
Monks				
Priests	5 rubles			
Deacons				
Servants (*slugi*)				

Civil Hierarchy (Court and Military Service, Government Civil Service)

The tsar and his family			
The upper upper-service class	Determined by the tsar		
Boyars	20	200 cheti	
Okol'nichie	15	150 cheti	
Kravchei s putem			
Chashnik			
Kaznachei			
Postel'nichei			
Counselor *dvoriane*	12	150 cheti	
Counselor state secretaries	10		
The middle upper-service class	Determined by the tsar		
Stol'niki	6 to 10	100 cheti	
Striapchie s plat'em	5 to 6	100 cheti	
State secretaries (*d'iaki*)	6	100 cheti	
The lower upper-service class	Determined by the tsar		
Moscow *dvoriane*	4 to 10		
Zhil'tsy	3 to 4	50 cheti	
The middle service class	Based on income		
Provincial *dvoriane*	3 to 4	70 cheti if serving in Moscow	
Deti boiarskie	2	10% of land entitlement	20 rubles per 100 cheti of land entitlement
The lower service class			
Musketeers (*strel'tsy*)			
Cossacks			
Artillerymen			
Soldiers (*soldaty*)			25 to 40 rubles
Cavalrymen (*reitary*)			25 rubles

TABLE 1.1 continued

Social Group	Payment for Injured Honor	Carts to be Provided to Postal Service	Moscow Province Land Entitlement	Captivity Ransom Sum
Civil Urban Hierarchy				
Stroganovs	100 rubles			
Wealthy merchants (1550); *Gosti* (1649)	50 rubles	5		
Merchants of 2d corporation (*gostinaia sotnia*)	10 to 20 rubles			
Merchants of 3rd corporation (*sukonnaia sotnia*)	5 to 15 rubles			
Townsmen	5 to 7 rubles			20 rubles
Postmen	5 rubles			
Urban slave-dependents (*zakladchiki*)				
Peasantry				
Landed peasants	1 ruble			15 rubles
Landless peasants (*bobyli*)	1 ruble			
Slave Society				
Elite slaves	5 rubles			
Registered (*dokladnye*) slaves				
Ordinary slaves	1 ruble			15 rubles
Hereditary (2d and subsequent generations)				
Full (1st generation)				
Limited service contract (*kabal'nye kholopy*; also 1st generation)				
Others				
Foreigners				
Wanderers	1 ruble			

*In 1649, dishonor sanctions (*bezchest'e*) depended on the status of the person who injured a churchman's honor: high cash payments for members of the upper orders, a beating and/or jail for those of low station.

the ninth century. These servicemen were supported by land grants that will be discussed in greater detail below. Land, which heretofore had been "free" and therefore of marginal value (because of the low population density and freedom of peasant mobility), became an object of value whose holding increasingly conferred status. What is particularly important here is that this greatly expanded service corps provided many new posts for people of indifferent origin, even for some who had been slaves, and contributed to the expanding and relatively fluid social order that persisted to the end of the sixteenth century.

Also important for the 1470-1550 years was the expansion of administrative and probably even court posts. These, plus military posts (for plunder), had been valued more highly than land before 1470 because they provided a more certain income: taxes could be collected, along with fees for administrative and judicial services, regardless of where people lived; rents, on the other hand, required that rentpayers live on seignorial land. Moscow had more posts, such as governorships (*namestnichestva*), to award as it annexed new areas; it also had some central administrative posts with the evolution of the court administration into a government and its creation of specialized chancelleries in the 1475-1575 century. These processes again created room at the top.

As time went by, these ranks took on attributes which one doubts that those who had created them could have foreseen. In the seventeenth century a protocol was worked out according to which officials of equal service rank had to communicate with their peers in forms different from those used for communicating with others, and an insulted party could sue the offender for compensation for the dishonor. This was a reflection of the increasingly rigid stratification of society that developed in the seventeenth century. Other indicators were rights belonging to ranks and the law's view of the individual as a potential violator of its norms.

In 1500, say, no such situation existed. The holding of a specific rank prescribed nothing about a person's right to own land or slaves, for example, two kinds of ownership that in the first half of the seventeenth century became privileged domains. The story of the abasement of the person of the peasant between 1565 and 1649 is well known and does not need to be repeated here. What needs to be emphasized is the fact that the possession of serfs, who increasingly were viewed as chattel, served as an automatic status elevator for members of the middle service class. (As we shall see in greater detail below, the possession of slaves was a significant status symbol for wealthier individuals on the labor-short east European plain, and the appropriation of an image of this possession—the serfs—was just one aspect of the rise of the middle service class.)

Also important in the developing conception of the Muscovite social order was the legal image of the potential culpability of a specific rank-holder. Such concepts cannot be found in the *Sudebnik* of 1497, but the conception of class justice and sanctions pervades the criminal norms of the *Ulozhenie* of 1649. In the latter document, the upper service class usually is ignored when the imposition of criminal sanctions is discussed; mild sanctions are prescribed for the middle service class, and brutal and barbaric ones for the lower orders. Similarly with torture, which became a favorite interrogation device in these years: it was applied first to the lower orders, then to members of the middle service class, and not at all to the magnates. In the government chancelleries, a wrong-doing state secretary would be beaten with a whip (*batogi*) but a clerk with a knout—which could be an instrument of capital punishment. The different penalties for insult have already been noted. Such a system of differential culpability potential and sanctions is expected in a caste society and constitutes a major part of its definition. There is every reason to believe that these norms, defined by the central government, were rapidly internalized by the populace. The situation even reached the point where special government offices were appointed to deal with litigation involving specific status groups—the Vladimir Judicial Chancellery handled disputes among members of the upper upper-service class, the Moscow Judicial Chancellery did the same thing for disputes involving members of the lower upper-service class and the middle service class.[9]

One of the remarkable aspects of the rise of Moscow was the absence of opposition, almost none of which has been recorded. A major reason for this was the "system of places" (*mestnichestvo*), a device of genius that assured in an orderly way that those who had been big fish in a small pond (a small principality) could expect that they and at least their first-generation offspring would be only slightly smaller fish in the big pond (Moscow). Potentially dissident elements whose territorial autonomy was being liquidated were aware of a stable alternative in which they could continue to enjoy the perquisites of social dominance and relatively high income. The alternative to independence was so attractive that there was no need to resist it—especially as resistance would have been hopeless anyway. This function has not been attributed to *mestnichestvo* by other students of Muscovy—a major omission, in my view. The "system of places" was an ordering of the Muscovite elite determined primarily if not exclusively (until about 1550) by service, and perhaps secondarily (and increasingly, as time wore on) by genealogy. Aristocratic pretensions were minimally heeded, at least in comparison with the neighboring Rzeczpospolita, and service was the crucial variable. Positions in the army, at court, and on ceremonial occasions were ranked (the right was higher than the left, for example), and, depending upon an individual's ranking in the "system of places," he could lay claim to a post, would refuse to serve under someone with a lower rank, and so on. (For some reason the towns to which governors—*namestniki*, *voevody*—were appointed "to feed" were not ranked. A person desiring such a post would petition for it but, to my knowledge, the operations of the assignment system have not been determined.) A person gained his place in the *mestnichestvo* hierarchy on the basis of merit and performance,

9. Peter B. Brown, "Early Modern Russian Bureaucracy: The Evolution of the Chancellery System from Ivan III to Peter the Great, 1478-1717." (Ph.D. diss., University of Chicago, 1978).

as evaluated by the monarch. (This resembles the operation of the service-land and monetary compensation entitlement system, *oklad*, discussed below.)

Clan relations came to be a crucial variable in the calculation of place. To some extent, a person rose and fell with his clan—regardless of his own merit. The performance and political influence of relatives also played some role in the assignment of rank and compensation—sort of a proto-collective-merit incentive system. Because of the manpower shortage, retirement was determined by physical incapacity, with little or no account taken of senility, functional obsolescence, and so on. Consequently the system must have been highly gerontocratic, leaving the sovereign little opportunity to appoint able persons to top posts. Ivan IV tried to get around this by decreeing that certain military campaigns and other occasions would be conducted "without regard to place," but nevertheless Muscovy lost several important battles in the second half of the sixteenth century because of place disputes among military commanders. Be that as it may, *mestnichestvo* served Muscovy well in its period of geographic expansion and provided a mechanism for the orderly resolving of disputes over precedence among the members of the upper service class. The lengthy extant records of suits to resolve *mestnichestvo* disputes intimate that servicemen were highly conscious of their rank in the system of places. This ranking was a status symbol that began to be appropriated by the middle service class in the first half of the seventeenth century. In 1662 the state secretaries gained the right to participate in the *mestnichestvo* system. Two decades later the system was formally abolished, with a great bonfire of the record books that recorded the occasions upon which place was determined. The passage of time (over two centuries) had made the necessary calculations increasingly tortuous and the genealogical elements had made the system unworkable as the ancient families died out and were replaced in the seventeenth century by new families to whom the system was both odious and irrelevant.

Muscovy knew many occupations, but throughout most of the quarter-millennium under discussion there seems to have been little concept of specialization or job-related expertise among the service classes. The situation was one that Lenin would have appreciated: everyone seems to have felt he could perform any job, if given the chance. A man's merit was determined by how well he performed a given assignment, but this merit (or, as far as one can tell, lack of it) was neither predictive nor prescriptive of future assignments. Thus it is not accidental that the government chancelleries, as they became increasingly developed and specialized, were staffed by lifetime professionals from milieus other than the service class. Similarly, when warfare became more specialized in the 1630s and on into the 1650s, evolving from cavalry shooting arrows to infantry shooting bullets in linear warfare, foreigners were hired to command and commoners were drafted to fill the ranks. Bureaucratic and military service continued to be meritocratic, but those with the merit, as well as those who developed it, were from outside the traditional service class, which looked down upon the newcomers—probably a protective reaction covering up their own obsolescence.

Below the landed upper and middle service classes were the various groups of the lower service class: musketeers, artillerymen, cossacks, and a host of others. They did not possess land or peasants, but were paid cash salaries, which they supplemented by gardening and (until 1649) petty trade and manufacturing. (Musketeers could trade after 1649, but were taxed on their endeavors.) Their officers were members of the middle service class, who often owned slaves. Members of the lower service class almost never owned slaves, but until 1675 they enjoyed at least the theoretical possibility of rising into the middle service class and acquiring its perquisites.

The urban classes, perhaps 2 percent of the entire population, occupied an intermediate position between the landholding-warrior service class and the peasantry.[10] There were dozens of identifiable urban occupations in Muscovy, with the highest status being enjoyed by the officially designated merchants of the first, second, and third corporations and the Stroganovs. Occasionally manufacturers enjoyed high status, but they usually were foreigners hired to produce weapons or luxury goods the Muscovites could not make themselves. Here, as elsewhere, rank and status were conferred by the government. The central power also meticulously ranked the rest of the urban tradesmen and artisans for tax purposes into the categories of "well-to-do," "middling," "poor," and sometimes "very poor," and then often demanded taxes high enough to put such persons in severe straits.

With the development of the central bureaucracy and the eschewment of central administrative service by the landed military service classes, the chancellery employees developed by 1640 into a distinct, hereditary subcaste of the town population when entry into clerkships (*pod'iachie*) became closed to outsiders. A boy whose father was in chancellery service would apprentice himself as a clerk in an office, and, demonstrating merit, would rise in the service. At the apex of professional bureaucratic service were the state secretaries (*d'iaki*), whose rivalry for status with the leading merchants, the *gosti*, was, we know, fierce. One can distinguish true first editions of the *Ulozhenie* of 1649, 1,200 copies published in the first half of that year and sold out immediately, from a second printing of 1,200 copies later in 1649 by the fact that the *d'iaki* are placed ahead of the *gosti* in the first edition; the situation was reversed under pressure from the *gosti* and a decree was enacted to that effect by the time of the new printing of the most important codification of Russian law prior to 1830.

The situation, however, remained fluid in the 1650s; whether commerce would be subordinated to bureaucracy remained undecided. In 1659 the boyars officially reversed the 1649 action in a case that had arisen in a manner typical for Muscovy. The *gost'* Matvei Antonov had been ordered to serve at a new mint (one probably established to coin the debased copper currency that was used to

10. Richard Hellie, "The Stratification of Muscovite Society: The Townsmen," *Russian History* 5, pt. 2 (1978): 119-75.

pay for the Thirteen Years War), and, upon being ranked lower than a *d'iak*, had filed a complaint. He cited the 1649 precedent. In the investigation that ensued, considerable reference was made to the service of each group—the *gosti* in the Moscow Administrative Chancellery and in the customs houses, the *d'iaki* in administrative work in Moscow, in the provincial towns, in the army, and on embassies. The case noted that people who held the rank of *gost'* (*gostinoi chin*) were "junior people" (*liudi molodye*), usually the offspring of common merchants, sometimes of churchmen. After an exhaustive investigation in several chancelleries (at a time when Muscovy was engaged in one of the most exhausting wars in its history), the conclusion was reached that *gosti* had always served under *d'iaki* on state business, the top merchants always had been ranked many notches lower than the state secretaries, and that the 1649 decision had been made incorrectly because of unprecedented and false representations by the *gosti*. Moreover, the state secretaries regularly served with the boyars on state business, whereas the first-corporation merchants never did, but only engaged in state commerce and customs collection.[11] Notable here is the maintenance of the old form—with its overarching idea that rank was based primarily on service and secondarily on lineage—in a trivial application to a status dispute between two groups totalling perhaps a hundred people who rarely ever encountered one another. The case also shows that the values and the conception of the social order laid down by the state permeated and were accepted by groups to which these things were not immediately relevant.

The famous petitions that led to the completion of the enserfment of the peasantry in the 1637-48 years are full of explicit and implicit conceptions of the social order. Among the groups mentioned were the state secretaries and clerks, who were condemned by the middle service class petitioners (obsolescent because of their unwillingness to adapt to the requirements of gunpowder warfare) for having enriched themselves through corrupt practices in a manner never before seen in Muscovy and for having adopted a life-style unknown even to members of the great clans—purchasing estates and even building themselves stone structures not befitting their rank. (This is not too unlike sentiments expressed about executives of major corporations that left New York City for exurbia by an executive who stayed in the city: "'It's not right for guys to have such big offices'.")[12] Explicit here is a conception that each rank had certain perquisites and that it was immoral to step out of that mold.

These petitions reveal the second half of the sixteenth century as a Golden Age, a time when we know that the government bureaucracy was just developing. Between that time and 1648 we know that the business of the chancelleries mushroomed, and so, while the years 1633-48 were known to be extraordinarily cor-

11. PSZ 1: 483-85, no. 247.
12. MS, pp. 167-205; William H. Whyte, "End of the Exodus: The Logic of Headquarters City," *New York Magazine*, 20 September 1976: 92.

rupt, it is also possible that regular business increased so much that those handling it were able to enrich themselves from the larger volume alone. Fees remained what they had been at a time when there was not much business, but I have observed that the 1590s were already a time when clerks were nearly the only non-landed elements who could and did buy slaves in the market, indicating that they even then possessed considerable excess income. If the sellers of literacy, the scribes, were able to do so well in the 1590s, the potential for enrichment was vastly increased half a century later. However, those living in the era of cavalry bow-and-arrow warfare seem to have been as out of touch with the reality of "big government" and its clerks as they were with the reality of gunpowder. The petitioners expressed (for posterity) a conception of the social order that probably went back in origin for generations. Until the advent of one aspect of "Westernization," the building of private stone houses, all the classes of Muscovy lived in dwellings that were not unlike one another, all made of wood and looking rather the same. This fact was noted by foreign travelers, who also noted the building of isolated stone residences in Moscow in the seventeenth century. Those residences symbolized the differentiation taking place under the combined pressures of Westernization, bureaucratization, and the formation of a caste society. Aspects of this development were distressing to more conservative elements, who voiced their discontent in collective petitions.

The urban classes served as part of a theoretical continuum of Muscovite society, between the landed service classes and the peasantry. It was theoretical because mobility into and out of the town probably was never very great, and was prohibited by law after 1649. Frequently the townsmen were in conflict with the supposedly salaried lower service classes, usually garrisoned in the towns, over the right to engage in trade and handicraft. While the urban areas of Muscovy in 1550 may have been partially organic economic manifestations of rural prosperity, decades of unwonted peace and good harvests, and relatively benign central governmental policy, all of this was no longer true for the century after, say, 1565. The cities and towns became administrative-military centers for the collection of taxes and the quartering of troops. The townsmen, usually at their own request, were gradually converted from free men expected to earn their own living into taxpayers and government servants existing to be squeezed. The townsmen accepted their prescribed place in the social order in collective petitions of the 1630s and 1640s, insisting only that they be given the wherewithal, through monopolies on commerce and handicrafts, to meet the demands made on them—and their requests were largely granted by the *Ulozhenie* of 1649. When pressed beyond endurance by the tax collector and demands for state service, all categories of townsmen took flight, and some participated in urban uprisings—actions tempered, one suspects, by the realization that the alternatives were little or no better elsewhere, whether in the service class, in the peasantry, across the frontier in the Rzeczpospolita or in Sweden, in Siberia, or on the southern frontier. The only other alternative was self-sale into slavery (either *zakladnichestvo* or *kho-*

lopstvo), and that, too, was forbidden in the mid-seventeenth century. Here, as elsewhere, the categories of 1550 served as a suitable framework for the nightmare of 1650.

Below the townsmen were the peasants. They were gradually enserfed, beginning in the second half of the fifteenth century, when their mobility was restricted to the two-week period around St. George's Day, November 26. A century later, beginning around 1581, some peasants were temporarily forbidden to move even on St. George's Day, and about 1592 this temporary injunction (which lasted until 1906) was extended to all peasants. Simultaneously, a five-year statute of limitations was imposed on suits for the recovery of fugitive serfs, which meant that flight was likely to be successful. It is only with the repeal of the statute of limitations in 1649 that the Russian peasants can be considered to have been fully enserfed: the peasant legally could not move, at any time he could be returned to his rightful lord, and serf dependency extended to both lineal and collateral relatives.[13] Moreover, as the peasant was being bound to the land, his social position was abased in the eyes of the law as it was gradually equated with that of the slave, a point that will be illustrated frequently throughout this work.

The social status, image, and esteem of the Russian peasant were low, even before he became a serf. To my knowledge, the East Slavic peasant was never glorified as a "free yeoman," which helps to explain why it was possible to reduce him to a chattel between the reigns of Ivan IV and Peter the Great. He played no significant part in military life (except in engineering battalions) until the late 1650s, after he had been fully enserfed. The official conception of the peasant's place in the social structure, from the time of the annexation of Novgorod and the creation of the middle service class on, was that his primary function was to provide natural support for the mounted cavalry. Peasants also paid taxes, and their tolerance of tax oppression in its various forms was limited: when sufficiently pressed, those that had lived for generations in the same place would quit it, often for newly opened lands; such movement resulted in the 80 to 90 percent vacancy rates noted, for example, in the Novgorod region at the time of the imposition of the Forbidden Years, 1581-92/3. To make the obvious point: the Muscovite peasant agreed that his function was to support the middle service class cavalry, but not at the expense of his own life.

At the bottom of Muscovite society, in many respects, were the slaves, comprising about 10 percent of the population and thus the second largest social group (after the peasants). The conception of their place in the social order altered considerably in the quarter-millennium under review. The problem is complicated by the continuing, but gradually diminishing, existence of elite slaves who served in the central government-palace administration and in provincial administration until the mid-sixteenth century, in the cavalry until probably the third decade of the seventeenth century, and as estate managers until the time of Peter the Great.

13. Hellie, *Enserfment*, chap. 7.

Many slaves, of course, were military captives and, certainly, the vast majority of them were Russians who sold themselves into slavery.

Muscovy had a ranked, hierarchical social order, a structure which was utilized by the state power under great stress to create a rigidly stratified, caste society. Most notable is the role of the hypertrophic central government in creating and advancing that structure and forcing the various classes to adhere to it and probably to internalize it. The ruling oligarchy desired that government service be the basic principle of society, and because of its control over so much of everyday life it generally succeeded. Opposed to the principle of service were notions of privilege and clan solidarity, even caste solidarity, which occasionally triumphed but did not become the primary conceptions of the social order, or the purpose of the social order, while serious threats to the very existence of the state continued. In a society in which resources were indeed very scarce, the state power used its authority to allocate as much as possible for defense, while a much smaller portion was used for spoils and incentive. The frequency of petitions by individuals for promotion indicates that the incentive system worked, that servicemen understood that meritorious service was the major road to advancement.

The surplus expropriated as spoils by the two to three thousand members of the upper service class and spent on conspicuous consumption and luxuries would not, if returned, have raised significantly the standard of living of the six to nine million at the bottom of the very flat Muscovite social pyramid. Life was cheap, for those at the top of society who did not live to marry off their daughters, and especially for those at the bottom of society who practiced infanticide on a large scale. The government, whose concern in the sixteenth century did not extend beyond defense, to which it added public order and law enforcement in the seventeenth century, did not have the knowledge or resources to worry further about public welfare in the Muscovite era. Social cohesiveness was minimal, with a force recognized as legitimate—the monarchy—providing the ties, both physical and emotional, that held the social order together. Lessened foreign danger and weaker monarchs permitted a diminution of the meritocratic principle and the expression of class pretensions and clan favoritism that got out of hand after the Time of Troubles. At the beginning of the eighteenth century Peter the Great found the Muscovite caste society he had inherited to be odious, so he reformed it by revitalizing the system in what I term the "second service-class revolution" of Russian history.[14] This did little to diminish social inequality but rather forced those who got more of society's product once again to serve for it.

While social cohesiveness was minimal, there was certainly a considerable degree of social consensus. The medieval consensus had a broad base, it seems, but a shallow one. It was probably based on the notion that the townsman or peasant could live in a Rus' principality if he would meet the periodic exactions of

14. Richard Hellie, "The Petrine Army: Continuity, Change, and Impact," *Canadian-American Slavic Studies* 8, no. 2 (Summer 1974): 237-53.

the tax collector. Those taxes included the old tribute (*dan'*), plus new ones. What the taxpayer expected in exchange is not clear. He certainly did not expect much conflict-resolution service, for that was a dyadic process in which the government's interest was its fee (note the simplicity of the 1497 *Sudebnik*). One may judge that the Eastern Slavs primarily expected their rulers to provide defense, a judgment based on the fact that nearly all social disorders prior to 1547 were provoked by a failure of the ruling elite with their retinues to provide such defense. Except as noncombatants in engineering battalions, ordinary persons had little experience in military affairs. Religion hardly played a substantial role in the medieval consensus, for even townsmen were largely pagans until the mid-fourteenth century, and after that there were hardly enough churches for all the Muscovites.

After the mid-sixteenth century, the social consensus was certainly deeper than it had been and was based on many more elements. To what extent the various categories of slaves shared in this consensus with the free (later enserfed) peasants and townsmen is something that I have been unable to determine. The symbols of Muscovite Christianity, with its emphasis on fear and obedience, provided one of the elements in the consensus and became gradually implanted in the minds of many of the populace. Christian holidays, usurping the pagan festivals, provided a sense of unity and relief from the boredom of quotidian life on the eastern European plain. Frederick Douglass, the former slave and great black writer of nineteenth-century America, noted about holidays that they "were among the most effective means in the hands of the slaveholders of keeping down the spirit of insurrection among the slaves." Had there not been relatively frequent holidays, Douglass observed, "the rigors of bondage would have become too severe for endurance, and the slave would have been forced to a dangerous desperation."[15] As the decades wore on in Rus' and awareness of Christianity increased while the masses were abased, holidays certainly assumed a roughly similar function to that noted by Douglass. This Christianization of the Muscovites was based, as the great historian V. O. Kliuchevskii pointed out long ago, almost exclusively on visual symbols and rituals, not on "content" or theology. The government was able to profit from the increasing hold of the church on the sentiments of the masses, until Nikon changed the symbols in the 1650s and thus, quite unintentionally, induced the populace to revolt against both the established church and the government. Moreover, he joined other churchmen in taking much of the "fun" out of holidays by persecuting popular music, minstrels, and other carnival aspects that had done much to alleviate the tedium of provincial life. We should note that, while the full Byzantinization of the Russian church did not occur until the seventeenth century, the Orthodox establishment had been able to enforce compliance with many of its norms (particularly those of family law and structure) by the sixteenth century. While one may

15. In Eugene D. Genovese, *Roll, Jordan, Roll*, p. 577.

question whether lower class cohabitation commenced only after a church marriage ceremony, before or even after 1550, one may be certain that such ceremonies (along with baptisms and funerals) became increasingly frequent as time went on. This elemental church presence no doubt had an impact on other areas, particularly that of the creation of the nuclear family, which was the dominant form of primary social organization in the 1550-1650 period, and probably for long before that.

Between 1450 and 1725, the relationship between the ruling authorities and the masses evolved from a weak, distant and perhaps consensual one based on taxes paid for defense to an efficient, coerced, nonreciprocal, and often nonconsensual relationship enforced by efficient organs of social control. Ever alert for new opportunities to enhance its legitimacy, the government in the quarter-millennium under review continuously expanded the area of its social control, both in breadth and in depth: social-estate (caste) membership, geographical mobility, range of choice in occupation and marriage, morals, possible intellectual horizon, as well as deviant behavior. Metaphorically, the wild Russian bear was put on a chain and muzzled. At the beginning of the period under review, a member of the lower classes had full legal opportunity to choose his social station and vocation, and might rise to a position of some authority. Limitations on opportunity were of a "sociological" rather than of a "legal" nature. After the mid-seventeenth century, such opportunity was absolutely out of the question. In the social order of the Muscovite service state, station and prestige were increasingly allotted by the central authority. One's service position to a large extent determined his prestige and the goods and services (and slaves) he could command. Almost the reverse was true for the urban taxpayers and peasants supporting the service classes, for whom the problem became one of trying to keep as much as possible of their own production for their own consumption, of thwarting the demands of tax collector and seignorial lord by appearing to diminish output and by concealing all assets and surplus. The government did everything in its power to control such disobedience as it strove to make itself the sole agency of social coordination.

Definitions of Slavery

What has just been described was the setting in which Muscovite slavery evolved in the period between 1450 and 1725. Let us now proceed to a definition of slavery, and conclude with a discussion of the international slave trade at the time.

The type of societies in which slavery appears is well known: those which have progressed beyond the most primitive level, and in which there are social differentiation (stratification), an economic surplus, a perceived labor shortage, free land (more generally, open resources), and some form of centralized governmental institutions (willing to enforce slave laws).[16] Most of these conditions were necessary for the existence of slavery, and rarely if ever was just one or two of them sufficient to determine its development.[17] Both medieval and early modern Rus' had achieved this level of middle-range social complexity, and so one would expect to find slavery there.

There is almost no sensible definition of a slave or the institution that would not encompass the Muscovite case. A few illustrations should suffice. Slavery is "a species of dependent labor [performed by a nonfamily member] and not the genus."[18] (I shall not go into the other forms of dependent labor—serfs, peons, debt pawns, indentured servants—which have been studied by others.)[19] "The superior has considerably more long-term legal rights than the subordinate, not only with regard to participation in political decision-making, but also with regard to participation in all kinds of social activities as well."[20] "Slavery is the institutionalized alienation from the rights of labor and kinship, the rewards of labor and natal descent."[21] "The essence of slavery lies in the control by others of the physical reproduction of the slave."[22] The slave's person is the property of another man, and his will is subject to his owner's authority. "Slavery is the legal institutionalization of persons as property."[23] A slave is a person deprived of the right of personal liberty, which "consists in the power of locomotion, of

16. Philip D. Curtin, "Slavery and Empire," *Comparative Perspectives on Slavery in New World Plantation Societies* (= vol. 292 [1977] of *Annals of the New York Academy of Sciences*): 7; Stanley Engerman, "The Development of Plantation Systems and Slave Societies," *Annals*, p. 66.

17. The open-resource theory advanced by Herman Merivale (1841), E. G. Wakefield (1849), A. Loria (1853), H. J. Nieboer (1900 and 1910), and Evsey Domar (1970), which holds that slavery is highly possible in the presence of free land and a gentry, that slavery as an industrial system can only exist where there is still free land, has been questioned by Frederick L. Pryor, "A Comparative Study of Slave Societies," *Journal of Comparative Economics* 1, no. 1 (March 1977): 37. Orlando Patterson has attempted to show that the correlation is even negative ("The Structural Origins of Slavery: A Critique of the Nieboer-Domar Hypothesis from a Comparative Perspective," *Annals*, pp. 12-34). A critique with a similar conclusion about the lack of predictive powers of the Nieboer thesis was made by C. Baks, J. C. Breman, and A. T. J. Nooij, "Slavery as a System of Production in Tribal Society," *Bijdragen tot de Taal-, Land- end Volkenkunde* 122 (1966): 90-109. For another view, see Sidney W. Mintz, "The So-Called World System: Local Initiative and Local Response," *Dialectical Anthropology* 2 (1977): 257, 268.

18. Moses I. Finley, "Slavery," *Encyclopedia of the Social Sciences* 14 (1968): 308. The material in brackets is from Pryor, p. 27.

19. I. J. Gelb, "From Freedom to Slavery," *Bayerische Akademie der Wissenschaften. Philosophisch-historische Klasse. Abhandlungen. N.s. no.* 75 (Munich 1972): 81-92.

20. Pryor, pp. 27-28.

21. Patterson, p. 15. On this subject, also see Wiens, p. 307.

22. Wyatt MacGaffey, review of *L'Esclavage en Afrique précoloniale*, ed. Claude Meillassoux (Paris: François Maspero, 1975), in *African Economic History* 5 (Spring 1978): 51.

23. Arthur Tuden and Leonard Plotnicov, *Social Stratification in Africa* (New York: The Free Press, 1970), pp. 11-12.

changing situation or moving one's person to whatsoever place one's own inclination may direct, without imprisonment or restraint, unless by due course of law."[24] Finally, the slave is usually kinless, has no ethnic ties or lineage, is an "outsider," a "marginal individual," a person who approximates "basic strangeness" to the dominant social group.[25]

Throughout history, slavery has been primarily of two types, productive slavery and household, patriarchal, or domestic slavery. There have also been other types, such as temple slavery, state slavery, and military slavery, but they have been relatively rare, and, by only a slight forcing of the issue, probably could be considered as varieties of household slavery. In productive slavery, the dominant impression created by the system is that slavery existed primarily as a profit-oriented institution to produce commodities for the market in mines or on plantations. Productive slavery as such was relatively infrequent, occurring primarily in classical Greece (specifically Athens) and Rome, and the post-Columbian New World. Other examples can be found, such as Iraq in the ninth century, perhaps among the Kwakiutl Indians, and a few rice-producing areas in Africa (prior to its internal colonization by Europeans, Arabs, and others who introduced plantations based on slave labor producing for the market), but such cases are few and far between. The dominant form of slavery has been household slavery, which is what one would expect to find in Muscovy. While domestic slaves sometimes were engaged in work outside the household, that was not their primary function. They often were a consumption-oriented status elevator for their owners, who in many societies invested much of their surplus in slaves. While some household slaves participated in harvesting, their primary function was that of menials for their owners. In many slave societies, patriarchal slaves often merged in varying degrees with the families of their owners. To the apparently very limited extent that this was true in early modern Russia, Muscovite slaves were the forebears of the well-known house serfs of imperial Russia.

With the Muscovite case in mind, it is important to clear up a few general misconceptions about slavery arising from our experience with the abnormal American situation. First, slavery is not necessarily involuntary. "Given the prospects of an economically precarious life as a free person and an economically secure life as a slave, it may be quite rational to choose the latter."[26] Not all slaves are miserable, and not all of them desire emancipation. Not all slaves necessarily oc-

24. Blackstone, cited in Rose, *Documentary History*, pp. 205-06.

25. For the concept of "outsider," see Finley, "Slavery." On "marginality," see Suzanne Miers and Igor Kopytoff, *Slavery in Africa*, p. 14 ff. On "basic strangeness," see Maria W. Piers, *Infanticide* (New York: Norton, 1978), p. 38. James L. Watson emphasizes the property aspect of slavery and the marginal status of slaves (*Asian and African Systems*, p. 4). The Russian varieties of slavery will be discussed further in chapter 2, but for a translation of *kholopstvo* as "slavery" in the sixteenth century, see AIS-ZR (1978), p. 111. Peter the Great occasionally used the most well-known word for slave, *rab* (PSZ 6: 302, no. 3708).

26. Pryor, "Comparative Study," p. 26.

cupy the lowest social status in a society. Elite slaves may have a higher social status than almost anyone else in a society except the ruler and his oligarchs, and even an ordinary slave may have more social esteem than an ordinary freeman if the former's owner enjoys an elevated social status. Finally, slavery is rarely if ever characterized by totally unlimited powers over the slave by his owner.[27]

This book is about slavery, but the reader should be aware of the fact that early modern Muscovites had a notion of what "freedom" was. This was expressed in the spring of 1651 by some Russians who refused to continue on an embassy to Georgia: "We are free people, whither we wish, there we go. . . . We are free people, we do not have to obey you." (*My de liudi volnye, kudy khotim, tudy i edim. . . . My de liudi volnye, a vas de ne slushaem*.)[28] The right to move about as one wishes and the absence of total subordination are recognized elements of freedom almost everywhere, and Muscovite slaves explicitly were denied both.

Early Modern Russia and the International Slave Trade

Between 1450 and 1725 the world witnessed many changes in slavery. The most notable were the abolition of slavery throughout most of Europe and the introduction of black slavery into the New World on a massive scale. To the east and south of early modern Russia, slavery in the Islamic world continued unabated, and the attempt to stop slave raiding by Turkic peoples, which dispatched hundreds of thousands of Russians into the international slave trade, was a major cause of the Muscovite garrison state. Comparisons with Africa are fruitful, for Africa and Slavdom have been the two chief sources of slaves for a longer period of time than have any other areas. Philip Curtin has described the two areas as "population reservoirs."[29]

In the Middle Ages the Turkic, Iranian, Ugrian, and Slavic peoples inhabiting the Caspian Sea and Black Sea drainage basins expended great effort to capture each other as human booty to sell as slaves.[30] Slavs appeared in the international slave trade about the tenth century, when, in Germany, the word *sclavus* began to compete with the Latin word *servus*, and an Arabic equivalent, *siklābi* (pl., *sakāliba*), appeared in Moslem Spain.[31] East Slavs felt no compunction about

27. Ibid., pp. 27, 30; Reuben Levy, *The Social Structure of Islam* (Cambridge: At the University Press, 1957), pp. 86-87.

28. M. Polievktov, ed., *Posol'stvo Stol'nika Tolochanova i D'iaka Ievleva v Imeretiiu 1650-1652 gg.* (Tiflis: Izd-vo Tiflisskogo Universiteta, 1926), p. 35.

29. Curtin, "Slavery and Empire," p. 9. For a discussion of the impact of slave raiding on political centralization in Africa, see Philip Burnham, "Raiders and Traders in Adamawa: Slavery as a Regional System," in Watson, ed., *Asian and African Systems*, pp. 59-64.

30. Zimin, *Kholopy*, p. 12; Verlinden, *Colonization*, pp. 31, 94.

31. Verlinden, *Colonization*, p. 35; Charles Verlinden, "Encore sur les origines de sclavus = esclave," in his *L'esclavage dans l'Europe médiévale*. Vol 2, *Italie—Colonies italiennes du Levant. Levant latin—Empire byzantin* (Gent: Rijksuniversiteit te Gent, 1977), pp. 999-1010.

dispatching each other into the international slave trade, but this practice was drastically curtailed with the consolidation of the Muscovite state at the end of the fifteenth century.[32] Around the mid-sixteenth century the Russians ceased providing other Slavs as slaves to the Tatars.[33] No such consolidation occurred in Africa, where, down to the 1930s, the various tribes continued to raid one another to capture slaves both for domestic use and to sell to outsiders. Moreover, in spite of the picture presented in Alex Haley's *Roots*, white slave traders almost never entered the interior in pursuit of prey but rather purchased their cargo from Africans at the ocean front; coastal Africans would not allow Europeans either into or through their own countries. On the other hand, the Tatars who raided Muscovy always penetrated Rus' on their own initiative, not by invitation, and the Muscovite government made the greatest possible effort to prevent Tatar incursions.[34]

On Russian slaves in the late medieval Italian world, see Verlinden's *L'esclavage. . . Italie*, pp. 221-24, 311-16, 470-71, 622-42. Omeljan Pritsak properly ascribes a major role to the international slave trade in the rise of the Kievan Russian state. However, one might question his apparent derivation of the name of the Slavs from an eighth-century "Mediterranean term *Saqlab = Sclav*" (*The Origin of Rus'* [Cambridge, Mass.: Harvard Ukrainian Research Institute, 1975], p. 18).

32. A. P. Novosel'tsev and V. T. Pashuto, "Vneshniaia torgovlia Drevnei Rusi," *Istoriia SSSR* 12, no. 3 (May-June 1967): 83, 85, 88, 95, 105, 107; A. L. Khoroshkevich, *Russkoe gosudarstvo v sisteme mezhdunarodnykh otnoshenii kontsa XV-nachala XVI v.* (Moscow: Nauka, 1980), pp. 30-32. Frequent references to the slave trade are scattered throughout Janet L. B. Martin, "Treasure of The Land of Darkness: A Study of the Fur Trade and Its Significance for Medieval Russia (X-XVI Centuries)" (Ph.D. diss., University of Chicago, 1980). Americans sometimes begin their legal studies of slavery with the case of a Russian slave in England in 1569, when, "in the eleventh of Elizabeth, one Cartwright brought a slave from Russia, and would scourge him, for which he was questioned; and it was resolved, That England was too pure an air for slaves to breathe in" (Catterall 1: 9). To my knowledge, the nationality of Cartwright's slave is unknown. It could have been a Russian, a Tatar, a Finn, a Pole, or a member of any of several other ethnicities.

33. P. O. Bobrovskii, *Perekhod Rossii k reguliarnoi armii* (St. Petersburg, 1885). The extent to which this ban was heeded may be questioned. A 1665 law, in response to a complaint from the governor of Kasimov who had seen going downstream on the Oka "Lithuanians" who had been sold in Moscow to Persians and Cherkassy of the Caucasus, brought a prohibition of the writing up of such sale transations and their approval in the Foreign Affairs Chancellery. The "Lithuanians" were probably booty acquired by the Muscovites in the Thirteen Years War (1654-67), brought to Moscow, and then sold to those particular Muslims. The captives were probably both non-Slavic Lithuanians and Slavic Poles (PSZ 1: 611, no. 374).

34. Rosemary Arnold, "A Port of Trade: Whydah on the Guinea Coast," in *The Slave Economies: Volume 1, Historical and Theoretical Perspectives*, ed. Eugene D. Genovese (New York: John Wiley & Sons, 1973), pp. 104-24; Joseph C. Miller, "Legal Portuguese Slaving from Angola. Some Preliminary Indications of Volume and Direction, 1760-1830," in Emmer, Mettas, and Nardin, p. 135. For a discussion of the "backwoodsmen caravan operators" (*sertanejos*) of Angola who "carried the European presence much further into the interior

The number of Africans sent into the international slave trade has been calculated at 10 million across the Atlantic between 1450 and 1870, 10 million across the Sahara between 850 and 1890, and 8 million from East Africa between 650 and 1905.[35] Alan Fisher has discussed the number of East Slavs captured by the Crimean Tatars and dispatched into the international slave trade for the years from 1468 to 1694, but arrived at no general totals. He also has some earlier figures, such as 2,000 slaves a year in the fourteenth century, with that figure rising in the fifteenth. Slave raiding into Muscovy reached crisis proportions after 1475, when the Ottomans took over the Black Sea slave trade from the Genoese and the Crimeans began slave raiding as a major industry, especially between 1514 and 1654. In the 1570s close to 20,000 slaves a year were being sold in Kafa, ten times the number that had passed through there in the 1540s.[36] In 1589, taxes were collected on the sale of 4,000 imported slaves in Istanbul alone.[37] For the first half of the seventeenth century, some have calculated that Muscovy lost an average of 4,000 slaves a year and that the Poles may have had losses at an even higher rate throughout the entire seventeenth century. Catherine the Great spoke of annual losses of 20,000.[38] No doubt she had in mind the number initially seized, not the much smaller number that ever made it to the sale block. Both African and Slavic losses can only be described as staggering.

While the impact of Muscovy's massive, involuntary involvement in the international slave trade on domestic political and social life is well known (the garrison state and a near-caste society were both second-order consequences of Muscovy's attempt to meet its defense needs against slave raiding), that participation seems to have had little impact on early modern Russian slavery itself. While there were Tatar slaves in Muscovy, the institution was shaped primarily by the fact that the vast majority of the human chattels in Muscovy were native Russians. This seems to be similar to the interpretation now forming about African

---

than was generally true in West Africa," see idem, "Some Aspects of the Commercial Organization of Slaving at Luanda, Angola—1760-1830," in Gemery and Hogendorn, pp. 5, 89-95. For governmental interviews of the Russian survivors whose family members and relatives were kidnapped in Tatar slave raids, see S. I. Kotkov, *Lingvisticheskoe istochnikovedenie i istoriia russkogo iazyka* (Moscow: Nauka, 1980), pp. 97-99, 142-43.

35. Curtin, "Slave Trade," p. 73; Ralph Austen, "From the Atlantic to the Indian Ocean: European Abolition, African Slave Trade, and Asian Economic Structure" (Paper presented at the Symposium on the Abolition of the Atlantic Slave Trade, the University of Aarhus, September 1978).

36. Halil Inalcik, "Servile Labor in the Ottoman Empire," in *The Mutual Effects of the Islamic and Judeo-Christian Worlds: The East European Pattern*, ed. Abraham Ascher, Tibor Halasi-Kun, and Bela K. Kiraly (New York: Brooklyn College Press, 1979), pp. 39-40.

37. Alan W. Fisher, "Chattel Slave Procurement in the Ottoman Empire" (Paper presented at the Twelfth Annual Meeting of the Middle East Studies Association, Ann Arbor, November 1978), p. 16.

38. Alan W. Fisher, "Muscovy and the Black Sea Trade," *Canadian-American Slavic Studies* 6, no. 4 (1972): 582, 593.

slavery. Before the appearance of the Miers and Kopytoff and Meillassoux volumes, some scholars claimed that slavery in Africa was a response to the international slave trade, but it is now obvious that slavery was an old domestic institution that was adapted for supplying the international market when it developed. The consequences of the massive losses of population for Africa are not as clear as they are for Muscovy. Philip Curtin even has suggested that the sixteenth-century contact with the New World led to the introduction of two new crops, manioc and maize, which helped to increase fertility and sustain a rise in population greater than the losses from the export trade.[39] Muscovy got nothing comparable from the Tatars.

Next, there is the matter of the abolition of domestic slavery in Muscovy while the international trade continued. Frederick Pryor has advanced the proposition that "slavery is less likely to occur if societies nearby are not carrying on a slave trade."[40] The reverse of the statement is also probably true, namely, that slavery is more likely to occur if societies nearby are carrying on a slave trade—which the Crimeans were until Catherine annexed them, long after the abolition of slavery by Peter the Great. Nevertheless, the proposition has not necessarily been refuted, for serfdom came to resemble slavery. However, no one would link the abolition of serfdom (or even its decline after 1797) with the liquidation of the Crimean Khanate. Here Russia seems to part company with Africa, for in Africa the abolition of domestic slavery was linked to the abolition of the international slave trade, although domestic slavery did outlast the international slave trade.

Finally, there is much evidence indicating that the Muscovites had considerable knowledge of the slavery practices of surrounding peoples. That information came from three basic types of sources: official dealings, written monuments such as legal codes, and the reports of individuals ransomed or fugitive from slavery in other lands. The use of that information varied widely, but certainly Muscovite slavery was "modeled" after none of the other systems. A few illustrations will suffice.

The Rusy and Russians had dealings of varying intimacies with Turkic peoples from the time of their arrival on the east European plain in the second half of the first millennium A.D. (see chapter 12). Among those Turkic peoples were the Bulgars and Khazars, who maintained large numbers of slaves, carried on a thriving slave trade, and may have served as a link between the practices of the Hellenistic world and Rus'. Later the Rusy had regular contacts with the Pechenegs, Polovtsy, and Mongols, all of whom gained much of their income by capturing East Slavs and putting them into the slave trade. In the period covered by this book,

39. Curtin, "Slave Trade," p. 79. For a discussion of whether the absolute monarchy of Whydah was a response to slave raiding, see Albert van Dantzig's "Effects of the Atlantic Slave Trade on Some West African Societies" in the Emmer, Mettas, and Nardin collection (p. 259).

40. Pryor, "Comparative Study," p. 32.

regular relations were maintained with the Crimea, and the early (around 1500) Muscovite records are full of references to Crimean slaves. Those slaves belonged largely to the khan, his wife, sultans, princes, and other members of the royal family, and were known to the Russians primarily because of their involvement in diplomatic activities as emissaries, aides, and the like. An archer is also mentioned.[41] All of these, typical for the Islamic world, had their counterparts in Muscovy.

The legal norms of Byzantine and Lithuanian slavery were well known in Muscovy because their respective legal codes, the *Procheiros Nomos* (867-79) and the *Statute* (1588), had relatively wide circulation and were materials the seventeenth-century chancelleries consulted while attempting to resolve trouble cases. This borrowing will be discussed in chapters 2 through 8, where it will be shown how the early modern Russians adapted those alien norms to local conditions.

Unquestionably the best source of information about neighboring slave practices was Russians who had been chattel and somehow managed to return to their homeland. In the early years, the major device for the recovery of slaves seems to have been diplomatic protest. For example, in 1500, sixty-four Russian merchants were seized by Crimean Tatars and Azov and Volga cossacks, and then sold into slavery in Azov and Kafa. Moscow filed a protest with the Crimean government, which apparently made a good-faith effort to retrieve the men, but only thirty-five could be located.[42] Over 150 years later, in 1661, the Kalmyks, who had migrated to the Volga steppe region from Mongolia a few decades earlier, agreed to return to Muscovy any Russian captives they acquired in combat with the Crimean Tatars, and a dozen years later the Kalmyks agreed to allow the ransom of any Muscovite captives they held and the transit back to Muscovy from Bukhara, Urgench, and Khiva of Orthodox Christians who had been held as slaves and released.[43] After 1551, the Moscow government by official policy ransomed

41. SIRIO 41 (1884): 30, 42-43, 52-53, 58, 64, 70, 84, 104-7, 115-16, 121-22, 124, 126, 134, 138, 142, 144, 146-57, 160-61, 164, 171-73, 176, 178, 183, 208, 216, 236, 401, 403, 415, 420, 441, 542-43, 549, 722, 731-32, 744.

42. Ibid., p. 332.

43. PSZ 1: 531-32, 925, nos. 300, 540. Russians also learned about slavery from those who managed to communicate their plight to Muscovite ambassadors abroad. For the case of icon painter Ivan Danilov enslaved in Georgia in the early 1650s and forced to paint frescoes on the wall of a Christian church there, see Polievktov, *Posol'stvo Tolochanova*, pp. 44-45. A list of seventy-seven Muscovite subjects who had been in captivity in Bukhara, Balkh, and Khiva and returned to Muscovy in 1678 was published in *Materialy po istorii Uzbekskoi, Tadzhikskoi i Turkmenskoi SSR*, pt. 1, *Torgovlia s Moskovskim gosudarstvom i mezhdunarodnoe polozhenie Srednei Azii v XVI-XVII vv.* (Leningrad: AN SSSR, 1932), pp. 386-97. The list gives the name of the returnee, his social position (most were peasants and Tatars, but there were many others as well), whence they came (primarily the Middle Volga region), how many years they had been in captivity (an average of fourteen years, with a range of from four to sixty years), by whom and under what circumstances they were enslaved (primarily by Bashkirs, while the individuals were farming), where they had spent their captivity (Central Asian cities), and how they came to be manumitted (many were ransomed by a

as many Russians as it could, expending tens of thousands of rubles, and, as we noted, the *Ulozhenie* set up a scale of sums that would be paid to free subjects from heathen captivity.[44] In addition to those ransomed, others managed to flee and returned home. Both categories were intensively interrogated upon returning to Muscovy, once at the frontier and again in the capital. The interrogations had two major purposes, to gather political and military intelligence, and to uncover those who were returning as foreign agents. The interrogations also brought out the nature and conditions of slavery in other countries.

For example, in 1656 the Military Chancellery in Moscow heard from Fil'ka Isaev Novokreshchenov how he had been captured in battle on the Don, taken to Azov, and sold to a janissary by the name of Delibaglit. Delibaglit took Novokreshchenov to Istanbul and sold him to a pasha of the galleys, one Kasymbey, and he rowed in the galleys for over three years, along with a dozen Russians, Belorussians, and Lithuanians. According to Novokreshchenov's account, the galley slaves murdered all thirty-five Turks on the vessel, and then Fil'ka got off at Venice. From there he went to Malta, Florence, Rome, Austria, Hungary, Poland, and back to Muscovy through Kiev.[45] No doubt such returnees told everyone they met for years thereafter about their experiences abroad, thus widely diffusing throughout Muscovy knowledge about slavery in other lands. This probably had a greater impact on generating social-consensus support for the government's defense measures than on the institution of slavery in Muscovy, although both are subjects that have not been explored. For example, the Russian language now contains the word *iasyr* (*iasyr'*, *esyr'*), "slave" or "captive," found in all Turkic languages, a word that was current in the Russian usage of the Muscovite period. In spite of that fact, the word seems not to have attracted the attention of lexicographers until the middle of the nineteenth century.[46]

Certainly the presence of slavery among neighbors helped to legitimize and perpetuate it in early modern Russia. While all the evidence may not be in, it certainly appears now as though only foreign legal norms had a measurable impact in Muscovy. The impact of the demise of slavery in countries to the west of Russia on the Muscovite institution itself will be discussed in chapter 18.

Russian ambassador, Vasilii Daudov, some were ransomed by others or "themselves," some were just set free by their owners); an average sum of 47 rubles was paid for each of the thirty-four persons for whom a ransom amount was listed.

44. A. A. Novosel'skii, *Bor'ba moskovskogo gosudarstva s tatarami v pervoi polovine XVII veka* (Moscow-Leningrad: Akademiia Nauk SSSR, 1948), pp. 440-42.

45. AMG 2: 549, no. 922; see also AMG 1: 628, no. 868.

46. E. N. Shipova, comp., *Slovar' tiurkizmov v russkom iazyke* (Alma-Ata: Nauka, 1976), p. 442; Polievktov, p. 42.

Part I

The Law of Slavery

2. Legal Varieties of Muscovite Slavery

Slavery is first and foremost a legal institution, and almost everywhere the law has devoted considerable attention to the subject. Muscovy was no exception. Moreover, law in general was a crucial indicator and instrument in early modern Russia because of the increasingly hypertrophic nature of the state power, which used law to effect its ends. Oligarchic government was the central feature of Muscovite life because no other institutions could restrain the government, no other institutions could command the power, allegiance, and popular feeling of legitimacy government enjoyed. The Muscovite government's objectives were similar to those of nearly all governments, regardless of their form or basis: defense of the national territory, maintenance of the position of the ruling elements, and preservation of domestic order. The government used law in the pursuit of these general goals by having it lay down rules for conduct; law has also been used intelligently by nearly all historians who make any attempt to understand Muscovite history.

Chapters 2-8 will lay out the principles of the Muscovite law of slavery in a comparative context to show that Muscovite legislators shared the concerns of lawgivers in other slave systems. Similarities and differences between Muscovite and other laws of slavery will be pointed out, and explanations will be advanced for them.

Muscovy was squarely situated in the Roman-Byzantine legal tradition in which property and its use were subject to public regulation. In the "Third Rome," with considerably less sophistication and splendor than in the first two Romes, the writer of the laws joined the soldier and the priest in serving the institutional ends defined by the oligarchy. The centrality of the Muscovite legislators' concern over slavery is statistically obvious when one bears in mind the fact that perhaps nearly a fifth of the 967 articles of the *Ulozhenie* of 1649 touch upon it. Chapter 20 of the code, on slavery, with 119 articles, is second in length only to chapter 10, on court procedure, with 287.[1] As we shall see, the institution of slave law was highly dynamic in Muscovy, with many decisions supporting and clarifying a regular stream of decrees. The general ignorance among modern historians of these developments is understandable, considering the subsequent importance of slavery's heir, serfdom, which eclipsed slavery in the minds of scholars.

---

1. Man'kov, *Ulozhenie*, p. 111. For a translation of chapter 20 of the *Ulozhenie*, see Richard Hellie, *Muscovite Society* (Chicago: The University of Chicago College Syllabus Division, 1967), pp. 255-99.

The Sources of Slave Law

First, a few words are in order about the slave laws themselves, many of which are integral parts of major law codes. At the beginning of our period, and down to about 1550, the major operational law code was the expanded version of the *Russkaia Pravda*, which began to be compiled in 1016 and was put together in its near final version in the mid-twelfth century. Later versions gradually were changed to reflect changing conditions and are sometimes known as the abridged version. As we shall see, the basic principles of slave law existing in the later fifteenth century differed little from those prevailing in Kiev many centuries earlier. The early law codes are so incomplete in their coverage of the normal trouble cases arising in any slave system that there must have been a relatively large body of common law developed for handling such instances that we simply know nothing about.[2] Much like students of U.S. slave law who note that in many respects sovereignty for the slave resided in the master, and thus lament the absence of thorough study of plantation codes, Russianists too may note that it would be entirely appropriate sociologically and anthropologically to study the popular notions of master-slave relationships. Americanists may some day determine those infractions for which slaveowners resolved that their chattel deserved so many strokes of the lash, but students of Muscovy probably will have to be content with such expediencies as projecting nineteenth-century norms (yet to be determined, however) back a quarter of a millennium into the past.

In 1497 appeared the first *Sudebnik*, primarily a brief compendium of 67 articles for court administration in which actual legal norms were present relatively incidentally. In 1550 the *Sudebnik* was expanded to 100 articles, and then in 1589 a version of the *Sudebnik* was compiled for the Dvina Land (White Sea littoral) area that had 231 articles. During the Time of Troubles a *Composite Sudebnik* was put together, probably during the brief reign of False Dmitrii I, ca. 1606, which reflected Lithuanian and Polish influence by dividing the code into twenty-five chapters containing 167 articles.[3]

During the era of the second and later *Sudebniki* the Muscovite chancellery system began to develop, and these *prikazy* kept their own records. Initially, slavery matters were handled by the Treasury, and new legislative norms were kept track of there in the Registry of Laws of the Treasurers' Jurisdiction. Sometime around 1571 the Slavery Chancellery was formed, and it began to keep its own records. One of its major acts was the promulgation of the 1597 slavery code, which, inter alia, formally changed the fundamental nature of Muscovite

2. S. V. Rozhdestvenskii, "Sel'skoe naselenie Moskovskogo gosudarstva v XVI-XVII vekakh," in M. V. Dovnar-Zapol'skii, ed., *Russkaia istoriia v ocherkakh i stat'iakh* (Kiev, 1912), 3: 67; Kolycheva, *Kholopstvo*, p. 202.

3. B. D. Grekov, ed., *Sudebniki XV-XVII vekov* (Moscow-Leningrad: AN SSSR, 1952); PRP 3: 346-73; PRP 4: 231-60, 413-42, 482-65.

slavery while mandating the compulsory registration of all slaves, both those in the possession of the slaveowner and those fugitive slaves the owner still wanted to claim. This compulsory registration, undertaken at no cost to the slaveowners, generated a large portion of the extant slavery contracts and other documentation available to the twentieth-century historian. A 1607 statute promulgated by Tsar Vasilii Shuiskii did much to set the tone for later Muscovite slave law.[4]

The statute book of the Slavery Chancellery became the basis of chapter 20 of the *Ulozhenie* of 1649, the most important codification of Russian law prior to 1830, and probably one of the most important codifications in human history. Most relevant for the study of Muscovite legal and social history, the *Ulozhenie* was the second or third nonreligious, civil book published in Muscovy, and its initial printing of 1,200 copies was immediately sold out. A second printing of 1,200 copies was ordered, and it too sold out rapidly. The consequence was that the document became widely known almost immediately, and, as will be shown throughout this work, was the post-1649 legal reference for everyone, from the tsar down to the person trying to gain his freedom from slavery.[5]

Legislation on slavery after 1649 survives only incidentally, most often in orders to fugitive-slave catchers. Regrettably, the archives of the Slavery Chancellery were burned on May 15, 1682, during the uprising of the *strel'tsy*, probably by fugitive slaves who wanted to suppress the records of their former status. Some of the post-1649 legislation was compiled by the Speranskii commission in its *Complete Collected Laws of the Russian Empire* (1830). As we shall see, that was the period of the decline of slavery, when serfdom increasingly resembled slavery. Slaves and serfs were often mentioned together in the legal material of that era.[6]

It is difficult to quantify the importance of slavery for Muscovite law. I have already noted the significance of slavery in the law compendia. Another approach would be to see what proportion of the actual practice of the courts involved slaves in one way or another. This can be done for one organ, the Novgorod Judicial Chancellery, in the years 1593/94 and 1594/95 (the Muscovite year after 1492 ran from September 1 through August 31).[7] (See table 2.1.) Thus it appears that slavery occupied about as much time of the courts as it did space in the written law, and was a major concern of the judicial system.

4. The *Ukaznaia kniga Vedomstva kaznacheev* and the *Ukaznaia kniga Prikaza kholop'ego suda* are in M. V. Vladimirskii-Budanov, *Khristomatiia po istorii russkogo prava*, pt. 3 (Iaroslavl': Tipografiia G. Fal'k, 1875), pp. 1-41, 90-115. For the 1597 law on slavery and the 1607 decree on slaves and peasants, see MS, pp. 137-41, 247-54.

5. PRP 6; M. N. Tikhomirov, and P. P. Epifanov, *Sobornoe Ulozhenie 1649 g.* (Moscow: MGU, 1961). The *Ulozhenie* is primarily a compilation of chancellery practice after the great Moscow fire of 3 May 1626, which destroyed many of the central government's records.

6. PRP 7: 185-206.

7. AIuB 2: 176-87, no. 139.

TABLE 2.1

Categories of Cases Handled by the Novgorod Judicial Chancellery in the Years 1593/94 (7102) and 1594/95 (7103)

	Years	
Type of Case	7102	7103
1. Felonies: murder, robbery, assault, theft	27.2%	23.5%
2. Peasants–disputes over their possession	9.1	11.8
3. Immovable property: land, city property	9.1	4.9
4. Other: debts (which could lead to debt slavery if not repaid), insults, etc.	3.0	20.6
5. Not specified (usually only the litigants were listed)	42.4	18.6
6. Slavery–mostly ownership disputes	9.1	20.6
Cases in which slaves are known to have been involved either as litigants or agents in types 1 through 5	12.1	2.0
N =	33	102

Source: AIuB 2(1864): 176-87, no. 139.

The Origins of Slave Law

Throughout this work attempts will be made to determine the origins of Russian practices. In the legal sphere, the Muscovite practices were of Byzantine, Lithuanian, and native origins. Byzantine sources were the bases of approximately 10 percent of the Muscovite laws on slavery and usually concerned the nexus between chattel status and the family or the church. It is not yet known precisely when these became Russian norms, but the work of Ia. N. Shchapov (following V. N. Beneshevich) indicates the late thirteenth century as the earliest time. There was a second Byzantinization of law (and even of other practices as well) in the 1640s and 1650s, in connection with attempts to purify the Russian Othodox church and the publication of the Church Statute Book (*Kormchaia kniga*) in 1653 as part of the Nikonian ascendancy. These norms had the same roots as did the Iberian law used in the New World.[8]

West Russian norms (themselves often originating still further west) entered Muscovite slave law via the *Lithuanian Statute* of 1588. While a very few of its norms seem to have penetrated Muscovite practice before the Smolensk War (1632-34), it was increasingly used as a handbook for solving trouble cases in the chancelleries in the 1630s, a form of "Westernization," as it were. Articles

8. Edwin Hanson Freshfield, ed., *A Manual of Roman Law. The Ecloga* (Cambridge: Cambridge University Press, 1926); E. E. Lipshits, ed., *Ekloga. Vizantiiskii zakonodatel'nyi svod VIII veka* (Moscow: Nauka, 1965); Edwin Hanson Freshfield, ed., *The Procheiros Nomos. Published by the Emperor Basil I at Constantinople between 867 and 879 A.D.* (Cambridge: Cambridge University Press, 1928); *Kormchaia kniga* (Moscow, 1653) (Photocopy of the Nikon redaction in the Lenin Library in Moscow).

of Lithuanian origin made up perhaps 5 percent of mid-seventeenth-century slave law, usually in the realm of felonies.[9]

The rest of Muscovite slave law, perhaps 85 percent of it, was of Russian origin. A very small portion of it, a few basic principles, went back to Kievan times. Most of the norms applied in the Moscow Slavery Chancellery or in the provincial administrative offices had originated within the previous hundred years or so. Muscovite slave law was among the most "national" areas of law, reflecting the government's attempt simultaneously to cope with and direct a dynamic social institution.

The Varieties of Slavery

Any typology of Muscovite slavery is open to revision and exceptions, but, for the purposes of discussion and comprehension, the following seems most appropriate.

Muscovy knew eight kinds of slavery (*kholopstvo*). The first major function of the law was to define these types of slavery, to establish their norms.[10] These types were: (1) hereditary, second-generation (*starinnoe*); (2) full slavery (*polnoe*), which was hereditary for offspring until very late in Muscovy; (3) registered (*dokladnoe*), for elite slaves, particularly estate managers; (4) debt (*dolgovoe*), worked off by defaulters and criminals unable to pay fines at the rate of 5 rubles per year by adult males, 2½ rubles per year by adult females, and 2 rubles per year by children ten and over; (5) indentured (*zhiloe*), into which a person sold himself for a term of years, upon whose expiration he had to be freed, often with cash, maybe a wife, and possibly other things; (6) voluntary (*dobrovol'noe*), into which an individual who had worked for someone for three to six months could be converted at the employer's request; (7) limited service contract slavery (*kabal'noe*), which prior to 1586-97 was a self-pawn for a year that became converted into self-sale and full slavery upon default of repayment, after that date was a self-sale for the life of the purchaser (I must apologize for this cumbersome, descriptive translation. However, *kabal'noe kholopstvo* seems to have been an unusual institution, and no adequate, unloaded translation has come to my attention. If in fact money changed hands, it went to the person who was selling himself; why he needed the cash, or what he did with it, remains unknown); (8) military captivity.

Until the mid-seventeenth century, when it was abolished, there was a special urban type of slave, the *zakladchik*, which might be suitably translated as "pawn." I have discussed that on another occasion. In brief, the *Ulozhenie*

---

9. I. Beliaev, ed., *Statut velikogo kniazhstva litovskogo 1588 goda* (Moscow, 1854); I. I. Lappo, ed., *Litovskii statut v moskovskom perevode-redaktsii* (Iur'ev, 1916).

10. 1550 *Sudebnik* 76; *Ukaznaia kniga Kholop'ego prikaza*, 1; 1649 *Ulozhenie* 20: passim.

ordered such people returned to the urban tax rolls, and that no other documents could be dredged up (forged?) subsequently to prove that the *zakladchik* was enslaved or was dependent for some other cause.[11]

My study of Muscovite slavery is concerned, in descending order of significance, with the *kabal'noe, starinnoe, polnoe*, and *dokladnoe* types of slavery, but it should be noted that there was little de jure distinction among any of them while the individual was enslaved. Few de facto differences are apparent either: the bundle of rights the Muscovite slaveowner held in his slave was not significantly determined by the category of the latter's bondage. While one might assume, for example, that the real-life existence of an elite estate-manager slave was considerably better in every respect than that of the most abased household slave, there is little evidence on this point. These varieties of slavery remind us of the situation in antiquity, in India, and in parts of Africa, where different forms of unfreedom were also known that in reality were very similar.[12] This is symptomatic of the well-known fact that the conception of slavery is much less different from one area to another, or one time period to another, than are the institutions regulating it. The things that slaves do and their relations with free people tend to be far less differentiated than are the legal norms governing those functions and relationships. Chapters 2 through 8 are concerned primarily with the Muscovite legal abstractions, while later ones will attempt to discuss more concrete details. However, more than thirty actual court cases will be discussed to illustrate particular aspects of Muscovite slave law. These illustrations should serve not only to make the law more vivid but to interject real-life elements into what otherwise might appear to be a rather abstract and lifeless catalog.

Some parts of this study are based on discussion and analysis of 2,499 cases that have been extensively subjected to computer processing. That aspect of the work encompasses the types and numbers of slaves shown in table 2.2. The types of documents in which the slaves are recorded are shown in table 2.3.

11. 1649 *Ulozhenie* 19: 13, 18; Richard Hellie, "The Stratification of Muscovite Society: The Townsmen," *Russian History* 5, pt. 2(1978): 140-44; N. P. Pavlov-Sil'vanskii, *Sochineniia*, 3 vols. (St. Petersburg, 1910), 3: 466-98; idem, "Liudi kabal'nye," pp. 226-29; idem, *Zakladnichestvo-patronat* (St. Petersburg, 1897). Apparently this type of slavery was available to medieval Germanic free men in times of distress (Wergeland, p. 20). Something like *zakladnichestvo* also existed throughout much of Chinese history, *t'ou-k'ao*, where people were not necessarily impoverished when they voluntarily subordinated themselves to influential households, often in search of tax and corvée exemptions (Wiens, pp. 296-97).

12. Moses I. Finley, "Between Slavery and Freedom," *Comparative Studies in Society and History* 6 (April 1964): 233-49: Seven kinds of slaves are listed in the Hindu *Laws of Manu* (4:415). On the Fulbe and Batoma of Benin, see Miers and Kopytoff, p. 450. On the Ashanti, see Winthrop Jordan, "Planter and Slave Identity Formation," *Annals* (1977): 36.

TABLE 2.2
Types and Numbers of Slaves

Type of Slave	No. of Slaves	No. of Documents	Average No. of Slaves per Document
Hereditary	483	91	5.3
Full	671	192	3.5
Registered	80	31	2.6
Limited service contract	4,009	2,116	1.9
Debt	13	5	3.3
Voluntary	1	1	1.0
Indentured	7	3	2.3
Unknown	311	60	5.3
Total	5,575	2,499	2.2

TABLE 2.3
Types and Numbers of Documents

Type of Document	Years	No. of Slaves	No. of Documents	Slaves per Document
Full slavery	1430-1554	210	100	2.1
Registered (*dokladnaia*)	1475-1600	52	28	1.9
Limited service slavery contract	1510-1702	3,942	2,091	1.9
Wills	1472-1597 + 1673	223	19	12.4
Gifts, dowries	1504-1598 + 1647	414	131	3.2
Marriage contracts	1512-1593	55	13	2.9
Manumission documents	1592-1673	63	22	4.2
Purchase documents	1575-1597	9	8	1.1
Court decisions	1518-1597	25	11	2.3
Property divisions	1546-1598	348	23	15.1
Out-of-court settlements	1534-1597 + 1673	11	5	2.2
Tsar charter	1577	4	1	4.0
Court cases	1620-1651	69	28	2.5
Memoranda	1592-1597	6	2	3.0
Debt memos	1684-1714	8	3	2.7
Indentures	1667-1695	13	5	2.6
Registrations of hereditary slaves	1593-1598	123	8	15.4
Unknown		?	2	
Total		5,575	2,499	2.2

These documents will be discussed in greater detail in later contexts. Three basic types of documents were generated in the process of enslaving free people: the full slavery, registered slavery, and limited service slavery documents. Purchase documents recorded a handful of sale transactions at the end of the sixteenth century. From the end of the Muscovite period other bondage instruments survive—indentures and transactions recording temporary enslavement for debt.

Hereditary slaves were recorded primarily in documents generated during the life cycle of the slaveowners; marriage contracts when nuptials were being arranged and dowries when they were consummated; wills and property divisions upon the death of an owner. Manumission documents also usually followed an owner's death. The judicial process is another source of information about slaves: out-of-court settlements were arranged to lower the costs of litigation, court cases recorded the process of litigation, and court decisions awarded the verdict to one of the litigants. A general registration of all slaves around 1597 recorded hereditary slaves. Miscellaneous documents were the memoranda and royal charters.

There is no way of knowing the actual percentages of each type of slave in Russian society at any given time. However, the books registering all slaves at the end of the sixteenth century present an idea of the relative proportions of the types of slaves being registered then (See table 2.4). The hereditary slaves were in wills, dowries, and like documents, some of them over a century old, whose heirs were still thereby enslaved in 1597-98. The same was true of the full slaves.[13]

TABLE 2.4
Types of Slaves Registered

	N	%
Hereditary	418	19.3
Full	601	27.7
Registered	52	2.4
Limited service contract slaves	1,097	50.6
Total	2,168	100

I shall first discuss the lesser forms of slavery—registered, voluntary, and indentured—and then the most important types—hereditary, full, and limited service contract slavery.

Registered Slavery

Registered slavery seems to have been reserved largely for elite slaves; the government entered the cases and perhaps even kept records at a date considerably earlier

13. These documents have been published in three collections: A. B. Lakier, ed., "Akty, zapisannye v krepostnoi knige XVI v.," *Arkhiv istoriko-iuridicheskikh svedenii, otnosiashchikhsia do Rossii, izd. Nikolaem Kalachovym* 2[1] (1855); A. S. Lappo-Danilevskii, ed., "Zapisnaia kniga krepostnym aktam XV-XVI vv., iavlennym v Novgorode d'iaku D. Aliab'evu," RIB 17(1898); A. I. Kopanev, ed., "Materialy po istorii krest'ianstva kontsa XVI i pervoi poloviny XVII v.," in *Materialy i soobshcheniia po fondam Otdela rukopisei i redkoi knigi Biblioteki Akademii nauk SSSR* (Moscow-Leningrad: Nauka, 1966).

than for other types of slavery, where its role was seemingly that of a neutral intermediary, for a fee. While the number of cases is small, one notable thing about them is that the sex ratio of children is normal—50 percent boys, 50 percent girls. This was not, in other words, a crisis-relief institution, but a service one. Competent people were being put in positions of trust, and the law required that they be slaves—"he who has the key shall be a slave" (*po kliuchu kholop*)—for reasons of subordination that will be discussed below. Moreover, as will be discussed in chapter 10, the price structure for registered slaves was apparently more rational than for any other type of slave until the end of the Time of Troubles.[14] The institution seems to have arisen around the end of the fifteenth century, and the last extant registered slavery document is dated before the end of the sixteenth century.[15] Nevertheless, the institution continued to be mentioned in the seventeenth century. A memorandum from Tsar Vasilii Shuiskii to the Slavery Chancellery of May 21, 1609, linked registered slavery with limited service constract slavery in that both were to end with the death of the slave-owner in whose name the document was made out. Recognizing the dependent condition that slavery put most individuals in, the law went on to note that registered slaves, manumitted on the death of their owners, were free to sign a limited service slavery contract with whomever they pleased, and that such documents were valid instruments, not the documents that had belonged to the deceased owners.[16]

The demise of registered slavery may be attributed partially to the decline in the role of elite slaves in the Russian system. Some of the major factors in that decline were the evolution of the central government from a royal household (managed largely by slaves) to an administration run by lay bureaucrats, a development notable in the mid-fifteenth century. Next was the abolition of the "feeding" (*kormlenie*) system of provincial-local administration. Each governor (*namestnik*) sent out his bailiffs to do his work for him, and the *pristav* was sometimes a slave. In the mid-sixteenth century this system yielded to one of local self-administration by the rising middle service class of cavalry archers, townsmen, and wealthy peasants, who purchased the right to manage some of their affairs themselves and thus escaped the oppression of the *namestniki* and *pristavy*. A third phenomenon was the radical decline in the reign of Ivan IV

---

14. V. I. Sergeevich thought that registered slaves were not a special category but the same as full slaves (*Drevnosti* 1: 148). I have tried to show briefly in this paragraph why I disagree with his judgment.

15. Man'kov, *Ulozhenie*, p. 114; Akty Iushkova, no. 259, is dated 1600.

16. PRP 4: 379. For a review of the issue of whether in the sixteenth century registered slavery was hereditary or terminated with the life of the owner, see Paneiakh, "Ulozhenie 1597 g. o kholopstve," p. 162. The issue is still unresolved: de facto, most such slaves were probably manumitted on the death of their owners; de jure, until 1597 they probably could be claimed by heirs, which explains the inclusion of such documents in the general registration of 1597-98.

of the large patrimonial estates (*votchiny*) needing stewards to manage them, in favor of an increase in smaller service estates (*pomest'ia*) that were increasingly managed by members of the middle service class living right on the estates. This was adumbrated in the 1550 law code by a move away from the old norm that a steward had to be a slave, to enslavement by consent only for rural stewards, and to no slavery at all for urban stewards.[17] (This was in turn probably caused at least partially by the economic expansion of the first half of the sixteenth century and its ramifications.)

A fourth noteworthy event in the demise of elite slaves was a decline in a number of armed slave retainers who accompanied their owners into combat on horseback. This process occurred rather quickly. As Muscovy strained to expand its armed forces, a shortage of retainers must have arisen, with a bidding up of prices for persons willing to sell themselves into that role. While magnates could afford the practice (but probably did not like the rising prices), lesser military men could not, so that in 1550 a fifteen-ruble limit was placed on, it should be noted, limited service contract slaves. Earlier higher-priced limited service slavery contracts were regarded as valid if immediately sealed by a boyar and signed by a secretary; if not so registered, the contracts could be contested in court.[18] A major impetus to the competition for slave cavalry retainers was the law of 1556 requiring one armed cavalryman to report from each 100 *chetverti* of land in one field, or 400 acres. This system was ultimately doomed by the gunpowder revolution, making the cavalry a secondary factor in warfare. However, the demise of the slaves' role in the cavalry was hastened by their extensive participation in the Time of Troubles: both Khlopko and Bolotnikov were probably fugitive elite military slaves, and the slaves played an important role in the siege of Tula. From this experience the government learned that slaves educated in martial arts posed a threat to the established order, and so, as soon as practicable, slaves were relegated to guarding the baggage train. The major point here, which will be elaborated on later, is that the demise of the cavalry slaves completed the demise of elite slaves as a significant force in Muscovy.

Registered slavery existed as a legal option in the seventeenth century, and one might assume that some estate managers were probably that type of slave—but I have no direct evidence to prove it.[19] Some estate managers are known to have been limited service contract slaves. We may also speculate that the demise of registered slavery was a function not only of the decline of elite slavery but also of the increasingly routinized bureaucratization of Muscovite administration. In theory, the registered slavery document was a personal report to the monarch, but, with the creation of the Slavery Chancellery and the increasing flow of paper generally, such practices became difficult and unwanted. Moreover, it was much

---

17. 1550 *Sudebnik* 76.
18. Ibid., 78.
19. 1649 *Ulozhenie* 20: 21, 32; MS, pp. 262, 267.

easier for the Slavery Chancellery to deal with only one form of slavery for Russians, the limited service contract, and that seems to be exactly what happened.

Voluntary Slavery

"Voluntary" slavery was perhaps the most bizarre form (or subform) of human bondage in Muscovy. It is mentioned in a law of 1555 in a rather elliptical fashion. As we shall see later, it has been customary in many societies for servants to be slaves, and Muscovy was no exception. However, it was possible for a person in most of the sixteenth century to serve a lord without formulating a strictly owner-slave legal relationship. Initially, the "voluntary slave" seems to have been such an individual, one person serving another without having formulated a contractual slavery relationship. The 1555 provision dealt with a suit by the lord against the departed "voluntary slave" for stolen property, and said that no lord could initiate such a suit. If a person was stupid enough to allow someone to serve him voluntarily and did not draw up a slavery document on him, then he could not sue the departed servant for stolen property, an action which was, said the law, probably only a ruse to force the return of the servant. By merely giving a caveat to the lord that he was being stupid in risking keeping servants without converting them into slaves, the government was tacitly permitting the practice. The government ordered the new law appended to the *Sudebnik* of 1550 and circulated to elected heads (*vybornye golovy*) in the provincial towns so that they would decide any such suits on this basis.[20]

"Voluntary" slavery seems to have flourished after a law of 1586 changed the nature of limited service contract slavery, making it less attractive. Between 1586 and 1597 "voluntary" slavery may have been quite popular, substituting for limited service contract slavery and causing a temporary decline in the numbers of persons selling themselves into *kabal'noe kholopstvo*.[21]

This was changed in 1597, when the general statute on slavery stated that free people who served someone voluntarily for over six months could be converted into limited service contract slaves by the employer. Initially, limited service contract slavery documents were to be formulated on such individuals no later than February 1, 1598. The reasoning behind the provision is worth quoting:

If someone says that he served voluntarily with someone for half a year and more, but does not want to give a limited service slavery contract on himself,

20. 1606 *Sudebnik* 100 (PRP 4: 514).

21. Koretskii, *Zakreposhchenie*, p. 212. Note that "voluntary slaves" were given manumission documents (NZKK 1: 267). The most useful discussions of voluntary slavery are found in the works of V. M. Paneiakh ("Dobrovol'noe kholopstvo," pp. 198-216; *Kholopstvo*, pp. 27-47, 131-45, 219-42).

and they [the responsible officials] discover that the voluntary slave served
with that man [the would-be slaveowner] for half a year, give a limited service
slavery contract on such a voluntary slave. Do not heed his petition [not to be
enslaved] on this matter because that man fed, clothed, and shod that voluntary slave; no one else except that lord shall take in [that person] as a voluntary
slave.[22]

The cost-of-maintenance argument is one that will be discussed further in
chapter 10. The thinking behind the provision was much like that of the 1497
Sudebnik, which provided that all stewards had to be slaves: ambivalence about
social status and occupation was, if not intolerable, at least to be avoided. In this
case, anybody who was a servant should be a slave. The text of the article makes
it clear that the government had servants in mind, operating on the assumption
that domestics and other lackeys did not earn their keep and were fundamentally
parasites on the lord's household. As we shall see in chapter 11, perhaps as many
as one-quarter of the limited service contract slaves at the end of the sixteenth
century were of voluntary slave origin.

Almost certainly the government did not intend initially for the law on voluntary slaves to be applied to wage earners, and could not have foreseen the second-
order consequences that such a provision might have had for the labor market.
One impact of the law, for example, seems to have been to allow lords to convert
desirable artisans into limited service contract slaves by forbidding them to
leave during the initial half-year of employment. The Stroganovs employed this
legislation (accompanied by the use of chains to ensure that the necessary time
had elapsed) to augment their workshops, particularly to distrain prized icon
painters.[23]

Whatever its intent, this legislation on voluntary slaves had a definite anti-
lower-class bias, for it had the potential to reduce to slavery almost anybody
who lacked independent means. This was recognized during the famous Bolotnikov rebellion during the Time of Troubles, and on March 7, 1607, Tsar Vasilii
Shuiskii abolished the mandatory provisions of the law. Consequently anybody
who was serving someone had the right to ask to be his limited service contract
slave; if he did not want to be enslaved, "even if he had served half a year, a
year, or more," such a person was not to lose his freedom. Perhaps trying to
conceal the reason behind the enactment—a desire to placate anti-Shuiskii senti-

22. UKKhP 1: 11; PRP 4: 274, 400; MS, pp. 253-54. For a court case in which the six-
month principle of "voluntary servitude" was used as part of the basis for returning a fugitive slave, see Voeikov v. Khilkov (1620), discussed in the manumission section of chapter 5
(Iakovlev, *Kholopstvo*, pp. 323-27, no. 2). A somewhat similar harshening of servile status
was evident in China, where a white contract slave who served the same master for over
three years was regarded in law as the more degraded red contract slave (Meijer, p. 330).
23. A. A. Vvedenskii, *Dom Stroganovykh v XVI-XVII vekakh* (Moscow: AN SSSR, 1962),
p. 86.

ment among the lower classes—the 1607 enactment treated the issue as purely a legal one and mandated that anyone who wanted to enslave someone should not keep a person even one day before formulating the slavery contract.[24]

The issue of voluntary slaves was one that would not go away. It arose again in May of 1609, when Tsar Shuiskii, in a memorandum to the Slavery Chancellery, noted that people had been serving lords for five, ten, and more years without having formulated limited service slavery contracts. He said that he would discuss the matter with the boyars, but, until he had resolved the issue, such people, if claimed as slaves by their masters, should be returned to them. A few months later the issue was resolved. On September 12, 1609, the 1607 enactment was repealed, restoring the situation to that prevailing in the 1597 slavery statute.[25] This reversal indicates that the 1607 repeal had been motivated by fear of Bolotnikov. In 1609 the time limit was reduced to five months, and the *Ulozhenie* reduced it to three months.[26] (It was by analogy with this provision that children born to limited service contract slaves were also enslaved: "issue limited service slavery contracts on such people, even though they do not wish to be slaves, because they have lived with them [the slaveowners] for many years.")[27] Why the time to convert a voluntary slave into a limited service contract slave was reduced has not been satisfactorily explained, but two reasons come to mind: (1) after the catastrophes of Ivan IV's reign had ruined the economy, the developing premium on free labor evident up to the time of the Livonian War disappeared; (2) with the formation of a caste society, a premium was placed on having everyone bound to an assigned station—taxpaying, government service, the church, or slavery. The creation of the Foreigners' Enclave (*Nemetskaia sloboda*) was in part a response proceeding from the same mentality: no one could be allowed to live in Russia without being ascribed, in today's Soviet terminology, to some "organization."

Debt Slavery

Another secondary form of servitude in Muscovy was debt slavery, perhaps the form of bondage known to the greatest number of societies. Debt slavery has often been linked with various forms of penal slavery, for default on payment of obligations is regarded as a form of theft. It was known in primitive societies, such as that of the Yurok Indians of northern California, a fishing and food-gathering people. In litigation a plaintiff who was found in the right could collect damages from the defendant. Should the defendant default, he had the option

---

24. PRP 4: 376-77.
25. Ibid., pp. 377, 380.
26. AI 2, no. 85; 1649 *Ulozhenie* 20: 16; MS, p. 261.
27. 1649 *Ulozhenie* 20: 30; MS, p. 266.

of becoming the plaintiff's debt slave, or of being executed by the plaintiff.[28] This example also reveals one of the original causes for slavery, the deferment of capital punishment, a subject that will be discussed in greater detail later. Debt slavery also was known in Babylonia, Assyria, Palestine, Greece, Egypt, Rome, China, India, Germanic societies, the Philippines, the Christian Assizes of Jerusalem at the beginning of the twelfth century, and was made illegal only in 1874 in Siam, where default on gambling debts was the chief cause of persons' selling themselves for debt.[29] Thomas Jefferson's passionate aversion to debt was based on the fact that it could lead to bondage, of which outright enslavement was the most graphic form. His sentiments were only a modern expression of those held by the Greeks and Romans, that any service obligation, such as working off a debt, was "slave-like."[30] Usually debt slavery was for a term, during which the principal was worked off, and little or no account was taken of interest on the debt.

The presence and role of debt slavery in Kievan Rus' is not totally clear. However, one may assume that the enactments by Vladimir Monomakh in the *Russkaia Pravda* after he became grand prince of Kiev in 1113 were made primarily with such slavery in mind. The contemporaneous Bulgarian *Zakon Sudnyi Liudem* that circulated in Kiev presumably envisioned a similar type of slavery when it provided that for the theft of a horse or weapon, or for riding another's horse without permission, the culprit should be beaten and then sold into slavery.[31] Perhaps this should be termed "penal slavery," but it is only a variation on the debt slavery theme—except that there was no provision for manumission after a term.

The *Sudebnik* prescribed slavery for the convicted first-time felon who had not the means to compensate his victim for the damages he had caused. After having been beaten with the knout, the miscreant of no means was turned over to the plaintiff as a slave. This provision was refined somewhat in the *Sudebniki*

28. E. Adamson Hoebel, *The Law of Primitive Man* (New York: Atheneum, 1973), pp. 53, 230.

29. Nieboer, p. 344; Wergeland, pp. 12, 14-15; James L. Watson, "Transactions in People: The Chinese Market in Slaves, Servants, and Heirs," in his *Asian and African Systems*, p. 223; Andrew Turton, "Thai Institutions of Slavery," in Watson, *Asian and African Systems*, pp. 251, 262-66; Hjejle, p. 109; D. G. E. Hall, *A History of South-East Asia* (New York: St. Martin's Press, 1968), p. 672; Verlinden, *Colonization*, p. 81; Pritchard, ed., p. 155, arts. 151-52; Mendelsohn, 13, 23, 27, 122; Westermann, pp. 4, 30, 44, 50-51, 59, 135; C. Martin Wilbur, pp. 87-88.

30. Edmund S. Morgan, "Slavery and Freedom: The American Paradox," *The Journal of American History* 59, no. 1(June 1972): 7-8; Finley, "Between Slavery and Freedom," p. 237.

31. M. N. Tikhomirov, ed., *Zakon Sudnyi liudem kratkoi redaktsii* (Moscow: AN SSSR, 1961), pp. 99, 108, art. 26 (hereafter cited as Short ZSL); idem, *Zakon Sudnyi liudem prostrannoi i svodnoi redaktsii* (Moscow: AN SSSR, 1961), pp. 159, 168-69, arts. 27, 30 (hereafter cited as Expanded ZSL).

of 1550 and 1589, with the notation that the slavery was for a term, until the sum due the plaintiff had been satisfied; moreover, the plaintiff had to post a bond guaranteeing that he would return the slave once the sum had been worked off. This form of slavery was still viable in the Felony Statute of 1669, whose article 22 permitted the conversion of a felon (but not his wife) into a debt slave to satisfy tortious losses at the rate of five rubles per year.[32]

On October 1, 1560, the government forbade creditors to get full and registered (*dokladnye*) slavery documents on debtors, and gave debtors whose houses had been destroyed in a June 17, 1560, fire a five-year grace period before creditors could press their claims for debts. In the next reign, on February 8, 1588, a fifteen-year statute of limitations was imposed on the filing of suits to recover defaulted loans.[33] The measures give the appearance of a government "program" directed toward curtailing debt slavery.

The *Lithuanian Statute* of 1588 prescribed that those who sold themselves or other members of their families during a famine should be temporary debt slaves, not perpetual slaves (as was the Muscovite practice). After the famine was over, such debt slaves were to repay the cash, or else work it off at a prescribed rate, and then be set free again.[34]

In the *Ulozhenie* of 1649, an individual who defaulted on legal obligations (debts, fines, payment of suits for stolen property) could be claimed by his creditor for a term to work off the debt: 5 rubles per year for men, 2½ rubles for women, and 2 rubles per year for children over the age of nine. Stating a prohibition that seems to have been a norm in other slave societies, the Russians declared that "children under the age of 10 do not perform slave labor."[35] If the creditor died before the debt was repaid, the debtor and his obligations were transferred to the heirs of the deceased until the redemption was completed.

32. 1497 *Sudebnik* 10; 1550 *Sudebnik* 55; 1589 *Sudebnik* 103; PSZ 1: 780, no. 441, art. 22.

33. Vladimirskii-Budanov, *Khristomatiia* 3(1875): 29-30, 41, *Ukaznaia kniga vedomstva kaznacheev*, nos. 16, 21.

34. 1588 LS 12: 19 (p. 359 in Lappo edition).

35. 1649 *Ulozhenie* 20: 39-40; MS, pp. 268-69. For an operational description of enslavement for inability to pay fines, see Adam Olearius, *Travels*, p. 141. Kotoshikhin also discussed debt slavery in some detail, noting that the owners were not to starve, leave unclothed, swear at, or assault such slaves; on their part, the slaves were to serve their masters faithfully, to be totally obedient in everything, "as befits a slave before his lord" (*kak godittsa rabu* [n.b.] *pered gospodinom*). The owner was answerable for damages inflicted on a debt slave, and the state would inflict an appropriate penalty on an erring debt slave slaveowner. At the expiration of the term, the owner had to return the debt slave to the government office that enslaved the victim, who was formally manumitted by the government (Grigorii Kotoshikhin, *O Rossii v tsarstvovanie Alekseia Mikhailovicha* [St. Petersburg, 1909], pp. 119-20). The relative value of slave labor was similar to that reached by calculations used elsewhere. Thus in West Africa adult male slaves farming on their own account in the nineteenth century had an obligation double that of adult female or child slaves (Gemery and Hogendorn, p. 191).

While the specific terms of this form of slavery were written in 1560, the principle was much older.[36] If the debt was incurred not because of negligence but because of an accident (robbery, fire), the debtor could be enslaved for a maximum period of three years. Similar provisions, including shipwreck (irrelevant in land-locked Muscovy), were known in the Kievan period. An attempt was made, probably in the 1630s, using the *Lithuanian Statute* of 1588, to institute debt slavery (presumably in preference to limited service contract slavery) as a charity vehicle in famine times: a starving person would have to work off the value of the sustenance conveyed (at grossly inflated prices?) according to the above norms, rather than becoming a slave for the life of his owner.[37] I do not know whether debt slavery was actually used as a charity surrogate, but, considering the vitality of limited service contract slavery, it would appear as though slave-owners were unwilling to use a less advantageous form of bondage.

Indenture

What is here referred to as "indenture" was an old form of temporary bondage well known in the *Russkaia Pravda*, and the inclusion of some but not all of the old provisions in the Abridged Version indicates that this form was surviving only feebly (if at all) at the end of the fifteenth century. Its survival was stronger in West Russian law, and then indenture was reborn in the seventeenth century as the older Muscovite forms of bondage became inflexible. In the *Russkaia Pravda* the indentured laborer (*zakup*) was a semifree man, as elsewhere. During the time of his servitude, he was in some cases the agent of his master, and at other times his own man. The master could not sue his indentured laborer for theft. On the other hand (articles 57 and 58), indentured laborers were responsible to their masters for negligence. Reciprocally, indentured laborers had rights vis-à-vis their owners. The lord could not seize the laborer's property, sell the indenture to a third party, or sell the laborer into slavery (articles 59-61). Moreover, the lord could reasonably chastise his indentured laborer, but if he did it without cause the laborer could collect damages from the master (article 62). Most important, the *Pravda* specified sanctions for violations by the master, and also insisted that the indentured laborer had the right to complain to the prince or other officials in case of violations by the master. Again, reciprocally, if the indentured servant ran away, his master could convert him into a slave (article 56). A sign of the waning of the indenture as an institution by 1500 was the omission of article 56 from the Abridged Version of the *Pravda*. However, the sanctions of articles 59 through 62 were still present.

The indenture (*zhilaia, zhiteiskaia zapis'*) was revived in late Muscovy as a form

36. AI 1, no. 154-xvi.
37. 1588 LS 12: 19-i; 1649 *Ulozhenie* 20: 43; MS, pp. 270-71.

of servitude related in some respects to debt slavery. I have five of them in my data, dating from 1667 to 1695. Indenture existed as a legal form of slavery somewhat earlier, perhaps borrowed from Lithuania in the 1630s.[38] Its virtue from the point of view of the slave was that the indenture was usually for a specific term, the sum of money was large (25 to 200 rubles), and the slave was to be freed with cash. Given the general labor shortage in Muscovy, it is not clear how limited service contract slavery could compete with indenture. Perhaps limited service contract slavery remained a relief institution for the desperate, while indenture was an avenue open to people unwilling to try to survive entirely on their own (or desirous of escaping inscription in the castes of peasants or townsmen), yet capable of commanding the purchasing power of someone wanting to take them (three of my cases were married, two were single) in as slaves.

Legislation on the indenture was scanty, and does not correspond in profile precisely to the handful of cases on it I now have—perhaps the institution evolved, or my sample is unrepresentative, or both. In law, the indenture seems to have been a device for permitting parents to relieve themselves of their children without having to sell them into other forms of slavery, and the document mentioned above in the paragraph on debt slavery for famine relief was called a *zapis'*, indicating its similarity to indenture; their common origin in the *Lithuanian Statute* of 1588 is another indication of their similarity. A debtor being beaten publicly (*pravezh*) could sell himself in an indenture to a third party to pay off a plaintiff trying to collect his money at the moment. Such indentures could be without term (*bessrochnaia zhilaia zapis'*) and legally had the potential for turning into a revived form of full slavery, inheritable and perpetual.[39] Another measure, dating from 1641, limited indentures to five years in cases where the lord himself was not a taxpayer.[40] This measure included the lowest ranks of church personnel (priests and deacons) and monastery servitors (*slugi*) forbidden to own limited service contract slaves but allowed to own indentured slaves. (Archpriests, archdeacons, and higher officials could own limited service contract slaves.)[41] A final law discusses parents indenturing their children for a term and requires them to guarantee their children's performance. Similarly, a person who was not a parent could guarantee an indenture and be required at law to enforce it.[42] A fugitive indentured slave could be claimed at law like any other slave if his contract had not expired.

The Muscovite indenture was somewhat similar to the American indentured servant, although there were some differences. For one, American masters could

---

38. 1588 LS 12: 22-i, ii. A marginal notation in the scroll copy of the 1649 *Ulozhenie* 20: 46 says that the article was written in 1634/35; MS, p. 272.

39. 1649 *Ulozhenie* 20: 46; MS, p. 272: Man'kov, *Ulozhenie*, pp. 127-28.

40. 1649 *Ulozhenie* 20: 116; MS, p. 298.

41. 1649 *Ulozhenie* 20: 104; MS, pp. 292-93.

42. 1649 *Ulozhenie* 20: 45; MS, pp. 271-72.

buy and sell the labor of their servants. On this point, the Muscovite situation is not clear, but the probability is that owners were expected to keep indentured slaves. Also in America, servants had the right of redress against a savage or incompetent master, and the presence of court records full of their complaints shows that his right was a real one. Muscovite legislation, unlike Kievan, said little or nothing on this score, but, as we shall see, making an analogy with debt slaves would probably force a Muscovite court to limit extreme cruelty toward an indentured servant that might result in his death. The most important parallel is that both the American and the Muscovite were temporary slaves.[43] American indentured servants could not sell themselves back into slavery, but, upon the expiration of their contracts, were thrust out into the competitive world. While the Muscovite indentured slave was also freed at the end of his term, he had the option of selling himself again, into limited service contract slavery. Legally he could sell himself again into an indenture, but knowledge of whether that ever happened awaits archival investigation. The degree of dependency indenture created in Muscovy is unknown, nor is anything known about the lives free men led after the expiration of the indenture. However, the example of the Chinese and Indians in the West Indies in the late nineteenth century, who frequently reindentured themselves, would suggest that freed Muscovite indentured servants probably resold themselves into slavery relatively often. Be that as it may, there can be little doubt that their being freed with cash or property put them in a much better condition to survive independently than could the majority of slaves, who were manumitted without anything.

Hereditary Slavery

Hereditary slavery (*starinnoe kholopstvo*) was the state of someone whose parents had been slaves, as a general rule. The documentation proving that someone was a hereditary slave, according to the *Sudebnik* of 1550, was a will "or other written document."[44] In the *Ulozhenie* of 1649 the list was extended to wills, marriage contracts, dowries, gift documents, and trial judgment charters.[45] When such slaves were transferred as part of a dowry, and the wife died without offspring, the surviving husband had to return the slaves (with their spouses) to the

---

43. Lawrence Friedman, *A History of American Law* (New York: Simon and Schuster, 1973), p. 73; David W. Galenson, "British Servants and the Colonial Indenture System in the Eighteenth Century," *The Journal of Southern History* 44, no. 1 (February 1978): 41-46; idem, *White Servitude in Colonial America* (Cambridge: Cambridge U. P., 1981).

44. 1550 *Sudebnik* 78. India also knew a variety of slaves. For a discussion of hereditary slaves, see Hjejle, p. 92. For a discussion of the varieties of Chinese slavery, beginning with hereditary slavery, see Wiens, pp. 296-98.

45. 1649 *Ulozhenie* 20: 61, 64, 81; MS, pp. 276-78, 285.

wife's kin who had provided the dowry.[46] A very large proportion, perhaps as many as half, of all slaves were hereditary slaves.

Perhaps it was by default rather than by design, at least initially, but Muscovite legislation from 1597 on often reveals an implicit desire to abolish hereditary slavery. The 1597 slavery statute prescribed that limited service contracts should be given in cases where other documentation was absent—one of the major signs that Muscovy was moving from an oral to a written society, for many claims to hereditary slaves were not written down and were based on traditional oral evidence. This is evident in many court suits. The 1597 provision may have been repeated at some time in the mid-1620s, for, in the 1630 case Malygin v. Voeikov (see below, chapter 8), the plaintiff testified that "when, by the sovereign's decree it was ordered that limited service slavery contracts should be taken on hereditary slaves, he had obtained a limited service slavery contract on that hereditary slave of his in Moscow in the year 1626" in support of his successful claim for a three-generation (at least) perpetual slave.[47]

Perhaps in spite of government intentions, hereditary slavery was very much alive throughout the seventeenth century. Moreover, in many respects, it was still the premier form of slavery, for the owner with hereditary claims to a slave had precedence over nearly all other claimants.[48] The sole exception was the case in which a hereditary slave fled, and then resold himself as a limited service contract slave to someone else. According to the *Ulozhenie* of 1649, if the plaintiff in a suit for that fugitive based his case on a purchase document of his grandfather's, and the purchase document had not stated that the slave(s) and his(their) offspring were being purchased for grandchildren, then such a fugitive belonged to the defendant who had a limited service contract on the slave.[49] This article is almost certainly a hasty abstract of a particular case that arose in the Slavery Chancellery, and both its intent and its applicability are not totally clear. As we shall see in chapter 15, one of the unusual features of Muscovite slavery from a comparative view was the fact that it was in many cases perpetual. Had the intent of that article been to limit hereditary slavery to two generations, no one would be particularly surprised. However, the article is so specific that one can only surmise that certain Muscovite jurisprudents were beginning to think seriously about limiting hereditary slavery. The confusion of Muscovite thought on the matter is represented in another article of chapter 20 of the *Ulozhenie*, which noted that wills, gift documents, marriage contracts, and dowries could transfer "full, registered, and purchased slaves and military captives" from their present owner, to "wives, children, grandchildren, and great grandchildren."[50] While

---

46. 1649 *Ulozhenie* 20: 62; MS, pp. 276-77.
47. Iakovlev, *Kholopstvo*, p. 446, no. 18, xi.
48. 1649 *Ulozhenie* 20: 13, 77; MS, pp. 260, 283.
49. 1649 *Ulozhenie* 20: 101; MS, pp. 291-92.
50. 1649 *Ulozhenie* 20: 61; MS, p. 276.

"full" slavery was an anachronism by 1649 for first-generation slaves, it might have served as the basis for the enslavement of a "great-grandchild" who was living at that time. Moreover, the article was not a mindless repetition of a past practice, for its purpose was to contrast those legitimate hereditary slaves with limited service contract slaves, who could not be conveyed in such legal instruments and in fact were to be freed if they were.

Whatever the government's intention, hereditary slaves were still present and were the subject of transactions at the end of the seventeenth century.[51]

Full Slavery

Full slavery originated before the Muscovite era. The *Russkaia Pravda* (article 110) knew three origins of full slavery: (1) self-sale for at least half a grivna before witnesses and the payment of a fee to an official; (2) the marriage of a free man to a slave woman, without the explicit prior stipulation of her owner that the husband-to-be was to remain free; (3) becoming a steward or housekeeper without stipulating in advance that the employee was to remain a free man. In the Muscovite period, full slavery became almost exclusively self-sale into perpetual bondage. By what date this had happened is unclear. Most full slavery documents list no seller of the slave or recipient of the funds, some state outright that the slave is selling himself, and it seems safe to assume that most instances of full slavery at the time of the extant documents, between 1430 and 1554, were instances of self-sale. The sole context of full slavery in the law code of 1550 seems to be self-sale.[52] Whether full slavery existed in real life after 1554 is unknown, although its continued mention in seventeenth-century law indicates that it well may have, for Muscovite legislators did not waste inordinate quantities of time on meaningless anachronisms. The scholarly consensus seems to be that the full slavery contract (*polnaia gramota*) itself ceased to exist by the beginning of the seventeenth century. Some of the obviously current laws in the law code of 1649 recognized only hereditary slaves and limited service contract slaves, but other provisions mentioned full slaves.[53] Perhaps this was to encompass descendants of full slaves. Chapter 20, article 7, of the *Ulozhenie* may be construed as forbidding further entry into full slavery, for it mentions only limited service contract slavery in the context of fresh recruits. A marginal notation on the scroll copy of the code dates this article to 1647/48, but exactly what aspects of the nearly two-hundred-word article were thought to be new cannot be determined, for all of the procedures had been current practice for some time. Perhaps only the total formulation was new. The spirit, if not the name, of full slavery

---

51. PSZ 2: 919-21, no. 1293.
52. 1550 *Sudebnik* 76. See also Kopanev, "Materialy," pp. 174, 176-78.
53. 1649 *Ulozhenie* 20: 4, 21, 115; Valk, "Polnye gramoty," p. 118.

lived on in the legal reality of Tatar slaves, which is discussed in chapter 3. The offspring of full slaves were perpetual hereditary slaves. As far as can be determined, when Muscovites sold themselves, they usually did it in the family units existing at the moment. The possible variations on that theme practiced elsewhere, from Africa to the Middle East to China, of a household head either selling himself and leaving the rest of the family free, or selling the rest (or some) of the family and leaving himself free, seem to have been unknown in Muscovy.[54]

One of the theses of this work is that full slavery and limited service contract slavery, in spite of their juridical differences, were otherwise very similar. They embraced the same types of people, and served similar functions: status elevation and labor for the slaveowners, relief for the slaves. Remarkable statistical similarities in the two forms of slavery will be demonstrated throughout this essay to show that, except for some juridical differences, they were nearly identical institutions.[55]

Limited Service Contract Slavery

The term *kabal'noe kholopstvo* has as its basis the term *kabalá*, a written contract. The word derives from the Hebrew *gabhālah* and the Arabic *ḳabāla*, obligation, contract. It appeared in written documents in Rus' at the end of the thirteenth century. It is thought to have made its way via the Tatars to Muscovy.[56] In Muscovy, to the very end of the period, a *kabala* was a written contract, which did not necessarily have anything to do with slavery. The term *sluzhilaia kabala* means "service contract," with the service being in the form of slavery, in lieu of paying interest on a loan.

Exactly when limited service contract slavery appeared in Muscovy is not known. The first mentions of the phenomenon are last testaments of royal personages toward the end of the fifteenth century in which they order the manumission of their *kabal'nye liudi*. In early 1481 Prince of Vologda Andrei Vasil'evich, brother of Grand Prince Ivan III, wrote in his will: "Concerning my full and limited service contract slaves, and the elite executive slaves [*prikaznye liudi*] who managed

---

54. A decree of May 21, 1609, mentions holding slaves on the basis of limited service slavery contracts and registered (reported) slavery documents that belonged to the slaveowners' parents, who in 1609 were deceased, but the slaves had been declared freed by the law of 1597 limiting such slavery to one generation of slaveowners (PRP 4: 379). That it does not speak of full slavery does not necessarily mean that full slavery was extinct, as V. I. Koretskii thought (*Zakreposhchenie*, p. 216). On the selling of other family members by Chinese fathers and husbands, see Meijer, p. 331.

55. Richard Hellie, "Reply to a Comment," *Russian Review* (January 1977): 70-75.

56. E. N. Shipova, *Slovar' tiurkizmov v russkom iazyke* (Alma-Ata: Nauka Kazakhskoi SSR, 1976), pp. 145-46; P. I. Petrov, "K voprosu o termine *kabala*," *Narody Azii i Afriki* 1965, no. 1: 113-15.

my revenues for me: they are all to be set free."[57] The next mention is again a last testament, that of Volok Prince Fedor Borisovich, written about April 1506, in which he commands: "Concerning my full and limited service contract slaves: those slaves of mine are to be set free."[58] The third and last will (of the twenty-five such wills extant) in which slaves of that type are set free was that of Uglich Prince Dmitrii Ivanovich, brother of Grand Prince Vasilii Ivanovich, written in early 1521, in which he wrote: "Concerning my elite executive, full and limited service contract slaves, would the grand prince grant [that] those slaves be set free."[59] Judging by these documents, limited service contract slavery must have been a fairly well-established institution in Muscovy by the end of the fifteenth century.

The oldest extant limited service slavery contract dates from 1510 on the south-eastern frontier of Muscovy, Riazan'. By 1550 limited service contract slavery was recognized as a fledgling and legally inferior form of slavery in the central legal code, the *Sudebnik*. It was available to any free person, defined as someone not already a full, registered, or hereditary slave.[60] To prevent confusion, the code specified that it was legally possible to borrow money at interest without becoming enslaved, and that anyone who tried to enslave an ordinary borrower risked losing his principal.[61] Thus it is completely clear that limited service contract slavery was not debt slavery; it was far more "slavelike" than debt slavery, and must not be confused with it. For a while, full and limited service contract slavery competed. At some point limited service contract slavery became exclusive, but when that happened is not clear. No full slavery documents are extant after the 1550s, but as I have already noted, the institution is mentioned for yet another century in the law. A notation in the *Ulozhenie* of 1649 indicates that a decree may have been issued making limited service contract slavery the replacement for full slavery in 1647-48.[62] Limited service contract slavery was the type of slavery that was repealed for agricultural workers in 1679 and for house slaves in 1723, when both were put on the tax rolls as serfs.[63]

The predominant forms of Muscovite slavery were full slavery and limited service contract slavery. As we have seen, a person could become a full slave by several routes, but the most common one seems to have been self-sale into perpetual bondage. Limited service contract slavery was different in that people could enter it only of their own volition. Free people initiated the contract by

57. DDG, p. 277, no. 74.
58. DDG, p. 409, no. 98.
59. DDG, p. 414, no. 99.
60. 1550 *Sudebnik* 78.
61. Ibid., art. 82.
62. 1649 *Ulozhenie* 20: 7.
63. PSZ 6: 506, no. 3901, art. 3; P. N. Miliukov, "Kogda 'zadvornye liudi' stali gosudarstvennymi tiagletsami?" *Trudy Riazanskoi uchenoi arkhivnoi kommissii* 12, pt. 1 (1897): 97-99.

taking a loan for a year (the initial limitation), agreeing to serve for the interest and to pay back the principal at the end of the year. In case of default, they became full slaves. In 1586 (or 1597) the institution was changed, presumably because almost everyone had defaulted: the "borrower" no longer had the option to repay the loan, and was enslaved for the life of the "creditor"; the owner was expropriated of the right to pass the slave to his heirs, or otherwise alienate him.[64]

There has been a considerable historiographic debate about whether a limited service contract slave was really a slave before he defaulted, in the initial year of his contract. The answer seems to be an almost unambiguous "yes," except that certain limitations were implicitly placed on his owner's right to alienate him.[65] These limitations were somewhat similar to the Middle-Assyrian laws which forbade a creditor to sell a person who had been pledged to him. The Assyrians, unlike the less precise Muscovites, even provided sanctions for violations: a forfeit of the debt plus the value of the pledge and a scourging for the violator, who then had to render twenty days of forced labor for the king.[66]

The repayment rate is almost impossible to determine with any degree of accuracy, for upon repayment the owner had to return to the slave the document that served as evidence of his indebted status. Nevertheless, the available evidence indicates that repayment was rare. Thus in one set of twenty-four documents, one man had succeeded in repaying 40 percent of his debt at the time of his death, and in another case a son had succeeded in repaying only 60 percent of a debt incurred by his deceased father thirteen years previously. Nine of the con-

---

64. PRP 4: 372-73; MS, pp. 250-52, arts. 6, 7. There is an extended historiographic debate on when limited service contract slavery was changed to the life of the owner, with 1586 being advocated by M. A. D'iakonov, B. D. Grekov, and V. I. Koretskii (Koretskii, *Zakreposhchenie*, p. 211). Yet Koretskii also said that loans secured by slavery pledges could be repaid in the 1590s (ibid., p. 192). Most other scholars have opted for 1597 as the date when the change was effected. For a review of the historiography of the issue, see Paneiakh, "Ulozhenie 1597 g. o kholopstve," p. 161. The descent into full slavery of the defaulting limited service contract slave parallels the fall into perpetual slavery of the Germanic debt slave who refused to work or otherwise satisfy his obligations (Wergeland, p. 17). The Thai redeemable slave also could fall into the status of nonredeemable slavery (Turton, p. 265). There was a modification of the status of the Chinese slave (*nu-pi*) in 1588 whose tendency also was to limit such slavery (Wiens, p. 303), but certainly the Chinese and Muscovite events proceeded totally independently of one another.

65. V. I. Sergeevich averred that prior to 1597 the *kabal'nyi kholop* in the first year of his contract was not a slave because he had the right to repay the loan and thereby escape his dependent position (*Drevnosti*, 1: 163). That was also the position of B. D. Grekov, who desired to minimize the importance of slavery in sixteenth-century Muscovy (*Sudebniki*, p. 286). Such an argument is not convincing, for the situation is much like that of the slave who has the right to buy his manumission, a not uncommon feature of many slave systems. The comment by Nieboer at n. 92 below is very relevant to this discussion. For the position of the leading Soviet specialist on *kabal'noe kholopstvo*, see V. M. Paneiakh, "Iz istorii kabal'nogo kholopstva"; *Kabal'noe kholopstvo*, pp. 85-86; *Kholopstvo*, p. 12.

66. Driver and Miles, *The Babylonian Laws* 1(1952): 219.

tracts bear notations that the debtors died without repaying anything. The only recorded complete repayment was by Ivan Ivanov Zhilin, who noted when selling himself (with his wife and daughter) in 1596 that at some earlier time he had sold himself, served for about three years, repaid the money, and retrieved the contract. After that Zhilin had served no one. This is a plausible story, for he was forty in 1596, and probably was about twenty when he sold himself the first time, well before 1586.[67] As will be shown later, repayment of the loan was unlikely not only because it was difficult to accumulate capital while serving someone full-time but also because slavery established a dependency syndrome that made it uncomfortable for the slave to leave and in fact, when he was forced out of slavery by an event such as the death of his master, even made him want to return. Repayment was no easier elsewhere. In Thailand few redeemable slaves for debt actually redeemed themselves, or were redeemed by others.[68]

Not only did the legislation of 1586-97 forbid the slave to repay the loan, it also essentially forbade anyone else to repay it for him, i.e., for the slave to sell himself to another owner before the expiration of the default date, a year after the conclusion of the agreement. We have seen that repayment by the slave himself seems to have been a rare event, but his purchase by someone else is recorded more frequently. The second oldest limited service slavery contract (1515) records that Iurii Podivnikov borrowed 2 rubles from Aleksei Kozha, which he, Iurii, used to repay his former creditor Nazar Nechai Mikhailov Minin. (This document is interesting in that it allows Iurii to pay 20 percent interest if he doesn't want to serve, for the first year, although the default option, at the expiration of a year, is still perpetual slavery. This feature, which was present in other early limited service slavery contracts as well, exhibits the flexible nature of the contracts.)[69] The same arrangement was made in the fourth oldest limited service slavery contract: sometime in 1515-17 one Timosha borrowed 3 rubles from Iakov Alekseev to repay his old creditor Ni[kolai] Ul'ianov Matov.[70] In the fifth such document, a military captive, Eufim Antonov, with his wife Ovdot'itsa and their son Ivanets, borrowed 10 rubles from Vasilii Olabin to repay the priest Fedor Dolgoi Afonas'ev. This document had the added feature of noting that any of the three bore responsibility for the entire sum.[71] Again in 1519 we find that Malets Stepanov borrowed 10 rubles (probably, for only the first letter is in the text) to move himself, his wife, and his son from Timofei Tikhan Semenov to Vasilii Pod'ius Ivanov Kobiakov. Like the others, they also had the option of

67. Koretskii, *Zakreposhchenie*, p. 192; V. G. Geiman, "Neskol'ko novykh dokumentov, kasaiushchikhsia istorii sel'skogo naseleniia Moskovskogo gosudarstva XVI stoletiia," *Sbornik Rossiiskoi publichnoi biblioteki* 2(1924): 285-86; NZKK 1: 395.

68. Turton, p. 265.

69. Akty Iushkova, p. 79, no. 93.

70. Ibid., p. 83, no. 98.

71. Ibid., pp. 85-86, no. 102. .

paying interest or working, and whoever remained was responsible for the entire obligation.[72]

By a quirk of the 1597 law whose import is not fully understood, a limited service contract slave could "upgrade" his dependency to that of registered or full slave. Perhaps he might have wanted to do this for more money, but this can be only speculation because no such case of "upgrading" is extant. The permission to "upgrade" could be granted only by a chamberlain (*postelnichii*) or the governor (*namestnik*) of a Moscow borough (*tret'*), the former being one of the tsar's intimates and the latter often one of his brothers. If a slave made a request to "upgrade" his slavery status in this manner in the Slavery Chancellery, he was to be denied his request and sent back to his owner as a limited service contract slave.[73] The motivation of this statute is not clear, but it seems to be an attempt to make transference out of limited service contract slavery to more permanent forms of slavery difficult by limiting the right to grant such a claim to the tsar's intimates, and to deny the Slavery Chancellery the right to grant such requests because the chancellery could be assumed to be coopted to the interests of the slaveowners and therefore liable to grant their requests even in the face of a slave's objection to such an "upgrading." Perhaps the central authorities wanted to leave the option of "upgrading" open but to deny it as an easy way to get around the generally desired restriction of self-sale to the life of the slaveowner.

After 1586 (or 1597), the slave borrowed the money, worked for the interest, but could not pay it back. Formally, this looked like a restoration of full slavery. However, the new form of slavery still remained limited—now to the life of the owner. Moreover, the owner in no way could alienate the limited service contract slave after 1586 (or 1597), another major contrast with full slavery.[74] Essentially, the owner was partially expropriated. Throughout the rest of the period during which limited service contract slavery existed, the government rigorously and successfully insisted that it be limited to the life of one owner, and that the slave be freed upon that owner's death.[75] In 1690, by analogy, the government ex-

72. Ibid., pp. 91-92, no. 107.

73. Vladimirskii-Budanov, *Khristomatiia*, 3(1875): 96-97; MS, p. 253, no. 10; Paneiakh, "Ulozhenie 1597 g. o kholopstve," p. 177.

74. UKKhP 1: 1. Half a century ago V. I. Veretennikov challenged established opinion by advancing the thesis that the law of 1597 repealed the borrower's right to repay and converted him into a slave for the life of his creditor only in the case of contracts concluded before that date, and made no fundamental change in the institution of limited service contract slavery as such. This, according to Veretennikov, explains why the terms of the contract remained the same for ninety years after 1597 as they had been before ("K istorii kabal'nogo kholopstva," pp. 169-72). Veretennikov's interpretation of the 1597 law has been concisely refuted by V. M. Paneiakh (*Kabal'noe kholopstvo*, pp. 127-28), but Paneiakh's analysis does not ·explain the persistence of the formula in the contracts of the one-year loan provision and the right to repay.

75. PRP 4: 373, 380; 1649 *Ulozhenie* 20: 9, 44 (originated in 1641/42), 52 (originated in

tended the provision to house serfs, the offspring of peasants who had been brought in from the fields to work in the master's household.[76]

This formal limitation on the disposition of a slave by his owner finds a counterpart in the Zaria (Islamic Nigeria) practice of forbidding the alienation of native-born slaves, a part of the process of mitigating the severity of thralldom for those who were no longer total "outsiders."[77] A twentieth-century freedom-loving perspective might lead one to expect that would-be slaves might have sought out older owners, a fact that cannot be checked but would seem to be a dubious proposition, for, as we shall see, those who really did not like subordination had the option of attempting to flee, and the rest sank into a dependency syndrome in which the life expectancy of the slaveowner did not matter, for, upon his death, the slave simply sought a new master and once again sold himself. Thus while the slave might seek an older master because Muscovite reality dictated that the latter probably would be a better provider than would a younger owner, the would-be chattel in such a case was taking the risk that he would sooner be forced to fend for himself again in a very hard world.

While there was no armed uprising by slaveowners or vote of confidence against Boris Godunov for expropriating their limited service contract slaves, nevertheless after 1597 many slaveowners tried to avoid such expropriation. One device was collective ownership, which will be discussed later. Yet another was to ignore the law. This is most apparent in the formula of the contracts, which for some time after February 1, 1597, continued to mention the date when the contract was concluded and to state that default occurred only after a year had passed. Moreover, lords continued to alienate slaves in the old way. A will dated September 8, 1597, ordered the executor (probably a slave) to free all of the deceased's limited service contract slaves living both in his household and in villages, except those he was transmitting to his wife for her lifetime. Another individual, in a dowry dated January 1, 1598, transferred both hereditary and limited service contract slaves to his brother-in-law for his sister.[78] The finest known example of attempting to avoid expropriation was the changing of the limitation from the life of one owner to the life of the slave, a trick one slaveowner tried to pull on his apparently illiterate subject![79]

At this juncture it might be worthwhile to leave the realm of the abstract for a

1608/9), 53, 61, 63 (originated in 1633/34), 81; MS, pp. 252, 271, 274, 276-77, 285; Vladimirskii-Budanov, *Khristomatiia* 3: 112.

76. PSZ 3: 82, no. 1383.

77. Michael Garfield Smith, *The Plural Society in the British West Indies* (Berkeley and Los Angeles: University of California Press, 1965), p. 127.

78. Koretskii, *Zakreposhchenie*, p. 194.

79. A. S. Lappo-Danilevskii, "Sluzhilye kabaly pozdneishego tipa," *Sbornik statei, posviashchennykh Vasiliiu Osipovichu Kliuchevskomu* (Moscow: Pechatnia S. P. Iakovleva, 1909), p. 735.

moment and briefly to show how a free person sold himself. Unfortunately, little evidence survives showing how the average would-be slave made contact with his would-be purchaser. A few documents have a statement such as "the purchaser met him while going along the road," but such statements are rare.

The details of what happened after the purchaser and the person about to sell himself agreed to conclude a transaction are well known. They first went to a scribe, who drew up the formal contract. At this point witnesses also may have joined the proceeding, although sometimes they appeared later. After the contract was drawn up, the parties took it to an official authorized to sanction such documents. He read the contract and then interrogated the person selling himself. This interrogation was quite detailed, and the relevant details were written in the official's record books. The most important point of the interrogation was the question about whether the person was selling himself of his own volition. If the government official was satisfied on these points, he would certify the sale document, which would be signed by the relevant officials and the witnesses. Fees were paid, and the original contract was kept by the slaveowner. (All of these matters will be discussed in further detail in chapter 8.) Now I shall quote from two original documents to illustrate the self-sale process.

On October 9 [1595] the scribes doing business on the public square of the Saint Sofia side [of Novgorod] —Kirilko, the son of Ivan Tryznov, Ondrei Dmitriev, and Grisha, the son of Vasilei Ushakov—brought to State Secretary Dmitrei Aliab'ev for registration a limited service slavery contract on Grisha, the son of Eremei, nicknamed Tormoshko, and they [also] brought that Grisha [himself] to the state secretary for the registration.

They said: "Having come, sire, to us on the public square, that Grisha ordered us to write on himself a limited service slavery contract in the amount of 10 Moscow rubles. He is going to serve in the household of Pervoi, the son of Ivan Onichkov. We, sir, at his, Grisha's, order wrote a contract on him, Grisha, called Tormoshko."

They placed before the state secretary that limited service slavery contract, and in the contract is written: "Be it known that I, Grigorei, the son of Eremei, called Tormoshko, have borrowed from Pervoi, the son of Ivan Onichkov, the sum of 10 Moscow rubles from the day of the holy Apostle James the Less, son of Alpheus, for a period of a year to the same day. For the interest I, Grigorei, shall serve my lord Pervoi every day in the household. When the monies come due on the specified date [and if I have not repaid them], I, Grigorei, shall serve him on the same basis every day in his household for the interest. Present as witnesses were Kirilo, son of Ivan Tryznov, and Ondrei Dmitriev. The contract was written by Grisha, the son of Vasilei Ushakov, on October 9, 1595."

Having heard that limited service slavery contract, State Secretary Dmitrei Aliab'ev asked Grisha: "Did you order the contract-writing scribe of the public square scribes and that witness to write that limited service slavery contract on yourself for the sum of 10 Moscow rubles? Did you take the sum of 10 Moscow rubles from Pervoi, son of Ivan Onichkov, and are you going to serve in his household for the interest? Heretofore have you served anyone else?"

Grisha Eremeev, called Tormoshko, said: "That, sir, is the limited service slavery contract that I ordered the contract-writing scribe of the public square scribes and the witness to write on myself in the sum of 10 Moscow rubles. I have borrowed the money, 10 Moscow rubles, from Pervoi Nichkov [sic], and for the interest I am going to serve him in the household. Heretofore I voluntarily served the middle service class cavalry archer [*syn boiarskii*] Grigorei Gordeev of Derevskaia piatina [one of the five provincial districts of Novgorod], and Grigorei, sir, died in Moscow about five years ago. After Grigorei's death his wife Ogaf'ia and his son Roman manumitted me and, sir, gave me a manumission document."

The slave's stature is average, he is about 50 years old, his hair is going gray, he has a long nose, a sharp face, and a long beard.

State Secretary Dmitrei Aliab'ev ordered that limited service slavery contract, having been copied into the permanent record books, returned to Pervoi Onichkov. He ordered the contract-writing scribe of the public square scribes and the witness to affix their signatures to the record books. He ordered the fees for that limited service slavery contract collected from Pervoi Onichkov by the sovereign Tsar's decree at the rate of 1 altyn per ruble [3 percent]. The fee of 10 altyns for the 10 rubles from that limited service slavery contract was collected from Pervoi Onichkov, and the contract was returned to Pervoi Onichkov. The contract-writing scribe Grisha signed this copy. The witness Ondrusha signed this note. The witness Kirilko, son of Ivan Tryznov, signed this contract note. [Source: NZKK 1: 274-76]

Be it known that I, Ignatei, son of Martem'ian, my wife, Matrena, the daughter of Ignatei, and my children, a daughter Orinka and a son Aleksei, have borrowed from Afanasei, son of Andrei Eremeev, the sum of 2 Moscow rubles from the day of the Holy Apostle James the brother of the Lord in the flesh until the same date a year hence. For the interest we shall serve every day in the household. When the date for the repayment of the principal lapses, we shall serve our lord on the same basis in the household.

The Nikola secretary of Peredol'skii pogost, Lazor' Semenov, witnessed this. The provincial administration [*zemskoi*] clerk, Zhdanko Gavrilov, wrote the contract, April 30, 1603.

The contract was entered in the books, and the fees collected.

The witness Lazarko affixed his hand.

In the interrogation the borrower Ignat said: "I was born, sir, in the household of Afanasei Eremeev."

In stature he is a man of average height, his complexion is ruddy, hair white, eyes gray, about 30 years old. His wife Matrenka is of average stature, swarthy complexion, gray eyes, about 30 years old. The daughter Orinka is 7 years old, has brown hair, gray eyes. The son Oleshka is 3 years old, has blond hair and gray eyes. [Source: NZKK 2: 327]

The Origin of Limited Service Contract Slavery

First appearing in early Muscovy, limited service contract slavery has been assumed to have been unique to Muscovy, something that the Russians had invented all by themselves. V. M. Paneiakh, for example, argues that it evolved out of the general loan contract of the period.[80] However, something exactly like Muscovite limited service contract slavery (prior to 1597) existed about 1,300 years earlier in Parthia, in Dura Europus on the Euphrates (Syria).

Roman law knew the institution of antichresis, "an agreement between creditor and debtor by which the former was granted the right to use the thing pledged (land or house) and obtain income therefore in lieu of interest. The creditor kept possession until the debt was paid."[81] In Syria, this institution which in the Roman world proper had applied only to immovables, was expanded to include human beings. (For movables, this type of pledge is known as a "pawn.")[82] The interesting thing about the Dura Europus development is that its features correspond in every respect to the Muscovite limited service slavery contract. It is even called by M. I. Rostovtzeff a "service contract."[83]

Self-sale into slavery was a not uncommon practice in the Ancient Near East. The secondary sources convey the impression that many of these people did not violate the "outsider" rule of slavery, for they were immigrants and others lacking kin to support them during difficult periods, persons who had no other option than to sell themselves or die.

> [In Ancient Babylonia] voluntary self-sale was a common phenomenon, especially among strangers who had neither kin nor friends to tide them over in times of distress; but even natives sometimes resorted to this desperate step. . . . From Nuzi we possess a number of documents relating to self-enslavement. These are mostly from the foreign immigrants, the Habiru, who, being unable to find employment, entered, "often of their own free will," singly or with their families, into the status of servitude.[84]

Having gotten over the psychological barrier of enslaving their own ethnos by

---

80. V. M. Paneiakh, *Kholopstvo v XVI-nachale XVII veka* (Leningrad: Nauka, 1975), p. 14: idem, "K voprosu o proiskhozhdenii," pp. 112-13.

81. Adolph Berger, *Encyclopaedic Dictionary of Roman Law* (= *Transactions of the American Philosophical Society*, n.s., vol. 43, pt. 2[1953]), p. 364.

82. H. C. Black, *Black's Law Dictionary* (St. Paul: West Publishing Company, 1968), p. 119. Lithuanian law also knew the antichretic mortgage, which was called *zastava*. One might speculate that the Muscovites borrowed the concept and applied it to movables. This seems unlikely, for the Muscovites did not borrow the institution for its initial application, to landed estates.

83. M. I. Rostovtzeff and C. Bradford Welles, "A Parchment Contract of Loan from Dura-Europus on the Euphrates," *Yale Classical Studies* 2(1931): 70.

84. Mendelsohn, *Slavery in the Ancient Near East*, pp. 14, 16.

gradually becoming accustomed to some self-sales of natives intermingled with the self-sales of immigrants, the people of the Ancient Near East then used free persons as pledges for loans. In Assyria, "as a setoff against the interest of the loan, the creditor would . . . enjoy . . . the labor of the pledged person. . . . In case the debt was not paid at the stipulated time, the pledge, slave or freeman, was foreclosed." The same was practiced later in Nuzi. "Wives, children, and often the debtor himself entered into the house of the creditor as a 'security' (ditennūtu) and remained there, working off the interest, until the loan was paid." The specialist on slavery in the Ancient Near East, Isaac Mendelsohn, thought that it would be best to define this institution as indentured servitude, a term that is more appropriate for another institution in Muscovy. He went on to note that "the service to be rendered by the ditennu was the most essential feature of the transaction and not the loan itself, which was of secondary importance." These contracts were of varied terms, some ten years, some as much as fifty years. Mendelsohn noted that it would be safe to assume that very few of the people so enslaved were actually freed.[85]

Using human beings as collateral for loans was an ancient practice in Syria. Antichresis-type loans with human beings as the collateral were common in Syria in the middle of the second millennium B.C. This was revealed in the Alalah (modern Atshana) excavations carried out in the years 1937-39 and 1946-49. Atshana lies south of the Lake of Antioch between the Aleppo road and the River Orontes. Among the items excavated were 460 tablets, of which 34 involved loans. As a surety for the loans, either the debtor himself or members of his family entered the service of the creditor (lived in his house and had to work for him), and were to be freed upon repayment of the debt. It is particularly noteworthy that some of the documents explicitly stated that the sureties were slaves until the loans were repaid. These loans differ however, from those two millennia later at Parthia in that the service was not in lieu of interest, which was mentioned in the documents.[86]

The use of antichresis for human collateral evolved in the Ancient Near East until it reached Dura Europus. Whether it evolved beyond that is unknown. But in Dura Europus the institution resembled that in Muscovy, especially in the stipulation that the initial period of the "loan" was one year. If we borrow the concept linguists use to define a dialect, "bundle of features," it is hard to see how we can fail to consider the Dura Europus and Muscovite institutions as identical.

In table 2.5 we see that Russian limited service contract slavery was like the antichresis of Dura Europus and Roman Egypt. Table 2.5 also makes evident

85. Ibid., pp. 28-32.

86. D. J. Wisemen, *The Alalakh Tablets* (London: The British Institute of Archaeology at Ankara, 1953), pp. 40-47, especially document no. 32 (= *Occasional Publications of the British Institute of Archaeology at Ankara*, no. 2).

Russian patterns of limited service slavery contracts. Numbers 1-8 are from Riazan' in the 1510s. Numbers 9-16 are typical of the abbreviated form in which earlier documents were registered in accord with the 1597 mandate that required the review and formal registration of all claims to slaves. Numbers 17-25 are typical current registrations from the Novgorod region. The clincher for the similarity of the Parthian and Russian forms of slavery, if one is needed, is provided by I. Sh. Shifman's comment that this form existed to get around the "impossibility" of enslaving a fellow citizen outright for debts or by any other means.[87] Whether the Muscovite limited service contract form of slavery was a case of spontaneous independent generation or an example of "discontiguous diffusion" is something that I cannot determine. The problem is made particularly difficult by the fact that slavery was rare in late Byzantium, and both there and in Islamic Persia of the fifteenth century the enslavement of coreligionists and fellow nationals was strictly forbidden. The problem is how the institution got from Dura Europus to Riazan' on the southern frontier of Muscovy in the early sixteenth century. If Byzantium and Persia are unlikely as sources, another possibility might be the Caucasus.[88]

While the Middle East provides a model for limited service contract slavery prior to the 1586-97 changes, the idea of limiting it to the life of the owner must have come from elsewhere. As we shall see in chapter 15, there have been throughout history many instances of a slave's bondage being limited to the life of one owner, but that was not the custom for those who sold themselves in the Near East.

The immediate inspiration for the 1586-97 change of limited service contract slavery to the life of the owner may have been a law of August 21, 1556, which prescribed that a military captive was to be enslaved only during the period of his captor's life, and could not pass as a slave to his children.[89] Consequently

---

87. A. P. Marinovich, E. S. Golubtsova, I. Sh. Shifman, and A. I. Pavlovskaia, *Rabstvo v vostochnykh provintsiakh Rimskoi Imperii v I-III vv.* (Moscow: Nauka, 1977), p. 117. An extensive discussion of the formulas of limited service slavery contracts can be found in Lappo-Danilevskii, "Sluzhilye kabaly," pp. 720 ff. The outright sale of natives was also against the law in China, although the law was not always observed (Wiens, p. 297).

88. Pryor, "Comparative Study," p. 32; George Ostrogorsky, *History of the Byzantine State* (New Brunswick: Rutgers University Press, 1969), pp. 393-94; Brauning, pp. 52-53. Contracts of *paramone*, a loan for which the debtor gives his services until the loan is paid, in most cases virtual sale of one's self into slavery, were known in Byzantine Egypt (Allan Chester Johnson and Louis C. West, *Byzantine Egypt: Economic Studies* [Princeton: Princeton University Press, 1949], p. 133 [= Princeton University Studies in Papyrology, no. 6]). Still another possible source for early modern Russian limited service contract slavery might have been India. A number of nineteenth-century Indian slavery contracts were remarkably similar to Muscovite limited service slavery contracts (see, for example, Hjejle, pp. 100-101, 122). However, I know nothing about Indian slavery in the fifteenth century.

89. AI 1, no. 154, V, 17.

TABLE 2.5

Features of Eastern Roman Antichresis and Russian Limited Service Slavery Contracts

Features	A	B	1	2	3	4	5	6	7	8	9	10	11	12	13	14	15	16	17	18	19	20	21	22	23	24	25
1. Official reporting	x	x	x	x	x	x	x	x	x	x									x	x	x	x	x	x	x	x	x
2. Borrower	x	x	x	x	x	x	x	x	x	x	x	x	x	x		x	x	x	x	x	x	x	x	x	x	x	x
3. Borrower's origins	x						x															x					x
4. Borrower's family							x	x	x	x				x	x											x	x
5. Creditor	x	x	x	x	x	x	x	x	x	x	x	x	x	x	x	x	x	x	x	x	x	x	x	x	x	x	x
6. Sum	x	x	x	x	x	x	x	x	x	x	x	x			x	x	x	x	x	x	x	x	x	x	x	x	x
7. Month and day	x	x	x	x	x	x	x	x	x	x			x						x	x	x	x	x	x	x	x	x
8. Period of loan	x	x	x	x	x	x	x	x	x	x			x						x	x	x	x	x	x	x	x	x
9. Other recipient of borrowed sum			x	x	x		x	x	x																		
10. Work for interest	x	x	x	x	x	x	x	x	x	x	x								x	x	x	x	x	x			
11. Will repay	x	x	x	x	x	x	x	x	x	x	x								x	x	x	x	x	x			
12. As comes due, will continue to work								x	x	x																	
13. Any person present responsible for debt								x	x	x																	
14. Fines for slave's absence	x																										
15. Won't sign another yearly contract			x	x	x	x	x	x	x																		
16. Won't agree orally to another contract			x	x	x	x	x	x	x																		

TABLE 2.5 continued

17. Master to feed and be liable for slave
18. Slave must renew contract on demand
19. Witnesses
20. Author of contract
21. Date of writing
22. Interrogation: Is slave compliant?
23. Slave's personal history
24. Slave's description

*Sources:

A. Dura Europus. Rostovtsev, p. 7; Wiedemann, pp. 42-44.
B. Egypt. Roak (1929), p. 48.
1. 1510. Akty Iushkova, p. 66.
2. 1515. Akty Iushkova, p. 79.
3. 1515. Akty Iushkova, pp. 79-80.
4. 1515-17. Akty Iushkova, p. 83.
5. 1516-19. Akty Iushkova, p. 85.
6. 1519. Akty Iushkova, p. 92.
7. 1519. Akty Iushkova, pp. 91-92.
8. 1519. Akty Iushkova, p. 91.
9. 1533/34. RIB 17(1898): 213, no. 558.
10. 1557. Kopanev, "Materialy," p. 157.
11. 1562/63. RIB 17(1898): 25, no. 71.

12. 1565. Lakier, "Akty," p. 48.
13. 1563/64. RIB 17(1898): 25-26, no. 74.
14. 1564. Lakier, "Akty," p. 48.
15. 1565/66. RIB 17(1898): 166, no. 450.
16. 1566/67. RIB 17(1898): 26, no. 75.
17. 1595. NZKK 1: 33-34.
18. 1595. NZKK 1: 34-36.
19. 1595. NZKK 1: 41-42.
20. 1599. RIB 15(1894): 1.
21. 1599. RIB 15(1894): 2.
22. 1599. RIB 15(1894): 2.
23. 1603. NZKK 2: 339.
24. 1603. NZKK 2: 339-40.
25. 1603. NZKK 2: 340-41.

captivity ceased to be a source of full slavery, for a time. While this idea failed to survive in the military sphere, it permanently changed the legal form of limited service contract slavery. The innovation persisted in the institution of limited service contract slavery because it was consonant with the changes in other parts of society at the time and in the government's needs. Peasants were bound to the land in the 1580s and 1590s, and the process was begun of binding townspeople to their towns. After the introduction of the St. George's Day limitation on peasant mobility in the second half of the fifteenth century, a peasant could move legally on or around November 26 by one of two means: by settling affairs with his lord and moving on (*vykhod*), or by another landlord making the settlement for him, with the understanding that the peasant would move to the second lord's land (*vyvoz*). The enserfment legislation of the 1590s forbade both options. Both options also were potentially available to limited service contract slaves before the changes of the 1586-97 period: before the expiration of the initial year, the slave could pay off the loan himself, or, with the slave's consent, another person could pay off the loan, and take the slave to his house. Both practices were prohibited by the law of 1597. After that, the slave could go free upon the death of his owner, something that was guaranteed. One may assume that the government was conscious of the parallels between *vykhod* and *vyvoz* (sometimes inelegantly translated as "exportation") and limited service contract slavery in its first year, but I have no evidence of this. Therefore it cannot necessarily be assumed that the government acted because it was made uncomfortable by the asymmetry of a prohibition against peasant geographical mobility and the lack of a prohibition against the slave equivalent.

Another possible motive for the government's alteration of the nature of limited service contract slavery may have been a concern for revenue. While there were some exceptions for slaves engaged in agriculture, as a rule slaves paid no taxes. It was obvious by the early 1580s that limited service contract slavery was fundamentally the successor institution to full slavery, which meant that perhaps as much as 10 percent of the population was perpetually and hereditarily removed from the tax rolls. In freeing the slave on the death of his owner, the state may have assumed that the slave element of society would largely self-destruct if the slaves were compulsorily manumitted once or twice every generation. What the state, at that time, did not understand was that slavery created dependency from which escape to a free status after any length of time in bondage was difficult if not impossible. Later, however, the government seems to have come to recognize that fact.

As will become clear in this essay, because slavery performed social functions for which there were yet no substitutes, the government could not simply abolish it in the 1580s or 1590s. We do not know whether the government considered abolishing slavery at the end of the sixteenth century, but it is fairly clear that, when it did take such legal action, alternative institutions were present to replace slavery. Perhaps unfortunately, the alternative institutions had borrowed much from the institution of slavery itself.

Yet another interpretation of the 1586-97 innovations in the institution of limited service contract slavery must be mentioned. That was the period of the ascendancy of the middle service class, something that I have described in *Enserfment and Military Change in Muscovy*. One might propose that the change in the nature of limited service contract slavery was instituted to safeguard the interests of the middle service class, whose members were at a disadvantage in competing with members of the upper service class for slaves. The latter, it might be claimed, were excessively vigorous in purchasing both would-be limited service contract slaves and those who had already sold themselves but who had not defaulted on the initial year of the contracts, and their actions so angered the members of the middle service class that they convinced Boris Godunov to make self-sale into slavery permanent, for the life of the owner.[90] Thus, the middle service class reasoning might have gone, its members would no longer have to suffer the indignity of buying a distressed person, financing his recovery (during which little service could be expected), and then witnessing the recovered individual's shopping around and selling himself to a wealthier (or otherwise more desirable) purchaser. This argument is very seductive, and in keeping with the tenor of the era. However, there is no evidence to support the hypothesis, either direct or indirect. It presupposes, moreover, that there was a shortage of individuals who wanted to sell themselves into slavery and who therefore, had to be competed for. Regrettably, there is no evidence to support this proposition either. Had that been a fact, as we shall see, slave prices would have been higher and fewer people would have died of starvation.

Another legal aspect of limited service contract slavery was regulation of the prices that could be paid for such slaves. This is the subject of chapter 10, but here I only need note that at some time in the 1620s the legal price was set at 2 rubles per slave, and then in the 1630s it was raised to 3 rubles, the price specified in the *Ulozhenie*.[91]

Not only are the Ancient Near Eastern, and specifically Parthian, analogues to limited service contract slavery unknown to students of Muscovite history, but more modern cases are unfamiliar as well: the Malayan, Thai, African. All of them shed very helpful light on the problem of defining and placing in a comparative context Muscovite *kabal'noe kholopstvo*.

Pawning of the debtor himself was a frequent occurrence in the Malay archipelago (the practice the Dutch called *pandeligen*), and the classical comparative student of slavery, H. J. Nieboer, made the point in discussing this that "as long as the debt remains unpaid, the pawn is in the same condition as a slave. He has not to perform a fixed amount of labor, he must serve his master without any

90. Koretskii, *Zakreposhchenie*, p. 233.
91. 1649 *Ulozhenie* 20: 19; MS, p. 262.

limitation; the master has over him a power that is, in principle, unlimited."
After pointing out that this was kind of *pignus* in Roman law called *antichresis*,
Niebor went on to note that:

> We may classify the pawns among the slaves if we can prove that sociologically
> a system of pawning performs the same function as a slave-system. And this
> certainly is the case. The same system of compulsory labor, the same subjection
> of the entire person exists, whether the subjected are perpetually slaves or tem-
> porarily pawns. Where pawns have a fixed amount of work to do, they are tem-
> porary serfs; but where (as is most often the case) no limit is put to the amount
> of work the master may exact from them, they are temporary slaves, and as
> long as they are slaves, take the same place as other slaves in the social system.[92]

This certainly describes the Muscovite case and helps justify calling the *kabal'nyi
kholop* a slave before as well as after default prior to 1597, and after 1597 as well.

The Pawn and the Problem of Mobility

While the Russian limited service slavery contract is almost an exact replica of
the Roman antichresis applied to movable property, the slave covered by it also
bears some resemblance to the more recent African pawn. The Vai of Liberia
and Sierra Leone allowed a man in debt to pawn his sister's children to his creditor until his debt was paid; the labor of the pawns was regarded as payment of
the interest on the original debt.[93] When Liberia in 1930 outlawed the practice
of human pawning, it was viewed as analogous to slavery.[94]

The African pawn is not considered a complete slave because, unlike most
African slaves, he is not kinless or an outsider, even though he is a marginal
individual in his society. The major distinction between the African pawn and
the slave is that the former remains among his kin, who can protect his honor
and render such services as kin are supposed to. Among the Igbo of Nigeria, for
example, the pawn, who was sometimes called a "debtor slave," was at the disposal of his master only for domestic use of his labor, but all other rights were
retained by the members of the pawn's lineage. Pawnship among the LaDagaa
of Northern Ghana, who fell into bondage under conditions of famine, is termed
"a kind of protective slavery."[95]

It is at this point that the Russian limited service contract slave parts company

---

92. Nieboer, *Slavery*, p. 40.
93. Miers and Kopytoff, p. 289. Sometimes Africans were panyarred to satisfy debts (Albert Van Dantzig, "Effects," p. 257). The word *penhor* means "pawn."
94. Miers and Kopytoff, p. 298.
95. Ibid., pp. 126, 131; Jack Goody in Watson, *Systems*, p. 27.

with the pawn. Among the data in the slave contracts are many indications of where the subject was born and his last place of residence. One can also determine the slaveowner's place of residence, which one may assume to be the final destination of the slave. About 235 such pairs (slave's birthplace, owner's home) can be discerned from the available data, and less than 10 percent (21) of them are identical. Mapping these data, one discovers that the Muscovite limited service contract slave was likely to have moved all over Russia before becoming enslaved, and thus was de facto kinless. This mobility is comparable in many respects to the enormous extent of geographical mobility among servants in the Old World (whose absence in the New World was one of the factors inducing the North American colonists to begin importing slaves as domestics).[96]

Not only does a map show that in fact the Russian slave was likely to be kinless, all other available information that I am aware of does nothing to contradict the conclusion that, geographically at least, the slave was an outsider. I have never read of a slave's relative interceding on his behalf in any manner, as happened both in the Ancient Near East and in Africa. When slaves had to post bail, their guarantors were not related to them. Slaves occasionally participated in legal inquests (particularly on matters of property ownership), and I do not recall ever seeing a situation in which a slave and free witness appeared to be related. The same was true in the notorious "mutual pledge" (*krugovaia poruka*) used by the government to force compliance with everything from elite loyalty to the payment of taxes, where slaves sometimes were used with free men, but again I do not recall members of the same family in both social categories.

On the other hand, the Muscovite limited service contract slave was not as kinless as some slaves have been at other times and places, when a chattel's sense of isolation was enforced by the denial of his right to use a patronymic. That was the case, for example, in the Ancient Near East, and specifically in Syria in the first through the third century A.D.[97]

Thailand knew a form of redeemable slave that bore some resemblance to the Muscovite limited service contract slave. Prior to 1805 there probably was a time limit on redemption in the Thai institution, at whose expiration the slave was regarded as definitely sold, much like the Muscovite case prior to 1597. The person of the slave represented the original capital sum loaned, his labor was for the interest and never paid off the principal. Unlike in the Muscovite case, in Thailand the amount of labor was expected to have some relationship to the amount of the capital sum. A more fundamental difference was that the person

96. Peter Laslett, "Fogel and Engerman on Family and Household in the Slave Plantations of the U.S.A." (Mimeographed paper prepared for the MSSB Conference on *Time on the Cross*, Rochester, N. Y., October 24-26, 1974), p. 17; published in his *Family Life and Illicit Love in Earlier Generations: Essays in Historical Sociology* (Cambridge: At the University Press, 1977), pp. 233-60.

97. Marinovich et al., p. 114. In 1701 the Russian government even went so far as to order that slaves should use full names, even in private correspondence (PSZ 4: 181, no. 1884).

enslaved for the debt commonly was not the debtor, and Thai law prescribed severe punishments for people who tried to sell themselves fraudulently when not in dire straits. It was possible for a debtor to initiate the transaction and sell himself, with a kinsman or someone else acting as guarantor, but in most cases someone else became the redeemable slave: an existing slave, or, more typically, a junior wife, a child, a grandchild, or younger sibling. That, of course, was not at all like Muscovite limited service contract slavery. Moreover, in the Thai case, there was a continuing relationship between the seller-guarantor, redeemable slave, and the buyer-owner. The guarantor could protect the slave against owner abuse, and could initiate legal action on behalf of the slave against the owner. Also unlike in the Muscovite case, the Thai redeemable slave was not released on the death of the buyer (or the seller, either), but was inherited by the heirs on both sides of the transaction.[98] Thus the Thai redeemable slave is somewhat like the Russian *kabal'nyi kholop*, but the differences are highly perceptible as well.

I have noted throughout my discussion of the varieties of slavery in Muscovy that each tended to have its birth, extended life-span, and gradual demise. This was true for full and registered slavery, although hereditary slavery seems to have remained relatively constant throughout the period. Limited service contract slavery gradually became the major institution for those who wanted to sell themselves, and perhaps even for some of the distant descendants of those born outside of East Slavdom as well. No precise date can be assigned to that moment when limited service contract slavery became the sole outlet for those who wanted to give up the struggle for an independent existence, but it is fairly clear that the codifiers of the Ulozhenie of 1649 expected that *kabal'noe kholopstvo* would be resorted to by such individuals.[99] Moreover, limited service contract slavery was usually the priority category of bondage. Tests were to be made to see whether its particular norms were applicable to a situation, and only if they were not could other forms of slavery be considered.[100] Throughout the 1680s the government insisted that limited service slavery contracts be formulated on domestic servants.[101] The demise of limited service contract slavery because of the military manpower and taxation exigencies of the Petrine era will be discussed in chapter 18.

---

98. Turton, pp. 264-65, 271-72, 290. An institution similar to that in Thailand existed in northern Sumatra. Specialists distinguish it from "slavery proper" by terming it "peonage." A sense of group responsibility was felt for the debtor, whose kinsmen often ransomed him immediately. The sense of community was a manifestation of a consciousness that kin belonged to an extended family and lineage, that all were descended from a revered ancestor (J. C. Vergouwen, *The Social Organization and Customary Law of the Toba-Batak of Northern Sumatra* [The Hague: Martinus Nijhoff, 1964], pp. 311, 315, 327, 335). There was no such sense of community, no ransoming of kin in Muscovy, that I am aware of.

99. 1649 *Ulozhenie* 20: 7, 8, 21; MS, pp. 257-58, 263.

100. 1649 *Ulozhenie* 20: 64; MS, pp. 277-78.

101. PSZ 2: 313-14, 588-89, 858-59, 909, nos. 869, 1073, 1246, 1278.

Military Captives

Military captives present a special problem in an examination of Muscovite slave law.

Military captivity probably has created more slaves in the history of mankind than all other causes combined. So it has been since the dawn of recorded history. "The earliest Sumerian terms for male and female slaves are the composite signs *nita + kur* 'male of a foreign country,' and *munus + kur* 'female of a foreign country,' indicating that the first humans to be enslaved in Ancient Babylonia were captive foreigners."[102] The same was true elsewhere, such as in Thailand, where war slaves were probably the earliest and often the most numerous human chattel. The word for "enemy" (*kha soek*, lit. "slave fight") intimates that adversaries were considered to be potential slaves.[103]

Muscovy, as Kievan Rus' had been, was part of a world in which captivity was a major by-product of warfare, and the right to take home captured slaves was one of the major incentives for almost every warrior. Right down to the eighteenth century, alien enemy peoples who fell into Muscovite hands could expect to be enslaved. A law borrowed in form from the *Lithuanian Statute* of 1588 on procedures for returning fugitive slaves includes in the list "hereditary slaves, limited service contract slaves, purchased slaves, or war captives of other lands."[104] This grouped military captives with the other types of slaves recognized in the *Ulozhenie* of 1649. There were, however, modifications of this type of slavery from time to time that distinguished it from the other forms.

We see the military captive mentioned in 1556 in a brief law that begins with the caption: "Add to the *Sudebnik* for use in resolving suits on slaveownership." Then it goes on to say: "If someone sues [to recover] a military captive as a slave, regardless of the origin of the captivity, and is awarded the verdict thanks to the evidence supplied by many witnesses, that military captive is his slave for the life of the owner. He is not to be a slave of his children. If the military captive has any children, they are not slaves of the slaveowner, and they are not the slaves of his children either." Thus the war captive is a very circumscribed form of slave, a point that is made clear by the rest of the 1556 decree: "If the military captive marries a slave woman, or gives another form of document on himself, then that military captive is a slave like others."[105] This provision, in the context of the captive who converts to Christianity, is repeated in the *Ulozhenie* of 1649.[106] Thus the war captive could choose to become a full or, later, limited service contract slave, and records of several who did choose to do that are ex-

---

102. Mendelsohn, p. 1.
103. Turton, pp. 255-56.
104. 1649 *Ulozhenie* 20: 89, borrowed in form from 1588 LS 12: 17-i.
105. AI 1: 257, no. 154, V, 17.
106. 1649 *Ulozhenie* 20: 37.

tant. If the military captive did not decide to become a regular slave, one may assume that the norms of slavery applicable to other slaves were applied to him as well, during the lifetime of his owner, while the law of 1556 was in effect.

As I noted already, this limitation on the possession of military captives itself was temporary but may have had a lasting impact on the institution of limited service contract slavery. At the time of the *Ulozhenie* of 1649, war captives were included with full slaves (probably an anachronism), registered slaves, and purchased slaves as those types which could be alienated in wills, marriage contracts, dowries, and gift documents. They were explicitly contrasted with limited service contract slaves, who in no way could be so alienated.[107] In 1690, however, the government returned to its position of 1556 and decreed that military captives were to be manumitted by the Slavery Chancellery on the death of their owners. The causes of the 1690 measure are not immediately apparent, but it may reflect either an attempt to curtail the institution of slavery after 1679 (in favor of augmenting the tax rolls) or a recognition that keeping perpetually enslaved the hordes of war captives that resulted from the Thirteen Years War and other engagements of the post-1654 period might tell negatively on the social structure of Muscovy.[108]

The situation of the military captive as slave is further complicated by the fact that he was subject to manumission by government decree at any time. This was particularly likely to happen as part of a treaty with a foreign power, one of whose clauses might be that all captured nationals of the other side could return home. Such events not infrequently expropriated the Muscovite slaveowner.[109] In 1558 the government ordered the manumission of any war slave who converted to Orthodoxy so that he might enter the tsar's service.[110] Military slaves were recorded in separate books in the Slavery Chancellery so that the government could keep track of them.[111]

Moreover, the government began to prohibit the enslavement of certain military captives as a part of the same process. Thus on October 9, 1634, after the conclusion of the Smolensk War, the government noted that, of the Poles and Lithuanians who had been seized during the war, some had been distributed throughout the country in the charge of governors and other governmental officials, some were being held in jails, and some were living with various private parties of sundry ranks throughout the country. No doubt the detainers in the last group had

107. Ibid., 20: 61.

108. PSZ 3: 82, no. 1383; N. A. Baklanova, "Dela o syske beglykh krest'ian i kholopov kak istochnik dlia istorii tiaglogo sel'skogo naseleniia v Povolzh'e vo vtoroi polovine XVII v.," *Problemy istochnikovedeniia* 11(1963): 320. See also the *iazyk/iazyki* entries in AMG 2: 773 and 3: 671.

109. *Opisanie dokumentov i bumag* 15(1908): 9, no. 5.

110. Man'kov, *Ulozhenie*, p. 116.

111. PSZ 2: 589, no. 1073; E. N. Kusheva, "O plene kak istochnike kholopstva," pp. 217-31; *Opisanie* 12(1901): 408, no. 346-IV.

probably seized the individuals in question and considered the captives as their slaves. However, the government ordered all such prisoners of war set free, either to settle in Muscovy or to return home, and prohibited the recording of slavery status for any of them. The government specified that this decree was to be made public in the usual fashion, by public criers announcing it frequently in all the public markets on market days. The government assumed that everyone who had possession of such military captives would hear the new law and would then bring their charges to the local government office for interrogation and manumission. The government wanted a list of all such people, including the name of each, his place of birth, religion, place of capture, whether he was a soldier or a peasant, and whether he wanted to return home or stay in Muscovy. The holders of those captives who wanted to return to the Rzeczpospolita were required to provide carts to transport them to the Novgorod Regional Chancellery office in Moscow, and those in jail were to be delivered by postal-system vehicles. As usual, Muscovy could not refrain from interjecting a class element into the scene: wealthy captives were to ride three to a wagon, poor ones five to a wagon. Any marriages that had been consummated by the captives were not to be broken up—the usual Muscovite practice, as we shall see.[112]

The captives taken during the Smolensk War continued to be a problem, in spite of the severe sanctions prescribed for violators of the 1634 statute. In 1637/38, according to a marginal notation in the original manuscript scroll of the *Ulozhenie*, another decree was promulgated on the military captives. It again insisted that such people had the right to choose whether to return home or stay in Muscovy, and dwelled on the issue of the captives' spouses of slave origin, who had to be freed with the captives themselves. The *Ulozhenie* went on to emphasize that the freed captives and their spouses of slave origin had every right freely to give themselves back as slaves to the people with whom they had been living at the time of the mandatory emancipation.[113] Nothing is known about the actual dimensions of this issue, about how many captives there were, how many chose to stay in Muscovy as free people, and how many chose to remain enslaved with their captors.

The perils to which war captives were potentially subject are revealed in the 1635 case of Krechetnikov v. Pozdeev, discussed in detail in chapter 4. There one of the slaves in dispute pretended to be a Lithuanian military captive, freed by the repatriation treaty and then enslaved by a limited service slavery contract which she pretended not to have understood.[114] While her story was subsequently revealed to have been feigned, one may well imagine that such situations actually occurred in real life, for otherwise the fugitive slave would not have attempted the ruse.

112. AAE 3: 389-91, no. 252.
113. 1649 *Ulozhenie* 20: 69; MS, p. 280.
114. Iakovlev, *Kholopstvo*, pp. 488-96, no. 24.

Ownership of military captives was additionally precarious for a special group of slaveowners, the non-Orthodox. In a proselytizing spirit, the government allowed any non-Orthodox slave who lived with a non-Orthodox slaveowner and was willing to convert to Orthodoxy to buy his own freedom. The slaveowner could charge up to 15 rubles apiece to free such slaves, but no more, even if higher prices were written in the purchase documents, for the government noted that the sums entered in such purchase documents were sometimes inflated.[115]

Purchased Slaves

Yet another category of chattel in Muscovy was "purchased slaves" (*kuplennye liudi*). As noted above, they were often mentioned in the same context as military captives (war slaves). No doubt slaves were bought and sold in Russia from the very dawn of the institution, but, as we shall see in chapter 10, by the sixteenth and seventeenth centuries the slave trade was very muted in Muscovy. The *Ulozhenie* of 1649 mentions "purchased slaves" in the context of Tatars of the Lower Volga and Siberia, but does not specify how the Tatars became enslaved. We know that Russians captured (and kidnapped) Tatars and sold them to each other, and also that Muscovites purchased Tatars from slave dealers in those Islamic frontier areas. In chapter 18 we shall see how the Muscovites began to curtail slavery in the areas they were annexing. Legally, purchased slaves were like other categories, and were alienable like hereditary slaves.[116] The major distinction between "military captives" and "purchased slaves" may well have been that the former were primarily, but not exclusively, Europeans, while the latter were non-Europeans. Moreover, the "purchased slaves" were appreciably less likely than the war slaves to be repatriated.

It would be fair to say that, by the reign of Vasilii III, the system of slavery was quite uniform for all of Russia. While I have data for over 350 different places from all of Muscovy and for 180 of the years between 1430 and 1714, I should mention that 92 percent of all the cases are from the northwest (Novgorod) region, and 80 percent are from the years 1581 to 1603, 743 of the 2,499 cases from that last year alone. Nevertheless, there can be little doubt that slavery was fundamentally the same throughout Muscovy.

A number of facts attest to the reality of a pan-Muscovite system of slavery. For one, there was a high degree of institutional uniformity throughout most of the period, as well as centralization enforced by requiring that major trouble cases be resolved in Moscow. Secondly, as we shall see, men from many parts of Russia were involved in the Novgorod region slave system as purchasers of slaves,

115. 1649 *Ulozhenie* 20: 71.
116. Ibid., 20: 61-62, 71, 74, 77, 89, 97, 98, 100, 115.

as witnesses to slavery contracts, and even as officials in charge of the system.

Even more telling may be the apparent patterns of mobility of the slaves themselves. Chapter 12 will discuss where slaves were born and where their owners lived, the most distant chronological pairs that can be established. The story seems to defy regionalization or the establishing of a hierarchy of central places. Slaves traveled in all directions all over Muscovy, from one frontier to the opposite one. Even more surprising are the places where slaves said they last lived before selling themselves. I am not yet prepared to argue that there was a pan-Russian market for slave labor, but it does appear as though these people did wander all over Muscovy. The pattern of peasant mobility was different: moving from one province to the next was the rule, jumping provinces was rare. Peasants of course were burdened with agricultural inventory, but future slaves had nothing. Some of the documents tell of owners picking up slaves on the road, say, from Moscow to Tver'. The image of Russians constantly migrating, constantly on the move, is a popular one in historiography and was advanced as one of the reasons why the government had to enserf the peasantry, which thereby lost the right to wander all over Russia. It is now known that most of the peasants were not at all migratory and usually remained in the same place for generations (as peasants are supposed to), and that they were enserfed for other reasons. It does appear as though there was a considerable amount of vagabondage among the social elements that tended to become slaves.

Mobility of people not bound to the land or a town, or not burdened with the cares and implements of agriculture or trades, was free because of the absence of political or geographic barriers in Muscovy. While some agricultural provincialism must have prevailed in Muscovy, there was no feudalism or feudal ties that might have bound a person physically or psychologically to any one place. This helps greatly to explain the uniformity of Muscovite slavery.

Slavery was fundamentally uniform not only throughout the land of early modern Russia but also across the eight types that have been discussed earlier in this chapter. This was much like the situation among the African Sena, where "the multiple patterns of recruitment did not generate separate systems of slavery, as they did in some [other] African societies. Whether purchased, stolen, or captured, slaves were grouped together with those who had voluntarily given up their freedom to form one rather ambiguous social category."[117] So it was among the Muscovites, as we shall see in the following chapters.

117. Miers and Kopytoff, p. 110.

3. Slaveowners and Slaves

A vast number of norms went into the making of Muscovite slave law. A primary set of those norms established who could be a slaveowner and who could be a slave. The slaveowners are the concern of chapter 17 of this work, so that here I shall restrict the discussion to formal definitions and limitations. In chapter 17 I shall discuss also the comparative aspect of slaveownership, and note that Muscovy was somewhere between societies in which only the royal family owned slaves and those in which a large portion of the free population consisted of slaveowners. In most societies slaveownership is not legally defined, and in this respect late Muscovy was unusual.

Legal Definitions of Slaveowners

In the reign of Ivan III there were few legal restrictions on who could be a slaveowner, but several were added in the course of the next two centuries. The situation was still completely unstructured at the time of the *Sudebnik* of 1550, which spoke of "princes, boyars, *deti boiarskie*, and sundry others" as slaveowners.[1] Toward the end of the sixteenth century the laws regulating the system of slavery became more specific, a fact embodied in the decree of February 1, 1597, on limited service contract slaves. That document lists the types of persons who might be slaveowners, such as: boyars, princes, *dvoriane*, chancellery officials, state secretaries (*d'iaki*), *deti boiarskie*, sundry servicemen, elite merchants (*gosti*), and sundry merchants.[2] It is fairly clear that such lists were descriptive, not prescriptive, for they were not universally consistent, and in fact at the time other categories of people, such as clergymen and elite slaves, owned slaves. In all probability such lists in the sixteenth century represent the process of the beginning of thinking on the matter of who was a slaveowner, and nothing more than that. Boris Godunov's 1603 law on freeing starving slaves still used the word "various" (*vsiakie*) in sufficient contexts to encompass almost any category of person in the ranks of slaveowners. The legal permissiveness of early Muscovite law on the ownership of slaves should be contrasted with the rules of other societies, such as the Ming and Ch'ing Chinese, whose 1397 and 1646 codes for-

1. 1550 *Sudebnik* 78.
2. PRP 4: 371; UKKhP 1597, arts 2, 4.

bade commoners to own slaves, which was a prerogative of the social elite and government officials.[3]

Real restrictions on Muscovite slaveownership appeared only in the second quarter of the seventeenth century and were an integral part of the stratification of Muscovite society. One, dated 1627/28, limited the ownership of Orthodox slaves to other Orthodox. Directed against Westerners who, it was claimed, were depriving Orthodox of the sacraments, it reflected the xenophobia of the post-Time of Troubles epoch. According to the *Ulozhenie* of 1649,

Orthodox Christians were suffering oppression and profanation at the hands of the heterodox, many were dying without confession, without spiritual fathers, and during the great fast [February 2-March 8 to March 21-April 24] and during other fasts they were involuntarily eating meat and various forbidden foods.[4]

The law prescribed that any Russian who tried to serve a non-Orthodox slave-owner as a regular slave or as a voluntary slave was to be "severely punished, to teach him and others like him not to do such things." No penalties were laid down for the non-Orthodox who tried to obtain, or kept in violation of the law, an Orthodox slave, probably because the government wished to avoid antagonizing that elite.

But what about non-Orthodox slaves who might desire to convert to Orthodoxy? Certainly such individuals' souls were as precious as those of slaves born in Orthodoxy. The logic of such an argument was impeccable, and the Muscovite government even took it one step further by proclaiming that any non-Orthodox slave in the household of a non-Orthodox slaveowner who desired to convert to Orthodoxy had the right to do so, whereupon the slave was to be freed, and the slaveowner was to be paid 15 rubles compensation for the loss of his chattel. Should the slaveowner be able to produce a document showing that he had paid more than 15 rubles for the slave, such documents were to be ignored "because

3. PRP 4: 373; MS, p. 252, art. 8; 1649 *Ulozhenie* 20: 10, 21, 32; MS, pp. 258-59, 263, 267; Wiens, pp. 293-94, 305, 330. Like many other social programs, the Chinese one was violated—by calling the slaves something else, adopted sons, daughters, daughters-in-law. For a discussion of slaveownership in Central Sudan, see Gemery and Hogendorn, p. 168.

4. 1649 *Ulozhenie* 20: 70; MS, pp. 280-81; A. S. Muliukin, *Ocherki po istorii iuridiche-skogo polozheniia inostrannykh kuptsov v Moskovskom gosudarstve* (Odessa: Tekhnik, 1912), p. 130. The 1627/28 law must not have been enforced, for Russian Orthodox house slaves in 1631 brought charges against the wife of the Scottish mercenary colonel Alexander Lesly in which they accused her of forcing them to eat meat on fast days and of throwing an icon into the stove. As a consequence, non-Orthodox were forbidden to possess service estates (N. G. Ustrialov, *Istoriia tsarstvovaniia Petra Velikogo*, 6 vols. [St. Petersburg, 1858-64], 1: 183; Samuel H. Baron, ed., *The Travels of Olearius in Seventeenth-Century Russia* [Stanford: Stanford University Press, 1967], pp. 244-45). See also a 1593 edict proclaimed in a rage of crusading Orthodoxy in Kazan' that also appears to have been ignored (AAE 1: 436-38, no. 358).

the sums are exaggerated in purchase documents." Finally, the slave was to pay the sum himself.[5] The difficulty a slave had in raising the cash to manumit himself can be imagined, although, as will be discussed in chapter 5, some slaves undoubtedly did possess property. One potential difficulty unanticipated by the authors of this law was that other, simultaneous developments were making it increasingly difficult for persons not members of the urban classes to engage in cash-earning activities of the type that might produce 15 rubles.[6] In reality, private persons sometimes put up the cash to buy such converts out of slavery, and the state treasury might pay if the converts were in government service.

Before the enactment of these articles, even Kazan' Tatars were allowed to buy Russian girls in Novgorod. Thus Muscovite law through the beginning of the seventeenth century was like that of the Code of Hammurabi in Ancient Babylonia, which did not distinguish between native and alien slaveowners. The Hebrews (Lev. 25: 39-42, 47-54) were the first to make that distinction.[7] The Muscovite restriction went a step further in defining slaveownership, and was similar to ones found elsewhere, such as in Byzantium, where Constantine forbade Jews to own Christian slaves; in the Crimea, where Jewish or Christian ownership of Muslims was forbidden; or in the New World, where non-Catholics were not allowed to own slaves in Brazil. In 1713 Peter the Great went to the extreme of forcing the conversion of Muslims in Kazan' and Azov provinces who had lands on which Orthodox peasants and slaves resided.[8] Such measures reflected a general recognition that slaves tended to adopt the religion of their owners. In Muscovy it reinforced the generally anomalous situation in which native Russians were owned by their own ethnos.

In the sixteenth century, and into the first quarter of the seventeenth, elite slaves owned other slaves.[9] As I shall discuss in greater detail in chapter 17, the fact of slaves owning other slaves (the latter were called in Latin *servi vicarii*) was a not uncommon phenomenon from at least late Assyrian times down to modern times, and its prohibition in places such as the U.S. South was atypical.[10] Muscovite slaves were somewhat restricted in their right to own other slaves in 1634/35, when they were forbidden to buy freemen in limited service slavery

5. 1649 *Ulozhenie* 20: 71; MS, p. 281. The spirit of this article, encouraging conversions to Orthodoxy, comes from the Byzantine *Procheiros Nomos* (39: 31) through the *Kormchaia kniga* (chap. 48). The Austrian traveler Sigismund von Herberstein saw the principle in operation, the freeing of foreign slaves who converted to Orthodoxy, in the 1520s (*Commentaries on Russia*, trans. O. P. Backus [Lawrence: University of Kansas Bookstore, 1956], pp. 50-52).

6. Hellie, "Stratification."

7. Mendelsohn, *Slavery in the Ancient Near East*, pp. 89-90.

8. Fisher, "Muscovy and the Black Sea Trade," p. 585; Buckland, *The Roman Law of Slavery*, p. 605; PSZ 5:66-67, no. 2734.

9. Kolycheva, *Kholopstvo*, p. 68. See also Zheliabuzhskii v. Lobanov-Rostovskii (1623) (from Iakovlev, *Kholopstvo*, pp. 356-57, no. 7), discussed below in chapter 8.

10. Mendelsohn, pp. 68-69; Catterall 2: 267.

contracts, and all such contracts outstanding were annulled. After that time slaves were permitted only to retain free men for a specified term in indentures. The *Ulozhenie* of 1649 repeated this prohibition and cited in the scroll copy a law of 1639/40 as its source.[11] This was a manifestation of the decline of the elite stratum of slaves and the formation of a caste society that was expressed also in a prohibition against slave ownership of landed estates and urban property.[12] The strictures of the 1630s were not, it should be emphasized, a blanket prohibition against the practice of slaves owning other slaves (such as hereditary slaves, war captives, and purchased Tatars), and slaves continued to own other slaves throughout the rest of the seventeenth century.

Perhaps following the practice laid down by the Byzantine Studion monastery, the church as an institution in Muscovy could not own slaves. In the twelfth and thirteenth centuries, monasteries had used slave labor extensively, but this practice had largely disappeared in the fourteenth century. However, leading church figures were permitted to own slaves. Through the beginning of the seventeenth century, priests in fact bought limited service contract slaves, although they paid less for them than did the average purchaser. The *Ulozhenie*, codifying an earlier law of unknown origin, forbade church officials below the rank of archdeacon and archpriest to own limited service contract slaves and specified that priests, deacons, other lower church officials, and monastery servants could only retain free people on the basis of contracts of indenture for a specific number of years.[13] This was in keeping with the general trend making slaveownership an elite prerogative.

The summary law of 1641 stated that taxpayers (*tiaglye liudi*, peasants and townsmen), priests, musketeers, artillerymen, monastery servitors, and slaves could not be issued limited service slavery contracts but only indentures for a specified term of years.[14] In the 1680s, potential owners were listed as members of the middle and upper service classes, servicemen of various ranks, and scribes (*pod'iachie*).[15] It is also known that elite merchants and clergymen owned slaves at that time.[16]

In chapter 17 I shall discuss the slaveowners in greater detail and note that one

11. 1649 *Ulozhenie* 20: 105; MS, p. 293; A. V. Romanovich-Slavatinskii, *Dvorianstvo v Rossii ot nachala XVIII veka do otmeny krepostnogo prava* (St. Petersburg, 1870), p. 279.

12. 1649 *Ulozhenie* 17: 41; 19: 15; E. D. Stashevskii, "Sluzhiloe soslovie," in M. V. Dovnar-Zapol'skii, ed., *Russkaia istoriia v ocherkakh i stat'iakh* (Kiev, 1912), 3: 5-7.

13. 1649 *Ulozhenie* 20: 104; MS, pp. 292-93; N. A. Rozhkov, *Gorod i derevnia v russkoi istorii* (Moscow: Gosizdat, 1920), p. 45; S. B. Veselovskii, *Feodal'noe zemlevladenie v severo-vostochnoi Rusi* (Moscow-Leningrad: AN SSSR, 1947), p. 220. In the later 1680s the restriction on owning slaves was modified for some middle-level church figures and elite priests and deacons of the Moscow Assumption Cathedral (PSZ 2: 688, 972, nos. 1136 and 1325; Arkhangel'skii, *O sobornom Ulozhenii*, pp. 71-72).

14. Iakovlev, *Kholopstvo*, p. 316.

15. PSZ 2: 644, no. 1099.

16. PSZ 2: 491, 688, 844, 972, nos. 985, 1136, 1229, 1325.

of the unusual aspects of the Muscovite system was the absence of corporate ownership of slaves. In other societies, ranging from Babylonia to the American South, the state, municipalities, temples, and churches owned slaves; there was none of this in Muscovy. There was no legal prohibition against such ownership on the east European plain, but the reason probably lies in the absence of any legal definition of corporations (other than for the Orthodox church) in a society that knew no autonomous institutions except the sovereign himself.

The government initiated conflict-of-interest limitations on those who otherwise were permitted to buy slaves. Thus persons under detention because of an ongoing criminal investigation could not be purchased as slaves by the investigators, and, in an article that a marginal notation of the original scroll copy of the *Ulozhenie* describes as "new," governors and central chancellery officials were forbidden to take limited service slavery contracts on anyone while they were serving in the provinces, or distant Siberia or Astrakhan'.[17] Conflict of interest seems to have been discovered by the Muscovites in the 1630s, and in this instance it was applied to officials who had great power over ordinary citizens and some of whom in the past had abused it to enslave persons under their jurisdiction.[18] Such abuse of authority was one of the major issues that concerned some of those participating in the disorders against the Morozov regime in the summer of 1648, and we may assume that these articles were enacted as part of the effort to quell such discontent.

It was a somewhat similar situation with the enslavement of those who had been participants and bystanders in the civil disorders that so plagued Muscovy. We may assume that the victors saw little difference between the vanquished, particularly when they were from the lower classes, and alien prisoners of war. The government of Aleksei Mikhailovich noted that the troops who had repressed the Razin uprising were carrying off the local people as they returned home. On February 14, 1671, the government forbade such actions and ordered the establishment of roadblocks to intercept the removal of the local populace, who were to be freed and sent back home.[19] Thus the government placed formal limitations on the use of military power to enslave the native populace.

Muscovite law of the late sixteenth century began to concern itself with the matter of joint, multiple ownership of slaves (a feature of many other slave systems), particularly in the context of limited service contract slavery. The ownership formula for full slaves was that the slave was owned by the purchaser and his children, but after the term of limited service contract slavery was restricted to the owner's lifetime, the listing of multiple owners became a way to outwit

17. 1649 *Ulozhenie* 20: 58, 117; 21: 104; MS, pp. 275, 298-99; PRP 7: 425, art. 87.

18. See, for example, the great case of Danila Dmitreev Big Beard v. Ulan G. Lodygin (Iakovlev, *Kholopstvo*, pp. 513-62, no. 26), which is discussed below in chapter 16. A primitive recognition of conflict of interest also can be found in the *Sudebniki*, whose first articles proscribe favoring one's friends.

19. *Vosstanie Stepana Razina* 3: 12, no. 11.

the law on the chance that one of the owners might outlive the slave. Although specifically outlawed in 1606, multiple ownership continued to be written into the contracts that the government recognized as valid until 1614.[20] (The 1606-13 period was one of general chaos, so it is remarkable that the new legal norms could be enforced so quickly after the Time of Troubles.)

The prohibition against multiple ownership, one of the laws taken from the Slavery Chancellery Statute Book, was repeated in the Law Code of 1649.[21] (An exception to this rule remained: if limited service contract slaves married and belonged to related owners, the surviving owner could inherit both slaves.[22] This followed the logic of the marriage law for slaves that forbade the breaking up of marriages. It is unknown how many slaveowners took advantage of this loophole to prolong the dependent status of limited service contract slaves.)

Legal Definitions of Slaves

The question of who could be enslaved is inherent in the law governing every slave system. The major point to be made here is that in almost every system the slave is an outsider, and the law is limited to defining and refining that concept. Thus the Spanish could not enslave Spaniards, and Arabs could not enslave Arabs. With the definition of religious ecumenae, it became illegitimate for Muslims and Christians of Europe to enslave their coreligionists.[23] One of the most bizarre aspects of Russian history is the fact that the prohibition against enslaving one's own kind has been ignored there, and thus the problem of who could be enslaved is discussed in terms almost completely different from those found in any other system.

One of the major changes instituted by law in the institution of slavery concerned who could be a slave. At the outset of the period, there was no limitation on who could be a slave. Even a peasant, whose mobility was otherwise limited to the period of St. George's Day by the end of the fifteenth century, had the right to sell himself into slavery at any time, for the obvious reason that, when he was in need of relief such as slavery provided, he could not wait for St. George's Day.

The first restrictions on who could be a slave, however, did not begin with the peasantry. Rather, as was the case in so many Muscovite instances, such restrictions were first applied to members of what might be termed "the upper classes." The problem of enslaving members of the armed forces became significant during and after the reign of Ivan IV. The issue had two parts, enslavement for debt and

20. PRP 4: 376; AI 2, no. 63; Wergeland, p. 29.
21. 1649 *Ulozhenie* 20: 9, 47-48, from UKKhP 4; MS, pp. 258, 272-73.
22. 1589 *Sudebnik* 106; 1649 *Ulozhenie* 20: 86; MS, p. 286.
23. Curtin, *Annals*, p. 6; Fisher, "Ottoman Slavery," p. 30.

selling oneself into full or limited service contract slavery. The *Ulozhenie* of 1649, borrowing a provision from the 1628 additions to the Statute Book of the Moscow Administrative Chancellery, did not allow members of the middle service class or the musketeers to fall into debt slavery. Recognizing that there might be recalcitrants among them unwilling to settle their just obligations, however, the *Ulozhenie*, in an effort to compel payment, allowed them to be beaten on the shins while locked up in the stocks (*pravezh*) for a month. If that had no effect, creditors could continue to try to collect from the debtors themselves "without any mercy," and they could also try to collect from slaves belonging to the debtor. As for the musketeers, the sums that they still owed after a month were to be deducted from their cash salary from the state, and they were to be paid only their grain allotments until the debt had been satisfied. (In 1683 the issue of indebted, retired *strel'tsy* who no longer had a salary came up. The government ordered that they be beaten in *pravezh* until their creditors were satisfied, but they were not to be converted into debt slaves.) Other members of the lower service class, cossacks, gunners, and others, as well as taxpayers (townsmen and peasants), after the month in *pravezh* was up, were to be handed over as debt slaves to work off their obligations for the creditors.[24]

The other aspect of the enslavement of members of the armed forces, self-sale into slavery, was much more complex. It was a problem recognized in law as early as article 81 of the *Sudebnik* of 1550, which forbade the enslavement of *deti boiarskie* and their children who had not been discharged by the tsar. The issue surfaced again after the Time of Troubles, and in 1620 *deti boiarskie* were forbidden to sell themselves into slavery. The 1621 provincial muster officers (*okladchiki*) were ordered to remove from their owners' houses *deti boiarskie* and cossacks who had sold themselves and to put them back into service. In the late 1620s the Military Chancellery demanded that the Slavery Chancellery permit the redemption of the wives and children of freedmen *deti boiarskie* who, while enslaved, had married slave women. Members of the middle service class kept the issue before the government in frequent petitions in the 1630s and 1640s, as part of their attempt to consolidate their social position in the face of a recognition of their military obsolescence, a point I have argued in detail in *Enserfment and Military Change in Muscovy*. The government responded in 1641 and 1649, for example, by forbidding *deti boiarskie* (along with townsmen and peasants) to sell themselves into limited service contract slavery. Acknowledging the impossibility of making effective servicemen out of individuals who had sold themselves into slavery before they had ever served, the *Ulozhenie* allowed such *deti boiarskie* to remain as slaves, but forbade the practice in the future. The system-of-places (*mestnichevstvo*) genealogical handbook edited by Iu. V. Tatishchev

24. UKZP 7; 1649 *Ulozhenie* 10: 264-66; PSZ 2: 516, no. 1003. For further discussion of *pravezh*, see H. W. Dewey and A. M. Kleimola, "Coercion by Righter (*Pravezh*) in Old Russian Administration," *Canadian-American Slavic Studies* 9(1975): 156-67.

shows that the self-sale by servicemen into slavery was a persistent problem at least between 1553 and 1673, in spite of the numerous attempts by the law to curtail the practice. Examples from the genealogical handbook will be discussed in chapter 11, but this prohibition against the enslavement of elite individuals resembles the 1803 Nepalese prohibition of the reduction to slavery of Brahmins and Rajputs.[25] In the Muscovite case, law initially had been a tool of military necessity but became the instrument for expressing caste and status ambitions, aspirations, and frustrations.

As the Muscovite caste society developed, other social groups were bound to their stations and forbidden to become slaves. Peasants were forbidden to leave their lands, regardless of circumstances, at the time of the Forbidden Years, which began in 1581 and were made universal about 1592, and lords were forbidden to convert their peasants into slaves. Should a lord have done so, and the peasant-slave later fled and sold himself to another master, by 1649 the law explicitly stated that the fugitive was to be returned to his former lord as a peasant, and that all of the slavery documents that might be presented in the case were irrelevant and void. The Slavery Chancellery was supposed to send lists of fugitive peasants throughout the empire to inhibit their selling themselves into slavery.[26] By 1681 a peasant could get only a two-year loan, nothing that juridically might be confused with a limited service slavery contract.[27]

Townsmen were bound to the *posad* beginning in the 1590s, and this became universal in 1637. Thus they could no longer sell themselves into any form of slavery, although they too still could become temporary debt-slaves. Those who were slaves were to be removed from that station and returned to their lawful urban taxpaying status. Those who tried to become slaves in the future were to be beaten with the knout in the marketplace and exiled to Siberia to live on the remote Lena River.[28]

A 1647/48 decree that was incorporated into the *Ulozhenie* of 1649 required that the potential purchaser of a limited service contract slave take the initiative to determine whether or not the person was eligible to become a slave, a "free person," and not a serviceman, urban taxpayer, or peasant.[29] There were no sanctions for failure to do so, and so one may assume that the government was only in the preliminary stages of thinking about the problem and was concerned

25. 1550 *Sudebnik* 81; Iakovlev, *Kholopstvo*, p. 315; PRP 5: 371; Hellie, *Enserfment*, pp. 65-66; 1649 *Ulozhenie* 20: 1-3; MS, pp. 255-56; Tatishchev, *Mestnicheskii*, pp. 11, 17, 49, 64, 72, 82: *Opisanie dokumentov i bumag* 15(1908): 50, no. 32-III; Lionel Cáplan, "Power and Status in South Asian Slavery," in Watson, *Systems*, p. 178.

26. 1649 *Ulozhenie* 11: 32; 20: 6, 113; MS, pp. 230-31, 256-57, 296-97.

27. PSZ 2: 313, 588, 674-75, nos. 869, 1073, 1128.

28. P. P. Smirnov, *Posadskie liudi i ikh klassovaia bor'ba do serediny XVII veka*, 2 vols. (Moscow-Leningrad: AN SSSR, 1947) 2: 291, 297; AAE 3, no. 297; 1649 *Ulozhenie* 10: 266; 19: 13 (from a petition of October 30, 1648), 20 (from 1642); MS, pp. 55-56, 58.

29. 1649 *Ulozhenie* 20: 7; MS, pp. 257-58.

that the potential purchasers of slaves do the most elementary screening of those offering themselves for sale. In the same article, the government expressed its reasons: law was being used to enforce its priorities, state service and tax payment.

Similar priorities were evident in the legal provisions on enslaving converts to Orthodoxy. If foreigners, either captives or immigrants who had converted to Orthodoxy, wanted to sell themselves into slavery, they could do so, provided they had been discharged from service or were not suitable for service. This law was first enacted in 1558, and was in force a century later.[30] Such people constituted one of the few manpower pools not rigidly bound to a caste by the mid-seventeenth century that had the option of becoming slaves. The others were Russians not bound anywhere (*guliashchie liudi*) and freedmen. On December 16, 1684, this law was repealed. Converts to Orthodoxy, whether in state service or not, as well as those Orthodox indigenes paying tax in furs or grain (*iasachnye*) and *posopnye liudi*), were henceforth forbidden to sell themselves into limited service contract slavery. The law was based on a specific example, and was not made retroactive, but any convert who sold himself after that date was to be freed from slavery and punished. No explicit sanction was specified.[31] In the Petrine era similar laws forbade the enslavement of Siberian peoples. The 1684 law does not say why it was enacted, but it is probably related to the general reluctance of colonizing states to permit the enslavement of the indigenes.

Age Limitations

A limitation on self-sale into slavery, initiated on September 1, 1559, in a decree from Tsar Ivan IV to the treasurers, was that a person who was the son of a serving *syn boiarskii*, but himself had not yet been inducted into service, had to be fifteen years of age to sell himself into slavery.[32] In the *Ulozhenie* of 1649 this was generalized to prohibit anyone under the age of fifteen from selling himself into slavery.[33] (This did not give those born in slavery leave to flee and sell themselves to someone else at age fifteen.)[34] The age rule had its roots in canon law. While generally observed, the rule was occasionally violated—people under fifteen were sold with no evidence that their parents were involved—sometimes the declaration was made that the person was an orphan. (It is not at all clear what other options were available to a minor orphan.)

30. UKVK 13; 1649 *Ulozhenie* 20: 37; MS, p. 268.
31. PSZ 2: 644-45, no. 1099.
32. AI 1: 263, no. 154-xii. Many commentators have failed to notice that the law of 1559 applied only to the children of servicemen, not to everyone. See, for example, Pavlov-Sil'-vanskii, "Liudi," p. 216.
33. 1649 *Ulozhenie* 20: 20; MS, p. 263.
34. 1649 *Ulozhenie* 20: 30, 83; MS, pp. 266, 285.

In an attempt to comply with the law, some probably falsified their ages, perhaps part of the reason why ages listed jump so radically from fourteen to fifteen, then fall to sixteen. Another reason for the jump is that ages tended to be grouped in five-year increments—age heaping was common in preindustrial societies. (See tables 3.1 and 13.6.)

TABLE 3.1
Reported Ages under Twenty-one of Slaves Selling Themselves (Out of 1,084 Cases in Which Ages Were Given)

Age	N	Age	N
		14	9
8	3	15	73
9	3	16	22
10	8	17	36
11	4	18	43
12	33	19	6
13	13	20	219

Parents had the legal right to sell their children, apart from themselves. This is hardly surprising in a society that allowed parents to kill their offspring with no sanctions whatsoever, until in 1649 penance was required. As noted, parents who sold their children had to guarantee that their children would serve.[35] This provision was adopted from the *Lithuanian Statute* of 1588, and its presence in the *Ulozhenie* indicates that a trouble case arose in Muscovy some time in the 1630s and was resolved by borrowing the West Russian precedent. In fact, however, cases of parents selling their children seem to have been very rare in Muscovy, and there are at most one or two in my collection that have such an odor.

Parents could sell their own children with themselves into slavery with no limitations if the children were under fifteen years of age. Children over fifteen years of age could not be sold in absentia but had to be still in their parents' household. Children who had attained their majority could not be claimed by those to whom their parents sold themselves if the children earlier had sold themselves to someone else or had established their own households.[36] That was a real issue, as can be seen by looking at the ages of the children sold into slavery in the age pyramid in chapter 13. Notable in the pyramid is the dramatic dropoff in the size of the fifteen-to-nineteen age cohort from that of the previous ten-to-fourteen age cohort. The fifteen-to-nineteen-year-olds had gone their own way before their parents sold themselves. Equally noteworthy is the sale of a number of older

35. 1649 *Ulozhenie* 20: 45; MS, pp. 271-72. The *Ulozhenie* (22: 26) threatened with execution women who killed illegitimate children. The concern there was fornication, not the lives of the children.
36. 1649 *Ulozhenie* 20: 5, 110; MS, pp. 256, 295.

children, some even in their late twenties, with their parents. In none of these cases was the child married, for the Russian family that became enslaved was seemingly always nuclear, never extended. In no way could children who were born prior to their parents' enslavement and who were no longer living with them be claimed as slaves by the progenitors' owners.[37]

Tatars

Tatars were a special category of slaves. They were genuine "outsiders," in the sense that they were neither Slavs nor Indo-Europeans, and they therefore perhaps serve as a sort of litmus test for theories of the interrelationships between slavery and racism. In my own data, less than 1 percent of the slaves can be identified as Tatars, although there may be more because Tatars were sometimes given Russian names.

My interpretation is that there was no racism involved, for the East Slavs had been dealing, even intermarrying, with Turkic peoples since at least the tenth century. (If one considers the relations between the originally Iranian, later Slavicized, Severiane and Poliane and the Khazars, these dealings go back even further.) Turkic people could enter the *mestnichestvo* hierarchy of the Muscovite empire just as anyone else could. The distinctions that were drawn between Tatars and Russians seem to have been primarily between Muslims and Orthodox Christians, and were not based on race.

In the law Tatars were dealt with separately because they were a distinct group. They could be captured, bought and sold, and given away as presents, in dowries, and in other instruments. The provisions of full slavery seemed still to have applied to them.[38] This traffic was forbidden in 1623/24 but was legally permitted again in 1648/49.[39] Tatar slaves were not automatically freed, after 1597, on their owners' death.[40] It should be noted, however, that Tatars, like Russians, could challenge the documents by which they were enslaved. They were entitled to every element of due process that native Russians were, including the right to be present when slavery documents on them were being formulated.[41] The kidnapping of Tatars in Astrakhan' and Siberia for the purpose of enslaving them was forbidden, and sanctions ("severe punishment") for violators were specified. But, if the kidnappers, before they were apprehended and convicted, had baptized the Tatars, they could keep their prey but had to pay the local market price for slaves to their next of kin.[42] (Obviously someone who had been "converted to

---

37. 1550 *Sudebnik* 76; 1649 *Ulozhenie* 20: 5.
38. 1649 *Ulozhenie* 20: 98-99; MS, pp. 290-91.
39. 1649 *Ulozhenie* 20: 117; MS, pp. 298-99.
40. 1649 *Ulozhenie* 20: 100; MS, p. 291.
41. 1649 *Ulozhenie* 20: 74, 100; MS, pp. 282-83, 291.
42. 1649 *Ulozhenie* 20: 118; MS, p. 299.

Christianity" could under no circumstances be returned to perfidious Islam, no matter what the cause of his conversion.) It is clear that by mid-seventeenth century the Muscovites were just as cautious about enslaving Tatars as they were about native Russians.

A major piece of evidence against seeing any racism in Russo-Tatar slave relationships is a law which forbade owners who had baptized their purchased Tatar slaves to resell them "because it has been ordered in a decree of the Sovereign not to sell baptized slaves to anyone."[43] This *Ulozhenie* article seems to have been of relatively recent origin, for it still contains the phrase that it was issued "by the sovereign's decree," something that tended to drop out as laws became customary norms with the passage of time. It is clear that what made the Tatar an outsider was not his race but his religion. Here also we see the civil law being used to declare and enforce the proselytizing goals of the Orthodox church.

I find it of some interest that the sources of none of these laws on Tatars have been discovered to date. There is nothing on this problem in the sixteenth-century corpus that I am aware of. I can only suppose that the issue arose because of Russian Orthodox missionary activity in the decades before the 1649 law code. I might close this section with a reminder that at the beginning of the seventeenth century Kazanis could purchase Russian girls in the Novgorod region to take to Kazan'. Can one imagine Africans being permitted to purchase Southern belles?

Freedmen

A final category of persons who could be slaves in Muscovy was the freedman, one who had been enslaved before but who by some device (usually either the death of the owner or outright manumission) had been set free. This topic will be discussed under several other headings as well, for the recirculation of ex-slaves was one of the most unusual features of Muscovite slavery. It is a truism that by the seventeenth century the freest person in Muscovy was the slave who had just been manumitted, for most other categories of the populace were bound to an increasing extent to a specific status. While in law the freedmen were the freest individuals in Muscovy, in reality they were trapped by their past. Consequently, freedom for many of them was short-lived, as they resold themselves into slavery.

The government was highly conscious of this dependency syndrome and took extensive measures to regulate it. By 1649 the chances were very good that anyone seeking to sell himself into slavery had been a slave before, and the authorities wanted to be sure that the person had been properly manumitted and was not really a member of some other social estate. Both the would-be slave buyer and the appropriate officials were obliged to attempt to verify the putative freedman's

43. 1649 *Ulozhenie* 20: 97; MS, p. 290.

claims about his status. A verifiable manumission document was always recognized as solid evidence of freedman status, but, given the nature of Muscovy, there were bound to be freedmen who lacked that essential piece of paper. The *Ulozhenie* tried to delimit the possible trouble cases by stating that anyone who claimed to have been manumitted by an owner who was still living had to produce a document signed by the manumitter before he could sell himself again to someone else. If the alleged manumitter was deceased, the freedman who wanted to sell himself into slavery but had no manumission document had to tell where and when he had formulated his last servitude, and then the government was to check to see whether the lord had died. If he had, and no other ownership claims on the slave were being pressed, then the freedman was to be allowed to sell himself again.[44] By 1681 the legislated stratification of society had proceeded to the point where about the only people who could sell themselves into slavery were freedmen.[45] Moreover, their dependency was legally reinforced in 1685 by a decree stating that freedmen and their children could not be issued regular loans but only limited service slavery contracts.[46] No reason was given for the new law, but it may have been enacted to parallel a prohibition that prevented peasants from selling themselves into slavery and forced them to take regular loans. The law also reflected existing reality.

As was so often the case in Russian history, military exigency forced a change in attitude toward freedmen. The authors of the *Ulozhenie* had realized that freedmen were not likely to make good cavalrymen, and thus allowed members of the middle service class who had been slaves to return to slavery if they found military service not to their liking. Not only was that a peacetime document, but in the next half-century the nature of warfare changed, the old middle service class cavalry was largely phased out, and the new formation army was institutionalized. In 1700, Peter the Great, faced with the Northern War, ordered that manumitted limited service contract slaves be enlisted in the infantry, and the order was repeated in 1703.[47] This partially broke up the cycle of perpetual dependency that slavery bred in Muscovy and was a major step in the direction of the abolition of slavery. A further step in the same direction was taken later in 1703 when the government for the first time in history moved to draft slaves into the army.[48]

Given the essence of Muscovite slavery, that the vast majority of the slaves were native Russians, a problem arose that was considerably less likely in systems where the slaves were outsiders: the illegal enslavement of persons who did not wish to abandon their free status. A stark example of such illegal enslavement is

44. 1649 *Ulozhenie* 20: 11, 12; MS, pp. 259-60.
45. PSZ 2: 313, no. 869.
46. Ibid., 2: 675, no. 1128.
47. Ibid., 4: 3, 209, nos. 1747, 1923.
48. Ibid., 4: 225, 369; nos. 1944, 2138.

discussed in the case of Danila Dmitriev Big Beard v. Uvar Lodygin, outlined in chapter 16. By the mid-seventeenth century, the government was beginning to express some concern about unlawful enslavement and to specify sanctions for violators. This concern was expressed in the context of the requirement that the identifying marks of slaves be listed, with the note that it was illegal to obtain a limited service slavery contract on a person by bringing one person in for the registration but writing the document on someone else. The person thus wrongfully enslaved was to be set free (no damages payable to him were specified), and the perpetrator of the illegal enslavement was to be punished by a beating with the knout.[49] One might surmise that such a sanction would be applied to anyone who illegally enslaved another person. The reality, as demonstrated in the case of Dmitriev v. Lodygin, was that a person could be convicted of illegally enslaving someone, suffer no such corporal punishment, and in fact continue to be a member of the tsaritsa's retinue. The method of the Muscovite legislative process would indicate that someone was beaten with the knout for illegally enslaving a person, but the applicability of that sanction to all other such malefactors remained a social program rather than a concrete reality.

Illegal enslavement was a matter of concern not only to free men but particularly to freedmen. The basic assumption of Muscovite law was that a freedman would sell himself back into slavery soon, an assumption that reflected very much the reality of the era. However, this may not have been the reality the government desired, so it took every measure possible to ensure that those who were legally freed from slavery could not be claimed as slaves under some guise such as a will. For example, a limited service contract slave was given every opportunity to prove his status in the face of slaveowner claims that he was some kind of perpetual slave.[50]

In 1500 almost anyone could have been a slaveowner in Muscovy, but in 1700 the ranks of those legally eligible to own slaves had been narrowed to members of the landed service classes, elite merchants, and clergymen. In 1500 almost anybody could become a slave, but in 1700 the ranks of would-be slaves were limited to foreign war captives and native freedmen. This limiting had been a gradual response to status needs and pressure from the slaveowners, the consignment of most of the Muscovite populace to closed castes, and the fiscal and manpower needs of the government. Moreover, by 1700 serfdom in many respects had come to look very much like slavery. Therefore it was relatively simple for the government to constrict slavery still further in favor of serfdom between 1700 and 1723, when slavery fundamentally disappeared as a legal institution.

49. 1649 *Ulozhenie* 20: 23; MS, p. 262.
50. 1649 *Ulozhenie* 20: 64; MS, pp. 277-78.

4. Family Law

The Slave in the Eyes of the Law

How the law has viewed the slave has varied widely throughout world history. He was usually the object of civil law, while less frequently he was the subject of criminal law. In the Ancient Near East, the slave was a chattel, yet there were certain restrictions on the owner's use of his property.[1] In Roman law, slaves were in the power and possession (*dominium*) of their owners. They were things (*res, instrumentum vocale*) without legal personality, not human beings.[2] This view was transmitted to early Byzantium, which considered a slave a thing whose use was regulated by law. Thus he was not the subject of family law and could not have personal property guaranteed by law. The revival of Roman law in modern northern Europe helped to perpetuate the classical idea of the slave as a personal possession totally subject to his owner's will. Later Byzantine legislation, perhaps reflecting the decline of slavery and the rise of serfdom, modified this view, as we shall see. Islamic law views the slave as both a person and a thing, a thing subject to the right of ownership, but a person capable of converting to Islam and thereby becoming worthy of freedom. The American Northwest Coast Indians, the Tlingit, Kwakiutl, and Oregon coast tribes, and the Dahomeans of West Africa, all viewed slaves as things with no rights or privileges.[3]

North American slave law, which began de novo because England lacked a positive law governing the ownership of human beings, often looks as though it had gone straight back to Rome in the first century B.C., the peak of classical slavery, for its inspiration. In the memorable words of a South Carolina judge in 1847, a slave "can invoke neither Magna Carta nor common law. In the very nature of things, he is subject to despotism. Law as to him is only a compact between his rulers."[4] However, other contemporary authorities such as Thomas Reade Roots Cobb denied this, claiming that, because the slave was protected by municipal law, he occupied "a double character of person and property."[5]

On the other hand, broadly speaking, Iberian and Muscovite slave law give the

---

1. Mendelsohn, p. 122.
2. Hopkins, p. 173; Rose, p. 198.
3. Siegel, pp. 366, 372.
4. Friedman, p. 198; Catterall 1: 14, 4: 1.
5. Rose, p. 198.

appearance of continuing the Byzantine tradition. While the medieval Russians in the *Russkaia Pravda* viewed the slave primarily as a personal object owned by his master, the Muscovite legal view of the slave varied, but the variations can be attributed to a combination of exogenous influences and the developing nature of Muscovite law in general, rather than to a coherent political attitude toward the institution of slavery.

Most legal systems distinguish between immovable and movable property, between the rights and duties of persons in relation to land and in relation to goods, animals, and people. In English law the distinction is between real property and chattels, in Roman law between *res mancipi* and *res nec mancipi*. A priori, one might imagine that slaves would always be chattels, movable property (as they were in medieval Germanic law and most New World slave law), but that was not so. Hindu law classified slaves with land, and the Romans also categorized slaves (along with horses and oxen) as *res mancipi*. The Romans thus distinguished things that were transferable only by a formal mancipation and things whose ownership changed hands by mere delivery. The Roman view of the slave was tried out in 1705 in Virginia, which declared the slave to be real estate, the same as houses, trees, or land, to assure uniform rules of inheritance "for the sake of justice to owners and heirs in settling and preserving estates" and for the settling of liabilities owed third parties. This view of the slave was dropped in 1792 for reasons that anyone who has bought or sold both a house and an automobile will appreciate: trading in movable chattels is simple, while trading in real estate is cumbersome and expensive. In spite of that fact, slaves always were treated as real property in Louisiana, with the result that the records of New Orleans slave sales are scattered among the real estate sales.[6] The Manchester anthropologist Max Gluckman has discussed the symbolic importance of objects such as slaves as immovable property in tribal systems which often have features which resemble the Roman law concept because slaves in those systems seem to be fixtures of the soil.[7] It is difficult to assign the Russian law of slavery to either category. For one, the Russians were not great legal theorists and have left us none of their considerations on the matter. This deficiency was compounded by the general weakness of the concept of property, and also by the fact that the domestic slave trade was very weakly developed. In spite of all of this, it would probably be appropriate to classify Muscovite slaves as movable chattels.

In 1853 the American antislavery writer William Goodell claimed that Southern slavery could be added to "the list of the strict sciences. From a single funda-

6. Wergeland, pp. 27-28; Caplan, pp. 181-82; H. S. Klein, *Americas*, p. 53; Catterall 3: 475, 496, 585, 609, 613; Stanley Engerman, personal communication, June 14, 1980. Kentucky in 1798 and the Louisiana Territory in 1806 also considered slaves to be real estate, not personal property. Slaves were treated as real property at some times also in Arkansas (Tushnet, "Law," p. 122).

7. Max Gluckman, *The Ideas in Barotse Jurisprudence* (New Haven: Yale University Press, 1965), pp. 130, 133.

mental axiom, all parts of the system are logically and scientifically deduced."
The axiom, according to Goodell, was that the slave was property, that he had
"no rights."[8] Muscovite slavery was not quite so simplistic, but its axioms were
few and the system was coherent.

Marriage

Some students assume that respect for the marriage bond and the institution of
chattel slavery are mutually incompatible.[9] They reason that a slave is property
but that the requirement of respect for connubial ties would so limit the disposition and use of that property that it would no longer be property, and human
beings so enmeshed could not be slaves. While this often has been the case, there
are sufficient historical instances in which marriage was respected to refute any
such broad generalization, and one of the purposes of this essay is to show that a
Muscovite slave was as much a slave as any other slave, even though his or her
marriage was respected by law.

The norm of productive slave systems certainly has been that a slave has no
right to marriage. Both Athenian and Roman law refused to recognize slaves'
capacity for marriage, yet tombstone inscriptions show that such chattels considered themselves to be married and even commemorated their dead spouses.
North American common and statutory law also refused to recognize the legality
of any slave marriage, but again, as is well known, the slaves themselves often
thought otherwise and kept in touch with one another after the breakup of
families; much of the migration after the Emancipation Proclamation and the
Civil War was by freedmen trying to reestablish family ties. Many U.S. slaveowners respected slave marriages, in spite of the law.[10]

On the other hand, Islamic norms often respected the sanctity of marriage.
When prisoners who had been taken captive during a jihad were distributed as
the spoils of war, surviving husbands and wives (and children as well) were not to
be separated. Moreover, Muslim slaves were competent to contract a marriage,
with the consent of the owners of each. When conquering China in 1618, the
Manchus issued an edict that ordered: "When people are captured in battle, don't
debauch their women, don't separate men from their wives."[11] Even the otherwise harsh 1755 *Règlement* of the Danish Virgin Islands permitted slaves to marry
and, furthermore, forbade the dissolution of marriages by any transaction what-

8. Friedman, pp. 196-97.

9. D. B. Davis, *Slavery in Western Culture*, p. 104.

10. Ibid.; Hopkins, p.174; Crawford, "Quantified Memory," chap. 5.

11. R. Brunschvig, "'Abd," *The Encyclopaedia of Islam*, vol. 1 (Leiden: E. J. Brill, 1960),
p. 27; Jonathan D. Spence, *Ts'ao Yin and the K'ang-hsi Emperor, Bondservant and Master*
(New Haven: Yale University Press, 1966), p. 6.

soever.[12] Another system in which one might expect that slaves would not have been allowed to marry was that of the Northwest Coast Indians, but in fact the Tlingit, Kwakiutl, and Oregon coast tribes allowed slaves to marry with the consent of their owners.[13] Both the Danish Virgin Islands and the Northwest Coast Indians had systems of the most ruthless forms of chattel slavery, by any definition.

Slave marriages were also inviolable in Carthage, Hellenistic Greece, and most of the Catholic medieval world, including converted Germanic societies and Spain, in its law of slavery dated 1263-65.[14] Matthew Vlasteres's collection of canon law in 1335 emphasized that the marriage of Byzantine slaves was inviolable. Similar norms passed to Muscovy, a fact acknowledged by its lawgivers: "In the canon of the Holy Apostles and Holy Fathers, it is ordered not to separate wives from their husbands: where the husband is, there also must be the wife; to whom belongs the wife, to him also belongs the husband."[15] With this principle, which I have never seen violated in Muscovy, early modern Russia escaped one of the major ravages of North American slavery. Moreover, the establishment of the norm that a slave marriage was inviolable facilitated greatly the logical and expeditious handling of many trouble cases, such as those involving fugitive slaves.

On the basis of the evidence presented here, the argument about whether marriage is compatible with the institution of slavery seems rather pointless. Certainly slave connubial bonds have been recognized at many times and places. It is of greater utility to see what meaning that recognition has. One may say, in general, that a slave marriage is not likely to be recognized in a dynamic, expansive, market-oriented slave system, and that it may be inviolable in a relatively static, household slavery system. Moreover, slave marriage often will not be recognized in systems that otherwise can be described as "harsh," while they may be in "milder" systems. Of course consideration of slave marriage is one of the major criteria for determining whether or not a system is "harsh" or "mild."

The Right to Marry

Some slave systems considered the matter of whether a slave had a right to be married. The Louisiana Code of 1824 explicitly stated that the slave had no such right, that a slave could marry only with a master's consent.[16] On the other hand, the Hanbali Muslims held that a slave could insist that his master marry him off.

12. Hall, "Virgin Islands," p. 177.
13. Siegel, p. 366.
14. Klein, *Americas*, pp. 61-63; Wergeland, p. 98.
15. Brauning, p. 48; 1649 *Ulozhenie* 20: 62. See also Canon 102 of the *138 Canons of the Regional Synod of 419* and *Procheiros Nomos* 9: 10.
16. Rose, pp. 176-77.

Slaves serving under the jurisdiction of the Spanish slave laws of 1263-65 also had the right to marry, to belong to one master, and to live together. Ming Chinese masters were obliged to select mates for their female slaves in their teens, for the males around age twenty. In Ch'ing times, the law said nothing about males, probably because they were in such a minority in what had become primarily a female institution. In India and nineteenth-century Nepal, the master was expected to find a spouse for his slave and to pay for the wedding. In Thailand, male slaves had the right to marry without owner consent, female slaves needed such consent.[17] It appears that Russian slaves also had the right to be married. The prominent abbot Joseph Sanin of the Volokolamsk monastery, creator of the Muscovite theory of autocracy, wrote at the beginning of the sixteenth century that slave boys of fifteen and girls of twelve should be allowed either to marry or to become monks or nuns.[18] It is highly doubtful that people of that age married in Muscovy, but interesting here is the statement by the most prominent clergyman of the time that slaves had the right to marry. More concrete both as a statement of demographic reality and as a legislative norm for the real world was the edict by Tsar Vasilii Shuiskii prescribing that a slave girl of eighteen, a slave boy of twenty, and a woman widowed two years had to be allowed to marry; if not, they could go to a Treasurer, who would manumit them. As a further sanction against lords who would not allow slaves to marry, the tsar decreed that such owners were not to be allowed to sue such slaves for stolen property. Otherwise, "fornication and immoral behavior would multiply among the slaves."[19] This moral concern is exactly like that expressed in Spanish law of the thirteenth century and the Spanish Code of 1789.[20] All had common roots in Byzantine enactments. The Law Code of 1649 did not repeat Shuiskii's decree, in all likelihood because it was not an issue of burning concern, for Muscovite slaveowners were not known to refuse their slaves permission to marry. On the other hand, a shortage of women in that bottom stratum of society, because of female infanticide, must have made the matter of finding a mate a matter of some concern for males. This is recognized in late seventeenth-century indentures specifying that the owner would marry the slave, a single male, to someone.

Even if the slave had a right to be married, it would seem doubtful that he or she had the right to choose the marriage partner. That is a relatively modern luxury, for most marriages in earlier times were arranged by parents, or by some other party in the parents' absence. Another such party might well be the slaveowner. This thesis corresponds with what is known of Russian reality. Never-

17. Wiens, p. 307; Meijer, pp. 332, 341-42; Caplan, pp. 175, 184; Turton, p. 269; Klein, *Americas*, p. 62.

18. Iosif Volotskii, *Poslaniia Iosifa Volotskogo*, ed. A. A. Zimin and Ia. S. Lur'e (Moscow-Leningrad: Akademiia nauk SSSR, 1959), p. 148.

19. Sergeevich, *Drevnosti* 1: 125.

20. Klein, *Americas*, p. 80.

theless, excessive compulsion was frowned upon. At the end of the eighteenth century, Radishchev, in his famous literary "journey from St. Petersburg to Moscow," cited forced marriages as one of the evils of serfdom, an institution that grew up out of slavery. More to the point, in the court case of Kuz'mishchev v. Satin, which is discussed at length in chapter 8, the plaintiff alleged that the defendant's wife had married off "by force" (*nasil'stvom*) the contested slave girl to one of their slave men. One can only suppose that Kuz'mishchev mentioned the "by force" element because there was some opprobrium attached to such a deed. This supposition may be supported by the fact that the entire purpose of that sentence in Kuz'mishchev's complaint is to discredit the accused, for the alleged wedding took place during the defendant's absence, at a time when he went to Persia "without getting royal permission," presumably another sign of Satin's satanic nature.[21] A similar sense of opprobrium is evident in Danilka Dmitriev Big Beard v. Lodygin, in which the plaintiff was forcibly enslaved by the defendant, and the former's son was forcibly married to one of the latter's slave women. The court awarded the verdict to the plaintiff and freed the entire family, including the daughter-in-law. The Slavery Chancellery regarded the forced marriage as a fact, and no attempt was made to undo it.[22] No doubt this reflected the Orthodox position that the sacrament of marriage created a bond that could not be broken.

I do not know whether any sanctions were invoked in the question of providing marriage partners for slaves, but it is clear that owners deliberately and expressly purchased slaves as marriage partners for chattel already in their possession. This could have led to slave breeding, but I am in possession of only one case that gives such an appearance: Voin Ofonasev Novokshchenov had four single males; he purchased four single females, and married them. Within four years, each couple had produced two offspring. This may have been simply slave-rearing under the best conditions. It has the same appearance as similar operations in the Ancient Near East, although the Muscovites were not quite so explicit as the ancients, who purchased female slaves "for wifehood" or for mating with specific individuals.[23] On the other hand, *Time on the Cross* seems to have refuted slave-breeding as a common, viable operation in the more favorable conditions of the U.S. South, and such breeding seems even less plausible for early modern Russia.[24]

Inviolability of Slave Marriage

The norms of Muscovite slave family law were most vividly expressed in in-

21. Iakovlev, *Kholopstvo*, p. 390.
22. Ibid., pp. 513-62, no. 26.
23. Mendelsohn, p. 54.
24. Fogel and Engerman, *Time on the Cross*, 1: 78-86.

stances of slave flight. The general norm was that the conjugal unit was to be preserved when the fugitives were returned to the rightful owner.[25] In the case of a fugitive married couple, or in a case where one spouse was a fugitive, the couple was to be returned to the lawful owner. In no case was a marriage to be broken up. The capitation fee was to be paid on each slave returned, even though only one of the slaves was a fugitive.[26] This rule of the church was codified as a civil law in 1631-32, according to a marginal notation in the manuscript copy of the *Ulozhenie*, but both before and after that date it was always carried out to the letter.

The principle of the inviolability of slave marriage extended to dowries. If the bride-wife to whom the slaves had been given as a dowry died without heirs (her own children), the dowry had to be returned to the donor in the wife's family—including all slaves, plus any marriage partners they might have acquired.[27] Muscovite owners almost certainly tried to arrange marriages between their own slaves, but often that was impossible because they had so few. Therefore marriages had to be arranged by different owners. The law requiring that married slaves be allowed to live together certainly forbade arrangements such as the inter-plantation visitation system that so plagued married chattel in the American South and also in some parts of India.[28] Whether virilocality or uxorilocality prevailed in Russia is unknown, nor is anything known about compensatory payments made to the owner who voluntarily surrendered his slave in a marriage compact. The handling of fugitives probably provides no guidelines for understanding voluntary situations.

The primary auxiliary principle in resolving trouble cases that might be related to the marriage sacrament was that no one was to accept or harbor another's human chattel. The receiving lord always lost the couple, even though one of the spouses may have belonged to him.[29] The object was to punish anyone harboring fugitives. Such situations could and did become complicated. The process of legal abstraction in Muscovy was a long and difficult one, and for decades norms were stated exactly as they had been set out in the resolution of an actual legal case. If a slave fled from his or her owner and abandoned his or her spouse (a not infrequent occurrence), subsequently remarried, and then returned to his or

25. 1649 *Ulozhenie* 20: 4, 88, MS, pp. 256, 287. A special law of 1634 that I have not seen apparently declared slave marriage to be inviolable (Iakovlev, *Kholopstvo*, p. 122, 128). As we have seen, the issuance of such a law, confirming a millennium-old principle, indicates that somebody must have violated or challenged it, forcing the government to reconfirm it. See also 1649 *Ulozhenie* 20: 31, 60, 62, 66, 69, 87, and 115.

26. 1649 *Ulozhenie* 20: 60; MS, p. 60.

27. Man'kov, *Ulozhenie*, pp. 113-14.

28. Caplan, p. 184; Crawford, chap. 5.

29. 1649 *Ulozhenie* 19: 37-38; 20: 84, 87. For illustrations of these laws in action, see Zheriapin v. Sheidiakova et al. (1627-28) and Zheliabuzhskii v. Lobanov-Rostovskii (1623), in chaps. 7 and 8, respectively (Iakovlev, *Kholopstvo*, pp. 359 and 389).

her first owner or was apprehended by him, the slave was to remain married to the first spouse. Torture could be used to force a slave to acknowledge a spouse. The second spouse was to remain with his or her owner, except if the first spouse had died during the runaway's absence. In that case, the second spouse was to be given to the lawful owner.[30] Another case stemming from Slavery Chancellery practice held that if a limited service contract slave married a free woman and the slave died—and subsequently she fled—then the widow was to be returned to the limited service contract slave's owner.[31] Moreover, if she remarried while a fugitive, the couple was to be returned to the old lord. Or, if a fugitive slave-woman married a free peasant, both were returned to the woman's lawful owner. Excepting instances involving people legally bound to a specific social stratum or position, the Muscovites followed the principle, one of the oldest in Russian law, that any free person who married a slave thereby automatically became enslaved (*po rabe kholop, po kholopu raba*).[32]

When a slave fled to a town and married a townswoman, the couple and any offspring they might have produced were to be returned to the slave's owner.[33] But if a townswoman fled and, while a fugitive, married a slave, the couple and their offspring were to be returned to the town and inscribed on the tax rolls.[34] This was one of the ways a slave could escape bondage, but the law's assumption was that he was essentially an innocent bystander, and his owner was being punished for having taken in an urban taxpayer.

A possibility not covered by the auxiliary principle was that of fugitive slaves who belonged to different lords marrying on neutral ground. In that case, the owners were to cast lots, the winner got the couple and paid the loser 10 rubles. The winning lord was not to consider the couple his purchased slaves, and both were to serve according to the document in the possession of the winning owner, either as hereditary slaves or as limited service contract slaves.[35]

The principles of Muscovite family slave law are best illustrated in legal cases that dealt with the issues themselves. Slave family law had many technicalities, and some of these were examined in the two cases I shall consider here.

Krechetnikov v. Pozdeev

I have just noted that one way to resolve the problem of fugitives who married on "neutral ground" was to cast lots. However, more sophisticated solutions were possible, as is evident in the 1635 case of Krechetnikov v. Pozdeev, tried in the Slavery Chancellery before director (*sud'ia*) Prince Ivan Fedorovich Volkon-

---

30. 1649 *Ulozhenie* 20: 26, 60, 84; MS, pp. 264, 276, 285-86.
31. 1649 *Ulozhenie* 20: 85; MS, p. 286.
32. Iakovlev, *Kholopstvo*, p. 430, no. 16, xxiii. See a discussion of the case Karsakov v. Borykov in chapter 8.
33. 1649 *Ulozhenie* 19: 37; MS, p. 61.
34. 1649 *Ulozhenie* 19: 38; MS, p. 61.
35. 1649 *Ulozhenie* 20: 115; MS, pp. 297-98.

skoi and the state secretaries Tret'iak Kopnin and Ivan Kostiurin. Both litigants were relatively typical members of the lower upper service class, based in Moscow. Plaintiff Vasilii Vasil'ev Krechetnikov̆ was a Moscow *dvorianin* at the time of the trial, a rank he held at least from 1629 to 1658. It is unknown when or at what rank he began his service (he may have been from Novgorod initially, judging by the fact that his guarantors at the trial were all from there), but the fact that he was not promoted for three decades reflects the fact that he did not distinguish himself in any way, as far as is known. His service is typical for men of his rank and time. He held one governorship, a two-year stint in Urzhum, a relatively minor western Siberian outpost about 160 kilometers northeast of Kazan'. Before his trial was over, he was sent there as governor and presided over a garrison of nineteen *deti boiarskie*, twenty-four Lithuanians and Cherkasy, twenty-one newly baptized Tatars, three translators, three artillerymen, eleven guards, smiths, gatekeepers; and houseslaves, and two hundred infantry *strel'tsy* under the command of two centurions. In Urzhum there were twenty-five tax-paying townsmen. Later, on April 16, 1651, Krechetnikov was part of a procession accompanying the tsar to the village of Pokrovskoe. In preparation for the Thirteen Years War, which recovered Smolensk and Kiev for Russia, Krechetnikov retooled and became commander of a unit of new formation cavalry. In all probability, Krechetnikov was killed or died during the war.[36]

The defendant in the suit, Matvei Ivanov Pozdeev, was somewhat younger than Krechetnikov. During the trial he was referred to by his rank, *zhilets,* the entry rating to the lower upper service class. The 1638 Moscow census noted that the counselor state secretary Ivan Fedotov Pozdeev, whose service career began at least in 1572, had a son Matvei, a *zhilets.* Both of them were out of Moscow at the time serving the tsar, and their slaves (perhaps including those involved in the litigation three years earlier) were with them. (The fact that M. I. Pozdeev was the son of a civil servant probably explains why he was not listed in the 1632 inventory of *zhilets* landholding, for those included were miliary servicemen, which, at the time, he was not.) Some time shortly after the census Pozdeev was promoted to the rank of Moscow *dvorianin,* a rank he held at least until 1677. In October 1638, M. I. Pozdeev was a palace sentry guarding the tsar day and night. In 1653, he was in charge of administering a section of Moscow, and in 1675-77 he may have served a term as governor of Balakhna, a center of the salt industry about twenty-five kilometers upstream from Nizhnii Novgorod on the Volga. When and whether Pozdeev saw combat is unknown, but given the fact that he did not follow his family tradition of chancellery service, one may assume that much of his later life was spent in regimental service, and that the

---

36. Ivanov, AUBK, p. 212; RIB 10 (1886): 7; Barsukov, SGV, p. 257; KR 2: 929; DR 3: 248; *Opisanie* 15: 524, no. 589, II. Other Krechetnikov clan members in the Novgorod region are mentioned in Ivanov, OPK, pp. 6, 47.

events that were noted in the surviving documents were highlights in an otherwise normal military career.[37]

The "facts" in Krechetnikov v. Pozdeev are difficult to sort out, for there
seems to have been more prevarication in the case than was normal. Numerous
state offices became involved in an attempt to resolve the dispute. The basic
facts seem to be that in 1630 Fedor (Fed'ka), son of Luka, a recidivist runaway,
fled from Pozdeev's house in Moscow with 32.75 rubles' worth of stolen property and ended up on the estate of Nikita Kireevskii, in the Kolomna region, where
he lived for nearly five years.[38] Kireevskii, who was not mentioned as a party in
this suit and seems to have walked away unscathed from the whole episode,
must have been one of the classic recruiters and harborers of fugitive slaves, for
he was alleged to have induced the other slave in the case, the widow Avdot'ia
(Dun'ka), daughter of Semen (or, Ignatei), to flee from Krechetnikov's village,
Dynevo, in the Moscow region to his estate as well. On his estate, Kireevskii
married Dun'ka to Fed'ka, setting the stage for an elaborate legal case. As appears to have been Fed'ka's wont, after nearly five years away, he returned to
his former owner, Pozdeev, and brought his new bride, Dun'ka, with him. According to Pozdeev's account, he brought the slaves to the Military Captives
Chancellery for interrogation and registration because Dun'ka claimed that
she had been a Lithuanian military captive freed by the 1634 Polianovka treaty
between Muscovy and the Rzeczpospolita in which the two freed each other's
nationals. From there, according to one account, the party went to the Great
Court, where Krechetnikov ordered the arrest of Dun'ka as his fugitive slave.
Krechetnikov later claimed that Pozdeev, because he had learned that he was
about to file suit to recover Dun'ka, ordered her to say that she was a Lithuanian
and brought her for registration to the Galich Regional Tax Collection and Administrative Chancellery, and that from there they went to the Great Court.

By another account, Krechetnikov found the couple on July 12, 1634, at Pozdeev's place in Temnikov (in Mordovia, one of the few other significant towns in
the Nizhnii Novgorod region, 215 kilometers south of Balakhna), had them arrested, and brought them to the Vladimir Regional Tax Collection and Administrative Chancellery. From there, they were taken to the Great Court because
of the allegation that Dun'ka was a military captive subject to repatriation and
thereby a free person who could choose her immediate fate. Before the fraud, in
which Dun'ka played an active and willing part, was discovered by the Great
Court—that in fact she was a Russian from Dorogobuzh (about 100 kilometers

37. Ivanov, AUBK, p. 328; RIB 10 (1886): 120; Izumov, "Zhiletskoe," pp. 118-19;
Beliaev, *Rospisnoi spisok Moskvy*, p. 124: Veselovskii, *D'iaki*, p. 417; DR 3: 365; Barsukov,
SGV, p. 13; DAI 9: 72-73, no. 21.

38. There were at least two Nikita Kireevskiis at this time. One, Nikita Suetin Kireevskii,
was a patriarchal *stol'nik* who died in 1635. The other was Nikita Dmitreev Kireevskii,
who held the rank of *striapchii* between 1627 and 1636 (Ivanov, AUBK, p. 183).

upstream on the Dnepr from Smolensk and outside the theater of military operations in the Smolensk War)—she was asked whether she wanted to be repatriated and said that she did not, that she wanted to remain with her husband. After the unmasking of the deception, the case went to a group of boyars headed by F. I. Sheremetev, who remanded the case to the Slavery Chancellery because it had nothing to do with military captivity.

About thirteen months after the arrest of the couple, the case went to trial in the Slavery Chancellery on August 22, 1635. There Krechetnikov presented a limited service slavery contract in the amount of 3 rubles negotiated between him and Dun'ka on May 3, 1635, and formalized in the Slavery Chancellery itself. While she was still feigning to be a military captive from Lithuania, Dun'ka claimed not to have understood the limited service slavery contract and said that Krechetnikov had told her that he could not keep her as a slave without such a formal registration. Krechetnikov, to support his claim to Dun'ka, noted that she had run away before, that he had found her cavorting with the infantry soldiers in Moscow in 1634, and that the Slavery Chancellery had returned her to him on the basis of the May 3 document.

Pozdeev claimed that Fed'ka's father, Luchka, had served his father and then him for forty years. In response to a decree issued about 1620 that forbade the keeping of hereditary slaves without registering them (a reiteration of the 1597 legislation), Pozdeev got a limited service slavery contract on the entire family. The document, dated April 30, 1620, was presented, and it noted that Luka Nikitin was originally from Velikie Luki, and the two adults and three girls and one boy (Fed'ka) sold themselves for the going rate of 2 rubles apiece, or 12 rubles for all. Pozdeev also cited the fact that Fed'ka had run away once before, in 1629, and had been returned to him after a trial in the Slavery Chancellery. There was no contest over the possession of Fed'ka.

The major issue of the case was what should be done with a slave couple who had married while fugitives. Resolution of this matter was entrusted to the Patriarch's Court, which contacted their priest. The priest reported that he had learned in the confessional (*v dukhovne*) that the couple had been married. (One of the reasons for contacting the priest was to check on Krechetnikov's allegation that the figure Nikita Kireevskii was an invention, that Pozdeev had married Fed'ka to Dun'ka, which of course would have cost the defendant everything.) The resolution of that aspect of the case was that "the great lord most holy Iosaf Patriarch of Moscow and all Rus' has ordered that Fed'ka Luk'ianov and his wife Dun'ka shall not be divorced, thanks to the testimony of their spiritual father." Then a precedent for this decision was cited:

On April 1 of the past year 1625 the great sovereign of blessed memory, most holy Filaret Nikitich, Patriarch of Moscow and all Rus', [considered] a court case concerning Vasilii Strelkov's limited service contract slave-girl Feklitsa and Prokofei Vraskoi's slave Danilko Iur'ev, in which he, Prokofei, had desired to marry his slave Danilko to Vasilii's limited service contract slave-girl Feklitsa, and then he did marry him, Danilko, to her. Having heard the summary of the court case, [Filaret] ordered that Prokofei's slave Danilko not be divorced from that slave-girl Feklitsa after the marriage [had been consumated]. The sovereign Patriarch ordered on the basis of the old document that the slave-girl Feklitsa and her bridegroom, that Danilko Iur'ev, should be given back to Vasilii Strelkov. The sovereign Patriarch ordered that Prokofei Vraskoi should be paid 15 rubles for the slave Danilko Iur'ev.

According to the sovereign Patriarch's decree, 15 rubles were taken from Vasilii Strelkov and given to Prokofei Vraskoi, and his slave Danilko Iur'ev was taken from Prokofei and given to Vasilii Strelkov.

With all of this information in hand, the Slavery Chancellery was unable to reach a verdict. So, it outlined the options, as it saw them, and on September 10 sent the case to the tsar again: (1) Should the woman be returned to Matvei Pozdeev with her husband as a hereditary slave or as a limited service contract slave? (2) Should Krechetnikov collect 15 rubles from Pozdeev, as specified in the 1625 decree, for Dun'ka on the basis of the limited service slavery contract? or (3) Should the slave and his wife be taken out of "hereditary limited service contract slavery" and be given to Vasilii Krechetnikov, and should Krechetnikov be forced to pay Pozdeev 50 rubles, according to a previous (uncited) royal decree? This inability to render decisions in anything other than black-and-white cases was mandatory for the Muscovite system and, as we shall see throughout this work, the exercise of independent judgment of the kind that would have been required to resolve this case was severely condemned.

A few weeks later, on September 24, 1635, Krechetnikov began to petition for a verdict because he had been ordered to go to Urzhum to begin his governorship. He repeated his request two days later and expressed the typical view that, after he departed from Moscow, the case would be decided against him. By the end of the month, plaintiff Krechetnikov left Moscow, and his brother Vasilii stood in for him when the verdict was rendered in October.

The case had been considered for the tsar after September 10 by boyars Fedor Ivanovich Sheremetev and Prince Ondrei Vasil'evich Khilkov, *okol'nichii* Stepan Matveevich Proestev, and counselor state secretaries Fedor Likhachev and Mikhail Danilov, who were sitting as sort of a "supreme court," not in the sense that they heard appeals of verdicts but rather in the sense that they rendered decisions in cases that the chancelleries felt were not clear enough for the making of obvious decisions. As was almost always the case, their decision was quite rational. They resolved that Fedor and his wife Ovdot'itsa should be given to defendant Pozdeev, who was to pay Krechetnikov 15 rubles, on the grounds that the former's limited service slavery contract, dated 1620, was older than Krechetnikov's, apparently a document dated prior to the 1634 one, probably around 1630. They also resolved that the two should be returned as hereditary slaves, in spite of the limited service slavery contracts. They noted that "the great sovereign most holy Iosaf Patriarch of Moscow and all Rus' had ordered, on the basis of the testimony of their spiritual father, that Fed'ka Luk'ianov and his wife Dun'ka shall not be separated." Thus the ancient principle was maintained, and a solution was found to the dilemma provided by the marriage of runaways belonging to different owners.

The decision was effected by the Slavery Chancellery at some time in October. Pozdeev paid the 15 rubles to the plaintiff's brother Andrei and claimed his slaves. However, he was only able to claim Dun'ka (for whom he paid the capitation fee of 3 altyns to the Slavery Chancellery) because Fed'ka had fled. The customary practice was to release slaves on bail after the trial, until a verdict resolving ownership was announced, at which time contested slaves would be turned over to their rightful owners. In this case, however, as we have seen, both slaves were recidivist fugitives, with the result that no one could be found who would post bail for them. In this circumstance, the contested slaves were turned over to a bailiff of the Slavery Chancellery who was responsible for keeping them available for the verdict, a feat usually accomplished by shackling them to a wall in his house. For this the bailiff was paid a "chaining fee." Such had been the fate of Fed'ka and Dun'ka. The husband decided that he could not tolerate it, and managed to escape. As the bailiff informed the Slavery Chancellery on September 29: "The disputed slave Fed'ka and his wife in the case Vasilii Krechetnikov v. Matvei Pozdeev sat in irons in my custody. On September 28 of the present year 1635, that disputed slave of theirs fled from me. He broke his irons and abandoned his wife. Now his wife is sitting chained in my custody." According to the law, the bailiff was responsible for finding the fugitive, or would have to settle the matter with the fugitive's rightful owner. Having signed the record in certification of the fact that Dun'ka had been turned over to him, Pozdeev observed that the bailiff had found the slave and turned the fugitive over to him.[39]

The case of Krechetnikov v. Pozdeev reveals how the Muscovites solved a trouble case involving fugitive slaves who married while both were absent from their owners. The marriage was preserved and the slaves were awarded to the owner who had the older document, and both slaves henceforth were to follow his status, in this case hereditary slavery. Assuming the falsity of Krechetnikov's allegations that Nikita Kireevskii did not exist and that Dun'ka actually had been married to Fed'ka by Pozdeev, there is every reason to see in the resolution of the case a typical example of Muscovite justice. The fact of Pozdeev's intimate connections with the chancellery milieu through his father and other relatives make this a particularly relevant circumstance in this case. In spite of his family ties, Pozdeev's claim that Dun'ka was a military captive (a claim that would have been easy to accept, given the tendency to place considerable credence in slave

39. Iakovlev, *Kholopstvo,* pp. 488-96, no. 24.

testimony) was rejected, and every one of the chancelleries involved in the case seems to have acted properly, expeditiously, and fairly.

Miakinin v. Velkov

Another issue involving married slaves was what kind of slaves they should be if each was of a different kind, a subject raised in the case of Miakinin v. Velkov tried in the Slavery Chancellery in 1643 before director Stepan Ivanov Islen'ev and state secretary Roman Bulygin. In this instance, a limited service contract slave married a military captive. The case was complicated by a number of other factors and is well worth discussing in some detail.

Plaintiff was Fedor Mikhailov Miakinin, a rather typical member of the lower upper service class. His career can be traced explicitly only between the years 1629 and 1648, when he held the rank of Moscow *dvorianin*. What he was and did before that time, and how he got that rank, are questions that cannot be answered. Fortunately for us, however, the zenith of his career coincided with the events of this case, so at least we know something about him during the time he was a slaveowner. (As will be seen in the discussion of other legal cases, this pattern was rather typical, for slaveownership was highly determined by the life-cycle; young and insignificant people often did not own slaves, older and more important ones, those likely to be recorded in extant documents, usually did.) The first entry in the military registers about his service is dated 1633, when he was a regimental scribe (*pismennaia golova*) in Kazan'. Later in the same year he was among the forces sent down the Volga to Astrakhan' for a "Tatar War," an unwelcome diversion during the Smolensk War. It must have been during that war that Miakinin captured the woman who is the subject of litigation in this case, and another Tatar woman as well. In the trial itself, Miakinin mentioned that the purpose of the Tatar War had been "to conquer, destroy, and take into captivity the Kazyev Tatars because of their disobedience and treason. And by the grace of God and your [the tsar's] royal good fortune we, your slaves, defeated and conquered the Kazyev Tatars and took their wives and children as captives."

We may assume that Miakinin distinguished himself in the Tatar War, for two years later he was dispatched as military governor to Krasnoiarsk, the last-mentioned place in the contemporary registers of such appointments. This did not make it the least significant such appointment in all of Muscovy, but it probably was considered the most junior post of its kind in Siberia. The Krasnoiarsk garrison consisted of 100 cavalry cossacks, 200 infantry cossacks, and 3 atamans. Miakinin served in Siberia for seven years. Early in that period his father-in-law, who had custody of the slave whose ownership was litigated in this case, wrote his son-in-law a lengthy letter that is itself a remarkable document. In the letter, the father-in-law, Ivan Ondreev Starinskoi, a man of Polish origin, told Miakinin about his slaves, mentioned that military recruits were being levied at the rate of one man from every ten peasant households and that four had been drafted from Miakinin's properties (telling us that he had about forty peasant households, a not insignificant number, but perhaps typical for a Moscow *dvorianin*), and that 17 rubles had been collected from his peasants to send the recruits into the army (*perekhozhie den'gi*). In passing, the letter mentioned that Miakinin had three other slaves (in addition to the two Tatar military captives), two of whom were to help convoy a large quantity of goods (some of which can only have been meant for trade) and 195 rubles in cash, along with the letter, to Miakinin in Krasnoiarsk. In with the business and family news, Starinskoi interspersed messages of a more poignant content, transliterated into Latin letters to escape understanding by eyes other than those of the addressee:

> Prince Mikhailo Temkin and his colleagues from Tobol'sk have written a denunciation against you. They sent along testimony gathered from torture sessions and normal interrogations of twenty fugitive Krasnoiarsk cossacks. In their interrogation testimonies it is written that they fled from your oppression. Thanks to divine kindness and the help and solicitude of Mikifor Ivanovich [Shipulin, state secretary of the Siberian Chancellery], four of them were ordered hanged and the rest, having been beaten with the knout, were exiled to farm in Kuznetsk. [News on slaves follows.]
>
> For God's sake, Fedor Mikhailovich, live carefully, without any misbehavior and publicity so that no one will initiate denunciations against you. Here in Moscow they are saying about the Siberian military governors: when there are petitioners against someone, and his illegal conduct is proved, he shall be ordered to serve [forever] in Siberia. For God's sake, protect yourself from that.

To this twentieth-century author, at least, such solicitude by a father-in-law on behalf of his son-in-law rings true. Miakinin's daughter stayed behind in Moscow during his governorship—apparently he did not want her to be a "Russian woman" two centuries before the wives of the Decembrists celebrated by the poet Nekrasov followed their husbands into Siberian exile.

That Miakinin would dare introduce such a document in the trial indicates either that he was desperate, or that he was totally sure that no one would be able to penetrate transliterated Russian. It turned out that the Slavery Chancellery assumed the passage was in Polish, which its members could not read. Expert witnesses testified that it was Polish, and no more was said about it. Nevertheless, the Slavery Chancellery, as we shall see, did not feel that the document was trustworthy, and ruled it out as evidence.

That Miakinin's conduct as governor of Krasnoiarsk cast a pall over his subsequent career seems to be shown by the fact that he was never promoted and never again held a governorship in his own right. In 1645 he was second governor of Putivl' and Trubchevsk under governor Zamiatnia Fedorov Levont'ev. Miakinin ended his career as a member of the honor guard (*pristav*) at receptions for foreign dignitaries. In 1647 he was a greeter at the reception of Adam Kisel, castellan of Kiev; in 1648 he participated in the reception of Conrad Burg, emis-

sary of the Prince of Orange; and in 1649 he attended the reception of the patriarch of Jerusalem.[40]

Defendant in the case was Ivan Stepanov Velkov, brother of Miakinin's mother-
in-law. This was not a unique family dispute over slaveownership; given the very
nature of Muscovite slavery, there undoubtedly were many of them. The Velkov
clan was of Greek extraction, the name was alien to the Muscovites and therefore
likely to appear in other than the most careful records as something else (for
example as "Venkov" or the very common "Volkov"). A contemporary with the
name of Ivan (L'vov) Volkov makes the records unclear when no patronymic is
given. Be that as it may, we can assume that Velkov was older than Miakinin,
although they were both listed as having the rank of Moscow *dvorianin* between
1629 and 1640, unless for some reason Velkov was an entire generation younger
than his sister. His father had a service landholding in Kashira province in 1622,
and in 1632 "Ivan Volkov" had a total of 374 cheti of service and patrimonial
land in the Vologda and Bezhetskii Verkh regions and was to render military
service himself on horseback with two combat slaves and two baggage-train
slaves. "Ivan Volkov" in 1633 was one of those sent to prospect for gold in the
Perm' region. On February 5, 1639, Ivan Stepanov "Vel'kov" participated in the
reception for an ambassador of the Persian shah passing through Moscow on his
way to Holstein. In 1639-40, Ivan Stepanov Velkov (also Volkov and Venkov)
served as governor in the southern frontier town of Riazhsk, 280 kilometers
southeast of Moscow. His tenure there seems to have been relatively uneventful,
the only recorded event being his receipt of a report on the compensation schedule of a novitiate in military service. The extant records tell us nothing more
about Velkov, but we should note how his career parallels that of his adversary,
Fedor Miakinin. They even had a similar taste for Tatar slaves, for Velkov's
other slave mentioned in the case was Aleksei Asmanov, obviously a Tatar.[41]
Such similarity in the contemporary careers of litigating slaveowners is a frequently observable phenomenon, leading me to conclude that slaves also developed certain tastes in owners. In this case, however, the decisive factor was the
mutual relationship of the litigants through Ivan Starinskoi's wife, Mar'ia Stepanova Velkova Starinskaia.

40. Ivanov, AUBK, p. 276; DR 2: 325, 411, 756; 3: 65-67, 94-96, 113-19; RK 1550-1638,
p. 344; RK 1550-1636, 2: 375; KR 2: 936, Barsukov, SGV, p. 116; Iakovlev, *Kholopstvo*,
pp. 506-7. For some reason, Miakinin is not included in the 1632 list of Moscow *dvoriane*
and their landholding (Stashevskii, ZMD, p. 156). Perhaps this omission is due to the
fact that he did not serve in the Smolensk theatre. It is tempting to see the Fedor Miakinin
who served as an officer (*golova*) at Kurmysh in 1584 (RK 1475-1598, p. 348) as this person, especially as F. M. Miakinin noted at the trial that he had not visited his Kurmysh
village for nine years, thanks to his service on the Volga and then in Siberia. However,
1584 service seems highly unlikely for F. M. Miakinin.

41. Ivanov, AUBK, p. 60; Savel'ev, 2: 40; ZKMS (=RIB 10 [1886]), p. 108; AMG 2:
119. On Ivan Volkov, see Stashevskii, ZMD, pp. 60-61; RK 1550-1636, 2: 375. On Ivan
Stepanov Volkov (Venkov), see Barsukov, SGV, pp. 197, 454.

The case was initiated on March 20, 1643, before two arbiters, Afanasii Ivanov Nesterov for Miakinin and state secretary Onisim Trofimov of the Petitions Chancellery for Velkov. Nesterov was the son of Mar'ia Stepanova Velkova Starinskaia's second husband, state secretary Ivan Minich Nesterov of the Musketeers Chancellery. Whether Trofimov had any connection to the litigants is not clear. The arbiters brought in opposing verdicts, each awarding the case to his litigant. The disagreement between the arbiters brought the case to the Slavery Chancellery for resolution on July 1.

In Miakinin v. Velkov the basic facts were not contested. In 1633, when the plaintiff had participated in the military campaign against the Tatars under the command of general *stol'nik* Vasilii Ivanov Turenin, it was his fortune to capture Zinoviia (Zinka) of the Kazyev ulus, whom he failed to register as his slave. Two years later Miakinin was again summoned into service to Krasnoiarsk. He deposited for safekeeping (or so he alleged at the trial) his slavewoman Zinoviia with his parents-in-law, Ivan Ondreevich Starinskoi and his wife Maria, daughter of Stepan Velkov. He emphasized throughout the case that he had neither given nor sold the Tatar slavewoman to his parents-in-law, but had only deposited her there, whereas the defendant claimed Miakinin had given her to his father-in-law. Be that as it may, without consulting their son-in-law, the Starinskois married Zinka to a Pole by the name of Semen Aleksandrov Kazimerskoi, whose baptismal name was Aleksandr (Oleshka). The plaintiff argued that Oleshka had agreed, as part of the marriage arrangement, that the couple would serve him when he returned from service, but that point was never proved definitely. The defendant argued that Oleshka was a slave belonging to Starinskoi, and that Oleshka's marriage to Zinka made Zinka Starinskoi's slave as well. The defendent's arbiter faulted Miakinin for not having left specific instructions with his father-in-law not to marry Zinka to one of his slaves but to hold her as a single woman until he returned from his governorship. This, by the way, is a very clear statement of the slaveowner's control of the marital status of his chattel. The arbiter also suggested that Miakinin should drop his suit against Velkov and, instead, sue his mother-in-law for having married off his slave without his consent.

The marriage of the military captive to the limited service contract slave set the scene for the subsequent dispute. The litigation was precipitated by the murder of the father-in-law, Ivan Starinskoi, by bandits. Okeshka was freed, as though he had been a limited service contract slave, on the death of his owner. Much was made of the fact that Mar'ia Starinskaia had not given the couple a manumission document upon her husband's death, but such a formality was not necessary. After Starinskoi's death, the slave couple lived for a while, as freedmen they assumed, in the household of the Tolochanovs (otherwise unidentified), and then on August 16, 1638, sold themselves for the regulation 6 rubles as limited service contract slaves to the defendant, Ivan Velkov. Oleshka noted his former slave status in the 1638 contract. Given the dependency created by Muscovite slavery, such self-sale again into slavery was an expected development. It is also not surprising that they sold themselves to Velkov, for he was the brother-in-law of the late Starinskoi, and we may assume that the parties were acquainted even prior to Starinskoi's death.

Miakinin argued that Oleshka and Zinka were not freed by Starinskoi's death but belonged to him because Zinka was a military captive and such people were not freed on the death of their owners. This principle was cited by Miakinin's arbiter in awarding him the verdict: "captured slaves are not freed after [their owners'] death, but belong to wives and children." He also noted that "captives, purchased slaves, and slaves given as a present [or dowry] are not manumitted upon their owners' death." Velkov did not deny that Zinka had been Miakinin's military captive, or that she had been married to Oleshka, but insisted that the rule of limited service contract slavery was the applicable one and that the slave was freed on the death of his owner.

Both litigants cited various forms of evidence to prove their cases. Miakinin cited two allegedly knowledgeable priests, Nikita, who had baptized the Tatar woman and was her confessor, and Aleksei, the spiritual father of both the Starinskois and Zinka, to prove his contention that when he had been sent into Siberian service he had left Zinka with his in-laws only temporarily (*na vremia*). He also noted that his mother-in-law had not manumitted either Zinka or her husband Oleshka because the captive slave Zinka belonged to him, and was not hers or her husband's. Also observed was the matter of intention, for Miakinin claimed that his mother-in-law had freed her other slaves and that Aleksei had signed the manumission documents for her. When interrogated by Miakinin's arbiter, Aleksei confirmed this version and added that Oleshka had come to him after Starinskoi's murder to ask the priest to intercede with the widow Mar'ia to free them, but that she had refused because the slave Aleksandrik Kazimerskoi and his wife, the Tatar Zinka, belonged to her son-in-law.

Miakinin also cited the lengthy letter his father-in-law allegedly had sent him in Krasnoiarsk, which was discussed above. About the marriage Starinskoi had written:

> I married off your Tatar slave-girl, Zinka. I had taken in the foreigner, the Lithuanian Kazimerskoi whose Russian name is Oleshka. By the sovereign's decree he was granted freedom [in the exchange of captured nationals at the conclusion of the Smolensk War], to go whither he wished. He came to us of his own volition and asked that we marry him to your slave-girl, the Tatar Zinka. I told him that that slave-girl is yours. He married her on the condition that he will be your slave. . . . I am going to take five of your slaves who have no families and settle them on waste lands in Gorki, Dmitrov province, in the Moscow area. I shall appoint Kazimerskoi to supervise them and shall set him up there.

Under interrogation, as reported in the arbiter Nesterov's case, the priest Aleksei claimed that he had been aware of Oleshka's promise to be Miakinin's slave if Starinskoi would allow him to wed Zinka.

The Slavery Chancellery awarded the verdict to defendant Velkov for a number of reasons. It found none of Miakinin's claims convincing. He had never registered Zinka as a military captive. He did not file a claim when she and her husband allegedly fled from the widow Mar'ia Stepanova Starinskaia (to which Miakinin replied that he had not been present, and Mar'ia was a woman with no one present to assist her in such affairs—the only male around was her brother, the one who had recruited the slaves for himself). Moreover, the Slavery Chancellery was not sure of the authenticity of the letter Starinskoi allegedly had sent to his son-in-law, for, it was not proved that the Russian had been written by Starinskoi, and the testimony proving that the transliterated Russian ["Polish"] was in Starinskoi's hand had been taken only by the plaintiff's arbiter, in the absence of the defendant's arbiter. Finally, the testimony of the two priests had been taken only by Miakinin's arbiter, in the absence of Velkov's, so it was ruled inadmissible. On the other hand, Velkov's limited service slavery contract was a valid document, and in it the slaves in question, Oleshka and Zinka, had said that they had been Starinskoi's slaves, not Miakinin's, who was not mentioned.

Velkov thus got to keep the slaves, although they were no longer those listed in the limited service slavery contract of August 1638. Oleshka had died, for unstated reasons, but the union of the Pole and the Tatar had produced a girl, Sashka, who was about five years old in 1643. Both of them were officially declared to be Velkov's limited service contract slave property, Zinka because she had been sold together with her husband in the 1638 contract, Sashka because she had been born in slavery.

When she was declared to be Velkov's property, Zinka was described as follows:

> The Tatar woman Zinka has a flat·face, a turned-up nose, distended nostrils, hazel eyes, her eyebrows are light brown. On her face and nose are pits from smallpox. Her left ear lobe has been gouged all the way across it. She is of average height.[42]

My own, twentieth-century sense is that, at least to a certain extent, there was a miscarriage of justice in Miakinin v. Velkov. In the first place, no one denied that Zinka had been captured by Miakinin. Secondly, the Starinskoi letter looks genuine to me. This is important because of its statement that Oleshka was a free person when he came to Starinskoi. Consequently the military-captive slave status of his wife Zinka should have been transmitted to him, a point made by Miakinin's arbiter. In that case, neither of them could have claimed the freedom due limited-service contract slaves on the death of their owners, and Velkov's

---

42. Iakovlev, *Kholopstvo*, pp. 496-513, no. 25. On the lowering of status in Chinese slave marriages, see Meijer, "Ch'ing," p. 347.

1638 contract would have been void. The validity of the Starinskoi letter and the priests' testimony supporting it constituted the central issue, for those forms of evidence were regarded as supportive of any legal claims. As we have seen, however, the Slavery Chancellery saw fit to disregard all of those points and, while noting that Miakinin had no documentation on Zinka, recognized Velkov's limited service slavery contract. (One may be sure, incidentally, that Zinka's extended residence with Velkov played no role whatsoever in the verdict, for the *sentiments* of slaves were never taken into consideration by the Muscovite authorities.)

It is unfortunate for us that this case was settled by resort to technicalities rather than by a resolution of the issue of the status of a military-captive slave and a limited service contract slave who married and had offspring. One may well surmise, however, that the more severe form of slavery would prevail for all of them, as in China at the beginning of the eighteenth century, when a white contract slave married to a red contract slave became herself a red contract slave. Nevertheless, the case demonstrates well the principle that the slave conjugal unit was to be preserved.

Orthodoxy did not acknowledge divorce. Nevertheless, a divorce could be arranged by a couple who sold themselves to different owners. For enslaved couples, marriage incompatibility was one of the major precipitants of flight from slavery, and may well have encouraged such flight because the deserting spouse had reason to believe that the owner would look after those who remained with him.

Slave Offspring

Offspring are another concern of slave family law. The problem has two major dimensions: what the status of the offspring will be and what liberties the slave-owner may take in disposing of them (how much he must respect the nuclear family).

Westermann was certainly correct when he observed that, in patrilocal societies, "customarily, in the eyes of the law the slave has no male parent."[43] (The principle is the same in matrilocal societies.) Thus the slave himself in patrilocal socieites is often kinless, which was completely true for some slaves in Muscovy, and partially true for most of the rest of them. In the next generation, the status of a slave's child can often be defined in terms of the principle that "the offspring follows the mother," from the Latin *partus sequitur ventrem*. This obviously has been the case in many slave systems, ranging from those in which slave marriages were not acknowledged and the child followed the status of the mother to those

43. Westermann, p. 20.

in which slaves were explicitly denied the right to have a patronymic.[44] The matter was dealt with somewhat poetically in India:

> As with cows, mares, female camels, slave girls, buffalo-cows, she-goats, and ewes, it is not the begetter (or his owner) who obtains the offspring, even thus (it is) with the wives of others.
> Men who have no marital property in women, but sow their seed in the soil of others, benefit the owner of the woman; but the giver of the seed reaps no advantage.[45]

Thus the principle was that the slave followed the mother.

In some slave systems, it does not matter which parent is a slave, for the offspring will be slaves in any case. Legislation in thriving slave systems, such as that for the New World in the sixteenth and seventeenth centuries, usually makes it very clear that the offspring of slaves themselves will be slaves.[46] Heritability of slave status is usually one of the signs of harsh systems, such as among the Northwest Coast Indians, where the children of slaves were always slaves. The same seems to have been true among medieval Germanic peoples and the Chinese.[47]

On the other hand, slave systems do not always prescribe that the children of slaves themselves must be slaves. Notable in this respect are many of the peoples of Africa, such as the Dahomeans of West Africa, the Ashanti of the Gold Coast (Ghana), or the Azande living between the Congo and the Nile, among whom slave children are free, ordinarily as part of the process of incorporating them into their new lineage. This was often true in Islam as well, for while the children of a married slave woman were legally slaves and belonged to her owner, the Koran recommended emancipation and thus effectively limited slavery to the generation of the person enslaved. This accounts for much of the virulence of Islamic slavery, for the system always had to be replenished by new recruits.[48]

44. Mendelsohn, p. 34; Martin Klein and Paul E. Lovejoy, " Slavery in West Africa," in Gemery & Hogendorn, p. 191.

45. *Laws of Manu*, IX, 55.

46. Mellafe, p. 117; Rose, p. 177. This principle, not English common law requiring the child's status to follow his father's, probably explains the 1664 Maryland law requiring the offspring of a free woman married to a slave to be enslaved (Catterall 4: 2).

47. Wergeland, pp. 22-23; Siegel, p. 366; Meijer, p. 331. Athenian slavery was generally "harsh," and offspring of two slave parents were also enslaved. However, the status of offspring of marriages in which one party was free, the other was slave is unclear, although it is possible that the Athenians also prescribed that the slave follow the status of the mother (A. R. W. Harrison, *The Law of Athens. The Family and Property* [Oxford: Clarendon Press, 1968], p. 164). Muscovy tried to avoid such ambiquity simply by insisting that any free party who had sexual relations with a slave was himself or herself enslaved. To my knowledge, Muscovite law did not deal with the problem of bastards issuing from free-slave liaisons.

48. Levy, *Islam*, p. 79; Siegel, pp. 374, 381, 385.

In Muscovy, children of any age living with their parents at the time when the elders became enslaved, or born while their parents were enslaved, themselves were slaves.[49] The *Ulozhenie* of 1649 upheld this ancient doctrine, with the additional note that the owners of such children were obliged to obtain limited service slavery contracts on them, regardless of whether the children were willing to be so registered.[50] Heritability of slave status was one of the major features of the Muscovite system, one that assigns it to the harsher systems of slavery.

Not infrequently, children who had been born in slavery fled, and then sold themselves to someone else. Their former owners had full legal claim to them when they found them.[51] Moreover, late Muscovite law established the procedures to be followed should a child of slaves flee and subsequently deny his parentage in an attempt to escape servitude: officials were to attempt to make children (they might be adults, of course) admit that they were related to their parents (or to siblings or to aunts or uncles who were enslaved) because of hereditary or limited service contract slavery by first arranging a visual confrontation between the apprehended fugitive and his relatives. If this did not produce an acknowledgment of slave status, the officials were to resort to torture. A second torturing might be used if the first did not produce a confession. Should the second torture session fail to produce a confession, the officials might turn the bloody victim over to a slaveowner who had a valid limited service slavery contract on him. In one of the many analogies extended to serfs from the Muscovite law of slavery, fugitive peasants were included in these provisions, and a special article on torturing fugitive serf children who denied their parents was included in the *Ulozhenie* at the request of the delegates to the 1648-49 Assembly of the Land.[52] This reminds us of the Ancient Near East, where the cruelest punishments were reserved for those who denied their slave status.[53]

The ravages of North American slavery and the abolitionist pictures of the child being sold away from its unwilling mother have led many people to assume that this was another natural part of slavery. And so it has been in many places. Peoples from the Babylonians and the Hebrews to the Tibetan-speaking Nepalese Nyinba and the Siamese thought nothing of breaking both the conjugal unit and the nuclear family.[54] In fact, however, the nuclear family was protected in some slave systems. Most unexpectedly, that was the legal norm in the 1755 *Règlement* promulgated for the Danish Virgin Islands, which proclaimed that no minor was to be separated from his parents by any transaction. A suitable sanction was also

49. Vladimirskii-Budanov, *Khristomatiia* 3: 112; 1550 *Sudebnik* 75; 1649 *Ulozhenie* 20: 87; MS, pp. 286-87; PSZ 2: 499, no. 992.

50. 1649 *Ulozhenie* 20: 30; MS, p. 266.

51. PRP 4: 379-80; 1649 *Ulozhenie* 20: 83; MS, p. 285.

52. 1649 *Ulozhenie* 20: 24-25; 11: 22; MS, pp. 227, 264.

53. Mendelsohn, p. 66.

54. Ibid., pp. 40-41, 53; Exodus 21: 4; Turton, p. 274; Nancy E. Levine, "Nyinba Slavery," in Watson, *Systems*, p. 203.

provided for a slaveowner who violated the norms: he had to give the remaining retained members of the family to the party to whom he had sold any one of the family members.[55] Islamic law forbade the separation of a child before the age of about seven from its slave mother.[56] Alabama law placed the minimum at age ten, with age five being the minimum only in extraordinary cases.[57]

In Muscovy, as in China, children of slaves could be disposed of freely, apart from their parents, and in fact were, when estates were divided among heirs. There also was some tendency in wills to split up the children of slaves among the various heirs. This violation of slave family ties may have been perpetrated with an eye to maximizing future marriage possibilities for the children while minimizing inbreeding, to increase the chances that slaves could be forced to marry other, nonrelated, slaves living with the same owner. Here Muscovy parted company with Byzantium, whose laws forbade the breaking up of the nuclear family.[58] Because owners could dispose of offspring regardless of family ties, the Russian hereditary slave in this respect was kinless. The law itself even occasionally prescribed the splitting up of a slave family. Thus when a slave fled from foreign captivity, he was granted his freedom. The government, intent on preserving consecrated marriages, insisted that the slave's wife be freed and returned to him "for his suffering in captivity." Their children, however, remained enslaved, the property of their parents' former owner.[59] Or, when a fugitive slave woman married a slave widower who had children by a previous marriage, the couple was returned to her owner, but the children remained with the person with whom they had been born in slavery.[60] A "compromise" situation for the slave nuclear family was created in 1700, as slavery was on its way to extinction: Peter the Great allowed a slave to flee from his owner and enlist in the infantry. Moreover, the slave could take his wife and children under twelve with him. (The age of majority was usually fifteen.) Children twelve and older born in slavery had to remain with their parents' former owner.[61] On the other hand, this was not always so. Generally, children were returned with their fugitive parents.[62] If a slave ran away, married a free woman, the couple had children, and subsequently he sold all of them with himself to a second master, his lawful first own-

55. Hall, "Virgin Islands," p. 177.

56. Brunschvig, "'Abd," p. 26..

57. Rose, p. 189.

58. Meijer, "Ch'ing," p. 332; Z. V. Udal'tsova, "Polozhenie rabov v Vizantii VI v. (Preimushchestvenno po dannym zakonodatel'stva Iustiniana)," *Vizantiiskii vremennik* 24 (1963): 26. For examples of the splitting up of slave families, see Kopanev, "Materialy," p. 159; Sergei Shumakov, "Obzor 'gramot Kollegii ekonomii', pt. 4: Kostroma 's tovarishchi' i Pereslavl'-Zalesskii," *Chteniia* 261(1917, bk. 2): 315, no. 949.

59. 1649 *Ulozhenie* 20: 66; MS, p. 278.

60. 1649 *Ulozhenie* 11: 13; MS, p. 224.

61. PSZ 6: 367, no. 3754.

62. 1649 *Ulozhenie* 20: 88; MS, p. 287.

er could claim the entire family.[63] Probably the motivation behind the law was to punish the second person for having received the fugitive, but its consequence was to preserve the nuclear family. To take another example, that of a problem which arose in 1625 and whose logical solution preserved both the marriage and the family of the slave: if a slaveowner unpremeditatedly killed another lord's slave, the victim's owner had the right to claim one of the killer's slaves in restitution. In addition, the bereaved owner also could claim the wife and children of the slave coming to him in compensation for the deceased.[64]

Peter the Great upheld the principle of family inviolability. In 1721, ready as always to compare his times with the barbarous past of his country, he noted that "there was a practice in Russia, which exists even now, of petty landholders selling their peasants and field and house slaves [*delovye i dvorovye liudi*] separately, like animals [*skot*], to whoever desired to buy them, something that is unheard of [*ne voditsia*] in the entire world. Out of a family a landholder sells a daughter or son away from the mother or father." The extent of such sales will be examined in chapter 10, where the point will be made that they were minimal. But be that as it may, Peter ordered that the sales of people be stopped. Recognizing, however, that it might not be possible to halt sales of human beings entirely, because a landholder might need the cash, Peter insisted that they be sold in whole families, not separately.[65]

Concern for the maintenance of the slave family did not diminish at the time when slavery was expiring, although such concerns had largely been transferred to the serfs. On April 6, 1722, Peter the Great repeated the principle that fugitive slaves were to be returned as families to their rightful owners. Reflecting the change in the nature of the family that was taking place, from the nuclear to the extended family, the law stipulated that not only children should be returned with their parents but sons-in-law who had fled with them, as well as grandchildren who had been born while the slaves were fugitives. The sole exception was for fugitive widows and girls who had been married, without the presence of their fathers, to slaves and peasants of the landowner with whom they lived as fugitives. The new lord was to pay the rightful owner 50 rubles apiece for such women. For daughters who had been born on the new lord's estate and then married there, 25 rubles were to be paid to the rightful owner, on the assumption that half of the increase was his. For granddaughters, the old lord got nothing. When two fugitives married, the couple and its offspring were to be returned to the husband's owner, who was to pay her owner 10 rubles.[66] Aside from this last minor modification, we see that the old rules for slaves were fundamentally preserved and transferred to serfs.

63. 1649 *Ulozhenie* 20: 87; MS, pp. 286-87.
64. PRP 5: 204-5.
65. PSZ 6: 377, no. 3770.
66. PSZ 6: 638, no. 3939.

Until near the very end of slavery as a legal institution, the Russians did not express much thought on the matter of the nuclear family. It could be broken up, and was, both in law and in life. The general practice, however, was not to separate children of slaves from their progenitors.

The ancient Mesopotamian laws of Eshnunna (ca. 1900 B.C.) were concerned with cases in which a slave mother by subterfuge gave away her child to someone of a high status, and provided that a rightful owner could claim such a child at any time. There were no such provisions in Muscovy, no doubt primarily because children were of little or even negative value there. Further along in the life cycle, a slave who gave his own daughter in marriage was considered by the Chinese to have cheated his owner of his rights.[67] A similar situation may have arisen in Muscovy, but its resolution is unknown.

Sexual Relations and Marriage between Slave and Free

Sexual relationships between slave and free were regulated or discussed in many systems. The purpose of such regulation often was to keep local people from being defiled by contact with outsiders. Relations between slave men and free women were usually of much greater interest than those between free men and slave women. In India a man who had sexual intercourse with a female slave could be charged with adultery and compelled to pay a small fine.[68] The reverse situation, of advances of a slave man toward a free woman, was not discussed. In China, no slave could legally marry the daughter of a free man. In Crete, adultery of a slave man with a free woman was punishable by a fine twice what a free man would pay in such a case. Slave women had to be manumitted before they could marry free men. At Athens such a slave would be punished by execution, and the same was certain in Rome if the woman was the slave's mistress. The Byzantines felt more strongly about the matter, and prescribed that a free woman who had had sexual intercourse with a slave should be executed, while the slave was to be burned alive.[69] However, Justinian repealed the classical law according to which a free woman who married a slave became herself a slave. Canon law picked this up and legitimized such unions.[70] By the fourth century A.D. in the Western Roman Empire the former conventions had broken down with the development of serfdom, and slaves and peasants began to intermarry.[71]

The regulations in the Spanish law of 1263 are of particular interest because of

67. Pritchard, *The Ancient Near East*, p. 136, arts. 33-35; Meijer, p. 333.

68. *Law of Manu*, VIII, 363. In more recent times, however, marriages of slaves and free persons were countenanced in India (as in Nepal), the principal condition being that the spouses were of the same or equivalent rank (Caplan, p. 184).

69. Westermann, p. 17; D. B. Davis, *Western Culture*, pp. 49, 61.

70. *Istoriia Vizantii* 1: 260; D. B. Davis, p. 93.

71. Jones, p. 198.

their presumed descent from Byzantine practice and because of the contrast provided with Muscovite legislation, much of which also descended from Byzantine practice. Thus the Spanish law of 1263 automatically freed a slave who was married by her master. Moreover, a slave could marry a free person without the owner's consent so long as the free person had been apprised of the chattel status of the spouse. Finally, if the owner consented to the union, the slave was freed.[72]

The situation in the New World is generally well known. In Latin America much attention was paid in the sixteenth century to the matter of sexual liaisons between the imported African slaves, the local Indians, and the European colonizers. In general, the restrictions imposed by the Old World legislators were not observed by those half a world away. Fewer African females than males were imported, and the Europeans, who came to the New World without women, tended to take the imported slave women as their wives or concubines. This left the African males with no mates, so they turned to the local Indians. The supposed melting pot of Brazil was the result. As often was the case in expansive slave systems, owners (and the law) held that the Indian mothers were slaves along with their African husbands.[73]

The situation was different when northern Europeans were involved. For example, in the Danish Virgin Islands the codes of 1741, 1755, and 1783 were all harsh when it came to mixing between slaves and whites. Slave women were not to be found in a white man's room at night unless they were performing household chores; a man who raped a slave woman was to be fined the enormous sum of 2,000 pounds of sugar, and any white woman who "indecently degraded" herself by having sexual relations with a black slave was to be fined, imprisoned, and then deported.[74] The North American history of this subject is well known, and its tone was set by the 1662 Virginia statute prescribing a double fine for anyone who "fornicated with a negro."[75] That northern Europeans were more race-conscious than others is well attested. For example, while contact with Orientals was restricted to Italians and Iberians, little distinction was noted; only when northern Europeans ventured to the Far East was it observed that the indigenes were yellow. Islam did not allow the death penalty that might be imposed on free people for fornication to be imposed on slaves of either sex because a slave was not capable of acquiring the particular legal condition of a spouse, which was reserved for free persons who had a legal marriage. Thus the punishment for slaves convicted of fornication was half that prescribed for an unwed free person, fifty lashes instead of a hundred. A Muslim could marry another slaveowner's slave women, but not his own.[76]

72. Klein, *Americas*, pp. 62, 64-65.
73. Mellafe, p. 117.
74. Hall, pp. 175, 177, 182.
75. Klein, *Americas*, p. 42.
76. Brunschvig, "'Abd," pp. 26, 29; Levy, *Islam*, pp. 64, 105.

One of the most extreme slave systems prevailed among the Northwest Coast Indians. Slaves were very much despised, a topic that will be discussed in a later chapter. Relevant here is the potential conjugal aspect of that attitude: marriage between a free man and a slave woman was simply unconscionable. Slaves were totally outside the social system, and never could attain any social status.[77]

Muscovy was an exception to the general attempt to isolate slaves from free people. In this it was not unique. In Babylonia and Nuzi, where insider-outsider sense was minimally developed, no stigma was attached even to the not infrequent marriages of slave men and free women. The Hammurabi Code was concerned about the subject only in the context of the dowry and offspring.[78] Ancient Gortyn also allowed unions between slave and free, as did even the later Roman Empire. If there was anything common to all of these places, it may have been a tacit ecumenical feeling of being a crossroads of humanity—that, and an absence of strong ethnic identity.

However, there was nothing "mild" about the Muscovite solution to the problem of slave-free sexual liaison, for the consequence of such alliances was the enslavement of the free party. This was not true in Babylonia, Gortyn, or the Western Roman Empire. The Muscovite situation, like that in many medieval Germanic societies as well as in the *Lithuanian Statutes* of 1529 and 1566, was normally handled by the very simple formula *po kholopu raba, po rabe kholop*: a person marrying a slave of either sex was thereby enslaved.[79] In the 1580s a royal decree modified this so that a free man marrying a slave woman lost his freedom, but a free woman marrying a male slave remained a free person.[80] The reason for this change is not evident to historians, and apparently the change did not seem rational to contemporaries, for the new law soon lapsed. Perhaps the innovation of the 1580s was made in an attempt to recruit wives into the overwhelmingly male slave world. Another possible explanation might be that someone in Moscow in the 1580s learned of the Justinian repeal of the provision enslaving a free woman who married a slave. I fear, however, that we shall never be able to penetrate the reasoning of the contemporaries who tried to change the customary practice, and failed.

Of greater interest than the reversal of the 1580s is the fact that Muscovy allowed slave-free marriages at all. Again, no contemporary explanation is at hand, but one may reason that this simply reflects the fact that the vast majority of Muscovite slaves were native Russians, and so therefore the general need to shelter the indigenous population from outside contamination was largely lacking. These

77. Siegel, p. 366.

78. Pritchard, p. 158, arts. 175-76; Mendelsohn, pp. 55-56.

79. 1550 *Sudebnik* 76; 1649 *Ulozhenie* 20: 31; MS, pp. 266-67; PSZ 2: 644, no. 1099; Wergeland, pp. 13, 19, 34; 1529 LS 1: [13] 12 (p. 118 in Iablonskis edition); Rafał Taubenschlag, *Wpływy rzymsko-bizantyńskie w drugim Statucie litewskim* (Lwów, 1933), pp. 19-20 (I am indebted to Peter Bowman Brown for this citation).

80. 1550 *Sudebnik* 76; 1589 *Sudebnik* 137.

slaves were, therefore, less outside the social system than most slaves elsewhere, a recurrent theme in this essay.

Because of the Muscovite solution to the problem of slave-free conjugal relations, there was no need to resolve the issue of the status of their offspring, who by definition were slaves. In other societies, ranging from the Ancient Near East down to the European Middle Ages, the children of free-slave unions were often declared to be free.[81] That led, in such societies, to a diminution of the number of native-born slaves, something that is not observable in Muscovy.

There were often exceptions to even the most hallowed Russian legal principles, if the principles conflicted with higher goals of the Muscovite administration. Thus the law allowed an unmarried slavewoman and widow to flee to a frontier town, marry a serviceman, and gain her freedom. Someone was supposed to compensate the slaveowner by paying him 50 rubles for the woman. Where the 50 rubles, ten times the annual salary of almost any frontier serviceman, were to come from is not specified. This article has the air of "compromise" for an impossible dilemma: the *po rabe kholop* principle and the rights of the slaveowners should not be infringed, but the expanding frontier had to be defended, and soldiers needed wives. The dilemma was "resolved" by prescribing a very high compensation payable to those whose interests were violated. Except for the fact that there was a great shortage of female slaves, one could see a slaveowner getting rich by buying single women in the Muscovite heartland for the regulation 3 rubles, "fattening them up" for several months, and then transporting them to the frontier and selling them for a high premium. Whether this ever happened is unknown. This provision for slaves was extended to single peasant women, with the difference that only 10 rubles had to be paid to compensate landholders for their loss.[82] In 1683 slaveowners raised the issue of returning their fugitive slave-women who married Moscow musketeers. They claimed the practice had been to return the couple as slaves. The government investigated the matter, and found that people with whom the fugitives had been living had offered the women in marriage, generalized the *Ulozhenie* provision on the marriage of servicemen and slave women (omitting the frontier aspect), and asked the rulers whether those who had married them off should have to pay the sum, and if so how much. In turning the case over to the tsars and boyars, whoever prepared the digest of the issues also noted that the *Ulozhenie* had forbidden enslaving musketeers and prescribed that the government was to pay the debts of such people. Resolving the issue, the tsars and boyars said that such slave girls should not be returned to their owners, that 10 rubles should be the redemption fee, and that the sum should be paid by those who married off the slave girls (if they could be found), or else by their husbands, the *strel'tsy*.[83]

81. Mendelsohn, p. 75.
82. 1649 *Ulozhenie* 20: 27; MS, pp. 264-65.
83. PSZ 2: 515-16, no. 1003.

This 1683 case makes it clear that the fundamental principle that marriage to a slave enslaved the other party was still intact as slavery was on the verge of being abolished as a legal institution. The slaveowners claimed to believe that principle, and the officials in charge of resolving the dispute (probably from the Slavery Chancellery, although that is not certain; they might also have been from the Musketeers Chancellery) obviously were not certain of the existence of any exceptions, other than that for frontier servicemen. Better evidence of both popular and official sentiment on an issue could hardly be found.

At this juncture in many slave systems a discussion of race would be relevant. Racial separation was one of the major functions of much of the New World legislation on slavery.[84] In Muscovy, however, that was not the case. None of the norms of Russian slave family law bears the slightest tincture of racism. More on the matter of race in Muscovite slavery has been said in chapter 3 in the discussion of Tatar slaves and will be said in chapter 10 on the price of slaves and in chapter 12 on ethnicity.

Muscovite slave family law was well within the mainstream of slave law, as determined by comparative examples. The slave was a movable chattel who usually could be married or not, as his owner desired. There was no limitation on whom a slave in Muscovy could marry, but, once married, the couple was enslaved, and Orthodoxy prescribed that the couple remain married until death did them part. The couple had no right to their children, who were also slaves, but the general practice was to respect the nuclear family.

84. Friedman, p. 196.

5. Legal Relations between Masters and Slaves

Sexual Access to Slaves

A transitional topic bridging family law and the legally defined relations between owner and slave is the sexual access to his slaves an owner enjoyed. Moses I. Finley has claimed that an owner's right of free sexual access to his slaves is "a fundamental condition of all slavery."[1] This has certainly been largely true since the dawn of history. In the Ancient Near East, females were often purchased expressly to be handmaids to their mistresses and concubines to their masters.[2] This was most true in Islam, where the law regularly allowed an owner to have sexual relations with his female slaves, and in fact forbade him to marry them, although he was not supposed to hire them out as prostitutes.[3] A captive woman pregnant with a Muslim's child could be kept enslaved. In traditional Africa, slave women were often the concubines of their owners, acquired and kept explicitly for the purpose of expanding the lineage. While some varieties of African slavery resembled Muscovite slavery in many respects, on this point they differed totally. Concubinage was also widely practiced in China, and a slave-owner legally had free sexual access to unwed slave women. However, a mild punishment of forty strokes with a light bamboo was prescribed for the slave-owner who raped a married slave woman.[4]

The New World situation also generally confirms Finley's observations. While late Southern antebellum legal theoreticians noticed the contradiction of legislating the crime of murder for owners who deliberately killed their slaves while excluding the charge of rape for those who had forcible carnal knowledge of their own or others' female slaves, nothing was done about it, as evidenced particularly by the "whitening" of the U.S. slave population between the censuses of 1850 and 1860.[5] Nevertheless, even for the thought to arise in North America

1. Moses I. Finley, "The Idea of Slavery: A Critique of David Brion Davis' *The Problem of Slavery in Western Culture*," in *Slavery in the New World. A Reader in Comparative History*, ed. Laura Foner and Eugene D. Genovese (Englewood Cliffs, N. J.: Prentice-Hall, 1969), p. 260.
2. Mendelsohn, pp. 8-9.
3. Brunschvig, "'Abd,'" p. 28. There were many refinements, such as forbidding an owner to use more than one sister as a concubine, but they need not detain us here.
4. Miers and Kopytoff, p. 14; Meijer, p. 333.
5. Rose, pp. 200, 204; Herbert Gutman and Richard Sutch, "Victorians All? The Sexual

that slaveowners might not enjoy automatic sexual access to their chattel is an important indicator that generalizers about slavery should consider. Moreover, as we have seen, the laws of the Danish Virgin Islands tried to deny such access, not, one suspects, out of concern for the female slaves but out of a desire to protect Europeans from contamination.

The Muscovite case, which was not unique, refutes Finley's proposition as one that is universally valid. East Slavic slaveowner access to female slaves was limited as early as a twelfth-century treaty between Novgorod and the Germans, which prescribed that a master who raped his slave had to pay a grivna fine for the offense, and furthermore set her free if she became pregnant.[6] This was not as far as the law of the Lombards went, however, which prescribed that if an owner raped his slave's wife, both the wife and her husband were to be emancipated.[7] In Muscovy, a woman who presented a child as proof of sexual assault had the right to complain to the tsar, and, according to provisions going back to the Byzantine *Canons of St. Basil the Great,* the *Ecloga,* and the *Procheiros Nomos,* he was to remand the case to the church for disposition. Some interpretations claim that church literature stipulated that the woman had to be manumitted forthwith, but the Russian *Kormchaia kniga* renditions of these sources prescribed that the victimized slave had to be sold to someone else.[8] Similar provisions of medieval Spanish law ultimately found their way to Latin America.[9]

I know of no instance in which the Muscovite sanctions were called upon. The extent of "consenting concubinage" also cannot be judged. The slave genealogies occasionally list children from others for whom no fathers are evident, but there is no easy way of knowing whether they were products of owner-slave unions. Flight was so common that no conclusions about why no father was present in a family are possible. Although Orthodoxy prescribed monogamy, the existence of a law stipulating that the fruits of such unions were to be freed, in consonance with the general worldwide norm that the offspring of free-slave unions should be manumitted, hints that at least in early Muscovy concubinage existed in reality. I have one case in which the owner purchased a number of young females, and no males. We may only speculate on whether the man was running a brothel or a harem, or was buying the females to marry them to males who are not recorded.[10]

As was typically the case throughout history since Babylonian times (except

Mores and Conduct of Slaves and Their Masters," in Paul A. David et al., *Reckoning with Slavery* (New York: Oxford University Press, 1976), pp. 152-53.

6. Sergeevich, *Drevnosti,* 1: 123.

7. Rose, p. 204.

8. AI 1, no. 134-xx; Sergeevich, p. 140; Kolycheva, *Kholopstvo,* p. 236.

9. Klein, *Americas,* p. 62. This was recommended for Southern law by T. R. R. Cobb in 1858 (Rose, p. 204).

10. NZKK 1: 246-49.

in parts of the New World), the offspring of a slaveowner and his concubine, according to the stipulation of article 98 of the *Russkaia Pravda*, were to be set free after their father's death. The law was used in Lithuanian court practice throughout the sixteenth century. One may surmise that the provision was not repeated in sixteenth- and seventeenth-century statutes either because most of the Russian populace (particularly the upper, slaveowning classes) was Christianized by that time and therefore was reasonably monogamous, or because such aspects of family law were turned over to the church. Be that as it may, a provision parallel to article 98 is to be found in the canon law of the Russian Orthodox church; one may assume that it did not motivate the *Russkaia Pravda* but did provide norms for later Muscovy.[11]

The *Pravda* declared such children to be essentially illegitimate and disinherited. This might be contrasted with Babylonia or India, where a son begotten by a free man on a slave woman could be included in his inheritance either if the father recognized the child as his own or prescribed the child as an heir. Both China and Islam, which legitimized the right of sexual access to slave women, logically legitimized the children of such alliances as well by making the offspring of concubines equal in status and privileges to those of free wives.[12]

Because Muscovy frowned upon the sexual exploitation of slaves, legislation on the topic is as sparse as in any slave system. Muscovite law did not concern itself with many of the topics that consumed much of the attention of lawgivers since at least the time of the Hammurabi Code, such as what rights a slaveowner has in the children begotten by his slavewoman and a man to whom the slave was rented, or what the relationship should be between a free woman who brought a slavewoman into a marriage as part of a dowry and the latter if she became the husband's concubine.[13]

Sic utere

The rights of a slave vis-à-vis his owner are often defined by the "sic utere" doctrine: *sic utere tuo ut alienum non laedas*, "use your own property in such a manner as not to injure that of another." Or, in other words, a person may use his property in any manner so long as it will not hurt a third party. Rights in-

---

11. Mendelsohn, pp. 50, 75; Inalcik, "Servile Labor," p. 33; Kolycheva, *Kholopstvo*, pp. 235-36.

12. Pritchard, p. 157, arts. 170-71; Mendelsohn, p. 50; *Laws of Manu*, IX, 179; Brunschvig, "'Abd,'" p. 29; Meijer, p. 333. It is doubtful that Russia ever knew the extreme disinheritance of owner-slave/concubine offspring that graced the Louisiana scene in 1861; as one planter put it, 'There is not an old plantation in which the grandchildren of the owner are not whipped in the field by his overseer." (Cited by Gutman and Sutch, "Victorians All?" p. 153.)

13. Pritchard, pp. 151, 154, arts. 119, 146-47.

here in persons, not in objects, which can have no rights. For his owner, the slave was an object. While legal systems may regulate the use of property, that does not give the property any rights. In this sense, vis-à-vis his owner, the Russian chattel slave had minimal rights. The rights a slaveowner had in relation to his full and limited service contract slave were hardly defined.[14] A Muscovite legislator would have concurred with the author of section 18 in the Louisiana Black Code of 1806 who declared that a slave "owes to his master, and to all his family, a respect without bounds, and an absolute obedience, and . . . is . . . to execute all . . . orders."

Murder of a Slave

Many legal systems did not provide, or did not desire to provide, meaningful guarantees to slaves against being murdered by their owner. An owner could kill a slave with impunity in Homeric Greece, ancient India, the Roman Republic, Han China, Islam, Anglo-Saxon England, among the Northwest Coast Amerindians, and in many parts of the U.S. South before 1830. Medieval Russian law, such as the 1398 Dvina Land Charter and the Metropolitan's Law Book, also made it explicit that a slaveowner was not guilty of a crime if he killed his own slave; he could not be tried by a lay governor for such an act but answered for it only to God.[15] There is little doubt that there was a strong homologism between cattle and slaves in such societies.

Other societies have placed some restrictions on the right of slaveowners to take the life of their human chattel. Among them were the biblical Hebrews, the Athenians, and the Romans under the principate (owners could not kill their slaves after 12 A.D., a right which Emperor Hadrian a century later formally turned over to the court).[16] The Roman jurist Gaius noted that as squanderers were forbidden to dispose of their property, so slaveowners were forbidden to kill their slave without cause.[17] The Muscovites inherited this Roman sense that the regulation of the use of property was a proper function of law.

The Byzantine emperor Constantine decreed that an owner who willfully

14. Sergeevich, *Drevnosti*, 1: 105.

15. D. B. Davis, *Western Culture*, p. 60; Rose, p. 204; Tushnet, "Law of Slavery," pp. 119, 135-37; Levy, *Islam*, p. 79; Wergeland, pp. 40-41; PRP 3(1955): 428, art. 30; Vernadsky, *Medieval Russian Laws*, p. 59, art. 11 (the Vernadsky translation is mistaken on the matter of intent) (Veselovskii, *Feodal'noe zemlevladenie*, p. 218).

16. Westermann, pp. 17, 115; D. B. Davies, *Western Culture*, pp. 60-61. Thai law prescribed a trial for homicide for the owner who killed his slave in any fashion (Turton, pp. 269-70). In Madagascar, slaves were totally at the disposal of their masters, except that they could not be killed without royal permission (Maurice Bloch, "Modes of Production and Slavery in Madagascar: Two Case Studies," in Watson, *Systems*, p. 107).

17. Shtaerman, p. 79. U. S. Southern slave law also assumed that the slaveowners' property interest would deter them from excessively damaging their slaves (Rose, p. 210).

killed his slave was to be punished for homicide. This provision was further developed in the Justinian Code, which changed the view of a slave from a thing to a person, and categorically forbade premeditated murder of a slave by his owner.[18] The *Procheiros Nomos* (39:85) elaborated on this thought:

> If someone beats his slave with a strap or a rod, and the slave dies from this, the lord shall not be tried as though it were murder; but if the lord without measure tortures him or kills him with poison, or sets him on fire, he shall be executed as a murderer.[19]

The distinction between careless and intentional homicide was also the program of seventeenth-century Muscovite jurisprudence, particularly after the publication of the Church Statute Book (the *Kormchaia kniga*) in 1653, which contains the *Procheiros Nomos*. That Byzantine code was used in the compilation of the *Ulozhenie* and the Felony Statute of 1669, and one can only speculate on why chapter 39 article 85 was not written down in the civil law. Two reasons might be advanced: the Muscovites, whose view of the slave as a thing had not evolved as far as the Byzantines' had toward the view of the slave as a person, simply did not really believe the provisions of 39:85; no trouble case involving the willful murder of a slave by his owner had arisen in the chancelleries, and so therefore the occasion never arose to go to the *Kormchaia* to borrow 39:85 and enter it in the statute book of the chancellery. Jurisdictionally, this would have been an interesting case. Matters concerning slaves usually were handled by the Slavery Chancellery. Serious felonies were the business of the Felony Chancellery. Bizarre cases from the provinces were also sometimes handled by the Military Chancellery, which in the seventeenth century had become the personnel office for provincial administration because of its control over the governors. Of interest here is the fact that chapters 21 and 22 of the *Ulozhenie* and the Felony Statute of 1669 (which integrated chapters 21 and 22, and updated them, often with explicit borrowings from the *Procheiros Nomos*) were products of Felony Chancellery practice, and thus would not necessarily have reflected what was done in the other central bureaus of the Muscovite government.

A reflection of Lithuanian norms on slaves can be found in the *Ulozhenie* arti-

18. Udal'tsova, p. 22. The Christian church in the West inflicted penalties for homicide of a slave (Rose, p. 205).

19. Freshfield's rendition of this seems to be in error, for it has the lord being punished if the slave dies under correction (p. 157). U. S. law after 1830 was similar to that of Byzantium in prescribing a charge of murder in the second (or even the first) degree for the owner who maltreated his slave and killed him (Rose, pp. 192, 198). Late Chinese law made somewhat similar distinctions: a slaveowner who beat to death a disobedient slave was not to be prosecuted, but he who intentionally killed his red contract slave was subject to sixty strokes of the heavy bamboo plus a year's penal servitude; he who intentionally murdered a white contract slave was subject to the punishment of strangulation (Meijer, p. 333).

cle on the return of a fugitive slave to his owner. Attempting to limit the lord's vengeance, the law prescribed that the owner was not to kill, maim, or starve to death a returned fugitive. However, this borrowing from the *Lithuanian Statute* of 1588, which must have been relevant thousands of times in the Muscovite slave experience, provided no sanctions for slaveowners who violated the law. Neither did the prototype, which did specify that chaining up (*viazen'*) was to be the slaveowner's instrument of punishment.[20] The presence of this article in the *Ulozhenie*, moreover, highlights the absence of general norms applicable to slaves who did not run away. That the Muscovites were conscious of this problem is also evident in the legal provision that creditors awarded debt slaves for a limited term had to post a bond guaranteeing that they would not murder or maim their temporary chattel.[21] While explicit sanctions also were not provided in this article of the *Ulozhenie*, it did prescribe that the debtors were to be presented in the chancellery after they had worked off their debt—presumably for inspection to see that they had not been abused. Nothing in this article would prohibit the creditor from "correcting" his debt slave. Once again, the contrast between the stated norms for debt slaves and the unstated norms for ordinary slaves is telling, and hardly lends support to the "assumption" of V. I. Sergeevich, the great nineteenth-century historian of Russian law, that premeditated murder of a slave by an owner in Muscovy did not go unpunished. Premeditation is hard to prove, and one may assume that the Muscovite legislators did not dwell on this issue because they did not want in any way to diminish the control slaveowners could exercise over their slaves. While the written legal norms tell us little about whether a slaveowner could execute his chattel, the Austrian traveler Sigismund von Herberstein wrote in the 1520s that only the grand prince had the right to execute slaves.[22] Unfortunately, he failed to say what sanctions would be imposed on a lord who deliberately executed his slave.

Homicide of a Slaveowner by His Slave

Almost no slave system had much sympathy for slaves who acted against their owners. The Romans prescribed that a slave who contemplated any action against his owner was to be burned alive. The slave who was so bold as to ask a fortune-teller about the health and life of his master was to be crucified. Moreover, the entire family of a slave was to be put to death if one of its members killed their owner. That terror was the purpose of this edict is clear from the inclusion even of minors among the proscribed if they were suspected of having

20. 1649 *Ulozhenie* 20: 92; MS, pp. 288-89; 1588 LS 12: 22(Lappo, p. 361).
21. 1649 *Ulozhenie* 10: 266.
22. Sergeevich, *Drevnosti*, 1: 139; Herberstein, *Commentaries on Russia*, p. 55.

participated in, or had been present with the master, at the time of the murder. The rest of the victim's slaves were subject to torture, as were slaves belonging to the spouse of the deceased. Emperor Hadrian included as accomplices slaves who did not come to the aid of their owner when he was threatened by danger.[23] Chinese law of the Ch'ing era prescribed death by slicing for the slave who deliberately killed his owner, and immediate strangulation for the chattel who accidentally killed his master. In the U.S. the principle that a slave had to be executed for killing his owner was articulated in terms of petty treason, that a slave could only be tried for murder if he killed his owner, and that the slave could not be tried for manslaughter because the law could under no circumstances recognize that the owner's conduct might give the slave sufficient cause to slay him.[24]

Middle and late Muscovite law recognized little ceremony for slaves who killed their owners: they were summarily put to death "without any mercy."[25] The *Lithuanian Statute* of 1588 also prescribed the death penalty for the servant who wounded his master, but this provision was not borrowed by the Muscovites. The Lithuanians specified that the slave was to be hanged (*gorlom kàrat'*) and then drawn and quartered.[26] This savagery, as we have seen, was modified by the Muscovites. For contemplating (sic) the murder of his owner or for raising his hand with a weapon in it against his owner, the slave's hand was to be amputated. This gratuitous barbarism was borrowed from the *Lithuanian Statute* of 1588, but it had antecedents in Roman and Byzantine law as well.[27]

Slave Obligations to the Master

Muscovite law placed few explicit obligations on slaves, but the most central one was to protect the mistress of the house. For failing to protect her from an invader who wanted to rape or kidnap her, and for assisting in the crime, the slave was to be put to death by the state. A marginal notation in the manuscript edition of the *Ulozhenie* of 1649 says that this was taken from Byzantine law, and the 1669 Felony Statute cited the Byzantine sanction: "A slave knowledgeable of and assisting in the rape of his mistress shall be burned alive." A provision similar to the *Ulozhenie* can be found in the *Lithuanian Statute* of 1588.[28]

23. Shtaerman, pp. 76-77.
24. Meijer, p. 335; Rose, pp. 234, 239-41.
25. 1550 *Sudebnik* 61; 1649 *Ulozhenie* 22: 8, 9; PRP 7: 426, art. 93.
26. 1588 LS 11: 9 (Lappo, pp. 306-7).
27. See UKRP, suppl. XV (Vladimirskii-Budanov, *Khristomatiia*, 3: 87), borrowed from the *Lithuanian Statute* prior to 1631. See also 1649 *Ulozhenie* 22: 8, which cites in a marginal notation [1588] LS [11: 9].
28. 1588 LS 11: 12; 1649 *Ulozhenie* 22: 16; PRP 7: 428, art. 102, whose marginal citation refers to the *Kormchaia kniga* as its source.

It is not surprising that such a measure should be found in slave systems where household slavery prevailed.

Another obligation the late Muscovites imposed on slaves was to remain in military service with their owners. Many slaves were military retainers of their owners, serving either as combat forces or in the baggage train. After the commencement of the Thirteen Years War, Tsar Aleksei on May 27, 1654, prescribed hanging for any slave who stole his owner's property and fled while they were in the army.[29] The theft seems as important as the flight, for a serviceman could no longer serve after his supplies were gone.

To speak of "slave obligations" would seem to be a contradiciton in terms, for one cannot legislate the obligations a horse or cow has to its owner, and most slave systems take a similar view of the human chattel. Such sentiments were expressed only in late Muscovy, when it was clear that in fact slaves had many human attributes.

Brutality

Far more slave systems imposed sanctions against owners who brutalized their slaves than against those who murdered them. This is not surprising, for dead men tell no tales, but there is no telling what a survivor of cruel treatment will do. But it took some time for legislators to reach that point. While the high incidence of slave flight in Babylonia was due in part to owner cruelty, the Hammurabi Code said nothing on the subject, and in fact specified brutal sanctions (perhaps in lieu of homicide, although it is not clear) for certain slave offenses: an apprehended fugitive slave might be chained and have the words "A runaway, seize!" incised upon his face, and the owner of a fugitive slave was allowed to cut off his chattel's ear if he denied his master.[30]

The biblical Jews prescribed punishment if a slave died while being beaten, but said that there should be no sanction if the slave lived a day or two, "for it [the slave] is his money [property]."[31] The Greeks also in no way restricted a slaveowner's right to punish his own slaves.[32]

This tradition was altered by the Romans. The Roman jurist Gaius said that unbearably cruel lords were obliged to sell their slaves, and Ulpian noted that the state power was obliged to intervene in instances where a lord was cruel to his slaves, or forced them to do anything that was shameful.[33] Justinian extended

29. PSZ 1: 340, no. 127.
30. Pritchard, p. 167, art. 282; Driver and Miles, *The Babylonian Laws* 1 (1952): 488-89; Mendelsohn, pp. 65-66.
31. Exodus 21: 20-21.
32. Westermann, p. 17. At Athens an abused slave had a right to take asylum in certain places and beg a third party to buy him from his owner (Harrison, *Law of Athens*, p. 172).
33. Shtaerman, *Krizis*, pp. 79-81.

these provisions, and deprived cruel owners of their human property. However, the owner had the right to beat his slave, and bore no responsibility if the slave died under the lash. The ancient Franks and Germans allowed slaveowners to exercise the right of life and death over their slaves, but warned against cruelty.[34]

We see the direction that Justinian legislation could take in the Spanish *Las Siete Partidas* of 1263-65, which prescribed that an owner who abused his slave would forfeit his chattel: either the slave would go free or he would be given to a new master. Moreover, if a slave died from a chastisement, the cruel owner was to be banished to an island for five years. If the punishment could be proved to have been deliberately inflicted so harshly as to kill the slave, the matter would be punishable as a homicide. A later law of 1573 observed that some slaveowners were terribly cruel, to the point of making their slaves want to commit suicide, flee, or rebel, and prescribed that such slaves were to be taken from the owner and he was to be put on trial.[35] The Black Code of Louisiana of 1806, which also came out of the Spanish legal tradition, made cruel punishment of slaves a crime. The Louisiana Civil Code of 1824 (article 192) prescribed that a mistreated slave belonging to an owner who had been convicted of cruel treatment, at the order of the court, could be sold to another master.[36]

A spirit similar to the Roman consideration of the slave as property and the Byzantine notion of correction can be found in the Virginia law of 1668 which prescribed that the death of a slave during correction under the lash could not be considered a felony, which was defined by intent, for no man would ever deliberately destroy his own property.[37] This position still was held by the Texas penal code of 1856, which allowed the slave owner "to inflict any punishment upon the slave not affecting life or limb . . . which he may consider necessary for the purpose of keeping him in . . . submission." On the other hand, by that date, ten southern codes decreed that mistreatment of a slave was a criminal act and imposed sanctions that included the forced sale to another owner or even emancipation.[38]

Two cases presided over by Judge Ruffin of North Carolina are notable for expressing the evolution of the view that the slaveowner was responsible before the law for his treatment of slaves. In the 1829 case of State v. John Mann, where the slave girl Lydia had been rented by Mann from Elizabeth Jones, Ruffin stated that a master was not liable to an indictment for a battery committed upon his slave, no matter how cruel and excessive, because the former had a right to all the means of controlling the conduct of the latter. He concluded that "The

34. Rose, p. 205.
35. Klein, *Americas,* pp. 60, 63-64, 74-75.
36. Rose, pp. 176-77.
37. Ibid., p. 210; Klein, *Virginia,* p. 48.
38. Rose, pp. 200, 203; Friedman, p. 198.

power of the master must be absolute, to render the submission of the slave perfect. . . . The end is the profit of the master, his security, and the public safety. . . . The slave, to remain a slave, must be made sensible, that there is no appeal from his master."[39] But a decade later, in the 1839 case of State v. Hoover, Judge Ruffin acquiesced in the conviction of a slaveowner for murder who had tortured to death a pregnant slave and held that it was a wrong. The judge expressed horror at Hoover's conduct ("He had beat her with clubs, iron chains, and other deadly weapons, time after time; burnt her; inflicted stripes over and often, with scourges, which literally excoriated her whole body" etc.) and found no substance in the defendant's claims that he was only responding to her attempts at arson, poisoning, theft, and impudence. Similarly, in 1843 the Alabama Supreme Court upheld the conviction for second-degree murder of one William H. Jones, who had been indicted after he had beaten a slave girl, Isabel, to death with clubs, sticks, and whips.[40] (Lest anyone imagine that Southern enlightenment on this issue grew steadily I might mention Jacob [a slave] v. State, a Tennessee case from 1842, which upheld the Ruffin 1829 position in affirming the verdict that Jacob should be hanged for killing his master, in spite of intense provocation: "The right to obedience. . . in all lawful things. . . is perfect in the master; and the power to inflict any punishment, not affecting life or limb,. . . for the purpose of . . . enforcing such obedience. . . is secured to him by law. . . . [T]he law cannot recognize the violence of the master as a legitimate cause of provocation.")[41]

Treatment of slaves in medieval and early modern Rus' seems to have been more a moral than a legal issue. The *Russkaia Pravda* had nothing to say on the subject, but medieval church sources did. In the twelfth century, Kirill of Turov, famous for his sermons, urged lords not to oppress their subjects. The *Kormchaia kniga* at the end of the thirteenth century in one of its earliest redactions forbade priests to accept donations in church from cruel lords. Such slaveowners were not to receive confession, and were equated with heretics, fornicators, thieves, murderers, bootleggers, magicians, and similar reprobates. Finally, the *Kormchaia* prescribed that slaves be treated kindly, that they not be punished cruelly, but rather as one's own children.[42] The only sanction was to deny the rite of confession to the cruel slaveowner. These moral imperatives, of course, continued to be repeated in Muscovy a quarter of a millennium after their compilation, but their efficacy is unknown.

Muscovite legislators discussed the treatment of slaves and forbade abuse in a

39. Rose, pp. 220-23, 234; Catterall, 2: 57; Tushnet, "Law," pp. 140-42.
40. Catterall, 2: 85-86; idem, 3: 151-52; Friedman, p. 199; Tushnet, p. 127, n. 32.
41. Catterall, 2: 516-17; Rose, p. 234.
42. Sergeevich, *Drevnosti*, 1: 122-23. Nineteenth-century Chinese law also made the analogy between slaves and children in the meting out of punishment and prescribed that the owner was to treat the slave humanely (Meijer, p. 332). This was a manifestation of the quasi-kinship master-slave relationship, something that was not prevalent in Muscovy.

few instances, but certainly this was not one of their major concerns. A creditor awarded a debt slave for a term had to post a bond guaranteeing that he would not murder or maim his temporary chattel.[43] Or, if a slave petitioned for his freedom on the ground that his owner was starving him, the slave's claim was denied and he was returned to his owner, and the owner was not to hurt the slave. Similarly, in a provision of Byzantine origin, an owner was not to beat to death, maim, or starve a returned fugitive slave.[44] No sanctions were listed for infractions, indicating that these were moral aspects which, if violated, were to be dealt with by the tsar and his counselors personally. This subject will be discussed further below in the context of the slave's right to complain against his master.

The reasons why societies generally could not tolerate gross mistreatment of slaves are obvious. Brutalized slaves demoralize an entire milieu—not only the remaining slaves of the cruel slaveowner but other slaves as well who might hear of the mistreatment. Such slaves were liable to flee, or even rebel. Mistreatment was perhaps the major precipitant of all types of slave resistance. Even neighboring slaveowners, upon occasion, were wont to denounce a brutal slaveowner to the authorities simply because they wanted such a contagion removed from their midst. The theoretician of Southern slave law, T. R. R. Cobb, was particularly adamant in demanding that cruel slaveowners be punished, and recommended that anyone so convicted be forced to sell all of his slaves and be forever disqualified from owning or possessing any more.[45]

The Soviet historian E. M. Shtaerman raised an interesting issue about the consequences of limiting the slaveowner's right to kill or brutalize his slave by jailing him in a ergastulum, shackling him for life, or freezing or starving him to death. Shtaerman thought that this would deprive the owner of the possibility of making his slave work and would thereby compel the owner to change the way in which the slave was exploited and along with the type of economy in which the slave was employed.[46] One might suggest that Shtaerman reflects the excessive pessimism about human nature and the consequent zeal for compulsion that marked the Lenin and Stalin era of Soviet history, but the problem she posed is nevertheless central to any system of forced labor. The solutions have been many, from what might be termed the "fine tuning" of compulsion to the arrangement of a system of incentives that might result in manumission. For Muscovy, however, the problem was somewhat different, simply because production for the market or even domestic consumption was not the major function of slaves. Compulsion was required to overcome the inertia which in all likelihood had propelled them into slavery in the first place and was perpetuated by

43. 1649 *Ulozhenie* 10: 266.
44. Ibid., 20: 92, from *Ecloga* 14: 2.
45. Rose, p. 203.
46. Shtaerman, p. 81.

their current lot. Almost any slave system allowed the employment of that degree of compulsion, and Muscovy was no exception.

It might be expected that I would now discuss the reciprocal of state concern over owner brutality directed against a slave—the assault or battery of an owner by a slave. In fact, the Ottomans and Ch'ing Chinese seem to have been among the few peoples willing to listen to charges made against slaves who assaulted their owners.[47] Muscovy, along with most other societies, knew no such provisions, just as there are few laws designed to protect an owner from being bitten by his own dog or gored by his own ox.

The Right to Food

Food has been one of the slave's basic concerns from antiquity right down to Soviet slave-labor camps. The Greek Peripatetic Pseudo-Aristotelian *Oeconomica* claimed that the life of the slave consisted of three elements: work, punishment, and food.[48] All works on GULag convey a similar impression.

Comparatively speaking, the lot of the Muscovite slave was probably easy, if only because he was a domestic slave for whom production (work) was not his raison d'être. Also, in households, punishment was perhaps less frequent than in industrial systems of slavery. This leaves food, whose scarcity was the cause of much Muscovite slavery.

One of the Muscovite slave's few basic rights seems to have been the right to food. Similar programs were established in many other slave systems, whether the Greek city-state world of the pre-Christian era, the latifundian ranch-type slave system of Sicily in the first century A.D., or the Roman prefecture of Egypt at the same time. Some places even went to the extent of mandating the food rations a slave could expect, such as in Judea in 200 B.C., Sicily in 135-32 B.C., or the Nile in 46 A.D. Iberian norms for the New World also expressed concern that slaves be properly fed. So did the Chinese, and so did Islamic law, which even provided sanctions: a slaveowner who could not feed his slaves was obliged to sell them. A similar concern was shown in Islamic law for animals.[49]

Even the Danish Virgin Islands, after a period of initial hesitation during which the slave had no rights at all, even to food, in 1755 forbade filling slaves up with untreated rum (locally known as "kill devil") and prescribed what were assumed to be adequate rations of flour, meat or fish. Six southern states re-

47. Fisher, "Ottoman Slavery," p. 30. The Chinese prescibed immediate decapitation for the slave who beat his master or fornicated with the owner's main wife or daughter and strangulation for abusive language against a master or fornication with a master's concubine (Meijer, p. 335).

48. Moses I. Finley, "Was Greek Civilization Based on Slave Labour?" in *The Slave Economies,* ed. Eugene D. Genovese, 1: 39.

49. Brunschvig, "'Abd," p. 25; Westermann, p. 21; Klein, *Americas*, p. 74; Wiens, p. 307.

quired owners to feed their chattel adequately, although, as Fogel, Engerman, Sutch, and others have shown, this was not as burdensome as would have been a similar requirement on the eastern European plain.[50] Nevertheless, even the *Lithuanian Statute* of 1588 required that slaveowners feed their chattel, and if they did not want to and drove them out during a famine, the slaves were to register their situation with the government and were declared thenceforth free forever.[51]

There was a greater logic in Muscovite law for legislative statements about the slave's right to eat than elsewhere. Other societies were concerned about the moral obligations of their slaveowners (sometimes in the same manner as they were concerned about the moral obligations to domestic animals), or they had in mind public safety considerations of the type discussed above on the topic of cruelty. In Muscovy, on the other hand, the provision of sustenance was the raison d'être for the existence of full and limited service contract slavery. Thus any owner who refused to provide the relief that his slave had a right to expect, forfeited him. On August 16, 1603, during the great famine of 1601-3, Tsar Boris Godunov ordered slaveowners to feed their chattel and forbade that the latter be sent out to beg. All such evicted slaves were to be freed, either if the victims complained to the authorities and their owners agreed that they could not feed them, or if the preponderance of evidence supported the slaves' claims. Tsar Boris ordered that the decree be frequently announced in the provincial towns so that slaves would know their rights, and in the last months of 1603 and in 1604 a number of slaves were freed under this provision.[52]

This provision was incorporated into the *Ulozhenie* of 1649, and is worth quoting in full:

> Chapter 20, article 41. If people of any rank, during a famine or at any other time, not wishing to feed their slaves, drive them from their house, but do not give them manumission documents or do not surrender the slavery documents [to the slaves (signifying that they are no longer slaves)], and desiring to keep them for themselves, order the slaves to feed themselves, and no one else will receive in his house these slaves because they have no manumission documents; and if the slaves petition against them for this, the officials of the Slavery Chancellery, on the basis of the slaves' petition, must send for their lords who drove the slaves from their houses and question these lords directly whether or not they drove away the slaves from their houses. If in the investigation the lords say that they dismissed their slaves from their houses, henceforth they

50. Friedman, p. 198; Hall, "Virgin Islands," pp. 175-76; David, *Reckoning*, pp. 231-301.

51. 1588 LS 12: 20 (Lappo, p. 360).

52. UKKhP 2; AI 2, no. 44; PRP 4: 375; Kusheva, " K istorii kholopstva," p. 92. The Indians invented a bizarre twist to the principle that owners should feed their slaves: they only had to feed them when they employed them. Otherwise, the slaves could look for employment elsewhere, but had to return as soon as their owners demanded (Hjejle, p. 96).

will have no claims to those slaves. Order them to sign their testimony. If [the lords] are illiterate, order them to have someone whom they trust sign their testimony in their stead. If, out of obstinacy, they will not sign their testimony, order them to sign their testimony involuntarily.

When they have signed their testimony, give the slaves their freedom after the slaves have been registered in the record books of the Slavery Chancellery. Give the slaves manumission documents from the Slavery Chancellery. If they petition [to sell themselves] to someone else, they are those people's slaves. Do not grant slaves freedom without questioning the people against whom the slaves have petitioned.

Chapter 20, article 42. If the lords of the slaves who are petitioned against say about these slaves that their slaves are petitioning falsely against them, that they did not send them away from their houses, give those slaves back to their lords. Order their lords to feed them during a famine so that they will not die of hunger. [The lords] must not do any harm [to the slaves] for having petitioned against them.

In the context of this discussion, the most noteworthy change between 1603 and 1649 is in article 42, which essentially allows the slaveowner the right to deny that he was starving his slave, and thereby put an end to the slave's case against his owner. In 1603, the slave had considerably greater protection than he did nearly fifty years later. We also should note other features of these two articles. One is the extreme centralization inherent in allowing only the Slavery Chancellery to hear such complaints. There is a logic to this, for, besides an owner, only the Slavery Chancellery had the right to grant manumission documents, but it is not at all clear how a starving slave was supposed to get to Moscow to present his case. Other assumptions of the law should be pointed out as well. One is that the slave is a domestic, someone living in the household of his owner. Another is that the manumitted slave was likely immediately to seek out another master, something that was in fact true and will be discussed in greater detail. Given the nature and role of law in Muscovy, we may be sure that almost all slaves and slaveowners knew of the government's understanding that the latter were required to feed the former. This was assured by the wide publicity given Godunov's 1603 announcement and the great prominence enjoyed by the *Ulozhenie* almost immediately after its publication. Ability and willingness to live up to prescribed norms do not necessarily follow from awareness of them, of course.

Whether there is any element of reciprocity expressed in the slave's right to eat is something that might be debated. One might argue, for example, that, in exchange for the right to make the slave engage in any legal occupation—in the words of the contracts, to make him serve "day and night in the household"— the slaveowner was reciprocally guaranteeing that he would feed his slave. While this may have been tacitly assumed by the slave, the contract clearly stated that what the slave was owed was the money he got, and nothing was ever said about maintenance. The state saw the matter as a defensive police issue: either the owner fed his slave, or the slave would steal, flee, or even rebel.

Muscovite law, unlike that of many other systems (Iberian, Nepalese Nyinba, Danish Virgin Islands, U.S. South), never went further than the matter of food in defining a slave's needs, and thus, for example, did not concern itself with a slave's clothing or shelter.[53] While the law itself did not deal with anything other than food, the slaves themselves did. In 1600 Peter Aisin, owner of Nechaiko Trufanov, his wife, and daughter, died. Nechaiko was a limited service contract slave who, by law, should have been freed upon Aisin's death. He was not, however, and petitioned to the authorities that Aisin's widow, Anna, was detaining them "and was not giving them drink, feeding them, clothing them, or providing them with footwear, but was starving them to death." It happened that Anna was lying ill, and could not give them a manumission document. Instead, the government returned to Nechaiko his slavery contract in lieu of a formal manumission document, and charged him the manumission fee of 9 kopeks apiece (total, 27 kopeks). The manumission was probably granted Nechaiko because of the death of his owner, not because he was being starved. Nechaiko probably mentioned the matter of food and clothing to stress the urgency of the situation, rather than because he thought he had a legal claim, although we cannot be sure. In any case, the government heeded his plea.[54]

Sickness and Old Age

Some slave systems prescribed that owners were responsible for their slaves when they became sick or old. That seems to be the import of articles of the Hammurabi Code which discuss the fees a slaveowner had to pay a physician for treating his slave.[55] Old-age assistance was assumed to be implicit in Indian slavery at the time of the English takeover, although sundry colonial officers reported that the assumption was not always honored. Regardless of such breaches, no category of Indian laborer enjoyed the measure of security that most slaves did.[56] North American slavery, which totally repressed the slave's spiritual needs and capacities, was very generous when it came to the slave's material needs, a fact that is often attributed to the abundance of resources to meet those needs. The article from the Alabama Slave Code of 1852 is worth quoting in full on this point:

53. Goldin, pp. 41-42; Hall, pp. 176, 183; Nancy Levine, p. 205.
54. NKK 7108 (=RIB 15^2[1894]), pp. 53-54. This case is discussed by Lappo-Danilevskii, "Sluzhilye kabaly," pp. 754-55.
56. India, Law Commission, *Report on Indian Slavery* (1841), p. 200; Caplan, pp. 175, 183.

The master must treat his slave with humanity, and not inflict upon him any cruel punishment; he must provide him with a sufficiency of healthy food and necessary clothing; cause him to be properly attended during sickness, and provide for his necessary wants in old age.[57]

A sanction of a fine of not less than 25 or more than 1,000 dollars was prescribed. However, the law allowed jurors to determine what were violations, and two-thirds of the jurors had to be slaveholders.[58] In spite of the relief function of Muscovite slavery, a concept such as maintaining sick and old slaves was totally alien to the Muscovite mind, although it became part of the relief function of serfdom in the eighteenth century. In fact, as I shall show later, one of the few reasons for which a Muscovite slaveowner ever emancipated a slave was to rid himself of an ill or decrepit subject. This reminds us of the Tlingit Indians, who simply executed and threw into the Pacific Ocean superannuated or otherwise superfluous slaves.

Time and Labor Rights

The Muscovite slave had little right to dispose of his own time or labor, which were expropriated by his owner. This was made explicit in the limited service slavery contracts, all of which stated that the slave was to labor every day in his owner's house. This was a nearly universal feature of slavery. In South India, for example, the owner had "an absolute right" to whatever labor his chattel was able to render. However, some slave systems placed limitations on the owner's use of slave labor, such as on the number of hours per day or number of days per week that the slave could be exploited.[59] Throughout most of the period, Muscovy knew none of this, nor was there any provision for holidays for slaves. However, a law of June 7, 1669, implied that slaves had the right to Sundays off, for *stol'nik* Prince Grigorii Venediktov Obolenskoi was jailed because on the day before he had forced the slaves and peasants in his household to perform manual labor *(chernaia rabota)*. Moreover, he had verbally abused them.[60] One may assume that this provision stemmed, as did so many others improving the slave's lot, from the equation of peasants and slaves. The former were abased, but the latter were recognized as human.

Some slave systems specified age limitations on the exploitation of slaves, something Muscovy hinted at in the regulation of debt slavery by noting "that children under the age of 10 do not work [do not perform slave labor]."[61]

57. Rose, p. 187.
58. Ibid., p. 192.
59. Hjejle, p. 93; Rose, pp. 192-93.
60. PSZ 1: 825, no. 453.
61. 1649 *Ulozhenie* 20: 40.

Occupational Legislation

Someone not acquainted with the Muscovite system might be surprised by the absence of limitations on or regulations of slave occupations (with the exception of the job of steward). This may have been due to the heritage of elite slavery, an absence of fear of slaves, the usual shortage of labor, minimal specialization, and lack of a tradition of assigning jobs to social categories. Many of the seventeenth-century restrictions that impinged on slave commerce or artisanal activity stemmed from a successful attack by the townsmen on tax-exempt activities, which included those of some slaves.[62] The slaves were not attacked as slaves, who could compete unfairly with free labor because of their lower overhead and consumption, as was the case, for example, in the American South.[63] Thus the creation of a caste society in the mid-seventeenth century did little to limit the sphere of competition from slaves—as long as they paid taxes on their enterprises along with the other taxpayers.

In a similar vein, it might be noted that Muscovite law did little to regulate the slave, either at work or at play. The absence of sanctions against slaves who in some manner damaged the economy indicates that the vast majority of Muscovite chattel were not engaged in production, a point that will be developed at considerable length later.[64] There was no such thing as a curfew in Muscovy for slaves. Thus none of the savage punishments for being absent from a plantation were meted out that were so common in the New World, such as the Danish Virgin Islands 1755 *Règlement*, which prescribed amputation of both ears and branding for a slave who had been absent from his plantation for a month, the loss of both legs for a second offense, and capital punishment for a third.[65] Muscovy not only had no plantations but was not concerned with helping the slaveowner to force his slave to produce, because production was not the primary function of slavery there.

Slave Property

The issues of whether slaves could own or inherit property and their standing in court are discussed in nearly all slave systems of record. As I shall show later, Muscovite slaves *de facto* could and did possess almost anything until the 1630s

62. Hellie, "Stratification: Townsmen," p. 130.

63. Goldin, pp. 38-40.

64. Kolycheva thought that the theft of slaves (along with the theft of horses) was punished by death because it weakened the economy (*Kholopstvo*, p. 226). That is an interesting idea, but perhaps farfetched, for slaves were not that central to the Russian economy and, moreover, the sanction was universal throughout most slave systems, both productive and household.

65. Hall, pp. 174, 178, 181.

although the *de jure* status of their ownership was never spelled out. I have no knowledge of any slave peculium, inheritance, or last will in Muscovy, although they may have existed in reality. The ownership of the clothes on a slave's back might be debated. This issue was raised in fugitive slave cases, especially when a suit was being filed for property the slave had allegedly stolen when he departed. Sometimes it was made clear that the clothing belonged to the slave and consequently was not the subject of litigation.

In this respect, Muscovite slavery was, at best, in the tradition of Roman, Islamic, and North American laws in which, in principle, the slave was incapable of owning property other than that assigned to him in his peculium (if even that), a tradition which contrasts with the situation in Roman Egypt, as well as in Ancient Egypt, Babylonia, Assyria, in Talmudic law, in the Greek law of Gortyn, probably in much of medieval Germanic society, in Thailand, Mongol and Ch'ing China, medieval Spain, and the northern Nigerian emirates, where slaves had the right of property ownership.[66] One of the major late Muscovite juridical distinctions between the slave and the peasant serf was that the latter was assumed to possess property, whereas the former was assumed to be without any.

Often, as in late Assyria or among the Tuaregs, the right to accumulate and enjoy property was a privilege granted by the slaveowner that he could withdraw at will.[67] One might have expected Muscovy to be in the more liberal tradition, given the nature of Muscovite slavery; that it was not probably reflects the generally underdeveloped state of Russian property law rather than any deliberate desire to restrict slaves.

This is a retrogression from medieval practice, as expressed in article 7 of a treaty concluded between Smolensk and the Germans in the first half of the thirteenth century which assumed that slaves had their own property and that this property was inheritable.[68] Whether this was a Latin or a Russian norm is unknown, but it represents just one of the discontinuities between medieval and early modern Russian slavery. What unites the periods is the norm that slaves could not sue their owners, which meant that there was no guarantee even of possession of whatever was acquired by a slave.[69] In reality, the Muscovite slave, because of the absence of any protection, was in the same condition as was the slave in India: "A Brahman may seize the goods of his slave, for as the

---

66. Mendelsohn, pp. 66-74; Westermann, pp. 16, 19, 122; Jones, p. 198; Wergeland, pp. 88-91, 94; Meijer, p. 336; Brunschvig, p. 28; Gluckman, p. 100; Klein, *Americas*, p. 60. The harshness of some Caribbean and North American law in forbidding slave ownership of anything, and even explicitly denying the right to possess personal property, was extraordinary (Klein, pp. 49-53; Hall, p. 175). See also Rose, pp. 176, 182-83, 203. Thai slaves were able to transmit property by inheritance (Turton, p. 296).

67. Mendelsohn, p. 70; Levy, *Islam*, p. 87.

68. PRP 2: 60-61, art. 7.

69. Sergeevich, 1: 137, 140.

slave can have no property, his master may take his possessions."[70] This was expressed also in a Muscovite decree of 1628 on the debts of slaveowners. If an owner refused to pay his debts while being tortured (*pravezh*), the debts could be distrained from his slaves and peasants.[71] Not only did this statute abase peasants by equating them with slaves, but it did not make any distinctions about the type of property a slave might possess, indicating that any or all of it could be seized to satisfy his owner's liabilities.

The repeal of the right of slaves to own landed estates and urban properties in the 1630s indicates that until that time such ownership was both possible and an accepted practice.[72] Other laws convey the same impression. Whether or not a slave could own property became especially important in the context of manumission, for the potential to be able to purchase his own freedom was one of the major incentives for slave accumulation in many societies. For example, slaves of the Manchus purchased on white contract after 1722 could purchase their freedom. In Cuba, one of the slave's most important rights, which made the island's slave system significantly less harsh than U.S. Southern slavery, was to *coartación*, a procedure that forced owners to free any slave who offered 50 pesos for his freedom or to set with the slave a price that could not be increased for which the master would agree to free his chattel. This subject will be discussed further in the context of manumission in chapter 15, but here I shall only note in passing that one article of the *Ulozhenie* assumed that a slave could accumulate property when it stated that a slave-foreigner who converted to Orthodoxy could purchase his freedom for 15 rubles. The law said that he had to pay the money himself, a statement that only could have been made under the assumption that the slave somehow could earn that sum and keep it for himself.[73]

On the other hand, the law made it abundantly clear that the slave himself had no legal interest in any property, other than perhaps his clothing, that happened to be in his possession. If the slave in question was a fugitive, the legal issue was whether the property belonged to one litigating lord or the other. Whether it might belong to the slave himself was not even considered. Moreover, a slave had no right to be manumitted with property. (Voluntary manumission was rare in Muscovy, and manumission with property even rarer.) Thus when a limited service contract slave was freed on the death of his owner, he could not sue the wife and children of the deceased for turning him out without any property. While there is no date on this article of the *Ulozhenie*, one may surmise that a

70. *Laws of Manu* VIII: 417; S. D. Skazkin et al., *Istoriia Vizantii*, 3 vols. (Moscow: Nauka, 1967), 1:260.
71. AI 3: 101, no. 92, xv; UKZP, 7; UKRP XI, 9; PRP 5: 214-15; 1649 *Ulozhenie* 10: 264; MS, p. 164.
72. 1649 *Ulozhenie* 17: 41; 19: 15, 16.
73. 1649 *Ulozhenie* 20: 71; MS, p. 281; Meijer, p. 337; Knight, p. 130.

freedman at some time after 1597 was turned out by his owner's survivors and deprived of property he had assumed was his, and that he filed suit. The government responded: such complaints are not to be received.[74] This contrasts starkly with the Roman tradition, as expressed in the Ethiopian *Fetha Nagast*: "A master shall not give his slave liberty, but then make him go out naked of his wealth."[75] Given the Muscovite norm, it is not surprising that slaves thus legally manumitted had little choice other than to sell themselves to another owner. In this manner the law reinforced the welfare dependency condition of slaves.

While Muscovite slaves had no right to anything they accumulated, one may assume that, as was also true in Islam, a number of them in fact were relatively well-to-do. The historical record is fairly well sprinkled with examples of slaves actually possessing significant assets. Their ownership of other slaves is discussed in chapters 3 and 17. Slaves also owned and traded in land, as was evident in a court suit of the 1460s in which a gift document to a monastery was presented as evidence showing that the slave Kharia Lagir', who belonged to Prince Iurii Dmitrievich of Zvenigorod, had purchased the property in question from Mikula Mishen' and another slave, Zherebil, who belonged to one Ivan Volodimerovich. The property consisted of wasteland, a forest, and a meadow, all of which he had donated to Metropolitan Iona. Earlier the land had been farmed by another of Prince Iurii's dowry slaves, one Borten'. (Borten' probably had cleared the land initially, for it bore his name.) Kharia, with his wife Kovernitsa, a slave (*roba*) of Princess Nastas'ia, had farmed the land for about a decade. What happened between the tenure of Borten' and Kharia is unclear, as is how the property passed from Borten' to Mikula and Zherebil. It is clear, however, that the judges, relying on oral witnesses who claimed to know the history of the property for the past fifty years, accepted the ownership claim of Kharia and affirmed his right to give it to Metropolitan Iona. Moreover, the document conveying the gift says nothing about the fact that Kharia was a slave, which only becomes evident in the trial testimony. Thus it is clear that Kharia was not conveying property that only formally belonged to him but really belonged to his owner, Prince Iurii. The land was really Kharia's.[76]

Slaves also occasionally possessed enough surplus to be able to make loans. This is evident in the last will of Aleksandra, daughter of Vasilii Ondreevich and wife of Fedorov Ivanovich Bezzubtsov, whose adopted name as a nun was Efrosin'ia and who wrote her will in June of 1546: As was customary, she first listed her liabilities, 15 rubles owed to five parties, then her credits, 41 rubles due from four parties. One of her creditors was Isup, the slave of Prince Dmitrii Ivanovich, to whom she owed 3.50 rubles, a sum she ordered paid out of her assets.[77]

74. 1649 *Ulozhenie* 20: 65, 88; MS, pp. 278, 287.
75. *The Fetha Nagast*, p. 178.
76. AIuB 1: 635-39, no. 103, I.
77. AIu, p. 450, no. 419.

Few slave systems guaranteed a slave's property against his owner's greed, and Muscovy's was no exception. The only ordinance was a self-denying one; any owner who took too much of his slave's property risked killing the goose that might lay golden eggs. Some elite slaves either held or managed considerable property, and we may assume that the line between ownership and possession was often blurred in the minds of both the slave and his owner.

No law states whether or not a slave might inherit in Muscovy, but one assumes that legally he could not. The Ethiopian *Fetha Nagast*, which was based on many of the same sources as were later Muscovite laws, more than once explicitly forbade slave inheritance and stipulated that any such property belonged to the slaveowner. Islam, which had an attitude toward slave ownership not totally unlike the one prevalent in Muscovy, specifically proscribed inheritance by slaves. (Islam also forbade non-Muslims to inherit from Muslims.) Among the Tuareg, any property left by a deceased slave passed to his owner, not to the slave's offspring. A similar prohibition against inheritance was expressed in the 1824 Louisiana Slave Code.[78] As far as is known, there were few if any slave "dynasties" in Muscovy, and the general inability to transmit property from one generation to the next may have been at least partially a factor contributing to their absence.

The Slave as an Extension of His Owner

Not only could the slave's property be used by his owner, his person as well was assumed to be the owner's property. The Muscovite law of slavery generally viewed the slave as an extension of his owner. I have already noted this in the 1628 law making the slave responsible for his owner's debts. Similarly, the slave was viewed as a lever that might be used to compel his owner to render military service or to comply with a bailiff's directives. In the military sphere, the government was constantly on the lookout for new devices to compel reluctant cavalrymen to report for and remain in military service. In 1629 the government decided that one method might be to jail two or three slaves and rich peasants while their owners, absent servicemen, were being sought.[79] Once again we see peasants being equated with slaves, who are viewed as property that can be manipulated to force owners to comply with their service obligations. No thought is taken of the slave's own person or responsibility, but rather a thing is being impounded until its owner appears.

While there were many manifestations of the slave as an extension of his own-

78. *The Fetha Nagast*, pp. 227, 245, 317; Rose, p. 176.

79. AMG 1: 225, no. 233; MS, p. 165. Jailing slaves and peasants to force their lords to render military service became standard policy. A 1662 edict put no time limit on how long slaves and peasants should be held in jail (PSZ 1: 567, no. 323).

er, nowhere was this so explicit as in various aspects of the judicial process. The *Ulozhenie,* in discussing the serving of an arrest warrant, a summons to a trial, a request for the posting of a bail bond, or resistance to any of these, talks about the defendant and his slave together. If a slaveowner ignored a court bailiff's orders, his slaves were to be arrested and forced to post bail for him, or else remain under arrest until their owner appeared.[80] In the 1622 case of Dedkov v. Dolgorukii, the defendant refused to appear in court for the verdict, so the judges ordered one of his slaves arrested in an attempt to force his appearance. The slave was held overnight (at Dolgorukii's expense), and, when it became apparent that his seizure would not force compliance, the verdict (against Dolgorukii) was read in his absence and the slave was released.[81]

The Muscovites even found it fitting to amplify a provision of the *Lithuanian Statute* of 1588 imposing sanctions on a person who boasted that he would kill someone, who was told by a court not to do so, and who then did it anyway. The *Ulozhenie* added an article about what to do if slaves of the principals take up their respective owners' cause, and "without the knowledge of their lords, in the market place, on a road, or in a tavern collide, have a great fight, and kill one another, or wound one another." The owners were not to be held responsible for such an event as a violation of the interdict on their own dispute, but they could go to court to recover damages for injuries the slaves had inflicted on one another.[82] What greater expression of loyalty could a household slave exhibit than to carry on a fight with the chattel of his master's enemy?

Slaves regularly took the oath for their owners, a ritual in which the minimun age was twenty. Slaves took the oath for their owners even in cases where other slaves were being contested. A number of formalities came to be associated with that ritual, as is evident in the following excerpt from the 1634 trial of Kozlova v. Kozlova et al., which is discussed in greater detail in chapter 17.

Sovereign tsar, the impoverished widow Fedorka, widow of Ivan Kozlov of Suzdal', petitions. In the present year 1634, sovereign, my brother-in-law, Andrei Kozlov, having seized with a police officer my limited service contract slave Timka Vasil'ev and calling him his own slave, sued me, bitter widow, in the Slavery Chancellery before Prince Fedorovich Volkonskoi and before your royal state secretary Ivan Kostiurin. And that same brother-in-law of mine, Ondrei, having sworn a false oath, sovereign, sued me, pitiable widow, for stolen property worth 20.50 rubles. In that suit, sovereign, I, impoverished widow, took my slave Ivashka Filipov to kiss the cross for me, but, sovereign, that Andrei said that my slave is too young to kiss the cross. He petitioned, sovereign, that they order my peasant Pavlik Alekseev to kiss the cross. But, sovereign, I,

80. 1649 *Ulozhenie* 10: 139-41. A peasant could substitute for a slave (art. 141).

81. Iakovlev, *Kholopstvo,* p. 352, no. 6. For a discussion of Dedkov v. Dolgorukii, see chapter 8.

82. 1588 LS 1: 25-vii; 1649 *Ulozhenie* 10: 134.

pitiable widow, at that time had no other slaves. Earlier I had a slave Fil'ka Savel'ev, the father of that Ivashko, but he fled. But now, sovereign, that Fil'ka has returned, and, sovereign, that peasant of mine, Pavlik, who was to kiss the cross, lies near death. Merciful sovereign, grant me, pitiable widow, order, sovereign, my slave Fil'ka Savel'ev to kiss the cross in Andrei's suit. He is the father of that Ivashka I chose to kiss the cross for me. Sovereign tsar, have mercy, grant this.

[A note on the reverse side:] November 7, 1634. Add to the case. Present Ivashko's father Fil'ka for the cross-kissing in his, Ivashko's, place. Prince Ivan Fedorovich and the secretaries Tret'iak and Ivan, having heard the petition, ordered it added to the case. They ordered the bailiff Kuz'ma Golovachev to present Ivashko's father Fil'ka for the cross-kissing in his, Ivashko's, stead.[83]

This document shows the slave as moral extension of the slaveowner. The son was his owner's first choice, but, as he was a minor, his returned fugitive father did just as well, the assumption being that he was an extension of the son, and therefore expressed the slaveowner's will as well. (The extension of this ancient principle of slavery to peasants was another mark of the abasement of the peasants-becoming-serfs by analogy with the slaves.)

Muscovite slaves could serve as the ultimate extension of their owners by representing them in court. This attitude must be contrasted with that found in the Ethiopian *Fetha Nagast*: "A man cannot be represented by his slave in bringing a lawsuit before the judge, since a slave is not equal in honor to a free man."[84] A sharper contrast to the Muscovite opinion would be hard to find, no doubt because the Ethiopian conception of freedom and honor greatly differed from that found in early modern Russia. This is a stark example of how two legal systems, both based to a considerable extent on the Byzantine *Ecloga* and *Procheiros Nomos,* could diverge.

The great student of Roman law, W. W. Buckland, noted in the Preface to his study of Roman slave law that "There is scarcely a problem which can present itself, in any branch of the law, the solution of which may not be affected by the fact that one of the parties to the transaction is a slave, and, outside the region of procedure, there are few branches of the law in which the slave does not prominently appear."[85] The same could be said about Muscovite law, with two very important reservations: as we have just seen above, slavery was important

---

83. Iakovlev, *Kholopstvo*, p. 485, no. 23, VII. The Chinese made slaves a more formal extension of their owners by attaching kin-like titles to them, thus including them in the masters' family circles. As a contemporary source put it, "'A bondservant is called "adopted son," so the relationship between father and son exists in that of master and bondservant'." (Wiens, p. 294). The Muscovite family was much less permeable, and no such fictions were created there.

84. *The Fetha Nagast*, p. 258.

85. Buckland, *The Roman Law of Slavery*, p. v.

for procedure in Muscovite law; and the solution to cases in Muscovite law often was not affected by the involvement of the slave, either because he was in certain circumstances totally identified with his owner or because he could act on his own account. The Muscovite custom of utilizing slaves as extensions of their owners also was evident in the fact that the law of agency was minimally developed.

Complaints Against the Slaveowner

A major formality is necessary for a slave to have any rights vis-à-vis his owner, the right to complain to someone who can impose sanctions in case of violations. That right was implicitly or explicitly denied in many slave systems. An extreme expression of this norm was Gratian's ruling in the late fourth century A.D. that a slave who lodged any complaint against his owner for any wrong other than high treason should be burned alive immediately, in spite of the truth of the charge. The Ming Chinese also allowed slaves to accuse their owners only of treason or rebellion.[86]

Recognizing that conflicts between master and chattel were bound to arise, some slaveholding societies provided formal channels for resolving them. In very limited circumstances, Ancient Near Eastern slaves who suffered cruelty or gross injustice could appeal to the courts.[87] In Greece, an aggrieved slave could flee to a temple of the gods (Thesus) and initiate his complaint. The priests were supposed to hear him out, and then propose a resolution. The Athenian priest might return the slave to his owner forthwith, grant him the protection of the temple, or recommend that the slave's demand to be sold to another owner be heeded. A similar custom prevailed in Rome, where an aggrieved slave even before the time of Seneca, and by the constitution of Antoninus, could seek refuge by fleeing to the imperial statues; the magistrates were then obliged to examine his claims, which, when substantiated, would result in the sale of the slave to another owner.[88]

In Byzantium, the *Ecloga* allowed slaves to file complaints against their owners in instances where the latter were keeping them illegally enslaved by concealing a will in which the slaves had been manumitted, by not permitting them to buy their freedom with their own funds, or by failing to set them free when ordered to.[89] While these norms circulated in Muscovy in the church *Kormchaia kniga*, there is no evidence that the Muscovites found them congenial or applicable to their trouble cases.

86. D. B. Davis, *Western Culture*, p. 61; Wiens, pp. 302-3.
87. Mendelsohn, p. 65.
88. Shtaerman, pp. 78-79; Westermann, p. 17; Rose, p. 204.
89. *Ecloga* 14: 3 (Freshfield, p. 96; Lifshits, p. 63).

In Kievan Rus', if the indentured slave was abused, he had the right to complain to the prince. This is a stipulation common for slaves of native origin (such as debt slaves) in many societies when the societies are reluctant to place such slaves in the nearly rightless legal condition that is normal for ordinary slaves almost anywhere. The same was true for the Muscovite debt slave, whose owner had to post bond guaranteeing that he would not harm him. Such people were not considered to be "total outsiders" but rather "temporary outsiders," individuals who could be expected to return at some time to the ranks of citizens and thus were deserving of some protection.

The New World was not noted as a place where a slave's welfare was closely tended to. Nevertheless, in Brazil a royal order dated 1688 allowed a slave who was being treated "excessively cruelly" to denounce his owner to the authorities, who might force the owner to sell his slave.[90] This, of course, is different from systems that wanted to repress slaveowner abuse but relied on the slaveowners themselves to denounce one another.

Muscovite law had little to say on the subject of enforcing a slave's right to complain against his owner. As we have seen, the law requiring a lord to feed his slave insisted that the former was not to harm the latter for having filed a complaint about inadequate sustenance, and the owner was not supposed to beat to death his returned fugitive, but no sanctions were specified.[91] There are few records of slaves' successfully bringing charges in court against their owners in Muscovy, a situation not inconsistent with that in other slaveowning societies. Slaves generally were unable to resist oppression legally, but they did seek refuge in those devices which are the subject of chapter 16. (The problem of slaves' lodging accusations of treason against their owners will be discussed there as well.)

By keeping silent on the matter of slave rights against the owner, except in cases of rape that produced an offspring, Muscovite jurisprudence tacitly affirmed the Roman position. No one knows, obviously, why the Muscovites provided no institution of asylum for slaves, but we may assume that there were two major reasons: treatment, as in most systems of household slavery, was comparatively mild, for Muscovy did not exploit slaves in mines or use them in field gang-labor, situations which were much more conducive to abuse; the Muscovite slave could take asylum in flight, something that will be discussed in considerable detail below.

Slaveowner Rights of Alienation

Certainly in a comparative context, the right of alienation is one of the most im-

90. Mellafe, p. 106.
91. 1649 *Ulozhenie* 20: 42, 92; MS, pp. 270, 288–89.

portant prerogatives of a slaveowner.[92] Until the change in the nature of limited service contract slavery mandated in the late sixteenth century, there were few formal restraints on Muscovite slaveowners in this context.

No doubt this was the most fearsome part of being a slave. Everyone fears change, but slaves were insulated from most change by their owners. Slaves became adjusted to their owners, but they never knew what living with someone else might bring. (As will be discussed in chapter 16, manumitted Muscovite slaves, to reduce the threat of change, probably chose to sell themselves to new owners who were as much like their former owners as possible.) Moreover, partially because they were insulated from the threat of change, slaves became highly dependent upon their owners. This was doubly so in Muscovy, where slavery was primarily a relief institution. Thus the matter of alienation was one of absolutely crucial importance not only in formal law but in the lives of its objects.

A comparative discussion of this subject need not be lengthy, for the norms almost everywhere were that most slaves could be sold, given away, passed to heirs in dowries and wills and otherwise alienated. For example, in the U. S., in general, there were few if any restrictions on the way in which a slaveowner could alienate his slave property. Besides the more customary forms of alienation, a slave could be used even as the stakes in a wager on a horse race. However, exceptions did exist, such as a 1794 Virginia law which held that a slave was the last item that could be sold to satisfy an owner's debts, after all other personal property had been disposed of.[93]

As chattel, Muscovite slaves were passed to heirs and other parties in wills, dowries, marriage contracts, and gift documents.[94] Included in these provisions were debt slaves who had not worked off their obligations at the time of the death of the creditor.[95] The only type of slave exempted from such transfers was the limited service contract slave after 1597. As a rule, according to E. I. Kolycheva, slaves in the sixteenth century were not transmitted to lateral heirs— brothers, cousins, and so forth.[96] While this was true for wills, it was less so in marriage contracts and dowries.

Of nineteen beneficiaries of wills, eleven inherited from their fathers and six from their mothers. A similar picture prevailed in property divisions—seven inherited from fathers, six from mothers. Of marriage contracts, five were given by fathers, three by mothers, two by brothers, and one each by an uncle and grandfather. Much more information is available about dowries. Only barely more than a third were granted by fathers, fifty, and a tenth by mothers, thirteen. Just half (56.4 percent), in other words, were directly from parents. This is not at all

---

92. Shifman, "Syria," in *Rabstvo* (1977), p. 111.
93. Friedman, p. 197.
94. 1649 *Ulozhenie* 20: 61.
95. Ibid., 20: 40.
96. Kolycheva, *Kholopstvo*, p. 146.

surprising, given the demographic fact that in many preindustrial societies most people did not live to see their grandchildren (or even to marry off their children) and the added life-span reducing element that slaveowners were a warrior caste. Listing in any one of these documents was recognized in law as valid evidence of slave status.[97]

After 1597, limited service contract slaves could not be passed to heirs, but the law recognized what was in reality the natural tendency—people continued to serve the same family. Limited service contract slaves had to be manumitted formally, and if they wanted to continue serving an offspring of their owner, a manumission document had to be attached to the new contract.[98] Extant information indicates that this provision, dating from 1606, was rigorously enforced.

The transactions of exchanging slave property in marriage contracts and dowries served as part of the social cement (along with land) holding the propertied classes of Muscovy together. This is emphasized even as late as the law code of 1649, which repeats the traditional formula on the return of dowry slaves to the donor when the wife died childless.[99] The tendency of much of the legislation after 1597 was to diminish gradually the property available for such transfers, and with it the social cement holding the upper classes together. This in turn put pressure on the government to convert peasant serfs into chattel who could (and ultimately did) replace slaves. An aristocratic society must have, or certainly would like to have, gifts to use in establishing relationships. The budding Muscovite autocracy forgot this when it changed the nature of limited service contract slavery at the end of the sixteenth century, just after it had almost abolished land (the *votchina*) as a form of property that could be transferred to others. As we know, however, within a century both forms of social cement, land and human chattel, were restored.

Manumission

Manumission of any slave by his owner was allowed in Muscovy, and, as we saw in chapter 2, was legally compulsory for all limited service contract slaves after 1597. The general topic of manumission will be discussed in greater detail in chapter 15, and here only certain aspects of manumission will be touched upon. A father in his will was allowed to set free his son's limited service contract slaves, a reflection of the broad power parents had over offspring in Muscovy.[100] The law was always insistent that a valid manumission document had

97. 1550 *Sudebnik* 76.
98. 1649 *Ulozhenie* 20: 9.
99. Ibid., 20: 62.
100. Ibid., 20: 106; MS, pp. 293-94.

to be respected by anyone and everyone.[101] Obviously manumission documents extorted from slaveowners during disorders such as those that occurred in 1682 were not valid, nor were those issued by such figures as Ivan and his son Andrei Khovanskoi, who were subsequently executed as rebels.[102]

In one of the laws concerning manumission, dated 1556, a seemingly curious rider was attached: a manumission document was voided if the freedman again served his old lord (*gosudar'*).[103] The sense of this provision becomes clear if one considers the tendency for slaves to develop a dependency syndrome that frequently induced them to sell themselves back into slavery rather than try to compete as free people in the harsh Muscovite world. This law of 1556 simplified the judicial process by removing from a slaveowner the onus of having to formulate new documents on a manumitted slave who came back to live with his former master. My basic data set contains numerous instances of manumitted slaves selling themselves back into thralldom but not one case of a freedman selling himself back to his former owner, no doubt because this law made unnecessary the formulation of any document that might have survived to the twentieth century. When a freedman sold himself to someone else, the manumission document was to be appended to the new service document.[104] This requirement, which ensured the survival of several manumission documents that otherwise certainly would have been lost, was made so that the freedman could no longer claim to be free because he did not have possession of the document and so that the new owner, by the same token, could prove immediately that the new slave had surrendered his freedom.

Novokshchenov v. Nazar Polikarpov

Various aspects of manumission legal practice are revealed in a case tried in the Slavery Chancellery before director Prince Ivan Fedorovich Volkonskoi and the state secretaries Tret'iak Kopnin and Ivan Kostiurin in late 1634, Novokshchenov v. Nazar Polikarpov (or perhaps, Dionisii v. Nazar). The case seems to have been an unusual one, and is worth discussing in some detail.

The first unusual aspect of this case is that both litigants can be cited by their first names, the plaintiff because he was a monk, the defendant because he was a slave who, like other members of the lower classes in Russia until the nineteenth century, did not have a last name. The defendant's full name was Nazar, son of Polikarp Makidonskoi, or Nazar Polikarpov Makidonskoi. (When he or his forebears came from Macedonia, in the Balkans, is not stated.) The plaintiff, represented at the trial by his highly paid nephew, state secretary Vasilii Sergeev Prokof'ev of the Chancellery for Ransoming Russians from Foreign Cap-

101. PRP 4: 372; 1649 *Ulozhenie* 20: 14, 15; MS, p. 250 (art. 5), 260-61.
102. PSZ 2: 499, no. 992.
103. AI 1: 257, no. 154, v, 16.
104. 1649 *Ulozhenie* 20: 8, 10; MS, pp. 258-59.

tivity,[105] before he became a monk had been counselor state secretary Nikolai Nikitich Novokshchenov.

Novokshchenov provides a classic illustration of the Muscovite meritocracy at work. His forebears were probably Tatars who joined Russian service, were baptized (thus the name, shortened from Novokreshchenov), and assigned service lands in the Novgorod Votskaia piatina region. It is unknown how or why he moved to Moscow, but in 1599 he was a clerk (*pod'iachii*) in the Military Chancellery, where he wrote up a precedence (*mestnichestvo*) dispute trial. He held that post until 1605, when he was elevated to the rank of state secretary and sent out of Moscow to administer the Northern Dvina land. In 1608 he returned to Moscow and became a state secretary in the Service Land Chancellery, a post he held at least nominally for many of the next dozen or so years. During that period he was a state secretary in the Military Chancellery for roughly a year (1611-12) and was involved in negotiations with Sweden between 1614 and 1617 that led to the Stolbovo Peace Treaty. He also negotiated with the Englishman John Merrick in 1616, and worked in the Military Chancellery for awhile again in 1618. For all of these services, he was promoted to the highly distinguished rank of counselor state secretary in 1618, one of three or four men in Muscovy who held the rank at that time. He was at the peak of his career.

As in any meritocracy, those who rise can also fall, and this Novokshchenov did: in 1619-20 he made a mistake in copying a royal decree, and for that lost his title of counselor state secretary, and probably the influence that went with it. This was not the end of the line for Novokshchenov, however, for he was granted the title of Moscow *dvorianin* in 1627, and in 1630 was appointed governor of Perm'. He was not listed in the 1632 inventory of Moscow *dvoriane* prepared on the eve of the Smolensk War, probably because he was never a combatant and therefore was not expected to render military service. He was tonsured in 1633, an event of major importance for this case, and died in 1637. He had service estates in Rzheva Vladimirskaia and in Moscow province, and in 1634 was able to donate the not insignificant sum of 150 rubles to the Trinity Sergiev monastery.[106]

The case began in the Slavery Chancellery on October 26, 1634, with the submission by Prokof'ev of a limited service slavery contract dated January 18, 1620, in the amount of 3 rubles between Novokshchenov and Nazar, which the latter admitted had been a valid document. Nazar claimed that Prokof'ev was trying to enslave him as he allegedly had enslaved, by force, Dionisii's cook, one

105. Bogoiavlenskii, *Prikaznye sud'i*, p. 288; Veselovskii, *D'iaki*, pp. 431-32.

106. RK 1550-1636, 2: 170, 213, 282, 289-90; Barsukov, SGV, p. 177; Veselovskii, *D'iaki*, p. 376; Storozhev, "B. S." (1909), p. 84; DR 1 and 2: passim; Ivanov, AUBK, p. 294; Bogoiavlenskii, *Sud'i*, p. 280; Samokvasov, AM 1: xxxiv, 48; KR 1 and 2: passim; RIB 28 (1912): 255, 268; Akty Iushkova, pp. 300, 303, 309; Shumakov, *Obzor* 2 (1900): 40, 336, nos. 192, 983; Shumakov, *Sotnitsy* 7 (1913): 4.

Vas'ka Matveev. Prokof'ev retorted that he had no claim to Nazar, was acting only on behalf of his uncle Dionisii to enforce the 1620 contract, and that Vas'ka had come voluntarily to him and negotiated a limited service slavery contract. (As we shall see in chapter 11, that last claim was highly plausible. It is partially substantiated by Nazar's own fate as well.)

However, Nazar at first based his claim for freedom on the fact that Novokshchenov had become a monk and thus "died" as far as "the world" was concerned. This claim had two bases: the 1597 law manumitting limited service contract slaves on the death of their owners; some precedents, in which other slaves had been manumitted by order either of the Slavery Chancellery or of Patriarch Filaret after their owners (in the two cited cases, Ondrei Golubovskoi and Prince Luka Scherbatoi) had taken monastic vows. Prokof'ev rejected those precedents, cited contrary ones in which Pafnutyi Zagriaskoi and Bogolep Redrikov had been allowed to keep their slaves upon entering a monastery, and submitted a petition by Dionisii to Patriarch Filaret dated August 14, 1633, in which, noting that his slaves would no longer obey him and wanted to leave him, he asked that the slaves be forced to tend him until his death. Filaret had ordered a *striapchii* to go to Dionisii's place and compel his slaves to serve him.

Then, at the trial, Nazar shifted his ground, and claimed that he was not subject to Dionisii because earlier Dionisii had manumitted him in favor of his son Nikita, who had subsequently died. Prokof'ev, suing for Dionisii, denied that any such events had taken place. The Slavery Chancellery searched its archive, and found a limited service slavery contract dated February 16, 1628, between Nazar and Nikita Nikolaev Novokshchenov. The following was written in the contract:

Nazar has a round face, a straight nose, is somewhat snub-nosed [sic], has gray eyes, a pockmarked face and nose resulting from smallpox. The hair on his head is light brown, his moustache is black and light brown, his beard and sideburns are sparse. The thumb on his left hand has been amputated. He is of average height. He said he is a hereditary slave of his [Nikita's] father.

Nikita Novokshchenov's slave Gavrila Varlam'ev handled the transaction for his owner, and paid Nazar 3 rubles in silver. (The claim that Nazar had been/ was a hereditary slave of Nikita's father is not necessarily contradicted by the existence of the 1620 contract, which may have been entered into because of the edict that owners of hereditary slaves were supposed to get limited service slavery contracts on their chattel.)

On November 16, 1634, the Slavery Chancellery ruled that any claim to Nazar made on the basis of the 1620 contract was void because of the existence of the 1628 contract, and on the twenty-fifth this verdict was read to the plaintiff and the defendant. Nazar, his wife Mar'itsa, and their daughter Malashka were declared freed of any claims by Dionisii. The death of the younger Novokshchenov had freed Nazar and his family from the 1633 order of Filaret, because they were free people at the time. (Technically, it would be important to know the date of the younger Novokshchenov's death, and whether Nazar had served the older Novokshchenov for any length of time after his son's death, for, if he had, he might have been enslaved by the five-month rule, had old Novokshehenov asked that it be applied. Apparently he had not, or else it was not relevant in the case.) Nazar paid the capitation fee of 9 altyns (3 apiece) for the decision on himself, his wife, and daughter.

That left a suit for stolen property in the amount of 122.90 rubles, which the Slavery Chancellery decided should be resolved by the taking of an oath. The issue of casting lots arose, and the Slavery Chancellery responded that this method of conflict resolution was reserved by law for clergy; since Dionisii had not sued on his own behalf, but his nephew, the state secretary Vasilii Sergeev Prokof'ev, a layman, had sued for him, the cross-kissing oath should be used. Nazar and Prokof'ev appeared to kiss the cross on November 29, December 1, and then on December 2 they announced that they had settled the matter, out of court. Whether any cash was involved in the settlement is not known, but Nazar agreed to pay the court costs, 10 percent of the verdict. One can only imagine where a house slave was to get such a sum of money.

It happened, however, that Nazar did not pay the court costs. In fact, throughout the trial he was the limited service contract slave of *boiarin* Boris Mikhailovich Saltykov, brother-in-law of Tsar Mikhail and de facto ruler of Muscovy after Filaret died in 1633. One of Nazar's defenses against the charge that he had deserted Dionisii after Filaret's *striapchii* arrived was that the family already was at Saltykov's. It is not at all clear why Dionisii did not sue Saltykov for having received a fugitive slave, but he did not, and the entire process was conducted as though Nazar were a free man maintaining his claim to freedom, even to the point of paying his own capitation fees (the sums paid by the winner of a slavery case). Saltykov's presence was felt first in the out-of-court settlement of the stolen property issue, and then only in a minor way: his slave Sergeev signed the agreement with Vasilii Prokof'ev at Nazar's behest.

At the end of the month, however, Saltykov's presence was expressed more strongly. On December 30, Nazar brought to the Petititons Chancellery his owner's petition that the court fees be dropped, and state secretary Kollistrat Akinfeev noted on the back that Tsar Mikhail granted the request. The next day Nazar delivered the document to the Slavery Chancellery, effectively ending the case. As I read it, the petition confessed that Nazar had stolen the property in question, for Saltykov said that the conciliation agreement had been signed because he had not wanted to commit perjury (*ne khotia dushevredstva sotvorit'*).[107] Other than through his intervention in the matter of the court

107. Iakovlev, *Kholopstvo*, pp. 473-79, no. 22.

fees for the stolen property, however, the presence of Saltykov was not felt at the trial.

Dionisii v. Nazar shows operationally how the manumission law of Muscovy was enforced. The law of 1597 said that all limited service contract slaves were to be freed on the death of their owners, and they were. This principle was even extended, if somewhat inconsistently, to "the death in the world" of a layman who entered a monastery. The case also reveals that a slaveowner who ceded his slave to another owner could not renege on the agreement, at least not without the slave's consent.

Voeikov v. Khilkov

The manumission document could be used not only by a freedman to maintain his freedom but by a subsequent owner to keep him enslaved. This fact, not too bizarre a one, given the nature of Muscovite slavery, is evident in the case of Voeikov v. Khilkov, tried in the Slavery Chancellery in January and February of 1621, to determine the ownership of the slave Semen (Sen'ka) Murza Nesterov. Both litigants were minor notables of early seventeenth-century Muscovy. Aleksandr Bogdanov Voeikov seems to have been so well known in his own day that he did not even have to use his patronymic, a fact we only learn in the case itself when it is said that Semen had been with Aleksandr's father, Bogdan, while the latter was governor of Kholmogory, one of the most prestigious posts in Muscovy, commanding, as it did, the White Sea trade into the Dvina River. On this basis, we may assume that the Aleksandr Voeikov who delivered a large payroll for the cossacks in the southern fort of Belev in November 1618 was the plaintiff in this case a year and a half later. Earlier, in 1602-3, he occupied the rank of *zhilets*, beginning his tenure in the upper service class, and from 1611 to 1616 he was already recorded as one of the sixty men who had the rank of *striapchii s plat'em*, meaning that he worked in the tsar's palace. In 1611, when he happened to be ill and was on a leave of absence from service, his land compensation schedule was 700 cheti and his cash salary schedule was probably 30 rubles, both considerably higher than provincial levels but average for those in capital service. These were increases from 600 and 20 prior to that time. In 1626 he held the rank of *stol'nik*, at some time in the 1620s was raised to the rank of Moscow *dvorianin*, and from 1627 to 1632 served at court.[108] One may assume that he died of old age at some time after that.

The defendant in the case, Prince Boris Andreev Khilkov, was of the twenty-first generation of a long, noble line. His career ran roughly parallel to Voeikov's, although he seems to have spent more of his life in the army and in the provinces

---

108. KR 1: 538; AMG 1: 79, 142; Storozhev, "B. S." (1909), pp. 83, 109; BS 1: 195; Sukhotin, ChSV, p. 204; Ivanov, AUBK, p. 69; DR 1 and 2: passim. It is possible that the Aleksandr Voeikov who was *golova* in Belev in 1632 was the same man (AMG 1: 399-407), especially considering the mutual association with Belev. However, such a task was usually assigned to a younger man.

than did his adversary, who spent far more of his time at the court in Moscow. Khilkov was recorded in the army as early as 1604, and in 1606-7, with the rank of *stol'nik*, he reported to service at Kaluga with thirteen recruits. Between 1613 and 1631 he occupied rotational posts for two or three years as military governor of some of the leading cities of Muscovy—Ufa, Belaia, Kazan', Riazan', Toropets, and Vologda, where he was in charge of taking a census. Only toward the end of that period, from 1626 to 1629, did he spend much time at court. He first appeared in 1613 as a *stol'nik,* ranking higher than Voeikov, and in the mid-1620s was raised to the rank of Moscow *dvorianin*. Khilkov's compensation probably ran ahead of Voeikov's. Prior to 1611, his land compensation entitlement was a hefty 800 cheti, and his cash salary 80 rubles per year. Moreover, his actual landholding was unusually close to his entitlement: in 1613 he had 273 cheti that he had inherited from his father's patrimony, plus service land-grants totalling 500 cheti from court lands in the Vologda region.[109] Thus Khilkov was an example of a typical, successful Muscovite elite military figure. In spite of his greater social prominence at the time of the trial, he lost the case.

The case opened on May 18, 1620, with Voeikov's declaration that, six days before, his slave Sen'ka Murza had fled and stolen 30 rubles in cash, personal property worth 32.50 rubles (pearls, silver bowls, three guns, much clothing), and about eleven of Voeikov's limited service slavery contracts—a large theft. The taking of the slavery documents was a major goal of slaves resisting their enslavement, for it deprived their owners of one of the major tools for their recovery. At the time of his flight Sen'ka had been a steward (*khodil v kliuche*), with ready access to his owner's wardrobe and strongbox, whose contents revealed that Voeikov was a comparatively wealthy man. The plaintiff filed his declaration of loss with the two directors of the Slavery Chancellery, Semen Mikhailovich Koltovskoi and Ivan Kuz'mich Begichev, and its state secretary, Filip Mitrofanov.

About seven months passed, during which time Voeikov looked for and found his slave Sen'ka, who was living with Khilkov. The fugitive was seized, arrested, and detained in the Slavery Chancellery for five weeks before the trial began. Khilkov did not appear at the trial, but was represented by his slave advocate, Fedor Dmitriev. Advocate Fedor presented a limited service slavery contract that the fugitive Sen'ka, on November 21, 1620, had arranged with another of Prince Khilkov's slaves, Fedor Sorokin, in exchange for 4 rubles. During the interrogation that preceded the signing, Sen'ka had claimed that at that time he was a free man but that he had been a slave a decade earlier, serving one Grigorii Mikulin and then his son Matvei, who, having been mortally wounded by cossacks in 1610, had manumitted him. The slavery contract had been signed and sealed in

---

109. Petrov, IRRO 1 (1886): 148; RK 1550-1636, 2: 270-349; BS 1: 249, 2: 29; Barsukov, SGV, pp. 25, 263; Ivanov, AUBK, p. 435; Opisanie 15 (1908): 17, 67; Storozhev, "B.S.," p. 78; AMG 1: 140; DR 1 and 2: passim; RK 1 and 2: passim; APD 1: 198, 203; Barsukov, "Dokladnaia vypiska 121" (1895), p. 6; RIB 28 (1912): 800-1.

the Slavery Chancellery itself before the same three officials to whom the plaintiff Voeikov had complained a half-year earlier. The fact that the fugitive slave was arrested three weeks after the signing of the new contract indicates that the officials of the Slavery Chancellery may have tipped off Voeikov as to the whereabouts of his runaway. The fugitive, knowing that he had stolen the contract he had signed with Voeikov, apparently felt secure in arranging another servitude relationship three months after he had fled from Voeikov. It is not clear why Semen, having stolen cash and property equivalent to at least ten years' pay for a good worker, had to sell himself again so soon, but it is likely that he was so dependent that he simply could not manage on his own—the result of having lived for so many years as a slave. It is also typical that the fugitive resold himself to someone who was very much like his previous master.

To his undoing, however, the slave Semen had forgotten to steal the manumission document from Mikulin, which apparently he had deposited with Voeikov upon selling himself to him. The dimension of the theft, and particularly the fact that all the slavery contracts were stolen, would indicate that Semen really hated Voeikov, or, perhaps, because he was illiterate, that he had taken all the documents just to ensure that he got his own. In any case, he overlooked the manumission document. Voeikov submitted the manumission document on the second day of the trial, and it became the center of attention. Sen'ka and his father, Nester Pavlov, had been hereditary slaves of Grigorii [Ivanov] Mikulin, a relatively prominent figure at the end of the sixteenth century and during the Time of Troubles. He first appeared in 1571 and 1572 as a junior member of the suite of tsarevich Ivan. In 1582 he was number 139 on an incomplete service list of figures at the tsar's palace. Mikulin seems to have fallen out of favor with Boris Godunov, who relegated him to secondary assignments such as commander (second-in-command, *golova*) in the new fort of Pelym' in Siberia on the river Berezova in the years 1596-97. Nevertheless, he kept his very high land-compensation entitlement of 600 cheti of land, of which he had 499 1/12 cheti in Viaz'ma province, due west of Moscow, in 1595. When False Dmitrii I invaded in 1605, Mikulin was commander of a detachment of *strel'tsy* stationed in Orel, the southern frontier district where his father had held a small service estate. He was shifted from Orel to Belgorod, whence he deserted for the forces of Grigorii Otrepov, the first pretender.

False Dmitrii I recognized a willing and useful collaborator, and elevated Mikulin to the rank of *dumnyi dvorianin*, in which capacity he accompanied the pretender from Putivl' to Kromy on his march to Moscow. In the capital, Mikulin was put in charge of the *strel'tsy*, and according to a gross story about the pretender's ambition to implant Roman Catholicism in Muscovy, promised that he personally with his own teeth would tear off the heads and rip out the guts of any *strel'tsy* who proved to be disloyal to Dmitrii. Unfortunately for Mikulin, and Russia as well, Dmitrii was overthrown, and Mikulin lost the fruit of his ambition.[110] Mikulin's career probably explains his son Matvei's death at the hands of the cossacks in 1610. The slave Sen'ka probably experienced many of these events, and chose successive owners whose profiles in many respects were like that of Mikulin.

Prince Khilkov's advocate, Fedor Dmitriev, asked that the writer of the manumission document be summoned to testify. He was, and announced that he had written the document. Once this happened, the verdict was awarded to Voeikov. The judges announced two basic reasons for the verdict. For one, Voeikov had the manumission charter in his possession, something that the fugitive Sen'ka could not deny. This forced Sen'ka to change his story. He admitted in a preliminary investigation that he had lived with Voeikov for four years but claimed that he had never sold himself to Voeikov. In other words, he had been a voluntary slave. During the trial, he changed his testimony and said that he had lived with Voeikov only for six months. However, the damage had been done. Sen'ka had admitted that he had lived with Voeikov for over six months, a term long enough to make him a slave even without selling himself, because of the 1609 decree on voluntary slavery. Thus the manumission document had trapped Sen'ka into admitting that he had been a voluntary slave of Voeikov, and so the fact that his owner no longer had the limited service slavery contract in his possession did not matter. Moreover, Sen'ka was trapped in other ways as well, particularly by the fact that Voeikov was able to produce many witnesses who knew that the slave had accompanied Voeikov's prominent father, Bogdan Borisov, while he was governor in Kholmogory in 1617-19, and many other people who knew Sen'ka had been Voeikov's slave in Moscow. Of course the slave was unable to refute any of this, and he was turned over to Voeikov. The case makes no mention of the stolen property.[111]

Slaves could be manumitted not only by their owners but also by the state when it desired to punish a slaveowner. This was part of the confiscation of a disgraced person's possessions. Such manumission was not infrequent during the reign of Ivan IV and through the Time of Troubles. This subject will be discussed in greater detail below, but here we should note the the *Ulozhenie* of 1649 repeated a law of 1608 affirming the freedom of any slave emancipated because of his owner's treasonous conduct. Moreover, if a person returned to the good graces of the sovereign, he could not claim any slaves so manumitted. On the other hand, if the manumitted slaves desired to return to him, they were free to sell themselves to him once again.[112]

The Muscovite state also prescribed that slaves who were taken into foreign captivity and then fled back to Russia were to be freed. That made good sense, es-

110. RK 1550-1636, 2: 123, 157, 226; RK 1475-1598, pp. 240-244, 505, 514; RK 1559-1605, pp. 73, 80; Belokurov, RZ 7113-21, pp. 5, 238; Storozhev, "B. S.," p. 60; PKMG 2: 651-53, 969; AAE 2: 109, no. 48; Platonov, *Ocherki Smuty*, pp. 220-22.
111. Iakovlev *Kholopstvo*, pp. 323-27, no. 2.
112. 1649 *Ulozhenie* 20: 33; MS, p. 267; Vladimirskii-Budanov, 3: 108-9.

pecially when we recognize that many slaveowners were military men who took some of their chattel with them to the military theater, either as combat troops or as baggage-train auxiliaries. Such people were as likely as their owners to fall into captivity. Tacitly recognizing the dependency that slavery created, the law allowed such returnees to serve their old masters if they wanted. This was to be noted on their old slavery documents, and a fee of 1 altyn was to be charged. Acknowledging that such a provision might be abused, legislators decreed that a slave could not flee to another state and then return to Muscovy and claim his freedom. Presumably, an owner could enforce his claims by proving that no witnesses had seen the slave's seizure into captivity. Moreover, freedom was not offered to a slave who had fled from his lawful owner, been taken into captivity, and then escaped back to Muscovy.[113] Another law of 1634, repeated in the *Ulozhenie*, reiterated these principles and, taking into consideration the Balash rebellion that had harassed the Muscovite rear during the Smolensk War, added that someone who had not been fighting with the government forces when he fell into captivity could not claim freedom when he escaped back to Russia.[114] One may assume, finally, that the slave the Muscovite authorities ransomed from foreign captivity for the sum of up to 15 rubles would not be granted his freedom, for the manumission articles explicitly state that the slave had to flee from foreign captivity in order to qualify.[115] As we have seen throughout this essay, many of the norms of slavery were applied to the peasants as they became enserfed. This was true as well for the manumission convention, used initially for seignorial estate peasants and later on applied to all peasants.[116]

It is appropriate to end this brief section on alienation and manumission of slaves with a reminder that slaves were rarely resold in Muscovy, that the domestic slave trade was very weakly developed even prior to 1597 and the change in the form of limited service contract slavery. This matter will be discussed below in chapter 10. Here I shall only make the comparative point that while the West regards an unlimited right of resale as a sine qua non of slavery, other societies do not. Thus many African and some Asian societies have often excluded the unlimited right of resale from their practice of slavery.

The Slave As Private Property, Recoverable at Law

The major point of the master-slave relationship in Muscovy was obviously that the owner could recover his chattel at law, more or less like any other piece of property. In recognizing the slaveowner's right to claim a fugitive slave on the basis of official documents registering ownership, the Slavery Chancellery assumed that the slaveowner had located and apprehended the runaway him-

113. 1649 *Ulozhenie* 20: 34-36; MS, pp. 267-68.
114. 1649 *Ulozhenie* 20: 66; MS, pp. 278-79.
115. 1649 *Ulozhenie* 8: 7; MS, p. 32.
116. 1649 *Ulozhenie* 15: 3; MS, p. 232; PSZ 2: 313-14, no. 869.

self.[117] By the middle of the seventeenth century the general practice was for a slaveowner to locate his slave and then have a court bailiff arrest the alleged fugitive, but it was still possible for a person to do everything himself. The law specified that such a slaveowner had immediately to bring the contested slave, together with all movable property claimed, to the Slavery Chancellery and initiate a suit to recover the contested slave.[118]

These procedures were a recognition of the slave as the property of his owner. The government also acknowledged ownership when it exempted slaves from the town tax rolls, for slaves were private property too important to confiscate just to give the townsmen a monopoly on urban income.[119]

Master-slave legal relations in Muscovy could be described as typical for slave systems. The slave owed nearly total submission to his owner and had few rights that he could claim from him. This was the legal image of the slave advanced by Zinovii Otenskii in the 1560s when criticizing the views of Feodosii Kosoi, a fugitive slave who was critical of the Orthodox church and the Muscovite social system (see chapter 16). Zinovii claimed that Feodosii could not be a "teacher" because he was a slave, for slaves had no civil rights, could not be witnesses in court, and were required to be absolutely submissive instruments of their owners and in their own right had no claim to anything.[120] Zinovii's view of the slave seems to have been quite accurate, although the logic of his claim that a slave could not be a "teacher" is not immediately obvious: perhaps he was trying to say that a teacher had to be respected, recognized as an authority, a complete human being, which a slave was not. Be that as it may, through the sixteenth century the personality of the slave in Muscovy hardly existed in the eyes of the law in case of conflicts with the owner, a view that was somewhat modified in the seventeenth century under the impact of the Byzantinization of Muscovite law, the use of the *Lithuanian Statute* of 1588, and particularly the ongoing enserfment of the peasantry. By 1700 the slave had more legal rights vis-à-vis his owner that he did in 1500, although it is by no means apparent that this made any difference in the slave's day-to-day life. In that same period the owner's legal control over his slave, especially in his right to alienate his limited service contract slaves and war captives, was appreciably diminished. Again, however, because of the household nature of Muscovite slavery and the dependency such an institution created, and also because of the enserfment of the peasantry, one cannot be sure that legal changes made much difference in the lives of the slaveowners.

117. PRP 4: 373; MS, pp. 252-53, art. 9.

118. 1649 *Ulozhenie* 20: 88; MS, p. 287. Several petitions (complaints) initiating suits in the 1620s for the recovery of fugitive slaves and the property they allegedly stole can be found in S. I. Kotkov et al., eds., *Moskovskaia delovaia i bytovaia pis'mennost' XVII veka* (Moscow: Nauka, 1968), pp. 45-47.

119. 1649 *Ulozhenie* 19: 5; MS, p. 53.

120. R. G. Lapshina, "Feodosii Kosoi—ideolog krest'ianstva XVI veka," TODRL 9 (1953): 249.

6. Legal Relations between Slaves and Strangers

Systems differed in their recognition of a slave's individuality. In the Roman system, one of the most severe, the slave ideologically had no individuality, no legal personality apart from that of his owner.[1] The same was fundamentally true in North America.[2] In Muscovy, on the other hand, this was not the case.

One test of the recognition of a slave's individuality lies in the realm of relations between slaves and third-party strangers. Some slave systems considered only the slaveowner's interests in third-party matters, while others considered the slave himself a human being with his own interests vis-à-vis strangers. Everywhere only an owner could recover for injury inflicted by a third party on a dog or a cow, the animal itself could not. So it was in the slave law of some societies but not in others. Thus, while the North American slave, for example, enjoyed the right of personal liberty vis-à-vis third persons in that the latter could not ordinarily at any time restrict or direct the former's movement, as allowed by his owner, the right was essentially meaningless because the slave himself could not recover any damages when it was infringed—only the master could recover for the trespass.[3]

Muscovy did not so limit slaves, with the consequence that the slave had considerably more rights in relation to third-party strangers than he did in relation to his owner; he was not defenseless against them and he had to answer for offenses he committed against them.

Personal Honor

A most significant right of the slave in relation to third persons was his dishonor payment, a sum he could claim if his personal honor was offended by anyone other than his owner. This is one of the clearest recognitions a slave's humanity found in any slave system. Thus after 1550 if any third party insulted a slave by word or deed, the slave could go to court to sue the offender and collect recompense for his injured honor. As shown in chapter 1, the dishonor sums were quantitative designations of Muscovite social stratification. In the reign of Ivan

1. Westermann, p. 20.
2. Rose, p. 200.
3. Ibid., pp. 206-7.

IV, the important presence of high status elite slaves is·shown by the fact that they could have a dishonor value (*bezchest'e*) as high as 5 rubles, the same as that for an ordinary free townsman. Estate managers (*tiuny*) and governmental assistants (*dovodchiki*) could have even higher compensation for injured honor, in amounts equivalent to their annual incomes. Even a common slave's honor had value, 1 ruble, the same as that of a poor townsman or a well-off or middling peasant. The sums for wives were double those for their husbands.[4] A century later, the situation in monetary terms had not changed much. The dishonor sum for elite slaves (*boiarskie sluzhilye liudi*) was still 5 rubles, that of ordinary slaves (*delovye liudi*) was still a ruble, the same as for peasants.[5] However, one can perceive a decline in slave status, which probably represented a decline in the role of elite slaves in society. The *Ulozhenie* no longer provided for compensation to an elite slave equal to his annual income. Moreover, 5 rubles was the compensation for the injured honor of the lowest category of townsman or for a postal driver, also a decline from the relative rankings of a century earlier.

Compensation for a slave's injured honor was something new to Muscovy. It was not present, for example, in Iaroslav's medieval Church Statute, which prescribed compensation only for free people.[6] Moreover, a concept such as the injured honor of a slave was not yet present in the *Sudebnik* of 1497. The appearance of the concept of injured honor epitomizes the evolution in the status of a slave from an object, a thing, to a kind of human being.

The protection of a slave's honor was evident in the 1622 Slavery Chancellery case of Dedkov v. Dolgorukii. While the litigation over the ownership of two slave girls was in process, they were entrusted to agents of the court for keeping. One of the agents, a bailiff (*nedel'shchik*) by the name of Zhdan Peresvetov, asked one of the young runaways, Var'ka, whether defendant Dolgorukii "had done anything shameful with her" (Peresvetov presumably was preparing to rape her). She complained to the Slavery Chancellery, which ordered her transferred to the custody of another bailiff (*pristav*) of the court, then had Peresvetov beaten "unmercifully" with a whip and denied him the "chaining fees" (*pozheleznye dengi*) he should have been paid for his custodial services.[7] Certainly many twentieth-century judicial systems have less regard for the honor of their charges.

Muscovy was not unique in protecting the honor of its slaves. In ancient Crete, for example, a slave had to be indemnified for homosexual or heterosexual rape, or for false arrest and detention, at one-half the rate specified for free men.[8]

---

4. 1550 *Sudebnik* 26; 1589 *Sudebnik* 48, 49, 51.
5. 1649 *Ulozhenie* 10: 94.
6. PRP 1: 269, art. 28.
7. Iakovlev, *Kholopstvo*, pp. 346-47. For a discussion of Dedkov v. Dolgorukii, see chapter 8 below.
8. Westermann, p. 17.

Rome and Byzantium reveal another possible variation on this theme. There no one was allowed to offend another person's slave, for such offense was taken as an insult to the slave's owner.[9] Similar norms were prevalent in parts of Africa. The end result of such strictures was some protection for the dignity of the slave, but the motivations were contrary: in Muscovy and Crete some thought was given to the slave, in Byzantium and Africa the consideration was solely for the slaveowner. The third possibility is to provide no consideration whatsoever for the slave for any reason, as was the case in North America. This was the case among the Yurok Indians of northern California, where slaves were equated with bastards and denied a right to maintain personal status or prestige; among the Tlingit and other Indians of the Northwest Coast; and among Africans imported into the South.[10]

A corollary of the fact that slaves had personal honor in Muscovy was the fact that they did not owe deference to anyone. The extremes to which that could go elsewhere are evident in the 1733 slave code of the Danish Virgin Islands, where a slave's menacing gestures or insulting words directed at a free person were punishable by a triple application of glowing pincers, and then branding. If the insulted person so desired, the offending slave's right hand could be amputated. The greatest manifestation of deference was demanded when slaves encountered whites on foot or on horseback: the former had to yield the way deferentially, or be subject to immediate corporal punishment.[11] Muscovy did not demand such deference or resort to such sanctions against its slaves, not because it was squemish about mutilation or corporal punishment but simply because slaves were not perceived as real or potential threats to the established order.

Homicide of a Slave by a Stranger

Homicide was a topic of concern in many legal systems that considered relations between slaves and strangers. There were two aspects to this problem: the law's view of a homicide and its consequences (1) when a person who was not the slave's owner killed him, and (2) when a slave killed a stranger.

In the Mesopotamian laws of Eshnunna, the owner of an ox or dog that caused the death of another's slave had to compensate the owner in cash.[12] In the Hammurabi Code and in Islamic practice, the person responsible for a slave homicide had to pay compensation to the owner.[13] Thus, in those ex-

9. Buckland, pp. 79-80.

10. E. Adamson Hoebel, *The Law of Primitive Man* (New York: Atheneum, 1973), pp. 53, 230; Siegel, p. 366.

11. Hall, p. 174.

12. Pritchard, p. 138, arts. 55, 57.

13. Ibid., pp. 162-65, arts. 213-14, 219, 231, 252; Levy, *Islam*, p. 79. Germanic law knew the *sclavenwergeld* (Wergeland, p. 75).

amples, the slave was a thing whose owner was to be compensated for its loss. The law expressed no sense that a crime had been committed, that the public order was in any manner offended by such a deed.

Roman law introduced the concept that killing a slave could be a crime. In *Lex Cornelia* the term *homo* included slaves, whose killing could be punished by death. Moreover, in private law, the killer had to compensate the slaveowner as for injury to other chattels. The *Lex Aquilia* has dozens of provisions on the liability for the death of slaves and who is to be compensated what sums.[14]

According to the provisions of the Justinian Codex, a free man was held criminally responsible for killing another's slave. The *Ecloga* and *Procheiros Nomos*, which circulated in Muscovy in the church *Pilot Book*, dictated death by the sword for anyone who committed premeditated murder, and one may assume that this would include murder of a slave by a stranger.[15]

The same was true in the Danish Virgin Islands, according to the code of 1783, which made the murder of a slave a criminal offense to be tried not before the colonial courts but the metropolitan courts.[16] (This latter measure was added because the legislators recognized that colonial courts were unlikely to enforce sanctions against the violation of norms involving slaves.) Similar norms developed even in North America, where in the period 1770-1830 the killing of a slave was held in the common law to be equal to the murder of a white man. Later this was incorporated into statutory law.[17] The matter of homicidal owners has been mentioned in chapter 5. In the case of strangers, however, the law was much less ambiguous: they could be convicted for the killing of a slave who belonged to someone else. One might argue that the concern developed simply because the slave was property, but the framework of prosecution and the sanctions invoked indicate that in fact the slave was considered as human. Manslaughter and murder cases were graded according to whether they were accidental or willful, and the penalties ranged from lengthy imprisonment to capital punishment, sanctions that were not imposed for the destruction of other property equal in value to that of a slave.[18]

Exactly the same arguments about the condition of the slave, whether he was a thing or a person, can be applied to the Russian situation. There is a great

14. Buckland, pp. 29, 31; Charles Henry Monro, trans., *The Digest of Justinian*, 2 vols. (Cambridge: Cambridge University Press, 1909), 1: 117-44.

15. *Ecloga* 17: 45 (Freshfield, p. 113; Lipshits, p. 72); *Procheiros Nomos* 39: 79 (Freshfield, p. 157).

16. Hall, p. 181.

17. Rose, pp. 192, 201. The 1851 Georgia Supreme Court ruling which held that it was not a common-law felony for a stranger to murder a slave was aberrational (Tushnet, "Law of Slavery," p. 131; Catterall, 3: 27-28).

18. Catterall, 2: 70-71; Rose, pp. 202, 220, 236. For additional discussion of the issue of the murder of slaves, see Mark V. Tushnet, *The American Law of Slavery 1810-1860. Considerations of Humanity and Interest* (Princeton: Princeton University Press, 1981), pp. 73-104.

controversy about the *Russkaia Pravda*'s sanctions against third persons who killed slaves. Article 16 states that the person (or his community) must pay a bloodwite of 5 grivnas for the killing of a peasant or a slave, and 6 grivnas for a female slave. The corruption of some texts in which "peasant or slave" (*smerd' i kholop,* or *smerd'i kholop*) is confused because of the practice of not dividing words by spaces; the former means "peasant or slave," the latter "the peasant's slave." I prefer the former interpretation, if only because peasants as a rule did not have slaves.

Further controversy surrounds the question of who receives the bloodwite. Supposedly that was a fine imposed on a killer to forestall the exaction of the traditional blood vengeance. But in that case, who collects for the slave, who is a person without kin? One may suppose that in article 16 the prince collects for the death of the slave, who may have been farming the prince's estates in Kievan times (and thus *smerd'i kholop* might mean "peasantry/farming slave," as opposed to a retainer or household slave). Article 16 was one of the initial articles of the *Pravda*, and may have lost its meaning by the time of the Mongol conquest. Certainly article 89 was the one operative in the early Muscovite period: "There is no bloodwite for either a male or a female slave." This corresponds to the fact that the slave is kinless, and that no kin have to be assuaged by a cash payment out of fear of their trying to exact vengeance from the killer and his kin. The bloodwite sum in article 16 became an outright fine of 12 grivnas in article 89. Although the slave is kinless, his master's interest had to be considered. Article 89 takes care of that by stating that the killer of a slave who did not provoke his own murder had to compensate the slave's owner for the loss. Similarly, the Anglo-Saxons required that the killer of an innocent slave pay to the owner the sum of 1 pound in compensation.[19]

Perhaps most important, if we return to Babylonia about 1760 B.C. for comparison, is the fact that a wronged free man had the absolute right without premeditation to kill a slave who had provoked him, and, even if he was not provoked, the killer only had to compensate the owner for the loss of his chattel. As discussed elsewhere, however, article 65 of the *Russkaia Pravda* did not allow a free man, with premeditation, to hunt down and kill a slave who had assaulted him; for such a killing the free man was fined.

The Soviet scholar E. I. Kolycheva has raised the issue of the similarity of sanctions for the murder of a slave and a free peasant in the first half of the sixteenth century.[20] The problem might be phrased in terms of whether the status of the slave was being elevated or that of the peasant was being abased, or perhaps some of both. Yet another possibility exists: that this is a nonissue. Kolycheva has noted that there was no distinction between the punishment for the murder of a free man and of a slave at the end of the fifteenth century,

19. Rose, p. 204.
20. Kolycheva, *Kholopstvo*, p. 238.

except that no bloodwite was paid for the murder of the latter. In cases of what we would term accidental homicide by someone not known to be a criminal, there was no sanction; where there was premeditation, the killer paid a 4-ruble fine to the authorities and compensation of 4 rubles to the free man's next of kin or to the slave's owner. Where the homicide was committed by a known recidivist, he was subject to the death penalty.

Only in late Muscovite law was the life of the slave explicitly protected in law. The Felony Statute of January 22, 1669, first prescribed that anyone who killed another person with intent was to be executed. The *Procheiros Nomos* (39:79) was quoted: "If an adult willfully murders someone, execute him with a sword," but (idem, 39:80), "If a child under seven or a madman kills someone, he is not guilty of murder."[21] It is not clear whether this encompassed an owner who murdered his own slave, a matter that has already been discussed, but the following article makes it clear that others are included.

> If a townsman, court peasant, or post driver kills someone's slave or peasant; or if some's slave or peasant kills a townsman, court peasant, or post man; and if such murders are committed without intent: pay for such murdered people 50 rubles in cash per person. If someone kills someone intentionally, and this is proved, execute such killers.[22]

Thus if a slave was accidentally killed, the killer had to pay the owner for the loss. This article apparently was borrowed in form from the *Lithuanian Statute* of 1588, which probably explains why members of the service classes and the clergy are excluded either as potential killers or potential victims of homicide. Such codification defects were not uncommon in Muscovite law. In all probability, had a trouble case arisen involving someone other than a townsman, court peasant, or postman, it would have been referred to the tsar for resolution, and he would have resolved it by analogy with this statute. Here, once again, we see the status of the slave in the eyes of the law being elevated by equation with enserfed seignorial peasants.

Further,

> If someone in a violent rebellious mood, with criminal intent, breaks into someone's house during a civil disturbance and murders the lord, his wife, children, or slaves, and this is proved: execute that person himself who committed the murder. Beat his accomplices with the knout and send them into exile wherever the Sovereign decrees.[23]

Here the murder of a slave by a stranger is equated with the murder of his

21. PRP 7: 423, art. 79.
22. Ibid., art. 80.
23. Ibid., p. 424, art. 84.

owner. Note the assumption that a slave may well be living in the house with his owner. The state, having taken over completely by the inquisitorial process the prosecution of murder, included slaves among those whose lives were protected by law against third parties. Equally important, the slave was held to be no more culpable than a free person in an instance of accidental homicide, and equally culpable in case of deliberate murder. In neither case was the slave singled out for special interrogation or torture, but rather he had the same legal position before the court as did a member of the lower classes. This may be attributed to the fact that the slave was not an outsider but a native Russian, as well as the fact that a compromise modus operandi for dealing with all members of the lower orders seems to have been the goal of Muscovy as the rigid stratification of society came to be expressed in such legal norms.

Assault of a Slave by a Stranger

The problem of third-party assaults on slaves aroused less concern on the part of lawmakers than did homicide, probably because only the latter was irrevocable and caused the slaveowner permanent loss. The American legal theoretician Thomas R. R. Cobb noted the difficulty in handling the battery of a slave, which could not be prosecuted without special laws, and pointed out that the owner's right to sue for civil damages was the only mode of redress against a stranger who trespassed a slave. [24] South Carolina law explained this by noting that the slave was not "within the peace of the state, and therefore the peace of the state [was] not broken by an assault and battery on him."[25]

In spite of such (contrived?) theoretical difficulties, many slave systems found ways to force strangers to think twice before they assaulted slaves. Mesopotamian law at Eshnunna explicitly forbade a third party to rape a slave girl, and prescribed that the owner was to be compensated for the injury, while retaining the slave.[26] The Hammurabi Code implicitly protected a slave against third-party assault by legislating that an individual who destroyed a slave's eye or broke a slave's bone had to pay the slaveowner one-half of the victim's value. However, the slave is viewed strictly as a chattel, for the owner is compensated for damage to his property, not the slave for the harm he had suffered.[27]

Athenian law forbade a third-party stranger to beat or otherwise assault another person's slave. The Roman Twelve Tables made breaking a slave's bones a crime, punishable by a fine half that for free men. The Justinian Code also explicitly limited the physical abuse third parties could heap on slaves. Norse law

24. Rose, p. 200.
25. Ibid., p. 232.
26. Pritchard. p. 136, art. 31.
27. Ibid., p. 161, art. 199; Mendelsohn, p. 65.

prescribed that a slave could collect monetary damages from a stranger who molested him.[28]

Even Southern sophistry was ultimately overcome, and the discovery was made that a stranger could be indicted for battery of a slave. The landmark case was State v. Hale (sometimes also State v. Hall [2 Hawks 582]), presided over by Justice C. J. Taylor in North Carolina in December of 1823. The sheriff had indicted Hale and the jury issued a special verdict in which it found that Hale had committed personal violence on the slave by striking him; the jury asked that the judge decide whether that was a crime. The court held that it was not a crime, whereupon the state appealed the verdict, won in Taylor's appellate court, and Hale was jailed on the grounds of battery without defense.[29] Late antebellum Alabama law stated that any person other than the master or his agent who committed assault and battery on a slave was guilty of a misdemeanor punishable by a fine of not over $2,000 and six months' imprisonment. (Assault of a free man was a felony.)[30]

As far as can be determined, the slave was never the special concern of Muscovite general criminal law on battery. Perhaps Byzantine laws circulating in the *Kormchaia kniga* might have been consulted had such a trouble case arisen, or laws about the damages payable to an owner for injury to livestock might have been invoked. The slave himself could have collected his dishonor payment for physical injuries (*uvech'e*).[31] The slave was included along with his owner if he was injured during a house break-in during a civil disorder. The culprit was to have his hand amputated, his accomplices were to be beaten with the knout and placed on bond, and the victim was to collect double his dishonor payment.[32]

Crimes Committed by Slaves against Strangers

A system's view of the slave is also made explicit by the manner in which it handles criminal acts commited by slaves against third-party strangers. The slaveowner and his chattel are often called upon to share responsibility in such cases, for the society wants to assign responsibility for the slave to his owner but nevertheless cannot fail to recognize that the slave may have been capable of exercising his own volition.

When sanctions have been imposed directly upon slaves, they were often more severe than for free people who committed the same offense. In Babylonia, free men were fined for assaulting one another, while a slave who struck such a per-

28. Westermann. p. 17; Buckland, p. 31; Wergeland, p. 19.
29. Catterall, 2:45; Rose, pp. 221, 232; Tushnet, "Law of Slavery," p. 140; idem, *American Law*, pp. 104-8.
30. Rose, p. 192.
31. 1649 *Ulozhenie* 10: 94; MS, p. 14.
32. 1649 *Ulozhenie* 10: 199.

son was liable to having his ear cut off.[33] (The reason for this is twofold: the slaves had to be kept in check, and the law could not assume that they possessed the means to pay a fine.) Similarly, in classical Greece, a slave might suffer corporal punishment for small infractions, while a free man did not have to suffer that indignity. Throughout Chinese history, slaves who committed offenses against free men were punished more severely than were ordinary citizens.[34]

In Latin America, for felonies such as robbery, rape, and murder, the penalties for offending slaves were extreme. Castration was often the prescribed form of punishment up to the middle of the sixteenth century; mutilation and slow death were also meted out to felonious slaves. The idealistic Spanish code of 1789 made the punishment of all crimes committed by slaves equal to that for free people, "an extremely unusual feature for slave societies."[35]

That slaves and their owners did not universally suffer for the wrongs of the former was evident in the Danish Virgin Islands, where in 1755 slaves themselves were indictable for offenses, but their owners were in no way responsible unless they had participated in the crime. The slave himself in that most harsh of slave systems had no access whatsoever to the state's judicial system should he be the object of offense, and was subjected to sanctions (beating, branding, hanging) more severe than those imposed upon free people for his crimes.[36]

In the U. S., slaves were more answerable than free whites for crimes, whether of homicide, arson, rape, or theft, and sometimes might be tried without a jury. Stealing was a capital crime in Georgia in 1806.[37] For theft in Virginia, a slave might be whipped, branded, or even hanged.[38] Whipping (followed by branding) was perhaps the favored penalty for crimes that did not command the death penalty (or its alternative, castration) because of its terror-inspiring properties and because it was cheap, both for the state, which did not have to feed someone in jail, and for the owner, who could put the chastised individual back to work in a relatively short time. Moreover, American slaves typically had no property or peculium, so fines had no meaning, and imprisonment was considered to be of little deterrence for those who in a sense were already prisoners and might have welcomed a break from work.[39]

Most American states recognized the property interest of slaveowners in their

33. Pritchard, p. 162, art. 205.

34. Westermann, p. 17; Wilbur, pp. 147-51; Wiens, p. 302; Meijer, p. 335. The Indians cut off the noses of slaves for minor offenses, a sanction that was not imposed on free men (Hjejle, p. 95).

35. Klein, *Americas,* p. 82.

36. Hall, pp. 175, 178. This was similar to the situation among the African Barotse, where a man was responsible for the delicts of his children but not for the actions of his "servants" (Gluckman, pp. 178-79, 188).

37. Friedman, p. 200.

38. Rose, pp. 242-43.

39. Ibid., pp. 193-94, 243-45; Friedman, p. 200.

chattel, and the reluctance that this might engender in them to surrender felonious slaves, by compensating them out of the public purse for delivering accused slaves.[40] This did not remove all of the incentive for the slaveowner to keep his chattel obedient, for, in some cases, such as in Alabama in 1824 and 1852, the jury in a capital case had to assess the value of the slave, and then half that sum was paid to the slaveowner in the event the slave was executed or transported.[41] Moreover, as was the case in Louisiana, the master was answerable for all damages caused by his slave, unless he was willing to surrender the slave to the party who had been wronged. If the owner had ordered the crime, he had to pay all damages, including those that might exceed the value of the slave.[42]

A particular problem was presented by homicide. No system condoned a deliberate murder of a stranger by a slave, but life presented instances in which a charge of first-degree murder offended the sensibilities of the legal system. Such was the 1834 North Carolina case, State v. Negro Will (slave of James S. Battle), presided over by Justice William Gaston. The slave Will had been disciplined by his overseer, Richard Baxter, who then shot him in the back and pursued him. Will stabbed Baxter with a knife during the pursuit, and Baxter died. The question was whether it was manslaughter or murder. Justice Gaston determined that Will had killed the overseer while in fear for his own life, without malice, that it was a manslaughter, and ordered Will sold to Louisiana. The situation was further complicated by Baxter's position, which was viewed as an extension of the master. Gaston ruled that neither owner nor overseer "has the right to kill a slave for a simple act of disobedience."[43]

The situation was still unresolved in Tennessee in 1845, when a local court held that it knew of no punishment it could inflict for manslaughter when a slave killed a free man, and that therefore a slave could only be tried for murder. In this case the murdered man was a total stranger, not the slave's owner or overseer, and had brutally assaulted the slave. The Supreme Court of Tennessee, in Nelson v. the State, in 1850, agreeing with the North Carolina verdict in State v. Hale that "an assault and battery [wantonly committed] upon a slave by a stranger is indictable," overturned the lower court's verdict and held that a manslaughter verdict was possible for a slave and remanded the case for a retrial.[44]

Sanctions in Islamic law were usually the same for free men and for slaves, part of the recognition that the slave is expected soon to be integrated into the society as one of its members. Thus, while a slave would be put to death for murdering a Muslim but a free Muslim would not be executed for killing a slave,

---

40. Goldin, p. 145.
41. Rose, p. 195. (The owner received no compensation when he was to blame for the offense, or when the slave was executed for insurrection or rebellion.)
42. Ibid., p. 176.
43. Shtaerman, p. 81.
44. Catterall, 2: 543-44; Rose, pp. 228-38.

for theft both could expect to have a hand cut off, for apostasy both would be put to death.[45] This is a part of the Mosaic lex talionis tradition, which tried, by resorting to "an eye for an eye, a tooth for a tooth" punishments, to overcome stratified sanctions that depended upon the social positions of the criminal and the offended. Thus lex talionis did not apply between slave and the free, but both suffered similar sanctions for offenses outside of that sphere. In pre-sixteenth-century Crimea, court status depended upon whether a person was a Muslim or a non-Muslim, and was the same for both slave and free in each category.[46]

Advanced legal systems elaborately differentiate civil and criminal wrongs. That was not the case in the abridged *Russkaia Pravda,* where the dyadic nature of the legal process considered what we could call criminal offenses to be torts, remediable by monetary compensation. That being the case, the early Muscovite (like the Roman and German) slaveowner's responsibility for his slave's criminal deeds was minimally distinguishable, as we shall see, from his responsibility for any other delict committed by his chattel.

The slaveowner was thus responsible for theft by a fugitive slave (article 120). In case of robbery, the owner had a choice: he might surrender the slave to the victim or compensate him. The article (121) is not totally clear about what is to happen should the robber be married and have offspring and they were not implicated in the crime. Apparently the slaveowner either had to surrender the entire family to the victim or redeem all of them. The *Pravda* provided that thieves were not to be fined, but rather they (or, most likely, their owners) had to pay double damages to the victims (article 46). This reflects the traditional fact that slaves, as things, cannot be punished by the civil authority, which barely recognizes their existence. In the last versions of the *Pravda*, article 46 was changed to require that slave robbers be surrendered to the jurisdiction of the court of the grand prince and his boyars, not for the imposition of sanctions against the slave but just to determine the fine the slaveowner would have to pay.[47] The slaveowner still had to compensate the plaintiff for his losses. Here we see some unraveling of the dyadic justice framework, but the refusal to recognise the slave as a responsible party still remains an established principle. This norm of slaveowner responsibility for his irresponsible chattel's criminal acts was made explicit in medieval Germanic law and in Lithuanian law, such as the *Sudebnik* of 1468.[48]

45. Brunschvig, p. 29. For lesser infractions, such as drinking wine, slander, or whoredom, slaves were subject to half the punishment of free persons, forty or fifty stripes instead of eighty or one hundred (Hamilton, *The Hedaya*, pp. 178-79, 196-97).

46. Fisher, "Muscovy," p. 585.

47. Kolycheva, *Kholopstvo*, pp. 227-28.

48. Ibid., p. 230; Wergeland, p. 35. In China, the slaveowner was made responsible for his slave's acts by analogy with a father's responsibility for his sons' criminal acts (Meijer, p. 334).

In cases of assault, the slaveowner who refused to surrender the offending slave had to pay a fine of 12 grivnas for him (article 65). That did not put an end to the matter, however: the offended free man had the right to apprehend the slave and lash the culprit himself (a perfect expression of dyadic justice: the state power, which barely exists, does not step in, even to mete out justice), or else he might accept a grivna in compensation for the offense.

Khovanskoi v. Skobel'tsyn

We may assume that the slaveowner would try to surrender a convicted thief to whom he felt little attachment to the plaintiff whenever the damages awarded exceeded the value of the slave. However, the extant evidence indicates that throughout the sixteenth century this was not permitted, and in all instances the slaveowner was obliged to repay the value of whatever his slave had stolen.

In a 1517/18 case tried before the governor of Dmitrov, *boiarin* Danilo Fedorovich Vel'iaminov, one Iakushka Ugrimov (initially of Novgorod), while a slave of Il'ia Fedorov Skobel'tsyn, had stolen 30 rubles' worth of property from Ivan Vasil'evich Khovanskoi. Litigating for Khovanskoi was Misha Iur'ev, no doubt his elite slave. The plaintiff was a minor dignitary of the first half of the sixteenth century whose clan claimed to have descended from Lithuanian Prince Gedymin and then come to Muscovy in the early fifteenth century. The plaintiff himself had been a boyar of Prince Boris Vasil'evich Volotskii and gave the great monastery at Volokolamsk 100 cheti of grain per year.[49] I know nothing about the defendant, and what role the apparent inequality of the litigants played in the verdict is not evident. Usually such cases were decided on their merits, and we may assume that this was the case in this instance. Iakushka was turned over as a surety slave to Khovanskoi, until that time when Skobel'tsyn might ransom him. Judging by the verdict, we may assume that an attempt was made to force Skobel'tsyn to pay the entire sum and take back Iakushka, even though he was not worth 30 rubles and Skobel'tsyn probably would have preferred to surrender the slave rather than to pay the sum.[50]

Metropolitan's Peasants v. Okinfov et al.

A 1521 case tried before the boyars Grigorii Fedorovich Davydov and Mikhailo Iur'evich Zakhar'in also illustrates this point of slave law and elucidates other aspects of slavery as well. For these reasons, as well as for the flavor of early Muscovy that it conveys, the case is worth summarizing in some detail. Eight peasants subject to the Metropolitan, the head of the Russian Orthodox church, filed a suit against one Pavel Chudinov Okinfov, his slave Sukhoi, three of his peasants, and a priest, Ivan Semenov. The plaintiffs charged that the defendants

49. "Rodoslovnaia kniga," *Vremennik* 10(1851): 80, 136, 225; Petrov, IRRD 1(1886): 173; Zimin, *Krupnaia*, p. 107.
50. Kolycheva, *Kholopstvo*, p. 228; RIB 17(1898): 113-14, no. 314.

had attacked them and in the course of the raid had stolen 15 rubles' worth of property in the form of horses, coats, shirts, axes, plows, grain, and cash, all of which were itemized. The attackers also were charged with breaking one man's arms and legs, although during the course of the trial, when the victim was brought in, it appeared as though only both of his legs had been broken (the right one had a compound fracture).

During the trial Okinfov initiated a countersuit on behalf of another of his slaves, Iakush, claiming that earlier the Metropolitan's peasants had come to Okinfov's father's village during the son's absence and assaulted Iakush. During the raid they had plundered the slave's house and stolen 7 rubles' worth of property in the form of three horses, two oxen, implements, a sheepskin coat, and some oats. During the trial Okinfov admitted that his slave Iakush had no evidence to prove who had plundered him and, moreover, had not sent for an agent of the court (*pristav*) after the alleged attack to hunt down the culprits. Okinfov thus was trying to make it look as though the raid that was the subject of the initial suit (of which he had disclaimed knowledge) might have been in retaliation for an earlier raid by the Metropolitan's peasants against another of his slaves. His inability to substantiate the charges of an earlier raid against his slave Iakush seems to have left the judges in a dubious frame of mind. Nevertheless, that was an inadequate basis for resolving the case.

Muscovite judges needed more solid evidence for awarding a verdict, if they could get it, and an appeal to divine justice was one such avenue. Both litigating sides in the case of eight peasants of the Metropolitan v. Okinfov et al. agreed to resolve the case by appeal to God's justice, either through kissing the cross or trial by combat. The judges ordered that a trial by combat be held in Moscow, and the Metropolitan's peasants were to fight Okinfov's two slaves and the three peasants. Okinfov was for some reason excused from the combat. Nothing was said about the priest, who should have been excused according to canon law, and the priest appeared 'on the field of battle along with Okinfov's two slaves and the three peasants. All appeared for the trial by combat, as ordered, and all but one remained there eight days. Apparently no combat was initiated. About the second day, Okinfov's slave Iakushko, the alleged victim of the putative initial raid, apparently fearing God's wrath, fled from the field, and his owner confessed that he did not know where his slave had gone. Twentieth-century readers skeptical about the efficacy of appeals to divine justice should note that it apparently worked in this case; justice was revealed, and the verdict was awarded to the Metropolitan's peasants.

The judges awarded the full 15 rubles claimed, and assigned shares of 5 rubles to the two slaves (even though only one, Sukhoi, had been charged in the peasants' suit). The other 10 rubles in damages were assessed against the peasants and the priest, who also were made to pay an additional 2 rubles to the maimed peasant. The cash was paid. For my purposes, I note that the slaveowner Okinfov had to pay the damages for his slaves, even though at least one of them,

Iakush, apparently was in possession of sufficient property to satisfy a 2.50-ruble verdict.[51] I should also stress again that the slaves were persons in every other respect in the eyes of the court: the terminology of Okinfov's suing for his slave Iakush is exactly the same as if the slave had been suing for his owner, or as it was in the case of the one peasant plaintiff who was representing the others. Moreover, a priori, one might not have expected the slaves to participate in the trial by combat.

Roughly the same group had another encounter four years later. This time Grand Prince Vasilii Ivanovich himself tried the case. The same peasants of the Metropolitan initiated a complaint against slaves of Chudin Okinfov (Pavel Chudinov Okinfov's father)—Kozel, the familiar Sukhoi, Andreiko Khromoi, and a group of Chudin's peasants were accused of stealing four cows and twenty sheep. The aggrieved peasants had gone to Kozel, Okinfov's steward, to complain, but he and his fellows assaulted them, set their dogs on them and killed one of the peasants. They also stole the deceased's horse with saddle and bridle, his clothing, and cash he was carrying. The plaintiffs also observed that the deceased had left debts totalling 4.25 rubles in cash plus grain debts of 10 chetverti of rye and 7 chetverti of oats. The theft amounted in value to 4.48 rubles, plus the deceased's debts and the value of his person. Again a trial by combat was proposed, and the accused, who had denied the accusations, accepted the challenge.

Slaveowner Chudin Okinfov then filed the customary countercharges: forces of the Metropolitan had come with a "thousand axes," invaded his property, chopped down a forest, plowed up the land, taken possession, and settled it. Okinfov had filed charges, but the Metropolitan's *deti boiarskie* had not bothered to appear for the trial.

Then he added the 1521 story, changing some of the details: after the attack by the Metropolitan's peasants, Okinfov claimed, Iakush had called a constable (*pristav*) from Moscow to pursue the culprits. The trial by combat was held, Iakush had gone to the Neglinnaia River for water and disappeared. Pavel Okinfov had asked for permission to hunt for Iakush, but this had been denied. We also learn that the governor of Iur'ev had charged 10 rubles for the trial.

Okinfov claimed that he then had initiated a hunt for his fugitive slave Iakush, who had disappeared from the dueling field, and that another slave, Gavrilko, had found him chained under a grain drier in a distant village near Rostov belonging to the Metropolitan. Gavrilko allegedly had freed Iakush but was pursued by the Metropolitan's peasants, who assaulted Gavrilko and, it is implied, again kidnapped Iakush. This was the very serious charge of "slave theft," one

---

51. Kolycheva, p. 228; AFZKh 1: 13-17, no. 1a. On the institution of trial by combat, see H. W. Dewey, "Trial by Combat in Muscovite Russia," *Oxford Slavonic Papers* 9(1960): 21-31.

of the few capital crimes in early Muscovy. Okinfov noted that his losses on the case so far had amounted to 38.50 rubles. The slave Gavrilko repeated the story for the court, noting that he had been walking by the grain drier when someone called out, and it just happened to be Iakush—obviously a suspicious coincidence.

Grand Prince Vasilii Ivanovich ordered the Metropolitan's forces to answer the charges, which they denied. A slave by the name of Danilko represented the Metropolitan's *syn boiarskii* Fedor Manuilov. They accused Chudin of fabricating the case to offset their charges of murder and robbery.

Gavrilko, Chudin's slave, admitted that he had no evidence in the matter of finding Iakush, and said that he had not filed charges about the matter in the area of the grain drier because it belonged to the Metropolitan. Note again that a slave is not only testifying in court but also had the authority on his own to file charges in court. At this moment the 1521 judgment charter was read.

Then Grand Prince Vasilii issued his verdict, in favor of the Metropolitan's peasants and *deti boiarskie*, against Chudin, his peasants, and his slaves. He declared that the countersuit was a ruse, unsupported by evidence. Later in Muscovite legal history such perjury as was obvious in the "slave theft" fabrication would have been treated far less lightly, for those who initiated false charges were liable to suffer the same penalties as those they slanderously accused—in this case, capital punishment. However, in 1525 state interest in the legal process had not progressed to the point where such a concept could be envisaged, with the consequence that sanctions were prescribed only for known felons who made false accusations.[52]

Chudin's slave Kozel and his peasants were ordered to pay the damages: 4.48 rubles for the robbery, 4 rubles for the murder, the murdered man's debts of 4.25 rubles, the 17 chetverti of grain, and the court costs. Here, it should be noted, the costs were assessed directly against Kozel, with no mention being made of his owner, Chudin, who happened to be in the court at the time of the trial. Whether this was an oversight on the part of Grand Prince Vasilii, or a recognition of Kozel's full judicial capacity to answer for his own crimes, is not clear. (The Grand Prince also ordered that the boundary dispute be resolved in the favor of the Metropolitan's peasants, that the boundary be marked by the setting out of markers and the digging of pits.) However, regardless of the verdict, the sums were all collected from slaveowner Chudin Okinfov, both for the slave Kozel and for the peasants. He paid not only those damages, but the costs run up by his other slave, Gavrilko, in the matter of the expenses connected with the trial borne by the Metropolitan's peasants and *deti boiarskie*, including the slave Danilko.[53]

52. 1497 *Sudebnik* 39; 1550 *Sudebnik* 59; 1589 *Sudebnik* 113.
53. Alu, pp. 31-37, no. 17; AFZKh 1: 17-22, no. 2a; Dewey and Kleimola, *Private Law*, pp. 121-27. The surveying of the boundary between Okinfov's and the Metropolitan's properties was effected (AFZKh 1: 136-38, no. 156).

We should also take note of the fact that, while Okinfov was not charged with responsibility for his slave Kozel, he paid the damages assessed against not only Kozel and his other slave Danilko, but also the damages for which his peasants were responsible. The reasons for his doing so are clear. While the peasants were in no ways serfs, or otherwise legally dependant upon Okinfov, one may assume that they were unable to pay the damages; had Okinfov not paid them, the peasants would have been seized as debt slaves by the Metropolitan's peasants and *deti boiarskie*, and Okinfov then would have lost their rent.

In a third case from 1519/20, slaves and peasants belonging to M. I. Sudimantov were accused of systematically plundering monastery peasants. The court held that Sudimantov had to pay all of the damages, thereby applying to the peasants norms traditionally reserved for slaves. While it may have happened in this case as a matter of expediency (I have only Kolycheva's telegraphic summary to go by), by an inability to differentiate what was stolen by the peasants from what was stolen by the slaves, it was this kind of thinking that led ultimately to the abasement of the peasantry (and their enserfment) by analogy with slaves.[54]

It is striking that in these cases where fighting between slaves and free people occurred, no damages were assessed against the slaves for assaulting the free people. In the medieval *Russkaia Pravda* (article 65) a slave could be killed, or later publicly beaten or forced to pay compensation, for such an offense, but in the first half of the sixteenth century not even any monetary compensation was due the free man who had been so wronged by a slave. In the still primarily dyadic judicial process of the era, the state did not yet feel that it was worth its while to become involved in the fighting and brawling that probably were a feature of everyday Muscovite life.[55] Moreover, because so many slaves were native Russians, no need was felt to single them out as aliens who specially threatened the peace. Only with article 26 of the *Sudebnik* of 1550 on personal honor did the state power begin to become involved with such matters as brawling.

The motivation of all these laws, of course, was to induce owners to keep control of their slaves. It also should be apparent that the crime rate must have been relatively low during the *Pravda* era, for otherwise no one would have been able to afford the risks of slave ownership.

An illustration of Muscovite slave law in the case of a homicide was provided by the German mercenary Heinrich von Staden, who was in Muscovy during Ivan IV's Oprichnina. Suspicion of the murder of an arquebusier (*strelets*) fell on von Staden's slave, who was wearing the coat of the deceased. In his memoirs von Staden claimed that the *strelets* had given the coat to the slave in exchange for drink. Whatever the facts were, the court found the slave guilty of murder. The chief of the *strel'tsy*, who in all likelihood was a slaveowner himself, served

54. Kolycheva, p. 229.
55. Ibid., p. 209.

as next-of-kin in the prosecution, and therefore was the beneficiary of the verdict. The chief realized that the monetary compensation he would get for the dead musketeer was insignificant. The value of a murdered peasant was only 4 rubles, and the court probably would have held that the value of a *strelets* was only little higher, perhaps the amount of his annual compensation, which would have been about 5 rubles. Therefore the chief claimed that the *strelets* at the moment of his death had on his person gold worth 60 rubles. Von Staden was forced by the court to pay this sum for his servant.[56] At that time the traditional restraints that had held medieval society together were breaking down, and Muscovites were distressed by an apparent "crime wave." In spite of that fact, cash compensation still could be made for murder, for the law code of 1589 decreed capital punishment only for the crimes of horse theft, theft in a church, and theft (kidnapping) of another's slave.

The reign of Ivan IV was a great watershed in many realms of Muscovite law, but the responsibility of slaveowners for the criminal conduct of their slaves did not change. This is evident in two directives to provincial felony administrators (the *guba* system), one for Medyn', dated 1555, and the other for Zubtsov, dated 1556. In the realm of criminal law, a change was taking place, for the directives prescribe that slaves who confessed to having participated in robberies were to be executed. Thus the private vengeance possible in article 65 of the *Russkaia Pravda* was replaced by explicit state sanctions. But in conformity with former practices, tort damages in civil suits for robbery (only half of the sums claimed, however) were to be collected from the slaveowners either when the slaves had been apprehended, tried, and excuted, or when the slaves had been denounced but could not be apprehended for trial because they had fled or were otherwise inaccessible. Moreover, the slaveowners had to post a bond guaranteeing that they would surrender the slaves should they appear.[57]

Roughly the same provisions became part of the criminal law after the Time of Troubles. On June 25, 1628, the government of Patriarch Filaret consulted with boyars and issued a law on the responsibility of slaveowners to present their chattel for trial when the slaves were accused of horse theft or theft of other property of considerable value. They decreed that the owners had to present the slaves for a visual confrontation with their accusers on the appointed date, and prescribed a fine for the owner who refused. He was also to be held responsible for the plaintiff's claims. In a further attempt to force compliance, the boyars proposed that the slaveowner's richest slave be seized in the absence of the accused and tortured to learn the whereabouts of the absent slave, whether the accused slave was being concealed or had fled with-

---

56. Ibid., pp. 225-26; Heinrich von Staden, *The Land and Government of Muscovy*, trans. and ed. by Thomas Esper (Stanford: Stanford University Press, 1970), pp. 123-24.

57. PRP 4: 181-82, arts. 3, 4; Dewey, *Muscovite Judicial Texts*, p. 38; Akty Iushkova, p. 157; Kolycheva, p. 230.

out his owner's knowledge. These terms were also to be applied to peasants, should the person accused of the felony be a peasant.[58] This law became part of the *Ulozhenie* of 1649, where it was generalized: the specific criteria of the theft of a horse or property of considerable value became the theft of "anything." The clause about fining the slaveowner for the nonappearance of his slave was omitted.[59] Thus, while the slaveowner still was materially responsible for compensating the plaintiff for any damages his slave may have caused, between 1628 and 1649 slaveowners ceased to be materially responsible to the state for producing their accused slaves, and in fact the responsibility for determining the whereabouts of the slave was transferred by the state power to another slave. Once again provisions universally applicable to slaves here were transferred to the peasants as part of the enserfment process. The slaveowner was also held materially responsible for his chattel's wrongs even if the latter died before the case had been resolved.[60] The law assumed that some slaves living outside their owners' households might have property, and so prescribed that that property should be used to satisfy claimants, whether the slave was living or deceased.[61] All of these norms are typical of slave law in most systems.

If both slaves and their middle service class owners were accused of a felony, a visual confrontation with the accusers was to be arranged first. If torture seemed necessary to elicit the truth, the slaves were to be tortured first. But if warranted, *dvoriane* and *deti boiarskie* could be tortured as well. Nothing was said about slaveowners who were members of the upper service class based in Moscow in this law from the practice of the Felony Chancellery of 1616/17, which the *Ulozhenie* of 1649 ascribed to a 1596/97 origin. Once again, the same provisions in the extant seventeenth-century versions were extended to peasants as well as slaves, and one may surmise that this was true in the late 1590s as well.[62] This is a perfect example of class-structured criminal legislation: the lower classes were most suspect, the middle service class was less suspect but considered capable of felonious conduct, and the upper service class was omitted

58. UKRP 7; PRP 5: 205-6.

59. UKRP 13; 1649 *Ulozhenie* 21: 45; MS, pp. 299-300. Muscovy did not know so formally the two classes of slave rights that were present in Jamaica: rights *in rem* vis-à-vis other slaves on the plantation with respect to material possessions, and rights *in personam* against the slaveowner for future allowances, usufruct, and holidays (M. G. Smith, *B. W. I.,* p. 104). One may assume that a slaveowner adjudicated disputes over possession between his own slaves and that, in cases where there were many slaves, such tasks were probably assigned to one of the elite slave managers. As we saw in chapter 5, only very late in Muscovy did slaves enjoy rights *in personam,* such as holidays. As we shall see below, Muscovite slaves often got allowances, but they had no claims at law for them, other than the right to eat, which might be jeopardized by the cutting off of a monthly allowance.

60. UKRP, suppl. art. 1 (1624); 1649 *Ulozhenie* 21: 67; PRP 7: 419, art. 63.

61. 1649 *Ulozhenie* 21: 68 (also from UKRP 1624); PRP 7: 419, art. 64.

62. UKRP 15; 1649 *Ulozhenie* 21: 47; MS, pp. 300-301.

from regularly defined norms, which meant that the tsar could deal with its members in whatever arbitrary manner he felt most fitting.

The slaveowner also had to pay in instances where his slave without premeditation killed another slave. This is one of the few instances in which Muscovite law mentions one slave offending another (another was the barroom brawl involving slaves of different owners carrying on their masters' feuds discussed in chapter 5); one may assume that other cases would be handled as though the owner of one was injuring the owner of the other. Be that as it may, in this case of unpremeditated manslaughter the slaveowner had to turn the killer over to the owner of the deceased, or else pay 50 rubles should the bereaved owner claim that the killer was a confirmed felon and refuse to take him. Moreover, the owner of the killer had to surrender the latter's wife and children, and could not get back in exchange any wife and children the dead man may have left. However, the killer himself did not get off scotfree any more, for the state assumed him to be a person with volition. Let us quote the original, to get some of the flavor of late Muscovite legal philosophy:

If a homicide is committed somewhere in the towns, the posads, and settlements, in the villages and hamlets in the provinces, one slave beats to death another slave, torture that killer who committed the homicide to determine whether it was done with intent, or while drunk, but without intent. If the killer says under torture that he killed without intent, in a fight while drunk, then, having beaten that killer with the knout, write up a written pledge on him guaranteeing that he will not in the future commit any felonies, and, having gotten the pledge on him, give him to the person whose slave he killed, with his wife and children, as slaves, and do not take away the wife and children of the deceased slave from the slaveowner whose slave was killed. If the plaintiff begins to petition about a debt he was owed by the murdered man, reject the claim for debt.

If that person to whom they begin to hand over the killer to replace his deceased slave says that the killer is a habitual felon, and that he is unable to take him into his household, he shall exact 50 rubles for his deceased slave from the person whom the killer is serving.[63]

These laws, dating from 1625, thus make the slave pay for unintentional homicide in three ways: (1) Muscovite torture certainly was unpleasant enough; (2) a beating with the knout was enough to kill almost anyone, but not quite, for that would have deprived the plaintiff of his slave; (3) being transferred to a new owner also contained its own traumas, as did having to live near the dead man's wife and offspring. Given the nature of the Muscovite legislative process, one may assume that these norms arose from actual practice. No doubt the initial case arose during a drunken brawl, and hurried compilers of the *Ulozhenie*

63. 1649 *Ulozhenie* 21: 69-70.

assumed that this was typical enough to allow those rather specific circumstances to remain in the generalized summary norms. The Byzantine norm of the inviolability of marriage is preserved here.

For the sake of comparison, I might note that the Alabama Slave Code of 1852 also dealt with the slave who was guilty of manslaughter of another slave, and prescribed that he be beaten for up to one hundred stripes, or branded in the hand, or both.[64] Under other provisions of the law, the slaveowner whose chattel was killed had to sue the killer's owner for the lost value of his deceased slave. Certainly the Muscovite solution was more expeditious, but then we must recall that the early modern Russians did not have hordes of lawyers who had to make their livings from the complexity of the law.

In cases of deliberate felonious assault, slaves were held by late Muscovite law to be more culpable than nonslaves. If an ordinary person invited someone to his house, or dragged him there by force, and then proceeded to beat him with a cudgel, a knout, or a whip, he was to be beaten with the knout in the marketplace and then jailed for a month. Moreover, the person so assaulted had the right to claim from his tormentor a double dishonor payment.[65] If a slave did the same thing, however, he was first to be tortured to learn whether he had acted on his own initiative. If he had acted at his owner's, or another person's, behest, all parties were to be beaten with the knout and jailed. But if the slave acted on his own volition, he was to be tortured and then put to death.[66] As we have seen, more severe punishment for slaves is by no means unusual in slave systems. What is apparent is that Muscovite legislators had not made up their minds on the issue.

These principles were generalized in norms consciously borrowed from Lithuanian practice. When a slave killed or wounded a third party while defending his owner, the slave was not to be accused of any crime, and the slaveowner was to be interrogated about the murder.[67] But if the slave killed someone without his owner's knowledge, and the owner brought the slave in and reported the homicide, the owner was not to be accused of the murder, and the slave was to be executed.[68] The article contains the assumption that the owner was generally responsible for his slave's actions, that other people in fact believed the same, but an exception was to be made for murder.

The slaveowner's power of life and death over his slave was epitomized in a 1616/17 law from the practice of the Felony Chancellery which allowed slaveowners to bring in their chattel (including peasants) and accuse them of a

64. Rose, p. 194.

65. 1649 *Ulozhenie* 22: 11; PRP 7: 427, art. 95.

66. 1649 *Ulozhenie* 22: 12; PRP 7: 427, arts. 96-97.

67. 1649 *Ulozhenie* 22: 21. A marginal notation says that this was borrowed from [1588] LS [11:1, 25].

68. 1649 *Ulozhenie* 22: 22. A marginal notation on the scroll copy says it was borrowed from [1588] LS [11: 25].

specific robbery, theft, or membership in an outlaw gang. No other accusation was necessary. The authorities were supposed to interrogate the accused slave, torture him without having conducted the usual preliminary investigation, and promulgate an appropriate verdict. This was a fundamental law of Muscovy throughout the seventeenth century.[69]

Slaveowners had to surrender to criminal authorities their slaves accused by strangers of committing the major felonies of robbery and theft. If they refused, they had to pay for the crimes and post a bond guaranteeing that they would produce the accused slaves, as had been required in the *guba* charters a century earlier.[70] A landholder who investigated a felony case himself, involving his slaves (or his peasants) and then executed them because he did not want to turn them over to the *guba* authorities, was to have his service estate confiscated and to pay damages that were due because of the criminals' behavior. If the same offense was committed by a person who did not have a service estate, he was to be ruthlessly punished for the offense by means of a public lashing with the knout in the marketplace, and then assume responsibility for material damages. Finally, if a lord's peasants or slaves themselves put someone to death for having committed a crime without their lord's knowledge, they themselves were to be executed "without any mercy."[71] This reminds us of Roman law's assertion for the state of the sole right to impose on slaves major sanctions such as the death penalty or exile to the mines.[72]

Procedurally, a medieval treaty between Novgorod and its princes prescribed that no slave was to be tried before a court except in the presence of his owner. This protection of the master's interest was not spelled out elsewhere or in later Muscovy, although one may assume that it was practiced.[73] This was the norm in other slave systems as well. Notice to slaveowners about the prosecution of their slaves by the state was required in Louisiana in 1824.[74] When Muscovite slaves were examined by a court, they had the right to confront their accusers.[75] Accused slaves could be tortured in the criminal process, and, if they denounced their owners, the latter could in turn be tortured to learn of any complicity.[76] The assumption there, as in other provisions concerning offenses committed by slaves against strangers, was that there was a good chance that the deed had been

---

69. UKRP 16; 1649 *Ulozhenie* 21: 48; PRP 7: 412-13, art. 42. The last did not allow lords to accuse hired housemen and articulated a fear that the law might be used to convert such individuals into slaves or serfs.

70. 1649 *Ulozhenie* 21: 45-46, 66.

71. UKRP 60 (of 1619); PRP 5: 200; 1649 *Ulozhenie* 21: 79-80; PRP 7: 413, art. 43.

72. Buckland, pp. 91, 94.

73. Sergeevich, *Drevnosti*, 1: 118, 120.

74. Rose, p. 176.

75. UKRP 7 (1628); 1649 *Ulozhenie* 21: 45, 74.

76. 1649 *Ulozhenie* 21: 47.

committed at the behest of an owner, that the slave was not acting on his own volition.[77]

We may assume that the slaveowner was totally responsible for his dependent's behavior and was expected to correct the slave and punish him for every infraction other than those major felonies over which the state had assumed jurisdiction. This was an integral part of chattel slavery. Except in the most egregious instances, the state disregarded the personality of the slave and his capacity for both moral and immoral actions, control of which was thereby committed to the owner. Muscovite law had no special provisions about a slave's injuring the honor of free men. Germanic law found that to be a contradiction in terms: the abusive language of a slave could not injure anybody's honor, except when the assumption was made that the slave was the mouthpiece of his owner.[78] We may assume that the Muscovite free man whose honor was injured by a slave could try first to collect from the slave but ultimately would probably collect from the slaveowner.

The *Ulozhenie* described a situation which is known to have occurred many times in Muscovite history and which further illustrates the semiautonomy vis-à-vis strangers that slaves came to enjoy in the eyes of the law. When an agent of the court, or the local people he had selected as witnesses or otherwise deputized, appeared to serve a summons, deliver a verdict, or present any other official documents, the citizenry were supposed to be decorous and obedient. However, as the law observed, sometimes slaves and peasants, both with and without their owners' and landlords' knowledge and approval, assaulted the governmental agents, or took away and ripped up their precious written documents. If the lord himself engaged in such activity, or directed his subjects to, he was to be beaten with the knout, jailed for three months, and required to pay a double dishonor payment to the offended governmental official; if the official died, the killer had to pay the recorded debts of the deceased and was to be executed. However, if the dishonor or assault occurred while the lord was absent, and the official sued him and he disclaimed any knowledge of the event, a trial had to be granted to determine the facts. If it was determined that the slaves and peasants had acted on their own initiative, they were to be beaten with the knout, and they had to pay the damages. This law, consciously adapted from the *Lithuanian Statute* of 1588 to late Muscovite conditions, also contained sanctions for officials who filed false accusations of this type: the offending officials were to be beaten with the knout and fined 2 rubles.[79] In this law nothing is stipulated about a

---

77. Ibid., 22: 12.

78. Klein, *Americas,* p. 48; Wergeland, p. 36. The slave was also held personally responsible when, without his owner's knowledge, he led a horse through the tsar's palace grounds. The slave was to be beaten with a knout, no sanction was imposed against his owner (Kotoshikhin, pp. 29-30).

79. 1588 LS 1: 24, 4: 11-i, ii, iv (Lappo, pp. 50, 126-27); 1649 *Ulozhenie* 10: 142-43.

slaveowner's being responsible for the conduct of his slaves, who themselves were held both corporally and materially responsible for their own wrongs. As in so many other instances in late Muscovite law, the peasants were abased by being equated with slaves, who in turn were elevated in law to the level of responsible human beings. This was one of the paradoxes of the development of early serf-dom. The precise influence of the *Lithuanian Statute* of 1588 cannot be deter-mined, but it well may have been significant, for that West Russian code no long-er recognized slaves but only peasants (*slugi i poddanye*), and prescribed that they be jailed for six months when a trial supported their lord's contention that he had not been involved in the assault on the official. Thus simply by analogy with the Lithuanian situation the late Muscovite slave may have been made re-sponsible for his own actions, in this instance. The provision for slave responsi-bility was consistent with seventeenth-century Muscovite practice, dating from at least 1624, assigning material responsibility for felonious acts to slaves who lived outside their owners' households and had their own assets.[80]

There is some evidence of crime committed by urban slaves, qua slaves, in the seventeenth century, particularly to get commodities to sell, but the Muscovite state never went to the lengths that some New World lawgivers did. For example, many restrictions on slave engagement in commerce had as their purpose not only securing preferment for whites but, particularly, curtailing opportunities for slaves to dispose of stolen goods.[81] The Muscovites had no grounds for as-suming that slaves were potentially more culpable than other members of the lower classes, from whom slaves ordinarily could not be differentiated, and so taking steps similar to those taken in North America would have been pointless.

The person familiar with the American law of slavery might well wonder where the Muscovite statutes on the rape of nonmistress women were in Muscovy, for that seems to have been one of the major concerns of Southern law.[82] The fact is that Muscovite law did not worry about this topic in the criminal law. Rapists, of whatever origin, were dealt with summarily by church law, which made no distinction between free and slave rapists.

The selling of illegal spirits was of much greater interest to late Muscovite legislators, for the state's monopoly control over the sale of alcohol was one of its major sources of revenue. Slaves, judging by the law, were involved in the illegal sale of spirits, and elaborate investigations and sanctions were prescribed. The first task was to determine whether the slaves were selling the alcohol with their owners' knowledge, or whether the former had stolen it from the latter (who had the right to brew specified amounts for their own consumption). The slaves were to be tortured to determine what their owners knew. If they knew nothing about it, then the slaves were to be beaten with the knout in

80. UKRP, supp. art. 5; PRP 5: 203; 1649 *Ulozhenie* 21: 68.
81. Goldin, p. 47.
82. Friedman, p. 200.

the marketplace and returned to their owners, who were advised to take more care that their dependents (including peasants) did not sell spirits. But if a second offense occurred, the recidivists were again to be beaten with the knout in the marketplace and jailed until the tsar ordered them released. Their owners were to be fined 10 rubles for each slave involved.[83] Once again, slaves were thought to have volition that their owners might not be able to control and should not be held responsible for the first time. But, in a spirit of compromise that recognized both the slave's volition and the fact that he was his owner's property, the owner was held responsible for his chattel's wrong after a warning had been given.

The position of the slave in the criminal law at the time of the *Ulozhenie* was considerably different from what it had been two centuries earlier. Two largely independent developments were responsible. First, the state assumed a much larger role in the criminal process in general, which was no longer dyadic but had become almost completely triadic. This was true for everyone, whether free or slave. Second, the slave changed, in the eye of the law, from a largely volitionless chattel not responsible for most of its own actions to a human being whose actions could be controlled by a combination of inner motivation (which could be partially created by the state) and owner compulsion.[84]

The Slave in Civil Transactions with Strangers

Wide differences are notable among slave systems in the degree of latitude they allowed slaves to deal with third parties in various transactions. There was also a considerable range in the responsibility assigned to the slaveowner in those systems that permitted such transactions.

Slaves in the Ancient Near East were allowed to engage in business transactions, and dealt with all parties (their owners, the temple, and other third parties) on a basis of equality.[85] On the other hand, the ancient Athenians made slaveowners responsible for all *delicta* committed by slaves. While slaves were allowed to engage in transactions and might be cited as defendants in litigation, the persons benefiting from possessing the slaves were held to be legally responsible.[86]

These principles became elaborately refined in the Roman Principate. The owner was held responsible for all debts and contracts of his slaves, unless he had openly disclaimed responsibility beforehand. In the latter event, procedures were

83. 1649 *Ulozhenie* 25:6.
84. Kaiser, "Transformation." On slave material responsibility for insult, assault, and robbery, see Novosel'skii, *Votchinnik*, p. 64.
85. Mendelsohn, p. 68.
86. Westermann, p. 10.

prescribed whereby the creditor could collect either from the stock of the business or the slave's peculium. In other cases, the Roman slaveowner's liability for his slave was limited to the value of the slave, and he could free himself from liability by handing over the chattel.[87] In Islam, a master was held not to be responsible for debts incurred by his slave, presumably on the theory that creditors should have better sense than to lend to a slave. However, when such debts were incurred, the schools of Islamic law were split on the remedies available to the creditor. Some held that the creditor might seize the person of the indebted slave, others that the debtor should settle with his creditors after he was emancipated.[88] Louisiana practice was similar. A master was responsible for a slave's business transactions at his command, but he was responsible only to the extent that he had benefitted when the slave was acting without authorization.[89]

The *Russkaia Pravda* provided that a person who loaned money to a slave could not collect at law from the slave if he knew the borrower was a slave; if he did not, however, the slave's owner had to settle with the creditor, or else surrender the slave (article 116). When an owner authorized his slave to trade for him, the former was responsible for the latter's debts and had the right to pay them in cash, rather than surrendering the person of the slave to a creditor (article 117). The real danger inherent in slaveownership was obvious in a stipulation that a master was responsible for any debts his slave might incur while a fugitive; the fact that the owner, claiming the slave and paying the obligations, could also take the goods involved would have been small consolation in the likelihood that the purchases had been dissipated (article 119).

A mortgage document dated 1529 illustrates the civil capacity of slaves in the sphere of transactions. One Vlas Nikitin Friazinov, together with his two slaves, Ivashko Ivanov and Ontsifor Shchiga Ivanov, borrowed 4 rubles in cash from a servitor (*sluga*, a near-slave) of the Kirillov monastery, one Dementii Ivanov. As surety, they mortgaged a hay meadow, which the monastery was permitted to mow in lieu of interest, a form of antichresis. In case Friazinov did not have the money on the date due, the monastery could continue to mow the meadow. In form, this of course is much like the limited service slavery contract: the creditor has use of the property until the loan is repaid. In this case, both Friazinov and his slaves were answerable for the principal by the same terminology that was used for partnerships of free men: "I with my slaves [am responsible] for the cash."[90] Thus the slaves are equal partners with their owner in the transaction, and any of them can answer for the others in court.

87. Jones, p. 195; Buckland, p. 123.
88. Brunschvig, p. 29.
89. Rose, p. 176.
90. AIu, pp. 261-62, no. 237; RIB 32(1915): 197-98, no. 120. For an example of a loan to a slave, see the mid-sixteenth-century 15-ruble loan to Gus', slave of a governor (*namestnik*), I. V. Polev (A. I. Kopanev, *Krest'ianstvo russkogo Severa v XVI v.* [Leningrad: Nauka, 1978], p. 206).

In the final reckoning, however, Muscovite lawmakers assigned unconditional responsibility to owners for losses caused by their slaves. A 1571 directive on the management of the *guba* system in Beloozero, north of Moscow, expresses the frequent suspicion of plaintiffs' claims for damages and allows creditors to collect only half of their losses from the slaveowners. In the *Ulozhenie* of 1649, however, no limit is placed on claims or the payment of damages.[91] While this is a chapter on felonies, one may assume that the same principle was applicable in civil affairs as well. Analogously, in a provision dating from 1642, the law held that, when felonies were committed by slaves living outside their owners' households, damages were to be collected from their own properties.[92] Usually, one may assume, slaves had no assets, and owners were held responsible for the deeds of their human chattel. Even in those cases, however, slaves answered for themselves in court and were permitted to take an oath.[93]

Muscovite civil law assumed that a slave could speak for himself in court, and forbade an opposing litigant to call the slave's owner in the case. (This follows an article forbidding a litigant to call his opponent's wife to testify, a principle known in modern jurisprudence as well.)[94] The reason for these exemptions is obvious: the Muscovites, like other civilized peoples, had no desire to atomize the family, and considered that forcing intimate family members to testify against one another was not worth the price. On the other hand, the law did allow parents to be summoned by the opponent in litigation.[95] This shows that the slave was considered to be a closer member of the Muscovite nuclear family than were parents, who usually lived in separate domiciles.

Muscovite law allowed slaves on their own behalf to sue not only free people but other slaves. The defendant in such a case had to take the oath himself. Whereas a free man could have a slave take the oath for him, the law did not allow the defendant's owner to pick another slave to take the oath for him.[96]

For contrast, one must compare this with practices elsewhere. The laws of Eshnunna (about 1900 B.C.) forbade slaves to make investments or take out mortgages. Thai law forbade a slave to enter into contracts without his owner's permission.[97] The Louisiana Slave Code of 1824 prescribed that "the slave is incapable of making any kind of contract, except those which relate to his own

---

91. Sergeevich, 1: 113-14; 1649 *Ulozhenie* 21: 66.

92. UKRP, supp. art. 5; PRP 5: 203; 1649 *Ulozhenie* 21: 68.

93 AI, 1, no. 134–xx; Sergeevich, 1:140. An exception to the rule that the slave usually answered in court for his actions was provided in the case Zheliabuzhskii v. Lobanov-Rostovskii (Iakovlev, *Kholopstvo*, pp. 344-59). It is fairly clear that the real defendant in the case was Lobanov-Rostovskii's slave Ivan Kozimerov, who did not appear. What went on at the trial seems to explain Kozimerov's absence: Lobanov-Rostovskii thought he could bluff the case, something that even an elite slave probably would have had difficulty doing.

94. 1649 *Ulozhenie* 10: 178.

95. Ibid., art. 177.

96. UKRP 11: 12; PRP 5: 216; 1649 *Ulozhenie* 14: 7.

97. Pritchard, p. 134, arts. 15-16; Turton, p. 270.

emancipation."[98] The suppression of the slave's personality in civil law was also complete in Alabama. Slaves could not make contracts, own property, sue, or be sued. In Creswell's Executor v. Walker (1860), the slave's legal status was described as "a complete annihilation of the will." The slave, held the court, had "no legal mind, no will which the law can recognize. . . . Because they are slaves, they are incapable of performing civil acts."[99]

"Keeping Their Place"

While Muscovite law regulated relations between individual slaves and individual nonslaves, no attempt was made to regulate relations between all slaves as a class and nonslaves. The fact that there were no formal legal sanctions against slaves who did not "keep their place" indicates that there was no fear of slaves, as well as the fact that the slaves were primarily Russians who were indistinguishable from the rest of the populace.

Noteworthy is the fact that there was no known system of marking, tattooing, or otherwise identifying (by such means as special clothing) slaves in Muscovy, as was done in other societies from China to Rome. The Chinese mutilated and tattooed their slaves to mark them as a base and ignoble class.[100] Slaves were also tattooed, branded, and tagged throughout the Ancient Near East, but not by the Greeks.[101]

The Muscovites never dreamed of making slaves wear badges, a common practice in cities of the American South.[102] In Muscovy there was no limitation on movement, as was the case in a number of slave societies.[103] There were no systems of passes or curfews. No attempt was made specifically to control drinking or other slave amusements.[104] Had thought been given to the matter, literacy would have been encouraged rather than forbidden. No attempt was made even to keep arms out of the hands of slaves.[105]

We may assume that no system of marking or of controlling slave mobility or assembly was instituted because slaves, as a class, were not viewed as a threat to the established order.[106] In fact, making slaves "keep their place" was impossible. Even their diversions were usually those of the rest of society, not alien ones

98. Rose, p. 176.

99. Catterall, 3: 247; Friedman, p. 197; Tushnet, *American Law*, pp. 213-15.

100. Pulleyblank, pp. 205-6.

101. Driver and Miles, 1: 306-9; Pritchard, p. 163. arts. 226-27; Mendelsohn, pp. 42-50, 104; Westermann, p. 19.

102. Goldin, p. 38.

103. Mellafe, p. 116; Klein, *Americas,* p. 48; Rose, p. 180.

104. Hall, pp. 174, 178-80, 182; Klein, p. 49; Rose, pp. 191, 225-26.

105. Hall, p. 177; Klein, p. 48; Friedman, pp. 75, 196; Rose, p. 182.

106. Rose, pp. 181, 183, 206-7.

that needed "correction." The Muscovites, unlike the Danes in the Virgin Islands in the first half of the eighteenth century, had no need or desire for conformity, predictability, and total regimentation of the slave community.[107] Most Muscovite slaves were natives of the lower classes who needed the relief provided by slavery, and the government's inaction in the sphere of controlling the slaves represented a recognition that there was little to fear from the lumpen of Muscovite society. As for the elite slaves, they were trusted—until the Time of Troubles; then they were phased out as rapidly as possible.

The Muscovite law of slavery was like that of other systems in that it devoted considerable attention to the legal relations between slaves and third party strangers. There seems to have been an evolution in the Muscovite law from the late *Russkaia Pravda,* which considered such relations primarily from the perspective of the slaveowner and the stranger, to the *Ulozhenie,* which complicated the issue by interjecting the state as well as the slave as a quasi-human being. This evolution conflicts with the general image of Kievan Rus' as a place perhaps "more humane" than Muscovy. In that respect, Kievan Rus' was perhaps more like Athens, where the free and wealthy elite were "really free," while slaves were almost totally deprived of any human rights or attributes. Continuing this analogy, we find that Muscovy was more like the Ancient Near East, "a world without free men, in the sense in which the West has come to understand that concept."[108] The evolution we have seen was caused by many factors, but certainly chief among them were the central importance of elite slavery in early Muscovy, the change from a dyadic to a triadic form of law, the likely diminution of war captives as the major source of slaves and their replacement by Russians selling themselves, the development of increasingly slavelike serfdom, and the influence of the Byzantine *Procheiros Nomos* and the *Lithuanian Statute* of 1588, two documents compiled at a time when slavery was on the wane in their respective societies. These factors combined to give the mid-seventeenth-century Muscovite slave a much more active role in judicial conflicts with strangers than the slave had had two centuries earlier. This evolution was facilitated by the fact that slaves as a class were not feared or segregated and thus were not for that reason prevented from participating in general Muscovite society, of which the judicial sector was a part.

107. Hall, p. 176.
108. Finley, "Greek Civilization," pp. 44-45.

7. Legal Relations between Slaveowners

Because the slave was viewed primarily as an object in Muscovite law, he was the object of contention between owners, and the legislators had to try to resolve such conflicts. These conflicts usually involved fugitive slaves in one way or another. Here I shall discuss also the legal ramifications of slaves who fled without involving third parties.

Slave Theft

Before discussing fugitives, I shall examine the issue of "slave theft," one of the classic concerns of slave law. In Mesopotamian Eshnunna, a person apprehended with a stolen (kidnapped) slave had to return him, and any official who seized a lost slave and failed to return him or her to the rightful owner within a week could be charged with slave theft. One may assume that there, as in later Babylonia, the penalty for slave theft was death.[1]

The issue was revived in the Mediterranean world. In ancient Corinth and Athens drastic penalties were prescribed for the person who stole another man's slave.[2] The problem was a live issue in the Roman Empire as well, and especially during the Principate, when a shortage of slaves occurred and kidnapping of others' slaves became a major tactic for trying to overcome the labor shortage. The great legal thinkers even came up with the brilliant notion that a fugitive slave was a thief of himself.[3] Medieval Ethiopian law required a person guilty of slave theft to return the stolen slave, plus another one of equal value. If the thief could not provide a second one or a cash equivalent, he himself was converted into a slave of the claimant. The Ottomans prescribed a fine for those who "stole or lured away" others' human chattel.[4] Slave theft was also an issue in American law, but the sanctions were highly variable: from two to five years imprisonment in the penitentiary in Virginia and Mississippi to the death

1. Pritchard, pp. 137, 140, arts. 7, 49-50.
2. Westermann, p. 15.
3. Buckland, p. 31; Max Weber, "The Social Causes of the Decay of Ancient Civilization," in *History of Western Civilization. Selected Readings,* topic 3, "The Christain Empire" (Chicago: The University of Chicago Press, 1953), p. 49. Even a perhaps less than great thinker, the author of *Athelstan's Laws,* had the same idea (Wergeland, p. 3).
4. *The Fetha Nagast,* p. 178; Fisher, "Ottoman Slavery," p. 31.

penalty without benefit of clergy in colonial Virginia, Alabama, and perhaps the District of Columbia.[5]

Theft of slaves was also a concern of medieval Lithuanian law.[6] In Russian law, it was the subject of articles 38 and 47 of the *Russkaia Pravda,* which allowed owners of stolen slaves great latitude in recovering them, and prescribed the maximum fine, 12 grivnas, plus court costs, for those who stole slaves. Article 38 was not included in the abridged redaction of the *Pravda.*[7] In the *Sudebnik* of 1497, the death penalty was prescribed for slave theft, as well as for theft from a church, and for the slave who killed or plotted against his owner (or is this regicide and rebellion?), the arsonist, the traitor, and the incorrigible recidivist felon.[8] The filing of charges of slave theft in the 1525 case of Metropolitan's peasants et al. v. Okinfov et al. was noted in chapter 6 above in the context of slaveowner responsibility for his chattel.

The death penalty for the person who stole from a church or kidnapped a slave was repeated in the *Sudebniki* of 1550 and 1589.[9] In 1589, however, the provision no longer made any sense for slave theft, perhaps because of faulty codification, perhaps because there was very little slavery in the Russian White Sea littoral region, perhaps because of all three reasons. The provision does not seem to have found its way into the *Ulozhenie* of 1649. Its parallel provision, punishment for church theft, was still viable, and in fact had been stepped up to provide that the person who stole from a church be executed "without any mercy," a gratuitous addition unknown to the *Sudebniki.*[10] One may surmise that the concept of "slave theft" had become obsolete in the second half of the sixteenth century.

A similar evolution had occurred in the Ancient Near East, where the crime was punished by severe sanctions in ancient Babylonia but seems to have become obsolete in the later neo-Babylonian period.[11] Moreover, as I noted, the same development happened in Virginia. The motivation of both the earlier and the later changes is not apparent, but in Muscovy the crime of slave theft was the product of a time when the slave was considered to be property with little or no volition of his own. By the second half of the seventeenth century, however, this view no longer prevailed, and the law seems to have concluded, in this respect, that slaves were human beings who could not be "stolen" but rather

5. Catterall, 1: 157, 219; 3: 141, 358; 4: 188.

6. 1468 *Sudebnik* 24; 1529 LS 12: 8; Kolycheva, *Kholopstvo,* p. 266.

7. Kolycheva, *Kholopstvo,* p. 223.

8. 1497 *Sudebnik* 9. This is a very controversial article. The problem is whether it involves felonious acts against the state, individuals, or both (Grekov, *Sudebnik,* p. 58; PRP 3: 347, 359; Dewey, MJT, p. 10).

9. PRP 4: 246, 426, 505; 1497 *Sudebnik* 9; 1550 *Sudebnik* 55; 1589 *Sudebnik* 107; 1607 *Sudebnik* 8: 55.

10. 1649 *Ulozhenie* 21: 14.

11. Mendelsohn, p. 62.

were volitional creatures who either fled from their owners to other ones, or at least minimally collaborated in their "abduction," and thus that the situation should be handled as a form of slave flight rather than as theft. Throughout the history of medieval and early modern Russian law many slaves were native Russians, but this type probably began to predominate by the second half of the sixteenth century, particularly with the lessening of the number of military captives. One can conceive of the "theft" of an alien slave, who had no command of Russian and was linguistically marked and helpless in a foreign milieu. Certainly, however, this would be true to a far lesser extent for native Russians who were fully at home in Muscovy, and in fact well may have traveled rather widely before selling themselves into bondage. For these reasons one may surmise that the ancient concept of "slave theft" lost its meaning in later Muscovite history. (One might also surmise that the relatively low price of slaves had something to do with the disappearance of the concept of slave theft. However, this seems unlikely, for the cost of a slave was still a not insignificant sum, as is shown in chapter 10. Moreover, the relative price of slaves did not change significantly throughout the period. The development of serfdom might also be considered in the context of the demise of the concept of slave theft. Much of the Muscovite law of slavery was applied to the evolving institution of serfdom. Had the law of slave theft been applied to kidnappers and enticers of other lords' serfs, capital punishment would have seriously depleted the Muscovite upper and middle service classes. That never happened, although the analogy must have been obvious. This might be another reason why the crime of slave theft disappeared in the late sixteenth century.)

Fugitives

The problem of fugitives occupies much of the attention of any legislator on slavery. At this point he confronts the major dilemma presented by slavery: is the issue one of property or of human beings with volition? If it is the former, slaves can be primarily the object of civil legislation, as was the case in classical Greece.[12] But if they are human beings, then they tend to become the subject of the laws, a concern for political legislation. That was what happened when the ancient Greeks prescribed that the fugitive, after recapture, be branded.[13] Roman law, on the other hand, provided no sanctions for fugitive slaves, unless they pretended to be free. In normal circumstances, fugitive slaves were simply returned to their owners.[14]

While the supply of slaves from Africa was strong, New World laws dealt es-

12. Westermann, p. 15.
13. Rose, p. 209.
14. Buckland, p. 268.

pecially harshly with fugitive slaves. In Spanish colonies a slave was hanged if absent longer than six months, and the same penalty for an absence of thirty days was applied in the English colony of Barbados until the year 1819.[15] Almost half of the clauses of the 1733 Danish Virgin Islands slave code dealt with the problem of fugitives. Actual or contemplated marronage that involved leaving the colony evoked terrible sanctions: torture with red-hot pincers at three separate public locations was to end in capital punishment for the major conspirator. Secondary figures in plots to flee were to have a leg amputated, should the owners consent. If their owners pardoned them, fugitives were still to get 150 strokes of the lash and be marked by the amputation of an ear.[16]

In New York, a slave found traveling by himself forty miles from Albany, in 1705, could be executed, while in the immediate antebellum period, the fugitive slave in the South was to a limited extent an outlaw who might be detained and imprisoned by anyone, like a criminal.[17]

Muscovy generally kept on the tack that slaves were property, even as fugitives, except in instances when their flight caused a dispute among slaveowners, and thus they could be beaten. Otherwise, fugitives for most of the Muscovite period were the object of civil suits, with the slave a relatively passive intermediary. The major question is why this was so.

Muscovite law was not squeamish about inflicting any form of punishment, but terror was resorted to less than it might have been in an attempt to solve the very serious problem of fugitive slaves. No doubt there were many reasons for this. Primary, certainly, was the very nature of Muscovite law and the conception of slavery, which was only beginning to take the slave out of the realm of property law and make him a matter of state concern. Then again, slaves were a minority in Muscovy, the state and social structure and the economy were not based upon them, and whatever they did (other than as outright rebels, who were simply done away with) could not possibly threaten the established order. One might be tempted to assign the difference between New World and Muscovite sanctions to racism, but that would not really be appropriate, for the Russians meted out sanctions to their own outlaws (burying alive, roasting on a spit, pouring molten metal down the throat, sacking) that were no less savage than those the Europeans applied to their outsider slaves of African origin.

Sanctions were imposed upon a fugitive slave if he petitioned to live with another lord, and that caused a dispute between the lords. In such a case the offending slave was to be beaten mercilessly with the knout on the rack in front of the Slavery Chancellery "so that those witnessing the scene will learn not to commit such an offense."[18] It was in provisions such as this that later Musco-

15. Rose, p. 209.
16. Hall, p. 174.
17. Rose, p. 208.
18. 1649 *Ulozhenie* 20: 22; MS, p. 263.

vite legislators expressed their dawning cognizance of the slave's humanity and his volitional capacity, for one would search in vain the earlier statutes for similar provisions, just as one would search any statutes in vain for sanctions against domestic animals which caused disputes between human beings. This article, of unknown origin, expresses the didactic-deterrent function of late Muscovite sanctions. Retribution was the major function of Muscovite criminal law, with the state the avenger rather than the person wronged, but deterrence increasingly was stated to be an objective of punishment as well. Finally, this article also tells us a bit about the social life of slaves in the capital: some of them could be expected to be present, either in the normal course of their everyday life as they passed through Red Square by the Kremlin, or as part of the audience that would assemble to watch any of the executions that were part of the entertainment in seventeenth-century Muscovy. Many slave systems did not acknowledge the human capacities of slaves to that extent, nor did the central organs become so involved in chastising disobedient slaves, but rather left the matter up to the discretion of the owner, as might be done for the owner of a stray dog or cow. For Muscovy, this was part of a general reliance in the law on corporal punishment to effect sanctions, combined with an emerging sense that sanctions should have a deterrent effect.

As slavery throughout the Muscovite period was primarily a private matter, so was the recovery of fugitives. For this reason the government did little to impose sanctions, other than the ancient penalty of capital punishment for slave theft, on those who recruited or received others' slaves. Between, say, 1550 and 1648, it is dubious whether the state power did anything to a person who used another person's slave. Almost certainly the government's thinking on the subject of fugitive peasants outran its concern for fugitive slaves. This was reflected in the stipulation that a recipient of a fugitive serf had to pay 10 rubles per year to the rightful lord to compensate him for his labor. A somewhat similar, but more restricted, compensation was scheduled for the person who kept a fugitive slave as a slave (*derzhal dlia raboty*): he had to pay the lawful slaveowner .07 rubles per week, which would be only 3.64 rubles per year. The difference between 10 and 3.64 rubles may be a consequence of the fact that the compensation sanction for the fugitive slave was taken directly from the *Lithuanian Statute* of 1588, along with the entire article, and thus embodied an obsolete sum.[19] That the Muscovites did not update it would indicate how fundament-

19. 1588 LS 12: 17; 1649 *Ulozhenie* 11:10; 20: 90; MS, pp. 223, 288; PSZ 2: 491-92, no. 985. In fact the 1649 sum was slightly less than the 1588 one because of rounding: the *Lithuanian Statute* prescribed 2 and one-half altyns (0.075 rubles) which the *Ulozhenie* rounded off to 2 altyns and 2 dengas (0.07 rubles). If rational calculation was present in setting the 10-ruble sum, account may have been taken of the fact that the lord lost not only his income but probably had been required (in one way or another) to pay the runaway serf's taxes as well.

There is a problem in interpreting the *Ulozhenie*'s use of the word *rabota*, which now means "work." If it had at all anything like the same meaning in the seventeenth century,

ally irrelevant the issue was. Moreover, unlike the serfs, most slaves did not produce income. Peasant flight deprived a lord of a productive, income-producing asset whose absence caused real loss, whereas the slave was probably a household domestic whose absence caused his owner at most inconvenience but probably saved him money on his keep.

After 1649, the matter of fugitives (primarily serfs, but slaves as well) became a more serious matter. According to an edict of 1662, officials of court lands, town, postal system, and rural elders who had taken in fugitive slaves after 1658 were to be beaten with the knout. If an estate manager took in a fugitive slave without his superior's knowledge, he was to be beaten with the knout, and in 1667 a year in jail was added to that. In 1681, the rules were changed again, and in a penalty going back to the *Ulozhenie*, the illegal possessor of someone else's slave had to compensate the rightful owner a grivna per day for his court expenses (*proest' i volokita*), calculated from the time the trial began until the slave was handed back to his rightful owner. As is evident in the case of Danila Big Beard v. Uvar Lodygin, discussed in chapter 16, that sum of 0.10 ruble per day could soon mount to an awesome figure. Besides that, a losing defendant had to transport the slave back to where he belonged on his own vehicle.

All of these rules were made primarily to deal with fugitive peasants, with slaves added more or less incidentally. Futhermore, one of the sanctions for receiving fugitive peasants had been to take additional peasants as well as the fugitive from the receiving lord to the lawful lord. This was repealed in 1681, which brought forth a howl of protest from members of the lower upper service class and the middle service class, who declared that once the repeal had been announced, landlords again began to receive fugitives. On December 1, 1682, the government restored the four-for-one sanction, and specified that it was applicable to fugitive slaves as well as peasants.[20] Needless to say, this provoked immediate cries of anguish, expressed in a lower upper service class petition dated December 20, 1682, that such a measure could not be enforced. (I have not examined the signatures on the 1681 and 1682 petitions.) It proved very difficult when owners found their own fugitives, for they had trouble in getting the provincial governors and other officials to enforce the penalties. Moreover, not everyone who received fugitives had four peasants. Therefore, on January

---

then the recipient of a fugitive slave had to compensate the rightful owner only if he worked the slave. This might not be illogical, for most slaves did not "work," at least in the sense of producing income, as peasants did. Therefore the slaveowner was not deprived of income when his slave was absent and did not have to be compensated for his loss of nothing. This might also explain the use of weeks as the accounting term rather than years, as for serfs. However, such a calculation may well be unnecessary, if only because it would have been impossible for Muscovites to determine which weeks a slave "worked" and which weeks he was merely a domestic servant. The meaning of *rabota* is discussed further in chapter 18.

   20. 1649 *Ulozhenie* 10: 229; PSZ 2: 356, 481-83, no. 891, 972.

3, 1683, the government abolished the four-for-one rule, and instead demanded that those who received either fugitive peasants or fugitive slaves pay the lawful lord 20 rubles apiece. That seems to have settled the issue at least as far as compensating the rightful owner went. In 1721 Peter the Great canceled the order that such fugitives had to be transported back to their rightful owners, and said that they had to be simply expelled. He had expected that they would go back to their old lords, but instead they went to Poland and southern Ukraine. In 1722 he restored the "free-ride return" requirement, specifying a 100 ruble fine (above the 20 rubles per year) for every slave so turned out. If stewards and elders on their own initiative so expelled fugitives, they were to be beaten with the knout, have their nostrils slit, and exiled for life to slavery in the galleys, but no 100-ruble fine was to be collected.[21]

Aiding and Harboring Fugitives

Sanctions against aiding fugitive slaves were a customary part of Russian law, as of other systems.[22] By no means, however, were the Russians as harsh as the Babylonians or the Romans, who, viewing it as a form of theft, prescribed the death penalty for aiding the escape of or harboring a fugitive slave.[23] The *Russkaia Pravda* provided that a person who aided a fugitive slave's escape had to pay 5 grivnas for a male and 6 grivnas for a female (article 112); for concealing a fugitive who did not escape and was found by his owner, the culprit had to pay a fine of 3 grivnas (article 32). The abridged version of the *Pravda* exculpated completely the person who would testify under oath that he unwittingly had aided a slave's escape (article 115) or who purchased unknowingly another's slave and got a refund after the rightful owner claimed his chattel (article 118).

In later Muscovite law, those who harbored fugitive slaves assumed in the eyes of the law the responsibility for the slave that ordinarily resided in the slaveowner.[24] This particular piece of legislation was a period piece reflecting the struggle for labor of the 1649 Law Code era, for it mentions fugitive slaves who returned to the estates of their formers owners to encourage and recruit additional fugitives (both slaves and serfs), and looted and burned out their former tormentors when leaving. There were at least two reasons for this provision: to define liability, and perhaps more important, to intimidate would-be appropriators of another's human chattel.

21. PSZ 2: 491-92, no. 985; 6: 359, 639-41, nos. 3743, 3939.
22. Rose, pp. 182, 208; Short ZSL 32, Expanded ZSL 36.
23. Pritchard, p. 141, arts. 15-16; Driver and Miles, 1: 105; Mendelsohn, p. 58; Buckland, p. 32. The death penalty was prescribed for harboring a slave in Malaya in the early nineteenth century, a sanction unknown in Islamic law (M. B. Hooker, *Adat Laws in Modern Malaya* [Kuala Lumpur: Oxford University Press, 1972], p. 73).
24. 1649 *Ulozhenie* 20: 4; MS, p. 256.

In another attempt to make the harboring of fugitive slaves as unattractive as possible, the *Ulozhenie* repeated a law of 1639, borrowed from the *Lithuanian Statute* of 1588, making a person who harbored a fugitive responsible to the rightful owner even if the slave subsequently fled further. The first order was that the one-time harborer had to find the fugitive and turn him over to the Slavery Chancellery. Such persons were to be given three allotments of time to find the fugitive, first two months, then four months, and finally six months. If a year passed and the fugitive had not been found, the person who had harbored him had to pay the rightful owner 50 rubles, a sum far greater than slaves cost on the "open market." If the harborer eventually found the fugitive slave and turned him over to his owner, the 50 rubles were to be returned.[25] This form of sanction was like that in Sumerian law, where the person who harbored a fugitive was fined 25 shekels of silver or one slave. The same was true in Nuzi. These sanctions were significantly less severe than the one imposed by the Christian Assizes of Jerusalem at the beginning of the twelfth century, which reduced to slavery the person who hid a fugitive slave.[26]

In chapter 16 I shall discuss in greater detail the patterns of fugitive-slave mobility. Here I only need note that slaves often chose a new owner very much like their old one, and that, while there were exceptions, the general pattern of mobility was probably the same as for fugitive peasants and serfs: from lesser owners of the middle service class to magnates of the upper service class (under whom exploitation was less intense). The major evidence to support this contention lies in the petitions of the middle service class from 1637, 1641, 1645, and 1648 demanding the completion of the enserfment. These petitions, along with other "literary evidence" on fugitive serfs and the missions of the fugitive-serf hunters, often contain parallel references to fugitive slaves.[27] The provisions of the laws on fugitives, however, do not overtly express any bias in favor of one group of owners over another. One can only speculate that the 1639 law on the 50-ruble fine for not being able to produce a once-harbored fugitive slave may have been enacted in response to middle service class pressure.

Ownership Disputes

Disputes arose in Muscovy over the ownership of slaves, as over any other form of property. Resolution of conflicts over the ownership of slaves was one of the major points of the treaties between the Rusy (the slavicized Iranian Poliane and their Viking mercenaries) and the Byzantines, and this concern remained central for the institution of slavery until the time of its demise.[28]

25. 1588 LS 12: 18; UKMSP 14; 1649 *Ulozhenie* 20: 50-51; MS, pp. 273-74.
26. Mendelsohn, pp. 58, 63; Verlinden, *Colonization*, p. 81.
27. MS, p. 179.
28. PRP 1: 9, art. 12. For an interpretation of the Rusy as a multi-ethnic trading operation

The first principle in the resolution of conflicts over fugitive slaves was that the person who could prove that his was the prior ownership was the one to whom the law awarded the verdict. This idea had been formulated in the *Russkaia Pravda* (article 118) and persisted to the very end of the institution of slavery. There is nothing extraordinary about this, and one would be hard put to find a slave system in which some other principle operated. Therefore what is of interest is how the Muscovites handled it, and some of the myriad variations on that theme.

Initially, oral claims had precedence. But, as Muscovy became a society that relied more on writing, there was rigid insistence that claims of prior ownership be formulated in terms of documentary evidence. A great deal of legislation was devoted to providing rules for determining which documents were the older. As was true also in Roman law, in Muscovy there was no statute of limitations on the recovery of fugitive slaves.[29] That was a matter of extreme importance for the Muscovite slaveowner, for the recovery of slaves was often a task that took years to accomplish. This principle was also applied initially to the recovery of fugitive serfs, and then became a matter of great concern from the 1590s until 1649, when fugitive serfs could again be recovered without limit of time. On the other hand, some systems prescribed that a slave who was absent from his owners for a length of time was considered free. Among the Lombards, for example, thirty years' absence made a slave free.[30] That no such statute of limitations existed for a slave, or his heirs, was one of the harsh features of Muscovite slavery. On the other hand, a comparative perspective suggests that Muscovy was typical of most slave societies in that respect. The reasoning should be obvious: hardly any slave society would want to hold out to runaway slaves the prospect of freedom because of the passage of time, no matter how lengthly, and Muscovy almost never did.

Zheriapin v. Sheidiakova et al.

The fundamental principle that the older document wins the verdict was expressed in the Slavery Chancellery case of Zheriapin v. Sheidiakova et al. tried by the directors Stepan Ivanov Volynskii and Ivan Fomich Ogarev and the state secretaries Nikita Leont'ev and Iakov Kliucharev in December 1627 and January 1628 to resolve the question of who owned the slave Andrei (Ondriushka) Esipov (Osipov).

The parties to the dispute were an interesting lot. The plaintiff, Grigorii Mikhailov Ushatoi Zheriapin, in 1629 held the rank of Moscow *dvorianin*. He

---

based in France, see Omeljan Pritsak, *The Origin of Rus'* (Cambridge, Mass: Harvard Ukrainian Research Institute, 1975), pp. 19-20. The basic commodity of trade was Slavic slaves.

29. For a brief exception, see Shuiskii's 1607 law (MS, p. 140).

30. Rose, pp. 208-9.

was one of three brothers serving under Tsar' Mikhail who were probably descended from Starodub princes. At the trial, he was represented by his brother Mikhail Ushatoi Zheriapin, a *stol'nik* who later held the lower rank of *dvorianin*, and seems to have been slightly more prominent in the next three decades.[31] The defendant was Princess Alena (Olena) Khanmenatevna Sheidiakova, wife of the probably deceased Ortem Sheidiakov. Codefendants were her children, Misha and Fedka, diminutives for Mikhail Artem'ev and Fedor Artem'ev Sheidiakov, who were not in fact juveniles at the time of the trial but rather adults with the rank of *stol'nik*. They were presented by Kanai murza Kineevich Sheidiakov, probably the same as Kanai Enaleev Sheidiakov, who in 1613 had the very high cash-compensation schedule of 80 rubles. He was assisted at the trial by a Tatar slave, Kurmash Abalev (Obalev). The Sheidiakovs were descendants of a Nogai Tatar clan, the Kutumovs, who had joined Muscovite service in the sixteenth century.[32] Politically and socially, the litigants were approximately equals.

While certain facts in the case are clear, the veracity of some claims remains opaque. The decisive factor was the limited service slavery contract between Prince Grigorii Zheriapin and Andrei Osipov, dated March 9, 1626, that was submitted at the trial on January 15, 1628. In that document, which was contested by no one, Ondriushka, who was eighteen years old and had a pierced right ear, said he was a free man and sold himself for 2 rubles, the mandated sum at the time, in the city of Iaroslavl'. The transaction was conducted by another of Zheriapin's slaves, Tomil Ondreev. It also was not contested that Ondriushka had fled from Zheriapin about ten weeks before the commencement of the process and had moved to the estate of the defendant Sheidiakova. Apparently the Zheriapins set out in search of him, and Prince Mikhail Zheriapin had found him in the village of Pozhar (presumably, a place in the Iaroslavl' region) and ordered his arrest. At the time of his arrest, Ondriushka had in his possession a horse and sleigh, a bear rug, and a sky-blue cloak that belonged to Kanai murza Kineevich Sheidiakov, whose slave Kurmash came and took them back for his owner. After he had been arrested, an inventory was made of Ondriushka's clothing: a heavy coarse gray cloth coat, a fur coat, a dark-green cloth cap, something else (perhaps a lap robe) with down and sables, and a pair of worn-out sky-blue cloth pants. The claim was made that the coats were his but that the hat and pants belonged to Princess Alena, whose slave Mikhail Zakhar'ev came and took them.

Prince Mikhail Zheriapin, who signed his own testimony, claimed that a slave by the name of Ileika, belonging to Kanai murza Sheidiakov, had instigated Ondriushka's flight. At the pretrial hearing on December 21, 1627, Kanai murza

31. Petrov, IRRD 1 (1886): 151; Ivanov, AUBK, p. 139; Storozhev, "B.S." (1909), p. 115; DR 2: 956, 3: 232, 380; AMG 2: 699.
32. Petrov, IRRD 1 (1886): 214; Ivanov, AUBK, p. 469; Sukhotin, ChSV, p. 310.

Sheidiakov's slave advocate, Kurmash Abalev, told another story, namely, that Ondriushka and his father much earlier had been hereditary slaves who belonged to Princess Alena. She had also had a limited service slavery contract on Ondriushka and his father, but that document had burned up in the village of Kurbino in Iaroslavl' province when Kanai murza's palaces burned to the ground. They claimed that they made declarations in the Slavery Chancellery about the loss of those documents two years before the Moscow fire, probably in 1625. (The importance of such declarations is discussed in chapter 8 in the case of Tatishchev v. Selekhovskii, 1624.) Ondriushka had fled with a dowry slave girl who belonged to Alena, Aniutka Fedorova, in 1623. While Ondriushka was living with Prince Grigorii Zheriapin, Kurmash claimed, the limited service contract of 1626 had been forcibly taken on by him. Zheriapin married Ondriushka to Aniutka, but the woman fled and returned to Princess Alena two years prior to her husband's return to his old owner. After that, it was claimed, the Sheidiakovs had gotten a limited service slavery contract on Ondriushka and Aniutka.

However, it was too late. On January 14, 1628, Kanai Sheidiakov's slave Kurmash signed an out-of-court settlement for Princess Alena and her sons with Prince Grigorii Zheriapin in which he ceded the two slaves, Ondriushka and his wife Aniutka, to the plaintiff. Kurmash acknowledged that they were bound to Zheriapin by the limited service slavery contract. Three days later the court returned its verdict. Recognizing the out-of-court settlement as the third element, the Slavery Chancellery rank-ordered its reasons for turning Ondriushka over to Zheriapin: first was the limited service slavery contract of 1626, and second was Ondriushka's confession that the contract was legal. The plaintiff paid the 3-altyn capitation fee for the trial and took his property, Ondriushka, away with him.[33]

Why the Sheidiakovs did not pursue their claims to Ondriushka can only be surmised. The sociology of Muscovite slavery would support their claims that Ondriushka had been born a slave belonging to the defendants. At the age of fifteen, the Muscovite definition of majority, he got tired of living at Princess Alena's and ran away. The new place suited him even less than the one he had been used to, so he returned. In spite of what may have been the justice of their claims, the Sheidiakovs probably realized the claims would have been unsupportable, without a long court fight that would have cost more than the slave was worth to them. No doubt their claim of 1625 had perished in the great Moscow fire of 1627, and so was only of rhetorical avail to them, especially as they had not renewed their claim immediately after the 1627 fire. The Sheidiakovs could have demanded an investigation in the Iaroslavl' region to prove that Ondriushka and his father had been their slaves, but memories would have been fogged by his four-year absence. The only incontestable fact was that the plaintiff Zheria-

33. Iakovlev, *Kholopstvo*, pp. 387-90, no. 13.

pin had the older document, and the law was explicit on the legitimacy of such instruments. They agreed to return Ondriushka's wife Aniutka because of the Orthodox dogma of the inviolability of marriage. No capitation fee was paid for her because she had not been listed in the suit.

Muscovy knew collective ownership (by father and sons, by brothers, and by groups of other kinds) of slaves. Oddly, however, there seems to have been no legislation, as there was in other societies, about how conflicts should be resolved that might arise from such ownership, ranging from the disposition of offspring to what should be done when one owner freed a slave but the other owner(s) did not want to.[34]

The Slave-Catcher

Mandatory rewarding of third parties who returned fugitive slaves is common in many slave systems. The Hammurabi Code prescribed that the person who apprehended a fugitive slave and returned him to his owner was to be paid 2 shekels of silver (1 shekel equals about 8 grams); if a Babylonian kept the fugitive slave for himself and was detected, he was to be put to death as a slave thief. The Alabama Slave Code of 1852 mandated a compulsory reward of 6 dollars for turning a fugitive over to his owner.[35] And the *Russkaia Pravda* established a fee of 1 grivna for the same service (article 113).

Regrettably, I know nothing more about Muscovite slave catchers than is written in the *Ulozhenie* of 1649, and that was borrowed from the *Lithuanian Statute* of 1588. If an owner made a public declaration that he would pay a reward for the apprehension of his fugitive slave, he had to pay the sum he offered, plus a sum of two dengi (a kopek) per day for feeding the slave. The slave-catcher was to return the fugitive to the lawful owner. If the slave-catcher kept the fugitive and put him to work on his own estate, the rightful owner had to sue to recover his chattel from the slave-catcher. The lawful owner was also entitled to compensation of two altyns two dengi per week (a kopek per day) from the person who apprehended his slave and refused to return him.[36] Muscovite law knew none of the procedural refinements about the apprehension of a fugitive slave by his owner or a third person (such as when it was or was not trespass to enter another's dwelling in pursuit of a fugitive) that developed in North America from the law of apprentices.[37]

There seems to have been some presumption that the slave-catcher might in

34. Udal'tsova, "Raby v Vizantii," pp. 8, 17.
35. Pritchard, p. 141, arts. 17-20; Mendelsohn, p. 59; Rose, p. 183.
36. 1588 LS 12: 17, 18 (Lappo, pp. 358-59); 1649 *Ulozhenie* 20: 89-90; MS, pp. 287-88.
37. Rose, p. 208.

fact be another slave, a reality that was discussed already in chapter 6, in the case of Metropolitan's peasants v. Okinfov, in which Okinfov's slave Gavrilko had found Iakush, who had fled from the field of trial by combat. This reality was abstracted in a law of September 1, 1558 (7067), on the subject of initiating a suit for a fugitive slave. The preamble assumes that the slave has apprehended another slave, that the former proclaims that the latter belongs to his own master, or another party, but that the documentation to prove ownership, how much the slave was worth, or matters concerning stolen property, is not at hand. Therefore the slave-catcher has to find the evidence. Tsar Ivan ordered that the apprehended fugitive was to post a 15-ruble bond, and the slave-catcher was to be given time equal to 100 versts a week to go to the service landholding or hereditary estate of the fugitive's owner, or to find him in service. When the slave-catcher returned with the evidence, a trial was to be held and a verdict rendered according to the laws of the *Sudebnik*.[38]

Only in the 1580s and 1590s did the state begin to provide the police power to search for fugitive slaves. The 1607 code promulgated by Tsar Vasilii Shuiskii after the crushing of the Bolotnikov uprising was a central monument in the development of slave law, for it regularized the state interest in fugitives by ordering local officials to keep track of everyone.

The Purchase of Fugitive Slaves

A problem that naturally grew out of the fugitive slave issue was that of what should be done if a third party purchased a fugitive slave. It was "natural" only for Rus', however, because the law assumed that the slave was selling himself. Therefore there is little comparative perspective on the problem. The *Russkaia Pravda* (article 118) dealt with the subject in a way that was consonant with the spirit of the times: the rightful owner could claim his fugitive, but had to pay the person who had bought the fugitive without knowing he was a fugitive. The logic of the provision was clear: as we have seen, the owner was responsible for the actions of his fugitive slave, including the deceit of another person who purchased the fugitive believing that he was a free man.

Article 118 was explicitly repealed by the *Sudebnik* of 1550, no doubt because of the increasing importance of written evidence as the old oral society declined; repealed with it was the chance of getting a refund after being deceived by a slave who claimed to be a free man. Proclaiming that the second purchaser loses his money, the repeal reflected the values of a more commercial society: caveat emptor. The change in liability from the owner of a slave in the *Russkaia Pravda* to the purchaser in the *Sudebnik* is a manifestation of the great change that was occurring in Muscovite society and its law at this time. Richard A. Posner's posi-

38. AI 1: 263-64, no. 154-xii.

tive economic theory of law sheds light on that process. For a number of reasons, the *Russkaia Pravda* assigned strict liability to the slaveowner for his chattel's conduct. Most important, because the society of the *Russkaia Pravda* was an oral one and because record-keeping and other such activities of the modern state did not exist, the cost of gaining information about whether a person was enslaved was so high that society simply assigned all the risk to the owner. The development of record-keeping made it less efficient for the slaveowner to bear all the risk of slaveownership as the decline in the cost of information precipitated "a movement away from strict liability and toward negligence as the dominant rule of liability." By 1550 it was possible for potential buyers of slaves to learn whether or not a person was already enslaved before purchasing him, so the state lawmaker deemed that the person who did not check on a person's status prior to purchasing him was negligent, and therefore he was forced to absorb the risk. It was no longer assumed that the price of information was so high that the buyer should not be expected to be liable for the consequences of his making a purchase. (The fact that those who were responsible for enforcing the *Sudebnik* did not always adhere to the new doctrine prior to the general registration of all slaves in 1597-98 indicates that some officials felt that the law's assumptions were overly optimistic, that in fact the system of keeping track of slaves was not yet good enough for the purchaser to be forced to bear all the risks. Such decisions also may represent a recognition of the chaos and decline in governmental efficiency caused by Ivan IV's paranoid adventures.) Moreover, the fact that the *Russkaia Pravda* proclaimed a rule of no liability for the purchaser of a slave dispensed with a need to determine questions of motive and care, questions that medieval Russian law in general could not hope to answer. The fact-finding procedures of the *Sudebnik* era, however, changed that situation. A minor element in the strict-liability provision of the *Russkaia Pravda* may have been the insurance factor: it is generally assumed that injurers on average are wealthier than victims, and the *Russkaia Pravda* legislator may have assumed that the person who already owned a slave was wealthier than the person who did not have one and thus was in the market to buy one; consequently, the slaveowner could more easily afford the loss than the deceived buyer could. It would seem doubtful that this possible *Pravda* consideration changed much in the *Sudebnik* era.[39] A final factor in the *Sudebnik* legislator's thinking may have been a recognition that the slave was a person with volition, that his owner should not be held materially responsible for every act of his chattel. This thinking was also a major change from the *Pravda* era.

39. 1550 *Sudebnik* 78, 79; UKKhP 1597, art. 1; Richard A. Posner, "A Theory of Primitive Society, With Special Reference to Law," *The Journal of Law and Economics* 23 (1980): 48-51; idem, "Retribution and Related Concepts of Punishment," *The Journal of Legal Studies* 9(1980): 90-91; idem, with William M. Landes, "The Positive Economic Theory of Tort Law" (University of Chicago offset publication, April 13, 1981), p. 32. I am indebted to Bart Goldberg for bringing this to my attention.

Pushkin v. Artsybashov

Nevertheless, according to Kolycheva, article 118 continued to be used in practice until the end of the sixteenth century.[40] This is evident in two limited service slavery contracts that were registered on January 15, 1598, by Iurii Iakovlev (Bulgakov) Pushkin. Pushkin was a prominent *syn boiarskii* on the court list from Votskaia piatina of the Novgorod region who by 1605 reached the top of the compensation scale with 600 cheti of land. In 1582 he already had possessed with his brother Andrei 120 cheti of land, and no doubt later acquired more. In 1604 he was paid his cash salary of 10 rubles, also a rather high amount. About the same time he attained the only post of note he ever held: in 1603 he was appointed siege defense chief (*osadnaia golova*) in Ladoga.[41] The earlier of the two documents he registered in 1598 was a limited service slavery contract that had been issued in 1583 when Petrusha Dmitriev, his wife Ul'ianka, their son Tomilko, and their daughters Okulinka and Mashka had sold themselves to Pushkin for the large sum of 15 rubles. About two years later the son Tomilko fled, and sold himself to Fedor Nevzorov Artsybashov for the sum of 10 rubles.

The second document Pushkin presented was the contract, dated April 23, 1585, between Tomilko and Artsybashov, who was in 1596 one of the leading servicemen of Derevskaia piatina of the Novgorod region and the elected director of the muster of servicemen (*okladchik*).[42] Tomilko apparently lived with Artsybashov for over a decade, when he was finally discovered and claimed by his rightful owner, Pushkin, in December of 1595. Pushkin paid Arstybashov back his money, and the latter signed the documents to that effect.[43] It is not clear whether Pushkin, the rightful former owner, paid back the money because it was felt that he had to, or because he for some reason wanted the slave back and paid Artsybashov his 10 rubles to avoid litigation. Having both contracts in his possession gave Pushkin clear title to Tomilko.

Obolnianinov v. Krevoborskii

Several of the principles applying to Muscovite fugitive slaves were manifest in a court case initiated on June 7, 1593, before the state secretary Piatoi Kokoshkin. Ignatii Petrov Obolnianinov sued Fedor [Ivanov?] Krevoborskii for the return of two fugitive slaves, Silka and Vaska, sons of Overkii Krivoi. Obolnianinov's case was based on a full slavery document that he had in his possession on their grandmother, Fedositsa, the mother of Overkii Krivoi.

The case was tried in Moscow, probably because the principals were from different regions of Muscovy. Obolnianinov, the plaintiff, was a *syn boiarskii* from Votskaia piatina of the Novgorod region who acquired at least twenty-two

40. Kolycheva, *Kholopstvo*, pp. 221-22, 239.
41. DVP, p. 470, no. 19; RK 1598-1638, p. 144; Sukhotin, ChSV, p. 27; Ianitskii, p. 183.
42. DN 1596, p. 198; Koretskii, *Zakreposhchenie*, pp. 37, 170.
43. RIB 17 (1898): 106-7, nos. 298-99.

slaves in eleven transactions during the years 1565-96. He first acquired three slaves in 1565 when he married, as part of his wife's dowry, and apparently did not purchase any himself for another sixteen years, until 1581. Beginning in 1589, he was involved in one slave transaction or another, almost annually, for the next seven years, a not unusual rhythm. We can see that he prospered in his later years, for his purchases of 1596 were made for him by other slaves. He laid out slightly more than average for his slaves, a bit over 5 rubles per transaction, or 3 rubles per slave. When he died at some time in 1604-5, his land-compensation entitlement was 400 cheti, seemingly a middling level for someone who had been in service about forty years. Very little is known about other aspects of his life. How much land or how many peasants he had cannot be determined. Toward the end of his life, he was probably one of the leaders of his community: he witnessed a document in 1602, and two years later he testified to the government about the impoverishment of his region, the Korelskaia polovina of Votskaia piatina. Judging by the fact that he was a plaintiff in another suit two years later for fugitive peasants, whose resolution is unknown, we may surmise that the lower orders apparently found living on his properties not always desirable.[44]

Unfortunately, less is known about the defendant, Fedor Krevoborskii. The fact that his patronymic is not given in the case indicates that he was known in Moscow. He is not mentioned in Novgorod records, and probably did not live there—indicating that the slaves being contested may have fled a considerable distance (perhaps to Suzdal'), a fact which also may account for the apparent considerable lag between the time they ran away and the time their rightful owner filed a suit for them: he had to find them himself, and it took him years to do so. That Krevoborskii was a man of substance is indicated by the fact that he did not even litigate the case himself, but rather his slave Ivashko Obramov did it for him. If this Krevoborskii was Fedor Ivanovich Krevoborskii, then indeed he was a prominent man. From the late 1560s to the end of the century he is mentioned quite frequently in the military record books (*razriadnye knigi*) as holding various military command positions, and in his later years he also was a census taker and local commander and governor.[45]

The facts in Obolnianinov v. Krevoborskii are fairly straightforward. Silka and Vaska fled from Obolnianinov to Krevoborskii. Initially, when apprehended, the fugitives denied knowing the documentary basis of enslavement of their forebears, but later admitted that they did. While a fugitive, Silka had sold himself into limited service contract slavery with Krevoborskii and married one of his hereditary slave girls, Aniutka Martinova. He had deserted a first wife, Annitsa

---

44. AIuB 2: 180; DVP, p. 504, no. 754; RIB 22 (1908): 587, 830, 836; Koretskii, *Zakreposhchenie*, p. 224.

45. RK 1475-1598, p. 567; RK 1559-1605, p. 399; RK 1598-1638, p. 362; Markevich, p. xcix; PKMG 3: 343; AFZKh 3: 398; DR 1, passim; BS 1: 124.

("Utka," "the duck") Elizarova Pozniakova, who had remained with Obolnian-inov. For all we know, Silka had fled to get away from his first wife, a not un-common precipitant of flight. Annitsa was living at the time of the case, and so by law Silka had to divorce Aniutka, who remained with Krevoborskii, and he was returned to his first wife, Annitsa. The judge ordered Silka returned to Obol-nianinov. A special decree by Tsar Fedor Ivanovich, which may have been gener-ated earlier, or composed for this occasion, said that Krevoborskii was not to be refunded the money that he had paid to buy Silka, as had been the practice in the *Russkaia Pravda* (article 118) but had been repealed by the *Sudebnik* of 1550. Why a special decree was issued on this point has mystified scholars for a long time.[46] If it was a special decree for this case, it may have been called for by the social standing of the defendant. Unfortunately, we shall never know the answer.

The defendant's advocate, his slave Ivashko Obramov, claimed that there had also been a limited service contract document for Silka's brother Vaska, but he was unable to produce the document. One may assume that the claim was ad-vanced in an attempt to seek reimbursement according to article 118. Vaska de-nied that he had sold himself to defendant Krevoborskii, but claimed rather that he had served with him voluntarily; in other words, he was a "voluntary slave," as discussed in chapter 2. State secretary Kokoshkin ordered Vaska returned to plaintiff Obolnianinov with his brother on the basis of the full slavery document and his own testimony. The verdict, which bore the seal of Tsar Fedor Ivanovich as well as the signature of Kokoshkin, was delivered on July 24, or about a month and a half after the case had been initiated.[47]

The case is typical for such suits for fugitives. The old full slavery document was recognized as the legitimate document, even though it had been issued two generations earlier, to Obolnianinov's grandfather, in the 1550s at the earliest. The plaintiff did not say whether he himself had ever owned the grandmother, Fedositsa (we may assume that he did not), an issue that was irrelevant in any case. Thus the law recognized the heritability of full slavery. It is also important to note that the case was decided both expeditiously and justly, in spite of the apparently superior social standing of the defendant. This also seems to have been relatively typical for Muscovite jurisprudence. The document itself was reg-istered by Obolnianinov on January 19, 1599, along with thirteen other docu-ments, during the compulsory registration of all claims to slaves.

Obolnianinov v. Viazemskii

June 1593 was a busy month for Ignatii Petrov Obolnianinov in court. On June 6, the day before the case just discussed began to be heard, he argued an-other one before state secretary Piatoi Kokoshkin. The defendant was Prince

---

46. Kolycheva, *Kholopstvo*, p. 223; Koretskii, *Zakreposhchenie*, p. 224.
47. RIB 17 (1898): 154-55, no. 421.

Ofonasii Viazemskii, the fugitive slave in question was Isachko Overkeev Krivoi, a brother of Silka and Vaska, whose fate has just been discussed. Again we are handicapped by the absence of a patronymic for Viazemskii, but it well may have been Ivanovich. There seem to have been two Ofonasii Ivanovich Viazemskiis, one who was an intimate courtier and general of Ivan IV, another who was second general at Kazan' under Ivan Mikhailov Vorotynskii in the years 1593-96. It seems fair to assume that the defendant in question here was the Kazan' general.[48]

The slave in question, Isachko, claimed that he belonged to Viazemskii and was married to Viazemskii's full slave Aniutka Makarova. He further claimed that he had served only Obolnianinov voluntarily, had not given any slavery documents on himself, and had not married a dowry slave woman. Obolnianinov presented the full slavery document on the grandmother, Fedositsa, and Isachko confessed that he was a full slave thereby, had run away, and had stolen Obolnianov's property and taken it with him. The resolution of this case was not so expeditious: the verdict was awarded to Obolnianinov only three years later, on August 14, 1596.[49] One may surmise that the delay was due to Viazemskii's service in Kazan', for which postponements were mandatory.

The judgment in Obolnianinov v. Viazemskii was also registered by the former on January 19, 1599, as part of the compulsory registration of all current claims to slaves. Typically, after the judgment charter had been registered, the recording officials entered the demographic events that had transpired in the lives of Overkii's three sons after the composition of the original judgment charter. Silka had been forcibly returned to his first wife, Annitsa ("the duck"), and they had produced a son, Senka. Vaska had married one of Obolnianinov's hereditary slave women, Ovdotitsa. Isachko was married to Aniutka (here mistakenly called Annitsa), and they had produced three children—two boys, Mikita and Aleksandrets, and a girl, Aksenitsa.[50] The results were four children, three boys and a girl. As we shall see later, this imbalance was not exceptional.

An undatable article in the *Ulozhenie* of 1649 that certainly was a digest of an earlier Slavery Chancellery case reveals how complicated such matters could get. A limited service contract slave fled from his owner, sold himself to a second lord, and then returned to his lawful owner. When the first owner died, the slave was automatically freed, but, unable to endure the rigors of a free existence in Muscovy, he sold himself to a third lord. The second lord filed a suit, claiming that the slave was rightfully his, probably on the grounds that his contract was older. However, the Slavery Chancellery awarded the verdict to the third lord,

48. Samokvasov, *Materialy* 2: 465, 470-71; RK 1550-1636, 1: 162; Petrov IRRD 1: 53; SIRIO 129: 187; RK 1550-1636, 2: 98, 110; Savel'ev, 2: 155; RK 1475-1598, pp. 277, 486, 494, 504; SIRIO 71 (1892): 353-64, 428-32, 434, 440, 452, 551; Koretskii, *Zakreposhchenie*, p. 307.

49. RIB 17: 155-56, no. 422.

50. Ibid.

and declared that the second lord's contract was void because it had been obtained illegally while the slave was a fugitive.[51]

Stolen Property

Accompanying suits for fugitive slaves almost always were suits for property allegedly stolen by the fleeing slave (*snos*). There is little comparative legal material on this issue either, because the Muscovite laws were based on the fact that the fugitive slave who had taken the property subsequently sold himself to someone else. Such assumptions are not to be found in other slave systems.

These suits yield interesting ethnographic material, for they list, inter alia, the slave's clothing. The legal tactic of suing a slave for stolen property could not be used to enslave a "voluntary slave" after he had departed, if the employer had neglected to formalize his enslavement before the departure "because he had trusted the slave and had kept him in his own home without a formal bondage document."[52]

When the issue of stolen property could be legitimately raised, the initial reaction of the law was that the person proved to have taken in a fugitive was automatically responsible for the stolen property.[53] A century later, however, in a provision borrowed from the *Lithuanian Statute* of 1588, Muscovite law expressed what seems to have been the hope that it would not be necessary to make that assumption, and that the parties could decide among themselves to whom a slave's property belonged. But, if mutual agreement was not possible, the government was only too willing to grant a trial to resolve the issue of stolen property.[54] This is not surprising, considering the revenue that the government gained from such litigation, which ordinarily far exceeded the minimal capitation fees charged for resolving slave ownership disputes. In case of perjury, when a disputed slave subsequently turned up in the possession of a defendant who had denied possessing a fugitive (or had claimed the fugitive had fled further), the plaintiff was awarded both the runaway and his suit for stolen property. The defendant was to be punished "as the sovereign ordered."[55]

A law originating in 1648 specified that suits for stolen property had to be initiated at the same time a suit was filed to recover a fugitive slave.[56] The reason for this becomes clear when we consider what was involved. A developing tactic on the part of plaintiffs was to sue first for the fugitive slave and then, depending on the outcome of that process, to decide whether to sue for the stolen

51. 1649 *Ulozhenie* 20: 114; MS, p. 297.
52. 1649 *Ulozhenie* 20: 17; MS, p. 262.
53. 1550 *Sudebnik* 79.
54. 1588 LS 11: 14; 12: 17; 1649 *Ulozhenie* 20: 88, 93; MS, p. 289.
55. PRP 4: 378, no. 3.
56. 1649 *Ulozhenie* 20: 57; MS, p. 275.

property. A person who lost a suit for a fugitive slave was highly likely to lose a suit for stolen property, although this was not universally true. (An exception might be a case in which the defendant won the case on the basis of a technicality, as when the plaintiff neglected to formulate documents on hereditary slaves, but yet the contested slave confessed that he was a fugitive and had stolen the property in question.) Because of the structure of the fee system of the Muscovite courts, the safe thing to do was to await the outcome of the suit for the fugitive. The capitation fees for fugitive slaves were low and were paid by the person to whom the court awarded the slaves; but the fees for stolen property were high (10 percent) and had to be paid by the loser of a case. Moreover, should the litigants reach an out-of-court settlement, no capitation fees had to be paid but the 10 percent fee on the value of the stolen property had to be paid on the value of a suit once it had been filed, regardless of its subsequent outcome.

The suits for stolen property often involved huge sums. Of the twenty-two cases in my data set, the smallest suit was for 9.50 rubles, the largest for 130 rubles. The median suit was 35 rubles, the average 45.13 rubles (with a standard deviation of 31.55 rubles). We must remember that the legal price for a limited service contract slave was 3 rubles. Suits covered almost everything the slave was wearing, garments that probably belonged to the owner, jewelry, and largely objects a person on the run could take with him. (Peasants, on the other hand, "stole" cattle, seed, and tools.)

Proshchevskii v. Aridov

Much of the suing for stolen property may well have been posturing and maneuvering to gain a position in the real suit at hand. This almost certainly was the case in a 1623 suit tried in the Slavery Chancellery before the directors Prince Nikifor Iakovlev Meshcherskoi and Ivan Kuz'mich Begichev and the state secretaries Patrekei Nasonov and Filipp Mitrofanov to recover the fugitive slave Fedor (Fed'ka) Moseev (Mokeev). The plaintiff was a Lithuanian in Muscovite service, an officer in the mounted musketeer corps, Matvei Iur'ev Proshchevskii. The defendant was Aleksei Nikitin Aridov, a cossack with a service land grant in Peremyshl' uezd. Sociologically, these people were on about the bottom rung of slaveownership in Muscovy. Besides the slave, at issue was stolen property that Proshchevskii claimed was worth 70.70 rubles, while Aridov claimed that he was owed 20.50 rubles for various expenses.

The facts of the case seem relatively clear. In 1619 Fed'ka had been a peasant living on land belonging to *boiarin* Prince Ivan Borisovich Cherkasskii, one of the most influential figures at the time, who became de facto ruler of Muscovy after the death of Filaret in 1633. The Poles seized Fed'ka and made a military captive out of him. About two years later, Fed'ka escaped from captivity, and, by one of the many analogies borrowed from the institution of slavery to define serfdom, he was freed from any claims that Cherkasskii might have had on him. In the 1623 trial, one of Cherkasskii's slaves, Neusypai Vladimirov, put in an appearance to say that his owner had no claim to Fed'ka because the latter had returned to Muscovy from captivity.

Apparently he had been rescued by the cossacks from Polish captivity, and lived with them in the vicinity of Komarichi for about eighteen months as a beggar. He left the cossacks in Elets and found his mother in Kaluga on Cherkasskii's estate, where he lived for awhile. Then his mother sold (*torgovala*) him in Kaluga, according to Fed'ka's story. However, according to a limited service slavery contract in Proshchevskii's possession, Fed'ka sold himself to the Lithuanian in October 26, 1622, for the sum of 2 rubles (the sum set by law at the time), and Fed'ka, prevaricating, claimed that both of his parents were deceased when interrogated about his past at the time the contract was formalized in the Slavery Chancellery in Moscow. Having taken the 2 rubles, Fed'ka shortly thereafter fled, apparently to Aridov, whom he said he had known in the cossacks. Plaintiff Proshchevskii claimed that Aridov had seduced Fed'ka away from him. The case does not make it clear whether Fed'ka was pretending that his mother had sold him to Aridov, although that seems to be implied. Aridov, on the other hand, did not lend support to Fed'ka's story at the trial and did not contest Proshchevskii's ownership of Fed'ka. In fact, he seemed to imply that he had incurred many expenses of the type that might be due a slave-catcher in turning the fugitive slave over to the Slavery Chancellery.

The Slavery Chancellery awarded custody of Fed'ka to Proshchevskii, who paid the capitation fee of 3 altyns, a logical move because, as the officials noted in the verdict, no one else claimed ownership of Fed'ka. That left the large suit by Proshchevskii for stolen property, and Aridov's preposterous claim for expenses. The litigants resolved their suit and countersuit out of court, probably because each had been satisfied, in his way, by the verdict, and felt that to pursue the cash suits would be counter-productive. Proshchevskii's suit was considerably larger than the average suit for stolen property (which was about 40 rubles), and it seems likely that it did not reflect reality for other reasons as well. For one, there was no list of things that had been taken, only the sum of their declared value. Second, while a slaveowner might have given a newly purchased, untested slave access to that much property shortly after the acquisition, it would seem to be unwise to do so, and therefore probably unlikely. Third, a Lithuanian officer with the rank of groom in the mounted musketeer corps might have owned 70 rubles' worth of easily stealable property, but that also seems implausible, especially for someone who appears to have been so insignificant as to have left no other trace in the historical record besides this suit.

One may surmise, therefore, that Proshchevskii filed a suit for so much stolen property in order to intimidate the defendant Aridov. Proshchevskii knew that he had the limited service slavery contract in his possession and that almost certainly he would be awarded the verdict. Adding on the suit for 70 rubles was a way to ensure that Aridov would not contest ownership of Fed'ka, as he easily might have by referring to Fed'ka's own perjured testimony that his mother had sold him in Kaluga. Further stories could have been concocted to show Fed'ka was known to have been Aridov's slave while still in the cossacks, before the date of Proshchevskii's document. The resolution of such a suit would have taken a long time, for it would have been necessary to take the testimony of hundreds of cossacks who were on the frontier in 1621 and might have known about events there. But by holding the threat of a property suit over Aridov, Proshchevskii was able to get the defendant to forego that gambit. Losing such a suit would have forced Aridov into slavery, for he hardly possessed assets enough to satisfy a judgment of 70 rubles. On the other hand, by suing for "expenses" incurred while "returning" Fed'ka to the Slavery Chancellery, Aridov held a threat over Proschevskii. Proving that Aridov had seduced away Fed'ka, as claimed, would have been nearly impossible, while the fact that Aridov had delivered Fed'ka to the Slavery Chancellery was known to every official who worked there. Be that as it may, once the slave had been awarded to Proshchevskii, he was sure that he would not have to engage in a long-drawn-out suit to establish title to the runaway, and that Aridov was able to drop the pretense that he had incurred large expenses in delivering the fugitive to the authorities. Sure of their positions, each litigant was willing to drop the suits for monetary losses, which is what they did.[57]

Treskin v. Zykov

The use of the suit for stolen property as a ploy was also evident in the case of Treskin v. Zykov of 1628, tried before the Slavery Chancellery directors Stepan Ivanov Volynskii and Ivan Fomich Ogarev and the state secretaries Nikita Leont'ev and Iakov Kliucharev. At issue were Demid, son of Semen Parfen'ev, his wife, Arina, daughter of Arist, and Demid's stepson Dmitrii Alekseev. Suit was also filed for 50.50 rubles' worth of stolen property, a sum judiciously chosen to force adjudication of the suit right away in Moscow.

The plaintiff, Bazhen Ovdokimov Treskin, was a provisioner (*sytnik*) in the royal Provisions Chancellery. Little more is known about him. He had a piece of land in Kashin province, in the Tver' region northwest of Moscow, which he had inherited as part of his deceased wife's legacy. (Why the wife's legacy did not revert to her clan is unknown.) She, Fetin'ia, daughter of Ivan Romeikov, had gotten the parcel from her father's patrimonial estate as part of her dowry. In the trial Treskin presented two pieces of evidence to show that the slaves were his. The first was a manumission document dated 1606-7, issued by Anna, daughter of Stepan Chirikov, for her deceased husband, Roman Kipreianov Palitsyn, setting free a female slave and her two girls and two boys, one of whom was a son, Demid. The second document was a limited service slavery contract that Demid had signed on January 24, 1620, with Treskin, in the amount of 2 rubles, the le-

57. Iakovlev, *Kholopstvo*, pp. 359-64, no. 8.

gal sum of the time. It was typical for children who had been born as slaves to
sell themselves at some later time to another slaveowner.

The defendant, who had the contested slaves at the time the case opened, was
Tikhon Ivanov Zykov, a Kashin *syn boiarskii.* Later, in 1651, he served as governor of Ladoga, and the major issue during his term seems to have been how to
handle peasants who lived in the frontier region and were accustomed to moving
back and forth across the border that changed hands in the Russo-Swedish wars
of the era.[58] He had been married the year before the suit, in 1626, to Oksin'ia,
daughter of Kiril Romeikov, and had received, as part of a dowry given by Kiril's
widow, the nun Sundaleia, the village in which Dem'ka Semenov was living. On
the basis of this document, which also mentioned Dem'ka's stepson, Mit'ka, the
defendant Zykov was claiming them as his peasants, who could be proved to
have lived there for eight years.

One may assume that Treskin lived in Moscow, and did not frequent the provinces. In all probability, Dem'ka was a slave farmer who paid his owner rent.
Dem'ka's wife, Orinka, was Treskin's manager in the area. (It was rare for
women to be managers.) When Treskin discovered that his village had been given
away to someone else because of confusion over the Romeikov patrimony, he petitioned on September 6, 1627, for permission to arrest his slaves. (Because of his
position in the government, he did not have to pay the fees ordinarily levied on
such a request.) The Slavery Chancellery, heeding his request, ordered that the
slaves in question be seized and sent to Moscow on a horse that Zykov was to
provide. An officer of the Slavery Chancellery (a *nedel'shchik*, elsewhere *pristav*)
went to Kashin province, drafted local priests, deacons, and peasants, and proceeded to hunt for the disputed slaves. The defendant Zykov and the disputed
slave Dem'ka hid and could not be found, but the arresting party found and
seized the wife Orinka and her son Mit'ka. Mother and son were brought to the
Slavery Chancellery in Moscow on a ten-year-old chestnut bald horse that belonged to Dem'ka.

In Moscow, the horse was put in the safekeeping of plaintiff Treskin's slave
Ondriushka Khoritonov, who provided three guarantors (one worked in the Provisions Court with Treskin, a second was a petty merchant) who pledged on
September 26, 1627, that they would pay the Slavery Chancellery a forfeit of 5
rubles in cash should Ondriushka fail to surrender the horse upon demand. (Note
that the 5 ruble value of the horse was greater than the value of a slave.)

Then the legal maneuvering began. Defendant Zykov filed five petitions, beginning on September 29 and ending on October 9, noting that some time had
passed since the slaves who were under arrest and "dying of hunger" had been
seized, but that plaintiff Treskin had neglected to file a suit. (For a further dis-

---

58. DR 3: 276; DAI 3: 289, no. 82; RIB 38: 424-25. I could find nothing about B. O.
Treskin.

cussion of this strategy, see Epanchin v. Leont'evs, 1627, in chapter 8.) Finally, after a bailiff had gone to look for Treskin on the ninth and reported that he was in Moscow, the plaintiff lodged his suit on October 16. In the trial that followed Treskin reported that Orinka was his stewardess of the property where she was living, and that she had without authorization given away 50.50 rubles' worth of property to Zykov. When it came time to take the oath, Treskin's slave Ondriushka kissed the cross for his owner. In addition to presenting the dowry agreement as evidence, Zykov cited three persons who could prove that Dem'ka, Orinka, and Mit'ka had lived in that area as peasants for eight years, and then asked for a general interrogation (*poval'noi obysk*) of everyone living in the vicinity, all the *dvoriane, deti boiarskie*, their slaves and peasants. Here we see, incidentally, the comparatively unusual role that slaves played as witnesses in the Muscovite judicial process. The slave woman herself seems to have best understood what the real problem was: two claims were rooted in the confused claims to the village in which the slaves were living.

Next Zykov presented a document that had been signed by both litigants on July 2, 1627, in which Treskin ceded to Zykov possession of the disputed village and also, until the ownership of the land could be definitively determined, possession of the peasants and slaves living there. A forfeit of 100 rubles payable to Zykov was prescribed should Treskin violate the agreement. Not surprisingly, the document was the product of the violence that was so typical of Muscovy in that era. At the trial, Treskin admitted that he had signed the document, but only under duress: all thirty villagers had seized him and forced him to sign it by threatening to drown him. After that bombshell, the court ordered the litigants each to post a bond guaranteeing that they would appear for the verdict and pay the fees.

At this moment the litigants decided on an out-of-court settlement. Zykov ceded the slaves to Treskin, who dropped his claims for stolen property but agreed to pay the court costs. The reasoning is clear: Treskin had the valid documents, the old manumission document and the limited service slavery contract, and was likely to win, something the Slavery Chancellery noted when closing the case. However, the plaintiff could not prove the stolen property charge, which of course the defendant could not disprove, either, and thus it was a negotiating instruments in the hands of the plaintiff to force the defendant to yield on the main issue, the slaves.

This left one matter unsettled, the court costs. The Slavery Chancellery, totaling them up, found that they amounted to 5.27 rubles. Treskin's guarantors were required to pledge that they would pay the sum, which, by November 11, 1627, the plaintiff still had not paid. This, of course, was an enormous sum of money, considerably more than most people were paid for working a year, more than the cost of two slaves. While the government was very hungry for cash, apparently it was not always diligent in collecting its judicial revenues, for fifteen years later, in January of 1643, the Slavery Chancellery sent out another memo asking a bailiff to collect the fees from Treskin's guarantors.[59]

Hiring Out of Slaves

Another area of relations between slaveowners was the hiring out, or renting, of slaves. In some systems laws on this subject were highly developed because of the frequency of the practice. Generally, the rule seems to have been that the authority of the slaveowner was transferred in toto to the renter. The doctrine of bailment applied when the slave was somehow damaged by the hirer.[60]

It is not clear whether the rent-a-slave institution existed in Muscovy. An ambiguous article of the *Ulozhenie* of 1649, borrowed from an equally ambiguous article in the *Lithuanian Statute* of 1588, implies that it may have existed, at least on paper. That law seems to imply that the owner of the slave (not the renter) was responsible for the actions of his chattel. In case a guaranteed slave who had been rented out fled, the owner had to find and return him or else pay 50 rubles to the renter, plus the value of any property the slave may have stolen and court costs. The hiring out of slaves was a common practice from the Athenian Laurium silver mines and Byzantium to medieval Germanic countries, Zanzibar, India, and the American South. I know of no such cases in Muscovy, although they may have happened. If they did, the law was ready.[61]

In another provision borrowed from the *Lithuanian Statute* of 1588, parents were declared to be responsible for any children they put out on term indentures, when the indentures were registered in the Slavery Chancellery. Similarly, individuals who had guaranteed the indentures of unrelated third parties could be held liable should the indentured slaves misbehave, flee, or steal anything before the expiration of the indenture.[62]

Distraint and the Use of Slaves as Collateral (Pledges)

Distraint, the seizure of a debtor's property to satisfy a creditor's claims, has been practiced since ancient times. In Eshnunna the law implicitly allowed the distraint of slaves, and went on to discuss what should happen should the distrainee cause the death of the slave (he had to replace the deceased slave with

59. Iakovlev, *Kholopstvo*, pp. 373-82, no. 11. For additional discussion of the subject of guarantors, see H. W. Dewey and A. M. Kleimola, "Suretyship and Collective Responsibility in pre-Petrine Russia," *Jahrbücher für Geschichte Osteuropas* 18(1970): 337-54.

60. Rose, pp. 220-21.

61. 1588 LS 12: 22; 1649 *Ulozhenie* 20: 91; Udal'tsova, pp. 10-11; Hjejle, pp. 93, 109; Wergeland, p. 29; Gill Shepherd, "The Comorians," in Watson, *Systems*, p. 80.

62. 1588 LS 12: 22-i, iii; 1649 *Ulozhenie* 20: 45.

two slaves.)[63] Distraint of slaves was common in Babylonia, slaves could be foreclosed to satisfy debts, and the Hammurabi Code prescribed a cash compensation and the forfeit of everything that was lent should a pledged slave die from beating or abuse.[64] Distraint was also applicable to slaves in Rome and the American South.[65]

Slaves were not pledged as collateral and distraint generally was not practiced in Muscovy because of the unwillingness to recognize slaves as market commodities. The exception was the state itself, which distrained slaves (and, by analogy, serfs) to compel desired owner conduct. If a person served as a guarantor for another, but failed to meet his responsibilities and rode off, the sums owed the government could be collected from his slaves and peasants, along with the fees due the court bailiff for the collection.[66] By analogy, private debts could also be collected from a debtor's slaves and peasants.[67] However, the slaves and peasants themselves could not be seized.

Commercial Transactions

Most systems of slave law devote considerable attention to the law of commercial transactions. Such laws are noticeably absent in Muscovy. After the *Russkaia Pravda* went out of use in the first half of the sixteenth century, there seems to be no law regulating slave sales by one private party to another.[68] Even before that time one notices the absence of Russian laws on the responsibility for physical (leprosy, epilepsy) and moral (tendency to steal, flee, rebel) defects in slaves such as appeared in Babylonian, Athenian, Roman, Germanic, and Ethiopian law. Islamic law gave the purchaser of a slave three days to discover any "faults" in a slave, and he could request his money back from the seller at any time within a year in case insanity or leprosy developed. Thai law required a seller to make a full refund if the slave fled or became seriously ill within a month of the sale, or if the slave committed a major felony against the new owner within three years. American slave traders developed a system of warranty, enforceable at law, for which they charged a higher price when selling slaves. The Hammurabi Code even provided that a former owner was responsible when claims were made against a slave who had been sold after the event that stimulated the claim had occurred. Chinese law at the beginning of

63. Pritchard, p. 135, art. 23.
64. Ibid, pp. 150-51, arts. 114, 116, 118; Driver and Miles, 1: 215-17.
65. Buckland, pp. 128, 558; Catterall, 3: 228, 281, 422-23.
66. 1649 *Ulozhenie* 10: 122.
67. Ibid, 10: 262, 264 (from UKZP 7 and 13: 9 of 1628; see also AI 3, no. 92-xv of 1629).
68. Kolycheva, *Kholopstvo*, p. 221.

the eighteenth century required a slave seller to have a guarantor.[69] There were no such laws in Muscovy.

Unquestionably slave sales occurred in Muscovy, but the number of surviving sale documents is strikingly small. The absence of regulation is further evidence that sales of slaves were few. Customs books report no human cargoes passing through. Muscovy seems to have been unlike the Ottoman Empire, where immense documentary evidence on the slave trade provides not only much quantitative material but vast amounts of qualitative and descriptive material about the entire slave system.[70] Moreover, the sparseness of sales may explain the absence of Muscovite written norms on the splitting up of families by sale.

Because slave sales were so few, Muscovite law did not have to concern itself with a subject that was of paramount concern in many other slave systems, the law of commercial transactions. The most elementary form of such law is found in the Mesopotamian laws of Eshnunna, which provided that a man who purchased a slave (or an ox or any other valuable good) without evidence that the seller had the right to alienate the commodity was liable to be charged with theft. Muscovy knew no such law. Nor did Muscovite law concern itself, as did the Ethiopian *Fetha Nagast*, with exotica such as whether a person could sell what he did not have, a fugitive slave or an unborn child.[71] Muscovy was devoid of such commercial law concerns and the law was based almost exclusively on the assumption that sales transactions were between a person selling himself and the future slaveowner. To my knowledge, there was no other such system in all of human history. The Muscovite case makes one question the high generalization "that there is no slavery without the slave trade."[72]

Selunskii v. Borkov

While commercial transactions involving slaves were rare in Muscovy, they were carried on in one fashion or another, and some of them involved the legal system. One such device was the out-of-court settlement, a device that allowed slaveowners to negotiate between themselves the disposition of slaves even though a court had awarded a verdict that would have had a contrary effect. An example of this was the case litigated in the Slavery Chancellery before its di-

---

69. Pritchard, p. 167, art. 278; Mendelsohn, pp. 9, 38-39; Westermann, p. 16; Shtaerman, p. 81; Brunschvig, p. 26; *The Fetha Nagast*, p. 187; Gluckman, p. 202; Turton, p. 270; Wergeland, p. 32; Meijer, p. 346; Catterall, 3: 601, 668-69; Pritchard, p. 167, art. 279. In New Orleans, premia on fully guaranteed slaves were 31.9 percent for males, 26.0 percent for females (Laurence J. Kotlikoff, "The Structure of Slave Prices in New Orleans, 1804 to 1862," *Economic Inquiry* 17 [October 1979]: 505). Muscovy knew nothing of such practices.

70. Fisher, "Ottoman Slavery," pp. 27-29.

71. Pritchard, p. 137, art. 40; *The Fetha Nagast*, p. 188.

72. Jack Goody, "Slavery in Time and Space," in Watson, *Asian and African Systems*, p. 41.

rectors Semen Mikhailov Koltovskoi and Ivan Kuz'mich Begichev and state secretaries Petrikei Nasanov and Filipp Mitrofanov in the first months of 1621 over the slave Tit Vladimirov by Ivan Dmitriev Selunskii and Bogdan Semenov Borkov. As usual, other interesting aspects of Muscovite slave law and practice are revealed in the case as well.

The plaintiff, Ivan Selunskii, was a Greek who worked in the Chancellery of Foreign Affairs as a translator, a fact that was important in the last phase of the case. How and when he came to Muscovy is unknown, and it is even possible that he may have been born there. Be that as it may, in 1577, already he (and his two brothers, Avram and Paleolog) held the rank of Moscow *dvorianin*. In 1604, the three brothers reported for combat service. In a service list of 1616 Ivan and Avram each had a land compensation salary schedule of 750 cheti, and were also scheduled to receive the enormous annual salary of 75 rubles. Ivan Selunskii did not spend his entire career as a translator, for as soon as this case was concluded, he was appointed governor of Pereiaslavl'-Zaleskii, where he served a normal term of two and a half years. During his term there he supervised the compilation of a land cadastre. Being replaced in that post in 1624, he returned to Moscow, where, in 1628 he and his brother Avram were recorded as performing twenty-four-hour sentry duty in the tsar's palace. The following year Ivan Selunskii still had the rank of Moscow *dvorianin*, one he had held for over half a century. After that, no more was heard of him.[73]

The defendant, Bogdan Borkov, was also nearly at the peak of his career at the time of this case. In 1611 he had been a provincial *dvorianin* appointed to serve on rotation in Moscow from Meshchovsk, a small town southwest of the capital whose nearest big town was Kaluga. He also had the enormous land compensation entitlement of 850 cheti, and a very high cash salary of 25 rubles. Even though he was illiterate, he was at the top of the provincial service hierarchy. Probably while serving in Moscow, he managed to wangle a post as a court provisioner (*sytnik*), but nevertheless in the 1620s he was never able to rise above the rank of provincial *dvorianin*.[74]

The facts of Selunskii v. Borkov are relatively straightforward. It seems highly likely that Borkov was correct in his claim that the disputed slave, Tit Vladimirov, had been born in his house and had been his hereditary slave. Unfortunately for Borkov, however, he had never bothered to have that fact formulated in a written document, for which Slavery Chancellery officials reprimanded him in their verdict. Borkov claimed that Titko had fled from him to Selunskii, who on July 1, 1598, formulated a limited service slavery contract on him, a document that was presented at the trial, twenty-three years later. In 1615 Titko fled from Selunskii, and, according to Borkov, spent a year and a half in the cos-

73. BS 1: 183, 255; 2: 90; AMG 1: 40, 143; 2: 271; Storozhev, "B.S." (1909), p. 87; DR 1: 1016; KR 1: 758, 868, 924, 1033; Ivanov, AUBK, p. 374.

74. Storozhev, "B.S.", p. 131; RIB 28 (1912): 383, 695; Ivanov, AUBK, p. 40.

sacks. Much of the trial was devoted to efforts by Borkov to prove that Titko had joined the cossacks, for in those records Borkov claimed that Titko would have said that he was a runaway slave who belonged to Borkov. However, two trips to the Cossacks Chancellery and one to the Military Chancellery failed to produce the payroll or sustenance records that Borkov claimed would have proved that Titko had been his hereditary slave. After Titko had spent some time in the cossacks, in 1617 he returned to his old owner, Bogdan Borkov. His first wife, Mar'itsa, had died, and Titko remarried Luker'itsa, a hereditary dowry slave belonging to Borkov. Still Borkov did not formulate ownership documents on Titko, probably because he assumed that the oral tradition would support his claims, should they be challenged.

Challenged he was, and the court awarded the verdict to the plaintiff, Ivan Selunskii, because he presented the only solid evidence at the trial, his twenty-three-year-old limited service slavery contract. The defendant was upbraided by the panel because he had trusted a slave and had not documented his property. Borkov was also informed that, by law, he was to lose the wife, Luker'itsa, because he was in violation of the law for having kept someone in his house for more than six months (a voluntary slave) without formulating slavery documents on her, and furthermore that he had violated the law by marrying off to someone a person claimed as a slave but not formally registered. The Slavery Chancellery officials went rudely on to say that no one should believe anything Borkov said, for he did not formulate his slave claims and his cossack claims had been unsubstantiated.

Because of technicalities, the Slavery Chancellery ruled that it could not turn Luker'itsa over to the plaintiff with her husband because the suit had not mentioned her. They suggested, however, that, if Titko wanted his wife, he himself should submit a petition to Filaret, patriarch and cosovereign with his son Mikhail. This Selunskii did, in a petition to Filaret signed by Ivan Taras'evich Gramotin, his superior, head of the Foreign Affairs Chancellery and simultaneously head of the Novgorod Regional Chancellery, one of the most influential men of the time. (Filaret granted the petition immediately.) Then the court noted that the matter of 9.50 rubles' worth of stolen property was still pending, which the plaintiff alleged had been taken and which he was holding the defendant responsible for, and suggested that the matter be resolved by an oath, kissing the cross.

Everything was going in Selunskii's favor. Had he taken the oath, Borkov would have had to pay him the sum and all the court costs for the property as well. (Selunskii paid the inconsequential sum of 3 altyns for the decision on the slave.) Instead, the litigants presented the Slavery Chancellery with a surprise. They announced that they had reached an out-of-court settlement in which Selunskii ceded the slaves to Borkov, and they agreed on an undisclosed property settlement. One can only guess why the contentious old men did this. Certainly the incomes of both were adequate to manage any settlement, as well as to acquire more slaves, if they had wanted them. Perhaps they asked the slaves what they wanted, and settled on that basis. There is no way of knowing.

It is clear, however, that some cash must have changed hands, for Selunskii agreed to pay the court costs resulting from the out-of-court settlement. Had Selunskii prosecuted the suit to its logical conclusion, Borkov would have had to pay the costs, so one may assume that Borkov must have given Selunskii something. Selunskii's agreement to handle the court costs led to the last part of the case.

The entire court costs were 39 altyns, or 1.17 rubles, to pay for the various fees, trial costs, and "legal tenth" to be paid on the value of the stolen property. Selunskii, who had been living in Muscovy for at least half a century, petitioned that he be required to pay only half of those sums, or 0.585 rubles, because he was a foreigner. This forced the Slavery Chancellery to correspond with the Foreign Affairs Chancellery, which supported the translator's contention. Selunskii carried the communications in both directions and paid the sums, thus ending the case.[75]

The case of Selunskii v. Borkov illustrates several points of early seventeenth century Muscovite slave law. The first is that the party which had the documentary evidence was almost certain to win the dispute. Borkov presumably could have referred to more traditional forms of evidence such as eyewitnesses, as will be shown in the case of Buturlin v. Netes'ev (see chapter 8), but he knew that he had no chance to win in face of Selunskii's possession of a valid piece of paper. The second point is that the ancient point of the inviolability of a slave marriage was supported. A final point is that the judicial process was used to disguise what almost certainly was a market transaction. Why outright market transactions were rare events is something that will be discussed in chapter 10.

In this chapter on legal relations between slaveowners, we have seen that the Muscovite rules on disputes over the ownership of slaves, primarily fugitives, were much like those found in other systems. On the other hand, the Muscovites lacked a corpus of laws on the sale of slaves by one slaveowner to another because such transactions were insufficient to generate them. In this respect the Muscovite law of slavery was unusual but not unique. The explanation for the unusual nature of Muscovite law in this respect probably resides to a certain extent in the fact that many of the slaves were native Russians. However, as we shall see in chapter 10, there were probably other, equally important, reasons as well.

75. Iakovlev, *Kholopstvo*, pp. 330-38, no. 4.

8. Procedure and Evidence

Procedure is central to the legal process, for it is the machinery that regulates the steps and conduct of any action. It is the body of rules whereby rights are effected, and includes pleading, process, evidence, and practice. Although procedure is generally distinguished from the law of evidence, both will be discussed in this chapter. After a few words on the course of the Muscovite process, I will discuss particular aspects of procedure and evidence that were notably important for the institution of slavery.

A judicial process could be initiated by anyone to whom an official would listen. The official (who was also a judge, for there was no separation of powers in Muscovy) decided to hear out or receive the plaintiff's petition or not, and, if he did, the case was under way. In the early period, while much of the process was still dyadic, we may assume that officials automatically agreed to begin a case as part of the consensual process that similarly compelled the accused defendant to respond. Whether this prevailed after, say 1550, and especially in the big towns, is anybody's guess. Again, one may assume that a desire to collect their fees compelled most officials to initiate a process, although the frequent injunctions in the law against favoritism indicate that there were such problems at every stage of judicial actions. On the other hand, it seems fairly clear that petitions properly filed in central Moscow chancelleries in the seventeenth century were acted upon.

When a case was docketed, the judge then moved into action. A bailiff informed the defendant that he had been sued, and when the trial would begin. All litigants were responsible for presenting their entire case, including mobilizing most of the evidence. There was no professional bar, and litigants presented their own cases, or had someone else do it for them. The judge had in hand the plaintiff's charges, or heard them orally. He repeated them to the defendant, and then, according to the trial transcripts, shouted to the defendant: "Answer!" A cardinal rule was that all accusations and evidence had to be responded to, either accepted or refuted. A frequent defense tactic was to file a countersuit, and the judge would usually hear and rule on both simultaneously. The verdict was usually announced to the litigants or their representatives within several days. Depending on the nature of the case, the defendant was released on his own recognizance, forced to post bond, or jailed from the time the case was initiated until the verdict was announced. A losing defendant was expected to satisfy the plaintiff immediately, or make arrangements for doing so. Failure on that count might lead to enslavement.

Slaves as Witnesses

All slave systems with written law devote some attention to the potential role of the slave at court, especially as witness. The matter seems to have two distinguishable aspects: The slave as witness in cases involving his owner and in cases where third parties were involved. Once again, North Americans are likely to have assumptions on this topic based on U.S. practice, where the rule against slaves as witnesses was nearly absolute, a principle whose inutility was noted in the antebellum South.[1]

Other societies have had different norms. The slave could appear as a witness in court in the Late Assyrian period.[2] In Greece, testimony might be taken, with the agreement of the slaveowner, from a slave under duress—by the bastinado or the rack.[3] The Romans changed this to a requirement that slave testimony, which could not deal with a master, could be given only under torture, and this custom was passed to Byzantium. The judge was not responsible if the slave died under such torture.[4] In Byzantium, slaves could be used as witnesses against their owners only in cases of murder, sacrilege, fornication, the kidnapping of girls, pederasty, and falsifying a census. The general rule was that "a slave or freedman shall not be a witness for or against his master."[5]

The Bulgarian *Court Law for the People (Zakon sudnyi liudem)*, a work with Byzantine roots that later circulated in Russia, said that slave testimony was suspect and could be used in court only when the object of litigation was a slave, and only under torture.[6] The same principle was operative in the Danish Virgin Islands, where slave testimony was admissible as proof only when the slave witness had been baptised and was testifying against another slave.[7] The Spanish law of 1263 noted that slavery made its victims desperate, and therefore their testimony might not be reliable. Slaves could not testify at all (except in treason cases) against their owners, although they could testify in defense of them when they had been accused of treason, murder, or adultery.[8] With limited exceptions, Islamic law generally does not admit slave testimony.[9] In India no slave by birth could be a witness in either criminal or civil cases except in extraordinary cases, where there were no other witnesses.[10] The Thai prohibition against slaves acting as witnesses seems to have been absolute.[11]

1. Friedman, pp. 199-200; Rose, pp. 176, 194, 203, 210, 230.
2. Mendelsohn, p. 71.
3. Westermann, p. 17.
4. Buckland, pp. 86-88.
5. *Ecloga* 14: 5 (Freshfield, p. 97; Lipshits, p. 63).
6. Short ZSL 20; Expanded ZSL 22.
7. Hall, pp. 178, 182.
8. Klein, *Americas*, p. 65.
9. Brunschvig, p. 29.
10. *Laws of Manu* 8: 66.
11. Turton, p. 270.

In the *Russkaia Pravda*, the situation concerning slave witnesses was much the same as in ancient India. Article 66 explicitly forbade slaves to be witnesses, with the exception of cases in which there were no free witnesses. In that case, an elite slave who was an estate manager could serve. This epitomizes the dilemma that any society which uses elite slaves is likely to find itself in: many of the decisions on which litigation might subsequently occur were made initially by slaves, and without their testimony society simply could not function. Thus there can be little doubt that elite slave testimony was frequently admitted as evidence in early Muscovy of the fourteenth and fifteenth centuries, and that this was the wedge that opened up the judicial system to other slave testimony.[12] Article 85 elaborated on the use of slaves as witnesses: in the dyadic judicial process, the plaintiff was responsible for bringing the accused to court. When he did so, he might refer to the slave's testimony, but it had to be explicit that the free man, not the slave, was initiating the process. Should the plaintiff fail to win the case, whether by ordeal or some other means, he had to compensate the accused by paying him a grivna "for the pain inflicted." The reason given in the law for the compensation was that the accused had been wrongly singled out by a slave. This exhibits the customary distrust of slaves, who were assumed to be outside the basic social fabric and thus uninterested in its preservation. One well imagines that a person wrongly accused by a slave had other avenues of recourse against the free man who initiated the prosecution, but that is not spelled out in the *Pravda*.

A highly significant change occurred in the judicial capacity of slaves between the era of the *Russkaia Pravda* and 1649. Earlier I noted the participation of slaves in judicial processes of the first half of the sixteenth century, but in those cases the slaves were litigants rather than witnesses. (Recall, for example, the trial by combat in Metropolitan's Peasants v. Okinfov et al., discussed in chapter 6.) At the same time, slaves began to be used in such important areas as witnessing documents.[13] Moreover, the institution of what we might call "the slave lawyers," which will be discussed further when we consider the occupations of slaves in chapter 14, seems to have made significant progress during the reign of Ivan IV, and the presence of slave advocates at court became an accepted practice.[14] Similar developments occurred in Germanic society, where a lord could send his slave to court, and the slave was admitted to the ordeal, trial by combat, as any free man.[15]

Equally important in legitimizing the presence of slaves in the Muscovite judicial process were decrees on judicial procedure promulgated on August 21, 1556. One of them demanded that the country's elite landholders issue orders

12. Kolycheva, *Kholopstvo*, p. 232.
13. Ibid., p. 234.
14. AI 1: 271, no. 154, xx.
15. Wergeland, pp. 86-87.

to the inhabitants of their villages (slaves and peasants) not to lie in judicial investigations, but to tell the truth. The decree went on to threaten with disgrace boyars and *deti boiarskie* whose slaves or peasants were found to have lied in an investigation, and the slaves and peasants were to be punished as in major felony cases. The lords could escape disgrace by telling the truth directly to the tsar, and the verdict was to be delivered on the basis of their testimony.[16] Not only is the taking of testimony from slaves of interest here, but also the fact that slaves and peasants are mentioned in the same context. While peasants were being abased in this period by such measures as this, linking them with slaves, they still enjoyed the right to move at St. George's Day and were not enserfed. It is also noteworthy here that a slaveowner could short-circuit the entire judicial process by going directly to the tsar.

The process of admission of the slave to the judicial process was completed by the *Ulozhenie* of 1649, which noted that his testimony could be taken in any judicial proceeding (*obysk* or *dopros*). The slave was to be put under oath in front of an icon and enjoined to tell the truth with a reminder that he would suffer at the Last Judgment if he lied under oath.[17] In this article the slave is linked with peasants and persons "of the female sex," a typical homologism. No direct source for this article is known, but its content indicates that it is a relatively new creation.[18] It is a logical development of the 1556 decree, and by 1649 the peasants had been enserfed and were increasingly linked in the government's mind with slaves. If peasants were entirely excluded from the judicial process, then the state might have followed the sixteenth-century Lithuanian practice of concerning itself solely with the gentry and nobility, and turned the lower classes over to them. The Muscovite state did not do this, however, and admitted both peasants and slaves to relatively unlimited participation in the judicial system. Women were admitted too. It should be noted, however, that slaves could not testify against their owners, and this provision was extended to manumitted slaves, who also could not testify against slaveowners' children.[19]

In late Muscovy, slaves could testify not only on their own account but in lieu of their owners as well. The logic of this is patent: the slave was an appendage, an extension of his owner, and so could be assumed to represent him. Moreover, in the real world, a household slave could be assumed to know the affairs and doings of his master. Thus owners in litigation could select a slave to take the oath on their behalf, a practice frequently seen in the cases discussed in this work. In another article that certainly arose from actual experience, we learn that if a slave an owner had selected to take the oath on his behalf fled or died before he could do so, another slave had to replace the fugitive or deceased. The

16. AI 1: 256, no. 154, v, 10-11.
17. 1649 *Ulozhenie* 10: 173.
18. The same point was made by Kolycheva (*Kholopstvo*, p. 235).
19. 1649 *Ulozhenie* 10: 174.

second slave apparently was to be selected by the court, and if the owner said that he did not have confidence in that slave, and suggested another one, the court was to insist that the person it had chosen should take the oath.[20] The reason behind this is clear: truth as revealed in divine justice does not depend upon particular individuals.

Karsakov v. Borykov and Dubenskoi

That the testimony of slaves, particularly those being contested, could be decisive is evident in one of the few nearly complete trial transcripts of a slavery case from the first half of the seventeenth century, Karsakov v. Borykov and Dubenskoi. The cases were initiated in the Slavery Chancellery in May of 1628 before the directors Stepan Ivanovich Volynskii and Ivan Fomich Ogarev and the state secretaries Ivan Eremeev and Andrei Stroev, and concluded there on December 29, 1631, before a new chief, Ivan Federov Volkonskoi, and state secretaries Stroev and Ivan Kostiurin.

There were really two cases, which were treated as two during the actual trials, but as one most of the rest of the time, probably so that the plaintiff could save on scribal fees. The plaintiff, Petr Stepanov Karsakov, was certainly one of the more prosperous individuals of his time, but how he achieved that prosperity cannot be determined. Records available to me do not reveal that he ever distinguished himself, but the case itself makes it quite clear that he had been a serviceman for some time prior to 1628. Apparently he had been a western frontier serviceman in the Smolensk region who had been resettled after the loss of that area to the Poles during the Time of Troubles, and one may surmise that his status was acquired for services rendered prior to 1611 and registered in documents now lost. For all the time that he was listed in the records now extant, he had the rank of Moscow *dvorianin*, from November 27, 1625, when he was one of fourteen of that rank who dined with Tsar Mikhail and his father, Patriarch Filaret, through 1632, when he stood guard at the Iauza gates to Moscow, until his retirement in 1643. On the eve of the Smolensk War, in 1632, an inventory was made of the Moscow *dvoriane* (see chapter 17), in which he was listed as having the very high cash salary of 47 rubles and at least 700 cheti of land, including 260 cheti of service land in Kineshma, 100 cheti of waste in Iur'ev Pol'skii, 200 cheti of patrimonial estate land in Kineshma, and 143 cheti of waste patrimonial dowry land near Moscow. His brother Ivan's cash salary was 59 rubles and his land compensation was 950 cheti, so one may assume that Peter was entitled to roughly the same amount of land, perhaps 850 cheti, and that he possessed a large fraction of it. Unfortunately the inventory does not list his peasants, but there must have been many of them, judging by the service he was supposed to render: "himself on an ordinary cavalry horse, 3 slaves on Nogai horses (one with a lance [*rogatina*], one with bow and arrow, one with a hand-

20. Ibid., 20: 96; MS, p. 290.

gun [*pishchal'*]), and as many baggage train slaves as are required."[21] These resources and requirements placed him near the peak of the Moscow service system.

His opponents were not as well endowed, but the fact of their inferior sources certainly had no relationship to their loss of their cases, although it was relevant to the way they were able to handle the verdicts. Mikhail Semenov Borykov was a *zhilets*, the entry rank into the upper service class, from Kolomna, although for some reason he was not on the 1632 inventory of *zhil'tsy* (see chapter 17), which did include eight men from Kolomna province. A number of years prior to the trial, in 1615, he had guaranteed the service of one of his fellow servicemen from Kolomna, indicating that he was by that time one of the more prominent members of his community, and so he must have been promoted to the rank of *zhilets* by 1628 as a reward for regular and meritorious service.[22] The other defendant, Matvei Matveev Dubenskoi, was also from Kolomna province and in profile much like Borykov. He held the rank of provincial *dvorianin,* the upper crust of the provincial service class. In 1628 he had been one of those chosen by his peers to direct the military levy (*okladchik*) from his province, an honor (and a burden) usually reserved for those at the peak of their careers.[23] People of this kind were almost always slaveowners.

The suits were remarkably similar. Karsakov v. Borykov concerned the identity and possession of Arina (Orinka), daughter of Isai (or Ivan), her husband and children. Karsakov v. Dubenskoi concerned the identity and possession of Ivan (or Luka), son of Pavl Postnikov, his wife and children. Both cases were consequences of the Time of Troubles, which threw the population of Muscovy into turmoil as people moved here and there in an effort to survive.

The facts of the first case seem to have been as follows. Orinka was the daughter of Iváshko Aleksandrov Molozhenisov, and both he and his daughter were listed in declarations of slave holdings that Karsakov had made in 1613 after the destruction of Moscow in 1611. (On this procedural point, see Tatishchev v. Selekhovskii, 1624, below.) In 1617 Orinka Ivanova, her husband (who died shortly thereafter), and their two boys, Kharitonka and Kondrashka, who had been registered as hereditary slaves in Smolensk, fled from Karsakov's Kineshma property, 350 kilometers northeast of Moscow, which presumably he had been assigned after the fall of Smolensk. The flight was in the winter, and they rode away in style, in a sleigh pulled by four horses (a gray gelding, a bay gelding, a chestnut gelding, and a chestnut mare with mane and tail lighter than its body) wearing horse collars, all worth 25 rubles. Their clothing and various small items were worth 20.50 rubles, for a total theft of 45.50 rubles. They ended up 350

21. DR 1: 759; Tatishchev (1910), p. 12; Ivanov, AUBK, p. 209; Stashevskii, ZMD, p. 130.

22. RIB 28(1912): 475; Iziumov, "Zhiletskoe zemlevladenie," p. 36.

23. Savelov 3: 115; Ivanov, AUBK, p. 121.

kilometers away, on a service estate that at the time of the trial belonged to the widow Ografena Borykova, the mother of the defendant, Mikhail Borykov, near Kolomna, 100 kilometers southeast of Moscow. Borykov's defense was that in Smolensk Orinka had been a vagrant beggar (a typical occupation for those who later sold themselves into slavery), who had never served Karsakov, that she was legally a peasant woman with a name different from that of the individual Karsakov was suing for. It is not clear why it was necessary to admit in Kineshma that she was from Smolensk, but perhaps her dialect or pronunciation made that a necessity.

The usual maneuvering followed the initial presentation of positions. Karsakov referred to the declaration he filed with the Slavery Chancellery in 1613, after the destruction of Moscow in 1611, about his ownership of Orinka and her father, Ivashko son of Aleksandr Molozhenisov, and then to another declaration he had filed after they had fled. He also cited individuals (one of them being an Ivan Petrov Lenin) and their slaves and peasants residing in the Kineshma area who knew that Orinka and her children had been his slaves and that they had fled from him. He also cited everyone else for ten and more versts around his estate, the *dvoriane*, *deti boiarskie*, other slaves, peasants, and clergymen, excepting members of the Bezstuzhov clan (apparently his enemies). Borykov responded that all those cited were the plaintiff's friends, all men of Smolensk, presumably those who had been given land in the Kineshma region after the fall of Smolensk. He also claimed that the contested slave woman was Orinka, daughter of Isai, not the daughter of Ivan, and cited her priest to prove the point. Another piece of evidence was the census which included her (second) husband, the peasant Mishka Semenov. Finally, he cited everyone in his region of Kolomna province to prove that she and her children had come from Smolensk province and had been living on his property as peasants since 1616, the year before Karsakov claimed that they had fled.

Woe to Barykov, all of his prevarications and distortions were in vain! The panel of the Slavery Chancellery next interrogated Orinka: whose hereditary slavewoman was she, what was her name? Her answer was reported as indirect speech:

> Her name is Orinka, daughter of Ivan, wife of Obram Filipov. They were the hereditary slaves of Petr Korsakov. During the destruction of Smolensk she had left Petr with her husband and children, Kharitonka and Kondrashka, and they had begged as vagrants. Her husband Obram died. Having left Petr, she remarried in Smolensk a free man, Ishka Semenov. Having left Smolensk with the second husband to seek employment in the various towns, they came to Mikhail Borykov. They had lived as peasants with Mikhail for about ten years. Now her husband and children are on Mikhail's land.

Thus she contradicted every one of Borykov's claims. She was the daughter of Ivan, not Isai. They had come to his place ten years earlier, not twelve or more. What is surprising is the fact that she did not claim that she and her family left Karsakov because of his inability to feed them; she didn't claim this, probably because it was not true, and perhaps because the Slavery Chancéllery looked askance on such claims in any case. One may assume that she supported Karsakov's claims out of a fear of being tortured.

After her testimony, Orinka, who had been arrested without resistance two weeks earlier, petitioned that she be released on bail to Borykov. (On bail, see Bormosov v. Berechinskii, 1627-29, discussed below.) In spite of Borykov's obvious untrustworthiness, the request was granted, probably because the bail system was so effective that those enmeshed in it were almost certain to fulfill its terms.

In 1617 Ivashka Pavlov Postniakov (Posnikov), his wife Maritsia, and three small children also fled from Kineshma. They stole property worth 35.50 rubles: three horses (a chestnut stallion worth 8.50 rubles, a bay stallion worth 5.50 rubles, and a mare worth 4.50 rubles), two cows (one black, one red, worth 5 rubles), plus clothing worth 12 rubles. Except for silver beads worth a ruble and some expensive coats claimed to be worth 2 and 3 rubles, the clothing was probably what the slaves wore every day. Judging by their theft, these slaves give the appearance of not having had access to their owner's wardrobe or cash box, as did household slaves, but rather of being farmers. The trial of Karsakov v. Dubenskoi to determine the possession of Ivashka and family was not held at the same time, in late May, as was Karsakov v. Borykov, because Dubenskoi had to report immediately for summer service. Using his own initiative, the bailiff, who after a small battle arrested the putative fugitive Ivashka, immediately released him on bail, guaranteed by five other Kolomna servicemen. Plaintiff Karsakov later implausibly lamented that this was a violation of the arrest order (*nakaznaia pamiat'*), made purposely to befriend Dubenskoi by entangling him, the defendant, in bureaucratic red tape and delay. Six months later on November 6, 1628, Dubenskoi reported to the Slavery Chancellery, noted that his service in Pereslavl'-Riazanskii was over, and asked that his presence be noted lest he lose the case for having violated the bail agreement. That was done, and he was ordered to produce a new bail agreement, according to which he would appear for trial between November 15 and 18.

Two weeks later, on November 20, Matvei Dubenskoi appeared in the Slavery Chancellery to report that, when he was bringing the contested slave for the trial, plaintiff Petr Karsakov and his slaves forcibly had kidnapped the contested Ivashka from him. As we know, slave theft at one time had been a capital felony. In spite of his claim, on December 3 the Slavery Chancellery announced that it was planning to fine Dubenskoi 50 rubles because he had not presented Ivashka between November 15 and 18. He was held responsible for fulfilling his agreement, and excuses were not tolerated.

The Slavery Chancellery's next tack was to order Dubenskoi to present Ivashka's second wife, Matrenka (whom he had married already in Kolomna), and their children. A new set of five guarantors then pledged that Dubenskoi would present the remaining contested slaves, plus the 50-ruble fine, in one week, on December 8. Not on the eighth, but on the seventeenth, Matrenka and her two children, a son Kuz'ka and a daughter Man'ka, were presented for the trial in the Slavery Chancellery. Finally, seven months after the initial actions, the trial was held.

Karsakov presented his claims, Dubenskoi denied them and alleged that once again it was a case of mistaken identity. The plaintiff wanted Ivashka, but the defendant had Lukashka. Karsakov's evidence was similar to that in the trial for Orinka: neighbors, their slaves and peasants, who knew the facts. Moreover, in 1613 he had filed a declaration of ownership after the destruction of Moscow. Dubenskoi's claims were lame indeed. Besides repeatedly claiming that Karsakov wanted the wrong man, he referred to the records of the archbishop of Kolomna to prove that Lukashka had married the peasant woman Matrenka in his house. To this Karsakov responded that he was suing for Ivashka, not Lukashka. Dubenskoi also claimed that Lukashka had been his peasant since 1614, two years prior to the purported flight of Ivashka.

Then the Slavery Chancellery panel called Matrenka to testify, and she gave it all away:

> The woman said that her name was Matrenka, daughter of Iakov. She was born in Dorogobuzh province [between Moscow and Smolensk]. She went from Dorogobuzh province to Matvei Dubenskoi's service landholding [a distance of about 350 kilometers], where she married a man who had come there from elsewhere. That migrant said that he had been the slave of Petr Karsakov of Smolensk, and his name was Ivashka. Matvei had married her to that slave, Ivashka, and Matvei had been calling him Lukashka already for ten years. She said that she has four children: [three boys] Mikitka, Ivashka, and Kuzemka, and a daughter Marinka. The priest Ivan of the church John the Baptist in Kolomna province married them in Matvei's service landholding. The priest left that place for Khuton, where he later died.

After the trial, the litigants posted bail, and Matrenka's bail was provided by persons not associated with either litigant.

Six weeks later, acting on a warrant sworn out by Karsakov, the bailiff Fedor Levashov brought in the primary object of Karsakov v. Dubenskoi, Ivashka, whom he had arrested just outside of Moscow. Ivashka again supported plaintiff Karsakov's case:

> The slave who was brought in said under interrogation that his name is Ivashka, son of Pavl Posnikov. He is the hereditary slave of Petr Karsakov. He fled about fifteen years ago from Petr with his wife Mar'itsa. His wife died in Kolomna about ten years ago. Having fled from Petr, he went to Matvei Dubenskoi in Kolomna, and there he married at Matvei's a girl who had come

from elsewhere, Matrenka. They had four children, boys Mikitka, Ivashka, and Kus'ka, and a daughter Mar'itsa. Since that time he had lived at Matvei's. Matvei had brought him from Kolomna to Moscow, and he, Ivashka, had fled from Matvei about thirteen weeks ago, and had been living by begging [*kormilsia*] in the villages of Moscow province. Having returned to Moscow, he was seized just beyond the Chertol'skie gates. When he lived at Matvei's, he changed his name to Luk'iashka, son of Pavl.

Again, the slave gave it all away. He supported Karsakov's claim for the stolen property by noting that he had gone directly to Dubenskoi's, but he let the latter off the hook for the 50-ruble fine by noting that he had run away from him, and thus Dubenskoi was not to blame for the slave's not being present for the November 15 trial. Note also that he did not support Dubenskoi's claim that Karsakov had seized (kidnapped) the slave from him.

A comic episode followed. Dubenskoi appeared at the Slavery Chancellery, obviously unaware that Ivashka had confessed. He repeated his claim that Ivashka was his peasant, and furthermore announced he had filed suit against Petr Karsakov in the Moscow Judicial Chancellery for purportedly having taken Ivashka away from him on the way to trial. (The "kidnapping" or "slave theft" charge was subsequently forgotten, probably because of the slave's testimony.)

Less comic was the handling of Ivashka, who by the time he was brought to trial was a notorious runaway. Rather than being released on bail to one of the litigants, or being released to a private entrepreneur who kept detainees for a "chaining fee," he was sent to jail. The Muscovites, as already noted, had an abhorrence of jails, and Ivashka's case brought the issue to the minds of the Slavery Chancellery, which on March 30 ordered a clerk to compile a list of those being held in jail at its behest, whether before or after a trial. Ivashka/ Lukashka proposed that he be let out on bail in the care of neutral parties, and this was done. While the slave was in jail, Dubenskoi got a continuance on March 6, 1629, because of a call to frontier service in Riazan'. (Simultaneously he himself was a plaintiff in another case before the Chancellery, suing Ermolai Gvozdev of Riazan' to recover three of his sister's dowry slaves. The trial had been held, but no verdict had been rendered.)

For absolutely unknown reasons, "the law's delay" seized the case. On November 21, 1629, Karsakov asked the tsar that verdicts be rendered in his two cases. Eighteen months had elapsed since the May 28, 1628, trial of Karsakov v.Bory-kov, and ten months since Ivashka's confession in Karsakov v. Dubenskoi, and nothing had been done in the interim. He noted that he had been in Moscow for three months since his discharge from service in Valuiki, trying to get justice in his cases, and that the delay was favoring the defendants. On November 24, he repeated his petition, and made the traditional claim that the defendants were using their leisure to bribe witnesses in the countryside. Then the Slavery Chancellery panel asked for the law on continuances (see Mortkin v. Gur'ev, below), decided that the defendants had had ample time to report to the Slavery Chancellery, and announced verdicts in favor of Karsakov on November 29. They noted that Kolomna "is a town not far from Moscow," so that there was no excuse for violating the law on continuances. "Their disobediance was great." Moreover, it was obvious that the defendants had not come to Moscow because they knew that the testimony of the slaves had cost them the verdicts. "These slaves, Ivashka Pavlov and his wife, and Orinka, in the preliminary interrogation [*privod*] and at the trial said that they were Petr's hereditary Smolensk slaves, and on this ground Matvei and Mikhail lose the case. On the same grounds they lose the cases in the stolen property disputes." The formal verdict was announced on December 9.

The consequences of the verdict were formidable. Plaintiff Petr Karsakov collected ten slaves that he did not have before. He had to pay the capitation fees of 3 altyns apiece for the adults in the dispute with Dubenskoi, 6 altyns for Ivashka and Matrenka, but he did not have to pay anything for their four children, three boys and a girl, because they were not present at the trial and in the official transference ceremony. On December 16 Borykov turned over his people to Karsakov, who had to pay 21 altyns for a population explosion: Orinka's son Kharitonka had married one Marfutka Ivanova, and they had begotton two boys, Petrushka and Vaska, and a girl, Dunka. Her other son had married one Ofim'itsa. So, Karsakov had to pay for seven persons, but he was excused from paying for two of them, Khariton's children, Vas'ka and Dun'ka, who were still at the breast. From Borykov, Karsakov got nine slaves. For the total sum of 27 altyns (= 0.81 rubles), he took home fifteen slaves.

That was not all, however. The slaves' confessions also allowed him to collect his total claims for stolen property, 79 rubles, an amount approximately equal to his annual cash compensation. In addition, the losing defendants had to pay 8.34 rubles in court costs. Often, apparently, suits for stolen property were a ploy to force concessions on the main issue, the slaves (see Proshevskii v. Aridov and Treskin v. Zykov, above). Karsakov, however, wanted every kopek of his claim, in blood, even it if had to be beaten out of the defendants. (His motivations are not apparent: perhaps he was mercenary, perhaps he was angered by the great length of time it took him to find his fugitive slaves, and by the obstinacy of the defendants in the face of the facts.)

On December 13, 1629, the Slavery Chancellery bailiff Fedor Levashov was ordered to collect 33.50 rubles for Karsakov and 3.57 rubles in court costs from Dubenskoi, and 45.50 rubles for Karsakov and 4.77 rubles in court costs from Borykov. The plaintiff's due was to be turned over to him, the sovereign's due was to be turned over to the treasurey of the Slavery Chancellery. Bailiff Levashov then got five men of Kolomna to guarantee that Dubenskoi would not leave Moscow and would appear at the first hour of every day in the Slavery Chancellery to be tortured by having his shins and feet beaten (*na pravezhe*) until the sums due were paid. The same five men, plus another four men of Kolomna, made the same guarantee for Borykov. The guarantors swore that each was responsible for the sums should the debtor default. At some time later in the month, the debtors had not paid the court costs, and Levashov was ordered to collect them from the guarantors. For some reason he failed to do so, but on January 13, 1630, Dubenskoi and Borykov paid them, and the sum of 8.34 rubles was dutifully noted as having been received.

The court costs had priority over the plaintiff's suits, which still had to be paid. We must again recall that 79 rubles was no mean sum, a figure that would buy at least twenty-five limited service contract slaves at the current government-set price. Borykov and Dubenskoi each had to pay Karsakov sums that for them must have been equivalent to roughly what the government paid them in cash for five years. Such sums did not just lie around, obviously. But Karsakov wanted his due. On January 30, 1630, he petitioned Tsar Mikhail (in care of the Petitions Chancellery, which then forwarded it immediately to the Slavery Chancellery) for his money, or whatever had been collected so far. He noted that both Borykov and Dubenskoi had endured, so far, two months of torture "hoping to escape having to pay" (*izvolochit'*). That was probably an unjust claim, especially in light of the fact that so far only 19 rubles had been paid. Karsakov signed a receipt for the money.

On April 13, 1630, Karsakov again petitioned for his money. By this time another 46 rubles had been collected, which on April 17 were duly signed for by the plaintiff. Somebody in the Slavery Chancellery noted that the records should be kept straight, and the calculation was made that 10.50 rubles were still due from Borykov, and 3.50 rubles from Dubenskoi.

The summer campaign season intervened, and then a whole year inexplicably went by, and Karsakov was still owed 14 rubles. Tiring of the delay, on December 3, 1631, he asked that the remaining sums be collected from the guarantors. The Slavery Chancellery obliged by ordering the 14 rubles collected from them. On December 29, one of the guarantors (Prov) Volodimerov Kusterskoi, paid the 14 rubles, which was signed for by Karsakov's slave Ivashka Iakimov. (For some reason Iakimov was given only 6.985 of the 14 rubles.)[24] Thus ended a case that had begun with the flight of two slave couples fifteen years earlier, and had been resolved by trials in the Slavery Chancellery three years earlier.

The case is clear evidence of the centrality of slave testimony in the Muscovite system of slave law. Getting the two women before the panel in the Slavery Chancellery resolved everything. One had been a fugitive herself, the other had married a fugitive whose wife had died. Because of the passage of time and the migration of the plaintiff and his slaves eastward after the fall of Smolensk, there can hardly be any doubt that the defendants would have won their cases had the fugitive slaves been able to sustain their stories. Facing certain torture, the wo-

24. Iakovlev, *Kholopstvo*, pp. 414-37, no. 16.

men told the truth, which resulted in the transference of fifteen people into slavery, of whom only five had actually been slaves, the rest being enmeshed by marriage and birth. Moreover, the confessions forced the defendants to pay ruinous monetary damages, costs that were so high that they well might have caused enslavment of the debtors by default had there not been a law forbidding the enslavment for debt of members of the middle service class.

One view of the testimony of a fugitive slave was expressed by the arbiter Anfanasii Ivanov Nesterov in the 1643 case of Miakinin v. Velkov: "There is no reason to believe him, for the fugitive slave is free to say whatever he wants to."[25] However, this did not correspond to the official view, set down in 1623/24 and reiterated in the *Ulozhenie* of 1649: in a dispute over the ownership of a slave, the testimony of the slave was to be believed. Recognizing that a slaveowner might attempt to speak in court on his slave's behalf, the *Ulozhenie* explicitly denied a defendant the right to testify on behalf of a fugitive slave, and prescribed that a slave had to answer for himself any questions put to him by a plaintiff.[26] This is a long way from slave systems which so denied the human capacity of slaves that they excluded them from any role in the judicial process.

Already noted in chapter 6 was the fact that the slave seems to have been a nearly equal party in cases involving his property disputes with third party strangers. This was not the case, of course, in suits between owners over what a fugitive slave had stolen from the lawful lord and taken to a defendant. In such cases the judge recognized the slave's rational capacities and took his testimony in disputes over what he had actually taken when he left his lawful lord and what he had acquired while in flight, but such testimony was rarely decisive, and the oath was often resorted to in stolen-property matters.

One may assume that the testimony of slaves was either not taken at all, or only on a very limited basis, in most slave systems, for two reasons. First, to preserve the fiction that a slave was more of a thing than a person, it was important to limit in every way possible his capacity to act as a human being. Such considerations were of secondary importance in a society such as Muscovy, where there was little concern for such niceties as human capacities. In this sense there was a significant change between medieval and early modern Rus'. Second, most legal systems considered that a slave was much like a spouse, who is never forced in civilized societies of whatever degree to testify against a mate; a slave, therefore, should not be forced to testify against his owner. The testimony of spouses against one another is taken only in judicial systems willing to violate the natural restraint of the family. Atomization and destruction of the family is the reward for any society willing to go against that taboo. Similarily, slaves who might have information worth bearing in court or elsewhere against their owners were usually part of a household. Slaveowners would have been unwilling

25. Ibid., p. 502, no. 25, III.
26. 1649 *Ulozhenie* 20: 54; MS, p. 274.

to tolerate confiding in their slaves (as many of them did), or allowing them to witness everyday life (as was inevitable), if they thought that at some time that slave might be used against them. For that reason slave societies have been very unwilling to allow testimony by slaves against their owners, for it would have undermined the basic function and utility of slavery itself in the eyes of the vast majority of slaveowners. This concern Muscovy shared with other slaveholding societies.

Other Witnesses

Both in conjunction with and in spite of the increasingly paper-flow spirit of later Muscovy, insistence on witnesses remained vigorous in the law. Witnessed wills conveying slaves were generally assumed to be valid documents, although they could be overturned by a limited service slavery contract that had been properly registered in the official records.[27] Given the proper circumstances, witnesses in a trial could overturn written documents.[28]

The presence of witnesses to the actual sale of slaves seems random, so I tried to make sense of the use of witnesses by an examination of the numbers involved.

TABLE 8.1
Relationship of Witnesses and Price of Slaves per Document

No. of Witnesses	Price per Document	N
1	3.25R	1,549
2	5.14	426
3	7.09	78
4	5.80	10
5	10.67	3

There seems to have been some relationship between the number of witnesses to a document and the price paid for the slaves in the document (see table 8.1). (The relationship is not strongly linear, however, for the correlation coefficient is only 0.3900.) There is, on the other hand, absolutely no relationship between the number of witnesses and the number of slaves per document (corr. coeff. = 0.0594). The relative importance of the two independent variables (cost and number of slaves) on the dependant variable (witnesses) seems to be confirmed by regression analysis also (price–Beta = 0.32656; number of slaves–Beta= 0.01686).

27. 1649 *Ulozhenie* 20: 64; MS, pp. 277-78.
28. 1649 *Ulozhenie* 20: 108; MS, p. 294.

The General Investigation

One of the less well-known forms of evidence used in Muscovite legal cases was the "general investigation" (*poval'nyi obysk*), an interrogation of everyone (ordinarily all adult free males, but slaves, women, and others might be included as well) in a community to discover their knowledge of certain facts. Such investigation often involved hundreds of people, but according to the law twenty or thirty were enough if no more people lived within a 10-kilometer radius of the site.[29] In many respects the general investigation was the supreme form of evidence in Muscovy, as shown by the fact that it could overturn a limited service slavery contract by proving that a litigant's hereditary slavery claims had precedence.[30] The general investigation, along with the physical descriptions in the various slavery documents, were the primary evidentiary bases for proving ownership of slaves, while land cadastres determined where peasant-serfs were required to reside.[31]

The procedures of the general investigation were outlined in an order sent in the name of the tsar to a governor (*voevoda*) in September 1650.

You are ordered to send a reliable *syn boiarskii*, whoever is fitting, throughout the town of Insar and its province to conduct a grand general investigation. He is to question archimandrites, hegumens, and monastery elders under the monk's oath, priests and deacons under the priestly oath; *dvoriane, deti boiarskie,* sundry servicemen and townsmen, patrimonial estate and service landholding stewards [who might be slaves], elders, sworn men (*tseloval'niki*), and peasants according to our oath on the cross; and princes, murzy, Tatars, Mordovians, and sundry tribute payers [*iasachnie liudi*] according to the oath [*shert'*] of their faith. [The questions to be answered were placed here. That will be discussed below.]

All people of the sundry ranks shall be questioned face to face; each person is to be interrogated individually. The investigator[*syshchik*] shall write down the testimony he gathers in the presence of the witnesses, not in their absence. He shall obtain the signatures of the witnesses, but if witnesses are illiterate their spiritual fathers shall sign their testimony in their stead. You shall order the investigator to write down what the witnesses say in the investigation; he shall enter their names and testimonies on the record by name, individually, and by social ranks. The testimony of the *dvoriane* and *deti boiarskie* shall be taken separately; the *dvoriane* and *deti boiarskie* shall not register their testimony together with their slaves and peasants.

Order the investigator to tell the witnesses specifically that they must tell the truth in the investigation directly, fearing no one and favoring no one by any means. But if the witnesses testify falsely in the investigation, they shall be in great disgrace with us and shall be punished.

29. 1649 *Ulozhenie* 20: 95; MS, pp. 289-90.
30. 1649 *Ulozhenie* 20: 108; MS, p. 294.
31. Man'kov, *Ulozhenie*, p. 135.

Order the investigator firmly, and in the order to him include this decree of ours which is written in this communication, that he shall write down exactly, with great precision, the truth that he finds in the investigation under our oath. He shall not befriend a friend or take vengeance on an enemy. He shall watch out for and take firm precautions that the witnesses, colluding in family groupings, do not lie in the investigations. If people begin to tell lies by family groupings in the investigation, and he, the investigator, learns of this, or if people begin to waver [*oslushatisia*], and they refuse to give their testimony, the investigator shall write about that to us in Moscow, about who specifically will not give his testimony. The investigator shall send lists with names of those who testify falsely in family groupings in the investigation, and he shall sign the lists.

If he, the investigator, begins to conduct the investigation unjustly for his own avarice, or he favors a friend or takes vengeance on an enemy in the investigation; or, if people prevaricate in family groupings in the investigations and others refuse to give their testimony, and the investigator fails to write to us about this, favoring the plaintiff or the defendant; and this becomes known to us in spite of him, the investigator: he, the investigator, for that shall be in great disgrace with us and shall be punished.

If a plaintiff or a defendant who loses a case because of this investigation petitions us against the majority of the witnesses and says that the majority of the witnesses lied in the investigation, and the minority of the witnesses told the truth in the investigations: on the basis of the petition take from both groups of witnesses two well-to-do people per hundred from the townsmen and servicemen; court villages, patriarchal, metropolitan, archiepiscopal, episcopal, and monastery estates; and the hereditary estates and service landholdings, belonging to boyars, *okol'nichie*, men of counselor rank, *stol'niki, striapchie*, Moscow *dvoriane, zhil'tsy*, provincial *dvoriane* and *deti boiarskie*, and sundry service landholders and patrimonial landowners. If there are less than one hundred, take one person each. Arrange for them a visual confrontation and thoroughly investigate them using every means to discover which faction lied in the investigation.

If a petitioner and the minority of the witnesses expose the fact that the majority lied in the investigation, then fine the majority of the witnesses for our [treasury] for the false evidence (or for refusing to testify) according to the following schedule:

Rank	*Fine in Rubles*
Archimandrite	50
Hegumen, cellarer	40
Treasurer, steward, elder	30
Ordinary monk	5
Large-monastery servant	20
Small-monastery servant, slave [*detenysh*]	5
Archpriest	40

Protodeacon	30
Priest	20
Deacon, church deacon	10
Stol'nik, striapchii, Moscow dvorianin, zhilets, provincial dvorianin, syn boiarskii	30
Town elder	20
Townsman, postman, estate steward [probably a slave]	10
Elder, sworn man	5
Peasant, bobyl'	1

Moreover, select the stewards and wealthy peasants from the witnesses and beat every tenth man with the knout.

Send the archimandrites, hegumens, priests, and deacons who lie in the investigation for penance to the patriarch, metropolitan, archbishop, or bishop in whose diocese they are.

If someone, a plaintiff or defendant, suffers losses, expenses, and delays [ubytki, proesti, volokity] from perjured investigations, we order all that exacted from those people who lied in the investigation and given to the person who suffered the damages. If some people because of perjured investigations are tortured, we order those tortured people to collect fourfold their dishonor and maiming compensation fee from those people who lied in the investigation so that henceforth they will not lie.

When the investigator brings the investigation testimony to you in the town hall [s"ezzhaia izba], you shall send those investigations, over the signatures of the investigator, the witnesses, and their fathers superior, to us in Moscow with whomever is suitable and order them forwarded to the Slavery Chancellery, to our stol'nik Vasilii Bogdanov Volkonskoi, and our state secretaries, Semen Kliucharev and Greznoi Akishev.

If you fail to execute the investigation according to our former and this present order and do not quickly send the investigations to us in Moscow c/o the Slavery Chancellery, we shall send out the bailiff at your expense, and we shall order that the cost of the investigation and the travel expenses of the bailiff be collected twofold from you.

Three levels of knowledge were recognized in the general investigation: personal knowledge, probably by seeing the event, v vedomo; knowledge that one might have, although he did not gather it personally, v znat'e; and hearsay, rumor, v slukh.

The evidence gathered by such a procedure led to the freeing of an artilleryman who had been forcibly enslaved twenty years earlier in the case of Danila, son of Dmitrii Big Beard, v. Lodygin (April 1649–June 1651). In that case the plaintiff's claim was that his father had been a gunner in Temnikov for sixty years and he himself had been a gunner there for twenty years before the defendant's father, Gavrila Lodygin, Temnikov governor in 1631, forcibly enslaved him in Alatyr'. The defendant's position was that the plaintiff had voluntarily sold himself into slavery as a free man (i.e., not as a gunner, in this case) from Temnikov whose full name was Danilka, son of Dmitrii Elagin (i.e., not Big Beard), as stated in a limited-service slavery contract on the plaintiff. The plaintiff agreed that the limited-service slavery contract was taken on him, but said that he had been terrorized into assenting to it. Moreover, the contract was inherently flawed because of the "free man/Elagin" content; it could be proved that such a person had never existed in Temnikov while the gunner Big Beard was well known. He asked for a general investigation of the entire population of Temnikov and its by-town Insar (in Mordovia, 135 kilometers southeast of Temnikov; 275 kilometers south of Nizhnii Novgorod, 170 kilometers south of Arzmas).

The tsar and the boyars ordered a general investigation, but at first nothing was done because the governors of Temnikov and Insar argued that the general investigation was a private-law discovery process that had to be arranged by the litigants. The Slavery Chancellery remained neutral in the matter, saying it would do whatever was ordered by the tsar. The plaintiff did not dispute the claim that the general investigation was primarily a private-law institution that had to be conducted by the litigants, but observed that the nature of the case required an exception: although he was the plaintiff, he was being treated as a fugitive slave who could not get bail and consequently was chained to the wall in the house of a Slavery Chancellery bailiff. This fact made it difficult for him to arrange a general investigation as a normal plaintiff might. As I shall argue in chapter 16, high government figures (including some in the Slavery Chancellery) must have found the entire case shocking and outrageous, with the result that the plaintiff's position was upheld, and the general investigations were ordered in spite of (or, perhaps, because of) his position. This maneuvering dragged out the case for much of its 636 days.

When the general investigations were conducted, the following four questions were put to the general populace:

1. Did you know Danilo's father, Dmitriko [dim. of Dmitrii] Big Beard as a gunner in Temnikov during the reign of former tsars, and that he died as a gunner in Temnikov?
2. After Dmitriko's death, was his son Danilka [dim. of Danila] a gunner in Temnikov prior to 1636? Was the Danilka you knew as a gunner "the son of Big Beard?"
3. Did you know a Danilka, son of Dmitrii Elagin, who was a free man, not a Temnikov gunner and not the son of Big Beard?
4. Did you know that when Gavrilo Lodygin was governor in Temnikov he fettered Danilko, sent him with his son Kondrat'i Lodygin to Arzmas, where he took a limited service slavery contract on him and thereby forcibly enslaved him, his wife and children?

The responses are tabulated in tables 8.2 and 8.3.

TABLE 8.2
1650 Temnikov Response to General Investigation of Status of Danilka Big Beard

Social Position of Respondent	1A. Knew Dmitriko Big Beard personally	1B. Knew of Dmitriko Big Beard by rumor	2. Knew Danilka Big Beard as a gunner in Temnikov prior to 1631	3. Knew free man Danilka, son of Dmitrii Elagin	4. Knew of forced enslavement of Danilka and his family	5. Knew nothing of entire case
Monastery hegumen	0	0	0	0	Not asked in Temnikov	1
Cellarer	0	1	1	0		0
Monastery treasurer	0	1	1	0		0
Monastery elder	0	5	5	0		0
Archpriest	0	0	0	0		1
Priest	0	2	4	0		1
Deacon	0	1	1	0		0
Gunner and messenger	19	0	19	0		0
Gatekeeper	6	0	6	0		0
Town elder	1	8	10	0		0
Town ten-man	1	1	3	0		0
Townsman	21	0	38	0		0
Peasant	14	34	51	0		0
Tatar	0	67	67	0		0
Mordva	0	3	38	0		0

TABLE 8.3
1651 Insar Response to General Investigation of Status of Danilka Big Beard

Social Position of Respondent	1A. Knew Dmitriko Big Beard personally	1B. Knew of Dmitriko Big Beard by rumor	2. Knew Danilka Big Beard as a gunner in Temnikov prior to 1631	3. Knew free man Danilka, son of Dmitrii Elagin	4. Knew of forced enslavement of Danilka and his family	5. Knew nothing of entire case
Priest	0		0	0	0	1
Deacon	0		0	0	0	1
Baptized Cherkas	6		6	0	6	0
Musketeer fifty-man	1		1	0	1	0
Musketeer	45		45	0	45	0
Gunner (*pushkar'*)	8		8	0	8	0
Artilleryman (*zatinshchik*)	4		4	0	4	0
Messenger	7		7	0	7	0
Gatekeeper	6		6	0	6	0
Watchman on fortified line	6		6	0	6	0
Cossack fifty-man	0		0	0	0	1
Cossack	6		6	0	6	159
Tatar	14		22	0	0	25
Mordva	0		0	0	0	62

These tables are fascinating because they give the social composition of the two towns and their surrounding areas. They also tell us something about geographical mobility and even demography in the relevant areas, for those who knew nothing about the case were required to tell why. The three churchmen of Temnikov gave no response because they had not been there in 1631. The hegumen of the Purdyshevskoi monastery had only arrived in 1649, and the archpriest and priest of the Temnikov cathedral church had come to the town only in 1641. (Such infusions of clergy from the outside were necessary in frontier regions, whereas in more established areas there was less circulation between the center or elsewhere and the periphery.) One can gain a notion about the age groupings of the population as well, for some who said they had no personal information claimed that it was because they had been too young at the time. The tables also show the relative degree of assimilation of the indigenous conquered populations: the Tatars were more in communication with the Russians than were the Finnic Mordovians. Finally, the tables tell us that the area was well pacified, for the garrison (except for the influx of 159 cossacks) had changed little in the course of two decades and was permanently stationed in the area.

The government also tabulated the responses by comparing town and countryside, and then by the general grouping of answers. Thus in Temnikov, 3 knew nothing about the case, 62 knew the father and son personally, 123 knew the father by rumor and the son personally, and 59 knew only the son, for a total number of 247 respondents. For Insar, 103 people knew about the case, and 249 did not. As is evident from the tables, the responses supported the plaintiff's case completely and denied any support whatsoever to the defendant's case: no one had heard of or knew of Danilka Dmitreev Elagin, an allegedly free man of Temnikov listed in Uvar Lodygin's limited service slavery contract. Thus, on the basis of the general investigation, Danilka and all of his family (including a daughter-in-law, one of Uvar Lodygin's slaves forcibly married to Danilka's son) were freed, and he was sent back to the gunners under the jurisdiction of the Kazan' Regional Administrative Chancellery.[32] In this case the general investigation proved to be a very effective instrument for verifying the veracity of a litigant's claim.

The Slave as Litigant

While many societies allowed slaves to appear in one capacity or another as witnesses in court, probably fewer permitted them to be litigants on their own behalf. Nevertheless, in societies where slaves were allowed to own property, they often were allowed to litigate in court as well. This was true, for example, in

32. Iakovlev, *Kholopstvo*, pp. 513-62, no. 26.

ancient Nuzi.[33] It was also true in Muscovy, and in that respect the seventeenth-century Russian slave system was among the most "progressive" in history.

Guarantors (Sureties) and Bail

The Muscovite period of legal history saw the creation of jails and other forms of detention, but they were still at a relatively primitive level. In some cases detention was a form of private enterprise, with those being detained entrusted to a government official, who supposedly maintained the detainee as long as the judicial process remained unresolved. This seems to have been the fate of most slaves whose ownership was being contested, as is evident in the extant cases. The process went as follows: a plaintiff initiated his complaint, the slave in question was seized and held by the bailiff until the case had been resolved, whereupon he was paid the "chaining fee" for his services. Unquestionably there were abuses in that system, primarily underfeeding by the bailiff. In spite of its drawbacks, the "chaining" system may well have been preferable to a formal system of incarceration, where the accused and contested were thrown in with the convicted in a warren of vice and disease. By the 1660s the jails and prisons in Muscovy were such an embarrassment that the government in the Felony Statute of 1669 did its best to curtail incarceration.[34]

There was, however, an alternative to incarceration in its various forms for slaves whose ownership was in question—the use of bail. From the slave's point of view, no doubt this was preferable to private-enterprise "chaining" or jailing. From the point of view of the authorities (whose officers could not collect the "chaining fees" when a slave was on bail) as well as of the slaveowners as a class, however, bail may have been less desirable, for it was less of a deterrent to flight than was chaining or incarceration (providing the lawgiver was viewing the slave as a rational human being). But when the legislator was concerned about his constituents, the slaveowners as individuals, he had to think in somewhat different terms. Chaining and jailing were expensive, and perhaps as subject to abuse as was the system of bail. For that reason the government prescribed that a contested slave should be released on bail with either litigant if a long time was likely to elapse before a trial could commence, such as when relevant evidence or the principals were distant from the capital. Moreover, bail was formally prescribed for slaves during the period between the conclusion of a trial and the time when the decision was handed down. In this instance bail was to be provided by someone unrelated to the litigants. Only if no one could be found to provide bail was a bailiff to keep a contested slave chained either before a trial began (while waiting distant evidence) or during the interim between the trial

33. Mendelsohn, p. 72.
34. PRP 7: 396-434.

and the verdict.[35] These articles reflect the general reality of the period, for the Slavery Chancellery attempted to release contested slaves on bond in many instances, and seems to have succeeded in cases where the slave was not a recidivist runaway.

All of the known cases of slaves on bail are essentially civil cases involving fugitives. The Muscovites permitted bail for those people accused of crimes, and it appears likely that no distinction was made between free and slave in such instances.

Strange as it may seem, on this point there was little difference between the Muscovite and American legal positions. An American slave suing for his freedom was allowed to post bond and to list individuals as his sureties.[36] Apprehended fugitives were usually kept in jail, although habeas corpus was available.[37] The practice of allowing bail for slaves accused of crimes in Alabama in 1852 was seemingly about the same as in Muscovy. There, slaves were "bailable before conviction, except for capital offences, when the proof [was] evident or the presumption great."[38] In an 1839 Kentucky case, the court held that a slaveowner had the right to bail his slave "if the offence with which he was charged would have been bailable in the case of a free man."[39] The American practice was motivated by the tradition of habeas corpus, which did not exist on the east European plain. The Muscovites' motivation was somewhat different: an insufficiency of jails, and an abhorrence of those that existed.

In court suits over slaves and stolen property all parties had to post guarantors to assure their subsequent appearance. In six cases involving from 25 to 120.90 rubles of stolen property (average: 49.81 rubles), the slaves posted from 3 to 9 guarantors, with an average of 5. In nine cases ranging from 20.50 to 50.50 rubles (average: 33.52 rubles), plaintiffs posted from 2 to 6 guarantors, with an average of 4.2. In ten cases ranging from 20.50 rubles to 50.50 rubles (average: 32.32 rubles), defendants posted from 3 to 9 guarantors, with an average of 5.1. For only the defendants was there the slightest linear relationship between the value of property stolen and the number of guarantors posted (corr. coeff. = 0.4784); there was none for the plaintiff (corr. coeff. = 0.1111), and essentially no relationship between those variables for the guarantors posted by the slaves (corr. coeff. = 0.0333).

These relationships did not hold in the same suits over the slaves themselves, at least in terms of the number of slaves. For plaintiffs, the correlation was quite high (0.6779) in twelve cases with from 1 to 6 slaves (average: 3.1) and 2 to 5 guarantors (average: 4.1). On the other hand, for the defendants, the correlation was negative (- 0.1396) in fourteen cases involving between 1 and 6 slaves (aver-

35. 1649 *Ulozhenie* 20: 59, 112; MS, pp. 275-76, 296.
36. Catterall 3: 593.
37. Stanley W. Campbell, *The Slave Catchers. Enforcement of the Fugitive Slave Law, 1850-1860* (New York: Norton, 1972), pp. 115-22.
38. Rose, p. 196.
39. Catterall 1: 347.

age: 3.1) and 4 to 9 guarantors (average: 5.4). For the slaves, the correlation was also low (0.1644) for eight cases with from 2 to 6 slaves (average: 3.9) and 4 to 9 guarantors (average: 6). In both instances, the independent variables of slaves and property, the plaintiffs posted the fewest guarantors—a sensible arrangement, for the purpose was solely to force them to pursue the suit, not to initiate a case and then hope to ruin a defendant by dragging it out endlessly.

Bormosov v. Berechinskii

The use of bail is illustrated by the case of Bormosov v. Berechinskii that occupied the attention of the Slavery Chancellery from some time prior to November 1627 until some time after September 1629. Unfortunately, the beginning and the ending of the case have been lost, so some of the issues are not totally clear. Nevertheless, it appears as though a widow, Okulina, called Pelageia, had sold herself to Mikhail Karpov Berechinskii for 2 rubles in a limited service slavery contract. She acknowledged the contract, written in Vladimir and dated March 6, 1625, and claimed that she had come to Berechinskii about half a dozen years earlier. Okulina had been a peasant living on properties belonging to the archbishop of Tver', and had married and been widowed twice, both times to peasants. For reasons that are not clear, Okulina, pregnant (she gave birth to a girl, Matriushka), moved from the Upper Volga-Tver' region about 1619 and settled in the Suzdal' region on the lands of Berechinskii, who was probably a young *syn boiarskii* at the time. Because some of the record is missing, Ivan Bormosov's claims are not clear, and it is not even clear who he was, because no patronymic is given. In all probability he was Ivan Vasil'evich Bormosov, who began service at the Moscow entry rank of *zhilets* in 1613, and by 1627 had achieved the rank of Moscow *dvorianin*, the rank he held as a sentry at court in September 1636 and on February 5, 1639, when he was part of a huge greeting party to receive the Persian ambassador, who was on a trip to Holstein. I. V. Bormosov died later that year.[40] We know from the case that Bormosov lived in Moscow. It seems strange, however, that he was represented at the trial by Iakim Zamortsov, a clerk of the Chancellery of the Great Court, for usually advocates were slaves or relatives of the litigant, or someone otherwise related to him by some occupational or geographic association. In this case, perhaps Bormosov simply hired Zamortsov for his expertise. The defendant, Berechinskii was represented by his uncle, Fedor Vasil'ev Sechenov.

The trial was held on November 3, 1627, and Bormosov seems to have claimed that Pelageia had been his hereditary slave who fled from him just prior to March 1625. She denied ever having known him or his father. Bormosov presented no documents to support his claims. On the same day the Slavery Chancellery released the slave woman on bail in the custody of the defendant, Berechinskii. The bail document is worth quoting in full:

40. Sukhotin, ChSV, pp. 102, 250, 329; Ivanov, AUBK, p. 40; RIB 10(1886): 17; DR 2: 953. There is no additional information about Mikhail Karpov Berechinskii.

After the trial they [the officials of the Slavery Chancellery] ordered the bailiff [*pristav*] Semen Dedevshin to obtain guarantee notes on the plaintiff and on the defendant, and they ordered the woman, on her petition, given on bail to Mikhail Berechinskoi. The police officer Semen Dedevshin submitted the guarantee notes, and in the notes is written:

Be it known that I, Iakov, son of Ivan Kozhekhov, of Suzdal'; and I, Tit, son of Mikhail Shilov, bailiff [*nedel'shchik*] of the Moscow Judicial Chancellery; and I, *zhilets* Iakov, son of Nikita Tregubov; I, tsaritsa's *syn boiarskoi* Davyd, son of Vasilii Bludov; and I, Prince Gavrila, son of Prince Ivan Gundarov; and I, Bogdan, son of Sidor Miagkov; and I, Elezarei, son of Rodion Miushiukov, of Borovsk; and I, Aleksei, son of Matvei Krotkoi, of Suzdal'; and I, Ivan, son of Iurii Tironov, of Suzdal'; and I, *zhilets* Mikhailo, son of Osip Bastanov; and I, *zhilets* Ivan, son of Fedor Kozinskoi, have pledged a guarantee with the bailiff Semen Dedoshin [sic] of the Slavery Chancellery for Fedor, son of Vasilii Sechenov, for the trial. Under our guarantee he shall appear in the Slavery Chancellery every day, upon request, before the [codirectors] Stepan Ivanovich Volynskoi and Ivan Fomich Ogarev, and before the state secretaries Nikita Levont'ev and Iakov Protopov. With himself he shall present the woman Okul'ka [dim. of Okulina], called Polaga [dim. of Pelageia], and her daughter Matriushka because he is representing his nephew Mikhail Berechinskoi [in the case] against Ivan Bormosov. If he, Fedor, fails to appear under our guarantee and fails to present that woman Okul'ka and her daughter Matriushka, we, the guarantors, shall be responsible for that woman Okul'ka and her daughter Matriushka as the sovereign decrees. Those of us, the guarantors, who happen to be present are the ones responsible for the guarantee on these slaves. This was witnessed by Ivan Fedorov. Vasiuk Timofeev wrote the note in the year 1628.

This bail bond is rather typical and tells us a good deal about the institution of Muscovite slavery, as well as about the law of bailment. First, even though we seem to possess no information about the defendant, his eleven guarantors tell us about him, for presumably they are his friends. They are upwardly mobile servitors from Suzdal', for *zhilets* is the entry rank of those beginning to serve in the capital service or because they were promoted from provincial to capital service.[41] We can surmise that Berechinskii is young because he is being represented in the litigation by his uncle.

Also striking in this bail bond is the statment by the officials of the Slavery Chancellery that it was granted because the slave herself had asked for it. It is difficult to imagine such consideration in most other slave systems.

Finally, one should note that the penalty forfeit for violation of the terms of the bail was not specified but rather was to be "as the sovereign decrees." I noted earlier that a 5-ruble penalty was provided for failure to present the horse that Orinka had ridden to Moscow in Treskin v. Zykov (1627), and in other instances the penalty was simply loss of the case. In Bormosov v. Berechinskii,

41. Iziumov, pp. 30-31, 96-97.

however, we see expressed that built-in arbitrariness for which Russian law was so famous: the tsar himself could decide the penalty. The provision for that arbitrary sanction was not uncommon in Muscovite law when members of the upper class were involved. It may have been borrowed from Lithuanian practice. While it allowed lesser penalties to be applied to the elite than to ordinary mortals, that was not its primary purpose. The reality of Muscovite history indicates that such arbitrariness was introduced not with the intention of providing the elite with a way to escape the savagery of early modern judicial sanctions but in order to keep the elite in control. Muscovy was not the Rzeczpospolita, where the elite had rights, but rather the place in which the elite was the first element of society to fall under the rigid control of autocracy. Institutionalized arbitrariness was a device to terrorize the elite, for its individual members could never know what sanctions might be applied. Ivan the Terrible used capital punishment as his sanction. Tsar Mikhail, as noted in the discussion of Tatishchev v. Selekhovskii (see "Evidence," below) did not shrink from ordering his elite *stol'niki* to be beaten with the knout.

Unfortunately, we do not know what sanction, if any, was applied in this case. After Okul'ka was released on bond, the plaintiff Berechinskii submitted three petitions between October 23 and November 11 asking for a verdict. The first petition was addressed to both Tsar Mikhail and Patriarch Filaret, but the last two, recognizing the real nature of the Muscovite government, were addressed solely to Filaret. Berechinskii noted that he was being detained in Moscow by the failure to grant a verdict, and that this was a burden for him, a provincial, a burden which Bormosov was using to bankrupt him. Apparently the Slavery Chancellery was delaying while searching for precedents to make its decision. Filaret noted on the second petition that the Slavery Chancellery should stop looking for precedents, if it couldn't find them with dispatch, and make a report to him, on which, presumably, he would render a decision. For some reason, however, nothing was done. Nearly two years passed, and plaintiff Bormosov on September 30, 1629, submitted another petition in which he made a number of complaints. One was that he had asked for a general investigation (*poval'nyi obysk*) of the population of Suzdal' and Torzhok to prove that Okul'ka had been his hereditary slave, and nothing had been done. He also objected that defendant Berechinskii's limited service slavery contract had been improperly granted, that it had been authorized in spite of his, Bormosov's, objections, by a fortifications offical (*gorodovoi prikazshchik*), rather than the proper officials: governors (*voevody*), siege defense heads (*osadnye golovy*), or *guba* elders. Finally, he objected that Okul'ka had been released on bond and was living on Berechinskii's service landholding in Suzdal' province. She had not been presented in the Slavery Chancellery, a requirement that Bormosov knew would have bankrupted the defendant.[42]

42. Iakovlev, *Kholopstvo*, pp. 383-87, no. 12. Another case of a slave woman's being released on bail is Kuz'mischev v. Satin (ibid., pp. 390-401, no. 14).

Thus we see that the institution of bailment existed in Muscovy, and that its granting and use was seen as benefiting one party at the expense of the other.

In most cases, sureties in bailments were Russians. However, there was no requirement that they be so, and sometimes in fact they were foreigners. This was so, for example, in the case of Kozlova v. Kozlova et al., discussed in detail in chapter 17, where Ivan Iakovlev Roganovskii, "a foreigner," guaranteed the bail instruments for both litigants.[43] Perhaps Roganovskii was a Pole, or perhaps his name was converted at the Muscovite equivalent of Ellis Island from something like "John Jacob . . ." to what we see. The importance of the willingness to allow foreigners to serve as guarantors of Russians lies in its witness to the fact that in this realm, as in so many others, the Muscovites did not manifest any national exclusiveness.

Documentation

A study such as this one must devote space to a discussion of the rules of documentation and evidence, for they held a central place (sometimes one might think *the* central place) in the Muscovite law of slavery. This almost banal truth has several dimensions to it. Most simply, these rules amounted to at least a quarter, and perhaps even a third, of the laws on slavery.[44] This was so because Muscovy was passing from an oral to a written stage of law.

This was comparable, in a way, to the writ stage of English law, when proper documentation, not conflict resolution, became the seeming end-all of law. This evolution is evident in the 1550 *Sudebnik*'s ordering the older document to be recognized in disputes over slaves, while simultaneously recognizing the legitimacy of the customary nondocumentary witness (*znakhor'*).[45] A century later, only the documentary part of this remained, reflecting what seems to have been a considerable increase in at least elementary, functional literacy.[46] Manumission documents improperly executed (and not paid for) were invalid, even if in the slaveowner's own handwriting.[47] One assumes that it was primarily this evolutionary process that motivated the government to order the registration of all slaves in 1597-98, many of whom had been serving on the basis of oral contracts. Many of the norms of the law code of 1649 existed also for the purpose of enforcing the point that documentation had to be complete and accurate.

43. Ibid., pp. 482-83, no. 23, IV.
44. On documentation, see, 1649 *Ulozhenie* 20: 28-30, 32, 38, 48, 56, 72-76, 78, 103, 107; on evidence, 20: 54; on procedure, 20: 45, 55, 57, 59, 79, 88, 93-96, 109, 111-12, 119.
45. 1550 *Sudebnik* 79.
46. 1649 *Ulozhenie* 20: 10; MS, pp. 258-59.
47. 1550 *Sudebnik* 77.

Failure to comply with the formalities, almost regardless of the realities of the situation, meant loss of a case by a previously negligent plaintiff.[48]

This development was linked to an administrative one, the evolution from a royal household to a hieratic, bureaucratic government. One may assume that the development of literacy and the writ mentality is both cause and effect of the development of bureaucracy. To attain and then to retain their authority, the bureaucrats must control mysteries and be able to work miracles beyond the capacity of the average illiterate. When such matters came to a trial in Muscovy, the officialdom insisted on the niceties of documentary accuracy and bureaucratic technicalities that must have boggled the mind of the poor illiterate seeking "justice," who ended up befuddled by the mysteries of "the law" and the miraculous ability of the wealthy to win in court. The pitiful souls who thought that law had something to do with conflict resolution undoubtedly found that trials were often procedural rather than substantive. This, miraculously enough, led to further resort to the written word, and the employment of just those people who could (for a fee, of course) manipulate the mysteries of the written word to the satisfaction of those who passed on the legitimacy and correctness of the formal procedures. Thus it is by no means accidental that the written procedures used to enserf the peasantry made great strides at the same time that slavery made the great transition from an essentially oral to a written institution. The landmark decade for both was the 1590s: slaveownership had to be formulated in written instruments. Cadastres, service estate assignments, and similar documents were the evidentiary basis for binding the peasants to the land.

The conflict between the oral and the written tradition was evident in the Slavery Chancellery in 1608. The codirectors of the chancellery, Ivan Andreev Solntsov and Kazarin Davydov Begichev, and their state secretary, Doroga Khvittskoi, presented the following dilemma to Tsar Shuiskii: *dvoriane* and *deti boiarskie* are suing for the return of their fugitive hereditary slaves on whom they have no documents. The slaves at a trial admit that earlier they were the plaintiffs' hereditary slaves. Defendants, on the other hand, place in evidence limited service slavery contracts, which the slaves admit that they agreed to. What should be done, how is the conflict between prior oral and subsequent documented claims to be resolved? Tsar Shuiskii heard the question and resolved it on March 19, 1609: "Return the slaves on the basis of the limited service slavery contracts to those to whom they, having fled, gave the contracts on themselves. Order rejected those who keep them in hereditary slavery without documents. Why would anyone keep a slave in his house ·[*u sebia*] without documentation?"[49] This principle of the priority of documentation was nearly always subsequently adhered to.

The priority of the written over the oral was made explicit in a law of 1642/

48. 1649 *Ulozhenie* 20: 18; MS, p. 262.
49. PRP 4: 379.

43 arising out of a conflict between two purchasers of the same limited service contract slave. The earlier purchaser had given money to the would-be slave and had received his oral promise that henceforth he would be his chattel. Apparently the slave did not find that individual to his liking, departed, and sold himself again to someone else. The second purchaser had the presence of mind to formulate and register a limited service slavery contract on the recipient of his money. When the case was tried in the Slavery Chancellery, the verdict was awarded to the more recent claimant because he had the valid document. The *Ulozhenie* summarized this case in one of its didactic homilies: "If someone gives money to a slave, but fails to obtain a limited service slavery contract, he will lose a court suit in which the ownership of the slave is contested because of his own doing: do not give money to a slave without obtaining a limited service slavery contract."[50]

The insistence on formal documentation was expressed in the *Ulozhenie* of 1649 in another context that almost certainly was codified into law on the basis of a relatively recent, and now no longer extant, legal case. A literate person had been working for someone, and signed himself as his employer's slave. Then the employee moved, and sold himself to another person. The employer sued for the return of the person to him as his slave on the grounds that he had signed himself as such. The Slavery Chancellery held differently, arguing that the limited service slavery contract was the legal criterion for determining slave status, not the fact that a person merely had signed himself as someone's slave.[51] By 1681, while the society was still largely illiterate, the awareness of documentation had progressed to the point that the government could simply state that no one was to keep slaves without having formulated the proper contracts, that undocumented claims to slaves were invalid.[52] In 1684 this was repeated, and extended to military captives and purchased slaves.[53]

It was not enough merely to have the appropriate document properly formulated on someone. The document also had to be registered in the Slavery Chancellery or it was not a valid document.[54] The logic of the provision is clear: without it, a slaveowner could escape paying fees that oiled the wheels of Muscovite administration. But, if the books containing such records were known to have perished and the records had recognizably valid signatures, they were still valid documents.[55] Record books extant in 1649 that had not been signed by the relevant officials prior to 1640 were recognized as valid if they had not been

50. 1649 *Ulozhenie* 20: 78; MS, p. 284.
51. 1649 *Ulozhenie* 20: 18; MS, p. 262.
52. PSZ 2: 313, no. 869.
53. Ibid., 2: 588, no. 1073.
54. 1649 *Ulozhenie* 20: 38, 45; MS, pp. 268, 272.
55. 1649 *Ulozhenie* 20: 56; MS, 275. This article dates from 1621/22 (K. Verkhovskii, "Istochniki Ulozheniia tsaria Alekseia Mikhailovicha," *Iuridicheskii vestnik* 3, bk. 2[1889]: 113-14, 387).

contested in the intervening years.[56] Such statutes of limitations were relatively frequent in Muscovy and reflected the government's attempt to rein in a generally litigious society. The recording of a limited service slavery contract in the official record books could be to a slave's advantage when his owner died, for he could refer to the books to claim his freedom in case his owner had illegally tried to convey the slave to his heirs in a last testament.[57] This provision was consonant with the Byzantine tradition that allowed a person who had been freed every opportunity to claim his liberty.

Part of the transition from an oral to a written society requires the development of standards for determining the accuracy of written documents. This can be seen in the 1622 case of Dedkov v. Dolgorukiis, when a point was raised about the authenticity of a document. The following gives an idea of the type of documentary analysis that the Muscovites were capable of.

> The scribes noted that there were changes in the letters: at first it was written Iushko Fofonov, but later changes were made in the letters, and it became Iashku Fofonov. Where at first the letter "iu" was written, a lower bar was added, making it the letter "ia." Where earlier had been written the word "he" [on], it was altered into "they" [oni] – "ik" had been added to "onu" with two upper bending lines. The old "sha" above and the abbreviation mark over "shami" were replaced in new ink for those two words, "iku" and "ia" when they were altered. . . . If it in reality had been written "Iashku," then they would have written after Iashku "Fofonova" [genitive singular] and not Fofonov [nominative singular]. In the name Fofonov the letter "V" [vedei] was written with the letter "A" [az], and not with the letter "E" [er]. Throughout the entire document there is no such "iku" written anywhere, but throughout the entire document "iki" is written with straight lines, not curved ones.[58]

An article of the *Ulozhenie* dating from 1621/22 on the veracity of documents written prior to the destruction of the records in Moscow in 1611 went further into the matter of establishing the authenticity of a given contract. If the persons whose signatures were on the document had died, then a handwriting comparison should be made with other documents allegedly written and signed by the same people. If they were similar, the contested document was pronounced genuine.[59]

Concern about the forgery of manumission documents seems to have arisen among the Muscovites rather late, and only in the context of the massive hunts for fugitives that were launched in the second half of the seventeenth century. In 1665 that possibility was mentioned in the instructions to the

56. 1649 *Ulozhenie* 20: 107; MS, pp. 293-94.
57. 1649 *Ulozhenie* 20: 64; MS, pp. 277-78.
58. Iakovlev, *Kholopstvo*, pp. 349-50, no. 6. For a discussion of Dedkov v. Dolgorukiis, see pp. 269-72 below.
59. 1649 *Ulozhenie* 20: 103; MS, p. 292.

serf- and slave-catchers, who were supposed to investigate such documents. In the 1683 instructions, sanctions for such forgeries were added: if the fugitive slave (or peasant serf) had committed the forgery, he was to be beaten with the knout. If the recipient of a fugitive did it, he was to be beaten with the knout and fined for receiving the fugitive as well.[60] Such a development reflects the increasing spread of literacy and the availability of paper in the second half of the seventeenth century, as well as a consciousness that the fugitive slave was a person who should be punished for his wrongs.

Late Muscovite law required that full descriptions of the slaves be given.[61] The surviving documentary corpus indicates that this practice was begun in 1592 by *gubnoi starosta* Lev Knutov of Zalesskaia polovina, Shelonskaia piatina (due west of Novgorod). The most striking thing about this seeming fact (who knows what went before, for which no evidence survives?) is that Knutov was illiterate, in violation of the law (unless no one else was available), and the sole major official in my data set who could not read or write—a fact noted every time he had anything to do with official documents. (Clerks compiled the actual documents.) The apparent spread of this practice of describing the slaves' features is an interesting case of cultural diffusion. The following year, 1593, another *gubnoi starosta*, Stepan Aleksandrov, of Bezhetskaia piatina (due east of Novgorod), copied the practice apparently begun by Knutov. In 1594 many other provincial areas of Novgorod were doing it; there was another lag of a year or so for documents written by church scribes in out-of-the-way places, and then the practice was followed in Novgorod itself. After that, it spread throughout Muscovy.

By 1641 description of the slaves's features became mandatory, and claims for disputed slaves were to be rejected if a slave in person did not coincide with the slave described in a document.[62] Another law originating in 1641/42 insisted that if a newer document with the correct description of a slave conflicted with an older one lacking an accurate description, the former was the valid instrument.[63] The authors of the *Ulozhenie* had great faith in the value of such descriptions, and proclaimed that there would henceforth be no disputes over slaves if their distinguishing traits were accurately recorded.[64] In the second half of the seventeenth century these descriptions became very elaborate—scars, birthmarks, chest hair color, hair styles. The more traditional descriptions were simply of hair- and eye-color, shape of face and complexion, and height. These data are shown in tables 8.4-6.

---

60. PSZ 2: 506, no. 998, article 18; PRP 7: 191, 224, 235.
61. 1649 *Ulozhenie* 20: 8; MS, p. 258.
62. Iakovlev, *Kholopstvo*, p. 316; 1649 *Ulozhenie* 20: 8, 23; MS, pp. 258, 263.
63. 1649 *Ulozhenie* 20: 75; MS, p. 283.
64. 1649 *Ulozhenie* 20: 76; MS, p. 283.

TABLE 8.4
Stature and Physical Build of Slaves

	N	%
Short-thin,	1	.1
Short-average	193	17.6
Short-fat	2	.2
Average	754	68.9
Average-thin	8	.7
Average-fat	3	.3
Tall-average	127	11.6
Tall-thin	2	.2
Tall-fat	4	.4
Total	1,094	100.0

Missing N = 1,405, or 56.3% of all cases.

TABLE 8.5
Slaves' Hair Color

	N	%
Red	84	6.2
Black	198	14.8
Brown	984	73.5
Gray	5	.4
White	59	4.4
Total	1,330	100.0

Missing: 1,169, 46.5%

TABLE 8.6
Slaves' Eye Color

	N	%
Gray	996	73.6
White [sic]	28	2.1
Hazel	145	10.7
Black	154	11.4
Dark gray	12	.9
Light gray	6	.4
Hazel-gray	2	.1
Brown	7	.5
Red [sic]	3	.2
Total	1,353	100.0

Missing: 1,146, 45.9%

In addition to these data, 345 cases contain descriptions of the slaves' faces (round, oval, sharp, flat, full, etc.) and 647 contain complexion information (pock-marked, swarthy, ruddy, pale, tanned, etc.).

Zheliabuzhskii v. Lobanov-Rostovskii

The central record-keeping, with full descriptions of slaves, that was developed in Muscovy came to play a major role in resolving disputes over fugitive slaves. This was evident in the case of Timofei Sidorov Zheliabuzhskii v. Prince Ivan [Ivanov] Lobanov-Rostovskii, tried in the Slavery Chancellery before its directors, Prince Nikifor Iakovlev Meshcherskii and Ivan Kuz'mich Begichev, and the state secretaries Patrekei Nasonov and Filip Mitrofanov, in January and February of 1623, to resolve the ownership of the slave woman Ofimka Ondreeva.

The case is particularly noteworthy because of the inequality of the litigants. Plaintiff Zheliabuzhskii at the time of the trial was a lower-ranking Moscow serviceman. During the Time of Troubles his cash salary was 19 rubles, and then in 1614 he got a raise to 23 rubles, at which time he held the capital service entry rank of *zhilets*. One may assume that he held that rank at the time of the trial, and was promoted to the rank of Moscow *dvorianiñ* four years later, in 1627. Nothing more seems to be known about Zheliabuzhskii, except that he had some property in Kozel'sk uezd in 1631, until the outbreak of the Smolensk War. Then he was put in charge of gathering horses and wagons from part of the Belyi Gorod section of Moscow to transport artillery. In November of 1632 he was second in command of the advance regiment, which was stationed at Dedilovo. After the Smolensk War, Zheliabuzhskii may have been serving in the Astrakhan' region in some capacity, and in 1636 and 1641 he was one of the *stol'niki* performing sentry duty in the tsar's palace. The last mentions of Zheliabuzhskii are ones a student of slavery might expect to find more frequently, i.e., grotesque examples of sadism. One of Zheliabuzhskii's fugitive peasants became a monk, and then, under interrogation, accused Zheliabuzhskii of having constructed a wooden cross with nooses, with which he tortured his peasants. One of the peasants, caught fornicating with a household slave girl, had been tortured to death in this appartus by Zheliabuzhskii, who then forged the death certificate.[65] How different Zheliabuzhskii's trajectory was from Lobanov-Rostovskii's! One can only wonder whether the trial had anything to do with it.

At the time of the trial, the defendant, Ivan Lobanov-Rostovskii, was no one special. In fact, the earliest mention of Ivan Ivanov Lobanov-Rostovskii is four years after the trial, when he was a *stol'nik*. No patronymic is mentioned for the defendant, and thus he might have been Ivan Semenov L-R, who flourished between 1584 and 1633, or Ivan Iur'ev L-R, father of Ivan Ivanov, who died in 1639. Around the time of the trial, Ivan Semenov was a wealthy man with a large estate of over 1,700 cheti and a cash entitlement (*oklad*) of 80 rubles, who held the rank of Moscow *dvorianin*. For military service, he was supposed to report with four combat slaves. Nothing seems to be known about Ivan Iur'ev.

<hr />

65. RIB 28(1912): 406-8, 479, 494, 499; Tatishchev (1910), p. 27; ZKMS (= RIB 10): 19, 42, 211; AMG 1: 368; DAI, 2: 149, no. 61; RK 1550-1636 2: 377; DR 2: 323; KR 2: 693-94, 708-10; Samokvasov, AM 1: 257; *Opisanie* 15(1908): 194, 212.

The omission of the patronymic leads me to believe that the defendant must be Ivan Ivanov Lobanov-Rostovskii, who came to be one of Muscovy's wealthiest and most prominent men. In 1632 he had a cash *oklad* of 70 rubles, a land *oklad* of 800 cheti, and total landholding of 2,405 2/3 cheti scattered throughout six provinces, from which he was supposed to provide seven combat slaves, plus as many baggage-train slaves as he wanted. His biography could occupy a small essay, but it suffices to say that he rose from the rank of *okol'nichii* to *boiarin* in 1658, his cash salary was raised to 380 rubles, and until his death in 1664 he was one of the most prominent governmental and military figures in Muscovy.[66] Whether he used his influence to suppress Zheliabuzhskii after the 1630s is something we may only surmise.

The surviving transcript of the trial proceedings opens in January 1621, when the contested slave woman was already in the custody of the Slavery Chancellery, having been delivered there by Lobanov-Rostovskii. Zheliabuzhskii's complaint alleged that Ofimka had fled in 1621 at the instigation of the defendant, who had married her off to one of his subjects in the interim. Ofimka denied that she had ever been a slave of Zheliabuzhskii, and claimed that for the past four years she had been living with Lobanov-Rostovskii's slave Ivan Kazimerov, who had married her to one of his slaves, Frol'ko Prokof'ev.

Zheliabuzhskii offered two kinds of defense. First, he cited at least ten people who had seen Ofimka in his custody as a slave. The Slavery Chancellery interrogated two of the witnesses and they supported the plaintiff's allegations. Second, he claimed that he had taken a limited service slavery contract on her in 1620 in the town of Shatsk, over 330 kilometers southeast of Moscow. Ordered to produce the contract, Zheliabuzhskii said that the original was still in Shatsk, and asked that the records of the Slavery Chancellery be searched to save him the trouble of getting the original.

Lobanov-Rostovskii claimed that Zheliabuzhskii might be able to produce such a document, but that it would be a fraudulent piece of paper drawn up by the plaintiff's other slaves, Vas'ka Olturov and Patrushka Vasil'ev, in collusion with the local fortifications officer (*gorodovoi prikashchik*). Bluffing completely, Lobanov-Rostovskii demanded that an investigation be made of the contract. Further, he suggested that the slave Petrushka Vasil'ev be tortured to see whether a confession could be extracted from him. If Petrushka denied the charges under torture, Lobanov-Rostovskii would pay him his dishonor sum and compensate him for any mutilation he might have suffered. In discussing Zheliabuzhskii's career after the trial I observed that he became a sadist. At the trial itself,

66. Petrov, IRRD 1: 104; Barsukov, SGV, p. 556; RK 1550-1636, 2: 354-63; Stashevskii, ZMD, p. 136; DAI 3: 97, 286, 386; AI 4, passim; *Opisanie* 12 (1901), passim; *Opisanie* 15(1908), passim; DR, passim; KR 1, passim; Novosel'skii, RP (1950), pp. 60-61: AMG 3, passim; Ivanov, AUBK, p. 233. Robert Owen Crummey kindly shared with me his file on I. I. Lobanov-Rostovskii.

we see Lobanov-Rostovskii essentially taking the same role, asking the authorities to torture a slave essentially for his pleasure. Lobanov-Rostovskii was a wealthy man and would have found no difficulty in locating a ruble to compensate Petrushka for the dishonor, or even another 4 rubles to pay for permanent damage. Besides, the gambit might pay off: to get the torture to stop, Petrushka well might have confessed to anything.

Torture was not resorted to, thanks to the records of the Slavery Chancellery. Lobanov-Rostovskii had claimed that, while a slavery contract may have been drawn up, it was done so secretly, without the slave girl Ofimka's being present. Yet when the records of the Slavery Chancellery were checked, a record of the transaction was found, and the description of the slave matched in every respect the appearance of Ofimka. Thereupon Ofimka confessed that she had lied at the instigation of Ivashka Kazimerov, and that she had negotiated the limited service slavery contract with Zheliabuzhskii.

The matter of Ofimka's marriage came up during the trial when it was asked whether Zheliabuzhskii had told the priest that she was his slave. The plaintiff stated that others of his slaves had communicated that fact to the priest, but the man of God had done nothing because he feared Lobanov-Rostovskii. The husband, Frol'ko Prokof'ev, had been a vagabond before the marriage, and by the marriage he of course was converted into a slave. As a result of the verdict, Frol'ko ceased to be the slave of Ivashka Kazimerov and was transferred to Zheliabuzhskii as part of the settlement. The Slavery Chancellery noted the law: "Do not marry off your own slave to someone else's fugitive limited service contract slave woman and, without verifying [her true identity], do not receive another person's fugitive slave woman." Zheliabuzhskii paid the fee of 6 altyns for the judgment and presumably later sued for property that he claimed Ofimka had taken from him when she fled. Lobanov-Rostovskii refused to appear to hear the reading of the verdict.[67]

Once again, this case exemplifies the thoroughness and honesty of the Slavery Chancellery. Obviously the defendant, Lobanov-Rostovskii, was at the time of the trial a more intimidating person than was the plaintiff, Zheliabuzhskii. The defendant intimidated the local priest and was willing to have an innocent slave tortured, just to see what might happen. In spite of that, the Slavery Chancellery checked its records, which it easily could have "lost," had it so desired, found that indeed the contested slave woman belonged to the plaintiff, and awarded him the verdict. Finally, one should note in this case the presence of other slaves. Lobanov-Rostovskii's elite slave Ivashka Kazimerov apparently was the real defendant, although he did not appear at the trial. Zheliabuzhskii had other slaves, too, such as those who had warned the priest at the time of the wedding that Ofimka belonged to Zheliabuzhskii.

67. Iakovlev, *Kholopstvo*, pp. 354-59, no. 7.

Malygin v. Voeikov

The importance of the registered features of disputed slaves was also revealed in the case of Malygin v. Voeikov, tried in the Slavery Chancellery before director Prince Ivan Fedorovich Volkonskii and state secretaries Andrei Stroev and Ivan Kostiurin between April 20, 1630, and May 13, 1631. Other principles of slave law are revealed as well.

As in so many of the other cases discussed in this work, Malygin v. Voeikov reveals a regime of law at work in the resolution of conflicts over slaveownership. The defendant was almost unquestionably socially superior to the plaintiff, yet the latter was awarded the verdict in both his own suit and a countersuit. The plaintiff, Vasilii Mikhailov Malygin, was an ordinary *syn boiarskii* from Iaroslavl'. That information comes from the suit, and extant records seem to contain little else about him, except that in January of 1612 he may have been part of a group that petitioned the boyars in Móscow not to levy fur coats for the army (the rate was 27 per sokha) from their ruined service lands because their slaves and peasants had all either been killed or fled.[68] His adversary, on the other hand, was a relatively prominent figure from the lower upper service class, a Moscow *dvorianin*, Ivan Prokhorov Voeikov. He is one of the few slave-owners about whose name there is some confusion, for he is also called Ivan Bogdanov Voeikov in some records that independently mention events recorded at the trial. (There was also an Ivan Prokof'ev Voeikov whose career seems to have coincided at some points with what the defendant in this case is known to have done). Be that as it may, the general profile of Voeikov is clear enough. In 1624-25 he probably served in Ustiug, and in 1627 he dined with Tsar Mikhail. Then on January 21, 1630, he accompanied Patriarch Filaret in a procession to Zvenigorod, and on May 2 of the same year he accompanied Filaret to Vladimir. After that he was sent to Nizhnii Novgorod to be military governor, where he was in charge of a garrison of 1,528 men: 500 musketeers and their 5 centurions, 85 Cherkasy with a centurion, about 275 Poles, Lithuanians, and Swedes in Russian service, 10 Crimean Tatars, a fortifications commander, 11 gate keepers, 35 gunners, smiths, and carpenters, 138 treasury honey collectors (*bortniki*), and 482 Mordvy. One of his assignments in Nizhnii Novgorod was to confiscate service land amounting to 250 cheti from someone who had refused ro report for the Smolensk campaign and to transfer that land to another serviceman who only had 41 cheti of his scheduled compensation of 800 cheti of land. He also handled more routine tasks such as verifying limited service slavery contracts, contracts on the sales of shops, and a draft of bricklayers for the town-of Viaz'ma. Nizhnii was one of the major governorships of Muscovy, from which Voeikov returned to Moscow at the end of his term in 1632. Thus at the time of the trial Voeikov had the ear of the real ruler of Muscovy, Filaret, and he then

68. Veselovskii, *Akty 1611-13* (1911), p. 67, no. 53.

held one of the most prestigious command posts. (None of this helped him at the trial, however.) June 21, 1633, found him in command of the area outside of the Tver' gates along the Neglinnaia in the defense of Moscow, in anticipation of a Crimean Tatar attack. He was in charge of defending the Petrov gates during the rest of the Smolensk War period. In addition to having lands in Tver' and Kashin Provinces, Voeikov had a house in Moscow that was occupied by at least one slave. For his services, he was promoted to the rank of *stol'nik*. He died in 1642 and was buried at the Trinity Sergiev monastery.[69]

Malygin v. Voeikov opened on April 20, 1630, with the plaintiff suing to reclaim Ignatii (Ignashka), son of Stepan Nuryshevskii, Ignatii's wife and children, and stolen property worth 32.50 rubles. Ignashka's testimony (in the form of indirect speech) tells the story of the case well:

They call him Ignashka, son of Stepan Nuryshevskoi. He is the hereditary peasant of Ivan Prokhorov Voeikov of the village D'iakovo of Tver' province. At an earlier time, Voeikov's village belonged to Tsar' Simeon [Bekbulatovich, Ivan the Terrible's creature], and his, Ignashka's, father was among the peasants in that village D'iakovo when it belonged to Tsar' Simeon. Lithuanians killed his father Stepka in that village D'iakovo. He, Ignashka, wandered to Kashin, and he lived in Kashin province as a hired worker of Timofei Rozhnov for about one and a half years. Ivan Voeikov, learning of his presence at Timofei Rozhnov's, captured him at Timofei's. He then lived with Ivan Voeikov in Kashin province in the village Kuz'modem'ianskoe for about four years. Ignashko, who did not have any friends in Kuzmodem'ianskoe village, learned that Ivan Voeikov's peasants were living in Iaroslavl' province, and made his way to Iaroslavl' province. There he married Ivan Voeikov's fugitive peasant Orinka Olekseeva, the sister-in-law of Sen'ka Piatyshov. The fugitive Sen'ka did not live on the property of Ivan Prokshin, in Iaroslavl' province. Then Vasilii Malygin hired him, Ignashka. Ignashka lived with him, Vasilii, as a hired worker for a year, and then desired to leave him. Then Vasilii Malygin obtained by coercion in Moscow a limited service slavery contract on him, Ignashka. [This was in 1624, when Ignashka implausibly claimed to be nineteen years old.] Ignashka then lived with him on the basis of that limited service slavery contract for a year. He fled from that Vasilei Malygin already five years ago [in 1625-26] and returned to his ancestral place in Tver' province, the village D'iakovo, with his wife and two children, a daughter Man'ka and a son Romashko. His wife died in Ivan Voeikov's village. His children, the daughter Man'ka and his son Romashko, are now in Ivan's village.

This testimony, taken at the trial on May 29, 1630, was never contested to any

69. DR 1: 878; 2: 109, 132, 337; RK 1598-1638, p. 351; Barsukov, p. 149; Storozhev, "B.S.," p. 112; RK 1: 1035, 1152; 2: 266, 333, 518, 527, 662; S. I. Arkhangel'skii, ed., *Nizhnii Novgorod v XVII veke*, pp. 77-78, 294, 345; Savel'ev, 2:90; Ivanov, AUBK, pp. 70-71.

extent, except on the stolen property point. The man in dispute, Ignashka, was a marginal agriculturalist and for a while had worked as a hired laborer for the plaintiff Malygin, who then had taken advantage of the "voluntary slavery" law to get a limited service slavery contract on Ignashka. Throughout the judicial process Voeikov kept insisting such an action was perfidious, but Ignashka had not objected when the contract was written on him in the Slavery Chancellery itself, and it had taken him a year to run away. Therefore, it should be safe to conclude that Ignashka's objection to enslavement arose only after the fact.

The case was complicated by the fact that Ivan Voeikov on May 29 filed a countersuit to recover Kuz'ma (Kuzemka), son of Mikhail Denisov, who was at the time in Malygin's possession. It is not clear whether Voeikov's story was true, or merely a ploy. He claimed that Kuzemka was his hereditary slave and that on December 6, 1609 (over twenty years earlier), he had been sent from Moscow to collect the rent from the peasants in Voeikov's village of D'iakovo. Having collected a sum in the amount of 25 rubles, Kuzem'ka was returning with it to Moscow toward the end of January when he decided to flee with the cash. He settled on the estate of Malygin, where he married. Voeikov's countersuit was only for Kuzemka, but he announced that he would sue for the stolen property later, probably to escape the costs that would be incurred should he lose the case. (As I noted in chapter 7, this tactic was subsequently disallowed.) Kuzemka denied that he had ever had anything to do with Voeikov.

The case was considerably prolonged because of its coincidence with the height of Voeikov's career. During his own appearances in Moscow he tried to take advantage of the law on guarantee notes by noting Malygin's absences from Moscow, motivated, claimed Voeikov, by his opponent's desire to bribe potential witnesses and to kidnap the ill Ignashka on the road when he was well enough to travel to the capital for the trial. He submitted such petitions on April 26 and 29. Malygin's turn to file a similar petition came on May 6, four days after Voeikov had left for Vladimir (something not mentioned by the plaintiff).

On May 19 Malygin presented Kuzem'ka to the Slavery Chancellery, and reviewed his claims to him. Both Malygin and Kuzemka contended that Kuzemka was at least a third-generation slave, that Kuzemka's grandfather and father had died in the possession of the Malygins, and that Kuzemka had been born in Malygin's house. Moreover, Vasilii Malygin had gotten a limited service slavery contract on Kuzemka dated March 14, 1626, because, according to testimony at the trial on May 29, a royal decree had "ordered that limited service slavery contracts should be taken on hereditary slaves." When that document was excavated from the files of the Slavery Chancellery, it revealed that Malygin at least nominally had paid 12 rubles for Kuzemka, his wife Katerina (deceased by 1630) and their three children, Ovdokim (then age seven), Semen (five), and Luker'ia (one). Moreover, in the document it had been observed that they had been hereditary slaves.

On May 21, Malygin filed another complaint against Voeikov, who had failed to present Ignashka in the Slavery Chancellery. He also accused Voeikov of avoiding the other suit, with the result that Kuzemka was "being tortured by being kept in chains, in irons, by the bailiff, and he is dying of starvation." On the twenty-fourth, Malygin repeated his petition of three days earlier. Five days later Voeikov presented Ignashka, noting that he had been ill and that his wife had died. Moreover, Malygin himself had been in the Patriarch's procession, and then personally accompanied Ignashka to Moscow so that Voeikov would not kidnap him on the road. After the preliminary testimony in which Ignashka and Voeikov presented their positions, two trials were held, also on May 29. On the matter of the alleged stolen property, the litigants agreed to let an oath on the cross decide the matter. Malygin's slave Oleshka Ovdokimov was to kiss the cross for him, Voeikov's slave Zamiatinka Filin was to do the same for him.

Then the litigants introduced other evidence that they claimed would support their cases. Voeikov said that his father had given Kuzemka to him in 1602, and claimed that he had submitted written declarations to the Slavery Chancellery and to the Robbery Chancellery in 1609/10 in the matter of Kuzemka's flight and theft of the rent monies. He also said that Kuzemka's grandfather had served his family, and that the forebear had been registered in Viaz'ma land cadastres. Finally, he proposed a general interrogation of the populace of Viaz'ma province to prove that claim. Malygin cited the limited service slavery contract of 1626 and the fact that Kuzemka's features were those of that slave. He also cited Iaroslavl' tax payment books (*platezhnye knigi*), which showed that Kuzemka's father had served Malygin and his father in the household, and had paid taxes. He also asked for a general interrogation of the populace of Iaroslavl' to prove that Kuzemka's grandfather at least fifty years ago had been born in Malygin's grandfather's house, that the same had been true for their respective fathers, and that Kuzemka was born in his house and had served him there up to that moment.

On some date in June the Slavery Chancellery ordered the limited service slavery contracts to be located on them. This was done, and Kuzemka's contract, dated March 14, 1626, was found to say the following: "he has a round face, a straight nose, dark gray eyes, the hair on his head is dark brown, his mustache and beard are light brown, he has no sideburns, there are pock marks on his face because he had smallpox, he is of average height." The contract on Ignashka, dated February 20, 1624, said that he had "a long face, a straight nose, dark gray eyes, the hair on his head is brown, he has a graying light-brown mustache, no sideburns or beard; he says he is nineteen years old, and has been living with Malygin for five years and gave a limited service contract on himself for 6 rubles" (for himself and his wife Orina). On July 28, 1630, Kuzemka was physically brought in for a comparison with the contract, was found to match it, and was released on bail in the custody of those who also guaranteed Malygin. This was repeated again on August 17 in the presence of the guarantors, and again Kuzemka's features were found to match those in Maly-gin's contract. Ignashka was also compared in person to the contract.

On August 18 the Slavery Chancellery returned verdicts in both suits in favor of Malygin. In the case of Ignashka, the judges noted that his features had been compared with and were found to match those of the slave described in the limited service slavery contract of 1624. They took cognizance of Voeikov's claims that Ignashka was his peasant, but noted that he had not done what was necessary to protect his claims. Between the years when the peasant had fled in 1619 and allegedly returned in 1626, the defendant had failed to file a petition declaring his absence, a practice borrowed from the institution of slavery by the developing institution of serfdom. Moreover, they noted that there was a five-year statute of limitations on filing for the recovery of fugitive peasants. Thus, through his own negligence Voeikov lost his peasant to Malygin, who had had the foresight to formulate a precise slavery contract on him.

Similar grounds were noted for allowing Malygin to keep Kuzemka. The defendant had been able to present his limited service slavery contract written in 1626, the man was compared with the document, and they matched. On the other hand, Voeikov had presented no documents. His "evidence" could not be substantiated. There were no declarations in the Slavery Chancellery from 1610, an investigation had revealed. Moreover, Voeikov had failed to state whether Kuzemka's grandfather was registered as a slave or a peasant in the Viaz'ma land cadastres. There was no point in following up on Voeikov's plea for a general investigation of the populace of Viaz'ma province because the plaintiff was suing imprecisely, stating that the grandfather's name was Denisko, son of Kuz'ma (called Goriainko), but Kuzemka said his grandfather was Denis, son of Vasilii (Zhuk), and the Slavery Chancellery took Kuzemka's word for it. On September 22, 1630, the verdicts were read to Malygin and one of Voeikov's guarantors (Voeikov himself by that time was governor of Nizhnii Novgorod), the slaves were turned over to Malygin, and he paid the capitation fees of 6 altyns (3 apiece) for them.

Two details were left unsettled, Ignashka's children and the matter of stolen property. (Malygin already had custody of Kuzemka's children.) On September 26, 1630, Malygin petitioned for a continuance because he had to report for service in Viaz'ma. It was granted, and five guarantors pledged that he would appear within a month after discharge. On March 5, 1631, he petitioned for a resolution of the two matters, and repeated the request on March 9 and 15. Voeikov of course was not in Moscow, but on March 29, 1631, the Slavery Chancellery ordered that his guarantors be presented for a resolution of the case. Nothing happened, and on March 31 Malygin noted that Voeikov was not presenting his slave who was supposed to kiss the cross to resolve the stolen-property dispute. He also claimed that his adversary had left to be governor in Nizhnii without asking for a continuance. Malygin noted that the case was entering its second year and he was perishing because of the expenses (*proesti*) and bureaucratic delay (*volokita*) and that he had been forced to abandon his house (*otbyl svoego iurtshka*, literally, "little tent"). On the same day the bailiff presented Voeikov's guarantors, who were released on bond with a directive to present Voeikov's slave for the oath (cross-kissing) ceremony. The slave was in Nizhnii with his owner and was given five weeks to appear. On May 13 the slave had not appeared, and Voeikov's guarantors were granted a two-week extension. At the same time, Malygin was readying his food supplies for the summer campaign.[70]

At this point the record breaks off, unresolved. The delay in the resolution of the stolen-property issue at first glance might appear pointless: Malygin had been granted the slaves, therefore, one might reason, he should win the stolen-property dispute. However, that was not the case. Ignashka had denied having stolen anything, an important factor in resolving such matters.

Malygin v. Voeikov clearly reveals the importance the Slavery Chancellery attached to the physical descriptions of slaves in the limited service slavery contracts. All other considerations in this case were definitely subordinate to that one. While the Slavery Chancellery troubled to refute Voeikov's claims, it did not even bother to examine Malygin's supporting evidence, for the slavery contracts were sufficient.

The way in which the Slavery Chancellery considered the physical description of a fugitive slave is revealed in the 1634 case of Kozlova v. Kozlova et al., discussed in detail in chapter 17 below. One of the litigants contended that a woman had not been present at the drafting of the limited service slavery contract in which she was included with her husband. The contested woman was brought in for examination, and the Slavery Chancellery wrote up the following:

The features and distinctive characteristics of the slavewoman Matriushka were compared with those in the limited service slavery contract, and neither she nor they coincided with the disputed features listed in [litigant] Andrei [Kozlov's] petition. Andrei said that she has a crooked nose, and in the limited service slavery contract it is written that her nose is blunt, but on examination she has a straight, snub nose. The other features, which Andrei's petition did not name, [also] do not coincide with the limited service slavery contract. In the limited service slavery contract it is written that she is of tall stature, but upon inspection her height is average. It is written that she is emaciated, but upon inspection she is neither emaciated nor fat, but a typical, average slave. It is written that her hair is light brown and eyebrows are light brown tinged with black. It is written that her eyes are black, but upon inspection they are hazel. It is written that a hair is growing out of her left eye [sic], but upon inspection no hair is growing out of her eye, both eyes are the same.

One may assume that the Slavery Chancellery did not continue its comparisons, for it felt that enough had been said. (More could have been said, for the original

70. Iakovlev, *Kholopstvo*, pp. 440-57, no. 18.

limited service slavery contract also claimed that Matriushka's face was pock-marked from smallpox [something relatively common], that she had a mole under one eye by the nose, and that the middle toes on her feet were joined—all in all, a very distinctive person.)[71]

One of the basic rules of later Muscovite slave law was that he who had the oldest document won a contest for a slave whose ownership was in dispute.[72] While this principle is obvious to the modern mind, it was by no means so to those in a society in which documentation was just being introduced. It was a principle that had to be restated frequently.

Stuneev v. Eropkin

The application of this principle is evident in a suit between *sytnik* Fedor Petrov Stuneev and *zhilets* Mikhail Fedorov Eropkin for the possession of Pavl, son of Semen Nikiforov (Pavl Semenov). The matter was litigated between May 11 and June 14, 1620, before Slavery Chancellery directors Semen Mikhailovich Koltovskii and Ivan Kuz'mich Begichev and state secretary Filipp Mitrofanov. Almost no information seems to be available about plaintiff Stuneev, outside of the material provided by the trial record. His title, *sytnik,* meant that he was perhaps head of the Sytnyi Dvorets, the office responsible for providing the palace with beverages. His friends were of the same milieu, as evidenced by the fact that his three guarantors were also palace provisioners (*striapchie*): one who also worked in the Beverage Office, and two others who worked for the Comestibles Office (Kormovoi Dvorets). Stuneev had a residence in Moscow.

A great deal of information is available about defendant Eropkin. He also had a Moscow residence, which in 1638 was kept by his slave Piatunka Ivanov, who was armed with a long gun (*pishchal'*). However, his basic residence was in Meshchovsk, near Kaluga, south of Moscow, where many of the events narrated in the trial took place. He first appeared late in the Time of Troubles, he was at Smolensk in November 1613-February 1614, had killed many of the enemy, was wounded, and was discharged. Note was made at that time that his cash compensation had been 20 rubles during the time of Tsar Vasilii Shuiskii. He recovered, and in 1616 was sent to Moscow, probably at that time being appointed to the capital service entry rank of *zhilets* as a reward for his service at Smolensk. In 1618 he was sent to Iaroslavl', to levy troops that then served in Astrakhan'. The years 1625-26 found him occupying the post of military governor (*voevoda*) of Riazhsk, a frontier town southeast of Riazan'. For his service there he was promoted to the rank of Moscow *dvorianin* in 1626/27. He was in palace service in 1630 (on Christmas he dined in the presence of Tsar Mikhail), and again in 1633. That was interrupted by a term as *voevoda* in 1631-32 in Novgorod Severskii, an outpost in Ukraine, where his major function seems to have been funnel-

---

71. Ibid., pp. 479-80, 486, no. 23, I, VIII.
72. 1649 *Ulozhenie* 20: 8; MS, p. 252, among many others.

ing intelligence about the Rzeczpospolita to Moscow on the eve of the Smolensk War. He hindered the Muscovite military effort in the war itself by refusing to send reinforcements to the front at Trubchevsk because of his hostility to General Baim Boltin. That action may have been what took him out of the records for the next decade, but he appeared again as governor of the northern town of Ustiug Velikii in 1641-42, where he played a major role in conducting a census.[73] Eropkin is a typical example of the Muscovite meritocracy at work, a person with a career typical for a provincial slaveowner who succeeded in the military and administrative service world.

The judicial case at issue opened when Stuneev filed a document in which he noted that he, with assistance of a bailiff, had apprehended his fugitive slave Pavl Semenov, a typical private initiative to recover a runaway. Pavl admitted that he signed a slavery contract with Stuneev, who wanted the slave turned over to him. Pavl had sold himself to Stuneev in October 1614, had fled in 1615, and five years later, around Easter, Stuneev had found the fugitive living with Eropkin, who, it turned out, had in his possession a limited service slavery contract on Pavl dated September 25, 1606, signed by the *guba* elder of Kaluga. The contract had been written by a Kaluga clerk of the civil (*zemskii*) administration and witnessed by a clerk of the Kaluga *guba* administration. Pavl had fled from Eropkin in 1612/13. Pavl confessed that the 1607 document was valid, and that he had hoped that the document had perished during the Time of Troubles. The luckless slave, who had sought refuge first with one slaveowner (Eropkin), then another (Stuneev), then with the first (Eropkin), claimed that he had not mentioned the 1606 document when Stuneev had apprehended him because he no longer wanted to live with Eropkin. The verdict was awarded to Eropkin because his contract was prior, and because Stuneev, knowing that he was going to lose the case anyway, left town and did not appear for the verdict. A fee of 3 altyns (9 kopecks) was paid for the trial, which, lasting only a month, was expeditious by any standards. The case was concluded definitively on July 22, 1620, when Eropkin was given a judgment charter showing that he had been awarded the verdict.[74]

Evidence

In the mid-seventeenth century the sources of evidence used to resolve conflicts over slaves and slave property were primarily written documents, witnesses, and

73. RIB 28(1912): 405, 411-12; Beliaev, *Rospisnoi spisok 1638*, p. 119; AMG 1: 204, 334, 348-49, 387, 409, 451-53; AMG 2: 41; DR 1: 732, 819, 845, 849, 866, KR 1: 920, 1028, 1114; 2: 433, 675, 731; Ivanov, AUBK, p. 133; *Opisanie* 15(1908), p. 84; Savelov, 3: APD 1: 390-94, 406-7, 478.

74. Iakovlev, *Kholopstvo*, pp. 318-23, no. 1.

visual confrontations.[75] As a check against forgery, not only was the original document considered in litigation but a copy of it was supposed to be in the record books. If there was no copy in the record books, an original document with a valid signature was still good. When the absence of a copy in the record books was due to an official's negligence, he was to be punished "as the sovereign decreed," a formula that, because of its uncertainty, was useful for maximally terrorizing the elite.[76] This was also the time when violence was being introduced into all spheres of law, and the law of slavery did not escape the trend. As we have seen, one of the unusual features of Muscovite law was that the slave could serve as a witness in the judicial process. He could even be forced to serve as a witness against himself. Thus fugitives, enslaved by reason of birth from slave parents but denying their parents to escape enslavement, could be tortured to force them to acknowledge their parents, and thus their slave status.[77]

A major concern for Muscovites as they entered the paper era was what should be done when those precious pieces of paper perished. This was a real concern in a land that was regularly experiencing foreign invasions, civil disorders, and just ordinary fires of the kind that regularly burned down as much as whole cities in "the land of wood." The solution was for those afflicted by such a loss to file a declaration (*iavka*) about the loss as soon as was practicable, and subsequently the declaration could play a substitutive role in resolving a conflict. As we shall see, woe befell the individual who neglected to file a declaration about a loss of documents. The 1597 law that redefined the nature of limited service contract slavery cited a previous law of March 1593 on the restoration of various documents (full slavery contracts, marriage contracts and dowries, wills, and the like) lost in the Moscow fire of 1571 or subsequent conflagrations, or lost for other reasons. The 1593 law provided that new documents were to be given the slaveowners, but it is not clear whether they were to be duplicates of the old hereditary slavery documents or new limited service slavery contracts.[78] Judging by practice in the first half of the seventeenth century, it was probably the latter.

The chaos of the Time of Troubles engendered many difficulties for the Muscovite slavery system. Not only were vast numbers of master-slave ties undone, but the records to prove claims were destroyed, both the originals in the possession of individuals and copies made and preserved by official organs. The paper revolution was dealt a severe blow, and resort often was had to more traditional forms of evidence. Once again, in an attempt to compensate for the loss of records, the government provided that interested parties could make declarations about the loss of their documents, and those declarations could later be used in

75. 1649 *Ulozhenie* 20: 24; MS, p. 264.
76. 1649 *Ulozhenie* 20: 20; MS, p. 263.
77. 1649 *Ulozhenie* 20: 25; MS, p. 264.
78. PRP 4: 372; MS, pp. 249-50.

litigation. Failure to make declarations could result in the loss of a case, although resort to other forms of evidence such as a general investigation was still possible to prove hereditary slave status.[79]

Tatishchev v. Selekhovskii

An illustration of that principle was provided by a case tried between August and December of 1624 in the Slavery Chancellery before the codirectors Stepan Ivanov Volynskii and Andrei Ivanov Baskakov and the state secretaries Ivan Shevyrev and Patrikei Nasonov. Iurii Ignat'ev Tatishchev sued Vasilii Mikhailov Selekhovskii for the possession of the slave Nikita Iur'ev, his wife, Ovdot'ka Eremeeva, and their two children, a boy Fed'ka and a daughter Ovdot'ka. The case was complicated by the fact that the slave used slightly different names, in one instance claiming he was the son of Iurii Iakovlev and in another of Iurii Skobel'tsyn, but this changing of his grandfather's name (the matter of Iakovlev and Skobel'tsyn) did not confuse the litigants and need not concern us either.

The litigants were social and moral equals. The plaintiff, Iurii Ignat'ev Tatishchev, did not advance princely pretensions, although he was a descendant of Vladimir Monomakh and Ivan Kalita. His father, Ignatii Petrov Tatishchev, had been a distinguished general and diplomat in the reign of Ivan IV. The son seems to have been less illustrious. The first reference to him seems to be as a delegate (with the rank of *striapchii*) to the 1598 Assembly of the Land that chose Boris Godunov as tsar. By 1604 he had been elevated to the rank of *stol'nik*, and was part of an embassy to Georgia in the Caucasus. He seems to have sat out the Time of Troubles, perhaps because of his connections with Godunov, but came out of the disaster in 1613 with enormous landholdings totalling 1,083 1/8 cheti. He continued to dabble in diplomacy. In 1617 he dined at court with the English ambassador, and in 1619 settled boundary disputes with the Rzeczpospolita in the Toropets region and also discussed the matter of exchanging military captives. He held two minor military governorships, one in Kursk on the southern frontier in 1613-16, and then in Viaz'ma west of Moscow in 1626. He must not have been highly regarded by his superiors, for he was never promoted above the rank of *stol'nik*. This may well have been connected with his personality, which seems to have made him somewhat more litigious than many of his peers. Not only was he involved in this case, which resulted from the fact that his new slave, a highly dependent person in reality, fled from him almost immediately, but he also was involved in three precedence disputes. The most notorious of them was his refusal to go to Kaluga in 1618 at the order of Tsar Mikhail to inquire after the health of Dmitrii Pozharskii, the hero of the liberation of Russia from the Poles in 1611-13, claiming it was beneath his dignity. He fled, his slaves were seized to make him appear (which he did) in the Military Chancellery

79. 1649 *Ulozhenie* 20: 29; MS, pp. 265-66.

before the tsar. The tsar and boyars ordered that he be beaten with the knout in the Military Chancellery for his disobedience and for insulting Pozharskii. The sentence of beating with the knout, known somtimes to kill its victims, was carried out, and then Tatishchev was sent to do penance before Pozharskii.

Tatishchev seems to have gotten into additional trouble, for by 1622 he had been demoted to the rank of Moscow *dvorianin*. Perhaps he failed in his Toropets negotiations, perhaps he did not get on well with Filaret after he returned in 1619, perhaps a decision was made to punish him additionally for the insult to Pozharskii. Be that as it may, he was not a favorite in Moscow at the time of this trial. [80]

The defendant in the trial, Prince Vasilii Mikhailov Selekhovskii, was a twenty-first generation Russian noble whose ancestors for some time had served in Lithuania but had joined Muscovite service after Olgerd confiscated their lands in 1436. Selekhovskii seems to have been somewhat younger than Tatishchev, for in 1611 he was on a list of *zhil'tsy,* the entry rating of capital service, entitled to compensation of 400 cheti of land and 5 rubles in cash. Somewhat significantly, as we shall see, he claimed that during the reign of Vasilii Shuiskii, 1607-10, he had been entitled to 600 cheti and 25 rubles, but the records were lost during the destruction of Moscow in 1611. In any case, for some reason he was disgraced and sent into exile in Siberia at the beginning of Mikhail's reign. In the trial, he referred to his stay in Siberia but said that he had been in service there! Thus Selekhovskii was a person whose word was not worth 2 kopeks, and perhaps he was as unpleasant as Tatishchev to boot. Be that as it may, in 1619 he was made governor for a year of the small northern town of Tot'ma on the Sukhona River, his last such assignment. For reasons that are not at all clear, by the years 1627-29 he had been promoted to the rank of Moscow *dvorianin*, the rank to which Tatishchev had been demoted half a decade earlier.[81] Thus this is a dispute between two of Muscovy's lesser, and less savory, members of the lower upper service class.

Certain of the basic facts in the case are clear. In the early years of the Time of Troubles, Nikita had been an hereditary slave first of Selekhovskii's grandfather Ivan, and of his cousin-once-removed, Petr Ivanov Selekhovskoi, in Medyn' province, in the Briansk region south of the Oka River. Petr Ivanov Selekhovskoi had died during the reign of Tsar Vasilii Shuiskii, 1607-10, and the defendant claimed that the slave Nikita, who was at that moment a free agent, had

80. Petrov, IRRD 1: 54; AAE 2: 44, no. 7; Hulbert, p. 394; Belokurov, RZ 7113-21, p. 25; Ovchinnikov, "BS 1607," p. 78; Markevich, p. cxxx; Barsukov, "Dokladnaia vypiska 121," 9-10; KR 1:78, 195, 558, 1115, 1230; RK 1598-1638, p. 294; RK 1550-1636 2: 269, 280, 300, 311, 330, 339; AMG 1: 158, no. 130; SIRIO 142(1913): 27; *Opisanie* 15(1908): 9, 37; DR, passim; Veselovskii, APD 1: 449, no. 219; Barsukov, SGV, pp. 55, 122; Ivanov, AUKB, p. 406.

81. Petrov, IRRD 1: 56; Sukhotin, ChSV, pp. 231-32, 239; Barsukov, SGV, p. 248; DR 1: 425; KR 1: 661; Ivanov, AUBK, p. 372; APD 1: 135-36, no. 63.

come to him and given a limited service slavery contract on himself. During the destruction of Moscow by the Poles in 1611, Selekhovskii and Nikita lost track of each other, and the slavery contract was lost as well. (Here we recall the purported loss of service records as well.) Then Selekhovskii was in service, he claimed, first in Lithuania, then Siberia (official records report he was really in exile there); when he returned from Siberia to Moscow in 1617, he reported at the trial that he had been told that declarations on documents lost during the Time of Troubles were no longer being taken. That probably was not true, and in any case led to his undoing.

The movements of the slave Nikita after 1611 do not quite add up because of various contradictions, but it appears that he then served with Mikhail Zakhriapin voluntarily, at which time he got married. In March 1616, Nikita and Ovdot'ia (who changed her patronymic to Fedorova) sold themselves for the sum of 3 rubles to the plaintiff in this case, the *stol'nik* Iu. I. Tatishchev, whose slave Erofei Aleksandrov Tigorskoi managed the transaction for his owner. Apparently the new slaves and Tatishchev did not get along well together, for they fled from him almost immediately. Then they served voluntarily with the foreigner Matvei Kholoimov in the Arzamas region for about six years, and finally sought out the defendant, Vasilii Selekhovskii, and sold themselves to him on October 9, 1622, for the sum of 4 rubles—2 rubles apiece. During the sale ceremony, they claimed that they had been his hereditary slaves. The return of former slaves to their old owners, or heirs of their owners, seems to have been a relatively common event in Muscovy. Mikita and Ovdot'ia seemed to do well as Selekhovskii's slaves, and had two children. However, two years later, their former owner Tatishchev discovered them, had them arrested, and filed suit.

The reasoning behind the verdict in favor of Tatishchev is no longer part of the case, but it is apparent that the judges in the Slavery Chancellery made their decision on the basis of the plaintiff's older document. Defendant Selekhovskii cited six specific witnesses, plus the entire population for twenty miles around Petr Selekhovskii's village, Burdakovo in Medyn' province, to prove that the slave Nikita had become his, Vasilii Selekhovskii's, slave after Petr's death, but the Slavery Chancellery officials probably noted that such memories were over a decade old and that those cited were all from the defendant's friends, besides. The crucial point was that Selekhovskii had never filed a claim about the limited service slavery contract he said he had lost in 1611, which, in the officials' eyes, cast doubt on the veracity of his testimony. He also was not helped by Nikita's testimony during the trial that Selekhovskii had ordered him to be silent about the 1616 contract with Tatishchev when the 1622 contract was being formulated.

For some unknown reason, this case dragged on unnecessarily. It is fairly clear that it was basically concluded in less than a week, when the Slavery Chancellery ordered the defendant to post a bond in which he guaranteed that he would not leave Moscow. Six weeks later Tatishchev summarized the case and asked for a verdict in his favor. He also noted that Nikita was being held in chains by a court bailiff, and that those expenses were mounting. A week later the slave, Nikita petitioned, noted that he and his family had been fettered and starved for twelve weeks, and asked for a resolution. Only in another week and a half did the Slavery Chancellery finally get around to awarding the verdict to the plaintiff.[82] Once again, the logic of Muscovite slave-law justice was clear. The litigants were, as was so often the case, social equals. Neither was favored by the court. Tatishchev had the older contract, Selekhovskii had the newer contract and had failed to comply with the requirements, of which he had been aware, that those who had lost documents during the Time of Troubles were supposed to declare their losses for future reference.

Declarations were called for in 1681 when a freedman came to someone with a manumission document and, having stated his intention to sell himself, fled. The would-be purchaser could take the manumission document as evidence and declare what had happened. Subsequently he was in a position to claim the freedman as his slave should the freedman reappear. Such a declaration had priority over a limited service slavery contract with a later date in someone else's possession.[83]

Buturlin v. Netes'ev

Even though Muscovy was making great progress in what one might call the "paper revolution," there were times when a slaveowner could not produce any written documents because his evidence had perished. In such cases the plaintiff had to resort to more traditional evidence, such as knowledgeable witnesses and eyewitnesses. This was evident in a case tried in December 1620, when Mikhail Kirillov Buturlin sued in the Slavery Chancellery before its codirectors Semen Mikhailov Koltovskoi and Ivan Kuz'mich Begichev and the state secretary Filipp Mitrofanov for the return of his slave Fedor (Fed'ka) Mitrofanov, called Sheliapin.

Mikhail Buturlin was not an overwhelmingly significant personage in Muscovy and may have shone partially in the light cast by his distinguished uncle, Efim Okhromeev Buturlin, about whom more will be said in a moment. Mikhail lived in Suzdal', north of Moscow, and in 1610 his salary was supposed to be 11 rubles per year. He distinguished himself late in the Time of Troubles in a battle at Voronezh, was wounded twice, and by 1613 his pay had been raised to 23 rubles. In September 1619 he was one of the officers sent to Iaroslavl' for reinforcements to lift a siege of Moscow. For his service in the Time of Troubles he was promoted to the rank of Moscow *dvorianin*, which he seems to have held for the rest of his apparently uneventful life. In 1624 and 1625 he served as part of the bodyguard assigned to protect one of the two leading boyars in Moscow, Fedor Ivanovich Sheremetev.[84]

82. Iakovlev, *Kholopstvo*, pp. 364-70, no. 9.
83. PSZ 2: 314, 589, 859, 909, nos. 869, 1073, 1246, 1278.
84. Sukhotin, ChSV, pp. 282-83; AMG 1: 204; DR 1: 616, 750; Ivanov, AUBK, p. 52.

The slave in question, Fed'ka, earlier had belonged to Buturlin's uncle, Efim, a luminary of the second half of the sixteenth century. In 1579 he was military commander (*voevoda*) in Orel, and held similar positions in other cities and towns of Muscovy and Siberia for the next three decades. He also from time to time commanded one or another of the divisions (advance, left, rear guard, central, or right) of the Russian army. In 1582 he was no. 107 in an incomplete list of the important personages of Muscovy, and by 1605 he was an *okol'nichii* and accompanied Tsar Boris Godunov and his son tsarevich Fedor on a religious procession. He quickly joined the forces of the pretender, False Dmitrii I, and in 1606 convoyed Ivan the Terrible's mock tsar, Simeon Bekbulatovich, to a forced tonsuring and exile in the Kirillov monastery north of Moscow. Not of royal birth himself, Efim was one of the more contentious individuals of his time, always willing to sue a prince for precedence in a military campaign. In 1603 Buturlin was one of the commanders dispatched to put down the slave uprising led by Khlopko. When the uprising by Bolotnikov broke out, he again was on the front lines. At Putivl' in 1606, now working for Tsar Shuiskii, Buturlin fell into the hands of the rebels on the field of combat and, along with at least a dozen other distinguished military figures, was tortured to death in a variety of gruesome ways that may be symptomatic of class warfare, or perhaps just of any civil war.[85] His death set in motion this case.

Fed'ka had been a hereditary slave belonging to Efim Buturlin, who apparently had not left any will ordering the disposition of his property. Efim's death threw Fed'ka, who was sixteen, his wife, Verka, and their son, Volod'ka, plus the members of five other families, into a state of limbo. Had there been a will, Efim's nephew Mikhail Kirillov Buturlin could have claimed all of the slaves as his hereditary property. There being none, they came to young Mikhail and sold themselves to him in Suzdal' as limited service contract slaves. Things seemed to have gone well for quite some time, the slaves multiplied in the course of about nine years (the court transcript says eleven years, but that does not agree with other dates), and then, for some unknown reason, in 1615, they fled from Mikhail Buturlin's place in Suzdal'. They took with them considerable property, including three horses, a cow, two saddles, two guns, and a considerable quantity of clothing, much of which they wore. They traveled about 350 kilometers, from Suzdal' to Arzamas, east-southeast of Moscow. Fed'ka had been Mikhail Buturlin's lackey and had accompanied him on military campaigns, and one assumes that he and the others were domestic house slaves. In Arzamas, however, they turned themselves into farmers, and tilled land assigned as a service estate to Stepan Ivanov Netes'ev.

85. Storozhev, "B.S.," p. 59; Markevich, p. lxvii; AIuB 1: 154, no. 48; RK 1550-1636, pp. 16, 124, 189, 234; RK 1475, passim; Belokurov, RZ 7113-21, pp. 8, 131, 133, 210, 212; AAE 2: 97, no. 41; Smirnov, *Vosstanie Bolotnikova* (1951), pp. 78, 163; A. I. Kopanov and A. G. Man'kov, ed., *Vosstanie I. Bolotnikova. Dokumenty i materialy* (Moscow: Sotsekgiz, 1959), pp. 77, 88, 110, 241, 346.

Netes'ev's career somewhat resembled that of Mikhail Buturlin, although his origins were almost certainly more humble. Netes'ev's father, Ivan Istomin, had been a frontier serviceman whose land entitlement was only 150 cheti of land at the time of his retirement in 1593. Ivan petitioned the government that he was old and lame, wanted to retire and asked to transfer all of his land, his full 150 cheti, to his son Stepan. That was granted. Stepan seems to have been a relatively unscrupulous individual, at least judging by the fact that he was accused of usurping a widow's property in 1608; then he left the camp of False Dmitrii II and joined the forces of Tsar Vasilii Shuiskii. Moreover, as we know, he received Fed'ka and other fugitive slaves in 1615, and then drove them out by force for unknown reasons four and a half years later—keeping their inventory (implements and seed), clothing, livestock and their grain in the ground. It is not clear what services he performed, but he was one of the 138 Arzamas servicemen awarded a gold den'ga for distinguished service in the Time of Troubles. He was promoted to the rank of provincial *dvorianin*, a rank he held in the 1620s.[86]

Netes'ev's expulsion of Fed'ka forced the latter to work for a while as a hired laborer in the villages of Arzamas province, but that did not suit him, so he returned to Moscow, "to save himself," perhaps in search of his old lord, Mikhail Buturlin. Buturlin and a policeman arrested him and brought him to the Slavery Chancellery, where Buturlin sued to have Fed'ka declared his slave and to force Netes'ev to compensate him for the property that Fed'ka had taken from him five years earlier.

A problem arose because Buturlin had no documentary evidence to prove that Fed'ka had been his slave, for his house in Suzdal' had burned in 1617, and the slavery contracts had been reduced to ashes. However, he had made the required declaration at the time that he had lost his documents. Lacking written evidence, Buturlin referred to the evidence that people who knew that Fed'ka had been his slave could provide. These included those who had seen Fed'ka as Buturlin's military lackey since Buturlin had entered the service at the age of fifteen, people in Kaluga who had seen Fed'ka and Buturlin together, plus the military servitors, townsmen, and merchants of Suzdal' and its province, "from the greatest to the smallest." Fed'ka cited the same people. Had he contested the issue, the Slavery Chancellery would have ordered an interrogation of all the people cited by Buturlin.

Stepan Netes'ev, who had received the fugitive slaves in Arzamas, was brought into the case. He testified in the Slavery Chancellery that he had had no connection with the fugitive slave Fed'ka, and, in an act of extraordinary impudence that seems entirely in keeping with his character, even refused to sign his testimony, saying that he did not know the slave Fed'ka. Perjury was illegal in Muscovy but seems to have been overlooked in civil cases such as this one. Netes'ev's

86. Veselovskii, "Arzamas," *Chteniia* 1916, pp. 394-95, 605-6: RIB 28(1912): 772; Ivanov, AUBK, p. 291.

testimony meant that no one else was claiming ownership of Fed'ka besides Buturlin, and so the court awarded him the verdict. The fee of 3 altyns was paid and the suit for the possession of the slave Fedor Sheliapin was resolved within two weeks after its initiation.

Several strands were left to be unravelled, however. One of them involved Fed'ka's family—his wife, son, and daughter. Nothing more was said about them and one may assume either that they had perished or, more likely, that Fed'ka had abandoned them. The other matter was that of the property that Fed'ka had stolen, for which Netes'ev, as his recipient, was liable, plus members of two other slave families who had accompanied Fed'ka to Arzamas. On that subject Buturlin and Netes'ev reached an out-of-court settlement that was accepted by the Slavery Chancellery. Unfortunately, the terms of the settlement are unknown. A final matter was documentation on Buturlin's ownership of Fed'ka. Even though the slave confessed that he belonged to Buturlin, the Slavery Chancellery forced Buturlin to post a surety bond signed by six men of Suzdal' guaranteeing that he would present the document he had obtained in 1617 after his house had burned and that the slaveowner would present Fed'ka in the Slavery Chancellery upon demand.[87]

The Continuance

The continuance was one of the unavoidable jurisprudential banes of the Muscovite service state and resulted from the nearly annual military service required of all landholders. Unfortunately I do not have any comparative material on this subject, but one may well imagine that nowhere else was the continuance so frequently resorted to as it was in Muscovy. A continuance was automatically granted whenever a litigant received a call to report for service. The general rule was that he was to report back to the court within a month after being discharged from the service.

Mortkin v. Gur'ev

For violating the terms of a continuance a litigant could lose a case. This was revealed in the case of Mortkin v. Gur'ev, tried in the Slavery Chancellery before codirectors Stepan Ivanov Volynskii and Ivan Fomich Ogarev and the state secretaries Nikita Leont'ev and Iakov Kliucharev, and then concluded before Prince Ivan Fedorovich Volkonskoi, Ogarev, and the state secretaries Ivan Varganov and Andrei Stroev between April 1628 and December 1629. The objects of contention were Pozniak (Pozniachko), his son, Kuz'ma, his wife, Akulina (called Liubka) Mitrofanova (or Ulanova), and their daughter, Aksin'ia. As in most litigation over slaves, the parties were servicemen, but in this case,

87. Iakovlev, *Kholopstvo*, pp. 327-30, no. 3.

while they may have been nearly coevals, they were not approximate service equals, as was so often the case. At the time of the case Prince Iurii Nikitich Mortkin, the plaintiff, was already a *stol'nik* in the service of Patriarch Filaret. His lands were located in the Maloiaroslavets region south of Moscow. After the death of Filaret he was transferred to the state service system and seems to have been a *stol'nik* in 1636, a rank that he apparently held to the end of his life about thirty years later. His life after the lawsuit seems to have been focused on three activities: in the period 1636-1640 he was often a sentry in the tsar's palace; in 1646 he was a census taker in Zubovo region, probably in the North, and in 1652 he was a surveyor (*mezhevoe delo*) in the Shatsk area, probably southeast of Riazan'; and in the early 1660s he was military governor of Putivl' and then Novgorod. He was in Putivl' from late 1660 to late 1662, at the time when it was a major center during the Thirteen Years War. From there he sent intelligence information to Moscow (he was literate), and was accused of dishonoring a front-line commander by refusing to send draftees who were quartered in Putivl' to the front for training; he sent artillery and powder to the Zaporozh'e cossacks, and tended to the postal communications system. Then he was accused of murder and treason, and was replaced. Apparently there was inadequate substance to the charges, for the following year, 1663, found him as commander in Novgorod. By this time Mortkin must have been quite an old man, but he was still alive and recorded as a *stol'nik* in 1668.[88] Far less is known about the defendant in the case, Batrak Ignat'ev Gur'ev, other than what is available in the case itself: he was an illiterate *syn boiarskii* from Tarusa, south of Moscow, who died about November 11, 1629, leaving behind his widow and small children—indicating that he himself was a comparatively young man, probably about the same age as Mortkin, or perhaps a few years older.

The facts in Mortkin v. Gur'ev were only partially in dispute, with the major contention being over the origin of the slavewoman Liubka. Plaintiff Mortkin claimed that she had belonged to his maternal grandfather, Vasilii Markovich Buturlin (a person who seems to have left few if any traces in the historical record), and, on his death, had passed to him. Then, according to Mortkin, she had run away from him, something not unexpected, for changing owners was often stressful. Defendant Gur'ev claimed at first that the woman Liubka had been manumitted by Buturlin but had come to him without a manumission document. Then he changed his story slightly, and claimed that her mother, Koterinka, had given Liubka to him when the contested slave was a small girl, a story not really inconsistent with the first one except in explaining Liubka's motivation at the time. Be that as it may, Liubka served Gur'ev for about two decades,

88. Petrov, IRRD 1(1886): 77-80; Ivanov, AUBK, p. 271; DR 2: 940; 3: 291; supp. 238, 347, 377-78; ZKMS (RIB 10): 16, 41, 140, 172, 212, 356; Shumakov, *Obzor* 4(1917): 440-41, 457, 528, 554; Sokolova and Fon-Meik, RKiSPP, p. 199; Barsukov, SGV, p. 190; *Opisanie* 12(1901): 513, 545; AMG 3: 220, 247, 371-74, 512.

"since the time when Pan Molottskoi [Andrei Mlotskii] burned the city of Ser-pukhov" (1610). (Her recollection was that she had left Mortkin and gone to Gur'ev "during the destruction of Moscow" [1611].) After Liubka had lived with Gur'ev for a while, she married the latter's slave, Pozniachko, and they in time produced the girl Aksin'ia. Pozniachko, at the time of the trial, claimed to have been a slave for Gur'ev's father, Ignatii, and then of Batrak Gur'ev himself for forty years (perhaps even before the slaveowner reached his majority). We may surmise that Pozniachko was somewhat older than Liubka, but by how much is not clear.

For reasons that we cannot determine, marital disharmony caused Liubka to abandon her husband on the Thursday before Easter, 1627. Gur'ev was away in service in Briansk, and during the night Liubka and her daughter crept out of the house and ran away. Where was she to go? Back to her prior owner, or her prior owner's son, of course! Gur'ev lived near Tarusa, and Mortkin lived in the Iaroslavets (Maloiaroslavets) region, so Liubka and her daughter fled about 70 kilometers to get away from her husband. Initially, at the trial, Gur'ev said that he had no idea where she had gone, he could not find her. And if that version is correct, no doubt he never would have found out, if a year later Mortkin had not sued to claim her husband, Pozniachko, as well. Why he did so is unclear. Perhaps the couple had been in contact with one another, and de-cided that they wanted to be reunited. That seems likely, for otherwise Mortkin would simply be asking for more trouble in his house than any rational person would want: a quarrelling slave couple. In any case, when Gur'ev learned the whereabouts of Liubka, he filed a countersuit to recover her as his slavewoman.

In the first extant document from the case, dated April 22, 1628, Gur'ev noted that Mortkin had initiated the case against him some considerable time earlier but then did not file the formal charges to open the court case. Finally, the litigants had agreed on the issues to be tried and a court date, but Mortkin did not appear for trial. In December Gur'ev filed another complaint in which he noted that Mortkin had not presented Liubka in the Slavery Chancellery, which he apparently had agreed to do in a continuance he must have gotten in the spring, in which they agreed to renew the suit after the summer campaign was over. He begged relief so that he, "exhausted by bureaucratic red tape, would not perish completely." Nothing happened, except that two weeks later Mortkin filed a similar complaint, claiming that Gur'ev had not presented Pozniachko either. He also claimed that his opponent was trying to bankrupt him by stalling tactics. The Slavery Chancellery apparently set a trial date, a week before Christmas, 1629, but nothing took place.

On January 20, 1629, Mortkin again asked for a trial, and it was held on that date. It was followed immediately by a trial for the countersuit. The conflicting testimony discussed above was presented. The basic problem of the case was that neither litigant had any written documentation proving to whom Liubka be-longed. They therefore resorted to the traditional knowledgeable witnesses. In this, of course, Gur'ev had the advantage, for many people could remember that Liubka had been living in his household for nearly two decades. Mortkin, on the other hand, was at a disadvantage, as he himself noted, in trying to find witnesses who could recall what had happened nearly twenty years earlier. He cited everybody for twenty and more versts around his Iaroslavets estate to prove that it was known that her mother, Koterinka, had died as his slave, and that people knew by rumor that Liubka had fled from his estate. Gur'ev followed tradition and, to prove his point—that Liubka's parents had not served Mortkin—cited the same witnesses, "excepting Prince Iurii's friends, relatives, and lackeys." Then he proceeded to point out who was thereby untrustworthy, and why. Gur'ev's claims were certainly all true: Liubka had lived in his household as a single woman, Gur'ev had married her to his hereditary slave Pozniachko, and she had fled with her daughter. At this point in the trial Gur'ev introduced some new information: apparently he had discovered the whereabouts of Liubka relatively soon after the flight, and had sent another one of his slaves to consult with Mortkin's steward, also almost certainly a slave, Ivan Ashiurok. Prince Iurii Mortkin agreed to return her, and she was returned. (How she again fell into Mortkin's hands is not discussed.)

The case of Mortkin v. Gur'ev reveals the interrogation process. One litigant proposed a question to the Slavery Chancellery panel, which then posed it. For example:

The plaintiff Prince Iurii petitioned that they ask Batrak Gur'ev: "With whom did the mother of that slavewoman Liubka serve after the death of Vasilii Buturlin?" Batrak said that he did not know with whom her mother served.

The plaintiff Prince Iurii petitioned that they ask him, Batrak: "On what basis is that long-term slavewoman Liubka his?" Batrak replied that she is his long-term slavewoman on the basis of the fact that she has served him for about twenty years.

Batrak petitioned that they ask him, Prince Iurii: "For how many years did the neighbors know [that the slavewoman Liubka] was in hereditary slavery in his house?" Prince Iurii replied that he does not remember, but it was few, for she was growing up with him at that time.

Then the Slavery Chancellery panel itself interrogated the slaves:

They asked the slave man: "What is your name, whose son are you, and whose hereditary slave are you?" The slave man answered that his name was Pozniachko, the son of Kuz'ma. He was the hereditary slave of Batrak Gur'ev's father, Ignatii Gur'ev. Since his father died, he has been serving Batrak as a hereditary slave for over forty years. Batrak had married him, Pozniachko, in his household to the slave girl Liubka, daughter of Stepan, over twenty years ago. He, Pozniachko, had never served anyone else anywhere. That woman Liubka for whom Prince Iurii Mortkin is suing as a slave is his, Pozniachko's, first wife.

The slavewoman Liubka said that she was the hereditary slave of Prince Nikita Mortkin. After Prince Nikita had died, she had served his son Prince Iurii Mortkin. While yet an unmarried girl she had left Prince Iurii during the destruction of Moscow and had come to Batrak Gur'ev. Batrak had given her in marriage to his own slave, to that Pozniak Kuz'min.

After the trial was held, all four parties, the litigants Mortkin and Gur'ev and the slaves Pozniachko and Liubka, posted bail. (On bail, see Bormosov v. Berechinskii above.) Mortkin and Gur'ev had the same four guarantors. Nine men guaranteed the slave Pozniachko, eight more again guaranteed Gur'ev (with the sanctions being "as the sovereign decrees" for violations), and six men (including another of the patriarch's *stol'niki*) guaranteed Liubka.

The trouble began on February 4, 1629, two weeks after the trial, when both litigants requested a continuance until a week before Easter. But then, on March 20, 1629, Mortkin asked for another continuance because he had to report for service in Tula, the main staging area for the southern frontier. Five men guaranteed that he would report for the trial a month after the summer service for the army (called annually in anticipation of Tatar raids) was discharged.

On November 2, 1629, Mortkin petitioned Tsar Mikhail that Gur'ev had not appeared, was living on his estate, and was bribing witnesses. He submitted a similar petition two days later, and the Slavery Chancellery ordered the case placed on the docket. Nothing was done, so Mortkin petitioned again, on November 6, and claimed that he had already brought in "many petitions" on the matter. This brought no results, so he again wrote the tsar, in care of the Petitions Chancellery, on November 6 and November 12. The last petition finally hit home, the state secretary of the Petitions Chancellery, Ivan Dedkov, noting on the back that the tsar had ordered the case to be resolved and then sending that petition to join all the others in the records of the Slavery Chancellery. The officials of the Slavery Chancellery then copied out the legislation on continuances:

> When plaintiffs and defendants are released on written bail documents for continuances, they are to appear in Moscow a month after their service has been completed. If they fail to appear a month after service is over, grant plaintiffs or defendants by royal decree a second trial date which shall be set at the rate of a week per one hundred versts to the [litigant's] service estate. If some one does not appear on the second date, the boyars have proclaimed that he will forfeit the case.

The officials of the Slavery Chancellery then ordered those who had guaranteed Batrak Gur'ev's continuance to report to the Slavery Chancellery. Five days later, on November 18, one of Gur'ev's guarantor's appeared and reported that he was not in Moscow, that he was living in the countryside at home. The following day, on November 19, 1629, the Slavery Chancellery returned the verdict in favor of Prince Iurii Mortkin because Gur'ev had violated the terms of his continuance. Once more, it can only be said that the Slavery Chancellery was judiciously enforcing the law.

An odd twist in the case reveals again the Slavery Chancellery's striving for fairness. It just so happened that Gur'ev had failed to appear not because he was in contempt but because he was dead. Obviously the Slavery Chancellery did not know that when it issued its verdict, particularly as one of Gur'ev's guarantors had said the day before that he was "living in the countryside." However, two days after the verdict, on November 21, Gur'ev's widow, who apparently was unaware of it, notified the Slavery Chancellery that her husband had not been bribing witnesses, as Mortkin had charged, but had been dying, and finally expired on November 14.

This unexpected event upset the plaintiff, Iurii Mortkin, who on November 23 asked that the decision of November 19 be reaffirmed. Not only had Gur'ev been in contempt, but the decision was rightly his anyway. The case had been further complicated by Gur'ev's deathbed manumission of Pozniachko, but Mortkin claimed that he belonged to him (Mortkin) because of his marriage to his slave woman Liubka. This was followed on November 29 by a petition from the deceased's brother, Ofonasei, asking that the decision be set aside. He noted that his brother's children were too young to carry on the case, that the family had no slave advocate (*a chelovechka tokovskova net*) to pursue the case for them, and that he would do so. On December 2 the Slavery Chancellery set aside its verdict that had been based on the continuance default. At this point the record ends, and the outcome of the case is unknown.[89] One may assume that the Slavery Chancellery resorted to a general investigation of the inhabitants of the region, and then awarded the verdict to Mortkin because the investigation supported his contention that Liubka had been his slave before running away to Gur'ev. This, however, is only speculation.

Mortkin v. Gur'ev shows Muscovite legality in action. The rules for continuances were known to litigants, and for grievous disregard of them they risked forfeiting a case. This was also noted above in the discussion of Karsakov v. Borykov and Karsakov v. Dubenskoi (1628-31), the trial transcript of which has a document showing that occasionally the Slavery Chancellery took the trouble to verify service claims made in the request for a continuance. Thus the Slavery Chancellery wrote on June 1, 1628, to the Military Chancellery to discover whether Mikhail Borykov of Kolomna had been ordered to report for service in Valuiki, 550 kilometers distant on the southern frontier, and on June 8 it received a memorandum that he indeed had been so ordered, as one of thirty Kolomna *deti boiarskie* drafted to convoy an exchange of ambassadors.[90] Such efficient verification was rather typical for Muscovy.

89. Iakovlev, *Kholopstvo*, pp. 401-14, no. 15. On the continuance for military service in criminal matters, see UKRP 10, 11 (PRP 5: 209-10).

90. Iakovlev, *Kholopstvo*, pp. 419-20, no. 16, vii, viii.

Expeditious Judgments

Muscovite law became increasingly concerned, almost frenetically so, with the expeditious resolution of disputes. It is clear that by the mid-seventeenth century this had become of paramount importance to legislators, of even greater importance than the attainment of justice. Shakespeare's concern with the injustices of "the law's delay" was by no means something that was alien to the Muscovites.

Within the law of slavery, such sentiments were expressed, presumably, because they had been part of the operating norms of the Slavery Chancellery. Unfortunately, when they were written down cannot be determined with any precision, but one may assume that it was at some time in the seventeenth century. One article requires that a verdict must be based on the evidence produced during the trial of a suit, that the litigant who at that time presented no evidence or did not claim that he had such evidence to support his claims for a disputed slave could not later produce such evidence and have it considered.[91] The other article dealt with appeals to traditional evidence (oaths [*opchaia pravda*] and massive interrogations of the local populace [*poval'nyi obysk*]) in distant towns of Siberia or in Astrakhan' on the lower Volga. If either litigant objected that his opponent was citing such evidence merely to delay the case, then the administrators in those distant places were not to be asked to generate such evidence, and the dispute had to be resolved on the basis of the evidence that was available without resorting to such distant appeals, "so that no one will suffer because of superfluous delay and bureaucratic red tape."[92]

Epanchin v. Leont'evs

In an effort to avoid "the law's delay," Muscovite lawmakers required that litigants prosecute their cases expeditiously. One of the many facets of this problem was evident in an aborted case before the Slavery Chancellery throughout most of the year 1627, Epanchin v. Leont'evs.

The problem arose because plaintiffs had to locate their fugitive slaves themselves, get a court bailiff (*pristav*) to serve notice to the accused, and then file formal charges. In this case, Tit Ivanov Epanchin, who was either a *syn boiarskii* or a provincial *dvorianin* from Tula at the time of the suit and who in 1623 had been a centurion (*sotnyi golova*) at Mtsensk, a southern frontier town, in January of 1627 located what he claimed were his fugitive slaves Terentei Vasil'ev, Afansii Nosik, and the latter's wife, Dar'ia, on properties belonging to Aleksandr and Lavrentii Leont'ev in Riazan' province.[93] One can imagine the difficulties

---

91. 1649 *Ulozhenie* 20: 79; MS, p. 284.
92. 1649 *Ulozhenie* 20: 109; MS, pp. 294-95.
93. On Epanchin, see DR 1: 558; Ivanov, AUBK, p. 131. No precise information seems available on the Leont'evs, especially as patronymics are lacking in the case.

Epanchin must have encountered in finding his fugitive slaves (if in fact they were his), in provinces over one hundred miles away from his home.

Epanchin filed notice of his intent to sue for the return of the three fugitive slaves, plus stolen property worth 50.50 rubles. The Leont'evs were forced to post a bond signed by six of their colleagues from Riazan' province that the defendants would remain in Moscow and be ready for trial at any moment. Of course that was a great hardship for provincial servicemen who did not have slaves or others they could leave in Moscow as their advocates. This hardship was supposed to be lessened by the requirement that plaintiffs initiate suits right away, which is what Epanchin failed to do. The defendants first pointed this out in a petition to the court dated April 13.

Apparently Epanchin had been summoned to military service, and got a continuance for that. He posted a bond in which he guaranteed, according to the traditional formula, that he would initiate the suit as soon as the army was discharged (literally, as soon as they dismounted from their horses). There were no unusual campaigns in 1627, Epanchin was discharged, but he failed to file the suit. Then again on November 8, 9, and 10 the defendants asked that the case be dismissed because no charges had been filed. There is no way to determine why Epanchin failed to file suit, but he did not. On December 12 the officers of the Slavery Chancellery issued a verdict in which they declared that Epanchin had forfeited the case because he had not filed his suit within the time limit of a week or two prescribed by a decree of the tsar and boyars. Moreover, Epanchin was prohibited from initiating a suit on this matter in the future.[94]

Nashchokin v. Kireevskaia

Another illustration of the same theme is provided by Nashchokin v. Kireevskaia, which was before the Slavery Chancellery codirectors Prince Ivan Fedorovich Volkonskoi and Ivan Fomich Ogarev and the state secretaries Ivan Varganov and Andrei Stroev in early 1629. On May 16, 1628, Fedor Nashchokin got an arrest warrant in Belev from the governor, Petr Streshnev, for the arrest of a fugitive slave he alleged was Pervyi Vasil'ev, his wife, and his children. The slave was freed on bail, and Nashchokin announced his intention to sue for the slaves, plus two horses they had allegedly stolen. The putative defendant, Tatiana Kireevskaia, widow of Ivan Kireevskii, had to post a bond for the horses and guarantee that she would answer the charges. One assumes that the case was postponed for the campaigning season.

On January 10, 1629, the widow's son, Dmitrii, appeared at the Slavery Chancellery, denied that the slave was in his mother's possession, and claimed that the person who had been arrested was not Pervushka but Kost'ka. (Mis-

---

94. Iakovlev, *Kholopstvo*, pp. 370-73, no. 10. This strategy did not always work, as evidenced in the case of Treskin v. Zykov, discussed above, where six weeks elapsed but the case was not forfeited (ibid., pp. 373-82).

taken identity was also alleged in Karsakov v. Borykov and Dubenskoi, discussed above.) Dmitrii had to post a new bond, guaranteed by six men from Kashira, Kozlov, and elsewhere, with the rank of *zhilets* and patriarchal *stol'nik*. On January 18, Dmitrii Kireevskii noted that he had been appearing in the chancellery but that Nashchokin had failed to file suit. He repeated this on January 20, and again on the twenty-fifth. A month later, on February 27, he noted that he was running out of funds and that Nashchokin had failed to sue. Finally, on March 9, the Slavery Chancellery dismissed the case because Nashchokin had failed to file a suit, and he was forbidden to open the case at a later time.[95] By such measures, the government hoped to expedite justice.

This expeditiousness was formalized in a provision that the 1649 *Ulozhenie* manuscript copy attributed to 1628: any plaintiff who failed to initiate his suit within a week after he had asked a bailiff to arrest an allegedly fugitive slave lost the case. Similarly, a defendant was declared to be in default and lost the case if he failed to appear for a trial within a week after he had posted bond.[96] As we have seen, the law was not enforced with quite such rigor, but in general this aspect of reducing the law's delay was enforced. However, expeditiousness penalized those who lacked the resources to cope with that demand of the legal system. This was one of the complaints of the middle service class in 1648—that its members were unable to comply with such rigorous schedules. Trying to satisfy all parties, the *Ulozhenie* stated that cases which prior to that time had been forfeited because of delay could not be reopened, but that no slavery cases were to be so forfeited in the future and that a trial had to be held in every instance before a verdict could be awarded.[97] Regrettably, I do not know how this contradiction was resolved.

The Muscovites took a number of other steps to try to ensure that justice was meted out expeditiously. One such measure was to declare that the trial, when it was held, was the place and time where a litigant's evidence should be presented. After the trial was over, no litigant could bring in fresh information, and the verdict had to be rendered on the basis of what was presented at the trial.[98] Moreover, in an article dating from 1645, but part of much older Russian law, no case that had been resolved on the basis of a decree from the tsar and a verdict from the boyar counselors could be reopened or discussed in the future.

95. Ibid., pp. 437-40. no. 17. The patriarchal *stol'nik* who guaranteed Dmitrii Kireevskii was Ivan Ignat'ev Kireevskii, mentioned in Ivanov's lists of Boyar Record Books for 1627 and 1629 (AUBK, p. 183). The *zhil'tsy* are found in the Iziumov list for 1632: Vasilii Ondreev Pavlov, of unknown domicile, had a small service landholding of 50 cheti, was supposed to report for service himself, on a horse. Taras Mikhailov Pavlov had 288 cheti of service land in Kozel'sk, Likhvin, and Riazan' provinces, and 240 cheti of patrimonial land in Likhvin and Galich provinces. He was supposed to report for service mounted on a horse, with a mounted cavalry slave ("Zhiletskoe," pp. 110-13).
96. 1649 *Ulozhenie* 10: 110; 20: 55; MS, p. 274.
97. 1649 *Ulozhenie* 20: 111; MS, pp. 295-96.
98. 1649 *Ulozhenie* 20: 79; MS, p. 284.

This was true not only for slavery cases but for all other litigation as well.[99] Once the supreme authorities of Muscovy had resolved an issue, there was nothing more to discuss.

Other Formalities: Sobriety, Appearance For Trials

There were a number of other procedural formalities and requirements that grew up to expedite and refine the Muscovite legal process concerning slaves.

Dedkov v. Dolgorukiis

One of the procedural requirements for self-sale into slavery was that the parties be cognizant of what they were doing. There is every reason to believe that the officials administering the slavery system made a good-faith effort to assure that this requirement was met. That was one of the primary functions of the interrogation that occurred in the presence of the official who formalized such transactions, and also for the interval that occurred between the drawing up of a slavery contract by scribes and the registration of the contract in the official record books by responsible officials. Drunkenness, the bane of Russian life, was not tolerated during the sale of someone into slavery. This was a central issue in the case of Ivan Titovich Dedkov (Detkov) v. Timofei and Fedor Vasil'evy Dolgorukii, tried in the Slavery Chancellery before the codirectors Semen Mikhailov Koltovskoi and Ivan Kuz'mich Begichev and the state secretaries Patrikei Nasonov and Filipp Mitrofanov between January and March 1622 for possession of three fugitive slave girls and 44.75 rubles' worth of stolen property. The case is interesting for a number of reasons and therefore worth summarizing briefly.

Typically, most of the basic facts were not in dispute. The plaintiff, Ivan Dedkov, a government clerk, lived three doors down the street from the defendant, Timofei Dolgorukii, a scion of the legendary founder of Moscow, who at the time of the suit held the rank of *stol'nik*. At the time of the trial, the widow Matrenka Gerasimova was living at Prince Dolgorukii's house, and her two daughters, Mar'ia and Aksin'ia, were in the custody of the Slavery Chancellery, into which they had been delivered by Dolgorukii. Plaintiff Dedkov claimed that the girls belonged to him because, claiming to be free vagabonds, they had sold themselves to him and he had limited service slavery contracts on them. The girls had fled from him in 1621, and Dolgorukii's peasants had transported them to Dolgorukii's property in the Periaslavl'-Riazan' area, over 175 kilometers southeast of Moscow.

Dolgorukii resorted to a number of dodges and subterfuges to try to win the case. He tried to discredit Dedkov's witnesses by claiming that they were the latter's obedient parasites (*khleboiazhtsy*), even though they were such people

99. 1589 *Sudebnik* 199; UKZP 37; *Ulozhenie* 15: 4, 20: 119; MS, p. 299; PSZ 2: 314, no. 869.

as State Secretary Ivan Mizinov of the Moscow Judicial Chancellery and the relatively important military figures Bogdan Voeikov and his son Oleksandr (a litigant in other cases discussed in this work).

Dolgorukii's first claim was that the two girls had been his peasants because their father, Iakov Fofanov, had been a peasant on an estate in Dmitrov province, north of Moscow, that had been given to Dolgorukii in a property division. Dolgorukii presented the 1613/14 property division document, whereupon its authors were sent for. They subjected it to intensive, sophisticated handwriting analysis, and observed, inter alia, that the name of the putative father, Iakov, had been altered from Iushko to Iashku in the document. The Slavery Chancellery officials sent the altered document to the boyars to determine who had committed the forgery.

Then Dolgorukii claimed that the girls were his because he had taken limited service slavery contracts on them in 1608, after their father died. He failed to present these, and the Slavery Chancellery officials pointed out that they would have been void in any case, for the law forbade taking slavery documents on one's own peasants, who thereby would have escaped taxation and the payment of the rents due military servicemen. Moreover, Dolgorukii had failed to file a complaint at the time, in 1620, when he claimed the two girls had fled.

Dolgorukii had yet another trick up his sleeve. He, supported by the two fugitives and their mother, claimed that the last had been drunk in the Slavery Chancellery when her two daughters had sold themselves into slavery. The story was somewhat garbled, depending on who told it, but everyone claimed that the plaintiff Dedkov had gotten Matrenka drunk for the self-sale ceremony, while Dedkov claimed she had been there of her own free will. Matrenka added that Dedkov had tried to get her to sell herself as well. The Slavery Chancellery officials would not buy that argument, either, for, had it been accepted, it presumably would have voided Dedkov's limited service slavery contracts on the two girls. For one, they stated flatly that it was not the customary practice for such documents to be compiled when one of the parties was in a severe state of intoxication. But, allowing that it just might have happened, they noted that three years had passed since the event, and that no complaint had been lodged either with the tsar or the Slavery Chancellery, until after the girls had fled. Matrenka said that she was only a simple long-time peasant woman who had had to give her daughters away because of extreme poverty, but that she had told Dolgorukii about it. The court noted that Dolgorukii had taken no action, either, and concluded that he had coached the three women to tell such a tale.

The officials also observed that, according to Matrenka's declaration recorded in the sale documents, Man'ka had been serving Dedkov for a third of a year, and Var'ka half a year, before the slavery transactions had been arranged, and that, during the ceremony, no one had objected to those statements. They noted as well that Dolgorukii had made no declarations to the authorities that his peasants or slaves were "missing" after they had gone to live with Dedkov and then sold themselves to him, that he must have been aware of the fact that the girls and their mother visited each other down the block, and that he had concealed the girls on his distant estate and then had lied to the authorities who came searching for them as to their whereabouts. Certainly nothing looked good for Dolgorukii, and the officials decided the case against him.

Dolgorukii decided that he was above the law, that he would not come to hear the verdict. After the court bailiff had looked for him numerous times, the Slavery Chancellery ordered one of the Dolgorukii slaves apprehended to force Dolgorukii to appear (see chapter 5), and the young slave boy Savka Timofeev was arrested. The verdict was awarded to Dedkov, who paid a fee of 6 altyns a-piece, double the usual fee, for the two slaves. Dolgorukii finally appeared in the Slavery Chancellery and announced that he was not going to listen to its verdict. Then he appealed to higher authority in a petition addressed to Patriarch Filaret, asking that the case be transferred to another chancellery.

Dolgorukii based his appeal on a claim that the officials of the Slavery Chancellery were biased against him, plus the fact that the verdict had been read in his absence![100] Perhaps he had some evidence that is not available to a late-twentieth-century historian, but his claim of bias seems totally unfounded. It is true that the plaintiff, Ivan Dedkov, was of the chancellery milieu, but at the time of this suit he was only a minor figure, a clerk in the Chancellery of the Great Court. It well may have been this case that brought Dedkov to the attention of the authorities and into relative prominence in governmental circles. From about April 24, 1623, to 1631 he was first the junior, then the senior state secretary under the director, F. L. Buturlin, of the Petitions Chancellery, the office set up to process popular grievances against the government. This made him a central figure in the administration. He acquired a service estate, and he spent considerable time dining with the sovereign and accompanying him on religious processions.[101] But at the time of the suit, that was something for the future, and Timofei Dolgorukii was at least as socially prominent as his accuser, which probably explains his incredible contempt for the judicial process that he revealed in his case. At the time of the suit he was a lower-ranking *stol'nik*, number 148 out of 217, who as recently as 1616 had not yet been assigned a service land entitlement or cash-compensation ranking. We may also judge that he was young at the time of the suit by the fact that even three years after the suit he was waiting on table, one of twelve serving the drink at the tsar's table. He spent much of his subsequent career in palace sentry service. Never was he promoted in rank. Only once, in 1636, is he listed as having a military command post, commander of 19 *deti boiarskie*, 24 Lithuanians and Cherkasy, 21 newly baptized Tatars, 3 translators, 3 artillerymen, 11 guards, smiths, and slaves, 2 cen-

100. Iakovlev, *Kholopstvo*, pp. 344-54, no. 6.

101. Veselovskii, *D'iaki*, p. 150; DR 1 and 2, passim; Samokvasov, AM, xxxvii; SIRIO 137: 15; Bogoiavlenskii, PS, p. 249.

turions and their musketeers in the western Siberian outpost of Urzhum, 160 kilometers north of Kazan'.[102] Thus at the time of the suit he was a brash young
man, perhaps full of conceit because of his name and inherited wealth, who
thought he could bluff the court. It seems to have been typical of his career that
went nowhere, and in the future his service superiors were no more likely to be
fooled than had been the professionals running the Slavery Chancellery.

While the outcome of this suit in the hands of the boyars, whither it was transferred by Patriarch Filaret, coruler with his son Tsar Mikhail, is unknown, we
well may imagine that they supported the professionals in the Slavery Chancellery. The legal reasoning and judgment of the latter were absolutely correct.
In addition to the other points of law they made in awarding the verdict to
the plaintiff Dedkov, there can be no doubt that drunkenness was not permitted in the enslavement process, that those making the decision to pass into
the state of unfreedom were supposed to be fully possessed of their faculties
when the decision was being made.

Another such formality was that a litigant who failed to appear automatically
lost the case, with a default judgment being awarded to his opponent. That principle is evident in the following case.

Gubachevskii and Tulub'ev v. Lodygin

A case tried in Moscow before state secretary Piatoi Kokóshkin in the autumn
of 1595 illustrates several important points of slave law and procedure. The case
had been initiated earlier, on September 4, before the ambassadors (heads of the
Foreign Affairs Office?) *okol'nichii* Prince Ivan Samsonovich Turenin and Ostafii
Mikhailovich Pushkin and state secretaries Grigorii Klobukov and Posnik
Dmitreev. Judging by the fact that Dmitreev was working in the Foreign Affairs
Office, and that Turenin, Pushkin, and Klobukov in 1593 had been sent on a
special ambassadorial assignment to Novgorod, one may assume that the case
had originated for unknown reasons in the Foreign Affairs Office, and then been
transferred to Kokoshkin in the Slavery Chancellery for disposition.[103]

Turenin's slave Grisha Zaitsov had brought the case to Kokoshkin. Torkh
Gubachevskii and Grigorii Vasil'ev Tulub'ev, about whom I have no information
other than that in this case, sued Ivan Vasil'ev Lodygin of the Novgorod region
for ownership of the slave Sava Grigor'ev. The plaintiffs, who must have been
cousins, claimed that they owned Sava because his father, Grisha, his mother,
Olenka, and his sister had been given as part of a dowry (which was presented as
evidence) to Gubachevskii's mother by Tulub'ev's grandfather, Dmitrii, and
father, Vasilii. They did not know who Sava's paternal grandfather had been because that was so long ago, but claimed that he had been a full slave. They

102. AMG 1: 141; Storozhev, "B.S.," pp. 82, 110; ZKMS (=RIB 10): 16, 41, 90; DR 1:
692, 1015; KR 2: 929; Ivanov, AUBK, p. 118.
103. Anpilogov, *Novye*, pp. 44, 55, 60; DAI, 1, passim; RK 1550-1636 1: 108, 111.

claimed that they had owned Sava, but that he had fled at the time that the Swedes had taken Rakobor (1580). At the time Tulub'ev had been captured but later filed a suit for the recovery of Sava. Perhaps Sava had been Tulub'ev's attendant at the front, or had taken advantage of his owner's absence to flee.

Sava denied that he had ever belonged to the plaintiffs and said that initially he had been a free man, then had lived as a landless peasant (*bobyl'*) with one Neustroi Kaltashev. Then he moved and lived with a peasant by the name of Stepanko in Peluskii pogost of Obonezhskaia piatina. At that time he had married Fevronitsa (Tat'iana) Stepanova, probably Stepanko's daughter. Then, nine years before the initiation of the suit, they sold themselves as limited service contract slaves for 7 rubles to Lodygin.

Ivan Vasil'ev Lodygin must have been a fairly young man at the time of the suit, 1595, and also atypically wealthy. He had been married five years earlier, and his wife's dowry contained seven slaves. Perhaps because of the added stress of being given away, two of the slave husbands in the dowry fled; their deserted wives were remarried to two voluntary slaves that also belonged to Lodygin. An unmarried young woman in the dowry was married off to yet another of Lodygin's slaves, who then took flight. Still other slaves belonging to Lodygin purchased single slaves for him, one for the large sum of 10 rubles in 1593, another for 5 rubles in 1594. One of those married a slave widow belonging to Lodygin. Sava and Fevronitsa had been his first slaves purchases of record. By 1598, when all of this was recorded in the compulsory registration of all slaves of that year, Lodygin owned at least fourteen adult slaves and nine children (six boys and three girls) and had legal claim to three adult male fugitives. This is an atypically large number of slaves for someone who had been married only five years.

It may be that Lodygin's marriage of 1590 was a second one, but it seems unlikely, based on the limited information about him. Unfortunately "Ivan Lodygin" is not an uncommon name in Russian history, but it seems as though a person by that name who might have been the defendant in this case was a commander of *strel'tsy* when Ivangorod was stormed in 1590. Other than that, no previous likely entries exist for Lodygin, indicating that he must have been an ordinary rank-and-file cavalryman before that time. It is clear that in 1604 Ivan Vasil'ev Lodygin was paid his full salary of 10 rubles, a sum suitable for a fifteen-year veteran.

Right after the Time of Troubles, Ivan Vasil'ev Lodygin was second military commander of Iaroslavl' in the years 1616/17, at which time he played a role in suppressing the rebellious cossacks under the command of Lisovskii. Thus he was destined, in 1595, to become a rather prominent man.[104]

Kokoshkin rendered his verdict in November, about two months after the case

---

104. Tatishchev (1910), p. 30; Sukhotin, ChSV, p. 29; Barsukov, SGV, p. 286; RK 1550-1636 2: 275; KR 1: 75, 181; RK 1598-1638, p. 295; AMG 1: 88-89; AI 3: 13, 57; DR 1: 149.

had been initiated. The litigants had pledged to show up for the verdict, but the plaintiffs did not appear. Kokoshkin gave the verdict to the defendant Lodygin for two reasons: Sava had said that he and his wife were Lodygin's slaves, and the plaintiffs Gubachevskii and Tulub'ev did not appear. Kokoshkin also noted that the plaintiffs did not present their documents, presumably meaning the full slavery document they claimed was the basis of Sava's grandfather's bondage. In January 1598, Lodygin registered the judgment charter Kokoshkin had given him twenty-six months earlier to support his ownership claims to Sava, his wife, Tat'iana, and the three children they had given birth to, two boys and a girl.[105]

Kokoshkin's judgment is not totally transparent. Both litigating sides had presented their claims in the form of written documents. However, nothing in the possession of the plaintiffs apparently proved that the slave Sava was really related to Grisha and Olenka. If one judges by the plaintiff's claims that Sava had fled at the time of the fall of Rakobor and Sava's own account of his life, it does not seem totally implausible that the plaintiffs' claims were justified. If so, it shows how long it sometimes took for owners to locate their fugitive slaves, especially when they fled from one region of Muscovy to another. However, nothing in the possession of the plaintiffs definitively proved that the slave Sava was related to Grisha and Olenka. The defendant Lodygin was probably convinced that he was right, for Sava may never have confided to him his prior history. The judge was probably partly convinced by Sava's story, although it was one he would have been expected to tell even if he were lying. What really convinced him must have been the fact that Gubachevskii and Tulub'ev did not appear for the verdict, indicating to him that they knew that they were wrong, or at least that they were not going to win. In that sense, the requirement that the litigants appear for the sentencing had the same effect as a trial by combat or an oath: the party in the wrong was expected to cede to the party in the right.

Perjury

An attentive reader of this work so far must have asked himself several times whether the concept of perjury existed in Muscovy, and what sanctions were imposed for its commitment. Obviously this was a major problem, and in 1617/18 attempts were made to come to grips with the issue, at least in its most obvious manifestation: the case when a person testified that he did not have in his possession a fugitive slave and subsequently that slave turned up on his estate and the plaintiff had him arrested there. In such an instance, the plaintiff was to be awarded the fugitive slave, plus his claims for stolen property. But that was not all:

105. Lakier, pp. 36-38.

Punish him severely for the crime of taking an oath falsely: beat him with the knout in the market place for three days so that it will become known to many people why such a punishment was meted out to him. Having beaten him with the knout in the market place for three days, jail him for a year. Henceforth do not believe him on any matter, and do not grant him a trial against anyone for anything.

The same sanction was provided for harboring a fugitive peasant.[106]
Even that was not all. Presumably the regular perjury statute was also applicable:

> If a magnate [*velmozha*] kisses the cross untruthfully, or orders someone else [his slave, in most cases] to kiss the cross untruthfully, the clergy shall not admit such people into the church of God, shall not enter their houses, and shall not chant the divine liturgy in houses belonging to them. If a priest has begun to chant the divine liturgy in someone's house, and such perjurers [*rotniki*] who took a false oath are present, they shall expel them from that temple. Concerning the person who took a false oath, Basil the Great in his own canon 64 placed a 10-year interdict on them. . . . On the same subject Emperor Leo the Wise in his New Canon 72 ordered the tongue of the perjurer cut out . . . . [etc.][107]

This was all pretty strong medicine, but one may doubt that it was frequently used. Almost certainly the beating with the knout was inflicted on somebody at least once, and it is more in keeping with the Muscovite style than lengthy excommunication or tongue amputation. But even the corporal punishment sanction is relatively specific and, given the extent of prevarication in the Slavery Chancellery after 1618 and the fact that sanctions were not usually imposed even on the most blatant liars, it is fairly clear that a program of such savage severity deterred almost no one because the Muscovites lacked the enforcement will to make it credible.

Arbitration

It was not absolutely necessary for conflicts over slave ownership to be resolved by official organs, for Muscovy knew a formal system of arbitration, borrowed from the *Lithuanian Statute* of 1588. The *Ulozhenie* of 1649 repeated the *Statute*'s provision, and added that arbitration verdicts could not be appealed to the chancelleries.[108] The workings of the system are known from earlier cases that

106. 1649 *Ulozhenie* 11: 27, 14: 9, 20: 49; MS, pp. 229, 273.
107. 1649 *Ulozhenie* 14:10.
108. 1588 LS 4: 85; 1649 *Ulozhenie* 15:5.

failed and were appealed to the Slavery Chancellery for proper resolution. This is in some respects comparable to knowledge of local court practice in the U.S. South, which is largely mirrored in the appellate process.

Moskotin'ev v. Vysheslavtsev

One case, Moskotin'ev v. Vysheslavtsev, was tried in the Slavery Chancellery between September 15 and December 15, 1630, before director Prince Ivan Fedorovich Volkonskii and state secretaries Andrei Stroev and Ivan Kostiurin. The litigants, Fedor Posnikov Moskotin'ev and Rakhmanin Vasil'ev Vysheslavtsev, from Meshchera, about 170 kilometers southeast of Moscow, were contesting the ownership of Davyd Ignat'ev, his wife, Anna Mikhaileva ("Dosadka"—"vexatious"), their two children (Iakushka and Ovdiushka) and Davyd's stepchildren (Mikiforka and Filimonka). Also at issue was 23.50 rubles' worth of property alleged to have been stolen when the slaves fled. In an attempt to resolve the dispute, the litigants had chosen arbiters, Moskotin'ev his brother Vasilii Posnikov Moskotin'ev, and Vysheslavtsev one Aleksei Mamleev Mal'tsov. All four of these men were listed in the 1615 military register (*desiatnia*) from Meshchera, which revealed that they were approximately equal coevals. Of 294 servicemen in the list, Fedor Moskotin'ev was number 121 (with compensation entitlement of 450 cheti of land and 12 rubles in cash), his brother Vasilii was number 76 (550 cheti of land and 14 rubles), defendant Vysheslavtsev was number 89 (500 cheti of land and 14 rubles), his arbiter Mal'tsov was number 71 (550 cheti of land and 14 rubles)[109] No more specific information seems to be available about them, but it would be safe to assume that fifteen years later, at the time of the trial, they were near the pinnacle of the Meshchera service pyramid.

In resolving the case, the Slavery Chancellery made two criticisms of that arbitration, criticisms of who did it and of how it was done. The first thing that might strike a modern observer is that choosing one's brother as an intermediary to resolve a dispute might not be the wisest thing to do. The panel of the Slavery Chancellery had the same sentiment, and criticized the choice of a blood brother to occupy that role.

More important, however, was the way the arbitration proceeding had been conducted and resolved. The Slavery Chancellery repeatedly emphasized that it should be as close to an actual trial as possible in all of its formalities. This, apparently, had not been observed. The worst offence, however, lay in the fact that Vasilii Moskotin'ev had drafted his verdict in the case to read as though his brother had submitted a 1604 limited service slavery contract, in which it was claimed that the contested slaves had been his hereditary slaves, when in fact no such document was presented at the hearing. The arbitrators had ordered Fedor to send a slave to fetch the contract and not to leave the proceedings himself.

---

109. Iu. V. Got'e, "Desiatni po Vladimiru i Meshchere 1590 i 1615 gg.," *Chteniia* 236 (1911, no. 1): 77-79.

He had failed to do that, and presented a document only some time after the arbitration hearing. In the interval, it was alleged, Fedor Moskotin'ev had forged such a document. Vasilii Moskotin'ev's arbitration verdict was presented in the Slavery Chancellery, and it reads in every respect like a genuine state document: "On the basis of that old limited service slavery contract . . . on the basis of the testimony concerning the hereditary slave status . . . and on the basis of this, Fedor's, sworn testimony, the plaintiff is justified in his claim for those slaves and the stolen property; and the defendant has no claim to those slaves . . . because his limited service slavery contract is new . . . and for this reason he loses the case." The arbitration verdict was dated February 6, 1627. It is not clear why it took three and a half years for the case to reach the Slavery Chancellery.

The Slavery Chancellery declared Vasilii Moskotin'ev's verdict to be null and void, as well as his brother's allegedly forged limited service slavery contract. They recognized instead Vysheslavtsev's 1624 contract, and on September 29, 1630, about two weeks after the beginning of the process in the Slavery Chancellery, awarded him the verdict, turned the slaves over to him, and collected the capitation fees of 12 altyns from him. This left the matter of the stolen property suit, which the litigants agreed would be resolved by an oath. Plaintiff Moskotin'ev's slave Min'ka Ivanov was to kiss the cross for his owner. After the expiration of a month's continuance granted both men to report for military service, Vysheslavtsev on November 29 appeared in the Slavery Chancellery and asked that the case be concluded. On December 3 he began to ask for a default verdict because Moskotin'ev had not appeared. He observed that he was being exhausted by the delay, suffering great losses and incurring enormous expenses for food (*kharchi*). He repeated this petition on December 8 and 15, and on Christmas day, 1630, he was given a present by the Slavery Chancellery: a default verdict in his favor. A check had been made with the Military Chancellery, which confirmed that the army had been demobilized, and therefore the plaintiff had had time to appear. In addition to dismissing the suit against Vysheslavtsev, the Slavery Chancellery ordered that court costs in the amount of 2.05 rubles (10 percent of the value of the suit, 20.50 rubles) be collected from the five men who had guaranteed the plaintiff Moskotin'ev's continuance bond. On the thirty-first, a bailiff was sent out to collect the money, and the case ends there.[110]

Moskotin'ev v. Vysheslavtsev tells us what arbitration was supposed to be like, and indicates why some litigants might have preferred it to a more formal process before official organs. In the words of the Slavery Chancellery verdict, the arbitration procedure was to mimic a formal civil suit (*protiv sudnogo dela*), and its judgment was modeled on the government's formulae. A written version of that judgment served as evidence in case of further dispute. No doubt this method of conflict resolution was preferable for many reasons. Certainly it was less formidable than going before a government body. It was also easier to have the case

---

110. Iakovlev, *Kholopstvo*, pp. 457-64, no. 19.

resolved locally, rather than having to venture to Moscow. Finally, it was certainly cheaper. Traveling to Moscow was not cheap, and staying there seems to have been deemed expensive, at least by provincials who did not have quarters there. Most important, the court costs, in this case the capitation fees of 0.36 ruble and the "legal tenth" of 2.05 rubles, would have been avoided entirely.

Unfortunately, I know of no way to calculate the frequency of resort to arbitration. By any standards, Muscovites were quite litigious (somewhere between the Japanese, who have abhorred litigation, and many African peoples, who look upon it as a form of entertainment), and therefore we may assume that they resorted to arbitration quite frequently. The paucity of records for such proceedings forces us to concentrate our gaze on the more formal, state-based methods of conflict resolution.

Belikov v. Tolstoi

The beginning of the utilization of an arbitration award by the Slavery Chancellery is evident in the case of Belikov v. Tolstoi, tried before director Prince Ivan Fedorovich Volkonskii and the state secretaries Andrei Stroev and Ivan Kostiurin between May 1631 and March 1632. At issue were the slaves Foma, son of Erem (also called Ivan, son of Ermolai Shanin), his wife, his son, Petrushka (also called Pershutka), and 13 rubles' (30.50 rubles') worth of stolen property. The drama of the case was primarily in the southern frontier area, south of Tula. The plaintiff, Mikhail Zinov'ev Belikov, was an army chief (*golova*) from Odoev. His arbiter had been Maksim Botavin, and he was represented in his arguments both in the arbitration proceedings and at the Slavery Chancellery by his uncle Petr Kolupaev. The defendant, Daniil Vasil'ev Tolstoi, was from Mtsensk, about 100 kilometers south of Odoev; his arbiter was Grigorii Shetalov.

Like Moskotin'ev v. Vysheslavtsev, this case took some time to reach the Slavery Chancellery. Shetalov died in 1624, about the time the arbitration, which had awarded the slaves to Belikov, was completed. For some reason, Tolstoi did not turn them over, and five and a half years later, in 1630, Belikov got a warrant from Moscow which he took to the governor, Vasilii Tarbeev, in Chern', about 25 kilometers north of Mtsensk, to enforce the decision by a confirmation verdict in the Slavery Chancellery. After the typical continuances for a military review and service in May of 1631, the case got under way again in January of 1632. Apparently Tolstoi arrived in Moscow before Belikov, and he filed the usual declarations of appearance in hopes that he could win the case by default.

This was not to be, however, for on February 5, 1632, Belikov arrived and opened the case with a review of the arbitration proceedings of 1624. On the eighteenth he submitted the arbitration verdict of December 16, 1624. In this instance, things seem to have been done properly:

During the trial the arbiter Maksim took testimony under oath from the plaintiff and the defendant in the case and investigated [the case] in every possible way. The arbiter Maksim Botavin conducted interrogations under oath, heard the case, and on the basis of the trial, the investigation, and the testimony under oath, awarded the verdict to Petr Kolupaiev in the matter of his nephew Mikhail Belikov's slaves.

The arbitration summary noted that Tolstoi used the frequent alibi that it was a case of mistaken identity, that Kolupaiev was suing for Foma, but he, Tolstoi, claimed to have Ivashka. Ivashka, he alleged, had been living with him for about fifteen years, and had married one of his hereditary slave women. Before that, Ivashka and his son Pershutka had lived with one Stepan Gubanov for about fifteen years.

As was often the case, the clergy became involved in Belikov v. Tolstoi when Kolupaiev asked who the slave's confessor was. The defendant identified him as Sergei of the church of St. George, who was then sent for. The priest took the clerical oath, and testified that

> [the] slave is living as a peasant in the village Svina, which belongs to Danila Tolstoi. Before that, he lived with Stepan Gubonov and Ivan Skuridin. When he married at Danilo Tolstoi's, he told me that his name was Ivashka. But in 1624 during Holy Week in the village Vostra, at the house of the *syn boiarskii* Ontip Skuridin, walking behind an icon of the Mother of God [*khodechi za prechistoiu*] he asked me for a blessing with his name as Foma. [The text shifts to indirect speech.] He, the priest, told him that he was committing a crime, that he had said his name was Ivashka at the wedding. That man has been living at Danilo's for ten years. Whose son he is, and who his grandfather was, he, the priest, does not know.

Thus we see that allowing Russian slaves to participate in the rites of their society, something that by no means every society allows its slaves, was not always to the advantage of the subject, for the Orthodox priest nearly always considered himself an establishment figure and was ready, willing, and able to use the priest-worshipper relationship to undo the worshipper. The arbiter noted the two contradictions, the names Foma and Ivashka, the durations of ten and fifteen years, and awarded the verdict to Belikov, whose claim was that Fomka and his father, Eremka, had been house slaves of Mikhail's father, Zinovii, and then Mikhail himself. However, the arbiter Maksim Botavin was not so sure about the stolen property, and awarded Belikov only 6.75 rubles.

Unfortunately, the case breaks off on March 19, 1632, with the Slavery Chancellery ordering the arbiter brought in and the placing of the case on the docket.[111] While the Slavery Chancellery's decision in the case is not extant, we may surmise that, if the arbiter Botavin confirmed orally what he had written down in his verdict, then the central organ would have put its imprimatur on it. Defen-

111. Ibid., pp. 464-70, no. 20.

dant Tolstoi had been caught lying twice, and while Belikov's evidence had not been checked, the former had said that he would admit it all as evidence. It was a misfortune that Tolstoi's arbiter, Shetalov, had died, but the defendant did not make much of a point of that, nor did he claim that Botavin had been biased. Therefore the extant record would seem to indicate that the arbitration proceedings had summarized the case accurately and would serve as the basis of a similar verdict by the Slavery Chancellery.

A third arbitration case, Miakinin v. Velkov, of 1643, has been discussed in chapter 4.[112] The arbiters disagreed on the verdict, and the case was resolved by the Slavery Chancellery. The plaintiff's arbitrator noted that they were supposed to handle the case just as though it were a formal legal proceeding, and cited a statute on the subject which is otherwise unknown. No mention was made by the Slavery Chancellery that Miakinin's arbiter, *striapchii* Afanasii Ivanov Nesterov, was his step-father-in-law's son, perhaps because he was Velkov's brother-in-law's son, thus neutralizing any kinship bias of the kind noted above in Moskotin'ev v. Vysheslavtsev. In rejecting the report of the plaintiff's arbiter and accepting that of the defendant, the Slavery Chancellery was using its best judgment and following principles of fairness that certainly would be recognized almost anywhere. Had the case not been submitted to arbitration first, one may assume that the errors that made some of Miakinin's evidence inadmissible would not have occurred. One might suppose that the Slavery Chancellery could have corrected the technical mistakes in the case, but, then, that would have made the very purpose of arbitration redundant. Arbitration was a legal mechanism for uncluttering the formal legal system, and the Slavery Chancellery wisely preserved it by taking cases from it as the final word. If technical mistakes were made in the arbitration procedure, that was the responsibility of the arbiters themselves and those who chose them, not of the central organ called upon to resolve disputes that could not be reconciled in the arbitration process.

Failures

The general picture that has been portrayed in this essay is of a system that worked. Norms were established that interested parties could agree with, and trouble cases generally were resolved with expeditiousness and a sense of fairness. Obviously there were exceptions, for the system with zero defects has not yet been invented. For reasons that are not clear, the system of conflict resolution occasionally broke down in the Slavery Chancellery.

Kuz'mishchev v. Satin

One example was Kuz'mishchev v. Satin, initiated in January of 1628 and still

112. Ibid., pp. 496-513, no. 25.

unresolved in December of 1631. The case was initiated before chancellery codi-rectors Stepan Ivanov Volynskii (in office from 17.IV/24 to 8.VI/28) and Ivan Fomich Ogarev (13.XII/25-29.XI/29) and the state secretaries Nikita Leont'ev (27.V/27-22.IV/28) and Iakov Kliucharev (6.VI/27-22.IV/28) and continued be-fore Prince Ivan Fedorovich Volkonskii (29.VIII/28-20.VII/37) and Ogarev and a new set of state secretaries, Ivan Varganov (30.V/28-22.VI/29) and Andrei Stroev (30.V/28-2.I/33).

As is evident, there was a considerable churning of personnel in the Slavery Chancellery in that period, but, under normal circumstances, both Volynskii and Ogarev would have been in office long enough to resolve the case. What went wrong is anybody's guess.

The dispute was over the ownership of the slave woman Anna (Oniutka), daughter of Emel'ian (Meleshka) Bogdanov. Both litigants had land in the Tula region. The plaintiff, Prince Osip Mikhailov Kuz'mishchev, at the time of the trial was a bailiff (*nedel'shchik*) for the Judicial Chancellery. The defendant, Roman Ivanov Satin, seems to have left slightly more tracks in the historical record. About the time of the trial he probably held the rank of provincial *dvorianin* from Solovl'. Toward the end of the Smolensk War, in February of 1634, he was a camp commander (*stanichnik*) in Mozhaisk, midway between the capital and the battle front, and from there sent a message to the tsar re-porting on the horrors of the war. A man of some upward mobility, in 1651 Roman Satin was governor of Krapivna, formerly a southern frontier outpost not far from Tula, but by 1651 an irrelevant backwater, thanks to the con-struction of the Belgorod fortified line even further south. His term as gover-nor was marked by contention over the draft (selection) of two persons to assist him in administration in his home town of Solovl'. Unfortunately there were only three townsmen (*posadskie liudi*) in Solovl', and they happened to be beggars unfit for public service, so Satin chose instead two servicemen from Krapivna. For this he was severely condemned, rebuked, and told in no uncer-tain terms that he was under no circumstances ever to use his own initiative, that he was not to do anything except what the tsar specifically had ordered him to do.[113]

How much Satin had used his own initiative, a quality that was the bane of Muscovite officialdom, in the dispute over Anna cannot be determined. Most of the facts in the case were in dispute, and Anna denied that she had ever known the plaintiff Kuz'mishchev, but, as I read the case, that seems unlikely. According to Kuz'mishchev, Oniutka's father, Meleshka, had been a war captive of the plaintiff's grandfather, and upon the grandfather's decease became the slave of the plaintiff's father. Mikhail Kuz'mishchev died about 1618, and his

---

113. On R. I. Satin, see KR 2: 627; AAE 3: 370, no. 243; DR 3: 273; Barsukov, SGV, p. 115; AMG 2: 285, no. 459. I could find no additional biographical information about Prince Osip Mikhailov Kuz'mishchev.

son claimed that Meleshka had been serving him in the decade since then. The daughter, Oniutka, was also his hereditary slave. Then, according to the plaintiff, around Easter of 1621 Oniutka fled from him at the instigation of Roman Satin. Some years later, while Satin was in Persia on his own initiative ("without an order from the Sovereign," presumably also a culpable exercise of individual initiative, as Kuz'mishchev tells it), the defendant's wife married off "by force" (also something that was frowned upon) Oniutka to another slave, Grishka Leont'ev.

The defendant admitted that Oniutka's father, Emel'ian, had served Osip Kuz'mishchev's father, Mikhail, but exactly what the relationship was (presumably, whether he was a hereditary slave or a limited service contract slave) is not stated. Satin further claimed that Mikhail had manumitted Emel'ian, who then gave his daughter Oniutka as a slave to the defendant. Then he, Roman Satin, got a limited service slavery contract on her in Tula on November 1, 1621, in the presence of the *guba* elder for the prescribed price of 2 rubles. At the sale Oniutka claimed that she had been living with Roman Satin for three years, and that previously she had been living with her father, who was a free man. (This was technically true, if he had been manumitted.) Roman Satin, when asked, said that he did not possess a manumission document for Oniutka (see Voeikov v. Khilkov, 1620-21, for the significance of that point).

At the trial on January 11, 1628, Osip Kuz'mishchev cited six witnesses, the last of them being Oniutka's putative father, Meleshka, to prove that Oniutka had belonged to his father and then to him. The other witnesses, besides the father, were from Tula and included the members of the cited individuals' families, particularly the females, indicating that Oniutka was a house slave who would have been known in that capacity to other female members of the community. In his defense, Roman Satin cited seventeen witnesses to prove that Osip's father had manumitted Oniutka (and presumably her father as well). His witnesses also were women of Tula, including female house slaves, plus a number of clergymen. The last were to prove that Mikhail in his testament had ordered those slaves manumitted and were supposed to have effected his wish. At this point the court case degenerated into name-calling, with Osip admitting that the cited priest had been his sire's spiritual father, while claiming that the priest was his, the son's, enemy. Osip said the the priest was a forger against whom he had earlier complained and won a court case in Tula over the possession of another slave woman.

After the trial, the contested slave woman, Oniutka, asked the Slavery Chancellery that she be released on bail to the defendant, Roman Satin. (Recall Bormosov v. Berechinskii, 1627-29, discussed above.) This the Slavery Chancellery, which had inquired whether the husband belonged to Satin, did. At this moment the system seems to have broken down. According to later repeated claims of Kuz'mishchev, she had been released on bail without the knowledge of either the plaintiff or the defendant, and the guarantors befriended the defendant, and turned the slave over to him. (That is not what the guarantee note on

Roman Satin says, rather that she was explicitly released into his custody.) The bail bond on Satin was the traditional kind. Seven men of Tula, three of whom were *zhil'tsy*,[114] the rank above Satin's probable rank of provincial *dvorianin*, guaranteed that they were responsible for presenting the slave woman Oniutka and for paying the court costs. The sanction for noncompliance was "as the sovereign decrees," the significance of which was discussed above in Bormosov v. Berechinskii. The bail system for some reason did not work.

On February 26, 1628, plaintiff, Osip Kuz'mishchev, initiated a campaign to get his due in court that in three years proved to be unsuccessful. He told the panel before whom the case had been argued that the defendant, Roman Satin, had left Moscow with the slave woman, charged that he had done so to bribe witnesses and to forge a will, and asked that the guarantors of Oniutka be required to report on her departure from Moscow, a violation of the bail document. The next day the guarantors appeared, and reported that they did not know the whereabouts of Roman Satin. The Slavery Chancellery did nothing.

On May 24, 1628, the Slavery Chancellery heard the last from Roman Satin for a while. He petitioned that the unresolved suit be postponed so that he could report for military service. This was granted, and seven men, different from those in the January group, from Solovl' and Tula, guaranteed that Satin would report for the trial a month after the summer campaign was over and the commanders had dismissed the army. Nothing was done about enforcing this promise, and on December 14, 1628, Osip Kuz'mishchev petitioned to point this out, and to note that the trial was now about to begin its second year. By now Ogarev was the only original Slavery Chancellery panel member. The new panel (Volkonskoi, Ogarev, Varganov, and Stroev) asked that the validity of Satin's limited service slavery contract be verified, and got back a report that it could not be, for the Tula record books had been burned up in a Moscow fire of 1626 in the Investigations Chancellery.

On January 9, 1629, Kuz'mishchev repeated his futile petition of December 14. On January 14 the Slavery Chancellery ordered that Satin's guarantors be presented to discover the whereabouts of the defendant and the slave woman Oniutka. A few days later, on February 1, 1629, it looked as though things were going to become serious. Levontii Petrov Rtishchev, the first-listed guarantor in the May 24, 1628, bond issued in response to Satin's request for a postponement while he was in military service, was himself ordered to post a bond guaranteeing that he would appear every day in the Slavery Chancellery to be tortured (*na*

---

114. Only one of the three *zhil'tsy* appeared in the 1632 inventory of *zhil'tsy* landholding. Savelii Ivanov Durov was not mentioned at all. Kiril Iur'ev Arsen'ev's brother Fedor Iur'ev Arsen'ev was mentioned. Only Demid Timofeev Kriukov was listed: he possessed 78 cheti of service land in Tula province, 50 cheti in Dedilov province, and 75 cheti in Kineshma province. Only the last was populated, with one peasant and two *bobyl'* households. Obviously a poor serviceman, he was supposed to serve on horseback with bow and arrow. He brought no slaves (Iziumov, pp. 74-75).

pravezhe—beating of the feet or shins while the victim sits in stocks) to force Satin's appearance. Six more servicemen of Tula all signed a note guaranteeing that Rtishchev would so appear, and would not leave Moscow. By this time twenty people had become enmeshed in the net of Satin's guarantors. Each of them individually guaranteed that he was responsible for Kuz'mishchev's claims, as the sovereign might determine. Again, nothing seems to have happened.

On December 13, 1629, Kuz'mishchev submitted another petition, his fourth, noting that the trial was about to enter its third year. He now began to see the handwriting on the wall; Moscow bureaucratism was depriving him of his slave woman. Exaggerating, he went on to claim that he was about to perish completely because of the red tape and delay of the Slavery Chancellery. The officials of the Slavery Chancellery were not impressed, and wrote "Add to the case" on the back of the petition, which was then glued to the scroll with the rest of the records. The inaction began to drive Kuz'mishchev to distraction. On December 23, 1629, he presented another petition. "Add to the case" was the response. Five days later, on December 28, he presented another petition. This time the response was: "Add to the case, and get new guarantors." Three days later, on December 31, the frantic Kuz'mishchev submitted his seventh petition on the Slavery Chancellery's delay in the case. Now the response was: "Add to the case and place the case on the docket [on the table] ." By now, Kuz'mishchev apparently was in a frenzy. He submitted an eighth petition on January 1, 1630, ("Add to the case") and a ninth on January 2—at this point he himself began to keep count. The response was: "Add to the case and place the case on the docket."

A week later, on January 9, 1630, the Slavery Chancellery heard again from defendant Roman Satin, for the first time in over a year and a half. He claimed that Kuz'mishchev was slandering him by his claims that he was not in Moscow, that in fact he had been in Moscow since he was discharged from the last campaign and that he had been litigating a service land dispute. He probably cited the dispute to prove that he had been in Moscow, not that he had been unable to appear in the Slavery Chancellery because he was tied up in other government offices. The Slavery Chancellery added that to the case, and again ordered that new guarantors be obtained for the defendant. That was done, and six more men of Tula and of Solovl' agreed to be responsible for Satin and his case.

Again, the implausible happened. Another year went by, and on December 2, 1631, Kuz'mishchev filed his tenth petition, making the old claims: Satin was living the countryside at home bribing witnesses and enjoying the services of the slave woman Oniutka. "Add to the case." The next day, December 3, Kuzmishchev submitted his eleventh petition, repeating the one of the day before, asking again for a verdict. The Slavery Chancellery noted: "Add to the case and place the case on the docket."[115]

At this point the case breaks off. How many more petitions Kuz'mishchev had

115. Iakovlev, *Kholopstvo*, pp. 390-401, no. 14.

to file, and whether he ever got justice, are unknown. It is obvious, however, that, in his own mind, he had already been deprived of justice, simply because for some reason the system had broken down. It is important to note that this could happen, although not to the extent that it did, for example, in the reign of Nicholas I.

Illegal Enslavement

A major failing of Muscovite slave law was that it failed to devote sufficient attention to illegal enslavement. Thoughts on this subject have been part of legal codes since the dawn of history. The Hammurabi Code and the codes of the Old Testament prescribed the death penalty for the kidnapping of minors and the selling of them as slaves. The death penalty was also applied to those who illegally enslaved free men in the ancient Greek world. The Chinese strictly enforced the law prohibiting the kidnapping and sale of children by persons other than their progenitors.[116]

Muscovy enacted similar legislation in 1558, at a time when an attempt was being made to curtail the institution of slavery, and then seems to have forgotten about it. In the midst of other laws, the Statute Book of the Treasury Department under November 30, 1558, noted that the death penalty was to be applied to anyone who forged full or registered slavery documents on a free man. The penalty was to apply both to the would-be slaveowner and to the official (in this case, customs officials were mentioned) who engaged in such an endeavor. An analogy was made with slave theft (literally, the person who stole a slave, *golovnoi tat'*).[117] As the crime of slave theft was forgotten, so, apparently, was the crime of illegal enslavement, for no laws against it seem to exist after 1558, even in the codifications of slave law.

In many systems such provisions might not be necessary, for slaves were outsiders, and thus at least a native who was illegally enslaved could easily make his plight known. An immigrant, however, might well need such protection. Moreover, Muscovite law never stated explicitly the assumption, as did the law of Gortyn (Crete), that in case of a dispute over the status of a man, the testimony of those who swore that the man was free was to be accepted.[118]

---

116. Mendelsohn, p. 5; Buckland, pp. 427-31; Meijer, p. 331; Westermann, p. 6. For a discussion of the forcible enslavement of native free men, see Yoram Barzel, "An Economic Analysis of Slavery," *The Journal of Law and Economics* 20, no. 1 (April 1977): 108-9.

117. UKVK, no. 14, in Vladimirskii-Budanov, 3:27. The Muscovites might have found U. S. Southern legislation on illegal enslavement relatively congenial. Such acts were a felony, but courts were willing to do little more than free those illegally enslaved. An 1855 Virginia case even implied that twenty years' possession justified ownership, regardless of the legality of its origin (Catterall 1: 80, 151, 177, 239). We may assume that racism motivated Southern lack of concern about illegal enslavement.

118. Westermann, p. 18.

The case of Danila Big Beard v. Uvar Lodygin, presented above ("The General Investigation") and discussed in detail in chapter 16, shows that illegal enslavement could occur, and that mid-seventeenth-century Muscovy knew of no sanctions for such an action. Under the rubric of conflict of interest in chapter 3 I noted that officials were forbidden to enslave people, but no sanctions were provided for someone who did, and no compensation was provided for the victims of such illegal action.

The existence of the legislation intimates that such instances of illegal enslavement were perceived as a problem, but the historian can only speculate about why no laws were drawn up to deal with the issue after 1558. The facile answer would be that oligarchs running Muscovy were indifferent to what their peers did to the lower classes, and therefore they closed their eyes to problems such as illegal enslavement. Perhaps; but this seems unlikely. It is doubtful that the Muscovite elite was any more contemptuous of the lower classes than was the Babylonian or Chinese elite. Moreover, as we shall see in the further discussion of Danila Big Beard v. Uvar Lodygin, the ruling elite was almost certainly horrified by what had happened, and regarded Danila's illegal enslavement as an anomaly, not daily reality. Perhaps illegal enslavement was so rare that post-1558 legislators and codifiers simply forgot about the issue. That, however, also seems unlikely.

I would speculate that illegal enslavement was not made the subject of a general law after 1558 because the lawgivers did not want to publicize it as something that was possible and preferred to deal with the rare instances of it on an ad hoc basis. Given the categories of the population that owned slaves, by 1649 only members of the upper classes could have committed the crime of illegal enslavement. The government sometimes preferred to deal with relatively rarely occurring problems involving such individuals outside of the formal legal system. Under such a regime, the potentials both for leniency and for creative terror were much greater than they might have been were crimes defined and sanctions specified. This was one way the ruling oligarch controlled the individual members of the upper classes.

The tendency of the evolution of Muscovite slave law is clear. It was primarily to facilitate the resolution of conflict between slaveowners, while simultaneously generating income for officialdom. There was also an occasional sense that the interest of the slave might be considered, but that is often ambiguous. For example, the strictures against multiple slaveownership were rigorously enforced. This might be considered of interest to the slave, who could be manumitted earlier than if he belonged to several owners. Or, a man with blue eyes could not be claimed by a slaveowner trying to recover a fugitive if the document said he had brown eyes. Such measures were in the slave's interest, but they were also in the state's interest, which was hungry for taxpayers and, very late in the legal life of slavery, for military recruits. But while the state was interested in taxpayers and soldiers, it tried to secure them by forbidding self-sale into slavery, rather than by assuming in a dispute that the contested individual was (or should be) a taxpayer rather than a slave. What had to be proved was not whether a person was a slave but what kind of a slave he was, and to whom he belonged. The preservation of the slaveowner's property rights in their chattel was the law's basic concern, and other considerations were subordinate to that one.

We might remind ourselves again here that the extent of the tension and latent conflict between the Muscovite authorities and the slaveowners was perhaps considerably greater than in most other slave systems, primarily because elsewhere slaves were an exogenous factor, while at least in later Muscovy most of them were natives who, were they not slaves, would have been subjects of the government.

Elsewhere, such as in Latin America, administrators consciously understood that registers and statistics were a sine qua non of social control and order. Census-type events were used to keep count and control of slaves (and their owners), parish priests were instructed to include slaves in their registers of marriages, births, and deaths.[119] The relationship between the development of record-keeping and control of slaves in Muscovy was far less deliberate, far more accidental. This was so primarily because early Muscovy was a dyadic, oral society, in which the impact of government on the individual was minimal. The degree of interaction between the government and individuals of the lower classes proceeded at about the same pace for everyone—townsmen, peasants, and slaves. Thus record-keeping was introduced for its own sake, not in order to control slaves. The pace of this practice was greatly accelerated in the 1586-98 years. For slaves, that meant the end of an era in which slavery must have been to a high degree a consensual phenomenon, and the beginning of one in which the slaveowner could use the law and its devices to ensure that his slave was his chattel. The state itself probably did not take slavery very seriously, but utilized the experience it gained for larger purposes, the control of all society.

A discussion of the Muscovite law of slavery in comparison with other systems places the Muscovite case firmly among them. While the early modern Russian law of slavery had its idiosyncrasies, it clearly tried to cope with most of the same problems that were prevalent in other slave systems.

During the medieval and early modern periods of Russian history, the legal attitude toward the slave underwent a substantial change. Initially the slave was a thing, an object of the law, something without any rights and for whom the very concept of having any rights was unthinkable. While native East Slavs were slaves, the image of the average slave painted by the law is that of an outsider, perhaps a captive taken as war booty.

Under the impact of the consolidation of the Russian state around Moscow, the decrease in number of war captives, and the lessening influence of the presence of elite slaves, the image of the slave in the eyes of the law gradually changed. The impact of norms borrowed from Lithuanian law, which abolished slavery in the sixteenth century and therefore dealt largely with enserfed peas-

119. Melaffe, p. 108.

ants, must also be considered. The consequence was that the slave was gradually humanized; he became a real person in a few respects, a semiperson in most respects. Nevertheless, the goal of the Muscovite law of slavery was to keep the slave in his place, to ensure that he remained, as long as he was enslaved, an object whose possession would elevate his owner's prestige, provide him with service for leisure, and even provide him with income either in cash or in kind. The function of the law was to try to ensure that this subordination was as smooth as possible, to resolve any conflicts that might arise about whether the person in question was a slave, who was his owner, or who was responsible in case of offenses. Late Muscovite law reflects an experience with most of these problems and stands as a relatively coherent set of guidelines for the resolution of most conflicts. What distinguishes later Muscovite law from other systems is the fact that it was dealing primarily with natives who had sold themselves into slavery, rather than with outsiders who had been coerced against their will into living in unfreedom in another land.

Another, although less clearly focused, tendency of the Muscovite law of slavery from the end of the sixteenth century on seems to be directed toward the gradual liquidation of the institution of slavery. Not only was the intake of slaves legally constricted, but their prerogatives and the uses to which they could be put were limited as well. When suitable alternative institutions were in place, the government was able to abolish slavery by fiscal fiat, by converting all slaves into tax-paying serfs, and not a murmur of protest is known to have issued from the mouths of the expropriated slaveowners. As we have seen, serfdom, which was the legal fate of the slaves when slavery was abolished, borrowed much from the institution of slavery.

As a chattel, the slave was primarily an object of the law, rather than its subject. This was a near-universal fact in slave law, although the degree to which slaves were dehumanized varied widely from system to system. Almost nowhere, for slaves, was there total deprivation of the rights of personal security, private property, and even personal liberty, and in Muscovy such deprivation diminished noticeably in the course of a quarter-millennium.

In most societies this treatment was rationalized partially because the slaves were outsiders, a condition that was the logical conclusion of such well-known phenomena as gradations of citizenship; residency, age, sex, and property qualifications for franchise; or the denial of civil rights to felons and the insane. For Muscovites, however, it must have required a greater leap to convert slaves into objects, for many of them were native Russians. This fact, which will be examined in detail in the second part of this book, was unquestionably responsible for much of the ambivalence of Muscovite slave law on the issue of the slave's rights and responsibilities. Nevertheless, those being converted into chattel were primarily relief or welfare cases, about whose capacity to manage themselves and participate in civic affairs there is often some question, even in modern societies.

9. Slavery Offices and Officials

The central place of slavery in early modern Russian life is evident not only in the formal laws but also in the institutions that enforced (and in many instances created) those legal norms. Muscovy is one of the few countries in recorded history to have special institutions to enforce its slave norms. Moreover, slavery was a relatively uniform, pan-Muscovite institution for a number of reasons. Among the most important was the uniformity imposed by the law as effected by central institutions and personnel and provincial institutions and personnel directed by the center. The law codes and updates spelled out the administrative organization controlling the slavery system. Stereotypical directives played a major role in ensuring uniformity of administration throughout Muscovy.[1]

A few details about the offices which ran the system may be of interest. Such information is basically lacking in the documents dating from before the mid-sixteenth century. In the centuries of the *Russkaia Pravda*, the act of sale into slavery was performed before a customs officer (*mytnik*—articles 45 and 48). In the sixteenth century, according to the *Sudebnik* of 1550 (article 66), only the highest officials, those with the right "boyar court," could issue full and registered slavery documents. A definition of "boyar court" was given in the *Sudebnik* of 1497 (article 1): officials who were entrusted with a commission allowing them to resolve cases involving murder, theft, and disputes over slaves. In practice, prior to 1586, this seems to have meant that those slavery instruments could be compiled in any Muscovite town where there was a governor (*namestnik*). The few records from that earlier era were kept by the Treasury, along with the major decrees regulating the institution of slavery. (Article 14 of the Statute Book of the Treasury Department, dated November 30, 1558, noted that customs officials also might legitimate full and registered slavery documents.)

After 1586 the law specified that full and registered slavery documents could only be compiled in Moscow, and in a form different from that used earlier. This is interpreted by the Soviet scholar V. I. Koretskii as a deliberate attempt by the central authorities to limit the use of the institutions of full and regis-

---

1. See the record book of the Slavery Chancellery (*Ukaznaia kniga kholopego prikaza* = UKKhP), the numerous directives to *guba* officials (*Gubnye i zemskie gramoty, otkaznye ustavnye* in *Chteniia* 1895, no. 3; A. I. Iakovlev, *Namestnich'i, gubnye i zemskie ustavnye gramoty Moskovskogo gosudarstva* [Moscow, 1909]), and the working orders to governors (such as DAI 3: 231-39, 243-49, nos. 65, 67).

tered slavery.[2] Judging at least by the surviving slavery documents, the 1586 legislation reflected, rather, the fact that full slavery had already gone into limbo, for the last extant document is dated 1554. Registered slavery was still a viable institution, and the last extant documents show that the measure attempting to centralize the compilation of those instruments in Moscow was successful; unfortunately, the Moscow archives have perished. This centralization was part of the sixteenth-century leashing of the magnates, the type of persons who would have tended to own the elite registered slaves.

The centralization of record-keeping was nothing new, for the Treasury earlier had preserved certain of the slavery contracts. In the 1580s and early 1590s, copies of the limited service slavery contract record books, along with the fees collected during the process of making these registrations, were sent semi-annually to the Treasury. In 1598 both were transferred to the Slavery Chancellery, and after 1641 provincial officials had to submit the records and revenues only on an annual basis.[3]

After June 1, 1586, only limited service slavery contracts could be compiled outside of the capital. They were recorded in the chancellery offices (*izby*) in the provincial towns and the *guba* (felony administration) offices in the provinces. They were also registered in the Slavery Chancellery in Moscow, of course.

The extant published documents tell where about half of these documents were written. Of these, over two-thirds (69.7 percent) were written in the *guba* institutions, the *gubnaia izba* (N=839) or the *gubnoi stan* (N=49). That was the center of provincial governmental activity in the second half of the sixteenth century. In the seventeenth century it was replaced by the *prikaznaia izba* (2.5 percent; N=32). In places remote from *guba* institutions, documents were written in churches or monasteries (6.1 percent; N=78). After the reforms of the 1580s, documents which earlier had been written up by church officials were composed by *zemskii* (provincial civil administration) officials. Documents from Novgorod itself were often composed by a public scribe and made official by the state secretary (*d'iak*), who governed Novgorod after the 1478 annexation by Moscow. Documents of Moscow province came from the grand princely court (7 documents) or from the Slavery Chancellery (47), a body founded about 1571, when it took over the records kept by the Treasury. The Slavery Chancellery functioned until 1681, when it was replaced by a special department of the Judicial Chancellery; it was reopened in 1683, and then it was finally closed and its business was turned over to the Judicial Chancellery in 1704. As table 9.1 reveals, there was a relatively high correllation between the type of document and where it was issued.

2. Koretskii, *Zakreposhchenie*, p. 216.
3. Iakovlev, *Kholopstvo*, p. 316.

TABLE 9.1
Slavery Documents and Place of Execution

	Full Slavery	Registered	Limited service contract[d]	Will	Dowry	Manu- mission	Property Division	Total[e]
			Type of Document					
Grand Princely court 1515-19			7					7
Slavery Chancellery 1598-1696			20					48
Unspecified Novgorod 1478-1600[a]	6	3	103	2	2	9	2	136
Gubnaia izba 1591-1701			839					839
Gubnoi stan 1593-96[b]			49					49
Prikaznaia izba 1643-98			32					32
S"ezzhaia izba 1639-89			9					9
Church or monastery 1541-98			61	6	6		4	78
Town Square 1667-94[c]			6	1				11
Written by Slave 1540-95			4		2			6
Written by Own- er 1524-98				2	19			26
Total	6	3	1,131	11	29	9	6	1,250

Notes:
[a] 1 other document in 1647
[b] 1 other document in 1668
[c] 1 other document in 1583
[d] 1 other document in Prikaznaia palata (1682-94)
[e] Includes:
   Marriage contracts—1 in a church, 1 by slaveowner

Purchase documents—4 written by slave-owner
Judgment charters—5 in Novgorod
Court cases—28 in Slavery Chancellery
Debt memorandum—1 in Prikaznaia palata (1682-94)
Indentures—3 compiled on town square
Registrations—1 in Novgorod
Gift—1 in Novgorod

Uncertainty coefficient = 0.58213 with type of document dependent

The law code of 1550 provided that manumission documents could be issued only in the three major cities of the realm, Moscow, Novgorod, and Pskov.[4] This high degree of centralization was also prevalent in the slavery statute of 1597, which assigned the Slavery Chancellery that task. The latter organ may have as-

4. 1550 *Sudebnik* 77.

sumed that duty right away, although evidence of its manumission activities dates only from 1603.[5] The law code of 1649 reaffirmed this practice.

A major theme of this essay, and of Muscovite history generally, is the increasing control that the center had over the periphery in slavery matters. This calls to mind the many parts of the New World, which the metropole tried to fashion according to its standards and values, something that was especially true in the cases of the Iberian and Danish possessions. The overland expansion of Muscovy often has been compared with the overseas expansion of Western Europe, and the obvious comparative question is whether these attempts at central control yielded similar results. Here I shall only pose the issue, and give a summary answer, the details of which will be examined later. In the case of the Old World trying to direct the New, the tendency was to make the norms of slavery considerably milder than the colonists wanted them to be. The general explanation for this is that the Old World legislators did not understand the conditions of New World slavery, where Europeans were often outnumbered by hostile slaves of African origin.[6] In some cases, the metropole legislators succeeded in mitigating New World slavery, but, on the whole, the institution was run by the minority whites on the spot.[7] In Muscovy, on the other hand, most of the slaves were native Russians, so the situations were not at all comparable. More comparable were the areas of territorial expansion, the middle and lower Volga inhabited by Tatars and Finnic peoples, and then Siberia with its myriad races. As will be shown in the "Imperialism and Slavery" section of chapter 18 below, Moscow control of the periphery was not always successful, but certainly it mitigated the harshness of slavery there.

The Muscovite system of centralization contrasts most starkly with that of the North American South. There was no federal slave law, with most norms that existed being state laws. In day-to-day reality, most extra-estate matters were handled in a summary fashion by the justice of the peace, or by the notorious slave patrol. Muscovy had no federal system and therefore no states, and local officials were loath to get involved with anything.

The Slavery Chancellery

To my knowledge, early modern Russia was the sole country to assign slavery matters almost exclusively to one specialized central bureau. This reflects both the high degree of centralization and the importance of slavery in Muscovy. Nevertheless, the available evidence indicates that the Slavery Chancellery was a relatively subordinate body in its early years. In 1590 *syn boiarskii* Aleksei

5. Koretskii, *Zakreposhchenie*, p. 203.
6. Melaffe, p. 109; Klein, *Americas*, p. 78.
7. Rose, pp. 182, 191, 211-12.

Nekrasov submitted a petition to the directors of the Slavery Chancellery, *okol'nichii* Mikhail Glebovich Saltykov and state secretary Dorofei Bokhin, in the matter of a limited service contract slave who fled from him in 1588. The case was unresolved, so in 1598 Nekrasov petitioned Tsar Boris Godunov that the matter be transferred to the Treasury (*kazennyi dvor*), headed at the time by state secretary Piatoi Kokoshkin. Two years later, in 1600, state secretary Afanasii Vlas'ev examined the Nekrasov case and sent interrogatories to the Slavery Chancellery, then directed by Leontii Ivanovich Aksakov and state secretaries Mikhail Unkovskii and Bogdan Grigor'ev. According to V. I. Koretskii, this means that the Treasury was a higher instance for the Slavery Chancellery in the 1590s.[8] It may have meant that, or merely that central administration was still a relatively personal matter, that rigid bureaucratic assignment of functions was still not the rule. We know that to be the case in other instances, as in the 1592 case where the director of the Kazan' Regional Chancellery (the eastern frontier) was put in charge of certain reconquered areas on the western frontier.[9] This was also the time when some chancelleries were still referred to by their directors' names rather than by their function.

In the first half of the seventeenth century the Slavery Chancellery was not one of the central concerns of the ruling elite, probably because slavery was an ancient institution that was "there," a relatively uneventful fact of daily life that was susceptible to regulation and from which income could be derived. The leading central organs were the chancelleries of Foreign Affairs (*Posol'skii*), Army and Central Personnel (*Razriadnyi*), Service Estates (*Pomestnyi*—it was also in charge of recording and enforcing peasant-serf residence), and Felonies (*Razboinyi*), and they were run almost exclusively by professional, lifelong state secretaries. The Slavery Chancellery did not command that category of personnel. It also was not an organ from which vast personal enrichment could be derived, or one that was pivotal in the governance and control of Muscovy (such as the Petitions or Musketeers chancelleries). Those bodies were usually run by members of the ruling clique, as exemplified by B. I. Morozov, who, prior to the disorders of 1648, was in charge (at least nominally) of six central chancelleries. Rather, the Slavery Chancellery had the normal turnover of second-level bureaucratic personnel who performed their jobs disinterestedly and competently, a point that is evident in the court cases discussed throughout this work. It is not surprising that the elite was little concerned with the Slavery Chancellery during much of its existence, for most of its functions were of a "house-

---

8. Koretskii, *Zakreposhchenie*, p. 203. The formation of the Slavery Chancellery out of the Treasury in the third quarter of the sixteenth century is discussed in detail by A. K. Leont'ev in his distinguished *Obrazovanie prikaznoi sistemy upravleniia v russkom gosudarstve. Iz istorii sozdaniia tsentralizovannogo gosudarstvennogo apparata v kontse XV–pervoi polovine XVI v.* (Moscow: Moskovskii Universitet, 1961), pp. 179–92.

9. MS, p. 34 ff. For some reason, the Slavery Chancellery was the sole central office mentioned in a 1607 boyar list (Ovchinnikov, p. 75).

keeping" nature: the registration of slaves and the resolution of disputes over slaves. Record keeping is inherently boring. Rulers and their entourages have almost always been disinterested when it comes to matters of conflict resolution, "disposing of society's garbage," as it is sometimes called. While financial gain was inherent in the early modern conflict-resolution process, the maintenance of the principle of disinterested resolution of private law trouble cases was in everyone's interest, for no one knew when his own turn to become enmeshed in the machinery would come. Generally, the fees collected went into the state coffers, not private pockets, and the society seems to have been sufficiently litigious that almost everyone of some means could expect to be involved in a judical process at one time or another. For that reason the risks of wrecking the conflict resolution machinery must have been so great that the potential gains to be derived from making the Slavery Chancellery into an object of political contention simply made any such effort unworthy of the sociopolitical elite. Moreover, the Slavery Chancellery did not make policy. When unprecedented cases had to be resolved, the employees of the Slavery Chancellery were obliged to convey them to higher authorities.

The situation changed in the second half of the seventeenth century, when certain serf affairs began to be administered in the Slavery Chancellery, in addition to the more traditional slavery matters. Then names such as Nashchokin, Streshnev, and Ordin-Nashchokin appear as directors. However, serfdom is not the central concern of this work.

The normal personnel complement in the Slavery Chancellery was two codirectors (*sud'i*) and two state secretaries (*d'iaki*), plus a number of scribes. Directors were usually members of the upper service class who worked in the Slavery Chancellery as one of many assignments throughout their careers. Their role was to see that administration policy was effected, that the bureaucracy was "responsive" to the demands of the reigning oligarchy, that the career civil servants did not take over the system. Such *sud'i* were more important in other chancelleries than in the *Kholopii Prikaz*, where they sat to provide income for themselves and training in supervision, and for the sake of symmetry with the other offices, not because the oligarchs felt that slavery was a matter that needed outside direction from day to day.

The state secretaries were professional bureaucrats, men who had worked their way up from posts as clerks and may have had aspirations to become counselor state secretaries, the handful of bureaucrats who were so central to the running of Muscovy that they had the adjective *dumnyi* (counselor) added to their title and joined the boyars and *okol'nichie* in advising the tsar on the establishment of policy. The second-level significance of the Slavery Chancellery is manifested by the fact that a sitting *dumnyi d'iak* never worked there.

The gross statistical service profiles of the directors and state secretaries of the Slavery Chancellery are astonishingly similar, as is evident in table 9.2, computed from the list of such individuals compiled by S. K. Bogoiavlenskii.[10]

TABLE 9.2
Lengths of Service Terms of Slavery Chancellery Officers

	Directors	State Secretaries
Average (months)	32.7	32.4
Standard deviation	32.6	33.3
Minimum (months)	3	3
Maximum (months)	146	160
N	38 men	57 men
Those who later served in other chancelleries (%)	23.7	45.6

Essentially the professional state secretaries held their posts in the Slavery Chancellery for the same length of time as did the more amateur directors—about the same length of time the latter held other temporary posts such as governor. For most of the officers, this was their last chancellery assignment, although a considerable number of the state secretaries went on to similar positions in other central bureaus. There is no perceptible change in any of these variables throughout the seventeenth century.

The longest tenured director was Ivan Ivanov Streshnev, a *stol'nik* who headed the slavery Chancellery from May 18, 1662 to July 1674. That was only a segment of his career, which extended from at least 1627 to 1692. The Streshnevs were related to the Romanov dynasty by marriage; Tsar Mikhail's second wife (1626) was Evdokiia Luk'ianovna Streshneva, the mother of Tsar Aleksei. Ivan Ivanov Streshnev seems to have benefited less than did some of the other members of his clan from the alliance. He began his career as a *dvorianin* but almost immediately became a *stol'nik*, the rank he held for the rest of his life. He also served at the palace, in addition to the Slavery Chancellery, and ended his career as a personal servant of Tsar Peter.[11] Streshnev's tenure was unusual in that he did not have a codirector, at the time when the subject of fugitive slaves and serfs was particularly heated. It is not apparent that an "especially loyal" person had to be appointed to that post at that time, if only because much of the action on fugitives, for example, was concentrated in other offices.

The state secretary with the longest service in the Slavery Chancellery in the seventeenth century was Ivan Gavrilov Andrianov, who began to work there about October 17, 1664 and was last reported there on January 7, 1678. These years largely coincided with the years Streshnev worked in the Slavery Chancellery, although the mutual tenure was probably coincidental. There were almost

10. Bogoiavlenskii, *Prikaznye sud'i*, pp. 203-9.
11. Ivanov, AUBK, p. 393; DR, 5: 241.

always two state secretaries, and Ivan Stepanov worked for eight years with Andrianov. Andrianov's known career stretched over more than three decades. In 1645 he was a palace clerk, and eleven years later he was state secretary in newly-reconquered Smolensk. From there he moved to full-time service in the chancelleries; at the end of the 1650s he was state secretary in the Vladimir and Galich Regional Taxation chancelleries, and from 1659 to 1663 he was a state secretary in the Spirits Chancellery. Next he served for a year in the Moscow Judicial Chancellery, and then moved to the Slavery Chancellery, where he ended his known career. Andrianov's career was typical for that of a state secretary, as was his salary: 60 rubles in cash and an entitlement to 600 cheti of land in 1660.[12]

The Slavery Chancellery also employed a rather large staff of clerks. The names of sixty-two of them are known for the seventeenth century. Its personnel roster ranged from thirty-five such persons in the 1630s to a low of eight during the plague of the 1650s. The high figures should be reduced by half to account for those who were on assignments outside the Slavery Chancellery, not working at the moment ("ne sidit"), or perhaps not even on the payroll. The normal working complement of scribes seems to have been somewhat less than twenty at any given time. This presumably indicates something about the level of business in the bureau.

Salaries for the top clerks were good, but the compensation for those at the bottom was more an apprentice stipend than a living wage. The top clerical salary was 25 rubles during the early reign of Tsar Mikhail, and 33 rubles toward the end of that era. The standard top salary in the second half of the century was 30 rubles. Toward the end of the century, one or two of the clerks may have been entitled to some land as well as a cash salary. Whether they had any land is not known. At the bottom, one or two clerks were listed as receiving 2 rubles, or even 1 ruble; they certainly were apprentices. The annual wage bill for clerical help of the Slavery Chancellery varied from 119 to 200 rubles, the cost per clerk from 9.15 to 12.50 rubles, with most known years toward the upper end for both figures.[13]

Finally, the Slavery Chancellery employed bailiffs, who played a role in almost every judicial case, and guards. In 1668/69 there were six bailiffs being paid 12 rubles apiece and four guards earning 7 rubles each.[14] As is apparent in the discussion of the Slavery Chancellery court records, the bailiffs had considerable opportunity to earn extra money by keeping disputed slaves chained to

12. Veselovskii, D'iaki, p. 25; Bogoiavlenskii, p. 233.

13. I am indebted to Peter Bowman Brown for having provided me with a list of Slavery Chancellery clerks from TsGADA Fond 210.

14. Petr Ivanov, ed., Opisanie gosudarstvennogo razriadnogo arkhiva, s prisovokupleniem spiskov so mnogikh khraniashchikhsia v onom liubopytnykh dokumentov (Moscow, 1842), p. 68. I am indebted to Peter Brown for bringing this item to my attention.

the wall in their houses and by feeding such individuals, for which they were additionally compensated.

The Slavery Chancellery was a "budget operation" whose expenses almost unquestionably were recouped many times over from the fees it charged. The income from about two dozen average suits for stolen property was enough to keep the entire chancellery for a year. One may assume that "excess income" ordinarily was turned over to the Treasury for general disbursement, a step that had not been necessary before the creation of the Slavery Chancellery when the Treasury itself handled slavery matters. An example of another way of expending surplus Slavery Chancellery funds is presented by the 1646 case of Ivan Kurtseev, who deserted from Lithuania to join the forces of Muscovy. In Moscow Kurtseev was entered on the service rolls and dispatched to his post in Kazan' (chosen to make return to Lithuania as difficult as possible). The travel expenses of Kurtseev and his family from Moscow to Kazan' were covered out of fees that had been paid to the Slavery Chancellery.[15]

Other Central Chancelleries Active in Slavery Matters

In the seventeenth century, other central offices besides the Slavery Chancellery played a role in slavery matters. It is quite apparent that all cases involving native Russian slaves were always handled by the Slavery Chancellery, that all another chancellery had to do was hear the word "slave" and it would send the case there. As we shall see, the matter of juridiction was more complicated when war captives were involved.

Turgenev v. Miasoedov

There were numerous reasons why the Slavery Chancellery had to involve other bureaus in its affairs. One of them was that the figures involved in a slavery case might well have generated relevant evidence elsewhere that could be called upon to aid in the resolution of a suit. This is evident in the fragment of a case, Turgenev v. Miasoedov, heard in the Slavery Chancellery before the director, Prince Ivan Fedorovich Volkonskii, and the state secretaries Tret'iak Kopnin and Pervyi Neronov in the spring of 1633.

As was so often the case, the litigants were approximate social equals; in this case they both held the rank of Moscow *dvorianin*. Of the two, plaintiff Ivan Iur'ev Turgenev probably began at a lower point but seems to have earned a more notable position in the historical record. About 1614 he petitioned Tsar Mikhail that he be allowed to begin a service career and noted that his father, who had been murdered at the behest of Boris Godunov, had enjoyed a compensation schedule of 750 chetverti of land and 40 rubles in cash. The petition

15. *Opisanie dokumentov i bumag* 15(1908): 494-95, no. 562-III.

was granted. Young Turgenev was himself assigned a compensation schedule. About the same time he petitioned that no taxes be collected from him because of his ruined condition, and that was granted too. In addition to routine military service, Turgenev seems to have held two types of jobs in his life. For one, he was a diplomatic and court functionary who escorted Cherkas murzas in January and March 1631, and the Persian ambassador in October 1636. He was commander of 51 *zhil'tsy* assigned to meet foreigners in February 1635; in April 1637 again escorted a Persian ambassador; and in May of 1649 accompanied the Jerusalem patriarch, Paisius, from Moscow to Putivl'. At the royal court in 1636 he served as a palace sentry. In September and October 1650, he accompanied Tsaritsa Mar'ia Il'ichna on processions to Kolomenskoe and the Trinity monastery, and in April 1651 was part of the tsar's procession from Moscow to Pokrovskoe. As was typical for men of his station, he also served as a military governor: in Murom in 1625/26, in Tiumen' in 1646/48, and in Vologda in 1650. The Murom post (in command of a garrison of 19 retired *deti boiarskie* who rendered defensive siege service, 2 messengers, and 9 artillerymen) seems to have been a failure for him, since he went there and was recalled in the same year. The Siberian post evidently was uneventful, and a highlight of the Vologda position seems to have been a roundup of aliens who had illegally crossed the Swedish frontier in violation of the Stolbovo treaty of 1617 and a forced return, with all their property, of those who had crossed in the previous two years. He served as a Moscow *dvorianin* from at least 1627 to 1658. Why he was never promoted is not clear. About the time of the trial, in 1632, Ivan Turgenev had 200 cheti of service land in the vicinity of Riazan', Dedilov, Vorotynsk, and Beloozero, plus 60 cheti of *votchina* land he had been granted in Vorotynsk for service during the Polish invasion of 1618 and another 98 cheti of purchased waste in the Moscow region. His service requirements were high: a horse for himself, three mounted combat slaves, and two baggage-train slaves. His luck as a slaveowner was not outstanding. When he was in service in Valuiki in 1632, four of his slaves took all of their gear (*sluzhbishka*) and fled to the Don, "ruining" him. The following year, 1633, he purchased some military captives, and Tatars abducted them from him. Two decades later, in 1660-61, some of his slaves fled, were apprehended, and sent from the Military Chancellery to the Petitions Chancellery.[16] One may assume that the fugitives were apprehended by people subordinate to the Military Chancellery, but why they were sent to the Petitions Chancellery, and what role it played in the disposition of fugitive slaves, is unknown.

The defendant in the case, Vasilii Ermolin Miasoedov, had a career that was

16. Sukhotin, ChSV, p. 199; idem, *Stolptsy pechat*, p. 140, no. 438; RIB 10(1886): 17; DR 1: 731, 2: 69, 183, 194, 416, 536, 3: 120, 189, 201, 248; Tatishchev (1910), p. 49; Ivanov, AUBK, p. 420; RK 1550-1636, 2: 358; Barsukov, SGV, pp. 47, 143, 254; KR 1: 1217; DAI 3: 152, no. 46; AAE 4: 63, no. 43; Stashevskii, ZMD, pp. 204-5; *Opisanie* 15 (1908): 81, 357.

somewhat like that of Turgenev, except in the very beginning of it. His father, Ermolai, was still alive at the time of the trial, and figured in it. Ermolai had 660 cheti of service land in Kineshma, Vereia, and the Moscow region, plus 130 cheti of hereditary land. The father's service requirements were also substantial: a horse for himself, as well as a sabre and handgun, three combat slaves (one specifically was to be armed with bow and arrows, another with a handgun), and two baggage-train slaves. Vasilii, according to Turgenev, was registered for service from his father's holdings. Vasilii himself was a patriarchal *stol'nik* in 1629, and in the records of 1639 and 1658 was listed as a Moscow *dvorianin*, as his father had been. In 1639 he was part of a convoy for an ambassador from the Persian shah, and in 1652 accompanied the tsaritsa on a procession to the Trinity monastery. It may have been this Vasilii Miasoedov who accompanied an arms shipment to Iablonovo, the southern frontier headquarters, in 1653.[17] Other than that, Miasoedov seems to have left no traces in the record, and thus, for example, he probably never held a provincial governorship. Ultimately, his career was less luminous than Turgenev's, although at the time of the trial that could not have been projected, for the plaintiff was probably a bit older than the defendant.

The allegations in Turgenev v. Miasoedov are fairly clear. Turgenev was suing to recover his fugitive slave Arina Fedorova Pospelova, whose grandfather and father had belonged to Turgenev's father and then to Turgenev himself near Vorotynsk on the Oka, not far from Kaluga. The plaintiff alleged that Arina had fled to Miasoedov's, where she apparently married a free man (*vol'novoi chelovek* [freedman?]), Ontipka, son of Vasilei Almametev, obviously of Tatar origin. Fleeing, she was alleged to have stolen 50 rubles' worth of property and cash.

The defendant claimed, as was so often the tactic, that it was a case of mistaken identity, that the woman in his possession was Arina Fedorova Bezzubova, his hereditary slave. She apparently accompanied Ermolai Miasoedov on a military campaign to the Terek, in the Caucasus. Judging by Turgenev's general preciseness and Miasoedov's evasiveness, I would say that the latter was prevaricating. Be that as it may, Miasoedov's slave Ondriushka Vasil'ev Olmametev, probably Arina's brother-in-law, kissed the cross to prove that his owner was telling the truth. The case was complicated by the issue of whether Ermolai's son-in-law, Odinets Mikhailov Beklemishev, had earlier, in August 1632, won a suit against Fedor Khomutov on Miasoedov's behalf to reclaim Arina Bezzubova, or a hereditary Tatar slave woman, Antipka Almametova. The former was alleged by Miasoedov, and would have served as evidence that Arina was earlier adjudged to have been his slave. The latter was alleged by plaintiff Turgenev, perhaps attempting to show that Miasoedov was trying to use the closeness of names (Arina, Antipka, which might look somewhat similar, at least to an illiterate) to pass off a verdict for another woman (probably Arina's sister-in-law) as though it

17. Ivanov, AUBK, p. 277; DR 2: 959, 3: 317; AMG 2: 347.

concerned his slave. Later he claimed that Beklemishev had changed the slave's father's name in the suit.

Further evidence discussed at the trial involved other government offices besides the Slavery Chancellery. Turgenev pointed out that Miasoedov had gotten a certificate of ownership (*zname*) at the office of the patriarch (*patriarkhov dvor*), and in it he had written that Orinka was a documented (*krepostnaia*, perhaps a military captive who had converted to Christianity) slave, and not a hereditary (*starinnaia*) slave, as he was claiming at the trial. Unfortunately, this document was not introduced at the trial, so nothing more is known about it, and the defendant did not respond to the charge. In the matter of the suit by Beklemishev, Miasoedov challenged Turgenev to check the court cases of all the chancelleries in Moscow to see whether Beklemishev had sued for Arina Fedorova Pospelova.[18] Of course that was not something that Turgenev had claimed, but the point here is that the defendant apparently assumed that such suits might be possible, for otherwise he would not have issued the challenge. Unfortunately, again, no other contemporary records seem to be extant that would support such a supposition, for after the Time of Troubles resolution of conflicts over slaves seems to have been concentrated in the Slavery Chancellery. Recalling the sketch of Turgenev's life, we will remember that the Military Chancellery and the Petitions Chancellery played a role in the matter of fugitive slaves in the 1660s. The Petitions Chancellery throughout the period distributed to the proper organs petitions addressed to the tsar, usually on the same day. Finally, it might be noted that suits were sometimes filed in the Robbery Chancellery when slaves stole property while fleeing, although resolution of such matters usually was in the hands of the Slavery Chancellery.

While the role of other central chancelleries and their agents in the resolution of slavery conflicts is not always completely clear, their assistance to the Slavery Chancellery is well documented. This assistance was necessary because the Slavery Chancellery itself had only a small staff in Moscow, and lacked sufficient bailiffs to send them out to the provinces to check on every point that might be raised in a Moscow suit. Moreover, there were certain jurisdictional problems, particularly involving clergymen, that were more easily resolved by having their central coordinating offices issue the needed instructions. Pertinent illustrations are available in the 1634 case Kozlova v. Kozlova et al., which itself is discussed in chapter 17.

By the 1630s the Muscovites had developed very strict rules of evidence, as was discussed above. In the trial of Kozlova v. Kozlova et al., allegations were made that a slave woman had not been present during the drafting of a limited service slavery contract in Shuia, and that a priest had obtained information about the nature of another slave woman's flight in Suzdal' and whether she had taken stolen property with her. The panel of the Slavery Chancellery proceeded to

18. Iakovlev, *Kholopstvo*, pp. 470-73, no. 21.

check on both allegations through the good offices of other Moscow chancelleries and their deputies.

In the matter of the composition of the limited service slavery contract, the Slavery Chancellery itself wrote, in the name of the tsar, to the governor of Shuia, Mikhail Nikonov Kolzakov, asking him to check on the matter with the *guba* elder, Frol Kishkin, before whom the contract had been signed.

> When this document of ours reaches you, having placed the *guba* elder Frol Kishkin before yourself, accurately conduct an interrogation under our oath on the cross: Did Timka Vasil'ev and his wife Matriushka petition [to serve] the widow Fedora, wife of Ivan Kozlov, in her house, and did they give her a limited service slavery contract on themselves? Was his, Timka's, wife Matriushka before him at the registering of the limited service slavery contract on themselves? Was his, Timka's, wife Matriushka before him at the registering of the limited service slavery contract, or not? Having written down what Frol Kishkin says about this, you are to order his testimony sent to us in Moscow over his, Frol's, or his spiritual father's, signature, for the resolution of this court case.

The governor was ordered to send the information directly to the Slavery Chancellery.

The evidence from the priest was solicited through the good offices of Patriarch Iosaf. He passed the request to *boiarin* Semen Vasil'evich Koltovskoi, director of the Patriarchal Court, and his state secretary, Maksim Bogdanov. They in turn were to send a request to the archbishop of Suzdal' and Tarusa Serapion, who was to interrogate according to church rules the priest Ofanasei of the village Sidorovskoe:

> Did the widow Fedora, wife of Petr Kozlov, and her sons Ondrei and Lavrentei, send back to her daughter-in-law, the widow Fedora, wife of Ivan Kozlov, her unmarried slave woman Irishka with the priest Ofonasei? Did he, the priest, interrogate that unmarried slave woman about who had induced her to flee? Did the unmarried slave woman tell him that slaves of the widow Fedora, wife of Petr Kozlov, and her sons had induced her to flee, or not? Having induced her to flee, did they carry away to Fedora stolen property, or not?

Having learned the answer, the archbishop was to send the testimony over the signature of the priest Ofonasei to Patriarch Iosaf, and another copy to the Slavery Chancellery.[19] While no demand was made for speed, the Slavery Chancellery acted in an expeditious manner in sending out its requests for information, and arranged its requests in such a fashion that they could be fulfilled in a businesslike manner and reported back directly. Moreover, while litigants paid a great deal for court services, no charges were added when the Slavery Chancel-

19. Ibid., pp. 486-88, no. 23, IX-X.

lery solicited this kind of information. When a special bailiff was sent out, litigants had to pay him a mileage fee, but requests of this type seem to have been dispatched by the regular government post system without fee to the litigants. Such efficient coordination was usually the order of the day among the Muscovite chancelleries.

Another example of the utilization of numerous central offices in the resolution of a complex case was discussed in chapter 3, Krechetnikov v. Pozdeev. In that dispute, which involved the issues of whether one of the contested slaves was a military captive and what should be done when fugitives belonging to different owners married on "neutral territory," at least five of the major central bureaus were involved: the Military Captives Chancellery, the Vladimir (or Galich) Regional Tax Collection and Administrative Chancellery, the Great Court, the Patriarch's Court, and the Slavery Chancellery. In addition, a group of the boyars (acting in the name of the tsar) was called in twice to resolve major issues.[20]

As in any government, jurisdictional problems sometimes arose. This was particularly true on frontiers and in combat zones. For example in May 1650 the Military Chancellery sent an order to the Slavery Chancellery announcing that the Military Chancellery had exclusive jurisdiction over all cases in frontier (*pol'skie*) towns, and that the Slavery Chancellery's writ did not run in such places.[21]

The Officials of the Slavery System

The job titles of the major officials are known in 90 percent of the slavery documents. The earliest documents were attended by governors (N = 36), postal officials (67), a steward (2), a bailiff (3), or a *tretnik* (4). All of the 25 registered slavery cases for which there is information were attended by governors and postal officials. The same was true in 74 of the full slavery documents, and the rest were serviced by the other pre-1560 officials listed.

In the second half of the sixteenth century, when limited service contract slavery became the dominant form of bondage, a *gubnoi starosta* was usually in charge of the system from the issuance of new contracts to the resolution of ownership disputes (N = 1,079), but sometimes in the years 1564-1700 the major official listed was the *zemskii d'iachok* (N = 123).[22] Church or monastery scribes handled about 10 percent of the work between 1553 and 1592. The state secretary was the major official in Novgorod (N = 399), and the town-square scribe was the only official listed in 120 cases. There was a great continuity of

20. Ibid., pp. 488-96, no. 24.
21. *Opisanie dokumentov i bumag* 15(1908): 298, no. 272-I.
22. N. E. Nosov, "Gubnaia reforma i tsentral'noe pravitel'stvo kontsa 30-kh−nachala 40-kh godov XVI v.," *Istoricheskie zapiski* 56(1956): 217.

these provincial administrators in the second half of the sixteenth century, with the same individuals often serving together for years on end. At the end of the sixteenth century, an army officer directed 24 of the extant cases. Slavery Chancellery cases were directed by a state secretary or director (N = 25). In the provinces, after the Time of Troubles, the governor was the major official in charge in 47 cases.

There was a considerable correlation between an official's position and the type of document he handled, as evidenced in table 9.3, which is based on an analysis of the data in my basic data set.

The *Ulozhenie* of 1649 and other documents frequently mentioned the officials involved in the slavery system and made some attempt to outline their functions. Those discussed were the governor (*voevoda*), state secretary (*d'iak*), chancellery employees (*prikaznye liudi*), *guba* elder, fortifications official (*gorodovoi prikashchik*), bailiff (*pristav*), and town-square scribe (*ploshchadnyi pod'iachii*). The fortifications official clearly antedated the governor, and was mentioned in the list of officials (along with the state secretary and *guba* elder) who could sign slavery contracts prior to the seventeenth-century court cases discussed above (Bormosov v. Berechinskii and Zheliabuzhskii v. Lobanov-Rostovskii), in the former case with the claim that a document signed by such a person should no longer be considered valid, that in 1629, only governors, siege defense heads (*osadnye golovy*), and *guba* elders could sign such documents. That claim seems to have made no impact on the Slavery Chancellery, and in the latter case it is clear that in 1621 the fortifications official still could legalize self-sale documents.[23] As for the other officials, the *Ulozhenie* makes it clear that limited service slavery documents were valid only when signed (not just sealed) by state secretaries, other chancellery employees, governors, and *guba* elders, and goes on to require specifically, therefore, that the *guba* elders be literate so that they could execute their job properly. The same requirement was specified for the books recording such documents that were sent periodically to Moscow.[24] Manumission documents could only be signed by state secretaries.[25] Limited service slavery documents were written by town-square scribes, but no monopoly was stipulated.[26] The bailiff was the link between the Slavery Chancellery and the outside world, the person who was supposed to bring those accused of not allowing manumitted individuals their freedom and contested slaves into the office for trial. As evident throughout this work, he was also the person to whom a contested slave might be entrusted for safekeeping if bail could not be arranged and jail was not necessary. For such services, the bailiff was paid a "chaining fee" and a boarding fee.[27]

23. 1649 *Ulozhenie* 20: 103; MS, p. 292.
24. 1649 *Ulozhenie* 20: 28, 48, 72-73; MS, pp. 265, 272-73, 282.
25. 1649 *Ulozhenie* 20: 8; MS, p. 258.
26. 1649 *Ulozhenie* 20: 19; MS, p. 262.
27. 1649 *Ulozhenie* 20: 14, 94; MS, pp. 260, 289.

TABLE 9.3
Major Officials Involved in Slavery Transactions and Cases, with Dates

Type of Document	Tsar, 1576	Chancellery head, 1635-96	Chancellery state secretary, 1591-1694	General or governor (voevoda), 1575-1701	Guba elder, 1591-1674	Governor (namestnik), 1475-1594	Slave steward (tiun), 1543-54	Postal official, 1471-1597	Clerk/scribe (pod'iachii), 1493-96a	Townsquare scribe, 1576-1698	Stol'nik, 1626-51	Palace office clerk, 1585-96	Moscow tretnik, 1465-89*	Slave, 1540-97	Court officer (pristav), 1467-1517	Priest or deacon, 1572-93	Metropolitan of the church, 1593	Army officer (golova), 1582-97	Novgorod state secretary (d'iak), 1564b-1602	Musketeer (streltsy), 1591	Fortifications official (gor. prik.), 1613	Document supervisor (Nadsmotr krepostnykh del), 1714	Zemskii clerk, 1564-1600c	Church or monastery scribe, 1472-1598d	Junior clerk, 1534	Total
Full slavery						12		64	3				4		3				1							87
Registered slavery						21		3																		24
Limited service	14	7	42	1,079					1	109		1						24	382		2e		114	167		1,942

Document type																									Totals
Will																	1	1				1	10		13
Marriage contract																						3	4		7
Dowry							5			3													1	41		51
Manumission			3							2f									9				3	1		18
Purchase										1						1							1			3
Judgment charter			2 1					4 2											2							11
Property division							3												2					3		8
Conciliation (*mirovaia*)							1			1														1		3
Tsar charter	1																									1
Court case								2																		2
Debt memo			1													1										2
Indenture										4									1							5
Registration of slaves																			1							
Gift registration																		1								1
Totals	1	14	10	47	1,079	37	2	67	4	118	2	2	4	5	3	4	1	24	398	1	2	1	123	228	1	2,181

Notes:

[a] 1 other in 1588

[b] 1 other in 1430, 2 in 1686, 1687

[c] 1 other in 1671

[d] 1 other in 1668

[e] 1 gorodovoi prikashchik, 1 gorodnichii, 1642

[f] 1 naemnyi diachok, 1670

Uncertainty coefficient = 0.61628, with type of document dependent

I know the official rank of only a handful of these officials. In eleven documents the major official was a boyar (in the 1510s, with a few later), in six a *postel'nik* (in 1588-94, all in registered slavery cases), in two a *syn boiarskii* (in the 1580s, for limited service contract slavery), in twenty-five a *stol'nik* (mostly in the second half of the seventeenth century), in two a *dumnyi dvorianin* (in the 1680s), and in seven an *okol'nichii* (mostly in the 1680-90s). On the basis of this scanty evidence, it would seem as though slavery was of least interest to the ruling elite at the time when the institution of slavery was the most dynamic, in the second half of the sixteenth century. This impression may well be misleading, however, although it is certainly correct that most *guba* elders (flourishing at the end of the sixteenth century) were members of the middle service class, and most governors (flourishing in the pre-1556 and post-1613 periods) were members of the upper service class.

Fees

Officials were interested in slavery matters because it was fairly big business. Tax exemption charters issued prior to the end of the fifteenth century indicate that at that time a fee (*stavlenoe*) may have been collected on the sale of full slaves.[28] In the sixteenth century, however, with the near disappearance of the domestic slave trade, such fees are no longer heard of. Later on, the end of the semiannual limited service slavery contract books reported the sums of money taken in, and their disposition. One of the major purposes of the law in almost every system is the enrichment of the ruling class, including those who have custody of the legal system. Muscovy was no exception, particularly as government posts were often more desirable and a more reliable source of income than land, thanks to the usual scarcity of labor. The law prescribed what each official was to earn from each transaction, and in many cases this amounted to considerable sums. This also helps to explain why clerks (*pod'iachie*) could own as many slaves as they did: they had a large cash flow from their near monopoly on the writing of documents.

28. ASEI 3: 42, no. 23, art. 9. I have no idea what the annual revenue generated by the institution of slavery was, either in absolute terms or as a percentage of total revenue. Alan Fisher has calculated that in Ottoman Kefe, in 1529, the tax on the purchase or sale of slaves amounted to about 23.6 percent of the total taxes levied on the province for all activities ("The Ottoman Crimea in the Sixteenth Century," *Harvard Ukrainian Studies* 5, no. 2 [June 1981]: 139, 143). Certainly that was many times greater than the governmental revenue generated by all slave-related activities in Muscovy. Had there been a significant slave trade in early modern Russia, certainly the officials from the time of Ivan IV to Peter the Great would not have let it pass as a source of revenue. The fact that no such revenues appear in the government records is one of the indicators that the slave trade was nearly nonexistent.

Fee schedules were established for everything. Fees had to be paid, for an example, for the writing, signing, and sealing of manumission documents.[29]

TABLE 9.4
Fee Schedules

Paid to	Amount per Person in a Document
The *boiarin* (in Moscow) or governor (in Novgorod or Pskov)	9 d.
The secretary	6 d.
The scribe	3 d.

Or, the state secretary was to be paid 6 dengi per person for renewing the slavery document on a slave who returned from foreign military captivity to his old owner.[30] A century later, fees were recognized as so important that an entire chapter, 18, of the *Ulozhenie*, with 71 articles, was included in the code to regulate that important aspect of administrative-judicial work. Fees had to be paid to initiate suits, for arrest warrants, for court judgments, and for judicial verdicts requiring the losing party to fulfill his obligations.[31] Articles in chapter 10 regulated the incomes of officials from fees exacted from the populace, for documents, suits, and other services.

Throughout the seventeenth century, three altyns (0.09 rubles) per person had to be paid to the Slavery Chancellery for each slave it processed, whether it was a fugitive slave being returned to his rightful owner after a trial, a slave being manumitted, or a military captive being registered as someone's slave. When hereditary estate peasants were sold at the end of the century, the same sum was collected for them. Landowners wanted to record such transactions in the Slavery Chancellery, but the government tried to insist that such records be kept in the Service Land Chancellery.[32] Although the enserfed peasants were becoming more like slaves almost every year, the government recognized and wanted to preserve the distinction between the two categories of the dependent population.

As is evident in the court cases discussed throughout this work, the court bailiff was a central figure. Besides his salary, one of his major sources of income was derived from chaining and feeding contested slaves from the moment a slave was arrested until bail could be arranged, the trial was held, or a decision was handed down, depending upon the circumstances. The fee for keeping the slave under guard (the "chaining fee") was 3 dengi (0.015 rubles) per day. In addition,

29. 1497 *Sudebnik* 17; 1550 *Sudebnik* 77; 1589 *Sudebnik* 139; Verner, pp. 35-36.
30. 1550 *Sudebnik* 80. 1589 *Sudebnik* 144 prescribed no fee, just a note on the original slavery document.
31. 1649 *Ulozhenie* 18: 43, 44, 46, 58.
32. PSZ 2: 590, 919-21, nos. 1073, 1293; NZKK 1: 29.

the losing litigant had to pay a fee of 4 dengi (0.02 rubles) per day for feeding the slave.[33] Since a slave-catcher was to be paid only 2 dengi per day for feeding the slave, the bailiff may be assumed to have been making a good profit on feeding, as well as chaining, a contested slave. A person who ordered the arrest of a slave and had him lodged with a bailiff had to pay the latter's fees even if he renounced his claims to the slave and resolved not to pursue the case to trial.[34]

Muscovy, of course, was not unique in prescribing that its officials be well paid for performing their jobs in regulating the slavery system. Thus the Alabama Slave Code of 1852 prescribed that the justice of the peace was to share in a reward of $20 for apprehending fugitive slaves, while a probate judge was to be paid the sum of $5 for certifying the emancipation of a slave.[35]

A comprehensive comparative examination of the varieties of offices and officials and their records and the reasons for those records would occupy far too much space, so here I shall make just a few points. Muscovy compiled and kept various records on slaves primarily to garner the revenues such activities generated, and to have evidence for conflict resolution over and control of the slave population. At some point it also began to try to keep lists of war captives so that they could be returned at the time of a peace settlement. No general census of slaves was taken, nor were they included in regular censuses, for such instruments were laboriously compiled to record only those who paid taxes and later were liable for military service. In the Ancient Near East, on the other hand, registers of slaves were kept so that chattel could be forced, along with free men, to render corvée.[36] Muscovy never demanded anything of slaves, who on that account were the purest form of private property, and when the government did resolve to ask for something (taxes, in 1679 and 1722), records were kept, but the consequence was to abolish slavery by merging the slaves with the serfs. The sole partial exception to the general governmental policy of excepting slaves from statistical compendia was the result of military convenience, when combat and baggage-train slaves were occasionally listed (by number, never by name) along with their owners in provincial muster lists, and when slaves capable of bearing arms were listed (often how many, sometimes as individuals) in the Moscow military census of 1638. Enumeration in the former was at the discretion of the compiler and the latter document was apparently unique, so they are hardly exceptions to the general rule that the government statistically ignored the slaves living in its domain.

The attention that Muscovite officialdom devoted to developing and maintaining a network of offices and officers to run the slavery system is indicative of the

33. 1649 *Ulozhenie* 20: 94; MS, p. 289. It was also possible for litigants to feed the contested slave held in the custody of a bailiff (1649 *Ulozhenie* 20: 112; MS, p. 296). These articles were taken from a statute dated 1630 in the UKMSP, art. 5.

34. 1649 *Ulozhenie* 20: 102; MS, p. 292.

35. Rose, pp. 183, 188.

36. Mendelsohn, p. 99.

important place the institution of slavery occupied. Other concerns, such as war and taxation, were more pressing than was slavery, but the latter was unquestionably one of the primary second-level interests of early modern Russians. No other society, to my knowledge, had a central organ comparable to the Slavery Chancellery. Moreover, the Muscovite provincial administration of slavery was as well developed as that found anywhere else. This concern for administration of the slave system can be explained as a manifestation of the general Muscovite tendency to solve problems by resort to administrative measures, by the fact that perhaps a tenth of the entire population was composed of slaves (this made the institution important), and by the fact that the majority of the slaves were natives. How these factors should be rank-ordered is anybody's guess.

Part II   The Sociology of
                           Slavery

10. The Image of the Slave, Slave Prices, and the Domestic Slave Trade

The Image of the Slave

Students of slavery in the New World have recently carried out several studies of the image of the slave, largely in an attempt to explain present-day problems. History itself has given us several homologisms for slaves, the most prominent of them being women, children, and animals. Less prominent analogies for the slave have been the apprentice, the pauper, the harlot. The scholars have created for us the equivalent of a concentration camp inmate, the complex image of "Sambo," and I am putting forth the late-twentieth-century dependent American welfare recipient as perhaps the most suitable Muscovite equivalent.

In many societies slaves, women, and children were discussed in similar terms because all were dependent upon the adult males who defined society, its members, and social roles. Frederick Pryor, in his seminal article, "A Comparative Study of Slave Societies," observed the frequent homologisms between wife and slave, the role of both being to relieve the husband of work and to provide him with an opportunity to exercise power, and the fact that in the Bismarck Archipelago male slaves were required to dress as women.[1] Slaves were equated with women (and also with metics, alien residents) in Athens, where none of them had the right to appear before the assembly (the *boule*).[2] In Han China "slave" is a later derivation from the original meaning of "child" or "wife and children."[3] In South China in the early twentieth century, slaves were considered to be stupid, uneducable, and childlike.[4]

Among the Hausa, the slave had the status of a legal minor, like free women and children.[5] The ancient Indians, in the *Laws of Manu*, expressed this view several times: "A wife, a son, and a slave, these three are declared to have no property; the wealth which they earn is aquired for him to whom they belong."[6] The Indians denied the slave the right to be a witness along with "one of bad

---

1. Frederick L. Pryor, "A Comparative Study of Slave Societies," *Journal of Comparative Economics* 1, no. 1(March 1977): 45.
2. Westermann, p. 17.
3. Pulleyblank, pp. 194-95.
4. James L. Watson, "Chattel Slavery in Chinese Peasant Society: A Comparative Analysis," *Ethnology* 15, no. 4(October 1976): 365-66.
5. M. G. Smith, p. 127.
6. *Laws of Manu*, pp. 416-17.

fame, . . . one who follows forbidden occupations, an aged person, an infant, . . . one deficient in organs of sense, a woman. . . . "[7] Finally, reflecting the household nature of Indian slavery, the lawgiver said: "With his father and his mother, with female relatives, with a brother, with his son and his wife, with his daughter, and with his slaves, let him not have quarrels."[8]

Of all the analogies, the Muscovites would have found the female one most acceptable. In the expanded redaction of the *Russkaia Pravda* the article on the killing of a slave (89) was placed after the statute on the killing of a woman (88), and both were under the section "On Women." The mid-sixteenth-century work *Household Management* (*Domostroi*) was completely in keeping with the traditional dependent image of the slave:

> The master himself must teach his wife and children and slaves [*domochadtsy*] not to steal, deceive, lie, slander, envy, bear grudges, malign, be inhospitable to strangers, be grasping, rebel, mock, dwell upon evil, or be wrathful to another person, but to be obedient and submissive to the great, loving to the middling, and considerate and merciful to the weak and the wretched.[9]

Another chapter lectures both wives and slaves on drunkenness.[10] Other sections of the *Domostroi* on the directing and managing of slaves persist in viewing them as educable but probably low-grade human beings.

While there was significant evolution in the condition of the slave between, say, 1450 and 1650, the *Ulozhenie* still retained the view of the slave as womanlike (or childlike), at least occasionally. Thus chapter 22, on felonies, discussed first patricide, the killing of children by their parents, various insults by children to their parents, fratricide and soricide, and then the killing by a slave of his owner and the assault by a slave against his owner (articles 8 and 9). In this context, the slave is the last member of the household. More to the point is the article on interrogations, where "slaves, peasants, and females" are "to be interrogated under the sovereign's oath before a divine icon in all cases so that they will tell the truth, as though they were standing at Christ's Last Judgment."[11]

The view of the slave as like a child was expounded in Babylonia, the Danish Virgin Islands, and upon occasion in the U. S. South.[12] This view was expressed in the Byzantine *Ecloga*, which circulated in Muscovy, and also in the Bulgarian *Court Law for the People* (*Zakon sudnyi liudem*), which was also known in Rus'.[13] That view is not totally alien to either the *Domostroi* or the *Ulozhenie*, as we have just seen.

7. Ibid., pp. 66, 70.
8. Ibid., p. 180; Nancy E. Levine, p. 210.
9. A. Orlov, ed., *Domostroi*, pt. 2, p. 18, chap. 21.
10. Ibid., p. 34, chap. 36.
11. 1649 *Ulozhenie* 10: 173.
12. Pritchard, p. 140, art. 7; Driver and Miles, 1: 85; Hall, p. 177; Rose, pp. 190, 221..
13. *Ecloga* 14: 4 and 5 (Freshfield, pp. 96-97); Short ZSL 20; Expanded ZSL 22. See also

The other popular homologism for slaves was animals. The view was expressed in Mesopotamian Eshnunna and Babylonia, where the slave was equated, in various contexts, with an ox, donkey, or sheep. This was also articulated in the tags and markings put on both slaves and various animals.[14] In the T'ang period of Chinese history, slaves were equated with domestic animals and property.[15] In medieval Siena, Italy, the same fine was paid for damaging a slave and a cow. Islam also equated the slave and animal as classes of property that the owner was required to maintain.[16] The basic analogy in the West Russian *Lithuanian Statute* of 1529 was also between slave and cattle. There, as in Hindu and Roman law, some slaves were grouped with the land in the law, were seen as part of the estate, no doubt accounting for such an image.[17]

While the Muscovites valued the horse and the slave similarly, in other respects the animal analogy probably had little life in Muscovy because most of the slaves were natives, not "dumb" outsiders. Nevertheless, there is a sense of value and interrelationship between human beings and animals expressed in the 1628 complaint by the service landholder Grigorii Shurinov against the forces of *boiarin* I. N. Romanov, who stole from him: over two dozen peasants and their families; the peasants' movable property; Shurinov's male house slave Sozonko Pashkov; a dozen horses; and finally, Shurinov's female house slave Oniutka.[18] In general, this is probably a fair seventeenth-century Muscovite ranking: peasants, peasant property, male slaves, horses, female slaves.

The Middle Assyrian treatment of the slave girl as a harlot (both had to appear unveiled in public places) would have been inappropriate because prostitution was not legalized in Muscovy. More appropriate would have been the equation of

the Byzantine *O poslusekh* (*Witnesses*, part of the *Knigi zakonnye*), arts. 19, 21, 25, 27, 28. The nexus between wives, children, the family, and slaves was discussed by Catherine the Great in her 1783 *Book on the Duties of Man and Citizen*, as translated by Elizabeth Gorky in J. L. Black, *Citizens for the Fatherland. Education, Educators, and Pedagogical Ideals in Eighteenth Century Russia* (Boulder: East European Quarterly, 1979), pp. 237-38.

14. Mendelsohn, p. 47; Pritchard, p. 137, arts. 40, 50; p. 140, art. 7.

15. Pulleyblank, p. 212; Wallace Johnson, ed., *The T'ang Code*, vol. 1, *General Principles* (Princeton: Princeton University Press, 1979), p. 29.

16. D. B. Davis, *Western Culture*, p. 61; Brunschvig, p. 26; Charles Hamilton, *The Hedaya, or Guide. A Commentary on the Mussulman Laws* (New Delhi: Kitab Bhavan, 1979), pp. 149-50.

17. K. I. Iablonskis, ed., *Statut velikogo kniazhestva litovskogo 1529 goda* (Minsk: Akademiia nauk BSSR, 1960), pp. 54, 64, 84, 121; IV, extra article; V: [8]7, VII: 7, XII: 7 and 8; Lionel Caplan, p. 171; Hjejle, "South India," pp. 75, 84.

18. E. D. Stashevskii, "K istorii kolonizatsii Iuga. (Velikii boiarin Ivan Nikitich Romanov i ego slobody v Eletskom uezde)," *Drevnosti. Trudy Arkheograficheskoi kommissii imp. Moskovskogo arkheologicheskogo obshchestva* 3(1913): 273. The 1627 last testament of Panteleimon Misiur' Solovtsov essentially equated slaves and animals. He prayed that the Lord would multiply his son's estates and villages and fill up his house with male and female slaves and sundry cattle (*da razbogateet dom ego raby i rabyniami i skoty vsiakimi*) (AIuB 1: 559, no. 86).

the slave with the pauper, as was occasionally done in the U. S.[19] While pauperism was at the root of perhaps most Muscovite slavery, the analogy could not very well be made because the early modern Russians were only on the threshold of dealing with the problem of poverty in any fashion and had hardly intellectualized the problem at all. If someone was in trouble, he could beg, sell himself into slavery, or starve to death. Other options were not yet considered.

In addition to these homologisms, free people usually express other forms of contempt for slaves. Probably nowhere were slaves more despised than among the Northwest Coast Indians, where they simply were thought to be outside the social system completely, incapable of ever attaining any social status, with whom marriage was unthinkable, and completely disposable in a potlach or other exhibition of contempt for property.[20] This view was extreme; elsewhere they were simply regarded as a subspecies of human being—childlike, womanlike, idle, slow as workers, boorish, lascivious, untrustworthy, and so on. This view, especially in Africa, was (and in fact still is) passed on to freedmen and their heirs.[21]

Views differentiating slaves from free men are hard to come by for Muscovy because of the society's general lack of reflectiveness and absence of intellectual tradition. Nevertheless, some images come through in the literature. As is typical in many other systems, the Muscovite slave was viewed in the *Domostroi* as perhaps more likely to prevaricate and slander than were free people.[22] The slave was also viewed as a natural prevaricator by one of the parties in the 1643 case of Miakinin v. Velkov: "There is nothing to believe when a fugitive slave is talking, for he is free to say whatever he pleases [without the slightest regard for the truth]."[23] We must bear in mind, however, the discussion in chapter 8, where it was shown that the Muscovite slave was allowed to be a witness in litigation far more frequently than in most slave-owning societies. Nowhere, to my knowledge, is it said that the slave will automatically lie simply because he is a slave. The Balkan immigrant Ivan Peresvetov, advising Ivan IV in the mid-sixteenth century to reform his army, noted that many Muscovite cavalrymen were slaves and recommended the phasing out of slave soldiers because of their basic fault, cowardice.[24]

Another immigrant, Iurii Krizhanich, a century later observed that slavery was a manifestation of sin, one of the social instruments for controlling and compelling insolent and disobedient human nature. He concluded that "while Russia

19. Mendelsohn, p. 61; Friedman, p. 187.
20. Siegel, p. 366.
21. Rose, pp. 204, 216; Miers and Kopytoff, p. 290; Wergeland, p. 17.
22. Orlov, *Domostroi*, p. 20, chap. 22.
23. "I tomu verit' nechem: beglomu kholopu vol'no skazattsa, chem khochet." Iakovlev, *Kholopstvo*, p. 502, no. 25, III.
24. I. S. Peresvetov, *Sochineniia* (Moscow-Leningrad: Akademiia nauk SSSR, 1956), pp. 174-75.

preserves its law of slavery, during that time, by the grace of God, it will succeed in preserving its greatness, liberty, and independence. But if the law of slavery someday should fall, then danger will arise, and such disorders, licentious morals, xenarchy, and ignominy in the eyes of others as have befallen the Poles will overtake the Russian people."[25]

Another view is that slavery is shameful, particulary in its contamination of descendants and those who have contact with slaves. This view was expressed early in Russian history, when Feodosii, founder of the Kievan Caves monastery, was chided by his mother for working with slaves because it brought reproach upon himself and his relatives.[26] The discomfort felt even by elite, ministerial slaves was noted in the famous late-twelfth-century work, *Lament of Daniel the Exile:*

Just as it is unfitting for a swine to have rings in its ears, so it is for a slave [to be clad] in fine garments. Even if a kettle has gold rings in its ears, its bottom is still black; and so it is for a slave: if he has any reason for pride, his name is still slave.[27]

It is not clear whether, or how, this image of slavery as a source of shame passed through the late medieval period in Rus', but it surfaced again in the second quarter of the seventeenth century. Elsewhere I will discuss defamation suits filed at that time by descendants of slaves who were freed and converted into Novgorod landholding cavalrymen at the end of the fifteenth century. The descendants, publicly shamed by being reminded that their clan was of slave origin, initiated a suit because of the "dishonor" stemming from the accusation and lost when government records revealed that the accusation was correct. This recalls similar situations elsewhere, such as among the Ibo of Nigeria, where slaves were never absorbed into the dominant society and the stigma of slavery has not disappeared.[28]

At this juncture it is only fitting to mention the "counterimage" of the slave, if only to note that such an image hardly existed in Muscovy. The first known writer to stress the humanity of the slave was he who spoke in the person of the philosopher Job:

If I disregard the rights of my male and female slaves when they argue with me, what shall I do when God appears? When he looks upon me, what shall I an-

25. L. M. Mordukhovich, ed., "Iurii Krizhanich o 'rabstve'," *Trudy Otdela drevnerusskoi literatury* 33(1979): 152.

26. Zimin, *Kholopy*, p. 154.

27. Ibid., p. 253.

28. Markevich, p. 168; Watson, *Systems*, p. 11. The contemporary West African attitude toward freedmen was noted by Flora Lewis in *The New York Times* (April 24, 1981, p. A31): "On occasion, others complained somewhat peevishly about American blacks sent as diplomats because 'You ask us to receive these former slaves with high honors'."

swer him? Did not he, who created me in the womb, create him and fashion us equally in the womb?[29]

A couple of centuries later Aristotle noted that the slave was a "kind of possession with a soul."[30] The Romans had a negative attitude toward the institution of slavery, viewing it as a product of war, and thus as accidental, not a condition that was naturally fitting for any man. For this reason, the Romans viewed any slave as capable of freedom. A millennium later, this view was expressed in a more developed form in the Spanish law code compiled between 1263 and 1265, which said that slavery was against natural reason because it was "the most evil and the most despicable thing which can be found among men."[31] The views of the Abolitionists are generally well known, although they were complicated by a strong infusion of racism. Such attitudes toward slavery, found from the time of Job to that of the Abolitionists, were very rarely expressed in Muscovy.

Prices

There is a vast quantity of information about the price of slaves in Muscovy, but making sense of that information presents difficulties. In this section I shall begin a general discussion of prices, which will then be continued in later chapters under other rubrics, such as the origins and occupations of slaves, slave demography, and the slaveowners and their incomes.

As we have seen, Muscovy.was not alien to the idea of the legal regulation of the institution of slavery, of which slave prices were a constituent part. Government regulation of slave prices in Byzantium went back to the time of Justinian, and was repeated in the *Procheiros Nomos* (34:11), a code well known in Muscovy as the *gradskii zakon*.[32] Whether this had any direct influence on the Muscovite regulation of slave prices is unknown.

The first such limitation in Muscovy was in article 78 of the *Sudebnik* of 1550, which placed a 15-ruble maximum on the amount that could be paid to a borrower who was going to serve for the interest, i.e., a limited service contract slave. This provision was repeated in the *Sudebnik* of 1589 (article 141) and the *Composite Sudebnik* of 1606 (article 77).[33] A decision was handed down on September 1, 1558, asserting that no trial was to be granted if a limited service

29. Job 31: 13-15.
30. Westermann, p. 15.
31. Klein, *Americas*, p. 59.
32. Udal'tsova, p. 6; Charles Verlinden, *L'esclavage dans l'Europe médiévale* (Ghent, 1977), 2: 50; Caplan noted that slave prices were statutorily fixed in nineteenth-century Nepal (p. 176).
33. Grekov, *Sudebniki*, pp. 169, 399; PRP 4: 512.

slavery contract for more than 15 rubles was presented.[34] No limited service slavery contract for more than 15 rubles seems to be extant, so the law was obviously enforced effectively. Most contracts were for much less, as we shall see.

There is no firm consensus as to why the 15-ruble maximum was enacted in 1550. V. I. Sergeevich linked this with article 91, which forbade merchants to live on monastery land, and saw it as an attempt to avoid competition with the old institution of mortgaging onself, *zakladnichestvo*.[35] The more popular thesis is that such a limit was enacted to regulate the bidding for elite slaves, especially those willing to serve as military retainers. The problem with that hypothesis is that the real scramble for military retainers presumably began only after 1550 in connection with the 1556 law requiring that all land (both service land, *pomest'e*, and patrimonial land, *votchina*) provide cavalrymen, one for each 100 cheti.[36] A struggle for competent warriors after 1556 would explain the 1558 judicial ruling, which indicates that 1550 limitation had been ignored.

The next step in the direction of price regulation was taken at some time around the end of the Time of Troubles, when a law seems to have been passed stating that 2 rubles had to be paid for each slave in the limited service slavery contract. Until that time, there had been no minimum that had to be paid for a slave, and "the market" had determined every price under the 15-ruble maximum. The sum of 2 rubles was less than a single slave previously had ordinarily cost, but often amounted to more than a married couple had been paid for selling themselves in the sixteenth century, and almost certainly more than a family had received. This enactment almost certainly had an impact on the demographic composition of slavery, making it harder for families to find buyers. Be that as it may, 2 rubles was too low a price for a single slave, and about the mid-1620s the official price was raised to 3 rubles for each slave in a document. The 2- and 3-ruble prices coexisted for a few years, and then the latter became the norm accepted by everyone. The *Ulozhenie* of 1649 stated that 3 rubles was the legal sum.[37] This price ceiling may have stimulated the revival of the indenture.

Three rubles remained the standard sum until 1680, when documents appeared that listed no sums at all. The government issued some decrees in 1680 forbidding the listing of principal or interest sums in the slavery documents, but apparently it was either not a universal decree or was not heeded everywhere. The practice of listing no sums coexisted with the 3-ruble per person norm until 1691, which was the last date (to my knowledge) a price was listed in a limited service slavery contract, when 6 rubles were paid for a widow and her four-year-old son. My data set contains contracts without prices down to 1701.[38]

34. AI 1: 264, no. 154, xii.

35. Sergeevich, *Drevnosti*, 1: 161.

36. Tatishchev, IR, 6: 253, 255; 7: 262, 332-36; Paneiakh, "Opyt," p. 552.

37. 1649 *Ulozhenie* 20: 19.

38. AIuB 1: 98, 598, 2: 32-34, 37; I. D. Beliaev, "Zakony i akty, ustanavlivaiushchie v drevnei Rusi krepostnoe sostoianie," *Arkhiv istoricheskikh i prakticheskikh svedenii, ot-*

The disappearance of stated prices from the contracts has never been explained. This is a relatively important matter, for it touches on the basic issue of why Muscovites sold themselves (particularly for so little money), why they needed the money once they had sold themselves, whether they received the cash sum listed, and what they did with it if they were paid it by the person who bought them. It is tempting to try to associate the occasional disappearance of prices in 1680 with the essential abolition of agricultural slavery after the census of 1678-79, but the actual linkage, causal and otherwise, if any, remains veiled. The coexistence of stated prices and no prices between 1680 and 1691 indicates that during those years some slaves were getting the cash while others were not. One may further assume that prior to 1680 most persons who sold themselves got the money, but that perhaps some of them did not. By 1680, however, as society became rigidly stratified, increasingly freedmen were the sole Muscovites who could become slaves, and apparently the interested parties felt that there was little sense in their being paid to sell themselves back into slavery. After 1691, "self-sales" for no stated cash became universal. That is what the government seems to have expected freedmen to do. It is perhaps significant that of the 42 extant slavery sale-documents from the 1680-91 period, 10 of the 11 for whom a sum is listed were stated to have been free before selling themselves, the eleventh was a manumitted slave. Of the 31 for whom no prices are given, 15 seem to have been free previously, 9 had been slaves, and the status of the remaining 7 is unknown. This seems to indicate that those who received money when they sold themselves in the 1680s probably had been free men, and that freedmen were considerably less likely to receive money for selling themselves. Once again, this expresses the dependency that slavery was likely to create in slaves, who had little option other than to resell themselves.

The legal material discussed in the previous chapters legislated a number of slave prices that I might summarize for the sake of comparison with the actual prices paid for slaves. Starting at the bottom, a Petrine edict of 1722 stated a

---

nos. k Rossii, 1859, bk. 2: 100; M. A. D'iakonov, Sel'skoe naselenie Moskovskogo gosudarstva v XVI-XVII vv. (St. Petersburg, 1898), p. 135; Rukopisnyi otdel Gosudarstvennoi publichnoi biblioteki im. Saltykova-Shchedrina, Obshchee sobranie gramot, nos. 3833, 3926, 4117, documents provided by Peter B. Brown; Materialy istoricheskie i iuridicheskie raiona byvshego prikaza Kazanskogo dvortsa, 6: 85; I. Preobrazhenskii and N. Al'bitskii, Podrobnaia opis' 962 rukopisiam nachala XVII do nachala XIX stoletii 'Linevskogo arkhiva' (St. Petersburg, 1895), pp. 38-39; Russkii Vestnik, 1841, vol. 3: 477-78; N. N. Selifontov, Podrobnaia opis' 440 rukopisiam XVII, XVIII i nachala XIX stol. pervogo sobraniia 'Linevskogo arkhiva' s dvumia prilozheniiami (St. Petersburg, 1891), p. 32; idem, Podrobnaia opis' 272 rukopisiam kontsa XVI do nachala XIX st. vtorogo (shevliaginskogo) sobraniia 'Linevskogo arkhiva' (St. Petersburg, 1892), p. 20; Trudy Orlovskoi uchenoi arkhivnoi komissii 6(1889): 16-18; Trudy Saratovskoi uchenoi arkhivnoi komissii 25:80; Vladimirskie gubernskie vedomosti 1858, no. 7, unofficial section, p. 28, no. 12; Lappo-Danilevskii, "Sluzhilye kabaly," pp. 758, 760. For a discussion of the new form for limited service slavery contracts sent to governors in 1680, see Veretennikov, "K istorii kabal'nogo kholopstva," p. 162.

negative price of 10 rubles for raising children.[39] The most realistic nonpunitive, trouble-solving price for a single slave at the time of the *Ulozhenie* was 10 rubles, payable when fugitive slaves of different owners married and the masters cast lots to decide ownership, the winner getting the couple in exchange for 10 rubles to the loser.[40] This may have been set somewhat high so that the owner who lost his slave would have no complaint. A heterodox slave could buy his freedom for 15 rubles if he would convert to Orthodoxy. This provision noted that exaggerated sums were registered in purchase documents, and claimed that no foreigner could possibly be worth more that 15 rubles. Again, the sum was set high enough so that no expropriated owner could possibly have any complaint.[41]

Another group of slave prices was clearly punitive, all for 50 rubles. That was the sum a person who guaranteed a slave might have to pay if the slave fled.[42] The person who aided a fugitive in his escape might also have to compensate the rightful owner in the amount of 50 rubles.[43] The government was probably thinking in similar terms when it stated that a frontier serviceman could keep his fugitive slave wife if he would pay 50 rubles. This article embodies the ambivalence the government felt about populating the frontier in the first half of the seventeenth century: on the one hand, the expanding frontier had to be populated, but on the other the heartland could not afford to lose people to populate the frontier. That this sum was clearly punitive was tacitly stated in the 1680s when the government required *strel'tsy* to pay only 10 rubles apiece to keep fugitive slave women.[44]

The most realistic price of all for a lower-class human being in Muscovy was the 4 rubles placed on the life of a murdered peasant. An identical sum was established in 1558 as the amount a guarantor had to pay a slaveowner in case a disputed slave on bond escaped during a trial.[45] The 1558 law seems to have been largely forgotten in the seventeenth century.

The pricing of slaves in some systems is very precise. For example, a knowledgeable onlooker in New Orleans in 1850 could probably predict with an error of no more than 20 percent, plus or minus, how much a slave on the sale-block would sell for.[46] That kind of precision is unattainable for Muscovy, where the student is confined to looking for patterns and general regularities.

39. PSZ 6: 638, no. 3939.
40. 1649 *Ulozhenie* 20: 115; MS, p. 298.
41. 1649 *Ulozhenie* 20: 71.
42. Ibid., 20: 91.
43. Ibid., 20: 27; MS, p. 265.
44. 1649 *Ulozhenie* 20: 51; MS, pp. 273-74.
45. PRP 5: 210; 1649 *Ulozhenie* 11: 25; MS, pp. 159, 228; UKVK, no. 14 (Vladimirskii-Budanov, 3: 27).
46. Laurence J. Kotlikoff, "The Structure of Slave Prices in New Orleans, 1804 to 1862," *Economic Inquiry* 17(October 1979): 502-10. See also Fogel and Engerman, *Time on the Cross*, 1: 72. Verlinden, *L'esclavage*, 2: 625-36.

Certain structural regularities become apparent when one examines the slave price systems. These prices were usually paid for an individual or a nuclear family, and occasionally for other groupings. Almost never were extended families involved. Table 10.1 shows the range of prices paid for slaves, ranging from a half-ruble to 200 rubles. Almost all, however, were for 15 rubles or less, with the median price just over 3 rubles. The table also shows the tendency for prices to be in round numbers. Table 10.2 shows the structure of prices paid per slave. The figures are arrived at by dividing the sums in table 10.1 by the number of slaves in each transaction. The utility of the data on price per slave is limited, although it is useful in pointing to some of the structural regularities of the system of slave prices. The prevalence of round numbers is again notable. The relationship between the price paid per document and the price paid per slave in each document is quite strong (r = 0.68; N = 2,192), but it is useful to bear in mind that the relationship is by no means linear.

TABLE 10.1
Amounts Paid per Document for Muscovite Slaves

Sum (rubles)	N	%
0.50	1	0.0
1.00	248	11.3
1.50	11	0.5
2.00	581	26.5
2.25	1	0.0
2.50	4	0.2
2.75	1	0.0
3.00	419	19.1
3.50	3	0.1
4.00	152	6.9
5.00	481	21.9
6.00	69	3.1
6.67	1	0.0
7.00	47	2.1
7.25	1	0.0
8.00	32	1.5
9.00	8	0.4
10.00	80	3.6
12.00	8	0.4
15.00	37	1.7
25.00	1	0.0
30.00	1	0.0
50.00	3	0.1
70.00	1	0.0
200.00	1	0.0
3.02 (Median)	2,192 (Total)	100.0
Documents without prices	307	

TABLE 10.2
The Structure of Prices Paid Per Slave

Price (rubles)	N	%
0.14–0.43	27	1.3
0.50	90	4.1
0.56–0.88	137	6.1
1.00	433	19.8
1.14–1.43	69	3.2
1.50	72	3.3
1.60–1.75	54	2.4
2.00	372	17.0
2.25–2.40	15	0.7
2.50	141	6.4
2.67–2.75	7	0.3
3.00	302	13.8
3.33–3.75	36	1.6
4.00–4.50	79	3.6
5.00	249	11.4
6.00–8.33	55	2.6
10.00	36	1.6
15.00	14	0.6
17.50–50.00	4	0.2
Mean = 2.58	Total 2,192	100.0
Median = 2.00		
Mode = 1.00		

Table 10.3 presents the price per document paid, differentiating the different types of slavery instruments in which slaves were sold. The full, registered, limited, and purchase documents were in one price category, the debt slavery and indenture instruments in another. Of special interest is the ratio between the average cost of the documents by each type of slavery and the mean cost of each slave in the documents. Once again, the similarity between full (61.2), registered (61.2), and limited service contract (67.3) slaveries is striking, as is that between

TABLE 10.3
Prices of Muscovite Slaves by Types of Enslavement Instrument

Type of Document	Price per Document (Rubles)	Price per Slave in Document (Rubles)	Ratios–Price per Slave/Price per Document	N
Full slavery	3.23	1.98	61.2	99
Registered slavery	3.07	1.89	61.2	27
Limited service slavery contract	3.80	2.56	67.3	2,033
Purchase	4.25	4.14	97.4	7
Debt slavery	21.67	7.78	35.9	3
Indenture	75.00	25.00	33.5	5

debt (35.9) and indenture (33.3). Table 10.4 shows a slightly larger picture, for it includes slaves for whom prices were given in instruments other than sale documents, such as court records.

TABLE 10.4
Type of Slave by Price, in Rubles

Type of Slave	Price per Document	Price per Slave	Ratio	N
Full	3.32	2.12	63.7%	107
Registered	3.07	1.89	61.2	27
Limited service contract	3.84	2.56	66.8	2,049

One of the fundamental contributions of this work is to show the extent to which full and limited service contract slavery were successive institutions. This is evident in table 10.5, where we can see a quite remarkable similarity in the individual sums expended on the two types of slaves.

TABLE 10.5
Cost per Document, in Rubles

	Full Slavery		Limited Service Contract Slavery	
Cost	N Cases	% of All Cases	% of All Cases	N Cases
1	12	12.2	11.2	228
1.50	8	8.2	–	–
2	26	26.5	26.8	544
3	21	21.4	19.2	389
4	7	7.1	6.8	139
5	8	8.2	23.1	470
6	4	4.1	3.1	62
7	–	–	2.2	45
8	4	4.1	1.3	26
9	–	–	.4	8
10	2	2.0	3.6	73
12	–	–	.2	5
15	1	1.0	1.8	36

Note:
A small number of fractional cases have been omitted.

A further attempt to probe the meaning of slavery prices is made in table 10.6. There the three basic types of slavery are compared by examining the average amount paid per document (and later per slave). The general rule for all three types of slavery is that more slaves cost more money. The relationship was strongest of all ($r = 0.839$) when each slaveowner's total expenditures are considered in terms of the total number of slaves he purchased. By type of slavery,

TABLE 10.6
Slave Prices, in Rubles, by Types of Slavery and Number of Slaves per Document

No. of Slaves per Document	Full Slavery			Registered Slavery			Limited Service Contract Slavery		
	Price Paid per Document	N	Interval Ratios	Price Paid per Document	N	Interval Ratios	Price Paid per Document	N	Interval Ratios
1	2.63	52	1:2 = 56%	2.21	17	1:2 = 64%	3.43	1,072	1:2 = 54%
2	2.94	24	1:3 = 38%	2.83	3	1:3 = 50%	3.69	492	1:3 = 44%
3	3.00	2		3.33	3		4.56	245	
4	4.00	13		5.67	3		4.65	137	
5	4.00	2		—			5.69	54	
6	6.50	2		—			5.86	21	
7	8.33	3		10.00	1		4.60	10	
8	8.00	1		—			3.00	1	
9	—			—			5.00	1	
	Mean = 3.23	99		3.07	27		3.80	2,033	
	r = 0.50			r = 0.65			r = 0.21		

No. of Slaves per Document	Full Slavery		Registered Slavery		Limited Service Contract Slavery	
	Price Paid per Slave	Interval Ratios	Price Paid per Slave	Interval Ratios	Price Paid per Slave	Interval Ratios
1	2.63	1:2 = 56%	2.21	1:2 = 64%	3.43	1:2 = 54%
2	1.47	1:3 = 38%	1.42	1:3 = 50%	1.85	1:3 = 44%
3	1.00		1.11		1.52	
4	1.00		1.42		1.16	
5	0.80		—		1.14	
6	1.08		—		0.98	
7	1.19		1.43		0.66	
8	1.00		—		0.38	
9	—		—		0.56	
	Mean = 1.98		1.88		2.56	
	r = -0.39		r = -0.19		r = -0.40	

the relationship between price paid and number of slaves purchased was strongest for registered slavery, and weakest for limited service contract slavery. The relationship would be stronger for the latter if one stopped at six slaves per document. The bottom half of table 10.6 shows that each successive slave usually cost less, down to the eighth one in the case of limited service contract slaves. Also striking in that table are the interval ratios for all three types of slaves between the price for one slave and a second slave, or between one slave and three slaves. It is also somewhat evident that, after the first person in a contract, the third person is most important in determining the price, especially for limited service contract slaves. This fact became evident in regression analysis, and will be discussed further in chapter 18. For the time being, I shall only note that the major determinant of price was the father, the second determinant was the first child, and the mother and subsequent children made less difference.

It is noteworthy that the price structure of contemporaneous full and limited service contract slavery documents was so similar. While they were competing institutions, between 1510 and 1554, the mean price of the 52 extant full slavery documents was 3.69 rubles, the median price 2.98 rubles, and the mode prices 2.00 and 3.00 rubles. For the 9 extant limited service slavery contracts of the same period, the respective sums were 3.33, 2.67, and 2.00 and 3.00 rubles. The median price of each full slave was 2.00 rubles, of each limited service contract slave 2.03 rubles. Almost certainly contemporaries considered them to be similar instruments. One may assume other similarities as well, one of which was that full slaves fled with the same frequency that later limited service contract slaves did, and that the earliest buyers of limited service contract slaves expected them to default, which would convert them into full slaves.

The annual average fluctuations in the prices of slaves (both per document and per slave in each document) are shown in figure 10.1. The general movement is a rise in prices from the fifteenth century to the Oprichnina years of Ivan IV's reign. The drop in 1581 may show a glut of slaves resulting from the temporary success in the generally failing Livonian War. The next peak is in 1592, the year the Forbidden Years were instituted and in general a very bad year for Muscovy.[47] After that prices fell continuously until the glut produced by the 1601-3 famine, and then they rose in the seventeenth century with the institution of mandatory prices. The spread between the top and bottom lines represents the varying numbers of slaves per document. (The number of cases for sixteenth-century years in figure 10.1 can be found in the "N" column of table 10.7. For the remainder, N = 57 for 1430-1500, 1 for 1601, 88 for 1602, 654 for 1603, 18 for 1606-26, and 61 for 1630-1714.)

47. Hellie, *Enserfment*, pp. 98-99.

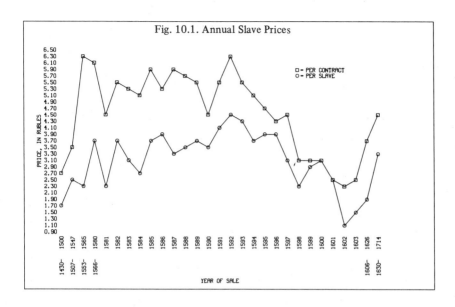

Fig. 10.1. Annual Slave Prices

The general fall in the price level in the 1580s and 1590s is striking, especially if one would like to believe that slaves were used appreciably in farming. At some time between 1584 and about 1590, a law was passed making seignorial demesne, that land belonging to or assigned to a lord and farmed for him personally, exempt from taxation. There is almost no question that this caused an increase in demesne, as lords took for their own land which previously had been farmed exclusively by peasants, and from which the lords had collected rent and paid taxes. The question has been where the lords got the labor to farm their increased demesne. They could not do it themselves, for they were usually in military service during most of the farming season, and therefore others had to farm it for them. One answer has been that the change in ownership (or possession) was only nominal, that the peasants continued to till the land as before, saving on taxes and probably paying higher rent. In a sense, it was a form of corvée labor, but again only nominally, for really little had changed. The other answer was that the increased demesne was farmed by slaves.[48] This issue will be discussed further in chapter 14, but here the obvious point will be made that such a demand for slaves should have raised the price. Instead, as we see, the price fell. This would tend to indicate that the demand was not for slaves as agricultural workers, and therefore one should not be at all surprised that the making of demesne tax-exempt had little if any impact on the price for slaves.

48. V. M. Paneiakh, "K sporam o kholop'em nadele v XVI veke," *Istoriia SSSR* 1973, no. 3: 57-63; G. V. Abramovich, "Novgorodskoe pomest'e v gody ekonomicheskogo krizisa poslednei treti XVI v.," *Materialy po istorii sel'skogo khoziaistva i krest'ianstva SSSR* 8(1974): 14.

TABLE 10.7
Indices of Prices of Slaves, Rye, and Composite Grains (Rye, Oats, and Barley) for the Sixteenth Century

Year	Slaves	(N)	Rye	Grains	Livestock
1500	53	2	15	20	36
1501	53	3			
1502	26	1			
1503	79	1			
1504	53	1		19	34
1507	40	2		[1505]	34
1508	79	2			
1509	26	3			
15.10	69	5			
1511	87	5			
1512	46	2			
1513	106	1			
1514	92	2			
1515	60	4			
1516	53	2			
1517	79	7	48	48	
1518	66	2			
1519	106	1			
1520	106	3	38	38	
1521	53	1			
1523	219	1			
1524	168	3	15	22	44
1525	79	3			
1526	101	3			
1527	99	4			
1528	53	1			
1529	79	1			
1531	86	2			
1532	132	2	66	37	
1533	132	1			
1534	26	1			
1536	330	2			
1546	79	1			
1547	132	1			[1550] 70
1553	79	1	101	103	[1552] 82
1554	79	1	100	84	82
1557	264	1	106	106	138
1563	145	2	114	114	71
1564	264	1	69	64	
1565	219	1	60	57	64
1566	52	1	57	57	
1567	99	4	69	49	63
1568	165	4	86	99	60
1569	159	1	76	100	71
1570	132	1	519 (sic)	435	100
1571	132	9	108	304 (sic)	

Year	Slaves	(N)	Rye	Grains	Livestock
1572	159	3	103	92	129
1573	205	4	79	79	92
1574	145	2	74	74	97
1575	203	6	77	94	58
1576	159	6	55	67	66
1577	182	8	55	49	120
1578	137	6	56	55	94
1579	221	6	77	66	123
1580	138	9	90	90	43
1581	114	17	87	94	83
1582	144	20	120	120	94
1583	142	37	121	136	114
1584	139	44	129	146	106
1585	159	53	129	146	64
1586	137	34	118	126	92
1587	159	8	158	152	139
1588	147	32	182	179	68
1589	144	48	171	138	90
1590	115	14	126	126	
1591	146	29	140	127	
1592	171	21	117	122	167
1593	149	57	102	92	
1594	130	121	62	54	109
1595	123	171		78	101
1596	116	133	72	69	67
1597	119	155	88	85	100
1598	79	7	100	100	90
1599	80	45	92	96	100
1600	79	115	100	100	

Note:
Slaves, 100 = 3.78 rubles, the average cost of all slave contracts; grains, prices in 1600 = 100; livestock, price in 1597-1600 = 100 (from Man'kov, *Tseny*, pp. 114-15, 118-19, 136-37).

An attempt is made in table 10.7 and figure 10.2 to index the price of slaves and compare that index with grain and livestock indices prepared for the sixteenth century by A. G. Man'kov, the Leningrad historian. (I am not aware of comparable indices for the fifteenth and seventeenth centuries.) What is evident is that, crudely, the prices of slaves followed the price of grain, and was considerably less sensitive to those forces that dictated the price of livestock. This is not at all surprising. As is well known, livestock prices, historically, have been much less volatile and expressive of the cost of living than have grain prices. However, the grain and slave indices do not always move in the same direction, but, on an annual basis, sometimes move in the opposite direction (see, for example, 1584, 1588, 1592, and 1598). This is also not difficult to explain, for the same factors which caused higher grain prices were likely to cause lower slave prices. The most well-known example is the famine of 1601-3 (unfortunately not in

Man'kov's book on prices in the sixteenth century, and therefore not in my tables), when the price of grain went sky-high, and the price of slaves plummeted. A shortage of grain drove the price of grain up and simultaneously drove more people to sell themselves in an attempt to survive, either because they no longer had the means to pay for grain or, in the case of farmers, had none of their own left to eat. Moreover, slaveowners were willing to pay less than usual at such times because of the increased cost of feeding slaves. A somewhat similar situation was observable in Mexico in the eighteenth century, when maize prices and real wages were inversely correlated, when high prices for maize coincided with a decline in demand for labor.[49]

It is also not at all surprising that low prices for slaves, indicating a glut, should coincide in Muscovy with a perceived shortage of labor. Two different pools of people were involved. As we shall see in chapter 11, relatively few agriculturalists sold themselves into slavery. Peasants were not "footloose" but moved only when pushed by disaster: crop failure, war, increased taxes and rent. In consequence of such mobility, lords perceived a labor shortage. The same phenomena produced more slaves, and lower slave prices—people driven by a serious downturn of the economic cycle to sell themselves in hope of survival. This meant not only that less grain could be purchased for the same amount of labor and income but also that there was less charity, less capacity of lords to feed the menials in their households, less work for day laborers. These were the people who sold themselves into slavery in Muscovy.

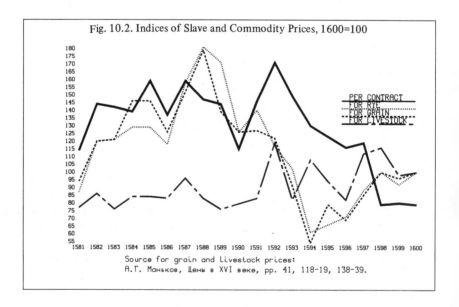

Fig. 10.2. Indices of Slave and Commodity Prices, 1600=100

PER CONTRACT
FOR RYE
FOR GRAIN
FOR LIVESTOCK

Source for grain and livestock prices:
А.Г. Маньков, Цены в XVI веке, pp. 41, 118-19, 138-39.

49. John H. Coastsworth, personal communication, May 7, 1979.

As I have noted previously, a major problem in the discussion of Muscovite slave prices is the determining of patterns and other elements of rationality. Most striking patterns of rationality appear when the limited service slavery contract prices in the eight major extant collections are examined. As one can see in table 10.8, the collections reveal once again the constant fall in prices from the 1580s to the famine of 1603. Even more interesting is the fact that average prices in different places at the same time were only a few kopeks apart.

TABLE 10.8
Average Prices of Limited Service Slavery Contracts in Eight Major Collections

Collection	Average Price, in Rubles	N
1. Lakier (retrospective)	6.13	48
2. RIB 17 (retrospective)	5.27	349
3. Kopanev (retrospective)	5.26	150
4. NZKK 7100-4 (1938-1)	4.69	395
5. NKK 7106 (RIB 15-1)	4.72	102
6. NKK 7108 (RIB 15-2)	2.96	115
7. Egorov 7108 (LZAK 24[1912])	2.91	33
8. NZKK 7111 (1938-2)	2.16	737
Mean of all contracts	3.80	2,033

The three retrospective collections caught the generally higher prices of the pre-1597 period. The next two (4 and 5) reflect the fall of current prices in the mid-1590s, and the next two (6 and 7) the post-1597 further decline by 1599/1600. Collection 8 mirrors the plunge of prices during the Great Famine. The similarities of the grouped pairs (2 and 3, 4 and 5, 6 and 7) would tend to indicate that some kind of a market was working to make prices at about the same time relatively uniform.

Table 10.9 attempts to examine the impact of legislation on the relationship between the number of slaves in a document and the price paid for a group of slaves in a document. Also examined is the assumption that the highest prices may have been paid to purchase quality rather than quantity. In the case of registered slaves, there is a rather strong correlation between quantity and price. This is surprising, considering the fact that most registered slaves were estate stewards, for whom one might assume that the quality of the steward was the important element and that the number of persons in his family would have been irrelevant (a fact that would be expressed with r = 0.0).

TABLE 10.9
Correlation Coefficients of Slaves and Prices Paid for Slaves

Cost	Registered Slaves	Full Slaves	Limited Service Contract Slaves			
			Before 1586	1586-97	1597-1610	1610-92
Under 10 rubles	0.67471 (N = 28)	0.4922 (N = 95)	0.2527 (N = 200)	0.2197 (N = 597)	0.2631 (N = 1077)	0.6304 (N = 70)
Under 15 rubles		0.4908 (N = 97)	0.3110 (N = 226)	0.2300 (N = 648)	0.2805 (N = 1080)	0.7151 (N = 74)
Under 16 rubles		0.4792 (N = 98)	0.3166 (N = 242)	0.2343 (N = 666)	0.2660 (N = 1081)	0.7614 (N = 75)

For full slaves, the correlation coefficient declines as the price increases, indicating that the relationship between price and number of slaves purchased was less for the higher prices than for the lower prices. However, the sample is not large enough to be conclusive, and the changes are so small that they are not of statistical significance.

For limited service contract slaves, the correlation between the price listed and the number of slaves purchased is very strong for the seventeenth century, after 1610. This is expected, for, as we have seen, the government seems to have decreed either a 2- or a 3-ruble price until the 1680s, which is precisely what the numbers tell us—that discreet sums usually were being paid for each slave in a contract.

Most interesting are the limited service slavery contract prices for the century from 1510 to 1610. As we know, in the first period (here, before 1586, the date of the initial major legislation on limited service contract slavery), limited service contract slavery competed with and drove out full slavery. In many respects, as shown throughout this work, the two forms of slavery were much alike. In these particular statistics, however, they are somehow different; the relationship between price paid and number of slaves purchased is stronger for full slaves than for limited service contract slaves. The reason for this difference is unknown.

The impact of the 1586 legislation seems to have been to reduce even further the relationship between quantity and price. Both before and after 1586 quality assumptions in the determination of price for limited service contract slaves seem unwarranted, at least on the gross level I am discussing here. This generally surprising fact will be generally confirmed and elaborated on in chapter 11, where we shall see that a person with skills often commanded no more than a person without. Considering that we are dealing with a system of household slavery, this is not too surprising: a former garment-worker or butcher does not necessarily make a more valuable lackey than does someone who was a beggar before he sold himself into slavery.

The modest increase in apparent price rationality after 1597 is surprising. Also noteworthy is the fact that there were only four slavery contracts for over 10 rubles in the 1597-1610 period, a period, as we have seen, of generally falling slave prices. This is also the period when almost certainly patent fictions appear; when, for example, 5 rubles was stated as the selling price for entire series of slave contracts, regardless of how many people of whatever demographic profile were being sold. This would seem, judging by the published document collections, to be the era of greatest chaos in prices, but in fact it differs little from the pre-1586 period, or the regulated 1586-97 years. [50]

A major reflection of the crisis character of Muscovite full and limited service contract slavery is the seasonal nature of self-sales.[51] As shown in table 10.10, during the severe winter months (December to March), when life was most difficult on the east European plain, the number of persons for sale was the greatest. Over 60 percent of all full slavery and nearly 54 percent of all limited service contract slavery documents were written in that third of the year, and once again it is worth noting the similarity of the two succeeding types of slavery in this respect. For limited service contract slavery, the months August through November are the low third of the year, when only 15 percent of all the documents were written. The pattern is about the same for full slavery (17 percent), but it is not quite so clear because of the low numbers involved. The intermediate months were spring and early summer, April through July. The seasonality of sales indicates that those selling themselves were not people dispossessed from agriculture, for peasants usually were able to survive the months following the harvest and had difficulty only in early summer, when they might run out of grain before a new harvest. Rather, those who sold themselves into slavery were not agriculturalists but individuals who had no food supplies of their own and sensed their crisis with the onset and development of the winter season.

50. I trust these discussions show the probable inaccuracy of I. Novombergskii's claim that the legislation of 1597 caused a drop in slave prices ("Vymuchennye kabaly," p. 302). His thesis was that the expropriation of the owner by the freeing of the slave on the death of the former would naturally cause a fall in the price. The logic is not flawed, but the data do not support the conclusion. While prices had been falling for some time prior to 1597 (along with the price of grain), they did not fall further after 1597 until driven down by the famine of 1601-3. Buyers were aware of the 1597 expropriation, but other factors seem to have been more important in determining what to pay for a slave.

51. One might think that these seasonal results were biased because three of the major documentary collections (Lakier, Kopanev, and RIB 17) that recorded the registration mandated by the 1597 law on slavery were compiled in December 1597 and January 1598. However, that is not the case: 23.3 percent of the 607 documents dated by month in those three collections were from December and January, whereas 27.9 percent of the 1621 documents in all the other collections were dated in those two months. Both the three collections of retrospective registrations and the óther, current, documentations exhibit the same pattern: the most documents in December through March, an intermediate number in April through July, and the least number in August through November.

TABLE 10.10
Seasonality of Slavery Transactions

Month	All Dated Transactions		Full Slavery		Registered Slavery		Limited Service Contract Slavery	
	N	%	N	%	N	%	N	%
January	286	13.0	5	6.3	3	12	260	13.2
February	238	10.8	15	18.8	1	4	210	10.6
March	355	16.1	17	21.2	5	20	311	15.8
April	164	7.4	3	3.7	4	16	149	7.5
May	190	8.6	2	2.5	2	8	175	8.9
June	197	8.9	5	6.3	3	12	176	8.9
July	128	5.8	6	7.5	2	8	114	5.8
August	83	3.8	3	3.7	0	0	76	3.9
September	78	3.5	6	7.5	0	0	66	3.3
October	93	4.2	5	6.3	1	4	77	3.9
November	90	4.1	0	0	2	8	79	4.0
December	307	13.9	12	14.9	2	8	281	14.2
Total	2,208	100.1*	81	100.0	25	100	1,974	100.0
Undated (by month) documents	291		19		3		116	

*Rounding error.

At least at first glance, it is somewhat surprising that registered slavery transactions follow the same pattern, although the documents are really too few in number to allow any definitive judgments. As we shall see, registered slavery was not a crisis institution but primarily something for estate stewards. What may be noteworthy in the seasonal statistics is the generally declining number of sales during the agricultural season, when an estate owner would want his manager to be working. While the amount of information that can be extrapolated from these data is limited, we can see that the peak for registered slave sales is early spring, the time when both the agricultural and military campaign seasons began. As Ann Kleimola has remarked, this may well have been a "crisis" period for a serviceman about to leave his estate for military service who was in need of a manager during his absence. This also may have been the time when elite combat slaves were most in demand.

A final general point about the seasonality of slave sales needs to be made. During the period of peak sales the slaveowners were usually not in service, and thus were available to buy slaves. This was less true during the April through November period, when servicemen were usually in the army. However, they were ordinarily in military service for only half of this period, and the availability of purchasers would not explain the significant difference in sales between April–July and August–November. For this and other reasons, it is fairly clear that the bulge in slave sales was during the winter not so much because buyers were available as because those who sold themselves experienced a crisis then that led to their momentous decision. If the crucial variable were the presence or absence of the servicemen because of their service obligations, one might think a far greater percentage of the transactions during the campaigning season would have been conducted by slaves in the stead of their masters than during the dead of winter. However, this seems not to have been the case: 4.8 percent of all February transactions were conducted by slaves, and 6.25 percent of all June transactions were. Thus slaveowners were able to buy in person just about as well in the summer as in the winter.

Also observable is a seasonality of prices, at least for limited service contract slaves (see figure 10.3). Roughly speaking, it looks as though prices reflected supply and demand. Lowest prices coincided with the largest supply, in the severe winter months, and the highest prices were to be found in the warmer summer months, when the supply of slaves was the lowest. The same pattern seems to be evident for full slavery as well, when lower than average prices generally coincided with the larger supplies of slaves. However, the numbers are really too low to make any certain judgments, and that is even more the case with registered slavery.

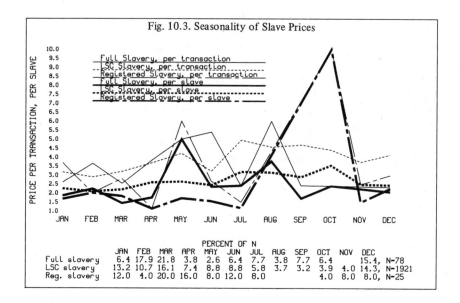

Fig. 10.3. Seasonality of Slave Prices

	JAN	FEB	MAR	APR	MAY	JUN	JUL	AUG	SEP	OCT	NOV	DEC	
Full slavery	6.4	17.9	21.8	3.8	2.6	6.4	7.7	3.8	7.7	6.4		15.4,	N=78
LSC slavery	13.2	10.7	16.1	7.4	8.8	8.8	5.8	3.7	3.2	3.9	4.0	14.3,	N=1921
Reg. slavery	12.0	4.0	20.0	16.0	8.0	12.0	8.0			4.0	8.0	8.0,	N=25

PERCENT OF N

Almost certainly the supply and demand factor was the one determining the seasonality of slave prices, but another argument is possible. Muscovite slaves frequently ran away, perhaps as many as a quarter to a third of them. Thus a slaveowner might have assumed when purchasing a slave that he would not own him for more than a year, and have set his price accordingly. Moreover, so we might assume, slaveowners purchased slaves to help in the harvest, the usual bottleneck in Muscovite agriculture. The lower prices more remote from the harvest season reflected the cost of feeding slaves up to the time of the harvest. While this argument is somewhat seductive, it is probably flawed in several respects. For one thing, harvesting was over in October and the agricultural year ended on November 26 (St. George's Day), so one would expect the price decline which began in November to be pronounced in December, which it was not. Secondly, most slaves seem to have been purchased to be household domestics and lackeys, not farm laborers.

The cost of slaves in relation to urban and rural locales is examined in table 10.11. The purchaser of the slave had that information at hand when concluding the transaction, for it all came from the sale documents. What differences, if any, the variables made, and why purchasers responded to them in any given way, are questions that cannot be answered definitively. It appears as though buyers were willing to pay more for slaves born in rural areas, not because they knew how to farm but, perhaps, because they were assumed to be more docile, less likely to run away. It is apparent that whether the person selling himself had previously lived in a large city or a rural area made no difference to the buyers. It is also quite clear that slaves purchased in a large city cost more than did those purchased in a medium-sized city, who in turn were significantly dearer than were those purchased in a rural area. Much of the lower price for slaves purchased in rural areas is probably attributable to the fact that the 1601-3 Great Famine slavery contracts are from rural areas (see figure 10.1), but even so rural prices are usually lower. This may have been the case because those who sold themselves into slavery in urban areas had qualities such as literacy and other urban traits that the purchasers valued. Finally, most purchasers lived in the countryside, but this seems to have made little difference in how much they would pay for slaves. This is not surprising, for most slaveowners in this study lived off government salaries and land grants that had relatively little to do with where they lived.

TABLE 10.11
Rural vs. Urban Indicators

	Slave's Birthplace		Slave's Previous Residence		Place of Sale		Purchaser's Home	
	Rubles	N	Rubles	N	Rubles	N	Rubles	N
A. Cost of Each Slavery Document (Transaction) at Time of Sale								
Large city	3.18	68	3.86	124	4.46	691	4.10	111
Medium city	2.77	15	3.30	50	4.08	30	2.73	184
Rural	3.83	176	3.60	376	3.45	1,462	4.18	1,412
Mean	3.60	259	3.63	550	3.78	2,183	4.02	1,707
B. Price per Slave at Time of Sale								
Large city	2.63	68	2.79	124	3.36	690	3.08	111
Medium city	2.13	15	2.27	50	3.08	30	1.72	184
Rural	3.16	176	2.74	376	2.13	1,462	2.77	1,411
Mean	2.96	259	2.71	550	2.53	2,182	2.68	1,706

In chapter 8 (table 8.1) the relationship between the number of witnesses to a transaction and the cost of that document was discussed, and while the correlation coefficient was relatively low (r = 0.39), because of wide differences, the general observable trend was for more costly slaves to have more witnesses to the transaction.

A comparative perspective provides some additional useful vantages on the problem of Muscovite slave prices. There is no universal rule about how much a slave should cost, whether in terms of horses, grain, or, as far as I can tell, eggs, to use Braudel's universal constant.[52] The value of slaves in relation to horses, at various times and places, is shown in table 10.12.[53]

52. Fernand Braudel, *Capitalism and Material Life* (New York: Harper and Row, 1973), p. 145.
53. Ibid., pp. 251, 254-55, 331; Mendelsohn, p. 41; A. P. Novosel'tsev and V. T. Pashuto, "Vneshniaia torgovlia Drevnei Rusi (do serediny XIII v.)," *Istoriia SSSR*, 1967, no. 3: 85; Wergeland, pp. 30, 100.

TABLE 10.12
Comparative Values of Slaves and Horses

Place and Time	Value
Assyria	3 slaves = 1 horse
Raffelstetten, upper Danube, beginning 10th century	1 slave = 1 mare
Medieval Sweden	1 slave = 2 horses
Sudan, beginning 16th century	12 slaves = 1 horse
Goa, 16th century	20 slaves = 1 horse
Moors, 1728	15 slaves = 1 horse
Morocco, 19th century	3 slaves = 1 horse
Buenos Aires, end 18th century	1 slave = 1 mule
	(horses were free)
Muscovy	1 slave = 1 horse

It is not even universally true that males were worth more than females; they were in Muscovy, as in most other places, but not in many parts of Africa.[54] I have observed, however, that the price of slaves in Muscovy seems to follow the supply, with the price falling at times of tremendous glut such as in the terrible famine year of 1603, as well as at times of greatest seasonal supply, during the winter months of December through March.

Perhaps more interesting is the question of whether slaves were comparatively cheap or dear in Muscovy. A. H. M. Jones provides certain guidelines for discussing this issue by comparing the cost of a slave with the cost of maintaining an individual for a year. On this basis he concludes that slaves were "fantastically cheap" in the fourth century B.C. at Athens and in Rome in the first century B.C., when a slave could be had for the equivalent of a year's keep. At other times, such as the second century A.D., they were expensive, costing eight to ten times a year's living expenses, or, from the third century onward, four to five times a year's keep.[55] If this comparison has any value, then ordinary Muscovite slaves were cheap, for the average cost of a single adult male around the year 1600 was 3.3 rubles (N = 458). According to the calculations of S. G. Strumilin, this was about the same amount as the cost of a year's food in the first half of the seventeenth century, 3.486 rubles. His figure for the second half of the century is 5.275 rubles.[56] The *Ulozhenie* of 1649 prescribed that the owner of a

54. Philip D. Curtin, *Economic Change in Pre-Colonial Africa: Senegambia in the Era of the Slave Trade*, 2 vols. (Madison: University of Wisconsin Press, 1975), 1: 176. Women had a higher "honor" value because of their presumed fragility and inability to protect themselves.

55. Jones, pp. 191-92, 194, 197.

56. S. G. Strumilin, *Ocherki ekonomicheskoi istorii Rossii* (Moscow: Sotsekgiz, 1960), p. 55. Strumilin's costing of the grain part of the diet, 1.496 rubles, is very similar to the more recent calculation of 1.55 rubles made by G. V. Abramovich ("Novgorodskoe pomest'e v gody ekonomicheskogo krizisa poslednei treti XVI v.," *Materialy po istorii sel'skogo khoziaistva i krest'ianstva SSSR* 8[1974]: 19).

slave was to pay a slavecatcher 2 dengi per day for feeding an apprehended fugitive slave, or 3.65 rubles per year. The bailiff who held a contested slave was supposed to make a profit from his effort and was paid 4 dengi per day.[57] Perhaps not surprisingly, according to the figures of the Czech Jesuit Jiri David, the cost of basic keep in the 1680s seems to have been in the range from 4 to 6 rubles per year: "Servants are expensive in Moscow. Foreigners have to pay each a ruble a month, without food; with food, 6, 7, some 8 rubles per year."[58] Elite slaves, costing 15 rubles, or five times as much as ordinary slaves, were obviously dear.

The conclusion that ordinary slaves were cheap appears astonishing, at first, in light of the well known perceived shortage of labor in Muscovy. Their price, however, probably reflected several factors. The first must have been the fact that no immediate return of any kind could have been expected from someone who had been purchased out of starvation. It would take some time for such a person to become even marginally effective as a domestic. Also, the skill level of the slaves was very low; only 20 percent of them had any kind of occupation before they sold themselves into slavery. Most of them had been beggars, day laborers, or some other form of dependent before they sold themselves into slavery. This reminds one of the Skid Row types sent out by "missions" to wash dishes and peel potatoes in American restaurants: their value as any kind of worker is very low. To continue the modern analogy, the Russian slaveowner was willing to pay a dollar an hour for this type of person but not top wages, which were reserved for the elite slaves. A notion of the perceived value of slave labor is expressed in the provision of the *Ulozhenie* on the compensation the person who illegally employed someone else's slave had to give the rightful owner—only 1 kopek a day.[59] This is a very low figure, particularly when one considers that the figure is supposed to be punitive as well as compensatory. Moreover, it is only a third of the the sum due for the illegal use of a peasant.

The important element in determining the cost of a slave in Muscovy was the cost of the slave's upkeep, not the value .of his labor or marginal productivity. The soundness of this conclusion will be developed later, especially when I show that slaveownership was highly determined by the slaveowner life cycle, for younger persons usually lacked the means to keep slaves. Moreover, one might recall at this juncture the discussion in chapter 2 on the cost-of-maintenance argument and voluntary slaves from the 1597 slavery statute: if a master had fed, clothed, and shod a "voluntary slave" for six months or longer, he had in-

57. 1649 *Ulozhenie* 20: 89, 94; MS, pp. 287-89.

58. Georgius David, *Status Modernus Magnae Russiae Seu Moscoviae (1690)* (The Hague: Mouton, 1965), p. 93. The price of servants was also relatively high in China, and consequently many people purchased female slaves because they were cheaper than maids (Meijer, "Ch'ing," p. 344).

59. 1649 *Ulozhenie* 20: 90; MS, p. 288.

vested enough in the slave to call him his own.[60] I know of no other slave system where the cost of maintenance was so important relative to the expected value of labor. Presumably this was true in most household slave systems, although none of the others articulated their concern as well as did the Muscovites.

Finally, such slaves as I am discussing here had a high propensity to run away, and their owners often could not recover them. The agricultural economist, Professor Theodore Schultz, looking at the prices of slaves and other price data, remarked that, judging by the data presented, "the slaves must have been manumitted within a few years after they were purchased." In fact, Muscovite slaves were almost never manumitted. They did, however, have a high propensity to flee, after they had recovered (at their owners' expense), and this must have been considered in the prices purchasers were willing to pay for them.

No doubt it still may seem hard to believe that Muscovy experienced simultaneously an intense demand for labor and low prices for slaves. However, one might note that a similar situation existed in the fifteenth century Ottoman Empire, although the causes were much different. During the period of Ottoman expansion, slaves were plentiful and comparatively cheap, yet there was also a general shortage of agriculture labor at the same time.[61]

One of the notable features of those who sold themselves into slavery in Muscovy was that they often moved considerable distances before doing so. Maps 10.1 and 10.2 compare the distance traveled from the slave's birthplace to his owner's home with the sum paid for the slave. The sums are grouped into least expensive (3 rubles and less), intermediate (3.01 to 5 rubles), and most expensive (over 5 rubles). The greatest distance (190 kilometers) was traveled by the most expensive slaves. We may hypothesize that they were the most desirable slaves, those least in need of relief, those capable of moving the farthest to get the best price for themselves. However, the least expensive slaves moved an average of 185 kilometers and the intermediate 160 kilometers, distances not significantly different from the greatest one. Thus there seems to have been relatively little relationship between mobility and price.

60. MS, pp. 253-54, art. 11.
61. Inalcik, "Servile Labor," pp. 31-33.

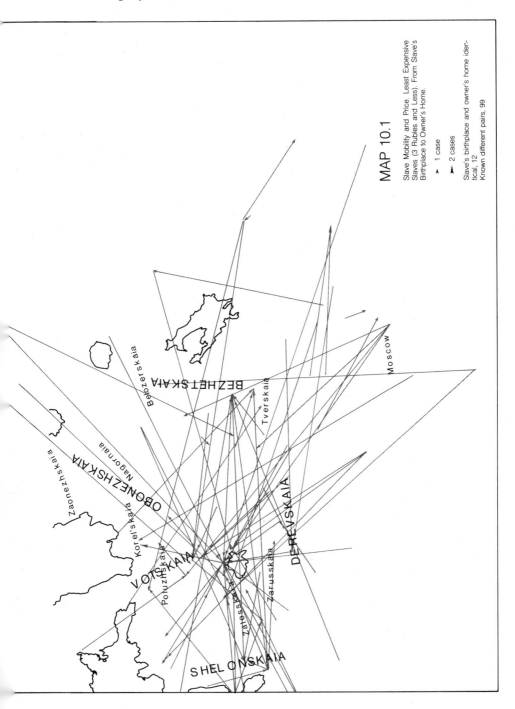

MAP 10.1

Slave Mobility and Price. Least Expensive Slaves (3 Rubles and Less). From Slave's Birthplace to Owner's Home.

▲ 1 case
▲ 2 cases

Slave's birthplace and owner's home identical, 12
Known different pairs, 99

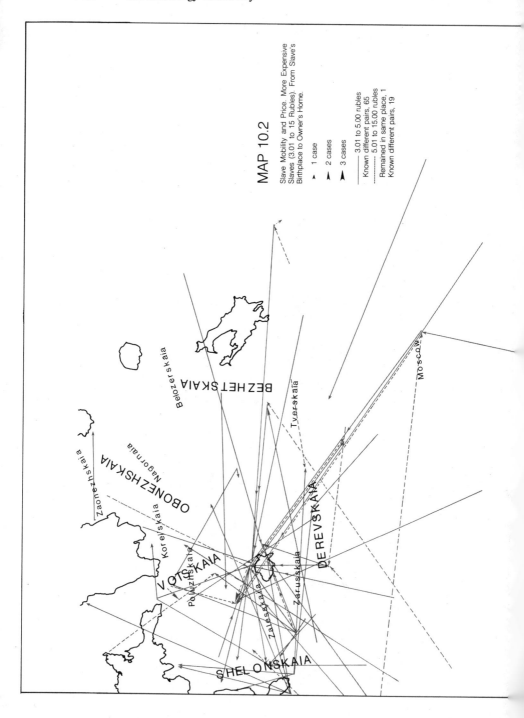

MAP 10.2

Slave Mobility and Price. More Expensive
Slaves (3.01 to 15 Rubles). From Slave's
Birthplace to Owner's Home.

➤ 1 case

➤ 2 cases

➤ 3 cases

———— 3.01 to 5.00 rubles
Known different pairs, 65
- - - - - 5.01 to 15.00 rubles
Remained in same place, 1
Known different pairs, 19

The Domestic Slave Trade

The domestic slave trade in Muscovy was very weakly developed. While there probably were many reasons for this, an initial one well may have been the fact that much of the function of a slave trade was performed by those who sold themselves. As we have just seen, free men were likely to have moved considerable distances before selling themselves, thus absorbing for buyers much of the cost inherent in acquiring slaves in other societies. One might speculate that this would have allowed purchasers to pay more to the slave directly than would have been the case had there been high acquisition, transportation, and transaction costs as well. Comparatively rock-bottom prices were paid for most Muscovite slaves, which probably had one of two meanings, or perhaps a combination of both: prices were so low partly because the purchaser's acquisition cost included only the price of the slave, with nothing paid for acquisition or profits to dealers; the slave received more for himself than he would have had the buyer been forced to pay in addition the "normal costs" associated with slave acquisition in most other societies. I know of no way to apportion these considerations. Perhaps we can get some help by considering what appear to have been prices at the Siberian frontier outposts of Tara and Tobol'sk between 1648 and 1691, when 282 almost exclusively non-Russian slaves were declared to be worth 1,581.50 rubles, or 5.60 rubles apiece. That is nearly double the 3-ruble price decreed for limited service contract slaves in the *Ulozhenie* of 1649, which was largely adhered to between the 1630s and the 1680s. The lower prices for native Muscovites may reflect both the lower acquisition costs and the fact that they had to be freed upon their purchaser's death, whereas purchased foreigners were hereditary property.[62]

---

62. *Materialy po istorii Uzbekskoi, Tadzhikskoi i Turkmenskoi SSR, Part 1: Torgovlia s Moskovskim gosudarstvom i mezhdunarodnoe polozhenie Srednei Azii v XVI-XVII vv.* (Leningrad: AN SSSR, 1932), pp. 380-85. I am aware of no calculations of the value added at each stage of enslavement (for example: the amount paid to the slave raider in Africa or Russia; the cost of transportation from the locale of the raid to a major slave market; the markup at the first slave market; transportation costs [perhaps a sea voyage] to the locale of the slave's ultimate employment; another markup in a slave market; transportation costs to a plantation or the slaveowner's house), but it is certain that the ultimate purchaser paid far more than the initial raider got. It was probably of the same order of magnitude that a modern house burglar gets from a fence for what he steals, perhaps 10 percent of an item's value. Some prices relevant to such a calculation are available from the world slave trade. Muscovite slaves that sold for roughly 3 rubles at home cost 20 to 30 rubles in bulk at the Crimean Kaffa slave market. In the seventeenth century slaves in Africa sold for about 4 pounds at the dock, but cost 22 pounds in the British Caribbean (Fisher, "Muscovy and the Black Sea Trade," p. 583; H. A. Gemery and J. S. Hogendorn, "Elasticity of Slave Labor Supply," in *Annals*, pp. 74-78). Almost certainly Muscovite slaveowners were getting a considerable bargain when buying their own kind.

The extent of this mobility is further evidenced in a consideration of central places of registration of slave transactions. It is possible to study the mobility of free men who became slaves in my data set from birthplace or last declared place of residence to Moscow, Novgorod, and provincial centers, and then to trace their movement as slaves to their owners' residences. Maps 10.3, 10.4, 10.5 show that the reach of Novgorod was greater than that of its provincial centers, and that all of these areas had extensive hinterlands. These four places (Novgorod, Borovichi, and the administrative centers of Derevskaia piatina and Zalesskaia polovina) were locales where self-sales into slavery were registered, with the free men who sold themselves absorbing the major costs of acquisition and transportation that prevailed in most other slave systems. There were no known slave-trading centers or markets in the sixteenth- and seventeenth-century Muscovite heartland. (The same was true in Thailand, which, like Muscovy, also had a well developed slave system.)[63] Concomitantly, as in the Ancient Near East, there were no slave merchants.[64] Even prior to the dramatic changes of 1597, extending limited service contract slavery to the life of the owner and fundamentally prohibiting him from alienating his slave in any manner, the slave trade was seemingly almost nonexistent. This remained true after 1597, even for hereditary slaves and slaves gained as a result of military conquest.

While some full and defaulted limited service contract slaves were sold prior to 1597, the number was very small. Less than a dozen such cases are extant. The number of extant seventeenth-century transactions seem to be even smaller. Moreover, there is no body of developed law or extant court cases adjudicating disputes over the sale of slaves, as there is for other types of property, and as there certainly would have been had the domestic slave trade been extensive. Muscovy knew in neither original creation nor translation any works advising purchasers of slaves, such as circulated widely in Islamic lands.[65] For probably good reasons, medieval Rus' knew a lively domestic slave trade that died out in Muscovy. Novgorod witnessed a great slave trade, and the famous Novgorod excavation under the direction of A. V. Artsikhovskii were carried out on *Kholop'-ia ulitsa*, "Slave Street," the location, one may assume, of the slave market, a place where many people congregated and public scribes and readers wrote and read aloud the birch-bark charters that have been discovered there. We might also speculate that the trade in serfs in the eighteenth century became considerably livelier than was the Muscovite domestic slave trade.

63. Turton, p. 276.
64. Mendelsohn, p. 96.
65. Kai Ka'us Ibn Iskandar, "On the Purchase of Slaves," which is chapter 23 of his *A Mirror for Princes. The Qābūs Nāma*, translated from the Persian by Reuben Levy (London: The Cresset Press, 1951), pp. 99-108.

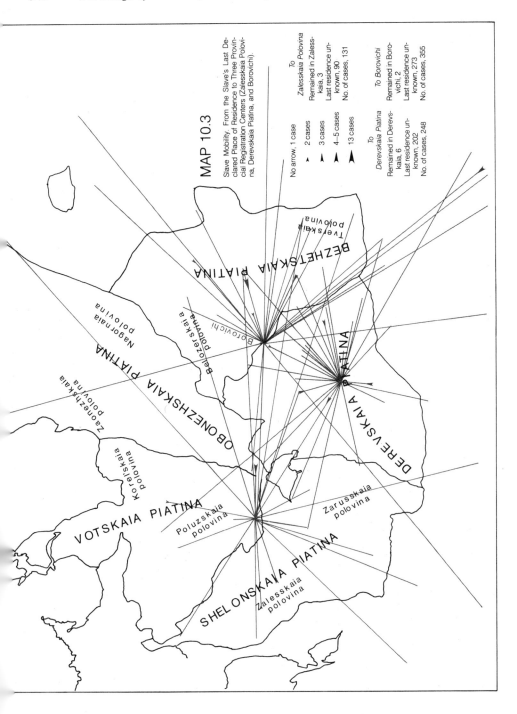

MAP 10.3

Slave Mobility. From the Slave's Last Declared Place of Residence to Three Provincial Registration Centers (Zalesskaia Polovina, Derevskaia Piatina, and Borovichi).

No arrow, 1 case
2 cases
3 cases
4–5 cases
13 cases

To
Zalesskaia Polovina
Remained in Zalesskaia, 3
Last residence unknown, 90
No. of cases, 131

To
Derevskaia Piatina
Remained in Derevskaia, 6
Last residence unknown, 202
No. of cases, 248

To
Borovichi
Remained in Borovichi, 2
Last residence unknown, 273
No. of cases, 355

BEZHETSKAIA PIATINA

Tverskaia polovina

Nagornaia polovina

Belozerskaia polovina

Borovichi

OBONEZHSKAIA PIATINA

DEREVSKAIA PIATINA

Zaonezhskaia polovina

Korel'skaia polovina

VOTSKAIA PIATINA

Poluzskaia polovina

Zarusskaia polovina

SHELONSKAIA PIATINA

Zalesskaia polovina

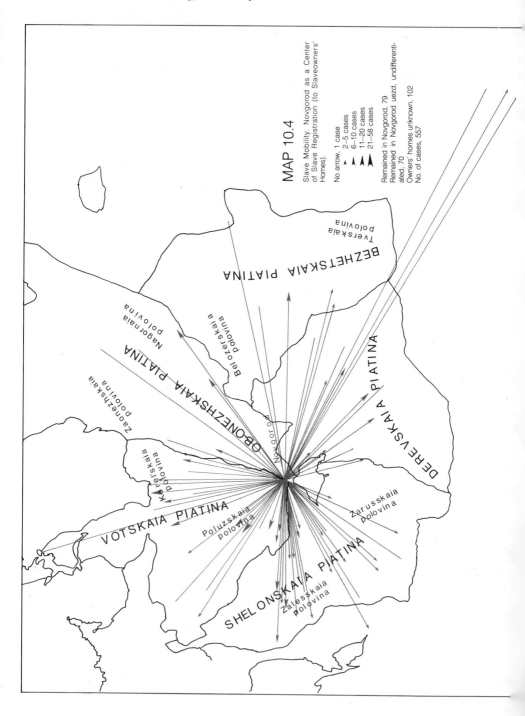

MAP 10.4

Slave Mobility. Novgorod as a Center
of Slave Registration (to Slaveowners'
Homes).

No arrow, 1 case
2–5 cases
6–10 cases
11–20 cases
21–58 cases

Remained in Novgorod, 79
Remained in Novgorod uezd, undifferenti-
ated, 70
Owners' homes unknown, 102
No. of cases, 557

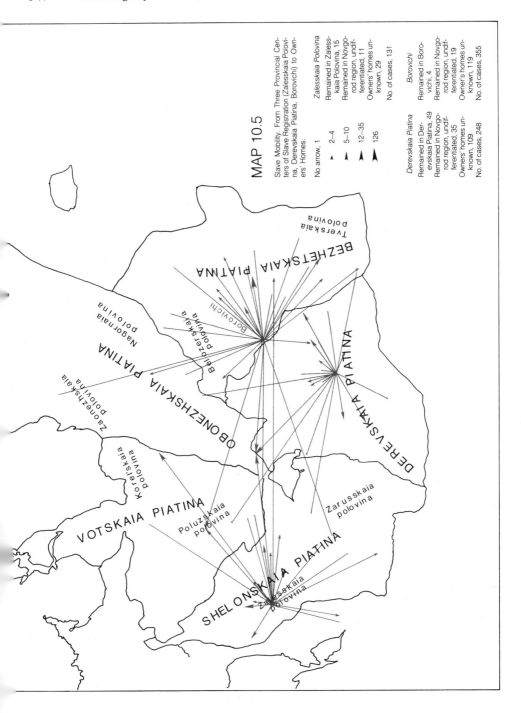

MAP 10.5

Slave Mobility. From Three Provincial Centers of Slave Registration (Zalesskaia Polovina, Derevskaia Piatina, Borovichi) to Owners' Homes.

No arrow, 1

▴ 2–4

▲ 5–10

▲ 12–35

▲ 126

Zalesskaia Polovina

Remained in Zalesskaia Polovina, 15
Remained in Novgorod region, undifferentiated, 11
Owners' homes unknown, 29
No. of cases, 131

Borovichi

Remained in Borovichi, 4
Remained in Novgorod region, undifferentiated, 19
Owner's homes unknown, 119
No. of cases, 355

Derevskaia Piatina

Remained in Derevskaia Piatina, 49
Remained in Novgorod region, undifferentiated, 35
Owners' homes unknown, 109
No. of cases, 248

As noted at the beginning of this section, apparently there was some kind of small slave trade on the Muscovite frontier. Customs records from the Siberian towns of Tara and Tobol'sk, on the Irtysh, are extant from the 1640s to 1691. The records tell who brought in the slaves (often Bukhara merchants, sometimes Kalmyks or local Siberian Tatars, rarely Russians), whence came those slaveowners (often from the Kalmyks, further upstream on the Irtysh, or Middle Asia), the slaves' ages (adults usually predominated) and nationalities (usually not stated, sometimes Chinese, one Russian woman from the entire group of 282 slaves), and some price information (an average of 5.60 rubles apiece). It is not stated what the prices meant, whether they were sums declared for purposes of payment of import duties, or whether they were transaction prices. Moreover, it is not clear whether the slaves were sold or, if so, to whom. Be that as it may, the number of slaves was rather small: 13 in one seven-month period and 65 in another, 13 in a two-week period, 104 in a half-year period, 41 in a one-year period, 59 in another. Most of the trade, if that is what it was, seems to have involved local indigenes (Moscow was just annexing Siberia at that time) and foreigners, with relatively little Russian participation. Thus this picture of the slave trade is one of a frontier phenomenon that had almost nothing to do with Russia proper, which was almost 2,000 kilometers away, except that Moscow agents were keeping the records.[66] To my knowledge, no such records ever existed for the heartland.

In Muscovy proper, eight slave purchase-sale (*kupchie*) documents are extant from the years 1575 through 1597. They were registered in the 1598 compulsory recording of all claims to slaves, and were distributed among the three extant collections of such documents. The prices paid were in the same range as those paid people who were selling themselves, from 1.50 to 10 rubles, with an average of 4.25 rubles. Seven of the transactions were between seemingly unrelated parties, while in the eighth two brothers exchanged a slave for 6 rubles. In all but one of the cases it was noted that the slaves were military captives. The exception was a Russian, while one of the imports was from Lithuania, the rest from Livonia. Five of the transactions involved single women, the other three transferred ownership of three men and a single woman.[67] Atypical for Muscovite slavery were the ethnicities and the sex ratios of the slaves.

Also recorded is the resale of a family of limited service contract slaves. In 1595 Fedor Zhdanov Korytkov purchased a man, his wife, and their daughter for 10 rubles. Subsequently he sold them to Shavruk Murav'ev, whose son registered the ownership of the slaves for his father in 1598. Unfortunately it is not clear when the Korytkov-Murav'ev transaction occurred, for Murav'ev may have simply been repaying the loan and assuming ownership. However, this

66. *Materialy po istorii Uzbekskoi* (1932), pp. 380-85.

67. Kopanev, "Materialy," pp. 160, 163; Lakier, p. 42; RIB 17(1898): 64, 142, 165, 169, 212.

seems unlikely, for in that case a manumission document and a new self-sale contract should have been drawn up. Moreover, the document says that Korytkov "ceded" (*postupilsia*) the slave to Murav'ev, indicating that it was a transaction between the two of them.[68] Another of the 1598 registration collections contains the resale of a family of seven full slaves for the sum of 7 rubles that had occurred about 120 years previously.[69]

A concealed sale may have been present in a case involving a couple of limited service slavery contracts. In February of 1589 Nazareiko Ivanov, called Kazarin, a native of Pskov from Gdov uezd, and his wife, Annitsa Vasil'eva, and their son, Iakushko, sold themselves for 5 rubles to Ondrei Kushnikov Paiusov, a landholder who in 1585 had 115 cheti of land in Gdov uezd.[70] A few months later, on November 14, 1589, Nazareiko, who was literate, sold himself again to Petr Ondreev Tushin, a prosperous member of the middle service class who by the early 1580s had 615 cheti of land in Novgorod's Shelonskaia piatina, and by the beginning of the seventeenth century had acquired still more land in Votskaia piatina.[71] One strange aspect of the case was that in November Nazareiko had a different wife, Annitsa Nikitina, and children, Mikhalka, Efimko, Irinka, and Okulinka. This time he sold himself for the large sum of 10 rubles, which he received from Tushin's slave Veresshchaga (sic) Pavlov. The coincidence of the given name, Annitsa, for Nazareiko's two wives is obvious, and one might assume that it was actually the same woman, that the patronymic of one or the other was mistaken, were it not for the fact that the children were all different.

Adding to the mystery of these documents is a statement appended to the February document, a statement by Paiusov dated May 28, 1596, that he had given up his claims to Nazareiko and his family. Tushin registered the two documents on January 19, 1598, in response to the 1597 law that all documents had to be registered.

How do we interpret what happened here? Almost certainly Nazareiko found living in Gdov uezd not to his liking, and fled to Votskaia piatina. Perhaps his first wife and child had died, and Paiusov manumitted him, but all of this seems implausible. One suspects, rather, that Nazareiko had a series of domestic spats with his wife, and decided to abandon her. To do so, he had to flee from Paiusov. He fled some distance, about 225 kilometers, remarried, and, being a dependent type resold himself almost immediately. Paiusov set out in search of Nazareiko, but it took him six and a half years to find him. One may assume that he threatened to file a suit against Tushin to recover the fugitive but that instead

68. RIB 17: 123, no. 338.
69. Kopanev, "Materialy," p. 182; ASEI 3: 420, no. 407; Kolycheva, *Kholopstvo*, p. 68.
70. PK po Pskovu, pp. 240, 243, 246.
71. NPK 5: 555-56; Ianitskii, pp. 100, 203; Andreiiashev, *Materialy*, p. 89; DVP, p. 470; Ivanov, OPK, p. 67; RIB 22(1908): 790, 824, 836.

they settled the matter out of court. Whether this was a concealed sale is unknown, although that has been suggested.[72]

Nothing seems to be known about how slaves sales were arranged in Muscovy. The following, from the Nepalese Nyinba system, may be suggestive:

> [S]lave sales were not conducted 'crassly,' in the offhand manner one might sell a goat or a cow. Rather, a prospective buyer would bring an offering of beer and humbly request the privilege of purchasing a particular slave. The agreement would be reached after deliberation on the part of the owner, and excessive bargaining was not allowed.[73]

Eight sale documents, two resales, and a concealed sale transaction hardly constitute a vigorous slave trade. The weakness of the slave trade in the presence of a well-developed slave system cries out for explanation. No easy explanation is at hand. One possibility might be that Muscovites were inhibited from selling their slaves because of the fact that they were primarily ethnic Russians, or at least Orthodox Christians. For example, Islamic law did not allow Muslims to trade in other Muslims, but then it also forbade them to enslave them at all, a principle that was totally alien to the Muscovites when it came to enslaving their kin. Moreover, while Christianity may have played a role in the demise of slavery among Western Europeans, it certainly failed to inhibit those people from enslaving white Christian Poles and Hungarians (as well as Orthodox Slavs and Greeks) and keeping enslaved nonwhite Christians for generations after their conversion. It is also curious that the Muscovite Orthodox were willing to offer freedom to enslaved Muslim Tatars who converted to Orthodoxy, but they felt no pangs whatsoever about the perpetual enslavement of their own kind. Perhaps in the late 1640s Tsar Aleksei Mikhailovich forbade the sale of non-Muscovite slaves who converted to Orthodoxy, a move that would indicate that such sales were practiced.[74] There are, however, no such strictures for those who were born Orthodox, or those who refused to convert. The primary objection to any theory based on ethnicity or religion in explaining the absence of a domestic Muscovite slave trade would be the fact that the Russians rarely traded in non-Orthodox Swedes, Poles, or Lithuanians, or even in Islamic Tatars.

The trade in Poles and Swedes may have been dampened by the practice, common after 1550, of including in peace treaties a clause allowing the free return of all military captives, a fact which would have expropriated any purchaser of a captive slave. To my knowledge, there were no such treaties with the Tatars, however.

---

72. RIB 17: 161-62, nos. 436-37; Paneiakh, *Kabal'noe kholopstvo*, p. 113.
73. Nancy E. Levine, p. 206.
74. 1649 *Ulozhenie* 20: 97.

Some students of slavery consider that the right to alienate his slaves is one of the major prerogatives of a slaveowner, and they might be inclined to downgrade or even exclude any slave system which in any manner limited that right.[75] While Muscovites passed on to heirs in various devises (property divisions, wills, marriage contracts, and dowries) all of their slave chattel until 1597, and hereditary slaves and military captives after that time, they admittedly did not sell or mortgage them with any great frequency. Here, once again, a comparative perspective may assist us. While slaves were traded in most systems, Muscovy was not the sole exception. For example, Ch'ing bannermen and officers who bought public slaves could not resell or pawn them.[76] Locally born slaves could not be sold on the Comoro Islands off the east coast of Africa. The Vai of Liberia and Sierra Leone rarely sold domestic slaves, and the few exceptions were farm slaves living by themselves in villages, not members of the owner's household.[77] On the Gambia, custom forbade the sale of slaves born into captivity.[78] And, in nineteenth-century Adamawa (now northern Cameroon) masters of household and court slaves were morally, although not legally, barred from selling them.[79] As we shall see in chapter 14, most slaves in Muscovy also served in the household.

There may be several other explanations for the absence of a domestic slave trade. It might be yet another manifestation of the generally acute labor shortage in Muscovy. The mentality created by this shortage may have persisted, or even have been reinforced, during the "good times" of Muscovy, such as the reign of Vasilii III (1505-33). Although the shortage of peasant cultivators and taxpayers was eased during such periods, the availability of slaves to serve in the household was probably even further curtailed at those times because diminished military activity lessened the supply of foreign slaves while domestic prosperity radically reduced the number of Muscovites forced to sell themselves into servitude in search of relief. In consequence slaves were always valued in Muscovy, both for the domestic service they performed and for the prestige their possession conferred on their owners. This meant that slaveowners were unwilling to sell their slaves at any time. (A sole exception might have been times of famine, when owners could not feed their slaves. But at those times buyers were inundated with potential slaves, and would not have to pay very much to acquire another's chattel.) This argument seems to be relatively unsatisfactory, for the emerging picture seems to be one of a general plenitude of slaves usually available at relatively low prices. The increase in demand for slaves was less than the increase in supply, although the number of those desiring to have slaves was

75. Marinovich, p. 111.
76. Meijer, p. 329.
77. Miers and Kopytoff, p. 290; Burnham, p. 50; Shepherd, pp. 77, 82.
78. Klein and Lovejoy, in Gemery and Hogendorn, p. 187.
79. Burnham, p. 50.

greater than the number of those who possessed the resources necessary to maintain them.

Another explanation for the absence of a slave trade may have been the fact that the inability to maintain one's slaves, made visible to all by their sale, was considered so humiliating that a slaveowner was simply unwilling to make such a spectacle of himself. He may have preferred to turn them out for nothing rather than endure the loss of face caused by selling them. Somewhat similar considerations apparently inhibited the sale of some slaves in the Old South in places where slaves were primarily domestics rather than cogs in productive enterprises. A similar situation prevailed in Africa, where domesticated slaves were rarely sold except under duress, and, among the Duala, for example, a loss of face resulted for those reduced to such extremities. In both India and Nepal slaveownership was a major prestige symbol; a family's respectability was measured by the number of its dependents, and the discharging or sale of slaves told against the owner's prestige and could bring disgrace.[80] It is safe to assume that the Muscovite situation was very similar. Thus if the Muscovite slaveowner turned out his domestic slaves, he could say that they had run away; if he sold them, it would be obvious to everyone that he himself had fallen in social prestige. Here one might notice the importance of "servants" in defining a person's wealth and social status in Russian fairy tales, where they are often linked with the hero's hoard of gold, silver, and precious gems. One might also note that the centrality of slavery in defining prestige was enhanced by the fact that Russians did not practice polygamy, as did many otherwise very similar societies, in which a man could use the number of his wives to demonstrate his wealth. The Russians had only their slaves. The values of the Muscovite era persisted into the Petrine period, as noted by the foreigner Vockerodt, secretary of the Prussian Embassy in Russia toward the end of Peter's reign: "A Russian nobleman is not interested in owning precious garments and furniture or enjoying fine dinners and foreign wines. He requires a plenitude of food and drink of Russian origin, a large staff of servants, and horses."[81] Unlike in the Old South, in Muscovy the role of slaves was far more central in expressing both to oneself and to the rest of the world the slaveowner's individual volition and merit, for the rest of his social indicators were determined and awarded almost exclusively by the state. The serviceman-slaveowner's service status correlated highly with his ownership of chattel, and no doubt this was apparent to contemporary Muscovites as well. Nevertheless, a man's position in service was determined by others, but he himself determined whether or not he owned slaves, and how many. To part with what he himself had achieved, one of his major status symbols, was probably something that the Muscovite slaveowner could not bear. Thus the ab-

---

80. Caplan, pp. 177, 185. In Indian Tamil country of the Madras Presidency agrestic slaves were seldom sold or mortgaged (Hjejle, p. 75).

81. Vasilii Klyuchevsky, *Peter the Great* (New York: Vintage, 1958), p. 102.

sence of a domestic slave trade in Muscovy can best be attributed to the shared values of the slaveowners.

These shared values may have been expressed by the author of chapter 60 of the *Domostroi*, who advised that a slaveowner who had a lazy, unimprovable slave on his hands should free the slave and let him go. In other societies, such a slave would have been flogged, and then sold. Considering the reality of Muscovite slavery, the *Domostroi*'s advice was perhaps most effective: a person who had been rescued from starvation or other intense stress almost certainly found the prospect of being thrust out into the harsh world a much more terrifying sanction than either being beaten or being sold to another owner.

Finally, the Vai analogy cannot be pressed farther than to show that Muscovy was not absolutely unique in having no slave trade. The Africans incorporated their slaves into their lineages, which obviously the Muscovites did not. While some Russian slaves became part of the family (the point of the Old South analogy), as any domestic is liable to do, others must have always been relatively remote from their owners and some must have been hated by their owners. The fact that not even these were sold is what I have tried to explain.

One might be tempted to argue that the price of slaves was so low that it made a domestic slave trade impossible, that the transaction costs would have been so high relative to the price for which the slaves could have been sold that no one would bother. This argument is highly seductive but certainly can be refuted. For one, there was a national market for horses, which cost the same as slaves. For another, the transaction costs of regional slave markets would have been close to zero, for the people who owned slaves in Muscovy were in the habit of traveling to regional centers, at least annually, for army musters and reviews and to engage in litigation. The servicemen-slaveowners were essentially unoccupied during the time of the annual winter court date, around New Year, and the cost of taking along an unwanted slave to sell on such an occasion would have been negligible. Yet there is not the slightest evidence that this happened even once, which would cast serious doubt on a "transaction costs" theory in an attempt to explain the absence of a domestic slave trade.

In considering the slave a subhuman being, in the same category as women and children, the Muscovites were in the mainstream of slave systems. The general level of prices paid for slaves, while low, was well within the boundaries of other slave systems' experience. Unusual was the minimal development of a slave trade, a fact that may be attributable to the shared values of the slaveowners.

11. Origins of Slaves and Precipitants into Slavery

The origins of human slavery are unknown, but it has been theorized that the institution began as a form of delay; a delay in execution for military captives or convicted felons, a delay in sacrifice of war captives and others in societies where that form of ritual was practiced, or a delay in cannibalism where human war prizes and similar victims might otherwise have been converted into nutritional supplementation. This theory was articulated in Islamic theology millennia after the first enslavement: "Slavery is, in the last analysis, only a kind of substitution for actual death."[1]

It is fairly safe to assume that most slaves throughout history were products of warfare, or warlike activities such as piracy and slave raiding. Certainly this was true for the slaves of classical Athens and Rome, medieval Germanic societies, the slaves who had been so prominent throughout Islamic civilization, the Slavs who gave their name for slave to so many languages beginning about the tenth century, and the millions of Africans who found their way into the domestic and international slave trade for a millennium. The Latin term for slave, *servus*, was derived from the verb *servare*, "keep, retain, preserve"—applied, one assumes, to the life of the war captive. War captives made up a significant portion of the slaves in Muscovy, too, while that form of incentive and compensation for military service persisted.[2]

Of course there were exceptions to the general rule that warfare generated the majority of slaves in any system. One such exception seems to have been the societies of ancient Mesopotamia, where "the great majority of slaves came from the ranks of defaulting debtors, originally free members of the same community." This meant that the slave was generally "the same 'race,' color, speech, and religion as his master."[3]

The Muscovite case seems to have been similar to the ancient Mesopotamian, in that the great majority of the slaves were natives. As we have seen, however,

---

1. Richard Turnwald, *Economics in Primitive Communities* (Oxford: Oxford University Press, 1932), p. 219. For similar ideas, see Wergeland, p. 3. See also Fisher, "Muscovy," p. 575; Udal'tsova, "Raby v Vizantii," p. 5. Ideas similar to the Islamic one have been stated in the twentieth century as "The loss of power is the loss of self. Whoever cedes his arms cedes all—life, liberty, even identity" (Wergeland, p. 8).

2. Iu. A. Tikhonov, "Pomeshchich'ia usad'ba i pomeshchich'e khoziaistvo v Rossii posle Sobornogo ulozheniia (1649-1679 gg.)," *Istoriia SSSR*, 1978, no. 4: 144, 146.

3. Mendelsohn, p. 122.

they were not "defaulting debtors," for there was a special category for them, and there was a specific limit to their enslavement. Muscovite full slavery was direct sale into a permanent state of bondage, not only for oneself but for one's descendants, forever. Muscovite limited service contract slavery initially was perpetual only when the borrower defaulted on his obligation to repay the loan at the end of the year, but this provision almost certainly was transparently a fiction to everyone, both creditor and borrower, as evidenced by the striking similarity between it and the old full slavery. Default was expected, and that is what occurred. I shall have occasion to say more about the enslavement of natives, but nowhere else did this occur on the scale that it did in Muscovy.

The known status of the slaves in my data set prior to the document recording their enslavement is listed in table 11.1. One must bear in mind, again, that most of these data were generated by the compulsory registration of all slaves as a result of the law of 1597 and annual registrations of sales in the Novgorod region between then and 1603. However, I have little reason to believe that the data in both tables 11.1 and 11.2 would not be representative (with a few exceptions) of the years from, say, 1450 to 1680. Perhaps the portion of military captives should be greater, although by how much is totally unclear. The first large impression that one gets from table 11.1 is that about two-thirds of the slaves had been free earlier, either persons taken as war captives or never before enslaved individuals selling themselves into slavery for the first time. The other third was made up of individuals who had been enslaved previously and were either voluntarily or involuntarily being registered as slaves. The cause of the previous enslavement in the vast majority of cases is not known. Some are known to have been born as slaves, but others may have been first-generation slaves themselves (either because of self-sale or military captivity) who were transferred to another party in a legal transaction (such as a dowry or will) or else sold themselves after

TABLE 11.1
Status of Slave Prior to Enslavement, and Price, in Rubles

Prior Status	No. of Documents	No. of Slaves	Slaves for whom Prices are Available		N
			Price per Document	Price per Slave	
Free	805	1,332	3.27	2.43	778
Slave freed on owner's death					
(involuntary on owner's part)	21	32	3.11	2.58	19
Manumitted slave					
(act of owner's will)	119	211	3.70	2.81	105
Born a slave	24	139	3.77	1.89	10
Enslaved	305	1,167	4.25	2.71	112
Total	1,274	2,881	3.42	2.49	1,024
Unknown	1,225	2,694			1,475

manumission. Considering the prices paid for the slaves in these broad categories, we see that those paid for persons who had been free are slightly lower than are those for persons who had been enslaved previously. One may speculate that slightly lower prices were paid for free persons because of the difficulty of sea-soning them to slavery and their greater presumed propensity to flee.

The general reasons for enslavement are shown in table 11.2. More than four-fifths of the transactions involved persons who sold themselves. Only two were explicitly "voluntary slaves," although, as we shall see in tables 11.3 and 11.4 more than that figure actually were "voluntary slaves." Quite a few people were enslaved simply because their parents were or had been of a similar status, and a small fraction were sold by their parents. Military captivity is known to have generated some slaves, as did the position of steward, whose holders for a time were required by law to be slaves. As we know, marriage of a free person to a slave also produced slaves, and so could indebtedness. The second major reason for enslavement, after self-sale, was transference by one slaveowner to another of chattel in gift, property division, and other legal instruments.

TABLE 11.2
Reason for Enslavement and Price of Slaves, in Rubles

Reason for Enslavement	No. of Documents	No. of Slaves	Slaves for Whom Prices are Available		N
			Price per Document	Price per Slave	
Working over 3 to 6 months	2	2	2.00	2.00	1
Parents were slaves	66	250	4.05	2.32	41
Military captivity	39	148	4.67	2.95	13
Job-mandated slavery	25	46	3.06	1.94	24
Self-sale	2,067	3,914	3.87	2.60	2,003
Sale by parents	8	15	8.25	4.40	8
Indebtedness	7	13	12.00	4.83	6
Transferred in a gift, marriage contract, dowry, property division, will, or other document	155	756	NA	NA	0
Marriage to a slave	2	3	NA	NA	0
Total	2,371	5,149	3.91	2.60	2,096
Unknown	128	426			403

Table 11.1 conveys the impression that over half of the persons registered as slaves in Muscovy had previously at one time or another been enslaved. This impression is certainly correct, considering slaves who were passed from one owner to another via dowries, wills, and other such instruments. The picture alters slightly when we consider only the 3,942 individuals who sold themselves into limited service contract slavery. The prior status of 2,267 of them is unknown, 1,195

were known to have been free prior to their self-sale, and 480 stated that they had been enslaved in one of the ways listed in table 11.1 prior to the transaction. Thus about 30 percent of those who sold themselves into limited service contract slavery had been enslaved before. This explains quite well the dynamics of seventeenth-century Muscovite slavery: a large re-enslavement of previously enslaved individuals, the handing on from one generation to another of hereditary slaves, plus regular infusions of new people selling themselves and war captives. The numbers in the first three categories were adequate to minimize warrior pressure for fresh recruits to maintain the system. In this respect Muscovy differed markedly from most Islamic countries, where regular manumissions kept up pressure for a constant infusion of new war booty that could be converted into human chattel. In all likelihood this factor reduced the militancy of the Muscovite army and contributed to its well-known defensive orientation, although quantifying that thesis would seem to be quite impossible.

What is striking about the categories in table 11.2 is the way in which they resemble those in the ancient Indian *Laws of Manu*, which say that:

> There are slaves of seven kinds: he who is made a [1] captive under a standard, he who [2] serves for his daily food, he who is [3] born in the house, he who is [4] bought and he who is [5] given, he who is [6] inherited from ancestors, and he who is enslaved by way of [7] punishment.

These categories may be glossed as follows: (1) could be either a war captive or a person who became a slave by marrying a female slave; (2) might be a poor man who voluntarily offered himself to a rich person; (7) could be either for inability to pay a debt or a fine, or for leaving a religious order.[4]

Unfortunately I have not the slightest idea about the relative importance of those seven Indian categories or how many people there were at any given time in each. It is clear, however, that every one of the large Indian categories has a Muscovite counterpart. In Muscovy, category (4) is very small, and category (2) (really the essence of voluntary, full, and limited service contract slavery) is very large.

The relevance of the Indian and Mesopotamian comparisons may be that they reveal the essentially antique nature of Muscovite slavery. This is also clear when comparisons are made between native African slavery and Muscovite slavery. This should not be surprising, of course, for Muscovite slavery was of the household form, rather than productive (on plantations, in mines, factories, or galleys). It is not clear when it became part of the human social program that slaves (other than those enslaved for debt and crime) should be "outsiders," but that was certainly the case in the Greek world by 500 B.C. While Muscovy was in some respects part of the early modern world, intellectually it was medieval, at

---

4. *Laws of Manu*, pp. 253-54, 415.

best (until 1650). That some of its social practices should be comparatively premedieval might be expected in a land that was neolithic only half a millennium earlier.

The Social Origins of Muscovite Slaves

Because most of Muscovy's slaves were natives, one can determine what many of them were before they became slaves. Such information is available for no other system. For example, it is known that a few Roman slaves were literate Greek doctors and teachers, but that is about all. Similarly, almost nothing is known about the social origins of the millions of Africans who became internal and export slaves.

One of the most striking features of Muscovite slaves is their almost complete lack of skills. A handful of those who became slaves were skilled, but the vast majority had no skills at all. The contrast with the Moscow census of 1638 is striking, for the capital contained hundreds of different types of specialists.[5] This further reflects the fact that most slaves came from the very bottom of society. Nevertheless, in spite of that fact, scions of the elite and members of the "middle class" (using Western sociological terminology) occasionally found their way into slavery as well.

Very little is known about the origins of slaves who had been sociologically superior to the "working class" and the lumpen prior to their enslavement. In chapter 14, when I discuss occupations held by slaves, I shall speculate that elite managerial and combat slaves were probably not of lumpen origin, but there is little hard evidence to prove this point. Certainly one reason for the absence of such information is that by the 1630s it was increasingly considered shameful to be a slave, and therefore notable families probably took some pains to conceal the fall of their members into slavery. Nevertheless, evidence of such descent is fairly abundant in the genealogies, as well as in the statements by members of the middle service class that their numbers were being thinned by self-sale into enslavement, and the government's response to those laments.

In 1910 Iu. V. Tatishchev published what he termed a "precedence" or "system of places handbook" of the seventeenth century. While recording precedence was its purpose, it was also a genealogical history of over 550 of the most important Muscovite clans. Special evidence seems to be present for those who in some manner were connected with the musketeers, so one may assume such a provenance for the document. For our purposes, however, the interesting aspect of the document is the references to the slavery status of some clan members. Thus under the entry for the Kaftyrev clan, we read:

5. I. S. Beliaev, *Rospisnoi spisok*, pp. xviii-xxiii.

In 1553 Kostor Kaftyrev served as a slave on the basis of a limited service slavery contract with Mikhail Semenov Polozov of Kostroma. Kostor's sons Aleshka and Ofonka served as limited service contract slaves with Ivan Filipov Ivanchev and Semen Dmitreev Ivanchev of Kostroma. The limited service slavery contract was taken out on their father in 1553 in Kostroma in their presence, and on both of them in 1557 when Ondrei Akinfov and Ermola Iazykov served as *guba* elders.[6]

That stain on the Kaftyrev escutcheon persisted for over a century. Another entry concerns the Chirikov clan:

In 1640 Kostentin Chirikov petitioned to be the slave of Prince Osip Shekhovskoi and gave a limited service slavery contract on himself. At that time Prince Ivan Los' Volkonskii and Ivan Ogarev worked in the Slavery Chancellery. Kostka's relatives Ivan and Petr Gavrilov Chirikov filed a complaint against him. On the basis of their complaint, Kostka was freed from slavery with Prince Osip Shekhovskoi and given over to them so that he would render the sovereign's service and he was to assist them. The case in the Slavery Chancellery was written up by the scribe Nikifor Kolikov. In 1648 Kostka's son Ivashka petitioned to be a slave, gave a limited service slavery contract on himself, and served in the household of *boiarin* Il'ia Danilovich Miloslavskii until the death of the latter. After the death of *boiarin* Il'ia Danilovich, he again petitioned to be a slave and is now [ca. 1680] serving *boiarin* Prince Iurii Nikitich Boriatinskii.[7]

In this entry we see that the other Chirikovs felt so strongly against one of their member's being a slave that they sued in the Slavery Chancellery to have him forcibly manumitted. Their will was effected, no doubt on the grounds that Kostka Chirikov was supposed to be a serviceman. However, the die was cast, and Kostka's son Ivashka was molded a slave. No doubt nothing was done about Ivashka's case, for two reasons: his owners were among the most prominent figures in Muscovy, and since he had never (in all probability) been in service, he was essentially exempted under the article of the *Ulozhenie* which proclaimed that people of the perpetual slave-dependency type should not be forced to render state service.[8]

Other entries in the handbook record additional individuals from elite clans who fell into slavery. Thus we learn that Vasilei Bibikov served *boiarin* Vasilii Borisovich Sheremetev (flourished in the 1640s and 1650s) as a limited service contract slave in the latter's household, and Grigorei Ivanov Poltev served as a limited service contract slave in the household of Semen Luk'ianovich Streshnev (flourished 1630s-50s). The case of Taras Stepanov Rostopchin is

6. Iu. V. Tatishchev, "Mestnicheskii spravochnik," p. 11.
7. Ibid., p. 64.
8. 1649 *Ulozhenie* 16: 2, 3.

interesting, for in 1661 he was a slave of *boiarin* Il'ia Danilovich Miloslavskii, but in 1672 Rostopchin was a mounted groom and a steward of royal estates (*putnyi kliuchnik*). Rostopchin no doubt was manumitted on Miloslavskii's death in 1668, and, atypically, found the energy to return to official service. In 1675 mounted groom Rostopchin carried colored "palms" (*verby*) in the Palm Sunday procession, and on September 21, 1680, he was in another royal religious procession, this time with the title of choir master or more likely, keeper of the paper supplies (*stolpovoi prikashchik*).[9] Rostopchin seems to have been treated as a reformed prodigal son after he was manumitted, a rare case indeed.

The records of the Military Chancellery contain petitions from relatives distressed by the presence of their kin in slavery. For example, in 1626 Evnikiia Levashova, prioress of a nunnery, filed a complaint because her son, the Rzheva *syn boiarskii* Vladimir Grigor'ev Levashov, was a slave of *boiarin* prince Ivan Ivanov Shuiskii.[10]

Noteworthy about those slaves from elite families was the fact that they largely served other members of the elite. No doubt there were others who did not serve members of the elite. Moreover, there must have been dozens who sold themselves to other members of the middle service class. Unfortunately, except possibly by resorting to onomastics, there is no way to determine which of the slaves in my data set were of upper or middle service class origin. One may assume that some of the most expensive slaves were of elite origin, and destined for elite service, but this cannot be proved from the data at hand.

Why should scions of the important, genealogically ranked families have sold themselves into slavery? This fact positively baffles some twentieth century observers, and makes them question whether *kholopstvo* could have been slavery. For this reason a bit of discussion is warranted. Everyone is aware of the "dropouts" from the U.S. middle and upper classes. This seems to be especially prevalent when upwardly mobile parents have achieved higher status than did the grandparents. The children, who "have everything," feel pushed by their parents to rise even higher. Some do, but others don't; they simply lack the drive to sustain their parents' level of achievement, and they respond by "dropping out," by becoming "drifters," even by committing suicide. It may not be totally irrelevant to compare the internally motivated U.S. drive for success and status with the Muscovite externally motived drive for success and status. The early modern Russian governmentally structured meritocracy put pressure on its servitors of a kind that perhaps only a few Americans in the upper echelons of a relatively small proportion of highly aggressive businesses can appreciate: your "profit center" must produce, or you are out of a job. A failed "profit center" manager can take time off to reconsider his career, but the Muscovite serviceman was

9. Iu. V. Tatishchev, pp. 49, 72, 82; DR 3: 1305, 4: 180.
10. *Opisanie dokumentov i bumag* 15(1908): 59, no. 39-I.

required to report for service in every campaign. Moreover, labor is not compulsory for offspring of American millionaires, but no comparable cushion was available in Muscovy, where service was required of every person in every generation. Certainly not every Muscovite personality could tolerate such pressure, just as not every American can tolerate the pressure. In America the son of a professor can run a mimeograph machine, but there was no such option for Muscovites. The range of options open to low-energy scions of the Muscovite middle and upper service classes has never been studied, to my knowledge, but it must have been very narrow. Certainly such a person could become a monk. Until 1640, he probably could become a government copyist. I have never heard of such a person becoming a peasant, tradesman, or merchant (such events do not seem to be recorded in the service genealogies), but, given the nature of Muscovy, such social descents may have occurred. The most logical outlet in fact was slavery, particularly when we consider the full range of occupations open to slaves, from managerial and combat to household. Certainly that was preferable to most other options, including suicide.

Most of the people who sold themselves in Muscovy listed no occupation, almost certainly because they had none. It has been widely assumed that such people must have been peasants, an assumption that I shall try to prove later must be false. Table 11.3 lists all the occupations stated by people when they sold themselves. If no occupation was listed, but a former status was (such as voluntary servitor, probably the same thing, essentially, as voluntary slave), I listed that instead. Tailor was the most widely held trade prior to enslavement, and other tradesmen were hatters, bootmakers, shoemakers, tanners, carpenters, smiths. Then there were a handful of churchmen who sold themselves into slavery, and also those who claimed to have been hunters or trappers. As is evident from table 11.3, none of these skills commanded a significant price premium in the slave market, in all likelihood because the purchasing slaveowners had no intention of putting their chattel to work in those capacities, but rather employed them as household help. Another factor to consider about those occupations is that most of the people who sold themselves probably were not outstanding practitioners of their trades, or they would not have had to sell themselves in the first place.

In addition to the tradesmen, there were individuals who had been members of the lower service class (*strel'tsy* and *cossacks*), or had farm jobs, such as cowherd. Far more had been peasants, and twice that number had been landless peasants. With that category we move into the basic origins of Muscovite slaves. Also important were hired day-laborers. As we shall see, a person who sold himself into slavery was likely to have been a landless peasant and a hired laborer. In each case I coded the last-listed position. Once again, there is nothing unusual about the prices paid for such people.

TABLE 11.3
Prior Occupation or Status of Slave and Price, in Rubles

Occupation or Status	Cost per Document	Cost per Slave	N
Sexton (*ponomar'*)	6.00	2.40	2
Church scribe (*d'iachok*)	6.00	6.00	1
Groom (*koniukh*)	5.00	5.00	1
Cook (*povar*)	3.00	3.00	1
Barber (*krovopusk*)	2.50	2.00	2
Tailor (*portnoi*)	3.47	3.27	15
Tailor/seamstress (*shveia/shvets*)	5.50	5.50	2
Hatter (*kolpachnik*)	2.75	2.75	1
Bootmaker (*sapozhnyi master*)	4.78	3.78	9
Shoemaker (*chebotnik*)	2.00	1.42	3
Tanner (*ovchinnik*)	10.00	10.00	1
Carpenter (*plotnik*)	3.00	3.00	1
Smith (*kuznets*)	3.00	1.00	1
Cowherd (*korovnik*)	2.33	2.33	3
Monastery steward (*okladchik*)	3.00	3.00	1
Monastery/church hired hand (*druzhinnik*)	5.00	5.00	1
Trapper (*promyshlian*)	10.00	10.00	1
Hunter	5.00	2.50	1
Butcher (*miasnik*)	2.00	2.00	1
Strelets	1.50	1.17	2
Cossack	2.78	2.00	18
Unspecified townsman	3.09	2.41	11
Peasant	2.90	2.50	51
Landless peasant (*bobyl'*)	3.28	2.02	98
Nonfarming peasants (*nepashennye*)	5.00	3.13	2
Hired laborer (*naemnik*)	3.60	3.17	68
Beggar	2.00	1.73	30
Servitor (*posluzhilets*)	3.88	2.64	70
Voluntary servitor (*dobrovol'nyi posluzhilets*)	4.60	3.56	182
Parents were slaves	4.08	2.69	48
Enslaved before	3.55	2.24	99
Mean	3.73	2.78	Total 727

Note:
N = Number of documents.

The next category was that of beggar. They also, occasionally, had been both landless peasants and day laborers. The beggars' price was definitely lower than the prices for others. Whether they were the worst risks in the sense of future utility (they might die sooner than others, for example), whether their price was lowest because they were the most desperate, or whether they cost the least because they were mostly solitaries (see tables 11.5 and 11.6) cannot be determined.

The lowest category was probably the most dependant (and therefore dependable) category, those who had already experienced household service. As we can see in table 11.3, those types typically commanded near-average or above-average prices. Often such people were known to their purchasers, for they had served relatives and others known to them previously. This assured them of their reliability and trustworthiness, for presumably almost any slaveowner would prefer to buy someone, even to pay a higher price for that person, who he was fairly certain would not flee and would not steal excessively from him. On the other hand, such purchasers were able to take advantage of such people because they were aware of their dependance, their inability to make for themselves an independent life in Muscovy. Because the Muscovite slave did not have a peculium (see chapter 5), the price of none of these slaves included the value of a peculium, as was the case in Byzantium.[11]

Tradesmen seem to have become slaves at regular intervals throughout Muscovite history. This was not true for certain of the other categories. Most volatile were the landless peasants, who constituted 28.5 percent of all known self-sales into slavery in the famine year of 1602-3, but only 2.9 percent at other times. This is not surprising, for they were no doubt hardest hit by serious crop failure. In normal times, they were well taken care of because of the shortage of labor. By contrast, the percentage of peasants selling themselves less than doubled, from 4.6 percent of all known sales into slavery at other times to 8.6 percent in 1602-3. The category of declared beggars also rose sharply, from 1.6 percent to 6.9 percent. One may assume that this reflected the lessened availability of alms. These percentage increases were primarily at the expense of formerly dependent categories, whose proportion of all transactions fell to half the usual amount. For one reason, there are no wills, dowries, or other such documents in the 1602-3 data. For another, although this might have been offset to a certain extent by the fact that many owners drove their slaves away in 1601-3 because they could not feed them, owners died in the famine as well. The major factor was that the gross quantity of persons selling themselves rose dramatically during the famine. That increase came not from people who were normally recycling themselves back into slavery, but from people in other, marginal groups who lacked their own resources to cope with successive crop failures.

Table 11.4 groups the disparate elements in table 11.3 into intellectually more coherent categories. We see that less than one-fifth of the people who sold themselves into limited service contract slavery previously had held what one might consider regular, solid jobs. We may assume that most of these people were driven to sell themselves because of sudden disaster that other societies would

---

11. Udal'tsova, p. 17. In Byzantium the skilled craftsman-slave "always" commanded a higher price than did the unskilled slave (ibid., p. 11). I doubt whether most of these people could have avoided enslavement by paying a higher interest while offering an inferior security, as suggested by Yoram Barzel in his theoretical discussion of the issue ("An Economic Analysis of Slavery," p. 43).

have helped them to overcome by offering some form of relief. The next group, the *bobyli* and *naemniki*, were constantly in trouble, always ready to fall over the brink into beggary or starvation. They, plus the actual beggars, constituted over a quarter of those who sold themselves into slavery. The biggest surprise must be the last category, those who already knew dependence, who made up over half of those selling themselves into slavery. This category may be not completely representative for all of Muscovite history because of the bulge stemming from the compulsory 1597 registration of all those persons that owners wanted to claim as slaves, but it is probably not too exaggerated. One of the distinctive features of Muscovite slavery was its recycling of dependent people, and the inability of people caught up in that dependence to escape it. As we shall see, even the law assumed that people who had been enslaved would again be enslaved, and ultimately in fact offered no other real option.

TABLE 11.4
Occupational and Social Origins of Limited Service Contract Slaves

Occupation	N	%
Craftsmen, tradesmen	36	4.9
Musketeers, cossacks	21	2.8
Townsmen, undifferentiated	11	1.5
Churchmen	5	.6
Peasants	57	7.7
Landless peasants (*bobyli*)	98	13.2
Nonplow peasants	2	.3
Hired day-laborers (*naemniki*)	68	9.0
Beggars	30	4.1
Servitors (*posluzhil'tsy*; near-slaves)	73	9.9
Voluntary servitors (*dobrovol'nye*)	184	24.7
Offspring of slaves	50	6.7
Former slaves themselves	105	14.2
Total	741	100.0
Unknown	1,375	

The large number of "unknown" in table 11.4 has proved to be disconcerting to those who are aware of it. The Soviet historian V. M. Paneiakh has compiled data somewhat similar to mine, and his Leningrad colleague R. G. Skrynnikov objected to the data in the table and pointed to the unknown, claiming that they must be peasants who had concealed their origin.[12] The same assumption, a rem-

12. R. G. Skrynnikov, "Rabstvo i kabala v XVI veke [O knige V. M. Paneiakha *Kholopstvo v XVI–nachale XVII v.*]," *Istoriia SSSR* 20, no. 3(May-June 1976): 156; Koretskii, *Zakreposhchenie*, p. 190. This discussion has most recently been continued by V. M. Paneiakh, who reported his findings that the limited service contract slavery books of the Novgorod region for the 1630s and 1640s indicate that from 13 to 66 percent of those selling them-

nant of B. D. Grekov-Stalinist historiography, is inherent in A. I. Kopanev's title of his publication of one of the major registrations, "Materials on the History of the Peasantry."[13]

There are two fundamental objections to this position. The first one is that there was absolutely no reason whatsoever for a peasant to conceal his origin. Slavery was a crisis welfare-relief institution, and the Muscovites were not so cruel as to deny a starving person succor. Thus even after the institution of the St. George's Day moving limitations at the end of the fifteenth century, the law explicitly exempted the peasant who wanted to sell himself into slavery. The logic of that exemption was simple: few peasants who had resources would want to sell themselves into slavery; a peasant without resources who was denied that form of relief would obviously die; and a dead peasant could not pay taxes or rent to anybody.[14]

The second objection to the Grekov-Kusheva-Skrynnikov position is that the statistical evidence does not lend support to a thesis that the unknown in table 11.4 must have been peasants concealing their identity. Tables 11.5 through 11.8 represent an attempt to provide an answer to this problem. As is obvious, many of the data in these tables are ahead of the general story I am discussing, for such issues as slave demography and the slaveowners are the subjects of later chapters. Nevertheless, the presentation of all this information here in the context of the origins of the Muscovite slaves will help to make the point that the slaves of unknown origin were probably not peasants. The reader may refer back to these data in connection with the social origins of other groups. Here I am concerned with two rows in these tables, "Unspecified peasant" and "Unknown."

---

selves were of peasant origin. Paneiakh gives no mean for the entire period, but his figures make it appear as though 30 percent would be a good estimate ("Iz istorii zakreposhcheniia krest'ian v kontse XVI–pervoi polovine XVII veka," *Istoriia SSSR* 1981, no. 5: 172).

13. A. I. Kopanev, "Materialy po istorii krest'ianstva," pp. 143-86; Hellie, "Recent Soviet Historiography," p. 17; G. V. Abramovich in AIS-ZR (1974), p. 195.

14. 1550 *Sudebnik* 88. One might surmise that peasants would have tried to sell themselves into slavery after the introduction of the Forbidden Years, beginning in the early 1580s, to escape the burdens of the Livonian War and its aftermath. However, there was risk in this because agricultural slaves sometimes were assessed for taxes. The main objection to this suggestion is that the profile of those who sold themselves as slaves just did not match those known to have been peasants previously.

TABLE 11.5
Social Status of Slave Prior to Enslavement—Known Compared with the Unknown

	No. of Slaves Per Document				Slave Prices in Rubles		Average Month of Sale	N
	All Slaves	Boys	Girls	Na	Per Document	Per Slave		
White collar (clergy, official)	1.56	0.00	0.33	9	5.44	4.22	April	8
Blue collar (tradesman, craftsman)	1.53	0.15	0.03	40	3.91	3.35	May	39
Military	2.10	0.30	0.20	20	2.65	1.92	April	20
Unspecified townsman	1.27	0.09	0.09	11	3.09	2.41	April	11
Unspecified peasant	1.41	0.12	0.04	51	2.90	2.50	April	51
Landless peasant (bobyl')	2.00	0.26	0.12	100	3.31	2.04	April	100
Day laborer	1.42	0.06	0.06	67	3.28	2.84	May	67
Beggar	1.21	0.06	0.00	34	2.09	1.91	April	34
Servitor	2.00	0.46	0.23	70	3.88	2.64	May	70
Voluntary servitor	1.76	0.25	0.18	182	4.60	3.56	July	182
Parents were slaves	1.90	0.31	0.17	48	4.08	2.69	August	48
Enslaved him/herself	2.15	0.46	0.29	99	3.55	2.24	May	97
Unknown	1.95	0.41	0.22	1,456	3.80	2.42	May	1,324
Mean	1.93	0.36	0.20	2,187b	3.80	2.53	May	2,051

aN is for both number of slaves and prices.
bOnly those documents for which there are prices.

Demographically, the number of persons per sale-transaction is definitely different for peasants and unknown in table 11.5 (This is more useful in this context than the similar information in table 11.6, which includes all the documents, sales plus dowries, wills, and other nonmonetary transfers; the latter category by definition includes considerably more individuals who were slaves earlier than does the sale category.) Not only is the total number of individuals for the peasants only three-quarters of the unknown, but the average number of boys and girls is only a quarter as much. The price paid per document for peasants is also considerably less, reflecting the lesser number of individuals as well as the earlier time of sale in the year. We see also (in table 11.6) that peasants who sold themselves tended to be younger than were the unknown. While the numbers may be too few to mean much in this context, peasants seem to have had their first surviving child at a slightly younger age than did the unknown (table 11.7). Again the numbers may be too small to be significant, but it appears as though those who purchased peasants as slaves had considerably more land than those who purchased the slaves of unknown origin (table 11.8). This should not be too surprising, for they may have purchased the peasants to farm for them, rather than to serve in the house. The land and cash compensation schedules probably do not tell us anything in this context.

TABLE 11.6
Social Status of Slave Prior to Enslavement—Known Compared with the Unknown

	No. of Slaves per Document				Ages								
	All Slaves	Boys	Girls	N	Major Person	N	Husband	N	Wife	N	First Child	N	
White collar (clergy, official)	2.60	0.10	0.40	10	31.4	7	20.0	1	15.0	1	7.0	1	
Blue collar (tradesman, craftsman)	2.58	0.29	0.11	45	26.2	25	29.3	7	30.0	5	7.0	3	
Military	2.05	0.29	0.19	21	30.3	17	33.3	9	25.8	6	7.0	7	
Unspecified townsman	1.27	0.09	0.09	11	18.6	9	23.0	1	—		—		
Unspecified peasant	1.45	0.15	0.04	53	21.6	38	28.1	8	26.4	7	7.0	7	
Landless peasant (bobyl')	2.00	0.26	0.12	100	27.3	89	30.1	31	25.2	29	10.8	24	
Day laborer	1.41	0.06	0.06	68	26.5	59	30.8	13	27.5	12	5.8	6	
Beggar	1.21	0.06	0.00	35	21.0	32	34.5	4	28.8	4	6.0	1	
Servitor	1.97	0.45	0.21	75	28.0	48	34.1	17	28.9	15	10.9	21	
Voluntary servitor	1.78	0.25	0.20	184	26.8	160	30.5	48	26.2	45	9.5	36	
Parents were slaves	3.19	1.28	0.55	67	25.6	43	29.6	19	28.0	17	7.9	10	
Enslaved him/herself	4.29	0.95	0.64	286	28.7	74	30.1	27	26.9	21	9.6	32	
Unknown	1.98	0.40	0.23	1,544	24.3	484	29.6	155	26.5	108	10.2	131	
Mean	2.23	0.45	0.26	2,499a	25.4	1,085	30.1	340	26.6	270	9.8	279	

aBased on every document in data set.

TABLE 11.7
Social Status of Slave Prior to Enslavement–Known Compared with the Unknown

| | Age at Birth of First Child | | |
	Husband	Wife	N
White collar (clergy, official)	–	–	–
Blue collar (tradesman, craftsman)	29.5	27.0	2
Military	26.7	25.0	3
Unspecified townsman	–	–	–
Unspecified peasant	24.3	21.0	3
Landless peasant (*bobyl'*)	25.7	20.3	12
Day laborer	31.5	22.8	4
Beggar	44.0	29.0	1
Servitor	27.1	22.8	8
Voluntary servitor	25.8	20.4	27
Parents were slaves	26.3	25.6	7
Enslaved him/herself	23.4	18.0	14
Unknown	25.4	21.5	37
Mean	25.9	21.3	118

TABLE 11.8
Social Status of Slave Prior to Enslavement (Known Compared with Unknown) and the
Slaveowner's Compensation Schedules and Landholding

Slave's Status	Landholding (Cheti)	N	Land Compensation Schedule (Cheti)	N	Cash Compensation Schedule (Rubles)	N
White collar	443.0	1	483.0	1	8.00	1
Blue collar	117.8	10	423.1	13	14.20	5
Military	–	–	550.0	3	25.00	1
Unspecified townsman	45.0	1	250.0	2	9.00	1
Unspecified peasant	320.0	8	443.8	16	16.83	6
Landless peasant	151.7	16	285.7	14	15.86	7
Day laborer	252.4	17	434.6	13	11.40	5
Beggar	160.7	6	375.0	4	11.75	4
Servitor	196.9	20	407.5	12	9.00	9
Voluntary servitor	246.1	46	532.2	45	22.95	22
Parents were slaves	154.4	13	458.3	18	19.45	11
Enslaved him/herself	178.1	64	453.0	77	13.36	28
Unknown	228.1	383	477.8	446	15.23	203
Mean	218.7	585	469.0	664	15.50	303

Note: The variables "Peasants" and "Peasant Households" are too few to list.

If one goes through tables 11.5 to 11.8 again, it appears as though the unknown are much more like the various formerly-dependent categories. Also, they are much like the overall averages. This is true partially because the unknown make up a large part of the averages, and also because the unknowns are probably a relatively random representation of the entire known set, with perhaps a nod toward the formerly dependent categories. What is almost certain is that the unknown do not conceal primarily hidden peasants.

Throughout this section I have observed that many of those who sold themselves into slavery had been formerly dependent in one way or another. In 86 cases those people mentioned how long they had served with their masters before finally selling themselves to them. These data are presented in figure 11.1, along with the prices paid for the slaves. We first note that the precision of the data may be questioned, for they tend to heap in the 1, 5, 10, 15, and 20-year categories. Nevertheless, such imprecision is not crucial for averages, and certainly there was no reason to prevaricate, unless perhaps those who had served a long time exaggerated their length of service for various reasons, such as proving personal loyalty. Be that as it may, the average length of prior service was 8.3 years. The relationship between the prior length of service and the price paid for slaves is by no means linear, although it is apparent that lower prices were paid for slaves with considerably less service, and generally higher prices were paid for longer service. As is evident in figure 11.1, there was some tendency for contracts involving those who had served longer to contain more people. Because very little additional was ordinarily paid for any slaves in a contract besides the major one prior to 1613, the price per slave in these instances had little linear relationship to the length of service (r = 0.13). Thus, if these prices have much meaning, they reflect the fact that older people who had served longer were somewhat more likely to include more family members with them in the contract, and purchasers were willing to pay a bit more for "seasoned" slaves known to be reliable and less likely to flee than "fresh" slaves.

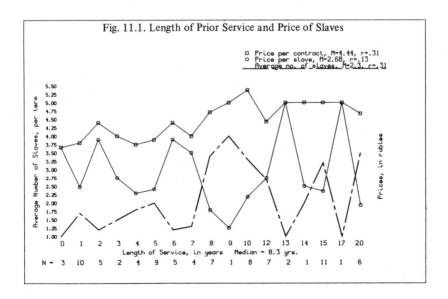

Fig. 11.1. Length of Prior Service and Price of Slaves

Precipitants of Slavery in Muscovy

I have just discussed the social origins of the people who became slaves in Muscovy, and now I shall turn to an examination of the causes that precipitated slavery there.

As discussed earlier, in Muscovy, as in Ancient Mesopotamia, a certain portion of the slaves and their descendants were prisoners of war.[15] Unlike Europe in the Middle Ages and the New World, Muscovy got few slaves generated by other peoples and transmitted to it by the slave trade.[16] Rebellion by peoples subjugated by the Muscovites, such as the various Turkic peoples, could very well have had as its consequence the enslavement of those peoples upon their reconquest. We saw such an operation in the case of Miakinin v. Velkov, discussed in chapter 8 above.[17] It was also true elsewhere that rebellion on the part of peoples of a different race was punished with slavery, as in the Middle Ages, for the conquered Moslems in Spain, and for Amerindians who revolted against European subjugation.[18] As I noted in chapter 2, Tatars for much of Muscovite history were a special category of people, who could be "outsiders" or "insiders," depending upon the circumstances. They could be captured and registered as slaves by their captors, or they could be purchased in the Don frontier area and then registered as slave property.[19]

The nature of the sales of Tatars on the Don is not entirely known, but one may assume that many of the sales were of children by their parents. Tatars relatively often sold their children to Christian merchants in the Middle Ages, and there is no reason to assume that this practice stopped forever after the Genoese and Venetians were driven out of the Black Sea. The *New Chronicle* observed the persistence of that old practice when it noted that Boris Godunov had sowed so much dissension among the Nogai Tatars that they laid waste many of their own uluses in civil war, and fathers from the devastated communities sold their children into slavery in Astrakhan'.[20] Presumably many of those children were sold to Russians.

The *New Chronicle*'s account of the fathers selling their children seems to express a certain amount of horror at that act, which is not surprising because that seems to have been something that Russians generally did not do. The sale into slavery of children that parents did not want or were unable to provide for was not a rare event in the history of mankind, especially in societies that experienced frequent shortfalls of food, as did Muscovy. For centuries the Chinese (often illegally) and Indians sold children when food was short as a result of condi-

15. Mendelsohn, p. 5.
16. Verlinden, *Colonization*, p. 28.
17. Iakovlev, *Kholopstvo*, p. 503.
18. Verlinden, p. 43.
19. 1649 *Ulozhenie* 20: 99; MS, p. 291.
20. Verlinden, pp. 45, 85; PSRL 14[1]: 52.

tions ranging from widespread natural calamities to individual improvidence.[21] However, instances of the sale by Muscovite parents of their children were very rare, less than ten being recorded. Instead of selling their children, the Musço-vites seemed to have preferred to let them die, as will be shown in chapter 13. The reasons for that preference can only be speculated on. Certainly, there was no legal prohibition against the selling of offspring: it was illegal for people un-der fifteen to sell themselves, a prohibition known to have been violated only in the depths of the 1601-3 famine, but nothing was ever written forbidding par-ents to sell their children. It is also possible that the market for children simply was very small. As I mentioned above, the law noted that there was a negative price for children, and this fact seems to be generally reflected in a point shown by regression analysis (see chapter 18), namely, that children added very little to the value of a slavery contract. This does not violate the laws of logic, for chil-dren are probably a liability in domestic slavery: they have to be fed, and they distract the slave mother from tasks that she might otherwise perform. In spite of that fact, however, the Muscovites occasionally did purchase parentless chil-dren of the same ethnos, and presumably brought some of the Tatar children as well. In all likelihood, the prohibition against parents selling their children was internally generated, one of the numerous manifestations of the general Musco-vite reluctance to engage in any form of trade in human beings at all.

The oldest extant document on the sale of children is dated December 30, 1500. Ivan Fedorov Novokshchenov's slave Matfeiko Okulov purchased for his owner from Ivashko Pavlov the Novgorodian his sons Fedotko and Obrosimko as full slaves for the sum of a Novgorodian ruble.[22] Novokshchenov, himself either a Tatar convert to Orthodoxy or the offspring of one, was a prominent landhold-er in Votskaia piatina according to the 1495-1505 land cadastres who possessed 405 cheti of land inhabited by sixty-seven peasants living in thirty-eight house-holds. His transactions were conducted for him by other slaves, and it is known that he owned at least seventeen slaves.[23] The document in question was regis-tered, along with twenty-six others, ninety-eight years later by Novokshchenov's heir, Voin Ofonas'ev Novokshchenov, a prominent *syn boiarskii* of Votskaia piatina on the court land register who was entitled to the maximum 600 cheti of land, was serving as the elected director of the military levy, and possessed at least twenty-four slaves.[24] Whether Voin registered the 1500 document as an an-tiquarian, or because he was claiming offspring of the two boys, is not clear.

---

21. Watson, *Systems*, pp. 232, 236; Wiens, p. 297. Parents who sold their children into slavery in the Ch'ing period were supposed to be punished with forty blows of the heavy bamboo (Meijer, p. 331).

22. RIB 17: 129, no. 834; ASEI 3: 438, no. 444.

23. Gnevushev, *Ocherki*, pp. 96, 99; ASEI 3: 425-53.

24. DVP, pp. 468, 470; Ivanov, OPK, p. 56; Barsukov, SGV, p. 132; RIB 22(1908): 103, 700-702, 708, 825; Samokvasov, *Materialy* 2(1909): 553, no. 72; DR 1: 248, 297, 646, 826, 923; KR 1: 81, 197, 1108, 1217, 1262, 2: 347, 736; *Opisanie* 15(1908): 22, 88, nos.

The apparent absolute power parents held over their children in early Muscovy
is evident in a document dated 1510. A slave by the name of Gridia Ivanov purchased for his master, Grigorii Fedorov Novokshchenov, from Tat'iana Zenov'-
eva her son Grid'ia Gordeev, his wife Ogaf'itsa Eremeeva, and their son Mikitka
the Novgorodian as full slaves for the sum of 4 rubles. Grigorii, like his brother
Ivan Novokshchenov, lived in Votskaia piatina, but he had more land (410 cheti)
and fewer peasants (sixty-one living in thirty households).[25] What the actual arrangements in that case were is unclear, whether Grid'ia and his wife and son
agreed to be sold, or whether his mother just sold them by right of mater famil-
ias.[26] The document was registered in 1597 by Andrei Riumin Novokshchenov,
in 1605 a *syn boiarskii* on the court land compensation list from Votskaia piatina who was entitled to 550 cheti of land.[27]

The last extant sale by a parent of his offspring into full slavery was dated
1525. On December 11, Piatoi Dobrynin, the slave of Nekliud Dmitreev Buturlin, purchased for his master Dmitreits the barber (*krovopusk*) from the latter's
father, Ivan Nazar'ev of Gorodenskii pogost, for the sum of 3 rubles. Nothing
more is known about Buturlin, for information about people who flourished in
the 1520s and 1530s is scarce. We may assume that Dmitreits was already an a-
dult, or else he would not have had the appellation of *krovopusk*. The document
was registered in 1598 for obvious reasons by the initial purchaser's son, Fedor
Nekliudov Buturlin, a leading Votskaia piatina *syn boiarskii*, an elected muster
director, on the 1605 court list entitled to 600 cheti of land: on the basis of the
1525 document he was laying claim to Dmitreits's grandson, a cook by the name
of Oleshka Grigor'ev, who was a fugitive.[28] This was a typical example of the
perpetual nature of Muscovite full slavery. Certainly it must be atypical that in
two of the three extant cases of sale by parents of their offspring into full slavery, the latter were already adults—unless by some circumstance this reflects the
fact that the market for children in Muscovy seems to have been very small.

The practice of parents selling their children seems to have died out after 1525,
or at least no records of such sales are extant. Whether the provision of the 1529
Lithuanian Statute forbidding parental sale of children into slavery had any impact in Muscovy is unknown, but the West Russian law may have expressed an

14, I, 65; RIB 35(1917): 772; AAE 3: 282; Ardashev, RKiSPP, pp. 108, 227; Shumakov,
Obzor 4(1917): 207, no. 709; Veselovskii, APD 1(1913): 522, 524, 528, nos. 248-49, 253;
idem, APD 2(1977): 31, no. 8; Belokurov, RZ 7113-21, p. 255; Ivanov, AUBK, p. 294; RIB
22(1908): 700-1, 711.

25. Gnevushev, *Ocherki*, p. 96.

26. RIB 17: 35, no. 102.

27. DVP, p. 473.

28. RIB 17: 80, no. 227; DVP, pp. 468, 470; Ianitskii, p. 115; Samokvasov, *Materialy*
2(1909): 28; Ardashev, RKiSPP (110), p. 59 (questionable); Sukhotin, ChSV, p. 275; RK
1598-1638, p. 328; DR 1: 343, 418, 616, 743; KR 1: 527, 939, 1152, 1247; Samokvasov,
AM 1: 49.

East Slavic consensus on the issue. At any rate, the sale of children was revived, in a modified form, during the famine of 1603, the type of event that had the capacity to change, at least temporarily, established institutions. Four otherwise relatively obscure landholders in the Novgorod region (including one woman, Onos'eia Sofontieva Okliacheeva) purchased children for 2 rubles apiece. Three of the children were girls (two of them age twelve, the third not specified), and the fourth was a boy of seventeen. (Why the last, legally an adult, did not sell himself is not clear.) In each case one parent was involved in the transaction (the father in the case of the girl of unspecified age, mothers in the other cases), one of the cases said that the other parent was deceased, and we may assume that this was true in the other transactions as well. The verbs used were that the parent "gave away" (*otdal, otdavala*) the child, "ordered" (*velila*) the limited service slavery contract written, or "was present" (*stoiala*) at the transaction.[29] In none of these cases was it stated that the parent sold the child or received the 2 rubles. Therefore, it is not clear whether these are actually cases of parents selling their children or rather legitimizing their sale during a famine. I should be inclined to favor the latter interpretation.

In spite of apparent Muscovite revulsion at the thought of selling children, such an expedient could not die in a land where parents still had the power of life and death over their offspring. The following 1647 document is the sole evidence in my possession of the sale of children after the famine of 1603, but one may assume there were others, although probably few of them. This is not unlike similar transactions going back to the dawn of written human history.

On May 5 the elite Novgorod merchants [*gosti*] Semen and Ivan Stoianov petitioned orally to governor Prince Semen Andreevich Urusov and state secretary Luk'ian Talyzin and submitted [to them] for registration, for recording, a gift memorandum [*dannaia zapis'*], that [they] would order the memorandum recorded in the limited service slavery contract record books.

Governor Prince Semen Andreevich Urusov and state secretary Luk'ian Talyzin, having heard the oral petition and the gift memorandum of Semen and Ivan Stoianov, ordered that memorandum registered in the limited service slavery contract registration books. In the memorandum is written:

Be it known that I, Nikula Leontiev, a Novgorod gardener, have given a memorandum to the elite Novgorod merchants Semen and Ivan Ivanovich Stoianov because I, Nikula, owe them recorded and unrecorded debts totalling 50 rubles, and I, Nikula, have no means to pay them my debt of 50 rubles. I, Nikula, for my debt of 50 rubles have given them, the elite Novgorod merchants Semen Ivanovich and Ivan Ivanovich Stoianov, my children [to serve] in their household. The children are my boy Senka and another boy, a two-year-old, Ivashka, and three daughters, Natalka, Oksiushka, and Ovdot'itsa. All my children are to serve them in their household until their [presumably, the Sto-

29. NZKK 2: 231, 317, 338-39.

ianovs'] death. They are to perform whatever servile obligations they compel them to, and my children are to obey and be submissive to them. Semen Ivanovich and Ivan Ivanovich are free to chastise those children of mine with any chastisement for a fault, and they are to keep them from doing ill. I, Nikula, will in no way intercede [*ni v odnogo ne vstupat'sia*] for my children, and I will not submit a petition about them to the sovereign tsar and grand prince Aleksei Mikhailovich of all Rus' in any town. I have absolutely no resourses to provide food, drink, clothing, and shoes for my children. If I, Nikula, petition the sovereign about my children or intercede for them, the Novgorod elite merchants Semen Ivanovich and Ivan Ivanovich Stoianov shall exact from me, Nikula, 100 Moscow rubles on the basis of this memorandum. Henceforth, on the basis of this memorandum, my children are bound to serve them in the household. For flight and theft by my children I, Nikula, provide them complete guarantee of responsibility. I, Nikula, have presented this gift document on my children as evidence of these intentions.

The document was witnessed by Grigorei Stepanov and Fedotov Nikiforov. The gift memorandum was written by the town square scribe Vaska Okhanatkov on May 5, 1647.[30]

This was followed by physical descriptions of the children, who ranged in ages from two to sixteen.

Several things are noteworthy about this document. The first is the sum. Why two elite Novgorod merchants, who are known to have run a fishery on the Volkhov River, to have brought gifts from the Swedish queen to the tsar after one of their trips abroad, to have testified on the 1648 Moscow fire and uprising, and to have been the object of the wrath of the Novgorod rioters in 1650 because they allegedly were exporting grain and meat during a famine, would have loaned the enormous sum of 50 rubles to a Novgorod gardener is unclear.[31] Perhaps entrapment was their motive. But why would they want parentless infants and teenagers running about their houses? It also is not clear why two owners were allowed here, when the clear preference of the law was for only one. One may suspect that this option of settling debts by selling children was relatively unused, so the issue of joint ownership may not have arisen. On the other hand, it seems to have been used sufficiently for a formula to be present that the Novgo-

30. I. D. Beliaev, "Zakony i akty, ustanavlivaiushchie v drevnei Rusi krepostnoe sostoianie," *Arkhiv istoricheskikh i prakticheskikh svedenii otnos. k Rossii* 1859, bk. 2: 100-102. On the selling of children into slavery in other societies (such as Nepal, India, China, and Thailand), see Watson, *Asian and African Systems*, p. 27. The available evidence does not seem to support foreign claims that many Russian parents sold their children into slavery (Ioann Georg Korb, *Dnevnik puteshestviia v Moskoviiu* [*1698 i 1699 gg.*], trans. and ed. by A. I. Malein [St. Petersburg: Suvorin, 1906], p. 240).

31. RIB 35(1917): 1084, 1086; AAE 3: 464; AI 4: 246; AMG 2: 472; DAI 3: 182, 240-43, 500-1, 503; LZAK 19(1903): 42, 238; RIB 5(1878): 121-22, 146-47, 165, 222, 243, 688-90, 1023; V. M. Paneiakh, "Novye materialy o Novgorodskom vosstanii 1650 goda," *Voprosy istorii* 1981, no. 2: 83, 88, 99.

rod scribe could copy, or at least work up out of what he knew. It is also not clear why Nikula did not use the device of debt slavery to handle the problem, for the six of them could have worked off the 50-ruble obligation at the rate of at least 11 rubles per year. Perhaps he was recently widowed and had lost control, perhaps he himself did not want to be a slave, perhaps the Stoianovs did not want him. A final point is worth making: Nikula certainly was expected to put considerable distance between himself and his children. This is logical, for the slave is supposed to be kinless. However, some students of slavery exempt debt slavery from this requirement, for often the debt slave has kin nearby. As we saw in chapter 2, the relatives of the African pawn could intercede for him. This 1647 document explicitly denies the right of intercession, a distancing mechanism that unquestionably made Muscovite slavery precisely that, rather than some more benign form of servitude.

While the Muscovites may be assumed to have practiced infanticide (in all of its dimensions, including allowing other children [those no longer infants] to die selectively), there is no evidence that this produced slaves. Exposure was one of the devices whereby the Greeks legitimized the sale of their own people. Certain African tribes exposed children of "a fateful birth" whose teeth first appeared in the upper jaw, and then other Africans picked up such infants and kept them or sold them as slaves. The peoples of both the classical Mediterranean lands and of Africa had more use for children than did the Muscovites, so it is not surprising that they took exposed children as slaves, whereas the Muscovites did not.[32]

Debt produced a number of slaves in Muscovy, but, judging by the available statistical and judicial information, such cases were relatively few. Many peasants borrowed money (crop loans, essentially) every year, but they seem to have been able to repay them regularly. V. O. Kliuchevskii advanced the famous "indebtedness theory" about the origins of Russian serfdom, but this has been effectively refuted. Thus Muscovy was not like the Ancient Near East, where insolvency inevitably led to the debtor's enslavement, and such slaves were the large majority of all slaves. Nor was early modern Russia like India, where low caste younger relations were occasionally sold into slavery by their elders who had no other way to pay their debts, or Thailand, where debt slaves were often the debtor's wife, children, or other close junior kin. Although the Muscovites are known to have used the courts to force one another into debt slavery, they did not do it frequently enough to develop an aphorism such as that from Northern Sumatra: "The clever one wins the law suit, the stupid one goes to the slave-stand in the market."[33]

As far as I am aware, a criminal could not sell himself into limited service contract slavery to escape criminal punishment. A criminal who could not pay a

32. Westermann, p. 6; Miers and Kopytoff, pp. 268, 439, 443-45, 455.
33. Mendelsohn, p. 23; Hjejle, p. 91; Turton, in Watson, *Asian*, p. 265; Pulleyblank, pp. 191, 207; Wilbur, p. 85; Raj Chanana, p. 68; Vergouwen, *Customary Law*, p. 293.

fine might default into debt slavery, a provision prescribed in article 55 of the *Sudebnik* of 1550. Earlier, as stated in a 1353 will, the 1397-98 Dvina Land Judicial Charter, and article 10 of the 1497 *Sudebnik*, crime might lead more directly to enslavement, but the sixteenth century preferred triadic sanctions (corporal punishment, jailing, and regulated term debt-slavery).[34]

Once again, one is forced to note how unusual was the fact that the majority of the slaves in Muscovy were natives who sold themselves into bondage. In the Ancient Near East, voluntary self-sale was common among *strangers* in the land.[35] The rarity with which Hebrews became voluntary perpetual slaves among their own people is exemplified by the very complexity of the process. As we have seen, the biblical Jews prescribed a six-year limit on enslavement for debt. However, the lawgivers understood that debt slavery was likely to create a permanent dependency syndrome, and so allowed the debtors to remain with the creditors after the sixth year, whereupon the freedman became a voluntary, perpetual slave. This process had to be approved first by the judges, and then the master had to bore through the slave's ear with an awl, presumably for the purpose of affixing an ownership tag (Ex. 21: 2-6; Deut. 15: 12-17). The Ethiopian *Fetha Nagast*, borrowing from the practice of Roman law, allowed self-sale only by collusion.

> If a free man who has attained twenty years of age confesses to having bonds of slavery to another, consents to be sold, and then persists in this confession— so much so that his [purported] master sells him or gives him away as dowry to his wife—he becames a slave. Especially is this so if it is said that he has agreed with the one who sold him on his price.[36]

This article, based on the Justinian *Institutes* (I, 3, 3) and *Digest* (I, 5, 5.1), makes it difficult for a native to sell himself, a process only possible by the free man's fraudulently admitting that he is a slave and colluding with his alleged owner to split the sum the alleged new (and really first) owner is going to pay for him. A final illustration of the general reluctance of most societies to permit their own people to sell themselves into perpetual slavery may be taken from Lesser Armenia, in Asia Minor, dated March 31, 1279. A man agreed to pay 400

34. DDG, p. 14, no. 3 (the problem here is whether *vina* means "crime" or "debt"; Zimin, *Kholopy*, pp. 311-12); 1397-98 *Dvinskaia ustavnaia gramota* 28-29; 1497 *Sudebnik* 10; 1550 *Sudebnik* 55. The issue seems to have been overlooked in the 1649 *Ulozhenie*, but the Felony Statue of 1669 (article 22) permitted the conversion of a felon (but not his wife) into a debt slave to satisfy tortious losses at the rate of 5 rubles per year. While the Muscovites knew the doctrine of vicarious responsibility, it did not generate slaves, as in China, where wives and children of executed traitors were given out as slaves. The Chinese also enslaved criminals, who were banished to the frontier (Meijer, pp. 328-29).

35. Mendelsohn, p. 23.

36. *The Fetha Nagast*, p. 177.

Armenian dirhems for a woman, but the notary refused to recognize the transaction.[37]

For reasons that I shall attempt to explain in chapter 12, the Muscovites felt no compunction whatsoever about self-sale into perpetual slavery. The legislation of 1586-97 was probably enacted in an attempt to curtail the practice, but native habits won out, and finally the government was forced to recognize that aspect of Muscovite reality. First I shall discuss briefly why this practice was necessary in Muscovy, and then conclude the chapter with illustrations of the types of precipitants causing Muscovites to sell themselves.

Slavery was necessary in Muscovy because there were inadequate alternative relief or welfare institutions. The amount of relief available in Muscovy is unknown. The *Sudebniki* of 1497 (article 59), 1550 (article 91), and 1589 (article 184) repeat the old provisions from the medieval Church Statue of Yaroslav that widows who are living off church alms are subject to church legal jurisdiction. Article 189 of the *Sudebnik* of 1589 is somewhat enigmatic in a charity context. The first half of the article forbids merchants to live in monasteries and requires that they be dispatched from their tax havens immediately. Then the second half of the article says: "But the poor who are feeding off the church of God shall live at monasteries." Obviously this did not *require* them to live there, and much less did it require monasteries to provide alms for the poor. I would interpret this to mean simply that, besides monks and nuns, only those too poor to pay taxes could live in monasteries, and that everyone else was supposed to live somewhere where the tax collector could find him. As is well known, providing charity was not the self-prescribed function of the Muscovite church, and the Studion Rule (the ideological and practical basis of Russian Orthodoxy, and particularly of its cenobitic monastic practices) did not recognize almsgiving. Fedotov observed that charity, which had been the dominant ethical attitude in Kievan Rus', yielded in Muscovy to an ethics based on fear of God or men.[38] As a consequence, monasteries, which owned a third of all the cultivated land by 1550, worked for their own aggrandizement. Idiorrhythmic institutions existed on the sums that those who lived in them brought with them. Cenobitic ones were more entrepreneurial, often made at least some of the monks work, and invested their incomes in their own enterprises, which sometimes remind us of modern, vertically integrated conglomerates. Moreover, there were a vast number of monks, all of whom had to be fed, and it is by no means clear that most mon-

37. Verlinden, *Colonization*, p. 88. For a discussion of self-sale into slavery, see Yoram Barzel, "An Economic Analysis of Slavery," pp. 101, 105. For additional discussion of "voluntary servitors" throughout history who were not quite full slaves, see Iu. I. Semenov, "Ob odnoi iz rannikh nerabovladel'cheskikh form ekspluatatsii [kabal'naia ekspluatatsiia]," in *Razlozhenie rodovogo stroia i formirovanie klassovogo obshchestva*, ed. A. I. Pershits (Moscow: Nauka, 1968), pp. 250-90.

38. G. P. Fedotov, *The Russian Religious Mind*, 2 vols. (Cambridge: Harvard University Press, 1966), 1: 389.

asteries had any surplus to give away in the form of charity. Considering the fact that most monasteries received a state subsidy (the *ruga*), originally given in exchange for the cancellation of various immunities, we may assume that on balance most monasteries were deficit spenders.

This meant that the state was called upon to provide charity, and of course the state was almost always on the brink of bankruptcy because of its military expenditures. As we know, Boris Godunov tried to provide alms during the famine, and perhaps did little to help because people from all over Muscovy tried to get to the capital for a handout. Tens of thousands died before they could get there, a horrendous number died in Moscow as well.[39] After the Time of Troubles and after the recovery of Novgorod from the Swedes, the government in 1618 set up "new almshouses for the poor" (*novye bogadel'nye izby nishchim*), near the tsar's residence on Nikitina Street. The Novgorod almshouse had a budget of 3.50 rubles per year, or 50 kopeks for each of seven persons.[40] The sum was inadequate to feed a person for a year, as we have seen, and seven people was a ludicrously small number, considering the demand. Nevertheless, it was a step in the right direction. More will be said on this subject in chapter 18. Here the point to be made is that relief in 1618 was still on a minuscule scale, that one may assume even less was available before then, and that people needing temporary relief could only find it in selling themselves into slavery.

Full slavery and then limited service contract slavery were stress phenomena, historically an unusual response to the universal human phenomenon of psycho-physiological stress. In modern biological parlance, stress distorts the chemical balance of one of the catecholamines, norepinephrine (noradrenalin), and some Muscovites sought relief by selling themselves into slavery.[41]

A slightly different but perhaps ultimately similar case may have occurred among the Northwest Coast Amerindians. The comparativist Bernard J. Siegel, presenting the Indian case, noted that "although most chattel slaves are not obtained from the in-group, this is not invariably so. There have been a few cases among the Northwest Coast Indians of commoners of very low socio-economic status who, for want of prestige, have virtually fallen without the protection of their clan or village."[42] The economic stress of both the Muscovites and Ameri-

39. Konrad Bussov, *Moskovskaia khronika 1584-1613* (Moscow-Leningrad: AN SSSR, 1961), pp. 98, 346-47; V. I. Koretskii, "Golod 1601-1603 gg. v Rossii i tserkov'," *Voprosy istorii religii i ateizma* 7(1959): 218-56.

40. A. M. Gnevushev, *Sel'skoe naselenie Novgorodskoi oblasti po pistsovym knigam 1495-1505 godov* (? , 1911), pp. 134-35.

41. The popular American literature on stress is enormous. For a recent example, see Maggie Scarf, "From Joy to Depression. New Insights into the Chemistry of Moods," *The New York Times Magazine* (April 24, 1977): 30-34. For a recent scholarly Soviet treatment, see Iu. M. Gubachev et al., *Emotsional'nyi stress v usloviiakh normy i patologii cheloveka* (Leningrad: Meditsina, 1976).

42. Siegel, "Methodological Considerations," p. 376.

can Indians may have been similar, but, due to the differences in social structure of the two societies, one may imagine that the prestige element was less in Muscovy.

There were numerous stressful events of varying magnitudes that precipitated Muscovites into slavery. Crop failure and destruction, food shortages, and famine were perhaps the primary causes. As we have seen, marginal people dependent on agriculture, such as landless peasants, were propelled into slavery in great numbers during the famine of 1601-3. Peasants also suffered from crop failures, and it is not accidental that the *Sudebnik* of 1550 (article 88) allowed peasants to sell themselves at any time. As we know, ordinarily peasants could move only in the period of St. George's Day, around November 26, but obviously those needing welfare assistance could not be expected to wait for that two-week period. Another sign that self-sale into slavery was a stress phenomenon lies in the fact that the bulk of those events came during the harsh winter months, December through March, when people lacking their own food and shelter had to find relief, or starve and freeze to death.

Robert Best, an English traveler to Muscovy in the 1550s, comparatively good times on the east European plain, wrote the following about the poor:

> There are a great number of poore people among them, which die dayly for lacke of substenance, which is a pitifull case to beholde; for there hath beene buried in a small time, within these two yeeres, about 80. persons, yoong and olde, which haue dyed onely for lacke of substenance: for if they had had straw and water enough, they would have shift to liue, for a great many are forced in the winter to dry straw and stampe it, and to make bread thereof, or at least they eat it in stead of bread. In the summer they make good shift with grasse, herbs, and roots; barks of trees is good meat with them at all times. There is no people in the world, as I suppose, that liue so miserably as do the pouertie in those parts: and the most part of them that haue sufficient for themselues, and also to relieue others that need, are so vnmercifull that they care not how many they see die of famine or hunger in the streets.[43]

Note should be taken of the lack of private charity that Best observed. The stress that some of those who sold themselves were under is evident in the descriptions of the slaves, some of whom were going gray at the ages of twenty and twenty-five.[44] Another person had rotting feet, certainly a cause of stress.[45]

---

43. E. Delmar Morgan and C. H. Coote, eds., *Early Voyages and Travels to Russia and Persia* (London: The Hakluyt Society) 73: 376.

44. NZKK 1: 402, 414, 2: 24.

45. NZKK 1: 372. Whether the Muscovites were aware of their failure to be charitable and of the consequences of this failure is not clear. The test would be the Time of Troubles, precipitated in part by thousands of slaves and others who, lacking sustenance, drifted to the southern frontier and joined the attack on the established order (see chapter 16). Contemporary explanations for the disaster ranged from "God's wrath because of our sins" to some-

Strange as it may seem, self-sale into slavery was also a possible second-order consequence of other stressful events such as marital disharmony, the birth of a first child, and even lonelinesss, not to speak of such more expected causes such as orphanage. It appears as though limited service contract slavery was a vehicle that a couple could use to arrange a divorce, in spite of the legal principles of marriage inherited from Byzantium. In one instance for which the documents are extant, the husband and two children sold themselves to one slave buyer, the wife and a third child sold themselves to a different slave buyer.[46] That this was a divorce must have been apparent to the local officials who wrote and registered the documents. However, for all I know, it was not explicitly against the law, as Russians often understood it: nowhere did it say that spouses could not sell themselves to different buyers. For this to have been made a violation, someone would have had to bring the matter to the attention of the civil or church authorities. The officials writing the contracts would not be likely to do so, for they would have lost their fees. Divorce per se was not legal under Orthodox canon law, but the method of achieving it that I have just described was not specifically proscribed. It was a victimless crime with no one to complain, so nothing was done about it.

Marital difficulties must have served as a precipitant for still others to sell themselves into slavery. Desertion by the husband was an obvious precipitant for an abandoned wife to sell herself, for what else was she to do? Thus 68 of the cases in my basic data set feature a married woman as the major figure. Of the 68, 28 were alone, 26 had one child, 11 had two children, and 3 had three children. Widows were identified as such (see chapter 13), so one may assume that most of the 68 had been abandoned by their husbands. In a limited sense, at least, the existence of slavery allowed, or even encouraged, marriage separations: husbands could desert knowing that a slaveowner would (or might, depending on the circumstances) take care of an unwanted wife and children.

The birth of a child, particularly a first child, is a stressful event for almost any family, and so it was in Muscovy. Chapter 13 will show that the usual practice was for the parents suffering severe stress to allow (if in fact they had any choice) young children to die before they sold themselves into slavery. There were other cases, however, in which it is quite apparent that a couple did not want to let the child die, and so sold themselves into slavery almost certainly with the hope of forestalling such an eventuality.[47] (Whether the gamble was

what more earthly notions that the Muscovites had been insufficiently "friendly" and "socially harmonious." Whether those ideas embraced the fact that there was insufficient charity, that the well-to-do were indifferent to the impoverished, cannot be determined (A. I. Iakovlev, " 'Bezumnoe molchanie.' [Prichiny Smuty po vzgliadam russkikh sovremennikov ee]," *Sbornik statei, posviashchennykh Vasiliiu Osipovichu Kliuchevskomu* [Moscow, 1909], pp. 664-65).

46. RIB 17: 54, 105, nos. 155, 293.

47. Bychkov, LZAK, pp. 2, 4; NKK 7105, p. 4; NZKK 2: 304, 317; *Russkii vestnik*(1841):

successful is unknown, but at least the infant lived long enough to be formally registered as a slave.)

Death was another major precipitant.[48] Certainly single women could survive in Muscovy, but no doubt most of the 92 widows who sold themselves found life easier as slaves than they would have trying to make their own way on the alms provided by the church. Similarly, we may assume that the 83 contracts made by minor children were largely the consequence of orphanage.

The available illustrations of this fact are legion. "Their father died as one of Prince Timofei's peasants. Upon the death of their father, they and their mother Matrenka came to Moscow to live in Prince Timofei's household."[49] Or, "Timoshka's father Vasilii Aleksandrov was a peasant, and the Lithuanians killed him. After the death of her husband Vasilii, that Marfutka, with her son Timka, petitioned as a peasant to serve in the household of Ivan Kozlov, and she gave a limited slavery contract on herself and her son Timka to Ivan Kozlov."[50]

As we know, not only birth, death, and divorce could precipitate slavery, but marriage could as well by the ancient principle that any free person who married a slave became a slave. Muscovy was exceptional in that there were no formal restrictions on who could marry a slave, and on the harshness of the consequences for the person who did. Around 1501 Ivan Fedorov Novokshchenov presented his full slave Zakharets Gridtsyn for registration, and noted that Zakharets' wife, Ovod'itsa Ivashkova Kostygina, who had been a free woman, became his slave by marrying him.[51] In a Pskov judgment charter, dated 1540, we learn that Iakov Nekliudov Krasnoslepov filed a suit to recover Ondreiko Ivanov, who had fled and stolen his property. Ondreiko confessed that he had stolen the property, and that he was Krasnoslepov's slave by virtue of his marriage to the latter's military captive slave, Fedoska. Fifty-nine years later Krasnoslepov's son-in-law, Ivan Semenov Kartmazov, a *syn boiarskii* from Votskaia piatina who had numerous landholdings and was entitled to 500 cheti of land and 25 rubles in cash, registered the judgment charter to support his claims to Ondreiko's son Mikitka and grandson Semeika Iushkov, and Semeika's wife Fedoska Zakhar'eva and child Luchka, all of whom were fugitives.[52] Thus a free man's marriage to a slave resulted in the perpetual slavery of his lineage, here represented down to great-grandchildren.

·478; Gos. publich. biblioteka im. Saltykova-Schedrina, Obshchee sobranie gramot, no. 2406.

48. NZKK 2: 339.

49. Iakovlev, *Kholopstvo,* p. 345, no. 6, II.

50. Ibid., p. 385, no. 23, VI, Similar situations in China also produced enslavement of children. However, such orphans in China were adopted by their owners, something unheard of in Muscovy (Wiens, p. 298).

51. RIB 17: 131, no. 810.

52. RIB 17: 140, no. 381; Samokvasov, *Materialy* 2: 315, 318, 366; Nosov, *Ocherki,* p. 336; DVP, p. 471; Ivanov, OPK, pp. 43A, 44A; RIB 11(1908): 89-90, 824; RIB 28(1912): 102.

As we have seen, a high proportion of those selling themselves into slavery earlier had been dependents of one form or another. As far as can be determined, this was true prior to 1586. The available documentation makes it abundantly clear that this was also true between 1586 and 1603, and it was increasingly true through the rest of the seventeenth century. The surviving evidence for full slavery and limited service contract slavery prior to 1586 is very scanty on this point because such information was often omitted in the abbreviated registrations of such documents in 1597-98, but perhaps a quarter of those selling themselves at the time previously had been dependent. The proportion increased as a consequence of the legislation of 1586-97 which more or less mandated that "voluntary slaves," "servitors," and other such types should be formally registered as limited service contract slaves. The famine of 1601-3 changed the overall proportions of those selling themselves into slavery because of the abnormal infusion of agriculturalists and especially those marginally dependent upon agriculture. For the rest of the seventeenth century, the proportion of agriculturalists fell back to pre-1601 levels or less, as lords increasingly assumed responsibility for those farming their family and service estates, and the proportion of those selling themselves who had previously been enslaved seems to have risen to more than half of the total number.

Unquestionably this was true because the condition of slavery established such a degree of dependency that few had the capacity (or the desire) to overcome it. There was a high tendency for fresh slaves to flee within a year or two, after they had recovered at the slaveowner's expense from the crisis that had propelled them into slavery. But those who did not flee found their enslaved condition either congenial or compelling, supporting M. I. Finley's generalization that "victims once caught up in bondage had little hope of release."[53] This was no doubt true for the Hebrew debt slaves manumitted by law after six years, and it was equally true for persons manumitted by the deathbed testament of their owners or by the 1597 requirement that limited service contract slaves be freed on their owners' death. This was particularly the case because there was no requirement that slaves be manumitted with property, and because Muscovy had no transitional status between slavery and freedom for freedmen. One cannot determine the extent to which this dependency was the product of complusion (the slave manumitted without property simply could not survive in Muscovy) or congeniality (the slave was so accustomed to being dependent that independence was out of the question), but I should be inclined to assign more weight to the latter. Even fugitives who had stolen a great deal of property had a tendency to sell themselves back into slavery. Moreover, obviously some slaves were able to handle freedom, either as fugitives or freedmen.

The tendency to recycle slaves back into slavery was strong in Muscovy. During the Time of Troubles, the slaves of traitors were assumed to be accomplices of

53. Moses I. Finley, "Between Slavery and Freedom," *Comparative Studies in Society and History* 6(April 1964): 234.

their owners, and put in jail. This assumption follows from what we have seen about the owner-slave nexus. There was a great reluctance to hold people in jail, and so such slaves were let out on bail. Instead of treating them as freedmen, as might have been done, those who posted bond for them got limited service slavery contracts on them. The slaves of traitors were automatically freed (when it was proved that they had no complicity in the crime), but many such people willingly sold themselves back into slavery.[54]

While the probable purpose of the 1597 law on limited service contract slaves was to attempt to curtail perpetual dependency stemming from slavery (as had been the purpose of the biblical six-year limit on enslavement for debt), other Muscovite legislation recognized the reality that slavery did create perpetual dependency. This was expressed in several ways. The *Ulozhenie* recognized that fugitives often sold themselves to someone else, and in fact seems to have assumed that they would.[55] The law code also assumed that slaves who had been taken into foreign captivity (presumably primarily those who were combat and baggage-train slaves) and subsequently returned to Muscovy might not exercise their claim to freedom but might return to their old owners.[56] Similarly, as in fact frequently happened, the law recognized that slaves freed on the death of their owners or otherwise manumitted probably would resell themselves.[57] The appalled foreign visitor Jacob Reitenfels observed the tendency of manumitted slaves to resell themselves.[58] This was even reinforced by late Muscovite legislation that forbade the granting of traditional loans to freedmen, and instead prescribed that they be granted loans solely under the limited service slavery contract rubric.[59] Under such a regime it was difficult for a person manumitted without property to do anything but resell himself. The clearest recognition in the law of the dependency created by slavery was expressed in the article of the *Ulozhenie* that permitted *deti boiarskie* who had sold themselves, but were taken out of slavery and ordered to render military service, to return to their former owners if they wanted to do so.[60] Clearly, it would be hard to find a more explicit contemporary recognition of the fact that many slaves preferred that condition and that such dependency rendered them fit for little else.

54. PRP 4: 377-78.
55. 1649 *Ulozhenie* 20: 24-25; MS, p. 264.
56. 1649 *Ulozhenie* 20: 34; MS, p. 267.
57. 1649 *Ulozhenie* 20: 8; MS, p. 258; PSZ 2: 313, no. 869.
58. Reitenfel's, "Skazaniia svetleishemu gertsogu toskanskomu," p. 139. The secretary of the Austrian embassy in Moscow at the end of the seventeenth century made this same observation (Korb, p. 240). This contributed to the widespread foreign impression that Russians loved slavery and were unsuited for freedom (ibid., p. 241). When trying to understand this view, one must recall that the early modern Western Europeans knew of no other European country where such a large portion of the population was enslaved, and particularly no other society in which such a high portion of the slaves were natives.
59. PSZ 2: 313, no. 869.
60. 1649 *Ulozhenie* 20: 3; MS, pp. 255-56.

Certainly there was nothing absolutely unique about Muscovite freedmen discovering that slavery was in many ways better than freedom. This discovery has been made elsewhere, with the difference that most other societies have made it much more difficult for freedmen to reenter slavery than did Muscovy. For example, in North Carolina, free Negroes who desired to enslave themselves had to secure the passage of private bills, and the passage of such bills was by no means automatic.[61] The literature also conveys the impression that other freedmen and their descendants would reenslave themselves, if only they had the chance. Gill Shepherd has observed that "Comorian slave descendants in some ways are worse off than slaves, since no one is responsible any longer for their welfare."[62] Muscovite legislators had no qualms about placing welfare above freedom.

Throughout the more than a quarter-millennium of its history, Muscovy witnessed enslavement for just about every cause ever experienced by mankind. Warfare, crime, poverty, and birth all generated their share of slaves. What was notable about the Muscovite system of slavery was the fact that such a very high proportion of the chattel were natives, primarily from the lower classes, but also from the clans of the elite as well. Almost a century ago the Dutch ethnographer H. J. Nieboer, one of the best students of slavery the world has ever produced, observed that "it is worth inquiring what can be the reason why, while resources are open [i.e., while there is free land] and so everybody is able to provide for himself, there are people who throw themselves upon the mercy of men of power."[63] Having made the inquiry, we have found that, even though there was free land, free men at times found that they could not provide for themselves, and then found that they had become habituated to dependence. While some elite slaves (such as stewards and combat slaves) may have been opportunists deliberately improving their status, most of those who sold themselves into slavery did so because of stress, because they found the demands and conditions of existence in Muscovy more than they could bear as free men. The conditions that permitted so many native Muscovites to sell themselves into slavery will be examined in the next chapter.

61. John Hope Franklin, *The Free Negro in North Carolina, 1790-1860* (New York: Russell and Russell, 1969), pp. 218-20.

62. Shepherd, p. 96. Anyone who doubts that consensual slavery could possibly be attractive should read the *New York Times* article by Michael T. Kaufman, "Price of a Woman in India: $306 and Much Sorrow" (August 11, 1981, p. A2). While the purchased woman, Kamla, was not legally a "slave" because the state authorities would not have enforced her subordination had she chosen to run away, Kaufman reported that "Kamla . . . thinks it is up to the people who bought her to take care of her. . . . She wants to work for the people who bought her and she is proud that she commanded so high a price." Apparently she was sold by her husband. Kaufman observed that Indians consider it a family obligation to take care of the weak; but when family ties collapse, the absence of charity gives the underprivileged no recourse other than to barter their labor in bondage or allow themselves to be sold. This is much like the Muscovite story of slavery, except that there is no evidence of any early modern Russian sense of kinship obligation.

63. Nieboer, p. 430.

12. Social Barriers: Ethnicity, Poverty, Anthroponymy, and Geographic Mobility

The basic task of chapter 11 was to show why the Muscovites violated the general human norm against the enslavement of natives. This chapter will try to explain how it was done, the facts that made such a violation possible.

The Problem of Ethnicity

One fundamental "law of slavery" is violated by the Muscovite case, the fact that the slave is supposed to be an "outsider." In most systems, this means that the slave is of a different race, ethnicity, nationality, or religion than the slave-owner. This is true whether the situation under consideration is in one of the many African societies, Babylonia, Athens, Rome, Amerindian tribes, the Tibetan-speaking Nepalese Nyinba, or the New World. In cases where this was not true for every slave, such as poverty-stricken Athenian parents who were forced to sell their offspring, a fiction such as exposure was used to disguise the sale. When Chinese were forced to sell their children, buyer and seller did not meet, the use of an intermediary preserving some semblance of distance. In instances of enslavement of kin for debt or criminal behavior (the latter often reflecting inability to pay a fine), most societies advanced at least "the social program" that such enslavement should be temporary and of relatively short duration, such as the Hebrew six-year limitation decreed in Deuteronomy 15:12. In China, when natives sold themselves during a famine, or otherwise became enslaved, the government made every effort to have them freed as expeditiously as possible. In Western Europe during the reign of Louis the Pious, slave traders were supposed to acquire their human merchandise from beyond the frontiers of the realm, and sales were by law to be public and in the presence of certified officials to prevent the kidnapping and selling into slavery of natives.[1] In Muscovy, however, such was not the case, except for the few actual debt slaves serving for a precise term

---

1. The Gutians have the distinction of being among the first outsider slaves in recorded history. Babylonian king Hammurapi noted that fact when he said of the remnant Guti in the Persian foothills that their "hills are distant" and their "language is queer" (W. B. Henning, "The First Indo-Europeans in History," in *Society and History*, ed. G. L. Ulmen [The Hague: Mouton, 1978], p. 220). On the fact that slaves in the Carolingian Empire were supposed to be outsiders, see Heinrich Fichtenau, *The Carolingian Empire* (Toronto: University of Toronto Press, 1978), pp. 154-55. On the foreign origin of Germanic slaves, see Wergeland, p. 7; on Nyinba, see Nancy E. Levine, pp. 203, 208. On the Chinese situation, see Watson, *Systems*, p. 233.

while working off their indebtedness. While the Muscovites owned "outsider" slaves, such as Tatar, Polish, or Swedish military captives, the vast majority of them (about 98.5 percent in my data set) were ethnic Russians. These figures are presented in table 12.1. It is evident from the table that nationality did not make much difference in the prices slaveowners were willing to pay.

TABLE 12.1
Nationality of Slaves and Their Prices, in Rubles

Nationality	No. of Documents	Total No. of Slaves	Price per Document	Price per Slave	No. of Cases with Prices
Russian	2,401	5,350	3.89	2.57	2,140
Lithuanian	12	31	2.83	2.36	6
Polish	1	9			1
Swedish	2	5	3.00	3.00	1
German	3	5	3.00	3.00	2
Livonian	33	58	3.85	3.05	22
Belorussian	5	14	4.20	2.01	5
Greek	1	2			
Chud' (Finnish)	1	1	3.00	3.00	1
"Newly baptized"	1	3	10.00	3.33	1
"Foreigner" (inozemlets)	1	1	3.00	3.00	1
Tatar	6	10	3.50	3.50	4
Unknown military captive	4	40			
Unknown	28	46			
Total	2,499	5,575	3.89	2.58	2,184

The data of table 12.1 were based either on declarations by the slave of his nationality or on a consideration of what his name was. The latter judgment is somewhat limited in its accuracy because of the Muscovite tendency to Russify foreign names, or to give a Russian name to an effectively mute foreigner such as a military captive. There are, however, some checks, besides names, on a claim that over 95 percent of the slaves were native Russians. One such check is provided by the physical description that accompanied many slaves when they were sold, a subject that was examined in chapter 8 in tables 8.5 and 8.6. In theory, we should be able to match up the distribution of the 1,353 eye-color descriptions and the 1,330 hair-color descriptions in those tables with information generated by modern anthropologists to see whether those selling themselves in Muscovy were primarily a Russian population, like the Russian population of the twentieth century. The task is complicated by the fact that the Muscovites used color descriptions that we can recognize (hazel, brown, black), but Soviet scholars have opted for language that represents shadings for hair color from blonde to black; for eye color (and sometimes hair color as well) from bright or light (svetlyi) to dark (temnyi) with "mixed" in between. Moreover, they are not consistent in their terminology. Nevertheless, in spite of such difficulties, it is fairly clear that the hair color described by the Muscovite officials is similar to that of modern Russians, who average 1.6 percent blonde hair, with a range from 0 to 4 percent (comparable to the 4.4 percent noted in Muscovy). If one expands what the Muscovites called "white" to include some of what is now called "fair" (*svetlyi*), the twentieth-century range is from 5 to 30 percent, depending on location. At the other end of the spectrum, the Muscovites categorized 14.8 percent as black-haired, not far from today's average of 13.8 percent, and well within today's range for "dark" of from 5 to 31 percent, depending upon locale. It is not clear to me where redheads (6.2 percent in Muscovy) belong on the modern spectrum, although they probably belong among the browns (73.5 percent in Muscovy), who might average as much as 84.6 percent of the twentieth-century population.[2]

It is more difficult to match up today's terminology for eye color with Muscovy's. At one end of the spectrum, black, there is no problem, for the 11.4 percent of Muscovy is within the "dark" range of 6 to 16 percent. Unfortunately the Muscovites did not see eyes as "blue," which is part of today's "bright," as are various shades of gray. Today's northwestern U.S.S.R. population has about 56 percent, Latvians range from 56.4 to 60.9 percent, and Finns have 83 percent "bright eyes." It would be tempting to speculate that those selling themselves in Muscovy (73.6 percent of whom reportedly had "gray" eyes) had a large Finnic component, but there is no other evidence to support such a contention (Finnish hair color is 89 percent "fair"), thus leaving us with the sense that the Muscovites either were not very observant or else had a different understanding of "gray" than we do.[3]

Table 12.2 examines data for hair and eye color in cross-tabular form, with percentages of the whole given for each pair. It no longer seems to be the Soviet practice to present such data in this form, as was done in 1930 by D. A. Zolotarev for Karela, much of which was part of the Novgorod region at the time most of the data used in this study were compiled. There is a great problem of comparability, for Zolotarev uses the terms blond (*belokuryi*), brown (*rusyi*), dark (*temnyi*), and red (*ryzhii*) for hair color. Zolotarev found 39.5 percent blondes in Karela, 51.1 with brown hair, 8.6 with dark hair, and 0.4 with red hair. None of these is comparable to the corresponding figure in table 12.2. About 9.6 percent of the Karela population had dark eyes, not too distant from the 11.4 figure of table 12.2 for black. However, his 35.4 percent for "light" and 54.9 percent for "mixed" find no correspondences in table 12.2. Totally blonde males (light hair and blue eyes) constituted 20.9 percent of all males, totally brunette

2. V. V. Bunak, ed., *Proiskhozhdenie i etnicheskaia istoriia russkogo naroda po antropologicheskim dannym* (Moscow: Nauka, 1965), pp. 53, 103, 106, 135, 164, 171, 354. [= *Trudy Instituta etnografii*, vol. 88.]

3. Ibid., pp. 53, 108-9, 135, 164, 171, 223, 356.

males (dark hair and dark eyes) were 3.6 percent of all males.[4] All things considered, it seems fairly clear that those selling themselves in Muscovy were not primarily Karelians. The available evidence thus does not contradict the assumption that most of those who sold themselves in Muscovy were ethnic East Slavs, the forebears of today's Great Russians.

TABLE 12.2
Hair and Eye Color of Those Presumed to be Russians Selling Themselves into Slavery (Actual Numbers and Percentages of Total)

Eye Color	Hair Color						
	White (blonde?)	Gray	Brown	Red	Dark red (*chermen*)	Black	Total
"White" (light blue?)	6 0.5%	0	10 0.8%	0	4 0.3%	1 0.1%	21 1.8%
Blue (*krasnosery?*)	1 0.1%	1 0.1%	29 2.3%	0	1 0.1%	3 0.2%	35 2.9%
"Red" (*krasny*)	0	0	2 0.2%	0	1 0.1%	0	3 0.2%
Light gray (*belysery, prosery, svetolosery*)	3 0.2%	0	5 0.4%	0	2 0.2%	1 0.1%	11 0.9%
Gray	38 3.1%	3 0.2%	678 55.3%	1 0.1%	58 4.7%	77 6.3%	855 69.9%
Dark gray (*temnosery*)	2 0.2%	0	9 0.7%	0	1 0.1%	5 0.4%	17 1.4%
Gray-hazel (*servykary, vkarisery*)	0	0	2 0.2%	0	0	0	2 0.2%
Light hazel, light brown (*svetlokary, krasnokary, rus, svetlorus, solovoi*)	0	0	10 0.8%	0	0	0	10 0.8%
Hazel, brown (*kari, bury, smugly*)	2 0.2%	0	97 7.8%	0	10 0.8%	21 1.7%	130 10.4%
Black	1 0.1%	0	64 5.2%	0	1 0.1%	73 6.0%	139 11.4%
Total	52 4.2%	4 0.3%	906 74.0%	1 0.1%	80 6.4%	181 14.8%	1,222 100%

It should be of considerable comparative interest to discover how the Musco-

4. D. A. Zolotarev, *Karely SSSR po antropologicheskim dannym* (Leningrad: AN SSSR, 1930), pp. 13-14. For a discussion of various colors, and especially *krasny* and *smugly*, see N. B. Bakhilina, *Istoriia tsvetooboznachenii v russkom iazyke* (Moscow: Nauka, 1975), pp. 71, 168, 209.

vites managed to violate so flagrantly a fundamental social science "law," the law that, in the words of Moses I. Finley, "no society could withstand the tension inherent in enslaving its own people."[5] The concept of "outsider" is sometimes a relative one, as for example, in some African and Hindu situations,[6] and one of the problems in studying Muscovite slavery is to determine how much explanatory power the notion has for the Muscovite situation. The oddity of Russians enslaving their own kind was observed by mid-nineteenth-century foreign commentators on serfdom, but even that anomaly seems to have been ignored by students of Russian history until the recent work of Peter Kolchin.[7] On the other hand, the contrast between Hitler, who fundamentally abused "outsiders," and Stalin, whose primary targets were Soviets, has been noted both in the U.S.S.R. and abroad.

As I now perceive this problem of understanding how the Russians were able to enslave their own kin, it is one of determining the social distance between the slaveowner and his chattel. As David Brion Davis has observed, "slavery ultimately depends on real or simulated ethnic barriers."[8] The problem of this chapter, then, is to try to determine how the Russians simulated the ethnic barriers that allowed them to enslave their own people on such a massive scale.

In an attempt to solve the problem, I shall examine briefly the various ethnic groups that went into the Muscovite "melting pot," the role of Orthodoxy in defining Muscovite identity, and the genealogical pretensions of the slaveowners. I shall next delve into anthroponymy for clues to determine the possible extent of hardened class divisions in Muscovy, and then consider poverty as a social barrier and the extent to which the changing image of slavery between the end of the fifteenth century and the mid-seventeenth century contributed to the process. Finally, I shall consider the fact of geographical mobility as a contribution to the simulation of ethnic barriers.

It is a basic thesis of this work that much of the peculiar quality of Muscovite

5. Moses I. Finley, "The Extent of Slavery," in *Slavery. A Comparative Perspective. Readings on Slavery from Ancient Times to the Present,* ed. Robin W. Winks (New York: New York University Press, 1972), p. 4.

6. Joseph C. Miller, Review of *L'Esclavage en Afrique précoloniale,* ed. Claude Meillassoux (Paris: François Maspero, 1975), *African Economic History* 5 (Spring 1978): 50; Lionel Caplan, pp. 172, 182-83, 191, 194. In Greco-Roman Egypt, when a free man sold himself, "the word 'enslavement' [was] carefully and intentionally avoided" (Raphael Taubenschlag, *The Law of Greco-Roman Egypt in the Light of the Papyri 332 B.C.–640 A.D.* [New York: Herald Square Press, 1944], pp. 52-53). The Muscovites made no such pretense that a person who sold himself was anything other than a slave:

7. Peter Kolchin, "In Defense of Servitude: A Comparison of American Proslavery and Russian Proserfdom Arguments, 1750-1860" (Paper delivered at the American Historical Association Convention, San Francisco, 28 December 1978), p. 2; published in the AHR 85 (October 1980): 809-27.

8. David Brion Davis, *The Problem of Slavery in Western Culture* (Ithaca: Cornell University Press, 1966), p. 47.

slavery, the fact that most of the slaves were natives, must be at least partially attributable to a fundamental lack of ethnic identity and cohesion among the inhabitants of Muscovy. This is not the appropriate forum for an intensive examination of this problem, but a few facts will remind the reader of its essence. The starting point is that in the early Middle Ages almost none of what we now think of as Russia was inhabited by Slavs. Slavs only arrived in the Kievan area about the eighth or ninth century, and even at the time of the Primary Chronicle, Rus' (the core around Kiev) was inhabited primarily by slavicized Iranian Poliane. The ancestors of today's Ukrainians were the Drevliane, who lived west of Kiev, across the Dnepr, and were much despised for their backwardness by the Poliane. The diverse ethnic mix of the Kievan region was recognized in 980 by Prince Vladimir when he set up his pagan pantheon: three gods were Iranian in origin (Khors, Simargl, and Svarog), three were Slavic (Dazhbog, Stribog, and Mokosh'), one was probably Scandinavian (Volos/Veles), and Perun, the Thunder God, was an Indo-European deity of 5,000 years antiquity. Slavs moved into the northern Novgorod region also around the ninth century. That was an area inhabited by Finns and Balts, and the original three subdivisions of Novgorod were the homes of the three ethnic groups. Slavs moved to the Beloozero region, inhabited by Finns, only in the eleventh century. Blood-group typing in the twentieth century indicates that the population north of a line running from Leningrad to Kazan' is still fundamentally Finnic, in spite of extensive Slavic migration north of that line beginning in the second half of the sixteenth century.[9]

Slavs moved into the Volga-Oka basin from the west, beginning in the eleventh century, about to the area where Moscow is situated, and the current ethnographic thinking is that the ethnic mix there is about 95 percent Czech and 5 per-

9. P. N. Tret'iakov, "O drevneishikh rusakh i ikh zemle," in *Slaviane i Rus'*, ed. E. I. Krupnov (Moscow: Nauka, 1968), pp. 180-87; Marija Gimbutas, "Ancient Slavic Religion: A Synopsis," in *To Honor Roman Jakobson*, 3 vols. (The Hague: Mouton, 1967), 1: 741-53; I. I. Liapushkin, *Dneprovskoe lesostepnoe levoberezh'e v epokhu zheleza. Arkheologicheskie razyskaniia i vremia zaseleniia levoberezh'ia slavianami* (Moscow-Leningrad: Akademiia Nauk SSSR, 1961 [=MIA no. 104]), p. 181; idem, "Arkheologicheskie pamiatniki slavian lesnoi zony vostochnoi Evropy nakanune obrazovaniia drevnerusskogo gosudarstva," in *Kul'tura drevnei Rusi* (Moscow: Nauka, 1966), pp. 127-36; V. Bunak, "Genetic-Geographical Zones of Eastern Europe by ABO Blood Groups," in Yu. Bromley, ed., *Soviet Ethnology and Anthropology Today* (The Hague: Mouton, 1974), pp. 344-46. See also R. A. Stavrovoitova, *Etnicheskaia genogeografiia Ukrainskoi SSR. Gematologicheskoe issledovanie* (Kiev: Naukova Dumka, 1979) and V. A. Bulkin, I. V. Dubov, and G. S. Lebedev, *Arkheologicheskie pamiatniki drevnei Rusi IX–XI vekov* (Leningrad: LGU, 1978). Bohdan Strumins'kyj proposes that the Poliane were Pontic Goths ("Were the Antes Eastern Slavs ? " *Harvard Ukrainian Studies* 3-4 [1979-80]: 786-96). Whether they were Iranians or Goths is irrelevant to my argument. The Moscow scholar A. N. Robinson has observed that the Severiane inhabiting the region north of Kiev were slavicized Iranians (Lecture at the University of Chicago Slavic Department on April 21, 1981).

391 Social Barriers: Ethnicity, Poverty, Anthroponymy, Geographic Mobility

cent Finnish. Slavs reached the confluence of the Volga and the Oka in appreciable numbers only in the thirteenth century.[10]

In the area of Muscovy there was a mixture of agricultural Slavs and neolithic hunting and gathering Finnic people (the Meria and Muroma). There were also Balts (the Goliad').[11] But one must not neglect the Turkic Bulgars, with whom the population of Suzdalia had extensive contacts prior to the coming of the Mongols, ties that paralleled in many ways those further south between the Ol'govichi of Chernigov and the Polovtsy. Given this background, it is not surprising that Alexander Nevskii and his heirs found no difficulty in collaborating for over a century with the Mongol conquerors. The remnants of the Golden Horde added yet another element to the Muscovite imperial melting pot, which by the end of the sixteenth century included all manner of Tatars—Kasimov, Kazan', Astrakhan', Nogai, and Siberian.[12]

The ethnic situation did not remain static in the west, either. The Ottoman conquest of the Balkans motivated people to come to Muscovy.[13] The frontier between Muscovy and the Rzeczpospolita, Livonia, and Swedish possessions was constantly moving back and forth, while the inhabitants of the region were taken into military captivity or moved voluntarily back and forth. The Polish counter-reformation began to drive people out of Ukraine into Muscovy in the 1630s, a flow that increased after Ukraine's annexation at mid-century.[14]

The ethnic mix of Muscovy was further diversified by the arrival from time to time of peoples from western and northern Europe and the Caucasus. This is

10. V. P. Alekseev, *Proiskhozhdenie narodov Vostochnoi Evropy (Krainologicheskie issledovaniia)* (Moscow: Nauka, 1969), pp. 206-8; V. V. Sedov, "Rezul'taty izucheniia cherepov," in M. V. Sedova, *Iaropolch Zalesskii* (Moscow: Nauka, 1978), pp. 150, 152; Christa L. Walck, Review of M. V. Sedova's *Iaropolch Zalesskii* in *Kritika* 15, no. 2 (Spring 1979): 66-78.

11. G. A. Khaburgaev, *Stanovlenie russkogo iazyka* (Moscow: Vysshaia shkola, 1980), p. 98.

12. A. P. Smirnov, "Drevniaia Rus' i Volzhskaia Bolgariia," in *Slaviane i Rus'*, pp. 167-72; N. K. Baibulatov et al., "Vkhozhdenie Checheno-Ingushetii v sostav Rossii," *Istoriia SSSR* (1980, no. 5): 52-53; M. D. Poluboiarinova, *Russkie liudi v Zolotoi Orde* (Moscow: Nauka, 1978). See also the remarkable series of articles by N. A. Baskakov, "Russkie familii tiurkskogo proiskhozhdeniia," in (1) *Onomastika* (1969): 5-26; (2) *Izvestiia Akademii nauk SSSR. Seriia literatury i iazyka* 28, no. 4 (July-August 1969): 356-64; (3) *Onomastika Povol'zhia. Materialy I povol'zhskoi konferentsii po onomastike* (Ul'ianovsk, 1969), pp. 28-33; (4) *Sovetskaia etnografiia* 1969, no. 4: 14-27; (5) *Antroponimika* (Moscow: Nauka, 1970), pp. 98-l03; (6) *Vostochnoslavianskaia onomastika* (Moscow: Nauka, 1972), pp. 176-209; (7) *Etnografiia imen* (Moscow: Nauka, 1971), pp. 93-99; (8) *Russkaia rech'* 1970, no. 6: 85-90; (9) *Onomastika Povol'zhia* (Ufa, 1973), pp. 101-15; (10) *Tiurkizmy v vostochnoslavianskikh iazykakh* (Moscow: Nauka, 1974), pp. 238-85; idem, *Russkie familii tiurkskogo proiskhozhdeniia* (Moscow: Nauka, 1979).

13. Gustave Alef, "Diaspora Greeks in Moscow," *Byzantine Studies* 6(1979): 26-34.

14. V. V. Strashko, "Pereselenie ukraintsev v Rossiiu v period osvoboditel'noi voiny ukrainskogo naroda 1648-1654 godov," *Sovetskie arkhivy* 1979, no. 3: 13-17.

392   The Sociology of Slavery

most evident (and also claimed) among the upper classes, but no doubt others came as well.[15]

The consequence of this diversity seems to have been that the in-group ethnic bonding ties were minimized, and the in-group–out-group consciousness was simply overwhelmed by diversity. What this meant was that for the Muscovites, ethnically, there was no such thing as an "outsider," for any outsider simply by presence or a verbal declaration could immediately be an "insider." In the practical world, this was most evident in the absolute freedom natives of both the upper and lower classes felt about establishing marriage ties with any foreigner, whether a Pole, Tatar, or Georgian.[16] This meant that a Russian woman could be purchased by a Tatar with second thoughts by no one. This also meant that the insider-outsider identification process was very localized, as in the 1930s when Belorussians still recognized no common bond with anything outside their native village—a phenomenon that certainly can be projected back to Muscovy. For example, in the Pskov region in the 1590s, "outsiders" (*prishel'tsy*) were defined.in a most diverse manner: converts (*novokreshcheny*, who could be either Tatars or Swedes, Poles, Livonians, or Lithuanians), military captives (*polonianiki*), or Russians from Rzheva (*rzhevitin*) or Riazan' (*riazanets*).[17]

For these reasons it can hardly be accidental that "national consciousness" was usually expressed in religious, rather than national, terms.[18] The Muscovites defined themselves as *pravoslavnye* (Orthodox) more frequently than as *russkie* (Russians), which of course many of them were not. In that sense the Orthodox church played a central role in the rise and consolidation of the Muscovite state, for it provided the crucial sense of ideological unity that was so lacking among the thirteen East Slavic tribes (plus the Finns and Iranians) during the Kievan period, or among their offspring, the warring principalities of post-1132 Rus' that continuously took one another's subjects into slavery down to their annexation by Muscovy. The conversion to Orthodoxy by any foreigner automatically made him a Muscovite, fully accepted by the central authorities and seemingly the native populace as well. As far as I can determine, profession of Orthodoxy was the "test" for belonging in Muscovy, as profession of a civic belief in repub-

15. O. N. Trubachev, "Iz materialov dlia etimologicheskogo slovaria familii Rossii (Russkie familii i familii, bytuiushchie v Rossii)," *Etimologiia 1966* (Moscow: Nauka, 1968), pp. 3-53. See also the 4-part work by V. A. Nikonov, "Opyt slovaria russkikh familii," *Etimologiia 1970* (Moscow: Nauka, 1972), pp. 116-42; *1971* (1973), pp. 208-80; *1973* (1975), pp. 131-55; and *1974* (1976), pp. 129-57; A. V. Udal'tsova, Ia. N. Shchapov, E. V. Gutnova, and A. P. Novosel'tsev, "Drevniaia Rus'—zona vstrechi tsivilizatsii," *Voprosy istorii* 1980, no. 7: 59.

16. RIB 17(1895): 92-93, no. 259.

17. AIS-ZR (1978), p. 110.

18. It is regrettable that the Soviet scholars writing on the formation of the Russian nationality do not confront this issue. See, for example, *Voprosy formirovaniia russkoi narodnosti i natsii. Sbornik statei*, ed. N. M. Druzhinin and L. V. Cherepnin (Moscow-Leningrad: AN SSSR, 1958).

licanism has been a test for citizenship in the United States. While most of the American naturalization statutes since 1790 have prescribed a five-year period of residence, and the census takers have considered the process of Americanization to take two generations (respondents are asked where they and their parents were born, if not in the U.S.), conversion to Orthodoxy was instantaneous and gave the convert all the rights of a native-born Muscovite. Similar thinking persisted into the nineteenth century. During the reign of Nicholas I, for example, any Jew who converted to Orthodoxy immediately became an "insider." The inability of "nationality" to tag people was expressed in the 1897 census of the Russian Empire, which did not have a "nationality" category but asked only about language. The ambiguity of "Russian" ethnicity in today's Soviet Union has just recently been recognized by Western scholars.[19]

What is peculiar about the Orthodox "connection" in the history of slavery resides in the fact that it condoned, and in fact encouraged, the enslavement of Orthodox by other Orthodox. From a comparative perspective, we would hardly expect that. Islam, for example, does not condone the possession of coreligionists. In 1517 Crimean Tatar ruler Mehmed Giray I observed in writing to Russian grand prince Vasilii III that some Muslims reportedly had captured other Muslims in the Meshchera region and then noted that Islamic holy writings forbade the sale of coreligionists. The Muscovite practice did violence to the contemporary understanding of Hugo Grotius (1583-1645) that Christians as well as Muslims did not enslave members of their own faiths.[20] As we have seen in chapter 2, beginning in 1627/28 the Muscovite government insisted that only Orthodox could own Orthodox slaves, a concern motivated by the understanding that slaves tended to adopt the faith of their owners. Prior to that time, there were no limitations or restrictions on the race, nationality, or religion of slave or slaveowner. The point here is that the xenophobic stricture of 1627/28, the Muscovite form of "nativism," took on a religious hue rather than a national or ethnic one.

Muscovites simulated barriers between slaves and slaveowners in many ways. Thus, for example, it cannot be accidental that the expansion and change in the institution of slavery in the period of Ivan IV's later years and thereafter was accompanied by a development of all kinds of genealogical pretensions among many slaveowning families of claims of foreign origin for their clan: they were foreigners reigning over another people. The most notorious claim of foreign origin was advanced by Ivan IV in conversation with any foreigner who would listen, from English travelers to the Livonian King Magnus in 1570, that he was not a Russian

19. Edward Allworth, ed., *Ethnic Russia in the USSR. The Dilemma of Dominance* (New York: Pergamon Press, 1980), see especially chap. 2. On the national composition of the ancien regime gentry, see A. P. Korelin, *Dvorianstvo v poreformennoi Rossii 1861-1904 gg. Sostav, chislennost', korporativnaia organizatsiia* (Moscow: Nauka, 1979), pp. 44-50.
20. Sb. RIO 95(1895): 378, no. 21; D. B. Davis, *Problem*, p. 115.

but really a German ruling over an alien (and inferior) people. No doubt he got this idea from the Varangian legend in the Primary Chronicle. The sixteenth-century genealogies are full of claims of foreign origin of Muscovite clans, paralleling those made elsewhere in Europe at the same time.[21] Some of the claims were true, but many of them were not. An indication of the irrelevance of "foreign origins" from the perspective of the ruling elite is the fact that such people were not singled out by Ivan IV and his entourage during the Oprichnina, during the numerous hunts for spies and traitors. Although claims of foreign origin initially were made to make status distinctions within the ruling elite, the consequence of the process almost certainly was to distance the entire elite from the masses. The process was even more evident in the later eighteenth and nineteenth centuries, when the Europeanization of the French-speaking gentry contributed to the gulf between them and the peasantry, whose enserfed status increasingly resembled slavery. While claims of foreign origin helped to simulate ethnic barriers between the ruling elements and the masses, we must not forget that conquerors generally do not make chattel of the people they have vanquished, particularly when the conquerors live among the vanquished.[22]

Another barrier between some slaveowners and the lowest elements of Muscovite society was the princely origin of some of the former, usually through descent from East Slavic or Lithuanian dynasts. Western readers must not be overly impressed by this fact, however, for royal descent meant relatively little in the Muscovite service meritocracy. The Holstein astronomer and traveler Adam Olearius was astonished in the 1630s by the fact that a prince in Muscovy could be the social equal of a peasant, but that was true: royal origin was a stamp of presumed quality for a generation or two, and provided a sociological advantage; but a prince could fall almost to the bottom of society without continuous service inputs by every generation.[23] ("Almost," because I have never seen a claim by a slave to be of princely origin.) Nevertheless, princes always

21. Iu. N. Shcherbachev, "Kopengagenskie akty, otnos. k russkoi istorii," *Chteniia* 1916, bk. 2, pt. 2, p. 34; Berry and Crummey, *Rude*, pp. 126-27; "Sinodal'noi spisok Rodoslov-noi," *Vremennik* 10 (1951): 74-84, 89-90, 92-93, 97, 101, 107, 110, 113-18, 121, 123. (Nineteenth-century Russian tsars also grew up with feelings of ambivalence about their own national identity [Richard S. Wortman, "The Russian Empress as Mother," in David L. Ransel, ed., *The Family in Imperial Russia* (Urbana: University of Illinois Press, 1978), p. 73].)

22. Charles Verlinden, *Colonization*, p. 46. The current Soviet specialist on the Muscovite elite, V. N. Bochkov, opined that many of the stories ("legends") about the foreign origin of the early modern Russian upper service class are in fact true (" 'Legendy' o vyezde dvorian-skikh rodov," *Arkheograficheskii ezhegodnik za 1969 god* [1971]: 73-93). Recent personal conversations with Soviet emigrés have led me to believe that the view of the foreign origin of the nineteenth-century Russian gentry may be widespread in the USSR. The advantage for the Soviet regime of such a psychological distance between "the gentry" and "the people" should be obvious.

23. Adam Olearius, *Travels*, p. 221. See the same claim by Herberstein over a century earlier (*Commentaries on Russia* [Lawrence: University of Kansas Bookstore, 1956], p. 91).

used their titles, and unquestionably that must have placed considerable distance between them and slaves.

In discussing the social distance between masters and slaves, one must not lose sight of the fact that in some instances such distance was absolutely minimal, that in fact there was even a confusion between them. This was certainly true, for example, between elite slaves and landholding slaveowners of recent slave origin. The sixteenth century was a period of great mobility, with potential and actual slaveowners regularly rising and falling. While here the accent is on the differences between the two elements, one should also remember their many similarities. These similarities make the institution of Muscovite slavery all the more unusual.

A complementary development in establishing social distance between masters and slaves may have been the expression by slaveowners of the seventeenth century that to be of slave origin was shameful, a notion well developed among many African peoples and the Chinese. When Ivan III launched the first service class revolution, he converted a number of slaves into members of the middle service class. Those slaves must have been elite military slaves, but that was of little or no consequence to their heirs in the seventeenth century who sued for insult (*bezchest'e*) people who claimed that their clan was of slave origin. Rather, they wanted to pretend that they and their forebears had always been free men.[24] It must have been through a series of these often complementary pretensions that the Muscovite slaveowners created barriers between themselves and their chattel. Whether these pretensions can be linked with the greatest pretension of the age, the development during the reigns of Vasilii III and Ivan IV of the idea that the Muscovite sovereigns were divine vicegerents on earth, is unknown, but one should not be surprised were that the case.

Yet another social barrier, a distancing mechanism between master and slave, was poverty. Poverty, the major precipitant of most first-generation self-sale into slavery, has obviously created psychological distance between have-nots and haves since such distinctions first appeared in human society. The poor have often been treated very harshly, from being driven out of town to being confined in workhouses. However, while the poor are always with us, in most other societies they are not reduced to slavery. In those societies where slavery has been recognized as a last-resort rescue from starvation, the extremity of that act has been recognized. In places as diverse as Byzantium, Ethiopia, and Thailand there have been threats of severe punishment, even capital punishment, for those who sold either themselves or their children into slavery except in case of dire, extreme need.[25] There was no such concern in Muscovy. There, one may as-

---

24. Al. I. Markevich, *Istoriia mestnichestva v moskovskom gosudarstve XV—XVII veka* (Odessa: Tip. "Odesskogo Vestnika," 1888), p. 168.

25. William Julius Wilson, *The Declining Significance of Race* (Chicago: University of Chicago Press, 1978); Udal'tsova, p. 7; Turton, p. 264. Yoram Barzel has observed that voluntary slavery can be viewed as an extreme form of poverty ("An Economic Analysis of Slavery," p. 109).

sume, poverty was one of the factors contributing to the creation of social barriers between natives who sold themselves and those who bought them. Once again, however, we must recall that there was no absolute income-level barrier between slaves and slaveowners. There was a continuum at all times between the two, although direction within the continuum seems to have changed, from one of a movement from the slave stratum into the slaveowning group at the end of the fifteenth and on into the sixteenth century, to movement from the potential slaveowning element to the enslaved group at the end of the sixteenth and into the seventeenth centuries.

Anthroponymy

Onomastics may provide us with additional information about the institution of slavery, particularly about its distancing mechanisms. My study contains over six hundred different personal names. The precise number cannot be determined because often only diminutives are given, and there is no way to determine which full names were intended. My data are based on the names of 2,438 adult male slaves and 1,414 adult female slaves; 1,060 boy slaves and 626 girl slaves; 1,839 male slaveowners and 184 female slaveowners (including dowry recipients).

By and large, both the slaves and their owners used the same names, as shown in tables 12.3 and 12.5.[26] However, as is evident in tables 12.4 and 12.5, some names were unquestionably class-typed. The thesis here is that class-typing represented a chasm in society that both the upper strata (slaveowners were primarily from this group) and the lower strata (slaves were primarily from this group) were conscious of, and that this consciousness was one of the elements that permitted the upper elements to distance the lower elements from themselves and thereby enslave them.

26. On the names in the *dvorovaia tetrad'*, see V. B. Kobrin, "Genealogiia i antroponomika (po russkim materialam XV–XVI vv.)," in *Istoriia i genealogiia. S. B. Veselovskii i problemy istoriko-genealogicheskikh issledovanii*, ed. by N. I. Pavlenko et al. (Moscow: Nauka, 1977), pp. 87-90. In 1598 in Smolensk, 588 townsmen (*posadskie liudi*), 1,282 *strel'tsy*, 3 *strel'tsy* commanders, and 14 *strel'tsy* centurions, a total of 1,884 men, took the oath to Boris Godunov. The major names in frequency were usually between those of the adult slaves and the slaveowners (S. P. Mordovina and A. L. Stanislavskii, eds., "Smolenskaia krestoprivodnaia kniga 1598 g.," in *Istochniki po istorii russkogo iazyka*, ed. by S. I. Kotov and V. Ia. Deriagin [Moscow: Nauka, 1976], pp. 134-35).

TABLE 12.3
Names Used by Both Male Slaves and Slaveowners

Name	Adult Slaves	%	Child Slaves	%	Owners	%	% Dvorovaia Tetrad'
Afanasii	35	1.4	7	0.7	35	1.9	1.5
Aleksei	28	1.1	7	0.7	30	1.6	0.5
Andrei	77	3.2	27	2.7	68	3.7	6.0
Danil	21	0.9	8	0.8	23	1.3	1.6
Dmitrii	29	1.2	14	1.3	33	1.8	3.4
Fedor	75	3.1	19	1.8	108	5.9	5.7
Ignatii	20	0.8	8	0.8	17	0.9	0.5
Il'ia	14	0.6	3	0.3	11	0.6	0.4
Grigorii	74	3.0	31	2.9	79	4.3	4.6
Ivan	270	11.1	92	8.7	269	14.6	16.8
Leontii	19	0.8	7	0.7	14	0.8	0.3
Matfei	21	0.9	8	0.8	26	1.4	1.1
Mikhail	69	2.8	25	2.4	65	3.5	4.5
Nikita	37	1.5	13	1.2	37	2.0	1.4
Petr	35	1.4	18	1.7	57	3.0	3.1
Semen	76	3.1	29	2.7	56	3.0	4.8
Stepan	68	2.8	25	2.7	61	3.3	1.6
Timofei	35	1.4	19	1.8	23	1.3	1.6
Vasilii	104	4.3	31	2.9	100	5.4	8.5
	N = 2,437		N = 1,060		N = 1,839		

TABLE 12.4
Names Used by Male Slaves and Slaveowners—Class-Typed Male Names

Name	Adult Slaves	%	Child Slaves	%	Owners	%	% Dvorovaia Tetrad'
Bogdan	1	0.0	3	0.3	54	2.9	1.3
Filip	25	1.0	12	1.1	4	0.2	0.2
Foma	15	0.6	5	0.5	0	0.0	0.0
Karp	12	0.5	3	0.3	0	0.0	0.1
Kiril	21	0.9	12	1.1	3	0.2	0.1
Kondrat	17	0.7	5	0.5	3	0.2	0.0
Kuz'ma	31	1.3	14	1.3	6	0.3	0.2
Larion	16	0.7	6	0.6	1	0.1	0.0
Omel'ian	22	0.9	14	1.3	0	0.0	0.0
Posnik	0	0.0	0	0.0	10	0.5	0.3
Sergei	19	0.8	8	0.8	3	0.2	0.1
Sidor (Isidor)	16	0.7	4	0.4	1	0.1	0.0+
Spiridon	13	0.5	2	0.2	0	0.0	0.0

TABLE 12.5
Female Names Found in Slavery Documents

Name	Adult Slaves	%	Child Slaves	%	Owners	%
Anna (+ Annitsa)	105	7.4	42	6.7	16	8.7
Fedosia	44	3.1	18	2.9	9	4.9
Katerina	31	2.2	18	2.9	4	2.2
Marfa	35	2.5	8	1.3	8	4.3
Maria	125	8.8	47	7.5	24	13.0
Marina	21	1.5	7	1.1	1	0.5
Matrona	57	4.0	19	3.0	1	0.5
Ofim'ia	40	2.8	16	2.6	8	4.3
Ofrosina	18	1.3	11	1.8	5	2.7
Okulina (Akulina)	30	2.1	24	3.8	2	1.1
Olena (Elena)	16	1.1	3	0.5	6	3.3
Ovdotia	103	7.3	37	5.9	20	10.9
Paraskov'ia	28	2.0	18	2.9	1	0.5
Polagia	34	2.4	15	2.4	2	1.1
Solomanida	21	1.5	9	1.4	4	2.2
Tat'iana	37	2.6	15	2.4	10	5.4
Ul'iana	37	2.6	15	2.4	4	2.2
	N = 1,414		N = 626		N = 184	

Let us examine a few of these cases to sharpen our understanding of the issue. If we commence with the name Bogdan, we see that fifty-eight slaveowners had the name, but only one adult slave and three child slaves had it. The adult was Bogdan Nemchin, probably a Swedish military captive, who was listed in 1592 in a marriage contract in which Ovdot'ia Semenova Shuitina, widow of Istoma Shchulipnikov, agreed to marry Nikita Ivanov Kropotov. She had four slaves: Bogdan, his son Savluchko, Ivanko Gavrilov, and the widow Ul'ianka Mikulina.[27] Bogdan thus either got his name abroad or was assigned it by one of his Russian owners. As for the three child Bogdans, two were hereditary slaves, one of whom was a person serving in 1598 and descended from a person who had sold himself into full slavery in 1489, and the other was part of a property division made in 1588. The third child Bogdan was part of a limited service slavery contract concluded on February 25, 1588, between his parents, Kirilko Grigor'ev and Varvara Ivanova, and Mikhail Miloslavskii's slave Vas'ka Timofeev, acting for his owner. The sum was 5 rubles, higher than average, and there were two other children besides Bogdan, Gavril and Olferii.[28] Unfortunately we cannot tell anything from the document about Kirilko's origin or past prior to 1588, but several comments may be in order. The self-sale of entire families was not typical. Given the nature of Muscovite slavery, it would not be unreasonable to speculate that

27. Kopanev, "Materialy," p. 161.
28. RIB 17: 180, 190, nos. 495, 514; Kopanev, p. 154.

the family had been recently manumitted and was selling itself back into slavery in 1588, which would indicate that Bogdan himself might have been born in slavery. This thesis is supported by the fact that the entire family was still present at the time of the 1598 registration; that no one had run away would indicate that they were all accustomed to dependency. The only thing arguing against such an interpretation within the document itself is the fact that there were only boys, no girls. Judging by the fact that no additions to the family had been made in ten years, we may assume that it was a completed family already in 1588. While it is possible that Varvara Ivanova only gave birth to boys, another possibility is that she and her husband sacrificed their girls during hard times, and then finally gave up completely and sold themselves for a first time into slavery. Regrettably, then, there is no way to determine how or why the last Bogdan got his name.

What can we conclude from this examination of the name Bogdan? First, it is obvious that Bogdan is a class-typed name, chosen almost exclusively by the upper elements of Muscovite society and avoided by the lower orders. Bogdan is a calque created in Old Slavonic from the Greek name Theodotos, "given by the gods."[29] Apparently the elements of Muscovite society who sold themselves into slavery did not feel themselves to be gifts of the gods, whereas the members of the slave-owning class did. All that is relatively logical. But what about the children? Perhaps they were named after someone in the owner's family. Perhaps they were named by their owners, which indicates something (I should deem generally positive) about slaveowner sentiments for their chattel, or perhaps they were named by their parents, which would seem to show that slaves had a considerably better conception of themselves after they were slaves than they did before. This latter option seems entirely in keeping with the apparent nature of Muscovite slavery as a status at least as positive as landless peasant or beggar, and occasionally considerably higher.

Turning the situation around, one also can "explain" the presence of "lower-class names" among slaveowners. Kondratii was the given name of seventeen adult male slaves, but of only three slaveowners. Kondratii Ermolin was a recently arrived Crimean Tatar who had been converted to Christianity. He joined the Muscovite forces and prior to the 1580s was assigned lands (at least 70 cheti) in Koporskii uezd of Votskaia piatina—as usual, about as far from any Tatar frontier as one could be. On April 1, 1574, he married the Russian Maria Istomina Krekshina, whose grandmother Ofrosin'ia Ivanova Voronina, wife of Mikhail Pushchin, provided a dowry of four slaves—a woman Fetikha, her son Login, her daughter Mar'itsa, and an unwed girl Annitsa. Following a typical pattern, after nearly a decade had passed, Kondratii Ermolin considered himself affluent

---

29. N. A. Petrovskii, *Slovar' russkikh lichnykh imen* (Moscow: Sovetskaia entsiklopediia, 1966), p. 64; A. V. Superanskoi, ed., *Spravochnik lichnykh imen narodov RSFSR* (Moscow: "Russkii iazyk," 1979), p. 386.

enough on December 6, 1583, to spend 15 rubles to buy himself a slave, the woman Ovdot'itsa Stepanova Telezhnikova, who subsequently married and bore three slave children. He registered all of them in 1598. In 1597 he married his daughter Ovdotia to Stepan Ondreev Kosittskoi, perhaps the person recorded as a Novgorod cossack centurion in 1590/90, and provided her with a dowry of two slaves, a boy Mikita Trofimov and a girl Stepanka Ivanova. Where he acquired them is unknown.[30] Thus Kondratii was not a Russian but typically fit right into Russian society in his marriage arrangements. No doubt the fact that slaves could be given away in a dowry transaction aided his absorption into Muscovite society.

The second slaveowner named Kondratii was Kondratii Nesipov, also a recent convert to Orthodoxy, perhaps of Tatar origin. He had owned Olfimko Ondreev and his wife Ovdot'ia Eremeeva, both about age twenty, but had manumitted them during the Great Famine, a fact they reported when they sold themselves on March 13, 1603, to Pavl Dmitriev Zagoskin and his son Grigorii.[31] And the last Kondratii was himself of the lower orders, a priest, Kondratii Ivanov. He entered the slave market at the time when Kondratii Nesipov was leaving it; on April 13, 1603, the priest purchased Polagiia Borisova Onchiukhova for the current low price of 2 rubles. He was a typical famine purchaser—at other times priests are not recorded as buying slaves, at least in such numbers. He was from Bolonskii pogost of Bezhetskaia piatina, and literate—something that no doubt set him apart from other provincial priests.[32] Thus we may conclude that Kondratii was a strictly class-typed name, one that no member of the upper classes would ever give to one of his sons. Its presence among the slaveowners is another indication of the fluidity of the service class in the sixteenth century.

Similar discussions could be made about at least some of the other "lower-class names" used by slaveowners. For example, no biographical data seem to be available about either *Sidor* Ivanov Borodin or *Larion* Usliumov Kokovtsov, indicating that both were recent additions to the service class who remained insignificant.[33] Judging by Larion's patronymic, he was the son of a Tatar who had recently joined Russian service. The same was largely true for the name Kuz'ma, used by thirty-one adult slaves but only six slaveowners. One Kuz'ma was a scribe, another a newly baptized Tatar. Little or no biographical data can be found on three others.[34]

The sole exception to the generalization about slaveowners named Kuz'ma was Kuz'ma Osipovich Bezobrazov, one of the lesser distinguished figures of the last quarter of the sixteenth century, a typical trimmer ("lovkost'" was the word

30. RIB 17: 92-93, nos. 259, 261; ibid., 17: 101, no. 283; Ianitskii, *Novgorodskii*, app., p. 134; RIB 22(1908): 780; AIuB 2: 183; Nosov, *Ocherki*, p. 359.
31. NZKK 2: 93.
32. Ibid., p. 49; RIB 28(1926): 5.
33. NZKK 1: 185; 2: 91.
34. Ibid., 1: 205, 302; 2: 40, 147; RIB 17: 208.

contemporaries used) who managed to serve faithfully every sovereign from Ivan IV to Vasilii Shuiskii. What he did in his early years is unknown, but he appeared during Ivan's reign as a *dumnyi dvorianin*, one of the highest ranks. In 1572 he carried a message destined for the Swedish king as far as Oreshek. He was awarded the rank of *striapchii s kliuchem* (manager of the tsar's household) in 1581, and also participated in the Swedish campaign of that year. In 1588 he investigated an uprising in Livny, in 1594 was one of the officers in charge of building the fortified line along the southern frontier, and in the years 1593-95 also served as a census director in Belev and Kozel'sk provinces. He was in the tsar's regiment in 1597 when the Muscovites encountered Kazy-Girei at Serpukhov and Tula, and in 1598 joined Boris Godunov's army at Serpukhov and then signed the document electing Boris tsar. In true Muscovite fashion, he proved that he could serve anybody. He was ranked nineteenth at the wedding of False Dmitrii and Marina on May 8, 1606, and in 1606 he served as a surveyor in Kozel'sk province. At the appropriate moment, he joined the forces of Tsar Vasilii Shuiskii, who rewarded him with numerous properties (some of which had been confiscated from "traitors"!) and in 1609 promoted him to the rank of *postel'-nichei* (chamberlain). In 1609 Bezobrazov was entitled to 1,000 cheti of land, of which he possessed 936 cheti, making him one of the wealthiest men in Muscovy. His total slaveholdings are unknown, but it is noteworthy that he is the last person who is recorded as having purchased registered slaves, a nuclear family of four to manage his estate, the village Marfino in Borovsk province, and three brothers to manage his estate at Fefilovo village in Dmitrov province. Moreover, as was typical for such instances, Bezobrazov did not buy those slaves himself, but other slaves did it for him.

Are there any reasons that explain Bezobrazov's having the given name of Kuz'ma? There seem to be. At birth, he may not have been of the sociological origins that normally would have destined him for service in the landed, military-service elite. In fact, Bezobrazov was not primarily a military man, but an administrator, a person whose major functions were civilian. He went along on some campaigns but as part of the tsar's central regiment on what might be called "all hands on deck" occasions. Ordinarily, he occupied positions at court and elsewhere in the administration that a century or so earlier might well have been occupied by a slave. Lastly, Kuz'ma Osipov Bezobrazov (or his nineteenth-century biographer) apparently realized that his given name was not in keeping with his stature and created a hyphenated variation, Avraam-Kuz'ma (or Kuz'ma-Avraam). Nevertheless, the sources available to me always referred to him as Kuz'ma.[35]

35. Petrov, IRRD, 1(1886); 331; Akty Iushkova, pp. 246, 276-77, 299-300, 304, nos. 235, 259, 281, 285; Zimin, KFV (1977), pp. 215, 220; Koretskii (1975), p. 201; RK 1550-1636, 2; 114, 146; *Opisanie dokumentov i bumag* 16(1910): 153, no. 926, III: RIB 22(1908): 35; SIRIO 129(1910): 228; RIB 35(1917): 98-101, 103, 105-6, 112-14; AIu, pp. 82, 99-101; Belokurov, RZ 7113-21 (1907), pp. 82, 138, 184, 223; RK 1598-1638, pp. 23, 31, 43, 336;

Thus one may conclude that class-typing of male given names was a definite fact of Muscovite life.

An examination of the female names in table 12.5 supports the generalizations made about tables 12.3 and 12.4. Most names were commonly shared by both the upper and lower classes, indicating the general integration of Muscovite society at that level. There were, however, names that members of the upper classes used that the lower tended to avoid, and vice versa. In the case of "upper-class names," the preference for certain ones was hardly as marked for females as it was for males. The names Olena (Elena) and Tat'iana were only twice as popular among the upper class vis-à-vis the lower class, hardly as pronounced as the cases of Bogdan and Posnik for males. In their turn, the lower classes preferred the names Matrona, Okulina (Akulina), Paraskov'ia, and Polagia. The most class-typed name was Matrona (as it probably remains today: see Solzhenitsyn's story "Matrona's Home," where the heroine is presumably an archetypal peasant woman), followed by Paraskov'ia (the female patron saint of marketing and laundry), and then Okulina and Polagia. An examination of the cases explains the anomalies, at least to some extent. For example, on March 12, 1596, at her husband's verbal command, Matrona Ryndina (daughter of Ivan Boranov Ondreevskii) and her sons Ivan, Posnik, Vasilii, and Mikhail Ondreev Ryndin freed a hereditary slave, the unwed woman Natas'itsa Tarasova, who had belonged to her husband. (Typically, the girl proceeded to marry a slave, and was thereby herself reenslaved. They soon gave birth to a slave son.) Matrona's name seems to be explained by her father's surname, Ondreevskii, which is a name used by clerks and other such individuals. No other information about Ondreevskii seems to be available, so it is not clear what his service was. We may assume, however, that he was for some reason hired or promoted into the middle service class. Nothing is known about Matrona's husband, Ondrei Ryndin, either, how he became a slaveowner, or. what his service was. Thus the husband and father-in-law were of comparable obscurity. We may assume that Ryndin was also the first of his family to join the middle service class, a status that he transmitted to his sons, who served as *deti boiarskie*. The sons' service land-compensation entitlements (150, 200, 250, and 300 cheti, on the provincial town registry) in 1605 were low enough to indicate that the status of their father had been lowly as well, that of a first-generation serviceman.[36] This explains how Matrona Ryndina was the sole slaveowner with that given name.

The other anomalies are harder to explain. For example, Paraskov'ia was the daughter of Shavruk Mikitin Murav'ev. On November 5, 1585, he made a present of the unwed slave girl Oksen'itsa Ivanova Borasheva to his daughter. The

RK 1475-1598, pp. 416, 521, 527; Ovchinnikov, "BS 1607," p. 75; Storozhev, *BS* (1909), p. 77; AAE 2: 42, no. 7: Tatishchev (1910), pp. 15-16, 50; Hulbert, p. 253.

36. RIB 17: 24, no. 69; DVP 1605, pp. 480-82.

Murav'evs were a prominent clan of Novgorod slaveowners throughout the period after the Moscow conquest, and thus by, say 1565 (about the time we may assume Paraskov'ia to have been born and named), hardly of lower-class tastes. One other feature of the Murav'evs, however, may explain the choice of "Paraskov'ia" for a daughter: they also chose atypical names for sons. Thus we have not only her father, Shavruk, but also Akinf, Astafii, Feoktist, Gerasim (twice), Ianysh, Mordvin, and Trefil (in addition to the more typical Bogdan, Fedor (twice), Grigorii (four times), Ivan (three times), Matvei, Mikhail, Mikita, and Stepan), unquestionably the most "original" set of names I am aware of. One wonders what the infliction of such atypical names did to their holders, even Paraskov'ia. The gift of a slave girl to her is nearly a unique event, for most other female offspring of slaveowners got them as dowries. Is it possible that Paraskov'ia remained an old maid because no scion of a serviceman was willing to marry someone named after the patron saint of launderesses? If so, this must have been a blow to Shavruk, who at the beginning of the seventeenth century was a commander (*golova*) of *strel'tsy* in Ivangorod, entitled to the maximum land compensation of 600 cheti (he probably possessed most of it, in Votskaia piatina), and an annual salary of 22 rubles in cash. Perhaps the unusual name stimulated him to succeed as a male but destroyed his daughter as a female.[37]

I have tried to explain differences in the use of such names as Maria and Tat'iana by possible differences in the birth cycles of the upper and lower orders in Muscovy. The assumption was that conceptions were likely to occur at different times of year for different social classes, and the Muscovites named their children after the saint on whose day they were born, or baptized, a few days later. Agriculturalists traditionally are known to have had the highest level of conceptions after the harvest, when they were rested from their labors and more well fed. One may assume that those elements who sold themselves into slavery would be least likely to conceive children during the harsh winter months, December through March, when they tended to sell themselves. For the service classes the lowest season of conceptions would be the military campaigning season, from May through November. I tried to plot a natality cycle for the slaves and slaveowners, but it failed, as far as I could tell, because, for example, Maria is a saint's day on January 26, February 6 and 12, April 1, June 7 and 9, July 12 and 22, August 9, and October 29.

In spite of that specific inutility of anthroponymy, there seems to have been a clear class-typing of names in Muscovy. The consciousness inherent in such a phenomenon perhaps was one of the factors creating the psychological distance that was necessary for members of the slaveowning class to enslave members of the lower orders.

37. Kopanev, "Materialy," p. 184 [the document is misdated in ASEI 3: 424, no. 415]; Samokvasov, *Materialy* 2(1909): 36; RK 1598-1638, p. 127; Veselovskii, *Onomastikon*, p. 207; Sukhotin, ChSV, p. 13; DVP 1605, p. 469; Ivanov, OPK (1841), p. 53; RIB 22(1908): 411, 492, 580, 600.

Anthroponymy may provide one last service for us. V. B. Kobrin compiled the information in the top four rows of table 12.6, and I have added the rest.[38]

TABLE 12.6
Use of Noncalendar Names in Muscovy

	Total People	No. with Noncalendar Names	%
First rank of the *Book of a Thousand* (ca. 1550) and royal counselors	61	1	1.6
Second rank of the *Book of a Thousand*	86	2	2.3
Third rank of the *Book of a Thousand*	931	140	15.0
Court Register (Dvorovaia tetrad') (1551-52)	3,500	502	14.3
Female slaveowners	184	2	1.1
Adult female slaves	1,414	23	1.6
Adult male slaves	2,437	113	4.6
Male slaveowners	1,839	252	13.7

Calendar names are those of saints of the Orthodox church, such as Aleksandr and Aleksandra, Amos and Anna, Ivan and Irina, Stepan and Sofia. Noncalendar names are of two types, Russian nouns and adjectives, and foreign (especially Turkic) names. One popular type of Russian name was ordinals (perhaps from place in a birth order), Pervyi (First), Vtoroi (Second), Tret'ia (Third), Piatoi (Fifth), Deviatii (Ninth), Desiatii (Tenth), and so on. Then there were nouns: Byk (Bull), Arbuz (Watermelon), Ezdok (Rider), Gost' (Merchant), Guba (Lip), Karaul (Guard), Sobaka (Dog), Dosada (Vexation), Sotnik (Centurion), Topor (Axe), Voin (Warrior), Zloba (Spite), Zveria (Animal). Then there were various adjectives: Chernyi (Black), Gorbatyi (Hunchbacked), Griaznoi (Filthy), Nekhoroshii (Bad), Seryi (Gray), Svetlyi (Bright). There were also "traditional" noncalendar names such as Istoma, Posnik, Nezhdan, and Zhdan. Russians also took national designations (*nomina regionalia*) as given names: Cheremis, Cherkas, Kazarin, Latysh, Meshcherin, Mordvin, Rusin. And, finally, there were dozens, if not hundreds, of Turkish names: Ablai, Alai, Bakhterei, Bibars, Ianysh, Iumran, Kurbat, Mamet, Murat, Shevruk, Temir, Uslium, and on and on.

As we see in table 12.5, few of these names were applied to women. The ruling male elite also confined itself to Orthodox calendar names. Male slaves had a wider selection of noncalendar names, reflecting the lower orders whence they came, with their use of traditional Russian names, such as Dobrinia, Dudin, Ievka, Izotik, Kozel, Pozniak, Rudak, and the like. The broadest group of names was used by the rank-and-file servicemen (third rank of the *Book of a Thousand* and the *Court Register*), whose more prosperous members were the slaveowners

38. V. B. Kobrin, "Genealogiia i antroponimika," p. 82.

of Muscovy. They had such a high proportion of noncalendar names because their members were partially recruited from the lower orders, they had a genealogical consciousness of precedence and order, and there was a large infusion of non-Russians in their ranks. It seems appropriate that the percentage of slave-owners with noncalendar names should be slightly less than the broader service stratum represented in the third rank of the *Book of a Thousand* and the *Court Register*, and considerably less than the first two ranks of the *Book of a Thousand*, the very top service elite of Muscovite society. Probably everyone in these first two ranks was a slaveowner, whereas not everyone in the other ranks was.

In other slave systems, the use of names had more explicit functions. In societies ranging from Syria in the first centuries A.D. to the American South, slaves were forbidden to have surnames as part of the distancing process, to perpetuate their kinlessness and status as outsiders. In other systems such as medieval and Ch'ing China, slaves often assumed the owner's family name, a manifestation of the quasi-kinship relationship between master and chattel.[39] Muscovy was somewhere in between those extremes. No fetish was made of the slave's formal "outsider" status, and no attempt was made to incorporate him into the owner's lineage. Yet, it is apparent that the Russians were conscious of the utility of names in establishing distance between the dominent elements in society and those beneath.

Geographic Mobility

Geographic mobility was another distancing factor that helped to make those who sold themselves into slavery "outsiders." This factor was noted at the outset of this chapter when it was observed that people from Rzheva and Riazan' were considered "outsiders," along with converts and military captives, in the Pskov region. Those who later sold themselves into slavery often had wandered all over Muscovy before doing so. It is evident from the sources that some of them walked on foot, some rode horseback, others rode in carts and wagons. From the 2,499 documents (slavery contracts, dowries, wills, etc.) that were computer-processed for this study, the birthplace of the slave is known in 300 instances, his place of residence prior to the transaction in 736 cases, where the document was written in 2,489 cases, and where the owner lived in 1,960 instances. Cross-tabulations of any two of the four variables show where a slave (or slave-to-be) moved.

While this mobility made the slave into an outsider, it also contributed to the

---

39. Shifman, in *Rabstvo*, p. 114; Wiens, p. 198; Meijer, p. 332. Southern American reality was expressed by Huck Finn when he said: "I don't want to be a king and have only just a given name, like a nigger" (Mark Twain, *The Adventure of Tom Sawyer* [New York: Gabriel Wells, 1922], p. 202).

unification of the system of slavery throughout Muscovy. By the reign of Vasilii III, almost certainly, such uniformity existed. Here I should mention that, while the data on slavery come from 420 discrete places throughout Muscovy and 180 of the years between 1430 and 1714, 92 percent of all the cases are from the northwest (Novgorod) region, and 80 percent are from the years 1581 to 1603. Many facts attest to the reality of a pan-Muscovite system of slavery. First, the law imposed a structural uniformity as it developed. Second, people from many regions of Muscovy were involved in the Novgorod region as purchasers of slaves, as witnesses to slavery contracts, and as officials in charge of the system. Third, individuals from all over Muscovy traveled to the Novgorod region and sold themselves into slavery there, and Novgorodians sold themselves throughout Muscovy.

This extensive mobility was facilitated by the consolidation of the Russian lands by Moscow. People not bound to the land, a town, or burdened with the cares and implements of agriculture or trade were free to move because of the absence of political or geographic barriers in Muscovy. While some variety of agricultural provincialism must have prevailed in Muscovy, there was no feudalism or feudal ties that might have bound a person physically or psychologically to any one place. It cannot be determined whether there was a "pan-Russian market" at any time for those desiring to sell themselves, but it is clear that people could and did move great distances. Such movement certainly helped to make the slaves "outsiders" in the places where they sold themselves and served. Moreover, this makes them more like slaves than the African pawns mentioned in chapter 2, who were surrounded and even protected by their kin. Under this rubric I shall examine the general issue of slave mobility.

The documents of sale almost always say where they were written, and in the few that do not that information generally can be deduced from the officials and scribes listed in them. Thus we can be fairly certain of where 2,489 of the 2,499 documents I have processed were written. Three hundred of the documents say where the slave, or person selling himself into slavery, was born, and 736 of them say where that person was living prior to the conclusion of the contract. In some cases this was the same place where the prior owner was living, whose residences in 373 instances can be determined. It is assumed that most slaves ended up where their owners lived. This information is rarely stated in the documents on the slaves, but it can be gathered for 1,960 cases from other Muscovite historical sources. The major exception to the general assumption about the destination of the slaves concerns estate stewards selling themselves into registered slavery, for whom the documents usually named the estate where the slave was to be the manager. By making pairs of these places (birthplace, last stated place of residence, place of sale or registration, and slaveowner's home), one can determine slave mobility throughout the Muscovite state. By pairing a former owner's residence with the present owner's home, one can examine the role of geography in establishing marriage alliances. One can also determine the importance of central places by examining the flow into and out of the major registration centers.

Slave mobility at its broadest extent was from the slave-to-be's place of birth to his ultimate owner's home. The data provide 231 such pairs, of which 11 must be ignored because one or the other (or both) of the places cannot be located. Only 19, or less than 10 percent, are known to have been enslaved where they were born—itself an astonishing expression of geographic mobility. The data show that people moved all over Muscovy. Thus the slaves must have been without extended kinship ties in the places where they were enslaved and were truly "outsiders" there. The pattern of peasant mobility was different: moving from one province to the next was the rule, jumping provinces was rare. Peasants, of course, were burdened with agricultural inventory; future slaves had nothing. Some of the documents tell of owners picking up slaves on the road, say, from Moscow to Tver.[40] The image of Russians constantly migrating, constantly on the move, is a popular one in historiography, and was advanced as one of the reasons why the government had to enserf the peasantry, which thereby lost the right to wander all over Russia. It is now known that most of the peasants were not at all migratory and usually remained in the same place for generations (as peasants are supposed to); they were enserfed for other reasons. It does appear as though there was a considerable amount of vagabondage among the social elements that tended to become slaves.

I considered the problem of mobility in various time frames, and for this series I considered as the starting point not the slave's birthplace but rather the place he declared to be his last place of residence before selling himself. For the period prior to 1592 (N=118), almost all the slaves were confined to the Novgorod region; a little more than one-third sold themselves to an owner whose residence was near the last declared place of residence, but almost two-thirds moved some distance within the vast area of the five Novgorod piatinas. Most of the documents recording this information were from the 1597-98 registrations in Shelonskaia and Votskaia piatinas, which accounts for a concentration of cases there. One may surmise that, because of its proximity to the Livonian War theatre, few people moved into that area. The average distance a slave moved in that period was 160 kilometers.

The next period considered was the years 1593-97 (N=235), after the Livonian War and before the general slavery statute of 1597 could have had any impact. About the same percentages moved about and stayed in the same places as during the Livonian War, but the distance moved was much greater, an average of 260 kilometers. Also notable is movement into the Novgorod piatinas from outside the region. This probably reflects the recovery of the Novgorod region from the devastation of the Oprichnina, the famine of the late 1560s and the oppressive taxation and rent collection of the Livonian War era. In the years 1598-1601

---

40. NPKK 1: 291.

(N=78), the average distance moved was 240 kilometers in a period of continuing recovery and general peace in northwest Muscovy.

During the era of the Great Famine (1601-3; N=112), mobility was curtailed to some extent (the average move was 175 kilometers), but it appears as though there was still extensive moving about as the starving tried to find someone who would or could feed them. It is unfortunate that the number of pairs is only 15 percent of the number of transactions recorded at this time, making generalization somewhat hazardous. Nevertheless, it well may have been the fact that the smallest percentage of those selling themselves remained where they had been during the famine, simply because people sold themselves when they assumed that there was no food where they were. As noted in chapter 11, this was the time when people such as landless peasants and others marginally linked to agriculture sold themselves, and they had to do so precisely because there was assumed to be no food where they were. Unfortunately, mapping the data does not indicate where people thought the food was. The picture of a great milling about in an almost random search for something to eat is one that is also portrayed in the travel accounts, diaries, and other writings of the period.

The last period considered, the rest of the seventeenth century after the Great Famine, allows a move away from the Novgorod region for a look at all of Muscovy (N=61). While 47 percent of the slaves' owners resided in the same places where the slaves had been prior to the conclusion of the transaction, the others moved throughout the country, with the average move being 260 kilometers. The fact that 47 percent remained in the same place probably represents the increasing stratification of Muscovite society and the tendency of slaves when manumitted to recycle themselves back into slavery. General mobility was reduced, and freedmen usually lacked the resources to travel very far before they had to sell themselves again. (See map 12.1.)

I also examined the issue of seasonal mobility. Most of the self-sales were concentrated in the four winter months, December through March, the smallest number of sales was in August through November, and April through July was an intermediate period. The best travel time in Muscovy was the frozen winter months (the army called it the time of the "winter route," *zimnii put'*, when servicemen were to send supplies to the front; distances were shorter by the "winter route" than at other times of year, for they were much more "as the crow flies" than around bogs, across flowing rivers, and so on), but this may not have been the best time of year for people who were starving, in need of the relief that only slavery could provide in Muscovy. It is not apparent that time of year made any difference in how far a person moved before selling himself, for the average distance for the months December through March was 210 kilometers, for April through July 200 kilometers, and for August through November 205 kilometers. (These distances were between the slaves' birth places and their owners' homes.)

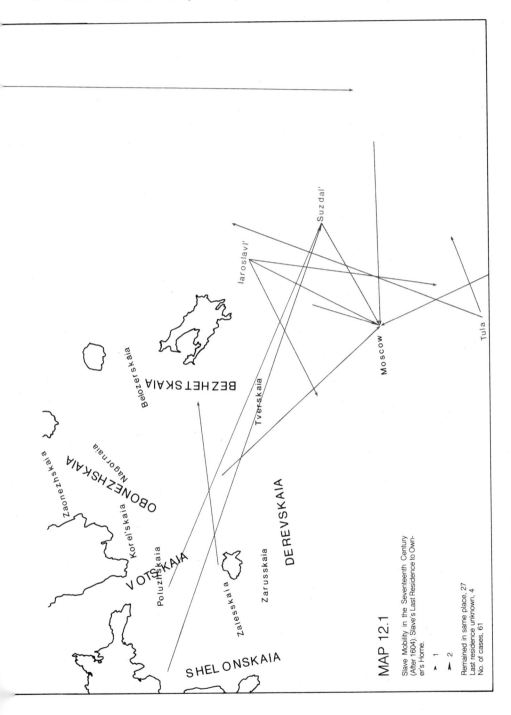

MAP 12.1

Slave Mobility in the Seventeenth Century
(After 1604). Slave's Last Residence to Owner's Home.

▲ 1
▲ 2

Remained in same place, 27
Last residence unknown, 4
No. of cases, 61

National Stereotypes

Societies that had extensive experience with slaves of many nationalities often created stereotypes of what those slaves were like. For example, the Ottoman image of the Russian slave was not very flattering:

> Some things which cannot happen: a Russian female slave who is not im-moral; Russian male slaves who are courageous. Cossacks from this race are all heavy drinkers; they are more depraved than the blackeyed Araps [Negroes] and they are continuously drinking wine and bozay [a fermented berry drink]. They are the worst scoundrels in the world.[41]

Mikalojus Tishkevicius noted a similar stereotype in the Crimea, where a slave auctioneer would shout out the virtues of his merchandise — that they were from Poland, not from Muscovy, "for Muscovites, considered dishonest and crafty, are lowly valued on the slave market."[42] These are just two examples of Ottoman and Crimean Tatar stereotypes. Different stereotypes can be found in other societies, often in publications of advice on domestic management.

To my knowledge, there are no such stereotypes of slaves in Muscovy. This is in spite of the fact that the Muscovites used slaves from China, Central Asia, the various Tatar peoples, Lithuanians, Poles, and Swedes. Had ethnic consciousness been developed, those slaves, contrasted with Russians, would have provided superb material for various ethnic stereotypes. Such stereotypes might have been reflected in the prices Muscovites were willing to pay, but, as far as can be deter-mined, they were not. They might have survived in some written form, but, to my knowledge, they did not. These voids would seem to support the thesis that ethnic consciousness was very minimally developed in Muscovy.

Ritual Distancing

In South Asia slaves at one time were "outsiders," when the invading Aryans

---

41. Fisher, "Ottoman Slavery," p. 40.

42. [Mikaloujus Tishkevicius], "Izvlechenie iz sochineniia Mikhaila Litvina," in *Memuary otnosiashchiesia k istorii iuzhnoi Rusi* (Kiev, 1890), p. 20. I am indebted to Alan Fisher for providing me with a copy of this work. The Latin original was: "Nam Moschorum genus, ut dolosum et fallax, ita vile habetur illic in mancipijs." (*Arkhiv istoriko-iuridicheskikh svede-nii, otn. do Rossii, izd. N. Kalachovym* 2²[1854]: 22.) The identity of the person who wrote under the pen-name "Michalonis Lituani = Mykolas Lietuvis" (previously attributed to Tishkevicius) has recently been reconsidered by E. Okhman'skii, who attributed it to a Lithuanian ambassador, Ventslav Mikolaevich, who signed himself as Venceslaus Lithuanus at Cracow University in 1506 ("Mikhalon Litvin i ego trakt o nravakh tatar, litovtsev i mosk-vitian serediny XVI v.," in *Rossiia, Pol'sha i Prichernomore'e v XV–XVIII vv.*, ed. B. A. Rybakov [Moscow: Nauka, 1979], pp. 106, 111).

conquered the aboriginal populations. But since at least the sixth century B.C., when the distinctions between the invaders and the indigenes disappeared in that area, slavery has been largely an indigenous system. This is possible because of, and is essentially required by, the Hindu religion, which demands that slaveowners know the ritual credentials of their chattel, precluding the use of "outsider" domestic chattel whose origins are unknown. The Hindus established distance between owner and slave by other, often ritual, means. This ritual distance was symbolized by the use of food, as is so often the case in India: custom required slaves to eat the food-leavings of their owners.[43] This presumably helped to equate slaves with animals. Curiously enough, the mid-sixteenth- century Muscovite *Domostroi* also discusses feeding table scraps, "leavings" (*ostanki*), to slaves.[44] Of course the early modern Russians knew little or nothing of Hinduism, but certainly the practice of feeding leftovers to slaves symbolized their distance from their owners.

Other societies practiced different forms of ritual distancing to convert the native into an "outsider." One was the exposure of infants in ancient Greece. Another was the use of middlemen in modern China, where the use of the go-between served to make the slave girls at least "quasi-outsiders" for their buyers.[45] The Muscovites, on the other hand, resorted to no such fictions, and bought and sold each other directly. The Chinese system of household slavery preserved the boundaries between master and slave by not permitting the slave to eat at the same table with the owning family or to address the owner with the pronouns "you" or "I."[46] As far as is known, the early modern Russians had no such special conventions for slaves, but then the Russians, unlike the Chinese did not make slavery into a quasi-kinship institution in which such barriers would be necessary.

The goal of this chapter has been to advance for consideration factors that together might explain convincingly how it could happen that Muscovites were one of the few peoples who freely and unabashedly enslaved their own kind. Because Muscovy was unusual in its willingness to enslave natives permanently on a massive scale, the comparative approach gives us almost no help. Moreover, the social science literature provides little help beyond narrative presentations of the obvious.

As we have seen, there was no one factor that allowed the Muscovites to simulate the ethnic barriers necessary to create a complete system for the enslavement of natives. We may assume that it was a combination of factors that permitted the creation of one of the world's most unusual slave systems. Rank-ordering these factors is a difficult task whose accuracy is by no means assured,

43. Caplan, pp. 188, 191.
44. *Domostroi*, pp. 55-56.
45. Meijer, p. 342.
46. Ibid., p. 332.

but, with that caveat, I shall proceed. Perhaps most important was the general uncertainty about who was an insider and who was an outsider. The society was sufficiently fluid ethnically, as far as one can tell, that it could take in anybody from another society or even of another race and make him a Muscovite through suitable employment, marriage alliances, and general acceptance as a peer. This easy social acceptance of seemingly any outsider must have had its counterpart in difficulty in determining who was an insider.

In this world of ethnic fluidity, identity was defined by religion, Orthodox and heterodox, and social standing. Religion was a clearly defined barrier but one that could easily be crossed by baptism. The barrier of social standing, of "we" and "they," was never minimal, but it was more easily bridged earlier than later. The class-typing of names indicates that such a consciousness existed throughout the Muscovite period, while the presence of exceptions shows the mobility presumably inherent in a service-oriented society. Less easily bridged were the pretensions of foreign origin (and presumably, therefore, of superiority) adopted by many clans in the late sixteenth century.

Finally, there were the simulated barriers provided by poverty and geography that created social distance between slaveowners and would-be and actual slaves of Muscovite origin. Many of them had traveled far, and thus were outsiders in the new communities where they were enslaved. Except for those who became elite slaves, those who sold themselves were also distanced from their purchasers by the have—have-not relationship.

These must have been some of the factors that allowed Muscovites to enslave one another. They were not the same as the later distancing features of Imperial Russian society (Westernization, serfdom, and the church schism) that enhanced the "we—they" distinctions which lent serfdom its slave-like character, nor were they like the political and other animosities that permitted the creation of the Soviet Gulag slave-labor system, all of which presumably built on Muscovite slave heritage. Certainly the elements examined in this chapter cannot pretend to be the definitive explanation of the fact that the Muscovite enslaved their own ethnos, but, one hopes, they constitute a beginning.

13. Slave Demography

The extant data permit a discussion of Muscovite slavery in most of the dimensions of interest to demographers, such as family composition and sex and age distributions. Regrettably, the data seem inadequate for more sophisticated demographic calculations, such as the compilation of life tables, but nevertheless the information on the slave population is the earliest and most complete available, prior to the eighteenth century and perhaps even later than that, on any segment of Muscovite society. Because comparable information for other segments of Muscovite society is lacking, comparisons between the slave population and those segments are usually impossible.

Such complete data are available on slaves because of the registration procedures requiring precise description of slaves so that owners could claim them should legal disputes arise. As we saw in chapter 8, the slaves were described when the contract was written up by a scribe, and then this information was verified during the formalization of the sale in front of the state secretary, *guba* elder, or other major government official. There was no comparable registration process for other segments of the society. The cadastres and censuses compiled in the late fifteenth and sixteenth centuries included only landed area and households (and sometimes heads of households or ablebodied males). In the mid-seventeenth century the taxation system began to shift away from landed area (which naturally had encouraged peasants to curtail cultivation) to the household, a process completed in 1678. The number of ablebodied males in the households was counted, and the government quickly discerned that the household tax caused families to double up to cut their taxes. This also artifically created the famous Russian extended family and reduced the number of solitaries, developments that almost certainly played a role in the demise of slavery. Be that as it may, in the 1720s Peter the Great abolished the household tax in favor of the soul tax, a sexist system which counted all males, from the youngest babe to the most decrepit geriatric. The assumption of the soul tax (which effectively abolished slavery) was that counting males would produce a representative sample of the community at any given time, an assumption that is probably not inaccurate, for in most societies about half of the population is made up of persons who are of working age, and the other half of those too young or too old to support themselves. The soul tax, as all the other systems, was only the basis for the government's collective assessment, and the tax commune had to meet the entire bill as it saw fit.

413

In all of these taxation systems the assumption was that only males were important, so females were listed only rarely. Moreover, the early census-type events did not list the ages of those counted. Thus the slave data are a truly unique source of demographic information for early modern Russia.

Heads of Households

Over half of the slave household units in early modern Russia were headed by single adults, most of them male, most of them solitaries.[1] As is evident in table 13.1, married males headed over one-third of the remaining households, and single minors (under the age of fifteen) the remainder. (Table 13.1 slightly exaggerates the proportion of all slaves in married-couple households, for in this tabulation only one type of family unit was coded per document, and in some documents, especially those transmitting hereditary slaves, there was often more than one family in a document. In those cases the largest unit was coded, which in fact was usually listed first. In the 1597-98 general registrations of all slaves and during the compilation of dowries, wills and the like, the general practice was to list families with children first, then couples, and lastly solitaries. The slightly erroneous impression of table 13.1 will be corrected in subsequent presentations.)

TABLE 13.1
Heads of Households in Muscovite Slavery

Type of Individual	Documents	%	Total Individuals	%
Adult single male	1,077	43.1	1,284	23.1
Minor boy	55	2.2	89	1.6
Adult male with children, no wife (widower)	73	2.9	220	4.0
Adult male with wife	913	36.5	3,362	60.4
Married female	70	2.8	137	2.5
Unmarried adult female	184	7.4	237	4.2
Widow	92	3.7	206	3.7
Minor girl	30	1.2	36	0.6
Unknown	5	0.2	?	?
Total	2,499		5,565	100.1

Most of the categories in table 13.1 are self-explanatory. However, one should

1. For a discussion of types of households, see Jacques Dapuquier and Louis Jadin, "Structure of Household and Family in Corsica, 1769-71" in *Household and Family in Past Time,* ed. Peter Laslett (London: Cambridge University Press, 1972), p. 287.

note that there are more than 1,078 individuals in the documents in which single males seem to be the major figure because occasionally a single male would sell himself (or be transmitted to another owner) along with a sibling or another solitary. The same was true for unmarried adult females and minor children. The category that needs some commentary is that of "married female," which is distinguished from that of "widow." The documents give the impression that they almost always say that a woman is a widow when her husband is deceased, and therefore we may assume that the remaining females who are said to be married and heading a household have been abandoned by their husbands. A desire to be rid of one's mate was a major cause of slave flight, and this seems evident in the group of 75 married females. On the other hand, the documents did nothing to distinguish males who no longer had wives because they were widowers or were otherwise separated.

The Muscovite slave world was an abnormal human community. Elsewhere in the early modern world married couples headed anywhere from 46 to 93 percent of households, single males from 1 to at most 17 percent, widows around 10 percent or more, and so on.[2] One of the functions of this chapter is to explain the peculiar demographic aspects of the Muscovite slave community.

Table 13.2 shows how these figures change when the types and nature of slavery are considered. Thus in full and limited service contract slavery, the two major first-generation varieties, by comparison with all slaves, the proportion of solitaries and single-adult headed households increases, the proportion of two-parent families decreases. This is symptomatic of the stress that forced people to sell themselves into slavery. Moreover, as usual, the statistical similarity between the two is striking. The marriage contracts and dowries are skewed more toward females because of the nature of the transaction, the provision of handmaidens and servants for the bride and her husband. Wills, property divisions, and registrations of complete slave holdings provide a fuller picture of what ongoing hereditary slavery was like. Especially this last will be discussed further in the "Family Composition" section.

Table 13.3 looks at these gross data from the perspective of price. Over 95 percent of the price transactions were for limited service contract slavery and weight the information heavily; thus, there are not enough differences in the price structures of full, registered and limited service contract slaveries to make it worthwhile to differentiate them. The prices paid per transaction (per document) and the prorated cost per slave in each transaction are not the same in the categories such as "adult single male" and "unmarried female" because sometimes (although rarely, as evidenced by the "% Ratio" column) individuals sold themselves with a sibling or an unrelated person. The same was true for the children. The figures make it clear that the cheapest slaves were the girls, then adult females, and then boys. Most expensive were single adult males. The

2. Peter Laslett, *Household and Family*, pp. 78, 317.

TABLE 13.2
Heads of Households by Type of Slavery Instrument

Type of Individual	Full Slavery				Limited Service Contract Slavery			
	No. of Documents	%	No. of Individuals	%	No. of Documents	%	No. of Individuals	%
Adult single male	57	57.0	64	30.5	953	45.6	1,070	27.2
Minor boy	2	2.0	4	1.9	50	2.4	76	1.9
Widower	6	6.0	19	9.0	59	2.8	160	4.1
Adult male with wife	31	31.0	112	53.3	748	35.8	2,209	56.2
Married female	2	2.0	3	1.4	56	2.7	101	2.6
Unmarried adult female	–	–	–	–	120	5.7	130	3.3
Widow	2	2.0	8	3.8	75	3.6	155	3.9
Minor girl	–	–	–	–	28	1.3	32	0.8
Unknown	–	–	–	–	2	0.1	?	?
Total	100	100.0	210	99.9	2,091	100.0	3,933	100.0

Type of Individual	Marriage Contracts and Dowries				Wills, Property Divisions, Total Registrations			
	No. of Documents	%	No. of Individuals	%	No. of Documents	%	No. of Individuals	%
Adult single male	22	15.3	62	13.2	5	10.0	42	6.1
Minor boy	–	–	–	–	–	–	–	–
Widower	3	2.1	19	4.1	3	6.0	18	2.6
Adult male with wife	52	36.1	254	54.2	40	80.0	630	90.8
Married female	8	5.6	27	5.8	–	–	–	–
Unmarried adult female	51	35.4	86	18.3	–	–	–	–
Widow	8	5.6	21	4.5	1	2.0	4	0.6
Minor girl	–	–	–	–	–	–	?	?
Unknown	–	–	–	–	1	2.0	?	?
Total	144	100.0	469	100.1	50	100.0	694	100.1

TABLE 13.3
Prices According to Major Figure in Transaction, in Rubles

Major Figure	Price per Document	Price per Slave	% Ratio	N
Adult single male	3.79	3.54	93.3	1,009
Adult married male	4.25	1.54	36.3	773
Widower	6.10	2.36	38.7	65
Minor boy	3.48	2.08	60.0	54
Married female	3.00	1.97	65.7	57
Widow	3.45	1.75	50.8	79
Unmarried female	2.69	2.57	95.3	123
Minor girl	1.64	1.45	88.0	28
Mean	3.89	2.58	66.2	2,188

prices of adult males with families were high, but the price per slave in each transaction was relatively low because the wife and children essentially were not paid for by the purchasing slaveowner. Regression analysis indicates that the major share of the price was for the adult male in such transactions, and the earlier children played some role in determining the price the buyer paid (see chapter 18). The wife and last children played very little role in determining the prices paid for families. This is not surprising, for the slaveowner was primarily interested in buying a lackey to serve him at home as a valet and accompany him on military campaigns. Wives and children could not fulfill these roles, and there was even less use for wives and children in cases when the slaveowner had more than one family, for there was a definite limit to how many people were needed to cook and clean in the Muscovite establishments. Such people served as examples of wealth and ostentatious consumption, which the slaveowners no doubt in fact valued.

It has not been unusual throughout history for males to cost more than females, although the reasons varied from place to place, and, of course, there were exceptions. In most "productive slave systems" men were worth more than women because slave labor usually required strength of the type more likely to be found in males than in females. It was not true in places such as Brazilian coffee plantations, where men and women could labor equally. Men were worth more in medieval Spain because slaves were employed in agriculture and industry, and males were deemed more suited for the work. On the other hand, in medieval Italy females cost more because they were preferred for urban domestic slavery.[3] In Africa, females had a higher value in the internal slave

3. Verlinden, *Colonization*, p. 29. It has been observed, however, that males and females were often substitutable in New World slave occupations, a fact expressed in the small price-differential between them (Herbert S. Klein, "The Cuban Slave Trade in a Period of Transition, 1790-1843," in Emmer, Mettas, and Nardin, p. 83).

trade, grown males were not wanted because of their tendency to flee and because they could not be used to expand lineages, and thus they were killed unless they could be sold into the export trade. In Muscovy, on the other hand, males were preferred because only they could be combat and baggage-train slaves and, as in recent south China, apparently, they made better household lackeys as well.[4]

Family Household Composition

The nuclear family predominated among those who sold themselves into slavery in Muscovy. As is evident in table 13.4, fully 95 percent of all cases readily and immediately can be seen as consisting of nuclear families, or parts thereof, ranging from solitary adults and groups of children no longer with parents to married couples, many children, and then numerous one-parent households. About a third of all the first-generation slaves lived in two-parent households with children, probably a smaller proportion than in the society at large. The proportion of solitaries was certainly much greater than in the society at large, and the same may have been true of the one-parent households and the groups of minor orphans. This reflects the crisis nature of Muscovite first-generation slavery. About the same ratio prevailed for hereditary slaves given away in marriage contracts and dowries, where no attempts were made by the slaveowners to keep families intact as they used slaves to provide "social cement" to bind together different families. While nearly three-fifths of other hereditary slaves (as registered in wills, property divisions, and the 1597-98 registrations of descendants of earlier first-generation slaves) lived in two-parent households with children, the high number of adult solitaries and married couples without children (over half of all families, more than a quarter of all slaves) indicates that marriage and procreation were probably discouraged by slaveowners. That Muscovy experienced primarily a system of household slavery should not make that lack of interest in children surprising.

The 5 percent "other groupings" are of some considerable interest. For the full slavery cases, two cases had four adults and two children, and three cases consisted of two single men. Two men, sometimes related but usually not, was also a frequent combination in limited service contract slavery, with 29 cases. There were also cases of three men; two women; two men and a sister; man, wife, and brother-in-law; man, wife, two children, and two sisters of the husband; and many others. The "other" group of those who sold themselves into limited service contract slavery can be broken down into 110 groups of which 63 were adult solitaries, 22 were married couples, 3 were couples with one child, 6 were couples with two children, and 1 was a couple with three children; there

4. James L. Watson, "Chattel Slavery in Chinese Peasant Society: A Comparative Analy sis," *Ethnology* 15, no. 4 (October 1976): 365; Goody, pp. 37-38.

were five couples with an unstated number of children; a man with one child; five mothers with one child, one with two children and one with three children; and two orphan children.

Notably absent from Muscovite slave society are extended families. There seems to be one example of a couple living with their son, daughter-in-law, and two grandchildren. Another couple had three children and a grandchild, but there was no daughter-in-law in the picture. There was also the case of a grandmother, her daughter and son-in-law, and their two children. A father and son sold themselves with two apparently orphan grandchildren. That is the extent of the three-generational families. Three more families were potentially extended families, with a daughter-in-law in the family married to one of the sons. Never do we find the classical example of the three-generational extended family: a patriarchal couple, two or more of their offspring and their spouses (usually wives), plus grandchildren. This absence of three-generational families, plus the general census figures of the period, lead me to believe that the three-generational family barely existed until the Muscovite government created it with the household (*dvor*) system of taxation.

The historian Lawrence Stone has discussed the absence of the extended family in England in the centuries 1500 to 1800 in the following terms:

> At the bottom of the social scale, the very poor possessed too little land to feed, and too few rooms to house, more than the members of the nuclear family: they just could not afford the extended or stem family, since they lacked the necessary resources to maintain it.[5]

Certainly most of those who sold themselves into slavery in Muscovy were very poor, although not because of absence of land, which was in many respects nearly a free good in many regions for much of the era. Moreover, housing was inexpensive (or even "free") in the Land of Wood, so that factor hardly deterred extended family formation. Rather, in Muscovy one may aver that those who sold themselves into slavery lived in nuclear families because that was the practice for nearly everyone.

The absolute size of all these slave families is only about two people apiece, much smaller than the 5.2 average the Soviet historical demographer Ia. E. Vodarskii advances for Russian townsmen (*posadskie liudi*) in the mid-seventeenth century.[6] As we saw in tables 11.5 and 11.6, the family size of those selling themselves into slavery was always much lower than 5.2, regardless of social origins. Moreover, the data in table 13.4 indicate that the completed family size for hereditary slaves was probably little more than four members. These

5. Lawrence Stone, *The Family, Sex, and Marriage in England, 1500-1800* (New York: Harper and Row, 1977), p. 25.

6. Ia. E. Vodarskii, "Chislennost'," p. 276.

TABLE 13.4
Family Composition by Type of Slavery

	Full Slavery				Limited Service Contract Slavery			
	Documents		Total Individuals		Documents		Total Individuals	
Family Composition	N	% = N	N	%	N	%	N	%
Single slave	53		53	25.2	1,041	49.8	1,041	26.4
Man and wife	13		26	12.4	355	17.0	710	18.0
Man, wife, 1 child	2		6	2.9	171	8.2	513	13.0
Man, wife, 2 children	10		40	19.0	108	5.2	432	11.0
Man, wife, 3 children	1		5	2.4	45	2.2	225	5.7
Man, wife, 4 children	—		—	—	15	0.7	90	2.3
Man, wife, 5 children	3		21	10.0	6	0.3	42	1.1
Man, wife, 6 children	1		8	2.9	1	0.0	8	0.2
Total: Man, wife, children	17		78	37.1	346	16.5	1,310	33.2
Man, 1 child	4		8	3.8	42	2.0	84	2.1
Man, 2 children	—		—	—	27	1.3	81	2.1
Man, 3 children	3		12	5.7	7	0.3	28	0.7
Man, 4 children	1		5	2.4	3	0.1	15	0.4
Total: Man, children	8		25	11.9	79	3.9	208	5.3
Woman, 1 child	2		4	1.9	47	2.2	·94	2.4
Woman, 2 children	—		—	—	21	1.0	63	1.6
Woman, 3 children	—		—	—	7	0.3	28	0.7
Woman, 4 children	—		—	—	1	0.0	5	0.1
Woman, 5 children	—		—	—	2	0.1	12	0.3
Total: Woman, children	2		4	1.9	78	3.7	202	5.1
1 child	—		—	—	60	2.9	60	1.5
2 children	2		4	1.9	27	1.3	54	1.4
3 children					5	0.2	15	0.4
4 children					2	0.1	8	0.2
7 children					1	0.0	7	0.2
Total: Children	2		4	1.9	95	4.5	144	3.7
Other groupings	5		18	8.6	97	4.6	327	8.3
Total	100		210		2,091		3,942	

	Slaves Given Away in Marriage Contracts and Dowries				Slaves Listed in Wills, Property Divisions, and 1597-98 Registration			
Adult solitaries	146	60.6	146	36.2	147	40.3	147	17.7
Man and wife	27	11.2	54	13.4	45	12.3	90	10.8
Man, wife, 1 child	12	5.0	36	8.9	13	3.6	39	4.7
Man, wife, 2 children	12	5.0	48	11.9	28	7.7	72	8.7
Man, wife, 3 children	9	3.7	45	11.2	15	4.1	75	9.0
Man, wife, 4 children	1	0.4	6	1.0	2	0.5	12	1.4
Man, wife, 5 children	–	–	–	–	2	0.5	14	1.7
Man, wife, 6 children	1	0.4	8	1.5	–	–	–	–
Man, wife, ? children[a]	3	1.2	12	3.0	70	19.2	280	33.7
Total: Man, wife, children	38	15.7	155	38.5	130	32.3	492	59.1
Man, 1 child	2	0.8	4	1.0	9	2.5	18	2.2
Man, 2 children	–	–	–	–	7	1.9	21	2.5
Man, 3 children	2	0.8	4	1.0	2	0.5	8	1.0
Total: Man, children	4	1.7	8	2.0	18	4.9	47	5.6
Woman, 1 child	7	2.9	14	3.5	11	3.0	22	2.6
Woman, 2 children	5	2.1	15	3.7	1	0.3	3	0.4
Woman, 3 children	1	0.4	4	1.0	1	0.3	4	0.5
Woman, 4 children	–	–	–	–	1	0.3	5	0.6
Total: Woman, children	13	5.4	33	8.1	14	3.8	34	4.1
1 child	15	6.2	15	3.7	5	1.4	5	0.6
2 children	–	–	–	–	3	0.8	6	0.7
3 children	–	–	–	–	1	0.3	3	0.4
4 children	–	–	–	–	2	0.5	8	1.0
Total: Children	15	6.2	15	3.7	11	3.0	22	2.6
Total	241	100.0	407	100.0	365	100.0	832	100.0
Transactions	144				59[b]			
Slaves per Transaction	2.8				14.1			

[a] Where no children have been listed, an average of 2 has been assumed.
[b] Includes 10 1597-98 registrations not counted before, with 159 people.

figures are considerably below the English mean household size of 4.75, and also below the mean household size for paupers (3.96) in England.[7] The slaves in Muscovy hardly reproduced themselves, and got infusions from that element of society that was not reproducing itself, either.

Table 13.5 examines these data from the perspective of the price paid for the slaves. Once again we notice the astonishing similarity between full and limited service contract slavery, especially if we consider that there was some inflation between the eras of the former and the latter. Also noteworthy are the similarities in the ratios of the prices of a single person and the price for each member of a couple, for a single person, and for each member of a couple with one child. Once again, the table reveals the very low value of children and women; most of what a slaveowner was willing to pay for was adult males.

It is possible to map and compare the mobility of those who became slaves in terms of family size, with solitaries, couples, and families of three or more being the units chosen. Perhaps somewhat surprisingly, the average distance moved (from birthplace to where the owner lived) was just about the same for all three categories: 230 kilometers for solitaries, 230 kilometers for married couples, and 220 kilometers for families of three or more. These data are compromised by the fact that, while the given documents state where the slave was born, they do not tell when the slave moved, whether it was before or after marriage or the birth of a child. With that caveat, it is nevertheless surprising that solitaries were only insignificantly more mobile than those in families. This picture is not contradicted by the court cases involving fugitive slaves, whose mobility also seems not to have been impeded by children. In this context, one might observe that single males congregated disproportionately in the big city, in this case Novgorod. While 26.4 percent of all documents (N = 2,499) were drafted or registered in Novgorod, 41.6 percent of all documents involving males (N = 1,005) were from Novgorod. Of all the Novgorod documents (N = 659), 63.4 percent of them dealt with single males. While they did not remain in Novgorod after enslavement, it is apparent that single males found the metropolitan center the best place to find someone to buy them.

Age Structure

Ages are available for about 40 percent of the people who sold themselves into slavery in Muscovy. Ages are unknown for hereditary slaves, although the data in table 11.6 on the origins of slaves tell us the ages of freedmen and other former dependents who sold themselves back into slavery. There we saw that dependent categories tended to be older than completely free men.

7. Laslet, *Household and Family*, pp. 126, 207.

TABLE 13.5
Social Composition of Slave Units, Type of Slavery, and Prices, in Rubles

Social Composition of Case	Full Slavery			Registered Slavery			Limited Service Contract Slavery		
	Price per Document	Price per Slave	N	Price per Document	Price per Slave	N	Price per Document	Price per Slave	N
Slave himself or herself	2.63	2.63	52	2.21	2.21	17	3.52	3.52	1,012
Man, wife	3.27	1.63	13	–	–		3.54	1.77	343
Man, wife, 1 child	3.00	1.00	2	2.50	0.83	2	4.02	1.34	169
Man, wife, 2 children	2.80	0.70	10	5.50	1.38	2	4.33	1.08	105
Man, wife, 5 children	8.33	1.19	3	10.00	1.43	1	4.50	0.64	6
Man, 1 child	2.63	1.31	4	3.00	1.50	1	4.83	2.41	41
Man, 2 children	–	–		–	–		7.08	2.36	26
Man, 3 children	8.00	2.00	3	–	–		4.33	1.08	6
Man, 4 children	–	–		–	–		7.00	1.40	3
Woman, 1 child	2.25	1.13	2	1.50	0.75	1	2.84	1.42	45
Woman, 2 children	–	–		–	–		4.19	1.40	21
Woman, 3 children	–	–		6.00	1.50	1	7.71	1.93	7
1 child	–	–		–	–		1.92	1.92	60
2 children	2.00	1.00	2	–	–		3.38	1.69	27
3 children	–	–		5.00	1.67	1	5.20	1.73	5
2 men	3.00	1.50	3	4.00	2.00	1	5.59	2.79	29
				Ratios of Price per Slave					
Man, wife: single	62%			–			50%		
Man, wife, 1 child:single	38.0%			37.6%			38.1%		

Table 13.6 is an age pyramid constructed for the last half of the era of Muscovite slavery. This is not the way demographers usually do it, for they prefer one place and one year, rather than areas widely diverse and a time span such as that from the 1590s to the 1680s. However, when I constructed an age pyramid from one source for the Russian year 7111 (the famine year 1602/3) in Novgorod province and compared it with another one that used all the rest of the data, they were so similar to each other and to table 13.6 that I decided to present only this table. The similarity of the three groups of data is evident in the summary table 13.8

TABLE 13.6
Age Pyramid for Muscovite Slaves

Age	N	%-age of Total Pop.	Single & Married Males	Single & Married Females	1st Child	2d Child	3d Child	4th Child
0-4	120	6.57			47	41	19	13
5-9	179	9.81	2	4	90	60	21	2
10-14	190	10.41	44	24	93	23	5	1
15-19	240	13.14	144	61	29	6		
20-24	333	18.25	227	89	14	3		
25-29	282	15.44	187	89	6			
30-34	213	11.66	136	77				
35-39	94	5.15	61	33				
40-44	115	6.30	86	29				
45-49	22	1.20	20	2				
50-54	31	1.70	20	11				
60-64	5	.27	5					
70-74	1	.05	1					
Total	1,825 of 4,594	100.03	933 of 2,119	419 of 1,290	279 of 660	133 of 353	45 of 128	16 of 44

Most striking about the age pyramid is the fact that it is not a pyramid at all but more like a diamond standing on a sawed-off point. The base of a typical age pyramid is the broadest part, portraying the newborn, infants, and young children in the 0 to 4 age group, and then it moves up to the peak, which is the oldest member of the society. In the age pyramid of those selling themselves into slavery, however, the broadest segment is not the base, but the 20-24 age group, that group of adults most prone to sell themselves and to be purchased by a slave buyer. The next most popular cohorts were those just above and below that group, those aged 25-29 and 15-19. One might note that there were still some offspring in those age groups who had lived with their parents and who had sold themselves with their progenitors. While the Muscovites defined majority as age fifteen, a fact that is very clear in table 13.6, nevertheless some children remained with their parents after that age.

The age pyramid is almost standing on a point, as we see in table 13.7, a breakdown of the 0-4 cohort. The number of infants (0 to 2 years) is very small. Once again, this reflects the fact that slavery was primarily a stress institution offering relief to those who sold themselves. Those people who sold themselves almost certainly had let their children die before they sold themselves, or perhaps had killed them because purchasers of slaves did not want their houses cluttered up with infants. Another factor to be considered is that their nutritional level was probably so low that their fertility was greatly reduced; both the chances of getting pregnant and bringing forth living young were far below normal.

TABLE 13.7
Children under Five

Age	1st Child	2d Child	3d Child	4th Child	Total
0-1	7	8	5	5	25
2	8	6	5	2	21
3	17	17	3	3	40
4	15	10	6	3	34

The gradations in the pyramid above the age group for 20-24 are relatively smooth, except for the dramatic fall off at 35-39. I cannot explain this, but note that it occurred in both the year 7111 data and the non-7111 data, perhaps because of the way Muscovites "heaped" their ages (see figure 13.2). Unfortunately the percentage differences between age cohorts are too large to match any life table. For example, only 84.7 percent "survive" from the 20-24 group to the next cohort. This probably represents two factors: a far higher mortality among that group of the Muscovite population than among any "normal" population ever recorded; a "mortality rate" further augmented by the fact of self-sale into slavery, for those who sold themselves were removed from the population (as though they had died), and were not available for sale again unless they fled or were manumitted. Another possibility may be simply that the population sample is incomplete because people who survived the crucial years around the age of twenty-five managed to cope with Muscovite reality better than they had earlier and thus did not need to offer themselves for sale, or, it may have been the case that those buying slaves simply refused to buy slaves over twenty-five out of proportion to their numbers in the society.

If one were to attempt a "demographic" explanation of table 13.6, it might go something like this. If early modern Russian society consisted of 10 percent slaves, half of them hereditary, half of them first-generation (full or limited service contract slaves), the first 5 percent would never appear in the life table because they could not sell themselves. (The table represents only that segment of society that could sell itself into slavery, obviously.) The second 5 percent, however, would disappear annually as each cohort moved along, just as though it had died. The figures 84.7 + 5 are close to the 90 percent survival rate that can be found in the $P_{(x)}$ life tables.

No matter how one attempts to explain table 13.6, the mortality level among those who sold themselves into slavery in Muscovy appears to have been very high; their life expectancy was very short. Whether it was as brief as the 17.5 years that the average slave in Rome lived is doubtful, but it probably was not much longer than the 25.5 year average life span of Roman slaves who lived outside the capital.[8]

While the Muscovite age structure is not a "normal" one, it is also certainly not unique in that respect. In fact, a "normal" age pyramid would probably be difficult to find in any slave society; the sole exception might be a society which cut off imports and denied manumission, such as the U.S. South in the nineteenth century. Although "bulges" stemming from the abnormal level of imports prior to 1808 kept working their way through the population (shortages of slaves, high prices, and a sense of paranoia accompanied the cutoff of imports in the 1810s and then in the 1830s and 1850s), by the 1850 and 1860 censuses there was no dearth of children or old people. In slave societies depending upon imports from Africa, for example, there was a great shortage of first-generation children under ten because the Africans kept that cohort for the expansion of their lineages, which complemented the fact that importers did not wish to bear the rearing costs of youngsters who could not work enough to earn their keep. For different reasons, slave demography was also "abnormal" in places such as the Roman Republic, which had no use for children, and perhaps in much of Islam, which had little use for old people.[9] As noted, the Muscovite abnormal pyramid was probably the consequence of owner preference combined with high child-mortality and infanticide. This last will be discussed further under the "Sex Ratio" rubric.

The major purpose of table 13.8 is to see what effect a demographic catastrophe had on the age structure of those selling themselves into slavery. In the table are all the categories of adults and children that appear in the data. The three columns of data are astonishing in their similarities. What this means, probably, is that it was always a time of grave crisis for those who sold themselves into slavery, and this was not changed by the Great Famine. The Famine did bring far more people into slavery, and somewhat different types (in chapter 11 we noticed particularly how it brought in individuals marginally connected with agriculture, such as landless peasants), but it seems not to have changed their ages. Once again I can only regret that I do not have data for the entire population for comparison.

8. B. Ts. Urlanis, *Evoliutsiia prodolzhitel'nosti zhizni* (Moscow: Statistika, 1978), p. 98, citing work of the Hungarian scholar Szilagyi.

9. Curtin, *Slave Trade,* pp. 19, 28, 41.

TABLE 13.8
Muscovite Slave Age Parameters

Sex, Marital Status, Children	All Known	All Except in 1602/03	1602/03
Adult single male			
Mean age	23.9	24.2	23.3
Median age	20.3	20.3	20.3
Age range	15 to 70	15 to 70	15 to 50
N	527 (of 1,077)	344 (of 843)	183 (of 234)
Adult married male			
Mean age	30.1	30.0	30.2
Median age	29.7	29.7	29.7
Age range	15 to 60	18 to 60	15 to 50
N	340 (of 914)	106 (of 587)	234 (of 327)
Widower			
Mean age	38.3	39.1	35.0
Median age	38.6	39.8	35.0
Age range	25 to 50	25 to 50	30 to 40
N	20 (of 73)	16 (of 66)	4 (of 7)
Minor boy			
Mean age	12.0	12.2	11.7
Median age	12.1	12.3	12.0
Age range	8 to 14	10 to 14	8 to 14
N	46 (of 55)	21 (of 30)	25 (of 25)
Adult single female			
Mean age	20.0	20.8	19.8
Median age	17.0	19.1	16.4
Age range	15 to 50	15 to 50	15 to 35
N	58 (of 184)	19 (of 134)	39 (of 50)
Adult married female (with husband)			
Mean age	26.6	27.8	26.1
Median age	25.1	25.4	25.0
Age range	15 to 50	15 to 50	15 to 50
N	270 (of 914)	79 (of 587)	191 (of 327)
Adult married female (without husband)			
Mean age	30.0	25.0	31.0
Median age	30.0	25.0	29.8
Age range	20 to 50	20 to 30	20 to 50
N	28 (of 69)	5 (of 34)	23 (of 35)
Widow			
Mean age	30.9	35.0	29.7
Median age	29.6	37.5	29.3
Age range	18 to 50	20 to 50	18 to 50
N	35 (of 92)	8 (of 54)	27 (of 38)
Minor girl			
Mean age	11.9	11.3	11.9
Median age	12.2	12.0	12.2
Age range	8 to 14	8 to 14	8 to 14
N	27 (of 29)	3 (of 4)	24 (of 25)

TABLE 13.8
Continued

Sex, Marital Status, Children	All Known	All Except in 1602/03	1602/03
First child			
Mean age	9.8	10.4	9.5
Median age	9.5	10.4	9.1
Age range	1 to 25	1 to 25	1 to 25
N	281 (of 660)	91 (of 443)	188 (of 217)
Second child			
Mean age	7.2	6.9	7.4
Median age	6.8	6.7	6.9
Age range	1 to 20	1 to 20	1 to 20
N	133 (of 353)	54 (of 259)	79 (of 94)
Third child			
Mean age	5.5	4.5	6.5
Median age	5.2	4.3	6.3
Age range	1 to 13	1 to 9	2 to 13
N	45 (of 128)	22 (of 101)	23 (of 27)
Fourth child			
Mean age	3.3	2.7	4.2
Median age	2.8	2.0	3.2
Age range	1 to 11	1 to 6	1 to 11
N	16 (of 44)	10 (of 37)	6 (of 7)

The Famine had a considerable impact on the type of household that sold it-self into slavery. This is also apparent in the data in table 13.8, but that table is somewhat misleading because not all the ages are reported (for the full population, see table 13.2, limited service contract slave section). The data of table 13.8 make it clear that while the personal age data shifted little for the Great Famine, the family composition of those selling themselves was altered by that phenomenon, from a concentration on solitaries toward more families (both two- and one-parent-headed) with children.

Another possible way to gauge the impact of the Great Famine on those who sold themselves into slavery might be to compare the physical descriptions of the slaves in 1602-2 with those from other periods. This comparison is presented in table 13.9. If these obviously subjective characterizations tell us anything, it is that fewer short people sold themselves during the famine, perhaps reflecting a greater proportion of fathers and fewer solitaries (who were often young) during the famine. The fact that the proportion of "thin" people actually declined during the famine indicates, as has frequently been stated, that selling oneself into slavery was always a crisis situation for the individual involved, and that the type of crisis could not be heightened or intensified on the personal level by a famine.

The health of the populace is also indicated by a description of the slave's complexion at the time of sale. When the remains of smallpox were present, this

TABLE 13.9
Physical Descriptions of Slaves at Time of Sale (% of Total Known Sales)

	1602/03 Famine	Other Times
Tall and fat	0.2	0.2
Medium height and fat	0.1	0.2
Short and fat	0.1	0.1
Tall and average weight	6.4	5.2
Average height and weight	37.0	32.0
Short and average weight	6.2	11.3
Tall and thin	0.1	0.1
Average height and thin	0.1	0.6
Short and thin	0.0	0.1
Unknown = remainder		N = 1,093

was recorded. Thirteen people who had had smallpox were recorded in 1602-3 and fourteen at other times. As is apparent in the table on height and weight, about half of such descriptive evidence comes from the famine year, the other half from other times, so we may conclude that the health of those selling themselves into slavery was about the same during the Great Famine as at other times.

Figure 13.1 plots various age parameters by the year in which the sale was made, particularly the dozen years from 1592 to 1603, and then groups the rest of the seventeenth century according to the era of 2-ruble prices (1606-26) and 3-ruble prices (after 1630). Most data are available for the major slave in the document, who may have been a married or single male, or a woman head of household. Out of that is extracted the data for married males, which should be contrasted with the wives' ages. Note that for the years 1600 and 1606-26, the age of wives is about the age of married males, something that could never occur in some societies. The same figure also compares the ages of husbands and wives at the birth of the first surviving child who is sold into slavery. The graph portrays no trends that I can discern, with all ages hovering about the mean, the exceptions being those for which there are very few cases. This seems to tell us that, demographically, slavery did not change very much throughout Muscovite history.

An attempt is made in figure 13.2 to show the number of births per year of adults and children. This figure is biased by two facts. The first is the tendency of early modern peoples to "heap" their ages, especially as they got older, into rounded-off ages, such as 15, 20, 25, 30 and so on. To my knowledge, it is not known how this was done (for example, whether those from 27.6 to 32.4 called themselves 30, or whether those 26 to 31 called themselves 30), and how, exactly this would affect the age pyramid (table 13.6) or the age averages used throughout this chapter. The second biasing fact is the dates of the collections with the available data—1595, 1597, and especially 1603. Thus one can see what look like major bursts of births at five- and ten-year intervals prior to 1603: 1553, 1563, 1568, 1573, 1578, 1583, and 1588. The intervals prior to 1597 are 1557, 1562, 1567, 1572, 1577, and 1582. The intervals prior to 1595 are 1560, 1565, 1570, 1575, and 1580. As the time of sale moves further from the date of birth, we see a tendency to heap in ten-year intervals, rather than the earlier five (see the upsurge at 1553 for 1603, 1557 for 1597, and perhaps even 1555 for 1595.) The curves for 1597 and 1603 look as though they were the "norm," with the latter being much higher because of the greater intensity of the crisis. The peak age for both 1597 and 1603 sales was twenty-five. (Why the shape of the 1595 curve is different and the peak at age twenty cannot be explained at the moment.) The curves for 1597 and 1603 further illustrate figure 13.5, which shows that age twenty-five was the crucial one for an adult to sell himself into slavery. I cannot say why age twenty-five was so difficult for Muscovites, but can observe that this was precisely the average age at which a husband had his first surviving child. As I noted in chapter 11, the birth of a first child was observed

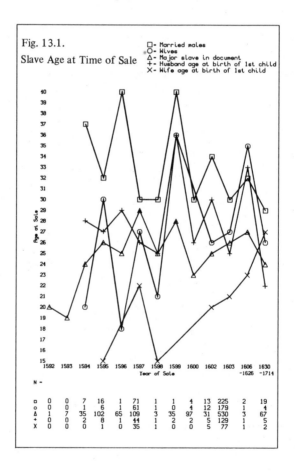

Fig. 13.1.

Slave Age at Time of Sale

□- Married males
○- Wives
△- Major slave in document
+- Husband age at birth of 1st child
X- Wife age at birth of 1st child

to be one of the stressful events that propelled, occasionally, individuals to sell themselves. Age-heaping is also observed for children in figure 13.2, although to a much lesser extent. The perceptible decline of surviving children born after 1600 who were sold into slavery with their parents in 1602 and 1603 is also visible. Finally, the gradual rise in the number of children born up to 1596 accompanies the maturation of those who sold themselves during the Great Famine of 1601-3.

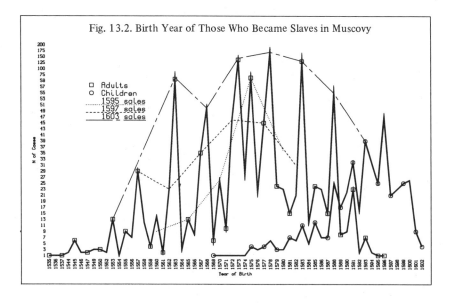

Fig. 13.2. Birth Year of Those Who Became Slaves in Muscovy

It would be interesting to discuss some of the individuals who make up the reality behind my demographic statistics. I have decided to present the youngest individuals in each category. What appears to be the youngest children without any parents were registered in Novgorod on December 17, 1597, by Ivan Mikiforov Obukhov. He purportedly paid 5 rubles to two sisters, Usten'itsa and Matrenka Petrova, ages ten and eight respectively, and another five rubles for an eleven year old boy, Grisha Andreev. All three claimed that they had already been serving him for about a year at the time the self-sales were registered. As is evident from the data in table 13.6, transactions involving such young people without any parents were comparatively rare. Is there anything that might explain why I. M. Obukhov might want to buy children? Judging by the fact that his father, Mikifor Fedorov Obukhov, was still alive and was also purchasing slaves in 1597 and 1598, we may conclude that Ivan himself was relatively young in 1597. The contemporary materials contain several mentions of "Ivan Obukhov," but, without the patronymic, any specific identification is difficult. His father almost certainly lived in Kositskii pogost of Shelonskaia piatina, and it seems likely that Ivan himself lived in Lazhinskoi pogost of Derevskaia piatina.[10] None of this tells us why Obukhov wanted children—perhaps he simply wanted children. To my knowledge, Muscovites did not adopt their slaves, as Africans incorporated slaves in their lineages, or as Chinese adopted them, to have a male heir. Or Obukhov may have regarded taking in what must have been orphans as an act of charity.

The youngest age recorded for wives is fifteen, and there are seven known such cases. They were reported to be married men of ages twenty (2), twenty-five (2), thirty, and forty, and one unknown. The two twenty-five-year-olds sold themselves into slavery in Novgorod in 1595 and 1597 for five rubles apiece, the other five sold themselves in provincial areas in 1603 for two rubles apiece. None of the seven couples declared any children. Thus the picture of very young wives is fairly clear. They had just recently (too recently to have had children) married men of disparate ages, who, otherwise, seem to have had little by which to be distinguished.[11] The number of very young wives also seems to have been disproportionately high during the Great Famine, perhaps reflecting orphaned females who tried to survive by marrying abnormally early, only to find that their husbands had no greater access to food than they did.

The youngest widow was Maria Malakhieva, who sold herself at age eighteen in Derevskaia piatina for one ruble on March 25, 1603, to Ivan Ivanov Onichkov, a *syn boiarskii* from Gorodenskii pogost of Derevskaia piatina. Unfortunately no more information is available about her—who her husband was, why he died, when they were married, and so forth. Little more is known about her buyer, either, except that he had a preference for solitaries; earlier he had purchased males in Novgorod (one for 7 rubles in 1595, a second for 3 rubles, and a third for 5 rubles in 1595) aged twenty (two of them) and thirty.[12] Perhaps Onichkov purchased Maria as a spouse for one of his males, although the age gap would have been rather larger than normal. Of course Onichkov may well have had other males that were listed in records now lost. We should note the low price paid for Maria, an expression both of the fact that she was a woman and that it was the period of the Great Famine.

The youngest married male, Ondrei Grigor'ev, was "about 15" (*let v 15*), two years younger than the next recorded age of seventeen. His wife was Ovdotia

10. RIB 15, pt. 1 (NKK 7106): 29-30; Ivanov, OPK, p. 57; RIB 22 (1908): 682; Sukhotin, ChSV, p. 167; RIB 28 (1912): 774; DR 2: 566. The high prices paid for these children almost certainly must be fictional. The documents in this series were primarily registrations of individuals who had been serving their purchasers for years and were being recorded as part of the compulsory process of late 1597-early 1598. Many of the other slaves registered at the time Obukhov registered these minors were also listed at 5 rubles per transaction. In processing the price data, I experimented with removing such cases from the data set, and discovered that it made no appreciable difference in the results.

11. RIB 15: 27; NZKK 1(1938): 85; NZKK 2(1938): 75, 78, 90, 249, 310.

12. Samokvasov, *Materialy* 2 (1909): 456.

Omel'ianova, whose age is not given in the document. On February 16, 1603, claiming to be free people (*vol'nye liudi*), they sold themselves at Borovichi, the great center of Bezhetskaia piatina, for one ruble to the brothers Petr and Oleksandr Sevriukov Pivtsov. Nothing more is known about their purchasers, perhaps because they were fundamentally insignificant servicemen who otherwise left no traces in the historical record. Once again we note the rockbottom price and can correlate it with the youth of the purchased slaves (who if they survived, could be expected with a high degree of probability later to run away) and, once again, the period of the famine.[13]

The youngest apparent widower, at age twenty-five, was Terentei Kuz'min, who had a son Osipko, aged three. On December 18, 1597, the two of them were purportedly sold for 5 rubles in Novgorod to Fadei Petrov Dirin. No more information is at hand about this particular Dirin, although his family is known to have furnished *deti boiarskie* who served as minor officials (*nedel'shchiki* and *pristavy*) in the Novgorod civil service. Terentei claimed that previously he had been the hereditary slave (*starinnoi*) of someone whose first name was Vasilei. To my knowledge, Fedei is not a nickname for Vasilei, so it is unknown who Terentei's previous owner was. There is also no information about who his wife had been, when they were married, and what had happened to her.[14]

One of the age features of Muscovite slavery that calls for some explanation is the presence of offspring age fifteen and over in slavery contracts with their parents. At age fifteen one theoretically reached his majority in Muscovy, and no slaveowner could claim a child of fifteen and over as part of a family if the offspring was living in his own establishment. Also, age fifteen was the youngest at which a person legally could sell himself, although events such as the Great Famine brought forth exceptions that the law winked at. The extent of Roman-style *patria potestas* is unclear in Muscovy, especially whether a father legally could force a child of age to sell himself into slavery. Probably he could not.

The existence of forty-nine instances of adult offspring being sold with their parents into slavery indicates, of course, that the age of fifteen was a formality, that in fact "children" up to the age of twenty-five continued to live with their parents as part of the parent-offspring household. The presence of such children does not destroy the late-twentieth-century orthodox doctrine that there was no adolescence until modern times, that in premodern times a person went immediately from childhood to adulthood. Be that as it may, the task at hand is to explain these forty-nine cases in more general terms than a narration of each one of them. Such generalizations seem quite possible. Twenty-one of the cases were two-parent-headed households, with one (6), two (6), three (6), four (2), and six children. Eleven of the cases were widower-headed households, with one child (4), two children (5) and three children (2); in nine of the cases the eldest child

13. NZKK 2 (1938): 30.
14. Nosov, *Ocherki*, p. 353.

was a son, and in the other two the second child was a son. Then there were four-teen widow-headed households, with one child (6), two children (5), three chil-dren, four children, and five children; in every case but the last, the eldest off-spring was a son, and in the last instance all five children were daughters. Finally, nearly all the known instances of three- (or proto-three-) generation households were included in this lot of units with adult offspring: a widow, her three sons, and the wife of one of the sons; a father, his son, and two orphan grandchildren of another child; a married couple, their three children, and a daughter-in-law who was wife of their eldest child. Thus twenty-seven, or well over half, of the forty-nine households, were single-parent-headed, a fact unusual even for the Muscovite slave population. Apparent in a number of these cases is the practice of the oldest child staying at home to look after the single parent. (The reverse, the oldest child leaving the home, setting up his own establishment, and then the single parent, with or without additional children, moving in with the oldest child seems unlikely simply on considerations of economy.) When times got es-pecially rough and no other relief was to be found, they sold themselves into slavery. Six of the forty-nine households were headed by widows of fifty, two of them by widowers of the same age. The attachment of a child to a single parent is evident not only in the twenty-seven cases mentioned but in some of the re-maining twenty-two as well. Nine of the two-parent-headed households give strong evidence that at most only one of the parents is the natural parent of the offspring in question, indicating that there was a considerable length of time when the one parent and the oldest child lived alone together. This is determined by noticing either impossible age combinations (the child being twenty, the mother thirty, and the father forty; or the child fifteen, no mother age, the father twenty) or a considerable gap between the ages of the first and second child-ren (twenty-five and twelve). Probably more of this would be possible were all parent and sibling ages recorded. There is also the fact that twelve of the child-ren in the twenty-one two-parent households were age fifteen (five more were sixteen), and considering the tendency to age-heap and the lack of precise knowledge about such things as ages, those children in fact may have been a year or two younger than stated. Thus, of the two-parent households, only four need to be explained, those with children twenty (3) and twenty-five years old. Two already have been explained (mother thirty, child twenty, father forty; first child twenty-five, second child twelve), and perhaps even a third (first child twenty, second child twelve, and both parents forty), leaving at most one or two "mysteries." In the last case (ages twenty, twelve, parents forty), the family had served with the person to whom they were selling themselves for twenty years. The fourth case is easily explicable: the two parents were forty years old, the child, twenty, was a widow, who presumably had returned to her parents after the death of her spouse.[15] Thus we may conclude that the normal practice in Muscovy was for children to cease being part of their parents' household at age fifteen.

Table 13.10 and figure 13.3 correlate the price paid for slaves first with the age of the major figure in the document, then with the age of just those cases involving single adult males. (The latter category is included in the former.) We see that there is a steady rise from 1 to 8 rubles that corresponds with the rise in ages from 22.3 to 35.0, in the case of heads of households. The situation is roughly comparable for single adult males, with the exception of the few cases at 6 and 7 rubles. This progression is interrupted for the slaves in the 9- to 15-ruble price range, in keeping with the general understanding that those higher sums were reserved for special cases, not run-of-the-mill individuals. The same data are presented with age as the independent variable on the right-hand side of the table, in keeping with the general practice of presenting such data in this form. The ages 20 to 37 were grouped nearest their respective five-year intervals to associate the few ages that were not actually given as 20, 25, 30, and 35 with their nearest figure in the customary age-heaping of the era. An examination of these data reveals two groups: for ages fourteen through twenty, the average price rose regularly for nearly every year (the exception being the few cases for age nineteen). This would seem to reflect greater worth of increasingly older individuals. Prices remained relatively constant for slaves in their twenties, and then rose regularly again for slaves over thirty. Part of this price rise reflects the addition of more family members, but it is worth noting that in several of the cohorts (23-27, 28-30, 40, 45, and 50) a single slave cost more than did a larger household. This again indicates that buyers may have assumed that they were paying more for expertise, although not of the type that could be determined by whether or not a person had a craft skill. The figures probably reveal a lack of concern for longevity, and may reflect the fact that, because of the high rate of runaways, owners did not expect to keep their slaves very long. Buyers may have been willing to pay more for older slaves because they assumed that there was less likelihood of their fleeing. While the crude trends of the age-price relationship seem clear, r (= 0.21 and 0.20) is low because of the great variance in prices.

15. Bychkov, LZAK 22: 5; RIB 15 (1894) sec. 3, p. 1: 14, 19-20, 27-29, 46, 50; NZKK 1: 8-10, 52-53, 150, 152-53, 158-59, 193, 244-45, 247, 282-83, 468-69; NZKK 2: 11, 34-35, 52, 64-65, 93, 99, 118-19, 123, 129-30, 138, 141, 148, 185, 194, 204, 223, 234-36, 240-44, 256-57, 279-80, 297-98, 325, 332, 339, 341-42, 384.

TABLE 13.10
Relationships between Slave Ages and Prices, in Rubles

Price per Document	All Heads of Households		Single Adult Males Only		Ages	Entire Households		Single Adult Males Only	
	Mean Slave Age	N	Mean Slave Age	N		Cost	N	Cost	N
1	22.3	178	21.9	103	8-14	2.10	72	–	–
2	24.9	346	22.1	161	15	2.01	68	1.98	64
3	25.5	177	23.6	113	16	2.42	19	2.29	17
4	26.5	45	24.1	26	17	2.58	33	2.44	29
5	27.8	246	25.2	117	18	3.28	39	3.26	35
6	28.1	14	21.0	5	19	3.00	5	2.25	4
7	31.4	11	24.0	5	20-22	3.32	224	3.30	174
8	35.0	4	35.0	4	23-27	3.18	211	3.30	98
9	29.0	2	–	–	28-30	2.93	160	3.24	68
10	33.6	17	31.5	10	33-37	3.81	67	3.22	23
15	22.7	3	22.7	3	40	3.46	93	3.76	21
					45	3.85	20	4.00	2
					50	4.00	27	4.50	8
					60	6.50	4	5.33	3
					70	5.00	1	5.00	1
Total	25.5	1,043	23.4	547		3.11	1,043	3.10	547
						r = 0.21		r = 0.20	

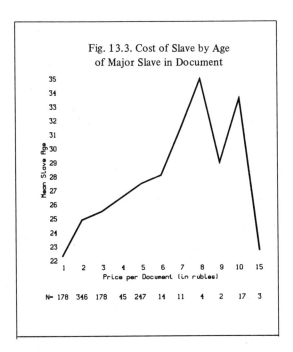

Fig. 13.3. Cost of Slave by Age
of Major Slave in Document

Marriage and Natality

European marriage patterns seem to have prevailed in Muscovy. Child brides did not exist, the average woman who was subsequently sold into slavery had married about the age of nineteen or twenty (see table 13.11). Her husband was four or five years older than she. Those who had been dependent earlier and thus presumably were somewhat more secure than were those trying to make it on their own seem to have married a year or so earlier than did those who claimed always to have been free prior to their enslavement. While precise data are lacking, the inference is drawn in chapter 17 that male slaveowners probably married at about the same age as did the males they purchased as slaves.

The mean age-spread between husband and wife, 4.2 years, was exactly the same as in Hingham, Massachusetts, prior to 1700, about the same as the Colonial Quakers, and more than the three years in England at the same time.[16]

16. Robert V. Wells, "Quaker Marriage Patterns in a Colonial Perspective," *William and Mary Quarterly* 29(1972): 429; Daniel Scott Smith, "The Contexts of Marital Fertility Change in Hingham, Massachusetts" (Paper presented at the American Historical Association, San Francisco, California, on December 30, 1978, and to the University of Chicago Economic History Workshop on January 12, 1979, p. 22 [table 2]). The Hingham male was 26.8 at first marriage, the female was 22.6. The Russian pattern was very much like that of

TABLE 13.11
Age at Marriage and Birth Characteristics

A. *Wife's Age at Marriage*: 19 or 20

Evidence: For 125 cases, the wife's mean age at the birth of a first surviving child is 21.1 years, the median age is 20.4 years, and the modal age is 20.0 years. By general rule of thumb, subtract one year from age at birth to determine marriage age.

For those always free previously, the age at birth of first child was 22.2 (N = 45); for those earlier enslaved, 20.7 (N = 57).

B. *Husband's Age at Marriage*: 23 or 24

Evidence: For 200 cases, the husband's mean age at the birth of a first child is 25.4, the median age is 24.8, and the modal age is 20 or 25 (20 instances of each). To calculate marriage age, see (A) above.

For those always free previously, the age at the birth of the first surviving child was 26.5 (N = 74); for those earlier enslaved, 25.2 (N = 84).

C. *Difference between Ages of Husband and Wife*: 4 to 5 years

Evidence: In 255 cases, the mean is 4.2 years, the median 4.8 years, and the mode 5 years.

For those always free previously, the difference was 4.1 (N = 108); for those previously dependent, the difference was 4.0 (N = 95).

D. *Intergenesic (Intergenetic) Intervals*: 4 years

Evidence: In 130 cases, the mean age difference between the first and second children is 4.1 years, the median is 3.6, and the mode 4.

In 44 cases, the mean age difference between the second and third children is 3.8 years, the median is 3.3 years, and the mode is 3 years.

In 16 cases, the mean age difference between the third and fourth children is 4.1 years, the median is 3.8, and the mode is 2 years (4 cases for 2 years, 3 cases of 3 and 4 years, 2 cases each for 5, 6, and 7 years).

In 38 cases where the parents previously had been free, the interval between the first and second children was 4.0 years; in 57 cases where they had been enslaved, the interval was 4.1 years.

Table 13.12 once again shows us that the number of teenage marriages among the population that became slaves in Muscovy was minimal. The presence in the table of only one teenage slave with a child does not mean that there were not more, for there probably were. The available data, however, only show six married male teenagers (ages fifteen, eighteen [4], and nineteen), and none of them had any children. Among the twenty-four known teenage wives, only two had any children. One was a woman of seventeen married to a man of twenty who had a child of unknown age. The other was the obvious stepmother of the eleven-year-old in the table below, a woman of eighteen married to a man of forty, the probable father of the child.[17] Some of the other statistical oddities

the Florentine countryside in 1427-30, when the bride's average age was 20.47, the groom's 24.79 (David Herlihy, presentation at the Newberry Social History Workshop, March 29, 1976, p. 7, table 00.1). See also Stone, *Family*, p. 60.

17. NZKK 2 (1938): 165, 394.

of the table (especially the 5.4 age for the 20-24 age cohort) are accounted for by remarriages, the ensuing adoption of others' children, the existence of a few hybrid families in which children were not the offspring of the parents, and the fact that 14.5 percent of the marriages were of couples in which the wife was older than the husband.

TABLE 13.12
Age Composition of Slave Household, by First Child

Adult Slave's Age	Husband's First Child's Age	N	Wife's First Child's Age	N
15-19	–	–	11.0	1
20-24	5.4	10	5.4	17
25-29	6.2	24	7.0	34
30-34	7.0	50	9.4	33
35-39	10.1	29	11.0	18
40-44	12.1	56	10.4	20
45-49	13.1	15	15.0	1
50-54	14.7	16	16.0	1
	M = 9.8	Total 200	M = 8.7	Total 125

These data seem to indicate that people from the stratum which ultimately sold itself into slavery in Muscovy did not marry at puberty but were mature adults when they did so. Moreover, the almost complete absence of stem families (newlyweds living with one of the in-law families until the former had the means to set up their own household) among this stratum of the population, as well as among the peasantry at least until the mid-seventeenth century, supports a contention that those who married in Muscovy were by and large already self-sufficient. The reasons for such "late" marriages remain to be investigated, but they probably were not the same as those that prevailed in contemporary northwestern Europe: there was no need to save to buy "necessary household goods," for Muscovite households had precious little of anything from the market. Nor was it necessary to wait to inherit a cottage, shop, or farm, for almost anyone could set up a cottage, start an enterprise, or begin farming at any time. While Muscovite marriages almost certainly did not wait upon either a lengthy period of saving or the death or retirement of a parent, it is not clear what they did wait upon. It is likely that some of the apparent "lateness" of Muscovite marriages resulted from late menarche and amenorrhea caused by malnutrition and other kinds of stress, which prevented women of the social strata that became slaves from having successful conceptions at an earlier age. This matter needs further consideration, probably from a comparative perspective.[18]

18. Stone, *Family*, p. 51; Rose E. Frisch, "Fatness, Puberty, and Fertility," *Natural History* 89, no. 10 (October 1980): 16-27. See also Jane Menken et al. , "The Nutrition Fertility Link: An Evaluation of the Evidence," *Journal of Interdisciplinary History* 11, no. 3

Modern marriage patterns seem to have prevailed in Muscovy when rural-urban distinctions are considered. If the place of sale can be taken as an indicator, those with a rural background seem to have married more than a half-year earlier than their urban cousins. Thus for 86 women for whom we have information about their ages and the ages of their children who were registered in rural areas, the mother was 20.8 years old at the time of the birth of her first surviving child. For the 39 women who sold themselves in large cities (Novgorod, Moscow), that figure was 21.6 years. For the 147 fathers from rural areas, the age at birth of first surviving child was 25.3, and it was 25.9 years for 53 fathers from the major cities.

Also corresponding to the "European pattern" is the fact that a significant portion, 37 of 255, or 14.5 percent, of the wives were older than their husbands. This is certainly more like the figure for an English community in 1599 of 21 percent or a 1778 French community of 27 percent than a 1733-34 Serbian figure of 0.5 percent or a 1713 Japanese proportion of 1.9 percent. The figures for the respective mean age gaps between husband and wife for the former two were 3.5 and 2.4 years, for the latter two 10.8 and 10.4 years.[19]

The population seems to copy neither the Western European nor the Serbian or Japanese pattern in the matter of who was married and who was single. In the Serbian population (1733) a third to half (1900) of the males from twenty to twenty-five were married, none were in the other populations. About 25 percent of the Muscovite males of that age were married. By the age forty, only 3 percent of the Serbian males were single, none of the Japanese were, but about a quarter of the Western Europeans and Muscovite slave males were.[20] J. Hajnal in his classic article noted that "in non-European civilizations there are scarcely any single women over 25."[21] That generalization is not completely true for Muscovy, at least for that stratum of the population which sold itself into slavery.

(Winter 1981): 425-41. The absence of twins in the slave population is also an indication of malnutrition (Frisch, p. 26). For a discussion of the problem of deriving age at marriage from the ages of surviving children, see Herbert G. Gutman, *Slavery and the Numbers Game: A Critique of Time on the Cross* (Urbana: University of Illinois Press, 1975), pp. 140-50.

19. Laslett, *Household and Family,* p. 75. The age pairs, with the wives older, were: 18 & 20 (2); 18 & 25; 20 & 25 (3); 20 & 30 (3); 22 & 25 (2); 23 & 25 (2); 23 & 30; 25 & 30 (8); 25 & 35; 25 & 40; 26 & 40; 30 & 35 (4); 30 & 40 (2); 35 & 40 (4); 40 & 45 (2); and 40 & 50. Note should be taken of the equal distribution. Thirty-two of the pairs, or 12.5%, found the wives 5 years or more older than their husbands, compared with 20% in "Europe" in the 17th and 18th centuries (Stone, *Family*, p. 193).

20. Laslett, *Household and Family*, p. 75; J. Hajnal, "European Marriage Patterns in Perspective," in D. V. Glass and D. E. C. Eversley, eds., *Population in History. Essays in Historical Demography* (London: Edward Arnold, 1965), p. 101. The "peculiar" Serbian demography was a response to Ottoman tax methods, much as Russian imperial peasant demography was a consequence of tax and other pressures (see chapter 18 below).

21. Hajnal, "Patterns," pp. 103, 106.

Of the 58 unmarried females in the data set for whom age data are given, 16 (28 percent) were age twenty-five and over. Of the 28 married females with no apparent husbands, 22 (79 percent) were age twenty-five and over. Of the 35 widows, 28 (80 percent) were age twenty-five and over. Of the entire female population age fifteen and over with no husband, 55 percent were age twenty-five and over. These women twenty-five and over with no husband constituted 5.2 percent of all women age fifteen and over living outside their parents' households. Whether that was true for the entire population cannot be determined. Two final observations are in order. Considering the low value placed on women by slave buyers, certainly that 5.2 percent must have been a lower bound, for many women without husbands of age twenty-five and over needed the relief provided by slavery but could not get it. But, in view of the apparent high rate of female infanticide in that stratum of the population, it is indeed astonishing that there were any single women of that age. Be that as it may, the nuptiality rate, the proportion of surviving children who married, seems to have been higher than England's 90 percent if these data about those who sold themselves into slavery tell us anything about the larger society.[22]

No doubt demographers will have difficulty accepting the marriage-age data, for it corresponds more to the "European pattern" than to the stereotypical "premodern" or "Eastern European" pattern that one might expect. This is the earliest such data available for Russia, as we have seen, nearly all of it from the end of the sixteenth century. No comparable quantity of such age data is to be found until the eighteenth century, when serfdom was fully entrenched and the marriage ages were considerably lower. My sense is not that my data are wrong, but rather that the eighteenth-century data reflect yet another perversion of serfdom (along with the extended family): landowners, thinking far ahead of their serfs, interfered dramatically in the family life of the serfs to raise more producers by arranging forced marriages at the earliest possible moment. We should note that in the eighteenth century, house serfs, the functional analogue and often direct descendants of the Muscovite slaves, had a higher age at marriage than did serfs who worked in the fields and elsewhere outside of the serfowner's house. In 1782, the modal age at marriage for serf grooms was 16, the average was 19; for brides, the modal age was 15, the average was 17.5. Those who married at the older ages were frequently indentified as house serfs. For males, this was sometimes over age twenty-five.[23] To the extent that serfowners could control the fertility of their chattel, this almost certainly represents a recognition that small children were not a household asset and that childcare distracted women from performing domestic service. Such attitudes, which

22. Stone, *The Family*, pp. 42-44.

23. Peter Czap, "Marriage and the Peasant Joint Family in the Era of Serfdom," *The Family in Imperial Russia*, ed. David L. Ransel (Urbana: University of Illinois Press, 1978), pp. 109, 111.

probably were present when Muscovites were buying slaves, may help to explain the preference for solitaries, and also the dearth of the very young children in table 13.7. Moreover, such an attitude makes clearer the reason for the legislation by Tsar Vasilii Shuiskii which stipulated that slaveowners were required to marry off their slaves or manumit them.

In the words of one demographer, "population statistics form an appropriate basis for probing into the subtlest nuances of social life."[24] One of the many strengths of *Time on the Cross* is the attempt by Robert Fogel and Stanley Engerman to use demographic data to uncover such nuances. For example, the intergenesic interval between surviving children of Muscovite women who subsequently sold themselves into slavery was four years (see table 13.11), close to the 3.5 to 4 years found in the British West Indies, much longer than the 2.5 years among Southern slaves (and whites).[25] This probably tells us quite a bit about the nutritional level, and perhaps the nursing and lactation practices, of lower-class Muscovite women. The primary inference to be drawn from such information probably is that there was high fetal wastage because of miscarriages and stillbirths, and then an immense number of the children born alive died in the first year, as continued to be the pattern in Russia until the first stage of the demographic transition (the reduction of infant mortality), that began in the mid-nineteenth century and was completed in the early 1960s. Such children obviously were not available to be sold with their parents (and thus to be counted in table 13.11), nor were the females who were victims of infanticide. Only secondarily, we may assume, was the apparent Muscovite lengthy intergenesic interval accounted for by prolonged nursing practices and extended amenorrhea stemming from severe malnutrition.[26]

Sex Ratios

One of the most astonishing features of Muscovite slave society was its sex ratio, nearly two males for every female. This ratio, even more surprisingly, held true for both adults and children, as shown in table 13.13. This is the count of the names from the anthroponymy study study of chapter 12. Slightly different totals are generated from different parts of the data, but the percentages remain remarkably consistent for the entire body of information on the Muscovite slave population. There are, however, significant variations among the various subgroups of the population that will occupy our attention in a moment.

24. William Peterson, *Population* (New York: Macmillan, 1961), pp. 2-3.

25. Herbert S. Klein and Stanley L. Engerman, "The Demographic Study of the American Slave Population: With Particular Attention Given the Comparison Between the United States and the British West Indies" (Paper presented to the University of Chicago Department of History Workshop in Comparative Social History [Paper no. 75-76-11], February 18, 1976, p. 23).

26. Stone, *Family*, p. 64.

TABLE 13.13
Ratios of Slave Males and Females, Children and Adults

	Children		Adults	
	N	%	N	%
Males	1,060	62.9	2,438	63.3
Females	626	37.1	1,414	36.7

Demographic statistics are available for many slave societies, and frequently such societies do not have normal sex ratios. Thus New World slavery based on African imports was heavily (60 percent, at least) male.[27] Because they correspond to the Muscovite ratios, I offer the comparisons shown in table 13.14.

TABLE 13.14
Slave Demographic Patterns in South Carolina and Cuba

	South Carolina		Cuba	
	1703	1708	1841	1860
Male	62.5%	62.1%	64.4%	59%
Female	37.5%	37.9%	35.6%	41%

The structure exhibited in the table complements almost perfectly that of internal African slavery, where the demand was primarily for women and children who could be used to expand lineages through incorporation, or for women alone, who played a vital role in African agriculture (adult males who could not be sold to a distant place simply would be killed to avoid the problems of resistance and flight inherent in the ownership of such males). The Chinese also could not overcome similar problems, with the consequence that by the twentieth century the purchasing of male slaves in the historical core of China ceased; male slavery was rare at the end of the Ch'ing as the institution became primarily a female one.[28] Or, to take another example, among *servi* adults on Saint Ger-

27. Franklin W. Knight, *Slave Society in Cuba during the Nineteenth Century* (Madison: The University of Wisconsin Press, 1970), p. 86; Peter H. Wood, " 'More like a Negro Country': Demographic Patterns in Colonial South Carolina, 1700-1740," in *Race and Slavery in the Western Hemisphere: Quantitative Studies,* ed. Stanley L. Engerman and Eugene D. Genovese (Princeton: Princeton University Press, 1975), p. 133.

28. Philip D. Curtin, "Major Trends in the African Slave Trade," *The Slave Economies,* ed. Eugene D. Genovese (New York: John Wiley, 1973), 1: 79, Miller, "Review," p. 49; M. G. Smith, p. 129; Herbert S. Klein, *The Middle Passage. Comparative Studies in the Atlantic Slave Trade* (Princeton: Princeton University Press, 1978), pp. 241-43; idem, "Cuban Slave Trade," p. 83; Joseph C. Miller, "Cokwe Trade and Conquest in the Nineteenth Century," in *Precolonial African Trade,* ed. Richard Gray and David Birmingham (London: Allen and Unwin, 1970), p. 191; Miers and Kopytoff, p. 297; Meijer, pp. 332, 338, 344.

main's seigneuries in ninth-century France, the overall sex ratio was an "incredible" 297.56 males to 100 women.[29]

We may assume that the Muscovite data are fairly accurate, for purchasers and owners had nothing to gain by concealing individuals of any age or either sex. The purpose of registration was to establish legal claim to property that experience showed was very likely to be contested (especially when slaves ran away). Moreover, the fees charged were a proportion of the amount paid for the slaves, not a capitation fee (as was the practice when a judicial dispute was resolved and the winning litigant had to pay a prescribed sum for each slave he had contested and was awarded). Thus no reason for falsifying the documents can be conceived, although mistakes were certainly possible. (The registration procedures, which were designed to check on what the scribes had written, presumably diminished errors.) Be that as it may, 767 (30.7 percent) of the 2,499 documents mentioned children; the mode was 1 child, the median was 1.8, and the maximum was one case (a will) with 27 children. In addition, 209 of the documents processed during the 1597-98 registration contain notations to the effect that, after the drawing up of the originals, a total of 422 children had subsequently been born. A particularly notable thing about figure 13.4 is its regularity. Most of the data through about the five-children category concern single families, almost all of which are in the study because they sold themselves. For this group, the ratio of boys to girls increases as the families get larger in size. Thereafter, generally, when the data come from documents relating to more than one family (wills, dowries, property divisions), the gap lessens.

Figure 13.5 shows the total number of slaves, then the number of boys and

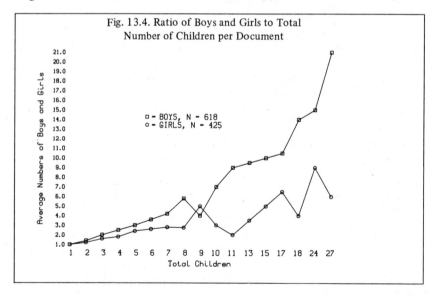

Fig. 13.4. Ratio of Boys and Girls to Total Number of Children per Document

29. Emily R. Coleman, "Medieval Marriage Characteristics," *Journal of Interdisciplinary History* 2, no. 2 (Autumn 1971): 212.

girls, included in the numerous recorded sale transactions throughout Muscovite history. The graph illustrates two noteworthy facts. The first is the tendency for the size of the average sale to decline throughout the sixteenth century almost to the point that self-sale slavery was becoming an institution for solitaries. Larger families seem to have been induced to sell themselves only by the more severe crises, such as the military reverses at the end of the 1580s, the well-known crisis of 1591-92 that led to the imposition of the Forbidden Years, and then the Great Famine of 1601-3. The 1590s after 1592 generally improved every year, and the distortions of 1597 and 1598 portray not a worsening of conditions but the mandatory registration of all claims to slaves, some of which were entered as self-sales by people who in reality had been hereditary and voluntary slaves for years. That the self-sale of families into slavery was unusual in "normal times" is specifically illustrated by one of the collections of current registrations, that for the year 1599-1600 (7108) of the Novgorod region. Of the 126 documents, only 4.8 percent recorded the sale of married couples. Adult single males were 75.4 percent of the total, widowers another 1.6 percent. Minors made up over a tenth of the collection (boys, 7.8 percent; girls, 3.2 percent). The rest were adult females (unwed, 3.2 percent; married without husbands, 1.6 percent; widows, 3.2 percent).[30] The other noteworthy fact shown in figure 13.5 is that there were only a few years in the quarter-millennium of Muscovite history when the number of girls exceeded the number of boys sold into slavery. While occasionally the spread widens or narrows, the consistency of the pattern throughout Muscovite history is quite remarkable. (The "Ns" are the same as on pp. 326-27 above.)

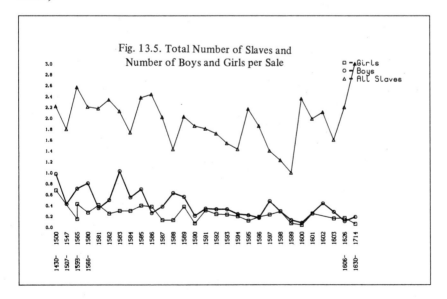

Fig. 13.5. Total Number of Slaves and Number of Boys and Girls per Sale

30. NKK 7108 (= RIB 15 [1895], pt. 3, sec. 2).

The discrepancy between the number of boys and girls was present not only on an annual basis but shows up in a comparison of the two major forms of self-sale, full slavery and limited service contract slavery. As is evident in table 13.15 not only is the child sex ratio practically identical in the two types of slavery but so are the proportions of each of the numbers of slaves (1 boy, 2 girls, and so on). This lends further support to my contention that, structurally and functionally, full and limited service contract slavery were successor institutions. Table 13.16 combines the types of first-generation slavery and compares the distribution of boys and girls according to the provenance of the document. The same information is presented for hereditary slavery. Again, the number of documents listing girls is always less than the number listing boys, and the number of girls per document is often less as well. The averages for each major locale, as presented in table 13.16, do not vary significantly from the overall mean for first-generation slaves.

The discrepancy in the boy-girl sex ratio also held constant throughout the major geographic subdivisions that the available data allow one to generate. We see in table 13.17 that these distinctions held, regardless of where the people who sold themselves had come from or where they were destined. Table 13.17 is more vivid than tables 13.16 and 13.18 in some respects, because the statistics take account of the fact that many documents did not list any children of either sex.

TABLE 13.15
Children per Family by Sex by Type of Slavery

	Full Slavery		Limited Service Contract Slavery	
	N	%	N	%
No. of boys				
1	14	63.3	297	63.3
2	5	22.7	117	24.9
3	2	9.1	47	10.2
4	1	4.5	7	1.5
% of documents with no boys		78%		77.6%
No. of girls				
1	10	66.7	224	74.7
2	4	26.6	64	21.3
3	1	6.7	9	3.0
4			1	0.3
5			2	0.7
% of documents with no girls		85%		85.7%
Sex Ratios	N 34:21		700:393	
Boys:Girls	% 62:38		64:36	

TABLE 13.16
Numbers of Boys and Girls per Document, Where Document Is Written, by Type of Slavery

Locale	Full and Limited Service Contract Slavery				Hereditary Slavery (Wills, Property Divisions)			
	Boys	N	Girls	N	Boys	N	Girls	N
Novgorod	1.6	101	1.4	62	2.7	9	2.1	7
Other large city	1.8	23	1.6	16	2.0	1	2.0	1
Medium-sized city	1.8	4	1.0	1	1.0	1	–	–
Bezhetskaia piatina	1.5	103	1.3	77	–	–	–	–
Derevskaia piatina	1.4	68	1.2	37	–	–	–	–
Obonezhskaia piatina	1.4	9	1.4	5	3.0	1	–	–
Shelonskaia piatina	1.3	82	1.2	45	3.0	2	2.0	2
Votskaia piatina	1.8	90	1.5	69	7.5	6	3.3	6
Other rural area	1.8	21	1.5	10	6.6	10	3.8	9
Total	1.6	501	1.3	322	4.9	30	3.0	25

TABLE 13.17
Rural vs. Urban Indicators

	Average Number of Slaves per Transaction at Time of Sale by							
	Slave's Birthplace		Slave's Previous Residence		Place of Sale		Purchaser's Home	
	People	N	People	N	People	N	People	N
Large city	1.50	68	1.77	124	1.64	690	1.61	111
Medium city	1.40	15	1.80	50	1.80	30	1.90	184
Rural	1.38	176	1.67	376	2.01	1,462	1.93	1,411
Mean	1.41	259	1.71	550	1.89	2,182	1.91	1,706

	Average Number of Male Children per Transaction at Time of Sale by							
	Boys	N	Boys	N	Boys	N	Boys	N
Large city	0.29	73	0.44	141	0.35	791	0.33	132
Medium city	0.06	17	0.19	63	0.35	40	0.26	200
Rural	0.32	210	0.57	531	0.50	1,659	0.52	1,627
Mean[a]	0.45	2,499	0.45	2,499	0.45	2,499	0.45	2,499

	Average Number of Female Children per Transaction at Time of Sale by							
	Girls	N	Girls	N	Girls	N	Girls	N
Large city	0.16	73	0.26	141	0.21	791	0.17	132
Medium city	0.12	17	0.19	63	0.10	40	0.18	200
Rural	0.18	210	0.31	531	0.29	1,659	0.29	1,627
Mean[a]	0.26	2,499	0.26	2,499	0.26	2,499	0.26	2,499

[a] Includes unknown.

The astonishing sex ratio among children is also evident in table 13.18, which examines the known destinations of all slaves, that is the places where the slave-owners lived. The documents used include not only sales but also court cases, marriage contracts and dowries, wills and property divisions, and so on. The rather larger means for Shelonskaia and especially Votskaia piatina are accounted for by the large numbers of hereditary slaves recorded there in the extant 1597-98 registration books. Most of the Bezhetskaia piatina documents are from the Great Famine years of 1602-3, when there was a tendency for a lesser proportion of solitaries and a greater proportion of families to sell themselves. In spite of all these variations, there is not a single place for which the absolute number of girls, the number of documents mentioning girls, or even the average number of girls per document is larger than it is for boys. After a while, the evidence becomes overwhelming that Muscovite slavery was predominantly a male world, that females were allowed to enter in lesser numbers and generally were far less wanted than males. It certainly may be posited that female infanticide was practiced on a large scale among most of those social elements that had had a tendency to become slaves. Considering the stress that they were under, that is hardly surprising.

TABLE 13.18
Geographic Distribution of All Slaves, Boys and Girls

Slaveowner's Home	All Slaves	N Cases	Mean per Case	Boys	N Cases	Mean per Case	Girls	N Cases	Mean per Case
Novgorod	131	86	1.5	29	12	2.4	14	9	1.6
Other large city	94	45	2.1	15	11	1.4	8	7	1.1
Medium-sized city	44	24	1.8	4	4	1.0	3	3	1.0
Bezhetskaia piatina	668	322	2.1	111	74	1.5	70	53	1.3
Derevskaia piatina	349	183	1.9	46	35	1.3	20	17	1.2
Obonezhskaia piatina	122	58	2.1	19	10	1.9	10	8	1.3
Shelonskaia piatina	833	343	2.4	161	92	1.8	55	45	1.2
Votskaia piatina	1,582	618	2.6	455	207	2.2	288	158	1.8
Other known rural area	579	278	2.1	97	64	1.5	56	43	1.3
Unknown	1,173	542	2.2	187	109	1.7	128	82	1.6
Total	5,575	2,499	2.2	1,125	618	1.8	653	425	1.5

There were other market aspects besides the rather impersonal one of geography, and they seem to have had some effect on determining the sex composition of Muscovite slavery. The most obvious one was money. Table 13.19 examines the relationship between the total sums owners are known to have expended on slaves and the number of boys and girls they purchased. Perhaps not surprisingly, the correlation is somewhat strong (r = 0.63) between the total sum a given owner spent on slaves and the number of boys he purchased. Once again, the relationship is somewhat weaker (r = 0.52) between the number of girls purchased and the amount expended, perhaps expressing the lesser overall concern

TABLE 13.19

Relationship between Sums Spent for Purchase of Slaves and Children in Slavery

Total Sum Expended per Owner on Slaves (in rubles)	No. of Boys	N	No. of Girls	N	No. of Children Later Born in Slavery	N
1-1.50	1.9	9	1.3	8	2.0	4
2-2.50	1.5	36	1.3	19	2.8	6
3-3.50	2.0	45	1.4	31	3.0	6
4	1.9	25	1.4	23	1.6	5
5	1.9	44	1.5	34	2.9	12
6-9	2.0	46	1.6	39	2.3	9
10-14	2.3	47	2.2	33	2.3	12
15-25	2.8	48	2.2	38	3.1	22
26-49	5.7	32	4.0	27	5.3	18
50-133	10.2	12	4.6	12	4.8	8
Total		344		264		102
	Mean = 2.7		Mean = 2.1		Mean = 3.2	
	r = 0.63		r = 0.52		r = 0.42	

for girls. (The relationship is weaker still between the sums expended and the number of children known subsequently to have been begotten by the slaves. That relationship probably is simply a reflection of the general rule that more money usually purchased more slaves, and more slaves were therefore likely to beget more slaves.) On the other hand, the discrepancy between the number of boys and the number of girls purchased seems to diminish with the increase of expenditures. If we move further ahead to other owner-linked variables that will be examined in greater detail in chapter 17, we can examine the relationship between the ranks (table 13.20) and positions (table 13.21) held by slaveowners and the numbers of boys and girls they owned. While the numbers are too small to permit the making of dogmatic declarations, certain patterns do seem to emerge. Among the ranks, those at the top (*boiarin, striapchii,* and so on) seem to have purchased approximately equal numbers of boys and girls. Those holding the bottom rank of the landed service class, *syn boiarskii,* purchased the most noticeably unbalanced mix of boys and girls. A consideration of the positions held by the slaveowners leads to the same tentative generalization: the upper elements of the slaveowning stratum were more likely to have about equal numbers of boys and girls. This was true for those who occupied major posts in the central governmental administration, and perhaps also for generals (*voevody,* sometimes also governors, but relatively infrequently in this data that concentrate primarily on the pre-1613 era). Thus we may conclude that the wealthiest elements among the slaveowners probably owned approximately equal numbers of boys and girls, perhaps because they enjoyed flaunting their ability to maintain equal numbers of males and females and of their probable offspring. The not so wealthy members of the slaveowning stratum were less likely to possess equal numbers of males and females. Perhaps this may have been because they lacked the means to maintain both themselves, their own families, and sexually balanced complements of slaves as well. It is also possible, of course, that these people only could buy what the market had to offer, but on balance, it does seem as though the purchasers had some hand in directing the market, and especially in selecting among what was available for sale.

The "literary" evidence on the owner capacity to maintain females is somewhat (but not totally) compromised by the available statistical indicators of wealth, which, without exception, tend to show that those who purchased boys were wealthier than those who purchased girls. As usual, one must note that the amount of evidence is small, and almost all of it is from the provinces (primarily the Novgorod region), whereas some of the rank and occupational data were from Moscow, the home base of the wealthiest elements of society, as well.

TABLE 13.20
Relationship between Slaveowner Rank and Slave Children

Rank	Boys	N	Girls	N	Children Born in Slavery	N
Boiarin	4.0	1	6.0	1	8.0	1
Dumnyi dvorianin						
Dumnyi d'iak			1.0	1		
Stol'nik	1.8	6	1.3	3		
Striapchii	2.4	5	2.3	3	2.5	2
Sytnik						
D'iak	1.0	1	6.0	2	1.0	1
Moscow *dvorianin*	1.0	4	1.0	1		
Zhilets	2.0	2	1.0	2		
Dvorianin	2.0	3	1.0	1	1.0	1
Reitarshchik						
Syn boiarskii, pre-1555						
Syn boiarskii, post-1555	4.0	129	2.7	110	3.4	67
Pomeshchik	2.3	77	1.8	55	2.4	24
Zemets, svoezemets						
Stroganov merchant	1.0	1				
Townsman	1.0	1	1.0	1		
Monastery elder	2.0	1				
Monastery treasurer	1.0	1	2.0	1		
Monk						
Nun	3.0	1	4.0			
Archpriest						
Priest	1.0	1	1.0	1		
Deacon						
Monastery servant	1.5	2				
Metrop. *syn boiarskii*	13.0	1	3.0	2	8.0	1
Archbishop's groom	1.0	1	1.0	1		
Murza						
Slave						
Total	3.2	239	2.3	186	3.2	97

TABLE 13.21
Relationship between Slaveowner Employment and Slave Children

Occupation	Boys		Girls		Children Born in Slavery	
	M	N	M	N	M	N
A. Servicemen in primarily military posts						
General	2.5	13	2.8	9	2.6	8
Unit commander	2.6	5	1.4	5	1.0	2
Member of selected 1,000	9.0	1	4.0	1	1.0	1
Strelets commander	1.6	5	3.0	1	3.5	2
Strelets centurion	2.9	7	1.4	7	2.0	3
Elected local commander	6.1	23	4.0	17	4.9	8
Siege service	2.2	12	1.2	5	3.0	1
Combat service	2.4	5	1.0	2		
Artilleryman	1.0	1	1.0	1	2.0	1
Subtotal	3.7	73	2.6	49	3.3	27
B. Servicemen in primarily nonmilitary posts						
Guba chief	2.9	10	1.8	8	4.1	7
Guba assistant	1.0	1				
Governor (*namestnik*)	15.0	1	10.0	1	4.0	1
Scribe	1.7	3	3.0	1		
Administrative assistant	1.5	6	1.2	6	2.0	4
Grantor of service lands	1.3	3	1.0	1	2.0	1
Census taker	2.0	5	1.2	5	1.3	4
Fortifications official	1.5	3	3.0	2	3.0	1
Collector	1.5	2	2.0	1		
Census director	10.5	2	5.0	2	8.0	1
Messenger	3.6	5	1.3	3	6.0	1
Surveyor	1.5	2	1.0	1		
Subtotal	2.9	43	2.0	31	3.3	20
C. Moscow government officials						
Chancellery director			1.0	1		
Chancellery state secretary	1.0	1	3.0	1	1.0	1
Palace service scribe			1.0	1		
Provisioner (*Putnoi kliuchnik*)	2.0	1	1.0	1		
Treasurer	1.0	1	2.0	1		
Chancellery official	3.0	1				
Palace official	2.0	1				
Ambassador	3.0	1	2.0	1		
Subtotal	1.7	6	1.7	6	1.0	1
D. Churchmen						
Priest or deacon	1.5	2	1.0	1		
Nun	3.0	1	4.0	1		
Church or monastery scribe	2.0	1				
Subtotal	2.0	2	2.5	2		
E. Others						
Widow	2.0	3	3.0	1	1.0	1
Slave	1.0	1				
Grand total	3.2	130	2.4	90	3.1	49

As table 13.22 shows, compensation correlated poorly with the total number of boys and girls purchased.

TABLE 13.22
Slaveowner Compensation and the Ownership of Boys and Girls

Compensation	Boys	N	r	Girls	N	r
Average land entitlement (*oklad*) in cheti	482.60	141	0.25	468.50	89	0.26
Annual cash salary entitlement (*oklad*), rubles	15.16	73	0.11	13.96	45	0.20
Actual landholding in cheti	200.70	93	0.17	170.60	50	0.02

Another way to look at the same problem is to consider the sex ratio of boys and girls in the most expensive transactions. Considering the 181 limited service slavery contracts for 9 rubles to 15 rubles, one finds that 105 (58 percent) of these had no children at all. The transactions that recorded children listed 115 (63.2 percent) boys, 67 (36.8 percent) girls, essentially the same ratio for the institution as a whole (see table 13.14). This again indicates that those with greater means to spend (in this sample, at least) did not expend them buying girl slaves.

There was clear selection for a boy among first children. Of the 58 children age 4 and under, 69 percent were boys. In three-person families, 114 consisted of a husband, wife, and boy, but only about half that number, 58 had a girl. In four-person families, 58 couples had one boy and one girl, but 52 couples had two boys and no girls, while only 15 couples had two girls and no boys, a ratio of nearly 3.5:1. Thirty-one single men (whose wives presumably had died or had fled) had one boy, but only seven had one girl. Such statistical patterns can hardly be accidental. On the other hand, among widows and women whose husbands had deserted them (a not infrequent occurance), 31 had a boy, 26 had one girl.

Among larger families, the gap grew wider. Families of six to eight members had a total of 123 boys (62 percent) and 76 girls (38 percent). This would indicate that, when times got bad, parents tended to increase their favoritism of boys (perhaps in the apportioning of food and clothing) at the expense of girls. The ratios continued to worsen as the number of children increased: 67 families had three boys, only 25 had three girls; 21 had four boys, only 7 had four girls.

Foreign nationality seems to have played little role in determining child sex ratio. In 72 documents embracing non-Russians, there was one Tatar boy and one Tatar girl. There were 30 boys (56 percent) and 24 girls (44 percent) of non-Turkic, non-Russian origin (Lithuanians, Poles, Swedes, Belorussians, Livonians, and Greeks).

Another test to apply in studying the wide discrepancy between boys and girls is the stated occupation or status of the parents. In my data are nearly a hundred occupations (estate manager, court bailiff, scribe, tailor, smith, cook, milkmaid) or largely nonoverlapping social categories (landless peasant, townsman, beggar, various kinds of slaves or servants) that the slaves used to categorize themselves. About two-fifths (950) of all the slaves were so identified. Among the more elite slaves, a lone bailiff had a boy and a girl. A former arquebusier had a girl. Many of the "professionals" and craftsmen were single men and had no children at all. Of 16 tailors and needle workers, only one had any children, two boys and a girl. Of 16 leather workers, 6 had children—eleven boys and four girls. Seven of the 53 former peasants had eight boys and two girls.

Moving further down the Muscovite sociological ladder, in 98 cases the major figure was identified as a landless peasant (*bobyl'*—usually poor, rarely a tax dodge for traders and the like who had become differentiated from agriculture), and they had 25 boys and 12 girls. A proximate status was that of hired laborer (*naemnik*); 95 percent of the 68 cases had no children at all, and those that did had the insignificant number of three boys and three girls.

The bottom of society consisted of those who identified themselves as beggars, (often the same people said they had been landless peasants, hired laborers, and beggars), and they were 96 percent childless: only 1 of the 30 had any children, two sons. As one might expect, as a person descended the Muscovite social scale, his fertility dropped, and it appears as though his propensity to keep girls vis-à-vis boys also diminished.

Other catagories were those who had been in some type of dependency earlier. In terms of freedom, they were even lower than landless peasants, hirelings, and beggars, but in material terms, and in terms of fertility, they were probably better off. I divided this heterogeneous cadre into four groups. The precise sense of the first two groups eludes me: (1) in Russian, *posluzhilets,* perhaps translated as "servitor," maybe even as "slave"; (2) *dobrovol'nyi posluzhilets*, "voluntary servitor," "voluntary slave." Remaining in the latter state for any length of time almost certainly led to the former, which often was discussed in the terminology of slavery, particularly "manumission." "Voluntary service" was for younger, usually single people. Claiming that origin immediately prior to enslavement were 184 slaves; 21.7 percent of them had children, 47 boys (57 percent) and 35 girls (43 percent). Among the 75 "servitors," 40.5 percent had children, 31 boys (64 percent) and 17 girls (36 percent). It may be that the insecurity and stress of this semidependent status forced them to take the final plunge into complete dependency, often with the same lord.

The other two categories were those whose parents had been slaves before them (67 cases) and those 286 cases who identified themselves as former slaves (or were so identified in wills, dowries, and similar documents). The fertility rates of the former were lower than those of the latter. The children of slaves had 67 boys and 28 girls, thanks largely to two cases containing 35 boys and 13 girls. Those who themselves were first-generation slaves had 255 boys (56 percent) and 203 girls (44 percent). I cannot differentiate children who were born while their parents were enslaved and those who were born while their parents were free, but in any case the ratios are somewhat less extreme than those encountered among other groups.

Another approach is to consider the source of the children's slavery, as shown in table 13.23.

TABLE 13.23
Sources of Children's Slavery

	Boys	%	Girls	%
Parents' job mandated enslavement (estate managers)	8	50	8	50
Military captivity	28	58	20	42
Present in a will, dowry, gift, property transfer	173	59	118	41
Self-sale (with parents)	714	64	395	36

When one recalls that the overall child sex ratio was 63:37, these data seem to confirm some of the previous suggestions. "Reported slavery" was not a disaster rescue operation, and the number of children was equal for both sexes. Less favorable was the environment of children whose source of slavery was military capture and deportation to Russia, which may have reflected either captors' preference or ratios in the devastated lands. The ratio for the transfer category somewhat surprises me, for most of those children probably were born in slavery, and I had expected that the number of boys and girls would be approximately equal. I think faulty counting and inaccurate listing should be ruled out, for the owner of a nonregistered slave had no claim to him in case of flight or other dispute. Thus one must tentatively conclude that either the parents or the owners (or both) had less use for girls than boys, and thus let them perish. (Another possibility is that females were emancipated in greater numbers than males. There is little evidence of this, that I know of, and, given the reluctance of buyers to take in girls, such a practice would be tantamount to murder.) As has been suggested, household slavery in Muscovy may have been conducive to such attitudes. As expected, the worst situation was self-sale.

Another set of statistics puts this into bolder relief: in 139 cases that had been enslaved previously, and then resold themselves (usually within a few days or months), there were 48 boys and 44 girls. Apparently those in this group found slavery compatible with their personalities, allowing them to lead a somewhat normal life. This situation can be compared with the exactly one thousand cases of people who claimed that they had always been free before selling themselves: they had 270 boys (67 percent) and 133 girls (33 percent). Speaking "with their feet" and "demographically," a certain sector of Russian society announced loudly that slavery was materially preferable to freedom.

Some evidence indicates that enslavement provided a solution to the "female infanticide" problem. Among those already enslaved who subsequently gave birth to one child, 26 girls and 22 boys resulted. Similarly, among those people there were twelve cases of two boys and twelve of two girls. These ratios are obviously far different from the one for those who sold themselves into slavery. This discussion could be continued, but my examination of 422 boys and girls known to have been born in slavery (coded as a separate variable) indicates that the sex ratio was close to equal. This is the best evidence that slavery was an effective form of social welfare for some.

On the other hand, even demographically, enslavement proved not to be favorable for all. In 188 cases of outright manumission (these are not the 139 cases that resold themselves), there were 40 boys (61 percent) and 26 girls (39 percent). There were any number of reasons for the rare phenomenon of manumission, but one was the owner's inability to provide satisfactory conditions for his slaves. During the 1601-3 famine, the government recognized the slaves' legal right to flee when their masters could not provide for them. My impression is that most manumitted slaves sold themselves again (often to the heirs of the manumittor), but some did not. These demographic statistics, the fact that some manumitted slaves did not reenter slavery, and the fact of numerous runaways and even open rebellion by slaves, all indicate that while Muscovite slavery may have had its material advantages, large numbers of the slaves would have preferred to be free.

It would be simpleminded to attribute the unusual sex ratio in Muscovite slave society to material conditions alone. Common social values must have played a role also. I have discovered no way to determine this, either with the aid of "literary" sources or by comparison with other social groups. To my knowledge, useful data of either type do not exist. There are peasant settlement contracts with lords, setting down the rights and obligations of both parties, but those I have examined so far lack the necessary specificity found in the slavery materials. My colleagues who study the upper classes seem to be unable to offer any comparative aid from that quarter, either. (Keeping track of the slaveowners has told me that their families were larger than those of their slaves, as was nearly always the case prior to recent times: the wealthier had larger families than did those at the bottom of the social pyramid. However, this tells us nothing about the sex ratio of the upper strata.) Census-type events in Muscovy tended to concentrate on taxpayers, and therefore on males. Some recently published census materials from Siberia list both sexes, which seem to be about equal.[31]

It seems probable that a number of forces combined to produce the unbalanced sex ratio that is so evident in Muscovite slavery. On the other hand, if one excludes the most elite elements, the members of the slaveowning class set the tone by declaring that females were of no worth and were unwanted, by their persistent practice of buying as slaves only half as many of them as males. The

31. Ia. E. Vodarskii, "Chislennost' russkogo naseleniia Sibiri v. XVII–XVIII vv.," in *Russkoe naselenie Pomor'ia i Sibiri (Period feodalizma),* ed. A.P. Okladnikov et al. (Moscow: Nauka, 1973), p. 213. Genealogical registers also rarely listed females.

lower classes, on the other hand, also found less use for girls than boys, and consequently killed them or let them die disproportionately to boys. I have no knowledge about the actual operation of the Muscovite "slave market," how potential slaves and potential buyers got together, but it seems quite certain that, when they did, their needs and means were in balance: those selling themselves had reduced their females (along with their very young) to numbers that purchasers were willing to buy.

There is some evidence that infanticide was practiced and that girls were singled out. The great early modern Russian law code, the *Ulozhenie* of 1649, for the first time in Muscovy specified sanctions (a year of penance) against parents who killed their offspring. This seems to have had some small impact, although my conclusions, shown in table 13.24, may be based on too small a sample.

TABLE 13.24
Impact of the *Ulozhenie* on Female Infanticide

	Children Born Prior to 1649	%	Children Born After 1649	%
Boys	1,088	65	26	59
Girls	631	35	18	41

At the beginning of the eighteenth century, Peter the Great continued to inveigh against infanticide.

Consciousness of the imbalanced sex ratio existed among contemporaries. This was expressed in indentures of the second half of the seventeenth century, when in at least two cases older teenage boys indentured themselves with the express stipulation that their lords would see that they got married.[32] I have no such evidence for girls. The slaveowners recognized that the institution of slavery was primarily a male world. In a petition to the government in 1658, they noted that fugitive slaves married "widows, unmarried women, and laboring [or slave?] women [*rabotnitsy*]."[33] (Fugitive slaves mirrored the general slave population, as shown in table 16.2.)

The legal sphere tends to confirm the Muscovite lack of interest in rearing children as slaves. In the Roman Empire, when a scarcity of slaves was sensed in the first century A.D., the law began to take an increasing interest in the offspring of slaves.[34] In Muscovy, on the other hand, a large body of slave law developed between 1550 and 1649, but little of it concerned children beyond the bare regulatory norms that in fact often antedated that century. The exceptions tend to confirm this lack of interest in making slaves out of children: the 1556 law cited

32. AIuB 3:35.
33. Novosel'skii, "Kollektivnye chelobitnye," p. 309, no. 2.
34. Jones, p. 193.

above limiting the slavery of military captives to the life of the owner also prescribed that any children born to military captives were not to be slaves at all.[35]

Muscovite full and limited service contract slavery were stress institutions whose primary purpose was the providing of welfare relief in a society excessively short of charity and kinship support. However, there were limitations on the number of people who could be supported in slavery, and one of the limitations was the exclusion of children, and to a certain extent, perhaps, of adult females as well.

Except for elite slaves, who exhibit a normal demographic profile, those who sold themselves into limited service contract slavery were destitute, and for them sale into slavery was probably a last resort. One may assume, therefore, that many of these people allowed their children to die before the parents finally sold themselves into slavery. As in India, for example, parents probably rationed their available food in favor of their sons, allowing the daughters to starve to death first. This would explain both the low numbers of children under five and the sex ratios. Infanticide was certainly widely practiced and, as usually has been the case throughout history, far more female infants were disposed of than male.[36] Widespread female infanticide among the lower strata of Muscovite society probably helps to account for the disproportionate number of adult males in slavery, which may have overtones of a skid-row phenomenon as well.

The alternatives for destitute adult women are not clear, for the few nunneries in Muscovy restricted their admittances to those whose families could pay for their keep, plus a few aging slave retainers who accompanied their tonsured mistresses or were sent "on pension" to die there by wealthy owners who lacked the gall to manumit and turn out slaves in such condition. Many single slave women throughout history have been prostitutes or concubines, and the fact that the Orthodox church forbade such practices may well help account for the small number, by comparison, say, with China or African or Islamic countries, of unwed adult females able to find men who would buy them out of destitution as slaves, along with the fact that men were preferred as military and baggage-train slaves, domestics, and farming slaves.

A necessary subsidiary issue in the discussion of infanticide from a comparative perspective is the sale of infants and children, the logical alternative to infanticide. In the Roman Empire from the third century A.D., on, for example, a severe shortage of slaves developed, prices rose dramatically, and there was a high demand for foundlings and newborn infants put up for sale by their parents, a practice which was even legalized. The sale of older children, already members of society and thus no longer "outsiders" (as newborn babies easily can be con-

35. AI 1, no. 154, V, 17.
36. Piers, *Infanticide*, pp. 16-17.

sidered psychologically),[37] remained illegal but was widespread.[38] While it was not illegal, to my knowledge, children were rarely sold in Muscovy.[39]

Earlier I have observed that the Muscovites established by law the prices that could be (and perhaps had to be) paid for slaves after the Time of Troubles. At first the sum was 2 rubles for each slave, and within a few years it was raised to 3 rubles, the sum that was the law of the land in the *Ulozhenie* of 1649 and remained so until the 1680s. Certainly this must have had a demographic impact, for wives had little value, nor did females in general and also second and subsequent children. Forcing slaveowners to pay equally for things that were not of equal value to them almost certainly would change their behavior, and this is what happened. As is evident in table 13.25, slaveowners responded almost exactly as one would háve expected them to, faced with structured prices that did not correspond with their sense of value. They cut down proportionally on their purchases of children (particularly girls) and females. Not surprisingly, however, those who had the good fortune to be purchased as slaves after 1613 differed little demographically (in this case, in age structure) from those purchased previously, for apparently the ages of the people needing such relief were not greatly different after 1613 from what they were before.

TABLE 13.25
Consequences of the Legal Structuring of Prices for Limited Service Contract Slaves

	Pre-1613	N	Post-1613	N
Adults per transaction	1.35	1,979	1.49	112
Boys per transaction	0.34	1,979	0.23	112
Girls per transaction	0.19	1,979	0.08	112
Children per transaction with children	1.87	569	1.85	20
Boys per transaction with boys	1.51	450	1.47	19
Girls per transaction with girls	1.32	292	1.13	8
Age of married males	30.68	339	29.05	21
Age of single adult males	23.80	450	21.78	40
Age of married females	26.57	265	27.40	5
Age of single adult females	20.07	54	18.80	5
Age of first child	9.87	263	8.06	16
Age of second child	7.93	125	6.22	9
Age of third child	5.68	41	4.00	4
Age of fourth child	3.20	15	4.00	1

37. Ibid., p. 38.

38. Jones, p. 196.

39. At the beginning of the twentieth century, Russians tried to give away their unwanted children. Thus the newspaper *Novoe vremia* on April 5, 1912 (p. 8) contained notices such as the following:

A girl, 1 year 8 months, I desire to give away as a daughter. Voronezhskaia street, 14, Apt. 6. . . . A boy, one month, I desire to give away for adoption. Kolozhevskaia street, 5, Apt. 98.

I wish to thank Louise McReynolds for bringing that regular feature of *Novoe vremia* to my attention.

Slavery in Muscovy normally was an institution that primarily provided relief, refuge, and a relatively secure place in an insecure world for young, single men. While some nuclear families were always selling themselves into slavery, their numbers rose appreciably during extraordinary disasters, such as the Great Famine of 1601-3. The statistics reveal a disproportionate ratio of boys to girls in such families. The reasons for the ratio are not obvious, but seem to be two: female infanticide was widely practiced by those at the bottom of society who needed the relief provided by self-sale into slavery; keeping domestic slaves who produced little or no income was expensive, and many of the less affluent buyers preferred not to buy girls, just as, apparently, they preferred not to buy single women. The consequence of such a marked buyer preference must have been the death from starvation and related causes of the females for whom a market did not exist.

14. Slave Occupations

The problem of slave employment is of central concern to the student of any slave system. Because of the nature of Muscovite slavery, however, the subject is not as easily discussed for that system as it is for those in which the primary function of slavery is to provide labor for profit-oriented agriculture or mines. Muscovite slavery was primarily of the household variety, but even within it there were many different occupations of varying status.

The data on which much of this work is based (the 2,499 contracts, dowries, wills, etc.) provide almost no information about what the slave was to do after he was purchased, something entirely in keeping with his chattel status. (A cow does not know what is going to happen to her after she is purchased, either. She may remain a cow, or she may become hamburger.) The only fundamental exception to this rule was the steward, whose contract in 23 cases noted that he was going to be a *kliuchnik* and usually stated the place as well. Three other cases mentioned that the slave might be a scribe (*d'iak*), tailor, or hatter (*kolpachnik*), and that is all.

It is probably fairly safe to assume that the occupations pursued by those who sold themselves into slavery were pursued after they had become slaves, but there is no firm evidence on this point. The lack of price differentiation for slaves with various "blue collar" skills vis-à-vis those totally lacking in skills would indicate that the purchasers' expectations were both very low and comparably undifferentiated. Therefore one must look at other sources of information to learn how slaves were occupied.

First, one might note a few distinctions between slaves and serfs, and remind oneself that the focus of this discussion is the former, not the latter. The duration of a slave's service was usually full-time, whereas a serf usually served his master only part-time.[1] The reality of the Muscovite situation was clearly outlined in the limited service slavery contract, which specified that the slave would serve his owner "every day in the household." One might note as well the general rule that the serf owned all of his means of production (except the land) and his lord had no right to expropriate his economic tools (livestock, tools, seed, buildings). In contrast, the slave had a legal right to nothing, even his own cloth-

1. Gelb, p. 87.

ing, not to mention his means of production or his product.[2] The Muscovite situation conformed fully to these norms.

Another general rule seems to be that the more autocratic the government is, the more opportunity there will be for slaves. Conversely, the more "democratic" the host society is, the less opportunity there is for slaves. Nearly all students agree that Muscovy in most of its quarter-millennium of existence became increasingly autocratic in the political sphere. There were few if any institutional restraints on the sovereign and his oligarchs. In a similar society, the Ottoman Empire, a complete continuum of slaves was found, nearly mirroring free society. A similar situation sometimes prevailed in Africa, where a slave often had more opportunity than the nonslave; before the slave was the possibility of substantial social mobility, and he could rise to positions of great wealth and power. Such a continuum can be found in Muscovy, but, curiously enough, most perfectly developed in the era before 1550. In such societies there are both "elite" high-status and "ordinary" low-status slaves, slave "ministers" working in the central government, and the most debased chattel working in private households. In Muscovy, high-status slaves were vastly outnumbered by those of low status, but, not surprisingly, there is far more information about the activities of the former than the latter. In this respect the student of Muscovite slavery finds himself in the same dilemma as does the student of any larger premodern society who has a comparative abundance of material with which to portray the life of the elite but a paucity of information about the broad masses.

Elite Slaves

The phenomenon of elite slavery astonishes most Americans, accustomed to the almost universally degraded condition of the Southern slave. The very thought that a slave might be in a managerial position such as an overseer generates disbelief. However, the American system was grossly atypical in its limitations placed on the role slaves could play in the society. Muscovy was much more typical. Americans are also misled by our enshrined dichotomy between "slave" and "free," which considers each category as a homogeneous status group. Throughout most of world history, there has been great differentiation within each group. The illusory antithesis prevents Americans from comprehending the fact that many societies had a full ranking of slaves, just as they had of free men.[3]

The Soviet historian E. I. Kolycheva combed the archives and published materials for data on the employment of slaves in Muscovy, and her findings are presented in tables 14.1 and 14.5.

2. Ibid.; Iu. V. Kachanovskii, "O poniatiiakh 'rabstvo' i 'feodalizm'," *Voprosy istorii* (1967, no. 6): 131.
3. Miers and Kopytoff, p. 128.

TABLE 14.1
Elite Slave Occupations

	First Half 15th C.	Second Half 15th C.	First Half 16th C.	Second Half 16th C.
Treasurer (*kaznachei*)	R*	R	R	
Administrative assistant (*tiun*)	R	R	R	
Bailiff (*dovodchik*)				R
Rural administrator (*posel'skii*)	R	R	P R	
Estate steward (*kliuchnik*)	R	P R	P	P
Administrator (*prikazchik*)			P R	
Salt boiler foreman (*varnishnyi prikazchik*)				P
Elder (*starosta*)			R	
State secretary (*d'iak*)	R	R	R	
Estate supervisor (*d'iak*)		P	P	P
Clerk (*d'iachok*)			P	P
Interpreter (*tolmach*)			R	
Falconer (*sokol'nik*)	R	P R	P R	
Trumpeter (*trubnik*)		R	P R	
Archer (*strelok, luchnik*)		R	P	P

Source: adapted from Kolycheva, *Kholopstvo*, p. 246.
*R = royal owner, P = private owner.

The utility of slave labor for the ruling family should be obvious, and roughly similar explanations can be advanced for the employment of elite slaves by other members of such societies as well. First, in some societies the principles of subordination are such that it is considered degrading for free people to take orders from anyone.[4] Thus, managerial functions have to be executed by persons not subject to this kind of degradation, such as slaves. Second, the employment of slaves frees their employer from the restraints inherent in free people such as loyalties to family or clan, social grouping or class. In this respect slaves are a suitable substitute for eunuchs or black clergy (monks) in government employ who owe their status and therefore their allegiance solely to their employer, who lack alternatives or any independent source of support. Slaves must obey, even slave ministers.

Prior to Ivan III (1472), state secretaries (*d'iaki*) managing the princely apparatus were primarily slaves in the households of the grand prince and appanage princes. The state secretaries employed by the fourteenth-century Moscow grand princes and mentioned by them in their wills were almost certainly slaves. Judging by these same testaments, palace treasurers were also slaves. This was true down into the reign of Ivan III, when Ostafii Arakcheev, a slave, was one of the keepers of the exchequer. The first treasurer known not to be a slave was V. G. Khovrin, a leading merchant and landholder, who was in office in 1450 and

4. Jones, p. 186.

sufficiently wealthy to found a stone church, and by 1457-58 was already a boyar. Not only were early Muscovite central administrators slaves, but those administering princely provincial properties were also—*dvorskie, kliuchniki, starosty, tiuny,* and *posel'skie.* The formulas mentioning these officials were repeated in princely testaments down to the beginning of the sixteenth century.[5] It is also recorded that Boris Godunov at the end of the sixteenth century had a penchant for slave servitors.[6]

These elite slaves remind one of the royal *ministeriales* of eleventh-century Germany, particularly during the Salian dynasty, who served as supervisors of the fisc, administrators of crown lands, and in general acted in the same capacities as their Muscovite counterparts did centuries later. Henry IV, surrounded by *vilissimi* and *infimi homines,* hardly outdid the Muscovite grand princes in ignoring the pretensions of the nobility and using his slave ministers to rule autocratically. (A precedent for this among Germanic rulers had been established by the Merovingian kings, who utilized slaves extensively in establishing despotic power.) In both Germany and Muscovy *ministeriales* were created by strong-willed rulers because of the absence of feudal vassals who could be relied on to obey, and Muscovy had the added incentive of the absence of a tradition of the use of churchmen to staff lay offices. In Germany such officials worked their way into the nobility by the thirteenth century, and even attracted free men to their ranks because of their near monopoly on the reins of power.[7] The same had happened in the Principate during the Roman Empire, and was to happen

5. AIuB 1: 169, 447; 2: 476; ASE 1: 281, 291, nos. 386, 398; 3: 465, no. 479; PSRL 12: 75, 112, 153, 199; DDG, pp. 8, 17, nos. 1, 4; Zimin, *Kholopy,* pp. 283, 312-16; Kolycheva, *Kholopstvo,* p. 65; Leont'ev, *Obrazovanie,* pp. 44-45; Kaiser, "Transformation," pp. 228-32; A. A. Zimin, "D'iacheskii apparat v Rossii vtoroi poloviny XV–pervoi treti XVI v.," *Istoricheskie zapiski* 87(1971): 231, 240; Demidova, "Biurokratiza'tsiia," p. 207; Sergeevich, *Drevnosti,* 1: 523; Kliuchevskii, *Sochineniia,* 6: 344; Veselovskii, *Feodal'noe zemlevladenie,* p. 221; V. A. Vodov, "Zarozhdenie kantseliarii moskovskikh velikikh kniazei (seredina XIV v.–1425 g.)," *Istoricheskie zapiski* 103(1979): 341; Nosov, *Stanovlenie. . . uchrezhdenii,* p. 483. Considering their origin, one should not be surprised to find that social prejudices against the state secretaries lingered in the sixteenth century (S. O. Shmidt, "O d'iachestve v Rossii seprediny XVI v.," *Problemy obshchestvenno-politicheskoi istorii Rossii i slavianskikh stran. Sbornik statei k 70-letiiu Akademika M. N. Tikhomirova,* ed. V. I. Shunkov et al. [Moscow: IVL, 1963], pp. 187-88).

6. *Skazanie Avraamiia Palitsyna* (Moscow-Leningrad: Akademiia Nauk SSSR, 1955), p. 107.

7. Geoffrey Barraclough, *The Origins of Modern Germany* (New York: Capricorn Books, 1963), pp. 80-84, 324-25; Josef Fleckenstein, *Early Medieval Germany* (Amsterdam: North-Holland Publishing Company, 1978), pp. 192, 209; Wergeland, pp. 53-58; Marc Boch, "A Problem in Comparative History: The Administrative Classes in France and in Germany," in his *Land and Work in Medieval Europe* (New York: Harper & Row, 1969), p. 96. Slaves were also used as officials by tyrants of ancient Greece (L. A. El'nitskii, "O roli rabov i otpushchennikov v nekotorykh formakh upravleniia gosudarstvom v Gretsii V–IV vv. do n. e.," *Vestnik drevnei istorii* 4(122) (October-December 1972): 101-6. Muhammad II the Conqueror used slave ministers after capturing Constantinople (Levy, *Islam,* p. 397).

again in Muscovy, although ennobling seems to have been more important in Germany and the attraction of free men to slave posts in the government more important in Rome and Muscovy.

Slaves were also known to have assisted the governors (*namestniki, kormlenshchiki*) in their administration of the provinces until that system of central control was abolished in the 1550s in favor of closely regulated local governance and ultimately was replaced by chancellery (*prikaz*) administration. It is particularly appropriate to assume that many of the provincial administrators (*volosteli*) were slaves of the governors, as were others of their auxiliary judicial personnel. Slaves played at least an equally important role in administering provincial Ch'ing China, where by the end of the seventeenth century slaves had served as prefects, subprefects, and magistrates, two had become governors, and one had become a governor-general.[8]

After government became more professionalized with the development of the chancellery system, some of the executive personnel owned slaves. Almost unquestionably most of them were household slaves, but some served their owners in the government. Thus on June 8, 1647, Peter Pushkin's slave Mishka Goriainov transmitted a memorandum from the Felony Chancellery to the Moscow Administrative Chancellery. "Peter" must be a mistake for *okol'nichii* Boris Ivanov Pushkin, director of the Felony Chancellery from March 1630 to August 1637, and again from 1642 through 1647. Pushkin also served as ambassador to Sweden, governor in Iablonovo, Mangazia, Briansk, and on the Dvina River. A person such as Pushkin was certain to have slaves, and while he was in chancellery service he used some of his chattel there to assist him in getting his missions accomplished. Almost certainly Mishka Goriainov nominally did not have the authority that some of his slave predecessors had possessed when serving the government, but undoubtedly many such posts were what their holders wished to make of them, or whatever the slaveowners allowed their chattel to make of them. Even at the end of the seventeenth century the personal secretaries of major government officials were their slaves.[9] The continuous employment of private slaves by their owners in government service is a Muscovite tradition that should not be overlooked. It might also be worthwhile considering the extent to which the employment of such slaves undermined the development of professional cadres and even professionalism per se in late Muscovy.

Thanks to the solid dynastic principles established in Rus' for over a half-millennium and the good fortune the dynasty had in being able to provide heirs, the elite slaves' access to power in the fifteenth and early sixteenth centuries was

8. Sergeevich, *Drevnosti*, 1: 454, 522-23; Kaiser, pp. 228-32; Kolycheva, p. 232; S. M. Kashtanov, "Po sledam troitskikh kopiinykh knig XVI v.," *Zapiski Otdela rukopisei B. I. L.* 40(1979): 52; Spence, *Ts'ao Yin*, pp. 14-15.
9. PRP 5: 384-85; A. N. Kazakevich and V. I. Buganov, eds., *Vosstanie moskovskikh strel'tsov 1698 god. (Materialy sledstvennogo dela.) Sbornik dokumentov* (Moscow: Nauka, 1980), pp. 232-35.

considerably more limited than it was in many Islamic societies, where slaves seized power at least fifty times. The Turkish elite palace administrative slaves took over power in the Central Asian Samanid domains, and one of their number, Sabuktigin, founded the Ghaznavid dynasty in A.D. 994, which then succeeded to the Samanid lands south of the Oxus.[10] In Mamluk Egypt, slaves became sultans. In the classical period of the Ottoman Empire, the Grand Vizir was usually of slave origin. Also in the Ottoman Empire, the value of slaves was increased by training in schools. Numerous Slavic slaves held high posts in the Ottoman Empire, usually after converting to Islam.[11] Whether the elite slaves in early Muscovite palace service were Eastern Slavs or from elsewhere is unknown. Judging by the fact that some of them were full slaves, we may assume that at least a few were East Slavic natives of their respective principalities.

Roughly a similar situation prevailed during the Roman Principate, when major posts were filled by slaves and freedmen because "no Roman of standing would have demeaned himself by becoming the Emperor's personal servant." In the Roman case, more than a century had to pass before "the major secretarial posts acquired sufficient status to rank as public offices and be acceptable to members of the equestrian order, although never to senators."[12] In Muscovy, members of the upper service class never became state secretaries, although in the seventeenth century they did assume positions as chancellery directors, particularly after it became apparent that the control of the *prikazy* was essential to that oligarchic clique with pretensions to managing the government, society, and even the sovereign himself in its own interest.

Other states from Babylonian to Soviet times have put slaves, particularly prisoners of war, to work on their great construction projects. In the Ancient Near East, such labor inputs were indispensable in the building of military fortifications, roads, irrigation projects, and temples.[13] In the Soviet Union prisoners of war were put to work building canals and railroads, universities and hydropower dams, as well as in logging, gold and coal mining, and other labor-intensive enterprises.[14] For reasons that are not clear, Muscovy rarely if ever exploited potential state slaves in this fashion. It certainly was not because of the absence of suitable projects: for example, the Smolensk fortress (1595-1602), the culminating project in the rebuilding of Muscovy's stone and brick fortifications, was the greatest construction undertaking in the sixteenth-century world. The 800-

10. Clifford Edmund Bosworth, *The Ghaznavids. Their Empire in Afganistan and Eastern Iran, 994-1040* (Beirut: Librairie du Liban, 1973), p. 37; Ann K. S. Lambton, *Landlord and Peasant in Persia* (Oxford: Oxford University Press, 1969), p. 52.

11. Fisher, "Muscovy," pp. 586-87; Inalcik, *Ottoman Empire*, p. 72. Elite slaves also were found throughout Africa (Maurice Bloch, p. 107).

12. Jones, p. 186.

13. Mendelsohn, p. 2.

14. S. Swianiewicz, *Forced Labour and Economic Development* (London: Oxford University Press, 1965).

kilometer Belgorod fortified line (1635-53) was another project that potentially could have absorbed (consumed) tens of thousands of state slaves.[15] According to some reports, Peter the Great's flotilla built in 1695-96 to attack Azov was constructed with slave labor, but his canals and capital, St. Petersburg, might have employed tens of thousands of slaves.[16] We may suspect that slave labor was not used on such projects because early modern Russia lacked the managerial talent to keep such a mass of forced laborers at work. Organizing the feeding of hordes of people was beyond the capacity of Muscovy, as evidenced by the fact that troops were responsible for bringing their own provisions to the combat zone. Muscovites preferred to regard prisoners of war as the private booty of their captors. Moreover, as I shall discuss further in relation to slaves serving in the army, Muscovy did not generate corporate forms to which such possessions could be entrusted. The church was the sole corporation, and everything else was owned individually. Even the state (until roughly 1613) was the personal patrimony of the sovereign.

Peter the Great changed this situation by forbidding individual soldiers to take military captives. His Military Statute of 1716 allowed Russian troops to loot the enemy at the appropriate time, but required that all human booty be turned over to the officer in command for state disposition. Deprivation of rank for officers and corporal punishment (running the gauntlet, *Spiessruten*) for enlisted men were the prescribed sanctions.[17] This was a radical departure from past practices, but was a logical concomitant of the professionalization of military service.

Another distinction of Muscovy was that the state rarely called upon privately owned slaves to do anything. In early Babylonia the state summoned slaves to perform corvée, and they were as subject to mobilization for public-works as were free men. In neo-Babylonia, the slave was subject to other state and church duties, in addition to the corvée. Ottoman slaves helped to build large state structures, including mosques.[18] The Muscovites frequently resorted to corvée for constructing fortifications and roads, for providing the royal court with its needs, but, once again, slaves seem to have been exempt from such obligations. That such work was considered the equivalent of slave labor is obvious from the verb used, *rabotat' vsiakie dela*, with "slave [*rab*]" as its root.[19]

15. Hellie, *Enserfment*, pp. 158-59, 178-79.

16. John Perry, *The State of Russia under the Present Tsar* (London, 1716), pp. 6, 28, 53. On the very limited utilization of slave labor (primarily Swedish prisoners) in the construction of St. Petersburg, see V. V. Mavrodin, *Osnovanie Peterburga* (Leningrad: Lenizdat, 1978), p. 92. On the use of slave labor in the shipyards of the new capital, see Marc Raeff, *Peter the Great*, p. 96.

17. PSZ 5: 352, no. 3006, chap. 14, art. 114.

18. Mendelsohn, pp. 38-39, 98. Slaves were also employed in corvée labor for state purposes in the American South (Catterall, 3: 448). Fisher, "Ottoman Slavery," p. 39.

19. Kotoshikhin, *O Rossii*, p. 88.

Slaves in the Army

Another locale of elite slave employment was the army, particularly after the 1556 law requiring all landowners to provide mounted cavalrymen according to the amount of land they possessed. (As this was precisely the moment when *kormlenie* was abolished, one may wonder how many slaveowners converted their administrators into cavalrymen.) The extent of utilization of slaves in the military forces of Muscovy has never been fully calculated, and a precise determination of the number of slaves, or their proportion of the total armed forces at any given time, cannot be made. Nevertheless, quite precise information for some periods is available and gives us a general notion of conditions as a whole.

A first point would be that the late A. A. Zimin's estimate that as much as three-quarters of the entire cavalry in the 1550s was made up of slaves must be excessive. His calculations were based on a fragment of the 1556 service register (*boiarskaia kniga*), which lists 180 *deti boiarskie* and their military slaves for grades 11 through 25 (13 and 14 are missing).[20] Slaves in military service were divided into two categories, those who participated in combat with their owners, and those who accompanied their owners mainly to guard their supplies in the baggage train. The 1556 register noted that 2 rubles were paid for each such slave supplied above the requirement. The sum of 4 rubles was paid as a premium for each combat slave beyond the required number who was outfitted with a quilted coat (*tegiliai*) rather than with full armor. A fine of 2 rubles was levied for each slave who should have been supplied but was missing. In 1556 the *boiarskaia kniga* recorded that 163 of the *deti boiarskie* were required by the extent of their landholdings to bring 593 combat slaves, but they brought 687, a surplus of 16 percent. The total number of combatants was thus at least 867 (the 687 slaves plus 180 *deti boiarskie*), and the slaves constituted 79 percent of that group of troops. The trouble with Zimin's projection is that other evidence indicates that the 180 servicemen in the 1556 list were not typical for the rest of Muscovy. While the 1550s were more prosperous than later times, there is little evidence that the free landholding cavalry had or could support such a large quantity of slaves.

The 1556 list also mentions 150 baggage-train slaves belonging to 71 owners. They were very important, for servicemen had to bring their own supplies to the front because the state did no provisioning for the cavalry (and there were not even private provisioners until the Smolensk War and later). When a campaign was planned in advance (in contrast to an immediate response to enemy incursion), cavalrymen were ordered to dispatch supplies for both men and horses to

---

20. Zimin, *Peresvetov*, p. 356; *Reformy*, p. 448 "Nekotorye voprosy," p. 108; N. Miatlev, "'Tysiachniki' i moskovskoe dvorianstvo XVI stoletiia," *Letopis' istoriko-rodoslovnogo obshchestva v Moskve* 8(1912, no. 1[29]): 60-61; Iakovlev, *Kholopstvo*, pp. 313-15; I. I. Smirnov, *Ocherki*, p. 420; Nosov, *Stanovlenie*, p. 397.

a frontal staging area by the "winter route" (straight overland, across frozen bogs and rivers) several months before the commencement of the campaign. The baggage-train slaves looked after their owners' supplies, and perhaps assisted in the defense of the baggage train with halberds and pikes (this is known for the second half of the seventeenth century). While secondary in a sense, the role of the baggage-train slaves was absolutely crucial, for no Muscovite army could fight effectively once its supplies had been exhausted, and the loss of the baggage train usually meant the loss of the campaign. It may be assumed that the 1556 list of baggage-train slaves is incomplete, for probably almost every serviceman on that list brought one. By later standards, the number brought (more than two for each listed serviceman) was high, and the reporting is almost certainly incomplete because there was no "state interest" in baggage-train slaves (in the sense that cash transfers were involved); moreover, the record-keeping was just in the process of being worked out.

A more complete, provincial, military register (*desiatnia*) is the one for Kolomna of 1577.[21] Over one hundred (perhaps as many as four hundred) *desiatni* are still extant, but this one is by far the most detailed that I am aware of. Certainly its recorder was a compulsive who felt he should note everything. The register lists 280 servicemen, of whom 195 (69.6 percent) were slaveowners. The latter brought with them 139 combat slaves and 184 baggage-train slaves, for a total of 323 slaves. This amounted to the totals noted in table 14.2.

TABLE 14.2
Slaveownership in 1577 Kolomna Military Register

	Slaves	N Servicemen
Combat slaves per serviceman	0.49	280
Combat slaves per slaveowner	0.71	97
Baggage-train slaves per serviceman	0.66	280
Baggage-train slaves per slaveowner	0.95	179
Total slaves per serviceman	1.15	280
Total slaves per slaveowner	1.66	195

The Kolomna figures seem not atypical for the era, and indicate that slaves made up approximately a third of the Muscovite combat forces. The armament of the sixteenth-century combat slaves varied but usually consisted of bow and arrow and saber. Riding ordinary horses, they often wore armor as well, sometimes chain mail (*pansyr'*), more frequently a thick quilted coat (*tegiliai*), and an iron helmet. The baggage-train slaves rarely had more than a horse or two. As befitted

21. V. N. Storozhev, ed., "Desiatni XVI veka. No. 1. Kolomna (1577 g.)," *Opisanie dokumentov i bumag, khraniashchikhsia v Moskovskom arkhive Ministerstva iustitsii* 8(1891), sec. 3, pp. 1-51.

their station, the slaves were almost never listed by name, although the description of the outfitting of each individual shows that a specific person was being described.

Moving into the seventeenth century, one finds that on the eve of the Smolensk War, in 1632, the government made thorough surveys of its forces; surveys of two groups of the upper service class, the *zhil'tsy* and Moscow *dvoriane* have been published. The rank of *zhilets* was complicated by the fact that it was awarded both to inexperienced scions of the upper service class and to experienced members of the middle service class who were being promoted to capital service. Such promotions were not infrequent and were certainly considered part of the cursus honorum for worthy provincial servitors. Among the 602 *zhil'tsy* in the list, 2 specifically stated that they had no combat slaves, 171 said they had one, 47 had two, 7 had three, and 1 had four.[22] As for baggage-train slaves, 3 said they had none, 208 had one, 30 had two, and 1 had three. Thirty-one men just said that they had baggage-train slaves, without stating how many (in my calculations, I assume that they had an average number, 1.13) The *zhil'tsy* had approximately 290 combat slaves and 313 baggage-train slaves. Over half (ca. 56.8 percent) of the *zhil'tsy* had slaves, as they reported in 1632 (see table 14.3).

TABLE 14.3
Military Slaveownership by *Zhil'tsy* in 1632

	Known No. of Slaves	N Servicemen	Calculated No. of Slaves	N Servicemen
Combat slaves per serviceman	0.48	602	0.48	602
Combat slaves per slaveowner	1.28	226	1.28	226
Baggage-train slaves per serviceman	0.45	602	0.51[a]	602
Baggage-train slaves per slaveowner	1.16	239	1.16[a]	270
Total slaves per serviceman	0.94	602	1.00[a]	602
Total slaves per slaveowner	1.65	342	1.75[a]	343

[a] Based on 270 known baggage-train slaves + an assumed 36 more.

The 623 Moscow *dvoriane* in the 1632 list were a less diverse and more prosperous group than the *zhil'tsy*. Among that group, almost 90 percent had combat slaves (a total of 1,302), and 75 percent had baggage-train slaves (a calculated total of 861). Befitting their higher status and wealth, they also had considerably more slaves per person than did the *zhil'tsy*, ranging from 177 with one and 198 with two, to 1 with nine and another with eleven. A similar distribution was true of baggage-train slaveownership: 108 Moscow *dvoriane* had one, 161 had two, 4 had six, and 1 reported seven. An additional 138 said that they

22. A. Iziumov, "Zhiletskoe zemlevladenie v 1632 godu," *Letopis' istoriko-rodoslovnogo obshchestva v Moskve* 8, nos. 3 and 4 [31-32] (1912): 26-163.

would bring as many baggage-train slaves as would be required.[23] Not counting the baggage-train slaves brought by those 138,579 of the 623 Moscow *dvoriane* brought an average of 3.3 slaves apiece (see table 14.4).

TABLE 14.4
Military Slaveownership by Moscow *Dvoriane* in 1632

	Known No. of Slaves	N Servicemen	Calculated No. of Slaves	N Servicemen
Combat slaves per serviceman	2.09	623	2.09	623
Combat slaves per slaveowner	2.35	556	2.35	556
Baggage-train slaves per serviceman	0.96	623	1.38[a]	623
Baggage-train slaves per slaveowner	1.89	318	1.89[a]	456
Total slaves per serviceman	3.06	623	3.48[a]	623
Total slaves per slaveowner	3.29	579	3.73[a]	580

[a] Based on 602 known baggage-train slaves + an assumed 259 more.

The relationship between the number of combat slaves and baggage-train slaves owned by a *zhilets* is strong ($r = 0.63$) but not overwhelming; for Moscow *dvoriane*, there was no linear relationship between the two ($r = 0.14$). It is of course not surprising that the ratio of combat slaves to baggage-train slaves rose with the increase in their absolute numbers, for a serviceman really had little use for more than one or two baggage-train slaves, whereas the government was able to use every combatant who could be raised. We might also note that even the Moscow *dvoriane* in 1632 did not bring as many combat slaves or baggage-train slaves as the *deti boiarskie* recorded in 1556 purportedly possessed.

The armaments of the combat slaves changed considerably between 1577 and 1632, with many of them discarding bow and arrow (and comparable armor) in favor of handguns (*pishchal'*), a change their owners were slower to make because of their resistance to technological change. A portrait of the required gunpowder-era armament of slaves is painted in an induction order dated December 4, 1698, telling slaveowning servicemen how their chattel were to be armed:

Your slaves, who will be with you in the regiments [in combat, as opposed to guarding the baggage train], shall carry firearms, fuses, and pistols in working order. They shall be mounted on Polish, Nogai, or domestic horses, or any other good ones which are accustomed to the shooting of firearms, so that they will not fear gunfire.[24]

Judging by the figures in tables 14.2, 14.3, and 14.4 for the years 1577 and 1632, it seems appropriate to calculate that in the era up to the Smolensk War

23. E. D. Stashevskii, *Zemlevladenie Moskovskogo dvorianstva v pervoi polovine XVII veka* (Moscow: T-vo "Pechatnia S. P. Iakovleva," 1911), pp. 40-237.
24. PSZ 3: 526, no. 1658.

there was about an average of one-half combat slave and another one-half baggage-train slave for each free landed serviceman of the middle service class and
lowest ranks of the upper service class. These numbers should be increased by a
multiple of three or four for the more prosperous members of the upper service
class, and no doubt increased even further for the most prosperous members of
the upper upper service class, the elite of Muscovite society.

These figures are not inconsistent with those of the Appendix of my *Enserfment and Military Change in Muscovy*, which indicates the number of slaves (undifferentiated) equal to the number of the middle service class in the second half
of the sixteenth century—17,500 rising to about 25,000. The Gunpowder Revolution, combined with middle service class desire that cavalry service be its domain and governmental fear of disorder created by elite combat slaves (Khlopko,
Bolotnikov, Vas'ka Shestakov, Balovnia, and others of the Time of Troubles who
had gained their military expertise as slave retainers) reduced the role of combat
slaves in the post-1613 era, particularly after the Smolensk War.

Grigorii Kotoshikhin noted during the Thirteen Years War (1654-67) that
slaves belonging to commanders (*golovy*) were serving as trumpeters (*trubachei*)
and drummers (*litavrshchiki*), important posts in preparing troops for combat
and maintaining morale and discipline. Neither was a combat position, it should
be noted. It seems not unlikely that in the Thirteen Years War and later, most
slaves were in the baggage train, about 10,000 in Sheremetev's army in Ukraine
in 1660, and 11,830 in the army in 1681. This degradation of the role of military slaves made them appear to be more like the slaves employed by the Byzantines in their armies.[25] What is striking about this change in that it coincided
with the "Byzantinization" of many other features of mid-seventeenth century
Muscovy ranging from criminal law to architecture. While the other changes were
seemingly a "medium revolution" stemming from the publication and wide distribution of the Church Statute Book (the *Kormchaia kniga*) in a general context
of efforts to "reform" Muscovy by Nikon and others, the lowering of the status
of military slaves certainly had primarily domestic causes, especially the discovery that townsmen and peasants could be drafted and that an army could be
composed of commoners led to a considerable extent by foreign mercenaries.

To my knowledge, no accounts exist of slave exploits on the battlefield. It
should be fair to assume that, unlike among the Manchus, where slaves were rarely used in actual combat, Muscovite combat slaves were as responsible as free men
for the victories and losses of early modern Russian arms. In this context one
should remember that traditionally slave-combatants have fought as ably as their
owners simply because they knew that as prisoners of war, their fate would ordinarily be worse than that of the free men. Adam Olearius noted in the 1630s
that the slaves were loyal to their owners and commanders, and fought well under foreign officers.[26]

25. Kotoshikhin, p. 131; Udal'tsova, p. 13.
26. Olearius, p. 152; Spence, *Ts'ao Yin*, p. 7.

The function of military slaves was not only the aggrandizement of Muscovite power but the personal enrichment of their owners as well. A larger slave contingent could extract and carry home more booty than a smaller one. This booty, one of the major objects of Muscovite warfare, was of all types—anything that could be moved, from precious objects to human beings. A 1684 court case recorded examples. Perhaps three decades earlier, slaves belonging to Ivan Alekseev Meshcherinov (a Moscow *dvorianin* who in 1671-73 was governor in Kozmodemiansk and in 1674-75 held the post of governor of Surskii ostrog, a fort on a Volga tributary that flows into the Syzran'), Sten'ka Ivanov, and others, had taken captive a Lithuanian boy near Shklov. The boy was brought to Moscow and registered as Meshcherinov's slave. He grew up in Mescherinov's household, married a Lithuanian slave girl, and they had three children. Being totally dependent on Meshcherinov, the slave said he always wanted to live in his household. The same case told of another person who had been taken captive by slave troops near Belaia Tserkov', lived five years as a slave, then fled and became a miller, but upon discovery was returned to Meshcherinov.[27] No doubt this was the optimum case: to go to war, send one's slave soldiers out on a raiding party, and return with human booty.

The existence of armed slaves surprises many familiar with slavery in the American South, where slaves were liable to a beating if apprehended with a hunting weapon. In Muscovy, according to the Moscow census of 1638, slaves possessed firearms in the homes of their owners, and seem to have been considered part of what we might call "the home guard."[28] This was articulated in the Petrine era, when a decree of January 5, 1708, declared that the entire population of Moscow, including slaves, was to be ready to bear arms in case of necessity.[29]

There was nothing unique about Muscovy's employment of slaves in the army. Military slaves were a feature of nearly all Islamic slave systems, although, as Daniel Pipes has shown persuasively, they were institutionally very different from their Muscovite counterparts. One major distinction between Islamic and Muscovite military slaves was that the former were owned by the state or ruler and recruited and trained for military service, whereas the latter were privately owned and, like their owners, were neither specially recruited nor trained to be soldiers. Military slaves also were found in many parts of Africa, and African slaves played a major role in the conquest of Latin America in the first half of the sixteenth century. Slaves were also employed in Asiatic military forces in such countries as Thailand.[30]

27. PSZ 2: 589-90, no. 1073; DR 3: 1551, 4; 422; Ivanov, AUBK, p. 261; Barsukov, SGV, p. 518.
28. Beliaev, *Rospisnoi spisok . . . Moskvy*. Southerners even went so far as to state that if slaves could be good soldiers, then their whole theory of slavery was wrong, essentially that the Africans should not be enslaved (Litwack, *Been in the Storm*, pp. 43-44, 66).
29. PSZ 4: 401, no. 2184.
30. Pipes, "From Mawla to Mamluk"; R. Stephen Humphreys, *From Saladin to the Mon-*

Contemporaries never articulated their reasons for such extensive use of slaves in the army, but several may be surmised. As we have seen earlier, the use of slaves at court in the medieval era was very common, and this no doubt was true for military personnel as well. *Dvorianin* meant "courtier," usually a slave, in the medieval era. *Syn boiarskii* is analogous to the Carolingian *puer regis*: the former was not a boyar's son, just as the latter was not the king's son; both were probably slave dependents.[31] The analogy between slave and child is frequent. By the sixteenth century both *dvorianin* and *syn boiarskii* had envolved to designate the free landholding military servitors who made up the bulk of the middle service class, the provincial mass cavalry. Their nominal progenitors, however, had been slaves, and the military use of slaves was a tradition.

Another factor dictating the employment of slaves in combat was a general reluctance in the sixteenth century to involve commoners in the martial arts. This required both the state and the larger landholders to look to slaves to supplement those holding the land in order to field an army of the maximum size that the government calculated the land could support. There was a general understanding in Muscovy that the priests prayed, the townsmen and peasants paid, and the landed element fought. But after the Time of Troubles this convention, which was still expressed in the second half of the seventeenth century, began to break down as landholders began to take peasants with them to war, or sometimes even to send them in their stead. Although this development is yet another example of the equation of peasants-becoming-serfs with slaves, here I want to emphasize that it represents the beginning of the disintegration of the long-held mystique that only landholders and courtiers (both free and slave) could render military service. This disintegration then led naturally into the development of the new formation army, based on foreign mercenary officers and Muscovite commoners. In all probability, tradition and the desire to maximize manpower while maintaining the military mystique of exclusiveness were the major reasons for the Muscovite use of combat slaves. The role of elite military-slave traitors during the Time of Troubles and the requirements of the gunpowder revolution also made the contribution of armed slaves much less important after 1650 than it had been a century earlier. Petrine legislation put an end to privately owned combat slaves by incorporating them in the state's army.

gols. *The Ayyubids of Damascus, 1193-1260* (Albany: State University of New York Press, 1977), pp. 76-79; Inalcik, "Servile Labor," p. 26; Lambton, *Lord and Peasant in Persia*, pp. 52, 56; Turton, p. 256; Shepherd, p. 89; Joseph Fletcher, "Turco-Mongolian Monarchic Tradition in the Ottoman Empire," *Harvard Ukrainian Studies* 3/4 (1979-80): 245-49; Miers and Kopytoff, pp. 170-71 and elsewhere; Mellafe, p. 26; Curtin (in *Annals*), p. 5; Fisher and Fisher, *Slavery*, pp. 62, 64, 154-63; Cooper, *Plantation Slavery*, pp. 190-95; Martin Klein and Paul Lovejoy, in Gemery and Hogendorn, p. 192; Daniel Pipes, "The Strategic Rationale for Military Slavery," *The Journal of Strategic Studies* 2, no. 1(May 1979): 34-46.
    31. Wergeland, pp. 54, 104.

Noncombatant slaves continued to be present in the Petrine armed forces until near the end of Peter's reign, and perhaps even beyond. These descendants of the baggage-train slaves were personal attendants, lackeys of the type known in almost all armed forces up to and including the U. S. Civil War.

Personal slave attendants (*slugi*) were discussed in the Military Statue of 1716. The *sluga* was forbidden to leave his owner (*gospodin*), and no other officer was permitted to recruit another's slave (*cheliadnik*, a variation on one of the medieval words for slave). The Russian *sluga* was translation of the German *knecht*, slave.[32] It is apparent in the 1720 Naval Statute that officers were entitled to have slaves (also called *slugi*) whose expense was borne by the government. An admiral was entitled to fifteen slaves, a doctor one. If anyone brought more than he was entitled to, he was subject to demotion.[33]

Slaves in Church Employ

Numerous societies had slaves that belonged to temples or cults, and such chattel do not fit neatly into either the "productive" or "household" categories. However, it is clear that they usually appear where household slavery is the predominant mode, and in that sense the temple was the household of such slaves. The tasks of temple slaves were often those of household slaves as well, to clean the temple, sweep its courtyard, and so on. But, on the other hand, a few temple slaves were forced to produce income for the cult. There were, for example, large numbers of temple slaves in Babylonia, recruited primarily from prisoners of war and by means of private donations but also by the dedication of free-born orphans and poor children. The Muscovite Orthodox church was not permitted to own slaves, by canon law, but it did essentially possess dependents who were in many respects "slavelike," although it is not clear that any of the norms discussed in chapters 2 through 8 were applicable to them. First were the *detenyshi* ("little children"), orphans and impoverished children who had found refuge in monasteries and then grew up there as dependent laborers; they remind one of the Babylonian case. Other *detenyshi* were hired laborers, often seasonal, casual laborers. Then there were, again, *slugi* ("servitors"), laymen who worked for the church in capacities ranging from laborer to armed retainer. Terminology links those people to slaves in secular life, but, again, it is clear that the *slugi* juridically were not slaves.[34]

---

32. PSZ 5: 340-41, no. 3006, chap. 9. arts. 73-75.

33. PSZ 6: 55, no. 3485, bk. 4, chap. 2.

34. Mendelsohn, pp. 101, 103-4, 106; V. A. Petrov, "Slugi i delovye liudi monastyrskikh votchin XVI v.," *Trudy LOII* 2(1960): 129-71. A census directive of January 26, 1678, declared that monastery peasants were not to be concealed under the names *sluzhki* and *detenyshi* (V. N. Sedashev, *Ocherki i materialy po istorii zemlevladeniia Moskovskoi Rusi v XVII veke* [Moscow: V. Rikhter, 1912], p. 208). Peasants were taxable, *sluzhki* and *detenyshi* presumably were not.

It is clear that the Orthodox church had an arm's length relationship with slaves. As a consequence of the Byzantine heritage, it did not permit slaves to be ordained as clerics unless they had been manumitted. Moreover, the law was very explicit in ordering the return to slave status of any slave who had illegally become a monk, priest, or deacon.[35] This practice might be compared with that of Islam, where, some scholars have maintained, slaves were readily accepted into the clergy. The frequency of such acceptances seems questionable, and one should note as well that no slave could act as an imam for free men.[36] Regardless, in Muscovy no slave was allowed to minister even to other slaves.

Privately Owned Elite Slaves

Muscovite private slaveowners held numerous other elite slaves in addition to combat slaves. These elite slaves served as the personal extensions of their owners in the capacities of advocate and steward. One of the themes of this work has been the extent to which slaves represented their owners. A good illustration of this in the public mind was offered during the Moscow uprising of 1547. The mob tried to get vengeance for the wrongs committed during Ivan IV's minority. An obvious target was Ivan's uncle, Iu. V. Glinskii, and, when the mob murdered him in the Kremlin on June 26, his slaves were all slain with him. Ivan the Terrible exhibited the same mentality, for during the Oprichnina, on at least nine occasions, slaves (sometimes forty or fifty of them, at least once over one hundred) were murdered at his behest along with their owners.[37] The same thinking was evident over a century later, with another twist to it. In 1682 *boiarin* V. V. Golitsyn complained to the cotsars Ivan and Peter that Ivan Andreev Khovanskii had tortured and personally interrogated the former's slave Rod'ka Chernov because of a dispute Golitsyn had with Khovanskoi's son, Andrei Ivanov Khovanskoi.[38]

Another illustration of the slave as personal extension of his owner was offered by the Muscovite judicial process, which permitted representation of litigants, if they so desired. Representatives were usually other members of the family— children, brothers, nephews, and so forth. The other possibility was to send a slave advocate, who was essentially a member of the family.

35. 1649 *Ulozhenie* 20: 67; MS, p. 279.

36. Fisher and Fisher, p. 50.

37. PSRL 4[1], vyp. 3: 620-21; PSRL 13: 154, 456-57; PSRL 29: 54; Hugh F. Graham, ed. and trans., "'A Brief Account of the Character and Brutal Rule of Vasil'evich, Tyrant of Muscovy' (Albert Schlicting on Ivan Groznyi)," *Canadian-American Slavic Studies* 9, no. 2(Summer 1975): 221, 224-25, 229, 240-41, 245-46, 250, 257, 263. Graham notes that no peasants were murdered in these orgies (ibid., p. 225, n. 69), a not surprising fact, for they had not yet been enserfed to the point where they could take on the slavelike attribute of being an extension of their lords.

38. N. G. Savich, ed., *Vosstanie v Moskve 1682 g. Sbornik dokumentov* (Moscow: Nauka, 1976), pp. 119-20, no. 73.

Shcheniateva v. Kolupaev

The court transcript of Shcheniateva v. Kolupaev in 1547 shows the slave advocates hard at work. The case was tried before the Moscow *tiun* Iakov Gubin Moklokov, who reported everything to the treasurers Ivan Ivanov Tret'iakov and Fedor Ivanov Sukin for final resolution. Moklokov was a free man, although certainly those who had held his post a century or two earlier were not, and even he was fundamentally slavelike in taking down the case for the treasurers' resolution. In dispute was Onisimko Onikeev Novikov, and his brother Kuzemka Ondreev (sic) Novikov.

Anna Shcheniateva was from one of the most prominent Moscow families, one descended from Lithuanian forebears. In the early 1550s, another clan member, Petr Mikhailov Shcheniatev, was a boyar. Her advocate was the slave Il'ia, sometimes referred to also as a *nedel'shchik*. Note that he is never given a patronymic. Defendant Mikhail Kolupaev seems to have been a landholder from the Rostov vicinity. Initially he was represented by Mikita Trofimov, whose name hints that he was a slave, although the case never says that he was. Trofimov introduced another of Kolupaev's slaves, Istomka Bolturov, who prosecuted his owner's case. Neither Shcheniateva nor Kolupaev appeared at the trial.

Although the case is lengthy, it can be summarized briefly. Bolturov claimed that Kolupaev loaned 3 rubles apiece to the Novikov brothers and that they became his slaves when they defaulted. Onisimko (who always spoke for his brother, who was still a fugitive) initially claimed that he belonged to Shcheniateva. Both advocates asked for a brief continuance to produce their documentation. Bolturov then brought an earlier court decision from the governor (*namestnik*) of Pereiaslavl', prince Ivan Vasil'ev Pozhar'skii, dated April 21, 1547, in which Kolupaev (in that litigation represented by still another of his slaves, Mitia Kovurtsov) was awarded ownership of the two brothers after they had confessed that they belonged to the plaintiff. The judge in that case had asked Onisimko whether he had a discharge (*otkaz*) from Kolupaev, and he responded incredulously: "A discharge? I just up and left Mikhail [Kolupaev]." (Later in the history of the limited service slavery contract, judges did not ask whether claimed fugitives had a discharge.) Il'ia presented no documentation on behalf of Anna Shcheniateva's claim. The treasurers awarded the verdict to Kolupaev on the basis of his earlier judgment charter. Moreover, Onisimko confessed that Il'ia's claims on behalf of Anna Shcheniateva—that he was the princess's slave and had stolen her property (12 rubles)—were slanders contrived to win the suit against Kolupaev.

A few other facts might be noted about the case. One may assume that the two brothers were combat slaves. Even in the Pereiaslavl' trial no one would post bail for them, presumably because of the perceived likelihood of their fleeing further upon being released from the custody of the bailiff, one Murzok (who may have been a slave himself, although the transcript does not say that he was). During the Moscow trial the issue of bail seems not to have been raised, and Onisimko, the recidivist fugitive (who was chained when he fled!) was simply kept in chains by an officer of the court. This implies that the case involved men in the prime of life who would not be bound by anything other than genuine fetters. Moreover, when fleeing, both times, Onisimko and his brother Kuzemka exhibited the tastes of cavalrymen. They stole a pair of horses each, Nogai saddles and bridles, sabers, bows and arrows, and expensive clothing. The total value of the first theft was 12.50 rubles, the second 15.25 rubles. The value of the thefts was added to the brothers' obligations to Kolupaev, and thus they were to be his slaves on that account as well, until they could pay off the 27.75 rubles. Kolupaev was also granted the right to seize the still-fugitive Kuzemka without the presence of a bailiff, further indicating that Onisimko's brother was an able person who might be able to get away if the usual formality of locating the fugitive and then getting an officer of the court to arrest him were adhered to.[39]

The case of Shcheniateva v. Kolupaev reveals an elite slave world that was almost totally encapsulated within the free world. The litigating advocates were slaves, the objects of contention were slaves. The hearing officer, the Moscow *tiun* Moklokov, was free but essentially slavelike in his position and functions. The officer of the court, Vaska, who tried to get bail in Pozharskii's court in Iaroslavl', was also a slave. The only really free men in the case were those who rendered the final decisions. One can wonder what all the other figures in the drama thought about such an order.

Slave advocates are mentioned throughout the period. A 1582 report to Tsar Ivan IV indicates how, in the absence of a professional bar, slave advocates seem to have taken control of the judicial system, or at least manipulated it to their advantage:

Many slaves are serving as advocates [*v dovodakh*] for their owners and are serving others for hire in the courts. The slaves are inflaming [the judicial climate] with slander and conspiracy, they are writing enormous sums in their suits, and, as is unfitting in court trials of civil suits, they tell lies and testify not to the point, distracting the court so that the decision will not be handed down for a long time. Or, they form conspiracies, bring up other previous cases, and prevaricate. Those hired by a plaintiff or defendant to stand in court behind him, stand there and collude with the opponent and sell out the person who hired them; they speak not to the case, or testify unnecessarily and thereby lose the case for the person who hired them. Others go around compiling complaints and suits for a fee, they entice people to join conspiracies, and they multiply superfluous litigation.[40]

Noting that such activity was not a crime, those writing the sovereign asked for a remedy. Always glad to oblige, the tsar prescribed various penalties for various

39. AIu, pp. 49-53, no. 22; Koretskii, *Zakreposhchenie*, p. 210.
40. AI 1: 271, no. 154, XX.

activities, ranging from exclusion from court to beating with the knout, exile, or death. The point is, of course, that a class of slaves had developed who not only could represent their owners but even counseled strangers about the judicial process, and at least occasionally seem to have been more in control of the situation than were the officials themselves.

The Statute Book of the Felony Chancellery in 1628 concerned itself with the subject of slave advocates. It stipulated that slaves could not represent their owners at the time an actual investigation (*obysk*) was being conducted, that the plaintiff and defendant themselves had to be present for that process. Further on, the Statute Book noted that the sovereigns (Filaret and Mikhail) had decreed that when the court ordered litigants to remain in Moscow for anything other than the *obysk*, it was legal to leave behind slave advocates for that purpose. The *Ulozhenie* of 1649, in an article of unknown origin, also recognized the slave advocate by stating that an opposing litigant could not demand that the slaveowner appear in court if the slave was there as his representative.[41]

There are perhaps countless examples of the use of slave advocates in the seventeenth century. In the late 1620s *boiarin* Ivan Nikitich Romanov was accused by southern frontiersmen of employing his slaves and peasants in Elets province to recruit others' peasants to settle on his properties. Some of the recruitment methods were "legal" (such as advising peasants of their right to move under the Forbidden Years laws), but most of them amounted to kidnapping and other uses of terror and intimidation. In addition to seizing labor, Romanov's minions stole horses, cattle, and personal property, and left a trail of assaults and arson in their wake. The petitioners' case was turned over to the Military Chancellery (*Razriad*, which was in charge of the southern frontier region) for resolution. Romanov, one of the half-dozen leading figures of Muscovy, as well as the uncle of Tsar Mikhail and brother of Patriarch Filaret, was much too elevated to appear in court, so his slave Pankratei Iaryshkin directed the Moscow defense. A full process was conducted, including a general investigation that interrogated 1,944 witnesses, but, in what seems to have been a miscarriage of justice, the verdict was awarded to Romanov, eight leading complainants were beaten with whips and jailed, and the petitioners were required to pay court costs of 54.20 rubles.[42]

In the 1670-80s, the slave Grigorii Shcherbachev handled *stol'nik* A. I. Bezobrazov's affairs (and those of his friends as well) in the Moscow chancelleries. When Ivan Bogdanov Lovchikov initiated a number of suits against Bezobrazov during his absence from Moscow in 1681, the latter's slave Mikhail Antip'ev, defending his owner, refused to affix his seal because his sealing ring was at home and his seal was in court; he also refused to sign documents on the grounds that his eyes hurt. For his obstinacy, Antip'ev was jailed for two weeks and nearly tortured. Thus throughout the Muscovite period slaves represented their owners

41. 1628 UKRP 11: 1, 3; AI 3: 100, no. 92, XV; PRP 5: 212-13; 1649 *Ulozhenie* 10: 178.
42. E. Stashevskii, ed., "K istorii kolonizatsii Iuga," cols. 253, 267, 271, 292.

in the judicial process. It was probably just such slave advocates who purchased copies of the 1649 *Ulozhenie* in the years 1650-64.[43]

With the demise of slavery in the eighteenth century, substitutes had to be found for the Muscovite slave advocates. This must have been a particularly a-cute institutional problem while mandatory service was required of landholders, a problem that should have diminished after the freeing of the nobility from compulsory state service in 1762, when individuals began to spend much of their time prosecuting their own litigation, and when foreign stewards began to be employed in the capacities held by elite slaves in Muscovy. When advocates were used, they seem to have been "marginal individuals in the judicial system, re-tired clerks practiced in the formalities of paperwork and the ways of bribery, or serfs and wealthy noblemen trained to watch out for their masters' interests."[44] They were not illogical successors to the Muscovite slave advocates, for slaves are sometimes called "marginal individuals," and serfs were in many respects the successors of slaves. Considering these antecedents, one should not be too sur-prised that, after the judicial reforms of 1864, the professional bar had some dif-ficulty in gaining popular respect.

The final major outlet for elite slaves was employment as estate stewards of the major landholders. In Greece, particularly Rome, and China this was the oc-cupation of many elite slaves.[45] The Muscovite records are full of the activities of these people, who purchased other slaves for their owners, negotiated tax and postal levies with governmental officials, defended their owners' peasants and or-dinary slaves from other landholders and official depredations, collected the tax-es and rent due from the peasants, and performed many other tasks.[46] In the words of a 1682 document summarizing the progress in hunting down Petr Ivan-ov Khovanskoi, which necessitated interrogating his slave Aleshka Komarov, such people "looked after the affairs" (*za dely khodit*) of their owners.[47]

43. Novosel'skii, *Votchinnik*, pp. 56-58, 60-61; S. P. Luppov, *Kniga v Rossii v XVII veke* (Leningrad: Nauka, 1970), p. 93. Slaves purchased 9 of the 664 copies whose purchaser is known. They also were 2 of 38 known purchasers of Smotritskii's *Grammatika*.

44. Richard S. Wortman, *The Development of a Russian Legal Consciousness* (Chicago: University of Chicago Press, 1976), p. 11.

45. Jones, p. 185; Wiens, p. 299; Meijer, pp. 335, 343. Abuse of power and revolts led to abandonment of the "bailiff" system of estate management in China in the 1662-1722 peri-od (Wiens, p. 334). In Muscovy there were abuses, but only the abolition of slavery led to the end of the system.

46. Kotoshikhin, p. 141; Iu. G. Alekseev, *Agrarnaia i sotsial'naia istoriia severo—vosto-chnoi Russi XV—XVI vv. Pereiaslavskii uezd* (Moscow-Leningrad: Nauka, 1966), p. 120. On the centrality of slaves in estate administration in the 1649-79 years, see Tikhonov, "Pomeshchich'ia usad'ba," pp. 143, 146.

47. Savich, *Vosstanie*, p. 148, no. 100. The published correspondence of the Khovanskoi family contains several reports from stewards on the conditions of various estates and the sending of food to Prince Petr. Some of the slave stewards were women (*kliuchnitsy*) (G. G. Luk'ianov, ed., "Chastnaia perepiska kniazia Petra Ivanovicha Khovanskogo, ego semi i rod-stvennikov," *Starina i novizna* 10[1905]: 384-94, 401-3, 436, 438).

As I have noted from time to time, many Muscovite slaves were purchased for their owners by other slaves. Certainly at least 5 percent of all slaves were purchased by elite slaves for their owners (and, occasionally, for themselves). Some individuals and clans did this to a great extent, others seem never to have done so. Obviously it was a question of resources. The Chertov clan (nine individuals) and Novokshchenov clan (twelve individuals) stand out in this respect as families that regularly resorted to elite slaves to buy additional chattel for them. Individuals who distinguished themselves in this respect were Nekliud Dmitreev Buturlin and Mikhail Ivanov Miloslavskii. Six purchases of full slaves were made in Novgorod for Buturlin in the years 1526-32 by other slaves belonging to him, Piatoi Dobrynin, Olesha Grigorev Chernoi, Panka Savluk, Mikita Dmitriev, Matfei Mikiforov, and a Vaska.[48] Miloslavskii was a *syn boiarskii* in the employ of the church (*syn boiarskii vladychnyi*) who in the 1580s and 1590s had a tax-exempt house in Novgorod and property in Liatskii pogost, Zalesskaia polovina, Shelonskaia piatina. He was closely associated with his brother Luka, and together in 1574 they had owned their father's patrimony in Moscow province which had on it two masters' houses, six inhabited slave houses, five inhabited peasant households (*dvory*), and five vacant peasant households. Right after the compilation of the Moscow cadastre they seem to have shifted their operations to the Novgorod region where, between 1574 and 1589, twenty-eight transactions were carried out in the name of Mikhail, seven jointly in the names of Mikhail and Luka, and one in the name of Luka. These slaves were purchased by Grigorii Vasil'ev Iazykov, Zubat Simanov, Fedor Vasil'ev, Vasilii Trofimov, Vas'ka Timofeev, and Semeika Ivanov. Ivanov was purchased in 1577 and Iazykov in 1581 by Miloslavskii for 15 rubles apiece, the maximum, but there is no evidence about where the other four came from. They were obviously trusted by Miloslavskii, for he allowed them to roam Shelonskaia and Votskaia piatinas spending large sums of money for other slaves.[49] Another probable "slave personnel director" was Dorofeiko Puzikov, who went to the Military Chancellery for his owner, counselor state secretary Emel'ian Ignat'ev Ukraintsov, to receive a returned fugitive slave who belonged to Ukraintsov, one Fedor Stepanov Sobolev, who had been beaten mercilessly with the knout on the rack for having fled to Voronezh. Dorofeiko was ordered to be prepared to return Fed'ka for further interrogation at any time.[50]

Elite slaves were of great utility to the landholders, who had to join their fellow members of the service class in the nearly annual obligatory service that consumed the lives of these people, forcing them to be absent much of the year from their estates. Such elite slaves were sometimes reported or registered slaves (*dok-*

48. RIB 17: 79-82.

49. Kopanev, "Materialy," pp. 151-55; Samokvasov, AM 1(1905): 46; PKMG 1: 138; RK 1475-1598, p. 260; Maikov, KPNV, p. 99; Sukhotin, ChSV, pp. 7, 10, 17, 18, 20; RIB 22(1908): 281-82, 608-9.

50. Savich, *Vosstanie*, p. 32, no. 15.

ladnye kholopy). Early in Muscovy all estate managers had to be slaves, but in the 1550 *Sudebnik* only rural estate managers did.[51] *Dokladnoe kholopstvo* expired with the sixteenth century, but it is apparent that estate managers still continued to be recruited from the slave element in the seventeenth century, although it is by no means clear that all stewards were slaves at that time. (On estates where there was little demesne, the preferred method of control often seems to have been to force the peasants to create a commune and then to elect an elder who was personally responsible to the landholder for the collective's rent, tax payments, and fulfillment of other obligations.)

The archives of two figures from the second half of the seventeenth century, Boris Ivanov Morozov and Andrei Il'in Bezobrazov, indicate that they relied heavily on slaves to manage their properties. Morozov is the more interesting figure and by now is widely known among students of Muscovite history as one of the most able men of his era. The tutor of Tsar Aleksei and actual head of government from 1645 to 1648, he was driven out because of his reforms and personal greed. More to the point here, he was one of the wealthiest men in Muscovy, with 9,100 taxpaying households and estates consisting of 274 villages, distributed widely throughout thirteen provinces. His correspondence with his stewards has been published, along with inventories of his properties compiled after his death in 1667. The inventories indicate that he had at least fourteen slave managers in 1667, and perhaps more than twice that many. Often they occupied their lord's manor house. During the two decades of his extant correspondence, Morozov dealt with literally dozens of estate stewards on issues ranging from the sick, state taxes, and the harvest to meting out punishment to peasants and making loans of thousands of rubles. Morozov even had elite slaves, two chief stewards, Stepan Nikitin Kiselev and Ivan Ivanov Lunin, slaves who were entrusted with all manner of functions, from transporting large sums of cash to affixing Morozov's personal seal (and sometimes their own) to documents. The designation of two chief slaves parallels governmental practice of dual direction of offices (the famous "collegiality" of Muscovite administration), an attempt to curtail corruption. Other stewards even referred to them as their master (*gosudariu moemu*) in corresponding with one or the other of them. In summary, Morozov's operation was a classic use of slave personnel to extend his own person and thereby manage relatively efficiently a large enterprise.[52]

The efficiency or inefficiency resulting from the management of the large Muscovite estates by slaves cannot be determined, as far as I can tell. Into any calculation of "efficiency" would have to go the cost of corruption, a hoary yet difficult subject. Corruption as a device for ensuring adequate compensation for the corrupted is hardly of major interest, but when it distorts the basis for rational decision-making it becomes of greater interest. Both must have happened

51. 1497 *Sudebnik* 66; 1550 *Sudebnik* 76.
52. *Akty Morozova*; *Khoziaistvo Morozova*.

in Morozov's economic world because of Lunin's bribe-taking. A complainant in 1651 wrote to Morozov that Lunin, for a consideration, was willing to determine that a murderer, blasphemer, or corrupt individual was a good man; that a peasant (taxed as 1) or a landless peasant (taxed as ½) was a pauper (*zakhrebetnik*, taxed as 0). On the other hand, if Lunin was not paid off, he would categorize the nonpeasant as a peasant. Moreover, the corruption, arbitrariness, and violence (such as flogging peasants without a trial) hardly can have stimulated the primary producers to maximize output.[53] If much of that went on, it must have distorted Morozov's attempts to be a rational, profit-maximizing entrepreneur.

Bezobrazov's archive comes to us because he was executed in Moscow on January 8, 1690, for participation in the Shaklovitoi-musketeers uprising, and all of his property, including his correspondence from the 1670s and 1680s, was confiscated. He operated on a smaller scale, befitting a *stol'nik*, than did *boiarin* Morozov, but his holdings in nine provinces were more than ample for a single individual, 2,452 cheti of land and 239 peasant households. He also had a stable of forty to fifty slaves (males, plus an unknown number of females) in his Moscow residence. In other words, this was a typical economy needing a number of managers, not only because of its scale but also because Bezobrazov, like Morozov prior to June 1648, was occupied much of the time with the governmental duties that entitled him to his compensation. His Moscow slave bailiffs (usually four of them) had every conceivable assignment. One of them was to scout Moscow for free plants and seeds that could be grown on one of the estates of their flower- and berry-loving owner. They also directed construction projects, hunted fugitive peasants and slaves, bought fish at distant points for the Moscow household, and investigated illegal activity of the provincial stewards.[54] Bezobrazov's elite slaves were known in all the elite houses of Moscow, as well as in the government itself, where they had connections, especially among the chancellery copyists (*pod'iachie*). They kept the supplies and doled out monthly rations to Bezobrazov's other Moscow dependents. While the elite slaves were Bezobrazov's chattel, they resented being called that by slaves lower than they, and they considered it an insult (*pozor*) to be called house slaves (*dvorovye liudi*). No doubt intelligent manipulation of the sense of hierarchy, of rank, among the slaves of Muscovy helped to keep them all more obedient.

An instance of a slave's carrying out his master's will in the ultimate sense was exemplified when one of Bezobrazov's slaves, Grigorii Shcherbachev, slashed another slave to death in their owner's presence (and presumably at his directive). For some reason the authorities intervened, Grishka was arrested, beaten with the knout, and jailed for two years. No sanction, other than the loss of Grishka for two years, was meted out to Bezobrazov.

In all his affairs Bezobrazov, like Morozov, tried to run everything personally, down to the last detail. His managerial slaves were to see that orders were car-

53. D. I. Petrikeev, *Krupnoe krepostnoe khoziaistvo*, pp. 61, 161.
54. On slaves functioning as slave-catchers, see 1649 *Ulozhenie* 20: 112; MS, p. 296.

ried out, not to make policy or even interpret directives. (This also mirrored government practice.) No doubt this was so both because of the personalities involved and because they lived in a milieu in which no one could count on anything being done properly. Slaves, of course, are particularly appropriate executors for such a person because they can be trained and beaten into precise obedience. Bezobrazov differed from Morozov, and also from Ia. K. Cherkasskii,[55] who had chief stewards and an office where administration was concentrated, in that he ran his domain out of his pocket, wherever he was. Bezobrazov tried to control his fifteen slave bailiffs (who usually directed eight of his eleven estates) by soliciting complaints against them from peasant individuals and collectives.

Most of Bezobrazov's estate stewards were hereditary slaves, members of families who had served the Bezobrazov family for generations. Bezobrazov as a general rule took the sons of his provincial bailiffs to Moscow to educate and train them, to ensure that they would understand him in the future. Morozov also seems to have used the children of his slave stewards in a similar capacity, although the matter of deliberate policy is not as clear. Bezobrazov's training school reminds one of those run by the Ottomans, although they tended to start afresh with each generation. By bringing children to Moscow and keeping them there (over their parents' objection, incidentally), Bezobrazov made them into Muscovites, and thus ultimately into outsiders when they returned to the provincial milieu, although he usually allowed them to return home for a Christmas vacation. Back in the provinces, they worked in accordance with general directives (a *pamiat'*), somewhat like those issued U.S. stewards (who were, however, free men) by absentee Southern landowners, plus a constant flow of ad hoc orders. Bezobrazov was usually less detailed in these instructions than was Morozov. A whipping awaited the slave bailiff who failed to execute his job properly. Corporal punishment and, especially, verbal abuse were frequently employed because of the relatively low level of some slave bailiffs' executive ability, their occasional dishonesty, an ignorance of formal record-keeping, and Bezobrazov's brutal personality.

Slave bailiffs also directed the estate court on Bezobrazov's properties. They functioned in conjunction with the elected communal elders in the presence of the entire community. A bailiff had the capacity to employ torture, including torture by fire, if it was deemed necessary to arrive at the truth. He also liberally applied the whip and knout to the accused. For less serious infractions, a bailiff struck or caned a recalcitrant peasant on the spot. The bailiff also had a hand in village matrimonial life and, reflecting the slavelike nature of Russian serfdom, could punish a peasant for marrying without permission. Making the peasants farm Bezobrazov's demesne and in general behave like obedient chattel was not an easy task, and it is not surprising that hard drinking was the vice of some slave stewards, who of course had no assurance of tenure in any post since that de-

55. Iu. V. Arsen'ev, "Blizhnii boiarin kniaz' Nikita Ivanovich Odoevskii i ego perepiska s Galitskoiu votchinoi (1650-1684 gg.)," *Chteniia* 205(1903, bk. 2): 53-64, 107.

pended on the whim of the slaveowner. Nevertheless, in spite of the difficulties that the slave stewards faced, and their personal shortcomings, they managed to provide a good life for Bezobrazov and his menage.[56]

An interesting illustration of an elite slave in action survives from the Thirteen Years War. Early in the war the Muscovite forces, while capturing Polotsk, took fifty Polish servicemen as prisoners of war. As was the customary practice, the prisoners were distributed throughout various towns. One batch of twenty was first sent to Velikie Luki, and then held in jail in Novgorod for a year and a half. The government provided monthly rations to the prisoners of war. In March of 1655 Moscow *dvorianin* Prince Ivan Andreev Golitsyn was appointed governor (*voevoda*) of Novgorod, and proceeded to violate the statute forbidding such individuals while on duty to enslave people. While visiting the jail handing out alms, Golitsyn asked two of the prisoners whether they would like to become his slaves and serve him in his household. They refused. The next day Golitsyn sent a freedman in his employ, his former slave Demidko Andreev Sofonov (who had been manumitted by order of the tsar, probably because his relatives had complained against the enslavement of a member of their clan), who took the Poles out of jail to Golitsyn's residence and attempted by compulsion to formulate slavery documents on them. In the household was another Pole, also forcibly detained, who was afraid to flee because he knew that he would be falsely accused of theft and then "legally" enslaved. The three of them wrote Tsar Aleksei and petitioned for their freedom.

Receiving the petition, Aleksei ordered a hearing. One of Golitsyn's slaves, Sten'ka Dymov, who tended his owner's business (*kotoryi za dely khodit*), on the day before Christmas, 1657, was summoned to answer for his owner.

Prince Ivan's slave Sten'ka Dymov was questioned: "By what documentation are Ivashko [Kuzmin] D'iachkovskoi and the [other two] slaves he brought [with him to the hearing] bound to Prince Ivan? How did they happen to come into Prince Ivan's household?"

Sten'ka under questioning said [that he did not know firsthand] how these slaves, Ivashko and his fellows, got [to Prince Ivan's], for he at the time was not with Prince Ivan in Great Novgorod. However, he had heard from Prince Ivan that Ivashko and Mishka [Aleksandrov Rymelt] from the jail had voluntarily asked Prince Ivan to be his house slaves. Prince Ivan at their request had baptized them in the Orthodox Christian faith. Sten'ka [Ivanov Kondyrev] had asked to be a house slave, and had been baptized of his own free will. They had lived in Prince Ivan's household voluntarily to this very day. Prince Ivan had no documents formulating their slavery status on them. He did not know whether Ivashka and his friends had been given their monthly rations [in jail], as prescribed by decree. Sten'ka also did not know for what reason they were sitting in jail.

56. A. A. Novosel'skii, *Votchinnik i ego khoziaistvo v XVII veke* (Moscow-Leningrad: Gosizdat, 1929).

Sten'ka signed his testimony, following the usual practice for elite slaves, and left the hearing. The government seems to have been outraged by Golitsyn's conduct. The prisoners of war were freed and ordered to serve in the Muscovite army, and Golitsyn seems to have received no more assignments or promotions after violating his trust in Novgorod.[57] All of these sanctions were applied without any consultation with Golitsyn, something totally consonant with the Muscovite notion that elite slaves were a part of the slaveowner himself.

Always on the alert for responsible persons who could be maximally intimidated and whose oppression would have the greatest effect on others, the government singled out stewards (along with wealthy peasants) for the assignment of liability in the judicial process. When provincials were suspected of prevaricating, stewards were to be selected and beaten with the knout. In so doing, the government recognized the authority over the peasants that the slave stewards acquired from their owners. Similarly, elite slaves known to be responsible for the collection of taxes were arrested, detained, and even tortured for failure to deliver what was expected of them.[58] In the post-Petrine era, after the effective abolition of slavery, lords turned to their serfs and trained them as estate administrators. Others imported foreigners, especially Germans, to work as stewards.[59]

Panov v. Kishkin

A glimpse into the world of the elite slave is provided by the case in which Buian Vasil'ev Panov sued Vasilii Ivanov Kishkin for the recovery of a runaway slave girl, Fekla, daughter of Fedor Berestov, in the late autumn of 1621. This might seem like any other case involving a fugitive slave, except that Panov himself was a slave who belonged to *boiarin* Prince Ivan Vasil'ev Golitsyn, one of the most powerful figures in the early reign of Tsar Mikhail. There is hardly any doubt that Buian was acting on his own behalf in this case, whose resolution is unknown. While the boundary line between master and slave is blurred in one instance where Buian is talking about another slave who was working for him, there is not the slightest intimation in the case that Buian was the agent of his owner Golitsyn. As we have seen, the slave advocate was a common figure in the Muscovite juridical process, but in this case it is clear that Buian was acting on his own behalf.

On August 28, 1621, Buian Panov initiated a suit for the return of Fekolka, who, he claimed, had been a dowry slave but had fled over ten years earlier, on

---

57. Arsen'ev, "Smes'," pp. 2-4.

58. AI 1: 255, no. 154, V; Novosel'skii, *Votchinnik*, p. 59.

59. Black, *Citizens for the Fatherland*, pp. 46-47. The sense that an estate steward was supposed to be slave-like persisted in the post-Petrine years. The instructions to a steward appointed to manage the Sheremetev estates in 1727 stated that he was to effect his duties "in a manner befitting a faithful slave" (*kak podobaet vernomu rabu*) (K. N. Shchepetov, *Krepostnoe pravo v votchinakh Sheremetevykh, 1708-1885* [Moscow: Ostankinskii Dvorets-muzei, 1947], p. 39).

Thursday in the fifth week of Easter, 1611. Such accuracy and record-keeping might be expected from an elite slave. Buian had traced her to Suzdal' and then initiated an action in the Slavery Chancellery for her recovery. His complaint alleged that, while fleeing, she had stolen a very significant sum of property from him. A listing of the property gives an idea of what an elite slave might possess, for one may assume that he would not submit totally preposterous claims. In addition to 20 rubles in cash, Buian claimed that she had taken a woman's cap made with golden cloth worth 5 rubles, a woman's silver chain with five gold-filled crosses on it worth 4 rubles; three gold-filled rings and a gold ring with a ruby, worth 3.50 rubles; a woman's white padded jacket lined with yellow oriental silk with silver gold-filled buttons, worth 10 rubles; and a woman's pearl necklace worth 10 rubles. Her total theft was claimed to have a value of 52.50 rubles. Moreover, as Feklitsa only took property fitting her sex, one may assume that Buian must have had a considerable quantity of other property as well, perhaps worth hundreds of rubles, a sum far greater than was ever paid for any slave in Muscovy. How Buian acquired his wealth is not evident, but certainly in the company of his owner, Golitsyn, he experienced many opportunities for enrichment. Such opportunities would not have been available to a free man, and this makes it clear why such elite slaves as Buian did not buy their freedom.

Buian had been fairly thorough in hunting down Feklitsa but had been unable to gather all the facts about what had happened to her during the course of the previous decade. He had sued Kishkin, who had accepted the challenge, although it was not clear that he should have. Kishkin himself was a *syn boiarskii* who for some reason was no longer serving, perhaps because of wounds or incurable illness. At one point he sent his father-in-law to represent him at the trial in Moscow because he was sick, and the officials in the Slavery Chancellery recorded the father-in-law as Kishkin's slave, probably because such emissaries almost always were. In reality, Feklitsa belonged to Kishkin's son Zakhar, who had acquired her as part of his wife's dowry in 1616 when Zakhar married Fedora, daughter of Ivan Andreev (Budikhin) Kazimerov.

Buian knew nothing about Kazimerov, a *syn boiarskii* serving from Suzdal', who testified at the trial and claimed that he had found Feklitsa begging and starving in Moscow in 1611, that he had taken her in, and that she had served him voluntarily, that is, she had been a voluntary slave. However, he had not obtained any documents on her, so that the first written evidence presented at the trial was the dowry, to which Feklitsa had not objected at the time. Nor did she object when she was married off in 1617 to one of Zakhar Kishkin's slaves. She supported her present owner's story completely, adding only that she and her mother had been washerwomen as well as beggars and vagabonds and that her mother had abandoned her. What the truth was, we cannot tell. However, Buian claimed that he still owned her mother.

Unfortunately the resolution of the case is unknown, but we do learn that Buian incurred considerable expense in trying to recover Feklitsa. Initially he said that he had delivered the documents suing Kishkin, but later it turned out that another of his slaves had done it for him. Be that as it may, on November 6, after the case had been under way for ten weeks, Buian noted that he had run up expenses of 2.25 rubles on signature and seal fees and transportation costs, a sum more than the current legal maximum of 2 rubles that could be paid for a limited service contract slave. The court told Buian not to worry yet about his monies.[60] If he had won the case, of course, he would have been able to recover them from the defendants, as well as Feklitsa and her husband and the 52.50 rubles.

The case of Buian Panov v. Vasilii Kishkin tells us several things that are useful to remember about Muscovite slavery. For one, Feklitsa's story about begging with her mother for alms at the time of the destruction of Moscow in 1611 is typical. One might have expected her to have found a wealthier lord than Kazimerov, if she actually had run away from Buian, but one well may imagine that she did not have much choice in 1611. That Kazimerov should have given her as a dowry slave to the son of a fellow provincial *syn boiarskii* was typical as well. Finally, the presence of the wealthy slave Buian is not unexpected in Muscovy, with its complete range of slaves from elite to the lowest. His property, in cash, valuables, and slaves, would have been exceeded by few in Muscovy, and his ability to command the attention of the Slavery Chancellery and to dispatch his own slave messengers to provincial towns with orders to produce defendants and witnesses was the mark of an elite member of Muscovite society.

Slaves in Commerce

Another group of slaves in Muscovy was composed of those engaged in various business activities. Such slaves have existed since practically the dawn of recorded history. In Babylonia they were well known and highly trusted by their owners, who allowed them to go about business on their own account, loaned them great sums of money at the going rate of interest, and collected an annual rent or tax called *mandattu*.[61] As part of the Roman-Byzantine tradition, the Spanish slave code of 1263-65 permitted slaves to engage in business, either on their own behalf or in their owners' enterprises.[62] In the Islamic world, in China, and in Africa, slaves were widely employed by their owners in commerce, both accompanying their owners' caravans and even directing them independently.[63] Not all societies, by any means, have allowed slaves to engage in commerce and other enterprises; some have forbidden such activities, largely out of fear that

60. Iakovlev, *Kholopstvo*, pp. 338-44, no. 5.

61. Mendelsohn, pp. 68-69.

62. Klein, *Americas*, p. 61.

63. Miers and Kopytoff, p. 169; Wiens, p. 301; Allan G. B. Fisher and Humphrey J. Fisher, *Slavery and Muslim Society in Africa* (Garden City: Doubleday, 1971), pp. 143-44; Klein and Lovejoy, in Gemery and Hogendorn, p. 194.

much of what slaves might sell would be stolen. Nevertheless, the Virginia prohibition enacted about 1800 forbidding slaves to peddle anything was unusual and extremely harsh.[64]

The Muscovites, until the 1630s, had a laissez-faire attitude toward slave employment, and even after that time restrictions were generally minimal. Judging by the records, some slaves were tax farmers. Artemii Vasil'ev Izmailov's slave Ivan Lobanov in 1615 paid 33.50 rubles for tax-farming a tavern and little market in Nizhnii Novgorod. Ivan Borisovich Cherkaskii's slave Fedor Sungurov paid 50 rubles for another tax farm. According to P. P. Smirnov, tax farmers of the lucrative posts were usually slaves (and also peasants) belonging to members of the ruling clique and some of the state secretaries and government clerks.[65]

The major activity of slaves in commerce was to expand the family firms of Muscovite merchants in their commerce with the Crimea, Siberia, and the White Sea littoral. Such commerce is known to have occurred from the end of the fifteenth to the end of the seventeenth centuries. Slaves belonging to merchants in Moscow and other major cities assisted their owners in their enterprises.

Intermediate- and Low-Status Slaves

As in most slave societies, the bulk of the Muscovite slaves were not elite individuals, but rather the lowest element of society, people fundamentally without talent, hopes, or many aspirations beyond mere survival. The jobs held by these individuals are listed in table 14.5.

TABLE 14.5
Ordinary Slave Occupations

	First Half 15th C.	Second Half 15th C.	First Half 16th C.	Second Half 16th C.
Household Help				
Groom (*koniukh*)		P*	P P	P
Kennel keeper (*psar'*)	R	P R	R	P
Cook (*povar*)		P R	P R	P R
Baker (*khlebnik*)		P R	P R	P
Kitchen helper (*kukhar'*)			R	
Forester (*poleschik*)			R	
Watchman (*storozh*)			R	
Nurse (*niania*)			P	

64. Hall, pp. 176, 178; Klein, *Americas*, p. 56.
65. RIB 28(1912): 124; P. P. Smirnov, "Ekonomicheskaia politika Moskovskogo gosudarstva v XVII v.," in *Russkaia istoriia v ocherkakh i stat'iakh,* ed. M. V. Dovnar-Zapol'skii (Kiev, 1912), 3: 394. The above illustrations of elite slave employment illustrate Yoram Barzel's theses that voluntary slaves were allowed more freedom of action and worked in occupations with more amenities than involuntary slaves often did ("An Economic Analysis of Slavery," *Journal of Law and Economics* [1977]: 105).

Occupation				
Wet nurse (*mama*)				P R
Pantry maid (*devka k lartsu*)			P	P R
Chamberlain (*detinka k posteli*)			P	
House girl (*sennaia devka*)				P
Clown (*skomorokh*)			P	
Musician (*zurnach*)			P	
Textile Workers				
Spinner (*domotkan, tonkopriaditsa*)		R	P	
Weaver (*bral', bral'ia*)		P	P R	
General textile worker (*khamovnik*)		P	P	
Wool worker (*sermiazhnik*)			R	
Garment Workers				
Tailor (*portnoi*)		P R	R	P
Seamstress (*shveia*)			P	
Detail worker (*strochnik*)		P	R	
Agricultural Workers				
Miller (*mel'nik*)		P R	P	
Honey collector (*bortnik*)	R	P	R	
Gardener (*sadovnik, ogorodnik*)	R	R P		
Cowherd (*korovnik*)		P		
Duck tender (*utiatnik*)		R		
Fisherman (*rybolov*)		R	R	R
Horse fodderman (*borovnik*)	R	R		
Metal Workers				
Smith (*kuznets*)		P	R	P
Armorer (*bronnik*)		R	R	
Sleigh-runner maker (*poloznik*)			R	
Bog iron-miner (*rudovshchik*)				P
Plowshare smith (*pluzhnik*)				P
Silversmith (*serebrianik*)		R		
Leather Workers				
Tanner (*kozhevnik*)			P	P
Bootmaker (*sapozhnyi master*)		P	P R	P
Shoemaker (*chebotnik*)		P	P R	
Furrier (*skorniak*)		P	P	
Sheepskin worker (*ovchinnik*)			R	P
Bowmaker (*sagaidachnik*)		R		
Knout maker (*knutnik*)			R	
Bridle maker (*uzdnik*)			R	
Saddler (*sedel'nik*)				P
Wood Workers				
Carpenter (*plotnik*)		P R	P R	P R
Tar maker (*dekhtiar*)			P	
Others				
Salt boiler (*tsyrennik*)				P
Icon painter (*ikonnik*)				P
Sexton (*ponomar'*)	P			

Source: adapted from Kolycheva, *Kholopstvo*, pp. 246-47.
*P = private owner, R = royal owner.

Many societies had what one might call intermediate-status slaves, those between the elite and the menial. Examples would be the silk weavers in Bursa,
Turkey, who worked for the international export market, and the armorers of
medieval Samarkand.[66] Muscovy probably had a lesser proportion of these than
did other societies, if for no reason other than that it did not have many such
skilled crafts. The major craft might have been that of icon painters, particularly
of the famous Stroganov school of the second half of the sixteenth century. It
is well known that many of these painters were slaves, and that the Stroganovs
made every effort to enslave desirable free artisans, even resorting to chaining
them to a wall should they try to depart before six months of service had passed
(the length of time after which an employer could legally convert a worker into
a slave). In Tula, the center of Muscovite ironworking in the second half of the
sixteenth century, 11 of the 144 smiths in 1588 were slaves (*dvorniki*). In Muscovy, as in West Africa, slaves involved in craft production and trade tended to
fit into the household model of slavery.[67]

Of relatively indeterminate status were slaves who worked as couriers. In the
government itself, messengers were honored quite highly, and by no means was
it the least significant people who carried important messages from here to there.
So it must have been for slaves who were messengers. On December 9, 1597,
Treshka Stepanov submitted a petition to the governor, Prince Daniil Ondreev
Nogtev, from his owner, Ignatii Posnikov Irettskoi of Bezhetskaia piatina.[68] In
September 1682 Sergushka Naumov delivered a petition from his owner, *boiarin*
Prince Fedor Fedorov Kurakin, to cotsars Ivan and Peter.[69] Such assignments re-
flected trust and responsibility, almost certainly would have not been given to
slaves at the bottom of the heap, and must have elevated the messengers above
other slaves.

Household Slaves

Most Muscovite slaves served as domestics and lackeys at the beck and call of
their owners. This has been the employment of most slaves in the majority of
slaveowning societies, from the Ancient Near East, Thrace, Byzantium, and Byzantine Egypt to China, Thailand, the Ottoman Empire, and medieval Europe,

66. Inalcik, "Servile Labor," p. 35, passim; R. G. Mukminova, "K istorii remeslennykh masterskikh—karkhana XVI (chugunoliteinaia masterskaia Samarkandskoi oblasti)," in *Sred-nevekovyi Vostok. Istoriia, kul'tura, istochnikovedenie*, ed. G. F. Girs et al. (Moscow: Nauka, 1980), p. 193.

67. A. A. Vvedenskii, *Dom Stroganovykh v XVI–XVII vekakh* (Moscow: Akademiia Nauk, 1962), p. 86; B. A. Kolchin, "Obrabotka zheleza v Moskovskom gosudarstve v XVI v.," *Materialy i issledovaniia po arkheologii SSSR* 12(1949): 193; Klein and Lovejoy, p. 193. For examples of forcible enslavement of artisans in the Islamic world, see Petrushevskii, "Rabstvo v Khalifate," p. 69.

68. RIB 38(1926): 153, no. 28, V, passim.

69. Savich, *Vosstanie*, p. 164, no. 118.

where Negro slaves were primarily domestic chattel.[70] Jewish law and custom discouraged employing free persons as servants, and in many societies, from Rome to the Arab Caliphate, personal servants were almost always slaves. Muscovy was no exception, a fact observed by contemporary writers, from the German mercenary Heinrich von Staden in the 1560s and 1570s to the Foreign Affairs clerk Grigorii Kotoshkikhin, who fled to Sweden in the 1660s.[71]

It cannot be accidental that these terms of enslavement were codified in the limited service slavery contract, where the slave agreed to serve in the household compound (*vo dvore*) of his owner. In 1646, when a person was proving that he was a free man, he said that he had not "lived on anyone's estate as a slave in the household" (*vo dvore on v kholopekh ni u kogo ne sluzhival*).[72] (The fact that slaves were rarely mentioned in the travel accounts of foreigners may be partially attributable to the fact that foreigners were not allowed to enter Muscovite homes. Also, as the slaves were mostly Russians, nothing in their appearance set them apart from the nonslave lower classes.)

At this juncture I might explain *dvor*, which is translated as "house," "household," "household compound," and so forth. Sometimes *dvor* is translated as "yard," which is not a bad rendition, either, except to say that a "slave served in the yard" would convert him into a dog or gardener, depending on the reader's experiences, and therefore that choice obviously is even less correct than the one that has been adopted. Let us look at what contemporaries called a *dvor*. The description comes from December, 1649, when Prince Nikita Iakovlev L'vov sold to *stol'nik* Vasilii Vasil'ev Buturlin his *dvor* in the Belyi Gorod district of Moscow, in the parish of Boris and Gleb, on Arbat street.

In the household compound [*dvor*] is a main residence [*khorom*]; the upper residential quarters [*gornitsa*] are subdivided into rooms over the first-story quarters [*podklety*]. The first story is finished [*sdelany*], but the second story above is rough-hewn squared beams, and the roof is also squared beams. The inside is not finished. The entry rooms [*seni*] leading into the residential quarters [*gornitsa*] and the main room [*komnata*] are covered with bast. Birch covers the planks on the roof. In the courtyard is a kitchen [*povarnia*], a little hut, a storage cellar [*pogreb*], over the cellar is a shed [*naves*]. There is also a well in the yard, the gates are planks covered with wicker, both gates have iron bolts. The fence [*gorod'ba*] on three sides is mine, and on the fourth is common with Ivan Chemodanov.[73]

70. Verlinden, *Colonization*, p. 47; Brauning, p. 42; Wiens, p. 299; Fisher, "Ottoman Slavery," p. 35; Allan Chester Johnson and Louis C. West, *Byzantine Egypt: Economic Studies* (Princeton: Princeton University Press, 1949), p. 132 (=Princeton University Studies in Papyrology, no. 6); T. D. Zlatkovskaia, "O kharaktere rabstva vo Frakii VII–V vv. do n.e.," *Vestnik drevnei istorii* 1(115) (January-March 1971): 54-64.

71. Petrushevskii, "Rabstvo v Khalifate," p. 67; Jones, p. 185; Heinrich von Staden, *Land and Government*, p. 122.

72. PRP 5: 61.

73. Arsen'ev, "Smes'," p. 1; S. B. Bogoiavlenskii, "[Dvorovye dereviannye postroiki XVI v.]," in his *Nauchnoe nasledie. O Moskve XVII veka* (Moscow: Nauka, 1980), pp. 192-232.

L'vov sold the property for 300 rubles, which, it was discovered about seven years later, Buturlin had stolen from the government.

As befits the subject, Grigorii Kotoshikhin ended his 1666 memoir *On Russia in the Reign of Aleksei Mikhailovich* with a discussion of house slaves:

> The boyars, counselor members of the upper upper service class [*dumnye*], and favorites [*blizhnie*] keep in their household slaves of the male and female sex, a hundred, two hundred, three hundred, five hundred, and a thousand, as many as they are able, depending on their rank and property. They give those slaves who are married an annual stipend of 2, 3, 5, or 10 rubles, depending on the person and the service they render. They also provide them with necessary clothing, grain, and various victuals, monthly. They live in their own rooms in the lord's house, or in separate houses. They, the slaveowners, annually send their married, honest slaves to their estates in the provincial villages and hamlets, in groups, in shifts, and order them to extract their stipend and all supplies that they need to live on from their peasants.
>
> Bachelor slaves of higher status are each given a small cash stipend, but those of lower status are not given a stipend. The bachelors are given various garments, hats, shirts, and boots. The senior bachelor slaves live in lower, distant rooms, the juniors live in upper rooms, and they drink and eat from the master's kitchen. They are all given two tankards of spirits apiece on holidays.
>
> Those of the female sex, widows, live in their husbands' residences. They are given an annual stipend and monthly rations. Some widows and unwed girls live with their owners' wives and daughters, in rooms [of the main house]. They give them their clothing, and they eat and drink from the lord's kitchen. When the girls reach maturity, they, the masters, marry off those girls and widows, with a dowry, to their house slaves, depending on who loves whom, or it sometimes happens, they are married off compulsorily. The wedding festivities take place at the residence of the slaveowner and depend upon the status of the slaves being married. The food, drink, and wedding clothing all are provided by the slaveowner. Girls and widows are not married off outside their owner's household, into the houses of other owners because the slaves they have, both males and females, are hereditary and limited service contract slaves.
>
> Regulations are established in their owners' houses for [the resolution of] any domestic disputes, income and expenditures, and for the investigation of trouble cases and their resolution involving slaves and peasants.
>
> In the same manner, people of other ranks keep slaves in their houses, as many as they are able to feed, hereditary and limited service contract slaves. It is decreed that no one shall keep nonslaves in his house.[74]

Kotoshikhin's is the sole account, to my knowledge, of domestic slave reality in Muscovy. Except possibly in its figures for the number of slaves owned by magnates, his picture coincides with that which is painted throughout this work. Particularly important is his point that the slaves do not produce income but live

74. Kotoshikhin, pp. 157-58.

as parasites off the slaveowners' peasants. While there is no doubt that many slaves rendered services to which a monetary value could be attached, there is equally no doubt that a vast number of Muscovite slaves were greatly underemployed, to use modern terminology. They were hardly atypical in Muscovy, where underemployment was the rule rather than the exception, if only because almost all occupations were so extremely seasonal. Neither the landholding cavalryman nor the peasant agriculturalist "worked" even half the year, so in that respect the slave was keeping good company. The entire Muscovite system contrasts with that of the Roman Empire, where "the urban population existed at the expense of the surplus product gained from intensive exploitation of slave labor."[75] In Muscovy, the peasant labored, and the slave was supported by peasant labor. As in South China around 1900, slaves were "luxury items that constituted a net drain on the economy."[76]

From a comparative perspective it would be interesting to know where the Muscovite household slave stood in the continuum of employment that might be established for the universal experience of human slavery. The full-employment end of the continuum would be occupied by those systems in which productive slavery was the prevailing order: Athens, Rome, the New World. Certainly the Ancient Near East seems to have allowed its slaves considerably less leisure than did Muscovy; slaves were used in state projects, temple activities, some mining, smelting, and casting, weaving, skilled activities, fishing, some farming, and domestic work.[77] Life among the larger slaveowners, where the emphasis was on visible consumption, must have been much like that in many African societies, where slaves (primarily children and females) were valued because they expanded the lineage of the slaveowner.

Yet this approach could be exaggerated. The vast majority of Muscovite slaves must have been compelled to do considerably more than make an annual trip to the slaveowner's peasants to collect their stipend and grain allotments. The impression conveyed by chapter 17 is that the modal ownership of slaves was 1. Certainly the slave who was the only slave of his owner, and even those belonging to an owner who had only one slave family, or a small number of slaves, could have been kept very busy, running errands, cleaning house, preparing meals, making repairs, and accompanying the master on military campaigns or wherever else he went. Such a life often represents not underemployment but double employment. The South China example just cited makes it more intelligible why males were preferred for household slavery in Muscovy, as they also were in the

75. V. I. Kuzishchin, "Nekotorye problemy izucheniia rabovladel'cheskogo sposoba proizvodstva," *Voprosy metodologii i istorii istoricheskoi nauki* 2(1978): 70.

76. Watson,"Chinese," p. 361. A. L. Shapiro and G. V. Abramovich have noted that the need to feed the slaves was a major reason why the income and produce from a lord's demesne exceeded the needs of the lord's family (AIS-ZR [1971], p. 351; [1974], pp. 222, 232-33). For a thoughtful discussion of slaves as luxury items, see Nieboer, p. 425.

77. Mendelsohn, pp. 67-117.

late Manchu period; males were more suitable for the heavy and demeaning work of hewing wood, drawing water, carrying out the slops, and heavy cleaning.[78] It is also fairly clear that household slaves were not "triple employed" by being forced to support themselves by subsistence farming, in addition to rendering their obligations, as was true for male slaves belonging to the Hausa, as well as for many slaves in the Caribbean monoculture islands.[79]

Fiction provides an illustration of the employment of household slaves in Muscovy. In the *Tale of Frol Skobeev* the hero hides himself in the house of the woman he is attempting to seduce, Annushka, the daughter of a wealthy member of the upper service class, *stol'nik* Nardin-Nashchokin. When Frol is discovered by Annushka's maid (*mamka*, probably a slave), the latter suggests that their many slaves could easily murder the adventurer and conceal his corpse. This solution does not appeal to Annushka, who yields to her seducer and elopes with him. Later on in the story, still other slaves play an important role as messengers in arranging a reconciliation between the *stol'nik* and his son-in-law.[80] Whether or not *Frol Skobeev* is a parody of actual events has been debated, but certainly the presence of large numbers of slaves in the households of the Moscow elite and their utilization as occasional assassins and regular messengers can hardly be doubted.

One of the many generalizations that has been made about slavery is that "prostitution is the inevitable fate of the female slave."[81] Certainly that has been the case in many slave societies, from the Ancient Near East, Greece, Rome, and the Ottoman Empire to Nazi Germany, which sent many of its female captives into houses of prostitution. On the other hand, beginning with Marcus Aurelius, provisions were enacted condemning this practice and setting free any women so employed. This attitude became enshrined in the Justinian Code, and from there went into the Spanish law of 1263-65.[82] The law was extended to prohibit a slaveowner from enjoying sexual access to his slaves both there and in Muscovy. This may well be the primary factor explaining the low demand and prices for female slaves in Muscovy. The available bits of information hint that the Muscovite authorities were aware of the law forbidding owners to rape their slave girls. One Andrei Bermatskii, a foreigner who in 1626-27 had dined with the tsar, in

78. Watson, p. 365.

79. M. G. Smith, p. 143; Sidney W. Mintz, "Was the Plantation Slave a Proleterian?" *Review* 2, no. 1(Summer 1978): 91-95.

80. *Izbornik. (Sbornik proizvedenii literatury drevnei Rusi)*, ed. L. A. Dmitriev and D. S. Likhachev (Moscow: Khudozhestvennaia literatura, 1969), pp. 690, 693-94; Serge A. Zenkovsky, ed., *Medieval Russia's Epics, Chronicles, and Tales* (New York: E. P. Dutton, 1974), pp. 477, 484-85.

81. Mendelsohn, pp. 11, 50.

82. Westermann, pp. 13-14, 118-119; Fisher, "Ottoman Slavery," p. 36; Ka-Tzetnik 135633, *House of Dolls*, trans. from Hebrew by Moshe M. Kohn (New York: Pyramid Books, 1955); Buckland, pp. 70-71, 603-4; Klein, *Americas*, p. 63.

1633 was tried before Patriarch Filaret Nikitich, boyars, and notables on charges of having fornicated with his limited service contract slave girl in the bathhouse, which caught on fire. Earlier, it was alleged, the slave girl had denounced the foreigner to the patriarch because Bermatskii had raped her, and apparently she had been returned to him, probably because the accusations were not believed. The truth of the bathhouse allegation is unknown, as is the outcome of the case, but this episode does reveal an awareness that raping a slave girl was a legal wrong.[83]

Similarly, there is no direct evidence that slave women were employed as prostitutes on any appreciable scale in Muscovy. On this subject, one may wonder why in 1595 *syn boiarskii* Ovsei Ivanov Pozdeev, an arquebusier centurion from the Bezhetskii Verkh region east of Novgorod, purchased four young women (ages 15, 17, and, for two of them, 20) for a ruble apiece, the rock-bottom price. This, however, is seemingly the sole hint in all the available sources that young women were being purchased on any appreciable scale for unknown purposes.[84]

There is also no evidence that infibulation or castration was practiced in Muscovy, where the slaveowners seem to have been rather less interested in the reproductive systems of their chattel and the manipulation thereof than many of their counterparts elsewhere have been. The Romans, Moors (who desexed Slavs from Rus' in the Middle Ages), the Maracatos in Africa, and many other peoples ventured into that realm, but Constantine, Leo, and Justinian inveighed against such practices, and probably their example and precepts were responsible for the absence of assault by Muscovite slaveowners against the genitalia of their slaves.[85]

Slaves in Muscovite Agricultural Production

This issue has two parts, the role of slaves in producing commodities for the market and the role of slaves in farming the arable demesne that belonged to their owners and which produced some portion of the food the slaveowners, their families, and household chattel ate. It is an issue related to a number of others, such as the extent to which peasants performed corvée labor on the demesne (*barskoe delo, barshchina*), the proportion of all slaves involved in that form of work and in the other occupations discussed here (particularly household service and military service), the introduction of tax-exempt demesne either

---

83. S. I. Kotkov et al., *Moskovskaia delovaia i bytovaia pis'mennost' XVII veka* (Moscow: Nauka, 1968), pp. 49-51, nos. 10-12; DR 1: 876, 881; Horace W. Dewey and Kira B. Stevens, "Muscovites at Play: Recreation in Pre-Petrine Russia," *Canadian-American Slavic Studies* 13, nos. 1-2 (1979): 190. Raping slavewomen was also considered a moral wrong, judging by the 1627 will of Panteleimon Misiur' Solovtsov, in which he begs forgiveness for having sexually assaulted his female chattel (AIuB 1: 558, no. 86).

84. Nosov, *Ocherki*, pp. 352, 360, SBV (1974), p. 251; Samokvasov, *Materialy* 2(1909): 229-30; NZKK 1: 243-49.

85. Buckland, pp. 602-3.

in the mid-1580s or shortly after 1590, and the development of serfdom.[86]

There seems to be no contention that slaves produced much if any of the grain that was marketed in Muscovy, whether the amount required to feed Moscow and the handful of other relatively large cities or the small amount exported to Denmark and other European states after the Time of Troubles. This reminds one of other times and places, beginning with Mesopotamia, where chattel slaves usually performed simple domestic tasks in the households of their owners and were rarely engaged in agricultural production, even on temple lands, although occasionally some slaves helped with harvesting. Agricultural slavery was also rare in Attica, where most slaves were domestics or employed in mining, trade, and manufacturing. Most of the land belonged to peasants, but some of it was owned by landlords, who had numerous small scattered farms and only the home farm, where the owner himself lived, was normally cultivated by slaves. In neither Pharaonic nor Greco-Roman Egypt, a major grain-producing area, did agricultural slavery exist. Slaves employed in agriculture usually have worked on industrial crops and those requiring intensive cultivation, such as figs, dates, olives, grapes, cotton, cane, rice, vegetables, mulberry cultivation, and silkworm rearing. Rarely have slaves been used in grain farming of the type that predominated in Muscovy—rye and oats, some wheat, groats, and so on. A comparative perspective would make one suspicious of claims that Muscovites purchased slaves to farm for them in order to produce cash income, and it seems as though they rarely did.[87]

As in Attica, the holdings of Muscovite servicemen were scattered, and the cadastres list slaves living in their own households at the central estate. That they did so indicates the weakness of the service land (pomest'e) system, which, in theory, was supposed to provide an income for the serviceman which would enable him to render state military and civil service. The 1570s and 1580s especially revealed the weakness of the system and the higher reliability of slave labor.

From the end of the fifteenth century on, the cadastres noted servicemen-pomeshchiki living in the provinces, with slave residences (liudskie dvory) adjacent to them.[88] At the end of the fifteenth century, roughly 2.6 percent of the rural taxpaying households in the Novgorod area were occupied by slaves, about the same percentage (2.8) as was occupied by landholders, who also paid taxes.[89] This meant, of course, that some servicemen had no slaves farming for them,

86. Some Soviet scholars perceive yet another issue, the movement of farming slaves out of barracks (the situation of farming slaves in Kievan Rus') and into their own houses, living thus much like peasants. This process, well under way by the fifteenth century, was completed when farming slaves were converted into serfs by including them on the tax rolls after the census of 1678-79 (Iu. G. Alekseev, "Kholop na pashne," pp. 435-38).

87. Mendelsohn, pp. 106, 109-10; Wiens, pp. 299-300; Hjejle, pp. 83-84, 86-87; A. L. Shapiro, "Barshchina v Rossii XVI veka," Voprosy istorii (1978, no. 11): 46.

88. Jones, p. 187.

89. AIS-ZR (1971), pp. 79-80, 199, 324.

others had more than one. At that time, servicemen probably got considerably less than one-fifth of their income from their demesne.[90]

Probably reflecting the prosperity of the first half of the sixteenth century, which permitted landholders to buy more slaves, the percentage of taxpaying slaves farming their owners' demesne fluctuated by the mid-sixteenth century between 5.7 and 8.3 in northwestern Rus'.[91] In Derevskaia piatina, of 135 service estates that had demesne in 1543, 25 were worked exclusively by slaves, 43 by slaves and peasants together, 12 by the servicemen themselves, and 55 by peasants alone. On those estates using slave labor in agriculture, 74 slaveowners exploited 198 households of slaves. In the 1580s, there were 134 service estates, and 54 of them had 67 slave households.[92]

Whereas slaves had farmed about a fifth of the demesne in Bezhetskaia piatina at the end of the fifteenth century, by the mid-sixteenth century they were farming two-thirds of it.[93] In Bezhetskaia piatina (Tverskaia polovina), in 1545-51, 231 service estates had 446 farming slaves. Those with the smallest demesne (36.4 percent) had one farming slave apiece, the next group (60.2 percent) had an average of slightly more than one and a half farming slaves apiece, and the remainder had just over three slaves each.[94] By 1582-84, this ratio had fallen, so that 367 estates had only 357 farming slaves.[95] According to the calculations of G. V. Abramovich, by the 1590s, when a lord's arable land was freed from taxation, 79.2 percent of the demesne was farmed by slaves, 0.9 percent by the lords themselves, 14.4 percent by peasants; who did the farming for 5.5 percent of the demesne was unknown.[96]

What was true for Bezhetskaia piatina seems to have been true for much of the rest of northwestern Rus' in the 1580s and into the 1590s. As is known, the region was greatly depopulated by the famines at the end of the 1560s, the depredations of Ivan IV's Oprichnina, and the ruinous taxation of the Livonian War. The consequence was that in the early 1580s about a fifth of the population that the census-takers could count was slaves, a radical increase above the mid-century level.[97] Even in the Pskov region, west of Novgorod, where the devastation was less severe, in the 1580s about 7 percent of all those in the inhabited house-

90. Ibid., p. 191.

91. AIS-ZR (1974), pp. 117, 186, 285.

92. Ibid., pp. 57, 72; N. A. Rozhkov, "Sel'skoe khoziaistvo Moskovskoi Rusi v XVI v. i ego vliianie na sotsial'no-politicheskii stroi togo vremeni," in his *Iz russkoi istorii. Ocherki i stat'i*, 2 vols. (Peterburg: Academia, 1923), 1: 165.

93. AIS-ZR (1974), p. 228.

94. Ibid., pp. 215, 221-22. Compare this with AIS-ZR (1971), p. 245.

95. AIS-ZR (1974), p. 230.

96. Ibid., pp. 231, 283. The claim by S. Tkhorzhevskii that the *pomest'e* system, which existed for a century without the benefit of serfdom, employed large numbers of slaves seems untenable ("Pomest'e i krest'ianskaia krepost'," *Trud v Rossii* 1, no. 1 [1924]: 75, 89).

97. AIS-ZR (1974), p. 285.

hold were slaves.[98] Slaves had not fled in as great a proportion as the peasants because of their dependence on their owners, and their owners in turn became increasingly dependent upon them for the greatly diminished income they received. The fact that a high proportion of the slaves did not flee may have taught the landholders to think that binding the peasants to the land, enserfment, would solve their labor problems.

While the evidence that has just been presented seems to be absolutely valid, it raises a number of questions. First, we must recall from table 10.7 that the price of slaves was continuously falling in the second half of the 1580s and in the 1590s. Had there been considerable demand to put such people to work farming the slaveowner's demesne in that period, one would expect a rise in the price of slaves as landholders discovered the utility of putting chattel to work on their holdings. However, precisely the opposite occurred. (One might argue that the price of slaves fell because the value of what they produced fell. However, as we have seen, what they produced was not marketed, so that argument seems largely irrelevant.) Moreover, the fact that lower than average prices were paid for peasants (and beggars), as shown in table 11.3, would hardly support a thesis that slaves were being purchased to farm for their owners.

There seems to be no way to sort out which slaves were purchased to farm the owner's demesne, which were to accompany him to war, and which were to serve in the household. The first two categories were presumably mutually incompatible, for the military campaign and agricultural seasons largely coincided, and the same person obviously could not be in two places at once. It is also likely that most household slaves, who were completely distinct from the farming slaves in that they lived in their owner's house or yard, paid no taxes, and were not counted in the census, did little farming. Olearius observed that some owners forced their slaves to make hay in August. In that respect they were like the Mesopotamian household slaves, who may have helped with the harvesting, or the South China slaves in the late nineteenth and early twentieth centuries, who aided in the planting and harvesting but for whom agricultural labor was a secondary occupation.[99] Such household slaves may be assumed to have been fully occupied with their tasks, and not to have had time to engage in much farming.

After the Time of Troubles, in the areas affected by the disorders of the era, farming slaves may have played a role in working their owners' demesne equal to the role they played in the 1590s, although the census takers presumably would not have noted them on tax-exempt land.[100] While agricultural slaves existed in 1678, when they were abolished as a special status and put on the tax rolls as

98. AIS-ZR (1978), p. 111.
99. Olearius, p. 151; Watson, "Chinese," p. 365.
100. The use of slaves as farming replacements for departed peasants after the Time of Troubles was discussed by A. I. Iakovlev ("Ocherk istorii krespostnogo prava do poloviny XVIII veka," in *Russkaia byl'. Velikaia reforma 19 fevralia 1861* [n.p., 1911 (?)], p. 14).

serfs (restoring their condition roughly to what it had been prior to the 1590s), their importance seems to have diminished by the mid-seventeenth century. Their diminished role as primary agricultural producers seems to be reflected in the law, generally a good mirror of Muscovite reality. In the *Ulozhenie* we read:

> If a service estate is confiscated from someone and redistributed [to other servicemen], and grain was planted by his *delovye* or *naemnye liudi*, the former landholder is to harvest the grain.[101]

Naemnye liudi were hired laborers. *Delovye liudi* are variously defined as "a category of people engaged in some activity [*delo*], either not working the land at all, or not having their own land." Sometimes the "or" was omitted, *delovye naemnye*, indicating that they were free hired workers.[102] (A century and a half earlier, in 1514, *delovye liudi* had been slaves who could be transmitted in a dowry, but they had precise occupations [*khamovnik*, textile worker or weaver; *koniukh*, groom; *bral'ia skatertnitsa*, tablecloth weaver; *tonkopriaditsa*, spinner or flax weaver; *ubrusnaia bral'ia*, scarfweaver].)[103] It is not clear whether the *delovye liudi* of the *Ulozhenie* were slaves, and, if so, what proportion of them were. In 1719 the Petrine Senate described the *delovye liudi* as people "who did not have their own arable, but farmed for their lords [*pomeshchiki*]." They were distinguished from slaves (*kholopy*) in 1722, who were described as "servitors (*slugi i sluzhebniki*) and others (*liudi*) who did not farm for themselves or for their landowners (*votchinniki*), but lived solely off cash and grain grants." The latter were also *boiarskie* (*barskie*) and *dvorovye liudi*.[104]

One cannot determine what portion of the slaves were primarily engaged in agriculture at any time, whether at the end of the sixteenth century or in 1678. Farming slaves were needed initially because landholders could not compel the free peasants to do more than pay them rent. The unreliability of peasant labor was confirmed in the latter third of the sixteenth century. However, the position of the peasants changed, beginning in the 1540s, and by 1678 they ordinarily could be compelled to perform such tasks as farming the demesne, which gener-

101. 1649 *Ulozhenie* 16: 38.

102. SRIa 4(1977): 208; *Akty Morozova*, 2: 31, no. 289. To complicate the issue, *delovye naemnye* might have been slaves rented from someone else, but the "rent-a-slave" business in Muscovy seems to have been too underdeveloped to support such an hypothesis.

103. ATN 2(1897) : 2, no. 2; ARG, p. 114, no. 111.

104. PSZ 5: 619, no. 3287; 6: 717, no. 4026; Rabinovich, "Ofitsery," p. 151; P. Sadikov, "K voprosu o rekrutskom nabore dvorovykh i delovykh liudei 1703 g.," *Arkhiv istorii truda v Rossii* 4, no. 2(1922): 49. For a discussion of *delovye* and *zadvornye liudi*, see A. N. Sakharov, *Russkaia derevnia XVII v. po materialam patriarshego khoziaistva* (Moscow: Nauka, 1966), pp. 89-90. Iu. V. Got'e saw *rabotniki* and *delovye liudi* as slaves (*Zamoskovnyi krai*, p. 203), and Anisimov also considers that *delovye liudi* were primarily slaves ("Izmeneniia," pp. 35-36).

ally remained a small portion of the tilled land.[105] In chapter 18 I shall discuss the total number of slaves in Muscovy, but here I shall only conclude that agricultural slaves must have been a relatively small portion of each serviceman's total holding of chattel.

It is also claimed that slaves were used in Muscovy, as they were in other societies, to expand arable by breaking in new land.[106] A comparative perspective may help to explain that situation. In Iran at the beginning of the fourteenth century the conquering Mongols would not allow peasants access to "dead lands" but had them cultivated by slaves.[107] In the Ottoman Empire, free peasants could not be moved to break in and develop new land, and this became one of the major uses of slaves. Moreover, sharecroppers could be forced to part with no more than an eighth of their produce as rent, a percentage that most lords considered too low, so that those who could, exploited slave sharecroppers to increase their rent, up to half of the harvest.[108] While the Muscovite ruling elite treated the native population as a conquered people in many respects, they did not try to restrict the peasantry's access to land. The Russians were much more flexible than the Ottomans, and ordinarily recruited peasants to break in new lands with settlement contracts containing temporary exemptions from the payment of rent and taxes. Additionally, Muscovite landlords were not so constrained as the Ottomans in the matter of how much rent they could collect from ordinary peasants; when they employed peasant sharecroppers, they made them part with from a quarter to one-half of the crop. Finally, when the employment of slaves to expand demesne would have made the most sense, in the 1590s, when peasants were bound to the land in the enserfment process (a process that made their recruitment more difficult just at the time when the exempting of demesne from taxation tempted some lords to expand such lands), the price of slaves seems to have fallen almost continuously. Thus, while we know that slaves were employed to break in wasteland (see the case of Miakinin v. Velkov, discussed above in chapter 4), considerably more information will have to be discovered before the real significance of such labor will be known.

The issues of profitability of slavery and the productivity of slave labor are largely, but not totally, irrelevant to Muscovy, for slavery's center of gravity lay elsewhere. However, the Leningrad group that produced the distinguised three-volume *Agrarian History of Northwest Russia* presented some findings that are ambiguous. One finding was that a peasant household produced the equivalent of only 0.69 rubles of income a year for the lord, but the slave generated about

105. Hellie, *Enserfment*, pp. 114-16; Iu. A. Tikhonov, *Pomeshchich'i krest'iane v Rossii. Feodal'naia renta v XVII—nachale XVIII v.* (Moscow: Nauka, 1974), p. 118, 120, 171, 173.

106. Abramovich, pp. 7, 11, 15; Petrushevskii, pp. 67-68.

107. Lambton, p. 91.

108. Inalcik, "Servile Labor," pp. 31-32; idem, *The Ottoman Empire: The Classical Age, 1300-1600* (London: Weidenfeld and Nicolson, 1973), pp. 112-13.

1 ruble.[109] On the other hand, by another calculation, a slave working demesne produced a surplus for his owner of 0.115 rubles, whereas the peasant produced 0.175 rubles. The difference lay in the fact that the peasant fed his own horse, whereas the owner had to provide the slave with a horse.[110] The second calculation seems to be the more likely one.

On this issue, one might note that historians of other slave systems have shown that slavery is ordinarily profitable only when the slave can be worked full-time the year around, or employed in industries such as sugar that are highly lucrative in spite of their seasonal nature or in occupations that free people will not practice.[111] Muscovy offered no such outlets for the employment of slave labor. In this context, it is telling that Tsar Aleksei often resorted to the employment of wage laborers for his enterprises created under the umbrella of the Secret Chancellery in the 1660s, rather than resorting to slave labor, as he certainly could have. Aleksei in 1662 ordered that fifty or sixty young Tatar slaves be purchased for him *secretly* in Zaporogi, but he employed them as domestic servants, falconers, millers, and stablehands, not as farmers.[112] (Observe here that the tsar did not want anyone to know that he was buying slaves, and that the market was on the distant southern frontier.) His mentor, Boris Morozov, who employed slaves as supervisors of agricultural labor (where they replaced one another weekly), also found hired labor very congenial, and he ordered the laborers to be worked "from sunup to sundown." Thus from Mesopotamia to Muscovy, the discovery was made that, except in the case of domestic labor, it was frequently cheaper to hire laborers than to own them.[113] Moreover, Ronald Findlay has argued that manumission should be more frequent in societies with higher interest rates, in those cases where economic production was important.[114] Muscovy had high interest rates and almost no manumission, indicating that early modern Russian slavery was of the "household" rather than the "productive" type, the type for which Findlay's economic model is relevant.

Slaves provided little, if any, competition with free labor in most of Muscovite history. As I have discussed elsewhere, the Russian townsman was in straits between 1613 and 1649 because of competition, perceived by him to be unfair, arising from the practice of granting tax exemptions to enclaves in urban areas and certain categories of the population, such as members of the lower service class (cossacks and musketeers, post drivers and artillerymen).[115] My profile of

109. Abramovich, p. 12.

110. AIS-ZR (1974), p. 282.

111. Mendelsohn, p. 96.

112. A. I. Zaozerskii, *Tsar' Aleksei Mikhailovich v svoem khoziaistve* (Petrograd: Petrogradskii universitet, 1917), pp. 163-65.

113. Mendelsohn, p. 118.

114. Ronald Findlay, "Slavery, Incentives, and Manumission: A Theoretical Model," *Journal of Political Economy* 83, no. 5(1975); 931.

115. Hellie, "Stratification," pp. 119-74.

the average Muscovite slave is of a person hardly able to keep himself alive, not of an individual who is about to threaten the livelihood of a healthy, honest, skilled workingman. For the unskilled, on the other hand, the picture well may have been somewhat different. The negative impact of slave competition on the unskilled has been noted in numerous societies,[116] and there is no reason to believe that another situation prevailed in Muscovy.

, As befit an autocratic society, Muscovy knew the extremes in the range of slave employment, from the lowest to the highest status. The period from the 1450s to the 1590s was one of considerable social mobility and fluidity, when seemingly anybody with ambition and talent could at least join the middle service class, become a landholder, and launch his heirs on the route to a relatively secure berth in Muscovite society. Slaves were included in this mobility, and enjoyed a full range of employment in the slave class. In the seventeenth century the range of slave employment diminished, coinciding with the general stratification of Muscovite society.

There can be little doubt that Muscovite slaves were as aware as free men were of status gradations. In East Africa "slaves partaking of urban life felt themselves superior to slaves in agricultural villages . . . , and slaves who lived in the houses of their masters . . . ranked highest."[117] Unquestionably, similar considerations prevailed in early modern Russia, where elite managerial slaves dined at the same table as their owners and even felt so good about themselves that they resented being reminded of their unfree status. The curtailing of opportunities for slaves in the seventeenth century must have had a negative impact on the entire slave community.

116. Mendelsohn, pp. 112, 116.
117. Shepherd, p. 92.

15. The Nature of the Muscovite Slave System: Treatment, Manumission, and the Transition to Freedom

One of the major problems of concern to comparative slavery students is the issue of whether the system under consideration was "mild" or "harsh." There are several components that enter into the formation of such an evaluation. Under the general rubric of "treatment," Eugene D. Genovese summarizes these components as (1) day-to-day living conditions, (2) conditions of life, and (3) access to freedom and citizenship.[1] The first category embraces such topics as quantity and quality of food, clothing and housing; length of working day; and the general conditions of labor. The second includes family security and opportunities for an independent social, cultural, and religious life. The meaning of the third category is clear, and will be discussed after a consideration of the subject of treatment.

In Muscovy in the sixteenth century, the situation was "mixed," but it almost certainly became "mild" in the seventeenth. In this context, one might reflect on David Brion Davis's observation that a harsh form of chattel slavery was more likely to appear in an expansive, fluid society such as the Roman Republic or the United States.[2] Certainly Muscovy was more expansive and fluid in the sixteenth century than in the seventeenth.

Physical Treatment and Conditions of Labor

Very little is known about the treatment of slaves in Muscovy, but probably it was as good as the owner could make it. While some societies were relatively indifferent to the killing of a slave by his owner, few were willing to tolerate sustained, premeditated, sadistic abuse of human chattel. In places ranging from Athens to Zanzibar, ill-treated, ill-used, or starved slaves enjoyed the right to seek the protection of a temple or the sultan, and, if they could substantiate their claims, could expect to be freed at once, or at least sold to another master. Byzantine legislation, expressing fear of civil disorder stimulated by maltreated slaves, not only deprived vicious owners of their slaves but also forbade them ever

---

1. Eugene D. Genovese, "The Treatment of Slaves in Different Countries: Problems in the Applications of the Comparative Method," in *Slavery in the New World. A Reader in Comparative History*, ed. Laura Foner and Eugene D. Genovese (Englewood Cliffs, N.J.: Prentice-Hall, 1969), p. 203.

2. D. B. Davis, *Western Culture*, p. 30.

again to buy others.[3] The fact that Muscovy had no formal institutions for resolving trouble cases stemming from owners' abusing their chattel, and did not
even borrow the Byzantine models, would seem to argue for the fact that relatively few such cases arose. Moreover, works on household management such as
the *Domostroi* (equivalent to the Greek *oikonomikos*) counseled humane treatment of slaves, advice that seems to have been heeded by the vast majority of
slaveowners.[4]

The exceptions seem to confirm the generalization that excessive physical brutality was not condoned in Muscovy. That Ivan IV began to assault slaves when
he was fourteen years old has always been viewed as one of his pathological
manifestations, not as a reflection of the normal Russian slave regime. Certainly
A. I. Bezobrazov, whose slave managers were discussed in chapter 14, was a
brute. However, we know about his activities because they were not condoned.
Every page recounting his activities glistens with blood drawn by the knout and
the whip. Cruelty and brutality were his everyday life. In 1679, during a military
review in Krapivna, he was accused of striking with his fists a tavern chief, Petr
Astaf'ev, who died from the blows. He was later alleged to have beated to death
with his fists (born in 1621, he must have been over sixty years old at the time)
a Borovsk *syn boiarskii*, Ivan Kul'ko, in addition to several of his own peasants
and slaves.

His wrath was exhibited in a 1681 episode, when two slaves, Ivan
Shcherbachev and Grigorii Markov, "unintentionally" and "while not drunk"
lost Bezobrazov's horse and ruined his cart. Certainly such an offense would
hardly go unpunished under any slave regime, but Bezobrazov's slaves feared the
worst, and hid. Shcherbachev approached counselor state secretary Vasilii
Grigor'ev Semenov and Kazan' Chancellery state secretary Mikhail Prokof'ev to
intercede for them, which they did. Their first task was to free Shcherbachev's
wife, who had been chained (*posadili na tsep'*) for her spouse's offense. Semenov
wrote a letter to Bezobrazov: "For God's sake, do not injure him in any way.
Pelageia [Semenov's wife], our children, and I fervently plead with you in this
matter. If you do not show him mercy, I will henceforth not intercede for [you
with the authorities]." Prokof'ev and his wife Praskov'ia also wrote in a similar
vein to Bezobrazov. Counselor state secretary Fedor Leont'ev Shaklovityi wrote
Bezobrazov on behalf of Grigorii Markov: "Show your mercy on them, as God
himself demands mercy."

---

3. Udal'tsova, pp. 22-23.
4. *Domostroi* (Orlov), p. 26, chap. 28. Muscovite works never went as far as did those of
the Ming Chinese, which advised masters to treat bondservants with courtesy, to refrain
from being pompous, to avoid cursing and flogging them: "To use severe punishment will
make bondservants lose their sense of shame, they cannot be governed by moral restraints
and hence they should no longer be kept in the household" (Wiens, p. 306). Of course
shame was not an instrument of social discipline in Muscovy, nor did the Russians regard
their slaves as semi-kin, "adopted sons," as did the Chinese.

Apparently Bezobrazov was excessively harsh in his punishment of the two miscreants, and his relatives and friends condemned him for his violence. Semenov wrote: "I was astonished that for such a small, unintentional offense you showed such lack of charity toward and wreaked such cruel punishment on your slaves. . . . For the sake of God's mercy, henceforth refrain from such cruelty. . . . God has preserved your health; that carts have been ruined is simply a matter of loss which they can work off for you."[5] The entire episode, and the personal intervention of three of the leading figures of the Muscovite government, would seem to indicate that such episodes were hardly condoned by Muscovite public opinion. One should not be surprised by the fact that aberrant individuals, totally unresponsive to public opinion, existed in Muscovy, nor should one by surprised by the fact that many of the revelations about this individual's conduct became part of the historical record during the trial that led to his execution for treason.

Exceptional cruelty by the slaveowner could hardly have any other impact than to encourage brutality from slave stewards in their dealings with underlings. In chapter 14 I noted that Bezobrazov's bailiff Shcherbachev murdered another slave in Bezobrazov's presence, for which Shcherbachev was jailed for two years. His estate stewards also were brutal, never spoiling the peasants by sparing the rod. In turn, if the stewards failed to live up to Bezobrazov's expectations, he had them lashed in public before all the peasants.[6] Once again, the degree of violence that accompanied and was generated by Bezobrazov seems to have been abnormal for Muscovy, seems to have been condemned both by the Muscovite authorities and by public opinion.

Some degree of physical coercion, of course, has nearly always been a common ingredient of human relations. For example, during Nikita S. Khrushchev's visit to the U.S. in September 1959, Americans witnessed directors of the late Soviet leader's entourage slapping assistants in the face in a fashion that was assumed to have ended with the revolution of 1917. That should be contrasted with the memoir of an American indentured servant, Elizabeth Sprigs of Maryland, who complained of "toiling day and night, and then [being] tied up and whipped to a degree you would not beat an animal, scarce anything but Indian corn and salt to eat and that even begrudged."[7] What I assume to have been rare in Muscovy was not the 1959 level of violence but rather the gross sadism exhibited by Sprigs's tormentor or by Bezobrazov, or that evident in the case of Danila Big Beard v. Uvar G. Lodygin, discussed in chapter 16. The early modern world was accustomed to far more interpersonal violence than are we of the twentieth century, and we must not confuse our standards with those of a bygone era. This is

5. Novosel'skii, *Votchinnik,* pp. 16-17.
6. Ibid., pp. 68-69.
7. Barbara Bigham, "Colonists in Bondage: Indentured Servants in America," *Early American Life* 10, no. 5 (October 1979): 83.

evident in the sale descriptions of the slaves in Muscovy, who were frequently observed to have been scarred by knives, dog bites, and other manifestations of violence.[8] The level of early modern violence probably was partly a result of poor nutrition, especially a lack of B vitamins, which made many individuals, particularly those of the lower classes, feel angry much of the time. To my knowledge, nutritional studies of the early modern world, such as those done by Robert W. Fogel and Richard Sutch for American slaves in the antebellum era, and by the Kiples for the Caribbean,[9] have yet to be undertaken, and consequently one can only speculate about the causes of violence in that era.

Unlike Athenian slaveowners, the Muscovites had no philosophers to warn them to treat their slaves well.[10] Sil'vestr, the putative compiler of the Domostroi, was a practical churchman who rose to be a personal adviser to Ivan IV, and his volume certainly had very limited readership.[11] The Muscovite slaveowner's teacher was the experience of life itself.

As a general rule, the Russian slaveowner was obliged to treat his slave with relative decency, or he would run away. The incidence of slave flight was significantly reduced in some societies because of a compact among owners not to receive or harbor others' slaves. In Muscovy, however, slaveowners were engaged in a "war of all against all" on many fronts, one of which was competition for slave labor. The slave could be expected to find a new owner with considerable ease, perhaps right down the street. It was difficult to recover a slave, since a court case initiated for that purpose, even if the slave had only moved across the street, and not 500 miles away, might last for years. Flight was easy, as witnessed by the fact that between a quarter and a third of slaves may have run away. This was also reflected in the prices of slaves, which may have had built into them the assumption that the slave might not necessarily be a chattel forever.

While one would not expect an individual who had complete dominion over another human being to be an angel, one may assume that, as among the Sherbro of nineteenth-century Sierra Leone, there were many self-denying ordinances restraining the Muscovite slaveowner, if he wanted to keep his slave, from treating him with the utmost savagery or from working him from sunup to sundown. As among the Nepalese Nyinba, "the ever-present threat of escape may have served

---

8. Lawrence Stone, *The Family*, pp. 98-99, 102; Andre Corvisier, *Armies and Societies in Europe, 1494-1789* (Bloomington: Indiana University Press, 1979), pp. 4-6. For Russian victims of violence who sold themselves into slavery, see NZKK 1: 155, 158, 182, 311, 313, 335, 436, 469; 2: 206.

9. Paul David et al., *Reckoning with Slavery*, chap 6; Kenneth F. Kiple and Virginia H. Kiple, "Deficiency Diseases in the Caribbean," *The Journal of Interdisciplinary History* 11, no. 2 (Autumn 1980): 197-215.

10. Hopkins, p. 175.

11. A. A. Zimin, *I. S. Peresvetov i ego sovremenniki* (Moscow: Akademiia Nauk SSSR, 1958), pp. 55-70; A. M. Sakharov et al., *Ocherki russkoi kul'tury XVI veka*, 2 vols. (Moscow: MGU, 1977), 2: 135.

to enforce equitable behavior on the part of the slaveowner."[12] The Muscovite slave never experienced a Northwest Coast Indian potlach, in which slaves were killed and thrown into the sea as an incidental aspect of a demonstration of contempt for wealth.[13] Moreover, certainly the Muscovite slave never knew "the living hell" that was the lot of some Athenian slaves in the Laurium mines, Russian slaves in the Crimea, or many African slaves on the plantations of colonial Brazil and Cuba.

A modification of one of the general rules of slave systems may have explanatory force here: slaves born within a tribe, of slave parents, usually were treated much better than those purchased or captured from foreign groups.[14] At present I can think of no way to test this basic generalization for Muscovy, to compare the lot of so-called hereditary slaves with that of military captives. I suspect, however, that the Russians who sold themselves into limited service contract slavery (the majority of the slaves) were closer to the hereditary slaves than they were to military captives. While the limited service contract slave had to be conditioned to absolute obedience, as did the captive, the fact that he "voluntarily" entered thralldom and knew the language and customs of his owner should have made him, on balance, much more like a slave born into his condition than like a foreigner suddenly cast into alien captivity. This generalization is reinforced by the data in table 11.4, which indicate that about 55 percent of the limited service contract slaves had already had some experience with extreme subordination before entering into their contracted servile relationship.

In this context, I might mention two of Frederic L. Pryor's generalizations about slavery that are certainly applicable to Muscovy. First, the relationship between master and slave need not be openly coercive.[15] While I am not aware of expressions of elements of mutual affection and love between master and slave in Muscovite literature similar to those common in Roman literature, I have no doubt that, given the nature of the institution, with one party having total dominance over the other (as in traditional husband-wife and parent-child relations), such sentiments existed. Second, much of Muscovite slavery did not include economic exploitation; rather, there was a symbiotic relationship in which the slaves received benefits from their owners, who in turn also benefited by the relationship.[16] Because of the potentially strong reciprocal element in the master-slave

---

12. Miers and Kopytoff, p. 191. The phrase "work them from sunup to sundown" was in fact used by B. I. Morozov in his correspondence with his estate stewards ("A na delo ikh velet' posylat', kak stanet solnyshko vskhodit', a z [sic] dela velet' spuskat', kak solnyshko siad[et]."), although it is likely that he was giving orders for the supervision of peasants on corvée (*Akty Morozova* 2:31, no. 289); Nancy E. Levine, p. 205.

13. Siegel, p. 366.

14. D. B. Davis, p. 47; Mendelsohn, p. 66.

15. Pryor, "Comparative Study," p. 27.

16. Ibid. On Chinese masters' affection for their slaves, the late Ming sense of reciprocal relationship between master and slave, see Wiens, pp. 294, 305. Reasonable treatment stem-

relationship, one would not expect many Muscovite slaveowners to brutalize their chattel, an assumption which seems to correspond with reality. This tendency may have been strengthened, moreover, by the very low rate of manumission, the fact that the slaveowner expected that he would always own and have to deal with his slave, unlike the American owner of an indentured servant or the Crimean owner of a Slavic slave, whose short period of ownership allowed him to abuse his chattel with little concern for the future.

Again one must recall that many, perhaps even most, Muscovite slaves were an integral part of the family with which they lived. This meant that the slaves knew what was going on in their owner's households. For example, this was the case in one aspect of Muscovite life described by Kotoshikhin, the arrangement of marriages, and it is known from other sources as well. At least among the upper classes, bride and groom did not meet before the wedding. As part of the arrangements, agents of the groom went to inspect the proffered bride. Given this system, apparently some Muscovites could not resist engaging in fraud, putting up a substitute for inspection, and then bringing someone else to the altar. The groom could cry "fraud" in case of substitution, and the patriarch and other church authorities would then interrogate the bride's neighbors and house slaves to determine the facts. If they said that the exhibited bride was the one who went to the altar, the groom was obliged to keep her. But if they said that a fraud had been perpetrated, the marriage was dissolved and sanctions were imposed upon the guilty.[17] The important point here is that Muscovite slaves were part of the family, and such slaves throughout history have been treated considerably better than those impersonally employed in temples, mines, or latifundia. Unquestionably it must have been the nature of the Muscovite family structure, with its rigid boundaries, that inhibited the Russians from going further and establishing kinlike relations with their slaves, as did the Chinese, or incorporating them, as did many African peoples.[18] This adherence to the European pattern of family structure was responsible for one of the distinctive features of Muscovite slavery, a feature particularly evident when Muscovite slavery is compared with slavery in parts of Africa and Asia.

Had they articulated their reality, the Muscovite slaveowners certainly would have echoed the rules of ancient India forbidding quarrels with chattel: "With his father and his mother, with female relatives, with a brother, with his son, and his wife, with his daughter, and with his slaves, let him not have quarrels."[19] This reflects the desired norm where slaves serve primarily in the household and

ming from the symbiotic relationship between masters and slaves has been observed in East Africa by Gill Shepherd (p. 89).

17. Kotoshikhin, p. 156.
18. Mendelsohn, p. 104; Wiens, pp. 294, 303, 307.
19. *Laws of Manu*, 4: 180.

are essentially members of the family. Russian history recorded some instances of slaveowners who suffered considerably because they forgot this fact.

Food is nearly always one of the slave's major concerns, and this was particularly so in Muscovy, where insufficient sustenance was the major factor forcing natives to sell themselves into slavery. The provisioning of food must have been at least equal to the presence or absence of physical brutality when the slave thought about his general treatment, and whether he should stay or flee. The record of the Muscovite slaveowners on that score was not outstanding. Even the usually mild-mannered *Domostroi* recommended feeding lower-level slaves table scraps and leftovers, while the better slaves (in this instance, garment workers) should be fed what the slaveowners themselves ate. The foreign traveler Adam Olearius noted in the 1630s that the "advice" of the *Domostroi* seems to have been followed by many slaveowners, that numerous slaves were poorly fed and thus were forced to turn to crime. Olearius's remarks were elaborated on by the traveler Augustin von Mayerberg two decades later:[20]

> Muscovites keep a relatively large number of slaves [*famulititium serviumque*], but do not expend much on them because they do not dress them in variegated liveries but clothe them in any cast-offs. [Moreoever,] they do not have the custom of providing them with regular rations or a monthy food supply [*duplicarios*]. By law there are many fasts. Besides those, to economize, the owners add several more on their own volition. They feed their slaves the very stalest bread, rotten or dried fish, and rarely any meat. They give them nothing but plain water to drink. When there is a holiday, water is dispensed more generously, being spoiled as near-beer [*kvas*] with a modest dash of malt to lift the spirits a bit. They give their servants no salary [*merces*] of any kind because the vast majority of them are slaves [*servi*] or serfs [*vernae*], and even the free people receive a very insignificant salary. Thus [sic] they never leave the dinner table with a full stomach, and, together with the idle paupers, of whom there are countless multitudes, they lounge about on the public squares without any work, hoping to acquire money to feed themselves and, especially, to buy drink. Not knowing, through their own fault, any honest

---

20. Kolycheva, *Kholopstvo*, pp. 80-81; *Domostroi*, chap. 55; Olearius (Baron edition), p. 149; [Adam Olearius], *Vermehrte Newe Beschreibung der Muscowitischen vnd Persischen Reyse* (Schleswig, 1656; reprinted Tübingen: Max Neimeyer Verlag, 1971), p. 198. (Olearius used the word *kostgeld* where Mayerberg later used *duplicarios*.) A. von Mayerberg, *Iter in Moschoviam* (1661); A. Maierberg, *Puteshestvie v Moskoviiu* (Moscow: Izdanie Obshchestva istorii i drevnostei rossiiskikh, 1874), p. 79. Probably most slaves throughout history have been underfed, and it is difficult to find exceptions or to generalize about them. U.S. slaves seem to have been comparatively well fed, and South Indian *pallans* in the vicinity of Trichinopoly, who were employed exclusively in rice paddy cultivation, were not undernourished or ill-treated, purportedly because of the self-interest of the brahman mirasidars, who also paid their marriage and funeral expenses for the same reason (Hjejle, p. 83). In both cases food was easily accessible, whereas in places ranging from Muscovy to the Caribbean it was not.

trade, they, as worthless good-for-nothings, pursue a life of crime. Either they burgle buildings that are poorly guarded or, having set fire to the dwellings of the wealthy, loot them as they feign to help them. At night, they fall on passersby with naked force and, with an unexpected blow, deprive them instantly of voice and life, so that they cannot cry out to the neighbors for help. Then they take from them their money and clothing. When they are sober, they are always at the ready to pick a quarrel and hurl foul insults, but when they are drunk, they often start fights for the most empty reason and then, grabbing their knives, plunge them into one another with extreme savagery.

No doubt this picture of the "lower depths" could be painted in many other slaveowning societies, for the observation that ill-fed slaves became criminals was by no means unique to observers of Muscovy. The unwillingness of some Muscovite slaveowners to feed their chattel adequately was another manifestation of the absence of generosity and charity already noted in chapter 11, of the ruthless individualism that made the enslavement of natives an absolutely essential element of the early modern Russian scene. Another factor that contributed to inadequate slave feeding was the fact that far too many slaveowners purchased more slaves than they had the means to keep. If slaves received the money listed in the self-sale contracts, they may have used it to tide themselves over the lean periods described by Olearius and von Mayerberg.

Clothing is often mentioned in the same context with food, as is evident in the Mayerberg quotation and from the discussion of legal aspects of the issue in chapter 5. There is little information on the subject for Muscovy. The *Domostroi* recommended that ordinary slaves should be given flax from which they would make their own clothing, while valued garment workers should be attired in lace and silk. The reality of the situation no doubt varied, from those poorly clad observed by Mayerberg to those dressed in finery appropriated from their owners by the fugitive slaves whose raiment was the object of court suits. In the eighteenth century, house servants were often better dressed than were the common folk, and we may assume that part of this conspicuous-consumption element of serfdom had its roots in Muscovite slavery, while some of it certainly was part of the "cost of Westernization."[21]

Slave Participation in Public Life

Numerous problems arise in societies where most slaves are "outsiders," such as whether the slave is to be allowed to keep any of his former identity, and how

21. *Domostroi*, chap. 56; John T. Alexander, *Bubonic Plague in Early Modern Russia. Public Health and Urban Disaster* (Baltimore: The Johns Hopkins University Press, 1980), p. 190; Arcadius Kahan, "The Costs of Westernization in Russia: The Gentry and the Economy in the Eighteenth Century," *Slavic Review* 25, no. 1 (March 1966): 40-66.

he is to be integrated into the new society. For Russians who sold themselves into full or limited service contract slavery, such problems like these probably did not arise. For others, such as Latvians or Tatars, linguistic and cultural friction unquestionably developed and seems to have been resolved by forced assimilation. While "outsiders" were not coerced physically to convert to Orthodoxy, the temptation must have been fairly strong at such times as the mid-seventeenth century, when conversion could lead to manumission. As far as can be determined, there was never any question of a foreign slave's preserving his independent personality or foreign culture in Muscovy. As has been stressed in chapter 12, Muscovy seems to have been flexible enough to incorporate almost anybody, and that seems to have been what happened to almost everybody.

Mitigating the harshness of slavery in Muscovy was the fact that the majority of the slaveowners and their chattel were of the same culture. M. G. Smith, contrasting slavery among the African Hausa and the Jamaicans, has posed the issues well:

> Among the Hausa, master and slave participated in the following identical institutions: religion, marriage, kinship and family, marketing, education and government. They also spoke the same language, shared the same technology, and took part in common economic processes. Both groups had a common lore, a common classical language, Arabic, in which the daily prayers were recited, common conventions, etiquette, and value systems.
>
> Among Jamaicans, masters and slaves professed and practiced different forms of the following institutions: religion, marriage, kinship, family, marketing, education, and government. They spoke different languages, operated different technologies, and took part in different economic processes. They were further differentiated as cultural sections in terms of lore, conventions, etiquette, and value systems. Latin was the classical language of the owners; slaves had none.
>
> It was forbidden for a slave to bear arms in Jamaica, the soldiery and command of Zaria included slaves in all ranks.[22]

In almost every respect the Muscovite pattern was that of the Hausa rather than that of the Jamaicans. Even the language, Middle Russian, was common for everyone.

Religion is an important feature in Smith's typology, and was important in Muscovy as well. The situation was just the opposite of that in the Danish Virgin Islands, where no slaves were admitted to church unless they were domestic slaves in attendance.[23] It is very evident that the slaves of Muscovy had the same religion as their owners and apparently practiced it with them. In the case of Miakinin v. Velkov we saw that the converted Tatar slavewoman Zinka and her

22. M. G. Smith, p. 145.
23. Hall, p. 177.

custodians (the Starinskois) had the same priest.[24] In the case of Voeikov v. Khilkov, one of the defendant's points in asserting his claim to own Sen'ka was that the slave had taken communion in Kholmogory with the priest Kostentin. Moreover, Sen'ka and Khilkov's father, Bogdan, had taken communion together, and the priest Kostentin was willing to testify that Sen'ka was Khilkov's slave.[25] Slaves were entrapped not only by participating in the formal rites of Orthodoxy, but also by church holidays. Lavrentei Kozlov seized his slave Timoshka Vasil'ev while the latter was attending a holiday celebration in honor of Nicholas the Wonder Worker.[26] Coming to the aid of one of his slaves who had been arrested in 1682, *boiarin* V. V. Golitsyn noted that at the time of the arrest his slaves had been in Butyrki celebrating the holiday (the birth of the Mother of God, September 8) as guests of some infantry soldiers.[27] These illustrations show how easy it was for the Muscovite slaves, both native Russians and converts, to join the religious mainstream, a fact that reduced the distance between them and their owners and, if the comparative perspective is valid, served to ameliorate the harshness of their lives as slaves.

We have also seen throughout this essay that Muscovite slaves had access to the legal system, in which they even served as advocates. They were allowed to bear arms, and served in the armed forces (in diminishing capacities) right down to the end of the institution of slavery. They partook of the same economy as did their owners, there were few restrictions on slave employment, and most slaves lived off peasant labor. In the earlier part of the era under discussion, slaves owned (at the pleasure of their masters) considerable quantities of land, which they might have owned before they became slaves, or which they might have acquired while enslaved. The slaves gave such properties to church institutions to provide for their souls, just as free men could. The ever-intensifying mobilization of land for state service after 1556 complicated slave ownership of land, but it still persisted until at least the end of the sixteenth century.[28] Some slaves partook of the same literacy that their owners possessed. Rules for marriage were the same for slave as for free. As far as is known, the corpses of dead Muscovite slaves were not simply thrown away, as they were in societies where slaves were totally despised and usually treated harshly, but were given the same burial as deceased free men received.[29]

24. Iakovlev, *Kholopstvo*, pp. 496-513, no. 25. The *Domostroi* urged slaves to go to church and to participate in holidays (p. 19, chap. 22).

25. Iakovlev, *Kholopstvo*, p. 326, no. 2.

26. Ibid., p. 481, no. 23, III.

27. N. G. Savich, ed., *Vosstanie v Moskve 1682 g. Sbornik dokumentov* (Moscow: Nauka, 1976), p. 119, no. 73.

28. Veselovskii, *Feodal'noe zemlevladenie*, pp. 217, 222-25, 228-29.

29. Nieboer, p. 433. To my knowledge, Muscovite slaves were not buried in their owners' family plots, as was the Chinese practice, presumably inherited from neolithic times, when slaves had their heads caved in so that they could accompany their lords to the other world (Wiens, p. 307).

The clothing worn by slaves did not differentiate them from the freer members of Muscovite society. The available evidence indicates that clothing distinctions were between wealthy and poor, metropolitan and provincial. The inventories compiled when a slave was entrusted to a bailiff in extant court cases make it evident that the wealthy tended to attire themselves in furs and imported fabrics, whereas the poor (including ordinary household slaves) were accustomed to sheepskins, coarse homespuns, and cheaper fabrics. Danilka Big Beard wore a sheepskin coat, a vest, blue summer pants, black cap with a feather, and a silver cross. His mature daughter Marina wore a white frock (*sarafan*), a silver cross, and copper earrings, while his wife Man'ka and daughter-in-law Dun'ka wore sky-blue dyed padded jackets and silver earrings.[30] As far as can be determined, this is the kind of clothing that the lower classes generally wore.[31] It was no doubt this type of clothing that Bezobrazov had in mind when he told his provincial stewards to send their children to him for education and training not in provincial garb but in what was fitting for the capital.[32]

The dress of the more prosperous elements of Muscovite society is revealed in the slaveowners' claims for what fugitive slaves had stolen from their wardrobes, another sign that most slaves served in or had access to the household. A 1545 case lists an overgarment of white Rzheva cloth, six caftans of varying colors and styles, and two white fur coats.[33] Even more elaborate garments (gold-embroidered cloth, silk, pearls) belonged to the elite slave Buian Vasil'ev Panov discussed in chapter 14. This is a far cry from those slave systems, such as in China and Ancient Rome, where slaves were required to wear distinct clothing to mark them off from the free population. Once again, we see that the tendency of Muscovy was to integrate its slaves into the mainstream of social life rather than to keep them isolated and at arms' length from the rest of society.

The Muscovite slave was an integral part of society in still other ways. In chapter 16 I shall look at slave participation in civil disorders, but here I should point out that slaves participated in the suppression of those disorders as well. This is clear in Grigorii Kotoshikhin's account of the Copper Riot of 1662, a disturbance evoked by the debasement of the currency and the counterfeiting during the Thirteen Years War. A group of petitioners went to Tsar Aleksei's residence at Kolomenskoe and appeared to threaten the monarch, whereupon he ordered those who had accompanied him, including slaves, to attack the petitioners. The unarmed mob took flight, over a hundred were drowned in the Moscow River, and about the same number were hanged in the vicinity of Kolomenskoe. Others

30. Iakovlev, *Kholopstvo*, pp. 516, 526-27.

31. G. N. Lukina, "Nazvaniia odezhdy v drevnerusskom iazyke XI-XIV vv.," in *Issledovaniia po slovoobrazovaniiu i leksikologii drevnerusskogo iazyka*, ed. R. I. Avanesov (Moscow: Nauka, 1978), pp. 221-45; G. G. Gromov, "Russkaia odezhda," in *Ocherki russkoi kul'tury XVI veka*, 2: 202-16.

32. Novosel'skii, *Votchinnik*, p. 53.

33. AIu, p. 50, no. 22.

were tortured and burned; hands and feet, fingers and toes were amputated. This was followed by a beating with the knout of the "rebels" and the branding of them with the letter "b" (for rebel, *buntovshchik*) on the right cheek; they were permanently exiled to Kazan', Astrakhan', the Terek, and Siberia. For assisting in the suppression of the Copper Riot, 118 slaves were each given a length of red calico (*kindiak*) cloth to make a hat, and 2 rubles in cash.[34] Muscovite authorities traditionally treated loyalists very well of whatever social standing. This integration even of slave elements into the enforcement arm of the Muscovite authorities was one of the factors that contributed to the viability of the regime and that mitigated the slave regime as well.

Muscovite slaves also assisted in the perpetuation of the regime by adding to their own numbers. Military slaves participated in the capture of foreign slaves abroad, managerial slaves purchased fresh full and limited service contract slaves at home. This reminds one of Africa, where, when slaves participated in raids to acquire additional slaves for their owners and were suitably rewarded, their actions contributed to the stability of their new homelands.[35]

Politically, however, Muscovite slaves remained outsiders. Total powerlessness in the political process is often typical for slaves, whether in the American South or among the Tibetan-speaking Nyinba of Nepal.[36] As far as we know, elite slaves in Muscovy were merely instruments of their owners, whether they were grand princes or landowning magnates. Military slaves certainly did not participate in the elections for local commanders (the *okladchiki* who mustered the troops and recommended compensation levels). On the local level, there is no evidence that either household or agricultural slaves participated in political life, either as electors or as candidates for office. Had slaves been considered full members of society, some of them would have been logical candidates for the elected provincial offices that Moscow demanded be held by literate persons. In listing categories of persons who might hold such offices (middle service class cavalrymen, peasants, townsmen, and others), the central chancelleries might well have included literate slaves, but, to my knowledge, they never did. Moreover, slaves never held such offices. In addition, slaves seem never to have been included in the lists of petitioners seeking redress from the government. Slave grievances were occasionally included in the petitions, but the signatories were the slaveowners. Thus exclusion from the political process was one of the marks of a slave in Muscovy.

34. Kotoshikhin, pp. 103-4; V. I. Buganov, *Moskovskoe vosstanie 1662 g.* (Moscow: Nauka, 1964), p. 86.

35. Burnam, p. 71.

36. Levine, p. 203.

Manumission

There are few, if any, slave systems that have not had to cope with the problem of manumission and the transition of freedmen to freedom. A number of the topics that have been discussed in this work were specific to early modern Russia, but that was hardly the case for manumission. Because of the universality of manumission, it is appropriate to examine Muscovite reality from a comparative perspective to highlight some of its general as well as its distinctive manifestations.

The comparativists have had interesting things to say on this subject. "The ease and frequency of manumission are the crucial standard in measuring the relative harshness of slave systems."[37] These words of David Brion Davis are suitably amplified by an earlier statement from the progenitor of Western hemisphere comparativists, Frank Tannenbaum: "The attitude toward manumission is the crucial element in slavery [, for] it implies the judgment of the moral status of the slave, and foreshadows his role in case of freedom."[38]

In the matter of access to freedom, the sixteenth-century Muscovite system was unquestionably "harsh" for such access was rare indeed. The early modern Russian "full slave" was heritable chattel, and I have slave genealogies lasting more than five generations. In 1597 slaveowners presented their claims to hereditary slaves whose thralldom had been initiated by their forebears as early as the 1430s. In the 1634 court case tried in the Slavery Chancellery, Kozlova v. Kozlova, a remarkable nine-generation genealogy was presented:

A slavery genealogy [*rod*]. Ivashko son of Pavl. Ivashko Pavlov begat Ileika, Ileika begat Fet'ka, Fet'ka begat Iakun'ka, Iakun'ka begat Mikitka, Mikitka begat a daughter Man'ka, Man'ka begat Marfutka, Marfutka begat Timoshka.[39]

This genealogy was not challenged by anyone as being ipso facto absurd, an indication that the Slavery Chancellery was used to such claims. Moreover, given the nature of Muscovite slavery, it does not appear ipso facto absurd, either. (This particular genealogy may have been fraudulent, but that is another matter.)

Owners rarely manumitted their slaves, and almost every known exception can be accounted for.[40] This is reminiscent of the Neo-Babylonian and Late and

---

37. D. B. Davis, *Slavery in Western Culture*, p. 54.

38. Frank Tannenbaum, *Slave and Citizen, The Negro in the Americas* (New York: Knopf, 1947), p. 69.

39. Iakovlev, *Kholopstvo*, p. 484, no. 23, VI. In 1598 Pskov slaveowners submitted claims to slaves that originated in 1512, the year Pskov was annexed by Moscow (AIS-ZR [1978] p. 110).

40. Iakovlev, *Kholopstvo*, p. 143; Kusheva, "K istorii kholopstva," p. 87.

Middle Assyrian eras, when manumission also was rare.[41] Some princes in the early Muscovite period freed their slaves, especially when they had no heirs, or when the slaves were elite palace operatives.[42] The absence of heirs also explains many, perhaps even most, of the private manumissions of the sixteenth century. It is also possible that at least some privately owned elite slaves were manumitted in the same period, a supposition based on the fact that the formula of the registered slavery document mentioned only the slaveowner, not his heirs (who were mentioned in the full slavery document). In the seventeenth century, however, if Bezobrazov was in any way typical, slaveowners were not wont to manumit even their stewards. I have examined twenty-two manumission documents in light of the variables that can be established for slaveowners (rank, position, compensation, landholding, and so on), and none of them seem at all predictive; from those perspectives the manumission of slaves seems to have been random. Eight of the documents manumitted a single slave, three of them two, four of them three slaves, six of them five slaves, and one set free seven slaves. Besides the eight solitaries, one married couple was set free, two couples with one child each, four couples with three children each, one woman with two children. There were also two cases of two children being manumitted, one case of three women, two couples with an unstated number of children (one with a mother-in-law), and one instance of a couple, their four children, and the husband's mother.

Slaves were also manumitted because they were sick or aged. The Hebrews freed slaves for these reasons, but elsewhere (as expressed in a South Carolina statute of 1800) such a practice was regarded as a social abuse and forbidden.[43] The real test of the Muscovite attitude toward manumission presented itself during the famine of 1601-3, when many owners discovered they lacked the means to feed their dependent chattel. In spite of that discovery, according to a contemporary, Avraamii Palitsyn, many slaveowners simply drove out their slaves but refused to give them manumission papers, hoping later to be able to claim the survivors who had managed to fend for themselves.[44]

Thus, a person who became a slave in fifteenth or sixteenth century Muscovy could expect that both he and his offspring would be slaves forever. Bernard J. Siegel helps to explain this from a comparative anthropological perspective: the existence of hereditary slavery is functionally interrelated with a kind of stratification based on a highly competitive system of prestige striving for wealth sysbols, with strong tendencies toward autocratic control.[45] While the generaliza-

41. Mendelsohn, pp. 83-84.

42. Zimin, *Kholopy na Rusi*, p. 311-12.

43. Mendelsohn, p. 65; Catterall, 2: 267-68.

44. *Skazanie Avraamiia Palitsyna* (Moscow-Leningrad: Akademiia Nauk SSSR, 1955), p. 107; I. I. Smirnov, *Vosstanie Bolotnikova*, p. 75. The fact that Iulianiia Lazarevskaia freed her slaves during the Great Famine was recorded as a noble act by her son (Ad. Stender-Petersen, *Anthology of Old Russian Literature* [New York: Columbia University Press, 1954], p. 385).

45. Siegel, p. 370

tion may not describe some societies, such as many Islamic ones, it certainly holds for Muscovy.

Absolutely central to an understanding of slavery is an awareness that a nearly total denial of freedom to slaves is relatively rare. This is particularly the case in systems of household slavery, where access to freedom was typically relatively easy. The reasons for this are not difficult to comprehend. In the first place, with the passage of time, the "outsider slave" becomes an "insider," whose continued enslavement would tend to unravel the social fabric. Second, the close human contact inherent in household slavery generates in many slaveowners a desire to free their chattel, at least in their wills. Third, many lawgivers have found large numbers of slaves not to their liking, and have enacted social programs to diminish the extent of such dependency in their midst.

The human endeavor to limit formally the duration of slavery was encountered first in the Hammurabi Code, which limited servitude stemming from debt to three years, requiring the reestablishment of freedom in the fourth year.[46] The Babylonians also unconditionally manumitted and released by adoption numerous slaves, especially house slaves. Moreoever, the slave in Babylonia could buy his freedom with his peculium, or might be ransomed by his kin. These practices significantly diminished the number of the unfree.[47]

The Hebrews were exceptionally conscious of the problem of extended periods of dependency, and promulgated the so-called "law of release," or "six-year bondage rule." At the time, this was probably applicable primarily to native debtors, although other people subsequently assumed that it had even broader implications. The problem was of major significance in the first millennium B.C., for Solon in ca. 594 and the Lex Poetelia Papiria in 326 completely forbade debt slavery for the Greeks and Romans (among whom it was called *nexum*), respectively.[48] The Muscovites never arrived at that level of consciousness, although they did limit indentures to five years in 1641 in cases where the lord himself was not a taxpayer, in addition to the more general norm discussed in chapter 2 of allowing debt slaves to work off their obligations at the rate of 5 rubles per year.[49]

Probably copying the Jewish so-called "six-year bondage rule," even the Crimean Tatars freed most of their slaves after a half-dozen years.[50] Islamic religious law (unlike Christian church law, which was centered on spiritual values rather than temporal conditions) advocated the testamentary granting of enfranchisement, which was widely practiced and may have been "perhaps the most

46. Pritchard, p. 151, art. 117.

47. Mendelsohn, pp. 46, 78, 104.

48. Exodus 21: 2; Deuteronomy 15: 12-18; Jeremiah 34: 8-16; Nehemiah 5: 2-5; Mendelsohn, p. 85; Adolf Berger, *Encyclopedic Dictionary of Roman Law* (Philadelphia: The American Philosophical Society, 1953), pp. 557-58 [= its *Transactions*, n.s., vol. 43, pt.2].

49. 1649 *Ulozhenie* 20: 116; MS, p. 298; Wiedemann, pp. 37-41.

50. Herberstein, *Commentaries* (1956), p. 109; Fisher, "Muscovy," p. 585.

important factor in eroding the Ottoman slave population."[51] In the classical Islamic world of the Middle East, the class of slaves usually was a relatively small and transitional group of foreigners, rather than a caste with a continuity of status from parents to children lasting for many generations.[52] In Mecca, house slaves ordinarily were manumitted at the age of twenty. In India, "Mussulmans" purchased Hindu children, and after three generations their descendants were considered to be "pure Mussulmans."[53] Islam had the same impact in Africa of encouraging manumission.[54] Among many traditional Africans, slaves (especially women and children) were assimilated into the lineage in that generation, the next, or at most in three.[55] This relative ease of access to freedom for many African slaves was made possible in large part because of the nature of the kinship organization and corporate lineages, with their possibilities for family fission and fusion and the widespread arrangement of fictional kinship.[56] Obviously no one ever heard of a Russian slave or his offspring being incorporated into the family or lineage line of the slaveowner. (Joseph C. Miller makes an important point when he notes that the execution or exportation of male captives in Africa "made impossible the reproduction of a permanent endogamous slave stratum in African societies"; after the overseas slave trade was halted, the wastage of so many males was recognized as a loss that could be coped with, and such a stratum of male slaves began to appear at the end of the nineteenth century. Moreover, there were some African exceptions to the general practice of incorporation and rapid emancipation, such as the Vai of Liberia and Sierra Leone, the Duala of Cameroon, the Nigerian Ibo, the Ashanti, and the self-reproducing endogamous Malagasy [Merina] of Madagascar.)[57] In Thailand, on the other hand, emancipation was considered a pious act and many slaves were enfranchised at their owners' death.[58] Chinese manumission practices varied throughout the centuries, but Ch'ing practice seems to have desired manumission practices of hereditary slaves after three generations.[59]

Naturally, practices were somewhat different in productive slave systems, where the slave not only had a cost but also a real value to be calculated. Nevertheless, Athenian slaveowners were not limited in their right to manumit slaves, and did so with "some frequency."[60] Even in the Roman Empire, slaves could

51. Inalcik, "Servile Labor," p. 35.

52. Curtin (in *Annals*), p. 5.

53. Levy, *Islam*, p. 84; Indian Law Commission, *Report on Indian Slavery*, p. 204.

54. Lovejoy, p. 346.

55. Miers and Kopytoff, p. 282.

56. Lloyd Fallers, in *Aspects of the Analysis of Family Structure*, ed. Marion J. Levy (Princeton: Princeton University Press, 1969), p. 78.

57. Miller, p. 50.

58. Miers and Kopytoff, pp. 115, 312; Watson, *Systems*, p. 31; Bloch, p. 108.

59. Turton, p. 288; Meijer, pp. 337, 342. In 1905-6 a government commission proposed that slavery should end in a person's twenty-fifth year (Meijer, p. 341).

60. Finley, "Between Slavery and Freedom," p. 239.

accumulate in the peculium (an institution unknown to the Muscovites) their own means that might even include other slaves and with their savings buy their freedom, a practice known 1,500 years later as *coartación* in Latin America. Roman slaves even could borròw the means to buy their manumission from clubs of ex-slaves or from a patron, practices unheard of in Muscovy. In general, slavery in Rome did not last as long as it seems to have done in Muscovy, down through the generations.[61] The Roman practice of allowing slaves to purchase their freedom with a peculium created from their earnings persisted into the High Middle Ages.[62] The same practices and ideals were present in medieval Germanic society, where slaves often used their peculia to redeem themselves in three years.[63]

Muscovy was like the Danish Virgin Islands in the eighteenth century or the rural American South, where the norm was not to manumit slaves but to keep generations of offspring in bondage forever.[64] In 1829 North Carolina Judge Ruffin expressed the prevailing opinion that "the slave is doomed in his own person, and his posterity, to live without knowledge, and without the capacity to make anything his own, and to toil that another may reap the fruits."[65] The reasons for the American pattern are obvious: a combination of racism, plantation-industrial exploitation of slaves for profit, the likely calculation that slaves allowed to purchase their freedom would be tempted to lower their value by willful misconduct, and the cutting off of new sources of supply after 1808. The Muscovite situation is more difficult to explain, except in the terms advanced by Siegel above, combined with the general Russian violation of the norms against enslaving one's own ethnos and the fact that the typical early modern Russian slaveowner had few personal alienable or heritable resources (often not even land), other than slaves. Of course Muscovy never went to the extreme of forbidding by statute the manumission of slaves, an incredible interference in the right to dispose of private property that graced the statute books of South Carolina in 1820, Mississippi in 1822, Arkansas in 1858, and Maryland and Alabama in 1860. As far as can be determined, there were no legal limitations on manumission in Muscovy. The law even allowed a father to set free his son's slaves.[66] There is no record, however, of that ever happening, a fact entirely consistent with the general reluctance of Muscovite slaveowners to part with their slaves.

61. Keith Hopkins, "Slavery in Classical Antiquity," in *Caste and Race: Comparative Approaches*, ed. Anthony de Reuck and Julie Knight (Boston: Little, Brown, 1967), p. 174; Knight, *Slave Society in Cuba*, p. 130.

62. Verlinden, *Colonization*, p. 87.

63. Wergeland, p. 94. The Muscovite case seems not to support Yoram Barzel's contention that voluntary slaves should more easily be able to buy their freedom than should involuntary slaves ("An Economic Analysis of Slavery," p. 105).

64. Hall, p. 177; Rose, pp. 187-88; Friedman, p. 195.

65. Rose, p. 222.

66. Barzel, p. 100; 1649 *Ulozhenie* 20: 106; MS, p. 293.

Michael Garfield Smith, comparing the differences in the frequencies of manumission in Zaria (Nigeria) and Jamaica, attributed the difference to dissimilarities in culture, particularly religious culture. In Africa, both master and slave shared a unified, relatively homogeneous culture formed by Islam; Jamaica lacked such a unifying agency, and the pluralistic system emerged there that emphasized the distance between owner and chattel.[67] The Muscovite case causes us to reflect not only about Smith's generalization but also about the nature of Orthodox Christianity and its impact on the various strata of Muscovite society.

At the end of the sixteenth century, the Russian legal situation changed. The government denied the limited service contract slave the right to pay off the principal of his debt (which apparently had been done very rarely, a failure paralleling Moses I. Finley's contention that, in antiquity, "victims once caught up in bondage had little hope of release"),[68] and decreed that he should be freed upon the death of his owner. This theoretically cut off the perpetuation of the generation-to-generation dependency of slave families on particular families of slaveowners. The author of the law of 1597 must go down in history with the author of the Hebrew six-year bondage rule, Solon, and the author of Lex Poetelia Papiria as someone who was aware of the dangers of excessive enslavement of natives, and tried to do something about it. As I have had occasion to observe earlier, all subsequent Muscovite officials rigorously insisted that limited service contract slaves be freed on the death of the owner.[69] In 1690 this was extended to war-captive house slaves and, typically, to peasants who had been brought in from the fields to serve in the household.[70] One would like to know whether the government's insistence on this point was mindless formalism or a persistent, conscious effort, after ignoring the issue for generations, to reduce the enslavement of Muscovites. However, given the nature of the Muscovite sources, it seems unlikely that the question will ever be answered.

A seeming oddity of late Muscovy was the written manumission by widows of their late husbands' limited service contract slaves. Thus from 1676 survives a document in which Fedosia Semenova, widow of Ivan Andreev Pustoboiarov, and her children set free, at her husband's command, his limited service contract slave Aleshka Ivanov; they declared that neither they nor any of their clan or tribe would ever have any claim on Aleshka, that he was free to live wherever he wished. A similar document survives from 1680, when Marfa Borisova, widow of Andreian Ivanov Suvorov, set free his limited service contract slave Iakim Ivanov, his wife, and his children. This was followed by the usual disclaimers for the future, and also the news that the emancipation was without property (*u nego ni*

67. M. G. Smith, pp. 126-29, 146, 159.

68. Finley, "Between Slavery and Freedom," p. 234.

69. PRP 4: 380; 1649 *Ulozhenie* 20: 44, 52, 61, 63, 81; MS, p. 252, art. 7, and pp. 271, 274, 276-77, 285.

70. PSZ 3: 82, no. 1383.

est' zhivotishkov). Although both emancipations were certainly gratuitous, they may have had a point: the formalization in writing of the manumissions probably made it easier for the freedmen to sell themselves again because they could prove that they legally could do so. And that is exactly what happened: Aleshka remained free for thirteen months, and then he, his wife, and three children sold themselves again for fifteen rubles to Aleksei Il'in Nozhnev; Iakim and his wife remained free for twenty-six months, and then sold themselves back to Marfa. The manumission documents were attached to the new sale documents.[71]

The law of 1597 also repealed what some specialists regard as one of the defining (but not essential) characteristics of the institution of slavery: "the right of the superior to transfer the subordinate at any time during his life to the possession of another superior without the subordinate's permission."[72] As we have seen, this right was exercised in only limited ways prior to 1597 anyway, a fact which was not unique to Muscovy. The new legislation, which the government rigorously enforced, made Muscovite practice for limited service contract slaves correspond to what Muslims for a millennium had believed was desirable, the grant of enfranchisement on the owner's death.[73] Moreover, an enigmatic "grandfather" clause, which seems not to have been observed, was placed in the *Ulozhenie* of 1649 prohibiting slavery that was based on earlier hereditary slavery from extending more than three generations.[74] These strictures made Muscovite slavery conform more to the general pattern of slave institutions elsewhere.

The expropriation decreed in the law of 1597 was resisted by some slaveowners but in a sly, devious, sometimes innovative fashion, rather than by actions or declarations that might well be considered treasonous. The most obvious form of resistance was to change the length of the contract so that it lasted not to the death of the lord, but to the death of the slave himself.[75] Then there was the service contract registration (*sluzhilaia kabal'naia zapis'*), one of which survives from 1675. It tried to undo the legislative history of the previous ninety years by having the person selling himself, Lazar' Ivanov, a sixteen-year old, declare that he will serve Vasilii Afonas'ev Grechin, his wife, and their children in their household until the last one of them dies. Lazar' guaranteed that he would not flee and would not steal anything, and, if he did, he agreed to pay them 50 rubles, plus whatever they said the property was worth. In accordance with the reality of late limited service slavery contracts, no sum was mentioned that he was to receive; apparently copying a clause found in indentures, the Grechins promised him that they would marry him to one of their

71. AIuB 1: 595-98, nos. 93, IV and V. See also *Materialy istoricheskie i iuridicheskie raiona byvshego prikaza kazanskogo dvortsa*, 6: 85, no. 64.
72. Pryor, "Comparative Study," p. 27.
73. Brunschvig, " 'Abd," p. 33.
74. 1649 *Ulozhenie* 20: 13, 77; MS, pp. 260, 283.
75. Lappo-Danilevskii, "Sluzhilye kabaly," p. 724, 735, 753.

slave girls or women. The document comes from southwestern provincial Alatyr', and whether it was replicated elsewhere is unknown.[76] It is known, however, that such deviations from the rule that self-sales were for a term were few and were not permitted to overcome the government's insistence on adhering to the 1597 norm.

The 1597 changes were palatable to the Muscovite slaveowning class for two reasons: the rest of society was becoming rigidly stratified, with the condition of the peasant coming to look more and more like that of the slave, particularly as the abasement aspects of serfdom developed; although in law the freedman was almost the sole person in Muscovy by the mid-seventeenth century who was not legally bound to one social estate or another, the reality of his compulsory emancipation, without property, greatly limited his real options. Such people after years of enslavement developed something analogous to what we today would call a "welfare dependency syndrome," in which an independent existence in a competitive society was simply out of the question for them. Emancipation without property, proscribed by other peoples, such as the Hebrews, whose law enjoined slaveowners not to let a manumitted slave "go away empty" but to "furnish him liberally" (*Deut.* 15:13-14), only reinforced the syndrome. Emancipation with property was also practiced in the Ottoman Empire, was found in a few sixteenth-century Muscovite testaments and came to be prescribed in seventeenth-century indentures, but it was not the custom for the majority of slaves, the full and limited service contract slaves.[77] The consequence was that, while some slaves may have used their manumission to become something else, a great number of them (what percentage is unknown) simply sold themselves back into slavery within a short time, often to other members of their former owner's family, such as a widow or son. This feature of Muscovite slavery was observed by the traveler Jacob Reitenfels in his 1690 account of life in Muscovy: "having been set free, many [freedmen] give themselves back into the power of new lords, so that they never become free, always passing constantly from one slavery dependence to another."[78] Had the Virginia planters known of this fact at the time of their debates on slavery in the years of the American Revolution, it would have reinforced their belief that slaves, accustomed to working only under compulsion, would not support themselves when the compulsion was removed.[79] In view of more modern comprehension of dependency,

76. *Materialy istoricheskie* (As n. 71 above), pp. 86-87, no. 65.

77. Inalcik, "Servile Labor," p. 28. Kashtanov, "Po sledam troitskikh kopiinykh knig," p. 56. For example, the will of Kunan Andreev Pisemskii, written in the year 1550/51, prescribed that some manumitted slaves (*delovye liudi*) were to get free grain for a year, others (*dvornye liudi*) could keep the horses assigned to them, and no one's clothes were to be taken away (ibid).

78. Reitenfel's, p. 139. Half a century earlier, Adam Olearius made a similar observation—that when a slaveowner died, his slaves soon sold themselves again (*Travels*, p. 151).

79. Morgan, "Slavery and Freedom," p. 13.

it might be appropriate to change "would not" to "could not," as the Muscovite case illustrates. Thus even compulsory manumission after 1597 was only a formality, but at least the option was present, perhaps mitigating the severity of thralldom for an optimistic few who managed to generate hope for the future.

Reality thus seems to explain what Grigorii Kotoshikhin meant when, in his discussion of the Muscovite chancelleries, he claimed that the Slavery Chancellery gave out "eternal service slavery contracts" (*vechnye sluzhilye kabaly*) on slaves.[80] As we have seen, that was not the case, legally they were "limited" service slavery contracts. In practice, however, a person caught in the slavery net was trapped "eternally" and had little chance of ever becoming an independent, free man again.

Slaveowner anxiety over the law of 1597 was also probably ameliorated by the persistence of what one might call "the worst-case determination of slave status." From chapter 3, we remember that anybody who married a slave became himself or herself a slave (*po rabe kholop, po kholopu raba*), and this formula remained unchanged to the final expiration of the institution. This meant that, for example, if a hereditary dowry slave married a limited service contract slave and the latter was freed by the death of the owner, the limited service contract slave would still be enslaved by virtue of marriage to the hereditary slave.[81] Moreover, their offspring would also be hereditary slaves.

That relatively few Muscovite slaves seem to have been manumitted must have had consequences for others besides the slaves themselves. Societies, such as Islam, which have suffered high attrition because of frequent manumission (or functional equivalents such as high death-rates among New World four-to-seven-year indentures in the mid-eighteenth century or among the slaves dispatched to the Sugar Islands) have exhibited strong tendencies to replace their losses by resorting to frequent slave raids or vociferous support for a continued slave trade.[82] The fact that Muscovy was able to satisfy its needs for slaves by recirculating those it had, with relatively small but usually regular infusions of new ones who sold themselves, probably was responsible for the fact that the early modern Russians placed minimal importance on captives as the major reward for military success and did not need a highly developed internal slave trade.

Part of the same rubric may have been the provision freeing slaves whose owners did not feed them.[83] For one thing such conduct created both potential and real disorder during such periods as the Time of Troubles, when masses of hungry slaves were trying to feed themselves by any means possible. Secondly, a slaveowner's refusal to feed his chattel violated the basic purpose of full and lim-

80. Kotoshikhin, p. 113.

81. RIB 17 (1898): 94, no. 262.

82. Lovejoy, p. 363; David W. Galenson, "British Servants and the Colonial Indenture System in the Eighteenth Century," *The Journal of Southern History* 44, no. 1 (February 1978): 52-53.

83. AI 1: 87-91, no. 44; 1649 *Ulozhenie* 20: 41; MS, pp. 269-70.

ited service contract slavery, the provision of relief for those unable to care for themselves.

While private owners were reluctant to free slaves in Muscovy, the government, for political, economic, religious, or military reasons, was willing to manumit the unfree.

It was Muscovite policy to confiscate the property of those guilty of political crimes, which meant that the slaves belonging to "traitors" were freed. This was a regular practice in the sixteenth century, especially during the reigns of Ivan IV and Boris Godunov, but became complicated during the Time of Troubles, when yesterday's traitor might well become today's hero.[84] That put strains on the traditional policy, but in 1608 the government of Vasilii Shuiskii decided to recognize manumissions made by the government of the First Pretender. However, as a compromise, Shuiskii's regime permitted dispossessed owners to reclaim their slaves if the latter could not produce the manumission documents they had been given by False Dmitrii.[85] The *Ulozhenie* of 1649 reasserted the tradition of freeing slaves of owners convicted of political crimes, and under this statute the Slavery Chancellery freed all of Bezobrazov's slaves after his execution in 1690.[86]

After the *Ulozhenie* of 1649, the government of Aleksei Mikhailovich seems to have wanted to maintain its urban centers and to have recognized that the towns, especially susceptible to such demographic disasters such as the plague of 1654, could only be maintained by infusions from outside. The "normal" process almost everywhere was for the urban concentrations to be constantly refreshed by infusions from the countryside, but this became difficult in Muscovy after the peasants were enserfed. In consequence, the government evolved for the first time in Russian history a modified *Stadtluft macht frei* ("town air makes one free") doctrine, in which from time to time it declared an amnesty for fugitive peasants and slaves living in a town, allowing them to become townsmen. The absolved fugitives were then added to the town tax rolls. Whatever economic motivation there may have been was complemented by the tradition of applying the concept of a statute of limitations to the initiation of judicial actions, as in the five-year limitation placed on the recovery of fugitive peasants in 1592/93 (for other examples, see chapter 8). Relying on the *Ulozhenie*'s directive that townsmen were not to be returned to the peasantry but were to continue on the town rolls, the government decreed in November of 1657 that fugitive slaves (and peasants) who had fled to towns along the southern frontier prior to 1652/53 (7161) were to be allowed to remain there.[87] This, of

84. *Skazanie Avraamiia Palitsyna* (Moscow-Leningrad: Akademiia Nauk SSSR, 1955), p. 109; NKK 7108 (=RIB 15): 13; NZKK 1: 5, 86, 128.

85. PRP 4: 378, art. 2; UKKhP 6; I. S. Shepelev, *Osvoboditel'naia bor'ba*, pp. 128-30.

86. 1649 *Ulozhenie* 20: 33; MS, p. 267; Novosel'skii, *Votchinnik*, pp. 54, 65.

87. PSZ 1: 444-45, no. 217. The story about the freeing of slaves who fled to towns in the second half of the seventeenth century is told in detail by A. G. Man'kov in his *Razvitie*

course, had defensive as well as economic ramifications. Throughout the rest of the century decrees continued to be issued that freed slaves who fled to towns.

Foreign captivity was another avenue to freedom for Muscovite slaves. Variations on this theme are almost as old as human history itself. The Babylonian Hammurabi Code (articles 280-82) decreed the freedom of a native Babylonian slave who was sold abroad and then fled back to his native land. Deuteronomic law granted freedom to Hebrews who fled from slavery in foreign lands.[88] The issue was an especially pressing one in Muscovy because of the role slaves played in the armed forces. The *Sudebnik* of 1497 (article 56) specified that a slave taken captive by a Tatar army was to be freed if he fled captivity. In 1550 (article 80) the provision was generalized to any military captivity, and, in recognition of the dependency created by slavery, permitted the freedman to return as a slave to his old master, whereupon, for the payment of a fee, the old relationship could be reestablished. In 1589 (article 144) the provision for the payment of a fee was dropped and replaced by a recommendation that a major official make a notation on the old slave document.

The *Ulozhenie* of 1649 further expanded the provisions of the *Sudebnik*. It was no longer necessary to have been taken by an army (*rat'*) into a foreign land; any agency was acceptable. Moreover, not only was the slave himself freed upon his return (it no longer applied just to escape) from captivity, but his wife and children were manumitted as well, "for his suffering in captivity." The 1550 provisions allowing for a voluntary renewal of the master-slave relationship were also repeated in 1649. Reflecting the increasing specificity of the law in general, the *Ulozhenie* went on to state that a slave who committed treason by going over to the enemy or by fleeing abroad would not be manumitted upon return to Muscovy, nor would a fugitive who fell into captivity while in the illegal custody of a second slaveowner.[89] The broadened coverage offered freedom to those who had been in foreign captivity and then were ransomed. Beginning in 1551 the government interjected a religious motif into the question (the likely profanation of Orthodox souls) and initiated a practice of trying to ransom Muscovites held in foreign captivity, and instituted a special tax (*polonianichnye den'gi*) to pay for it. In 1649 the government legislated the fact that it was willing to pay 15 rubles to ransom a slave (or peasant) from foreign captivity.[90] The government expended massive sums buying its subjects out of Tatar captivity, but how many of those so ransomed were slaves is not known. Moreover, influential military figures sometimes initiated special quasi-private efforts to recover their favorite slaves from foreign hands, as evidenced by the efforts of

---

krepostnogo prava v Rossii vo vtoroi polovine XVII veka (Moscow-Leningrad: AN SSSR, 1962).

88. Mendelsohn, pp. 63-64.
89. 1649 *Ulozhenie* 20: 34-36; MS, pp. 267-68.
90. 1649 *Ulozhenie* 8: 7; MS, p. 32.

Prince Semen Prozorovskii to recover his slave Sergei Ivanov from Swedish captivity in 1611.[91] In theory the slave could have asked for his freedom, but one may be relatively sure that a combination of gratitude and dependency forced him back into the arms of his owner.

The Orthodox church became involved in the issue of ransoming Muscovites from foreign captivity out of concern for the salvation of their souls. The tax for ransoming Orthodox from foreign captivity was a product of the 1551 Hundred Chapters church council.[92] Religious concerns also paved other roads to manumission as well. In an attempt to garner more souls, the Orthodox church persuaded the government to allow non-Orthodox slaves to convert to Orthodoxy and then buy their way out of slavery.[93] The measure, it should be stressed, was not an expropriation, for the slaves had to pay for their freedom or other Orthodox paid the redemption sum for them.[94] This spirit is reminiscent of papal concern in the 1430s over Genoese exportation of baptized slaves to Islamic Egypt. The government of Genoa replied that it was living up to its obligations: upon embarkation, Catholic representatives interviewed the chattel to sort out Christians and potential converts. The actual or would-be faithful were then taken off the ships and sold to Christians.[95] As in the Muscovite case, the servile condition of the Genoese human cargo was of no concern to the pope, who was aroused only because Christian souls might be lost to Islam. As we have seen in several instances throughout this work, in Muscovy prisoners of war and other captives converted to Orthodoxy and never were manumitted, and in fact never even contemplated manumission. On the other hand, during the Thirteen Years War some prisoners of war not belonging to private individuals were freed if they converted, and were even given a monthly ration to tide them over the adjustment period.[96] This was more in the spirit of the famous 1772 English case of *Somerset v. Stewart*, in which it was held that "a notion had prevailed, if a negro came over, or became a christian, he was emancipated."[97]

For the Orthodox church the issue was souls, not slavery. In this sense it

91. DAI 2: 56, no. 31.

92. *Stoglav*, pp. 224-45, chap. 70.

93. 1649 *Ulozhenie* 20: 70-71; MS, pp. 280-81. Without amplifying, Herberstein in the 1520s claimed that foreign slaves were freed in Muscovy if they accepted Orthodoxy (*Commentaries*, pp. 50, 52). It is not clear whether the expropriated owners were compensated for their loss, to what extent such a provision was utilized, or for how long it remained in effect. As noted in chapter 11, prisoners of war sometimes sold themselves into limited service contract slavery. For all one knows, they may have converted to Orthodoxy, been freed without resources, and then forced to sell themselves to survive.

94. Arkhangel'skii, *O sobornom Ulozhenii*, pp. 38-40.

95. Verlinden, *Colonization*, p. 93; Kenneth M. Setton, *The Papacy and the Levant (1204–1571)*, vol. 2, *The Fifteenth Century* (Philadelphia: The American Philosophical Society, 1978), pp. 46-48 (= APS *Memoirs*, vol. 127).

96. Iu. V. Arsen'ev, "Smes'," *Chteniia* 196 (1901, bk. 1), pt. 4, p. 4.

97. Catterall, 1: 15.

epitomized the otherworldly strain of Christianity, the concern for salvation and the neglect of earthly cares. Unlike Islam, Orthodoxy did not advocate private manumission as an act of faith. Like Father Antonio Vierira, who preached patience and martyrdom to plantation slaves in Bahia in 1633, the Orthodox church collaborated in every conceivable way to make it possible for the secular authorities to rule over a docile mass. In 1667 Virginia enacted a law repealing the understanding that baptism would free a slave, and in 1671 Maryland reversed its position that only pagans could be enslaved and decreed that baptism there would no longer produce manumission.[98] That, too, was the basic Orthodox position, although the Muscovites were willing to hold out the carrot of freedom to the heterodox who might be willing to convert and buy their freedom. Of course no such avenues were offered to those who were already Orthodox and might want to buy their freedom. On that subject, the Orthodox church had nothing to say.

Perhaps the major government-inspired route to freedom for Muscovite slaves was military service. The width of that route is a good gauge of the military pressure sensed by the oligarchs running the early modern Russian political establishment. The first major manumission of slaves for military purposes occurred after the annexation of Novgorod, when Ivan III needed additional forces to garrison northwestern Rus'. He partially solved the problem by assigning land grants (*pomest'ia*) to elite military slaves, who were thus converted into members of the middle service class.[99] It is safe to assume that similar manumissions followed upon the annexation of other regions. Among the 519 servicemen in the 1574 Smolensk muster list, not one is from a known family, and the assumption is that many of them were manumitted slaves.[100]

Prisoners of war were usually the booty of those who captured them. The major exception was elite prisoners, who were claimed by the state power as pawns to be held for extortionate ransom or exchange for major Muscovite figures. Another exception was made for prisoners who were willing to serve Moscow. Given the amorphous nature of what it meant to be a Muscovite and the perceived shortage of military manpower, such free access to service is not at all surprising. Ivan IV is known to have freed captives gathered in the Livonian War on condition of their service in the Muscovite forces. The same was true during the Thirteen Years War, when on December 22, 1657, the government issued an edict freeing Polish prisoners of war from slavery on the condition that they serve in Tsar Aleksei's army. These particular individuals had been captured as a group of fifty when Polotsk was taken, and had been distributed to various

---

98. Klein, *Americas*, p. 50.
99. RIB 22 (1908): 30-31; AIS-ZR (1971), pp. 334-37.
100. Makovskii, *Razvitie*, p. 184; M. V. Murav'ev. "Razbornaia desiatnia 1574 goda po Smolensku," *Letopis' istoriko-rodoslovnogo obshchestva v Moskve* 34 (1913, no. 2): 69-99. 69-99.

towns. They sat in jail on monthly rations provided by the state for about eighteen months in Novgorod, and then were forcibly enslaved by Ivan Golitsyn. In Muscovite service they were given ranks comparable to those they had held in Polish service.[101] One may assume that comparable terms were available to other prisoners of war.

The Time of Troubles, like any civil war, saw the stretching of concepts that would have been unheard of under other circumstances. On an ad hoc basis, P. P. Liapunov promised freedom to slaves who would join the militia that was attempting to liberate Muscovy from Polish occupation.[102] More enduring was a principle that fugitive slaves (and also peasants, according to the linkage that was becoming customary) who as cossacks had participated in the liberation of Moscow from the Poles prior to the election of Mikhail Romanov could claim their freedom for their service to the motherland. This principle was promulgated annually between 1613 and 1616, was noted in correspondence between the Slavery Chancellery and the Cossacks Chancellery, and was codified in 1620. The government assumed, naturally, that many of those fugitive slaves were dependent types who sooner or later would want to sell themselves back into slavery. It is clear that they could sell themselves back to their old owners, but, regrettably, the law breaks off before it states whether or not such fugitives who had been in the cossacks could sell themselves to someone else. However, the law seems to indicate that self-resale to another owner might be permissible.[103] The important point is that the principle was being established that military service to Muscovy could lead to freedom for slaves. The cossacks argued for adherence to this principle during the Smolensk War, but the government refused to grant freedom to fugitive slaves in their ranks until January 25, 1634, by which time the war had fundamentally been lost.[104]

The gunpowder revolution and the introduction of the new formation regiments, first during the Smolensk War and then during the Thirteen Years War, threw a different light on the role in warfare of the common man, even that most common man, the slave. We saw in chapter 14 that slaves had played a role in bow-and-arrow cavalry warfare, either as elite cavalrymen or as much more lowly, essentially noncombatant baggage-train slaves. But the new formation regiments, particularly the infantry, were different: there was no mystique about being drafted into the infantry and taught to fire a musket. During the Thirteen Years War, as Muscovy dipped ever deeper into its manpower pool for recruits, those responsible for finding cannon fodder for the military machine realized that slaves would do as well as anyone else. And so they proceeded to

101. Arsen'ev, "Smes'," pp. 2-4.
102. A. A. Zimin, "Nekotorye voprosy istorii krest'ianskoi voiny v Rossii v nachale XVII veka," *Voprosy istorii* 14, no. 3 (March 1958): 103.
103. AI 3: 90, no. 92, I; PRP 4: 381-82.
104. B. F. Porshnev, "Sotsial'no-politicheskaia obstanovka v Rossii vo vremia smolenskoi voiny," *Istoriia SSSR* 1, no. 5 (1957): 130-31, 133-34.

draft slaves into the new formation cavalry (*reitary*), dragoons, and infantry. This was the first time that slaveowners had been forced to part with their chattel, without compensation, to any significant degree. Of course slaveowners had been furnishing military personnel for decades, but in the new formation regiments the slaves and their owners did not necessarily serve together, as they had in the traditional "Russian formation" regiments. It is not clear why (perhaps it was by analogy with prisoners of war), but out of that service developed the principle that a slave should be freed upon discharge, even if no foreign captivity had intervened.[105] The same principle was applied to peasants drafted into the new formation regiments: they also did not have to return to their old lords upon completion of their military service. Thus arose the principle that two centuries later may have had such an important impact on the emancipation of the serfs: since military service was to be followed by emancipation, how were large, ready reserves based on short-term, universal service of all males to be created without thereby either freeing all males or sending worldly militants back to the volatile serf world? The 1861 solution was to solve the problem "backwards": free everybody first, and then run all the males through a relatively short course in the army. As for so many other post-Muscovite developments and features of Russian life, we should not be surprised to find an impact from the institution of slavery on the emancipation of the serfs.

A logical consequence of freeing slaves who had been drafted into the army was to manumit fugitives who performed comparable military service. This, of course, touched a raw nerve for the slaveowners, and they complained bitterly about it during and after the Thirteen Years War. The government, nevertheless, was beginning to assume that its needs for military personnel outweighed those of the slaveowners, and in late 1675 decreed: "without a special order from the sovereign, do not return [fugitives] to slavery [*kholopstvo*] or serfdom [*krest'ianstvo*], to their service landholders and patrimonial estate owners because those troops have been trained in the new cavalry, lancer, dragoon, and infantry formations and are required for present service and the [forthcoming] campaign."[106] The same provision was made in 1683 for fugitive slaves who had served in the Chigirin campaign against the Crimea prior to May 3, 1681, and in 1698 Peter the Great freed from a return to slavery all those (and their descendants) who had been registered in 1675 or 1680 in frontier military service. These seventeenth-century developments helped to set the stage for the abolition of slavery by Peter the Great.

There were two other routes to manumission in Muscovy. One, the freeing of prisoners of war at the conclusion of peace treaties, has already been discussed in chapter 2.[107] The route used by most slaves, of course, was flight, one of the topics of chapter 16.

105. Kotoshikhin, p. 138.
106. Novosel'skii, "Kollektivnye chelobitnye," p. 343.
107. 1649 *Ulozhenie* 20: 69; MS, p. 280.

The Transition to Freedom

A comparative perspective would lead one to predict the inability of freedmen to adjust fully to the requirements and exigencies of a competitive society in Muscovy. Many societies in which slaves were regularly manumitted had some intermediate status between slave and free for such people. In North Babylonia the freed slave became the adopted son or daughter of the manumittor.[108] The Roman freedman, or *libertinus*, had client ties lasting for three generations to his former owners, who protected him. The Romans accepted slavery as an established custom, the product of war, but felt that it was without moral foundation, was contrary to nature, and conferred no lasting stigma on its victims. Becoming an insider by gradual assimilation, the ex-slave was accepted as a Roman citizen.[109] In third-century Syria, a manumitted slave preserved ties resembling indentured service (*paramone*) to his former owner.[110] In China, as in Rome, it took three generations for a liberated slave to regain a completely free status with no dependency upon anyone.[111]

Among most Muslims, the freedman immediately enjoys the same full legal capacity as the freeborn, but both he and his male heirs in perpetuity remain attached to the emancipator and to his or her family by a bond of "clientship," in which the former owner is the "patron" of his client.[112] It is claimed that many freedmen preferred a continuance of supervision.[113] In Palestine, after the First Crusade, a freedman continued to be closely bound to his patron and could not initiate a suit against him.[114] The kinless Germanic slave also experienced various forms of clientage and a "half-free" transitional status that might last as long as three, or even five, generations.[115] Whereas late medieval English customary law "had little to say about slaves," it had "plenty to say about the recently freed man, how long he should have held land before he could claim hereditary title to it, who were his heirs, and if had had no heirs, to which lord his land should revert."[116] Muscovy knew none of this. Slavery was abolished in Portugal in 1869, but freedmen continued to exist as a distinct legal class until 1878.[117] (In all of these cases freedmen were in some respects only "quasi-free"

108. Driver and Miles, 1: 227.
109. Hopkins, p. 175.
110. Marinovich, p. 114.
111. *Encyclopaedia Britannica* 4 (1974): 408; James L. Watson, "Chattel Slavery in Chinese Peasant Society," *Ethnology* 15, no: 4 (October 1976): 370.
112. Brunschvig, p. 33.
113. Levy, *Social Sturcture of Islam*, pp. 81, 84.
114. Verlinden, *Colonization*, p. 82.
115. Wergeland, pp. 110-53.
116. Cicely Howell, "Peasant Inheritance Customs in the Midlands, 1280–1700," in *Family and Inheritance. Rural Society in Western Europe, 1200-1800*, ed. Jack Goody et al. (Cambridge, England: Cambridge University Press, 1976), p. 121.
117. Verlinden, *Colonization*, p. 40.

but not in the sense used by John Hope Franklin to categorize the racist restrictions placed on U. S. free Negroes.)[118] Even in the antebellum United States there were provisions for a transition to freedom. Article 188 of the Louisiana Slave Code of 1824 provided that "the act of emancipation imparts an obligation on the part of the person granting it to provide for the subsistence of the slave emancipated, if he should be unable to support himself."[119] Similar provisions were found in most U. S. state laws on emancipation. In much of West Africa, the transition process was taken care of by assimilation. Not only were offspring of slave concubines assimilated, but most other slaves were largely absorbed into the lineage in one to three generations. The freedman became a kind of relative and had a continuing association with his former owner, participating in family events while the ex-master helped the freedman's sons to get married and established.[120]

Kievan Rus' had a transitional status that could be resorted to by freedmen, that of *izgoi*, which relied on the church for succor. Medieval Rus', in one of the legal statutes that was borrowed from Byzantium, also recognized the special status of freedmen by forbidding them to testify against their former owners.[121] The Muscovites as well recognized the problem of the freedman when during the Thirteen Years War the government manumitted and gave a monthly ration to prisoners of war who would convert to Orthodoxy.[122] Other than that, however, the Muscovites evidenced little concern for the freedman. There was no transitional status for ordinary marginal individuals, a fact that greatly complicated the return of emancipated slaves to freedom. In this sense, Muscovy was like some parts of the Ancient Near East, where a man could be a slave one day and "freed the next, and, once freed, all ties with his former master were cut off."[123] Muscovy also was like Thailand, where there was no freedman status, except in the case where a free man married a slavewoman and redeemed her, and then she assumed a status below that of a second (free) wife and above a slave wife.[124] One might recall at this juncture that Muscovy, those parts of the Near East being considered here, and Thailand all shared the common feature of having many slaves who were natives.

The similarity between the condition of the manumitted Muscovite slave and that of freedmen in Jamaica at the beginning of the seventeenth century is striking:

118. John Hope Franklin, *From Slavery to Freedom. A History of Negro Americans* (New York: Knopf, 1974), chap. 11.
119. Rose, p. 177.
120. Klein and Lovejoy, in Gemery and Hogendorn, pp. 190, 192.
121. Zimin, *Kholopy*, p. 48; *O poslusekh* (part of the *Knigi zakonnye*), arts. 16; 28.
122. Arsen'ev, "Smes'," p. 4.
123. Mendelsohn, p. 122.
124. Turton, p. 269.

[T]he economic circumstances of the free blacks were usually such as to imperil their own subsistence and prevent [their purchasing their freedom]. On purchasing his freedom, the black slave surrendered all his rights to allowances of food, clothing, tools, housing, garden land, medical attention, and other benefits from his former master, and ceased to be a member of the estate community, setting forth, an isolated individual, with no rights in land on the grim task of earning his livelihood in a society which had little place for free labor.[125]

After 1649, the evironment was somewhat different, as serfdom developed, providing a comfortable position for the freedman in a state of continuing dependency on the master. This is somewhat analogous to the status of the first-generation *libertinus* in Byzantine legislation over a millennium earlier.[126]

Why Muscovy did not develop a special transitional status for freedmen, especially after 1597, remains a mystery. Given the nature of the Muscovite legislative process, however, one may surmise that nothing happened because no such trouble cases demanding resolution arose in the Slavery Chancellery. This was so because the solution for freedmen who could not adjust immediately to freedom was clear: sell yourself back into slavery. In one sense, no special status was necessary, for most of the slaves were natives of the culture anyway. This may have been the government's "reasoning" on the matter. But in another sense, a special status was needed (if the governmental oligarchs were really serious about reducing the number of slaves) to assist freedmen, particularly those manumitted without property, in overcoming the shock of independence. Since there was no transitional status, dependence was assured; the freedman had little choice other than to follow the dictates of his psychological condition and sell himself back into slavery.[127]

125. M. G. Smith, p. 101.
126. Udal'tsova, p. 28.
127. In this context, a comparison between the status and experience of the Muscovite freedman and the freedmen in the British Caribbean and the U.S. South may be relevant. The British usually provided for a transitional "apprenticeship" stage for those manumitted by the abolition of slavery in 1831. In the South, except for the activities of the Freedmen's Bureau, there was no transitional status. Yet the consequences for the freedmen were about the same in both places (Stanley L. Engerman, "Economic Aspects of the Adjustments to Emancipation in the United States and the British West Indies" [Paper presented at the University of Chicago Economic History Workshop, January 30, 1981]). Slaves who were freed in the New World grew up in a climate that placed a high premium on freedom, and they had little alternative but to adjust to it. For many freedmen, the adjustment was not easy, and hunger forced some of them to steal and to resort to other survival techniques (Steven Hahn, "The Roots of Southern Populism: Yeomen Farmers and the Transformation of Georgia's Upper Piedmont, 1850-1890" [Ph.D. diss., Yale University, 1979], p. 287; Litwack, *Been in the Storm So Long*). The Muscovite freedman, on the other hand, did not grow up in a climate that placed a premium on freedom. He had the cushion of slavery to fall back onto, and the cushion was often used.

From my perspective as a student of Muscovite slavery, the American slave system seems to have been legally and morally among the most harsh the world has ever known. This seems to have had two primary causes: (1) America claimed to be a democracy. This meant that free people had to be distinguishable from slaves, and the distinction was arranged by excluding slaves from certain spheres.[128] Initially, slaves were excluded from elite employments, and later this was extended even to blue-collar employment. "Democracy" gave free reign to the basest instincts of the free provincial and urban demos. (2) North America was settled primarily by northern Europeans, who unlike Mediterranean peoples, had no prior experience with nonwhites (Orientals, Arabs, Africans). Coming into contact with black Africans, they were afraid of them, a fact that engendered the particular racist and exclusionary aspects of North American slavery.

Muscovite slavery was poured into neither of these molds. Muscovy was not a democracy, and, far from fearing people of other nationalities or races, the Muscovites absorbed "outsiders" with comparative ease. Moreover, Muscovite slavery was conditioned by the fact that most slaves were "insiders," natives already accustomed to the society and in fact part of it. Much of the tension of early modern Russian slavery stemmed from the attempts to make "insiders" into "outsiders," and the fact that it was so easy for "outsiders" to become "insiders." In daily life the tension was resolved by relatively benign treatment of people who were in most respects part of the functioning society, distinguishable as much by wealth and social standing as by freedom or race. Not benign was either access to freedom or the transition to freedom. This seems to have been the consequence of the rulers-legislators' making the decision that slaves really were not worthy of freedom, a decision that was self-fulfilling, as freedmen and even many fugitives recycled themselves back into slavery.

128. On this topic, one might note the comment by the historian of medieval Germanic slavery: "[T]he free and omnipotent warrior needs the slave as his social contrast. . . [in] the North, untouched by Roman influences. . . , the slave[was]most absolutely subjected" (Wergeland, p. xii). On the U.S. Southern sentiment that it might be necessary to free slaves if they proved that they could fight, see Litwack, p. 43.

16. Slave Volition and Resistance to Slavery

To speak of the volition that a slave has seems to be a contradiction in terms, for theoretically a slave is a chattel, an extension of his owner. Reality, however, is different. The extent of slave volition varied greatly from society to society, and ranged from the possible choice of his own occupation (as we have seen, some slaves were told to produce a rent for their owners, and how they got it was of little concern to the masters) to the preservation, definition, and choice of his culture (most, but not all, slaves adopted the culture of their owners) to whether he would resist his enslavement. Except for the last issue, there is very little evidence on how much volition Muscovite slaves exercised. As I noted, the practice of turning slaves loose in exchange for an annual rent payment seems to have been unknown in Muscovy, although it was widely practiced in later serfdom.

Choice of Owner

There was one area of slave choice present in Muscovy that was not present in most slave systems, namely, the choice by the first-generation full or limited service contract slave of who his owner would be. As far as I can determine, at least some slaves were quite discriminating in their choice of owners. The fact that this was possible in itself says perhaps quite a bit about the nature of Muscovite slavery.

One might imagine that a person who was in such great stress that he was compelled to give up his freedom, who in all probability had allowed his girls to die for lack of food and clothing, would not be in a position to be very discriminating about the person to whom he was about to sell himself, would not be in command of a seller's market. In most cases the slave-to-be may not in fact have had much control over his destiny. Nevertheless, certain patterns of resales do exist, and it may be not illogical to extend some of the discretion exhibited there to initial sales as well.

For the 2,091 extant limited service slavery contracts, it can be determined in 282 (13.5 percent) of them that the slave was previously owned, and who the former owner was. In 85 percent of the cases, the prior owner was not related (as far as can be determined) to the purchaser of the document currently being registered. In the rest of the cases, the prior owner was the brother-in-law in one case, the brother in eight cases, the uncle in one case, the father in twenty-two

534

cases, the husband in two cases, the son in two cases, the son-in-law in one case, and an unspecified relative in six cases. That slaves would sell themselves to heirs or relatives of the deceased is certainly understandable. Most, however, sold themselves to a person with no visible links to the deceased. This seems most likely (but of course not certain) in cases where the owner died at the front or had his property confiscated. Slaves seemed to pick as a second owner a person who had traits similar to those of his first owner. If the first owner was a professional scribe, the second was very likely to be also. The same was true when the first owner was a member of the middle service class (primarily a *syn boiarskii*), or of the lower upper service class (Moscow *dvorianin, striapchii,* or *stol'nik*). Even more striking is the fact that Russians who had belonged to non-Russians (primarily Orthodox Tatars in Muscovite service) often resold themselves to the same type of person. It is also notable that a similar pattern can be detected for fugitive slaves: the litigants contesting in court over the ownership of a slave were often very much alike. (It is possible, of course, that some of the second purchasers had become acquainted with the slave while he was still in the possession of his first owner because of common associations among the various groups of slaveowners. Similarly, a defendant may have enticed a fugitive from the plaintiff's house. The extent of these associations remains veiled.)

Some of the dynamic of the dissolution of an estate on the owner's death is evident in the case of Stepan Istomin Rakhmanov, a centurion of Novgorod *strel'tsy* in 1591/92. He had lands in Gruzinskii and Soletskii pogosty of Votskaia piatina. He was a young man at the time of his death, in late 1599 or early 1600, if one can judge by the fact that his land compensation entitlement was only 250 cheti and the fact that he was married only in 1594 (at which time his father-in-law, Gerasim Ianysh Murav'ev, presented him with the woman Annitsa—Utka, "the duck"—as a dowry). Between 1594 and 1598, Rakhmanov purchased three other slaves, three adult males, in separate transactions, for the sum of 11 rubles. About 1600 Rakhmanov died, or was killed. It is unknown what happened to the four slaves he registered in 1598 (although one may assume that his wife kept Utka), but the records note the fate of three other slaves that had belonged to him: on January 20, 1600, a single male, age twenty-five, who had been orphaned when very small, sold himself to Rakhmanov's father-in-law, Gerasim Ianysh Murav'ev, for 2 rubles; a boy of twelve sold himself to Rakhmanov's brother-in-law, Trefil Gerasimov Murav'ev; and a lad of eighteen sold himself for 3 rubles to Nekar' Alekseev Obolnianinov. Nothing more about Obolnianinov seems to be known other than that he also lived in Votskaia piatina; whether he was related to Rakhmanov or the Murav'evs, for example, is not evident. One may assume from the fact that the beards of the black-haired eighteen and twenty-five-year-olds were going gray (*us vysedaet*) that these young men were under stress. Nevertheless, the system of slavery prevented them from breaking down completely, and it was particularly convenient that in-laws were right at hand to take over when a slaveowner died.[1]

A relatively high proportion of Muscovite slaves fled, but certainly the majority of them remained with their owners until they or the owners died. When an owner died in the seventeenth century, his limited service contract slaves were manumitted. Those who remained with their owner until the death of the latter were low-energy types whose wills became totally passive in their years of dependency. Upon manumission, they resold themselves, often within a few days, sometimes to the nearest party at hand, the wives or children of the deceased. Muscovite slavery confirms once again the obvious: abject dependency is not a school for freedom.

Resistance to Slavery

No work on slavery is complete without such a section as this. The standard types of resistance, ranging from theft and flight to arson, murder, and rebellion, are found in ample quantity in Muscovy. Because most of the slaves there were Russians, the more exotic varieties of resistance such as secret cults and native religions, common release and resistance mechanism of peoples enslaved in an alien society, seem to be absent.[2] The more subtle forms of resistance, such as lying, dissembling, shirking, and perhaps suicide, remain concealed from the historian of Muscovy, although he may infer that they were present because they are so well documented in other slave systems.[3]

One form of possible resistance that should not be overlooked is alcoholism. A fondness for alcohol among the Rusy was noted by the chronicler who discussed Vladimir's "shopping expedition" in the 980s for a religion, during which he ruled out Islam because "the Rusy love to drink and cannot be without it." This quotation has been a favorite of the denizens of the east European plain for nearly a millennium, while excessive drinking has been a major concern of thoughtful governments for a long time. Most analyses of the problem of excessive drinking conclude that excessive tension is one of its major causes. Almost certainly that should be the framework for considering the alcoholism of Bezobrazov's slave stewards, some of whom seem to have been drunk for most of their adult lives. One of them was described as "eternally drunk" (vechno p'ian), a sign of something more than "a love of drinking."[4] Leaving this world for an alcoholic stupor, the steward was almost certainly getting revenge on his owner, as well as stimulating Bezobrazov's wrath even further.

---

1. Nosov, *Ocherki*, pp. 360, 387; RIB 22(1908): 780, 809, DVP, p. 507; RIB 15[2](1894): 52, 72; NZKK 1: 413; RIB 17(1898): 26-27, 73; Bychkov, LZAK 22: 6.

2. Monica Schuler, "Slave Images and Identities: Commentary," *Annals*, p. 378.

3. Genovese, *Roll*, p. 598.

4. Novosel'skii, *Votchinnik*, p. 61.

Attacks against Owners

Muscovite legislation indicates that the murder of slaveowners by their chattel was a problem. There is no way, of course, to determine how much of this resulted from an owner's giving one too many reprimands to his lackey, and how much from a slave's sense that he was inherently wronged by the unequal conditions between his master and himself. I imagine that the domestic quarrel by far predominated. Because of the Muscovite monogamous family structure and the limitations on sexual access to female slaves, the incidence of murder was probably far less than in nineteenth-century Hausaland, where killings by concubines instilled great fear in slaveowners. Also, Muscovite slaves were not driven, as in the U.S., where Mississippi Valley overseers carried arms in constant fear for their lives.[5] Greater consciousness may have been prevalent in the cases where a slave refused to aid his owner under attack, or collaborated with third parties in assaulting his owner. Much of the Muscovite legislation on this problem originated in Byzantium, and the fact that it continued in use in Muscovy indicates that the Russians had the same type of trouble cases as had the Greeks eight centuries earlier.

Periods of civil disorder allowed slave hatred for owners to break out into the open. Such a period was the Khovanshchina of 1682. The slave Aleksei Stepanov on May 19, 1682, sent his owner, counselor *dvorianin* Semen Fedorov Tolochanov, the following note:

> Wide-open-legged mother [wife-whore, *rastokaia mat'*], Senka Tolochanov [sic], give us our limited service slavery contracts and manumission documents! If thou will not give them to us, we will beat thee to death, you wide-open-legged mother! How is it possible that you are never riding home to spend the night? It is intolerably disgusting [*liuto izvest'*] that we cannot exterminate you. If you try to get along with us [*khot' lesti*], or if you don't try to get along with us, we will slash you to pieces at night in your bedroom. Now there is no way out. Sooner or later we will get you. If you give us back the limited service slavery contracts, you will be glad that you returned [them], or your head will not be on your shoulders. We are hereby giving you notice! Give them back to us right now, if you desire to continue among the living. You give them back to us while you are still living![6]

The invective in this missive from a literate slave to his hated owner is a rare survival. It shows, of course, the importance of the slavery contracts and the manumission documents (only if the slaves had them in their possession could they go about as certified freedmen). (The demand also may have been for the

---

5. Genovese, *Roll*, p. 616. The sole murder of a free man by a slave that I am aware of was the instance in which a slave killed the eldest son of Iuliana Lazarevskaia (Stender-Petersen, *Anthology*, p. 383). On murder by slaves in Germanic society, see Wergeland, p. 69.

6. Savich, *Vosstanie*, p. 24, no. 5.

issuance of manumission documents by Tolochanov, but that seems less likely than that Tolochanov was holding earlier manumissions that had been given to Stepanov and his father.) The demand that Tolochanov hand them over while he lived is also intelligible, for upon his death the slaves were automatically freed (even if he was murdered), although of course the killers personally would suffer the supreme penalty.

Tolochanov, of course, was hardly intimidated by Aleshka Stepanov's familiarity, bluster, and threats. On May 20 he filed an oral complaint addressed to tsar Peter and the boyars with the Musketeers Chancellery. The boyars ordered the arrest and interrogation of Aleshka, who at first denied writing the threat. Soon, he confessed that it was his handwriting, that he had put it in Tolochanov's pocket among the papers that his owner had taken home from his job as codirector of the Treasury (*Kazennyi prikaz*). He admitted that he had hoped that Tolochanov would be frightened, and would free him and his father. He claimed that he had acted alone in a fit of absence of mind, and that Tolochanov's other slaves knew nothing of it. As befitted a house slave, he knew that the doors to his owner's bedroom were not locked at night. After the interrogation, Aleshka was turned over to the custody of a group of sentry *strel'tsy* for safekeeping, and he fled. He fled to Tolochanov's estate in Belev, was arrested, jailed, and fled further. Sixteen months later, on September 26, 1683, he was apprehended in Voronezh, over 550 kilometers south of Moscow. In the interim, he had lived for a month with the Don cossacks, and then, so he told his interrogator, the governor (*voevoda*) in Voronezh, had decided to return to Tolochanov, hoping for mercy from his owner, who in the interim had been promoted to the rank of *okol'nichii*. The arrest message reached Moscow on October 11, Tolochanov was informed, and wrote tsars Ivan and Peter reviewing the threats and requesting that a further investigation of Aleshka's conduct be undertaken. After further correspondence between the Musketeers Chancellery and the Military Chancellery, the case reached the corulers Ivan, Peter, and Sofia, and the boyars, who on October 31 decreed that Aleshka should be hanged in the presence of a large assemblage in Voronezh. In November, the sentence was effected, ending the story of Aleshka Stepanov's threats to his owner.[7] Not surprisingly, it apparently never once had occurred to Aleshka to ask himself why he, a freedman, had sold himself to Tolochanov in the first place. Why he did not ask himself this question is evident in his initial flight to his owner's estate in Belev, and then in his attempt to return to his owner after wintering with the Don cossacks in Cherkask: the experience of slavery had in fact made him so dependent that it was impossible for him to live as a free man.

Depending upon the general political climate, the Muscovite slave had one way of gaining his freedom while simultaneously getting even with his owner that was not available to chattel in less authoritarian societies, the way of political

7. Ibid., pp. 25-31, no. 6-14.

denunciation. This practice was rampant during Ivan IV's paranoid rout, when any denunciation was received with great favor. Occasionally "the Terrible" came to his senses, as in 1582, when he forbade the receipt of such communications. However, Boris Godunov revived the practice in 1586 by inciting slaves of the Shuiskiis to denounce their owners, and later on he used slaves against the Romanovs.[8] This was a fairly sure way of gaining freedom, and several of the slaves in my data set were selling themselves following their manumission from owners who had fallen into "disgrace" (*opala*).[9] Under the Romanovs, in the *Ulozhenie* of 1649, political denunciation by slaves was decreed to be unacceptable, and slaves who initiated such denunciations against their owners were to be "cruelly punished, beaten with the knout unmercifully," and then returned to their owners.[10]

This provision of the law must have been widely known in the chancellery milieu, for Kotoshikhin cites it in his memoir, but in a somewhat altered form. "If a slave petitions *falsely* [emphasis added] against his owner, or accuses him of treason because he no longer wants to serve him, and an investigation [has proved the accusation to be false], the slave will be beaten with the knout and given back as a slave to his owner: do not petition or concoct charges *falsely* [emphasis added] against your master."[11] Kotoshikhin's addition of the adverb "falsely" (*lozhno*) is much more in keeping with Muscovite reality than a general

---

8. V. N. Tatishchev, *Istoriia rossiiskaia* 7(1968): 362-65; PSRL 14[1](1965): 36-37, 52.

9. NZKK 1:5, 86, 128; NKK 7108 (=RIB 15): 13. For more information on *opala*, see Ann M. Kleimola, "The Muscovite Autocracy at Work: The Use of Disgrace as an Instrument of Control," in *Russian Law: Historical and Political Perspectives*, ed. William E. Butler (Leyden: A. W. Sijthoff, 1977), pp. 29-50.

10. 1649 *Ulozhenie* 2: 13. A dozen examples of slave involvement in "treason cases" ("the sovereign's word and business"—*slovo i delo gosudarevy*) in the years 1632-48 are among the 327 such cases published by N. Ia. Novombergskii. Usually such cases were "treasonous" only by a flight of the imagination, as the following examples will illustrate. In one instance, apparently an attempt at illegal enslavement, the would-be enslaver had announced that he would be the "sovereign" (*gosudar'*) of his intended victim; she denounced him as part of her successful escape strategy. In another case, slaves had fled from military service and their owner wanted them jailed. To get even, and hoping to escape slavery thereby, the fugitive slaves, when apprehended, accused their owner of having made derogatory remarks about Tsar Boris Godunov, who had reigned three decades earlier. Having been flogged by his owner (either because the slave accused the owner of arson, or because the slave's wife fled), a slave ran out into the street shouting that he knew a treason case involving his owner, a state secretary. In another instance, after a slave had gone berserk, his owner ordered him detained in jail; apparently in an attempt to escape incarceration, the slave announced that he knew of a treason case (N. Novombergskii, *Slovo i delo gosudarevy*, 2 vols. [Tomsk: T-vo "Pechatnia S. P. Iakovleva," 1909-11], 1: 69-73, 187-88, 191-92, 206-7, 347-51, 399-400, 458-64, 523-26, 535-36, 543-44, 571-72; nos. 55-56, 115, 117, 125, 199, 223, 252, 278, 284, 291, 316). The very low yield and obvious potential for mischief in permitting slaves to proclaim knowledge of treason cases may be why the *Ulozhenie* ordered that such denunciations no longer be received against slaveowners.

11. Kotoshikhin, p. 120.

prohibition against receiving denunciations at all. This was evident when the government of Peter the Great pressed treason charges against A. I. Bezobrazov. His slaves, desiring vengeance for their owner's savage treatment of them, filed into the Investigations Chancellery and accused their owner of desiring to kill Peter and his mother (they also accused him of witchcraft). For their testimony, which helped send Bezobrazov to the gallows, some of the slaves received 100 rubles apiece, and all of them were manumitted.[12]

Kotoshikhin noted that the government was willing to receive slave petitions against owners, and such was the case. This was true particularly in cases of illegal enslavement, such as of the Polish prisoners of war forcibly held by Golitsyn, discussed in chapter 15. The same was true for native Muscovites, as is evident in the astonishing case discussed below.

Danila Big Beard v. Lodygin

A successful struggle for freedom that lasted over two decades and involved two generations was portrayed in a massive and complicated case tried in the Slavery Chancellery between April 17, 1649, and June 6, 1651. This was the case of Danila, son of Dmitrii, Big Beard v. Lodygin. The trial began before directors *stol'nik* Prince Vasilii Bogdanov Volkonskii and Grigorii Aref'ev Neronov and state secretaries Sava Samsonov and Semen Kliucharev; toward the end of the trial, Volkonskii was replaced by Vasilii Timofeev Griaznoi and Kliucharev by Griaznoi Akishev. The case portrays graphically the potential abuse inherent in a system based on the enslavement of the native ethnos, the nearly insurmountable difficulties a person forcibly and wrongfully enslaved had in establishing his claim to freedom, and the highly professional conduct of the Muscovite officials in resolving what was apparently a relatively rare slavery conflict. For these reasons the case is worth extended discussion.

The case began in Temnikov, a Mordovian garrison town about 185 kilometers south of Nizhnii Novgorod and 380 kilometers southeast of Moscow that ensured the submission of the native Tatars and Finnic Mordovians. It was on the steppe road to Astrakhan', traversed winter and summer by horse traffic. By the 1630s Temnikov was a backwater, a place in which the plaintiff's father Dmitrii Sozonov Big Beard had served for sixty years as a gunner and had died in that occupation. His son, the plaintiff Danila, had already served twenty years as a gunner in Temnikov prior to the 1630s. The gunners lived in a special settlement, received no pay from the central government, but were supported locally.

In May of 1629 Gavrilo Vasil'ev Lodygin arrived in Temnikov as governor, a post which he held until 1633. This was his fourth governorship, for he earlier had held the same job in Sebezh (1612), Perm' (1617-19), and Galich (1625-27). It was relatively unusual for a man to hold four governorships. While he held only the rank of Moscow *dvorianin*, Gavrilo Lodygin in the year before his

12. Novosel'skii, *Votchinnik*, p. 65.

assignment to Temnikov experienced the heady atmosphere of the inner circles of the Kremlin, where he dined several times with Tsar Mikhail and his father, Patriarch Filaret, and attended Mikhail's wife's birthday and nameday parties. When he returned from Temnikov, he seems to have fallen from favor, and appears only twice in the records: on April 6, 1634, he had the privilege of dining in the presence of the "bright eyes of the sovereign," and on January 30, 1637, he was part of a massive reception for the Lithuanian ambassador in the gold chamber of the Kremlin.[13]

We may assume that Gavrilo Lodygin was a favorite of Patriarch Filaret, the actual ruler of Muscovy until his death in 1633. Lodygin's son, at the trial two decades later, noted that his father had done everything he could while in Temnikov to carry out what he deemed to be Filaret's policies. Those activities were perceived by the indigenous locals (no doubt including many of the 14 Cherkasy, 386 Tatars, and the Mordovians occupying 1,120 households, over whom Gavrilo was governor) as religious oppression, as when he razed the local mosques and expelled the horse-meat market from the town because it defiled the nearby Orthodox churches. In fact, his father so antagonized the local populace by his rigid policies that his son claimed two decades later that they still hated him and that they perjured themselves in the trial over Danilka's slavery status just to get· even with him. Unfortunately, information about Gavrilo Lodygin's comportment as governor elsewhere is unknown, but he certainly felt that he was God's vicegerent on earth in Temnikov, one to whom nothing was forbidden. Thus, he jailed Danilka for reasons that the victim alleged he did not know, and then resolved to enslave him as well. Thus began Danilka's travail.

Danilka claimed that it began in 1631, although he may have been off by a year. Gavrilo Lodygin turned Danilka over to his son Kondrat Lodygin, who carted him to Arzamas, 100 kilometers to the northeast. Danilka repeatedly emphasized throughout the trial that the Lodygins had thoroughly terrorized him during the jailing and subsequent events. In Arzamas Danilka was turned over to Uvar Gavrilov Lodygin, who took out a limited service slavery contract, dated February 18, 1630, on him. Subsequently Uvar Lodygin tried to make something of the 1630-31 discrepancy, but the Slavery Chancellery never expressed any interest in it. Of greater interest were two statements in the contract that eventually led to Danilka's freedom: the contract said (1) that the person being enslaved was Danilka Dmitriev Elagin (whereas Danilka said his father's patronymic had been Sozonov Big Beard) of Temnikov, and (2) that the person being enslaved was a "free man," a person legally bound to no occupation or social status (whereas Danilka proved that he had been a gunner). Danilka purportedly took the sum of 15 rubles from Uvar Lodygin's slave Ivan Vasil'ev for himself, his wife, Mar'ia Levontieva, and his three sons, Grigorii, Fedor, and Fatii. The

13. Barsukov, SGV, p. 510; KR 1: 405, 544, 661, 1141, 1246, 1353; 2: 199, 295, 361, 750; DR 1: 295, 740, 931, 934-35, 969, 1001, 1003, 1005, 1011, 1016, 2: 58, 867, 873.

Slavery Chancellery also might have been suspicious of the makeup of the unit represented by those in the contract. While the fact that there were only boys in the contract was not unusual, the self-sale of a man-wife-and-three children combination was rather atypical.

For the next dozen years Danilka seethed with rage while he worked in Lodygin's household as his personal servant. His two younger boys died, and his oldest, in 1641, at the age of twenty-three, was forcibly married to one of Uvar Lodygin's dowry slaves, Dun'ka Gavrilova Sidorova, who had been given to him by one of his in-laws, Ivan Kutuzov.

In 1643 Danilka managed to file a complaint with the Slavery Chancellery against his forcible enslaver, Gavrilo Lodygin. A visual confrontation between them was scheduled, but the director of the chancellery, Stepan Ivanov Islen'ev, "betrayed" him and did not arrange it, or so Danilka later alleged. The records of the Slavery Chancellery indicate that a bailiff had been unable to locate Lodygin to serve him with the warrant requiring him to appear for the confrontation, and then Islen'ev ignored Danilka's second petition. Gavrilo Lodygin was none too pleased by the complaint filed against him, and vowed revenge. He had his slaves take Danilka to Talyzina settlement in Alatyr', where he was led around the streets of the village three times and beaten with the knout by Uvar Lodygin's slave Kirilko Semenov. Then he was put in stocks for two years and kept alive on minimum rations. His wife was taken away from him and held in a Lodygin village in Dmitrov province. It almost appears as though the Lodygin forces were in training for the later martyrdom of Avvakum.

By 1649 Danilka's son Grishka was a grown man of thirty-one years, and he took up his father's cause. Having fled from Uvar Lodygin on March 11, 1649, he submitted a petition to the tsar signed by his father which got the case going by renewing the 1643 complaint. Tsar Aleksei on April 17, 1649, ordered that the case be looked into, a decision affirmed by the boyars I. V. Morozov, M. P. Pronskoi, and their colleagues, who turned the case over to the Slavery Chancellery. Upon hearing this, Uvar Lodygin immediately had Grishka arrested as a fugitive slave, which he was on two counts: he was listed in the 1630 contract, and he was married to one of Lodygin's slaves. Moreover; it turned out that Grishka had fled before, in 1639, when he joined the infantry. Lodygin had recovered him from the infantry on the basis of the 1630 contract, with no investigation being made of whether the document was legitimate. (In an attempt to avoid further complications, Uvar Lodygin had locked up Grishka's father in the stocks when the son fled.)

Having arrested Grishka as his fugitive slave, Lodygin brought him to the Slavery Chancellery, which turned him over to one of its bailiffs for safekeeping. The bailiff chained Grishka to the wall. Lodygin asked for a trial on the matter of Grishka, but, in one of those astonishing developments that sometimes leaves the historian speechless, the Slavery Chancellery refused, and, prodded by the tsar and boyars, said that it would consider Grishka's case only in connection with his father's case.

A facile explanation of the Slavery Chancellery's decision to take up Danilka's case would be that, after the momentous events of the summer of 1648, which shook the government to its foundations, central officials were more than ordinarily receptive to petitions from below. While there may be some truth to that, it seems more likely that the case was one of such glaring injustice that it cried out for rectification even to cynical members of the central hierarchy. This sentiment seems to be expressed in the way in which the 35,000-word record of the trial was kept, for Danilka's claims of grotesque abuse are always noted, even in summaries where a more neutral rendition of the facts would have served just as well.

Uvar Gavrilov Lodygin's tactic in the trial was to procrastinate and to prevaricate to the very outer limit that the Slavery Chancellery would tolerate. At this juncture, I might discuss his career briefly. I have noted that his father had held four governorships, an unusually high number, particularly by comparison with Uvar himself, who held none. There may be two reasons why he never held that office: his father's conduct cast an aura of distrust over his son, or the son was wealthy enough so that he did not have to petition for such posts, which often were arduous and full of discomfort for their holders. The second reason seems more likely, for Uvar Lodygin is revealed in this case to have had quite a few slaves and several estates scattered throughout Muscovy. Instead, he seems to have preferred service in the capital. He was listed in 1621-22 as a *stol'nik*, no. 161 on the list (his brother Kondratii was no. 116). He held that rank until about 1641, at which time he was demoted to the rank of Moscow *dvorianin*, which he occupied, as far as is known, for the rest of his career. It is not clear why he was demoted, but he was not the only one by any means who suffered that fate. In the 1620s and 1630s, Lodygin participated twice in the great ritual receptions of foreign ambassadors (in 1625 and 1635), served as palace sentry (in 1628, 1637, and especially in 1639), and dined with the tsar at least once, on May 19, 1635. This, certainly, was hardly a career as elevated as his father's had been. After his apparent demotion, Uvar Lodygin served as a palace sentry in December of 1649, and then seems to have disappeared from the record for awhile. The trial transcript notes that in 1643, when Danilka filed his first complaint, Uvar Lodygin was conducting an investigation in Pskov, and it was from there that he sent the order to Talyzina, over 1,150 kilometers away, on the torture that should be meted out to Danilka. Uvar Lodygin reappeared in Moscow on January 16, 1648, at the marriage of Tsar Aleksei to Mar'ia Il'ichna, where he accompanied her sleigh. After that, he seems to have become part of the tsaritsa's retinue, and is recorded several times between April 28, 1650, and June 2, 1652, as attending her in Moscow and on pilgrimages to Kolomenskoe and the Trinity Sergiev monastery.[14] The case under review here was resolved by June,

14. Ivanov, AUBK, p. 236, ZKMS (=RIB 10[1886]): 91, 117, 136, 142, 174, 182, 227, 230; RIB 28(1912): 732; Storozhev, "B. S.," p. 109; Beliaev, *Rospisnoi spisok*, p. 61; DR 1: 685, 1015; 2: 438, 462, 935, 943, 966, 975; 3: 81, 160, 174, 189, 231, 259, 317.

1651, so it seems to have had no impact on Lodygin's failure to appear in the records after a year had passed. Perhaps he died at that time.

Grishka's petition once again stimulated Lodygin revenge. Uvar Lodygin wrote about the matter to his wife, Pelageia Ivanova, in Alatyr'. Pelageia had six slaves in three shifts beat Danilka with knouts until he nearly died. Then she locked him in stocks and starved him from Easter (March 23) to May 23. Not content with that savagery, Pelageia Lodygina sent Danilka's wife to Uvar's estate near Moscow, where she was kept chained and fettered next to the millstones of a flour mill. While illegally enslaved, Danilka and Man'ka had given birth to two girls, Marinka and Oksiutka, and a boy, Eufimko. They were hidden on Uvar Lodygin's other estates in the Moscow region about the time when Danilka himself was finally brought to Moscow.

In structuring his claim against Uvar Lodygin for his freedom, Danilka asked that a check be made with the Kazan' Regional Chancellery for the records of his father's and his own service as gunners and of the land cadastres compiled by Ivan Usov, which would show that his father and he had lived in Temnikov and in its by-town, Insar, to prove that both his father and he had served as gunners and that the person listed in Uvar Lodygin's limited service slavery contract, the free man Danil Dmitreev Elagin from Temnikov, never existed.

The Slavery Chancellery complied with Danilka's first request, added some of its own, and on May 4-5, 1649, the Kazan' Regional Chancellery reported that Danilko Dmitreev was registered as a gunner in the 1613/14 census review books (*dozornye knigi*), but that the sobriquet "Big Beard" was not used. (A point of the latter observation was made by Lodygin, to which Danilko responded that no sobriquets at all were recorded in that document, but that note should be taken of his listing as a gunner.) The Kazan' Chancellery also reported that it could not check the payroll records for information about Danilka and his father because such documents were not submitted to that Moscow office. (They were not submitted because gunners were maintained locally, like *nedel'shchiki*.) Finally, the Kazan' Chancellery confirmed that Gavrilo Lodygin had been the governor in Temnikov in 1631. While this initial discovery was taking place, Danilka was not present; he was being beaten and starved by Lodygin's wife in the Alatyr' region.

Grishka's persistence kept the case alive. On May 28, 1649, he petitioned that Uvar Lodygin was delaying the case, which, among other things, was running up the bailiff's chaining fee. He also noted that the Slavery Chancellery had ordered Lodygin to present his father in its offices, and that he had failed to do so. At the same time defendant Lodygin asked for an extension to bring Danilka to Moscow and claimed that he had sent his slave Sen'ka (elsewhere, Vas'ka) Tatarin to fetch him but that the slave had been unable to travel because of floods and muddy roads. While that *may* have been true, it is dubious, and one may suspect that Lodygin really wanted time to repair the injuries his wife had inflicted on Danilka. Be that as it may, the Slavery Chancellery granted him another three weeks to produce him, and on June 12 Danilka was brought to the Slavery Chancellery. At that time he repeated the accusations made in his April complaint and elaborated on them. After the initial hearing, the Slavery Chancellery ordered Danilka released on bond, if he could raise it. As we have seen in chapter 8, this opportunity was allowed only the most trustworthy of accused slaves. The fact that it was offered to Danilka indicates that the Slavery Chancellery sympathized with him. However, he was unable to produce bond, so he was turned over to the bailiff Kondrashka Starkov, who presumably chained him to the wall next to his son Grishka. While no one would envy Danilka's position, all things considered, it cannot have been too bad. For one thing, Danilka and the other members of his family did not frequently utter the common lament that they were being starved while in the bailiff's custody. (In fact, it was Starkov who lamented—that he was being bankrupted and on the verge of falling into debt slavery himself because of the expenses he incurred feeding the captive slaves.) Secondly, Danilka seems to have been able to prosecute his case quite effectively, even though he was chained to the wall for over 600 days. He even was able to get counselor state secretaries to sign his petitions that were necessary to push the case along.

The case must have been rather unusual, for the boyars were kept apprised of each step as it went along. (It cannot have been unique, however, for there seems to have been a uniformity and sureness of vocabulary that would not be expected in a case that was absolutely the first of its kind.) A summary of the June 12 appearance was sent to the boyars, who six days later ordered that a visual confrontation be arranged between the litigants. On June 25, 1649, a trial was held. Such dispatch was not atypical for the Muscovite chancelleries.

At the trial, the old issues were rehashed, and the subject of stolen property was introduced. Danilka alleged that the Lodygins had usurped his house in the gunners settlement of Temnikov and stolen other property with a total value of 15.50 rubles. Lodygin introduced a countersuit against Grishka for 15.88 rubles' worth of stolen property. Danilka took the oath for himself, Lodygin's slave Garas'ka Gashukov kissed the cross for his owner. Under cross-examination on documents and such discrepancies as the absence of the sobriquet "Big Beard," Danilka noted that he was illiterate and not responsible for the imprecision of written instruments. His persecutor, Uvar Lodygin, did not suffer from the handicap of illiteracy, and Danilka noted that the defendant had been able to manipulate the skill to his obvious advantage. After the trial, defendant Lodygin was released on bail and produced the extraordinarily large number of eleven guarantors, an indication that the Slavery Chancellery considered him somewhat notorious. Had Danilka and Grishka been able to produce bail, they would have been released. They could not, however, so they were returned to the bailiff. That the Slavery Chancellery was again willing to offer them bail indicates some sympathy with their case.

Danilka's next move, on July 2, 1649, was to request that the rest of his family be produced in court for the trial as well. Perhaps he sensed sympathy for his position, and wanted them present when the verdict was issued to avoid complications and certain additional brutalization, for he noted that his wife was being forced to thresh grain and was chained next to the millstone. The tsar granted his request, and ordered the Slavery Chancellery to insist that Lodygin produce them. This initiated another long saga. On July 16, the Slavery Chancellery asked Lodygin where they were and he lied, saying they were on his estate in Talyzina settlement, near Alatyr'. Perhaps for obvious reasons, Lodygin did not sign this statement. Four days later, the Slavery Chancellery again ordered him to produce them. Fifteen people guaranteed that he would, under forfeit of 50 rubles apiece for failure to do so. It was noted that the distance to Alatyr' was 600 versts (kilometers). A month later, on August 22, 1649, Lodygin asked for more time because it was so far, and the farming season (*pashennaia pora*) was in progress.

On August 23, Danilka noted that six months had passed since the suit began, and asked that Lodygin be forced to present the rest of his family. He made a second request four days later, and on August 30 the Slavery Chancellery ordered its bailiff to ask the fifteen guarantors to present them. Nothing happened, and Danilka repeated his petition on September 3 and 4. This moved Lodygin to action, and he petitioned the tsar for another postponement. Noting the Slavery Chancellery's refusal to grant him one, and the August 30 order to the bailiff, he alleged that he had sent a slave to Alatyr' to fetch them and that some misfortune must have befallen him. The tsar granted his request.

As though to relieve the tension in a tragedy, the next actor was the bailiff Kondrashka Starkov, who appeared in the Slavery Chancellery on September 7, 1649, to complain that Danilka and Grishka were eating him out of house and home and drinking up everything he had. He noted that Lodygin, who was responsible for their presence in his house, was not providing food and drink for them and, of course, was not paying the bill, either.

At this juncture, still another member of Danilka's family became involved in the struggle for freedom. On September 9, his daughter Marina came to the Slavery Chancellery of her own volition, and repeated the story her father and brother had been telling. She had broken away from Lodygin and come to the Slavery Chancellery to find out about her father and brother. She told of the recent travails of the rest of the family. As I noted earlier, they were not in Alatyr', as Lodygin alleged, but had been brought to the Moscow-area village of Ermolina about the time their father had been brought to the Slavery Chancellery. They were held there, chained to the flour mill, until July 20, when they were moved to another of Lodygin's estates in the village of Osanova in the Pereiaslavl'-Zalesskii province. They were kept in chains there as well, until the Slavery Chancellery's order of August 30 threw a fright into Lodygin, and he moved them to Moscow, where they arrived on September 6. Again, the family had been chained to a millstone. Marina had been unable, she said, to endure the deprivation (*nuzha*), had sought a chance to escape, and took advantage of an opening in a fence, at a moment when she was unchained, and fled. Having heard her story, the Slavery Chancellery ordered her turned over to bailiff Starkov, where she was reunited with her father and brother.

Marina's appearance immediately put an end to Lodygin's lies that the family was in Alatyr', and the next day the Slavery Chancellery ordered him to produce the rest of them forthwith. He did, and had the gall to claim that Marina had stolen some property when she crept out through the fence, a half-hour before she arrived in the Slavery Chancellery. As far as is evident in the transcript of the case, the Slavery Chancellery made no move to censure or otherwise punish Lodygin when his lies were revealed.

Upon being produced in the Slavery Chancellery, the adults in Danilka's family were called upon to make a preliminary statement. His wife, Man'ka Levont'eva, repeated the story told by her husband and two children, Grishka and Marina, adding nothing other than the statement that Danilka frequently had been placed in the stocks and beaten by the Lodygins. Grishka's wife, Dun'ka Gavrilova Sidorova, noted that she had been the vicious Pelageia's dowry slave, had been married to Grishka for about a decade (actually, eight years), and noted that her father-in-law had been given the name Elagin after Lodygin had taken him to Moscow (in the early 1630s). She told how, after it had been learned that her husband Grishka had filed the complaint in the Slavery Chancellery, her owner Pelageia had beaten her with a whip while slaves were beating her father-in-law with the knout. Another slave, Danilo Reshetnikov, had taken her and Man'ka's daughter Oksiutka to Moscow, where they were kept at the house of Mikhail Kutuzov, Lodygin's in-laws. Her mother-in-law was chained while being transported.

After their appearance in the Slavery Chancellery, the new arrivals had their clothing inventoried, as was customary, and were turned over to the bailiff for safekeeping. Now there were seven: Danilka and his wife Man'ka, their children Grishka, Marina, Oksiutka, and Eufimka, and their daughter-in-law Dun'ka. At this juncture they were released on bail. How Danilka arranged it while chained to the wall is not clear, but he got five men to provide bail for him. One was a priest of a nunnery in the region where the Lodygin house was located (Dmitrovka), another was a townsman with the rank of centurion from the same region. A third guarantor was a townsman from Rostov, and the last two were municipal employees with the rank of decurion (*desiatniki zemskogo dvora*). Arranging bail took about ten days, and on the day the seven were released the bailiff Kondratii Starkov petitioned the tsar for his money for guarding and feeding them, with the note that they had left without paying their food bill. Within a week or so, Danilka and his family were back under arrest, where they remained for another eighteen months, and claimed that they were starving. No reason for the cancellation of their bail is given. Perhaps it was to guarantee that the bailiff would get his money. In his petition of October 2, 1649, Danilka asked that his case be resolved on the basis of the *Ulozhenie* of 1649, a document that was henceforth cited in almost every instance by the litigants and even by the tsar himself. It is interesting how rapidly knowledge of that great codification spread to all levels of society.

Once again, the case must have caught the attention of an important member of the Muscovite administration, for the Slavery Chancellery prepared a digest of the case and presented it to the boyars, who on October 18, 1649, heeding Danilka's request, ordered that a general investigation be conducted in Temnikov and Insar and their provinces. The conduct and results of this investigation have been discussed in some detail in chapter 8. The boyars specified that the two major questions were whether Dmitreiko and Danilka had been gunners in Temnikov, and whether their sobriquet was Big Beard. They also copied out the 1649 *Ulozhenie*, 20: 108, on conflicts over the name of a slave. On November 15, 1649, an order in the name of the tsar was sent to the governor of Temnikov prescribing the conduct of the general investigation, and on the following day the same order was sent to the governor of Insar.

Nothing happened. On January 1, 1650, relying on rumor that had reached him (while he was chained to the wall in the bailiff's house), Danilka submitted a petition to the tsar asking that the governors be nudged on the issue. He said that they were refusing to act because the general investigation was a private law matter that litigants were supposed to pay for, or else conduct themselves. But, the former gunner noted, he did not have the capacity to take depositions while he was chained to the wall, nor did he have slaves to do it for him. The head of the Slavery Chancellery had told him that he did not have the capacity to order governors to conduct general investigations, but that he would be glad to pass on a royal order should it be issued. Danilka's petition bore the signature of the counselor state secretary of the Foreign Affairs Chancellery, perhaps the highest official in the Muscovite civil administration. Tsar Aleksei ordered that the case should go forward and that any difficulties should be referred to the boyars for resolution. One might well wonder why the tsar was involved so frequently in this case. To my knowledge, Aleksei's thoughts on the case can no longer be recovered, but some likely explanations come to mind. The most prominent one must be that such cases were rare, and the Slavery Chancellery, like all other such organs, did not dare to take any routes that were not well marked by precedents. In innovative cases, the sovereign had to be consulted regularly. Moreover, Muscovy's population was small and widely scattered, so the total volume of business in the Muscovite chancelleries was not so great that consulting the ruler on major issues when they arose was difficult. Finally, there were few major pressing issues in these years, so the tsar no doubt had more free time than he did in years when the country was lurching from one crisis to the next.

Given this impetus, the Temnikov governor ordered the general investigation, which was conducted in mid-April, 1650, and delivered the results to Moscow on July 20. On August 9 the Slavery Chancellery quantified the depositions, none of which was unfavorable to the plaintiff. By August 12 Danilka had been informed of the results of the Temnikov investigation, and petitioned that the verdict be rendered without waiting for the report from Insar. He claimed the governor of Insar was purposely delaying to favor his friend Lodygin. Whether this latter allegation was true cannot be verified, and well may have been one of the scribal flourishes that were so stereotypically applied in Muscovy, even though often false. (They continued to be used in imperial jargon, with the difference that by the nineteenth century many people came to believe that they were true.)

On September 10, 1650, Tsar Aleksei asked the Insar governor for the results of the general investigation and threatened him with financial sanctions if he did not comply with this second order. This stirred the governor to action and the investigation was conducted at the end of January, 1651. On February 16, 1651, the results were sent to Moscow, where they arrived on March 4. The results from Temnikov and Insar were totalled, and it was observed that 346 respondents knew of Danilka's past, and 252 did not. No one knew of the fictive Danilka Dmitreev Elagin.

On March 10, 1651, the Slavery Chancellery was ready with its verdict: free Danilka and the whole family, assess Uvar Lodygin for the chaining and feeding fees due the bailiff. The family included eight members, those in the custody of the bailiff eighteen months earlier plus Vasiliska, a daughter of Grishka and Dun'ka. When the verdict was read to Danilka, Grishka, and Lodygin on April 14, 1651, Danilka noted that only seven were to be set free because his granddaughter Vasiliska had died. This cut his cost for the capitation fees, assessed against him as winning plaintiff in the suit, by 3 altyns. No doubt the high infant and child mortality noted in this case was typical for the era, something that further complicated the life of a man struggling to gain his freedom. The issue of stolen property still remained to be resolved, and the Slavery Chancellery decreed that the only way to get at the truth was for the litigants to take an oath. Dates were prescribed—April 16, 17, and 19 for Danilka's suit, April 21, 22, and 24 for Lodygin's suit. Apparently the litigants agreed to settle out of court, for on April 21 Danilka paid 1.55 rubles for his suit, plus the 0.63 ruble capitation fees, for a total of 2.18 rubles. On April 30, Lodygin paid the fee of 1.81 rubles for his suit.

Danilka and his family were now free. They were sent to the Kazan' Regional Administrative Chancellery and reenrolled in the gunners. Lodygin had lost not only Danilka and his direct family, but his dowry slave Dun'ka (Grishka's wife) as well, thanks to the Orthodox doctrine forbidding the dissolution of slave marriages. But now it was his turn. Although, apparently, there was no sanction for falsely enslaving someone—the 1558 law seems to have lapsed, another remedy appeared. Perhaps urged by the counselor state secretary of the Kazan' Regional Chancellery, who also signed the document, Danilka sued Lodygin for having initiated a false suit and then dragging out the process for almost two years. The

Ulozhenie of 1649 (10: 18) had prescribed a sanction of 10 kopeks a day for the litigant who prolonged a trial, with the cash to go to the other party. In suing for those damages, Danilka noted that he was in debt and had had to mortgage his children to meet his various expenses, among which were the three petitions to the tsar to get his case moving. This strange request went to Tsar Aleksei, who ordered the matter resolved according to the provision of the *Ulozhenie*. It is apparent that Tsar Aleksei felt that Lodygin's conduct was outrageous, for in this, as in every other instance we have noted, he ordered that the case be moved along. However, as we have seen, it was not so outrageous that Aleksei felt Lodygin should be removed from the tsaritsa's retinue. On April 30, 1651, the Slavery Chancellery totalled the bill, 63.60 rubles, for the 636 days from the beginning of the case (June 12, 1649, by its reckoning) until the slaves were freed on March 10, 1651. Technically, of course, Danilka had begun the suit, not Lodygin, although the Slavery Chancellery no doubt had in mind Lodygin's claims for Grishka.

Lodygin was not about to give up, for 63.60 rubles was a huge sum, the cost of twenty-one slaves. On May 12, 1651, Danilka again petitioned for his 63.60 rubles, and noted that his children were mortgaged. The tsar ordered him compensated. On May 15, Lodygin petitioned that he be excused from paying the fees due the bailiff and the money due Danilka because the law did not specify that those sanctions were to be applied in a case where a slave sued for his freedom. Technically, he was correct, for Muscovite law did not allow a chancellery to apply the doctrine of analogy; each case which was not precisely like a precedent had to be referred to the tsar and boyars for resolution. He also repeated his old story that he could not have gotten a fair hearing in the general investigation because the people hated him for his father's persecution of them, and then repeated his lies that Danilka was his lawful slave. He always referred to Danilka as his slave, and said that the laws being applied were not applicable to slaves. It is not clear why someone did not just tell him that Danilka was a gunner, not a slave, and that therefore his frame of reference was wrong, but no one ever did. Tsar Aleksei ordered the case resolved by the rules of the *Ulozhenie*, or else sent to the boyars, in spite of Lodygin's claims that the *Ulozhenie*, with its 10-kopek a day fine for false suits, was not applicable because a printed copy of it had not arrived from the Printing Office in the Slavery Chancellery until June 18, 1649, six days after the June 12, 1649, opening of the case. One might note that Lodygin never based any of his appeals on a claim that he was being discriminated against by either the Slavery Chancellery or the boyars, in spite of the ritual prescription that losers in judicial cases should automatically make such claims.

On May 30, 1651, Danilka again petitioned to the tsar that he was not getting his due. He claimed that Slavery Chancellery director Volkonskoi had not acted because he was about to be rotated out of the post, and that his successor Griaznoi had refused to act because he accepted the argument that the case had been initiated before the applicability of the *Ulozhenie*. Danilka countered that argument by asserting that the process had begun on July 2, 1649 (the date his family was brought into the case), after a copy of the document had been received in the Slavery Chancellery. Once again, Tsar Aleksei ordered the provisions of the *Ulozhenie* enforced.

Lodygin refused to give up. On June 6, he repeated his claim that slaves had no right to those remedies under the law, a position that reflected the post-1630s abasement of the slaves of Muscovy. He alleged that he could not understand why Griaznoi and the others of the Slavery Chancellery wanted him to pay the 63.60. Finally, he made the most telling point: if Danilka was allowed to succeed in this case, "our other slaves" would take note and flood the system with complaints in an attempt to sue their way out of slavery. Tsar Aleksei did not respond to this appeal to class solidarity, probably because he realized that it was fundamentally a rhetorical flourish irrelevant to the institution of slavery, where dependency was the norm, not a blazing desire for freedom. The tsar ordered the *Ulozhenie* enforced and the appropriate decree issued.[15]

That is the end of this incredible case. We may assume that Lodygin procrastinated further, that the bailiff was almost certainly paid, and that Danilka ultimately may have been paid. The case is worth recounting at length, for it illustrates clearly several points. The first one is that not everyone in Muscovy wanted to be a slave. That should be an obvious statement, yet because willing dependency is the basic theme of this work, a reader might get the impression that all Muscovites wanted to be slaves. They did not, and here is a case that proves it.

Danilka was a man willing to struggle for two decades to gain his personal freedom, and he infected two of his older children with that will as well. The odds against the success of such a struggle were enormous. Perhaps Danilka's major disadvantage was his illiteracy. Things could be written about him that he had no way to check, and when they were later revealed to him he could only reply that "they can write whatever they want." The system of justice in Muscovy could be very complex, and almost any official could cause fatal delays, whether through inadvertence or by design. For an ordinary member of society, such as a provincial gunner who knew nothing other than his settlement in Temnikov, to understand and to penetrate that system was a major feat, for when the case was stuck he had to know exactly where pushing was necessary to get it going again, or else he was lost. Moreover, a member of the lower classes had no natural friends in the system who could counter an oppressor who was related to and served with many of the elite members of the system. A person such as Danilka was also nearly overwhelmed by his personal lack of material resources (cash and slaves), and by the fact that most cases were still viewed as torts in which the litigants made up their own cases, and where the state was willing to become involved, ordinarily, only in the role of arbiter, for a very large fee. Finally, the Danilkas of late Muscovy were nearly helpless in collecting damages from an individual such

15. Iakovlev, *Kholopstvo*, pp. 513-62, no. 26.

as Lodygin, for the Muscovite system of remedying wrongs still had as its fundamental operating principle the notion of consensus, the idea that the person who wronged another would make amends when ordered to do so by the arbiter, in this case the state. The state was willing to go to any length to collect its fees from a litigant immediately upon the rendering of a verdict. If a litigant would not pay, his guarantors would be summoned immediately. The individual, however, had no such collection agency, and the person to whom damages were due could do little more than complain and petition for justice. A person such as Lodygin, who was not a party to the consensus, had the upper hand, for he was willing to try the judicial process again on the chance that he might win next time. Essentially, all he had to lose in so doing were more court costs. That a person such as Danilka could win a struggle for freedom against such odds is indeed remarkable.

This case also shows that there were Muscovites, like Lodygin, who were willing to go to pathological lengths to keep unwilling individuals enslaved. From an American comparative perspective, this seems particularly bizarre, for the obvious solution to the Danilka-Lodygin hatred was for the latter to get rid of the former by some means. As we have seen, Lodygin had a half-dozen other slaves who were named specifically in this case, and it is implied that there were others scattered throughout his Alatyr', Dmitrov, Pereiaslavl'-Zalesskii, and Moscow properties. He certainly did not "need" Danilka and his family, for the case makes it abundantly clear that while enslaved Danilka never did anything other than render personal service to Lodygin, and, in view of the amount of time he spent locked up in the stocks, he could have been readily replaced. The unwillingness of Lodygin to dispose of Danilka by some device will be discussed in chapter 17. Lastly, the process reveals that many officials in the Muscovite government were repelled by a case like this one. Such cases occurred infrequently, for clearly the Slavery Chancellery was not accustomed to handling matters of this kind routinely. When something so unusual did occur, some members of the Muscovite officialdom, from the tsar on down, were interested enough so that justice could be done, slowly. Because such cases were so rare, it was possible to overcome two decades of unlawful enslavement by dogged persistence.

One last point needs to be discussed in the case of Danilka Dmitreev Big Beard v. Uvar Lodygin: why did he not simply flee? It has been emphasized throughout this work that flight was a relatively simple matter, in most cases, and that perhaps a quarter to a third of Muscovite slaves did flee. The explanation for Danilka's unwillingness to flee is probably related to the fact that numerous runaways, after a period of absence, returned to their owners: while hiding in the vastness of Muscovy was not difficult, and there were even numerous "no questions asked" options for fugitives, making it on one's own was not easy, especially for those who had become dependent upon someone else. This probably describes Danilka's situation. He had spent his entire life in the gunner milieu, where his father had served for sixty years. Danilka was dependent upon that environment, which provided him with some income and a comparatively easy life. Almost certainly he had to supplement his income by a little gardening or even small-scale farming, but fundamentally he was taken care of—just like a household slave. Almost certainly that is what Gavrila Lodygin counted on when he impressed him into slavery: he was merely converting one of the "sovereign's slaves" (Danilka noted that he was one of the *gosudarevye liudi*) into one of his own. He did not anticipate a spirited resistance because he did not appreciate that personal dependence can be far more oppressive than the impersonal dependence of one of the tsar's distant military servitors. Moreover, we must consider that Danilka was already middle-aged by the time he was forcibly enslaved, past the prime runaway age, and he also was burdened by a family, which made flight much more difficult. Finally, his son Grishka did attempt to flee, but again was trapped by and therefore apprehended because of a dependency syndrome. Rather than fleeing to the frontier, he enlisted in the infantry in Moscow, and was caught when he was being registered there. That can only be described as a very unwise move on his part, but it was also one that was not unpredictable. Having become dependent during a decade of living in Lodygin's house, Grishka sensed that an occupation offering regular support would be to his liking, so he enlisted in the infantry. Unfortunately for him, the infantry kept records, and this made it possible for Lodygin to find him easily. Thus several factors made the slow struggle through the judicial process the only route to freedom for Danilka and his family. Fortunately, he was offered a position back at his old job in the gunners, where again they could be taken care of. Had that option not been available, Danilka might have been looking for a new owner rather soon.

Flight

While most Russian slavery was "voluntary," in the form of self-sale, the number of runaways was very high; perhaps as many as from a quarter to a third of all slaves seem to have fled. Of the 863 documents submitted in the compulsory registration of all claims to slaves in 1597, 235 of them mentioned fugitives; extant are collections from three different locales, with the percentage of fugitives (and their heirs, wherever they might be) claimed being roughly the same in each (see table 16.1).

TABLE 16.1
Proportions of Documents Claiming Fugitives in Three Registrations, Novgorod Region, End of Sixteenth Century

Collections	Total No. of Documents	Documents Listing Fugitives	% of Documents Claiming Fugitives
Lakier (1855)	98	25	25.5
RIB (1898)	532	127	23.9
Kopanev (1966)	233	83	35.6
Total	863	235	27.2

The statistical similarities would tend to show that the collections were typical for the region. These data tend to indicate that a considerable portion of those people who were supposed to be slaves were not, or at least were not living with their lawful owners. We should also bear in mind that the number of runaway slaves may have been considerably greater, for certainly some lords must have considered laying claim to fugitives an exercise in futility. Not one slaveowner registered only claims to fugitive slaves in the compulsory registration of all slaves and claims to slaves of 1597-98. All claims for fugitives were in addition to registrations of slaves who were still present. Certainly there must have been a number of slaveowners who had no slaves at all at the time of the 1597-98 registration because they had all fled. The apparent fact that claims solely for fugitives were not filed would indicate that the claims to runaways were incomplete, probably because of the pointless nature of the exercise. (A modern analogy is calling the police to report a crime: many people do not, because they know the chances of a criminal's being apprehended are slight, the likelihood of a successful prosecution even less—so that the cumulative result is that a felon has less than a 1 percent chance of going to jail. I do not know whether a slave owner had a much greater chance than this of recovering and retaining a fugitive slave.) As is well known, large numbers of slaves also fled in the seventeenth century, and many were returned by the fugitive-serf hunters in 1649 and later.

To my knowledge, there is no comparative work on fugitive slaves. This may well reflect the near impossibility of such an enterprise, if only because throughout much of human history this has been a private matter, for which public records often were not kept. Muscovy seems to have been much like the Ancient Near East, where the flight of slaves of both sexes probably was a common occurrence. Slave flight was also common in medieval Germanic society, over four-fifths of Thai nonredeemable slaves fled when they had the opportunity, and in Ch'ing China such a large portion of the male slaves fled (and in general were so difficult to control) that owners gave up on them, and slavery, by some reports, became largely a female institution.[16] Whether the causes of slave flight were similar is a separate topic. On the other hand, the incidence of slave flight seems to have been considerably less, for example, in many African slave systems where the treatment was benign or escape an exercise in futility, or in the U.S., where escape was difficult, recovery likely, and the sanctions severe.

One of the cumulative registration books gives thirty-three dates when slaves fled, plus the date when the contract in question was drawn up. (Most such documents just say that the slave [s] had fled, without giving any date.) One fled in the same year the document was written, and, at the other extreme, two fled after thirteen

16. Driver and Miles, 1: 105; Mendelsohn, p. 59; Wergeland, pp. 66-68; Meijer, p. 344; Turton, pp. 265, 286, Paneiakh, "Opyt tsifrovoi obrabotki," p. 555. The U. S. Census of 1850 and 1860 lists runaways, yet discussion is often based on ads for their recovery (Genovese, *Roll*, pp. 648, 789).

years. The average length of time in slavery before fleeing was 3.3 years, and the median and the mode both 2 years. Once again, this seems to record a "come in out of the cold" situation. Under stress, people sold themselves into slavery. Some recovered, and, no longer needing the relief provided by slavery, fled.

In many respects it is misleading to call much of the flight by slaves "resistance," for they were simply changing owners. In such cases, flight was a symbiotic arrangement between the slave and another master, not a change from a state of dependency to one of independence. As noted earlier, this was possible because Muscovite slaveowners were always willing to recruit and to receive another's chattel. The fact that, in Sierra Leone, Sherbro kin groups voluntarily returned one another's fugitives, whereas Muscovites, even members of the same family, litigated in court battles to resolve slaveownership questions, had obvious consequences. On the other hand, much of the slave flight, and the high volume of theft of valubles (cash, jewelry, expensive clothing–all indicating that the slave was a domestic with ready access to the owner's wardrobe) certainly represent hardened resentment against slavery. Halil Inalcik, discussing the Ottoman case, helps to explain the high rate of flight in Muscovy: "As a rule, lifetime slaves tended to run away or to be indolent."[17] No one knows why the Ottomans were unable to teach the Muscovites this lesson, not to have lifetime slaves.

For the thirty-nine cases about which I have information on how long the fugitives had been away, the average length of time was 10.6 years. Of interest may be a comparison between the types of slaves that fled and the general composition of the slave population. By comparison with some other slaveowners, the Muscovites seem to have been relatively unconcerned about the risk of flight, at least when they set out to buy slaves. Or, to put it another way, they distributed their risk evenly throughout the slave population, as is evident in table 16.2. The statistical similarity between the two sets of data is very high. Any slave population that consists, as did the Muscovite, primarily of males between the ages of fifteen and thirty-five is going to experience a large number of fugitives. In the U.S., over 80 percent of the fugitives were from that group.

We might compare the Muscovite situation with the African, where buyers were selective at the outset to avoid the problem of fugitives.[18] Women and children from remote areas were preferred. As has been emphasized earlier, adult men often had no buyers and would be killed unless they could be sold to a dealer in the international slave trade.

Thus the fugitives constituted a microcosm of the entire slave society, at least in many significant respects. If one looks at the same data from a slightly different angle, comparing those who fled with the entire population of slaves by head of household, a similar picture is seen, fundamentally, with the following differ-

17. Inalcik, "Servile Labor," p. 45.
18. Miers and Kopytoff, p. 92.

TABLE 16.2
Comparison of Fugitive Slaves with the Total Slave Population

	Fugitives		All Slaves	
	N	%	N	%
Single slave	99	51.0	1,181	53.1
Man and wife	28	14.4	389	17.4
Man, wife, and 1 child	13	6.7	189	8.5
Man, wife, and 2 children	5	2.6	128	5.8
Man, wife, and 3 children	4	2.1	55	2.5
Man, wife, and 4 children	2	1.0	18	0.8
Man and 1 child	6	3.1	48	2.2
Man and 2 children	7	3.6	27	1.2
Man and 4 children	1	0.5	4	0.2
Woman and 1 child	5	2.6	55	2.5
Woman and 2 children	1	0.5	24	1.1
Woman and 3 children	1	0.5	9	0.4
Single child	11	5.7	60	2.7
2 children	8	4.1	32	1.4
3 children	3	1.5	7	0.3
Total	194	99.9[a]	2,226	100.1[a]
Others (% of total cases)	30	13.4	273	10.9

[a] Rounding errors.
Statistics: r=0.9914 . Eta^2=0.999 with fugitive slaves dependent.

ences: 48.4 percent of the fugitives were single, 54 percent of the entire slave population was single. On the other hand, 51.6 percent of the fugitives had a person who was or had been married at the head, but only 46 percent of the total population did. These may well be insignificant differences.

Patterns for time of year of sale into slavery and for willingness to flee were also very similar. In 158 cases for which information is available, 53.8 percent of those who fled had sold themselves into slavery during the severe December-March season, 28.5 percent during the intermediate April-July months, and 17.7 percent during the mildest period, August through November.

In relation to the cost of slaves—there are nearly identical percentages for the total population and for those who fled: 1.2 percent of all fugitives cost a ruble or less, 2.9 percent of the entire pre-1597 population did; 31.5 percent of the fugitives cost 5 rubles, 27.5 percent of the entire population did; for 15 rubles, the respective figures are 3.1 and 3.4 percent. There is no discernible relationship between the price paid for a group of slaves and the number of those slaves who subsequently fled (r = 0.14; eta^2 = 0.18; N = 162). The nationality of the slaves seems to have made little difference in determining who would flee: 96.4 percent of the fugitives were Russian (N = 223), 96.7 percent of all the slaves in my basic data set (N = 2,484) were Russians. The other fugitives were Lithuanian, Swedish, Livonian, Greek, Tatar, and undetermined military captives.

It is even difficult to say that prior condition of servitude made much difference: for those about whom information is available prior to 1597, 48.9 percent had always been free before becoming slaves, and 52 percent of the fugitives (N = 64 and 123 cases) had not been in any way enslaved before. If the figures were larger, this might indicate definitively that those who had never been in any form of servitude before placed a higher value on freedom than did those who had experienced dependency earlier. This might be supported by the fact that 8.5 percent (N = 36) of all known slaves prior to 1597 had earlier been manumitted, and not a single one of these fled after having been reenslaved: having been enslaved once, then freed, they were unwilling to leave the known security of servitude again for the uncertain world of freedom. A similar situation can be seen in the case of slaves given away as presents: 4.5 percent of all documents were of such origin, but only 0.8 percent of the fugitives were. On the other hand, those who had never known freedom in other contexts were slightly more willing to try freedom than indicated by their representation in the total slave population: 0.7 percent of all slaves had been born as slaves (with no other qualification), and from these came 4.9 percent of all fugitives; 4.2 percent of all slave documents were wills, and 7.3 percent of all fugitives were from wills; 25.2 percent of documents were dowries, and 28.5 percent of the fugitives had been given away in dowries.

Looking at prior occupation, we see that one fugitive had been in the needle trades, four had been bootmakers, one had been a peasant, and two had been landless peasants. If we compare these figures with those in table 11.4 we find that former peasants, landless peasants, and beggars are underrepresented, tradesmen are present in higher percentages among the fugitives than among the general slave population, and that there was a slightly greater chance that formerly dependent elements would flee than would formerly free people.

The data reviewed seem inconclusive, as far as definite trends are concerned. One small point can be made: of those enslaved because their posts as stewards mandated that they be slaves, not a single one fled. Similarly, while 20.7 percent of all slaves had earlier been "voluntary servitors," only 2.9 percent of all fugitives were of that category, or only in one case (with five people) of 72 cases of voluntary servitors did such slaves prove dissatisfied enough with the owner to flee. Not surprisingly, those who had listed themselves as day laborers (7.5 percent of the total) did not flee either—they knew how difficult it had been for them to try to survive in freedom, and were unwilling to try it again.

Of all the fugitives whose slave status can be determined with some accuracy (N = 429), 16.6 percent were hereditary slaves, 16.3 percent were full slaves, 1.2 percent were registered slaves, 67.3 percent were limited service contract slaves, and 0.2 percent were "voluntary" slaves. These figures are quite representative of the entire slave population studied in this work (see table 2.2), for which the corresponding percentages are 8.7, 12.0, 1.4, 71.2, and 0.1 percent.

Considerable information is available about the owners from whom slaves fled.

If one looks at the matter impersonally, there seems to have been almost no way to determine from whom slaves would flee. The land compensation schedule is available in 125 cases (involving 253 people), with compensation entitlement ranging from 150 to 1,200 cheti. There seems to have been no relationship between the numbers who fled and the land entitlement ($r = 0.03$; $eta^2 = 0.10$). The same was true for cash salary entitlement ($N = 59$) and the amount of land the slaveowner had ($N = 81$). Whether or not a slave fled also seems not to have depended on where the slaveowner lived ($N = 211$; 431 fugitive individuals), what his rank was ($N = 188$; 386 fugitive individuals), or what his job was ($N = 83$; 174 fugitive individuals). The number of owners seems to have played little role in determining whether a slave would flee: 76.2 percent of the slaves were owned by a single male ($N = 2,499$), 78.8 percent of the fugitives were ($N = 224$); 6.2 percent were owned by two brothers, 5.8 percent of the figitives were; 1.8 percent of the slaves were owned by single women, 0.9 percent of the fugitives were. Ownership will be discussed further in chapter 17, and here I need only note that whether there was one or more owners seems not to have encouraged or deterred slave flight.

Real people were the losers of fugitive slaves, and 123 such individuals can be identified; 469 slaves ran away from these people on 224 occasions. Seventy-nine slaveowners had one loss experience, twenty-five had 2. Eight had 3, five had 4, two had 5 and 7, one had 6, and one slaveowner reported 21 cases of runaways. The biggest loser of slaves was Mikhail [Ivanov] Miloslavskii, from whom ran away 41 slaves in twenty-one separate episodes. He and his brother Luka jointly lost another six people (in five episodes). M. I. Miloslavskii himself owned a total of 63 slaves, and together with his brother another 13 more, which means that they lost 64 percent of the slaves that they owned. This was a considerably higher proportion than usual (twice as high, perhaps), but there seems to be nothing in his life (discussed in chapter 17) that would explain such losses.

Six other slaveowners reported four or more losses, with the total numbers of slaves fleeing ranging from 5 to 11. They were Ivan Eremeev Chertov (5 fugitives of 19 slaves registered), Ivan Il'in Korotaev (9 of 15), Stepan Petrov Kositskoi (10 of 33), Ivan Mikiforov Likhorev (11 of 46), Matfei Ivanov Meshcherskii (11 of 49), and Makarii Deviatyi Skobel'tsyn (8 of 10). They all possessed considerably more than the average 4.3 (median, 2.4) slaves belonging to the "average" slaveowner, and their losses ranged from 22 to 80 percent of total registrations. The eight "big losers" from slave flight lost a total of 101 of the 248 slaves they registered, or 40.7 percent. One might be inclined to attribute these higher than average losses to the impersonality of large slaveholdings, the alienation of the chattel from their owner, and the difficulties of supervision which typify large slaveholdings in every system. Whether this was completely true for the Muscovite situation seems doubtful. The dynamics of slave purchasing in the presence of such high numbers of fugitives will be discussed in chapter 17, but the point to be made here is that an owner such as Miloslavskii never owned many slaves at any one time (probably never more than seven). The import of these examples seems to be that some wealthier slaveowners provided more "relief" services for the lower elements of society than did the poorer ones; they "recycled" more slaves from the stress that caused them to sell themselves into slavery, bringing them back to a condition in which they felt steady enough to leave their dependent status and try life on their own. The profile of these eight slaveowners is not complete, but it does convey a general picture of who it was that had the resources to provide, whether willingly or unwillingly, the temporary relief that many who sold themselves into slavery were seeking: they were provincial *deti boiarskie* (from Pskov and the Novgorod area, they lived in various places in Shelonskaia and Votskaia piatiny in the last third of the sixteenth century), one of them (Meshcherskii) served a term as a governor (*namestnik*) in the small town of Oreshek, but the rest of them seem to have spent their careers in combat service. Their land compensation entitlements (500 to 600 cheti) were at the top of the scale, as were their annual cash salary entitlements (15 to 30 rubles). While Miloslavskii's landholding (162 cheti) was not very high, that of the others (450-58 cheti) was also in keeping with their profile and, in keeping with the requirements necessary to support quite a number of slaves.[19]

In general, it would have been statistically difficult to predict who would flee,

---

19. I. E. Chertov: RIB 17: 174-76, RIB 15[2]: 55; AI 2: 157; DVP, p. 474. I. I. Korotaev: RIB 17: 152-53; NZKK 1: 377; DVP, p. 506; Veselovskii (1976), p. 157; AIuB 2: 179, 186; SIRIO 129: 324-25; RK 1475-1598, pp. 477, 483. S. P. Kosittskoi: Kopanev, "Materialy," pp. 180-82; RIB 15[2]: 77; NZKK 1: 419; 2: 339, 344. I. M. Likharev: Kopanev, pp. 184-85; NZKK 1: 279, 281; 2: 323, 328-39; RIB 38(1926): 285-86, 292-93, 306; AIuB 2 (1864): 186; RIB 22(1908): 88-92, 369, 569, 618, 638; Ianitskii, pp. 98, 158; NPK 5: 513, 515; Andreiiashev, *Materialy*, p. 171; RK 1559-1605, p. 344, M. I. Meshcherskii: RIB 17: 44-49; RIB 15[1]: 21, 24-25; Markevich, p. cvii; DR 1: 890; DR 2: 668, 673; RIB 35: 191; Sukhotin, ChSV, pp. 11-12; RK 1475-1598, pp. 398, 411; RK 1598-1638, pp. 127, 144; RK 1559-1605, pp. 253-54; Samokvasov, *Materialy* 2: 426-27; AIuB 2: 176-77; RK 1550-1636, 2: 47; DVP, p. 469, Koretskii, *Zakreposhchenie*, p. 266. M. D. Skobel'tsyn: Kopanev, p. 168; Ivanov, OPK, p. 64; Sukhotin, ChSV, p. 371; Samokvasov, AM 1(1905): 49; Paneiakh, *Kholopy*, p. 46. Soviet archives purportedly contain the records of slaves who hoped to flee from D. M. Pozharskii, the hero of the Time of Troubles. Recognizing that they might be questioned en route to their destination, the Zaporozh'e cossacks, the slaves forged a safe-conduct letter in Pozharskii's name to a bailiff of a distant Meshchevsk estate and sealed it with their owner's ring, which they stole while he was taking a bath (A. L. Stanislavskii, "Oskol'skaia gramotka 1649 goda," *Voprosy istorii*, 1981, no. 1: 185). Carrying forged letters of safe-conduct may have been a standard fugitive-slave ruse. In May of 1634 a fugitive slave, one Ivan Semenov, the property of Mar'ia, widow of the famed publicist state secretary Ivan Timofeev, was detained outside of Moscow. On his person were three such letters. Under interrogation, Ivan Semenov admitted that he was on his way to join the cossacks in Roslavl'. Ivan was jailed by the Military Chancellery, and Mar'ia wrote the tsar a petition asking for his release, in which she claimed he was starving and would die without confession (S. P. Mordovina and A. L. Stanislavskii, "Podlozhnye pis'ma moskovskogo kholopa XVII v.," in *Pamiatniki russkogo iazyka. Issledovaniia i publikatsii*, ed. V. S. Golyshenko and A. I. Sumkina [Moscow: Nauka, 1979], pp. 99-104).

and who would not. One may assume that potential buyers simply avoided kinds of individuals they felt would flee, and therefore these kinds do not appear in the data because slavery as a form of relief, no matter how badly needed, would not be available to them. Even if the slave cost its owner no cash outlay, those taking in slaves would know that the overall rate of flight was high, and that a slave who fled probably would take some property with him. Not desiring to take unnecessary risks, slaveowners simply ignored those segments of the population that would have presented abnormally high risk. Such risks do not appear in the data, and, not surprisingly, none of the legislative measures on fugitives or stolen property are targeted at high risks. We may conclude provisionally that flight was a matter of serious concern for slaveowners, that the tendency to flee was statistically unpredictable, and that in fact there was little chance of recovering fugitives.

The length of time slaves had succeeded in being fugitives at the time they were claimed in registration by their owners is available for thirty-nine cases. The average length of successful flight was 10.6 years. Perhaps not surprisingly, it was in cases involving single slaves that runaways had been fugitives the longest, 13.5 years (N = 19); those from cases with larger numbers of slaves (4, 5, or 6) were fugitives for a lesser time period, 8 years (N = 7). Those in groups of two or three had been fugitives for 10.2 years (N = 13). Twenty-six of the fugitives had belonged to Mikhail Miloslavskii and had fled from Liattskii pogost. He was entitled to 500 cheti of land and 15 rubles cash compensation per year; he actually possessed 162 cheti of land. For at least thirty cases, there was a strong negative correlation between successful flight (years absent) and the amount paid for slaves: the lesser the amount paid, the longer the slave was absent from his owner (r = 0.72). It also appears as though units headed by males were more successful at fleeing than were females. The thirty-four units headed by males had been fugitives for an average of 11.0 years at the time they were claimed, the five by females had been absent 7.6 years.

Other variables, such as what the slave had been previously, or who his owner was, seem to have had no bearing on the success of slave flight.

It is too late in time to ask Muscovite slaves why they ran away, whether they were motivated by "political" or "personal" concerns, but the extant evidence gives us some idea. The general impression conveyed is that few fled because they felt slavery to be "unjust," or to register some kind of a personal protest against the regime that led to their enslavement. Rather, slaves fled because they were dissatisfied with their present status, or believed that some other might be preferable, from a personal point of view.

A perceptible, but unquantifiable, motive for slave flight was a desire to be somewhere else, to see more of the world than the inside of one slaveowner's household compound. This impression is strongly conveyed by the court cases discussed in Part I of this work in which a hereditary slave fled from his rightful owner, spent several years elsewhere, and then returned to his initial residence.

Such cases arose because the highly dependent slaves were unable to survive on their own for long, consequently sold themselves to someone else, and that second owner sued for their return after the slave had gone back to his first owner. Such "wanderlust" seems to have been less of a factor motivating first-generation slaves to flight, for, as we have seen, many of them had done considerable traveling before they sold themselves. Also unquantifiable is the claim by some slaveowners that their slaves fled to avoid having to accompany their masters in military service.[20]

The desire to escape one's spouse—effectively, to arrange a divorce—was one of the motives impelling people to sell themselves into slavery. It is equally apparent that a desire to escape an unwanted spouse was a major cause of flight by those who were already slaves. This desire, one may safely assume, was the cause of almost all the family formations headed by women not otherwise identified as widows. The deserting party was almost always the male, who abandoned his wife. (I would be inclined to doubt that in many such cases the women were concubines who had borne their owners' children.) The process of husband desertion is evident in the history of a dowry given by Dobrynia Tolmachev to Ivan Vasil'ev Lodygin in 1590 and registered by the latter in January of 1598. In the initial dowry were the couple Isachko Isakov and his wife Matreshka Kurbatova Nikitina. Some time after 1590, Isachko fled, and Matreshka was remarried to Lodygin's voluntary slave Zakharko Esipov, and they begat a daughter, Ofimka. A second married couple Tolmachev gave away was Emel'ianko Fedorov Budilko and his wife Ogrofenka Olekseeva. Emel'ianko also fled, and Ogrofenka was remarried to another of Lodygin's voluntary slaves, Fetka Vasil'ev, and they begat Romashka, Grishka, and Khovronitsa. Tolmachev also gave away two single slaves in the dowry. One of them, Aniushka Borisova, was married to another of Lodygin's slaves, Matreshka, and in 1598 that marriage was still intact.[21] We cannot be sure why Isachko and Emel'ianko fled. Perhaps they did not get along with their new owner, Lodygin, or, perhaps the strain of living with their wives was too much for them under new ownership. The fact that Lodygin so rapidly married off the deserted wives would indicate, of course, that he did not expect to be able to recover the fugitive husbands. Almost certainly Ivashko fled because he could not get along with his new wife.

Whether Ivashko was forcibly or voluntarily married to Aniushka is something that is not clear from the document. The matter of forced marriages is something that is discussed above in chapter 4, where it was argued that such practice probably was not illegal, although frowned upon. The fact of forced marriages in Muscovite slavery cannot be denied, and this fact undoubtedly made many marriages less compatible than they might have been otherwise. Another illustration can be found in the dowry presented by Ivan Fedorov Kultashev to his son-in-

20. Novosel'skii, "Kollektivnye chelobitnye," pp. 310, 335, nos. 2, 12.
21. Kopanev, "Materialy," pp. 159-60.

law Ondrei Grigor'ev Skobel'tsyn in 1581. The dowry contained three single slaves, Samulka Vasil'ev "Chiudinko" (probably "the Finn"), Mar'itsa Ivanova (a Russian woman), and Mar'itsa Latyshka *polonianka* (the Latvian military captive). This document was also registered in 1597, with intervening demographic events duly noted. The Russian Mar'itsa had been married to Filka Timofeev, who had fled. The Latvian Mar'itsa had been married to Omel'ianko Ivanov; he also, apparently, did not like the arrangement, and fled. Finally, for good measure, perhaps copying the Russian males, Samulka fled as well.[22] The origins of Filka and Omel'ianko are not stated, but we may assume that they were also slaves and fled because they found their compulsory spouses hardly to their liking.

That fugitive slaves often abandoned their spouses was noted in a slaveowner petition about fugitives dated December 19, 1682, and then in the government response of January 3, 1683, a decree by the tsar, patriarch, and boyars (the most powerful, authoritative combination the Muscovites could muster when promulgating legislation) on the sanctions to be imposed for taking in the runaways. The preamble begins: "those slaves and peasants, having abandoned their wives and children, fleeing as solitaries, are residing. . . ."[23] Of course the government did not discuss why slaves abandoned their families, much less do anything positive that might diminish the desire of slaves to flee, but at least it was aware of the problem and its potential social consequences (broken marriages and the like).

(The reader might wonder whether the government's concern was not misplaced, given the extreme sexual imbalance in favor of males in the institution of slavery. Certainly it does seem as though slaveowners were able to provide "an instant husband" for almost any woman, and thus few marriageable women who wanted husbands could have gone for very long without one. We must recall that this was still the era before warfare had a serious demographic impact on the lower classes.)

Another stimulus to slave flight must have been the fact of incompatibility between slave and slaveowner. As was discussed in chapter 15, the naked exercise of force and violence by slaveowners was not unknown in Muscovy. Slaves have been fleeing cruel masters since at least Babylonian times. Most studies of slave flight in the U. S. conclude that owner brutality (or the fear of chastisement) was its major impetus, and there is documented evidence in the case of Bezobrazov's slaves that they fled for the same reason. In another instance, slaves are recorded as having fled because they had been assaulted by their owner's son.[24] It seems unlikely, however, that experience or fear of owner brutality was the

22. Lakier, p. 43.

23. Novosel'skii, "Kollektivnye chelobitnye," p. 331, no. 10; PSZ 2: 491, no. 985. For another illustration, see the 1589 case of Nazareiko Ivanov (RIB 17: 161), discussed below in chapter 18.

24. Mendelsohn, p. 63; Genovese, *Roll*, p. 649; Novosel'skii, *Votchinnik*, p. 64; Kopanev, *Krest'ianstvo russkogo Severa*, p. 185.

major cause of flight in Muscovy. For one thing, there was probably less of it, and the Muscovites were more accustomed to it. For another, since flight was so easy, one may assume that far more causes precipitated it. While most slaves remained dependent, those who had physically recovered from the causes that forced them to sell themselves (or, even military captives who had become accustomed to their new land) were willing to flee for many causes besides an actual or potential hiding. One may surmise that, in addition to marriage disputes, almost any slight by an owner, insufficient food, or simply the desire to go somewhere else was often quite enough to put a slave on the road. The favorite time, of course, was when the owner was in service, an annual event for most of Muscovite history that most slaves could routinely count upon. While the wives, relatives, or slave stewards of some slaveowners were able to handle their affairs during their absence, in most cases the pursuit of slaves usually seems to have waited upon the return of the master himself from service. This is most evident in the many petitions for temporary discharge from military service requested and granted because of the flight of the serviceman's chattel.[25] By the time he got home, of course, the slave could be lost in the vastness of the east European plain.

There are a number of questions that can be asked about fugitive slaves for which no answers seem to be available. One would be about the seasonality of slave flights and their correspondence with self-sales. Unfortunately, the registration documents from 1597-98 that mention slave flights never state the dates when they occurred, and those instances from the court cases are too few to permit any generalizations. One might surmise that flights were the mirror image of self-sales, the most flights coming during late summer and autumn, the least during the four worst months of winter, but the extant data do not tell us that. Of course slave motivation, planning, and prior arrangements would also be tempting to investigate, but that seems impossible as well. It is also unclear whether first-generation or hereditary slaves had a greater tendency to flee. The general assumption is that the latter, those born and brought up as slaves, were more docile than those who had been free men, and then either sold themselves or were somehow forced (e.g., by war captivity) into slavery. The general impression created by the Muscovite data is that flights from the two groups were equally divided, but that cannot be checked precisely.

Destruction of Documents

It is often assumed by students of slavery that some degree of political consciousness and protest was exhibited by slaves who took the trouble to destroy or steal the documents formulating their slavery status at the time they fled. The

25. AMG 1: 585, no. 634.

destruction of documents might destroy a slaveowner's claim to his chattel. Such actions demonstrate that the act of flight was planned in advance and was not a spontaneous response to a family squabble or a beating by the master. Such forethought seems to have been comparatively rare in Muscovy. Information concerning at least 250 acts of slave flight is extant, and only two of them mention the destruction of documents. On February 27, 1592, Iakov Elisiev Krasnoslepov signed a marriage contract with Ivan Semenov Kartmazov for his daughter Fedos'ia, and gave away two families—one with two boys and a girl, the other with two girls and a boy—and a single male. At some time in the next six years one of the daughters, Okulsha Vashutina, was married to Fedor, and they begot a son, Kondratko. Prior to the registration of the document in December of 1598, Okulsha and her son fled. What happened to Fedor is not mentioned, nor is anything said about why she fled. It is noted, however, that she stole (*vykrala*) the dowry gift document, written on July 29, 1592, that confirmed the marriage contract executed five months earlier. Apparently she also stole, for good measure, another document on the slave Mitka Ondreev.[26] It is not stated when Okulsha and her son fled and took the documents, but they had not been recovered by 1598. (The other case of a slave stealing his documents while fleeing was discussed in chapter 8.)

The major instance of the deliberate destruction of documents was of course the setting fire to the Slavery Chancellery during the disturbances of 1682, an event that will be discussed further below.

The Lives of Fugitives after Flight

Information of what fugitive slaves did after running away is relatively plentiful. As noted earlier, many of them simply transferred to another owner. Sometimes this was by design, as when a slave moved down the street, at other times it was by necessity, when the runaway discovered that he lacked the internal resources to survive by himself. In other cases, however, sometimes changing their names, they passed themselves off as free men, and tried to support themselves as such.

A number of fugitive slaves joined the ranks of the poor, sustaining themselves in odd jobs of various kinds (*iaryzhnye*).[27] Others, who fled to the northwestern frontier Pomor'e region (bordering Swedish possessions), a favorite place of refuge during the Time of Troubles era, joined the cossacks under government command at the end of 1613 and the beginning of 1614 and tried to render military assistance to Pskov when it was besieged by the Swedish king, Gustavus Adolphus. After 1614 Tsar Mikhail Romanov's government assisted efforts of

26. RIB 17: 137-40, nos. 376, 380.
27. PSZ 2: 491, no. 985.

owners who sent agents to the front to recover their slaves in the region, with the consequence that the fugitives joined the forces creating disorder in the Belo-ozero-Vologda region in the early years of Mikhail's reign.[28] The trans-Onega region remained a place of refuge throughout the seventeenth century, and labor-short enterprises such as salt boiling offered no-questions-asked employment. Others who fled to the southern frontier tried to mingle in with the civilian or military personnel there. For example, in 1637 a slave who had joined the musketeers in Kozlov was taken out of those ranks and returned to his owner.[29] The region of the frontier, along the Belgorod and Saransk fortified lines, offered almost continuous refuge to fugitive slaves throughout the second half of the seventeenth century, and fugitive slaves were eagerly enrolled in the sundry lower- and middle-service class ranks and military occupations. The records of fugitives apprehended and returned in the 1660s reveal that most peasants fled in family groups, that many of the solitary fugitives were slaves who fled to the Don, to join the cossacks. The cossacks, and also the musketeers, were a place of refuge for fugitive slaves in the early 1680s.[30] The Volga region, from Kazan' to Astrakhan', sponged up fugitives, who worked on the boats plying the great river, in the potash industry (cutting over the land and burning the timber), and in other unskilled, day-wage occupations. Still another source of employment was offered by merchants engaged in intercity trade, who hired fugitive slaves to transport their commodities.[31] Others tried to find refuge in the ranks of the lower clergy. When found, they were defrocked and returned to slavery, as was nearly always done in any organized religion. (In the 1670s the same provisions were applied vigorously to fugitive peasant-serfs.)[32] Some fugitives with trades pursued them. A 1684 court case cites a Lithuanian prisoner of war who served his captors for five years, then fled. Apparently blending in well, he became a miller, but tiring of that he returned to his captor-master.[33]

28. M. N. Tikhomirov, "Pskovskie povesti o krest'ianskoi voine v Rossii nachala XVII v.," *Iz istorii sotsial'no-politicheskikh idei. Sbornik statei k 70-letiiu Akad. V. P. Volgina,* ed. N. M. Druzhinin et al. (Moscow: Akademiia Nauk SSSR, 1955), p. 186; V. A. Figarovskii, "Krest'ianskoe vosstanie 1614-1615 gg.," *Istoricheskie zapiski* 73(1962): 203.

29. On the case of a musketeer returned to slavery, see Brian Davies' 1637 Kozlov file, case no. 379. In the 1520s Herberstein reported that the recently annexed northeastern frontier region of Viatka-Khlynov was a favorite fugitive slave asylum (*Commentaries,* Backus edition, p. 97.)

30. A. A. Novosel'skii, "K voprosu ob ekonomicheskom sostoianii beglykh krest'ian na iuge moskovskogo gosudarstva v pervoi polovine XVII v.," *Istoricheskie zapiski* 16(1945): 58; Savich, *Vosstanie,* pp. 310, 314, no. 157, 199.

31. Novosel'skii, "Kollektivnye chelobitnye," pp. 309-10, 313-14, 316, 322-23, 334-35, 341.

32. 1649 *Ulozhenie* 20: 67, 68; MS. p. 279; PRP 3(1955): 423, art. 12; G. N. Obraztsov, "Ulozhenie 1649 g. i krest'iane votchiny Antonievo-Siiskogo monastyria," *Istoricheskie zapiski* 63(1958): 279-80; Arkhangel'skii, *O sobornom Ulozhenii,* pp. 45-46.

33. PSZ 2: 590, no. 1073.

Perhaps most notable about the postflight careers of slaves is that so few of them engaged in agriculture. When they fled, they did not take agricultural inventory with themselves, and, when apprehended, they were hardly ever farming. All of this once again indicates that relatively few slaves were individuals who had recently been engaged in primary agricultural pursuits.

In general, a fugitive slave was able to find employment of some kind very easily almost anywhere in Muscovy until at least the end of the seventeenth century. This fact, recognized by complaining slaveowners, unquestionably made flight a far more attractive proposition than it would have been otherwise.

Nothing is known about the mental condition of Muscovite fugitive slaves—whether they felt guilty, "hunted," or were joyful over being at least temporarily free. There are no Muscovite "slave narratives" (such as those in the American Fisk University and WPA compilations), and my sample of fugitives is limited to those who were apprehended or voluntarily returned to their former owners. That certainly biases the sample negatively, whereas those who were successful in fleeing must have felt more positively about the experience.

The Return of Fugitives

That slave societies have shown a nearly uniform severity in dealing with fugitive slaves is well known.[34] However, Muscovy ordinarily was far less harsh than some places, such as Babylonia, where the Hammurabi Code prescribed death, or Riyadh, Saudi Arabia, where the death sentence was carried out as late as 1960.[35] The Muscovites left the matter in the hands of the owner, who was instructed not to kill or maim his apprehended fugitive, but no sanctions were stated for violators. Until the mid-seventeenth century, Muscovy's slave-catching system was primitive by comparison with others, which is one reason why slaveowners had such difficulty in recovering their fugitives. The state only became involved in the apprehension and return of fugitive slaves in connection with the massive searches for fugitive urban taxpayers and then serfs in the mid-seventeenth century. The state probably did not get involved in the matter of runaway slaves earlier because that had always been a subject of private concern, because the state apparatus was insufficiently developed to undertake such a task, and because no one perceived it as a serious problem while slaves were cheap and replacements were available to those who had the means to maintain them.

In the mid-seventeenth century the Muscovite government began to concern itself increasingly with the matter of fugitive slaves. The subject of fugitives has been touched upon briefly in previous chapters, but here I shall discuss some

34. D. B. Davis, p. 56.
35. Winks, p. 191.

of the post-*Ulozhenie* measures on fugitives in the seventy-five years prior to the effective abolition of the institution of slavery.

A first point to be noted is that Muscovy did not develop extensive preventive measures, such as in Mesopotamian Eshnunna (ca. 1900 B.C.), where a branded slave could not go through the city gate without a pass from his owner.[36] Slaves later were marked by shaving, branding, or mutilation in Babylonia and elsewhere in the Ancient Near East, or by the wearing of badges in the U.S. South.[37] Moreover, Muscovy never developed an institution such as the infamous Southern slave patrol, although the frequent instructions issued to provincial authorities in the seventeenth century requiring them to observe all movements of unknown persons were intended to have the same effect.[38] (In 1658 the petitioning owners of fugitive slaves asked the government to enlist the local clergy as well in the task of monitoring the mobility of strangers.)[39] The reluctance of Muscovites to mark slaves has been discussed in chapter 6, but in general it was a manifestation of the relatively passive attitude of the government toward slaves, which can be characterized as at first a general "hands-off" position (a reflection of the dyadic nature of early Muscovite law and its aftermath), later a willingness to leave the option open for the slave to flee and to worry about what to do with him only after he did. In 1684 slaveowner petitioners wanted the government to enforce a modified form of internal passport systems (every worker would have to possess documents, either a manumission document [*otpusknaia*] or a pass from his owner [*prokhozhaia*]), but Muscovy was not yet ready for such police-state refinements.[40]

Decrees on fugitive slaves were issued in 1655, 1657, 1658, 1661, 1663, 1664, 1665, and 1681-83. These dates coincide with the tension of the Thirteen Years War and the period of interregnum prior to the assumption of power by Peter the Great. The series of decrees opened on March 11, 1655, a time when slaves were deserting their owners en masse in the Smolensk War combat zone, with a savage decree prescribing hanging for fugitives. On March 24, this was reduced to hanging for every fifth fugitive when groups fled, and a flogging with the knout and return to lawful owners for the rest.[41] Many of the subsequent decrees were promulgated in response to petitions from slaveowners complaining about the flight of their chattel (usually linked, of course, with the problem of fugitive serfs). The ending of the Thirteen Years War and the suppression of the Razin-

---

36. Pritchard, p. 137, arts. 51-52.

37. Driver and Miles, 1: 306-9; Mendelsohn, p. 49; Goldin, p. 38. An extensive pass system was also in use throughout the U.S. South.

38. Rose, pp. 178, 183; MS, pp. 140-41.

39. Novosel'skii, "Kollektivnye chelobitnye," p. 311.

40. Ibid., p. 334, no. 11.

41. The laws on fugitives were: PSZ 1: 359-60, 444-46, 556-58, 576-77, 583-84, 593-602, 611; 2: 355-56, 481-83, 488-92, 499, 502; nos. 150-51, 217, 220, 307, 333, 350, 364, 373, 891, 972, 981-82, 985, 991, 997. The capital punishment statutes were nos. 150-51. See also Novosel'skii, "Otdatochnye knigi," p. 130.

shchina noticeably diminished slave flight and were responsible for the quiescent 1670s.

In 1975 the late Soviet historian S. M. Troitskii published thirteen collective petitions dated between 1657 and 1694 on the subject of fugitive slaves and serfs that had been prepared for publication some time earlier by A. A. Novosel'-skii (1891-1967). The petitions are dated 1657, 1658, 1676, 1677 (2), 1681, 1682 (4), 1684, 1691, and 1694. The correlation between the dates of the petitions and the laws on fugitives is, of course, not accidental. The continuity in the petitioning process was deliberate and displayed a regularity of themes. The petitioners usually emphasized their military service and the fact that their slaves had used their absence to flee; taking advantage of the fact that the loyal manpower was at the front, the slaves first looted and then set fire to what they could not cart off of their owners' property, murdered the owners' wives and children, stole their horses, weapons, and other combat gear. Fugitives sometimes formed large gangs of a hundred or more, tried to lure other slaves, and engaged in highway robbery. They fled to the towns along the Belgorod and Saransk fortified lines, to towns of the Volga region, and even to Ufa in Bashkiria.

The early petitioners emphasized the near impossibility of recovering their own fugitives by themselves. When they themselves tried to return fugitives, or sent other slaves to do it for them, the runaways resisted, sometimes assaulting the would-be slave catcher, even shooting him with bow and arrow or a handgun. With the passage of time, as the government became increasingly involved in the location, apprehension, and return of fugitives, the laments about the futility of private efforts were dropped, indicating that the efforts were no longer made. Instead, the petitioners noted quite consistently that the regular officials, governors, census-takers, and the like could not be trusted to return fugitives because of lethargy, friendship, preoccupation with other tasks, or interest in keeping the fugitives in the area as servicemen or taxpayers. They recommended as the solution to the personnel problem the appointment of special fugitive slave- and serf-hunters. The petitioners also consistently recommended increasing the sanctions for receiving and harboring fugitive slaves, claiming that the penalties were so trivial that violators could ignore them with impunity.[42]

The government responded to the petitions by appointing investigators (*syshchiki*) to hunt for runaways. The first substantial attempt to do this was made at the end of the 1630s, when the Repnins were appointed to try to find fugitive townsmen (*posadskie liudi*) and return them to the places where they were registered on the tax rolls. The *Ulozhenie* decreed that townsmen should be registered on the tax rolls where they lived, and no attempt should be made to return them to a previous residence; but the precedent of sending out government

---

42. Novosel'skii, "Kollektivnye chelobitnye," pp. 304-41. For a discussion of the extreme rarity of apprehending fugitives in the pre-Time of Troubles era, see AIS-ZR (1978), p. 110.

agents to search for those fugitives was utilized to hunt down fugitive slaves and serfs. (The petitioners, be it noted, always mentioned slaves first, probably because that helped psychologically to legitimize a conception of their peasant-serfs as objects which could be pursued, returned, and treated by methods that previously had been used only for slaves.) The government issued instructions to the slave-catchers during the era of the Thirteen Years War which were subsequently summarized in a fifty-two-article legislative monument of March 2, 1683, that was promulgated explicitly in response to petitions of November 18 and December 1, 1682.[43]

The 1683 instructions to the fugitive slave-and serf-catchers were a summary codification of a combined, integrated approach to the problem of fugitives. The starting point of the codification, in many respects, was a repetition of an order of September 18, 1663, forbidding the temporary exemption or discharge from military service of servicemen who wanted to look for fugitives. Such practices were needed so long as the finding of fugitives remained a personal matter, but they were a continual problem. Under the pressure of the Thirteen Years War, however, the government decreed that slave-catching was the task of its appointed agents. (This did not rule out a slaveowner's hunting for his fugitives during his free time, or sending out other slaves to look for them.) The government-appointed slave-catcher was to do his work both on the basis of slaveowner petitions that noted where fugitive slaves were and on his own initiative: when he independently learned of the presence of fugitives, he was to investigate the population of a region and, following the procedures discussed in chapter 8, was to sort out the fugitives and prepare for their return. These methods resulted in the return of thousands of fugitives in the second half of the seventeenth century. For example, in 1664-65, 3,036 people were returned from Riazan' province. Of them, 660 were fugitive slaves, the rest fugitive peasant-serfs.[44]

While increased emphasis was placed on the discovery of fugitives, the government remained aware of the fact that flight was so common at least partially because it was so easy, and experimented with various methods of making the life of the fugitive less attractive and the receipt of fugitives less rewarding. Almost unquestionably it was initially inhibited in the attempt to find solutions by a priori conceptions that slaves were chattel fundamentally unaccountable for their actions and that slaveowners were by and large a category of individuals to whom the ordinary arsenal of governmental sanctions (capital and corporal punishment, mutilation, incarceration, fines) should not apply. However, in an

43. P. P. Smirnov, *Posadskie liudi*, 1: 455-87; PSZ 2: 502-13, no. 998; PRP 7: 184-201; Man'kov, *Razvitie*, pp. 31, 82-119.

44. Novosel'skii, "Otdatochnye knigi," p. 146. A list of the major fugitive slave and serf hunts can be found in A. P. Gudzinskaia, "Dokumenty sysknykh komissii vtoroi poloviny XVII v. kak istoricheskii istochnik," *Arkheograficheskii ezhegodnik za 1967 god* 11(1969): 116-18.

attempt to cope with the problem of fugitives, the government ultimately felt compelled to abandon most of those conceptions.

Possible solutions to the problem of fugitives would have been to make it more attractive for slaves to remain with their owners; to impede the process of flight by devices ranging from the establishing of roadblocks to the circulation of lists of fugitives; to punish the slave himself for fleeing; or to make it difficult for a fugitive to find refuge. The first solution was never tried, to my knowledge. Impediments, particularly of the surveillance type, were constantly being raised, and resulted in the creation of a proto-police state, but proved insufficient. The government, ultimately recognizing the volitional capacity of slaves, in 1665 decreed and prescribed hanging for fugitives and later effected the savage, "merciless" beating with the knout for slaves; this deterred few slaves from running away, apparently, since the chance of fleeing successfully remained high.

Comprehending the situation, the government concentrated much of its attention on denying refuge to fugitives by trying to make it unattractive for anyone knowingly to harbor a runaway. In the 1660s the approach was to beat with the knout seignorial estate stewards (themselves often slaves), and communal representatives elsewhere (on court lands, in towns, postal stations, and the like), but in a society accustomed to a high level of violence, that proved relatively ineffective. In 1663, the government added a year in jail to the beating, although that had no effect, and in 1667 it proposed turning the steward who received a fugitive over to the plaintiff as a peasant. Next, the oligarchs decided to impose sanctions on those who really benefited from the reception of fugitives, the landholders themselves (or peasant, town, or postal-system leaders, or an entire village), and switched to a policy of fines and confiscation of additional personnel (in 1661, one peasant for each fugitive, and in 1682 four peasants per fugitive), in addition to depriving the recipient of the fugitives themselves. In 1681 the policy of exacting peasants for the fugitives was temporarily dropped in favor of a fine of 10 rubles per year. The fine was temporarily abolished in 1682 and then in 1683 it was reinstituted and established as 10 rubles a year for each family or solitary taken in prior to 1662, and 20 rubles per year after 1662. The guilty were given a month in which to pay each 100 rubles of fine; if they could not pay, they were to endure a "cruel punishment" (*zhestokoe nakazanie*), a beating with the knout. The fines were inheritable if the heirs had shared the property prior to the major figure's death. Moreover, the recipient of a fugitive slave was supposed to transport on his own carts the runaway back to the rightful owner. These stiff sanctions imposed on those who received fugitives are thought to have been somewhat effective.

When a fugitive was denounced by a local landowner, steward, or communal official, or apprehended by a slave-catcher, he was taken to a regional center, interrogated, and jailed. Late Muscovite authorities abhorred jail, and the 1683 statute discussed the options: bail, or perhaps jailing only of the slave's wife and children. A local government was to pay for feeding jailed fugitives out of its revenues. Having learned who the owner of the apprehended fugitive was, the local detaining authorities were to inform the governors and other officials, and also to instruct criers to make public announcements in the marketplaces that they had custody of slave X belonging to this or that *dvorianin* or *syn boiarskii*, who was then supposed to fetch back his subject. If the lawful owner did not reclaim his slave (the appropriate interval is not stated, only a "long time" [*mnogoe vremia*]), then the person with whom the slave was living when apprehended could reclaim him—paying all the fees, of course.[45]

Thus as the system of slavery was about to expire, the Muscovites worked out an effective, formal system for the recovery of fugitive slaves. Of course it must be emphasized that, while slaves were always mentioned first (and probably lent a moral legitimacy to the procedure of fugitive-hunting), the impetus to the creation of a slave recovery system was given by the problem of fugitive serfs. One might plausibly argue, counterfactually, that the fifty-two-article 1683 legislative monument never would have existed had it not been for the serfs, for issues involving them galvanized the government in a way the issue of slavery had never succeeded in doing.

The 1683 codification on fugitives remained the fundamental law until the end of slavery. An obvious defect in the law of 1667 and in the 1683 codification that had to be remedied was the vagueness about the length of time a fugitive could be detained in jail before measures to recover him had to be initiated. In 1690 *mnogoe vremia* was reduced to a month, in 1691 to a week, and in 1694 its application was strengthened.[46] In 1699 Peter the Great observed that the problem of fugitives had not been solved and that the harborers of runaways showed contempt for the sanctions of previous decades; sending out a new crop of fugitive-hunters (even to the Don and Belgorod frontier regions), he combined all of those sanctions; a beating with the knout for stewards who took in the fugitives, a fine of 20 rubles per year, and an exaction of four peasants (plus their families) for each fugitive taken in.[47] Such draconian sanctions were typical of the Petrine era but had little effect. The humane mind might find it difficult to conceive of measures beyond those of 1699, but in 1704 Peter showed that escalation was possible: he decreed confiscation of landed property, the death penalty, and damnation for receiving and concealing fugitives.[48] Such sanctions were manifestly absurd, a fact realized two years later, when they reduced to confiscation of one-half of the fugitive harborer's landed property for the tsar, the other half for the owner of the fugitive.[49] In 1707 Peter, observing that people regarded his edicts with contempt and were ignoring them, went on

45. PSZ 2: 502-13, no. 998.
46. PSZ 3: 56-57, 91, 179-80, nos. 1368, 1396, 1495.
47. PSZ 3: 443-46, 474-78; nos. 1623, 1625, 1644-45. For petitions of the mid-1690s, see *Opisanie dokumentov i bumag* 17(1912): 368, no. 2550.
48. PSZ 4: 257-58, no. 1980.
49. PSZ 4: 341, no. 2092.

another tack: to find fugitives, the local peasants should be interrogated under oath and with the threat of the death penalty for perjury, and then the former sanctions should be imposed.[50]

The desperate Petrine legislation on fugitives coincided with the ruler's youth and the dark years of the Northern War. After Poltava, the situation changed, and the issue of fugitives became one of refining technicalities and introducing imperial standards and procedures into newly annexed areas of Ukraine.[51] Moreover, the institution of slavery was definitely waning, and in the early 1720s laws on fugitives began to be promulgated that did not mention slaves at all, or along with the issue of fugitive peasants in the context of the new census.[52] But the codifying spirit of the late Petrine era ultimately lit on the problem of fugitives, and slaves were included in the general law of April 6, 1722, on the problem.[53] Its norms fundamentally went back to the previous century, and prescribed the return of fugitives, heavy fines for lords, and a beating with the knout for stewards and peasants who took fugitives in. These remained the devices for trying to cope with fugitive serfs, who of course posed a problem down to the end of the serf regime. The new law also recognized the further demise of slavery by placing a three-year limit on reclaiming fugitives, who then became the property of the people with whom they had been living.[54]

The request by slaveowners late in the seventeenth century for tighter control of slave mobility was finally met by Peter, as the system of slavery itself was about to expire, with the beginnings of a formal internal passport system. Decrees of 1722 specified that no one could be rented night lodgings without the appropriate documentation (*iavnoe svidetel'stvo*) or hired for any job without documentation guaranteeing his status (*poruchnaia zapis'*).[55] Thus the origins of one element of the police state can be traced in part to demands by slaveowners for measures to control their fugitives.

Once again we see that the institution of slavery had a direct impact on the institution of serfdom. The recovery of fugitive slaves during and for a long time after the dyadic era of justice in Muscovy had been a matter of private concern, the business of the slaveowner. The state was willing to lend its services to resolve conflicts over the ownership of fugitives but took no part in their discovery or apprehension. With the development of the state system, however, governmental authorities were increasingly willing to become involved in ever-widening aspects of life, including the apprehension of fugitive slaves. In the second half of the seventeenth and the beginning of the eighteenth centuries these measures

50. PSZ 4: 378-79, no. 2147.

51. PSZ 5: 50-51, 87, 125-26, 150-51, 158; nos. 2706, 2783, 2846, 2891, 2910.

52. PSZ 6: 127-28, 234, 358-61, 460-61, 503-10, 525; nos. 3512, 3636, art. 3, 3857, 3901, arts. 15-16, 3936.

53. PSZ 6. 638-41, no. 3939.

54. PSZ 1: 577; 6: 640, nos. 333, 3939.

55. PSZ 6: 648, 732, 804-5, nos. 3958, 4047, arts. 20, 4130, art. 28.

were perfected as corps of fugitive slave and serf hunters were dispatched to discover runaways, and attempts were made (never very successful ones, regardless of how barbarous) to fine-tune sanctions both for slaves who fled and lords or officials who received them. These measures became the operating enforcement tools for serfdom.

Collective Disorders

All of the forms of resistance discussed so far have been primarily of an individual nature, similar to those in many other slave systems, including that in the American South. There is a major discontinuity between slavery and later nineteenth-century Russian slavelike serfdom, in which, as emphasized by Peter Kolchin, much of the resistance was in the form of communal, collective confrontation with the serfowners.[56] Professor Kolchin also observes that the response of the owners was different in the imperial Russian and American systems: the Russian was slow and bureaucratic, often through a chain of command beginning with the local steward and ending in St. Petersburg; the American was immediate and local.[57] The Muscovite response might be described as an intermediate one; owners and stewards certainly punished recalcitrants on the spot, but there was also considerable written correspondence between stewards and owners, as well as a tendency to appeal to the central authorities, because of the concentration of authority in the capital, for help in quelling relatively petty disturbances.

In some societies, slave revolts had a significant impact on the institution of slavery. China was such an example: extensive revolts at the end of the seventeenth and beginning of the eighteenth centuries caused a great diminution in the large number of massive slaveholdings and the liberation of many slaves by an official reclassification of them from "base people" to "free people." Slavery continued to exist in China, but became primarily an institution for docile females. In Muscovy, however, there were no "slave revolts," probably for the same reason that there were none in the Ancient Near East: there was no great concentrations of slaves in mines or on latifundia-plantations.[58] Where there were large numbers of slaves, such as in Moscow, perhaps in other major towns,

56. Peter Kolchin, "The Process of Confrontation: Patterns of Resistance to Bondage in Nineteenth-Century Russia and the United States," *Journal of Social History* 11, no. 4 (1978): 470.

57. Ibid, pp. 472-73.

58. Mendelsohn, p. 121. Moreover, to my knowledge, Muscovy had few messianic preachers, who "appeared in almost every slave revolt on record" (Eugene D. Genovese, "American Slaves and Their History," *The New York Review of Books* 15, no. 10 [December 3, 1970]: 35).

and in the army, they were generally diffused, and certainly a minority, among the greater numbers of free men.

Nevertheless, slaves played a noticeable role in many of the civil disorders in Muscovy, and their influence came to a climax during the Time of Troubles.

The nature of civil disorders changed about the mid-sixteenth century from typical medieval protests against the failure of officials to provide adequate defense to more modern disorders directed against outright corruption and occasionally against the very structure of society itself. (I intend to examine this evolution more fully in another forum, and shall not pursue it further here.) Little is known about the involvement of slaves in disorders prior to 1600. It was rumored that the 1547 fire in Moscow was set at the behest of some of the ruling elite, and presumably the incendiaries would have been slaves. In that case, of course, they were not exactly acting on their own volition. R. G. Skrynnikov has recently written that the 1586 reformulation of limited service contract slavery was preceded in May of that year by massive social disorders with slave participants in the capital. In 1591 the Crimean Tatars attacked Muscovy and burned the southern suburbs of the capital. It was later reported by the Dutchman Isaac Massa that a plot had been uncovered in which slaves had intended to burn Moscow itself during the siege by Kazy-Girei. About seventy conspirators, mostly slaves, were arrested and punished. (One may assume that they were executed, although Massa only says that "all these traitors received the appropriate retribution.")[59]

Slaves played a leading, sometimes catalytic role in the disorders of the Time of Troubles and the leaders of the major movements (Kholpko, Ivan Bolotnikov, Vas'ia Shestakov, and Balovnia) themselves were present or former slaves. According to the contemporary Avraamii Palitsyn, over twenty thousand fugitive slaves who had been driven out by their owners during the 1601-3 famines were concentrated along the southern frontier of Muscovy, where they had sought refuge and succor.[60] It is assumed that many of these men joined the army of Khlopko, which moved against Moscow, attacked the city, and was defeated in September 1603. Nothing is known about Khlopko, who he was or where he came from, although it is obvious that his name means "slave" (*kholop*). The attack of Khlopko's forces is often linked with Boris Godunov's law of August 16, 1603, setting free slaves who were starving and had been evicted, but not formally manumitted, by their owners. The assumption is, of course, that the measure was a demagogic move to diffuse the Khlopko movement, one obviously long overdue as the famine was in its third year.[61]

59. Isaak Massa, *Kratkoe izvestie o Moskovii v nachale XVII v.* (Moscow: Gossotsekgiz, 1937), p. 39; R. G. Skrynnikov, *Rossiia nakanune "smutnogo vremeni"* (Moscow: Mysl', 1980), p. 104.

60. *Skazanie Avraamiia Palitsyna* (Moscow-Leningrad: Akademiia Nauk SSSR, 1955), p. 108; I. I. Smirnov, *Vosstanie Bolotnikova*, pp. 74-75.

61. PSRL 14[1], p. 58 (chap. 84 of *Novyi letopisets*); V. I. Koretskii, "Iz istorii krest'ianskoi voiny v Rossii nachala XVII veka," *Voprosy istorii* 15, no. 3 (March 1959), pp. 128-33.

Basically nothing is known about any of the slave leaders of the Time of
Troubles other than in the case of Ivan Bolotnikov. Comparisons between him
and Spartacus, the leader of the Gladiatorial War (73-71 B.C.) against Rome, are
inevitable. Ivan Bolotnikov was an elite military slave who was captured by the
Tatars, sold in Kaffa, resold in Istanbul to a German trader, and transported to
Venice. From there he escaped back to Muscovy.[62] As leader of the rebels, he
was offered a bribe to join the forces of Vasilii Shuiskii, but refused.[63] His
forces besieged Moscow from October 7 to December 2, 1606, then were defeated. Vasilii Shuiskii's government made no concession to the slaves (many of
them survivors of famine eviction) among Bolotnikov's forces, and answered
with harsh legal repression after the rebellion had been crushed.

While the leader, Bolotnikov, was a slave, it is doubtful that the majority of
his troops had ever experienced similar civic disabilities. However, the rebels
did appreciate the potential for creating trouble inherent in the slave population
and the Englishman John Meyrick (the attribution is not certain, but likely)
noted that some of Bolotnikov's forces

Writt ltres to the Slaves wth in the Towne [Moscow], to take Armes against
their Masters and to possesse themselves of their Goodes and substance.[64]

Noteworthy about that quotation is the fact that the slaves of Moscow were
assumed to be able to read (as we have seen throughout this work, many of them
could), and that the rebels did not ask the slaves to join them but rather to
destroy the will of the capital to resist from within.

The role of slaves in the Bolotnikov rebellion has been subject to widely
varying interpretations. Lengthy discussion of historiographical issues is not
the function of this work. Nevertheless, the range of opinions on this important subject should be noted, even though they are inconclusive. For
example, D. P. Makovskii noted that slaves were not the motive force of the
Bolotnikov rebellion; they were disorganized, panicked easily, and were willing
to join whoever would pay them more.[65] This last aspect, the fact that the slaves
were as likely to be on the repressing side in Muscovite disorders, will be
noted in other contexts as well. On the other hand, N. E. Nosov assigned a
very important role to the slaves, and I. I. Smirnov saw slaves as one of the pri-

62. Fisher, "Muscovy," p. 587.
63. Bussov, pp. 140, 269; Makovskii, PKV, p. 336.
64. I. I. Smirnov, *Vosstanie Bolotnikova*, pp. 553, 555. Nearly the same news was sent by
Patriarch Ermogen to Metropolitan Filaret (AAE 2: 132, no. 58).
65. Makovskii, PKV, pp. 465-66. A. A. Zimin considered the peasantry to have been the
basic motive force of the Bolotnikov uprising (Zimin and Koroleva, "Dokument," p. 28).
Zimin's statement in his article "Nekotorye voprosy istorii krest'ianskoi voiny v Rossi v
nachale XVII veka,"*Voprosy istorii* 1958, no. 3: 98, 108-9, prompted a rebuttal by I. I.
Smirnov ("O nekotorykh voprosakh istorii bor'by klassov v russkom gosudarstve nachala
XVII veka," *Voprosy istorii* 1958, no. 12: 120) that clearly defined the issues.

mary forces of the Bolotnikov rebellion.[66] Aside from the matter of leadership, the issue may well be one of critical mass. Could any of the uprisings of the seventeenth century, from that of Bolotnikov to the 1682 Khovanshchina, have attained the scale (not only in sheer numbers, but in their capacity to frighten the ruling elements) that they did had it not been for the slave participation? The answer would be no, and the "proof" might well be furnished by the eighteenth century, when after the abolition of slavery, the character of uprisings changed. Of course there were other reasons as well for the diminution of domestic disorder in the eighteenth century, but the absence of the slave element is a fact that should not be overlooked.

The social origins of the second pretender, False Dmitrii II, are unknown, but, while headquartered in Orel (on the southern frontier) in the winter of 1607-8, he made a broader appeal to the slaves than had Bolotnikov. He made many promises, including a restoration of freedom to the slaves. He further promised, according to Konrad Bussow, that any slaves who would come to him and take an oath of allegiance could have the estates belonging to their owners. Moreover, if the slaveowners had left their daughters on the estates, the slaves could take them as well, for their wives. (The appeal to the predominantly male slave world is evident here.) The German adverturer reported that "many impoverished slaves thereby became lords, rich and powerful, and their owners, starving, streamed into Moscow."[67] After 1613, Mikhail Romanov's government voided all the False Dmitrii II land grants.

The Muscovite government suffered several distractions during the Smolensk War (1632-34) that contributed to the failure of what otherwise would almost certainly have been a sure victory. One such distraction was the disorders led by Ivan Balash (and then Anisim Chertoprud) beginning in October 1632. The "Balash movement" was probably primarily a peasant affair, but there is no doubt that it was joined by dissatisfied elements from Shein's army besieging Smolensk, cossacks, *deti boiarskie,* and considerable numbers of slaves, on whom the dissidents concentrated their attentions. In January 1633 the Balash army moved on Chernigov but was turned back, and in April the government offered an amnesty to all rebels who would join Shein. The appeal had some success, and Balash was captured. The movement continued. Chertoprud attracted Moscow slaves to his banner on a visit there, but his forces were further weakened by another amnesty in January of 1634; other leaders

66. N. E. Nosov, Review of *Feodal'naia Rossiia vo vsemirno-istoricheskom protsesse* in *Voprosy istorii* 1973, no. 12: 151; I. I. Smirnov, *Vosstanie Bolotnikova*, pp. 106-9.

67. Konrad Bussow, *Moskovskaia khronika,* pp. 149, 281; I. I. Smirnov, *Vosstanie,* p. 458, n. 3. For a Russian version of the rebel call to the slaves to kill their owners, with the promise of taking over the owners' estates, see AAE 2: 129, no. 57. Such statements unquestionably created the sentiment among the ruling elite in Moscow in 1610-11 that it was better to serve Polish Prince Wladyslaw than to be conquered by their own slaves (RIB 13[1891]: 1187).

were captured, and the movement was crushed after April.[68] No doubt the movement contributed to the ending of the war and the signing of the Polianovka peace treaty on April 12, 1634. The whole episode further showed the unreliability of the old "Russian formation" army, particularly its slave element, and gave further impetus to the introduction of the new formation regiments.

In some respects, the Moscow disorders of the summer of 1648 were the most important of the early modern period, for they brought together developments that had been in process for some time and caused them to be codified in the *Ulozhenie* of 1649: the enserfment of the peasantry, the stratification of urban society, the abolition of medieval enclaves in towns, and so on. I have outlined the course of the 1648 disorders and their consequences elsewhere.[69]

Slaves played a minimal role, largely one of looting, for which perhaps ten were hanged. They were no doubt the element S. V. Bakhrushin had in mind in his 1917 essay on the 1648 uprising:

> The revolt [*miatezh*] of 1648 was not the affair of society's dregs [*podonki*], the "rabble" [*chern*], in our sense of the word. Of course, as always during social disorders [*smuty*], such elements participated in plunder [*grabezh*] and violence [*nasil'e*].[70]

The Soviets published Bakrushin's works posthumously, and deliberately falsified the above passage:

> The uprising [*vosstanie*] of 1648 was not the affair only of the urban poor [*posadskaia bednota*]. Of course, they also participated in the movement [*dvizhenie*].[71]

This is one of the most remarkable examples of Soviet falsification of a historian's work. Bakhrushin's utter contempt for the gutter element of society has been changed into a romantic view of the poor, his revulsion at mob disorder has been elevated into approval of a sanctified revolutionary movement. Whatever one thinks of collective disorder, the role of the slaves in 1648 was better described by Bakhrushin in 1917 than by the posthumous perverters of his work in 1954.

A peculiar episode occurred in the mid-1650s. A clerk of the Slavery Chancellery, one Bogdan Nikitin, was appointed to patrol Arbat Street, and, while

68. B. F. Porshnev, "Sotsial'no-politicheskaia obstanovka v Rossii vo vremia Smolenskoi voiny," *Istoriia SSSR* 1, no. 5 (1957): 126-27, 129, 136, 138-39.

69. Hellie, *Enserfment*, pp. 135-37; idem, "Stratification."

70. S. V. Bakhrushin, "Moskovskii miatezh 1648 goda," *Sbornik statei v chest' Matveia Kuz'micha Liubavskogo* (Petrograd, 1917), p. 734.

71. S. V. Bakhrushin, "Moskovskoe vosstanie 1648 g.," *Nauchnye trudy*, ed. A. A. Zimin et al., 4 vols. (Moscow: Akademiia Nauk SSSR, 1952-59), 2: 68.

on duty, he was assaulted by slaves from the household of *stol'nik* Andrei Ivanov Pushkin.[72] This incident is difficult to interpret because of insufficient information, but it appears as though the slaves probably recognized an official from the central organ that was responsible for keeping them in bondage, and, taking advantage of the opportunity, vented their rage on a hated symbolic figure. It is possible, of course, that a group of slaves with excess energy just decided to assault someone, and the random victim happened to be an employee of the Slavery Chancellery.

The participants in the 1662 Copper Uprising were enumerated by Grigorii Kotoshikhin: "merchants and their children, cavalrymen, bakers, butchers, pastry cooks, peasants, wanderers, and slaves." He was astonished by the absence of Poles and other foreigners. That is the first disturbance from which survive the records of those interrogated after the event, and the evidence indicates that seventy-five of the participants were military men, forty-seven townsmen, forty-two slaves, thirteen peasants, seven churchmen, four landholders, and fourteen visitors. Of the 826 direct and possible participants mentioned in the extant archival sources, 62.8 percent were servicemen; 17.3 percent were townsmen; 6 percent were slaves; 2.6 percent peasants, 2 percent church servants, and the rest "others." V. I. Buganov, the latest Soviet specialist to work on the problem, estimates that the townsmen were grossly undercounted, that they probably constituted 70 to 80 percent of the actual participants, that perhaps 10 percent were military personnel, and that the remaining 10 to 15 percent were slaves, peasants, church servitors, and the like.[73]

Thus, certainly, the slave element was not insignificant among the participants. Judging by the frequency of torture sessions for the accused and the number of blows finally meted out as punishment, none of the major figures were slaves (rather, they were townsmen, peasants, churchmen, etc.). (Admittedly the sample was considerably depleted by the savage repression meted out immediately when Tsar Aleksei decided to crush the protest.) Among the looters, the most severely punished (with thirty-three strokes) was a slave Martynko Eremeev, the property of second corporation merchant (*gostinaia sotnia*) Volodimer Chanchikov, who confessed to having stolen two pairs of sables from the house of the elite Moscow merchant Vasilii Shorin.[74] Thus the slaves were a significant element in the Copper Uprising, but they were neither leaders nor probably even crucial to the existence of the protest. We must bear in mind that probably more slaves participated in the suppression of the uprising than had a role in creating or sustaining it; one contemporary account assigned to loyalist slaves the major

72. *Opisanie dokumentov i bumag* 15(1908): 468, no. 545-1.

73. Kotoshikhin, p. 104; V. I. Buganov, "O sotsial'nom sostave uchastnikov moskovskogo vosstaniia 1662 g.," *Istoricheskie zapiski* 66(1960): 313, 315.

74. V. I. Buganov, *Moskovskoe vosstanie 1662 g.* (Moscow: Nauka, 1964), pp. 116, 121; idem, ed., *Vosstanie 1662 g. v Moskve. Sbornik dokumentov* (Moscow: Nauka, 1964), pp. 187, 278-302.

role in the drowning and killing of the protestors who were trying to escape.[75] Again, it was this dispersion of forces on both sides that so contributed to the general stability of the Muscovite regime and to the system of slavery as well.

The next major disorder was the Razinshchina, the cossack movement led by Stepan Razin. It began in 1666 under the leadership of Vasilii Us, when cossacks from the Don River region tried to march to Moscow (their actual march was from the upper reaches of the Don to Tula and back) to ask Tsar Aleksei to take them into service (with pay) to fight the Poles in the Thirteen Years War. They suffered from an excess of numbers because of the addition of numerous fugitives in the 1650s and also because of diminished Muscovite subsidies and reduced opportunities to plunder the Crimean Tatars. Aleksei's government panicked, refused to meet with the cossacks, demanded that they surrender the fugitive peasants and slaves in their midst (how many there were is anybody's guess, although documents are extant in which slaveowners complained to the government about the flight of their chattel to the forces of Us),[76] and sent military forces under Iurii Nikitin Bariatinskii to turn back the rebels. The government also hastened to sign the Andrusovo Truce, ending the devastating Thirteen Years War.

The failure to meet the demands of Us led to the Razinshchina, which was concentrated mainly in the months from December 1669 to August 1670. If the phrase "peasant war" has any meaning for Russian history, the movement led by Stepan Razin was the first to contribute to that meaning. Certainly the Bolotnikov uprising was not such a war, a fact recognized by all but the most dogmatic of Soviet historians. The major element of the Razinshchina was the peasants and fugitive serfs, who were joined by Volga boatmen, townsmen, subjugated Turkic and Finnish indigenes of the Volga basin, oppressed frontier military forces, and others.[77] The records from the Razinshchina do note, however, the flight of slaves to the Don; they mention that slaves captured after the suppression of the uprising helped to inform the government about what had happened; and they list more than 175 slaves in the name indices of the four-volume (in five parts) collection of documents the Soviets published on the event.[78] Striking is the absence of slaves in either major leadership roles or as a numerically significant part of the masses engaged in the Razinshchina. One may aver that the absence of slaves in leadership roles is attributable to the gradual curtailment of the use of slaves in the Muscovite combat forces after 1613, a fact which definitely deprived the slave element of the experience needed to lead combat forces. The apparent absence of significant numbers of fugitive slaves

75. V. I. Buganov, *Moskovskoe vosstanie*, p. 89.

76. *Krest'ianskaia voina pod predvoditel'stvom Stepana Razina*, 1: 36, 47, nos. 10, 19.

77. A. A. Pronshtein, "Reshennye i nereshennye voprosy istorii krest'ianskikh voin v Rossii," *Voprosy istorii* 42, no. 7(July 1967): 158.

78. *Krest'ianskaia voina pod prevoditel'stvom Stepana Razina.*

among the followers of Us and Razin is more difficult to explain. In all likelihood, however, the gradual evolution of the institution of slavery greatly reduced the numbers of those with initiative, and those who had any initiative were statisifed with their status and spiritually allied with the status quo. The slave masses were largely reduced to "welfare-dependent" types whose major exertion was to go to their owners' serfs to collect their rations. Such individuals obviously did not have the energy to flee to the Volga, become self-sustaining cossacks, and then participate in a rebellion.

Slaves were in evidence during the disturbances in 1682 following the death of Tsar Fedor Alekseevich and the attempts by Sofia to take power from Ivan and Peter, the Miloslavskiis (Sofia's clan) to drive out the Naryshkins (Peter's clan). This was the occasion of the deliberate burning of the Slavery Chancellery (and also the Moscow Judicial Chancellery) on May 15, 1682, presumably with an eye to destroying the slaveownership records. An official decree of the following year noted further acts of slave violence in 1682: slaves forcibly extracted manumission documents from their owners by threatening to kill them. One such instance, the case of Aleshka Stepanov and Semen Fedorov Tolochanov, was discussed earlier. Another example was that of Ivan Mikhailov and Matvei Maksimov, military captives from the Rzeczpospolita who had been purchased by G. V. Solodovnikov, a merchant of the second corporation (*Gostinaia sotnia*). On May 27, 1682, the two fled to a regiment of musketeers commanded by Fedor Ivan Golovlenkov, one of whose number, a T. Emel'ianov, had incited them to flee. Their owner apparently discovered his slaves' whereabouts, whereupon over two hundred musketeers went to Solodovnikov's house "with lances and halberds to torture [*vymuchit'*] [manumission documents] out of him." Solodovnikov issued such documents, but did not return the purchase documents, claiming he had lost them. In the summer of 1682 the Investigations Chancellery, at the instigation of musketeers, formally freed Mikhailov. Maksimov apparently did not bother with the formality of going to a governmental office for manumission. (Later, on November 25, 1682, they were ordered reenslaved and given back to Solodovnikov.)[79]

Moreover, in an effort to win the favor of the slave element, Prince Ivan A. Khovanskii and his son Andrei were handing out manumission documents from their *strel'tsy* headquarters. True to form, the 1683 decree assumed that those slaves active in 1682 were actually highly dependent, had soon resold themselves; the decree annulled the 1682 manumissions and prescribed that those who had obtained them be "beaten mercilessly with the knout in front of the Slavery Chancellery." Those who resold themselves were to repay the cash they received from the second purchasers. (How was not specified, but perhaps out of their annual stipends, as discussed by Kotoshikhin.) If the old, legitimate owners did not want back their slaves who had extorted and otherwise illeg-

79. Savich, *Vosstanie*, p. 310, no. 157.

ally attained manumission documents, the latter were to be exiled (with their families) to Siberia, the Lower Volga, distant Ukrainian towns, or Ufa. This was to be a lesson for other slaves in the future. Apparently the lesson was well learned, for significant slave participation in civil disorders is not recorded in the post-1682 period.[80]

The civil disorders in Muscovy were of the "reactionary collective violence" variety, rather than either "primitive collective violence" or "modern collective violence," to borrow the typology worked out by Charles Tilly.[81] The rebels were protesting against the way power was held, not striving for well-defined objectives or rights due them. The rhythm of collective violence followed the rhythm of the assembly of communal groups, gatherings with collective petitions, court dates, military assemblages. Such violence was usually spontaneous, and often burst out at times when the dynasty was weak, when restraints were lessened. Urban disorders usually lasted about a week, rural disorders might last a year or more. The roles of slaves in Muscovite disorders is by no means totally clear, but the diminution of the role of slaves with the passage of time seems quite clear. Bolotnikov was the last major slave leader of social disorders, and by 1662 slave rebellion seems to have been reduced to looting activities. This reduction of the importance of slaves in disorders reflects the reduction of their role in society at large.

The inability of slaves to seize power, and especially the fact that magnates never used their slaves to seize power, is striking. Mamluks seized power in Egypt, and men of slave origins directed Islamicate governments more than fifty times.[82] That this never happened in Muscovy reflects the inherent legitimacy enjoyed by the Riurikid dynasty, the ability of the Romanovs to create a sense of legitimacy within two or three decades after their accession to power, and the degree of control the government exercised over the magnates both collectively and individually.[83]

80. PSZ 2:499, no. 992. For example, no slave participation is recorded in the 1698 musketeers' uprising (A. N. Kazakevich and V. I. Buganov, eds. *Vosstanie moskovskikh strel'-tsov. 1698 god [Materialy sledstvennogo dela] Sbornik dokumentov* [Moscow: Nauka, 1980]). On the other hand, the descendants of the house slaves, the eighteenth-century house serfs (who were even called by their Muscovite name, *boiarskie liudi*), were singled out as playing a notable role in the Moscow plague riot in 1771 (Alexander, *Bubonic Plague*, p. 198). By that time, of course, all memory of the savage repression of disorders a century earlier had faded.

81. Charles Tilly, "The Changing Place of Collective Violence," in *Essays in Social and political History*, ed. Melvin Richter (Cambridge: Harvard University Press, 1970), pp. 139-64; idem, "Collective Violence in European Perspective," in *The History of Violence in America: Historical and Comparative Perspectives*, ed. Hugh Davis Graham and Ted R. Gurr (New York: Praeger, 1969), pp. 4-45.

82. Pipes, "Rationale," p. 38.

83. A. M. Kleimola, "Up through Servitude: The Changing Condition of the Muscovite Elite in the Sixteenth and Seventeenth Centuries," *Russian History* 6, pt. 2(1979): 210-29.

582   The Sociology of Slavery

From a comparative perspective, Muscovite slaves seem not to have been at either end of a hypothetical "passive-militant continuum." Slaves in West Africa seem to have been the most passive because the regime there was generally benign; escape was almost impossible and other forms of resistance totally impossible; the claims that owners could make were fairly precisely defined; assimilation into the owner's lineage was likely; life was often better for slaves than for free men; most adult males were not kept but rather executed or sold to distant parts (these sanctions were always present before the eyes of malcontents); the slavery itself was often viewed by the slave as "legitimate," stemming from a "fateful birth."[84] Resistance of all types in the American South was also minimal, with only a handful of incidents (New York City [1712]; Stono, South Carolina [1739]; the Gabriel Prosser plot in Richmond [1800]; Louisiana [1811]; the Vesey conspiracy in Charleston [1822]; the Nat Turner uprising in Jerusalem, Virginia [1831]) to disturb the slaveowner's image of his chattel as "Sambo." Generally good treatment, minority status, the relatively small size of Southern plantations, and the certainty of savage repression curtailed flights and limited outright rebels to fanatics such as Denmark Vesy and Nat Turner, who, like their Muscovite counterparts, were also elite slaves in their society. The ancient Mediterranean world seems to have been akin to Muscovy in the degree and variety of slave resistance. The works of Joseph Vogt and his school have thoroughly disproved the view of the ancient slave revolts as in any way revolutionary, and the same can be said of the Muscovite civil disorders in which slaves played a role.[85]

The greatest resistance to slavery seems to have been in the sugar islands of the Caribbean and in Bahia, Brazil, where whites were in the minority and where control was possible only by resort to a combination of savage brutality (often shocking to Europeans in the mother country), the promotion of selected blacks to elite status, and the employment of Indians to pursue fugitives and repress uprisings.[86] The most famous rebellion, under the leadership of the former slave Toussaint-L'Ouverture, which brought independence to Saint-Domingue (Haiti), is well known. There were dozens of lesser uprisings throughout the rest of the region.

It seems unlikely that comparative historians will be able to determine which features of servitude led slaves to revolt. In Latin America, as we have just seen, chattel slaves, particularly first-generation slaves born in Africa, were most likely to rebel against their servitude. This was not true in Greek history, where chattel slaves did not revolt, and only between 135 and 70 B.C. did they revolt in Ro-

84. Miers and Kopytoff, pp. 445-46.

85. Joseph Vogt and Hans Ulrich Instinsky, eds., *Forschungen zur antiken Sklaverei* (Wiesbaden: Franz Steiner Verlag GmbH, 1967-); Eugene D. Genovese, *From Rebellion to Revolution: Afro-American Slave Revolts in the Making of the Modern World* (Baton Rouge and London: Louisiana State University Press, 1979), pp. 41-50.

86. Melaffe, pp. 102-4.

man history. In classical antiquity, the rebel elements were debt slaves, or the Spartan Helots—presumably people native to the milieu.[87] In Muscovy, the rebellious element seems to have been the natives, with perhaps a nod toward those who had been born in slavery. Thus the three places do not reveal any pattern as far as origin or longevity of servitude are concerned in determining who will rebel and who will not.

In every case that I am aware of, the death penalty was prescribed for slaves who conspired to rebel or participated actively in a rebellion.[88] The vengeance exacted after the Khlopko uprising (when five hundred were hanged), the Bolotnikov uprisings (when the rebels were shoved under the ice), the Copper Uprising (one thousand drowned, killed, hanged, or otherwise executed), or the Razinshchina (Razin was drawn and quartered, his followers were slain or enslaved) can only bring to mind the suppression of Spartacus's revolt, particularly the crucifixion of six thousand prisoners by Crassus along the Appian Way.[89]

The consequences of slave disorders seem to have been almost universally similar. After a savage repression, the ruling elements made life more difficult for slaves than it had been before the uprising. This has been most clearly demonstrated for the United States, where the status of the slave improved after the formation of the country in 1787 down to the Nat Turner uprising of 1830. The uprising in Haiti of 1792-93 halted that process temporarily, but then it resumed. The Turner rebellion coincided with other events (notably, the Abolitionist movement and the demographic downturn of the 1820s and the ensuing run-up in the price of slaves) to magnify the slaveowners' threat perception, and the screws were turned down on the slaves. While the situation was not entirely comparable in Muscovy, if only because peasants, not slaves made up most of the labor force, the response seems to have been somewhat comparable. The major event there was the Time of Troubles, which was far more threatening to the disintegrating Muscovite social order than was Nat Turner's escapade to the social order of the American South. The Smuta had two consequences for slaves. The first was the repressive legislation, initially Boris Godunov's (after defeating Khlopko) and then Vasilii Shuiskii's (after defeating Bolotnikov), which set the tone for much of the rest of the seventeenth century.[90] The second was the implantation in the minds of the Muscovite elite of the idea that society would be better off if fewer elite positions were held by slaves, especially in the army. This coincided, of course, with long-term trends diminishing the importance of elite slaves anyway, but the role of Bolotnikov and

87. Moses I. Finley, "Between Slavery and Freedom," *Comparative Studies in Society and History* 6(April 1964): 235.

88. Rose, p. 193.

89. I. I. Smirnov, *Vosstanie*, pp. 73, 492; A. G. Man'kov, ed., *Zapiski inostrantsev o vosstanii Stepana Razina* (Leningrad: Nauka, 1968), pp. 98, 100.

90. Koretskii, "Iz istorii krest'ianskoi voiny," pp. 133-34; Shepelov, *Osvoboditel'naia bor'ba*, pp. 156-57.

others in the early seventeenth-century disorders apparently convinced the ruling oligarchy that slaves should be taken off horseback as soon as possible. Obviously this could not be done overnight, but the gunpowder revolution and the induction of the masses into warfare helped to accelerate a diminished reliance on slaves as combatants.

Maroonage

In Latin America maroonage was a common phenomenon, with the communities of cimarrones (also called palenques, quilombos, columbos, mocambos, ladeiras, sometimes republics) resembling in many respects the cossack communities of Muscovy. (There were also a handful of maroon communities in various parts of Africa: Futa Jallon [Kondeeah], Guinea [1756]; Kukuna, Guinea and Sierra Leone [1836], Vitton and Mogogoni [Malindi, Kenya, 1867]; and Mozambique [1650-1900].) These communities lived primarily a parasitic existence, preying on settled communities and commerce, their members only occasionally having time to become sedentary farmers.[91] Fishing and some gardening were also common pursuits, as they were among the cossacks. The more successful quilombos, such as Palmares in Pernambuco, Alagoas, Brazil (1605-94), worked out a form of government, based on African principles, that brings to mind the cossack "circles" (krugi).

The responses of the respective governments to the cimmarone, or maroon, and cossack communities are interesting from a comparative perspective. Basically, both were usually minor irritants that had to be kept within tolerable bounds lest they spread, but upon occasion they were regarded as major threats that were worthy of large undertakings to try to exterminate them. There were also differences between the cossack and maroon communities that evoked different official responses. The cossacks were primarily fugitive taxpayers and serfs, the maroons almost exclusively fugitive slaves. The cossacks had much greater endurance than did the maroons, whose communities ordinarily endured for only a couple of years. The cossacks were occasionally of considerable utility to, even in the employ of, the Muscovite state, but, with rare exceptions (such as in 1738 in Jamaica, and with the Mandinga community in Mexico and the Bush Negroes in Surinam, where accommodations were worked out that even included the returning of fugitive slaves) maroons never were.[92] For most colonials, even accommodation with mocambos was unthinkable. In the long run, the Russians ex-

91. Melaffe, pp. 104-5, 108-9, 121-22; Richard Price, ed., Maroon Societies. Rebel Slave Communities in the Americas (Garden City: Doubleday, 1973); Klein, Americas, p. 69.

92. Price, Maroon Societies, pp. 228, 236-39, 294, 301; Patrick J. Carroll, "Mandinga: The Evolution of a Mexican Runaway Slave Community, 1735-1827," Comparative Studies in Society and History 19(1977): 499-500.

hibited a similar orientation toward the cossacks, but during the Muscovite era the state lacked both the will and the capacity to liquidate them. Official Muscovites even sometimes said that "a cossack is free,"[93] words that almost certainly were never formulted in any Latin American's brain. The differences must have been based primarily on racial perceptions of the respective fugitives. The cossack phenomenon served as a safety valve that protected the Muscovite heartland from considerable disorder. The Latin American cimarrone safety valve was kept too tightly closed, with the consequence that there were far more disorders in that part of the New World than there were in Muscovy's share of the Old World.

Antislavery Thought

Many books and articles have been written on antislavery movements in other societies, but probably no more than a few pages can be written about anything resembling such a phenomenon in Muscovy. Certainly there was no "movement" against slavery in early modern Russia, but there was some articulate opposition in favor of curtailing or abolishing it. The handful of individuals who formed this opposition flourished around the middle of the sixteenth century, but it is doubtful that they knew or influenced one another.

Ivan Peresvetov's opposition to military slavery has been noted in chapter 10; it was based on his sense that slave troops did not fight as well as did free men. Another "establishment" figure whose name has been linked to opposition to slavery was Ermolai-Erazm Pregreshnyi. Ermolai was first a cleric in Pskov, then archpriest of the palace cathedral Spas na Boru in Moscow. The most prolific writer of the four who will be discussed here, he was fundamentally a supporter of the Orthodox church. At the end of the 1540s he proposed social reforms that, among things, would have limited peasant rent to one-fifth of the crop, and taxes to another fifth. Observing that all men were descendants of the same Noah, he nevertheless was not an advocate of equality. His concern for the peasantry seems to have been motivated by a fear of civil disorders. It is perhaps in that context that he expressed his opposition to slavery, or rather to the enslavement of primary agricultural producers. In the years 1553-56 Ermolai criticized Ivan IV's policies, and this led to his disgrace. It was probably in that context that he was tonsured and adopted the name Erazm. In spite of his fall from

---

93. W. E. D. Allen, *The Russian Embassies to the Georgian Kings, 1589-1605*, 2 vols. (Cambridge: Cambridge University Press, 1970), 1: 213. The cossacks admitted that some of their numbers were fugitives "from eternal slavery, from involuntary slavery, from the sovereign's boyars and *dvoriane*" ("Povest' ob azovskom osadnom sidenii," in Stender-Petersen, *Anthology*, p. 363.)

favor, he apparently died peacefully.[94] It is not apparent that the thinking of either Peresvetov or Ermolai-Erazm would have eventually led them to advocate the manumission of all slaves.

It was different for the other two under consideration here, Matvei Bashkin and Feodosii Kosoi. Matvei Semenov Bashkin was a slave-owning member of the middle service class descended from princely servitors (who perhaps may have been slaves) settled on the land as servicemen in Pereiaslavl' province. Matvei rose above his humble origins and became a minor palace figure and a member of the Chosen Thousand from Borovsk in 1550. He preached against many of the practices of the established Orthodox church in the years immediately following the inauguration of Ivan IV. Basing his thought about slavery on the biblical injunction that people should love one another, he opposed full and limited service contract slavery. He destroyed the full and limited service slavery contracts on his own slaves, thereby effectively manumitting them. For his general proselytizing, he was arrested in 1553, incarcerated in the Volokolamsk monastery, inquired into by church councils of 1553 and 1554 (the "Bashkin heresy"), and probably burned during the Oprichnina.[95] Feodosii was a slave who fled Moscow at the end of the 1540s to Beloozero, where he became a monk. While still a slave, he had spread discontent among his fellow-chattel. In 1551 he began to propagate what he called his "New Teaching" (*Novoe uchenie*). In 1553 he was dragged into the Bashkin case and incarcerated in a Moscow monastery, whence he fled to Lithuania, changed his name, married, and continued to preach his views. Feodosii devoted most of his efforts to criticizing the Orthodox church (from an anti-Trinitarian perspective), but also advanced a notion of love, mercy, and universal equality that required the abolition of slavery.[96]

The accomplishments of these "abolitionist" thinkers were few. Peresvetov's suggestion on phasing out slave troops was at least a half-century premature, Ermolai-Erazm was totally ignored, and Bashkin and Feodosii were persecuted off the scene. It must be stressed that their thoughts on slavery were secondary, probably almost incidental, concerns. What impact they had on their contemporaries, or whether they had any successors, is unknown; such individuals, if there were any, were almost certainly few. Abolitionism was not yet a burning issue

94. V. F. Rzhiga, "Literaturnaia deiatel'nost' Ermolaia-Erazma," LZAK 33(1926): 180, 186, 191, 196; T. A. Kolesnikova, "Obshchestvenno-politicheskie vzgliady Ermolaia-Erazma," TODRL 9(1953). 257, 263; Sadikov, *Oprichnina*, p. 11; A. A. Zimin, *I. S. Peresvetov i ego sovremenniki* (Moscow: AN SSSR, 1958), pp. 135-36; A. I. Klibanov, "Sbornik sochinenii Ermolaia-Erazma," TODRL 16(1960): 188, 190.

95. N. A. Kazakova and Ia. S. Lur'e, *Antifeodal'nye ereticheskie dvizheniia na Rusi XIV—nachala XVI veka* (Moscow-Leningrad: AN SSSR, 1955), p. 223; Zimin, *Peresvetov*, pp. 169, 180.

96. R. G. Lapshina, "Feodosii Kosoi—ideolog krest'ianstva XVI veka," TODRL 9(1953): 245, 247; Zimin, *Peresvetov*, pp. 182-83, 210-16; Kazakova and Lur'e, pp. 202-3.

anywhere in the world, while in Muscovy many people benefited from the presence of slavery.

This chapter has shown that the Muscovite slave exercised about the same types of volition as did slaves in other systems. The major distinction between Muscovite slaves and those elsewhere was that the majority of Muscovite slaves had chosen to be slaves (for reasons ranging from a desire to attain an elite managerial position to a hope that starvation could be escaped), and this choice of an owner was an occasion for the exercise of considerably more volition than was possible in any other slave system on record. After enslavement, volition was reduced to protest. Some Muscovite slaves, protesting against enslavement, tried to gain vengeance against their owners, a few rebelled against the system and the reigning social order, but most had to be content with trying to flee. The government was unable to maintain perfect order among the slaves, but, with the assistance of many of the slaves themselves, the rulers of Muscovy were able to perpetuate the slave system as long as it was considered useful.

17. The Slaveowners

No study of a system of slavery is complete without study of the slaveowners, those who benefit from the subordination of their chattel. Biographical profiles of individual slaveowners have been scattered throughout this work in connection with the owners' participation in particular events, and the reader interested in representative individual careers is advised to consult those sketches. The focus of this chapter is primarily a prosopographical one, considering the slaveowners as an aggregate. We shall see that slaveownership was highly life-cycle determined, that it was often a perquisite of those who faithfully served the state as directed by the Moscow oligarchs.

First we might take a brief look at the general structure of slaveownership, as shown in table 17.1. The table shows the number of slaves owned by each of the 1,286 ownerships in my general data set, which is based on slave cases. (The 1,286 ownerships represent more than 2,000 slaveowners because many slaves had multiple owners, as shown in table 17.24 below.) The modal owner had

TABLE 17.1A
Distribution of Slaveownership

All Slaves Owned			Inherited Slaves				Purchased Slaves		
Slaves (N)	Owners (N)	%	Slaves (N)	Owners (N)	RF[a]	AF[b]	Slaves (N)	Owners (N)	RF[a]
1	430	33.4	1	38	3.0%	19.8%	1	425	33.0%
2	249	19.3	2	39	3.0	20.8	2	239	19.3
3	152	11.8	3	19	1.5	9.9	3	142	11.0
4	130	10.1	4	19	1.5	9.9	4	119	9.2
5-9	201	15.6	5-9	42	3.3	21.9	5-9	176	14.9
10-14	67	5.2	10-14	20	1.6	10.4	10-14	47	4.0
15-25	35	2.7	15-25	4	0.3	2.1	15-25	23	1.9
26-38	9	0.7	26-39	6	0.5	3.1	26-31	4	0.3
40-49	9	0.7	40-42	3	0.2	1.6	46	4	0.3
51-63	4	0.3	51-53	2	0.2	1.0	59	1	0.1
Total	1,286			192				1,180	
Mean: 4.3			Mean: 6.5				Mean: 3.6		
Median: 2.4			Median: 3.5				Median: 2.2		
Mode: 1.0			Mode: 2.0				Mode: 1.0		

[a] Relative frequency.
[b] Absolute frequency.

588

TABLE 17.1B
Distribution of Slaveownership

Slaves Owned per Slaveowner[a]	Inherited Slaves[a]	N[b]	Purchased Slaves[a]	N[b]	Boys Owned	N[b]	Girls Owned	N[b]	Children Born as Slaves	N[b]
1	0.04	430	0.96	430	1.00	8	1.00	7	1.93	15
2	0.19	249	1.81	249	1.67	36	1.53	23	2.41	24
3	0.28	152	2.72	152	1.11	54	1.16	31	2.72	18
4	0.50	130	3.50	130	1.60	60	1.23	48	3.67	9
5-9	1.11	201	5.20	201	2.10	133	1.60	98	2.04	27
10-14	3.28	67	8.49	67	3.19	62	2.63	54	3.62	21
15-25	3.49	35	14.83	35	5.35	31	3.31	29	5.44	16
29-38	20.22	9	12.33	9	9.67	6	3.00	7	1.67	3
40-49	21.33	9	23.67	9	13.25	8	6.67	9	3.00	4
51-63	32.25	4	24.25	4	15.00	4	5.50	4	9.00	2
Total		1,286		1,286		402		310		139
	Mean = 0.97		Mean = 3.33		Mean = 2.73		Mean = 2.04		Mean = 3.04	
	r = 0.68[c]		r = 0.73[c]		r = 0.81[c]		r = 0.63[c]		r = 0.31[c]	

[a] Inherited slaves + purchased slaves = slaves owned.
[b] N = owners.
[c] r = the linear relationship between the number of slaves in each category and the total number of slaves owned.

only a single slave, an important fact to keep in mind, something that goes far to explain the predominance of males discussed in chapter 12: if a person had the means to keep only one slave, a single male was probably more useful than a single female for the domestic tasks slaves performed—hewing wood, drawing water, cleaning the outhouse, running errands. The average slaveowner in this data set owned 4.3 slaves, but the median ownership is much lower, 2.4.

These slaves were either inherited or purchased. As shown in table 17.1, only 15 percent of those in my data set who had slaves inherited them, but over 90 percent purchased some. The modal inheritance was 2, the modal purchase was 1. The table also shows that small owners inherited few slaves, but the larger ones (those owning over 25) inherited more than half of their holdings. We also see that the unequal numbers of boys and girls prevailed at almost every level of slaveownership, and for some reason the numbers of children born in slavery seems not to have correlated highly with the total numbers of slaves owned.

Map 17.1 shows the location of the slaveowners' homes in the Novgorod area. Their siting correlates to some extent with what we may assume the population density of the region to have been.[1] There is a high concentration around Nov-

1. "Plotnost' naseleniia novgorodskikh piatin 1500 g.," map appended to *Agrarnaia istoriia severo-zapada Rossii. Vtoraia polovina XV–nachalo XVI v.,* ed. A. L. Shapiro (Leningrad: Nauka, 1971). A map from 1600 would have been more suitable, although there is little reason to believe that relative population densities changed significantly during the sixteenth century.

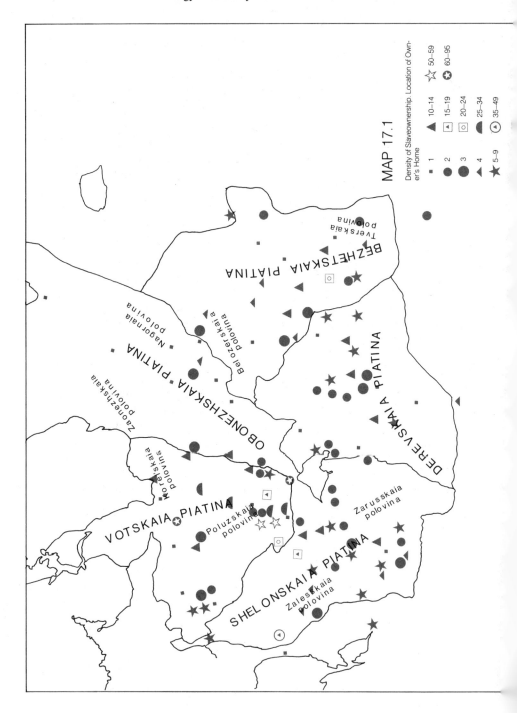

MAP 17.1

Density of Slaveownership. Location of Owner's Home

Symbol	Value	Symbol	Value
▪	1	◄	10–14	☆	50–59
●	2	◧	15–19	✪	60–95
●	3	◻	20–24		
●	4	◒	25–34		
★	5–9	◔	35–49		

BEZHETSKAIA PIATINA

Tverskaia polovina

Nagornaia polovina

Belozerskaia polovina

OBONEZHSKAIA PIATINA

Zaonezhskaia polovina

DEREVSKAIA PIATINA

Korelskaia polovina

VOTSKAIA PIATINA

Poluzskaia polovina

Zarusskaia polovina

SHELONSKAIA PIATINA

Zalesskaia polovina

gorod, some of the low-density regions of Obonezhskaia piatina correspond to low population density, the band of slaveowners running southeast to northwest through Derevskaia piatina mirrors the high density region of that province, and the greater presence of slaveowners in the southern (Tverskaia) half of Bezhet-skaia piatina reflects the considerably denser population there. The concentration in the southwestern section of Shelonskaia piatina also represents a region of high population density.The exceptions can probably be explained in terms of owner preference or military necessity. The quarter-circle ring of slaveowners northwest of Novgorod is in a low-population region, but owners probably congregated there to be near the great city. Then there are also large numbers of slaveowners along the line running from Ladoga and Oreshek to Kopor'e, Iama, and Ivangorod, regions of relatively low population density, but on the line of first defense against Sweden. (The circled star symbol in northern Votskaia piatina represents those living in the region, without further specification.) Thus one may conclude that slaveownership density corresponds with peasant population density. This makes sense because most slaveowners were cavalrymen living off service land grants (*pomest'ia*), which depended upon peasant population. The income from peasant agriculture was what permitted servicemen to own slaves. The exceptions to the determination of slaveowner location for population density were frontier locales, where servicemen were stationed to meet military needs, and the area northwest of Novgorod, where people preferred to live because of its relative proximity to the city.

Slaveowner Rank

Everyone in Muscovy had an official position in society, whether as boyar, townsman, or peasant. The major story of Muscovite social history is how the right to hold specific ranks became the prerogatives of specific categories of people. Society became rigidly stratified by 1649, and after that it was nearly impossible, legally, to leave the castes of peasant-serfs, bound townsmen, and servicemen. The vast majority of slaves were owned by members of the middle and upper service classes, the provincial and capital servitors who manned the army and held most of the higher governmental administrative posts. This subject will be discussed again in the context of the posts they held, and at that time I will discuss as well the nonservicemen slaveowners (merchants, clergymen, other slaves).

Within the service class, there were about two dozen ranks, from cossack and *strelets* of the lower service class to *syn boiarskii* and *dvorianin* of the middle service class to *zhilets* and *boiarin* of the upper service class.[2] Unfortunately, there

2. For a listing of the upper and middle service class rankings between 1616 and 1687, see PSZ 2: 857, no. 1243. My work on the slaveowner prosopography section of this work was greatly facilitated by a PL/1 sort program written for me by Fidelis N. Umeh.

seems to be no way to determine for any given time how many slaves significantly large groups of individuals owned. Such data can be gathered on variables such as landholding or numbers of peasant households in the possession of various ranks of servitors because the government carefully collected and kept that information, but the government's interest in slaves was much less manifest. The only complete inventories of slaveholding are those that were made during the compulsory registration of all slaves in 1597-98 and those made incidentally during the composition of wills and property divisions. Insufficient numbers of such documents are available to draw any conclusions about slaveownership by rank.

Here I shall present the information that can be gleaned from my data set of about 2,500 slave cases. There are approximately two thousand individual slaveowners in the data set for whom biographical information has been searched in all the approximately 150 major sources of data available to me. In many cases there was joint ownership of slaves, but for such instances the rank of only one owner (the senior, when it could be determined) was recorded. There are 1,286 different instances of ownership in my data set, and the ranks or social positions of 704 of them have been determined. Table 17.2 lists the 639 (90.8 percent) owners whose government service rank is known, along with the average number of slaves they are known to have had in their possession. Table 17.2 also lists the social position of 65 slaveowners whose service was not primarily governmental and their slave holdings and expenditures on slaves.

The distinction between *syn boiarskii* and *pomeshchik* is not clear, for the former is a definite rank and the latter means simply "service landholder." I assumed when reading the documents that *pomeshchik* would be a combination of *syn boiarskii* and provincial *dvorianin,* with properties of both. In fact, however, *pomeshchik* numerically seems to have been inferior to *syn boiarskii,* so the separate categories have been preserved in this discussion. In addition, there were 7 *deti boiarskie* in the service of the metropolitan who owned 10.7 slaves apiece and a groom (*koniushii*) in the service of an archbishop who owned 4 slaves. (The first number is so large because of the great number of slaves owned throughout his life by Mikhail Ivanov Miloslavskii, who has been discussed elsewhere.) There is also evidence of one local Novgorodian landholder (*zemets, svoezemets*) and a commander of Tatar forces (*mirza*) each owning one slave. These 10 men were also ordinarily available for government service, indicating that over 90 percent of the slaveowners were on the government payroll. All together, the individuals in government service owned 96.4 percent of the slaves (3,409 of 3,537) for whom I can determine the rank or social postition of the owner. Once again, it must be stressed that table 17.2 is not a complete profile of slaveownership, but rather a listing of those slaveowners about whose slaves something is known. Certainly, therefore, the figures for the Moscow ranks are much too low. Other data on the holdings of the Moscow *dvoriane* and *zhil'tsy* will be presented in a moment. Nevertheless, in spite of this deficiency, it is al-

TABLE 17.2
Relationships between Slaveowner Rank and Slaves and Sums Paid for Them, in Rubles

Rank	N	Slaves Owned (M)	Inherited Slaves	N	Purchased Slaves	N	Mean Sums Expended	Mean Sum per Slave	Mean Sum per Sale	N
Boiarin	5	4.8	4.5	2	5.0	3	16.33	3.57	4.89	9
Dumnyi dvorianin	1	1.0			1.0	1	3.00	3.00	3.00	1
Dumnyi d'iak	1	3.0			3.0	1	3.00	1.00	3.50	2
Stol'nik	23	8.9			3.9	23	12.75	2.64	3.52	23
Striapchii	10	4.5	4.3	4	4.0	7	8.00	2.53	5.42	7
Sytnik (?)	2	1.0			1.0	2	2.00	2.00	2.00	1
D'iak	3	3.7			3.7	3	8.00	2.81	6.00	4
Moscow dvorianin	16	2.3	2.0	1	2.1	16	5.10	2.85	3.83	12
Zhilets	6	3.2			3.1	6	4.75	1.78	3.17	6
Dvorianin	10	3.7			3.7	10	11.11	3.11	5.00	21
Reitarshchik	1	1.0			1.0	1				
Syn boiarskii, pre-1555	5	2.8	7.0	80	2.8	5	6.80	1.89	3.90	10
Syn boiarskii, post-1555	323	6.2	5.6	35	4.95	294	11.09	2.78	4.34	743
Pomeshchik	233	4.3			3.7	216	7.47	2.49	3.81	422
Zemets, svoezemets	1	1.0			1.0	1	2.00	2.00	2.00	1
Stroganov merchant	2	2.5	1.0	1	4.0	1	12.00	3.00	6.00	2
Townsman	21	2.0			2.0	21	7.81	4.00	5.11	37
Monastery elder	1	4.0			4.0	1	2.00	2.22	4.00	4
Monastery treasurer	1	5.0			5.0	1	3.00	0.60	3.00	1
Monk	1	2.0			2.0	1	3.00	1.50	1.50	2
Nun	1	14.0	14.0	1						
Archpriest	1	1.0			1.0	1	5.00	5.00	5.00	1
Priest	20	1.7			1.7	20	3.00	2.09	2.73	22
Deacon	2	1.5			1.5	2	2.50	2.00	2.50	2
Monastery servant	3	3.0			3.0	3	5.33	2.22	4.00	4
Metropolitan syn boiarskii	7	10.7	4.0	1	10.1	7	23.86	2.86	5.35	34
Archbishop's groom	1	4.0			4.0	1	3.00	0.75	3.00	1
Mirza	1	1.0			1.0	1	2.00	1.50	2.00	1
Slave	2	1.5			3.0	2	5.00	1.67	2.50	6
Total	704	M = 4.99	M = 6.4	125	M = 3.9	653	M = 9.21	M = 2.66	M = 4.17	1,383

most certainly correct that about nine-tenths of the slaveowners were in government service, and that they owned at least that portion of all of the slaves.

In 1632, in preparation for the Smolensk War, the government probably made careful inventories of all of its forces. To date, two of those inventories have been published, that for the *zhil'tsy* and that for the Moscow *dvoriane*.[3] *Zhilets* was the entry rank for the upper service class, and was complicated by the fact that it contained both scions of the upper service class just commencing their service and individuals from the middle service class who were being promoted to capital service. The list consisted of 602 individuals, of whom 226 had 1.3 combat slaves apiece, 239 had 1.1 baggage-train slaves each, and, counting both types of slaves, 342 had 2.2 slaves apiece. Moscow *dvorianin* was a more elevated rank whose composition was by no means uniform but certainly was more homogeneous than that of *zhilets*. Of the 623 Moscow *dvoriane* listed, 561 had an average of 2.3 combat slaves apiece, and 316 had 1.9 baggage-train slaves each. An additional 138 said that they would bring as many baggage-train slaves as would be required. Not counting the baggage-train slaves brought by those 138, 579 of the 623 Moscow *dvoriane* brought an average of 3.3 slaves apiece. (The respective slave holdings of the two groups will be considered further, below, in the context of their compensation and land and peasant holdings.) It should be safe to assume that the *zhil'tsy* and Moscow *dvoriane* owned perhaps twice as many slaves as mentioned here, for certainly only ablebodied males accompanied them to war, while women, children, the aged and the sick stayed at home.

The other ownership figures worth noting in table 17.2 are those for townmen (mostly scribes, as we shall see later) and priests. It is almost certainly the case that they owned fewer slaves than did the government servicemen.

Table 17.2 also examines the 125 individuals of known rank who inherited slaves and the 653 individuals who purchased them. The table also shows the amounts expended on slaves by rank, as well as per slave and per transaction. Looking at the larger numbers, we see a progression downward, from *boiarin* and *stol'nik* to *dvorianin* and *syn boiarskii*, in total sums expended on slaves and amounts paid per slave, as one might expect, but the numbers of cases are probably too small to be significant. We see a similar difference between the elite Stroganov merchants and the townsmen, and again among archpriest, priest, and deacon. One can only surmise that such patterns would also prevail if larger numbers of cases were available.

3. Iziumov, "Zhiletskoe zemlevladenie," pp. 1-231; Stashevskii. *Zemlevladenie Moskovskogo dvorianstva*.

Occupations

Perhaps more interesting than rank is the job held by the Muscovite slaveowner. For clergy, of course, it was the same as rank. For the major group, the members of the middle and upper service classes, however, the matter was considerably more complicated, for there was little sense of specialization throughout most of Muscovite history, a fact which allowed the government to keep its servitors on a short leash. While most of the servicemen indubitably spent most of their time after age fifteen in fundamentally undifferentiated roles as cavalrymen, some of them spent varying lengths of time in military command or "civilian" government posts. The "occupation" for servicemen in table 17.3 was, when it could be determined, the post held at the time of slaveownership; if that could not be determined, it was any occupation that could be found. Moreover, as noted in the brief biographies scattered throughout the text, slaveowners often had many jobs; the position assumed to be the more important and prestigious was the one assigned here (for example, general or governor [*voevoda*] was assumed to be higher than centurion, which in turn was higher than messenger). More refined choices would be likely to be arbitrary, for, as is well known, the Muscovites themselves determined the value of many assignments (excluding major military command postions, which had their own ranking) on the basis of the place of others—the "system of places." [4]

As was the case when ranks were considered, the small numbers for many occupations make interpretation of the data both difficult and tentative. In spite of such reservations, definite patterns do emerge, particularly when we consider the larger subgroups. Thus we see that servicemen who engaged in tasks that might be defined as primarily military both inherited and purchased more slaves and expended more acquiring them, on the average, than did those members of the middle and upper service classes in primarily nonmilitary posts. (Some of the generals were also governors in the seventeenth century, but otherwise the dichotomy between military and nonmilitary posts is generally valid. The categories "combat service" and "siege service" are listed for servicemen who were given special payments for one or the other at some time.) It would probably be fair to say that those for whom the larger numbers stick out held the more important posts: the elected local military commander (*okladchik*), the *guba* chief (local director of provincial administration, primarily felony administration, but including matters such as the slavery system as well), grantors of service lands, and census-takers. The figure for *voevoda* is probably too low, as represented by both the range of slaves owned (from 1 to 18) and the standard deviation (7.06).

4. Tatishchev (1910), pp. 15, 46, 50, 55, 58-59; A. M. Kleimola, "Boris Godunov and the Politics of Mestnichestvo," *Slavonic and East European Review* 53, no. 132 (July 1975): 355-69.

TABLE 17.3
Relationships between Slaveowner Occupation and Slaves and Sums Paid for Them, in Rubles

Occupation	N	Slaves Owned (M)	N	Inherited Slaves	N	Purchased Slaves	N	Mean Sums Expended	N	Mean Sum per Slave	Mean Sum per Sale	N
A. Servicemen in Primarily Military Posts												
General (*voevoda*)	43	4.8	11	6.1	41	3.4	41	10.00	36	3.02	4.31	85
Unit commander (*golova*)	19	6.1	2	16.5	19	4.4	19	9.52	19	3.05	2.92	60
Member selected 1,000	1	12.0	1	12.0								
Strelets commander (*golova*)	10	4.1	2	3.0	8	4.4	8	10.00	8	2.69	4.44	18
Strelets centurion (*sotnik*)	22	4.3	9	4.4	15	3.7	15	7.47	15	2.97	3.39	33
Cavalry commander (*porutchik reitarskoi*)	1	1.0			1	1.0	1					
Cossack commander (*golova*)	2	2.0	1	2.0	1	2.0	1	4.00	1	2.00	2.00	2
Cossack centurion (*sotnik*)	2	2.5	1	4.0	1	1.5	1	3.00	2	2.25	3.00	2
Siege service	26	4.0			25	4.0	25	6.56	25	2.00	3.49	47
Combat service	8	6.0			8	6.0	8	10.63	8	2.60	3.42	19
Artilleryman (*nariadchik*)	2	1.5			2	1.5	2	3.50	2	2.25	3.50	2
Elected local commander (*okladchik*)	42	12.2	10	16.9	41	8.3	41	21.18	40	3.14	5.72	148
Subtotal	178	6.4	37	9.0	163	5.1	163	12.28	156	2.90	4.39	416
B. Servicemen in Primarily Nonmilitary Posts												
Guba chief (*gubnoi starosta*)	30	4.8	7	3.9	28	4.1	28	9.21	28	3.29	4.50	57
Guba assistant (*gubnoi tseloval'nik*)	1	3.0			1	3.0	1	1.00	1	0.33	1.00	1
Governor (*namestnik*)	3	16.7	1	3.0	2	23.5	2	49.50	2	8.41	4.75	20
Zemskii clerk (*d'iak*)	1	1.0			1	1.0	1	1.00	1	1.00	1.00	1
Postal (*iam*) official	4	1.8			4	1.8	4	3.50	4	0.88	3.50	4
Scribe (*pod'iachii*)	21	2.4	1	3.0	21	2.2	21	7.71	21	3.85	4.49	35
Administrative assistant (*nedel'shchik*)	32	2.6	3	3.3	30	2.4	30	5.07	30	2.39	3.23	47
Grantor of service lands	3	9.7			3	9.7	3	26.00	3	3.28	5.23	13
Chief of provincial administration (*ob'ezzhaia golova*)	1	4.0	1	4.0								
Census taker	11	7.7	2	15.0	10	7.8	10	12.40	10	1.59	3.30	30
Novgorod administrator (*d'iak*)	5	3.6			5	2.6	5	11.25	4	4.38	5.63	8
Fortifications official (*gorodovoi prikashchik*)	3	9.0	1	4.0	3	7.7	3	15.00	3	2.12	5.00	9
Collector (of taxes? military personnel? *Sborshchik*)	5	3.6			5	3.6	5	7.00	5	2.65	3.89	9
Jailer (*reshetochnyi prikashchik*)	4	1.5			4	1.5	4	4.25	4	2.75	3.40	5

Translator	1	6.0	1.0	1	5.0	1	31.00	1	6.20	6.20	5
Tax collector (desiatel'nik)	1	2.0		1	2.0	1	10.00	1	5.00	5.00	2
Messenger	15	4.4		16	4.4	16	9.42	14	2.74	4.92	30
Surveyor (mezhevshchik)	2	6.0		2	6.0	2	8.00	2	1.56	2.67	6
Siberian service	1	5.0		1	5.0	1	5.00	1	1.00	1.67	3
Subtotal	144	4.4	4.8	17	4.0	138	8.99	135	2.94	4.19	285
C. Moscow Government Officials											
Chancellery director	2	2.0		2	2.0	2	3.00	2	2.00	3.00	2
Chancellery state secretary (prikaznoi d'iak)	2	4.5		2	4.5	2	6.00	2	1.21	5.33	3
Treasurer (kaznachei)	1	5.0		1	5.0	1	3.00	1	0.60	3.00	1
Chancellery official	1	5.0		1	5.0	1	15.00	1	3.00	15.00	1
Ambassador	3	1.0		3	1.0	3	1.83	3	1.83	1.83	3
Moscow palace official	2	3.0		2	3.0	2	3.50	1	0.88	3.50	1
Palace stol'nik	1	3.0		1	3.0	1	4.00	1	4.00	4.00	1
Palace secretary (dvortsovyi d'iak)											
Palace service scribe (dvortsovyi pod'iachii)	3	2.3		3	2.3	3	5.67	3	2.56	4.40	5
Subtotal	16	2.7		16	2.7	16	4.71	14	2.01	4.41	17
D. Churchmen											
Priest or deacon	17	1.8		17	1.8	17	3.06	17	2.02	2.74	19
Monk	1	2.0		1	2.0	1	3.00	1	1.50	1.50	2
Metropolitan	3	1.7		3	1.7	3	2.00	3	1.33	2.00	3
Monastery elder	1	2.0		1	2.0	1	2.00	1	1.00	2.00	1
Nun	1	14.0	14.0	1	14.0						
Church, monastery scribe	2	3.5		2	3.5	2	6.00	2	1.83	4.00	3
Official of Novgorodian archbishop	2	1.0		2	1.0	2	3.00	2	3.00	3.00	2
Archpriest	1	1.0		1	1.0	1	5.00	1	5.00	5.00	1
Subtotal	28	2.3	14.0	1	1.8	27	3.19	27	2.06	2.77	31
E. Others											
Shopkeeper	1	1.0		1	1.0	1	3.00	1	3.00	3.00	1
Widow	10	3.2	1.5	2	3.6	8	9.80	5	2.77	5.44	9
Slave	4	2.3		4	2.3	4	3.75	4	1.58	2.50	6
Subtotal	15	2.3	1.5	2	2.6	13	6.70	10	2.32	4.19	16
Grand total	385	5.1	7.6	57	4.2	362	9.69	347	2.81	4.49	761

The information on Moscow government officials is certainly incomplete and unrepresentative, as is that for all the churchmen listed except priests or deacons. Finally, the data for scribes are probably representative.

In Muscovy occupation seems generally to be a better predictor than rank. This is initially evident when we examine the two in relation to each other. Here there are two sets of data, one for former owners of slaves and one for current owners of slaves (those who owned them at the time of the formulation of the extant documents).

TABLE 17.4
Comparison of the Relationship between Rank and Job

	Former Owners (N = 104)	Current Owners (N = 732)
Lambda, with job dependent	0.300	0.200
Lambda with rank dependent	0.404	0.334
Uncertainty coefficient, with job dependent	0.420	0.305
Uncertainty coefficient, with rank dependent	0.632	0.571

The statistics in table 17.4 indicate that a slaveowner's job was far more likely to determine his rank than his rank was to determine his job. In fact, as we shall see, a serviceman's job was almost always a better predictor of anything than was his rank.

It is relatively easy, in the context of the Muscovite governmentally directed meritocracy, to understand why occupation was such an important determinant. In a world that, at least theoretically, almost began de novo with every person's birth, variables that were highly esteemed in other worlds with longer time-horizons were not necessarily so relevant. Thus service land (*pomest'e*) throughout most of the era under consideration here theoretically could not be inherited, and while occasionally a son did assume his father's grant (or part of it), that was certainly nothing that anyone could count on. The same was even more true for the peasants on the land, until serfdom was fairly well instituted. Rank also was not heritable, nor was compensation schedule, although the child of a high-ranking serviceman with a higher compensation schedule might not begin his career at the absolute bottom: he might, in fact, be initiated into service as a young adult with a land compensation entitlement schedule ranging from 100 to 300 cheti. Apparently, the theory was that the child of a distinguished serviceman would have learned more from his progenitor than would the offspring of an ordinary person and therefore deserved to commence his career with a bonus because of this head start. What mattered to a Muscovite first and foremost was the job he held, a conviction that the state did everything in its power to encourage and perpetuate. Other major facets of a serviceman's life depended on his job, those crucial things such as his rank, compensation schedules, and his land and peasant holdings. Upon those, in turn, depended what the Muscovites considered the finer things of life, such as slaveownership.

The serviceman's working life, as we have seen, can be subdivided into two fundamental types of employment, military and civil. Obviously the compartmentalization was not so neat in Muscovite reality, so that governors were responsible for the army in their areas upon occasion, census-takers were at work primarily because of military needs, messengers and the post system delivered communications of both military and diplomatic-civil import. Nevertheless, the dichotomy may serve at least some organizational purpose.

Military servicemen needed slaves for three basic functions: to manage their landed estates while they were in service; to fill their quotas for combat personnel that were based on their landholdings; to provide for their personal comfort and security, as lackeys, attendants, and guards both in service (especially in the baggage train) and at home.

Somewhat surprisingly, there is little evidence available about the military life of the servicemen. Nearly all the positions listed in table 17.3 are command posts. One gains the impression that provincial servicemen spent no more than three years of their lives in such command positions, with the rest of their days being spent in the ranks of the relatively undifferentiated cavalry. Ellerd Hulbert calculated that 42 percent of the "chosen (*vybornye*) *deti boiarskie*" (chosen to serve in the capital for a term, usually three years) appeared an average of 3.3 years in the military service records (*razriadnye knigi*) which listed the major personnel dispositions of the Military Chancellery; 12 percent of the *deti boiarskie* on the court register (*dvorovye*) appeared an average of 2.3 years in the service records; and only 3 percent of the provincial (*gorodovye*) *deti boiarskie* appeared at any time in the military registers (*razriadnye knigi*), and then only for an avarage of 2.1 years. Only 33 percent of the *dvoriane* and *deti boiarskie* at the 1566 Assembly of the Land appeared in the military service record books during the period 1550-80, and only for an average of 4.4 years each.[5] "Siege service" was usually for those who were retired from active, horseback service but were in some fashion still ambulatory. Other concerns of the military servicemen, besides winning battles and staying alive, are not apparent in the documents. For example, field commanders had no autonomy and were supposed to obey orders from Moscow. What the field commanders thought about this situation is completely unknown. I have listed as field servicemen those for whom I had that information but no other; one may safely assume that nearly all the other servicemen at one time rendered combat service, but specific information is lacking about the vast majority of such cases. I should add that, because of the defensive nature of much of Muscovite military history, not only the superannumated fulfilled "siege service" but the ablebodied were often found defending fortresses as well.

Military service was absolutely compulsory, and seemingly everything possible

5. Ellerd Hulbert, "Sixteenth-Century Russian Assemblies of the Land: Their Composition, Organization, and Competence" (Ph. D. diss., University of Chicago, 1970), chaps. 3 and 5.

was done to compel it. Perhaps the most powerful tool (aside from the threat of confiscation of a service estate) was the pledge or guarantee (*poruka*) signed by a serviceman's fellows certifying that he would appear for service. While the threats mounted against errant servicemen appear terrifying, it is not clear that the more gruesome sanctions were frequently invoked. Probably typical of actual service was the career of I. K. Rudakov outlined in table 17.6. He served 35 years without a promotion, and that may be explained by his less than satisfactory performance at Smolensk (1632-34). Muscovy could not invoke its terrible sancions against ordinary servicemen, or even expel them from the ranks, because the government perceived that it did not have sufficient manpower to treat more than a handful of them severely. Most slaveowners spent nearly their entire adult lives in military service, other aspects of which will be discussed later in this chapter.

Some remarks about the lives of the slaveowners in fulfilling their "civil" tasks are in order. Every one of the "civil" posts in my list held by a slaveowning serviceman was created, defined, and commanded by the central government. This was true right through the Muscovite historical experience, from the early governors (*namestniki*) to the seventeenth-century governors (*voevody*), from the postal (*iam*) officials to the host of officials who directed provincial administration (felony officials, primarily [*guba*] , and noncriminal officials [*zemskii*]) and conducted the censuses. The evolution of the duties of these posts can easily be traced, from an initial concentration on revenue generation to a later sharing of concern with provincial order, as the local native institutions for resolving conflicts were usurped, coopted, and gradually abolished by the centrally directed ones.

It seems fairly certain that nearly all of the holders of major executive positions were slaveowners, a fact that late Muscovites recognized as a situation fraught with potential for conflict of interest and abuse. We have seen an instance of such abuse in the case of Danila Big Beard v. Uvar Lodygin. A quite different instance of a governor's buying slaves while in office was that of Daniil Ondreev Nogtev, whose career has been discussed above. In 1596, while he was governor (*voevoda*) of Novgorod, three adult single males (ages 16, 20, and 20) were purchased for him by two of his other slaves, Ratman Stepanov and Ondrei Krisanfov Ostretsov. Comparatively high prices were listed for them (3, 5, and 10 rubles), and, at least as they told their stories to state secretary Dmitrii Aliab'ev (all three had been formerly dependent in some way, an element of owner-choice I shall discuss further below), no element of coercion seems to have been involved.[6] The fact that Nogtev was governor at the time was not mentioned, and seems to have been fundamentally irrelevant.

6. NZKK 1: 349, 422, 424; Samokvasov, *Materialy* 2(1909): 456, 484; RK 1550-1636, 2: 132-33; RIB 38(1926): 3-5, 9-11; RIB 22(1908), passim (136 citations); DAI 1: 238, 254; AIuB 2: 177, 179, 184, 187; RK 1475-1598, pp. 255-511; RK 1559-1605, pp. 101-

Provincial officials were under unrelenting and unceasing pressure from the center. The situation was such that, by comparison, the Soviet servitors in the third service-class revolution during the first two Five-Year Plan years would have felt almost positively relaxed. Impossible commands were routinely made, as in, for example, the postal system, the pride of Muscovy, which will be discussed under the subject of "Slaveowner Politics" below.

A nearly analogous šituation prevailed in the realm of revenue collection. Taxes were of various kinds, direct and indirect, farmed and directly collected. The central government's major fear was that it would not get its due from its agents, and so it resorted to severe sanctions to ensure collections. To my knowledge, servicemen did not volunteer for tax-collection responsibilities in Muscovy. Given the fallback that the government allowed itself, it would appear as though servicemen could not expect to enrich themselves at the expense of the tax system to the extent that was often typical elsewhere. Those who collected tax revenues were held materially responsible for turning over to the central authorities those sums that past experience indicated could be produced by a given place, be it a tavern, or a customs office, or could be raised by direct levies on the population. The sole exception to this rule was for those instances when a serviceman had officially renounced his post, and no replacement could be found. In such cases the serviceman had to keep the job, but was responsible only for what he actually could collect.

A related function was that of census-taker, a task that was entrusted to many of the Muscovite elite at one time or another. This was a crucial activity, for on it depended taxation of landed or sown area and, later on, of occupied households. The census directors went about their work under the threat of dire sanctions for malfeasance.

The other category of civil functions that engaged slaveowning provincial servicemen was "police functions," in a broad sense. During the Muscovite period these functions underwent a great expansion, from little more than concern for major felonies in an otherwise dyadic system of conflict resolution at the beginning of the period being considered here to a broad attempt to direct and regulate morality in many spheres by the end of the seventeenth century. The growth of these concerns went hand in hand with the government's capacity to manage them. Thus jails began to appear at the end of the sixteenth century, at first to detain suspects until a court had resolved the case. Some of the provincial slaveowners directed the lockups (*reshetochnye prikazchiki*). A century later incarceration was an integral part of the government's array of sanctions, and jail maintenance was one of the tasks that Moscow entrusted to the provincial elite. The provincial elite were also involved in keeping track of who was

292; RK 1598-1638, pp. 52, 80; Markevich, p. cxi; SIRIO 129: 389, 394; Abramovich, "Novgorodskoe pomest'e," p. 8.

coming and going, in pursuing felons, in bringing the accused to court (*nedel'-shchik* was an entry job for many younger servicemen; such employment lasted a year or two), and in trying court cases (often in the company of an official sent from Moscow). The same people were also charged with fire prevention and the maintenance of what Moscow determined was morality: the curtailment of drunkenness, the stamping out of tobacco chewing, gambling, and prostitution.

In directing provincial police operations, Moscow did not issue the hysterical threats of sanctions that were so common in the military and financial spheres. Not only were police functions of more recent and lesser concern than the others, but in general the central government was more tolerant of deviant personal behavior than it was of refusal or inability to pay taxes or render military-related services. Obviously it was of little concern to Moscow whether a murder was committed in Nizhnii Novgorod or someone was drunk in Novgorod, but it mattered a great deal when someone slipped through the taxation net or refused to pay or render his due.

My impression is that only a small fraction of the provincial servicemen played any part in "civil service." Muscovy did not expend significant resources on administration. By comparison with some other places, it was probably "under-administered." However, it was adequately administered: more officials might have produced better (and certainly more frequent) census records or collected more taxes or apprehended more felons, but the marginal improvement would not have been worth the cost. The Muscovite administrators felt they needed their servicemen in the army, and that is exactly where they were. Probably not more than 1 percent of the provincial servicemen were rendering "civil service" at any one time. This means that many of them probably never rendered any at all, and the terms of those who did were short, usually a year or two. Slaveowning elite servicemen probably spent more time in "civil service" than did rank-and-file servitors, for they were the ones both trusted and commanded by Moscow to undertake its assignments. The constant rotation of individuals in and out of civil-service-type posts had both pluses and minuses for the central regime. It meant that few gained much expertise in handling a specific function, but it also meant that few acquired any sense of vested interest or security in any position. The serviceman was thus always a tool, a person with no administrative, political, or economic base of his own. Moreover, any individual was totally expendable and could be treated arbitrarily, for there were many others equally qualified willing and able to assume his post. It also meant that there were few sinecures: every serviceman had to work in his post, often if for no other reason than to generate his own income. This tended to maximize government revenue while keeping administrative costs low. This was a perfect background for the development of autocracy, and differed markedly from the situation in Western Europe at the same time.

While exercising civil functions, servicemen could utilize their slaves in much the way low-paid menials are now employed by those in executive positions, as messengers, personal representatives, and aides of various sorts. For example, the translator Obliaz sent his slaves to carry out various assignments that were probably treasonous.[7] Slaveowners had a tendency to require their slaves to perform what the government considered to be the owners' jobs. Sometimes this was legitimate and sometimes it was not. Thus the *Sudebnik* of 1550 prescribed that slaves performing provincial administrative functions for their owners were not to take bribes, and further insisted that bailiffs had to deliver warrants in person and could not have their slaves do it for them. The same provision was repeated in the *Ulozhenie* of 1649.[8]

Certainly, however, most of the slaves owned by Muscovite servicemen were domestics serving in the household. This reminds one of the Ottoman Empire, and also the Crimean Khanate, where individual nobles and government officials purchased slaves for use in domestic tasks. In Ottoman circles, the number of chattel a slaveowner possessed was a major status elevator, one of the signs of his importance. Productivity was not considered. Fisher notes that "this was strikingly similar to the numbers game that Russian noblemen played with their serf holdings."[9] A nearer analogy would have been Muscovite slaveowners.

A transitional group of slaveowners was the scribes (*pod'iachie*), some of whom worked in the government, others of whom were private individuals available for hire to anyone who needed documents composed or private messages written. Some paid taxes with the townsmen (*posadskie liudi*), others probably did not. Most were an arm of the civil service, in that they worked in the government and were on the bottom rung of a *cursus honorum* that might lead to the rank of counselor state secretary (*dumnyi d'iak*); or, for a fee, they drew up documents at the behest of private individuals that came to be legal instruments when properly registered and signed.

A significant number of the slaveowners (twenty-one, over 1 percent) about whose slaves there is good information were laborers with the pen, and most of them were apparently government employees. This might appear astonishing until one reflects upon the role of literacy in Muscovy. In one of his many deprecatory remarks about that country, the papal legate Antonio Possevino commented on the "ignorance" of the Muscovites, who claimed to be "learned" if they could read and write.[10] Moreover, one may recall that in the late sixteenth and the seventeenth centuries Muscovy was making the transition from an oral to a documentary society, one in which the possession of properly and accurately executed documents was crucial for many aspects of life, from the tsar's sense

7. SIRIO 41(1884): 333, 335.

8. 1550 *Sudebnik* 47, 62; 1649 *Ulozhenie* 10:148.

9. Fisher, "Muscovy," p. 586.

10. Antonio Possevino, "The Missio Muscovitica," trans. and ed. Hugh F. Graham, *Canadian-American Slavic Studies* 6, no. 3(Fall 1972): 473.

of legitimacy (as in the case of Kotoshikhin) to valid claims at law. The scribes were the basic instruments of the initiation of the literacy revolution, and it is not surprising that they enjoyed high status, as reflected in the fact of slaveownership.

An equally important question is what people such as clerks and scribes did with slaves. They only rarely owned land, so they could not have employed them as farmers. Of the twenty-one scribe-slaveowners, thirteen are known to have purchased only one individual (usually a male), something that would lead us to believe that they were buying lackeys, house servants. Others, however, purchased more. The Novgorod scribe Pervii Karpov, working for the Court Chancellery (*Dvortsovyi prikaz*), in 1595 purchased a twenty-three-year-old man, in 1596 a fifty-year-old cossack and a twenty-five-year-old female voluntary servitor, and in 1600 a twenty-five-year-old male-hired laborer.[11] Perhaps he also was staffing his house with menials who were of some visible utility. But then there was Grigorii Dmitriev Kobel'ev, an energetic scribe in Novgorod who between 1595 and 1600 purchased eleven slaves in eight transactions. According to a 1583 tax list, he was a scribe and owned a shop, from which he paid a tax of 0.21 rubles, and a garden. Whether he was a public scribe or a government one at that time is not clear, but in 1584 he assisted in negotiations with the Swedes. By 1602-3 he had become a state secretary (*d'iak*), and worked in Korela. At some time he assisted in the taking of a census (*dozor*) of Lopskii pogost (Votskaia piatina) that was cited in 1613.[12] Kobel'ev purchased primarily previously-owned slaves, but what he did with them is by no means clear. It should be fairly safe to assume, however, that he was an example of a person who purchased slaves as a prestige symbol, to tell those looking on how successful he was, for this was one of the major functions of slavery in Muscovy.

Townsmen and merchants also owned slaves, in what were probably modest numbers that were determined by the amount of surplus they themselves enjoyed. Great merchants, such as the Stroganovs, members of the three official government-designated corporations (*gosti, gostinaia sotnia,* and *sukonnaia sotnia*) and those involved in international and the Siberian trade employed slaves of the elite or intermediate-status variety, not the low-status individuals who were so prone to flee.[13] For example, nearly all Russian merchants going through Smolensk to trade in Lithuania in the winter of 1588-89 and again in 1603-4 had slaves listed in their travel documents. Seventeenth-century customs books frequently recorded the collection of duties from slaves. In December,

11. NZKK 1: 143, 268, 436; RIB 15^2 (1894): 20; RIB 38(1926): 271, 279, 312; RIB 22(1908): 523.

12. RIB 15^2 (1894): 76; NZKK 1: 17, 41, 43, 290, 363, 417, 430; LKN-V 1583, pp. 38, 170; SIRIO 129: 360; RK 1598-1638, pp. 127, 144; *Kareliia v XVII veke* (1948), p. 28.

13. V. E. Syroechkovskii, *Gosti-Surozhanie* (=*Izvestiia Gosudarstvennoi akademii istorii material'noi kul'tury imeni N. Ia. Marra*, vypusk 127 [135]): 84-86; also information furnished by Charles Wilmot from TsGADA, f. 214, 1663, 11.128-32; Got'e, *Zamoskovnyi krai*, p. 203.

1677, the great merchant of the first corporation from the northern provincial town of Vologda, G. M. Fetiev, owned fifty-three slaves.[14] The merchant of the second corporation (*gostinaia sotnia*), G. V. Solodovnikov, purchased as military captives from the Rzeczpospolita Ivan Mikhailov and Matvei Maksimov.[15] Unquestionably some of the slaves were employed as domestics, but others were used in business. Here African comparisons are helpful: both native African and Arab merchants found the employment of slaves to be a major instrument for overcoming the inherent limitations of the family firm; they not only used slaves to man their caravans but even staked them to engage in what amounted to their own ventures. Similar situations may be found in Muscovy, both in the southern and Siberian trade spheres. No study has been made, to my knowledge, of the contribution slaves made to merchant income and capital accumulation in Muscovy. Moreover, there is little information on how merchants adjusted to the abolition of slavery, or on the impact the change had on their incomes and profits. Merchants were the primary group whose needs for subordinates were not satisfied by serfdom, and their desire to purchase serfs led to conflicts with the landed serfowners and also to the further abasement of the serfs. The fact that serfs were not always a suitable substitute for slaves possibly contributed to the rise of the use of significant quantities of free labor in the second half of the eighteenth century.

It is possible that manufacturers may have resorted to the occasional employment of slaves (as a supplement to domestic tasks), but I have little evidence on this point. The Russian situation may have been much like that of the Roman Empire in the fourth century A.D., where the employment of slaves in private industry was rare.[16] Possibly also arguing against the employment of slaves in industry is the absence of the practice of renting slaves and the practice of allowing slaves to work as independent agents in exchange for a fixed rent. Both practices were well developed in Athens, where slaves were an investment for their owners, who used one or the other device to supply mining and manufacturing interests with labor.[17] (There was no mining in Muscovy, of course.) The practices were well-developed elsewhere as well. In the towns of the Caliphate there were slaves who hired themselves out and paid rent to their owners. Many rich people first in Constantinople and then in Istanbul made a livelihood by

14. E. I. Zaozerskaia, "Vologodskii gost' G. M. Fetiev. (Iz byta torgovykh liudei XVII v.)," *Zapiski istoriko-bytovogo otdela gosudarstvennogo russkogo muzeia* 1(1928): 201; *Russko-belorusskie sviazi. Sbornik dokumentov (1570-1667 gg.),* ed. L. S. Abetsedarskii and M. Ia. Volkov (Minsk: "Vysshaia shkola," 1963), pp. 21-26, 55-60; *Tamozhennye knigi Moskovskogo gosudarstva XVII veka,* ed. A. I. Iakovlev, 3 vols. (Moscow-Leningrad: Akademiia nauk SSSR, 1950-51), 1: 314-22. Both of the latter two books have many other examples of slaves assisting their owners in commerce.

15. Savich, *Vosstanie,* p. 310, no. 157.

16. Jones, p. 197.

17. Ibid., pp. 188-89. On the Laurium (Laurion) silver mines, see Noel H. Gale and Zofia Stos-Gale, "Lead and Silver in the Ancient Aegean," *Scientific American* 224, no. 6 (June 1981): 176-92.

hiring out their slaves, and in the towns of the Crimea Muslim owners occasionally rented out slaves to Christian employers.[18] Both practices were also prevalent in the urban American South.[19] Why neither practice was prevalent in Muscovy is not clear, but the reason may be associated with the general norm that everyone was supposed to be bound to a specific station and that free agents, now working here, now living there, would be discouraged. No doubt there are other reasons as well.

The Moscow military census of 1638 reveals that others besides servicemen owned slaves (see table 17.5). (The census included in its listing, sometimes by

TABLE 17.5

Slaveowners in Moscow According to the 1638 Military Census (Excluding Military Servitors and Palace and Known Chancellery Personnel)

Social Position			N
Church personnel		*Nemchin* merchant	2
Monastery prior	2	Dutch merchant	2
Monastery prioress	1	*Inozemets* (foreigner, either	
		Western European or Tatar)	13
Nun	6	*Inozemets* translator	1
Monastery servitor (*sluga*)	1	Tatar	1
Archpriest	1	Kasimov tsarevich	2
Priest	7	Greek	4
Sexton	1	Craftsmen and others	
Patriarchal secretary (*d'iak*)	1	Singer (*pevchev d'iak*)	1
Patriarchal *boiarin*	1	Trumpeter	3
Patriarchal *syn boiarskii*	1	Psaltery player (*gusel'nik*)	1
Patriarchal clerk	2	Goldsmith	1
Patriarchal slave	1	Silversmith	2
Merchants		Mint master	3
Gosti	6	Steward (*kliuchnik*)	7
Member of *Gostinaia sotnia*	29	Sub-steward (*podkliuchnik*)	4
Gostinaia sotnia widow	2	Cooper (*vekoshnik*)	2
Member of *Sukonnaia sotnia*	13	Stoker (*istopnik*)	2
Sukonnaia sotnia widow	1	Scribe (*pisar'*)	1
Ordinary merchant	4	Green grocer (*ovoshnik*)	1
Foreigners		Furrier	1
Apothecary	2	Hatter	1
Diamond cutter	1	Female cowl maker (*kalpachnitsa*)	1
Salt petre master	1	Female dyer	1
Military officer	2	Taxpayer (*teglets*)	3
Nemchin (Western European)	32	Slave	5
Nemchin widow (*nemka*)	8	(Note: Some of the above may have	
Nemka widow of goldsmith	1	worked for the government either	
Nemchin priest	2	full or part time.)	
Nemchin translator	1		

Source: I. S. Beliaev, *Rospisnoi spisok goroda Moskvy 1638 goda.*

18. Fisher, "Muscovy," p. 585; Inalcik, "Slave Labor," p. 18; Udal'tsova, p. 10.

19. Goldin, *Urban Slavery*, pp. 18, 21, 25, 35-37, 39, 45. See also Stanley J. Stein, *Vassouras*, p. 75.

name, male slaves able to bear arms. One person, Prince Aleksei Ivanovich Vorotynskii, was cited as owning 30 such slaves [and possibly more]; two individuals owned from 20 to 29 slaves, ten owned from 10 to 19, one owned 9, three owned 8, three owned 7, four owned 6, twelve owned 5, fourteen owned 4, forty-five owned 3, 198 owned 2, and 525 owned 1. This was a total of 1,402 slaves, and does not include 333 instances in which the number of slaves owned was not specified.)

Men of the cloth, priests and monks, also were slaveowners. So too were nuns. The mid-seventeenth-century strictures, supposedly enacted in 1597, against slaveownership by priests and deacons were not yet operative during the Time of Troubles.[20] Clergymen seem to have registered few if any slaves during the compulsory registration of all slaves in 1597, so probably few of them were slaveowners in the sixteenth century. However, during the great famine years of 1601-3, when the price of slaves dropped to record low levels, a number of priests entered the market, usually paying the lowest price. (This was only one manifestation of the general expansion of the slaveowning class during major natural disasters: lesser members of the middle service class also tried to elevate their social prestige and domestic convenience by becoming slaveowners at such moments of opportunity.) This probably means that rank-and-file clergymen in ordinary times did not possess surplus adequate to buy slaves, but initiated the venture when the slave supply curve intersected with the priests' low ability and their unwillingness to pay for and maintain slaves. As is evident from tables 17.1 and 17.2, clergy paid lower than average prices and possessed fewer than the average number of slaves. Both observations would seem to be consistent with an image of the Muscovite clergy as a group that was generally not well-to-do. On the other hand, we should note exceptions such as the famous Old Believer autobiographer, archpriest Avvakum Petrov, who, during his exile travels to Siberia, seems to have taken his slaves at least part of the way with him, for he notes that at one juncture he left his wife, children, and slaves (*domochadtsy*), "about twenty people," in Iur'evets.[21] Ownership of twenty slaves would indicate considerable wealth. Clergymen in general were not landowners, and so one may assume that a certain minimum number of slaves could be employed as domestics and that any quantity above that must have been maintained as a symbol of opulence. (It would seem doubtful that clergymen might keep more slaves than they could "afford" as an act of charity, for it would have been quite possible for such men of the cloth to give alms for a while, and then send the recovered mendicant on his way, without enslaving him.)

The almost total absence of peasants among the slaveowners of Muscovy is

20. 1649 *Ulozhenie* 20: 104.

21. Avvakum, "Zhitie," RIB 39(1927): 14; N. K. Gudzii, ed., *Zhitie protopopa Avvakuma im samim napisannoe i drugie ego sochineniia* (Moscow: Goslitizdat, 1960), p. 64; Kenneth N. Brostrom, trans. and ed., *Archpriest Avvakum. The Life Written by Himself* (Ann Arbor: University of Michigan Slavic Publications, 1979), p. 50.

striking. Peasants had owned slaves in Byzantium, whose legal norms were read-ily available and were utilized in early modern Russia, although not on that issue. A comparison with the Ancient Near East may provide some explanations. In the societies ranging from Babylonia to Syria and Palestine the more prosper-ous farmers owned slaves, and some of those slaves were employed in agricul-ture. In general, however, the peasant household was self-sufficient; there was little need for extra help, either hired laborers or slaves.[22] In the case of Musco-vy, the "more prosperous farmers" were gradually abolished (if they ever existed) with the introduction of the service landholding system by Ivan III, and their place was assumed by the *pomeshchiki* in the provinces no later than the 1570s. Remaining were self-sufficient households, fearful of manifesting any overt sign of prosperity that would increase their rent or tax obligations. Thus in the sixteenth century, when the tax system (the *sokha*) was based on sown area, the peasants tended to decrease the area sown to the minimum, thus removing any reason whatsoever for employing slaves to expand tillage. Moreover, the reduc-tion of tillage combined with the abysmally low yields (in the vicinity of 3:1) prohibited the employment of household menials by peasants who derived their incomes from farming, simply because they barely had enough feed themselves.

The exceptions to the rule that peasants did not own slaves were few, and per-haps even can be questioned as exceptions. In the North, the White Sea littoral Dvina Land region, so-called *svoezemtsy* occasionally owned slaves in the begin-ning and middle of the sixteenth century. The origin of the *svoezemtsy* is often uncertain, but some of them may have been heirs of quasi-magnates in the fif-teenth century, when the region belonged to Novgorod. While nominally and le-gally peasants (or quasi-peasants), some of them possessed a number of villages, often holding as much land as did members of the middle service class. The Amosov family prior to 1527 owned seventy-nine hereditary slaves, used as do-mestics, craftsmen (tailor, carpenter), and agents (probably in the family fishing and salt-boiling interests). When the family property was divided, five brothers inherited fifteen to seventeen slaves. Further property division reduced each owner forty years later to only four slaves. Other *svoezemtsy* also owned slaves, some of whom were recorded as having been purchased in the sixteenth century. A few of those slaves farmed for their owners, others assisted them in their trad-ing operations. Slaveownership by peasants in the North declined with their homogenization on the road to serfdom under Muscovite power.

Other cases of "peasants" owning slaves are from late Muscovy, from the pro-perties of the magnate and statesman B. I. Morozov. Census records of 1647 and 1665 indicate that a handful of Morozov "peasants" owned a few slaves each. Thus Antrop Leont'ev owned the purchased Tatar slaves Danilko Danilov and his son Iakimko, and three house slaves (*dvorovye liudi*), Serezhka Trofimov,

---

22. Mendelsohn, pp. 109, 111; Udal'tsova, "Raby," p. 8. (Browning questioned whether peasants owned slaves in Byzantium [Brauning, p. 43].)

Mishka Fedorov, and Borisko Osipov. The peasants Nikita Timofeev Boldyr' (sic) and Ivan Andreev Kvasnikov also owned purchased Tatars. Eighteen years later, Leont'ev's sons Ivan, Semen, and Timofei owned five house slaves, two purchased Polish war slaves, and one purchased Tatar captive. At the same time Vasilii Petrov Muromtsev owned three house slaves and four Polish war slaves, Ivan Isaev owned eight house slaves, possibly also Polish prisoners of war.

Who were these slaveowners? The first thing that one should bear in mind is that they were subjects of and seemingly sponsored by Morozov, in 1647 probably the most powerful man in Muscovy, a person himself certainly "above the law," and one whose status was transferred to his subordinates. As for the "peasants" themselves, they were not ordinary agriculturalists. Antrop Leont'ev was a "non-farming peasant," sometimes called a "rent-paying landless peasant" (*obrochnyi bobyl'*), who owned warehouses, shops, lots, and a mill. In 1650 he contracted to deliver down the Volga to Astrakhan' 50,000 chetverti of rye, groats, oats, and oat flour. In the same year Morozov loaned him 1,000 rubles. Boldyr' ("half-breed"—mixed Russian and Tatar or Finn) and Kvasnikov (" seller of near-beer") are unusual because they had surnames, which most peasants did not; they were not surnames of the genealogically elite, of the type who typically owned slaves, but they were surnames nevertheless. (Boldyr' could be just a nickname, but it does not seem to be here.) One may assume that the sons of Antrop Leont'ev followed in the father's footsteps. Ivan, for example, while legally a peasant, was also a customs official (*tamozhennyi golova*) for the villages of Murashkino and Lyskovo, two of Morozov's major possessions. Muromtsev was again atypical because of his surname, and also because of his ownerhip of two warehouses and four shop-stalls. His brother Afanasii was a great grain-trader who annually sold over 20,000 chetverti of grain to Astrakhan' in the early 1650s. Isaev, another of Morozov's favorites, had a hand in administration, engaged in rather large-scale usury, was involved in the Astrakhan' salt business, and in general was a petty entrepreneur. It seems that, like the rest of these individuals, he did not do any farming and was only legally a peasant. Thus these "peasant" slaveowners seem to have appeared in late Muscovy after the legal stratification of society required that they be called peasants, although in reality they were equivalent to prosperous townsmen.[23]

Given the nature of Muscovite society and political life, one would expect that slaves themselves would be slaveowners. This was true in many other societies, ranging from Late Assyria, Nuzi, Palestine, China, and some African societies, to Byzantium, where slaves owned by other slaves had the special name of *ser-*

23. Nosov, *Stanovlenie soslovno-predstavitel'nykh uchrezhdenii*, pp. 265-67; Kopanev, *Krest'ianstvo Russkogo Severa*, pp. 36, 89, 99, 182-87. On slaveownership by Toropets *semtsy* (sic), see R. E. F. Smith, *Peasant farming in Muscovy* (Cambridge: Cambridge University Press, 1977), pp. 182-86. On Morozov's "peasant slaveowners," see *Khoziaistvo krupnogo feodala semńadtsatogo veka*, vol. 2; Petrikeev, *Krupnoe krepostnoe khoziaistvo*, pp. 166-68.

vi vicarii. The purchasing activities of four Muscovite slaves are preserved, all of them from the famine year of 7111 (one purchase in 1602, five in 1603). Unlike the clergy, slaves did not buy other slaves at rock-bottom prices but even during the famine laid out an average of 2.50 rubles per purchase. Three of the purchases were registered in Borovichi (Bezhetskaia piatina) by *gubnoi starosta* Ivan Salamykov, the other three in Derevskaia piatina by *gubnoi starosta* Mikifor Matiushin. The four slaves who bought slaves for themselves were Venedikht Grigor'ev (who belonged to Semen Moiseev Stromilov), Khariton Rodivonov (who belonged to Sharap Molozhaninov), Petr Rostovtsev (who belonged to Ivan Fedorov Meshcherskii), and Fedor Stepanov (who belonged to Il'ia Ivanov Butenev). There seems to be nothing that would distinguish the owners of these four slaves who purchased other slaves from any of the other two thousand slaveowners whose biographies have been compiled for this study. Four of the purchases were of solitaries (three males, one female), two of families (a husband twenty-five and a wife twenty; a husband thirty, a wife thirty-five, and a boy six). The only thing at all "exceptional" about this group of purchases is that two-thirds of the individuals involved had been previously owned by someone else, a higher than average ratio. However, because the numbers are small, little significance should be attached to the fact. It would appear doubtful that Muscovite slaves ever owned other chattel on the scale that slaves did in the Ottoman Empire, where Cafer Aga, who served as the chief white eunuch, owned 156 slaves when he died in 1557. Nevertheless, Muscovite medieval slave ministers or the slaves who belonged to magnates of the seventeenth century such as Romanov and Morozov must have owned more than the modal one slave recorded in the Great Famine purchases.[24]

Muscovite slaves unquestionably owned other slaves both before and after 1602-3, a fact reflected in the prohibition in the 1630s of the ownership by slaves of limited service contract slaves, a concession to the middle service class that was trying to enhance its position. The measures of the 1630s were not an outright prohibition against slave ownership of other slaves, and thus it is not surprising, for example, that A. I. Bezobrazov's elite managerial slaves owned other slaves in the early 1680s.[25] One may assume that elite slaves owned other slaves for much the same reasons that free slaveowners did: to provide them with personal service and the prestige that ensued from the ownership of other human beings.

Women constituted a final category of slaveowner. The standard image of the unmarried woman and of the wife was of someone who was absolutely helpless, who could not possibly do anything by herself.[26] Widowhood, however, often

24. Mendelsohn, pp. 68, 71-72, 74; Udal'tsova, pp. 9, 17-18; Wergeland, p. 97; Fisher, "Ottoman Slavery," p. 34; Fisher and Fisher, *Slavery and Muslim Society in Africa*, pp. 41, 49; Burnham, p. 50; Shepherd, p. 84; NZKK 1: 149; 2: 110, 113, 202, 222.
25. Novosel'skii, *Votchinnik*, pp. 81-82; Got'e, *Zamoskovnyi krai*, p. 203.
26. Iakovlev, *Kholopstvo*, p. 504.

seems to have brought about an abrupt reversal of this helpless and unequal stereotype, with the woman taking control of her husband's personal assets and trying to make a living from the portion (usually about 20 percent) of his land entitlement she was given after his death. Neither the image nor the sudden change was quite as dramatic as it appeared to be, for the wife of the average slaveowner must have spent half of her married life apart from her husband while he was in service. When she was young, she sometimes moved in with her parents, but when they were deceased she was on her own, running the estate as her husband's stand-in. This was especially the case in those many instances when the husband was not yet advanced enough in the service to have the means to acquire and maintain any slaves, and for longer still in those cases when the serviceman had only house slaves and no elite, managerial slaves. Thus the wives of most slaveowners must have embarked upon widowhood with considerable experience in directing slaves.

The Novgorod land cadastres compiled in 1582-84 list 2,745 landholders, of whom 64, or 2.3 percent, were women.[27] Those compiled in 1626-27 list 1,650 landholders, of whom 91, or 5.5 percent, were women.[28] Those census-type events bracket the vast majority of the cases in the basic data set used in this study. Both figures are higher than the proportion of the instances in which slaves were explicitly owned by women, 47 of 2,383 cases, or 2.0 percent. (This excludes the 4.6 percent of all cases that were dowries, in which the slaves were transferred from the father-in-law to his new son-in-law and seem to have become thereby the property of the latter. See "Multiple Ownership" section below.) While in only 15 of the 54 cases did the document explicitly state that the woman was a widow, it should be safe to assume that few married women conducted transactions while their husbands were still living, and that in most of the 54 cases the principal was a widow. Women paid slightly higher than average prices for slaves (4.08 rubles, N = 26; vs. 3.88 rubles, N = 2,163), perhaps because they were not as experienced at managing money or perhaps because slaves considered it a fall in status or projected a less secure status when they sold themselves to a woman. No documents are extant revealing whether women purchased full slaves; the first extant purchase was in 1575, and many purchases were made between 1593 and 1603, and then again between 1689 and 1701. Women purchased 72 of the 4,009 limited service contract slaves, or about 1.8 percent of the total.

An examination of the purchases made by twenty-five women indicates that they seem to have bought an approximate cross-section of the slave population: eleven single men, four single women, one girl (aged twelve), eleven married couples, two couples with one child, three couples with two children, and one

27. N. Ianitskii, *Ekonomicheskii krizis*, app. xiv, pp. 110-226.
28. Petr Ivanovich Ivanov, *Obozrenie pistsovykh knig po Novu-gorodu i Pskovu* (Moscow: Tipografiia Senata, 1841), pp. 37-71.

couple with four children. If we compare these figures with those for limited service contract slaves in table 13.2 we find that 45.5 percent of the purchases by women were adult solitaries, and 49.8 percent of the entire population of limited service contract slaves was; 33 percent of the purchases by women were childless couples, 17 percent of the entire population was; 18.2 percent of the purchases being discussed here were complete families, compared with 16.5 percent of the total population. The female slaveowners seem to have been reluctant to take in one-parent families and orphans, who made up 12.1 percent of the general population of limited service contract slaves but only 3 percent of the women's purchases. The ages of eighteen of the adult males were listed in the purchase documents, and they averaged 28.9 years of age, somewhat above the average of 26.6 for all 887 adult males of known age.[29] One might speculate that the women buying slaves were thus looking for people with greater experience than those the average male slaveowner wanted, but, other than the 10 percent difference in average ages, there is nothing much to support such a hypothesis. In general, women purchased the same slaves that men did, and probably primarily for the same reason: to have household help.

Compensation and Slaveownership

As we have seen, most slaveowners were government servicemen who maintained their slaves out of a surplus remaining from various forms of official compensation. Compensation existed in two realms, entitlement (*oklad*) and reality. A servicemen's *oklad* (a sum usually expressed both in terms of land and cash) reflected his deserts, based on official evaluation of his service and other factors, such as social origins and the attainments, primarily in service, of kin and peers. Compensation entitlement is a subject somewhat difficult to deal with because it was constantly changing for individuals, the norms were gradually inflated, and few men achieved (were granted) what they were entitled to. On the other hand, it was an important indicator of status, it unquestionably stimulated service achievements, and it had real meaning at times when it was the basis for rewards, pensions, and survivors' benefits. For example, a serviceman's widow might be given 20 percent of his *oklad* to live on after his death; if his *oklad* had been 600 *cheti* of land and he actually possessed 120 *cheti*, she would keep all

29. AIuB 1: 597; *Deistviia Nizhegorodskoi uchenoi archivnoi komissii* 6: 794-96; Rukopisnyi otdel Gos. Publich. Biblioteki im. Saltykova-Shchedrina, Obshchee sobranie gramot, nos. 3475, 3486, 3833; Kopanev, "Materialy," pp. 151, 184; *Materialy istoricheskie i iuridicheskie raiona byvshego prikaza Kazanskogo dvortsa*, 2: 85; NKK 7106, pp. 3, 5, 7-8; NKK 7108, pp. 25, 68; NZKK 1: 115, 187, 356, 360, 378; NZKK 2: 231, 282, 306, 314, 333; *Russkaia vivliofika* 1(1833): 404; *Sbornik starinnykh bumag, khran. v muzee N. I. Shchukina* 10(1902): 329; Selifontov, *Podrobnaia opis' 440 rukopisiam*, p. 31; *Trudy Saratovskoi uchenoi arkhivnoi komissii* 25: 79; RIB 17: 32-33, 162.

of it. On the other hand, had his *oklad* only been 300 *cheti* and he possessed 120 *cheti*, the widow could get to keep only 60 *cheti* for her maintenance and would have to surrender the other 60 *cheti* to an active serviceman.

The service pyramid in Muscovy was very flat, and the serviceman's progress up the cursus honorum very slow. While there were only two ranks (*dvorianin* and *syn boiarskii*) for provincial servicemen, there were many gradations, particularly within the rank of *syn boiarskii*. Thus a person could be serving at the expense of the central government (*dvorovoi*, literally, the court) or the provincial town (*gorodovoi*), and then be ranked by compensation entitlement. One of the problems was that there was some tendency for the level of compensation entitlement to inflate, something the government recognized in 1605 when it declared two men's schedule of 650 cheti illegal by noting that the top rate was 600, in spite of the fact that 700 cheti had been recorded as early as 1584 in Pereiaslavl'.[30] By 1610-11 the top compensation entitlement reached 950 cheti, and in 1621-22 it was up to 1,000 cheti.[31] On the other hand, entry-level entitlements did not change to any significant degree at least between 1596 and a formal systematization of the scale in 1652.[32]

A major statistical study needs to be done on this problem, but my sense is that the degree of inflation has been exaggerated, that for the century from the 1550s through the 1650s most of the provincial servicemen were held to the area of 200 to 400 cheti.[33] The servicemen received a lower percentage of their entitlements in the seventeenth century because their numbers increased from 25,000 to 40,000, a matter of 60 percent, and not so much because of progressive inflation of compensation schedules.

The cumulative impact on the servicemen of the ranking and formal compensation system and the possibilities of achieving one's entitlement is unknown. Promotions were achieved only by specific feats acknowledged by central bureaucrats in the Military Chancellery (*Razriad*), and certainly the ranking system served as an incentive to perform the type of feats required by the central authorities. On the other hand, the fact that servicemen could expect as time went on to hold a decreasing portion of their entitlement within a Muscovy of a constant size (this problem was solved for a time by usurping peasant lands and assigning them as service estates, but this expedient had run its course considerably before the middle of the seventeenth century) may have had harmful consequences for morale.

30. Miatlev, pp. 467-68; V. N. Storozhev, "Materialy dlia istorii russkogo dvorianstva," *Chteniia* 230 (1909, no. 3): 7-8.

31. Storozhev, pp. 98, 122.

32. PSZ 1: 278-80, no. 86; N. Likhachev, "Desiatnia novikov poverstannykh v 1596 godu," *Izvestiia Russkogo Genealogicheskogo obshchestva* 3(1909): 113-209. (Hereafter cited as DN 1596.)

33. Storozhev, "Materialy." See also idem, *Tverskoe dvorianstvo XVII veka*, 4 vols. (Tver': Tipografiia Gubernskogo Pravleniia, 1891-95).

In a system more responsive to its servicemen, the pressure on the land fund created by a combination of some inflation of compensation schedules, a considerable growth of the service class itself, and a perceived decline in the standard of living even of the provicial elite might have provided a built-in dynamic for wars of expansion. Such claims are made for other places. One's suspicions might even seem to be confirmed by the very fact that land-hungry servicemen were given grants after every major expansion of the Muscovite empire, whether in Novgorod in the last quarter of the fifteenth century, Kazan' in the 1560s, Livonia and Rzeczpospolita in the Livonian War and the Thirteen Years War, or into the chernozem and steppe as Muscovy moved southward.

It might even be possible to conceive of a dynamic system in which, during periods of weak government, when oligarchic cliques vied for support (such as Ivan IV's minority, the Time of Troubles, the post-Filaret years of 1633-45), inflated grants were made, and then in the ensuing period of stability, attempts were carried out to make real those grants. Unfortuantely, while such dynamic may be posited, it cannot be proved.

The possibility of getting more land may have served as an incentive for Muscovite servicemen to fight, but I know of no way that a desire for land could have been or was translated into pressure that was felt in Moscow. The formation of policy in Muscovy remains an unknown process. Moreover, the major issue in the period was not land but peasants to till the land. Warfare and its attendant taxation always caused great peasant dislocation, with concomitant stress for the provincial cavalrymen. Muscovite expansion, such as that both to the south and to the east, opened up new lands for peasant colonization, and the peasants had to come from the Volga-Oka mesopotamia, where most of the servicemen had their estates. The peasants moved into newly secured lands faster than the *pomeshchiki*, a fact that helped propel the middle service class to initiate the enserfment process. Thus it is not at all clear that Muscovite servicemen were a dynamic force compelling expansion; in fact, much of the evidence for the period after 1580 points in the opposite direction.

A serviceman's movement up the compensation scale was usually very slow. He had to petition for each advancement, citing his service, and the petition might or might not be granted. In the Novogorod region between 1596 and 1605 initial increments following initiation into service seem to have been quite regular, but in other times and places that was not so. As is evident in table 17.16, many servicemen died or retired at or near the entry ratings. Reaching the top took decades, in most cases. Thus Muscovy's meritocracy was also a gerontocracy. This is evident in the career of I. K. Rudakov, which is summarized in table 17.6. Material to illustrate similar situations is relatively abundant.

One may assume that Rudakov was a novitiate at about the age of fifteen, so he was nearly sixty when we last hear of him, riding off to the Thirteen Years War with his sabre and carbine. It is not unlikely that he perished during one of the major engagements between 1658 and 1661, when the flower of the middle service class was exterminated.

TABLE 17.6
The Career of Ivan Kamyshnikov Rudakov

	1616	1621	1631[a]	1634[b]	1649	1650[c]	1658[d]
Novitiate (*Novik*)	N						
Gorodovoi		G	G				
Dvorovoi				D	D	D	D
Land *oklad*, cheti	200	200	200	200	250	300	600[e]
Cash *oklad*, rubles	7	8	8	8	8		
Pomest'e size, cheti		196[f]		196 1/16	same?[f]		
Amount paid, rubles		8	20	20	14	10	

Source: V. N. Storozhev, *Tverskoe dvorianstvo* 2(1893): 137-38.
[a] He was supposed to serve on a horse and with a handgun (*na merine, s pishchal'iu*).
[b] He left the Smolensk front prior to being discharged, which probably explains why he received few raises for the next 20 years.
[c] Rudakov must have been literate, for he signed for his pay himself. A surprisingly high percentage of provincial servicemen were literate, at least to that extent.
[d] He was to serve with a sabre and carbine, on a horse (*na merine, s sableiu, da s karabinom*).
[e] The reason for this rapid rise in land *oklad* is not stated in the source, but one may assume that Rudakov performed several notable feats in the early years of the Thirteen Years War.
[f] While Rudakov held almost all the land he was entitled to, the crucial fact for him was that it was uninhabited. This may help to account for his being paid more than he was entitled to.

Real compensation was in both cash and land. The cash *oklad* was an annual entitlement but could only be paid when the treasury had the money, and efforts were made to make such payments when a campaign was about to be launched (presumably so that servicemen could buy service-related commodities, such as horses, sabres, and later, handguns), or when the loyalty of servicmen was desired, such as during the Time of Troubles.[34] Unquestionably cash *oklad* is an important status indicator. Its value as a predictor, however, varies from instance to instance.

The other aspect of compensation was land. The relative importance of cash and land fluctuated greatly from time to time and serviceman to serviceman, depending primarily upon whether the Treasury had funds and whether the land was populated with peasants. Land without peasants to till it was worthless, so that the number of peasants (calculated variably, but usually either by adult males or by households) was often just as important, or even more important, than the amount of land a serviceman held. Paying for the army in this "natural"

34. During the Time of Troubles entitlement seemingly often was listed only in cash terms. This may reflect the fact that land was essentially meaningless during a period of such turmoil and mobility, while some cash could still be collected, as in the pre-*pomest'e*, pre-Ivan III era, when land in general was not valued highly by government servitors because of the difficulty of collecting rent, whereas taxes, transit duties, and judicial imposts could be levied almost without regard for peasant mobility. Because the major surviving documents that support this hypothesis happen to be those of chancelleries that made payments in cash and were not concerned with land entitlements or allotments, the hypothesis may not be a valid one (see Sukhotin, *Chetvertchiki* [1912]).

way reflected a number of factors, one of which was the relatively primitive nature of much of the central administration. Another reason for paying troops directly, by the primary producers, was that this avoided the problem of "skimming" that inevitably occurred in any tax system; the crown was far more sure that the available surplus would be put at its disposal when demanded in kind, rather than in cash processed through a central apparatus.

While changes in land and cash entitlement were usually gradual, actual holdings of land and peasants were highly variable, depending upon availability. A few examples from the 1632 list of *zhil'tsy* will make this point. In that list Timofei Iazykov possessed no land, nor did he have any in 1631 or in 1634. But in 1638 he had 150 cheti of land and 7 peasant households.[35] In 1632 Petr Bogdanov Chiulkov possessed 70 cheti of apparently uninhabited service land; in 1638 that sum had risen to 402.5 cheti, inhabited by forty-five adult male peasants living in thirty households.[36] In 1632 Ivan Timofeev Usov had no land at all; by the end of the decade he possessed 421.25 cheti of land inhabited by twenty-eight male peasants living in twenty-seven households.[37] Such volatility was the natural consequence of the meritocratic nature of the service system in which nearly everybody began his career at a very low level of compensation, was awarded land and cash entitlements (*oklady*) according to deserts, and got those entitlements by luck (primarily by the death of senior servicemen). Luck cannot be programmed or depended upon, and that feature of the Muscovite slaveowner's existence makes statistical analysis of the available data difficult.

An attempt was made to assemble data on these variables for all servicemen-slaveowners in the data set (see table 17.7).

TABLE 17.7
Compensation of Slaveowners

	N	Mean	Median	Minimum	Maximum
Land entitlement (*oklad*), cheti	252	411.9	399.4	50	1,800
Cash entitlement (*oklad*), rubles	113	20.79	10.13	5	700
Landholding (cheti)	238	197.8	150.1	0	2,406
Peasants (adult males)	27	36.7	34.0	3	89
Peasant households	32	27.2	25.0	2	73

The total number of possible entries was 1,286, so that it is obvious that data could not be found for most servicemen. A few other remarks about table 17.7 are in order. A slaveowner in government service might have all of the five variables indicated, depending on his age, luck, and other factors. On the matter of the peasant holdings, official records sometimes enumerated adult males, at

35. Iziumov, pp. 160, 188.
36. Ibid., pp. 154, 187.
37. Ibid., pp. 142, 186.

other times households. The figure 1,286 includes about two thousand slave-owners, something that will become clearer when multiple ownership is discussed below. The figures in table 17.7 (especially land entitlement) reflect the total entitlement of the group, so that a father with an *oklad* of 400 cheti and two sons with known *oklady* of 150 cheti apiece were coded as 700 cheti, on the assumption that 700 cheti were the total resources at hand to buy and maintain the slave the three of them collectively purchased. (Such instances were rare and were excluded in the calculations that were made for an individual, such as the landholding of a *stol'nik* or a governor.) Moreover, one should note that the data came from different periods. Peasant-holding data are primarily from the end of the fifteenth century,[38] actual landholding comes primarily from the 1582-84 Novgorod land cadastres,[39] land entitlement figures rely heavily on the 1605 muster roll (*desiatnia*) of Votskaia piatina,[40] and perhaps the majority of the cash compensation entitlement sums come from the Time of Troubles period, specifically the years 1604-17.[41] Scattered data of course are found throughout the other sources that have been searched as well, but most of the data turned out to be highly concentrated in those few sources. The data do not coincide precisely with the time of the majority of slavery documents (1594-1603), and, given the volatility inherent in the Muscovite serviceman's career, this lack of synchroneity is probably responsible for many of the low correlations between the serviceman's economic status and his activity in the slave-holding realm. The importance of official arbitrariness and chance (if he lives, will the serviceman have a chance to prove his mettle? Will his service be recognized? Will populated land be available to reward him for meritorious service?) combined with the fact that most servicemen started at the bottom (with a low compensation entitlement and little or no land) to make the projection of career trajectories very tenous.

Table 17.8 shows how the compensation variables break down by rank, and table 17.9 shows the same thing in terms of the occupations the slaveowners held. Again, one must remember that while the ranks, jobs, and compensation belonged to the same individuals, they were not necessarily synchronous.

Calculations have been made of the total sums the various slaveowners are known to have expended in purchasing slaves. The structure of these expenditures is shown in table 17.10, as is the average number of slaves purchased for those sums. The relationship between total expenditures and total numbers of slaves purchased is among the strongest presented in this study (r = 0.84). The total sums known to have been expended on slave purchases do not, however, correlate highly with the known compensation variables, as presented in table

38. NPK; A. M. Gnevushev, *Sel'skoe naselenie*; A. M. Andreiiashev, "Materialy."
39. Ianitskii, *Ekonomicheskii.*
40. Miatlev, "Desiatnia Votskoi Piatiny."
41. Sukhotin, *Chetvertchiki.*

TABLE 17.8
Slaveowner Ranks, Compensation Schedules, and Land- and Peasant-Holding

Rank	Cash Entitlement (Rubles)	N	Land Entitlement (Cheti)	N	Landholding (Cheti)	N	Adult Male Peasants	N	Peasant Households	N
Boiarin										
Dumnyi dvorianin										
Dumnyi d'iak										
Stol'nik	15.00	1	533.3	3	953.7	3				
Striapchii	15.00	1	1,000.0	1	462.0	2				
Sytnik,	25.00	1	850.0	1						
D'iak			150.0	1						
Moscow *dvorianin*	18.00	3	687.5	4	254.0	2				
Zhilets	12.00	3	500.0	2						
Dvorianin	19.25	4	575.0	4	540.0	3				
Reitarshchik										
Syn boiarskii, pre-1555	14.63	45	409.3	209	463.5	2	10.0	1	40.0	2
Syn boiarskii, post-1555	11.65	20	311.8	17	155.7	84	3.0	1	9.3	3
Pomeshchik					195.6	127	39.1	25	28.6	26
Zemets, svoezemets			150.0	1						
Metropolitan *syn boiarskii*	15.00	1	500.0	1	162.0	1				
Mirza	120.00	1								
Archbishop's groom					70.0	1				
Means and totals	15.41	80	414.6	244	199.3	226	36.7	27	27.5	31
Eta	0.79		0.34		0.51					

17.11. This "poor fit" may well be the result of the asynchroneity of the data, discussed earlier. Table 17.12 shows that there was even less correlation between the amount a slaveowner paid for each slave he purchased and the five elements of compensation. Table 17.13 examines the relationships between the total number of slaves a slaveowner possessed and the relevant variables of his compensation.

TABLE 17.9

Relationships between Slaveowner Occupation and Major Compensation Variables

Occupation	Cash Entitle-ment (Rubles)	N	Land Entitle-ment (Cheti)	N	Landholding (Cheti)	N
General or governor (*voevoda*)	26.17	6	694.4	9	540.8	12
Unit commander (*golova*)	7.67	3	557.1	7	366.8	8
Siege commander (*osadnaia golova*)			516.5	2	331.5	2
Strelets commander (*golova*)	22.00	1	125.0	2	111.0	3
Strelets centurion (*sotnik*)	9.50	4	365.4	13	207.5	4
Cossack commander (*golova*)	15.00	1				
Cossack centurion (*sotnik*)			150.0	1	15.0	1
Siege service	9.76	21	375.0	10	90.3	4
Combat service	12.83	6	387.5	4	40.5	2
Artilleryman (*nariadchik*)			350.0	1		
Elected local commander (*okladchik*)	15.77	13	674.0	25	182.4	18
Guba chief (*gubnoi starosta*)			367.1	7	154.5	11
Governor (*namestnik*)	30.00	2	600.0	1	425.0	2
Postal (*iam*) official	8.00	1			400.0	1
Scribe (*pod'iachii*)	16.00	1			40.0	1
Administrative assistant (*nedel'shchik*)	16.00	1				
Grantor of service lands	22.50	2	500.0	1	162.0	1
Chief of provincial administra-tion (*ob"ezzhaia golova*)					255.0	1
Census-taker	7.33	3	466.7	3	162.0	1
Novgorod administrator (*d'iak*)			150.0	1		
Fortifications official (*gorodovoi prikashchik*)			250.0	1	102.5	2
Collector (*sborshchik*)	10.00	1	383.3	3	30.0	1
Jailor			350.0	3	137.5	2
Census director	15.00	1	600.0	1	128.0	1
Translator			400.0	1		
Messenger	10.00	1	487.5	4	100.0	1
Ambassador					65.0	1
Moscow palace official					440.0	1
Widow			900.0	1	24.7	3
Means and totals	14.29	70	475.2	113	230.4	89
Eta	0.68		0.69		0.54	

TABLE 17.10
Amounts Spent per Slaveowner and Number of Slaves Purchased

Rubles	N	%	No. of Slaves Purchased
1.00-1.50	97	8.6	1.3
2.00-2.50	212	18.7	1.7
3.00-3.50	176	15.6	2.1
4.00	101	8.9	3.0
5.00	161	14.2	2.5
6.00-9.00	148	13.1	3.8
10.00-14.00	104	9.2	5.0
15.00-25.00	83	7.3	7.1
26.00-49.00	39	3.4	13.1
51.00-93.00	11	1.0	32.3
133.00	1	0.1	59.0
Total	1,133	100.0	4,146.0

Expenditures per owner:
Mean = 7.30 rubles
Median = 4.10
Mode = 2.00

Relationship between
total expenditures and
total numbers of slaves
purchased   r = 0.84

These tables all reveal relatively low correlations between the numbers of slaves a person inherited, purchased, or owned in toto, and the variables of his compensation. As noted earlier, at least part of this variation must be due to the asynchroneity of the data. A low level of correlation is observable when one compares the compensation variables with each other. For example, for the forty-eight available cases in this data set when both land and cash entitlements are known, the relationship is very weak (r = 0.14), and it is not very strong either in the seventy-four cases where land entitlements and actual landholding are known (r = 0.45). It should be noted, however, that strong linear relationships are relatively infrequent even when the data are absolutely synchronous.

If we return to the distinction between military and civil service assignments made earlier, table 17.14 is of interest. As I interpret the data in table 17.14, there was relatively little difference between military and civil service in Muscovy. According to the Eta statistics, whether a man was in military or civil service did little to determine any of the other variables. The basic similarities, again, reflect the general absence of specialization in Muscovy, and the fact that all servicemen (except professional possessors of literacy, the scribes and state secretaries) were expected to spend most of their time in the army. They ventured forth into what I called 'civil service" to manage the postal system, conduct censuses, or direct the criminal justice system, but they could always expect to return to the army.

TABLE 17.11
Sums Expended on Slaves Compared with Slaveowner Compensation, Land, and Peasants

Total Sum Expended per Owner on Slaves (Rubles)	Cash Entitlement (Rubles)	N	Land Entitlement (Cheti)	N	Slaveowner's Land (Cheti)	N	Adult Male Peasants	N	Peasant Households	N
1.00-1.50	8.00	2	172.22	9	171.00	14	59.0	3	33.0	4
2.00-2.50	21.33	15	350.80	25	139.87	30	32.8	5	22.2	6
3.00-3.50	12.35	20	380.00	35	199.36	33	44.0	5	29.0	6
4.00	16.95	10	409.09	22	223.67	15	60.0	2	30.7	3
5.00	7.56	9	439.47	19	162.22	27	20.5	2	18.0	2
6.00-9.00	10.14	14	363.89	36	206.26	27	21.2	5	20.6	5
10.00-14.00	10.72	11	378.57	28	149.61	28	15.0	2	14.5	2
15.00-25.00	22.20	10	450.00	29	234.72	25	32.5	2	44.3	3
26.00-49.00	14.80	10	574.15	20	225.50	12	67.0	1	38.0	1
50.00-133.00	21.25	4	783.33	6	329.60	5		0		0
Mean	14.62	105	410.06	229	189.28	216	36.7	27	27.2	32
	$r = 0.09$		$r = 0.40$		$r = 0.16$		$r = 0.06$		$r = 0.27$	

TABLE 17.12
Prices of Slaves Compared with Slaveowner Compensation, Land, and Peasants

Price for Each Slave (Rubles)	Cash Entitlement (Rubles)	N	Land Entitlement (Cheti)	N	Slaveowner's Land (Cheti)	N	Adult Male Peasants	N	Peasant Households	N
0.20-0.43	10.00	1	150.00	1	250.00	1		0		0
0.50-0.92	11.91	11	305.00	12	175.57	23	36.6	5	26.5	6
1.00-1.43	9.52	17	298.44	32	202.50	42	58.2	5	37.8	5
1.50-1.89	12.60	10	409.38	16	204.29	21	34.0	2	23.3	3
2.00-2.45	13.48	24	369.82	38	169.08	37	35.0	5	25.7	6
2.50-2.86	10.00	4	450.00	21	161.00	16	39.0	2	17.0	3
3.00-3.92	10.95	20	392.93	58	204.11	37	24.4	5	30.4	5
4.00-4.67	30.00	1	356.25	16	192.43	7		0	28.0	1
5.00-5.75	12.60	5	453.85	13	199.65	17	21.0	2	18.0	2
6.00-9.50		0	372.22	9	97.86	7		0		0
10.00-15.00	19.00	3	600.00	1	248.88	8	31.0	1	31.0	1
Mean	12.06	100	376.75	217	189.28	216	36.7	27	27.2	32
	$r = 0.19$		$r = 0.19$		$r = 0.02$		$r = -0.24$		$r = -0.05$	

TABLE 17.13
Relationships of Slave Holdings and Slaveowner Compensation Variables

	Mean Cash Entitlement (Rubles)					
No. of Slaves	Inherited Slaves	N[a]	Purchased Slaves	N	Total Slaves	N
1	–		17.70	30	42.03	29
2	14.67	3	15.96	14	16.28	16
3	30.00	1	13.62	13	12.67	12
4	15.00	1	12.77	13	13.55	11
5-9	11.17	6	11.09	22	10.83	24
10-14	7.00	2	19.00	6	13.78	9
15-25	15.00	1	11.33	6	12.86	7
26-39			15.00	1		
40-49	25.00	1	30.00	1	27.50	2
51-63	10.00	1	15.00	1	13.33	3
Mean	13.75	16	14.80	107	20.79	113
	r = 0.06		r = 0.0008		r = −0.05	
	Mean Land Entitlement (Cheti)					
1	436.7	15	387.6	67	381.0	70
2	342.3	13	381.4	57	361.2	57
3	550.0	2	377.8	27	387.5	28
4	412.5	4	390.0	15	382.4	17
5-9	500.0	11	444.1	34	413.2	34
10-14	700.0	3	475.6	16	474.2	19
15-25	683.3	3	618.3	10	587.2	5
26-39	487.3	4	600.0	2	580.0	5
40-49	500.0	2	600.0	2	550.0	6
51-63	1,200.0	1	500.0	1	766.7	3
Mean	457.0	58	413.6	231	411.9	252
	r = 0.43		r = 0.23		r = 0.32	
	Mean Landholding (Cheti)					
1	184.8	9	197.3	66	196.8	67
2	206.8	9	197.8	46	207.6	47
3	233.3	3	153.9	26	147.2	26
4	150.0	8	185.0	21	197.2	24
5-9	143.1	9	239.0	37	222.2	39
10-14	114.2	5	199.6	9	170.3	16
15-25	379.0	2	143.1	7	167.3	10
26-39	162.0	3	108.0	1	170.5	4
40-49			459.3	3	419.5	4
50-63			162.0	1	162.0	1
Mean	177.6	48	199.5	217	197.8	238
	r = 0.03		r = 0.08		r = 0.06	

[a] N = number of owners.

TABLE 17.14
Comparisons of Military and Civil Service Jobs

	Military	Civil
Average number of slaves per slavery contract[a]	2.49	2.06
Land entitlement, chetverti[b]	569.55	439.91
Cash entitlement, rubles[c]	13.72	20.21
Actual landholding, chetverti[d]	213.72	220.72

[a] Eta = 0.069 with slaves dependent.
[b] Eta = 0.226 with land dependent.
[c] Eta = 0.254 with cash dependent.
[d] Eta = 0.017 with land dependent.

In spite of the limitations of the data presented, two regressions may shed some light on the numbers of slaves owned and the amounts paid for slaves. With total slaves owned as the dependent variable, the following variables contribute to r^2 the values shown:

Landholding	$r^2 = 0.378$
Rank	0.009
Job	0.020
Place of Residence	0.021
Land entitlement	0.556
Cash entitlement	0.015

With the total sum paid for slaves as the dependent variable, the determining variables have roughly the same values:

Landholding	$r^2 = 0.328$
Rank	0.036
Job	0.003
Place of residence	0.041
Land entitlement	0.465
Cash entitlement	0.126

These data may be interpreted as follows: the number of slaves purchased and the amounts expended to purchase them are known to be highly interrelated. In a society such as Muscovy, the amount of land a serviceman had was the crucial element in his well-being. The land entitlement was a prestige factor, an element that reflected a serviceman's position in his community. A major factor of prestige in Muscovy was slaveownership, and thus servicemen with the requisite amount of land did everything they could to become slaveowners.[42] This inter-

42. The greater contribution made by land entitlement than by actual landholding may be attributable to the fact that the former was closer (1605) to the basic slavery data (1594-1603) than the landholding data (1582-84).

pretation from the general study of 2,499 cases will be confirmed by the more specific cases that follow.

More precise indicators of the relationship between slaveownership and slave-owner rank and compensation can be found in sources that are synchronous, or nearly so. Most of these sources (the 1577 Kolomna military register, the 1632 listing of *zhil'tsy* and Moscow *dvoriane*) state only that "N N" had "x combat slaves and y baggage-train slaves," giving no names or other identification for the slaves in question. The slaves were as impersonal as the horses and bows and arrows that the servicemen brought with them; they were susceptible to being counted, and little more.

The 1577 military register (*desiatnia*) for Kolomna is the most complete available, and it lists not only the cavalrymen and their weapons grouped according to cash and land *oklad*, but also enumerates the combat and baggage-train slaves each serviceman brought with him.[43] There were 280 servicemen in the list, of whom 195 were slaveowners. Of the 323 slaves listed, 139 were combat slaves and 184 were baggage-train slaves. Table 17.15 presents the relevant data.

TABLE 17.15
1577 Military Register for Kolomna

	Per Serviceman	Per Slaveowner
Combat slaves	0.49	0.71
Baggage-train slaves	0.66	0.95
Total slaves	1.15	1.66
Land entitlement (*oklad*; in cheti)	194.50	215.90
Cash entitlement (*oklad*; in rubles)	9.10	10.37

In summary, the cash compensation scale (an amount actually paid in 1577) was a considerably better determinant of slaveownership on a campaign ($r = 0.75$) than was the land entitlement compensation scale ($r = 0.55$). It is not immediately apparent why this was the case, but in all probability the cash was paid, whereas by that stage in the Livonian War (1577) many of the peasants may have left the Kolomna region for points south and east because of unbearable taxation, thus making land possession (and also land entitlement, *oklad*) a poor determinant of income and thus of the ability to keep slaves. Not surprisingly, the slaveowners had higher cash and land entitlements than did the average serviceman.

Additional information can be gathered by correlating the muster roll of Votskaia piatina (the northwestern district of the Novgorod region, fronting the Baltic and Swedish possessions) from 1605 with data from the same region on slaveownership generated during slave registrations of the previous decade. Table 17.16 shows those of the 778 individuals (*okladchiki* are listed twice) on the

43. Storozhev, "Desiatni XVI veka. No. 1. Kolomna."

TABLE 17.16
Known Slaveowners on 1605 Muster Roll, Votskaia Piatina (Novgorod Region)

Rank	Land Compensation Scale (Oklad) in Chetverti													
	20	50	100 [+ 3 @ 120]	150	200	250 [+ 1 @ 270]	300	350	400 [+ 1 @ 420]	450	500	550	600 [+ 2 @ 650]	oklad-chiki
Dvorovoi spisok							2/1a	2/1	9/0	25/9	15/10	15/11	46/35	
Gorodovoi spisok		12/2		16/4	39/4	45/9	43/12	56/9	59/28	19/6	12/7	9/6	4/1	
Streletskie sotniki							1/0	3/2	3/1	2/2				
Nedel'shchiki						1/0	2/1							
With father				9/0	6/2	3/0	6/1	1/1	3/0	1/1	1/0			
Noviki		8/0	5/0	25/1	11/0	11/0	10/0							
Zemtsy	87/0		31/0											
Absent: deti boiarskie			3/0		6/0		1/0							
Absent: zemtsy			4/0		2/0		2/0							
Beggar/impoverished			3/0	3/0		1/0								
Unfit for service .			1/0					1/0		1/1				
Disabled: dvorovoi								1/0						
Disabled: gorodovoi				5/2		3/1	1/1		1/1		1/0			
Retired: dvorovoi							4/2			1/1	1/1			
Retired: gorodovoi							1/1						1/0	
Blind							1/1					1/1	1/1	
Deceased: dvorovoi						1/1	4/1	2/1	3/3	1/1	4/3	1/1		
Deceased: gorodovoi		12/0	5/3	11/0	6/3	10/4		1/1	4/3	2/0	2/1			
Total servicemen/ slaveowners	87/0	32/2	55/3	69/7	70/9	77/15	78/21	67/15	86/37	52/21	36/22	22/18	47/34	30/21
(%)	(0)	(6)	(5)	(10)	(13)	(19)	(27)	(22)	(43)	(40)	(61)	(82)	(72)	(70)
Mean number of slaves per slave-owner	0	2.5	4	2.1	3.1	2.8	3.2	2.9	4.2	3.7	13.9	5.6	13.4	13.2
(current)	0	2	3	7	9	13	21	11	36	20	20	17	30	18

Source: N. Miatlev, "Desiatnia Votskoi Piatiny 1605 goda," *Izvestiia Russkago genealogicheskogo obshchestva* 4(1911): 467-509.
aFirst figure represents number on rolls; the second, the number of slaveowners.

1605 Votskaia piatina muster roll who were known to be slaveowners by land entitlement and current status. Extant information indicates that 204 of the 778 (26.2 percent) were slaveowners, a ratio that is probably an absolute lower bound, for it is almost inconceivable that nearly 100 percent of the elite servicemen (those, say, with land entitlements of 550 to 650 cheti, and certainly the *okladchiki*) did not all own slaves. Moreover, of the 778, 158 were indigenous small holders (*zemtsy*), who almost never had slaves, and another 47 were adolescent novitiates, who also did not have slaves. This left 573 *deti boiarskie* who might have owned slaves, and the extant documentation indicates that at least 35.6 percent of them did. It would be safe to assume that others among the 1605 Votskaia piatina servicemen owned slaves as well, but no evidence of that fact survives. One may conclude, provisionally, that at least a third of the provincial servicemen in Novgorod were slaveowners. There is evidence that they owned an average of at least 6.9 slaves apiece, not necessarily at any one time but over the course of their careers. The number of slaves owned correlated highly with land entitlement ($r = 0.73$).

The most prestigious rank was that of a provincial *syn boiarskii* on the "court list" (*dvorovoi spisok*), meaning that the central government assumed responsibility for that serviceman's compensation. Such men were highly compensated, and a high proportion of them owned slaves. Most provincial servicemen were to be maintained locally (the *gorodovoi spisok*), and the probability that the more well-to-do of them would be slaveowners was also high. Centurions of the arquebusiers (*streletskie sotniki*) were chosen from the landed middle service class, and they often were slaveowners. *Nedel'shchiki* were usually relatively young servicemen rendering a term in civil service, as court bailiffs (where they have been seen before in this narrative), and general assistants to their elders taking their turn in provincial administrative service. The "with father" category were young men without their own land allotments, usually scions of more senior servicemen who could support their sons in military service from their own landholdings. These young men got slaves in dowries, or had the means to buy them on their own account. The novitiates (*noviki*) also were just beginning their service careers, but usually had little or no land, and lacked the means to maintain slaves. The *zemtsy* were descendants of Novgorodians who lived in the region before it was annexed by Moscow, and were allowed to have land allotments in exchange for limited military service (local, not distant, compaigns). They were also relatively poor and almost never owned slaves.

The next categories, those absent, impoverished, and otherwise unfit for service, could not think of owning slaves, and in fact might sell themselves into slavery, given the chance. The disabled were a disparate lot, the products of the chances of war.

The most interesting categories in table 17.16 are the last ones, especially the retired. Higher percentages of them were slaveowners than those with comparable land compensation schedules in active service, indicating that slaveownership was something that they strove for and finally achieved before their deaths. Fundamentally the same message is conveyed by the "deceased" category, lessened by the obvious fact that combat and other accidental deaths that removed younger people are not distinguished from deaths in advanced age. (The "mean number of slaves per slaveowner" category includes all slaves known ever to have been owned, not just those living in 1605. Most of them were those registered in 1598. The "current" category includes those I know to have been slaveowners about the time of the compilation of the 1605 Votskaia piatina muster roll. The few others had been slaveowners earlier, or were known to be later.)

If one graphs this material, as in figure 17.1, one sees that the probability was very high at the beginning of the seventeenth century that a person with the maximum *oklad* would be a slaveowner, whereas those at the bottom of the compensation entitlement scale rarely if ever had slaves. (The correlation between *oklad* and slaveownership was very high, r = 0.949.)

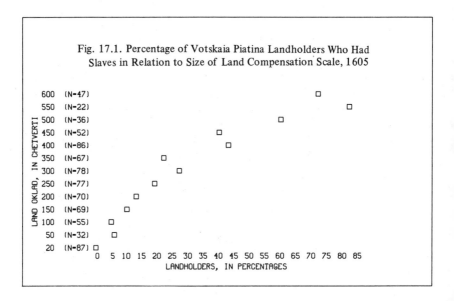

Fig. 17.1. Percentage of Votskaia Piatina Landholders Who Had Slaves in Relation to Size of Land Compensation Scale, 1605

In the previous section I discussed briefly the 1632 lists of 602 *zhil'tsy* and 623 Moscow *dvoriane*, and noted that they brought with them 0.9 and 3.1 slaves apiece, respectively. The members of those two Moscow ranks had the compensation profile shown in the table 17.17.[44]

Comparing table 17.17 with table 17.15, one finds that the *zhil'tsy* in 1632 were not too different from the provincial servicemen of Kolomna in 1577. Their cash salary entitlements were similar, and the number of slaves they

44. Iziumov; Stashevskii.

brought per serviceman also were relatively equal. The respective land entitlements, on the other hand, were quite different, and there are no comparable
data on actual service lands held, hereditary lands owned, or peasant holdings.

TABLE 17.17
Average Compensation of *Zhil'tsy* and Moscow *Dvoriane*, 1632

	Zhil'tsy	N	*Dvoriane*	N
Cash entitlement (*oklad*, rubles)	9.97	64	49.85	165
Land entitlement (*oklad*, cheti)	389.3	28	736.8	159
Service lands possessed (*pomest'e*, cheti)	127.6	573[a]	307.2	621[b]
Hereditary land owned (*votchina*, cheti)	89.0	220[c]	204.2	584[d]
Total land possessed (cheti)	213.6	434	505.8	613
Households of peasants and bobyli	9.3	309[e]	20.8	339[f]

[a] Includes 178 who declared they had no *pomest'e*.
[b] Includes 29 who declared they had no *pomest'e*.
[c] Includes 40 who declared they had no *votchina*.
[d] Includes 108 who declared they had no *votchina*.
[e] Includes 8 who declared they had no peasants or bobyli.
[f] Includes 6 who declared they had no peasants or bobyli.

The Moscow *dvoriane*, on the other hand, were in another league. Their cash
entitlements were five times those of the *zhil'tsy*, their other compensation variables were at least double those of the *zhil'tsy*. One notable correspondence is
the relationship between the number of known slaves the average *zhilets* (0.9)
and Moscow *dvorianin* (3.1) brought with them and the total landholdings of the
two groups, 92,715 cheti for the former, 310,061 cheti for the latter. The similarity of the ratios (0.9 to 92,715 and 3.1 to 310,061) is obvious. This lends support to one of the basic themes of this work, that slaveownership depended
strongly on the resources available to maintain it.

If one compares the figures in table 17.17 with those in table 17.14, for example, one again sees that the owners of the slaves that make up the bulk of the
concern of this work are an elite; while they were based primarily in the provinces, their compensation was somewhere between that of the average *zhilets* and
the average Moscow *dvorianin*. In chapter 18, when an attempt will be made to
estimate the total slave population of Muscovy, I shall make some comparisons
between the Moscow *dvoriane* and the members of the upper upper service class.

Tables 17.18 through 17.23 examine the relationships between the numbers of
combat and baggage-train slaves the *zhil'tsy* and Moscow *dvoriane* brought with
them, and the other quantifiable features of their service life—compensation
entitlements and actual land and peasant holdings. Certain general features are
notable about the tables. In the first place, the linear relationships (r and eta[2]),
for these synchronous data are generally quite low, which indicates that the low
numbers for the comparable data from the larger study of 2,499 cases may not
be due so much to the asynchroneity of the data as to other factors. The second

general feature is that the statistics for the Moscow *dvoriane* are always better

TABLE 17.18
Relationship between Military Slaveownership and Cash Entitlement

Cash Entitle-ment (Rubles)	Zhil'tsy				Moscow *Dvoriane*			
	Combat Slaves	N	Baggage-Train Slaves	N	Combat Slaves	N	Baggage-Train Slaves	N
1-4	1.3	4	1.0	5				
5-9	1.1	7	1.1	7				
10-14	1.8	16	1.4	14	1.4	5	1.5	4
15-19	1.3	3	1.0	4	1.8	11	1.3	7
20-24					2.2	25	1.8	10
25-29	1.0	1			1.7	13	1.9	8
30-49					2.5	43	1.9	25
50-99					3.3	42	2.1	18
100-250					5.1	20	3.3	8
Mean and total N	1.5	31	1.2	30	2.8	159	2.0	80
Total slaves	46		37		452		160	
r =	0.19		0.22		0.50		0.32	
Missing cases	571		572		464		543	

TABLE 17.19
Relationship between Military Slaveownership and Land Entitlement

Land Entitle-ment (Cheti)	Zhil'tsy				Moscow *Dvoriane*			
	Combat Slaves	N	Baggage-Train Slaves	N	Combat Slaves	N	Baggage-Train Slaves	N
250			1.0	1				
300			1.0	1				
350			1.0	2				
400	1.4	5	1.0	4	1.7	3	1.5	2
450					1.5	2	1.0	2
500	1.0	1	1.0	1	2.8	16	2.1	7
550					1.8	11	1.6	5
600	1.0	1			2.2	13	1.6	7
650					2.0	13	1.4	7
700					2.9	15	2.0	8
750					2.0	13	1.2	5
800					2.6	18	2.0	9
850					2.8	6	2.0	3
900					2.2	15	1.7	12
950					3.0	10	2.6	7
1,000					5.1	17	3.0	8
Mean and total N	1.3	7	1.0	9	2.7	152	1.9	82
Total slaves	9		9		411		157	
r =	-0.37		x		0.33		0.32	
Missing cases	595		593		471		541	

TABLE 17.20

Relationship between Military Slaveownership and Hereditary Landownership

Hereditary Lands (Cheti)	Zhil'tsy				Moscow *Dvoriane*			
	Combat Slaves	N	Baggage-Train Slaves	N	Combat Slaves	N	Baggage-Train Slaves	N
0	1.0	1	1.0	2	1.7	84	1.5	47
1-99	1.2	50	1.2	69	1.8	85	1.5	56
100-199	1.5	26	1.1	19	2.1	165	1.9	94
200-299	1.8	14	1.4	7	2.5	79	1.9	45
300-399	1.1	7	1.0	4	3.0	42	2.1	25
400-499	1.0	1	1.0	1	3.3	17	2.3	12
500-599	4.0	1			3.7	24	2.3	12
600-699					4.6	8	3.0	3
700-799					4.7	7	2.7	3
800-999	2.0	1			2.8	8	2.0	4
1000-1800					6.0	10	4,3	4
Mean and total N	1.4	101	1.2	102	2.4	529	1.9	305
Total slaves	142		119		1,249		570	
r =	0.27		0.02		0.53		0.37	
Missing cases		501		500		94		318

TABLE 17.21

Relationship between Military Slaveownership and Service Landholding

Service Landholding (Cheti)	Zhil'tsy				Moscow *Dvoriane*			
	Combat Slaves	N	Baggage-Train Slaves	N	Combat Slaves	N	Baggage-Train Slaves	N
0	1.1	11	1.0	12	1.6	22	1.1	11
1-99	1.0	22	1.0	46	2.1	45	1.8	30
100-199	1.2	74	1.1	91	1.7	105	1.5	72
200-299	1.4	71	1.2	56	1.9	118	1.8	68
300-399	1.3	30	1.1	24	2.2	105	1.9	62
400-499	1.7	11	1.1	7	2.6	76	2.0	39
500-599	2.0	3	2.0	1	3.2	36	1.9	18
600-699	4.0	1	3.0	1	3.1	23	2.5	13
700-799					4.1	17	2.5	8
800-999					6.3	10	4.5	4
1000-1800					5.0	2		
Mean and total N	1.3	223	1.1	238	2.3	559	1.9	325
Total slaves	287		265		1,297		602	
r =	0.36		0.25		0.46		0.33	
Missing cases		375		364		64		298

than for the *zhil'tsy*, almost certainly reflecting the dual nature of the latter, beginners and those being promoted to Moscow service from the provinces. The third major feature is the large degree of variation within each category, which is

TABLE 17.22
Relationship between Slaveownership and Peasants and Bobyli on Slaveowner's Lands

Peasant and Bobyl' Households	Zhil'tsy				Moscow *Dvoriane*			
	Combat Slaves	N	Baggage-Train Slaves	N	Combat Slaves	N	Baggage-Train Slaves	N
0					1.3	3	0.7	3
1-4	1.0	21	1.0	45	1.3	11	1.3	12
5-9	1.2	40	1.1	57	1.4	37	1.3	26
10-14	·1.0	33	1.1	39	1.4	49	1.7	34
15-24	1.5	38	1.2	22	1.6	94	1.6	67
25-49	1.5	17	1.4	11	2.4	84	2.0	44
50-99	2.0	1			4.7	14	2.7	6
100-120					6.0	2	4.0	1
Mean and total N*	1.2	150	1.1	174	1.9	294	1.7	193
Total slaves	186		187		587		325	
r =	0.38		0.32		0.67		0.31	
Missing cases		452		428		329		430

TABLE 17.23
Relationship between All Military Slaves and Total Land Held and Owned

Combat and Baggage-Train Slaves Combined	*Pomest'e* and *Votchina* belonging to *Zhil'tsy* (Cheti)	N	*Pomest'e* and *Votchina* belonging to Moscow *Dvoriane* (Cheti)	N
1	201.5	174	322.2	91
2	262.2	115	392.0	135
3	316.3	23	453.6	126
4	323.0	11	562.7	106
5	361.6	5	722.5	45
6			792.8	33
7	878.0	1	930.4	16
8			799.3	6
9			1,298.8	5
10			1,108.2	5
11			1,305.0	1
12			1,198.0	1
14			1,824.5	2
Mean and total N	239.3	329	516.8	572
r =	0.34		0.57	

reflected in high standard deviation and variance and wide dispersal on scatter-grams. This is easily seen in table 17.22, where the average total of *pomest'e* and *votchina* landholding increases in almost every case for every additional slave brought to military service, yet the linear relationships are quite low because of the wide variations in each group. In any individual case, landholding may not be a good indicator of income and capacity to support slaves, for the land may or may not have been populated. This is shown in table 17.22, where the most linear relationship in all the tables under consideration is between the actual number of peasant and *bobyl'* households possessed by the Moscow *dvoriane* and the combat slaves they brought to service with them. (These observations tend in the same direction as those made by the Soviet scholar E. I. Kolycheva, who noted that in the first half of the sixteenth century there was often a very high correlation [r usually over 0.80] between the number of slaves a man owned and the size of his estate and the number of peasants living on it.)[45]

One can also see in table 17.22 and elsewhere that the number of combat slaves was more variable than was the number of baggage-train slaves, no doubt because the amount of supplies and other baggage that needed tending was relatively constant for everyone, and thus differentials in available slaves were expressed primarily in the number of combat slaves an owner brought with him. In this context, we might note that the government got relatively more combat forces from the Moscow *dvoriane* than it did from the *zhil'tsy*. While the amount of land that supported each slave (lumping together combat and baggage-train slaves) was about the same for Moscow *dvoriane* (162.8 cheti per slave) and *zhil'tsy* (164.4 cheti per slave), the amount of land supporting each combat slave belonging to a Moscow *dvorianin* (238 cheti per combat slave) was considerably less than that supporting each combat slave brought by a *zhilets* (315.4 cheti per combat slave). This happened because slaveowners first tried to have someone tending the baggage, and only then, after that had been taken care of, would they add more combat slaves. (The figures we are dealing with here correspond quite well to government expectations, namely, that each 400 cheti of land should be able to support one cavalryman and one infantryman.)[46]

The Islamic system of employing military slaves was certainly more efficient than the Muscovite, for the Muscovites almost unquestionably had a much larger contingent of slaves supporting the baggage train than did Islamic armies. The Crimean Tatars marvelled at the size of the Muscovite baggage trains accompanying the farcical Golitsyn expeditions that tried to conquer the Crimea in 1687 and 1689.[47] However, one must judge that the relative Muscovite ineffici-

45. E. I. Kolycheva, "Opyt primeneniia korreliatsionnogo analiza dlia resheniia nekotorykh spornykh voprosov istorii kholopstva," *Istoriia SSSR* 1969, no. 4: 140-45.

46. Stashevskii, *Zemlevladenie*, p. 8. There seems to be little information on the number of slaves the elite brought with them to military service. A military inventory dated February 13, 1674, gives some idea about the relative number of slaves each rank brought. General *boiarin* Prince Iurii Petrovich Trubetskoi brought eighteen slaves, and General *okol'- nichii* Prince Danil Stepanovich Velikii Gagin had twelve slaves. Then *stol'nik* Fedor Ivanov Koltovskoi brought four slaves. All the other members of the unit (a state secretary, other *stol'niki*, *striapchie*, Moscow *dvoriane*, *zhil'tsy*, and commanders of Moscow *strel'tsy*) were accompanied by lesser numbers of slaves (*Sinbirskii sbornik. Istoricheskaia chast'* 1 [1845], pt. 4, p. 102, no. 97).

47. E. A. Razin, *Istoriia voennogo iskusstva*, 3 vols. (Moscow: Voenizdat, 1955-61), 3: 254-62.

ency was "worth it," for never did Muscovite military slaves succeed in overturning their masters and seizing the throne.

Certain individuals with the rank of Moscow *dvorianin* even went into debt to acquire and support their service horses and the slaves they brought with them to service. For example, Prince Fedor Ivanov Mortkin in February 1632 noted that he had 583 cheti of arable land worked by 21 peasant households (much of the land was vacant). He observed that he himself was serving, and that.he was bringing to the military theater two combat slaves and one baggage-train slave. Mortkin also claimed that he "lived in a very modest way [*v skudnom statke*] burdened with great debt." Both the horses and slaves he had in the sovereign's service were encumbered with debt.[48] Here perhaps we see the origins of the well-known Russian gentry practice of living in debt. We do not know to whom Mortkin was indebted, but, if he was like many of his peers, it was to a monastery.[49]

Slaveownership in Muscovy seems to have been diffused in about the same manner that it was in the Ottoman Empire. A few magnates may have owned as many as 260 slaves, but the modal ownership was a single slave. In my data (see table 17.11), thirteen owners acquired from 40 to 63 slaves. For six owners, this involved from 13 to 28 transactions. They spent from 1 to 133 rubles buying slaves, with the median being 4.10 rubles (table 17.10). The largest owners in the Novgorod area were Ignatii Ontonov Chertov with 60 slaves and Mikhail Ivanov Miloslavskii with 63. Five men gave away from 31 to 67 slaves in dowries and wills, sums that may be assumed to have represented nearly all of their slaves.

A century earlier, when Novgorod was annexed by Moscow in the 1480s, the land was parceled out as service estates (*pomest'ia*) to Muscovite servitors. Among them were forty-two estates parceled out to elite military slaves. Of the forty-two, thirty-one had slaves, about 70 of them. Eight of the service estates had only one slave; five had 2, five had 3, one had 4, two had 5, one had 7, one had 8, and four had an unknown number of slaves who lived in their owners' houses.[50] These figures are not unlike those for Edirne, Turkey, where between 1545 and 1659, slaves lived on forty-one out of the ninety-three estates there belonging to (depending upon which authority one reads) "members of the ruling class," members of the Askeri military service class, or government officials of a middle rank in the bureaucracy.[51] As in Muscovy, the modal slaveownership was 1 (N=14). Beyond that, seven estates had 2 slaves, eight had 3, two had 4, three had 5, and seven had more than 5 slaves. The forty-one estates had a total of 140

48. Stashevskii, *Zemlevladenie*, pp. 32, 35.

49. Ibid., p. 26.

50. K. V. Bazilevich, "Novgorodskie pomeshchiki iz posluzhil'tsev v kontse XV veka," *Istoricheskie zapiski* 14(1945): 76-77.

51. Inalcik, "Slave Labor," p. 9; idem, "Servile Labor," p. 27; Fisher, "Ottoman Slavery," p. 32.

slaves, 54 females and 86 males.[52] Here the sex ratio even approximated the general Muscovite ratio of 2:1 (males: females). One may assume that Ottoman grandees possessed slaves on the same scale as the Muscovites did, perhaps even to a greater degree.

There were vast numbers of petty servicemen who owned no slaves at all. This is immediately obvious from table 17.16. There must have been an analogous group of small servicemen in the Ottoman Empire, a group which could not possibly be included in the "ruling class." The Novgorod regional census of 1582-84 lists 2,745 landholders, many of whom at that time held land with no tenants; some of them were *zemtsy*, the lowest category, who almost never owned slaves. Of the 2,745 in the 1582-84 census, 204 were slaveowners of record in the late 1590s. Obviously many in the census had died by the end of the century, and the slaveownership records have not all survived. In my examination of the 1605 muster records from Votskaia piatina I noted that at least 35.6 percent of those servicemen who might be expected to own slaves in fact did. In Kolomna in 1577, the proportion of servicemen owning slaves was even higher, 69.6 percent. The same was true in 1632 for *zhil'tsy* (56.8 percent) and Moscow *dvoriane* (92.9 percent). The Votskaia piatina figure well may be too low, for the slaveownership data antedated the muster record by more than half a decade, and many changes occurred in Muscovite slaveownership in such a span of time. Moreover, Votskaia piatina was a relatively poor frontier area that had been severely devastated during the Livonian War. The Moscow *zhil'tsy* and *dvoriane* possessed slaves in higher than average numbers, for that is what Moscow service was all about—prestige and its visible manifestations, which were more in evidence there than in the provinces. One may also assume that the percentage of *zhil'tsy* owning slaves was as low as stated because, as has been noted in the case of the 1605 Votskaia piatina muster and will be discussed in some greater detail below, those who were just beginning military service often did not have slaves, and that included, of course, a significant portion of the *zhil'tsy*.

It should be safe to conclude that at least 20 percent of provincial servicemen ordinarily owned slaves, and probably it was an even greater proportion, a third or more. Of those who served from Moscow, certainly over half owned slaves, a figure rising to nearly 100 percent for members of the upper upper-service class, the counselor state secretaries, *dvoriane*, *okol'nichie*, and boyars. Thus the Muscovite pattern of slaveownership was more like that of the Ottomans, the early nineteenth-century Indians, or the African Sena and unlike that in Dahomey, Thailand, or in the Caribbean, where a very small proportion of the wealthiest

52. Inalcik, "Slave Labor," p. 9. Many distributions of New World slavery could be cited, but those for Jamaica will do. In 1829-32, the average urban slaveholding was 5.3. In 1832, 24.3 percent of all Jamaican slaves lived in holdings of 1–50; 14 percent in holdings of 51–100; 26.5 percent, 101–200; 21.4 percent, 201–300; and the rest, 14.7 percent, in holdings of 301–800 (B. W. Higman, *Slave Population and Economy in Jamaica, 1807-1834* [Cambridge: Cambridge University Press, 1976], pp. 58, 70).

proprietors owned the vast majority of the slaves, or in Han and fourteenth-century China or Hausaland of the Sokoto Caliphate, where slaveownership was more widely diffused and the ruling elite owned considerably greater numbers. At the beginning of the period discussed in this work, in the fifteenth century, rank-and-file masters may have owned as many as ten to twenty families, the great lords from seventy to a hundred, even as many as a hundred and fifty. With the expansion of the service class after the annexation of Novgorod and then in the reign of Ivan IV, average slaveholdings probably declined, along with landholdings and the general level of income. Less is currently known about the seventeenth century, but slaveholdings probably remained about the same, or even declined, with the supply of new recruits being cut off as society became more rigidly stratified. On the other hand, leading figures of the administration in Moscow such as I. N. Romanov and B. I. Morozov may be assumed to have owned from three to four hundred house slaves apiece.[53]

Slaveowner Volition

Chapter 16 discussed the exercise of volition by those who sold themselves into slavery in Muscovy, and some of the ways they continued to make choices while enslaved. In this section I shall examine some of the choices those who owned slaves explicitly made when purchasing slaves.

I have already had occasion to note that some purchasers exhibited a distinct preference for slaves who previously had been owned by someone else. This was notably true for Semen Andreev Lvov (eleven purchases, solely of solitaries, between 1593 and 1599),[54] Danil Andreev Nogtev (three purchases in 1596),[55] a number of the members of the Sekirin clan (Boris Stepanov, Ivan Stepanov, Andrei Asmanov, Fedor Mikiforov, Ivan Borisov, Mikita Girigor'ev, fifteen purchases between 1573 and 1598);[56] Neudacha Romanov Talyzin (two purchases in 1603),[57] Mikita and Stepan Vasil'ev Vysheslavtsov, and Mikita's son Iakov (four purchases between 1585 and 1600).[58] The logic of such deliberation is patent: it is nearly a truism that previously owned slaves are much easier to manage than those who have never experienced the total submission of slavery be-

53. A. A. Novosel'skii, "Krest'iane i kholopy," in *Ocherki istorii SSSR. Period feodalizma XVII v.* (Moscow: AN SSSR, 1955), p. 187; Paneiakh, "Iz istorii politiki tsarizma," p. 107; Zimin, "Otpusk kholopov," p. 71; Paul E. Lovejoy, "Plantations in the Economy of the Sokoto Caliphate," *Journal of African History* 19, no. 3(1978): 359; Hjejle, p. 90; Orlando Patterson, *The Sociology of Slavery* (London: MacGibbon and Kee, 1967), p. 37; Wiens, pp. 294-95; Wilbur, p. 166.
54. NZKK 1: 5, 146, 148, 187, 226-27, 288, 325; NKK 7108, p. 12.
55. NZKK 1: 349, 422, 424.
56. NZKK 1: 20, 128, 130; RIB 17: 198, 205; NKK 7106, p. 46.
57. NZKK 2: 50, 94.
58. NZKK 1: 113, 439, 441; NKK 7108, p. 7.

fore. On the other hand, some purchasers obviously preferred slaves who had never been owned before by anyone. One such individual was Matfei Ivanov Meshcherskii, who in twenty purchases between 1577 and 1597 is never recorded as buying a slave who had been previously owned by anyone.[59]

Another area of discretion was the amount paid for slaves. Some people paid only low prices. The Izmailov brothers (Dmetrii, Nesprashivai, and Ivan Alekseevy) in 1603 made five purchases of solitary slaves (four males and one female) for a ruble apiece.[60] In the same year Ivan Mikiforov Likharev and his sons Fedor and Antonii made eleven purchases for 2 rubles each: two brothers and the wife of one of them, two children, three male solitaries, three married couples, a couple with one child, and a couple with two children.[61] Five brothers, Pervyi, Vtoroi, Matfei, Ivan, and Matfei (sic) Semenov L'vov, made seven purchases in 1603, for which they paid 2 rubles apiece (two men, three women, and two families of a married couple and two children).[62] A number of other examples could be provided.

Some purchasers preferred to pay uniformly average prices, in this case 5 rubles per transaction. Grigorii Dmitriev Kobelev made eight purchases (mostly solitaries) at that price in the years 1594-1600.[63] Ivan Dmitriev Molevanov made four purchases in 1597 of previously dependent families, purchases of 5 rubles apiece.[64]

There were also slaveowners who paid uniformly high prices. One such person was Ignatii Posnikov Irettskii, who made eight purchases in 1594 and 1595 for sums ranging from 5 to 10 rubles, with an average of 7 rubles per contract. For the sum of 56 rubles he purchased: two solitary males, two married couples, three families with children (one each with one child, three children, and five children), and a woman with two children, a total of twenty-four people. The number of solitaries is atypically low and the number of families is atypically high. Nothing is stated about the skills or prior status of any of the slaves. The highest sum, 10 rubles, was paid for the family of five; the father was about sixty years old, but the ages of the other family members (the mother, a boy, and two girls) are not given. Two of the other family heads were about fifty years old, and the only other age given is for a girl who was twelve.[65] Another big spender was Voin Ofonas'ev Novokshchenov, who in the years 1585-93 made twelve purchases in the range of 5 to 15 rubles for an average of 6.73 rubles apiece. He preferred smaller units than did Irettskii, buying three solitary males, six married couples, a couple with two children, and two fathers (one

59. RIB 17: 44-49; NKK 7106, pp. 21, 24-25.
60. NZKK 2: 37, 74, 86-87, 98.
61. NZKK 2: 299, 328-31.
62. NZKK 2: 300-2, 306, 334.
63. NZKK 1: 17, 41, 43, 290, 363, 417, 430; NKK 7108, p. 76.
64. NKK 7106, pp. 1-3.
65. NKK 7108, pp. 163-64; NZKK 1: 249-51, 466.

with one child, the other with two). The documents list no ages or other information about Novokshchenov's purchased slaves. They do, however, reveal what
happened demographically to them between the time of their initial purchase
and re-registration in 1598: fourteen children were born. Also interesting is the
fact that the sex ratio of boys (10) and girls (9) was nearly equal. As I have had
occasion to note earlier, Novokshchenov was a prominent individual with a very
high land entitlement (600 *cheti*). There is no evidence available that would indicate why he paid such large sums, other than that he had the means to.[66]
Other examples of "big spenders" could be provided, as well as of those who
made purchases throughout the price spectrum.

Elsewhere we have seen other examples of explicitly discretionary slave purchases in such matters as the sex of slaves or their abilities. Such evidence of the
use of discretion is of course interesting by itself, but it also seems to have larger
implications: the fact that slavebuyers could exercise such discretion implies that
it was possible to make such choices, which in turn seems to indicate that the
supplies of people wanting to sell themselves exceeded the demand. Had that not
been the case, explicit choice would have been difficult to exercise. We know, of
course, that at times such as the 1601-3 famine the number of people willing to
sell themselves (rather than starve to death, as certainly hundreds of thousands
did) exceeded the number of purchasers, and the fact that some buyers could pay
only rock-bottom prices at that time is not surprising. What is surprising is that
not everyone did. The demonstration that choices could be made at other times
as well seems to indicate that there was nearly always a surplus of people willing
to sell themselves. (As we have seen in chapter 10, the price-level of slaves seems
to indicate the same thing.).

Forms of Slaveownership

The issue of multiple slaveownership was a major one at the end of the 1590s
and at the beginning of the seventeenth century, after the government decreed
that limited service contract slavery was to end on the owner's death. The natural slaveowner response to such a dictum was to try to avoid it by registering the
ownership of the slave in the name of as many owners as possible, to avoid expropriation. The government awoke to that tactic and successfully forbade it as
well.

Multiple ownership was not, however, concocted to cope with the change in
the institution of limited service contract slavery. It was allowed in Roman and
Islamic law, was inherent to some extent in the nature of marriage contracts and
dowries, and was part of the purchase formula for full slavery. It also appeared
early in the era during which limited service contract slavery became the prevailing form of self-sale slavery, a fact that is shown in table 17.24.

66. RIB 17: 131-34.

TABLE 17.24
Forms of Slaveownership and Prices Paid For Slaves

Ownership per Document	N	Dates	Price per Document (Rubles)	N	Price per Slave (Rubles)	N	Ratio of Price per Slave to Price per Document (When N Is Over 15)
1 man	1,903	1480-1714	3.90	1,760	2.64	Same	.676
2 brothers	154	1567-1603	4.22	143	2.54		.601
3 brothers	23	1575-1603	6.72	18	3.60		.535
4 brothers	8	1575-1603	3.86	7	1.11		
5 brothers	11	1603	1.81	11	0.96		
Father, 1 son	62	1571-1603	3.45	62	1.87		.543
Father, 2 sons	52	1595-1603	4.06	52	2.62		.645
Father, 3 sons	6	1586-1603	3.67	6	2.63		
Father, 4 sons	2	1603	1.50	2	0.83		
2 brothers, 1 son	3	1595-1599	6.00	3	6.00		
1 woman	44	1541-1701	4.32	22	2.44		
Mother, 1 son	6	1568-1603	2.75	4	1.88		
Mother, 2 sons	1	1599					
Mother, 3 sons	1	1533					
Mother, 4 sons	1	1596					
Wife, husband	116	1504-1668[a]					
Father, children	99	1430-1554[b]	3.17	96	2.04		.641
Man, wife, children	2	1567, 1675	2.00	1	2.00		
Wife, children	1	1472[c]					
2 related men	1	1575					
Unknown	3						
Total and mean	2,499	1595-1596	3.90	2,187	2.58		.662

[a] Marriage contracts, dowries.
[b] The formula of a full slavery contract.
[c] A will.

It can be seen from table 17.25 why it was necessary to issue the decree of 1606 that forbade multiple ownership and confined limited service contract slavery to the life of a single lord. The table shows that there was definitely an upsurge in the forms of multiple ownership after the law of 1597 that reformed the institution of slavery; this is a trend that almost certainly reflects a consciousness of expropriation that was inherent in the statute of 1597.

TABLE 17.25
Chronological Patterns of Multiple Slaveownership

Year	Cases of Multiple Ownership (N)	No. of Limited Service Slavery Contracts (N)	Multiple Slave Ownerships (%)
1510-1583	20	156	12.8
1584	5	44	11.4
1585	7	54	13.0
1586	7	36	19.4
1587	2	7	28.6
1588	3	28	9.7
1589	3	48	6.3
1590	0	14	0.0
1591	1	28	3.6
1592	1	20	5.0
1593	4	56	7.1
1594	9	120	7.5
1595	32	169	18.9
1596	17	128	13.3
1597	7	152	4.6
1598	1	8	12.5
1599	7	45	15.6
1600	9	116	7.8
1601	0	1	0.0
1602	17	89	19.1
1603	150	654	22.9
1606-1701	2	112	1.8
Total (1510-1701)	304	2,091	14.5

The benefits stemming from multiple slaveownership are not immediately apparent. Prior to the change in the legal nature of limited service contract slavery, the logic of the practice is not even immediately apparent, for if the borrower defaulted after the initial year and the owner died, the slave passed immediately to the owner's heir. The major reason for establishing multiple ownership might have been to avoid the natural inheritance process, to assure that the slave would pass to someone other than the legal heir.

In any event, collective ownership of slaves was a fact of life that might be explained by the prices paid for slaves. (See table 17.24.) A priori hypotheses offer little help because they are contradictory. On the one hand, collective ownership might have been advantageous because of the greater resources that could be pooled to buy slaves, thus enabling multiple owners to pay more than single purchasers could. Moreover, multiple slaveowners might be able to supervise slaves more efficiently, get more out of them, and reduce the threat of losses, thus increasing the sums they were willing to pay for what, as we have seen, was often a quite fleeting commodity. On the other hand, multiple ownership might offer greater security to the person under stress who was selling himself into slavery and who would, therefore, be willing to sell himself for less.

In a limited sense, the data seem to support the first hypothesis. Of the combinations for which there are over fifteen examples, one of two brothers and another of three brothers paid more than did a solitary male purchaser, but, regrettably, for the hypothesis, a father and a son together paid less than, statistically, either of them would have individually. Looking at the last column in table 17.24, we can see that in some abstract sense the solitary male slaveowner got the least for his money, in term of the ratio between the amount he paid for each transaction and the amount he paid for each slave in the transaction. Whether that fact has any real meaning remains to be determined.

Corporate Ownership of Slaves

Since Babylonian times, when the temple was a major slaveowner, corporate bodies frequently have owned slaves.[67] From a comparative perspective, it is striking that Muscovite ownership of slaves was largely restricted to individuals. There were, of course, minor exceptions, such as monasteries, which from time to time (probably in violation of church rules—the Studion monastery in Constantinople forbade the use of slaves as personal servants, monastery servants, or laborers on monastery lands, and the Russian Orthodox church adopted the Studion rule) seem to have owned a slave or two. When the treasurer of the Nizhnii Novgorod Monastery of the Caves, Andreian Sushnitsyn, purchased Grigorii Fedorov (of Kostroma), his wife Maria, their son Taras and daughters Mar'ia and Pelageia for 3 rubles in January of 1602, it is fairly clear that this was an institutional purchase, not a personal one, for they agreed to serve at the monastery's headquarters (*dvorets*), "or wherever the archimandrite orders."[68] Occasionally there was an exception, such as in the early 1590s, when the Joseph of Volokolamsk monastery officials resolved to make large profits from a usury operation and tried to enforce it by compelling peasants to sign limited service slavery contracts; the peasants soon rebelled, and the operation was halted.[69] In general, however, while the place of the church in Muscovy was

67. Mendelsohn, p. 100; Hjejle, p. 84; Indian Law Commission, *Report on Indian Slavery* (1841), pp. 203-4.
68. Pavlov-Sil'vanskii, *Akty* (1909), pp. 254-55.
69. Koretskii, *Formirovanie*, pp. 140, 217; Brauning, p. 46; K. N. Shchepetov, "Sel'skoe

comparable to that of the temple in much of the Ancient Near East ("the largest landowner, the greatest industrialist, the richest banker"), the many extant studies of the economies of the church and sundry monasteries are notable in their lack of discussion about slaves.[70]

Particularly striking is the fact that the state itself did not own military slaves, as was so common in Islamic states.[71] (It could not have owned galley slaves—until late in the Petrine era—or mining slaves because Muscovy had no fleet or mines.) In Eshnunna (1900 B.C.) the palace was a major owner of slavegirls,[72] but certainly there was no such phenomenon in Muscovy.

State slaves also existed in the Ancient Near East and in times since then.[73] In early Muscovy the elite slaves who performed "statelike" functions in either the military or civil sphere were distinctly the property of their owners (the sovereign himself, or other dignitaries) who could and sometimes did manumit their property in final testaments. Elite slavery of this kind expired with the conception of Muscovy as the sovereign's patrimony. After the sovereign's domains became conceptually distinct from "the state" itself, the former were managed by free men, even though great private estates belonging to magnates still continued to be administered by slaves. This failure to transmit slave management of the royal patrimony to the state itself is a subject worthy of further examination; perhaps it can be attributed to a number of factors. One of them would be the creation in the first half of the sixteenth century of the notion that the monarch was legitimate because of his divine assignation. This placed the ruler above all others, who became slavelike in their obedience and submission. Secondly, the creation of the meritocratic service class system, supported by service land, provided an always available pool of personnel for running both the state and the sovereign's personal possessions. Together, these factors made it possible to dispense with elite slaves, who certainly presented more problems in recruitment and control than did the members of the middle and upper service classes.

Municipalities have also owned slaves since Babylonian and then Roman times. Athens employed slaves as policemen, Constantinople used them as sanitation workers, and U. S. southern municipalities put them to work as firemen.[74] Ex-

khoziaistvo na imenii Iosefo-Volokolamskogo monastyria v kontse XVI veka," *Istoricheskie zapiski* 18(1946): 100-105. Monasteries did have tax-exempt slavelike individuals farming for them who went under the names *sluzhki* and *detenyshi*. See ch. 14, n. 34 above.

70. Mendelsohn, p. 100; N. A. Gorskaia, *Monastyrskie krest'iane tsentral'noi Rossii v XVII v.* (Moscow: Nauka, 1977); L. I. Ivina, *Krupnaia votchina Severo-vostochnoi Rusi kontsa XIV–pervoi poloviny XVI v.* (Leningrad: Nauka, 1979); A. N. Sakharov, *Russkaia derevnia XVII v. po materialam Patriarshego khoziaistva* (Moscow: Nauka, 1966).

71. Pipes, "Strategic Rationale," pp. 34-36.

72. Pritchard, p. 136.

73. Mendelsohn, p. 92; Udal'tsova, p. 11.

74. Mendelsohn, p. 94; Westermann, p. 64; Udal'tsova, p. 11; Richard C. Wade, *Slavery in the Cities; the South, 1820-1860* (New York: Oxford University Press, 1964), pp. 36, 45-46.

planations for the absence of municipal ownership of slaves in Muscovy do not spring out, but one might be tempted to ascribe the fact that Muscovite slave-ownership was personal to an absence of civil corporate definition or conceptualization in Muscovy: the state itself, as we have just seen, was often defined as the personal possession of the sovereign, and, administratively, "towns" were completely subordinate to the ruler first through his personal agents, then through the chancelleries. Even Moscow, the capital, enjoyed not the slightest autonomy but was administered (after 1564) by a bureau, the *Zemskii prikaz*, which was in no way distinct from the other chancelleries responsible for affairs in the rest of Muscovy. Moreover, Muscovite municipalities lacked the means to keep slaves and found it cheaper to compel the townsmen themselves to render the essential services.

The fact that nearly all slaves in Muscovy were owned by individuals also tells us interesting things about the ethos of the society in general. As I have had more than one occasion to observe about those who sold themselves into slavery, the Muscovite ethos was a highly individualistic one. Try as it might with its institutionalization of collective responsibility for both behavior and taxes, the state, until late in the seventeenth century, was unable to diminish the centrality of the individual as the basic unit in Muscovy. (This did not mean, however, that the individual was accorded any rights by the state.)

The Life Cycle of Slaveownership

Slaveownership in Muscovy was highly life-cycle determined, a fact that mirrored the government-engendered meritocratic ethos of the servicemen, who made up the bulk of the slaveowners. The pattern of acquisition of slaves was quite predictable.

The novitiate began his service career with no slaves, as is apparent from table 17.16. An exception to that general rule might be provided when a young serviceman's parents (or other relatives) died, in which case he might begin his adult life with some slaves in his possession. It is clear that such instances were few, even though the unpredictable factor of a serviceman's father's dying and willing slaves to his son could occur at any time.

The next major event in the slaveowner's life was his marriage. In the following section I shall discuss marriage contracts and dowries in some greater detail, but here I shall note that this was sometimes the moment when a slaveowner acquired his first slaves. There seems to be absolutely no way to determine the age at which servicemen married, although the impression given by the extant

In Tamil India communities, rather than individuals, often owned slaves (Hjejle, p. 75). To my knowledge, Muscovy knew no such communities.

materials is that some time elapsed between the moment when a novitiate began service and the moment when his marriage was arranged and then finally concluded, about six months later.

A relatively typical example of one pattern was provided by Bogdan Danilov Borkov. In 1565 he married Olena Ofonas'eva Sekirina, who brought into the marriage five slaves—three women, a man, and the man's son. Twenty-five years were to pass before Borkov himself had the means, 3 rubles, to buy a slave.[75] A similar example is provided by Savastian Stepanov Chiurkin. In 1565 he married Mar'ia Fedorova Khvostova, whose five brothers provided her with a dowry of two slave girls, one of whom was identified as a Livonian war captive. Savastian's next recorded transaction was two decades later (he was then a *strelets* centurion with 170 cheti of land), when he and his son Grigorii paid 12 rubles for a man and his two sons. His next purchase was twelve years later, in 1597, a single man purchased for 6 rubles. When registering these documents in 1597, Chiurkin also noted that he owned slave descendants of people that his forebears had purchased as full slaves around 1482, a couple and their offspring, three boys and two girls. It is not stated when he inherited these seven hereditary slaves.[76] More than a dozen other examples of a considerable time lapse between marriage and the first purchase of slaves were provided by Kondratii Ermolin (married 1574, first purchase in 1583),[77] Posnik Fedorov Iakimov (1578 and 1584),[78] Ivan Semenov Krasnoslepov (1573 and 1591),[79] Mikita Ivanov Kropotov (married first in 1582, a second time in 1592; first purchase in 1598),[80] Stepan Tret'iakov-Mikhailov Kuz'minskii (first married in 1569, second marriage in 1587; first purchase in 1594),[81] Matfei Ivanov Meshcherskii (1554 and 1576),[82] Ivan Ofonas'ev Meshcherskii (1590 and 1597),[83] Ivan Stepanov Murav'ev

75. RIB 17: 204-5.

76. RIB 17: 104-5; Ianitskii, p. 211; RIB 38(1926): 470; Samokvasov AM 2: 96; DVP, p. 508, no. 803.

77. RIB 17: 92-93.

78. Kopanev, "Materialy," pp. 162-63; Samokvasov, *Materialy* 2(1909): 539; Ivanov, OPK, p. 71; Maikov, KPNV, p. 100; AIuB 2: 177; RIB 22(1908): 247 and passim; Paneiakh, *Kholopy*, p. 46; Nosov, *Ocherki*, p. 356.

79. RIB 17: 138, 210-12; NZKK 1: 184; DVP, p. 472, no. 58; Ivanov, OPK, p. 47; RIB 22(1908): 245 and passim; Koretskii, *Zakreposhchenie*, p. 270.

80. Kopanev, "Materialy," p. 161; NZKK 1: 207; Nosov, *Ocherki*, pp. 365, 379; Paneiakh, *Kabal'noe*, pp. 32, 116; idem, *Kholopstvo*, p. 193.

81. RIB 17: 13-15, 18; NZKK 1: 108-10; NKK 7106, p. 36; Ianitskii, p. 146; Samokvasov, *Materialy* 2(1909): 147-48; DVP, p. 474, no. 77; RIB 22(1908): 682.

82. See n. 59 above.

83. RIB 17: 146-47; AMG 1: 89; DR 1: 308, 825-26; Sukhotin, *Chetvertchiki*, pp. 33, 35, 37; KR 1: 444-48, 452, 1039, 1261; RIB 35(1917): 233; Veselovskii, APD, 1: 534, 536, 543; AAE 2: 227, 360; KR 1: 1261; DVP, p. 471, no. 46; RK 1550-1636, 2: 187, 342; DR 1: 308, 825-26.

(1573 and 1589),[84] Ofonasii Ivanov Novokshchenov (1540 and 1554),[85] Ignatii Petrov Obolnianinov (1565 and 1581),[86] Semen Iakovlev Perepechin (1583 and 1589),[87] Ivan Isupov Samarin (1570 and 1584),[88] and Ontonii Silin Vypovskii (1596 and 1603).[89] This pattern seems to have been consistent throughout the sixteenth century. Some of these individuals may have acquired by testament or other means still other slaves between the time they married and the time they first purchased slaves; this must have been the case with Ivan Danilov Saburov, who wed in 1569, purchased slaves in 1586, and in 1597 registered twenty-five slaves that he did not record as having been given to him in a dowry or having purchased.[90] The general pattern, however, was that considerable time elapsed between marriage and the time when a serviceman had the means to purchase slaves himself. One might note that some of the individuals discussed under this rubric, such as Fedor Il'in Korotaev, probably had served some length of time before marrying. In his case, he married in 1580 and first purchased slaves in 1585. However, in 1582 he already had a very substantial service land grant in Votskaia piatina of 310 cheti, and in 1605 he was retired with the notation that he was "old, sick, henceforth unable to serve," and had been replaced by his two sons.[91] The same was true for Petr Danilov Skobel'tsyn, who wed in 1586 and began to purchase slaves only in 1597. Seven years prior to his marriage, in 1579, he had spent 5 rubles on a tax-exempt, unencumbered house with a number of out-buildings in Novgorod.[92]

There were other patterns besides the passage of a considerable length of time

84. RIB 17: 20; RK 1598-1638, pp. 81, 94, 111, 127, 144; AIuB 2: 178; RK 1475-1598, pp. 502, 511, 534, ASEI 3: 432, no. 431.

85. RIB 17: 130, 182-83; Likhachev, *D'iaki*, index, p. 56, app., p. 28; ASEI 3: 404; TK 1550, p. 363, list 153 on p. 85; RK 1559-1605, p. 65; Ianitskii, p. 174; PSRL 13[1]: 298, and 13[2]: 304; RK 1475-1598, pp. 171, 174, 184; RK 1550-1636, 1: 73, 76, 90.

86. RIB 17: 154-60; AIuB 2: 180, DVP, p. 504, no. 754; RIB 22(1908): 587, 830, 836; Koretskii, *Zakreposhchenie*, p. 225.

87. Kopanev, "Materialy," pp. 169-70; NZKK 2: 45; DN 1596, p. 199.

88. RIB 17: 162-65; NZKK 1: 172; Nosov, *Ocherki*, pp. 352, 388; Veselovskii, *Issledovaniia*, p. 485; RK 1476-1598, p. 483; Veselovskii, APD, 1: 389-90; Storozhev, "B.S.," p. 95; DVP, p. 506, no. 771, LZAK 19(1908): 41; RIB 22(1908): 200; AIuB 2: 180.

89. Kopanev, "Materialy," p. 174; NZKK 2: 349-50; PK po Pskovu, pp. 145-46, 166; Savelov 2(1908): 145-46.

90. RIB 17: 22-23; Samokvasov, *Materialy* 1(1905): 19; 2 (1909): 309; AI 2: 296; Ianitskii, p. 100; RK 1475-1598, pp. 250, 270, 300, 329; AIuB 1: 74, 182-84; Likhachev, *D'iaki*, app., p. 34; DVP, p. 468, no. 16; p. 470, no. 17; SIRIO 137(1912): 21; SIRIO 142(1913): 20; RIB 22(1908): 502, 506, 521; Andreiiashev, *Materialy*, p. 305; Koretskii, *Zakreposhchenie*, p. 137.

91. RIB 17: 66-67; DVP, p. 499, no. 724; Ivanov, OPK, p. 46; Ianitskii, p. 145; *Vremennik* 6(1850):13.

92. Kopanev, "Materialy," p. 174; NZKK 2: 310, AIu, pp. 130-31, no. 91; RIB 32 (1915): 562-63, no. 283; Ivanov, OPK, p. 64; RIB 38(1926), p. 474; RIB 22(1908): 281-82, 608, 626; RIB 17: 69.

between a serviceman's marriage and his first purchase of slaves. One variation was nearly simultaneous marriage and first purchase of slaves. A relatively typical example was Fedor Misiurev Bezstuzhev, who in 1587 married Fedora Starkova Neelova, whose dowry consisted of a slave girl. In the same year he purchased for 5 rubles a male slave who at some time between then and December 1597 fled. Bezstuzhev's next known slave purchase was in 1600.[93] We may assume that someone gave Bezstuzhev the 5 rubles as a present in 1587, and that he and his wife intended that the two slaves would keep house for them. Perhaps an attempt to marry them by force was the precipitant of the male slave's flight. Only thirteen years later did Bezstuzhev acquire the means to buy another slave. Tikhon Petrov Miakhovo also bought a slave soon after he married.[94] There are three other examples of nearly simultaneous marriage and first purchase of slaves, but the men in all three cases seem to have had significant service careers beforehand. Mikifor Kudeiarov Meshcherskii wed and first purchased slaves in 1596, but he almost certainly must have been well along in years by that time, for in 1605 he had the top service land entitlement (600 cheti) and was an *oklad-chik*. Moreover, in 1613 he was a signatory on the charter offering the Novgorod throne to the Swedish prince, Karl Philipp, and was the second signatory on a document promising the Swedish occupation authorities that certain Novgorodian landholders would not leave.[95] Andrei Semenov Parskii married and made his first purchases in 1585, but in 1582 he already possessed in Shelonskaia piatina 53 cheti of land himself, plus the 510 cheti jointly with three brothers, indicating that they had been already some time in service.[96] The same was even clearer in the case of Ivan Ondreev Pustoshkin, who purchased slaves and got married in 1592/93, for he had been assigned 153 cheti of land in Shelonskaia piatina in 1571.[97]

Another pattern was for a serviceman to marry, acquire slaves in the marriage contract or dowry, and then commence buying slaves within two or three years after that. Information about thirteen slaveowners who did that is available. For half of them (Bogdan Iur'ev Kosittskoi,[98] Roman Dmitreev Kushelev,[99] Gera-

93. RIB 17: 11; LZAK 24: 9; DVP, p. 477, no. 182; RIB 22: 811, 836; DAI 1: 309; 2: 79-82.
94. Lakier, pp. 44, 54; Ivanov, OPK, p. 53.
95. RIB 17: 104, 206; Tatishchev (1910), p. 27; Veselovskii, APD 1: 158; PSRL 14: 138; DVP, pp. 468, 470, nos. 18, 29; DAI 2: 7, 18.
96. Kopanev, "Materialy," p. 169; Ianitskii, p. 181; Ivanov, OPK, p. 59; RIB 22: 280-1, 613, 631-32; Nosov, *Ocherki*, pp. 350, 354, 385; SBV (1974), p. 239; KR 2: 517; Paneiakh, *Kabal'noe*, p. 46.
97. Lakier, p. 46; NZKK 1: 188; NPK 5: 458-59; Ianitskii, pp. 99, 188; Ivanov, OPK p. 61.
98. Lakier, pp. 41, 51; Samokvasov, *Materialy* 2(1909): 137; RIB 17: 69.
99. RIB 17: 85-86; DVP, p. 471, no. 51.

sim Enyshev Murav'ev,[100] Prokhor Ivanov Nazimov,[101] Stepan Istomin Rokh-
manov,[102] and Bogdan Vasil'ev Volkov-Kuritsyn[103]) there is little additional information available. For the other half, however, the extant information indicates that they had already established their careers prior to their marriages. Fedor Grigor'ev Buturlin was married in 1593 and made his first slave purchase in
1596, but he seems to have been active as a landholder and communtity leader
in Shelonskaia piatina already in 1585. Moreover, a Fedor Grigor'ev Buturlin
was active in inviting Gustavus Adolphus to take the Novgorod throne in 1611,
and a man with the same name was a general in 1619 in Ustiuzhna Zhelezopol'-
skaia and then in Kargopol' in 1625.[104] Zhdan Ushakov Kharlamov married in
1582, made slave purchases beginning in 1584, but was active as a Bezhetskaia
piatina landholder in 1564.[105] Poluekht Matveev Kolychev, who married in
1590 and began making purchases of slaves in 1591, also seems to have been
active earlier. That may in fact have been his second marriage, for he made
joint slave purchases with his son Matfei Poluekhtov (sic) in 1597 (to my knowledge, it was not customary for joint ownerships to be made with six-year-olds
as partners). A slave he purchased in 1596 said that he had already served Poluekht voluntarily for seven years. Poluekht Matveev Kolychev was also part of
the 1611 Novgorodian embassy that offered the throne to Gustavus Adolphus or
his son Karl Philipp.[106] A similar pattern of extensive premarital service activity can be observed in the career of Semen Ofonas'ev Meshcherskii. Married in
1592 (he began to buy slaves in 1594), he had been a military commander in
1584 in Chern'.[107] Ofonasii Vasil'ev Neelov was certainly not a young man
when he married in 1582 (he began buying slaves four years later), for, when he
was reviewed in 1604, it was noted that he had five sons, was "old" (over fifty,
probably), and was discharged.[108] Bogdan Semenov Pustoshkin was married in

100. RIB 17: 7-9, 20; Kopanev, "Materialy," p. 181; NZKK 1: 119; Samokvasov, *Materialy* 1(1905): 129-31; DVP, p. 468, no. 27; 470, no. 34; DAI 2: 17-18, 79; RIB 22(1908):
592, 596.
101. Kopanev, p. 171.
102. RIB 17: 26-27, 73; Bychkov, LZAK 22: 6.
103. RIB 17: 28; Petrov, IRRD 1 (1886): 354; DVP, p. 474, no. 78.
104. RIB 17: 79; NZZK 1: 404, 411; Storozhev, "B.S.," p. 92; Likhachev, *D'iaki*, p. 47;
Veselovskii, APD 1: 109, no. 83; Petrov, IRRD 1(1886): 265; Samokvasov, *Materialy* 2
(1909): 38, 137; Ivanov, OPK, p. 240; RIB 38(1926): 459; Opisanie 15(1908): 81, no. 60,
II; 315, no. 286, II; LZAK 19(1908): 30; RIB 22(1908): 88-90, 102, 206-7, 569; KR 1:
646, 868, 924; DR 1: 418; Tatishchev (1910), p. 63. It is not clear whether this is one person, or more than one.
105. Lakier, pp. 43, 57, 60; NPK 6: 1064-66; Nosov, *Ocherki*, p. 392; Ivanov, OPK,
p. 68; AIuB 2: 178.
106. Lakier, pp. 46, 59, 61, 63; NZKK 1: 351; DAI 1: 279-80, 282, 284; Ivanov, OPK,
p. 45; RIB 22(1908): 624, 644.
107. RIB 17: 63-64; NZKK 1: 1; Rozhdestvenskii, SZ, pp. 190, 217; DVP, p. 471, no. 43;
RK 1550-1636, 2: 8; RIB 22(1908): 780, 830; Paneiakh, *Kholopstvo*, p. 191.
108. RIB 17: 95-96; AIuB 2: 181; Sukhotin, ChSV, p. 30; Nosov, *Ocherki*, pp. 350, 352,
354; DVP, p. 501, no. 733; Ivanov, OPK, p. 55.

1586 and purchased slaves beginning in 1588, but he was already active in She-lonskaia piatina land matters in 1562; in 1582 he had a large holding of 400 cheti there and by 1598 he was deceased.[109] Ivan Borisov Sekirin was married in 1595 and made his first recorded slave purchase in 1597, but he must have been a man of some substance considerably before that time. In 1598 two dozen hereditary slaves, inherited from an ancestor who had purchased a full slave about 120 years earlier, were registered in his name. To maintain those slaves he must have possessed considerable resources, a probability indicated in his 1605 Votskaia piatina land compensation entitlement of 500 cheti. Sekirin was anoth-er Novgorod-area landholder who signed the 1613 invitation to Swedish prince Karl Philipp, another sign of high community standing.[110] The conclusion to be drawn from these cases seems to be that a certain segment of servicemen post-poned marrying until they had accumulated considerable resources, enough to permit them to maintain not only a wife but slaves as well. While there seems to be no evidence that a cash gift accompanied slaves in a dowry for their mainte-nance it seems likely that it did not. This meant that the marrying male not only had to support his new wife but the chattel she brought with her as well.

The remaining possible pattern would seem to be that of slaveowners who pur-chased slaves considerably prior to the time they married and acquired slaves in the marriage contract or dowry. That was the variant noted in the *Ulozhenie* of 1649, where it was observed that many people bought slaves prior to their mar-riage.[111] The available data present twenty-one examples of that pattern, which seems to have been the most popular. Combining these examples with those just discussed, one seems to be able to discern a pattern of late marriages among Mus-covite servicemen. An atypical late marriage was Gavril Savinov Beketov's. Dur-ing the years 1578-89 he was in Swedish captivity. Upon his return to Muscovy, he was ordered to serve in Ivangorod as a translator. In 1592 he purchased a male slave for 10 rubles, in 1593 he purchased a woman for 5 rubles, and in 1594 he purchased another man for 10 rubles. Later that year he married Orina Ivanova Peretrutova, whose dowry consisted of a female slave. Then in 1595 and in 1597 he purchased additional males for 3 rubles apiece.[112] More typical is the ex-ample furnished by Ivan Eremeev Chertov, who made five purchases that netted him thirteen slaves between 1576 and his marriage in 1596. He also made one re-corded purchase in 1600.[113] The career of Iumran Narbeikov presents another

109. Kopanev, "Materialy," pp. 157, 164; Ianitskii, p. 183; Samokvasov, *Materialy* 1 (1905): 9-10; Paneiakh, *Kholopy*, p. 46; Koretskii, *Zakreposhchenie*, pp. 38, 45; Ivanov, OPK, p. 60; RIB 22(1908): 282, 300, 641.

110. RIB 17: 197, 205; NKK 7106, pp. 13-15; Samokvasov, *Materialy* 2(1909): 57; RIB 22(1908): 652; Nosov, *Ocherki*, pp. 352, 359, 388; AIuB 3: 182-84; DVP, p. 474, no. 79; DAI 2: 7; Ivanov, OKP, p. 63; KR 1: 81, 197, 407, 762; DR 1: 248, 297; Barsukov, SGV, pp. 243, 253.

111. 1649 *Ulozhenie* 20: 100; MS, p. 291.

112. RIB 17: 55-56; DVP, p. 472, no. 59; RIB 22(1908): 194.

113. RIB 17: 174-76; NKK 7108, p. 55; AI 2: 157; DVP, p. 474, no. 86.

illustration. The year when he began his career is unknown, but he was allotted land in 1571 in Shelonskaia piatina that earlier had belonged to one Mikhail Korenev Il'in. He also purchased two slaves at that time. Two years later, in 1573, he married Ofem'ia Ivanova Ogareva, who brought six slaves into the marriage.

Apparently Ofem'ia died, and in 1589, he remarried one Polageia Lizar'eva Tyrkova, whose dowry consisted of four slaves, who, upon her death (if she were childless), were to revert to the donor, her uncle, Petr Ondreev Tushin.[114] Other examples of marriages concluded after the purchase of slaves are provided by Grigorii Petrov Esipov (first purchase 1563, wed 1575),[115] Petr Menshoi Glotov (1586 and 1595),[116] Ivan Semenov Kartmazov (1585 and 1592),[117] Ivan Andreev Kashkarov (1573 and 1578),[118] Stepan Petrov Kosittskii (1583 and 1597),[119] Liapun Ivan Kosittskii (conducted a disputed-slave court case in 1521, married in 1524),[120] Fedor Andreev Kultashov (first purchase made in 1586, wed in 1596),[121] Ivan Matfeev Kuzminskii (1584 and 1588),[122] Mikhail Matfeev Kuzminskii (1580 and 1594),[123] Iakov Zhukov Levshin (1531 and 1548),[124] Feoktist Mikitin Murav'ev (1586 and 1588),[125] Loban Osipov Nazimov (1595 and 1598),[126] Stepan Petrov Obolnianinov (1583 and 1592),[127] Bogdan Ivanov Skobel'tsyn (1576 and 1580),[128] Daniil Fedorov Skobel'tsyn (awarded a court verdict in a disputed slave case in 1530, married in

114. Kopanev, "Materialy," p. 175; Samokvasov, *Materialy* 1(1905): 24; SBV (1974), p. 379; Ianitskii, p. 172; Ivanov, OPK, p. 55; RIB 22(1908): 602; Samokvasov, AM 1: 106; Paneiakh, *Kabal'noe*, p. 46.

115. RIB 17: 24-26; Andreiiashev, "Materialy," pp. 349-50, 406-7; Ivanov, OPK, p. 41A.

116. RIB 17: 109-11; AIuB 3: 275; Ivanov, OPK, p. 43; Savelov 2: 182; RIB 22(1908): 630.

117. RIB 17: 136-41; Nosov, *Ocherki*, p. 336; DVP, p. 471, no. 50; Ivanov, OPK, p. 43A; RIB 22(1908): 89-90, 824; RIB 28(1912): 102.

118. RIB 17: 90-92; DVP, p. 506, no. 780.

119. Kopanev, "Materialy," pp. 180-83; NZKK 1: 419; 2: 339, 344; RIB 15³, pt. 2: 77.

120. Lakier, p. 36; NPK 4: 412.

121. Kopanev, "Materialy," pp. 166-67, 169; Samokvasov, *Materialy* 2(1909): 525; Ivanov, OPK, p. 48; Paneiakh, *Kabal'noe*, p. 46.

122. RIB 17: 14-15, 142; AIuB 2: 176; Nosov, *Ocherki*, pp. 350-51; DVP, p. 475, no. 107; RIB 22(1908): 1603; DAI 2: 19.

123. RIB 17: 16, 63; DVP, p. 475, no. 118.

124. RIB 17: 119; Samokvasov, *Materialy* 2(1909): 343; Ianitskii, p. 159; Maikov, pp. 19-20; NPK 5: 320; SBV (1974), p. 179; Andreiiashev, "Materialy," p. 15.

125. RIB 17: 60; Samokvasov, *Materialy* 2(1909): 526; Belokurov, RZ 7113-21 (1907), p. 255; Nosov, *Ocherki*, pp. 350-51; Ivanov, OPK, p. 53; RIB 22(1908): 780, 791, 809; DVP, p. 468, no. 26; p. 470, no. 20.

126. NZKK 1: 296; Kopanev, "Materialy," p. 179.

127. RIB 17: 117; Samokvasov, *Materialy* 2(1909): 137; Nosov, *Ocherki*, pp. 353-54; SBV (1974), p. 225.

128. RIB 17: 112-16; Lakier, pp. 54, 56, 59; Nosov, *Ocherki*, p. 389; Belokurov, RZ 7113-21 (1907), p. 303; Samokvasov, *Materialy* 2(1909): 533; DVP, p. 470, no. 26; KKKCh 1613-27, p. 26.

1540),[129] Gam Semenov Tyrtov (1524 and 1538),[130] Vasilii Fedorov Turov (1584 and 1591),[131] and Matfei Ofonas'ev Zenov'ev (1574 and 1577).[132] For the twenty-one cases that have just been mentioned, the average time between first slave purchase (or other slave-related activity) and marriage was 8.3 years. Examination of the cases also reveals that most of the slaveowners had been serving for some time prior to making their first purchases, as was usual.

At least two interesting conclusions emerge from this examination of the relationships among the times when a slaveowner married, when he first purchased slaves, and when he commenced his service. First, a beginning serviceman rarely owned slaves, almost certainly because he lacked the means to buy or keep them. Second, roughly the same constraint must have affected his decision in taking a wife: the beginning serviceman at age fifteen, or any time soon thereafter, lacked the resources to maintain a family. There seems to be no way to determine at what age a Muscovite serviceman typically first wed, but certainly one may surmise that it was not while he was a teenager or perhaps even in his low twenties. We have seen that the mean age of the male who sold himself into slavery was 25.4 at the time of the birth of his first surviving child; the evidence reviewed here makes it difficult to imagine that servicemen married much if any younger. (The data tell us nothing about their wives.)

Regardless of when Muscovites acquired slaves in relation to the time of their marriage, there can be no question that one of their basic aspirations until the moment they died was to keep possession of slaves, and, if possible, to augment their holdings. The response of Mikhail Ivanov Miloslavskii to his high rate of fugitives is indicative of this practice. While he owned at least sixty-three slaves during his lifetime, we know that many of them (twenty-one, at least) fled, with the consequence that he probably never owned many more than seven slaves at any one time.[133] This struggle to acquire and maintain a minimum of domestic service was no doubt increasingly characteristic of slaveowners as they aged, a major aspect of maintaining a fitting life style.

Muscovites knew two forms of death: going into a monastery or nunnery and undergoing physical death. We know that those who became monks and nuns liked to take slaves with them to the cloister, and the problem this created after the 1597 reform of limited service contract slavery is discussed in the 1634 case of Novokshchenov v. Nazar Polikarpov (see chapter 5).

129. Kopanev, "Materialy," p. 174.
130. Ibid., pp. 177-78; Zimin, TK, pp. 155, 413; SBV (1974), p. 77; Veselovskii, *Issledovanie*, pp. 53, 564; NPK 5: 570-78; Ivanov, OPK, p. 67.
131. Kopanev, "Materialy," p. 164; Skrynnikov, 1: 305, 325, 416; Barsukov, SGV, pp. 165, 205, 579; AMG 1: 722; KR 1: 178, 391, 642; DR 1: 416; KKKCh 1613-27, p. 66; Ivanov, OPK, p. 67; RIB 22 (1908): 307-9, 611-12, 629-30.
132. RIB 17: 40-42; Ianitskii, p. 89; RK 1598-1638, pp. 170-71; Samokvasov, *Materialy* 2(1909): 460; DVP, p. 476, no. 123; Ivanov, OPK, p. 43A; RIB 22(1908): 208.
133. Kopanev, "Materialy," pp. 151-55.

The ages at which Muscovite slaveowners died cannot be calculated, as far as I can determine. Some certainly lived to be quite old, but at least half, as we shall see in the discussion of dowries, died before their children were married. This is not surprising, considering that the vast majority of slaveowners were military servicemen. Freedmen reselling themselves often told how their former owners died, and death in combat was not the least mentioned. Others died from combat-related causes, particularly plagues and other diseases that took away many otherwise healthy men at the front.[134] Still others died, or were executed, for political reasons.[135] Of course, some slaveowners died "naturally" at home in their beds.[136] The death of the slaveowner ended the cycle but also began it anew: heirs inherited the hereditary slaves, while the manumitted slaves often began to scurry about to sell themselves to someone else.

The Use of Slaves in Establishing Marriage Alliances

Slaves were one of the major forms of "social cement" in Muscovy, for they were often given in marriage contracts and dowries by the bride's relatives to the groom. The exchange of objects is known to be important in cementing many social relationships, and slaves were of central concern when marriages were arranged. This has been typical of many societies since at least Babylonian times.[137] The available evidence forces one to concentrate on Novgorod in the sixteenth century, particularly in the second half of that century (86.6 percent of all the extant cases), but comparable forces presumably were at work throughout Muscovy in most of the early modern period. One should note, however, that the pressure to cement marriage alliances with slave transfers was probably the greatest in exactly this period because alienable land nearly disappeared in the second half of Ivan IV's reign in favor of service land; later, as the seventeenth century wore on, the alienation of land and also peasant serfs became increasingly possible. Slaves were still important in the 1660s, as noted by Grigorii Kotoshikhin, who wrote:

> When somebody considered marrying a woman, he inquired after her dowry, clothing, cash, patrimonial lands, and slaves [*dvorovye liudi*]. When a decision was made to conclude a marriage, a list was made of what the dowry would be, the cash, silver and other dishes, clothing, patrimonial lands, and slaves [*dvorovye liudi*].[138]

134. NZKK 1: 125, 281, 333, 340, 356, 410, 419.
135. NZKK 1: 5, 86, 128; NKK 7108, p. 13; Kleimola, "Disgrace," in *Russian Law: Historical and Political Perspectives,* pp. 29-50.
136. NZKK 1: 406. See also religious "death," when owners entered monasteries and freed their slaves (NZKK 1: 51).
137. Mendelsohn, p. 4.
138. Kotoshikhin, p. 149.

This section is based on 12 marriage contracts and 114 dowries written between the years 1504 and 1598 (with a lone one from 1668). The following families were involved:

Aprelev	Iakimov	Miakhovo	Samarin
Beketov	Iamskoi	Murav'ev	Savin
Beloselskii	Irettskoi	Myshetskii	Sekirin
Bezstuzhev	Kalitin	Narbeikov	Semichev
Bibikov	Kamenev	Nashchokin	Serkov
Birilov	Kartmazov	Nazimov	Shablykin
Blazhenkov	Kashkarov	Neelov	Shamsheev
Blekloi	Kharlamov	Neledinskii	Shekhovskoi
Boborykin	Khvostov	Nepliuev	Shepiakov
Boboshin	Knutov	Novokshchenov	Shuitin
Boranov	Kolychev	Obolnianinov	Skobel'tsyn
Borisov	Korin	Odintsov	Sorochin
Borkov	Korotaev	Ododurov	Snazin
Bukharin	Koshkar	Ogar'ev	Snoksarev
Buturlin	Koshkarov	Ogibalov	Solovtsov
Cherkasov	Kositskii	Okhlebaev	Temkin
Chertov	Kovezin	Okunev	Tolmachev
Chiudov	Krasnoslepov	Ozhogin	Tolstoi
Chiurkin	Krenev	Palitsyn	Tyrtov
Dolgorukov	Kropivin	Parskii	Turov
Dubasov	Kropotov	Pechenegov	Tushin
Dubrovskii	Kultashev	Perepechin	Uskovo
Elagin	Kushelev	Peretrutov	Uvarov
Eletskoi	Kuzminskii	Pleshcheev	Vel'iaminov
Eremeev	Levshin	Poiarkov-Kvashin	Volkov-Kuritsyn
Ermolin	Lodygin	Potilov	Volynskoi
Esipov	Lupandin	Potilov	Voronin
Esiukov	L'vov	Pushkin	Voronov
Evreev	Medrovtsov	Pushtoshkin	Vypovskii
Glotov	Malovo	Ragozin	Zavalishin
Golovachev	Martianov	Rokhmanov	Zelenin
Gubachevskii	Meshcherskii	Rostovskii	Zinov'ev
Gur'ev	Miakinin	Rumiantsov	Zmeev
		Saburov	

Most families were involved in only one of the 126 events, but 23 were involved twice, 12 thrice, 5 four times, the Murav'evs seven times, the Meshcherskiis and Nazimovs eight times, the Kositskiis nine times, and the Skobel'tsyn clan ten times. There were 120 different grooms and 116 different parties giving away brides.

The relationships of the persons giving away the 397 slaves to the grooms can be seen in table 17.26

TABLE 17.26
Relationships of Party Providing Slaves for Marriage Contracts and Dowries to Groom

Relationship	N	%	Average No. of Slaves per Transaction
Fiancée	4	3.2	4.5
Father-in-law	55	43.7	3.4
Mother-in-law	16	12.7	2.7
Brother-in-law	37	29.4	3.0
Uncle-in-law	11	8.7	2.4
Nephew	1	0.8	1.0
Uncle-in-law and brother-in-law	1	0.8	7.0
Grandfather-in-law	1	0.8	3.0
Total	126	100.0	3.2
$Eta^2 = 0.07$			

(The four cases of "fiancée" are women who married themselves off.)[139] Most noteworthy here is the apparent demographic fact that less than half, only 43.7 percent, of fathers lived long enough to marry off their daughters—not surprising when one considers the times and that one is dealing primarily with Muscovy's warrior caste. It is well known that before the Industrial Revolution most people did not live long enough to see their grandchildren—a fact evident here even among the society's elite. Ideally, a longitudinal study of these relationships would determine whether and to what extent they change in response to events such as major wars and plagues, but not enough cases are available over a sufficient length of time to be able to do that here. We can also see in table 17.26 that the size of the dowry was not statistically determined by the relationship of the donor(s) and the groom.

The annual dating of marriage contracts followed the rhythym of military service, as is evident in table 17.27.

TABLE 17.27
Months in Which Marriage Contracts Were Written

Month	N	Month	N	Month	N
January	5	May	4	September	2
February	6	June	1	October	6
March	10	July	4	November	4
April	4	August	0	December	3
Unknown	77				

Marriages were usually arranged before men went off to service in April and after

139. Kopanev, "Materialy," p. 161.

they returned in October. The task at hand is to try to determine what functions the granting of slaves performed in arranging these family alliances and what other social conceptions can be garnered from the alliances.

One might first note that these 126 exchanges encompassed 397 slaves, an average of 3.2 per transaction, ranging from 1 to 12 slaves per marriage contract or dowry. The mode donation was 2 slaves (32 cases). Later, 92 of these slaves, or their offspring, fled. Judging by the total number of slaves that comparable individuals left in their wills, we may assume that an average parent gave away about 20 to 25 percent (3 of from 12 to 15) of his or her slaves in providing a dowry, and a lateral relative or sibling may have had to part with up to half of his total holdings to provide a dowry. The extent to which Muscovites strained to provide ostentatious dowries is not immediately apparent. If the slaves were a productive asset (like land, in Kotoshikhin's list), parting with so many would certainly tell in a person's economy; if, on the other hand, slaves were primarily a consumption good (like silver and other dishes, in Kotoshikhin's list), then such generosity would cost the donor little while burdening significantly the recipient. As the latter seems to have been the case, it is hardly surprising that so many grooms were well along in their careers before they got married, for otherwise they would have lacked the means to support their brides' dowries.

The 126 documents had a single male adult slave as the major figure in 17 cases, an adult married male in 44 cases, a widower in 2 cases, a married female in 7 cases, a widow in 7 cases, and an unmarried female in 49 cases, in a total of 48 different combinations that I will not bother to list. The transactions involved about 116 adult males, 198 adult females, and 83 children. When one compares this with the sex ratio of the entire slave population (nearly two-thirds males, for both adults and children) and the general composition of all Muscovite slaves' family structure, two things stand out: the marriage contracts and dowries contained a lower ratio of single male adults than usual; the sex ratio in the transactions is extraordinary.

These facts may help to explain certain aspects of the dowry phenomenon. The slaves in a dowry technically belonged to the wife and were to be returned to her clan if she died without children. The same was true in the Hammurabi Code.[140] The granting of dowries in itself indicates that Muscovite women of the service class did no useful labor, as was generally posited by Ester Boserup in her *Woman's Role in Economic Development*.[141]

The value of the slaves to the groom is not immediately apparent. In the open market, men purchased slaves of a different mix than came with their wives, so one may assume that the dowries were intended at least partially for the bride's benefit. A major purpose of the slaves must have been to provide handmaidens for the women, who, as is well known, were generally isolated.

140. Pritchard, p. 156, art. 162.
141. Ester Boserup, *Woman's Role in Economic Development* (London: Allen and Unwin. 1970), p. 48.

More important, the slaves themselves make little sense in relation to the arranging of marriages. Their numbers are only randomly related to any of the other indicators I have. The principles of marriage alliances cannot be found in the number or variety of slaves granted. On the whole, the number of slaves granted reveals no strong statistical relationship to either the donor's or the recipient's rank or job, cash or land *oklad*, or actual landholding (see table 17.28).

TABLE 17.28
Statistical Relationships between the Number of Slaves Listed in Marriage Contracts and Dowries and Other Variables of Muscovite Slaveowners' Lives and Careers

		Grooms	In-laws
Rank	Uncertainty coefficient	0.088 (N = 95)	0.237 (N = 69)
Job	Uncertainty coefficient	0.504 (N = 43)	0.618 (N = 37)
Cash *oklad*	r	0.266 (N = 8)	0.420 (N = 5)
Land *oklad*	r	0.284 (N = 45)	0.081 (N = 25)
Landholding	r	0.097 (N = 39)	0.199 (N = 34)

The only statistic in the table that looks interesting is that for the in-laws' jobs, about which more will be said in a moment.

One tactic not tried for making this material more intelligible is to compare not the groom with his in-laws but the groom's father with the in-laws. That, of course, is the normal way for making such comparisons, but it is not possible here because of a shortage of data, and it probably would not work in Muscovy— as I shall discuss further in a moment. I do have data for the cases involving brothers-in-law, and it proves to be little more informative (see table 17.29).

TABLE 17.29
Relations between Slaves Granted in Dowries and Certain Statistics about Brothers-in-law

		Grooms	Brothers-in-law
Land *óklad*	r	0.000 (N = 16)	0.407 (N = 11)
Landholding	r	−0.278 (N = 13)	−0.334 (N = 9)

The numbers in the table are too small to be genuinely enlightening, but they indicate a slight, seemingly paradoxical tendency, to give less slaves in a dowry when either the groom or his brother-in-law has more land.

I had hoped to be able to show that the highly status-conscious Muscovites used slaves to improve their clan situation or accepted them in larger numbers when "marrying down." Attempts to analyze the meaning of dowries from that vantage point have proved successful for England and elsewhere. I have not been able to do this, and one reason may be the combined great fluidity of sixteenth-century Muscovite society and its meritocratic essence. High death-rates among the landed elements (in the constant wars and Ivan's Oprichnina) and the possibility of moving up may have made such calculations difficult, if not impossible for those involved in these marriage transactions.

While the use of slaves tells us very little about how arrangements of marriages among the landholding class were made, the data about the contracting parties themselves prove slightly more enlightening. As I have already mentioned, ideally I should compare father—father-in-law pairs, but I have been unable to gather the necessary data. The low percentage of fathers that survived to marry off their daughters makes one pause before he accepts a priori the modern, Western models for marriage arrangments. Once a serviceman died, most of his estate was disbanded, and his heirs both in theory and in reality began from the bottom, with perhaps the exception that heirs seem to have had a high-priority claim on the deceased's service land to satisfy their land compensation entitlements. A constant goal of the middle service class was to make its service estates hereditary (thus vitiating entirely the principle of the service land system), but little headway had been made in that direction in the last third of the sixteenth century, whence come most of the data.

Be that as it may, examination of the groom—father-in-law pairs is interesting, and, because of the frequent presence of stand-ins for the fathers-in-law, groom—brother-in-law and other pairs hint what the Muscovites had in mind when marriages were arranged. Rather than calculating in terms of upward or downward mobility, they seem to have been searching for stability in what was after all an absolutely chaotic world. They tended to marry into families relatively nearby and in the same circumstances they were at the moment. All of the alliances that I have any information about were in the middle and upper service classes, and the ranks of those marrying were quite similar, regardless of how many slaves were exchanged or the sex and family composition of the chattel. Although the job data are scarcer, a similar generalization probably can be made. In the one case where I have the cash *oklad* for both brothers-in-law, the groom's was 8 rubles and his brother-in-law's was 10 rubles.

Yet, while the above generalizations are correct in the large sense, one must not get carried away. One's interpretation here, as everywhere else, depends upon the precision he wishes it to have. Thus it is absolutely true that no landed servicemen in my 126 cases married peasants, merchants, or clergymen. They all married within the service class. But, within the service class itself, some precision is lost. Our contemporary conventional wisdom would expect the closest fitting pairs to be those of father—father-in-law, which I do not have. Yet consider table 17.30. The numbers (No.) are the positions of the servicemen in the *desiatnia*. Note that Gurev, No. 786, is almost adjacent to his father-in-law, Kalitin, No. 790. With such a wide possible range (see table 17.16), one would hardly expect a son-in-law to be so close to his father-in-law, or a nephew-in-law to be so close to his uncle-in-law. One might expect brothers-in-law to be close. However, for the group as a whole, neither generalization fits. While the situation is not totally random, there are no strong correlations, either.

TABLE 17.30
Selected 1605 Votskaia Piatina Land Compensation Scales for Servicemen Related by Marriage

	Land Entitlement in Chetverti		Land Entitlement in Chetverti
Grooms		Fathers-in-law	
Ia. S. Shepiakov, No. 522	350	M. I. Meshcherskii, No. 775	400
I. I. Gurev, No. 786	350	S. I. Kalitin, No. 790	350
I. O. Meshcherskii, No. 46	550	I. T. Voronin, No. 122	600
I. P. Obolnianinov, No. 754	400	Iu. I. Neledinskii, No. 93	450
		Brothers-in-law	
I. T. Kuzminskii, No. 107	450	F. M. Sekirin, No. 151	450
S. O. Meshcherskii, No. 43	550	S. M. Myshettskoi, No. 68	600
M. S. Boborykin, No. 736	500	I. F. Gurev, No. 81	500
		Uncle-in-law	
B. I. Skobel'tsyn, No. 26	600	F. M. Meshcherskii, No. 5	600

Considering the land *oklad*, the correlation between the groom—father-in-law pairs was very low (N = 5, r = 0.208), whereas those of brothers-in-law was somewhat higher (N = 10, r = 0.471). This explains the relationship of all the pairs, which is intermediate between those two major ones (N = 17; r = 0.349). There are a number of explanations for these statistics, but one of them is that a serviceman's compensation could hardly be anticipated, and there was little that was necessarily hereditary about it.

The amount of land actually held was apparently even less of a predictor of marriage alliances (N = 13; r = -0.067). Once again, the groom—father-in-law pairs show less correspondence (N = 5; r = -0.076) than do the brother-in-law pairs (N = 5; r = 0.281). The inferior status of landholding is hard to explain. Contemporaries may have realized that landholding depended more on luck (learning of available land some place in Russia, then being first to claim it and have the claim honored) than on merit or desert. Once again, the prediction and inheritance factors may have been relevant.

The rank data (N = 52) fail to tell much because nearly all the paired in-laws are either *deti boiarskie* or *pomeshchiki*, which were close to the same. Lastly, the data are too sparse to tell much about the relationship of landholders' posts to their marriage alliances. There are only sixteen pairs, and while the statistic looks good (uncertainty coefficient [asymmetric] = 0.636, with the groom's job dependent), that is too few to say very much about. The pairs do look almost predictive, however, as is evident in tables 17.31 and 17.32.

TABLE 17.31
Groom–Father-in-law Posts in Muscovite Marriages: Pairs

Groom	Father-in-law
voevoda	*okladchik*
streletskii sotnik	*gorodovoi prikashchik*
streletskii sotnik	*okladchik*
okladchik	*voevoda*

TABLE 17.32
Posts of Brothers-in-law in Muscovite Marriages

Groom	Brother-in-law
voevoda	*voevoda*
voevoda	*gubnoi starosta*
gubnoi starosta	*streletskii golova*

Once again, I must caution that the pairs are not necessarily synchronous.

The best predictor of marriage alliances seems to have been geographical proximity. I know where 123 of the 126 documents were written, where 110 of the grooms probably lived, and where 96 of the in-laws probably lived. The provenience of the document was taken from the source itself, the homes of the contracting parties were taken from the service records, land cadastres, and other information that has been searched for this information. In a handful of cases I had evidence that a person possessed his land in one area yet rendered service from another. I always chose the place chronologically closer to the marriage document in the case of such a conflict.

The data yield 96 pairs for which the dwelling places of the donors and recipients of the slaves in marriage alliance transactions are known. If one collapses the data into Novgorod and its five piatiny, one can generate table 17.33.

TABLE 17.33
Geographical Distribution of Marriage Pairs

Grooms	In-laws					
	Bezh	Derev	Obon	Shel	Votsk	Novg
Bezhetskaia piatina	2					
Derevskaia piatina						
Obonezhskaia piatina						
Shelonskaia piatina		1	1	14	3	1
Votskaia piatina		2		3	41	
Novgorod city						2

N = 70
Other known pairs, 26
Unknown pairs, 30

The same data are graphically presented in map 17.2.

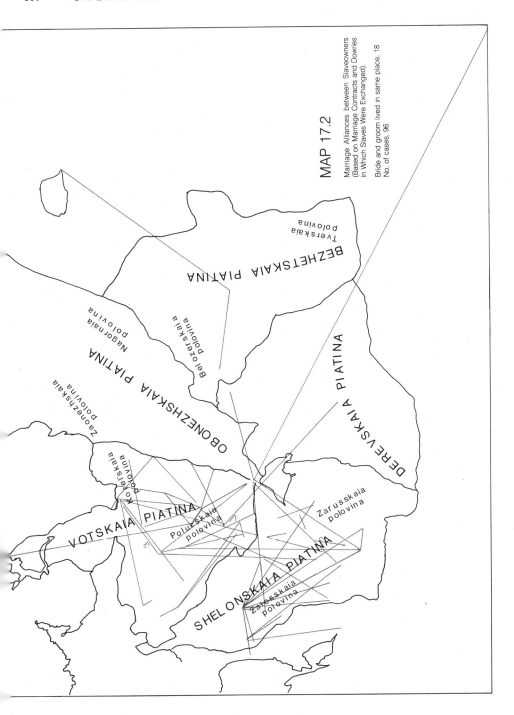

MAP 17.2

Marriage Alliances between Slaveowners (Based on Marriage Contracts and Dowries in Which Slaves Were Exchanged).

Bride and groom lived in same place, 18
No. of cases, 96

The average distance between the mapped pairs was 75 kilometers. That the exchange of slaves in marriage contracts and dowries in the Novgorod region was so piatina-bound is hardly surprising, for that was the major frame of government-enforced social intercourse. Servicemen were registered by piatina, and reported for muster and duty in the same regions. It is also safe to assume that they often fought in piatina-determined units. Provincial administration was organized in the same way. Most of the alliances shown on the map are either in Shelonskaia piatina or Votskaia piatina because that is where the three extant 1597-98 compulsory registration collections were compiled, the Lakier and Kopanev collections from the former piatina, the RIB 17 (1898) collection, edited by A. S. Lappo-Danilevskii, from the latter.

Muscovite marriages may have been arranged according to set formulas, but they cannot be discerned with as great precision as one might desire. I have no evidence that any marriage involving the exchange of slaves was made outside the service class, although one may assume that wealthy merchants also exchanged slaves in dowries. The precise function for the slaves in the marriage arrangements remains opaque; the available evidence does not permit a determination of why a particular person or category of persons gave a number or assortment of slaves. Nor can any relationship be established between the number of slaves in a marriage contract or dowry and the value of other things (immovable property of various kinds, icons, jewelry, clothing) often included in those marriage instruments, because in most of the extant records the slaves have been excerpted and the rest of such presents were ignored. One may be fairly certain that the women who were married with such dowries did little productive labor themselves. While all alliances for which data exist were made within the service class, calculations about the respective ranks, service compensation levels, and actual landholding of the paired in-laws do not prove to be statistically interesting. The information about the posts of the marrying pairs is the most interesting, and may reveal the actual unreliability of land as as source of income, a continuation of the old preference for jobs that themselves generated income rather than land which well might be depopulated (hence the development of serfdom in this period). I would attribute the lack of significance of the other variables partially to the relative newness of the service class in the sixteenth century, partially to the fluidity of the political and economic situation after 1560. More complete data might yield a different picture, but I doubt it. I suspect, however, that greater regularities could be established after 1649, with the enserfment of the peasantry and the creation of a more gentrylike mentality in the service class. However, such data are not at hand.

The marriage contracts and dowries had another instrument of social cohesion besides the slaves, the witnesses to the compacts. The legal function of the witnesses is clear: to serve as evidence that the transaction had taken place. As we have seen in chapter 8, witnesses had a long career and central position in Russian legal history. In marriage instruments they not only had a legal import, they also ceremonially bound together additional people outside the two contracting families and thus served as a device for maintaining the stability of the system. There were no formal prescriptions about how many witnesses there should be to marriage contracts and dowries, and the numbers on these instruments varied (see table 17.34). (The distribution of witnesses between the two instruments is not significant [uncertainty coefficient = 0.019].)

TABLE 17.34
Numbers of Witnesses to Marriage Contracts and Dowries

No. of Witnesses	No. of Marriage Contracts	No. of Dowries
0	1	22
1	2	35
2	7	37
3	2	13
4	0	1
Unknown	–	6
Mean	1.4	1.8

The question here is whether the witnesses were random, just people who happened to be around, or whether they were correlated with other objective facts which might serve as confidence indicators when marriage alliances were being concluded. Is there evidence that, because of lack of confidence in some trait of the other party, one of the contracting parties dictated that a certain number of witnesses attest to the arrangement? This can be checked by using the same variables that were used earlier. (First, it might be mentioned that the difference in the number of witnesses is not a subject of the passage of time. The numbers remained essentially constant throughout the sixteenth century, declining almost imperceptibly [slope = -0.00843].)

As one sees in table 17.35, the number of witnesses seems to correspond with the number of slaves in the marriage contract or dowry. Thus the number of witnesses seems to rise quite regularly with the number of slaves in the document. However, because the standard deviation is so high (0.93), the actual correlation is low ($r = 0.29$).

The correlation was slightly negative between the number of witnesses and the amount of land the groom had ($N = 36; r = -0.179$). In a rigidly stratified society one might expect a strong negative correlation—a person with great landed wealth could be assumed to be an honorable person to support his wife, with the opposite being assumed about a poorer landholder. Of course Russian society was not rigidly stratified in the last third of the sixteenth century, so it is not at all surprising that such assumptions do not seem to have been made by those arranging marriages. The relation between the donor's landholding and the number of witnesses is positive but insignificantly so ($N = 29; r = 0.175$). If there

TABLE 17.35
Relationship between Number of Witnesses and Number of Slaves in a Marriage Contract or Dowry

No. of Slaves	Average No. of Witnesses	N
1	1.1	28
2	1.4	31
3	1.4	21
4	1.9	18
5	1.4	8
6	1.5	4
7	2.3	4
8	2.0	1
9	3.0	1
11	3.0	1
12	1.7	3
	Mean 1.5	120

were questions about the donor's delivering the slaves, the relationship might have been different. However, this seems not to have been an issue either. (Essentially the same conclusions seem to be shown by partial correlation statistics on the number of witnesses, the number of slaves, and the amount of land possessed by the contracting parties. The number of slaves has some minor import, but the landholding is irrelevant.) The other variables here seem not to be determining either: groom's land *oklad* (N = 7; Somer's D symmetric = -0.229); the donor's land *oklad* (N = 5; Somer's D symmetric = 0). Confidence also does not depend on the relationships of the contracting parties. The number of witnesses is almost randomly distributed, regardless of whether the pairs were father-in-law—son-in-law, brothers-in-law, or something else (N = 120; uncertainty coefficient asymmetric [witnesses dependent] = 0.074). The same is true of the ranks and jobs of the contracting parties.

On the basis of these data, one may conclude that the warfare endemic to the service class was temporarily suspended at the time when marriage alliances were made. Obviously this is a thin reed to lean on, but I know of no other evidence to use. The question of the climate of marriage alliances seems to me to be a very important one, and I wish better data were available for a discussion of the issue. In any event, the number of witnesses was almost totally random, not chosen as an indicator of something. This shows little about the degree of atomization of society, but it may indicate that mutual confidence between the parties was high when the documents were drawn up. If the competitive atmosphere that often pervaded Muscovy was not present upon such occasions, that in itself would be significant.

Conflict Engendered by Slavery

One of the persistent themes of a study of slavery in Muscovy is that the existence of the institution pitted slaveowners against one another, rather than uniting them, as it is perceived to have done at least to some extent in societies where the institution of slavery was under attack. While transfers of slaves were useful in binding together generations and clans, that cohesive factor in the institution of slavery was almost certainly more than offset by constant conflicts over the ownership of specific slaves. At least in the period from the 1580s through 1649, the "peasant question" served to unite the middle service class, but there never was a "slave question," and the institution, on balance, tended to fragment members of the upper and middle service classes. If there was a gainer from the conflicts inherent in the institution of slavery, it was the increasingly autocratic government, which battened on the fees generated by slavery as it exercised its role of disinterested arbiter.

Kozlova v. Kozlova et al.

Conflict engendered by slavery not only encompassed unrelated slaveowners but sometimes took in members of the same family as well. Property not only can be used to bind together family members but also to alienate kinsmen, if they start to squabble over it. In this respect, slavery was an especially volatile form of property because of the slave's potential for volition. The disjunctive potential of slavery is illustrated in the case of Kozlova v. Kozlova et al., tried in the Slavery Chancellery before director Prince Ivan Fedorovich Volkonskoi and state secretaries Tret'iak Kopnin and Ivan Kostiurin in the autumn of 1634. The case features two suits, a countersuit, and a mother-in-law, and seems to be a perfect illustration of a domestic spat blown up to large proportions thanks to the institution of slavery. Unfortunately, not all of the case, including its resolution, is extant, but enough is available to show quite vividly what happened.

The plaintiff in the case was Fedora Kozlova, whose husband, Ivan Petrov Kozlov, had recently been killed in the Smolensk War. (She will be called henceforth Fedora I. P. Kozlova.) She was represented at the trial by her nephew Vasilii Nikitin Kozinskii of Suzdal'. The defendants were Fedora Kozlova, widow of the deceased Petr Andreev Kozlov (she will be referred to as Fedora P. A. Kozlova), and her two sons, Andrei and Lavrentii Petrovy Kozlov, also of Suzdal'. They were respectively, mother-in-law and brothers-in-law of the plaintiff. Andrei handled the case for the defense.

The first case (consisting of a suit and a countersuit) involved the status and ownership of Timofei Vasil'ev Aleksandrov, his wife Matrena Nikitina, and their two children, a girl Lukeria and a boy Vasilii. Timka's father allegedly had been a peasant who had lived in a village belonging to Petr Kozlov; the father died, and Petr Kozlov gave the young boy to his son Ivan Petrov Kozlov, who raised him and got a limited service slavery contract on him. (The same had been true of Matrena Nikitina, Timka's wife.) When Ivan Petrov Kozlov was killed at the front, his father, Petr Andreev Kozlov, manumitted the slaves, at his son's behest. This was the way things should have been done, according to the law of 1597, if they had been limited service contract slaves. On May 17, 1634, Timka (then twenty-two years old), his wife Matrena (about twenty-five years old), and their children, Lukeria (five) and Vasilii (four), sold themselves to Ivan Petrov Kozlov's widow, Fedora, for the sum of 3 rubles in the town of Shuia. Such a self-sale was entirely to be expected.

The initial suit was filed by Andrei Kozlov against his sister-in-law Fedora I. P. Kozlova. He and a bailiff had seized Timofei Vasil'ev and placed him under arrest. The suit alleged that Timka had fled from him and his mother and had stolen 20.50 rubles' worth of property. Furthermore, Andrei Kozlov claimed that the limited service slavery contract had been forced on Timka, and that Timka's wife Matrena had not even been present when the contract was drawn up. This last point seems to have been proved by comparing Matrenka in person with the person described as Matrenka in the document, a point discussed above in some greater detail in chapter 8. (Why she had not been present, and what the import of that omission—and probable fraud—was, other than that the law on the drawing up of such contracts requiring the presence of the slaves so described had been clearly violated, are not clear.) The major bone of contention seems to have been whether Timka had earlier been a peasant through his father, or a slave via his mother, Marfutka. Andrei Kozlov submitted a full slavery document on Marfutka, and then a manumission document in which she was set free, along with her son Timka and his wife Matrenka. (The manumission document had been written by Petr Andreev Kozlov's slave Fet'ka Sofontiev on March 21, 1634, and signed for the manumiter by his priest. This tells us that Kozlov's slave was literate but that Kozlov himself was not.) To prove his point that Timoshka was a slave, Andrei Kozlov presented a "slave genealogy" going back for nine generations through his mother, an amazing document in light of the general rule that most slaves throughout history were not enslaved for long, and supporting my contention that perpetual slavery was one of the unusual features of Muscovite slavery.

To uphold their claim that Timofei was of peasant origin, Vasilii Kozinskii presented a genealogy showing that Timka's father had been a peasant and his mother a free woman: her father had been a slave agriculturalist who belonged to Stepan Timerev Kaisarov and who later was the slave of his widow, "but that Marfutka was a free person (byla vol'naia)." The basis of that claim was not stated, but analogies made to prove the point discussed the current status of Marfutka's siblings. All had left Kaisarov's household, but only one of them managed to remain free. One brother was a peasant in Nizhnii Novgorod province, but a second brother and her big sister seemed to have been slaves in provincial Suzdal' households. Thus, while most of the family had been unable to escape from a slavery-dependency syndrome, at least Kaisarov and his clan no longer had claim to them. As for Marfutka herself, she and her son had been precipitated into slavery after the Lithuanians had killed her husband, Vasilii, and the family survivors signed limited service slavery contracts with Ivan Kozlov. They also claimed that Timka's wife, Matrena Nikitina, was the offspring of two peasants.

The countersuit in Kozlova v. Kozlova is missing from the case, but a reader of the rest of the case can surmise that it was filed by Kozinskii against Andrei Kozlov for possession of Timofei's wife, Matrena Nikitina, and their three children, Lukeria and Vasilii plus one not named, probably a very young child. The plaintiffs also claimed that 90 1/8 cheti of grain had been stolen and was due them.

The third suit in this obviously bitter case was over property allegedly stolen by Irina (Arishka) on Good Friday (*sbornaia piatnitsa*) 1634. Fedora I. P. Kozlova claimed that her mother-in-law, at the instigation of her sons, had sent slaves under the leadership of one Mit'ka (Ziat') to lure away Arishka, obviously a household slave, and that they stole 10 rubles and valuable property from her wardrobe: a woman's pearl necklace worth 12.50 rubles, a woman's cap worth 3 rubles, ten sets of underwear (*navina*) worth 5 rubles, five women's blouses worth 3.50 rubles, four scarves and two towels worth 2.50 rubles. The total value of the theft was 36.50 rubles. About six months later, claimed the plaintiff, the defendants had sent the girl back but had neglected to return the stolen property, for which she was suing. The defendants, on the other hand, denied that Arishka had been seduced away or had brought any stolen property, but rather claimed that she had fled from the plaintiff to visit her mother (this may have been a case in which a slave family had been split up), and that they had returned her to avoid further complications. As evidence, the plaintiffs cited a priest who purportedly had interrogated Arishka and knew thereby that she had been recruited to flee and had taken the property. The defendants denied that the priest had interrogated Arishka or knew anything of the kind, but alleged instead that he had accompanied her back to her lawful mistress.[142] (The Slavery Chancellery's attempts to check these claims are discussed above in chapter 9.)

The evidence presented in the extant part of Kozlova v. Kozlova does not make it possible to determine who was legally right in the three suits. What it does show, however, is that the institution of slavery had the potential for manifesting and generating intense hostility within the slaveowning stratum of Muscovite society. There was a far greater potential for the generation of such hostility by slave property than by ordinary property simply because of the fact that slaves had volitional capacity. In this case, that capacity was demonstrated by Timoshka signing the limited service slavery contract after leaving Fedora P. A. Kozlova and her sons, and by Irishka leaving Fedora I. P. Kozlova.

142. Iakovlev, *Kholopstvo*, pp. 479-88, no. 23.

The hostility of the case generated four guarantee notes (bail bonds) involving many people, and the Slavery Chancellery dispatched memoranda to the provinces to gain evidence to resolve the case. The resolution, which is unknown, was almost certainly very expensive, for the court costs on disposing of five slaves and claims for 57 rubles' worth of allegedly stolen property and a substantial quantity of grain had to be satisified, regardless of the outcome. Rendering the government its due of at least 6 rubles was almost certain to engender additional hostility in the Kozlov clan for years to come after the formal resolution of this particular case. It should be safe to assume that there were many other similar cases in Muscovy, pitting family members against one another over the issue of slaveownership.

Common Interests of Slaveowners

There seems to have been a minimal sense of common identity among the slave-owners of Muscovy stemming from the fact that they owned slaves. In *Enserf-ment and Military Change in Muscovy* I traced the creation of such an identity formation among the members of the middle service class of the Volga-Oka-triangle and the Novgorod area over the issue of serfdom.[143] In Kenya, slave-owners went so far as to agree not to receive each other's fugitives.[144] In the American South, they fought a war to maintain "the peculiar institution." That the Muscovites felt no need to develop a sense of mutual purpose and common identity is not at all surprising. First, anyone, in theory, could become a slave-owner, so that nobody of any political consequence was arbitrarily excluded from the benefits of the institution. Those owning slaves therefore did not have to defend themselves against those who did not own any. Second, while some slaveowners were greatly outnumbered by their slaves, slaves as a group comprised only a small percentage (perhaps 10 percent; see chapter 18) of the populace, and thus were no threat to society. Slaveowners did not have to develop the siege mentality common to societies in which there were vast numbers of chattel held in bondage by a small number of owners. Third, slavery provided a symbiotic situation for many of the slaves and their owners, the former attaining elite positions they could not have held as free men or else receiving much-needed relief, the latter achieving status elevation and manpower. Fourth, no outside group (other than the government) ever questioned or threatened the existence of slavery. When the government moved against the institution in 1597, it offered in exchange what seem to have been meaningful concessions to the slaveowners. When effectively abolishing agricultural slavery in 1679 and

143. Hellie, *Enserfment*, chapter 3.
144. Frederick Cooper, *Plantation Slavery on the East Coast of Africa* (New Haven: Yale University Press, 1977), p. 207.

household slavery in 1723, the government offered the landholders serfs and house serfs in exchange. (Thus only merchants who used slaves as a way to expand the family firm were inconvenienced by the abolition of slavery in Muscovy.) These factors explain why the slaveowners of Muscovy developed no common positions either among themselves or against the rest of society or the government on the issue of slavery.

Having made this point, I should note that the absence of a group consciousness among slaveowners was not absolute. I have found one exception and should not be astounded were a handful of others to arise as well. The case of Danila Dmitriev Big Beard v. Uvar Gavrilov Lodygin has already been discussed in two contexts, that of the "general investigation" (chapter 8) and the struggle for freedom (chapter 16). After more than two decades of unlawful enslavement, the artilleryman Danila was awarded his freedom, plus large damages against Lodygin. As the available transcript breaks off, Lodygin states his view that Danila should not have been freed because that might encourage other slaves to sue for their freedom.[145] Of course Lodygin might have been thinking solely of his own slaves, but it does seem probable that he had the larger universe of slaves and slaveowners in mind. One must recall again that this was only an argument, and a rather desperate one at that, which Lodygin made in the Slavery Chancellery. He did not, as far as is known, initiate a petition campaign or otherwise get other slaveowners to help him press his case. Lodygin's solitary act is a great distance from the collective petition campaigns that led to the enserfment of the peasants, or that subsequently motivated the government to hunt down fugitive slaves and serfs and increase the sanctions for harboring them.

Slaveowner Politics

Some people assume that politics do not exist in an autocratic society, such as later Muscovy was. This certainly was not true during the Time of Troubles, when there was no autocrat, and even at other times issues about who got what, when, and how arose that generated slaveowner expression of concern and action. As we have seen, almost certainly nearly every prominent serviceman was a slaveowner, so almost any major issue could be studied with consideration of the positions of slaveowners on it. Here I shall limit myself to three issues in which it is obvious that slaveowners played a major role: the choice of a monarch as the Time of Troubles was nearing an end, the initiation of the Forbidden Years that played such a crucial role in the enserfment process, and the operation of the postal system in the Novgorod region in the last quarter of the sixteenth century.

145. Iakovlev, *Kholopstvo*, p. 562, no. 26.

The Time of Troubles was one of the most dramatic episodes of early modern Russian history. It featured a dynastic crisis (the expiration of the Riurikovich dynasty, succeeded by the Romanovs), social discord (among others, the Khlopko and Bolotnikov uprisings discussed in chapter 16), and foreign "intervention" (invasions by Poles and Swedes, with the former taking Moscow, the latter Novgorod). Slaveowners played an active role in all phases of the trauma, but here I shall concentrate on the resolution of the dynastic crisis and associated aspects of the foreign intervention.

Many of the slavery documents are from the Novgorod region in the decade ending in 1603, where many of the slaveowners were still alive and active in various matters relating to the Swedish occupation of their part of Muscovy. Some seem to have collaborated actively with the Swedish occupation, others were passive in their cooperation with the Swedish authorities, while still others actively resisted. The first document I shall discuss was dated December 25, 1611 and invited Swedish King Charles IX Vasa to send one of his sons, Gustav Adolf or Charles Philipp, to rule Novgorod. This was just one of the many contemporary attempts to find a ruler for all of or various parts of Muscovy, and so no particular meaning should be attached to it—it was hardly "treasonous." Those involved were eight clergymen, forty-two servicemen, and thirty-four townsmen. Of the servicemen, there is evidence that at least half of them (22) owned an average of 5.7 slaves apiece, and it seems likely that that is an absolute lower bound.[146]

One may assume that political consciousness was somewhat different a year and a half later, when on July 27, 1613, a delegation of Novgorodians offered the throne to Charles Philipp. By this time the Muscovite Assembly of the Land had resolved on selecting Mikhail Romanov as tsar, so that actively to solicit someone else indicated a conscious rejection of Mikhail. Sixty-eight individuals were involved in the invitation to Charles Philipp, thirteen church figures, thirty-one servicemen, and twenty-four townsmen.[147] At least twelve of the servicemen can be identified as slaveowners who are known to have owned 8.2 slaves apiece. Metropolitan Isidor and *boiarin voevoda* Ivan Nikitich Odoevskoi were the major figures in both the 1611 and 1613 invitations, but only one known slaveowner, Ignatei Zhdanov Kharlamov, can be identified who was present in both episodes. The import of that fact is not clear. One should also note that this was a region that supported in the neighborhood of three thousand *pomest'e* servicemen.

The impact of the Swedish occupation on slaveowners can be seen in the matter of harvesting grain on lands of servicemen who deserted the Novgorod region for Moscow. At some time in 1612 or 1613 the Swedish occupation forces ordered such grain harvested. Of the figures working for the Swedes, about half

---

146. DAI 1: 283-85, no. 162. This document is supplementary to the original of July 1611 (SGGD 2: 553-63, no. 264), which was published without signatories.

147. DAI 2: 508, no. 4.

were known slaveowners, and two of the three who fled to the Moscow forces had been slaveowners.[148] The same issue again arose in September of 1614, and one of the two collaborators working for the Swedes was a slaveowner, while three of the five who had gone over to the Moscow side probably were slaveowners.[149] The "loyalists" owned 2.5 slaves apiece.

Collaborating with the Swedes had its dangers, as the life of Fedor Bestuzhev shows. He was one of those who reported to the Swedes for the harvesting in 1612-13, but in May of 1616 he almost lost his life. On April 27, 1616, two boats bearing ten townsmen slipped away from Novgorod, and the *deti boiarskie* Fedor Bestuzhev and Ignatei Skobel'tsyn (both slaveowners) were charged with having allowed them to flee. They were tried before the Russian collaborationist authorities, at least one of whom was a slaveowner, and Bestuzhev was sentenced to death. On May 1, Swedish general Jacob De la Gardie commuted the death penalty and ordered him beaten with the knout and jailed until further notice.[150]

People resisted the Swedish occupation not only by fleeing but in other ways as well. In November 1613 twenty-six prominent Novgorodians were required to guarantee that ten individuals would not leave their estates. Of the guarantors, twelve are know to have been slaveowners, and, as the guarantors as a group seem to have been among the most prominent servicemen of the region, we may assume that all of them were slaveowners. Only two of them, Nikon Fedorov Buturlin and Fedor Timofeev Obolenskoi, had signed the 1611 communication to King Charles, and only one, Gost' Mikiforov Kokovtsov, was involved in the 1613 offer to Prince Charles Philipp, so we may assume that the guarantors comprised both Swedish partisans and others, as would have had to have been the case for the mutual pledge to have had any deterrent impact. Half of those confined to their estates were women, who, one may assume, had been somehow criticizing the Swedish occupation, at least. Of the eight males involved (either as husbands, sons, or fathers, or else those personally confined to their estates), five at least are known slaveowners who owned an average of 2.3 slaves each.[151]

In a similar document, dated January 17, 1614, forty-four servicemen signed a guarantee that Eufim Fedorov Myshetskoi would not depart from Novgorod. Of the forty-four, twenty-one can be identified as slaveowners, and judging by the fact that the known slaveowners alternate in bunches with those individuals not known to be slaveowners, one may assume that they signed by regions; the unknowns were from regions for which I have no data about slaveownership.[152] Here the number of guarantors who had signed the invitations was somewhat

148. DAI 1: 309, no. 177.
149. DAI 2: 48, no. 23.
150. DAI 2: 77-82, no. 47.
151. DAI 2: 17-18, no. 9.
152. DAI 2: 18, no. 9.

greater: four slaveowners (Fedor Timofeev Obolenskoi, Zhdan Iakovlev Tyrkov, Fedor Ofonas'ev Odintsov, and Ignatei Kharitonov Kharlamov) had signed the 1611 invitation, and four other slaveowners (Vasilei Ivanov Motiakin, Matfei Semenov L'vov, Mikifor Kudeiarov Meshcherskii, and Gost' Mikiforov Kokovsov) signed the 1613 one. Again one may assume a mixture of pro-Swedish collaborators and neutrals or opponents of the occupation who decided to remain in the region.

Clearly not all Novgorodians decided to remain under Swedish occupation. In 1615 the Moscow Military Chancellery paid a reward of 2 rubles to each of the twenty-two Votskaia piatina servicemen who had left Novgorod and were then in Pskov. Only seven of the twenty-two can be identified as slaveowners.[153] This should be significant, for the slaveownership records of Votskaia piatina are the best extant. Moreover, the seven owned barely more than one slave apiece (two of them owned two), indicating that, at least in Votskaia piatina, the supporters of Moscow among the servicemen were the poorer element, those who had no slaves, or had very few slaves. Because, as we have seen, slaveownership was highly life-cycle-determined, leaving occupied Novgorod for Moscow-controlled Pskov may have been determined primarily by an "energy factor"; the younger and therefore poorer servicemen, with little to leave behind, were the ones who had the drive to leave the occupied area, whereas older servicemen did not. It should not be ruled out, however, that older and more experienced servicemen may have found Swedish hegemony more to their liking.

Another alternative during the Time of Troubles was Polish hegemony. There again one finds slaveowners active. In autumn of 1610, two known slaveowners, Onton Pavlov Zagoskin and Oksentei Fedorov Snazin, constituted the Bezhetskaia piatina contingent of the delegation to Poland with Filaret and Golitsyn.[154] In 1595 Snazin had purchased thirty-one slaves, and Zagoskin had bought two in two transactions in 1603. One may assume that in 1610 both had large numbers of slaves. About the same time, on August 17, 1610, seventy-four *dvoriane* and *deti boiarskie* from Tverskaia polovina of Bezhetskaia piatina swore allegiance to Polish Prince Wladyslaw. Of the seventy-four, at least sixteen of them were almost certainly slaveowners who are known to have owned an average of 5.7 slaves apiece.[155]

It is apparent that in the Swedish and Polish occupations, slaveowners from the Novgorod region could be found as partisans of either one or the other foreign hegemony, or as refusing to surrender independence to either. The other notable fact is that loyalist partisans opposed to foreign domination consistently were the lesser slaveowners, whereas the average person who chose either a Polish or a Swedish ruler is known to have possessed several times more slaves than did the

153. RIB 28 (1912): 331.
154. SIRIO 142(1913): 182-83.
155. SIRIO 142(1913): 82-83.

average "Moscow loyalist." Convincing explanations of this observation do not immediately spring out. In fact, the observation would seem to be contrary to what one would expect, for ordinarily one would assume that bigger slaveowners would be more vigorous supporters of the regime. The problem with the Time of Troubles, of course, was precisely that there was no "regime." It well may be that the more established slaveowners simply were grabbing for the straw that appeared to them to offer the greatest hope for stability and a restoration of order.

Another major political issue of Muscovy was enserfment. I have discussed this at length in my *Enserfment and Military Change in Muscovy* and hardly need review the issue at this point. Here I should like to mention solely that those who initially benefited from the binding of the peasants to the land in the mid-1580s were individuals who were to become substantial slaveowners.[156] In 1602 and 1603 Bogdan Ivanov Kropotkin purchased eight slaves;[157] at the same time Ivan Dmitriev Nepeitsyn purchased five slaves,[158] and in 1603 Boris Ivanov Somov also purchased five slaves.[159] Regrettably, no information is available about their slaveholdings (if there were any, and we may surmise there were) in the 1580s, but even the little information we have about their slave-related activites is unusual. The fact that they made their purchases during the Great Famine is itself a likely indication of possession of some surplus, but they also expended sums far greater than was typical during that grave period: Kropotkin laid out 16 rubles in five transactions, Nepeitsyn paid 7 rubles in two transactions, and Somov spent 5 rubles in one transaction. This would tend to indicate that, almost two decades after the initiation of the Forbidden Years, these men were at the top of the elite slaveowners.

The question of interest here is whether that condition can be projected back to the mid-1580s. As is well known, the universalization of the Forbidden Years in 1592/93 might well be called the Average and Poorer Servicemen's Relief Act of 1592/93, for its motivation was to stem the flight of peasants from the lands of those individuals so that they could collect rent from the peasants and thereby render military service. This does not necessarily mean, however, that poorer servicemen initiated or, benefited in the early years from, the binding of the peasants to the land, and in fact it would seem unlikely that the process began that way. The fifteenth-century limitation of peasant mobility to St. George's Day was initiated by significant institutions such as the Beloozero St. Kirill monastery, and it was the great Trinity-Sergiev monastery that obtained a temporary prohibition of any peasant movement from two of its estates in the mid-

156. R. G. Skrynnikov, *Rossiia posle oprichniny* (Leningrad: LGU, 1975), pp. 176, 185-86.
157. NZKK 2: 203, 273, 280.
158. NZKK 2: 205, 270.
159. NZKK 2: 169.

fifteenth century.[160] In the same way one may assume that more established
servicemen got their peasants bound to their lands as a private relief measure and
that, once the idea was in the air and it was observed to benefit the wealthier
landholders, it spread rapidly—ultimately to the great displeasure of the great
landowners, who were simultaneously, often, the great slaveowners.

A brief examination of the lives of the three men mentioned above should con-
vince one that they were leaders of their cohort not only in 1603 but two decades earlier as well. In 1582 Kropotkin possessed 70 cheti of land in Derevskaia
piatina, not a large holding but not an insignificant one, either. A few years
later, his service lands were in at least three pogosty, Berezaiskii, Kolomenskii,
and Mikhailovksii. The last was near Edrov, a major center and postal station at
the time. Some time later, he also acquired land near Edrov in Navolotskii pogost, Zaonezhskaia polovina, Obonezhskaia piatina, which in 1607 had thirty-
three taxpaying peasant houses. Extant documents from the Forbidden Years
mention thirteen peasants who had fled during the years 1584-87 from his
Kolomenskii pogost estate, Mar'in Riadok on the Berezaia River. It is not known
how many peasants Kropotkin had besides those who had fled. Another likely
sign, at least of Kropotkin's self-image in 1585, was his defiance of the postal
system authorities. When the postal system cart collector came to Mar'in Riadok,
syn boiarskii Kropotkin, claiming to be exempt from such levies, assembled his
slaves and peasants and drove him out. In his report, the cart collector noted
that most of the estates in the area were totally depopulated. In return, the cart
collector was ordered by his superiors to assemble a small army to levy the
carts "mercilessly and without showing favor to anyone." The outcome of the
fracas is unknown, but the gist of it all for my purposes here is that already at
the time of the initiation of the Forbidden Years Kropotkin was an important
slaveowner who was able to get privileges from the government and simultaneously to defy it.[161]

In 1582 Ivan Dmitriev Nepeitsyn had more land in Derevskaia piatina than
did Kropotkin—110 cheti. Aside from that, all that is known about him for
the 1580s is that two of his peasants fled from him to a monastery in Edrov
while he was in service in 1582, during the Forbidden Years. By 1596, he was
one of the thirteen elected local military commanders (*okladchiki*) of Derevskaia piatina, of whom ten can be identified as slaveowners.[162] Almost certainly he was a relatively substantial person in the 1580s as well.

160. MS, pp. 94-105.
161. Ianitskii, p. 146; Samokvasov, AM 2: 46, 47, 129; idem, *Materialy* 2(1909): 451-52,
530; Petrov, IRRD 1(1886): 61-63; Anpilogov, *Novye,* pp. 415-18; RIB 22(1908): 146-50;
Skrynnikov, *Rossiia,* pp. 176, 186-87, 197; Koretskii, *Zakreposhchenie,* pp. 97-98; Gnevushev (1911), p. 118.
162. Ianitskii, p. 171; Samokvasov, AM 2: 46; idem, *Materialy* 2(1909): 449-50; RIB 38
(1926): 104-8; AIuB 2: 184; DN 1596, p. 198; Koretskii, *Zakreposhchenie,* p. 97; Skrynnikov, *Rossiia,* p. 176.

The third figure, Boris Ivanov Somov, is less well documented in the early years. In 1558 his father, Ivan Ivanov Somov, had 135 cheti of land in Lokotskii pogost of Derevskaia piatina, and it is possible that Boris was serving from that holding in 1582. In 1585, when a figure responsible for collecting carts for the Krestetskoi postal station sent his slaves to Lokotskoi pogost to get them, Boris Somov was a landholder there and refused to provide them. About the same time, Somov was granted an additional 30 cheti of land, the village Moshnia on the Moscow road in Kholovskoi pogost, Derevskaia piatina; from that village his peasants (eleven households), plus a *bobyl'* household, provided three carts for the Zaechevskii postal station. There were two vacant households at Moshnia that had been abandoned during the Forbidden Years, 1582-85. A decade later, in 1594, Somov was one of the most prominent figures of Derevskaia piatina, for he was one of the elected *guba* elders, in charge of felony administration, slavery, property divisions, and so on. During the Great Famine, he had surplus grain, since an inventory dated September, 1603, shows that he was storing his grain at the Liatskii monastery. That is all that is known about Somov, obviously another substantial person who benefited from the Forbidden Years. One might note that the Somov and Kropotkin clans were related, as revealed in a 1613 document in which Prince Fedor Ivanov Kropotkin of Derevskaia piatina sold a Novgorod yard (*dvor*) with its buildings on Nutnaia Street that had belonged to his grandfather, Boris Somov (who can hardly be the Boris Ivanov Somov under discussion here).[163]

From the available evidence, one cannot tell precisely when the Forbidden Years were initiated, or by whom, but it does seem clear that the earliest beneficiaries were relatively substantial *deti boiarskie* who were to become shortly the leaders of their provinces and prosperous slaveowners. These were not individuals unable to render service because of the flight of their peasants, but landholders who were already doing well, of the type who, when they were able to collect additional surplus from renter-peasants, used it to buy and maintain additional slaves. Their success in using the Forbidden Years probably was the fact that motivated the universalization of the institution to enable marginal servicemen to render military service.

The last matter I shall discuss under the political rubric is the postal system, the marvel of foreign observers and commentators from at least Sigismund Herberstein in the 1520s right down to the latest American author of a book on Muscovy.[164] None of these observers seem to have realized fully what the purpose of the postal system was, particularly what its cost was.

163. *Materialy po istorii krest'ianskogo khoziaistva i povinnosti XVI–XVII vv.* (1977), p. 55; Petrov, IRRD, 1(1886): 82-83; Samokvasov, *Materialy* 2(1909): 499-500; RIB 22 (1908): 112, 144, 870-71; Nosov, *Ocherki*, pp. 350, 357; AIuB 2: 389, no. 148/vii; Skrynnikov, *Rossiia*, pp. 38, 97; Koretskii, *Zakreposhchenie*, pp. 38, 97; idem (1975), p. 138.
164. J. Michael Hittle, *The Service City. State and Townsmen in Russia, 1600-1800* (Cambridge, Mass: Harvard University Press, 1979), pp. 21-22.

The postal system, whose origin some scholars find in the Mongol heritage,[165] had two primary functions: to facilitate Muscovite military and diplomatic communications; to transport foreign embassies. While the first is both obvious and well known, the second seems to have been of at least equal concern to the authorities in Moscow during the reigns of tsars Fedor Ivanovich and Boris Godunov. Great concern was shown that large parties of a hundred and more foreigners should be whisked through the expanses of Russia "without stopping" and "without seeing anything." The death penalty was threatened for anybody who failed to meet the rigorous standards set by Moscow for the operation of the postal system, who caused so much as "even a one-hour" delay in the transportation of foreigners.[166]

A large number of the individuals who administered and were otherwise responsible for its maintainence were slaveowners. Many of the *deti boiarskie* sent in 1585 to superintend the Moscow-Novgorod road to the western frontier can be identified as slaveowners.[167] The first responsibility of those running the postal system was to keep Moscow informed about every river, brook, marsh, or other obstacle along the road, its length and condition, and then to make sure that every obstacle could be traversed at the required breakneck speed.[168] This was done by drafting those who lived for up to 50 kilometers on either side of the road to perform the corvée labor necessary to keep the way in top condition. Then the postal stations had to be manned and provisioned. The manpower was provided by drafting the most able peasants to serve as coachmen and drivers; and forcing them to give up farming and paying rent to servicemen and to move to a settlement (usually tax-exempt) of postal drivers. The remaining peasants mutually had to guarantee that those elected by their peers or drafted as postmen would fulfill their obligations, a necessary measure because forcing established peasants to leave their economies and assigning them to often unprepared and unprovisioned postal stations was much too frequently akin to a death sentence, which peasants fled if they could.[169] At first surprising is the fact that slaves were never, to my knowledge, conscripted as postmen, a fact that merely reflects the government's recognition of the sanctity of the slave form of private property. The servicemen-landholders strongly resented the conscription of their most productive peasants..

The postmen had to be provided with horses, wagons, and sleighs, which were confiscated from those living along the post road. The same cadastres that were employed in enserfing the peasants were used to determine what could be col-

165. For the early history of the Muscovite postal system, see Gustave Alef's article "The Origin and Early Development of the Muscovite Postal Service," *Jahrbücher für Geschichte Osteuropas* 15(1967): 1-15.
166. RIB 22(1908): 711.
167. RIB 22: 85.
168. RIB 22: 567-68, 572-73, 587-90, 599.
169. RIB 22: 623-26, 635-36, 681-83.

lected from each landholder, and detailed records were kept of requisitions.[170] As we saw in the discussion of Kropotkin and Somov above, these requisitions, made by men who were often slaveowners and worked under the threat of dire sanctions for failure, were resisted by landholders, themselves often slaveowners, who had the great misfortune to live in the post road's swath. The post road contributed to turning much of the region into a desert, a phenomenon observable in Byzantium centuries earlier. Pitched battles were not unheard of, with local landholders, their slaves and peasants, driving out the agents of the postal system desperately trying to execute their impossible commissions. The consequences of such a pressure-cooker environment was exactly what one would expect: those appointed by Moscow or elected locally to maintain the postal system submitted to the center an endless stream of correspondence detailing the local resistence and other factors that made it impossible for them to fulfill the demands made upon them, and the local residents responded with laments about illegal exactions, corruption in the granting of exemptions, and other oppressions visited upon them by the agents of the postal system.[171] No doubt there was exaggeration in much of the paper flow, but the findings of special agents dispatched from Novgorod or Moscow to review the situation tended to confirm what both sides had already informed the capital.[172]

Nearly every page that has been cited in this discussion of the postal system reveals the pitting of slaveowners against other slaveowners in the battle to meet Moscow's demands, or to escape those demands in an attempt to survive another day. There seems to be no pattern of well-to-do slaveowners vs. poorer slaveowners or nonslaveowners in the postal system. The issue was the state vs. everyone else; all were under pressure, with the heaviest pressure on those closest to the source of orders. That was typical of Muscovite history, a climate hardly conducive to the forming of "parties" along any lines. To a considerable extent the same was probably true on the issue of enserfment. If it was not true during the late Time of Troubles, one must recall that the issue was precisely the absence of a government, and what should be done to resolve that lack.

Idleness

A fitting conclusion to this chapter on the slaveowners of Muscovy would be a brief consideration of the problem of idleness. D. B. Davis has written that "occasionally men recognized that slavery was dangerous to the security of the state, that it provided some masters with too much idleness and too much power."[173] As should be apparent from what has just been discussed, such a state-

170. RIB 22: 102-5, 279-83, 778-81, 823-26, 836.
171. RIB 22: 88-89, 199-201, 203-6, 222-24, 283-88, 568-72, 590-94, 699-711.
172. RIB 22: 89-102, 202-3.
173. D. B. Davis, *Western Culture*, p. 62.

ment was not true for Muscovy, thanks to the service principle that forced nearly all of those who were slaveowners to work hard in the service of the state, as
well as to the fact that the Muscovite slave consumed his owner's wealth rather
than providing the conditions under which the latter could be idle. (The Davis
statement is more applicable in the Russian case to serfdom between 1665 and
1700, and after 1762.)[174] In at least one respect, the conditions of Muscovy
turned one of the major features of Southern American slavery on its head: in
the South, the slaves were driven, but in Muscovy the slaveowners were driven.

That explains much of the motivation for slavery in Muscovy. While subject
to some personal abuse and to treatment as a thing, an object, the person selling
himself into slavery perhaps was subject to abuse anyway; the "rights" enjoyed
by "free people" in Muscovy were not what we are accustomed to in the West,
and slavery normally provided adequate security and probably considerable
leisure as well. On the other hand, the person buying and maintaining the slave
acquired someone to perform household chores, someone he could dominate as
well. No doubt that lessened the psychological pressure of continuous domination by superior governmental authorites.

Categories of slaveowners have differed widely throughout history. In some
places slaveownership was open to anyone and was the aspiration of everyone.
This was true in Athens of the fifth century B.C., for peasant farmers with
small holdings as well as for wealthy Athenian citizens; in the later Roman Empire, for private soldiers in the imperial army as well as magnates in the Heaven-
ly City itself; and in Byzantium at the time of Justinian, for urban merchants
and artisans as well as for rural clerical and lay landholders and even peasants
and coloni.[175] Among the Crimean Tatars who raided the lands of the Slavs,
even "the poorest and simplest horseman" anticipated that he would at some
time be a slaveowner.[176] A similar situation prevailed in many parts of Latin
America, where virtually everyone with sufficient funds, including Indians,
purchased one or more slaves, even when they were not immediately required
and sometimes just as an investment.[177] In the American South, there were no
restrictions on which categories of free men could own slaves, but three-fourths
of them did not. In Africa, a full spectrum of people in some societies owned
slaves, whereas in others slaveownership was strictly limited to a few types of
people, even solely to members of the royal family. In the Hausaland Sokoto
Caliphate of the nineteenth century, officials had thousands of slaves, usually

174. Catherine the Great's remarks on the "idleness and sloth" of the Moscow gentry
are noted in Black, *Citizens for the Fatherland*, p. 70.
175. Jones, pp. 185, 188; Udal'tsova, p. 8.
176. Alan W. Fisher, "Chattel Slave Procurement in the Ottoman Empire" (Paper presented at the Twelfth Annual Meeting of the Middle East Studies Association, Ann Arbor,
November 1978), p. 8.
177. Mellafe, p. 94.

acquired during military campaigns; commoners owned a few they purchased in the market.[178] In neighboring Damagaram, a section of nineteenth-century Niger, anyone could buy and sell slaves, many peasants owned them and the aspiration of the young was to acquire fifteen or twenty slaves, go home, marry, and begin farming millet. In Zanzibar all free men owned slaves. The same was reportedly true in Gonja (Nigeria), where slaveownership was widely distributed, and in Merina (Madagascar), where most free men had slaves.[179] At the other extreme, among the people of Dahomey, who controlled and encouraged in every possible way the slave trade on the island of Whydah in the Bight of Benin off the Guinea Coast, slaveownership was a privilege limited to persons of rank.[180] The same was true in Madrid, where only the nobles owned Negro, Moorish, or Turkic slaves up to the mid-seventeenth century, and also in Thailand, where members of the ruling stratum (two thousand highly ranked people out of the population of two million) owned the slaves.[181]

More analogous to the Muscovite situation was that of the Sena in nineteenth-century Mozambique in the Zambese region. Slaves were plentiful, but only the most affluent (leading farmers and merchants, senior members of the royal family, and local village headmen) enjoyed the means to acquire and sustain them, and then only a half-dozen or so at most. According to Barbara and Allen Isaacman, "the inability to acquire a great following indicates the limit of capital accumulation, even at the upper levels of Sena society."[182] A somewhat similar situation prevailed among the Kerebe of Tanzania.[183] As far as I can tell, there are no features whose knowledge would permit a student to predict who the slaveowners in a given society would be. Of all the topics discussed in this work, that of the slaveowners seems to be the most fruitful for additional research.

Up through the Time of Troubles and even beyond, there were no restrictions on who could own slaves in Muscovy. In fact, however, only certain segments of society owned slaves. For example, slaves were never owned, to my knowledge, by farming peasants, because they probably did not possess enough surplus to be able to purchase and sustain slaves. (Either the farming peasantry was relatively undifferentiated economically, or else those who may have been able to purchase and sustain slaves calculated that visibly manifesting such wealth would only tempt a landlord, a tax collector, or those who apportioned the collective tax burden to relieve the well-to-do of their surplus.) Members of the lower service class (musketeers, cossacks, and so on) also rarely owned slaves, pro-

178. Paul E. Lovejoy, "Plantations in the Economy of the Sokoto Caliphate, " *Journal of African History* 19, no. 3(1978): 359.

179. Miers and Kopytoff, p. 167; Goody, p. 36; Bloch, p. 110.

180. Miers and Kopytoff, p. 115.

181. Verlinden, *Colonization,* p. 39; Turton, p. 253.

182. Miers and Kopytoff, p. 110.

183. Ibid., pp. 267, 269, 278, 281.

bably for the same reason. It is possible, of course, that the values of the peasantry and the lower service class were so different from those of their social superiors that they simply did not want to own slaves, but this seems unlikely.

Restriction on Muscovite slaveownership was primarily an economic reflection of the ability to buy and, particularly, to maintain slaves. It seems crucial to stress that slaves generally were not a productive asset, as they were in places such as Athens, where a person of limited means could buy a slave and expect the chattel to earn back the purchase price and produce a good return on the investment besides. The Muscovite slave, as a rule, as emphasized by Kotoshikhin, expected to be maintained out of his owner's income, thus ruling out as slaveowners all those whose own future income stream was precarious, a prospect that applied to most of the subjects of Muscovy. Consequently, only a relatively few townsmen (elite merchants and handfuls of other, more prosperous *posadskie liudi*), some members of the clergy, and persons in government military and civilian employ owned slaves. As we have seen, perhaps 90 percent of all slaves were owned by government servicemen. In some respects, these servicemen were analagous to the Tatars, not only in their military style but in their expectation of slaveownership, which in Muscovy was highly life-cycle-determined. There were major differences between the Crimean Tatars and Muscovites, however. The former expected to gather his slaves on raids into Muscovy and the Rzeczpospolita, the latter (who acquired some slaves by raiding the Tatars and in combat with western neighbors) primarily expected to buy Russians as slaves from the proceeds of peasant rent and government cash salary that increased as the serviceman demonstrated his merit. Whatever his success in earning merit increases and his luck in finding populated service land, the serviceman made every effort to acquire at least one slave. The acquisition of slaves determined the serviceman's level of comfort and his sense of self-esteem and prestige among his peers. On the other hand, slaveownership probably played little role in defining the political views of a serviceman—unless exhibition of martial prowess demonstrably advanced a serviceman and he therefore became more aggressively militant in an effort to gain more slaves. The institution of slavery was challenged significantly in Muscovy only by the government itself, and therefore the slaveowners did not need to coalesce in response to a lesser challenge. When the government challenged and ultimately abolished slavery, it had the good fortune to be able to provide meaningful substitutes.

18. The Importance of Slavery in Russia

As a summary and conclusion, this chapter will integrate the previous seventeen chapters. Emphasis will be placed on a calculation of how many slaves there were in early modern Russia, the functions of slavery, its abolition, and the long-term impact of the institution on the course of Russian history. I shall conclude with a synopsis of the system of early modern Russian slavery.

Number of Slaves

There is no way to calculate with precision the number of slaves in Russia at any time between 1450 and the abolition of slavery at the end of the reign of Peter the Great. In a moment some calculations will be made to show that slaves, although a small percentage of the total population, may have been the second largest social group, far inferior in number to the peasants, yet more numerous than the townsmen, servicemen, or clergy. Before making those calculations, however, I shall take a brief look at the numbers of slaves in other societies.

The percentage of the population constituted by slaves has varied widely from country to country and from era to era, often changing radically in the same country within short periods of time and from place to place. Many societies have almost no slaves, while in a few the overwhelming majority of the populace has been in bondage.

In the societies studied by Orlando Patterson the following percentages of population was slave:[1]

Less than 10% slave	41.7% of societies
10-24%	19.4%
25-49%	22.2%
50-74%	13.9%
75-100%	2.8%
	100.0% N = 36

In the Ancient Near East, the number of privately owned slaves was a small fraction of the free population, and the average slaveowner only owned from

---

1. Patterson, "Structural Origins of Slavery," p. 19.

one to four chattel. In places like Nuzi, only two or three slaves were in the possession of each owner; in the late Assyrian period the numbers rose to three or four in the city, five to eight in the country.[2] The situation was much different in Athens, where there may have been one slave to every three or four adult free persons, approximately half the ratio in the U. S. South.[3] In ancient China (second and first centuries B. C.), where slaves were used in domestic service and not as part of agricultural production or as other producers of wealth, they probably made up "well under 5% of the population, maybe not even 1%." In South China around 1900 perhaps 2 percent of the population were slaves, and in Nepal at the same time about 1 percent of the population were slaves.[4] In the English Domesday Book, 10 percent of the population were slaves, as was also the case among the Melanau of Sarawak. In Malabar, southwest India, about 15 percent of the population was enslaved in the nineteenth century, in Siam perhaps a quarter to a third of the population was so disabled. In the Crimea, there were reportedly twice as many slaves as Muslim free people—400,000 slaves, 100,000 commoners, and 87,000 soldiers—in 1667.[5] Similar ratios are reported for parts of Africa. Hausa slaves sometimes are estimated as high as 95 percent of the total population, but a more realistic figure might be something like 50 percent of the population in Zaria (northern Nigeria). It has been estimated that two-thirds of the total population on the north bank of the Gambia and on the islands of Zanzibar and Pemba were slaves. About a quarter of the population in the Wolof and Serer states of Senegambia was made up of slave warriors. Among the Vai of Liberia and Sierra Leone, in 1826, 75 percent of the total population were slaves.[6] Elsewhere in Africa, the proportion of slaves was considerably less. Similar ranges could be found in the New World. The population of Caribbean islands was sometimes 90 percent slaves. Keith Hopkins has observed that slaves in the societies where they played a major role in production (Athens in 400 B. C.; Roman Italy in 31 B. C; Brazil in 1800 and 1850; the U. S. South in 1820 and 1860; Cuba in 1804 and 1861) all hovered around 30 percent of the total population.[7] As we shall see, the slave population in early modern Russia was probably less than a third of that.

2. Mendelsohn, pp. 116, 119-21.

3. A. H. M. Jones, "Slavery in the Ancient World," *The Economic History Review* 9, no. 2 (1956): 187; Finley, "Between Slavery and Freedom," pp. 238-39, Stampp, 30; Lewis Cecil Gray, *History of Agriculture in the Southern United States to 1860* (Carnegie Institution of Washington, ca. 1932; reprint ed., Gloucester, Mass: Peter Smith, 1958), pp. 481-82.

4. Wilbur, *Slavery in China*, pp. 174-77, 216, 214; Watson, *Systems*, p. 250. Among the Nyinba, slaves may have made up 12 percent of the population (Nancy Levine, p. 200).

5. Inalcik, "Servile Labor," p. 34; Caplan, p. 185; Turton, p. 275; H. S. Morris, "Slaves, Aristocrats and Export of Sago in Sarawak," in Watson, *Systems*, p. 296; Hjejle, pp. 89-90; Banaji, pp. 195-203.

6. Miers and Kopytoff, p. 294; Burnham, p. 48; Shepherd, pp. 77, 80; Klein and Lovejoy, in Gemery and Hogendorn, pp. 207-8.

7. Keith Hopkins, *Conquerors and Slaves. Sociological Studies in Roman History* (Cambridge: Cambridge University Press, 1978), p. 101.

The number of slaves in Muscovy can be calculated by various means. The Moscow military census of 1638 included slaves among the adult males able to bear arms. In the provinces, slaves who lived in their own houses (*dvory*) and farmed sometimes were listed in the cadastres and censuses. The numbers of combat and baggage-train slaves brought from some locales and by groups of servicemen are available. Wills and property divisions reveal the number of slaves at the time of an owner's death. Total annual purchases for some areas are available, as are current purchases that can be aggregated for individuals. Regrettably, the extent to which these various categories overlap or are mutually exclusive cannot be determined. One may assume that farming slaves paying taxes were not in any way an over lapping category with household slaves, who paid no taxes. It also seems likely that the agricultural slaves were almost completely separate from the military slaves, for the agricultural and military seasons coincided, and the reason owners had farming slaves was because they themselves were at the front during the sowing and harvesting seasons. The degree to which household and military slaves overlapped also is difficult to calculate; while one may assume that a person owning a single slave might employ him both as a lackey at home and a baggage train slave at the front, the same assumption probably would be invalid for combat slaves. Moreover, it is known that the hordes of domestic slaves in some wealthy households never appeared at the front.

There is no way to determine the functional destination of purchased slaves (although it has been speculated that most of the higher-priced ones were military slaves). One may assume that slaves recorded in wills and property divisions encompass household, military, and agricultural slaves, but certainly the few slaves occasionally manumitted in such instruments were often hereditary slaves, and little mention is made of slaves who automatically were freed by law on their owner's death. With these reservations, I shall proceed to calculate the approximate proportion of the early modern Russian population that was enslaved.

The Moscow military (home guard) census of 1638 listed 7,672 households containing 10,787 adult males, of whom approximately 1,735, or 16.1% were slaves. About 15.1% of the households reported owning slaves, meaning that the average owner had one adult male, who sometimes was listed at the time of the census as being at the front with his master.[8] These figures are in the same range as those of Istanbul, where roughly a fifth of the population has been estimated to have been slaves and freedmen.[9] To my knowledge, a count similar to that made in Moscow in 1638 is not available for any other Russian town. There is, of course, fragmentary evidence, such as that generated by the surrender of Smolensk to the Poles in 1613, when lists were made of those captured. Only three instances of slaves were mentioned: one family with four slaves, one with five, and a third with an unspecified number. Certainly, others in Smolensk also

8. I. S. Beliaev, *Rospisnoi spisok*.
9. Inalcik, "Slave Labor," p. 9; idem, "Servile Labor," p. 26.

owned slaves, but we have no idea who or how many. Similar tidbits can be garnered for Novgorod, Iaroslavl', and other places, but they contribute little to my
purpose. One may assume, however, that the percentage of the adult male population constituted by slaves in other cities was smaller than in Moscow because
the amount of surplus to be expended on slaves was so much less elsewhere,
thanks to the high concentration of elite individuals and wealth in the capital.
We know that provincial servicemen in some parts of the country tried to
maintain "siege residences" in nearby towns, and the *Ulozhenie* of 1649
allowed them to leave one slave caretaker there. Well-to-do provincial merchants
also owned slaves. The Petrine revision of 1721 provides information that may
or may not be typical for the earlier era. In Cheboksary, on the Volga between
Nizhnii Novgorod and Kazan', 5 elite merchants owned 43 house slaves (*dvorovye liudi*); the remaining 335 households contained 86 additional house slaves,
with the result that *dvorovye liudi* made up 15.2 percent of the city's male
population. The smaller town of Vologda in the 1678 census reported that about
6.2 percent of the population consisted of slaves belonging to servicemen and
clergymen, and Petrine censuses of the Vologda province in the 1710s reported
4.4 percent of the population as slaves, a figure that fell to 3.7 percent in 1718-
22.[10] All things considered, perhaps 5 to 10 percent of the adult male population of the leading provincial towns was enslaved. In the smaller towns, where
there was relatively little income differentiation, there were probably very few
slaves.

In chapter 14 calculation was made that each cavalryman from the middle service class and *zhil'tsy* was accompanied by one military slave. Among the Moscow *dvoriane*, this rose to 3.1 combat and baggage-train slaves. Members of the
middle service class in 1638 were supported by an average of 5.6 peasant households, *zhil'tsy* by 14 peasant households, and Moscow *dvoriane* by an average of
29 peasant households.[11] This indicates that each military slave was supported
by 5.6, 8.2, or 14 peasant households. As one moves up the military service
hierarchy, perhaps 850 *striapchie* in 1638 had an average of 24 peasants apiece,
500 *stol'niki* had 78 peasant households apiece, and the 32 members of counsel-
or rank (boyars, *okol'nichie*, et al.—see table 1.1) for whom information is available had 759 peasant households apiece.[12] Certainly the relationship between

10. SIRIO 142(1913): 375, 377; M. Ia. Volkov, "Materialy pervoi revizii kak istochnik po
istorii torgovli i promyshlennosti Rossii pervoi chetverti XVIII v.," *Problemy istochnikovedeniia* 11(1963): 277; Ia. E. Vodarskii, "Vologodskii uezd v XVII v. (K istorii sel'skikh
poselenii), " in *Agrarnaia istoriia evropeiskogo Severa SSSR*, ed. P. A. Kolesnikov (Vologda,
1970 [=*Voprosy agrarnoi istorii evropeiskogo Severa SSSR*, vol. 3]), pp. 257-58.
11. MS, p. 217; Iziumov.
12. Ia. E. Vodarskii, "Praviashchaia gruppa svetskikh feodalov v Rossii v XVII v.," *Dvorianstvo i krepostnoi stroi Rossii XVI–XVII vv.*, ed. N. I. Pavlenko et al. (Moscow: Nauka,
1975), pp. 74, 85-104. A statistical examination of the peasant households in the possession
of the elite members of the tsar's inner circle from 1638 to 1700 reveals the great amount of
change in that period. The correspondence of peasant holdings between the years 1638 and

peasant households and military slaves was not linear for all landed cavalrymen, and to pick the extreme case, one may doubt whether a boyar on campaign brought either 54 or 135 military slaves, but nevertheless the ranks above Moscow *dvorianin* certainly brought more military slaves to the front than did those of lesser material resources. Be that as it may, the number of slaves employed as combat and baggage-train slaves prior to the introduction of the new formation regiments probably equalled 125 to 150 percent of their landed owners, who themselves numbered somewhere around 15,000 to 18,000 on active combat duty. (In the half-century between, say, the 1580s and the 1630s, there were another 10,000 to 13,000 members of the landed service classes who rendered garrison or "siege" service, often because they were too poor or too old to be sent on active duty. Presumably they brought no combat slaves with them, but may well have had baggage-train slaves accompanying them as lackeys.)

We saw in chapter 17 that both *zhil'tsy* and Moscow *dvoriane* brought one military slave for each 165 cheti of land they held in 1632. Were full information available, one might calculate both the total number of military slaves on the eve of the Smolensk War and an approximate ratio of military slaves to peasants. Complete data are not available for either calculation, but what there is may be indicative.

At about that time, around 1629-30, there were approximately 885,896 desiatinas (a desiatina = 2 cheti) of hereditary and service land (*votchina* and *pomest'e*) belonging to servicemen in sixteen of the thirty-six provinces (*uezdy*) in the heartland of the Muscovite state (*zamoskovnyi krai*, the area bounded by the Lake Beloozero on the north, Lakes Okhvat, Sterzh, and Selinger on the west, Serpukhov on the Oka on the south, and Nizhnii Novgorod on the east).[13] That sum of land, according to the 165 cheti-per-slave ratio, should have been able to contribute about 2,685 military slaves to the army. Using the relative proportions of peasant households in those sixteen provinces and the rest of the *zamoskovnyi krai* in the 1678 census, one might project that the entire region should have been able to produce at least 6,102 military slaves in the pre-Smolensk War period, an absolute lower bound for many reasons. When this analysis is extended to the northwest (Novgorod and Pskov),[14] at least another 1,283 military slaves should be generated, for a total of 7,385. When still other areas are added, it is not difficult to see how as many as 10,000 military (bag-

---

1647 is very low (r = 0.36; N = 15). This is not quite so true for the period 1678 to 1696 (r = 0.65; N = 15), although it is for the years 1678 to 1700 (r = 0.46; N = 10). Only for very short intervals is there a high correspondence or continuity of peasant holdings: 1647 to 1653 (r = 0.99; N = 26) and 1696 to 1700 (r = 0.98; N = 64). For longer intervals, such as between 1647 and 1678, the turnover of personnel was so great that no statistics can be calculated.

13. Got'e, *Zamoskovnyi krai*, pp. 252, 258.
14. Vodarskii, *Naselenie*, pp. 221-23.

gage-train and combat) slaves could have been fielded on the eve of the Smolensk War.

Making the other calculation, one may assume that approximately 22.7 percent of the 165 cheti were farmed in the 1624-40 period, the other 77.3 percent remaining fallow.[15] If 37 cheti were farmed, and the average peasant in this period farmed from 2 to 3 cheti, that could indicate that perhaps from 12 to 19 peasant households were required to support one military slave. This is very roughly consistent with the calculation that each *zhilets*, who had an average of 14 peasant households, brought one military slave, and each Moscow *dvorianin*, who had 29 peasant households, brought three military slaves.[16] On the other hand, we also know that provincial *dvoriane* and *deti boiarskie* supplied about one military slave apiece with only 5.6 peasant households. Very roughly speaking, again, the pan-Muscovite ratio must have been something like 1 military slave for every 10 seignorial peasant households.

Another category of slaves whose numbers can be counted were those engaged in agriculture. One may assume, as noted earlier, that there was very little overlap between them and the military slaves. This was unlike in many West African slave-producing societies, where there was no distinction between fighting slaves and farming slaves. The African slave warrior was compelled to farm, whether he wanted to or not.[17] Of course African agriculture was far different from Muscovite agriculture, permitting such combined roles. Russian farming slaves were discussed in chapter 14, where it was observed that almost every service estate in the Novgorod region from the end of the fifteenth through the sixteenth centuries had at least one farming slave household, although the figures ranged from perhaps .5 to 3, depending on the time and place. The same figures seem to have prevailed for the Moscow region in the seventeenth century. Iu. V. Got'e studied 120 estates for the 1620s-30s, and found 126 slave households; for the years 1684-86, he found 129 such households on those estates.[18] Perhaps the practice was for each estate holder to try to have one household of farming slaves to tend a kitchen garden for both master and slave while also contributing something to the grain requirements of the owner, just as each serviceman (= estate holder) tried to bring at least one slave to military service, as a lackey or a combatant. This is confirmed by the holdings of the upper service class, whose 59 members in 1647 only had an average of 3.7 farming slave households apiece, in marked contrast to their average of 700+ peasant households.[19]

15. Got'e, p. 116.

16. Tikhonov, *Pomeshchich'i krest'iane*, pp. 136, 138-39; Gorskaia, *Monastyrskie krest'-iane*, pp. 22, 256-57; Iakovlev, *Prikaz sbora ratnykh liudei*, p. 259.

17. Klein and Lovejoy, in Gemery and Hogendorn, p. 193.

18. Got'e, pp. 159-60.

19. S. V. Rozhdestvenskii, "Ropis' zemel'nykh vladenii moskovskogo boiarstva 1647-48 goda," *Drevnosti. Trudy Arkheograficheskoi kommissii imp. Arkheologicheskogo obshchestva* 3(Moscow, 1913): 193-238. The published list of the holdings of the upper upper-

While the number of farming slave households usually approximated the number of estate holders, it is more difficult to establish what proportion farming slaves were of the total agricultural population.[20] As we saw in chapter 14, that percentage fluctuated between 2.6 and close to 10. E. I. Kolycheva calculated that 8.5 percent of the 223 newly settled hamlets (*pochinki*, consisting of one or two households) of Shelonskaia piatina in 1539 were occupied by slaves. Of 3,545 farming households on service landholdings, 344 (or 9.7 percent) were occupied by families of slaves. At the end of the sixteenth century, according to A. M. Gnevushev, in the southern Orlov province, 6 percent of the agricultural workers were slaves, 94 percent were peasants and *bobyli*.[21] For the 120 estates in the Moscow region examined by Got'e, in the 1620-30s there were 1,005 peasant households, 802 *bobyl'* households, and 126 slave households, and the last were 6.5 percent of the total; in the years 1684-86, the figures were 4,412, 407, 129, and 2.6 percent. Kliuchevskii noted that the 1630s census of Belevskii uezd south of Moscow along the Oka River found 9 percent of the farming population to be slaves, a figure that rose to 12 percent in 1678.[22] Changing the terms slightly, Iu. A. Tikhonov in a study of the rent on 473 *pomest'e* estates found that 35 of them (7.4 percent) were worked without any peasants.[23] During the census of 1678, in ninety-three central provinces between 75,839 and 79,855 adult males were listed as *zadvornye* and *delovye liudi* out of a total rural population (excluding those on properties that belonged to the royal court) of between 1,988,622 and 2,041,277 males, for proportions of between 3.7 and 4.0 percent.[24]

These figures would seem to make it safe to assume that at most 5 percent of the farming of seignorial service and hereditary estates was done by slaves. (Recall that there were few such estates in the North, and that monasteries, which may have owned a third of all the cultivated land in Muscovy after 1550, as a rule did not own slaves.) In making such calculations, it is important to observe

---

service class in 1678 does not contain such breakdowns (A. A. Novosel'skii, "Rospis' krest'-ianskikh dvorov nakhodivshchikhsia vo vladenii vysshego dukhovenstva, monastyrei i dumnykh liudei, po perepisnym knigam 1678 g.," *Istoricheskii arkhiv* 4[1949]: 122-49).

20. V. I. Koretskii offered a range from 3 to 30 percent (*Zakreposhchenie*, p. 186).

21. Kolycheva, *Kholopstvo*, p. 108. Paneiakh calculated that there were 321 slave households, or 9.1 percent (*Kholopstvo*, p. 65). A. M. Gnevushev, "Zemlevladenie i sel'skoe khoziaistvo v Moskovskom gosudarstve XVI–XVII vv., " in *Russkaia istoriia,* ed. M. V. Dovnar-Zapol'skii (Kiev, 1912), 3:296.

22. Got'e, p. 160; Kliuchevskii, *Sochineniia*, 3: 170. I have been unable to verify Henry Kamen's statement that "in the steppe, where many estates had no peasants, slave labor was used, and the proportion of slaves to free peasants in some districts here was high as fifty per cent" (*The Iron Century. Social Change in Europe 1550-1660* [London: Weidenfeld and Nicolson, 1971], p. 418).

23. Tikhonov, *Pomeshchich'i krest'iane*, p. 102.

24. Vodarskii, *Naselenie*, pp. 198-211.

the circumstances and date of their origin. One example will suffice. When a census was taken along the southern frontier in 1646, 36,000 households of court and seignorial peasants, *bobyli*, and slaves (*zadvornye liudi*) were counted, of which only 26 were slave households. In 1678, when the census was again taken, 41,000 households were counted, but the number of slave households had risen to 12,000.[25] After 1649, peasants and *bobyli* were enserfed and becoming daily more slavelike. When the 1678 census was taken, lords obviously decided to "go all the way," and to claim that thousands of their peasants were slaves; this attempt to cheat the tax collector was carried out in the hope that farming slaves would not have to pay taxes. The government was even smarter, and, at a stroke of the pen, converted all farming slaves living in their own houses (*zadvornye liudi*) into serfs. For that reason, the 2.6 percent figure reported from the Got'e study for 1684-86 is probably the absolute lower bound, for, while the total of 129 slave households approximates one for each of the 120 estates, some slave-owners may have ceased to call those who had been real slaves by their former judicial appelation several years after it had been abolished. The 3.7 to 4.0 percent figure might also be slightly inflated, but it is probably more useful because the count well may be incomplete; moreover, it certainly does not reflect the mad rush to enslave juridically the serfs that was evident in the southern frontier figure of 12,000. Nevertheless, when one considers that there were roughly 21,000 landholders who owned or possessed 29,000 estates in 1678,[26] that figure of nearly 4 percent adult male farming slaves is somewhat more than one finds for the period, say, 1480-1640.

It is most difficult to find figures for the numbers of household slaves, for they ordinarily were not counted. For the ninety-three provinces mentioned earlier, the Soviet demographic historian Ia. E. Vodarskii has calculated that there were 83,400 *dvorovye liudi* in 1678 and 28,000 in 1719.[27] These figures are incomplete, as are those for the agricultural slaves given earlier. Both 1678 figures are close to one another, so that of the house slaves would be about 4.1 percent of the population. Not surprisingly, 4.1 percent is also the proportion that house serfs were of all serfs in the 1830s.[28] These figures, which are incomplete, indicate that the total slave population in 1678 was more than 8.1 percent, in the range of Vodarskii's calculation of 10 percent.[29]

A slightly higher figure in the same range can be generated for the end of the sixteenth century. About half the slaves in the Novgorod region between 1593 and 1603 were probably hereditary slaves, the other half were first-generation limited service contract slaves. Table 18.1 shows the annual dynamics of self-

25. V. M. Vazhinskii, *Zemlevladenie i skladyvanie obshchiny odnodvortsev v XVII veke (Po materialam iuzhnykh uezdov Rossii)* (Voronezh: Vorpedinstitut, 1974), pp. 54-55.

26. Vodarskii, *Naselenie*, p. 64.

27. Ibid., p. 94.

28. Blum, *Lord and Peasant*, pp. 455-60.

29. Vodarskii, *Naselenie*, p. 94.

TABLE 18.1
Annual Dynamics of Self-Sale into Slavery

Place	Time	N of Sales	Weighted for Annual Basis[m]	N of Households (Dvory) in Region (Year)[n]	% (Documents and Households)
Novgorod	Oct. 1594-March 1595[a]	30	49	ca. 5000 (end 16th c.)	1.0
Novgorod	Sept. 1595-Aug. 1596[b]	119	119	(end 16th c.)	2.4
Novgorod	Sept. 1599-Aug. 1600[c]	116	116	(end 16th c.)	2.3
Bezhetskaia piatina, Tverskaia polovina	March-June 1595[d]	39	95	1936 (1583)	4.9
Bezhetskaia piatina	Oct. 1602-Aug. 1603[e]	360	372	2719 (1582-83)	13.7
Derevskaia piatina	March-Aug. 1594[f]	21	41	1333 (1582-83)	3.1
Derevskaia piatina	Sept. 1594-Aug. 1595[g]	38	38	1333 (1582-83)	2.9
Derevskaia piatina	Nov. 1602-Aug. 1603[h]	245	273	1333 (1582-83)	20.5
Obonezhskaia piatina, Nagornaia-polovina	Sept. 1599-March 1600[i]	14	22	2861 (1582-84)	0.8
Shelonskaia piatina	Sept. 1594-March 1595[j]	10	15	1657 (1582-83)	0.9
Shelonskaia piatina	Dec. 1602-July 1603[k]	138	162	1657 (1582-83)	9.8
Votskaia piatina	Sept. 1592-Aug. 1593[l]	23	23	1014 (1582-85)	2.3

a NZKK 1: 1-52.
b NZKK 1: 263-367, 390-476.
c NKK 7108 (= RIB 15 [1895], sect. 3, pt. 2).
d NZKK 1: 237-63.
e NZKK 2: 1-160. This file is not complete for the time listed.
f NZKK 1: 52-80.

g NZKK 1: 80-149.
h NZKK 2: 163-292.
i Egorov, "Otryvki," in LZAK 24(1912): 10-27.
j NZKK 1: 223-28.
k NZKK 2: 293-350. This file is not complete for the time listed.
l NZKK 1: 179-92.

m The figures in this column are determined by calculating what fraction the "N of Sales" column is of a year, and, then, using the monthly percentages of sales of limited service contract slaves (see table 9.12), projecting what the annual rate might have been.

n These data are very imprecise for two reasons: there seems to be no agreement among those who have access to the census materials on how they should be counted; unquestionably, the regional demographics in the period 1592-1603 were different from what they had been in the early 1580s —some areas improved and the population probably increased, others deteriorated and the population unquestionably diminished. The major sources consulted have been A. P. Pronshtein, *Velikii Novgorod v XVI veke* (Khar'kov: Izd-vo Khar'kovskogo Universiteta, 1957), pp. 246-51, and SIE 10: 265; N. Ianitskii, *Ekonomicheskii krizis* (1915), tables 2-10; A. L. Shapiro, ed., AIS-ZR (1974), pp. 70, 95, 116, 171, 194, 242, 247.

sale into slavery for a dozen times and places in that decade. The last column, the percentage of households selling themselves, is based on the assumption that each slave contract was the equivalent of a household that might have been listed in the census. Because of the high number of solitaries who sold themselves, however, one may assume that the average household selling itself into slavery was about half the size of an average census household, and thus it would be fitting to reduce the percentage figures by half to determine the total percentage of the free population that sold itself into slavery every year. Very roughly speaking, then, perhaps 1 percent of the population sold itself into slavery in "normal years" (such as the 1590s), with the figure rising to between 5 and 10 percent in times of extraordinary stress (such as the Great Famine of 1601-3, when the household size rose considerably as far more families with children sought refuge in slavery from starvation).

To try to determine the total percentage of the population that was at any given time in first-generation slavery, one must first recall that perhaps a quarter to a third of all slaves fled and that most of them were never recovered. Then one must calculate the number of years a person who sold himself might expect to live as a slave. If the average adult male was about twenty-five years of age when he sold himself, one might assume that he could look forward to at least fifteen years of enslavement before his death. (Since those "selling" themselves in 1597-98 had already experienced an average of 8.3 years of dependency, it would not seem unreasonable to double that figure for the total period of slavery.) For women and children, the period would even be longer than fifteen years, so that should serve as a suitable lower bound. Multiplying 1% x 2/3 x 15 years, one might assume that at any given time 10 percent of the population was enslaved in the sixteenth century because of self-sale. After the law of 1597 restricting limited service contract slavery to the life of the owner, that percentage would have to be reduced on the assumption that owners often predeceased their slaves; and, in spite of the dependency caused by enslavement, some slaves probably remained free on the death of their owners. When one adds the number of those who sold themselves into slavery to the hereditary slaves and enslaved military captives, it is difficult to imagine that the slave population was much less than 15 percent of the total population in regions of Muscovy where slavery existed. For all of early modern Russia 10 percent would seem to be an absolute lower bound as a portion of the total population that was subject to the laws of slavery. Again, one may assume that a considerable majority of these were household slaves, although the proportion cannot be ascertained.[30]

30. Another approach to figuring the total number of slaves might be to examine total individual holdings. Events such as death and the 1597-98 compulsory registration of all slaves produced such data. More than a dozen wills are extant which list an average of 16.8 slaves apiece, and eight property divisions (apparently when a person died without a will) listed 27.8 slaves apiece. Regrettably, the typicality of these instruments cannot be determined. Moreover, eighteen registrations of all slaves averaged 15.4 apiece. Since slave ownership was

The proportion of the population that was legally enslaved in 1600 was probably greater than it was in 1678 for a number of reasons, the primary of which was serfdom. Serfdom both legally limited the possibilities for self-sale into slavery and realistically reduced the stress that forced people to sell themselves. Moreover, enserfed peasants could be, and sometimes were, forced to farm the lord's demesne, one of the primary functions of agricultural slaves prior to the enserfment. Along with serfdom went the stratification of most of the rest of society, which prevented townsmen and servicemen from abandoning their ascribed social positions. Another factor was the decline of elite slavery, particularly the use of slaves in the army.

If early modern Russia's population consisted of a 10 percent slave element, that would be more than probably has been often assumed but less than the 30 percent of the most well-known slaveowning societies. If the townsmen (*posadskie liudi*) made up only 2 percent of the population, and the various service elements constituted perhaps less then that, the slaves at somewhere in the 10 percent range would be the second largest element, after the peasantry.[31] That relative magnitude is perhaps more significant than the precise percentage of the total population that the slaves constituted. It is not surprising, then, that the law of slavery is such an important part of the legal legacy, or that slaves appear so frequently in other contexts as well.

The Functions of Slavery

The slaves I have just discussed performed many functions in early modern Russia. In a summary of the situation, the interests of three parties are worth considering: the government, the slaveowners, and the slaves themselves. Slavery was a legal institution as defined and enforced by the government, so I shall begin with it. The enduring interest of the government in slavery lay in the fact that it was a source of revenue, something that is true of most slave systems. Government officials were more than earning their keep by writing, registering, witnessing and sealing the paper flow inherent in the quarter of a millennium of Muscovite slavery. Adjudication of disputes over slaveownership, and especially over the property claimed to have been stolen by fugitive slaves, was another not insignificant source of revenue. The central government also derived benefits

---

highly life-cycle determined, these figures presumably represent end-of-career holdings. If the mortality rate of slaveowners were known, one might be able to project these figures to make a larger picture. It might also be possible to work them in with other figures, such as those from random data indicating that owners of full slaves are known to have purchased 4.8 slaves apiece, and limited service contract slaves 3.7 each. The figure of fifteen years has been suggested for the working life of the slaves in Africa (Gemery and Hogendorn, p. 154).

31. The same conclusion has been reached by A. G. Man'kov (*Ulozhenie*, p. 111).

from the supplementation that slaves provided in the administration of the provinces under the feeding (*kormlenie*) system until the 1550s and in augmenting the size of the army. No doubt such slaves were essential while they lasted, but ultimately the Muscovites learned to do without them. In early Muscovy, slaves also served as state secretaries (*d'iaki*) and other officials in the central government while it was still basically at the royal household stage, a situation that also prevailed in antiquity and in many Islamic countries. However, Muscovy interestingly diverged from the Ottoman Empire at this point: Ottoman sources explicitly stated that the absolute power of the ruler was based on his having slaves in his service in the administration and in the army. Muscovite military slaves belonged to individuals, not the sovereign. At the time when slavery was still a central element in Muscovite administration, the sovereign made no claims to absolute power, and the theory of Muscovite autocracy was developed in the first half of the sixteenth century quite independently of slavery and at a time when the administrative relevance of slavery to the central power was waning.[32]

For the slaveowners, early modern Russian slavery served approximately the same broad, general functions it has elsewhere. First, it provided labor, particularly domestic service, but also a small portion of the agricultural labor needed to raise food for the slaveowner and his household. There were no events in Muscovy like the introduction of sugar cane in Barbados in 1640, or the invention of the cotton gin by Eli Whitney in 1793, which stimulated slaveowners in other parts of the world to utilize slaves for the production of commodities for the market, and the Muscovite market remained a very limited one throughout the period. Somewhat paradoxically, or so it at first seems, the less well-to-do members of the middle service class were proportionately more dependent upon their slaves than were magnates, who were adequately endowed with rent-paying peasants and (after, say, 1592) serfs to provide them with more than sufficient income for their service and other needs. The utilization of domestic slaves made it unnecessary for free women to be overtaxed with work, and in fact made it possible for the women of the elite classes to remain in nearly haremlike conditions down to the time when Peter the Great had sufficiently "Westernized" Russia to force such women into public view.

Second, slaves were a source of prestige, a visible manifestation of an individual's disposable income in a society which provided few other such outlets. Land (which had its drawbacks after the promulgation of the universal service requirements in 1556), personal clothing, military gear, and precious objects (very few of them) are about the only other things mentioned, in addition to slaves, in

32. 1497 *Sudebnik* 17, 40-41, 43, and part I of this work; Inalcik, "Servile Labor," p. 25. The problem of the extent to which the autocratic government benefited from the atmosphere of slavery and was able to use the prevailing social attitudes to employ its servitors as "free slaves" rather than having to rely on "enslaved slaves" has been mentioned, but cannot be resolved in this work.

wills. Among the Ottomans, slaves formed the third most important component in the value of estates, following cash and properties.[33] A similar ranking might be appropriate for Muscovy. While Muscovites lacked the resources to wallow in the luxury of the hundreds or even thousands of chattel that so distressed the moralists of the classical world, the wealthiest among them employed slaves as personal servants in numbers lavish by modern standards, shocking to at least some contemporary (1660s) foreigners ("several of the wealthy have whole hordes of slaves of both sexes feeding in their houses"), and probably in excess of what a twentieth-century perspective might calculate as an optimal use of resources, considering the heavy demands always being made on Muscovy's resources.[34] Moreover, judging by the stress in the mid-sixteenth-century *Domostroi* on the necessity for slaveowners to maintain their chattel at an adequate level of nutrition and clothing, we may assume that a number of them were tempted to keep more than their resources could support.[35] This admonition well may have been directed particularly at the small, marginal slaveowner for whom slaveownership was almost certainly more necessary for his psychic well-being than it was for more affluent servicemen and merchants. In Muscovy, as in Byzantium and Danubian Bulgaria, a large retinue of slaves served as the most public manifestation of their owner's wealth; they did not necessarily represent his political influence because, as is known, personal retinues played no role in Muscovite capital politics, and wealth and standing at court were not highly correlated in early modern Russia. The prestige element of slavery is stressed for most systems, ranging from Han, T'ang, and Ch'ing China, to the Comorians and much of the Old South.[36]

The desire of the elite for slaves was never so strongly expressed as in the reign of Tsar Fedor Ivanovich, which certainly was the pinnacle for legislative activity on slavery as well. According to the publicist cellarer of the Trinity Sergiev monastery, Avraamii Palitsyn, writing in the second decade of the seventeenth century:

In the reign of Tsar Fedor, Boris Godunov and many other magnates, not only of his clan but his associates [*bliudomii*] as well, induced many people to serve them as slaves. Some they attracted into their houses with flattery and gifts, not only commoners of outstanding craft ability or extraordinary artistic talent, but people from the most distinguished, ancient families with patrimonial estates, service landholdings, and villages, the most elite sword-bearers and greatest combat fighters, the most handsome and fair in appearance and of prime age. Others were forcibly enslaved because they had been stewards;

33. Inalcik, p. 28.

34. Jones, p. 185; Iakov Reitenfel's, "Skazaniia svetleishemu gertsogu toskanskomu Koz'me tret'emu o Moskovii. Paduia, 1680 g.," *Chteniia* 214 (1905, no. 3): 139.

35. *Domostroi*, p. 26, especially chap. 28.

36. Udal'tsova, p. 13; Brauning, pp. 50, 54; Shepherd in Watson, *Asian*, pp. 84-86; Wiens, p. 299.

force and torture were used to extort slavery contracts in still other instances. The offense of some merely was to drink slightly to excess—three or four tankards were sufficient to convert a person into a slave.[37]

Avraamii's tale is one of a desire for subordinates, for dominance over others, gone berserk, but certainly at other times the desire was only slightly more subdued. Hereditary slaves also helped to serve as social cement, to be given away as part of marriage contracts, dowries, and wills, the transactional documents that served as the ritual linkages between generations and families. Finally, slaves served as a perfect outlet for the exercise of dominance in a society in which, considering the pressures from above, such an outlet was sorely needed by the members of the Muscovite service classes.

For slaves in early modern Russia, the institution often functioned differently than in other systems. For most first-generation slaves throughout world history, the institution served, at least initially, as a form of delay: a delay in execution for military captives or convicted felons, a delay in sacrifice in societies where that form of ritual was practiced, or a delay in cannibalism where slaves might otherwise have been turned into nutritional supplementation. For the typical Muscovite slave, however, the "delay" was from starvation, from dying of want in a society with pre-Carolingian grain yields that increasingly was trying to live in the early modern gunpowder world, a society that had few alms to provide and seems to have been singularly short of all forms of charity. G. P. Fedotov observed that charity, which had been the dominant ethical attitude in Kievan Rus', yielded in Muscovy to an ethics based on fear of God or men.[38] Only after the Time of Troubles were alms houses (*novye bogadel'nye izby*) set up in Novgorod, with an apparent total capacity of seven people—a figure that should be contrasted with the fact that many times that number, even in "normal times," annually sold themselves into slavery.[39] Limited service contract slavery was a stress phenomenon, the Muscovite social response to this universal human phenomenon.[40] A slightly different but perhaps ultimately similar case may have occurred among the Northwest Coast Indians. The comparativist Bernard J. Siegel, presenting the Indian case, noted that "although most chattel slaves are not obtained from the in-group, this is not invariably so. There have been a few cases among the Northwest Coast Indians of commoners of very low socioeconomic status who, for want of prestige, have virtually fallen without the protection of their clan or village."[41] The economic stress of both the Muscovites and Amerindians may have been similar, but, due to the differences in social

37. Avraamii Palitsyn, *Skazanie Avraamiia Palitsyna*, ed. L. V. Cherepnin (Moscow-Leningrad: AN SSSR, 1955), pp. 107, 255.

38. G. P. Fedotov, *Religious Mind*, 1: 389.

39. Gnevushev, *Novgorodskii dvortsovyi prikaz*, p. 134.

40. Gubachev, *Stress*.

41. Siegel, p. 376.

structure of the two societies, perhaps the prestige element was less in Muscovy. Someone who has wandered off a hundred miles has lost contact with his kin, who were far less supportive in Muscovy than in some of the other societies we have noticed. That provision of the means of existence was the primary function of slavery, at least from the slave's point of vew, was recognized by Muscovite legislators, who decreed that any owner who refused to provide the relief that his slave had a right to expect forfeited him: the law of 1602-3, at the time of the Great Famine, laid down the norm for seventeenth-century Muscovy that starving slaves were to be freed, either if the victims complained to the authorities and their owners agreed that they could not feed them, or if the preponderance of evidence supported the slaves' claims.

It is important to notice as well the fact that poverty tends to serve as a social barrier in many places. The difference lies in the nature of the barrier, whether society tries to take it down, ignores it, or, in the Muscovite case, make it permanent. One might compare Muscovy with France and England, where about 5 percent of the population at any given time needed welfare.[42] That percentage may be not too remote from the figure for those who needed welfare in Muscovy. As we know, definitions of "need" vary widely, and the fact that welfare exists probably increases the need. The French solution was to try to tide people over a crisis, the Muscovite was to turn them into chattel. Another; and perhaps less useful comparison, is between the attitudes of those with surplus in the U.S. South and in Muscovy. In the former case, the planting aristocracy considered it their social obligation to assist paupers, orphans and the physically and mentally afflicted. In Louisiana, planters supported great charities and relief associations.[43] In Muscovy, on the other hand, there were no private associations, and the only obligations wealthy estate owners recognized at times of food crises was to hold as much grain off the market as possible in order further to inflate the price, and then to purchase some of the social casualties as chattel. The market behavior of those with surplus grain was detailed by Boris Godunov in his famous edict of November 3, 1601, which attempted to cope with the first year of the 1601-3 famine; the response of landholders to the plight of the populace is evident in the dramatic increase in purchases of slaves during those years.[44] It is difficult to imagine that the hoarders and slave purchasers did not overlap, for those lords without sufficient grain dismissed their slaves, and it is even harder to conceive of someone buying slaves without the means to feed

42. Natalie Zemon Davis, *Society and Culture in Early Modern France* (Stanford: Stanford University Press, 1975), pp. 48, 63.

43. Rosser Taylor, "The Gentry of Antebellum South Carolina," *North Carolina Historical Review* 17(April 1940): 119; Roger Shugg, *Origins of Class Struggle in Louisiana* (Baton Rouge: LSUP, 1939), p. 59.

44. Grigorii Khilkov, *Sbornik Kniazia Khilkova* (St. Petersburg: Tip. br. Panteleevykh, 1879), pp. 165-71, no. 62.

them. (While the slave may, or may not, have gotten the money listed as his price, the officials who registered the documents had to be paid their fees.)

It is noteworthy that the type of person selling himself into ordinary limited service contract slavery hardly differed, whether it was the worst of times (such as 1603) or some other time. The major difference was that, in the worst of times, the number of persons selling themselves increased vastly, a few minors (orphans under fifteen) were present, and the proportion of families increased. The nature of the stress felt by the person who was a candidate to sell himself did not vary much from times that were for society at large "good" to times of total social disaster. The only other society in which the welfare element of slavery may have been as strong as in Muscovy was that of India, where the British Parliamentary Papers of 1841 noted that "Slavery may be regarded as the Indian Poor Law and preventive of infanticide."[45] The term "welfare" has also been applied, without much elucidation, to Kerebe slavery (south of Lake Victoria) prior to 1800.[46]

Other societies had provisions for the destitute to sell themselves into slavery, but I am not aware that any of them were as harsh as the Muscovite system, nor did they embrace as many people. The Law of Leviticus allowed Hebrews (nomads) to sell themselves, but prescribed that they were not fully slaves and that they had to be manumitted shortly. Genuine slavery was to be reserved for "the heathen that are around about you." If impoverished Jews sold themselves to "a sojourner or stranger," they had the right to redeem themselves or members of their clan could redeem them; failing that, the slave would be manumitted automatically by working off the debt. (This is comparable to the Russian "debt slave," a category quite distinct from limited service contract slavery.) Or, in sixteenth-century Genoa, the homeless poor sold themselves as galley slaves every winter.[47] Their purchasers freed them in the spring, rather than keep them in perpetual slavery, as was the practice of the Muscovites. Hugo Grotius found nothing shocking about an exchange of bondage for a perpetual certainty of food. But he was talking about the selling of children (who are still "marginal" individuals in adult society) by their parents, not self-sale by the latter.[48]

Why the Muscovites did not invent in the sixteenth century a short-term solution to the problem of stress is an interesting question, but unfortunately no definitive answer is available. Certainly that is what limited service contract slavery was supposed to do when it appeared late in the fifteenth century, but it was overwhelmed by the older tradition of full slavery, and the fact that those who took the year-length loans simply lacked the resources to repay them.

45. Dharma Kumar, *Land and Caste in South India* (Cambridge: Cambridge University Press, 1965), p. 48.
46. Miers and Kopytoff, p. 281.
47. Leviticus 5: 39-55; Braudel, *Capitalism*, p. 205.
48. D. B. Davis, *Western Culture*, p. 115.

Also striking is the high degree of individualism inherent in the Muscovite's selling himself into slavery. In Muscovy, everybody was on his own. In Africa, we have noted the kin institution of pawnage. Another possibility, in worse times, was exhibited by the Margi of Nigeria. Under conditions of severe deprivation, such as a famine, villages sold some of their members into slavery in exchange for food for the rest of them.[49] To my knowledge, no such development ever occurred in Muscovy. Or, the Igbo of Nigeria sometimes sold their own relatives into slavery for reasons such as delinquency or abnormality (recidivist boys and debtors, abnormal children), but these business transactions had to be preceded by a ritual that separated the slave-to-be from his lineage, and the perspective slave's agnates and his mother's agnates had to agree to the separation.[50] I am aware of no such rituals in Muscovy, where the slave-to-be (whether he be a full slave, limited service contract slave, or a debt slave) had to walk into marginality by himself.

Slavery proved to be so debilitating that its dependency was inescapable for many. Take the case of the brothers Mishka and Efimko Zakhar'ev, slaves of Grigorii Chiurkin. After their owner was killed in action, they remained with his wife. She remarried one Mikita Kalitin, who detained them against their will and took them to Ivangorod. In August of 1622 they fled from Kalitin, and sought refuge with another slaveowner, Ivan Tyrkov.[51] Apparently they fled from Kalitin because he had abused them, certainly not because they wanted to live on their own as free men. Early modern Russian slavery was so coercive psychologically and so seductive physiologically that it was unnecessary to have special terms or legal status for freedmen. Those who in other societies would have been freedmen were welcomed back into slavery with open arms in Muscovy.

Slavery provided not only welfare relief, but also was an avenue of escape from other undesired aspects of early modern Russia. It provided escape from military sevice, particularly for members of the middle service class. It also provided escape from taxation (as in most other societies) and from other government-imposed obligations (as it did not in some other societies).

The End of Slavery

Slavery has been ended by violence, by relatively abrupt legislative fiat, and by a process of gradual evolution. Muscovy chose the last route, and the similarities in the abolition of slavery there and in the Roman Empire are striking. Rome enjoyed a great infusion of slaves in the first century B.C., and then, because of the expansion of the empire, which reduced the number of captives, consumed a

49. Miers and Kopytoff, p. 92.
50. Ibid., p. 125.
51. RIB 38 (1926): 470.

greatly diminished number at much higher prices during its remaining centuries.. In the three centuries after the death of Jesus the conditions of the slaves gradually improved and evolved into serfdom. The reasons for this evolution are many, but most deserving of mention is the fact that the diminished supply of slaves coincided with the disintegration of the olive-oil- and wine-producing plantations of southern Italy in the face of competition from Spain, Gaul, and North Africa; wheat, less suitable for cultivation by slaves, appeared in the old olive groves and vineyards. Simultaneously, in the first three centuries A.D. law and practice lowered the legal and economic status of the free peasants and tradesmen toward that held by slaves. By the third and fourth centuries Rome was suffering a labor and cash shortage, the free agriculturalists were converted by legislative fiat into coloni bound to the land, and slaves increasingly were converted into taxpayers.[52]

The early modern Russians also witnessed a conversion of peasant and slave status in the new institution of serfdom, although not for precisely similar reasons. The Roman government was becoming weaker and more decentralized in the third and fourth centuries, while the Russian government was becoming stronger and more centralized in the period between, say, 1590 and 1725. Russia did, however, suffer from perceived population shortages, a growing appetite for taxes, and the need for military manpower. These were the major causes of the rise of serfdom and the demise of slavery.

In the land immediately to the west of Muscovy slavery died out or was abolished considerably earlier than it came to an end there. In all cases the institution seems to have merged with serfdom, as it did in Russia. Of the countries west of Russia, Poland was the first to witness the abolition of slavery. In the late Middle Ages, by the fifteenth century, the sale and purchase of slaves within the boundaries of the Polish state was forbidden. Slavery disappeared in Latvia at the end of the fifteenth century with the development of serfdom. In Lithuania, at the same time, slaves began to be given small plots of land, and by the first half of the sixteenth century the institution was dying out. It was abolished formally in the *Lithuanian Statute* of 1588.[53] As far as can be determined, the demise of slavery in those countries had no impact on its collapse in Russia, which was due to internal developments.

Slavery always was in a state of evolution in Muscovy. When one variety was done with, another arose to take its place. Full slavery was replaced by limited

---

52. Westermann, pp. 114-15, 133, 141-42; Udal'tsova, pp. 15-16. Serfdom also came to take the place of slavery in medieval Germany (Wergeland, p. xiii).

53. Kazimierz Tymieniecki, "Zagadnienie niewoli w Polsce," p. 522; idem, "Niewolni," p. 148. (I am indebted to Peter Bowman Brown for providing me with this information.) Gudavichius and Lazutka, "Protsess zakreposhcheniia krest'ianstva Litvy i Litovksii statut 1529 goda," *Istoriia SSSR* (1970, no. 3), pp. 82-90; 1588 LS 12: 21 (Lappo, p. 360); MS, p. 287. War captives could still be enslaved, but they and their children had to be settled on estates as peasants.

service contract slavery, which between 1586 and 1597 changed from a limitation of one year on the initial loan before default and perpetual slavery to a limitation based on the life of the owner. Hereditary slavery seems to have yielded to limited service contract slavery in the seventeenth century, and limitations at various times were also placed on enslavement of foreigners stemming from military captivity.[54] However, slavery was extraordinarily tenacious, and half-hearted measures were inadequate to do away with it. The 1586-97 measures may have been the result of concern over the perpetual enslavement of natives, but even there an interest in tax revenues may have been paramount.

Unquestionably the interests of the fisc were uppermost in the minds of pre-Petrine legislators who moved against the institution of slavery. Russians in the third quarter of the seventeenth century discovered two ways to escape the tax collector. Earlier, when tax levies had been based on tilled acreage, they reduced tillage. That was harmful to the national interest, so the government in the second quarter of the seventeenth century began to move in the direction of taxing not landed area but households (as was the practice in urban areas already). The Russians responded by cramming many people into one household, creating the extended family. Serf farmers and their lords also tried to cheat the tax collector by claiming that the former were slaves. Coping with both tax dodges fundamentally meant the abolition of slavery.

Seeing that farming peasants were calling themselves slaves, the government in a law of September 2, 1679, decreed that all such individuals (*zadvornye liudi*) were to be placed on the tax roles. This edict seems to have been issued in response to preliminary reports from the 1678 census.[55] In any event, after 1679, slaves living outside their owners' households and yards (*dvory*), in their own, separate yards, were to be included in the taxed population equally with the peasants.[56] There was some tradition for taxing slaves engaged in agriculture. The reform at the end of the 1670s, which insisted that all slaves who farmed like peasants be taxed, was the beginning of a strenuous attempt to differentiate slaves who had income from those who did not, and to enter the former on the tax rolls. In 1686, article 7 of the instructions to the census-takers again told them that slaves (*zadvornye, delovye,* and *kabal'nye liudi*) living outside their owners' households were to be included in the cadastres.[57] Statistical evidence from the late Petrine era indicates that these measures were successful, that less than 10 percent of the slaves at that time were engaged in agriculture.[58]

54. Iakovlev, *Kholopstvo*, pp. 401-13.

55. V. N. Sedashev, *Ocherki i materialy po istorii zemlevladeniia Moskovskoi Rusi*, p. 209; AAE 4: 336-37, no. 243; Veselovskii, *Soshnoe pis'mo*, 2: 254; M. A. D'iakonov, *Ocherki iz istorii sel'skogo naseleniia v Moskovskom gosudarstve (XVI–XVII vv.)* (St. Petersburg, 1898), p. 142. [=LZAK 12 (1901).]

56. Tikhonov, *Pomeshchich'i krest'iane*, p. 100.

57. PSZ 2: 746-47, no. 1169.

58. Anisimov, "Izmeneniia," pp. 39-40.

It should be noted that the status of farming slaves was not formally abolished, so that when Peter the Great decided to quarter the army on the peasantry, a census was taken in 1719 to determine the country's resources; it listed peasants, landless peasants (*bobyli*), and slaves farming their own arable (*zadvornye* and *delovye liudi*). Slaves (*delovye liudi*) who did not have their own arable but farmed for their lords were also to be enumerated, but separately. This was the beginning of the soul-tax census, which was to include all males, from those just born to the very oldest, and to list their ages.[59]

The effective abolition of household slavery by the conversion of such individuals into house serfs seems to have come about as an afterthought. In January of 1720 Peter surmised (correctly) that potential taxpayers were being concealed as house slaves, and so he ordered that *dvorovye liudi* also be counted in the census.[60] Two years later, on February 5, 1722, Peter again announced that landholders were to be informed that they were responsible for paying the soul tax (80 kopeks) for every male peasant and slave (*dvorovye* and *delovye liudi*; *liudi vsiakogo zvaniia*).[61] On June 1, 1722, however, a Senate decree announced a retreat from this principle of universal male taxation by stating that those who did not farm, but lived in someone's household by either a cash or grain grant, did not have to pay taxes (the *raspolozhenie na polki*).[62] The attempt to differentiate those who had income from those who did not was perceived to be open to abuse, for while cooks and coachmen were totally dependent on their owners and had no independent access to income, artisans and petty traders who also lived in their owners' households did have such income.[63] The dilemma was finally resolved in a Senate decree (article 8) of January 9, 1723, (confirmed by Peter on January 19) which prescribed that the soul tax was to be collected from all slaves, regardless of their status or income.[64] Peter himself, commenting on article 8, noted that this eternally equated house slaves (*dvorovye liudi*) with peasants.[65] The measure both placed a tax on slaveownership and formally put an end to the tax-exempt aspect of slavery by converting all house slaves into taxable house serfs. The inclusion of house slaves on the tax rolls as house serfs effectively meant the end of slavery, although the institution was never formally

59. PSZ 5: 618-19, no. 3287.
60. PSZ 6: 1, no. 3481.
61. PSZ 6: 505-6, no. 3901.
62. PSZ 6: 717, no. 4026.
63. Anisimov, "Izmeneniia," pp. 36, 38.
64. PSZ 7: 2-6, no. 4139, particularly art. 8; PSZ 7: 11, no. 4145.
65. Anisimov, "Izmeneniia," p. 50. Peter's action might be compared with that of the Chinese Yung-cheng emperor, who in two decrees of 1727 and 1728 emancipated the slaves by redesignating them as no longer "base people," but "free people" (Wiens, p. 338). The Chinese acts, which proved not to be definitive, were in response to extensive revolts, whereas the Russians responded to military needs. (The Chinese abolished slavery again on January 31, 1910 [Meijer, p. 345].) I am indebted to Ann Waltner for referring me to the articles by Wiens and Meijer.

abolished, to my knowledge, and, was referred to even after the reign of Peter the Great. It is fair to say, however, that by 1723 slavery had quite thoroughly been merged into serfdom and effectively abolished.

By the 1720s the cadre of house slaves already had been significantly reduced by recruitment into the army. That violation of the sanctity of private property was relatively new, for slaves who served in the army prior to 1632 usually remained the private property of their owners, reflecting the government's extraordinary reluctance to demand anything of privately owned slaves. That reluctance was overcome during the Thirteen Years War, when Kotoshikhin noted that slaves were drafted as infantry soldiers for the new formation regiments.[66] In chapter 15 I have already discussed military service as an avenue to freedom, and here shall only mention a few of the highpoints of the Petrine era. The Northern War and the initial defeats by the Swedes dissolved whatever inhibitions remained about recruiting slaves into the army, as military planners acted to diminish a perceived shortage of manpower. At first slaves were allowed to volunteer for military service, but soon they were drafted. The many calls made on the slave manpower pool must have played a major role in preparing for the abolition of the institution by greatly reducing the numbers affected when slaves were added to the soul-tax rolls.

Beginning leisurely, on February 1, 1700, over nine months before the humiliating defeat at Narva, Peter announced that owners who wanted to free their slaves should bring their chattel with the papers to the Slavery Chancellery, which was to send them to the Preobrazhenskii Chancellery for possible recruitment as infantry. If the freedmen were found unfit for infantry service, they were free to sell themselves again to whomever they desired. Typically, no assumption was made that they might like to pursue a free existence.[67] Three years later, this decree was extended to slaves freed because of the death of their owners, and service in the navy was added to that in the infantry. In February of 1705 Peter decreed that those slaves freed on their owners' death were to be brought to the Moscow Judicial Chancellery for registration. Wives, children, and executors of the deceased did not need to manumit such slaves or give them manumission documents because they were freed automatically. Heirs of slaveowners were not to keep those freedmen, as often happened, without written authorization from the Moscow Judicial Chancellery. Disgrace and other sanctions were provided for violators.[68] These measures persisted to the end of Peter's reign and meant that it was difficult for freedmen to sell themselves back into slavery; this put an end to the dependency cycle that was crucial to the perpetuation of early modern Russian slavery. The measures were enforced by the imposition of stiff fines on owners who manumitted their slaves in violation of

66. Kotoshikhin, p. 133.
67. PSZ 4: 3, no. 1747; Anisimov, "Izmeneniia," p. 48.
68. PSZ 4: 209-10, 291, nos. 1923, 2035.

the statutes and on those who took in freedmen who had not been considered for military service.[69]

At the same time the government began to allow slaves to volunteer for military service. After Narva, on December 3, 1700, the Preobrazhenskii Chancellery announced that fugitive slaves who had not committed any crime other than to flee from slavery might remain enlisted in the infantry. (Fugitive serfs were to be returned to their lords, a rare divergence in the treatment of the two categories.)[70] By any definition, this was a historic decree, for it meant that any able-bodied slave could find freedom in the army. Often service in the army was tantamount to a death sentence, but that fact almost certainly was unknown to an abused slave or to an owner abusing him. The December 3 decree must have put master-slave relations in a different perspective. The right of slaves to enlist in the army was recognized again in 1702, but kitchen help (*povary, prispeshniki,* and *khlebniki*) were excluded.[71] One may assume that this reflected a government recognition that preparing the food for the owner's family was the most essential slave occupation, and slaves who performed other functions could be dispensed with.

As the manpower crisis worsened while the war continued to go badly, in October of 1703 the Chancellery of Military Affairs required all servicemen and merchants who owned slaves to list them all with the chancellery, and then to produce for inspection every fifth household slave (*dvorovoi*) and every seventh production slave (*delovoi*). Those brought in for the physical, preliminary to being drafted, had to be between the ages of twenty and thirty and of sound mind and body. Tatars, Kalmyks, Poles, and Swedes had to be inventoried but not brought in for the draft. The death penalty was provided for failure to comply with the edict. Allowing slaves to enlist in the army, and then drafting them, was important for the success of Petrine arms in the Northern War, and especially in the early years. Peter's regular army depended to a significant extent on slave "voluteers" until the introduction of massive recruitment in 1705, for a law of 1699 had categorically forbidden the sending of peasants into the army. A decree of February 4, 1707, made further inroads into the slave population by mandating that every fifth house slave be presented for induction from households headed by retired servicemen, widows, minor males, and unwed girls. Nothing was stated about households that did not have at least five house slaves.[72] A year later, in March of 1708, another order was issued requiring all slaveowners to submit lists of all their house slaves, and, under the threat of the death penalty for noncompliance, required that they bring them all to the Preobrazhenskii Chancellery. If a slaveowner of the upper ranks pretended to be out of town

69. PSZ 7: 5, 10, 128, nos. 4139, art. 16, 4145, 4318.
70. PSZ 4: 92, no. 1820.
71. PSZ 4: 196-97, no. 1912.
72. PSZ 4: 225-26, 369, nos. 1944, 2138; Anisimov, p. 43.

and therefore unable to comply, but was discovered to be concealing his slaves thereby, he was to be fined; if of the lower ranks, he was to be cruelly punished without mercy. By 1711, 158,000 slaves had been given military physicals, and 139,000 of them were conscripted.[73] The 1703 measure was repeated in 1715, with slight changes. Cooks were subject to registration, but stewards (? *pervye slugi*) were exempt. All slaves over the age of ten were to be presented for inspection, and 2,000 were to be drafted from those aged thirteen to twenty.[74] These requirements, motivated by military necessity, undermined slaveownership and almost certainly must have helped to prepare the way for its abolition. The replacement of the mystique of bow-and-arrow cavalry by the reality of mass slaughter in gunpowder warfare made the ordinary slave eligible for manumission into the status of rank-and-file infantryman. Whether this reflected a changed image of the slave is somewhat doubtful, for the status of cannon fodder in the early modern world was not very elevated.[75]

How many slaves were freed by these measures is unknown, but large numbers must have been involved, judging by the fact that in the 1720-21 inventory of 2,245 military officers in the Russian Empire, 157 (7 percent) of them were freedmen. Only 1 of the 157 had been in the army as a slave prior to being manumitted and joining the regular army, and only 4 of the 157 had enlisted prior to 1700. An astonishing two-thirds of the 157 had joined the army in response to the call of 1700. Almost 60 percent of the freedmen officers had enlisted voluntarily, the rest were sent by their owners to meet draft calls. By 1720-21, the average freedman-officer had served 19.5 years, with the range from 16 to 24 years. Over 90 percent of them served in the infantry (57 percent of all officers were in the infantry), and literacy seems to have been one of the advantages that the slaves who became officers possessed. Others were promoted for the performance of meritorious feats. One freedman achieved the position of quartermaster, another the staff officer position of *podpolkovnik*. The others held senior officer ranks of *kapitan, poruchik, podporuchik,* and *praporshchik*. The nationality of the freedmen is unknown, but not all of them were Russians. D. Tatarinov had been a Black Tork taken captive on the Terek, *podpolkovnik* G. L. Baskakov was of Tatar origin.[76] Such mobility was typical of the Petrine era.

Those who sold themselves into slavery were primarily single males of prime draft age. Many of them married with the passage of time, but such slaves were still a ready pool of military manpower. The recruiting and drafting of slaves

---

73. PSZ 4: 403, no. 2190; Anisimov, p. 44. The 19,000 rejects were sent home because legally they were peasants, not slaves.

74. PSZ 5: 179-80, no. 2944.

75. Corvisier, *Armies*, pp. 44-46, 129.

76. M. D. Rabinovich, "Sosial'noe proiskhozhdenie i imushchestvennoe polozhenie ofitserov reguliarnoi russkoi armii v kontse Servernoi voiny," in *Rossiia v period reform Petra I*, ed. N. I. Pavlenko et al. (Moscow: Nauka, 1973), pp. 150-54.

may well have reduced their numbers in the prime-age male cohort by one-half to three-quarters. The fact that the census-takers in 1719-20 found 6.9 percent of the population of Kozel'sk province to be slaves, and in 1720 counted 11.5 percent of those in Meshchovsk, Mosal'sk, Kaluga, Medyn, Borovsk, Vereia, and Peremyshl' provinces as slaves, must be discounted to some extent and explained as a joint effort by serfs and their owners to reduce their tax liabilities.[77] That, basically, was Peter's appreciation of such figures, but the only way to be sure would be to compare those data in the archives with the demographic data of chapter 13.

In March of 1721 the government returned to the problem of fugitives who had enlisted in the army, and reaffirmed a March 1700 decree permitting them to remain in the infantry. They were also allowed to claim their wives and their children under twelve. Exceptions were made for those who had committed a crime, or whose owners had taught them seamanship: they were to be returned to their owners and to slavery. Peter went on to say that any slave could enlist in the infantry or navy at any time.[78] In March of 1722 a contradiction was perceived between allowing free enlistment of slaves in military service and their inclusion in the soul-tax rolls. It was noted that continuing the right of such individuals to enroll in the army or navy would throw confusion into the collective accounting for taxes and the quartering of troops. Consequently, the government repealed the right of such taxpayers voluntarily to join the army or navy.[79] This measure was possible because of Russia's victory in the Northern War. Nevertheless, there was much discussion of this problem in government circles in 1722, and ultimately the issue was resolved in favor of the armed forces: slaves were allowed to enlist in spite of the trouble it caused for the tax system. However, after Peter's death, in 1726, slaves were no longer permitted to volunteer for army service, because of the burden such enrollments placed on the remaining taxpayers; slaves were to be drafted like peasants. No longer could a slave escape his status; the last loophole that had permitted exit from slave status was closed.[80] The slave was converted into a serf.

The government still recognized that certain people were slaves at the end of the Petrine era, although it is not clear that, de jure, there was much difference between them and serfs. For example, on April 6, 1722, the government linked fugitive slaves and serfs who were apprehended but would not reveal their owners. They were to be resettled in St. Petersburg, and if their owners were discovered the fugitives were not to be returned and the owners were to be compensated with a cash payment.[81] In 1741 a lieutenant in Simbirsk province spoke the dreaded "sovereign's words" (*gosudarevo slovo*), which initiated a treason

77. Anisimov, pp. 39-40.
78. PSZ 6: 367-68, no. 3754.
79. PSZ 6: 518, no. 3923.
80. Anisimov, pp. 49-50.
81. PSZ 6: 640, no. 3939.

trial, "to prevent himself and members of his family from being enslaved as *kholopy*."[82] I have no other information about this incident, but it does indicate that the memory (and perhaps even the reality in some limited form) of slavery persisted after the basic extinction of the institution at the end of Peter's reign.

The demise of slavery in Russia was linked with the rise of serfdom, and particularly with the need of the state for tax revenues and military manpower. That is, however, basically a description of what happened, not an analysis of the factors that permitted the institution of slavery to die. Slavery fulfilled certain functions in early modern Russia, and either those functions no longer had to be performed or some other institution had to fulfill them in order for the government to be able to do away with the ancient institution.

Assuming that slavery performed essential functions for the government, the slaveowners, and the slaves, I shall examine briefly those changes that permitted the demise of the formal institution of slavery. Following the order of this functional discussion, I shall begin with the government. By the Petrine period, officialdom had found many other sources of revenue, and the sums collected from registering slaves and adjudicating ownership disputes paled in comparison with the many different forms of direct and indirect taxes and imposts that supported the state. In the military sphere, the new formation regiments of the seventeenth century and then the Petrine regular army showed that adequate manpower could be raised without using slave combatants.

The interests of the slaveowners must also be considered. Obviously they were offered appropriate substitutes, for no resistance on their part to the abolition of slavery is noted, other than fraudulent transfers of farming slaves to the status of house slaves, and then house slaves with income to the status of house slaves living on doles from their owners. For the owners, serfdom seems to have been an adequate, even generous, substitute for slavery. House serfs provided domestic service, status elevation, and objects for the exercise of social dominance. Agricultural serfs bound to land that was increasingly heritable provided the social cement in marriage contracts, dowries, and wills that the old slaves had once provided. The ease of Russian transition to other forms of exploitation is similar to that found in the Roman Empire, India, parts of Africa, the American South, and elsewhere.

Here again, the interests of the slaves demand the most consideration, for they "voluntarily" made early modern Russian slavery the unusual institution that it was.

Considering the primary function of slavery in Muscovy, one should not be surprised that it was abolished at a time when substitutes had been created. Over a century after Jean Bodin (1530-96) praised the wise legislator who could antici-

---

82. John L. H. Keep, "The Secret Chancellery, the Guards and the Dynastic Crisis of 1740-1741," *Forschungen zur osteuropäischen Geschichte* 25(1978): 184, n. 84.

pate problems and who would destroy a possible source of bondage by providing public houses where the poor could learn useful trades, Moscow opened its first almshouse.[83] In 1723, the government prescribed that freedmen who were unfit for military service and were so unsuitable for work that no one would employ them were to be registered in the almshouses.[84] A new consciousness of the need for public assistance was expressed during the Thirteen Years War, when the government required monasteries to maintain wounded soldiers who could not serve anymore and had no resources of their own, a measure that presumably applied primarily to the nonlanded elements of the new formation regiments.[85] Later in the eighteenth century still other welfare measures were enacted.[86]

The major developments enabling the abolition of slavery involved cutting off the sources of those who could sell themselves into slavery while simultaneously providing fundamentally compulsory support for those who in previous times would have sold themselves. Certainly the former could not have been effected independently of the latter.

By the Petrine era the stratification of Russian society had cut off most sources of recruits into slavery from outside the institution itself. In 1700 the government decreed that there were no "free" (vol'nye) people left, and unattached "wanderers" (guliashchie) had gradually disappeared as a consequence of everyone's being bound to one of the legal estates (peasant-serfs, townsmen, servicemen, clergy). Peter the Great rejoiced, noting that the state could not benefit from people who rendered no service, from whom only felonious behavior could be expected.[87] The consequence of this development was increasingly to restrict new enslavements to freedmen. The enlistment of so many slaves in the army during the first two decades of the eighteenth century greatly reduced this pool.

83. N. Z. Davis, pp. 113-14. A special Chancellery for the Construction of Almshouses existed in the decade 1670-80. At the time, there were seven or eight royal almshouses in Moscow with a capacity of 410 people (A. E. Ianovskii, "Bogadel'nia," *Entsiklopedicheskii slovar'* 4[1893]: 142). Almshouses also were built in provincial Muscovy in the second half of the seventeenth century. A census of 1669 noted that Prince Ofonasii Ivanovich Lobanov-Rostovskii was supporting an almshouse consisting of ten separate houses in Iaroslavl'. By the end of the century, there were a dozen almshouses in Iaroslavl', seven of which were of stone. Maintained by private donations, they must have had a capacity of from 250 to 500 persons (V. Lestnitsyn, "Iaroslavskie bogodel'ni v XVII i XVIII stoletiiakh," *Iaroslavskie gubernskie vedomosti* [1873, no. 1]: 12-13; *Trudy Iaroslavskoi uchenoi arkhivnoi komissii* 6, no. 3-4 [1913]: 281).

84. PSZ 7: 127-29, 139-41, nos. 4318, 4335.

85. Kotoshikhin, p. 138.

86. David L. Ransel, "Abandonment and Fosterage of Unwanted Children: The Women of the Foundling System," in his *The Family in Imperial Russia*, pp. 189-217; Alexander, *Bubonic Plague*, pp. 46, 94-95, 271, 277-78; J. Michael Hittle, *The Service City. State and Townsmen in Russia, 1600-1800* (Cambridge: Harvard University Press, 1979), pp. 123, 130, 142, 207.

87. Anisimov, p. 43.

The major factor permitting the abolition of slavery was the creation of the extended family by the Russians in an attempt to reduce the tax burden, as the government moved from a tax on sown area (and presumed equivalents in urban areas) to a household tax. Evidence of such a change in the seventeenth century is overwhelming, and so is the consequence of that development. Those who sold themselves into slavery, almost without exception, were from nuclear families, and there is only incidental evidence that slaves ever came from extended families. The same picture prevailed throughout Russia prior to 1646-48. In the Novgorod area around 1500 in one count there were 882 taxable males in 788 households.[88] The old and the new censuses taken in the Novgorod region at that time revealed 1.13 and 1.08 taxable males per household, respectively.[89] The same ratios prevailed throughout the sixteenth century in the Russian northwest area.[90] Similar signs of nuclear families predominated throughout central Russia in most of the first half of the seventeenth century. On *boyarin* F. I. Sheremetev's estate in Galich province in 1619 there were 346 males in 146 households. On one of I. N. Romanov's southern estates in 1628, there were 86 adult males in 86 households.[91] The Soviet historian of the seignorial peasantry, Iu. A. Tikhonov, counted 2.4 males per household prior to 1645, 3.3 in the years 1649-79, and 4.6 in the period 1680-1725.[92] Iu. V. Got'e found 1.7 males per household in the 1620-30s, and 4.0 in 1678, for the heartland region of Russia.[93] Along the southern frontier there were 2.6 males per household in 1646, 4.5 in 1678.[94] In the north, in Kevrol'sk province, there were less than an average of 2 males per household in 1623, but nearly 4 in 1686.[95] In the 1678-79 census, there were an average of 3.43 males per household in peasant households on church lands, 4.0 on lay seignorial lands.[96] While churchmen may have lagged behind in informing peasants of the advantages of larger households, they apparently made every effort to catch up. Thus, in one 1693 count, there were 239 males in 50 households, or nearly 4.8 apiece.[97] Such examples could be multiplied many times.

88. A. S. Khoroshev, "Ekonomicheskoe polozhenie prikhodskikh tserkvei v Novgorode Velikom," in *Russkii gorod. (Issledovaniia i materialy)* 2(Moscow: Moskovskii gos. universitet, 1979): 230.

89. AIS-ZR (1971), pp. 323-25.

90. AIS-ZR (1974), pp. 118, 185.

91. Iurii V. Arsen'ev, "Blizhnii boiarin kniaz' Nikita Ivanovich Odoevskii i ego perepiska s galitskoiu otchinoi (1650-1684)," *Chteniia* 205(1903, bk. 2), pt. 1, p. 129; Stashevskii, "K istorii kolonizatsii Iuga," col. 289.

92. Tikhonov, *Pomeshchich'i krest'iane*, pp. 99.

93. Iu. V. Got'e, *Zamoskovnyi krai v XVII veke* (Moscow: Sotsekgiz, 1937), p. 60.

94. Vazhinskii, *Zemlevladenie*, p. 54.

95. P. I. Ivanov, "Zametka o razmere okladnoi pashni i naselennosti dvorov v Kevrol'skom uezde XVII v.," *Drevnosti. Trudy arkheograficheskoi kommissii imp. Moskovskogo Arkheologicheskogo obshchestva* 2, pt. 1 (1900): 156-58.

96. N. M. Shepukova, "K voprosu ob itogakh podvornoi perepisi 1678-1679 gg. v Rossiiskom gosudarstve," *Istoriia SSSR* 4, no. 3 (May-June 1960): 146.

97. Gorskaia, *Monastyrskie krest'iane*, p. 45.

Thus was born the famous Russian extended household. The immediate impact was to remove solitaries from the scene, for few could afford to live by themselves and pay the household tax.[98] The household tax also made it unlikely that married couples or single-parents would find it economical to live by themselves. All of these people crowded in with others to escape the tax collector.

The government was not blind to the impact of the household tax, which is why the soul tax was introduced in 1719. Naturally, the question arises as to why the extended family outlasted the household tax. The answer seems to be twofold. First, taxes were assessed not on individuals but on a collective. The assessment of collective taxes resulted in the creation of the commune, which discovered that its members were much better able to pay their obligations when they were crowded together in extended households. The logic is simple: basic expenditures on housing and fuel were considerably reduced when 8 to 10 people lived in each house, rather than the pre-1647 norm of less than 4. This increased the per capita disposable income that could be paid in taxes. The serfowners made the same discovery, and added to the compulsion that preserved the extended family. The serfowners also made other discoveries about the utility of "the family." They forced all kinds of marriage alliances that never would have been made had serfs been left to their own devices.[99] They forced orphans, who in the pre-serf era would have become beggars or tried to sell themselves into slavery, to live with lateral relatives and nonrelated persons. The rise in the "welfare component" of serfdom is evident in the peasant household composition of Shelonskaia piatina as it changed between 1646 and 1678. In 1646, 4.7 percent of all households (N = 3,108, with 10,173 males) contained nonrelated persons. In 1678 that figure rose to 7.3 percent (N = 4,153, with 18,007 males). (The increase in mean household size from 3.3 males to 4.3 males should be noted as well.)[100] Thus the serfowners invented elastic household boundaries to overcome severe deprivation that the traditional Russian small nuclear family was unable to do independently.[101]

As should be obvious, all of these measures greatly reduced both the number of persons who might be needing the type of welfare that had been provided

---

98. For an analysis of such families, see E. N. Baklanova, "Perepisnaia kniga 1717 g. kak istochnik po istorii kres'ianskoi sem'i v Vologodskom uezde," in *Materialy po istorii evropeiskogo severa SSSR* (=*Severnyi arkheograficheskii sbornik*, vyp. 1) (Vologda, 1970), pp. 170-81. See also Peter Czap, Jr., "Marriage and the Peasant Joint Family in the Era of Serfdom," in Ransel, *The Family in Imperial Russia*, pp. 103-23.

99. Czap, "Marriage," p. 109.

100. Andrejs Plankans, "Parentless Children in the Soul Revisions: A Study of Methodology and Social Fact," in Ransel, *The Family*, p. 101; V. M. Vorob'ev and A. Ia. Degtiarev, "Osnovnye cherty razvitiia sel'skogo rasseleniia na Severo-Zapade Rusi v XVI–XVII vekakh," *Istoriia SSSR* (1980, no. 5): 177-78.

101. The terminology is from Herbert G. Gutman, *The Black Family in Slavery and Freedom, 1750-1925* (New York: Pantheon, 1976), p. 468.

by slavery as well as the very causes of that need. They were also probably responsible for the feeble development of indentured slavery after the introduction of the household tax in the mid-seventeenth century, for it began to be used just at the time when such relief assistance was beginning to be unneeded. As noted in the discussion in chapter 12 of Siberian population statistics for the Petrine era, serfdom and the extended family also probably combined to reduce female infanticide.

Another by-product of serfdom was that serfowners helped out the extended family and the commune with their grain reserves. Lords had kept grain reserves earlier but had selfishly used them to drive up prices during periods of shortage, and then spent the proceeds on slaves. After the peasants were enserfed, lords shared their stores with their serfs, with the consequence that the period 1700-1861 did not know the great famines such as that of 1568-70 and 1601-3 that had forced so many Muscovites to sell themselves into slavery. An edict of 1734 required a lord to feed his serfs during a famine. "Enlightened" Catherinian legislation passed in 1767 and 1772 admonished lords to provide for the subsistence of their peasants and forbade them to turn their charges out to beg. An edict of 1782 forbade freeing and turning out of the old and infirm serfs.[102] All of these were welfare functions that had been performed by slavery in Muscovy and in the century between, say, 1670 and 1770 had been assumed gradually by other institutions. Catherine's laws were not meant to fill the gaps left by the abolition of slavery but rather to admonish those who forgot to fulfill the obligations that had long been expected of them.

The institutions that had permitted the abolition of slavery in the Petrine era collapsed with the abolition of slavelike serfdom, and the conditions that forced people to sell themselves into slavery perhaps not unexpectedly reappeared. The immediate consequence of the removal of serfowner and communal elder authority in 1861 was the crumbling of the extended family. This fact alone should have been enough to tell students of the Russian family that the extended family was a product of compulsion, not a by-product of the "Slavic soul." As the great English observer of post-Emancipation Russia, Donald McKenzie Wallace, noted, the big families broke up because all wanted to live in their own nuclear family houses. To support themselves, some resorted to usurers and many became insolvent. Communal equality disappeared and income differentiation appeared.[103] Subsequently, those peasants prospered whose households most resembled the extended households of the serf era—fathers with grown sons still living at home; the poorest, who in Muscovy might have sold themselves into slavery, simply died without offspring.[104]

102. Blum, *Lord and Peasant*, pp. 430, 436.

103. Donald Mackenzie Wallace, *Russia on the Eve of War and Revolution* (New York: Vintage Books, 1961), pp. 264, 270, 341.

104. Teodor Shanin, *The Awkward Class. Political Sociology of Peasantry in a Developing Society: Russia 1910-1925* (Oxford: Clarendon Press, 1972), pp. 76-80, 90, and passim.

This should help to answer one of the basic problems that Soviet historians have about the longevity of slavery in Russia. They wonder if it persisted so long (compared to Western and Central Europe) because, perhaps, Russia was "Asiatic."[105] While the Marxist category of "Asiatic despotism" describes certain aspects of the Russian historical experience (particularly the introduction of major change because of exogenous influences),[106] the persistence of slavery can be explained without resort to such grand schemes. Russia was a comparatively poor country in which many people regularly needed relief, and for hundreds of years the Russians had used slavery as their major relief institution. Slavery was expendable only when an adequate substitute had been found. The odd thing about the solution was that, while the extended family and serfdom "freed" the slaves, these institutions actually kept them in bondage while simultaneously enslaving much of the rest of the population as well.

The Abolition of Slavery among Non-Russians in the Russian Empire

It has been observed that a nation that conquers another one to the point of dominating its territory almost never enslaves the defeated people. Similarly, in more modern times, nations that have embarked upon imperialistic ventures have tended to put an end to enslavement in the territories they came to control. This was true in Latin America, where, for example, the enslavement of Indians was forbidden in Brazil after 1680.[107] England in Africa is another illustration. This is not the place to argue whether England was drawn into Africa by a desire to put an end to slavery, or went into Africa and then put an end to slavery. The fact is that imperialism coincided with the beginning of the end of slavery in Africa. Charles Verlinden has generalized that "indigenous slavery and colonization are . . . contradictory. This is one of the great laws of colonial society in all times."[108] One seems to witness a similar development in Muscovy's relations with the various Turkic peoples that it was coming increasingly to dominate and include within the Muscovite state. This could, and no doubt will, be the subject of an entire monograph, so here I shall merely note the problem. The Turkic peoples and Slavs regarded each other as fair game for enslavement for a millennium, from the first encounters of the Bulgars and Khazars and then Pechenegs with the Eastern Slavs down to Catherine the Great, who liquidated the Crimean Khanate for what she declared was the

105. S. O. Shmidt, *Stanovlenie rossiiskogo samoderzhavstva. Issledovanie sotsial'no-politicheskoi istorii vremeni Ivana Groznogo* (Moscow: "Mysl'," 1973), p. 272.
106. Joseph Schiebel, "Pre-Revolutionary Russian Marxist Concepts of Russian State and Society," in G. L. Ulmen, ed. *Society and History* (The Hague: Mouton, 1978), pp. 311-28.
107. Curtin (in *Annals*), p. 5.
108. Verlinden, *Beginnings of Modern Colonization*, p. 46.

specific purpose of ridding the eastern European plain of that dread for all time.

The Muscovites were quite aware of some of the slavery practices among the southern and eastern peoples who ultimately became subjects of the Russian Empire. For example, we have already had occasion to observe the Russians taking note of slavery practices among the Astrakhan' Tatars during the reign of Boris Godunov. During the Time of Troubles, they noted that the natives of Siberia were selling their wives and children to raise money to pay the taxes imposed by Moscow (the *iasak*).[109]

Of greater interest here, however, are the attempts by the Russians to curtail the enslavement of, and limit slavery among, the non-Russians. In 1626 the government sent an order to the officials of Astrakhan' on the lower Volga forbidding them or anyone else to sell Nogai Tatars to the Persians "so that there will be no disputes between Us and the Persian Shah Abbas." The issue had been raised by the discovery and subsequent investigation in Astrakhan' of two Nogai female slaves who had been sold by state secretary (*d'iak*) Vasilii Iakovlev.[110] I do not know why Moscow feared complications with Persia over such transactions, but what is noteworthy here is that the Nogais, a Muscovite client horde, were thereby protected by this provision. A number of the articles of the great chapter 20, "On Slavery," of the *Ulozhenie* of 1649 are devoted to Tatar slaves. In those articles one can observe the beginnings of interest by the central government in protecting the subject peoples of the Muscovite empire from enslavement. Most noteworthy is a provision forbidding the kidnapping of Tatars for the purpose of enslaving them. Also of interest is a measure of 1623/24 (repealed in 1649) prohibiting anyone from buying Tatars.[111] In December of 1684 Turkic and Siberian peoples were forbidden to sell themselves to anyone, and they were to be punished if they asked someone to buy them.[112] This essentially reinstated the law of 1623/24, except that it placed the sanctions on the would-be seller (of himself) rather than on the would-be buyer. Russians were never categorically forbidden to sell themselves into slavery (the prohibitions were on certain estates: the peasantry, townsmen, members of the middle service class), and thus this prohibition for the colonials outran that for the Russians themselves.

Such measures did little to liquidate slavery among the non-Russians of the empire. Peter the Great concentrated his energies on the western front, and only later did the Russians have the energy and the means to move against slavery among the Bashkirs, Tatars, Turkomans, Uzbeks, and Kazakhs. Soviet collections of primary sources are full of information about post-Petrine slavery among

109. Gnevushev, *Akty*, nos. 115-17.
110. DR 1: 843-44.
111. 1649 *Ulozhenie* 20: 117-18; MS, pp. 298-99.
112. PSZ 2: 644-45, no. 1099.

the minority nationalities, and the efforts, successful a few decades prior to the Revolution of 1917, of St. Petersburg to liquidate the institution.[113] Thus the Russian Empire in its expansion to the south and east exhibited an attitude toward the enslavement of its colonial subjects similar to that of the Western powers in their expansion to the south and west.

The Heritage of Muscovite Slavery

Once again, this is a topic suitable for a separate monograph, so what follows can only be a suggestive, rather than an exhaustive, summary. It should be clear, however, that serfdom was slavery's most important legacy. Almost every important aspect of imperial Russian serfdom had antecedents in Muscovite slavery. It is this legacy that makes comparison between, for example, American slavery and Russian serfdom such a potentially fruitful undertaking. The parallels and continuities between slavery and serfdom are everywhere, from the complete dependence and helplessness of house serfs that sapped them of vitality to the possibility that a serfowner could accept for himself a government award granted for a valorous deed performed by his serf and say, when questioned about the propriety of such conduct. "What of that? Was he not my man? It is all the same."[114] That is what slavery was all about: the slave, who was ordinarily deprived of individuality, was an extension of his owner. That is what the serf became.

Certainly one of slavery's most grotesque legacies was that its norms, developed for the weak, unproductive, non-self-sufficient, dependent elements of society, were applied to the productive elements of society. As is now well

113. Dozens, probably hundreds, of examples could be provided, but these should be adequate for this illustration: *Kabardino-russkie otnosheniia v XVI-XVII vv.*, ed. T. Kh. Kumykov et al., 2 vols. (Moscow: Akademiia Nauk SSSR, 1957), 1: 84, 139, 141, 158, 172, 257, 259, 310, 403; 2: 158, 285; *Materialy po istorii Bashkirskoi ASSR*. Vol. 5, *1776-1800 gg.*, ed. S. M. Vasil'ev (Moscow: Akademiia Nauk SSSR, 1960), pp. 129, 183, 542-44, 549-50; B. I. Iskandarov, *Vostochnaia Bukhara i Pamir vo vtoroi polovine XIX v.* 2 vols. (Dushanbe: Akademiia Nauk Tadzhikskoi SSR, 1962-63), 1: 25, 31, 34: Arthur N. Waldron, Review of N. A. Khalfin, *Rossiia i khanstva Srednei Azii (Pervaia polovina XIX veka)*, in *Kritika* 14, no. 1 (Winter 1978): 33. On Russian attempts to abolish slavery in Middle Asia in the 1870s and 1880s, see Seymour Becker, *Russia's Protectorates in Central Asia: Bukhara and Khiva, 1865-1924* (Cambridge: Harvard University Press, 1968), pp. 55-57, 73, 86-88, 200.

114. Blum, *Lord and Peasant*, pp. 438-39, 458. For more on the merger of slavery and serfdom, see George Vernadsky, "Serfdom in Russia, " in Tenth International Congress of Historical Sciences, *Relazioni* (Firenze: G. C. Sansoni, 1955), 3: 267-71. For an earlier account, see N. I. Turgenev, *Rossiia i russkie*. Vol. 2, *Ocherki politicheskoi i sotsial'noi Rossii* (Moscow: Russkoe tovarishchestvo, 1907), pp. 68-69. On the parallels and similarities between Russian serfdom and U.S. slavery, see Peter Kolchin's articles listed in the Bibliography.

known, people often respond to negative images by confirming those images. Certainly the abasement of the peasantry by application of slave norms contributed to the development of the "infantile, passive, helpless, animal-like serfs" of the nineteenth century, for whom the image of the slave presented in chapter 10 is apposite. Whether slavery and serfdom had the consequence of creating the energy level in much of Russian society after 1861 that allows one to compare that level of effort with the welfare dependency syndrome in the U.S. is debatable. Certainly the proposition would be worth considering. Assuming that a causal connection exists, this may be one of the reasons why the productivity of labor is so low in Russia, why workers need to be driven to do anything. We must also recall that the very Russian word for work, "rabota," means the labor of an unfree man, coming from *rab*, "slave." (Americans know the word in the form of "robot," coined by the Czech playright Karel Čapek in 1920 from *robota*, "slave.") Whether Russians are still conscious of the fact that "work" is something done by slaves would have to be determined by in-depth interviews on the spot, but the consistent effort by the Soviets to overcome the popular aversion to "work" forces one to raise the issue.[115]

The social and psychological barriers that permitted the enslavement of the enserfed peasantry in Imperial Russia are more easily comprehended than those barriers discussed in chapter 12. The binding of the peasants to the land and the abasement of their persons that constituted serfdom differentiated the peasants from the landholders. This gulf was widened by the great Church Schism in the third quarter of the seventeenth century, in which the mass of the peasantry remained Old Believers while the landed elements went along with the reformed church. The gulf became an unbridgeable chasm as a result of Westernization, which altered the consumption appetites and some of the thought patterns of the gentry, who by 1800 spoke French while, of course, the serfs continued to speak Russian. It is difficult to imagine that this could have occurred had not the Russians for centuries been accustomed to enslaving their own people. The Soviet slave labor system of GULag was built on the foundations of the earlier slave and serf edifices.

The slave legacy must have been responsible for other Russian patterns of thought besides the permissibility of enslaving one's own people. The Russians, by holding slaves and their offspring in bondage for centuries, violated the ex-

---

115. Zimin, *Kholopy*, p. 67. For a late twentieth-century discussion of the meaning of *rabochii* (worker), with its "clear connotation of subordination" and *rabotnik* (a more subordinate worker), "a position which robs a person of his inner autonomy and independence," see Arcadius Kahan, "Some Problems of the Soviet Industrial Worker," in Arcadius Kahan and Blair A. Ruble, eds., *Industrial Labor in the U.S.S.R.* (New York: Pergamon Press, 1979), pp. 302-3. In northern Germanic law, the kind of labor that slaves rendered was called *verk* (Wergeland, p. 44). The Muscovites had several verbs that probably should be translated into English as "work." For example, chancellery employees were reported to "sit" (*sidiat*) in the *prikazy* (PSZ 1: 484, 828, 833; 2: 264, nos. 247, 462, 466, 820).

pected pattern that slaves should be manumitted within a period ranging from six years to three generations. The Muscovite view on this subject was expressed in 1811 by N. M. Karamzin in his memoir to Tsar Alexander I. Discussing the problem of emancipating the serfs, he claimed that "the serfs who are descended of slaves (the *kholopy*) are lawful property of the gentry and cannot be personally emancipated without the landlords receiving some special compensation."[116] In most other societies the offspring of the slave "outsider" in 1723 would have become an "insider" by 1811, but Karamzin, himself a great historian, expressed the peculiar Russian view of the capacity of slaves for freedom, a sense that perpetual unfreedom is fitting for human beings of one's own ethnos. It is certainly not a great leap from that view to the position that the people are absolutely without rights.

The memory of slavery lived on in other spheres as well. Such nineteenth-century Russian authors as Pushkin, Nekrasov, and Saltykov-Shchedrin had a good understanding of what slavery did to many of its victims, of the nature of the slave's soul.[117] The peasants also remembered. After 1861, the rejuvenated corvée (*otrabotki*) was called *kabala*, "slave labor."[118]

Slavery also had its impact on the "ruling class" of Russia. The medieval Muscovite employment of slave ministers curbed potential aristocratic pretensions by nobles and nonprincely elements surrounding the monarchs. Toward the end of the fifteenth century courtiers began to call themselves "slaves" (*kholopy*) when addressing their sovereign. Whether this was a tradition imported from Byzantium or Italy (with Ivan III's second wife Zoe), or a continuation of a previously unrecorded practice when servitors (*dvoriane*) and state secretaries (*d'iaki*) actually had been slaves, cannot be determined. It is only clear that the servants of the prince of Moscow were probably never full human beings with an independent sense of dignity. The same was true of those agents who controlled the periphery for the center, the governors and their aides. For this reason it was not an excessive labor for Ivan IV to convert his officials, in the words of English traveler Giles Fletcher, "not only into vassals, but *kholopy*, his very villeins or bondslaves."[119] One should not be surprised by the unanimous exclamations by all Western visitors to Muscovy on the slavishness of the Russians, for no other European society they knew had such a high proportion of slaves so widely distributed throughout society. For these and other reasons, claims by historians that the oligarchs surrounding the monarch had the capacity on an institutional level to oppose or restrain their creator are without merit.

Similarly, institutional restraint on autocratic will was unlikely to develop in the provincial countryside. Initially, the term *deti boiarskie* presumably meant

---

116. Richard Pipes, *Karamzin's Memoir on Ancient and Modern Russia* (New York: Atheneum, 1969), p. 164.

117. D.P. Makovskii, *Pervaia krest'ianskaia voina v Rossii* (Smolensk, 1967), p. 465.

118. Stepniak, *The Russian Peasantry* (London: Swan, Sonnenschein, 1888), 1: 59-60.

119. Berry and Crummey, *Rude*, p. 138. See also Olearius, p. 173.

"boyar slaves," and, as we know, many of the members of the provincial middle service class were of slave origin. Their primary function was cavalry warfare, which they shared with slaves. When they were commanded to take over provincial administration from the governors in the reign of Ivan IV, they assumed functions that had belonged to slaves. Thus it is not striking that the provincial middle service class was not born with gentry pretensions: they lived off state grants, having no land of their own, and performed military and civil administrative functions that were also rendered by slaves. That they were able to acquire gentry pretensions (while still addressing the sovereign as "your slaves") probably stems from the fact that in the sixteenth century they displaced not ordinary slaves but elite slaves, who also had pretensions, and from the fact that they confronted a dying dynasty in the 1590s and then a new and weak dynasty in the first half of the seventeenth century. There is also the fact that service class revolutions in Russian history have always tended to lose their élan once the initial threat that stimulated the creation of the service class has passed.[120] Because the capital upper service class and the provincial middle service class did not serve as institutional restraints on the monarchy, it is fair to say that the institution of slavery made a not insignificant contribution to the creation and perpetuation of Russian autocracy.

Slavery also helped to create the values of the members of the Russian landed class. As in Muscovy they highly valued having the service of and exercising dominance over as many slaves as possible, so in the imperial period they shocked foreigners with their large numbers of house serfs, "legions of superfluous servants," maintained for prestige purposes. The Russians maintained five to six times as many domestics as nobles of equal rank and income in other lands. As slaveowners had fawned before the tsar and occasionally brutalized their slaves, so their heirs scraped before the emperor or empress and tormented their serfs. As the slaveowners had occasionally traded in slaves, so their offspring sometimes bought and sold serfs, all the while believing that it was illegal.[121] This list of parallels and continuities could be extended considerably.

Is Freedom a Zero-Sum Game?

This is a twentieth-century question that is asked with increasing urgency, and upon which the history of slavery sheds considerable light. For example, Athenian democracy was possible because the extensive employment of slaves permitted the slaveowners the leisure to concern themselves about democracy, freedom for themselves, and similar problems. The same was true to a consider-

120. Hellie, "Structure," p. 4.
121. Richard Pipes, *Russia under the Old Regime* (New York: Schribner's, 1974), p. 187; Alexander, *Bubonic Plague*, pp. 73, 78, 128; Blum, *Lord and Peasant*, pp. 427-28, 456.

able extent for the antebellum American South: the freedom of the slaveowners was paid for by the unfreedom of the slaves. (The amount of freedom the non-slaveowning "free" whites possessed is a matter for discussion, especially as the slaveowning minority plunged the South into civil war.) The same can be said for the absentee slaveowners of the Caribbean who revelled in the freedom of London, and so on.

Early modern Russian slavery also looks like a zero-sum game. By Athenian or U. S. standards, free men had comparatively little freedom, but, by the same standards, slaves had comparatively quite a bit of freedom. In the early period they could hold elite governmental, military, and estate positions, they could pay taxes and appear in court, they could own land and other slaves.

The hypothesis of freedom as a zero-sum game was put to the test in the 1630s when the members of the middle service class and the townsmen began to claim that they had certain rights, ranging from exclusive privileges and monopolies to the right to advise that government on matters of war and peace and legislation. According to a zero-sum game theory of freedom, the rights of some other group(s) should have diminished. That is exactly what happened. The peasants were enserfed, and as elite slaves largely disappeared, limitations appeared on the former (unstated) rights of slaves to own other slaves, landed estates, and urban property. These were claimed as the prerogatives of the members of the middle and upper service classes and townsmen. The image of the slave probably also changed at this time, with the early sixteenth-century notion of a continuum of slaves paralleling free society being discarded in favor of the idea represented by the action of a member of the middle service class who felt insulted enough to launch a defamation suit against a person who noted (accurately, as government records proved) that the plaintiff's clan had been of slave origin 150 years earlier.[122]

The situation that was arising in the 1630s and 1640s calls to mind the extreme cases of Athens and the American South, where slaves were barred from elite employment and from civil and military service.[123] In those societies slaves were systematically excluded from certain positions and functions, which were reserved as perquisites for free men. Such segregation played a major role in distinguishing free from slave. The privilege of participating in actual fighting, as combatants in warfare, was a privilege connected with citizenship. (Athenian slaves who, in violation of the general rule, occasionally fought in civil wars were subsequently freed.)[124] In those most democratic of societies military and civil service, and, in the mid-nineteenth century, even many urban occupations, were reserved solely for free men; a major part of the definition of a free man was that he (and not slaves) had the exclusive right to such posts.[125]

122. 1649 *Ulozhenie* 17: 41; 19: 15; 20: 105; Markevich, p. 168.
123. Finley, "Between Slavery and Freedom," p. 239.
124. Westermann, pp. 15-16.
125. Goldin, p. 29.

The brief Muscovite experience with proto-democracy culminated in the Assembly of the Land (*Zemskii sobor*) of 1648-49, and its legislative product, the *Sobornoe ulozhenie* of 1649. Certainly against the will of the reigning oligarchy, the townsmen got their monopolies and the middle service class got the peasants enserfed and achieved a firmer grip on the land fund. Strictures against slaves were also part of the law code, particularly their exclusion from monopolized income-producing ventures.

The experiment did not last; as the government recovered its will to rule autocratically, the middle service class was replaced as the dominant military force by the new formation regiments, and both "victorious groups" in 1648-49 rested on their laurels and did not press the government further for a share in the decision-making process of ruling Russia.[126]

This was also the time when slavery began to decline and then disappeared as an institution. It is apparent, however, that it played an important role in the zero-sum game equation of the second quarter of the seventeenth century. The equation also operated after 1762 as the serfs provided the material support for the degree of freedom enjoyed by the gentry, and, for themselves, provided a level of support and material equality whose extent was revealed with the differentiation that appeared after the abolition of the institution in 1861. The topic of Russia as an embodiment of the thesis that freedom is a zero-sum game is certainly worthy of further consideration.

The Early Modern Russian Slave System

Throughout this work I have discussed the various elements of the Russian slave system as it existed between, roughly, 1450 and 1723, and compared the Russian elements with those of other slave systems. The Muscovite law of slavery dealt with most of the problems that occur in other systems, and the legal norms that defined the institution of Muscovite slavery were akin to those in other systems. Where there were differences, they can be described as making the system "milder" or less harsh than some others, and can be attributed to the presence of elite slavery and to the fact that a majority of the slaves were ethnically Russians. The Russian slave system, in sum, was not like any other, which should not be at all surprising, for Russian civilization in general has always been highly eclectic.

The most unusual feature of Russian slavery was the fact that so many of the slaves were Russians, combined with a general Muscovite reluctance to manumit slaves and the absence of kinlike titles or family ties between master and slave of the type that often existed in other household slavery systems. Slaves in Muscovy did not reproduce themselves, probably for the combined reasons that

---

126. For further elaboration on this subject, see Hellie, "Comparative," p. 181-83.

slaves often do not "multiply in captivity" and that owners probably discouraged reproduction because they preferred solitary males. This meant that the institution had to be refreshed constantly with new slaves. Most other systems replenished their supplies by direct resort to warfare and various forms of piracy, or by purchasing from peoples that did the direct recruiting. The Muscovites also recruited slaves by warfare and kidnapping, but their major source was natives who sold themselves into slavery because that was fundamentally the only kind of welfare relief that early modern Russia offered. Slavery was an outlet for individuals who somatized stress, a consequence of life in Muscovy and, particularly, of scarcity. Scarcity is often a major obstacle to social integration and a major cause of stress, but the Muscovite solution, the perpetual enslavement of the victim and his offspring, has been rare in human history. The enslavement of natives seemingly reflected a lack of ethnic specificity among the denizens of the east European plain and the fact that kinship obligations had receded but alternative forms of social insurance had not been created to take their place.

The government, at least occasionally, was not happy about an institution that seems to have enveloped perhaps 10 percent of the total population, and primarily concerned about a loss of tax revenues and a misallocation of human resources, took measures to restrict the number of slaves. Various measures were enacted that facilitated war captives' access to freedom and curtailed the enslavement of non-Russians who were part of the expanding Russian Empire. Major attention, however, was devoted to native Russians and those (possibly initially of non-Russian origin) who had been enslaved for generations. Full slavery yielded to limited service contract slavery, in which self-sale was first provisionally limited for one year, then, upon default, became hereditary and perpetual, and then, after 1586-97, was limited to the life of the slaveowner. Restrictions were also placed on other forms of slavery, including hereditary bondage, as limited service contract slavery became the preferred type in the seventeenth century. Around 1679 agricultural slavery, and by 1723 house slavery, yielded to serfdom.

The government, in spite of its incentives and prodding, learned that, in the words of a Soviet historian, "indeed, not every slave dreams of freedom."[127] The reasons why this was so were no doubt many, but the total dependency created by slavery was almost unquestionably the major one. Once a slave had been subjected to his owner's dominance for several years, an independent existence for him in the harsh reality of Muscovy was almost unthinkable. Thus, seemingly, most freedmen recycled themselves back into slavery almost immediately upon manumission.

That is not to say that Russians naturally loved slavery or that all slaves immediately became docile and dependent. They did not. Almost certainly many free men, in response to the stress of the moment, sold themselves because

127. Anisimov, p. 48.

slavery was the sole form of relief available, and intended to flee as soon as they had recovered. In the straits of the moment, others gave flight no thought at the time of self-sale, but discovered its possibility, the major form of resistance to slavery in Muscovy, within a short time. This accounts for the fact that perhaps from a quarter to a third of all slaves fled, in family compositions similar to those in which they entered slavery. While some slaves who fled were recovered, often after the passage of many years, most were not. This helps to account for the low prices paid for slaves, roughly the equivalent of the cost of a year's food.

There were other determinants of the price of slaves besides their propensity to flee.. The major one, of course, was their low skill level. (Prices five times higher were paid for the most desired slaves.) Most slaves were employed in the household, as lackeys, cleaners, cooks, messengers, and in other such assignments.

Males were preferred, females and small children were not desired. This owner preference dovetailed with the demographic reality of those who offered themselves for sale into slavery. Female infanticide must have been practiced on a massive scale among the beggars, hired laborers, landless peasants, and others divorced from agriculture who sold themselves for the first time into slavery. Household slavery was a man's world, entered by those of prime age, between fifteen and twenty-five.[128] Only the worst disasters, such as the famine of 1601-3, forced large numbers of two-parent families with·children, or minors, to sell themselves into slavery.

There are general patterns to Muscovite slave prices, but variances are often very high. The regression analysis of slavery prices presented in table 18.2 seems to correspond with what we know about the institution of slavery.

TABLE 18.2
Regression Analysis of Muscovite Slave Prices

	Rubles	R^2 Change
Constant (the cost of the average slave contract)	3.59	
Famine years	−2.66	0.23309
Price of grain	0.003	0.00009
Sex of first slave	0.62	0.00562
Age of first slave	0.01	0.00072
Wife	−0.29	0.00081
First child	0.71	0.03878
Second child	0.67	0.00809
Third child	0.59	0.00203
Fourth child	0.25	0.00009
N = 1824		

128. There is little validity in calculations that begin by assuming that half of the house slaves (*dvorovyne liudi*) were males, as was done by Tikhonov in his *Pomeshchich'i krest'-iane* (p. 171). See chapter 12 above.

The table may be interpreted as follows. The average slave family unit cost 3.59 rubles. If the family unit (which might have been a solitary individual) was headed by a male, the buyer was willing to pay 0.62 rubles more than if it was headed by a female. The age of the first slave had little to do with the price, 0.01 rubles per year of age over the average age of twenty-six. A wife contributed a negative price of 0.29 rubles. The buyer was willing to pay a little bit more for each child, but not much: 0.71 rubles for the first child, only 0.25 rubles for a fourth. The general price level for slaves followed that of grain, but in any given year the two were liable to go in opposite directions. Thus, overall, the price of grain contributed nothing to the price of slaves. The major determinate in the price of slaves was whether or not it was a famine year (7078 [=1569/70], 7079 [=1570/71], and 7111 [=1602/3] were coded as famine years, all others as non-famine years). A famine shifted out the supply curve as the quantity of people desiring to sell themselves into slavery increased greatly. When the price of slaves fell dramatically in famine years, buyers with surplus became relatively wealthier than they had been previously and scrambled to pick up greatly discounted chattel. A famine was the time, we may recall, when less prosperous servicemen, clergymen, and slaves entered the market. These variables account for 53.8 percent of the price of a slave contract, the highest I am able to account for by regression analysis. (Leaving out the price of grain from the analysis permitted raising the N to 2,184 cases. The contributions of the children changed slightly [first child added 0.75 rubles, the second child 0.46 rubles, a third child 1.15 rubles, and a fourth child 0.56 rubles], but the other contributions remained about the same.)

Slaves were also employed in agriculture, to farm the owner's demesne. Still others were used in the army, either as combatants or as attendants of the baggage train. They, like other slaves, were not corporately owned but were the property of individuals. In the earlier Muscovite era, slave employment (except for household help, which was largely a slave preserve), mirrored the occupations of free men. Slaves served in the central and provincial governmental administration, they administered estates, they were advocates in the judicial system. By 1700, however, elite slavery was largely a fact of history as the social functions of elite slaves were assumed by free men.

It would be useful to compare slavery in Muscovy with other varieties by resorting to Moses I. Finley's typology of the rights and duties that define a person's status in society:[129] (1) The Muscovite slave's claims to property, his power over things, was greater than that of slaves in many other systems, although it declined after the 1630s. (2) The same was true of his power over human labor and movement, both his own and others', particularly for elite slaves. (3) The Muscovite slave had little power to punish (except as this was part of the elite slave steward's control and supervisory authority); himself part of a

---

129. Finley, "Between Slavery and Freedom," pp. 247-48.

society in which few individuals of any status were immune from punishment, he was as liable to both just and arbitrary punishment by either the state power or his owner as any slave in human history. (4) On the other hand, the Muscovite slave had a greater capacity in the judicial process than did most slaves elsewhere; he had both privileges and liabilities, he could sue and be sued. (5) In the area of family privileges, the Muscovite slave was somewhere in the middle of a continuum, for (at least according to a decree of Vasilii Shuiskii at the beginning of the seventeenth century) he had the right to marry and his marriage was inviolable, although his nuclear family was not; in other respects, he was essentially kinless, for he had no formalized rights of succession and no one to look after his interests other than his owner. (6) The Muscovite slave had greater privileges of social mobility, while still remaining enslaved, than did most other slaves, although this social mobility was gradually curtailed in the course of time. (7) In the sacral, political, and military spheres, the Muscovite slave again had more privileges and duties than did most other chattel in world history; if a Russian, he was a "member" of the Orthodox church and could participate in its rites in the same fashion that free people could; if a non-Russian, he could convert to Orthodoxy and thereby attain the status of an Orthodox member of Muscovite society. In the conditions of Muscovite autocracy, an elite administrative slave had as many "political rights" as did a free person exercising the same functions, but it must be noted that the military slaves, so prominent in the sixteenth century, did not participate in the elections of their local military administrators (*okladchiki*).

Everybody benefited from slavery. The war captives lived, instead of being killed. Those who sold themselves also lived, instead of starving to death. Government officials benefited from the fees paid to register slaves and for adjudicating disputes over them. The slaveowners benefited from the captive labor the slaves rendered, the psychological dominance they were able to exercise over their chattel, and the prestige that accrued from visible ownership of property. Most slaveowners were either clergymen, wealthy merchants, or, primarily, military and bureaucratic government servitors who owned or possessed land. Slaveownership was highly life-cycle determined, sometimes commencing when slaves were inherited or acquired in a dowry at marriage, more often beginning after several years of service and the acquisition of adequate land and cash compensation enabled an owner to maintain slaves. There are high overall correlations between land- and peasant-holding and slaveownership. Slaveownership was so highly prized that almost all servicemen seem to have acquired slaves by the time of their death. Enough owners acquired them either without adequate income to maintain them or in excessive numbers so that the *Domostroi*, discussing household management, felt compelled more than once to caution owners about the evils that might ensue from inadequately maintaining one's slaves. While there were psychopaths among the slaveowners, slaves in general seem to have been subject to no more abuse than were other elements of the population. When they were abused, they fled. It is also quite clear that the slave trade in Muscovy was minimally developed, perhaps because most of the slaves were Russians and because to sell slaves would have degraded the slaveowners.

One may conclude that the Muscovite system was considerably milder than most of those that may be known to the reader of this essay. Many factors account for this. Perhaps most important was the fact that Muscovite slavery was primarily of the household or "patriarchal" type, oriented toward the generation of prestige, service, and leisure for the slaveowners, rather than toward profits from plantations, factories, or mines. A second factor was Muscovy's employment of slaves in all aspects of social life, the fact that there were both elite and common slaves, with subordination to the owner being the primary determinant of slave status rather than occupation, in a milieu in which all were increasingly subordinate to the autocratic monarch. A third important determinant of the Muscovite slave system was the fact, quite exceptional in the history of slavery, that the majority of the slaves were not "outsiders" in the formal sense but were Orthodox ethnic East Slavs. Only considerably later did the Russians learn to treat their own kind with utmost savagery. Related to this was a fourth factor, that while formal manumission was rare in Muscovy, informal manumission through flight either to another slaveowner or to an independent life was a possibility that placed real restraints on the conduct of any slaveowner. Lastly, Muscovy's slave system developed as it did at least partly because a number of its norms came from Byzantine laws that had been written when slavery was on the decline and that continued in force in an early modern European world that was increasingly learning to live without slavery within its borders. Slavery was perpetuated in Muscovy because of tradition and the presence of hereditary slaves, the possibility of some refreshening of the institution with new supplies of military captives, the fact that slavery was a major and flourishing institution among southern neighbors, and an unceasing need for relief and welfare in a society that was unwilling to provide it in any meaningful manner other than by enslaving those in need of charity. Muscovite slavery was abolished without severe dislocation or alteration of the social structure because of a decreasing need for the institutionalized subordination of people fulfilling managerial tasks, the discovery that peasants and townsmen could be forced to serve in the army, the needs of the fisc for additional revenue, the gradual abasement of the peasantry, and the development of alternative institutions to fulfill the relief and welfare functions of slavery. Long after 1723, slavery continued to have an impact on the peasants, the gentry, the government, and the minds and values of Russians.

Abbreviations of Works Cited

AAE. *Akty, sobrannye v bibliotekakh i arkhivakh Rossiiskoi imperii Arkheograficheskoiu ekspeditseiu imp. Akademii nauk.* 4 vols. + index. St. Petersburg, 1836, 1858.

AFZKh. *Akty feodal'nogo zemlevladeniia i khoziaistva XIV–XVI vekov.* 3 vols. Moscow: Akademiia Nauk SSSR, 1959-61.

AI. *Akty istoricheskie, sobrannye i izdannye Arkheograficheskoiu kommissieiu.* 5 vols. + index. St. Petersburg, 1841-43.

AIS-ZR. *Agrarnaia istoriia severo-zapada Rossii.* Edited by A. L. Shapiro et al. 3 vols. Leningrad: Nauka, 1971, 1974, 1978.

AIu. *Akty iuricheskie, ili Sobranie form starinnogo deloproizvodstva, izd. Arkheograficheskoi kommissii.* 1 vol. + index. St. Petersburg, 1838, 1840.

AIuB. *Akty, otnosiashchiesia do iuridicheskogo byta drevnei Rossii, izd. Arkheograficheskoi kommissieiu.* 3 vols. + index. St. Petersburg, 1857-1901.

Akty Iushkova. *Akty XIII–XVII vv., predstavlennye v Razriadnyi prikaz posle otmeny mestnichestva.* Published by A. Iushkov. Moscow, 1898.

Akty Morozova. *Akty khoziaistva boiarina B. I. Morozova.* Edited by A. I. Iakovlev. 2 vols. Moscow-Leningrad: Akademiia Nauk SSSR, 1940, 1945.

AMG. *Akty Moskovskogo gosudarstva, izd. imp. Akademieiu nauk.* Edited by N. A. Popov. 3 vols. St. Petersburg, 1890-1901.

APD. *Akty pistsovogo dela. Materialy dlia istorii kadastra i priamogo oblozheniia v Moskovskom godudarstve.* Compiled by S. B. Veselovskii. 2 vols. in 4 pts. Moscow, 1913-78.

ARG. *Akty russkogo gosudarstva, 1505-1526 gg.* Edited by A. A. Novosel'skii et al. Moscow: Nauka, 1975.

ASEI. *Akty sotsial'no-ekonomicheskoi istorii Severo-Vostochnoi Rusi kontsa XIV–nachale XVI v.* 3 vols. Moscow-Leningrad: Akademiia Nauk SSSR, 1952-64.

ATN. *Akty, otnosiashchiesia k istorii tiaglogo naseleniia v Moskovskom gosudarstve.* Edited by M. D'iakonov. 2 vols. Iur'ev, 1895-97.

BS. *Boiarskie spiski poslednei chetverti XVI–nachala XVII vv. i Rospis' russkogo voiska 1604 g. Ukazatel' sostava gosudareva dvora po fondu Razriadnogo prikaza.* Compiled and edited by S. P. Mordovina and A. L. Stanislavskii. 2 vols. Moscow: TsGADA, 1979.

Chteniia. *Chteniia v Obshchesvte istorii i drevnostei rossisskikh pri Moscovskom universitete. Sbornik.* Moscow, 1845-1918.

DAI. *Dopolneniia k aktam istoricheskim, sobrannye i izdannye Arkheograficheskoiu kommissieiu.* 12 vols. + index. St. Petersburg, 1846-75.

DDG. *Dukhovnye i dogorovnye gramoty velikikh i udel'nykh kniazei XIV--XVI vv.* Edited by L. V. Cherepnin and S. V. Bakhrushin. Moscow-Leningrad: Akademiia Nauk SSSR, 1950.

DN 1596. "Desiatnia novikov, poverstannykh v 1596 godu." Edited by N. Likhachev. *Izvestiia Russkogo genealogicheskogo obshchestva* 3(1909): 113-209.

DR. *Dvortsovye razriady, izdannye II-m otdeleniem sobstvennoi ego imp. velichestva kantseliarii.* 4 vols. St. Petersburg, 1850-55.

DVP. "Desiatnia Votskoi Piatiny 1605 goda." Edited by N. Miatlev. *Izvestiia Russkogo genealogicheskogo obshchestva* 4(1911): 467-509.

KR. *Knigi razriadnye po offitsial'nym onykh spiskam.* 2 vols. + index. St. Petersburg, 1853-56.

LKN-V. *Lavochnye knigi Novgoroda-Velikogo 1583 g.* Compiled by S. V. Bakhrushin. Moscow: RANION, 1930.

LS 1529. *Statut velikogo kniazhestva litovskogo 1529 goda.* Edited by K. I. Iablonskis. Minsk: Akademiia nauk BSSR, 1960.

LS 1588. *Litovskii statut v moskovskom perevode-redaktsii.* Edited by I. I. Lappo. Iur'ev, 1916.

LZAK. *Letopis' zaniatii Arkheograficheskoi kommissii.* 35 vols. St. Petersburg-Leningrad, 1862-1929.

MS. Hellie, Richard. *Muscovite Society.* Readings for Introduction to Russian Civilization. Chicago: Syllabus Division, The College, University of Chicago, 1967 or 1970.

NKK 7106. "Novgorodskaia kabal'naia kniga 7106 (1597) goda." *Russkaia istoricheskaia biblioteka* 15 (1894), III[1]: 1-62.

NKK 7108. "Novgorodskie kabal'nye knigi 7108 (1599-1600) goda." *Russkaia istoricheskaia biblioteka* 15 (1894), III[2]: 1-87.

NPK. *Novgorodskie pistsovye knigi, izdannye Arkheograficheskoiu komissieiu.* 6 vols. + index. St. Petersburg, 1859-1915.

NZKK. *Novgorodskie zapisnye kabal'nye knigi 100--104 i 111 godov (1591-1596 i 1602-1603 gg.).* Edited by A. I. Iakovlev. Moscow-Leningrad: Akademiia Nauk SSSR, 1938.

Opisanie. *Opisanie dokumentov i bumag, khraniashchikhsia v Moskovskom arkhive ministerstva iustitsii.* 21 vols. St. Petersburg, 1869-1921.

PKMG. *Pistsovye knigi Moskovskogo gosudarstva, izd. imp. Russkogo geograficheskogo obshchestva.* 2 vols. + index. St. Petersburg, 1872, 1877, 1895.

PRP. *Pamiatniki russkogo prava.* 8 vols. Moscow: Gosiurizdat, 1952-63.

PSRL. *Polnoe sobranie russkikh letopisei.* 35 vols. St. Petersburg-Moscow, 1841-1980.

PSZ. *Polnoe sobranie zakonov Rossiiskoi imperii.* 45 vols. St. Petersburg, 1830.

RIB. *Russkaia istoricheskaia biblioteka.* 39 vols. St. Petersburg-Leningrad, 1872-1927.

RK 1475-1598. *Razriadnaia kniga 1475-1598 gg.* Edited by V. I. Buganov. Moscow: Nauka, 1966.

RK 1475-1605. *Razriadnaia kniga 1475-1605 gg.* Compiled by N. G. Savich. 3 parts in 1 vol. Moscow: Akademiia Nauk SSSR, 1977.

RK 1550-1636. *Razriadnaia kniga 1550-1636 gg.* Compiled by L. F. Kuz'mina. 2 vols. in 3 pts. Moscow: Akademiia Nauk SSSR, 1975-76.

RK 1559-1605. *Razriadnaia kniga 1559-1605 gg.* Compiled by L. F. Kuz'mina. Moscow: Akademiia Nauk SSSR, 1974.

RK 1598-1638. *Razriadnye knigi 1598-1638 gg.* Compiled by V. I. Buganov and L. F. Kuz'mina. Moscow: Akademiia Nauk SSSR, 1974.

Sbornik Khilkova. *Sbornik Kniazia Khilkova.* St. Petersburg, 1879.

SBV (1974). Veselovskii, S. B. *Onomastikon.* Moscow: Nauka, 1974.

SGKE. *Sbornik gramot Kollegii ekonomii.* 2 vols. Leningrad, 1922-29.

SIRIO. *Sbornik imp. Russkogo istoricheskogo obshchestva.* 148 vols. St. Petersburg, 1867-1916.

ZKMS. *Zapisnye knigi Moskovskogo stola 1636-1663 g.* [= *Russkaia istoricheskaia biblioteka* 10(1886).]

ZSL (expanded). *Zakon Sudnyi liudem prostrannoi i svodnoi redaktsii.* Edited by M. N. Tikhomirov and L. V. Milov. Moscow: Akademiia Nauk SSSR, 1961.

ZSL(short). *Zakon Sudnyi liudem kratkoi redaktsii.* Edited by M. N. Tikhomirov and L. V. Milov. Moscow: Akademiia Nauk SSSR, 1961.

Selected Bibliography

Note: This bibliography lists only some of the materials used for the topic of slavery in Russia and elsewhere, and for Muscovite prosopography. Others are cited in full in the notes. The same is true for materials on general Russian history, law, demography, and other topics covered in this book.

Primary Sources for Slavery Contracts, Wills, Dowries, and Similar
   Materials

AAE, AFZKh, AIu, AMG, AIuB, Akty Iushkova, ASEI, NKK 7106, NKK 7108,
   NZKK
Arkhangel'skii, S. I. *Nizhnii Novgorod v XVII veke. Sbornik dokumentov i
   materialov k istorii N. Novgoroda i ego okrugi.* Gor'kii: Gor'kovskoe knizhnoe
   izd-vo, 1961. P. 77, no. 40.
Arkhiv Stoeva (= RIB 32 [1915]), p. 722.
Beliaev, I. D. "Zakony i akty, ustanavlivaiushchie v drevnei Rusi krepostnoe sos-
   toianie." *Arkhiv istoricheskikh i prakticheskikh svedenii, otnos. k Rossii* 2
   (1859): 98-101.
Borisov, V. *Opisanie goroda Shui i ego okrestnostei s prilozheniem starinnykh
   aktov.* Moscow, 1851. Pp. 398-99.
——— *Starinnye akty, sluzhashchie preimushchestvenno dopolneniem k opisan-
   iiu Shui i ego okrestnostei.* Moscow, 1853. Pp. 128-29.
Bychkov, I. A. "Otryvok Novgorodskoi kabal'noi knigi 1597 g." LZAK 22
   (1909): 1-6
Chteniia 1916, 2, Sec. 1, p. 123, no. 161.
Deistviia Nizhegorodskoi uchenoi arkhivnoi komissii 6: 237, 7: 133-41.
D'iakonov, M. A. "K voprosu o krest'ianskoi poriadnoi zapisi i sluzhiloi kabale."
   Sbornik statei, posviashchennykh Vasiliiu Osipovichu Kliuchevskomu. Moscow,
   1909. Pp. 317-31.
Egorov, V. A. "Otryvki iz Novgorodskikh kabal'nykh knig 7108 g." LZAK 24
   (1912), sec. 5, pp. 1-35.
Gosudarstvennaia publichnaia biblioteka im. Saltykova-Shchedrina v Leningrade.
   Rukopisnyi otdel. Obshchee sobranie gramot, nos. 1727, 1937, 1941, 2017,
   2019, 2348, 2406, 2635, 2672, 2761, 3026, 3081, 3120, 3392, 3475, 3486,
   3833, 3926, 4117, 4201; Sobranie kn. Mansyrevykh, no. 68; Sobranie Vyn-
   domskoe, no. 6. These documents, 25 in all, were copied by Peter B. Brown.

Iakovlev, A. I. *Kholopstvo i kholopy v Moskovskom gosudarstve XVII v.* Moscow-Leningrad: Akademiia Nauk SSSR, 1943.

Khoroshkevich, A. L. "Istochniki po istorii polnogo kholopstva kontsa XV-nachala XVI vv." *Sovetskie arkhivy.* 1974, no. 4, pp. 82-84.

———"Pskovskaia polnaia gramota 1511 g." *Arkheograficheskii ezhegodnik za 1967 god.* Moscow: Nauka, 1969. Pp. 68-72.

Kolycheva, E. I. "Polnye i dokladnye gramoty XV-XVI vekov." *Arkheograficheskii ezhegodnik za 1961 god.* Moscow: Nauka, 1962. Pp. 41-81.

Kopanev, A. I. "Materialy po istorii krest'ianstva kontsa XVI i pervoi poloviny XVII v." *Materialy i soobshcheniia po fondam otdela rukopisnoi i redkoi knigi Biblioteki Akademii nauk SSSR.* Moscow-Leningrad: Nauka, 1966. Pp. 143-86.

Lakier, A. B. "Akty, zapisannye v krepostnoi knige XVI." *Arkhiv istoriko-iuridicheskikh svedenii, otn. do Rossii* 2¹ (1855).

Lappo-Danilevskii, A. S. "Zapisnaia kniga krepostnym aktam XV-XVI vv., iavlennym v Novgorode d'iaku D. Aliab'evu." RIB 17(1898).

LZAK 5(1870), sec. 1, p. 98.

Loparev, Khr. *Opisanie rukopisei imp. obshchestva liubitelei drevnei pis'mennosti.* St. Petersburg, 1892. P. 189, no. 18.

Materialy istoricheskie i iuridicheskie raiona byvshego prikaza Kazanskogo dvortsa. 3: 85-86; 6: 156.

Pavlov-Sil'vanskii, N. P. *Akty o posadskikh liudiakh—zakladchikakh.* St. Petersburg: Tip. M. A. Aleksandrova, 1909.

Preobrazhenskii, I. and Al'bitskii, N. *Podrobnaia opis' 962 rukopisiam nachala XVII do nachala XIX stoletii "Dolmatovskogo arkhiva."* St. Petersburg, 1895. Pp. 36-41.

Russkaia vivliofika, ili sobranie materialov dlia otechestvennoi istorii, geografii, statistiki i drevnei russkoi literatury. Edited by Nikolai Aleks. Polevoi. 1(1833): 402-5.

Russkii vestnik. 1841, vol. 3, pp. 477-78.

Rubinshtein, N. L., editor. *Istoriia Tatarii v materialakh i dokumentakh.* Moscow: Sotsekgiz, 1937. P. 193.

Sbornik dokumentov po istorii SSSR. Vol. 3, XVI vek. Edited by A. M. Sakharov. Moscow: Vysshaia Shkola, 1972. Pp. 78-79.

Sbornik starinnykh bumag, khraniashchikhsia v muzee N. I. Shchukina. 2(1897): 121; 10(1902): 324-41.

Selifontov, N. N. *Podrobnaia opis' 440 rukopisiam XVII, XVIII i nachala XIX stol. pervogo sobraniia "Linevskogo arkhiva" s dvumia prilozheniiami.* St. Petersburg, 1891. P. 31, no. 176.

———*Podrobnaia opis' 272 rukopisiam kontsa XVI do nachala XIX st. vtorogo (shevliaginskogo) sobraniia "Linevskogo arkhiva."* St. Petersburg, 1892. Pp. 19-20.

Selivanov, A. V. "Materialy dlia istorii roda riazanskikh Selivanovykh, vedushchikh svoe nachalo ot Kuchibeia." *Trudy Riazanskoi arkhivnoi komissii.* 25(1912), issue 2, app., pt. II, pp. 50-51.

Sil'vanskii, N. P. "Akty o posadskikh liudiakh-zakladchikakh." *LZAK* 22(1910): 254.

Trudy Orlovskoi uchenoi arkhivnoi komissii 6(1889): 16-18.

Trudy Riazanskoi uchenoi arkhivnoi komissii 17(1902): 182.

Trudy Saratovskoi uchenoi arkhivnoi komissii 22: 162-63; 25:.79; 26: 13-14.

Vladimirskie gubernskie vedomosti 1858, no. 7, pp. 26-28.

Vremennik Demidovskogo iuridicheskogo litseia 52(1890): 194.

Vvedenskii, A. A. *Torgovyi dom XVI-XVII vv.* Leningrad: Atenei, 1924. Pp. 56-58.

Zhurnal zemlevladel'tsev 1858, no. 3, sec. II, p. 59.

The 2,499 documents that were coded and computer-processed were taken from the above materials.

Other Materials on Russian Slavery

Abramovich, G. V. "Novgorodskoe pomest'e v gody ekonomicheskogo krizisa poslednei treti XVI v." *Materialy po istorii sel'skogo khoziaistva i krest'ianstva SSSR* 8(1974): 5-26.

Alekseev, Iu. G. *Agrarnaia i sotsial'naia istoriia severo-vostochnoi Rusi XV-XVI vv. Pereiaslavskii uezd.* Moscow-Leningrad: Nauka, 1966.

——. "Kholop na pashne v svete dannykh toponomiki." *Trudy LOII* 7(1964): 435-38.

——. "Piatnadtsatirublevyi maksimum po sluzhiloi kabale, sluzhba s zemli i feodal'naia renta." *Trudy LOII* 12(1971): 110-17.

Anisimov, E. V. "Izmeneniia v sotsial'noi strukture russkogo obshchestva v kontse XVII-nachale XVIII veka (Posledniaia stranitsa kholopstva v Rossii)." *Istoriia SSSR* 23, no. 5 (September-October 1979): 35-51.

Arkhangel'skii, M. *O sobornom Ulozhenii tsaria Alekseia Mikhailovicha 1649 (7156) g. v otnoshenii k pravoslavnoi russkoi tserkvi.* St. Petersburg, 1881.

Arsen'ev, Iu. V. "Blizhnii boiarin kniaz' Nikita Ivanovich Odoevskii i ego perepiska s Galitskoiu votchinoi (1650-1684 gg.)." *Chteniia* 205(1903, bk. 2): 53-129.

——. "Smes'." *Chteniia* 196(1901, bk. 1), pt. 4, pp. 2-4.

Bazilevich, K. V. "Novgorodskie pomeshchiki iz posluzhil'tsev v kontse XV veka." *Istoricheskie zapiski* 14(1945): 62-80.

Beliaev, P. N. "Drevne-russkoe obiazatel'stvennoe pravo." *Iuridicheskii vestnik* 18(1917): 82-105.

——. "Kholopstvo i dolgovye otnosheniia v drevnem russkom prave." *Iuridicheskii vestnik* 9(1915): 115-52.

Berry, Lloyd E., and Crummey, Robert Owen, editors. *Rude and Barbarous Kingdom. Russia in the Accounts of Sixteenth-Century English Voyagers.* Madison: The University of Wisconsin Press, 1968.

728   Selected Bibliography

Blum, Jerome. *Lord and Peasant in Russia. From the Ninth to the Nineteenth Century*. Princeton: Princeton University Press, 1961.

Buganov, V. I. *Moskovskoe vosstanie 1662 g*. Moscow: Nauka, 1964.

———. *Vosstanie 1662 g. v Moskve. Sbornik dokumentov*. Moscow: Nauka, 1964.

Cherepnin, L. V. *Obrazovanie russkogo tsentralizovannogo gosudarstva v XIV-XV vekakh. Ocherki sotsial'no-ekonomicheskoi istorii Rusi*. Moscow: Sotsekgiz, 1960.

Debol'skii, N. N. *Grazhdanskaia deesposobnost' po russkomu pravu do kontsa XVII veka*. St. Petersburg, 1903.

Dewey, Horace W. *Muscovite Judicial Texts, 1488-1556*. Ann Arbor: Department of Slavic Languages and Literatures, the University of Michigan, 1966. (=*Michigan Slavic Materials*, no. 7.)

———, and Kleimola, Ann M. *Russian Private Law in the XIV-XVII Centuries. An Anthology of Documents*. Ann Arbor: University of Michigan, Department of Slavic Languages and Literatures, 1973. (=*Michigan Slavic Materials*, no. 9.)

D'iakonov, M. A. "K voprosu o krest'ianskoi poriadnoi zapisi i sluzhiloi kabale." In *Sbornik statei posviashchennykh Vasiliiu Osipovichu Kliuchevskomu*. Moscow: T-vo "Pechatnia S. P. Iakovleva," 1909. Pp. 317-31.

———. *Ocherki iz istorii sel'skogo naseleniia v Moskovskom gosudarstve (XVI-XVII vv.)*. St. Petersburg, 1898.

———. *Ocherki obshchestvennogo i gosudarstvennogo stroia drevnei Rusi*. St. Petersburg, 1912.

———. *Sel'skoe naselenie Moskovskogo gosudarstva v XVI-XVII vv*. St. Petersburg, 1898.

Egorov, V. A. "Kabal'nye den'gi v kontse XVI veka." ZhMNP. 1910, no. 7: 146-91.

———. "Zapisnie kholop'i knigi d'iaka Aliab'eva." In *Sbornik statei, posviashchennykh S. F. Platonovu*. St. Petersburg, 1911. Pp. 462-70.

Eroshkin, N. P. *Istoriia gosudarstvennykh uchrezhdenii dorevoliutsionnoi Rossii*. 2d edition. Moscow: Vysshaia shkola, 1968.

Froianov, I. Ia. *Kievskaia Rus'. Ocherki sotsial'no-ekonomicheskoi istorii*. Leningrad: Leningradskii Gos. Universitet, 1974.

———. "O rabstve v Kievskoi Rusi." *Vestnik Leningradskogo universiteta*. 1965, no. 1: 80-92.

Geiman, V. G. "O nekotorykh svoeobraznykh iuridicheskikh dokumentov XVII v." *Istoricheskii arkhiv*. 1962, no. 3: 185-92.

———. "Neskol'ko novykh dannykh, kasaiushchikhsia istorii 'zadvornykh liudei'." *Sbornik statei po russkoi istorii, posviashchennykh S. F. Platonovu*. Petersburg: Tip. im. Guttenberga, 1922. Pp. 39-48.

Got'e, Iu. V. *Zamoskovnyi krai v XVII veke. Opyt issledovaniia po istorii ekonomicheskogo byta Moskovskoi Rusi*. Moscow: Sotsekgiz, 1937.

Grekov, B. D. *Krest'iane na Rusi s drevneishikh vremen do XVII veka*. Moscow-Leningrad: Adademiia Nauk SSSR, 1946.

——, editor. *Sudebniki XV-XVI vekov*. Moscow-Leningrad: Akademiia Nauk SSSR, 1952.

Gudzinskaia, A. P. "Dokumenty sysknykh komissii vtoroi poloviny XVII v. kak istoricheskii istochnik." *Arkheograficheskii ezhegodnik za 1967 god* 11(1969): 107-18.

Hellie, Richard. "Muscovite Slavery in Comparative Perspective." *Russian History* 6, pt. 2(1979): 133-209.

——. "Recent Soviet Historiography on Medieval and Early Modern Russian Slavery." *The Russian Review* 35, no. 1(January 1976): 1-32.

Herberstein, Sigismund. *Commentaries on Muscovite Affairs*. Edited and translated by Oswald P. Backus III. Lawrence: University of Kansas Student Union Bookstore, 1956.

Iakovlev, A. I. *Kholopstvo i kholopy v Moskovskom gosudarstve XVII v*. Moscow-Leningard: Akademiia Nauk SSSR, 1943.

Kamentseva, E. I. "Zapisnye knigi krepostiam d'iaka Dmitriia Aliab'eva." *Trudy Istoriko-arkhivnogo instituta* 2(1946): 79-98.

Khoziaistvo krupnogo feodala-krepostnika XVI v. Edited by S. G. Tomsinskii and B. D. Grekov. 2 vols. Moscow-Leningrad: Akademiia Nauk SSSR, 1933, 1936.

Kleimola, Ann M. *Justice in Medieval Russia. Muscovite Judicial Charters (Pravye Gramoty) of the 15th and 16th Centuries*. Philadelphia: American Philosophical Society, 1975. (= *Transactions*, vol. 65, pt. 6.)

Kliuchevskii, V. O. *Istoriia soslovii v Rossii*. 3d edition. Petrograd: Lit.-Izd. Otdel Komissariata Narodnogo Prosveshcheniia, 1918.

——. "Podushnaia podat' i otmena kholopstva v Rossii." *Sochineniia*. 8 vols. Moscow: Sotsekgiz, 1956-59. 7: 318-402.

——. "Proiskhozhdenie krepostnogo prava v Rossii." *Sochineniia*. 7: 238-317.

Kolycheva, E. I. *Kholopstvo i krepostnichestvo (konets XV-XVI v.)*. Moscow: Nauka, 1971.

——. "Nekotorye problemy rabstva i feodalizma v trudakh V. I. Lenina i sovetskoi istoriografii." In *Aktual'nye problemy istorii Rossii epokhi feodalizma. Sbornik statei*. Edited by L. V. Cherepnin et al. Moscow: Nauka, 1970. Pp. 120-47.

——. "Opyt primeneniia korreliatsionnogo analiza dlia resheniia nekotorykh spornykh voprosov istorii kholopstva." *Istoriia SSSR*. 1969, no. 4: 140-45.

——. "Russkaia Pravda i obychnoe pravo o polnykh kholopakh XV-XVI vv." *Istoricheskie zapiski* 85(1970): 268-306.

Koretskii, V. I. *Formirovanie krepostnogo prava i pervaia krest'ianskaia voina v Rossii*. Moscow: Nauka, 1975.

——. *Zakreposhchenie krest'ian i klassovaia bor'ba v Rossii vo vtoroi polovine XVI v*. Moscow: Nauka, 1970.

Kormchaia kniga. Moscow, 1653. (The Nikon copy.)

Kotoshikhin, Grigorii. *O Rossii v tsarstvovanie Alekseia Mikhailovicha*. St. Petersburg, 1909.

Kusheva, E. N. "Epizod klassovoi bor'by soldat, krest'ian i kholopov na rubezhe XVII-XVIII vv." *Trudy LOII* 9(1967): 348-55.

——. "K istorii kholopstva v kontse XVI-nachale XVII v." *Istoricheskie zapiski* 15(1945): 70-96.

——. "O plene kak istochnike kholopstva vo vtoroi polovine XVII v." *Trudy LOII* 12(1971): 217-31.

Lappo-Danilevskii, A. "Sluzhilye kabaly pozdneishogo tipa." *Sbornik statei, posv. Vasiliiu Osipovichu Kliuchevskomu.* Moscow, 1909. Pp. 719-64.

——. "Vvedénie [k zapisnoi knige krepostnym aktam XV-XVII vv., iavlennym v Novgorode po Vodskoi piatine d'iaku D. Aliab'evu]." RIB 17 (1898): iii-xxx.

Lappo-Danilevskii, A. S., et al., compilers. "Katalog chastnykh aktov Moskovskogo gosudarstva." *Problemy istochnikovedeniia* 2(1936): 333-79.

Loewenson, Leo. "Escaped Russian Slaves in England in the Seventeenth Century." SEER 42(1963-64): 427-29.

Leont'ev, A. K. *Obrazovanie prikaznoi sistemy upravleniia v russkom gosudarstve. Iz istorii sozdaniia tsentralizovannogo gosudarstvennogo apparata v kontse XV-pervoi polovine XVI v.* Moscow: Moskovskii Universitet, 1961.

Lokhvitskii, A. *O plennykh po drevnemu russkomu pravu (XV, XVI, XVII veka).* Moscow, 1855.

Makovskii, D. P. *Pervaia krest'ianskaia voina v Rossii.* Smolensk, 1967.

Man'kov, A. G. *Razvitie krepostnogo prava v Rossii vo vtoroi polovine XVII veka.* Moscow-Leningrad: Akademiia Nauk SSSR, 1962.

——. *Ulozhenie 1649 goda. Kodeks feodal'nogo prava Rossii.* Leningrad: Nauka, 1980.

Miliukov, P. N. "Kogda 'zadvornye liudi' stali gosudarstvennymi tiagletsami?" *Trudy Riazanskoi uchenoi arkhivnoi kommissii* 12, vyp. 1(1897): 97-99.

Milov, L. V. "O drevnerusskom perevode vizantiiskogo kodeksa zakona VIII veka (Eklogi)." *Istoriia SSSR* 20, no. 1(January-February 1976): 142-63.

Miuller, R. B. "Nekotornye zamechaniia ob izdanii zakonodatel'nykh aktov vtoroi poloviny XVI v." *Problemy istochnikovedeniia* 9(1961): 333-40.

Mordukhovich, L. M., editor. "Iurii Krizhanich o 'rabstve'." *Trudy Otdela drevnerusskoi literatury* 33(1979): 142-55.

Nazarov, V. D. " 'Dvor' i 'dvoriane' po dannym novgorodskogo i severo-vostochnogo letopisaniia (XII-XIV vv.). In *Vostochnaia Evropa v drevnosti i srednevekov'e. Sbornik statei.* Edited by L. V. Cherepnin et al. Moscow: Nauka, 1978. Pp. 104-23.

Novombergskii, N. "Vymuchennye kabaly v Moskovskoi Rusi XVII stoletiia." ZhMIu 21, no. 5(May 1915): 288-338.

Novosel'skii, A. A. "Kollektivnye dvorianskie chelobitnye o syske beglykh krest'-ian i kholopov vo vtoroi polovine XVII v." In *Dvorianstvo i krepostnoi stroi Rossii XVI-XVIII vv. Sbornik statei, posviashchennyi pamiati Alekseia Andreevicha Novosel'skogo.* Edited by N. I. Pavlenko et al. Moscow: Nauka, 1975. Pp. 304-43.

——. "Otdatochnye knigi beglykh, kak istochnik dlia izucheniia narodnoi kolonizatsii na Rusi v XVII veke." *Trudy Istoriko-arkhivnogo instituta* 2(1946): 124-52.

——. "Pobegi krest'ian i kholopov i ikh sysk v Moskovskom gosudarstve vtoroi poloviny XVII veka." *Trudy Instituta istorii RANION* 1(1926): 325-54.

——. *Votchinnik i ego khoziaistvo v XVII veke.* Moscow-Leningrad: Gosizdat, 1929.

Novosel'tsev, A. P., Pashuto, V. T., and Cherepnin, L. V. *Puti razvitiia feodalizma (Zakavkaz'e, Sredniaia Aziia, Rus', Pribaltika).* Moscow: Nauka, 1972.

Novombergskii, N. "Vymuchennye kabaly v Moskovskoi Rusi XVII stoletiia." ZhMIu 1915, no. 5.

Olearius, Adam. *The Travels of Olearius in Seventeenth-Century Russia.* Translated and edited by Samuel H. Baron. Stanford: Stanford University Press, 1967.

Orfenov, B. "Kabal'noe kholopstvo v Moskovskom gosudarstve v kontse XV i XVI veke." *Uchenye zapiski Saratovskogo gosudarstvennogo pedagogicheskogo instituta.* Vyp. VI. *Trudy istoricheskogo fakul'teta.* Saratov, 1940. Pp. 51-56.

Orlov, A., editor. *Domostroi.* St. Petersburg, 1908.

Paneiakh, V. M. "Dobrovol'noe kholopstvo v zakonodatel'stve XVI-XVII vv. (1550-1649 gg.)." *Trudy LOII* 12(1971): 198-216.

——. "Iz istorii kabal'nogo kholopstva v XVI v." *Trudy LOII* 2(1960): 101-28.

——. "Iz istorii politiki tsarizma v kholop'em voprose v kontse XVI veka (pomeshchiki-vladel'tsy kabal'nykh kholopov)." *Trudy LOII* 8(1967): 100-9.

——. "K sporam o kholop'em nadele v XVI veke." *Istoriia SSSR* 1973, no. 3: 51-66.

——. "K voprosu o kholopakh-stradnikakh v XVI v." *Ezhegodnik po agrarnoi istorii Vostochnoi Evropy za 1960 god.* Kiev: Naukova dumka, 1962. Pp. 73-81.

——. "K voprosu o proiskhozhdenii kabal'nogo kholopstva." *Ezhegodnik po agrarnoi istorii Vostochnoi Evropy za 1964 god.* Kishinev: Kartia Moldoveniaske, 1966. Pp. 111-20.

——. "K voprosu ob ukaze 1601 goda." *Problemy istochnikovedeniia* 9(1960): 262-69.

——. "K voprosu o tak nazyvaemykh derevenskikh sluzhilykh kabalakh Spaso-Prilutskogo monastyria." *Problemy istochnikovedeniia* 5(1956): 210-30.

——. *Kabal'noe kholopstvo na Rusi v XVI veke.* Leningard: Nauka, 1967.

——. *Kholopstvo v XVI-nachale XVII v.* Leningrad: Nauka, 1975.

——. "Novgorodskaia zapisnaia kniga starykh krepostei 1598 g. (Opyt rekonstruktsii)." *Istoriia SSSR* 1960, no. 1: 175-81.

——. "Novyi istochnik po istorii kholopstva v XVI v." *Istoricheskii arkhiv* 4(1959): 203-11.

——. "O klassifikatsii i sostave kabal'nykh i zapisnykh knig starykh krepostei XVI veka." *Arkheograficheskii ezhegodnik za 1962* (1963): 397-400.

——. "O sotsial'nom sostave kabal'nykh kholopov v kontse XVI v." *Trudy LOII* 9(1967): 172-75.

——. "Ob odnom nesokhranivshemsia ukaze XVI v." *Trudy LOII* 7(1964): 390-97.

——. "Opyt tsifrovoi obrabotki materialov zapisnykh knig starykh krepostei XVI veka." *Trudy LOII* 5(1963): 542-56.

——. "Ulozhenie 1597 g. o kholopstve." *Istoricheskie zapiski* 77(1955): 154-89.

——. "Ukazy o kholop'ikh otpusknykh 50-kh godov XVI v." In *Iz istorii feodal'noi Rossii. Stat'i i ocherki k 70-letiiu so dnia rozhdeniia prof. V. V. Mavrodina.* Edited by I. Ia. Froianov et al. Leningrad: Leningradskii Gos. Universitet, 1978. Pp. 103-10.

——. "Zapisnye knigi starykh krepostei kontsa XVI v." *Problemy istochnikovedeniia* 11(1963): 346-63.

Pavlov-Sil'vanskii, N. P. "Liudi kabal'nye i dokladnye." ZhMNP 297, no. 1 (Jan. 1895): 210-39.

——. *Zakladnichestvo-patronat.* St. Petersburg, 1897.

Perel'man, I. L. "Novgorodskaia derevnia v XV-XVI vv." *Istoricheskie zapiski* 26(1948): 128-97.

Petrikeev, D. I. *Krupnoe krepostnoe khoziaistvo XVII v. Po materialam votchiny boiarina B. I. Morozova.* Leningrad: Nauka, 1967.

Petrov, V. A. "Slugi i delovye liudi monastyrskikh votchin XVI v." *Trudy LOII* 2(1960): 129-71.

P'iankov, A. P. "Kholopstvo na Rusi do obrazovaniia tsentralizovannogo gosudarstva." *Ezhegodnik po agrarnoi istorii Vostochnoi Evropy za 1965 god.* Moscow: Nauka, 1970. Pp. 42-48.

Polosin, I. I. "Drevnerusskii literaturnyi portret." In his *Sotsial'no-politicheskaia istoriia Rossii XVI-nachala XVII v. Sbornik statei.* Moscow: Izd-vo Akademii nauk SSSR, 1963. Pp. 246-62.

Rabinovich, M. D. "Sotsial'noe proiskhozhdenie i imushchestvennoe polozhenie ofitserov reguliarnoi russkoi armii v kontse Severnoi voiny." In *Rossiia v period reform Petra I.* Edited by N. I. Pavlenko et al. Moscow: Nauka, 1973. Pp. 133-71.

Romanov, B. A. "K voprosu o 15-rublevom maksimume v sluzhilykh kabalakh XVI v." *Istoricheskie zapiski* 52(1955): 325-35.

——. *Liudi i nravy drevnei Rusi.* 2d edition. Moscow-Leningrad: Nauka, 1966.

Rozhkov, N. A. *Sel'skoe khoziaistvo Moskovskoi Rusi v XVI veke.* Moscow, 1899.

Sadikov, P. "K voprosu o rekrutskom nabore dvorovykh i delovykh liudei 1703 g." *Arkhiv istorii truda v Rossii* 4, no. 2(1922): 45-49.

Savich, N. G., editor. *Vosstanie v Moskve 1682 g. Sbornik dokumentov.* Moscow: Nauka, 1976.

Seeley, Frank F. "Russia and the Slave Trade." SEER 23(1945): 126-36.

Sergeevich, V. I. *Drevnosti russkogo prava.* 3 vols. St. Petersburg, 1909.

Shapiro, A. L. "Kholopy-stradniki v XVI v." *Iz istorii feodal'noi Rossii. Stat'i i ocherki . . . k Mavrodinu.* Pp. 92-102.

——. *Problemy sotsial'no-ekonomicheskoi istorii Rusi XIV-XVI vv.* Leningrad: Leningradskii Universitet, 1977.

Shepelev, I. S. *Osvoboditel'naia i klassovaia bor'ba v Russkom gosudarstve v 1608-1610 gg.* Piatigorsk, 1957.

Shepukova, N. M. "K voprosu ob itogakh podvornoi perepisi 1678-1679 gg. v Rossiiskom gosudarstve." *Istoriia SSSR* 4, no. 3(April-May 1960): 145-47.

Shilov, A. A. "Postupnye zapisi." In *Sbornik statei, posviashchennykh A. S. Lappo-Danilevskomu.* Petrograd, 1916. Pp. 266-309.

Smirnov, I. I. "K probleme 'smerd'ego kholopa'." *Trudy LOII* 2(1960): 306-26.

———. "Novyi spisok Ulozheniia 9 marta 1607 g." *Istoricheskii arkhiv* 4(1949): 72-87.

———. *Ocherki politicheskoi istorii Russkogo gosudarstva 30-50-kh godov XVI veka.* Moscow-Leningrad: Akademiia Nauk SSSR, 1958.

———. *Ocherki sotsial'no-ekonomicheskikh otnoshenii Rusi XII-XIII vekov.* Moscow-Leningrad: Akademiia Nauk SSSR, 1963.

———. *Vosstanie Bolotnikova 1606-1607 gg.* Leningrad: Gospolitizdat, 1951.

Smirnov, P. P. "Chelobitnye dvorian i detei boiarskikh vsekh gorodov v pervoi polovine XVII v." *Chteniia* 1915, no. 3, pt. I, pp. 1-73.

———. *Posadskie liudi i ikh klassovaia bor'ba do serediny XVII veka.* 2 vols. Moscow-Leningrad: Akademiia Nauk SSSR, 1947.

Sverdlov, M. B. "Dvoriane v Drevnei Rusi." In *Iz istorii feodal'noi Rossii. Stat'i i ocherki k 70-letiiu so dnia rozhdeniia prof. V. V. Mavrodina.* Edited by A. Ia. Degtiarev et al. Leningrad: Leningradskii Universitet, 1978. Pp. 54-59.

———. "Ob obshchestvennoi kategorii 'cheliad' v Drevnei Rusi." In *Problemy istorii feodal'noi Rossii. Sbornik statei k 60-letiiu prof. V. V. Mavrodina.* Edited by A. L. Shapiro et al. Leningrad: Leningradskii universitet, 1971. Pp. 53-58.

Tatishchev, V. N. *Istoriia rossiiskaia.* 7 vols. Moscow-Leningrad: Akademiia Nauk SSSR-Nauka, 1962-68.

———. *Sudebnik gosudaria tsaria i velikogo kniazia Ioanna Vasil'evicha, i nekotorye sego gosudaria i blizhnikh ego preemnikov ukazy.* Moscow, 1786.

Tikhomirov, M. N., editor. *Sobornoe Ulozhenie 1649 goda.* Moscow: Moskovskii Universitet, 1961.

Valk, S. N. "Gramoty polnoe." In *Sbornik statei po russkoi istorii, posviashchennyi S. F. Platonovu.* Petrograd, 1922. Pp. 113-32.

Vashchenko, T. F. "Leksicheskie dannye kabal'nykh zapisei." In *Pamiatniki russkogo iazyka. Voprosy issledovaniia i izdaniia.* Moscow: Nauka, 1974. Pp. 246-57.

Veretennikov, V. I. "K istorii kabal'nogo kholopstva." *LZAK za 1926 g.* 1[34] (1927): 161-70.

Veselovskii, S. B. *Feodal'noe zemlevladenie v severo-vostochnoi Rusi.* Moscow-Leningrad: Akademiia Nauk SSSR, 1947.

Vodarskii, Ia. E. "Chislennost' naseleniia i kolichestvo pomestno-votchinnykh zemel' v XVI v. (po pistsovym i perepisnym knigam)." *Ezhegodnik po agrarnoi istorii vostochnoi Evropy za 1964 god.* Kishinev: Kartia Moldoveniaske, 1966. Pp. 217-30.

———. *Naselenie Rossii v kontse XVII-nachale XVIII veka*. Moscow: Nauka, 1977.

———. *Naselenie Rossii za 400 let (XVI-nachalo XX vv.)* Moscow: Prosveshchenie, 1973.

———. "Praviashchaia gruppa svetskikh feodalov v Rossii v XVII v." *Dvorianstvo i krepostnoi stroi Rossii XVI-XVII vv.* Edited by N. I. Pavlenko et al. Moscow: Nauka, 1975. Pp. 70-107.

———. "Sluzhiloe dvorianstvo v Rossii v kontse XVII-nachale XVIII v." In *Voprosy voennoi istorii Rossii. XVIII i pervaia polovina XIX vekov*. Moscow: Nauka, 1969. Pp. 233-38.

Zabelin, Iv., editor. *Domostroi po spisku imperatorskogo Obshchestva istorii i drevnostei rossiiskikh.* Moscow: Universitetskaia tipografiia (M. Katkov), 1882.

Zaozerskii, A. I. *Tsar' Aleksei Mikhailovich v svoem khoziaistve*. Petrograd: Petrogradskii universitet, 1917.

Zimin, A. A. "Kholopy drevnei Rusi." *Istoriia SSSR* 1965, no. 6: 39-75.

———. *Kholopy na Rusi (s drevneishikh vremen do kontsa XV v.)*. Moscow: Nauka, 1973.

———. "Otpusk kholopov na voliu v Severo-Vostochnoi Rusi XIV-XV vv." *Trudy LOII* 9(1967): 55-74.

———. *Reformy Ivana Groznogo. Ocherki sotsial'no-ekonomicheskoi i politicheskoi istorii Rossii serediny XVI v*. Moscow: Sotsekgiz, 1960.

Materials on Slavery Outside of Russia

Averkieva, Iu. P. *Rabstvo u indeitsev Severnoi Ameriki*. Moscow-Leningrad: Akademiia Nauk SSSR, 1941.

Banaji, D. R. *Slavery in British India*. Bombay: D. B. Taraporevala Sons & Co., 1933.

Blavatskaia, T. V., et al. *Rabstvo u ellinisticheskikh gosudarstv v III-I vv. do n.e.* Moscow: Nauka, 1969.

Bowser, Frederick P. *The African Slave in Colonial Peru, 1524-1650*. Stanford: Stanford University Press, 1974.

Brauning, R. "Rabstvo v Vizantiiskoi imperii (600-1200 gg)." *Vizantiiskii vremennik* 14(1958): 38-55.

Brunschvig, R. "'Abd." *The Encyclopaedia of Islam* 1(1960): 24-34.

Buckland, William W. *The Roman Law of Slavery*. Cambridge: Cambridge University Press, 1908.

Buckley, Roger. *Slaves in Red Coats: The British West Indian Regiments, 1795-1815*. New Haven: Yale University Press, 1979.

Catterall, Helen Tunicliff, ed. *Judicial Cases Concerning American Slavery and the Negro*. 5 vols. Washington: Carnegie Institution, 1926-37.

Cooper, Frederick. *Plantation Slavery on the East Coast of Africa*. New Haven: Yale University Press, 1977.

Craton, Michael, editor. *Roots and Branches. Current Directions in Slave Studies.* (= *Historical Reflections* 6, no. 1 [Summer 1979]).

Curtin, Philip D. *Economic Change in Pre-Colonial Africa: Senegambia in the Era of the Slave Trade.* 2 vols. Madison: University of Wisconsin Press, 1975.

Dandamaev, M. A. *Rabstvo v Vavilonii VII-IV vv. do n.e. (626-331 gg.).* Moscow: Nauka, 1974.

David, Paul A., et al. *Reckoning with Slavery. A Critical Study in the Quantitative History of American Negro Slavery.* New York: Oxford University Press, 1976.

Davis, David Brion. *The Problem of Slavery in Western Culture.* Ithaca: Cornell University Press, 1966.

——. *The Problem of Slavery in the Age of Revolution.* Ithaca: Cornell University Press, 1975.

Degler, Carl N. *Neither Black Nor White: Slavery and Race Relations in Brazil and the United States.* New York: Macmillan, 1971.

Driver, G., and Miles, J. C. *The Babylonian Laws.* 2 vols. Oxford: Oxford University Press, 1952-53.

El'nitskii, L. A. *Vozniknovenie i razvitie rabstva v Rime v VIII-III vv. do n.e.* Moscow: Nauka, 1964.

Emmer, Pieter, Mettas, Jean, and Nardin, Jean-Claude, editors. *La Traité des Noirs par l'Atlantique: Nouvelles Approches.* Special issue of *Revue française d'histoire d'outre-mer* 62, nos. 226-27(1975).

Engerman, Stanley. "Some Considerations Relating to Property Rights in Man." *Journal of Economic History* 33(March 1973): 43-65.

——, and Genovese, Eugene D., editors. *Race and Slavery in the Western Hemisphere. Quantitative Studies.* Princeton: Princeton University Press, 1975.

The Fetha Nagast. The Law of Kings. Translated from the G'ev by Abba Paulos Tzadua. Edited by Peter L. Strauss. Addis Ababa: Haile Selassie I University Faculty of Law, 1968.

Finley, Moses I. *Ancient Slavery and Modern Ideology.* New York: Viking Press, 1980.

——. "Between Slavery and Freedom." *Comparative Studies in Society and History* 6(April 1964): 233-49.

——. "The Extent of Slavery." In *Slavery. A Comparative Perspective. Readings from Ancient Times to the Present.* Edited by Robin W. Winks. New York: New York University Press, 1972. Pp. 3-15.

——. "Was Greek Civilization Based on Slave Labor?" In *The Slave Economies.* Edited by Eugene D. Genovese. 2 vols. New York: John Wiley, 1973. 1: 19-45.

Finley, Moses I., editor. *Slavery in Classical Antiquity. Views and Controversies.* Cambridge: W. Heffer & Sons, 1960.

Fisher, Alan W. "Chattel Slave Procurement in the Ottoman Empire." Paper Presented at the Twelfth Annual Meeting of the Middle East Studies Association, Ann Arbor, November 1978.

———. "Chattel Slavery in the Ottoman Empire." *Slavery and Abolition* 1, no. 1 (May 1980): 25-45.

———. "Muscovy and the Black Sea Trade." *Canadian-American Slavic Studies* 1972, no. 4: 575-99.

Fogel, Robert W., and Engerman, Stanley L. *Time on the Cross. The Economics of American Negro Slavery*. 2 vols. Boston: Little Brown, 1974.

Foner, Laura, and Genovese, Eugene, editors. *Slavery in the New World. A Reader in Comparative History*. Englewood Cliffs, N. J.: Prentice-Hall, 1969.

Franklin, John Hope. *From Slavery to Freedom. A History of Negro Americans*. New York: Knopf, 1974.

Freshfield, E. H., editor. *A Manual of Roman Law. The Ecloga, Published by the Emperors Leo III and Constantine V of Isauria at Constantinople, A. D. 726*. Cambridge: Cambridge University Press, 1926.

———. *The Procheiros Nomos. Published by the Emperor Basil I at Constantinople between 867 and 879 A.D.* Cambridge: Cambridge University Press, 1928.

Friedman, Lawrence. *A History of American Law*. New York: Simon and Schuster, 1973.

Gelb, I. J. "From Freedom to Slavery." *Bayerische Akademie Der Wissenschaften. Philosophisch-Historische Klasse. Abhandlungen. Neue Folge Heft* 75 (Munich 1972): 81-92.

Gemery, Henry A., and Hogendorn, Jan S., editors. *The Uncommon Market. Essays in the Economic History of the Atlantic Slave Trade*. New York: Academic Press, 1979.

Genovese, Eugene D. *Roll, Jordan, Roll. The World the Slaves Made*. New York: Pantheon, 1974.

———, editor. *The Slave Economies*. 2 vols. New York: John Wiley, 1973.

Goldin, Claudia Dale. *Urban Slavery in the American South, 1820-1860. A Quantitative History*. Chicago: The University of Chicago Press, 1976.

Gutman, Herbert G. *Slavery and the Numbers Game. A Critique of Time on the Cross.* Urbana: University of Illinois Press, 1975.

Hall, Neville. "Slave Laws of the Danish Virgin Islands in the Later Eighteenth Century." *Annals of the New York Academy of Sciences* 292(1977): 174-86.

Hjejle, Benedicte. "Slavery and Agricultural Bondage in South India in the 19th Century." *Scandinavian Economic History Review* 15(1967): 71-126.

Hopkins, Keith. *Conquerors and Slaves. Sociological Studies in Roman History*. Cambridge: Cambridge University Press, 1978.

———. "Slavery in Classical Antiquity." In *Caste and Race: Comparative Approaches*. Edited by Anthony de Reuck and Julie Knight. Boston: Little, Brown, 1967. Pp. 166-77.

Hurd, John Codman. *The Law of Freedom and Bondage in the United States*. 2 vols. Boston: Little, Brown, 1858-62.

Inalcik, Halil. "Servile Labor in the Ottoman Empire." In *The Mutual Effects of the Islamic and Judeo-Christian Worlds: The East European Pattern*. Edited by Abraham Ascher et al. Brooklyn: Brooklyn College Press, 1979. Pp. 25-52.

India. Law Commission. *Report on Indian Slavery*. London, 1841.

Istoriia Vizantii. Edited by S. D. Skazkin et al. 3 vols. Moscow: Nauka, 1967.

Jones, A. H. M. "Slavery in the Ancient World." *The Economic History Review* 9, no. 2(1956): 185-99.

Jordan, Winthrop D. *White Over Black. American Attitudes toward the Negro, 1550-1812.* Baltimore: Penguin, 1969.

Kachanovskii, Iu. V. "O poniatiiakh 'rabstvo' i 'feodalizm'." *Voprosy istorii* 43, no. 6(June 1967): 123-34.

———. *Rabovladenie, feodalizm ili aziatskii sposob? Spor ob obshchestvennom stroe drevnego i srednevekogo Vostoka, dokolonial'noi Afriki i dokolumbovoi Ameriki*. Moscow: Nauka, 1971.

Kallistrov, D. P. *Rabstvo na periferii antichnogo mira*. Leningrad: Nauka, 1968.

Klein, Herbert S. *The Middle Passage. Comparative Studies in the Atlantic Slave Trade*. Princeton: Princeton University Press, 1978.

———. *Slavery in the Americas*. Chicago: Quadrangle, 1971.

Knight, Franklin W. *Slave Society in Cuba During the Nineteenth Century*. Madison: Wisconsin, 1970.

Kolchin, Peter. "In Defense of Servitude: A Comparison of American Proslavery and Russian Proserfdom Arguments, 1750-1860." Paper Delivered at the American Historical Association Convention, San Francisco, December 28, 1978. Published in *The American Historical Review* 85, no. 4(October 1980): 809-27.

———. "The Process of Confrontation: Patterns of Resistance to Bondage in Nineteenth-Century Russia and the United States." *Journal of Social History* 11, no. 4(1978).

Kuzishchin, V. I. "Poniatie obshchestvenno-ekonomicheskoi formatsii i periodizatsiia istorii rabovladel'cheskogo obshchestva." *Vestnik drevnei istorii* 1974, no. 3: 69-87.

The Laws of Manu. Translated by Georg Buhler. New York: Dover Publications, n.d.

Lebedeva, G. E. "Kodeksy Feodosiia i Iustiniana ob istochnikakh rabstva." *Vizantiiskii vremennik* 35(1973): 33-50.

Lentsman, Ia. A. *Rabstvo v nikenskoi i gomarovskoi Gretsii*. Moscow: Akademiia Nauk SSSR, 1963.

Litwack, Leon F. *Been in the Storm So Long. The Aftermath of Slavery*. New York: Random House, 1980.

Marinovich, A. P., et al. *Rabstvo v vostochnykh provintsiakh Rimskoi Imperii v I-III vv*. Moscow: Nauka, 1977.

Meijer, Marinus J. "Slavery at the End of the Ch'ing Dynasty." In *Essays on China's Legal Tradition*. Edited by Jerome Alan Cohen, R. Randle Edward, and Fu-mei Chang Chen. Princeton: Princeton University Press, 1980. Pp. 327-58.

Mellafe, Rolando. *Negro Slavery in Latin America*. Berkeley: University of California Press, 1975.

Mendelsohn, Isaac. *Slavery in the Ancient Near East. A Comparative Study of Slavery in Babylonia, Assyria, Syria, and Palestine, from the Middle of the Third Millennium to the End of the First Millennium*. New York: Columbia University Press, 1949.

Miers, Suzanne and Kopytoff, Igor, editors. *Slavery in Africa. Anthropological and Historical Perspectives*. Madison: University of Wisconsin Press, 1977.

Nieboer, H. J. *Slavery as an Industrial System. Ethnological Researches*. The Hague: Martinus Nijhoff, 1910.

Patterson, Orlando. "On Slavery and Slave Formations." *New Left Review* 117 (September-October 1979): 31-69.

——. "Slavery." *Annual Review of Sociology* 3(1977): 407-49.

Petrushevskii, I. P. "K istorii rabstva v Khalifate VII-X vekov." *Narody Azii i Afriki* 1971, no. 3: 60-71.

Picheta, V. I. *Belorussiia i Litva XV-XVI vv*. Moscow: Akademiia Nauk SSSR, 1961.

——. "Institut kholopstva v velikom kniazhestve Litovskom v XV-XVI vv." *Istoricheskie zapiski* 20(1946): 38-65.

Pipes, Daniel. "From Mawla to Mamluk: The Origins of Islamic Military Slavery." PhD. dissertation, Harvard University, May, 1978.

——. *Slave Soldiers and Islam. The Genesis of a Military System*. New Haven: Yale University Press, 1980.

——. "The Strategic Rationale for Military Slavery." *The Journal of Strategic Studies* 2, no. 1(May 1979): 34-46.

Priotrovskii, B. B., editor. *Problemy antichnoi istorii i kul'tury. (Doklady XIV mezhdunarodnoi konferentsii antichnikov sotsialisticheskikh stran "Eirene")*. Erevan: Izd-vo AN Armianskoi SSSR, 1979.

Pritchard, James B., editor. *The Ancient Near East. An Anthology of Texts and Pictures*. Princeton: Princeton University Press, 1958.

Pryor, Frederick L. "A Comparative Study of Slave Societies." *Journal of Comparative Economics* 1, no. 1(March 1977): 25-50.

Pulleyblank, E. G. "The Origins and Nature of Chattel Slavery in China." *Journal of the Economic and Social History of the Orient* 1, pt. 2 (1958): 185-220.

Raj Chanana, Dev. *Slavery in Ancient India*. New Delhi: People's Publishing House, 1960.

Rose, Willie Lee, editor. *A Documentary History of Slavery in North America*. New York: Oxford University Press, 1976.

Rostovtzeff, M. I., and Welles, C. Bradford. "A Parchment Contract of Loan from Dura-Europos on the Euphrates." *Yale Classical Studies* 2(1931): 1-78.

Rubin, Vera, and Tuden, Arthur, editors. *Comparative Perspectives on Slavery in New World Plantation Societies. (= Annals of The New York Academy of Sciences* 292[1977].)

Shtaerman, E. M. *Krizis rabovladel'cheskogo stroia v zapadnykh provintsiiakh Rimskoi imperii*. Moscow: Akademiia Nauk SSSR, 1957.

——. *Rastsvet rabovladel'cheskikh otnoshenii v Rimskoi respublike*. Moscow: Nauka, 1964.

——, and Trofimova, M. K. *Rabovladel'cheskie otnosheniia v rannei Rimskoi imperii (Italiia)*. Moscow: Nauka, 1971.

Siegel, Bernard J. "Some Methodological Considerations for a Comparative Study of Slavery." *American Anthropologist* 47(1945): 357-92.

Smirnov, A. P. "Proiskhozhdenie rabovladeniia." In *Leninskie idei v izuchenii istorii pervobytnogo obshchestva, rabovladeniia i feodalizma. Sbornik statei.* Edited by P. I. Zasurtsev et al. Moscow: Nauka, 1970. Pp. 113-32.

Smith, Michael Garfield. *The Plural Society in the British West Indies*. Berkeley and Los Angeles: University of California Press, 1965.

Spence, Jonathan D. *Ts'ao Yin and the K'ang-hsi Emperor, Bondservant and Master*. New Haven: Yale University Press, 1966.

Stampp, Kenneth M. *The Peculiar Institution. Slavery in the Ante-Bellum South*. New York: Random House, Vintage, 1956.

Stein, Stanley J. *Vassouras. A Brazilian Coffee County, 1850-1890. The Role of Planter and Slave in a Changing Plantation Society*. New York: Atheneum, 1976.

Tymieniecki, Kazimierz. "Niewolni, wolni i przypisańcy w Polsce przed kolonizacją na prawie niemieckim." *Sprawozdania. Towarzystwo Naukowe we Lwowie* 16(1936): 146-52.

——. "Zagadnienie niewoli w Polsce u schyłku wieków średnich." *Prace Komisji Historycznej Poznańskiego Towarzystwa Przyjaciół Nauk* 7(1933): 498-537.

Udal'tsova, Z. V. "Polozhenie rabov v Vizantii VI v. (preimushchestvenno po dannym zakonodatel'stva Iustiniana)." *Vizantiiskii vremennik* 24(1963): 3-34.

Verlinden, Charles. *The Beginnings of Modern Colonization. Eleven Essays with an Introduction*. Ithaca: Cornell University Press, 1970.

Wade, Richard C. *Slavery in the Cities; the South, 1820-1860*. New York: Oxford University Press, 1964.

Watson, James L. "Chattel Slavery in Chinese Peasant Society: A Comparative Analysis." *Ethnology* 15, no. 4(October 1976): 361-75.

——, editor. *Asian and African Systems of Slavery*. Oxford: Basil Blackwell, 1980.

Wergeland, Agnes Mathilde. *Slavery in Germanic Society During the Middle Ages*. Chicago: The University of Chicago Press, 1916.

Westermann, William L. *The Slave Systems of Greek and Roman Antiquity*. Philadelphia: American Philosophical Society, 1955. (APS *Memoirs*, vol. 40.)

Wiedemann, Thomas. *Greek and Roman Slavery*. Baltimore: The Johns Hopkins University Press, 1981.

Wiens, Mi Chü. "The Origins of Modern Chinese Landlordism." In *Festschrift in Honor of the Eightieth Birthday of Professor Shen Kang-po*. Edited by Wang Pi-ch'eng. Taipei: Lien-ying ch'u-pan shih-yeh Kung-ssu, 1976. Pp. 289-344.

Wilbur, C. Martin. *Slavery in China During the Former Han Dynasty, 206 B.C.-A.D. 25.* (= *Publications of the Field Museum of Natural History*, 525. Anthropological Serieṣ 34 [January 15, 1943].)

Materials for a Muscovite Prosopography

Andreiiashev, A. M. "Materialy po istoricheskoi geografii Novgorodskoi zemli. Shelonskaia piatina po pistsovym knigam 1498-1576 gg." *Chteniia* 250(1914, no. 3): i-lxxviii + 1-544.

Anpilogov, P. N. *Nizhegorodskie dokumenty XVI veka (1588-1600 gg.).* Moscow: Moskovskii Gos. Universitet, 1977.

——. *Novye dokumenty o Rossii kontsa XVI-nachala XVII veka.* Moscow: Moskovskii Gos. Universitet, 1967.

Barsukov, A. P. "Dokladnaia vypiska 121 (1613) g. o votchinakh i pomest'iakh." *Chteniia* 172(1895, no. 1): 1-24.

——. *Spiski gorodovykh voevod Moskovskogo gosudarstva XVII st.* St. Petersburg: M. M. Stasiulevich, 1902.

Beliaev, I. D., editor. "Pistsovye Novgorodskie knigi 7090 i 7091 godov." *Vremennik* 6(1850): pt. 2, pp. 1-126.

Beliaev, I. S., editor. *Rospisnoi spisok goroda Moskvy 1638 goda.* Moscow: Tipografiia Moskovskogo universiteta, 1911. (= *Trudy Moskovskogo otdela imp. Russkogo voenno-istoricheskogo obshchestva*, vol. 1.)

Belokurov, S. A. "Razriadnye zapisi za smutnoe vremia (7113-7121 g.)." *Chteniia* 222(1907, no. 3): 1-311.

Bernadskii, V. N. *Novgorod i novgorodskaia zemlia v XV veke.* Moscow-Leningrad: Akademiia Nauk SSSR, 1961.

Bogoiavlenskii, S. K. *Prikaznye sud'i XVII veka.* Moscow-Leningrad: AN SSSR, 1946.

Bychkova, M. E. *Rodoslovnye knigi XVI-XVII vv.* Moscow: Nauka, 1966.

Danilova, L. V. *Ocherki po istorii zemlevladeniia i khoziaistva v Novgorodskoi zemle v XIV-XV vv.* Moscow: Akademiia Nauk SSSR, 1955.

Dolgorukov, P. V. *Rossiiskaia rodoslovnaia kniga.* 4 vols. St. Petersburg: Tip. K. Vingebera, 1854-57.

Glebov-Stretnev, F. P. "Spisok boiar, okol'nichikh i drugikh chinov, s 1578 do tsarstvovaniia Fedora Alekseevicha." *Arkhiv istoriko-iuridicheskikh svedenii, otnosiashchikhsia do Rossii* 2[1] (1855), sec. ii, pt. 4, pp. 130-41.

Gnevushev, A. M. *Akty vremeni pravleviia Tsaria Vasiliia Shuiskogo (1606-1610 gg.).* Moscow, 1914.

——. *Novgorodskii dvortsovyi prikaz v XVII veke.* Moscow: Russkaia Pechatnia, 1911.

——. *Sel'skoe naselenie Novgorodskoi oblasti po pistsovym knigam 1495-1505 godov.* Kiev, 1911.

Got'e, Iu. V. "Desiatni po Vladimiru i Meshchere 1590 i 1615 gg." *Chteniia* 236(1911, no. 1): 77-99.

Grekov, B. D. "Opis' torgovoi storony v pistsovoi knige po Novgorodu Velikomu XVI veka." LZAK 24(1912): pt. 4, pp. i-ix + 1-88.

Hulbert, Ellerd Miner. "Sixteenth Century Russian Assemblies of the Land: Their Composition, Organization, and Competence." Ph.D. Dissertation, University of Chicago, 1969.

Ianitskii, N. *Ekonomicheskii krizis v novgorodskoi oblasti XVI veka (po pistsovym knigam).* Kiev: Tip. imp. Universiteta Sv. Vladimira, 1915. See especially app. xiv, pp. 110-226.

Ivanov, Petr Ivanovich. *Alfavitnyi ukazatel' familii i lits, upominaemykh v boiarskikh knigakh, khraniashchikhsia v l-m otdelenii Moskovskogo arkhiva Ministerstva iustitsii.* Moscow: Ministerstvo Iustitsii, 1853. (Cited as Ivanov, AUBK)

———. *Obozrenie pistsovykh knig po Novu-gorodu i Pskovu.* Moscow: Tip. Senata, 1841. (Cited as Ivanov, OPK.)

Iziumov, A. "Zhiletskoe zemlevladenie v 1632 godu." *Letopis' istoriko-rodoslovnogo obshchestva v Moskve* 31-32 (1912, nos. 3-4): 1-231.

Khoroshkevich, A. A. *Torgovlia Velikogo Novgoroda v XIV-XV vekakh.* Moscow-Leningrad: Akademiia Nauk SSSR, 1963.

Likhachev, N. P. *Razriadnye d'iaki XVI veka.* St. Petersburg: Tip. V. S. Talanshova, 1888.

Maikov, V. V. *Kniga pistsovaia po Novgorodu velikomu kontsa XVI v.* St. Petersburg: Tip. M. A. Aleksandrova, 1911.

Markevich, Al. I. *Istoriia mestnichestva v moskovskom gosudarstve XV-XVII vekov.* Odessa: Tip. "Odesskogo Vestnika," 1888.

Miatlev, N. "Desiatnia Votskoi Piatiny 1605 goda." *Izvestiia Russkogo genealogicheskogo obshchestva* 4(1911): 467-509.

Nosov, N. E. *Ocherki po istorii mestnogo upravleniia russkogo gosudarstva pervoi poloviny XVI veka.* Moscow-Leningrad: Akademiia Nauk SSSR, 1957.

Novosel'skii, A. A., and Pushkarev, L. N., editors. *Redkie istochniki po istorii Rossii.* 2 vols. Moscow: Akademiia Nauk SSSR, 1977.

Obolenskii, M. A., editor. "Perepisnaia okladnaia kniga po Novugorodu Votskoi piatiny Korel'skogo gorodka s uezdom 7008 goda." *Vremennik* 11(1851): pt. 2, pp. 1-464; 12(1852): pt. 2, pp. 1-188.

Ovchinnikov, "Boiarskii spisok." *Istoricheskii arkhiv* 8(1953): 70-79.

Petrov, L. N. *Istoriia rodov russkogo dvorianstva.* St. Petersburg: K-o German Goppe, 1886. (Cited as Petrov, IRRD.)

Petrova, R. G. "Otryvok iz pistsovoi knigi kontsa XVI v. [Bezhetskoi piatiny]." *Istochnikovedenie otechestvennoi istorii. Sbornik statei 1979* (1980): 242-75.

Pistsovye knigi Obonezhskoi piatiny 1496 i 1563 gg. Leningrad: Akademiia Nauk SSSR, 1930.

Pronshtein, A. P. *Velikii Novgorod v XVI veke.* Khar'kov: Izd-vo Khar'kovskogo Gos. Universiteta, 1957.

742 Selected Bibliography

Pskov i ego prigorody. Moscow: Tip. Ministerstva Iustitsii, 1913. (= *Sbornik Moskovskogo arkhiva Ministerstva iustitsii* 5.)

"Rodoslovnaia kniga." *Vremennik* 10(1851): pt. 2, pp. i-viii + 1-286.

Rozhdestvenskii, S. V. "Rospis' zemel'nykh vladenii moskovskogo boiarstva 1647-48." *Drevnosti. Trudy Arkheograficheskoi kommissii imp. Arkheologicheskogo obshchestva* 3(1913): 193-238.

——. *Sluzhiloe zemlevladenie v Moskovskom gosudarstve XVI veka*. St. Petersburg: Tip. V. Demakova, 1897.

Rummel, V. V. and Golubtsov, V. V. *Rodoslovnyi sbornik russkikh dvorianskikh familii*. 2 vols. St. Petersburg: A. S. Suvorin, 1886-87.

Samokvasov, D. Ia. *Arkhivnyi material*. 2 vols. Moscow: Universitetskaia tipografiia, 1905, 1909.

Savelov, L. M. *Rodoslovnye zapiski*. 3 vols. Moscow: T-vo "Pechatnia S. P. Iakovleva," 1906-9.

Shumakov, Sergei. "Obzor 'Gramot Kollegii ekonomii'." *Chteniia* 190(1899, no. 3): i-vi + 1-170; 194(1900, no. 3): i-iv + 1-208; 242 (1912, no. 3): i-viii + 1-259; 261(1917, no. 2): i-ii + 1-336; 262(1917, no. 3): 337-700.

——. "Sotnitsy, gramoty i zapisi." *Chteniia* 247(1913, no. 4): i-vi + 1-46.

Skrynnikov, R. G. *Nachalo Oprichniny*. Leningrad: Leningradskii Universitet, 1966.

——. *Oprichnyi terror*. Leningrad: Leningradskii Universitet, 1969.

Smirnov, D. N. *Ocherki zhizni i byta nezhegorodtsev XVII-XVIII vekov*. Gor'kii: Volgo-Viatskoe knizhnoe izdatel'tsvo, 1971. P. 40.

Sokolova, A. A. and Fon-Mekk, A. K. *Raskhodnye knigi i stolpy Pomestnogo prikaza (1629-1659 gg.)*. Moscow, 1910. Cited as Ardashev, RKiSPP.

Stashevskii, E. D. *Zemlevladenie Moskovskogo dvorianstva v pervoi polovine XVII veka*. Moscow: T-vo "Pechatnia S. P. Iakovleva," 1911.

Storozhev, V. N. "Boiarskie spiski." *Chteniia* 230(1909, no. 3): i-iv + 1-222.

——. "Desiatni XVI veka. No. 1. Kolomna (1577 g.)." *Opisanie* 8³ (1891): 1-58.

——. *Materialy dlia istorii deloproizvodstva pomestnogo prikaza po Vologodskomu uezdu v XVII veka*. 2 pts. (= *Zapiski Rossiiskoi Akademii nauk po istoriko-filologicheskomu otdeleniiu. VIII seriia*. Pt. 1 is the issue for 1906; pt. 2, 1918.)

——. *Tverskoe dvorianstvo XVII veka*. 4 vols. Tver': Tipografiia Gubernskogo Pravleniia, 1891-95.

Sukhotin, L. M. *Chetvertchiki smutnogo vremeni (1604-1617)*. Moscow: Sinodal'naia Tipografiia, 1912.

——. *Pervye mesiatsy tsarstvovaniia Mikhaila Fedorovicha (Stolptsy Pechatnogo prikaza)*. Moscow: Sinodal'naia Tipografiia, 1915.

Tatishchev, Iu. V. "Mestnicheskii spravochnik XVII veka." *Letopis' Istoriko-Rodoslovnogo obshchestva v Moskve* 6, nos. 2-3 [22-23] (1910): 1-81.

Veselovskii, S. B. *Akty podmoskovnykh opolchenii i zemskogo sobora 1611-1613 gg*. Moscow: Sinodal'naia tipografiia, 1911.

———. "Arzamasskie pomestnye akty. 1578-1618 gg." *Chteniia* 256 (1916, no. 1): i-xvi + 1-736.

———. *D'iaki i pod'iachie XV-XVII vv.* Moscow: Nauka, 1975.

———. *Issledovaniia po istorii klassa sluzhilykh zemlevladel'tsev.* Moscow: Nauka, 1969.

———. *Nizhegorodskie platezhnitsy 7116 i 7120 gg.* Moscow: Sinodal'naia tipografiia, 1910.

Voskoboinikova, N. P., et al. *Materialy po istorii krest'ianskogo khoziaistva i povinnostei XVI-XVII vv.* Moscow-Leningrad: Akademiia Nauk SSSR, 1977.

Zimin, A. A. "D'iacheskii apparat v Rossii vtoroi poloviny XV-pervoi treti XVI." *Istoricheskie zapiski* 87(1971): 219-86.

———. "Spisok namestnikov russkogo gosudarstva pervoi poloviny XVI v." *Arkheograficheskii ezhegodnik za 1960 g.* (1962): 27-42.

———. *Tysiachnaia kniga 1550 g. i Dvorovaia tetrad' 50-kh godov XVI v.* Moscow-Leningrad: Akademiia Nauk SSSR, 1950.

Index

Most people in Muscovy did not have surnames. They were known by given name and patronymic, as, for example, Ivan Petrov *syn* (Ivan, Petr's son), which is rendered usually as Ivan Petrov. The feminine form, Anna Petrova *doch'* (Anna, Petr's daughter), is Anna Petrova. Such names are indexed under the patronymic, such as Petrov, Ivan, or Petrova, Anna. Persons with only a given name in the text have not been indexed.

Modern masculine patronymics usually end in "-ich," feminine in "-na," so that the Middle Russian Ivan Petrov *syn* is now Ivan Petrovich, and Anna Petrova *doch'* is now Anna Petrovna. In early modern Russia, only those of noble (princely) descent and certain members of the elite used "-ich" and "-na" patronymics. Many modern editors of published documents have tended to substitute "-ich" patronymics for the original "-'s son" form. Other editors, such as P. I. Ivanov, have opted for the "-ov" form, which usually has been followed in this book.

Most Russian spellings are in the modified Library of Congress system of transliteration. A few well-known names are used in the usual English form, such as Moscow, Peter the Great, or Alexander I.

Peoples of a given nationality are usually indexed under their country's name.

In instances where several members of a family are mentioned in the text, ordinarily only the leading member is listed in the index.